MODERN
LEGAL
GLOSSARY

by

Kenneth R. Redden, J.D.
Professor of Law
University of Virginia

and

Enid L. Veron, B.A., M.A., J.D., Ph.D.
Assistant Professor of Humanities
University of Virginia

THE MICHIE COMPANY
Law Publishers
CHARLOTTESVILLE, VIRGINIA

R
340
R 313

PREFACE

There are many good law dictionaries currently in print which adequately define words. This is the first one devoted exclusively to a definition of legal terms and related concepts, both old and new. It also includes other items of importance such as professional associations, government agencies, international organizations, foreign expressions, names of popular cases and statutes, famous trials, classic law books, ancient codes and biographies of outstanding people in the field of law. In fact, if we've done our job at all well, you'll even enjoy browsing through the pages on a rainy day as a valuable compendium of useful information presented in an interesting fashion.

Professors Kenneth R. Redden
and
Enid L. Veron

University of Virginia,
June 1, 1980

ACKNOWLEDGMENTS

The authors wish to thank Donna Callander for her invaluable editorial assistance. In addition, we are grateful for the contributions of the following students at the University of Virginia School of Law: Peter Bancroft, Edward Baxa, Jeffrey Butrico, Richard Cohen, Grayland Crisp, Michael Davis, Ronald Feinman, John Flood, Michael Frost, David Fudella, Gordon Fuller, Lewis Hassett, Josiah Henson, Michael Hollis, Robert Kaplan, Mary Kearney, Maynard Kirpalani, Robert Landau, Robert Littleton, John Martin, Elvire Marchandasi, Bringier McConnell, Matt Neperud, Linda Romano, Thomas Watson and Andrew Wright.

A TIP OF THE HAT

This book has been in preparation for half a century. It would have remained an unfinished manuscript gathering dust on a library shelf without the generous expression of confidence of Dean Emerson G. Spies and the University of Virginia Law School Foundation.

CONTENTS

A

A.A.A. See AMERICAN ARBITRATION ASSOCIATION.

A.A.C.S.L. See AMERICAN ASSOCIATION FOR THE COMPARATIVE STUDY OF LAW.

A.A.L.L. See AMERICAN ASSOCIATION OF LAW LIBRARIES.

A.A.L.S. See ASSOCIATION OF AMERICAN LAW SCHOOLS.

A.A.P. See ART ADVISORY PANEL.

A.A.U.P. (American Association of University Professors). Founded in 1915 by scholars to protect their legal rights and to advance the standards, ideals and welfare of higher education faculty. For over three generations, it has served professors and has grown to become the nation's largest, most active, most influential organization attending to the needs of teachers and research scholars in colleges and universities throughout the country. Today, the A.A.U.P. has members at more than 2,200 institutions with local chapters at 1,365 campuses, and 45 conferences, uniting chapter organizations on a statewide basis. Alone among faculty organizations, the A.A.U.P. has developed policies on academic freedom and tenure which are generally regarded as the fair standards of the profession. These relate to such vital matters as academic due process, re-appointment of non-tenured faculty, retrenchment in the face of financial exigency, proper notice, grievance procedures, the rights of teaching assistants, extramural statements, the political activity of professors, retirement, and many other concerns. The A.A.U.P. guards academic freedom and tenure by working to have its policies observed by the nation's colleges and universities. In most instances, when the A.A.U.P. communicates with an administration on a specific case of possible violation of A.A.U.P. policies, a successful resolution is attained. The A.A.U.P.'s advice is also sought in advance by both faculty and administrators in more than 1,000 cases a year. Administrative officers approach the A.A.U.P. to determine what standards and procedures they should follow. The A.A.U.P. is regularly called upon by institutions to assist in review and revision of their regulations so that institutional policies meet the high standards of the A.A.U.P. When mediation is resisted, and the case continues to pose serious unresolved issues relating to the principles of academic freedom and tenure, the A.A.U.P.'s General Secretary appoints a special investigating committee to examine it and prepare a report for publication. Sometimes it is necessary to draw public attention to the violations of academic freedom and tenure by censuring the administration involved. Since almost all institutions wish to avoid this, or take steps afterwards so that the censure will be removed, censure has proved to be an effective tool. The A.A.U.P. has done more than any other professional association to influence the hard law of higher education and of faculty rights enforceable in court.

A.B.A. See AMERICAN BAR ASSOCIATION.

ABANDONED AND MALIGNANT HEART. See MURDER ONE.

ABATEMENT OF LEGACIES. When an estate is insufficient to satisfy all legacies, bequests and devices, some or all may be abated to satisfy superior claims, such as expenses of administration or statutory shares asserted by a spouse or pretermitted heir.

ABATE v. MUNDT (403 U.S. 182 (1971)). A Supreme Court case concerning legislative apportionment. In *Abate,* the Court allowed an 11.9 percent deviation from population equality in the apportionment of a county legislature on the ground that the local body reflected close cooperation between the county and its constituent towns. However, the dissent regarded the decision as a weakening of the requirement of one man/one vote.

ABBOTT LABORATORIES v. GARDNER. See RIPENESS DOCTRINE.

ABBOTT LABORATORIES RULE. See RIPENESS DOCTRINE.

AB INITIO (Latin—from the beginning). A contract unsupported by valuable consideration, for example, may be said to be void Ab Initio.

A.B.L.A. See AMERICAN BLIND LAWYERS ASSOCIATION.

ABOOD v. DETROIT BOARD OF EDUCATION (431 U.S. 209, (1977)). A Supreme Court decision involving an agreement between a school board and a union, which required that nonunion employees pay the union a service fee equal in amount to union dues as a condition of employment. Rejecting the challenge to public bargaining in the public sector the Court justified the portions of the "service charge" used for collective bargaining, contract administration, and grievance adjustment purposes. However, the Court upheld First Amendment objections to those portions of the fee spent for purposes not directly related to collective bargaining.

ABRAMS v. UNITED STATES (250 U.S. 616 (1919)). See CLEAR AND PRESENT DANGER DOCTRINE.

ABORTION PAYMENT DECISIONS. A trilogy of Supreme Court cases in 1977 which held that public funds need not be given for therapeutic abortions unless the abortion is needed to protect the health of the mother. Dissenting Justices pointed out that these decisions are reminiscent of a "let them eat cake" attitude, in that women who can afford to have children can also obtain abortions, but poor women can afford neither alternative.

ABSENTEE VOTING. A privilege given by the states to qualified voters which enables them to vote in an election in the precinct of their home when they are temporarily absent on the day of the election. While there is no absolute right to absentee voting, this privilege is granted in a majority of the states. Each state varies somewhat in describing by statute those persons who may vote as an absentee. Virginia is, however, typical in permitting absentee voting by duly registered voters who are absent in the ordinary course of their business, profession, or occupation; on vacation; in the Armed Forces or Merchant Marine; regularly employed in a business, profession, or occupation outside the continental United States; students; or those who are ill or physically infirm. In order to ensure the verity of an absentee ballot, most states require that the ballot be opened, marked, closed, and sealed before some officer authorized to administer oaths and that an affidavit to this effect accompany the ballot. Failure of the voter to comply with these statutory requirements renders the ballot void.

ABSTENTION DOCTRINES. A group of related rules recognizing that, in certain circumstances, a federal court may decline to proceed even though it has jurisdiction under the constitution or federal law. It is more precise to understand the general abstention principle in terms of at least four distinct but overlapping doctrines, involving different lines of cases, factual situations, procedural consequences and treatment by the Supreme Court. The first of these Abstention Doctrines is the most clearly established, and is referred to as the Pullman Doctrine. It arises in cases where state action is challenged in federal courts as contrary to the federal Constitution but where the case may be disposed of on questions of state law in order to avoid the federal constitutional question. A second abstention rationale is that a federal court should refrain from exercising its jurisdiction in order to avoid needless conflict with a state's administration of its own affairs, as in the area of state taxation. A third type of abstention has been employed by the federal courts to avoid deciding difficult yet unsettled questions of state law, despite the availability of certification of an issue to the state Supreme Court. Finally, a fourth category of abstention—discussed by some federal courts but not by the Supreme Court—is that abstention may be ordered merely to serve the convenience of the federal courts and ease the con-

2

gestion of their dockets. To date, the various abstention principles have been only rarely invoked. As federal courts become faced with a greater number of difficult and complex issues, however, they may see fit to resort more frequently to the abstention technique, and it may become increasingly difficult to distinguish clearly between the various types of abstention rationales and their application.

ABSTRACTIONS TEST. Used in a copyright infringement action to determine substantial similarity between the copyrighted work and the alleged infringing work. The test, first enunciated in 1930 in *Nichols v. Universal Pictures Co.*, 282 U.S. 902 (1930), examines whether the defendant's work copies the expression of the idea—as opposed to borrowing the idea itself, which is permissible—contained in the copyrighted piece.

ABSTRACT OF TITLE. See TITLE ABSTRACT.

ABUSE OF PROCESS. See MALICIOUS PROSECUTION.

ACCELERATED CHRISTIAN EDUCATION (A.C.E). Packaged curricula used by over 2500 schools in which fundamentalist Christian philosophy permeates all academic learning. Many schools using A.C.E. programs are involved in lawsuits over state regulation of school curricula and standards. The fundamentalists view their schools as places of religious teaching, bringing into issue the doctrine of separation of church and state. States argue that the fundamentalists must meet certain minimal standards, such as those regulating teacher certification, in order to adequately equip their students with necessary skills. Resistance to state regulation has spawned at least two fundamentalist legal defense funds which finance court battles over the regulation issue.

ACCELERATED REMAINDER. The trust property which passes from a trust beneficiary to a subsequent beneficiary called a remainderman due to a failure of the trust property or the preceding

trust beneficiary. For example, if a trust is set up with X as its beneficiary, the creator of the trust might well be concerned about what will happen to the money in trust for X if X should suddenly die. To protect his wishes, the creator may designate Y to receive the benefits on X's death. In such a case, Y, the remainderman, is said to take an Accelerated Remainder due to the fortuity of X's premature death.

ACCELERATION CLAUSE. A provision in a contract or document which permits a party's expected interest in property to vest upon the occurrence of a specified event. For example, such a clause in a mortgage might provide that if the mortgagor shall fail to pay a note, interest or taxes, the entire amount of the mortgage shall become due. An Acceleration Clause is often found in installment contracts, so that the entire debt becomes due if a purchaser fails to pay an installment as agreed.

ACCESS-TO-PLANT CLAUSE. An agreement in a union contract relating to use of company property for union organizational activities. Such agreements generally limit the times and places available to union organizers for soliciting and distributing union literature. The Supreme Court has struck down such agreements where they operate to waive the rights of employees to communicate on non-working time and in non-working areas. The Court foresaw the danger in such situations that an incumbent union could become entrenched by limiting access of potential rival organizers.

ACCORD AND SATISFACTION. An agreement between an insolvent debtor and his creditor under which the creditor discharges the debtor of his debt in return for partial payment of money or property. An Accord and Satisfaction is distinguished from a Compromise and Settlement in that in the latter case the parties dispute the existence of the debt, while in the former case they do not.

ACCRUAL METHOD. An accounting method whereby income and expenses are reported when they are incurred or earned even though they have not actually been paid. The Accrual Method is the most widely-used method of reporting income.

ACCUMULATED DIVIDEND. A dividend which a corporation has not paid but which it owes.

ACCUMULATION TRUST. Common name for a trust which provides that trust income is to be accumulated rather than distributed to the beneficiaries in order to achieve tax savings for the beneficiaries.

ACCUMULATIVE SENTENCING. See SENTENCING PROCEDURES.

A.C.E. See ACCELERATED CHRISTIAN EDUCATION.

ACKNOWLEDGMENT OF CHILD. The father of an illegitimate child admits the paternity of the child or accepts the child as his by his statements or conduct. This is a particularly powerful weapon against the defendant in a paternity suit. The fact of acknowledgment does not have to be universally known, but most state statutes require that it be made known to the father's friends or acquaintances in order to be effective. The acknowledgment of the child becomes a very technical issue when a legitimation statute, enabling parents to legitimate their illegitimate children, has the requirement of acknowledgment.

A.C.L.U. (American Civil Liberties Union). A national organization dedicated to the protection of constitutional rights, especially those rights set forth in the Bill of Rights. The A.C.L.U. was founded in 1920 by Roger Baldwin, who brought together as original members Norman Thomas, Clarence Darrow, Helen Keller and Felix Frankfurter. It first achieved national prominence in 1925 in the so-called "Monkey Trial" in which John Scopes was tried for violating a Tennessee law banning the teaching of evolution in the public schools. Since that time the Union has been involved in many controversial cases, including the Sacco and Vanzetti, Scottsboro, Gideon, Miranda and Chicago Seven cases. The A.C.L.U. has de-fended unpopular groups such as the K.K.K., Nazis, Black Muslims and Communists as well as ordinary individuals who have had their rights abridged. The A.C.L.U. maintains, however, that it always has "the Bill of Rights as a client" and not a single individual. It now has over 200,000 dues-paying members and 5,000 volunteer lawyers with offices in 500 cities throughout the country and an annual budget of $7 million.

A.C.O. See ADMINISTRATIVE CONTRACTING OFFICER.

ACQUISITION CIRCULARS. See DEFENSE ACQUISITION REGULATION.

ACREAGE ZONING (Large-Lot Zoning). A land-use scheme which requires large building lots in order to reduce residential population.

ACTIO EX CONTRACTU. See ACTION EX CONTRACTU.

ACTIO EX DELICTO. See ACTION EX DELICTO.

ACTION AGENCY. Strengthens the impact and appeal of citizen participation in programs providing personalized services to people whose needs are compelling, both at home and abroad. It provides centralized co-ordination and administration of domestic and international volunteer activities sponsored by the federal government, and serves as an umbrella federal agency for other programs, such as the Peace Corps, R.S.V.P., S.C.O.R.E., and V.I.S.T.A. In striving to reach its goal of a system of volunteer service which uses to the fullest advantage the power of the American people to serve the purposes of the American nation, the Agency identifies and develops the widest possible range of opportunities for mobilizing the American spirit of service among all ages.

ACTION EX CONTRACTU. In both the civil and common law, an action on, or arising out of, contract.

ACTION EX DELICTO. An action, arising out of a contractual relationship, for the breach of a duty imposed by law and not by the contract. Assume that Jones installs a furnace in Baker's home pursuant to his contract with Baker. If the installation was negligently performed and thereby Baker is subsequently injured, Baker may choose to treat the wrong as a tort and sue Jones in an Action Ex Delicto, even though the relationship between the parties was governed by their contract.

ACTION GRANTS. See URBAN DEVELOPMENT ACTION GRANTS.

ACTIVE TRUST. A trust arrangement regarding which the trust trustee has an active duty to perform, such as to try to increase the value of the trust property. An active trust is usually designed for the maintenance or improvement of some designated asset—such as an estate of real property or a mansion. Many times a settlor will set up an active trust to pay creditors or make investments.

ACT OF GOD. A natural catastrophe, such as a hurricane or earthquake, which causes damage and yet the injured party cannot successfully sue anyone for the loss sustained.

ACT OF STATE DOCTRINE. The principle that the conduct of one independent government cannot be successfully questioned in the courts of another. In its traditional formulation, set forth in the famous 1964 case of *Banco National de Cuba v. Sabbatino*, 376 U.S. 398 (1964), the Act of State Doctrine precludes the courts of one country from inquiring into the validity of the public acts which a recognized foreign sovereign commits within its own territory. The doctrine, developed primarily in the United States and not widely recognized in international law, is generally invoked by a party to a lawsuit to argue that the court not examine the validity of the act of another sovereign government under either the "public policy" of that court's government or any principle of International Law. An example of an Act of State is the expropriation or taking away of private property by a state within its own territory.

ACTS OF BANKRUPTCY. For a debtor to be forced into Bankruptcy by means of an involuntary petition in bankruptcy filed by his creditors, he must be shown to have committed one of the six Acts of Bankruptcy in the four months preceding the filing of the petition. The six Acts of Bankruptcy are: 1) concealing or transferring property with intent to delay or defraud creditors; 2) making a preferential transfer of property to a creditor; 3) suffering a lien to be placed on property through legal proceedings; 4) making a general assignment for the benefit of creditors; 5) having a receiver or trustee appointed to administer the debtor's property, as happens in the case of dissolution of a corporation; and 6) the admission by the debtor in writing that he is unable to pay his debts. Creditors filing an involuntary petition in bankruptcy must allege the occurrence of one or more Acts Of Bankruptcy in their petition, and must prove the occurrence at an adjudication hearing if the debtor contests the proceedings. If the debtor performed one of the first two Acts of Bankruptcy—concealing or transferring property with intent to delay or defraud creditors, or making a preferential transfer of property—and is adjudged a bankrupt, the trustee in bankruptcy appointed by his creditors to administer the bankruptcy estate may be able to have the transaction revoked as a fraudulent transfer or a voidable preference. As a result of the enactment of the Bankruptcy Law of 1978, Acts of Bankruptcy no longer are required for cases brought after October 1, 1979.

ACTUS REUS (Latin—guilty act). The act which, when accompanied by criminal culpability, constitutes a crime. It includes positive acts, omissions to act, possession and being. Being refers to crimes such as vagrancy or drug addiction, which punish a status or personal condition. An omission to act constitutes a criminal act in certain cases. Examples are the failure to file a tax return and the failure of a parent to provide medical care for his sick child.

ADAIR v. UNITED STATES (208 U.S. 161 (1908)). See YELLOW DOG CONTRACT.

ADAMS v. TANNER (244 U.S. 590 (1917)). A Supreme Court case that invalidated a law prohibiting employment agencies from collecting fees from workers. *Adams* was one of a series of cases during the early part of the twentieth century in which the Court invalidated restraints on competition that restricted entry into a particular line of business.

ADAMS v. WILLIAMS. See INVESTIGATORY FIELD STOP.

A.D.B. (Asian Development Bank). A multilateral international organization created in 1966, headquartered in the Philippines and composed of 42 countries, including the United States, of which 28 are Asian. Its purpose is to foster the economic growth of the developing member countries in Asia, collectively and individually.

AD DAMNUM (Latin—to the damage). A technical legal term used in pleading that identifies that part of the document which contains a statement of the plaintiff's loss or the damages which the plaintiff claims he has sustained as a result of the defendant's wrongdoing.

ADDERLY v. FLORIDA (385 U.S. 39 (1966)). A Supreme Court case rejecting a constitutional challenge to a Florida trespass statute. To protest the arrest of fellow students, petitioners demonstrated on the premises of a county jail. They argued that this property was appropriate for their demonstration. However, the Court concluded that the state, "no less than the property under its control for the use to which it is lawfully dedicated."

ADD-ON CLAUSE. See FLOATING LIEN.

A.D.E.A. (Age Discrimination in Employment Act). A federal act, which became effective in 1967, designed to promote employment of older persons based on their ability, rather than their age, and to prohibit arbitrary age discrimination in employment. The Act makes it unlawful for employers, labor organizations, and employment agencies to refuse to hire or to discharge an employee, to reduce wage rates, or to segregate workers in any way solely because of age. Age can be the sole deciding factor only when an employer can show that age is a bona fide occupational qualification reasonably necessary to the normal operation of the particular business. Under A.D.E.A., an injured individual may obtain such relief as a court order for back pay and an injunction to stop the illegal practice, or the Department of Labor may intervene to represent the injured party's interests.

ADEMPTION BY EXTINCTION. Specific bequest or devise of property described by the testator, in his will, which is not found in his estate at his death and only applies to specific gifts by definition.

ADEMPTION BY SATISFACTION. Testamentary gift intentionally rendered inoperative by a gift of property to a donee in the will. Related to the doctrine of advancement in intestacy but the testamentary donee has no opportunity to come into hotchpot.

ADHESION CONTRACT. See TAKE-IT-OR-LEAVE-IT CONTRACT.

AD INTERIM COPYRIGHT. To gain statutory copyright protection, a book or periodical, if printed, must be printed and bound in the United States or Canada. Ad Interim Copyright provides a limited exemption from this manufacturing requirement for English-language books or periodicals first published in foreign countries. If a foreign edition work is deposited with the Copyright Office within six months of its first publication, it will obtain a five-year Ad Interim Copyright which will mature into a full statutory copyright if, during that five-year period, an edition complying with the manufacturing clause is published.

ADJOURNMENT SINE DIE (Latin —adjournment without day). Adjournment without setting a time for another meeting. Typically, it refers to the closing of a term of court, a legislative session or a convention.

ADJUDICATION IN BANKRUPTCY. A formal determination by a bankruptcy court that a person is bankrupt. Once the Adjudication in Bankruptcy has been made, the bankrupt must surrender his property to the bankruptcy court to be distributed among his creditors, and may apply for a discharge of debt. The Adjudication in Bankruptcy follows automatically from the filing of a voluntary petition in bankruptcy, but when an involuntary petition in bankruptcy has been filed and the debtor contests it, the Adjudication in Bankruptcy can be had only if the creditors prevail at an adjudication hearing held before the bankruptcy referee. As a result of the enactment of the Bankruptcy Law of 1978, adjudication in Bankruptcy no longer applies to cases brought after October 1, 1978.

ADJUDICATORY HEARING. In juvenile proceedings, the fact-finding process wherein the juvenile court determines whether or not there is sufficient evidence to sustain the allegations in a petition. An Adjudicatory Hearing occurs after a petition has been filed and after a detention hearing (if any). If the petition is not sustained, no further formal court action is taken. If it is sustained, the next step in the proceeding is a disposition hearing to determine the most appropriate treatment or care for the juvenile. For statistical purposes, the Adjudicatory Hearing ends when a finding is entered, that is, a juvenile adjudication is made. An Adjudicatory Hearing concerning an alleged delinquent is analogous to a trial in criminal proceedings since both proceedings determine matters of fact concerning alleged acts. An adjudication of delinquent requires proof beyond a reasonable doubt. An adjudication of a status offender requires that the preponderance of evidence support the allegations.

ADJUSTED BASIS. A taxpayer's investment in property, used to determine his gain or loss for tax purposes when the property is sold. To arrive at the Adjusted Basis the taxpayer adds to his original investment in the property the amount he has spent on capital improvement, and deducts the amount of amortization, depreciation and depletion allowances where applicable. Comparing the Adjusted Basis at the time of sale with the net proceeds from the sale reflects the amount of taxable gain or loss.

AD LITEM (Latin—for the suit; for the purposes of or pending the suit). A guardian ad litem is a person appointed to represent a party who is unable personally to prosecute or defend a suit because of an incapacity, such as infancy, or because the identity of such party is unknown or indeterminable.

ADMINISTRATIVE ADJUDICATION (Administrative Hearing). Agency counterpart to a judicial trial conducted by officials who are granted authority to conduct hearings. Generally, procedures in an Administrative Adjudication are comparable to those in federal or state courts. However, informal adjudications may dispense with the requirement of counsel or cross-examination. In addition, there is never a jury in an Administrative Adjudication, and the trial examiner is often an expert on the very question he must decide. Although concerned with adjudicative facts, administrative hearings are oriented toward development of policy to a greater extent than judicial trials and therefore the hearing officer's decision will involve considerations of the impact of his decision on the general public as well as on the particular parties.

ADMINISTRATIVE AGENCY. According to the Administrative Procedure Act "Each authority of the Government of the United States, whether or not it is within or subject to review by another agency, but does not include: (a) the Congress; (b) the courts of the United States; (c) the governments of the territories or possessions of the United States; (d) the government of the District of Columbia; (e) agencies composed of representatives of the parties or representatives of the organizations of the parties to the disputes determined by them; (f) courts martial and military commissions; or (g) military authority exercised in the field in time of war or in occupied territory." The title, i.e., "corporation," "administration," "department," "officer," "bureau," "board," etc. is irrelevant, as is the number of individuals exercising certain powers, as the President or a Governor may correctly be considered an Administrative Agency. Central to the designation is the performance of rulemaking or adjudicative or prosecutorial functions by bodies other than the legislature or the courts, which affect the rights of private parties. Administrative Agencies exist for a variety of purposes including distribution of welfare benefits, land management, taxation, law enforcement, and education among others. While the Veterans Administration and the Customs Office had their genesis in 1789 and the Patent Office was born one year later, the creation of the Interstate Commerce Commission (I.C.C.) in 1887 is often regarded as the starting point of the administrative process, due to the absence of an identifiable corpus of administrative or public law prior to the I.C.C. The F.T.C. was created 30 years later, but it was not until the New Deal that the federal bureaucracy began to take the form which we recognize today. Increasingly, Congress has adopted the administrative agency approach to handle narrow areas requiring specific expertise. The presence of an agency adds continuity and direction that legislative and judicial action are unable to supply. In one body both policy development and implementation can be achieved. Administrative agencies were thought to be peculiarly able to produce quick decisions on day-to-day matters where time is of the essence. Quaere whether O.S.H.A.'s estimated 18-month complaint-to-resolution cycle fulfills that goal.

ADMINISTRATIVE CONFERENCE OF THE UNITED STATES. Established as a permanent independent agency by the Administrative Confer-

ence Act of 1964. The statutory provisions prescribing the organization and activities of the Conference are based in part upon the experience of two temporary Conferences called by the President in 1953 and 1961, each of which operated for a period of 18 months. Although the Administrative Conference has the authority only to recommend changes in administrative procedures, the Chairman is authorized to encourage the departments and agencies to adopt the recommendations of the Conference and is required by the Administrative Conference Act to transmit to the President and to Congress an annual report and interim reports concerning the activities of the Conference, including reports on the implementation of its recommendations.

ADMINISTRATIVE CONTEMPT. See CONTEMPT OF COURT.

ADMINISTRATIVE CONTRACTING OFFICER (A.C.O.). In federal government contracting, a contracting officer at a contract administration office.

ADMINISTRATIVE DETAINEES. A euphemistic term given by the Israelis to their Arab political prisoners.

ADMINISTRATIVE LAW. Defines the authority and governs the practice of administrative agencies. The focus of this branch of jurisprudential inquiry concerns judicial review of administrative action. Substantive law developed by the agencies is not properly included under the heading Administrative Law. The term refers principally to what the agency looks like, what it does and how it can do it. The answers to these questions are supplied in part by the organic statutes creating the agencies (e.g., Federal Trade Act for Federal Trade Commission), but much of the picture is filled in judicially with justification rooted in constitutional or statutory interpretation or through application of the common law.

ADMINISTRATIVE LAW JUDGE (A. L.J.). The presiding and deciding official in hearings involving administrative agencies of the federal government. A.L.J.s collectively are often called the

Hidden Judiciary because of the low visibility of their positions. To become eligible for appointment as an A.L.J., one must pass a Civil Service examination and obtain a numerical rating from the Civil Service Commission; each agency then selects the individuals it wants. The neutrality of A.L.J.s has been attacked since an A.L.J. must review the actions of the agency to which he is assigned. For this reason, some commentators have suggested that A.L.J.s ought to rotate among agencies though this might sacrifice the expertise that is developed under the present assignment system. The Administrative Procedure Act created the position of Hearing Examiner in 1946. In 1972, the Civil Service Commission changed the title to Administrative Law Judge, which enhanced the prestige of the position. In the 1950s, salaries of examiners were approximately one-third those of federal district judges. Today, the salaries are nearly equal. The years have brought a shift in assignments as well. In 1947, there were 197 examiners for 18 agencies, the bulk of whom were in the Interstate Commerce Commission. By contrast, in 1979, 1,010 A.L.J.s served 35 departments, with the Social Security Administration utilizing over one-half of them, followed in number by the National Labor Relations Board, the Occupational Safety and Health Review Commission, and the Department of the Interior.

ADMINISTRATIVE OFFICE OF THE UNITED STATES COURTS (A.O.).

The housekeeping agent of the federal judiciary, created by Congress in 1939. The Director is the Administrative Officer of the United States courts, excepting the Supreme Court. Under the supervision and direction of the Judicial Conference of the United States he is required, among other things, to: (1) supervise all administrative matters relating to the offices of clerks and other clerical and administrative personnel of the courts; (2) examine the state of the dockets of the courts; prepare and transmit quarterly to the chief judges of the circuits statistical data and reports as to the business of the courts; (3) fix the compensation of employees of the courts whose compensation is not otherwise fixed by law; (4) exercise general supervision of federal probation officers, bankruptcy judges, magistrates, and public defender organizations.

ADMINISTRATIVE PROCEDURE ACT (A.P.A.).

Governs the procedures of all federal agencies and departments. The Act sets standards of conduct for hearings mandating a trial-type record; prohibits Ex Parte contacts between administrative law judges and agency staff; places the burden of proof on the agency; creates a duty to keep the public informed of agency rules and procedures; and clarifies procedural distinctions between informal rulemaking and more formal adjudicatory hearings. Although the earliest federal peacetime agencies—to estimate duties payable on imports and to provide pensions for injured veterans of the Revolutionary War—date from 1789, the Administrative Procedure Act was first enacted in 1946. The influx of agencies during the New Deal and the concomitant growth of their powers signaled the need for controls. Consequently, the Attorney General appointed Dean Acheson to head a committee to study administrative procedure. Congress, without dissent, passed the A.P.A., based largely on the committee's recommendations. The Act has been amended several times, most recently in 1976.

ADMINISTRATIVE REMEDY.

A remedy which is granted by an administrative agency pursuant to statutory authority. Such a remedy is designed to accord to persons relief, which is more quickly and easily available than judicial remedies, administered by the agency which has expertise in the matter. Where an Administrative Remedy is provided by statute, a party seeking judicial relief must pursue and exhaust all Administrative Remedies before the courts may act to grant relief. For example, if Jones is denied a liquor license under a statutory scheme which provides for appeals to the entire Alcoholic Beverage Commission, he must make such an appeal before seeking judicial review of the denial. This is known as the Doctrine of Exhaustion of Administrative Remedies.

ADMINISTRATIVE RULEMAKING. Quasi-legislative action in which a federal agency develops a statement of general or particular applicability and future effect designed to implement, interpret, or prescribe law or policy, or to describe the organization, procedure or practice requirements of the agency. Rulemaking is authorized by section 553 of the Administrative Procedure Act and is regarded as an inherent power of administrative agencies. In "notice and comment" or "informal" rulemaking, a proposed rule is published by the agency in the *Federal Register* for the purpose of affording interested parties the opportunity to comment on the desirability and ramifications of the regulation. Comments are evaluated by the agency staff and the proposed rule is modified accordingly. There is then an additional 30-day period for opponents to object to the final version. Military or foreign affairs activities, as well as matters relating to agency management or personnel or to public property, loans, grants, benefits or contracts are not included under section 553. Further, interpretive rules and situations where the agency finds and announces that notice and comment are "impracticable, unnecessary, or contrary to public interest," are excluded. "Formal rulemaking" involves the seldom-used procedure of conducting full trial-type hearings prior to the issuance of a rule. State administrative agencies have similar rulemaking powers.

ADMINISTRATOR CUM TESTAMENTO ANNEXO (Administrator C.T.A.; Latin—an administrator with will annexed). Where the decedent names no executor, or for any reason the person named fails to act as the executor, a probate court appoints an Administrator C.T.A. to perform the same functions. Courts usually appoint the residuary legatee or one of the principal legatees as an Administrator C.T.A. since such a person has the most to gain by an efficient administration of the estate.

ADMINISTRATOR DE BONIS NON (Administrator D.B.N.; Latin—an administrator of goods not administered). If an executor dies or is otherwise removed after partially administering an estate, the court appoints an Administrator D.B.N. to complete the administration.

ADMINISTRATOR'S DEED. Conveys property when an individual dies without a will.

ADMIRALTY JURISDICTION OF THE UNITED STATES. Jurisdiction extending to all admiralty and maritime cases, conferred upon the courts of the United States by the Constitution. The Judiciary Act of 1789, which implemented this constitutional provision, provides for exclusive original jurisdiction in such cases in the United States District Courts. However, a savings clause within this legislation preserves the right of a plaintiff to pursue a common law remedy in admiralty cases in a state court where such remedy exists. Admiralty Jurisdiction includes those things principally connected with maritime transportation, such as vessels, their cargoes and personnel, and extends to all navigable waters which may be used in interstate or foreign commerce.

ADMIRALTY LAW. See MARITIME LAW.

ADMISSIBLE EVIDENCE. May be considered by a judge or jury in order to resolve a judicial controversy. Although only Admissible Evidence may be so considered, not all such evidence must be admitted. For example, under the new Federal Rules of Evidence, a judge may exclude evidence if the probative value of the evidence is outweighed by the fact that it will consume too much time, confuse the issues or mislead or prejudice the jury. Thus, in a claim for damages resulting from fire, a party may not be permitted to introduce a photograph showing the grief-stricken family in front of the rubble of their home, since such an emotional photograph is likely to prejudice the jury. Similarly, a gory photograph of a nude victim is likely to be prohibited as evidence of the murder. In these instances, the judge may use his discretion to require that the fire and the murder be proved by less prejudicial evidence.

ADOPTEE REGISTRY. A clearinghouse for information to enable adopted children and their natural parents to locate each other.

ADOPTEES IN SEARCH. See A.I.S.

ADOPTEE'S LIBERTY MOVEMENT ASSOCIATION. See A.L.M.A.

ADOPTION BY ESTOPPEL. See EQUITABLE ADOPTION.

ADOPTION RESOURCE EXCHANGE. An agency which maintains files on children eligible for adoption and reciprocally exchanges this information with similar agencies in other states or within the state. The compassionate purpose, of course, is to increase the number of adoptions throughout the country.

ADULT ENTERTAINMENT CODE. See INVERSE ZONING.

AD VALOREM (Latin—according to value). An Ad Valorem tax is a tax on the value of the object subject to taxation, levied as a fixed percentage of its determined value. An Ad Valorem duty is a customs duty levied according to the value of the imported object.

ADVANCE APPROPRIATION. In the federal budget, an appropriation provided by the Congress one or more years in advance of the fiscal year in which the budget authority becomes available for obligation. Advance appropriations allow state and local governments sufficient time to develop plans with assurance of future federal funding. For example, the 1976 appropriation for the Washington Metropolitan Area Transit Authority was contained in the Department of Transportation and Related Agencies Appropriations Act for 1975. An Advance

Appropriation is sometimes mistakenly referred to as Forward Funding, which involves an agency in obligating funds in the current year for outlay to programs that are to operate in subsequent fiscal years.

ADVANCEMENT OF INHERITANCE. A gift or other transfer of property by a parent to one of his or her children which, if the parent dies intestate, is considered to be an advancement of the child's inheritance and deducted from the child's intestate share of the parent's estate. Generally, gifts of land or substantial amounts of personal property are presumed to be Advancements of Inheritance, the idea being that the parent was simply passing on what the child would receive anyway when the parent died. The doctrine of advancement has no application to ancestors who die wholly testate.

ADVERSE POSSESSION (Squatter's Rights). A process by which a person acquires title to land without paying for it. Adverse Possession ripens into title when the possession is open, hostile and continuous for the period of time which is stipulated by statute, usually 15 to 21 years. Such possession gives notice to all the world, including the owner of record, that claim is being laid to the land. For example, a tenant who pays rent is not in Adverse Possession because he is there by permission of the landlord, but if he ceases to pay rent, and continues to occupy the property in open, hostile and continuous possession, he becomes an adverse possessor. A title acquired by Adverse Possession is as good as one acquired by deed.

ADVERTISED BIDDING. The procedure for letting public contracts employed by the federal government and copied by many states and localities. The governmental unit desiring to contract for private goods or services publishes a detailed set of specifications to known suppliers and the public, inviting sealed bids to be opened at a given time and place. Once submitted, bids may generally not be withdrawn. Further, an accepted bidder must perform his contract. When the bids are opened, the contract is awarded to the lowest bidder who meets the specifications. While this system for placing contracts is fair to the bidders, it has the disadvantages of being time-consuming and expensive.

ADVICE AND CONSENT. The procedure specified in the federal Constitution (Art. II, Section 2) for Senate approval of presidential appointments and treaties. The Senate gives advice to the President by consulting with the Executive, by passing resolutions stating its position, or by assigning to some of its members the task of participating in treaty negotiations. Its consent is given by actual vote. Two-thirds of the Senators present must consent to the enactment of a treaty, but the Senate may confirm presidential appointments by simple majority vote. Citizens commonly speak of "treaty ratification" to describe the Senate's consent function in treaty-making. In the treaty context, however, ratification is actually performed by the President, who ratifies the form of the treaty approved by the Senate.

ADVISORY OPINION. An extra-judicial expression of legal opinion by a court or judge on some abstract question of law, outside the context of actual litigation. Although such a device has been sanctioned by several states, within the federal system there exists a long-standing rule against the use of Advisory Opinions. The rule was first enunciated in 1793 by the Supreme Court in response to a list of 29 questions submitted by Secretary of State Jefferson, dealing with international law, neutrality, and the interpretation of British and French treaties. In its rationale, the Supreme Court cited the separation of powers envisioned by the Constitution, and the fact that the Court was the court of last resort. The rule against Advisory Opinions in federal courts should not be confused with their ability to issue declaratory judgments. Where an actual controversy between real parties exists, a federal court may issue a declaratory

judgment setting out the respective rights and liabilities of the parties even though such a judgment cannot be executed.

A.E.C.B.C.A. See BOARDS OF CONTRACT APPEALS.

A.F.D.C. (Aid to Families with Dependent Children). Welfare program which provides monthly cash payments to families with at least one child who has been deprived of parental support or care by reason of the death, continued absence from the home, or physical or mental incapacity of one or both parents. The program involves state and federal cooperation in that while the Social Security Act of 1935 supplies the definition of "dependent child," state agencies determine what standard of need is to be applied and how much money will be paid. As a result, the size of welfare allotments varies significantly from state to state. The federal government contributes at least 50 percent of the amount the state deems appropriate. A.F.D.C. is the largest of the categorical assistance programs (others are for the blind, the disabled and the elderly). The federal contribution to more than 10 million A.F.D.C. recipients is several billion dollars a year.

AFFINITY RELATION. A close relationship between certain persons arising out of a marital relationship. The doctrine of affinity developed under the prevailing influence of religion, prohibiting incest. The Roman Catholic canonical concept is that marriage makes the husband and wife one. The husband thus has the same relations by affinity to his wife's blood relations as he has to her, and is therefore precluded from marrying one of them, such as a sister-in-law, even after the wife's death. Henry VIII legislation reduced the number of forbidden relationships to those found in the Bible and the statute prohibiting marriage to the deceased wife's sister was eventually repealed in England in 1907. In America, the states vary with respect to marriage impediments for relations by affinity and many had eliminated the concept entirely.

AFFIRMATIVE ACTION (Reverse Discrimination). A federal program under the auspices of the Department of Health, Education and Welfare (H.E.W.) to remedy past discrimination or special disadvantages faced by minority applicants seeking employment and educational opportunities. Sex, race, ethnic and national origin are the key variables. H.E.W. Affirmative Action applies only to employers and educational institutions having federal contracts or receiving federal support. Under the program, the employer or school must undertake a comparison of the composition of the relevant applicant pool and the makeup of the pertinent work force or student body. To the extent that a significant disparity is revealed, certain statistical changes must be achieved over a specified time period. Violators are required to specify numerical goals and timetables for achieving results in hiring, promotion, wages, and training programs. Otherwise, the government will withdraw its contract or support monies. A similar government program under the Equal Economic Opportunity Act of 1972 requires employers, labor unions and unemployment agencies to actively seek out minority and women candidates for employment in order to eliminate existing imbalances. Discrimination in employment practices was first outlawed by Title VII of the 1964 Civil Rights Act, but that legislation did not address the problems of past discrimination. Sometimes the term Benign Discrimination is used to describe Affirmative Action programs. This means that a minority group member is being selected discriminatorily but that the purpose of the discrimination is to aid a minority group member rather than to be invidious. Sometimes the method of such Benign Discrimination is by the use of racial quotas whereby certain levels of minority hiring or admissions are required, generally by a government agency, or are voluntarily adhered to by the institution involved. Serious constitutional challenges have been raised to Affirmative Action programs. Some scholars maintain that the Fourteenth Amendment's Equal Protection Clause is color blind and prohibits racial discrimination practiced against the majority as well as against a minority. Others argue that the purpose of the Equal Protection Clause is only to protect discrete and insular minorities who are unable to protect themselves by resort to the political process, while majority groups need no such protection because they can make their will known and protect themselves through the democratic process. In 1973 it appeared that the Supreme Court would render a decision on the benign use of racial criteria in special University admissions programs. In *Defunis v. Odegaard*, 416 U.S. 312 (1974), the petitioner claimed that he had been unconstitutionally denied admission to the University of Washington law school by use of an admissions program which gave preference to minority applicants over better qualified white applicants. However, the Court found the case to be moot because DeFunis had been attending the law school while the litigation was in progress and was ready to graduate. Justice Douglas was the only member of the Court courageous enough to render an opinion on the merits of the case. He strongly criticized racial considerations in admissions programs but also stated that there were possible cultural biases in the admissions process and suggested that the case be remanded for a new trial to decide, in part, if reliance on the L.S.A.T. (Law School Admissions Test) scores was inappropriate for minority group applicants. Supreme Court ruling in *Regents of the University of California v. Bakke*, 434 U.S. 810 (1978), which allowed race to be taken into account by admissions offices of educational institutions so long as Affirmative Action plans do not involve rigid numerical quotas. The Court ordered Allan Bakke, a white applicant, to be admitted to the fall class at Davis Medical School, while approving the principle of Affirmative Action programs designed to improve education and job opportunities for minorities and women. While the *Bakke* Ruling is narrowly applicable only to admissions programs, commentators have viewed this case as the Supreme Court's most important pronouncement on race since *Brown v. Board of Education,* 347 U.S. 483 (1954), and some see it as an expression of growing sentiment that government intervention cannot solve all social problems. In 1979, the Supreme Court ruled against *Brian Weber* in his reverse-discrimination lawsuit against the Kaiser Corporation. He had filed his suit when two Blacks with less seniority were picked ahead of him for a program to train semiskilled workers for higher-paying jobs. He charged that the affirmative-action plan violated Title VII of the 1964 Civil Rights Act, which bans employment discrimination based on race. But the Supreme Court rejected his argument, holding that Title VII was designed to improve opportunities for Blacks. Thus, the Kaiser employment program, which includes a quota system, does not violate the law.

AFFIRMATIVE DEFENSE. A defense to a charge of criminal activity, which places the burden of proof on the defendant. Examples of Affirmative Defenses include insanity, self-defense and intoxication. In some jurisdictions, the burden placed on the defendant is one of merely initially producing the relevant evidence. In other jurisdictions, the burden of persuasion is placed on the defendant. Often the burden amounts to establishing the defense by a preponderance of the evidence, but the Supreme Court has held that it is not a denial of due process for a state to require a defendant to prove insanity beyond a reasonable doubt.

A.F.G.E. (American Federation of Government Employees). A union, associated with the AFL-CIO, representing more than half the government's blue and white collar workers. The A.F.G.E. is strongly opposed to Civil Service reforms proposed by President Carter which may increase the possibility of being fired from a government job.

A.F.M. (American Federation of Musicians). A powerful union which negotiates employment contracts in such fields as recording, live entertainment, motion pictures, television, and advertising. The A.F.M. issues several booklets covering employer-employee relations. For example, "Booklet B" covers tours in the United States and "Booklet F" covers foreign tours.

A FORTIORI (Latin—with strong reason). Used to denote a point of logic that if one fact is proven to exist, another fact which is included within the primary fact or analogous to it, and which is less improbable than the primary fact, must also exist. In modern usage it means "all the more so."

AFRICA LEGAL ASSISTANCE PROJECT. Provides legal assistance to victims of racial repression in South Africa and to individuals and organizations in the United States working to promote human rights in South Africa. The Project is a branch of the Lawyers' Committee for Civil Rights Under Law and has developed considerably since it was first founded in the early 70s. The Committee has increasingly directed its efforts toward heightening the awareness of lawyers to the critical role of law in white-ruled Africa. It promotes involvement on the part of the professions in the United States and elsewhere.

AFRICAN NATIONAL CONGRESS. See A.N.C.

AGE DISCRIMINATION IN EMPLOYMENT. See A.D.E.A.

AGENCY FOR INTERNATIONAL DEVELOPMENT. See A.I.D.

AGENCY SHOP. See UNION SHOP.

AGENT ORANGE VICTIMS INTERNATIONAL. An organization formed by Paul Reutershan and other veterans who were exposed to "agent orange," a powerful chemical sprayed by the Air Force in Vietnam to defoliate the land and thereby make guerilla warfare more difficult for the Vietcong. In law suits which they filed against the United States and the Dow Chemical Company which manufactured "agent orange," they claimed damages for having developed cancer from the chemical.

AGENT PROVOCATEUR. A secret agent or undercover man; one employed to associate and sympathize with a suspected group for the purpose of inciting them to some illegal or harmful action, exposing them to apprehension and punishment.

AGGRAVATED BATTERY. Generally a battery that (1) results in serious physical injury; (2) is carried out with a deadly weapon; or (3) is perpetrated on a woman, a child or a police officer. Such crimes are usually punished with stiffer penalties than those imposed for ordinary batteries.

AGGRAVATED KIDNAPPING. Generally a kidnapping to obtain ransom or to commit other crimes, including sexual assault of the victim. Kidnapping a child is often considered Aggravated Kidnapping.

AGGRAVATED ROBBERY. Generally, robbery committed with a deadly weapon.

AGGRESSIVE PAYMENT. See INTERNATIONAL CORPORATE BRIBERY.

AGNEW, SPIRO. Disbarred lawyer and the only Vice-President of the United States to resign from office voluntarily and in disgrace in October, 1973, after being indicted for federal tax evasion.

AGREEMENT ON PREVENTION OF HIGH-SEAS INCIDENTS OF 1972. An international agreement that provides measures to assure the safe navigation of ships and planes of the United States and Russia on or over the high seas.

A.I. See AMNESTY INTERNATIONAL.

A.I.A.W. See TITLE IX OF THE EDUCATION AMENDMENTS OF 1972.

A.I.D. (Agency for International Development). A federal agency within the Department of State, which carries out assistance programs designed to help the people of certain less-developed countries develop their human and economic resources, increase their productive capacities, and improve the quality of human life, as well as to promote economic or political stability in friendly countries. Our foreign aid program began after World War II in a speech Secretary of State George Marshall gave at Harvard University, in which he spoke of our duty to rehabilitate the lands of both our enemies and allies of World War II. It was a generous gesture without precedent in recorded history. The first such program was named the Marshall Plan. Its successors have had various other names such as F.O.A. (Foreign Operations Administration) and I.C.A. (International Co-operation Administration).

A.I.D. See ARTIFICIAL INSEMINATION DONOR.

AID TO FAMILIES WITH DEPENDENT CHILDREN. See A.F.D.C.

A.I.H. See ARTIFICIAL INSEMINATION HUSBAND.

A.I.M. (American Indian Movement). A radical group whose activist efforts to lobby for the protection by law of the rights of American Indians and the elimination of all legal and illegal discrimination against them has occasionally resulted in violence.

AIR FORCE INTELLIGENCE. See UNITED STATES INTELLIGENCE GATHERING CENTERS.

AIRLINE BUMPING. The Civil Aeronautics Board requires airlines that are overbooked first to ask for volunteers to be bumped in exchange for a payment to be set by the airline. If there are not enough volunteers, those who were asked to volunteer but refused can be denied passage, but can recover denied boarding compensation. They must be paid the face value of their ticket up to $200 and put on another flight to their destination within two hours of the original departure. If this cannot be done, they must be paid double the ticket value up to $400. Foreign airline carriers are not covered by this rule.

AIRLINE DEREGULATION ACT OF 1978. A federal law which, among other things, in the elimination of control by the federal government over airlines provided for the automatic expansion of airlines by allowing each one to apply for one new route for each of three years.

AIRPLANE LAW. When your plane is late, the plane you are trying to catch leaves on time. By M. Stanton Evans, in *The Wall Street Journal*, February 20, 1975.

AIR QUALITY ACT (1967). Federal legislation which authorizes the Department of Health, Education and Welfare to establish interstate agencies to investigate and control air pollution.

AIR RIGHTS. Part of the bundle of property rights associated with the ownership of land which apply to the air above its surface. It is clear, for instance, that overhanging trees or buildings constitute a Trespass to Land. Less clear is just how high the possessory right extends above the property. While courts will generally not protect a landowner from aircraft flights at normal altitudes above his property, courts offer differing amounts of protection in that sensitive area of property rights associated with low-flying aircraft near airports.

A.I.S. (Adoptees in Search). A nonprofit volunteer organization founded to assist adopted adults who wish to ascertain the identity of their natural parents. It is part of the *Roots* movement. Although a handful of American states by statute give adoptees access to court records for this purpose, the rest of the Nation seals the records. The Supreme Court refused to open the state records as a matter of constitutional right in 1978.

A.L.A.R.A. See STEAM GENERATION JUMPERS.

ALASKA COALITION. An organization composed of 40 separate groups which lobbies actively and successfully at the local, national and international levels to protect the wilderness and environmental interests of our northernmost state.

ALASKA NATIVE CLAIMS SETTLEMENT ACT. See NATIVE CLAIMS ACT OF 1971.

ALASKAN NATIONAL INTEREST LANDS CONSERVATION ACT. A proposed federal bill which would determine how much of America's last frontier is to be protected. At stake is an area larger than the state of California.

ALBERTSON v. SUBVERSIVE ACTIVITIES CONTROL BOARD. See SUBVERSIVE ACTIVITIES CONTROL BOARD.

ALCOHOL SAFETY ACTION PROGRAM. See A.S.A.P.

ALEATORY CONTRACT (Latin — aleator: gambler). An agreement that depends on an uncertain event or contingency.

ALEXANDER, SADIE. First Black woman lawyer to earn a Doctorate of Laws degree. Still active in the practice of law after a half-century at the Bar, in 1981 she will chair the White House Conference on Aging.

A.L.I. See AMERICAN LAW INSTITUTE.

ALIAS OPERATION. Sponsored by the Federal Department of Justice, it encourages and protects endangered witnesses who testify against organized crime by relocating them and their families with new identities, including names, birth certificates, Social Security numbers, drivers' licenses and passports. The program has been a success although several participants have been tracked down and assassinated by the "Mob" and others have reverted to their former criminal careers.

ALIAS SUMMONS. A second summons issued when the first summons cannot be served.

ALIEN AND SEDITION LAWS. Congressional Acts in 1798 which provided criminal penalties for critics of the government or its officials, and which authorized presidential deportation of undesirable aliens. The Federalist Party sponsored the laws in an attempt to silence public criticism of the Adams Administration. About twenty-five people suffered imprisonment or fines under the laws, which contributed to the Federalists' defeat in the presidential elections of 1800. Thomas Jefferson, the new President, pardoned the critics convicted under the laws. The laws, which were repealed between 1800 and 1801.

ALIEN REGISTRATION ACT OF 1940. See SMITH ACT.

A.L.J. See ADMINISTRATIVE LAW JUDGE.

ALLEN INSTRUCTION. A jury instruction given in criminal cases when the jury is deadlocked in order to persuade jury members to reach a verdict. Minority jurors are instructed to re-examine their positions in light of the majority's view, and, in some courts, they are told to consider the expense and inconvenience of a retrial. Although approved by the Supreme Court in 1896, the instruction has been the subject of much controversy and twenty-three states have disapproved it. The Supreme Court of California has criticized the instruction as telling the jury to consider matters irrelevant to the issues to be decided and as circumventing a defendant's right under state law to a unanimous jury verdict.

ALLGEYER v. LOUISIANA (165 U.S. 578 (1897)). A Supreme Court case involving a Louisiana statute prohibiting anyone from doing an act in the state to affect insurance on any Louisiana property from any marine insurance company which has not complied with Louisiana law. The Court invalidated the statute on the ground that it infringed upon liberty of contract without due process of law. *Allgeyer* illustrates the Court's adherence to substantive due process, a view which it has since abandoned.

ALLIANCE FOR DISPLACED HOME-MAKERS. Formed by Tish Sommers and Laurie Shields in 1975 in recognition of startling statistics that an American woman has a fifty-fifty chance of being divorced or widowed in her middle age. She then finds herself too young for Social Security, too old to be hired, and not eligible for welfare or unemployment insurance. With federal funding, these organizations around the country provide counselling and assistance for these women, especially to help them obtain employment.

ALLOCUTION RIGHT. Permits defendants to speak in their own behalf in criminal cases prior to sentencing and to present any information in mitigation of punishment. This is an ancient right, long recognized under the common law. It is expressly granted to a defendant by Rule 32(a) of the Federal Rules of Criminal Procedure.

ALLODIAL OWNERSHIP. Possession of real property by individuals. In certain periods of time, such as the Middle Ages, individuals were not permitted to own real property.

ALLOWABLE COST. With respect to federal government contracts, this term refers to those incurred expenses which the government deems acceptable for payment. For example, in Department of Defense contracting an allowable cost is one which is reasonable, allocable to the contract in question, in consonance with standards promulgated by the Cost Accounting Standards Board (if applicable), or otherwise in harmony with generally accepted accounting principles, in compliance with the requirements of the Defense Acquisition Regulation Section XV, and in accord with contractual provisions.

ALL-RISK INSURANCE. A misleading term used to describe a type of insurance policy which provides protection against all fortuitous losses, except those specifically excluded. It is misleading in that no insurance policy covers every conceivable peril. For a loss to come within the coverage of such a policy, it must result from a fortuitous event and it must not be caused by an excluded peril. At the other end of the spectrum is Named-Peril Insurance which provides protection only for losses caused by the perils listed in the policy.

As the protection accorded by All-Risk Insurance is much broader than Named-Peril Insurance, the premium is typically higher.

A.L.M.A. (Adoptee's Liberty Movement Association). A national private organization which helps adopted children to locate their natural parents and lobbies with state legislatures to unseal the three basic documents of birth certificates, court records and adoption agency records.

A.L.R. (American Law Reports). A selective annotated reporter of important appellate court decisions. Begun in 1919, the A.L.R. system was designed to report and annotate only those cases which the editors thought would become "leading" or significant cases. The heart of A.L.R. consists of the annotations which follow each reported decision. The annotations are expository essays on the significant legal topics contained in the decision. In addition to the commentary on selected legal topics, the annotations discuss and cite all previously reported state and federal decisions on those topics. In short, A.L.R. is a useful introduction to most important topics in the law as well as a comprehensive case-finding tool. The A.L.R. set is only a part of a larger family of interrelated legal reference books, known as "The Total Client Service Library." A.L.R. itself has gone through three editions: A.L.R. covers the period 1919-1948; A.L.R.2d covers 1948-1965; and A.L.R.3d covers 1965 to date. In 1969, a new service, A.L.R. Fed., began reporting and annotating important federal cases in the same manner, although federal cases continue to be reported in A.L.R.3d. There are basically three ways to find cases in A.L.R.: the table of cases, the fact approach (through the A.L.R. "Quick Index" volume), or the analytical topic-headings in the A.L.R. Digest. In order to provide updated service as to cases reported after an annotation was published, the editors published a Blue Book of Supplemental Decisions to A.L.R. and a Later Case Service for A.L.R.2d. With A.L.R.3d, however, each volume has an annual cumulative pocket supplement. Finally, it should be noted that the newer A.L.R. volumes occasionally provide supplementary or superseding annotations, which are indexed in the A.L.R.2d and 3d Quick Indexes.

A.L.R. DIGESTS. A set of analytical topic-heading indexes designed to accompany A.L.R. and A.L.R.2d. The Digests were discontinued with A.L.R. 3d in 1965, in favor of the more compact "Quick Indexes," which began with A.L.R.2d. The Digests to A.L.R. and A.L.R.2d have no word index. Some paragraphs in the Digest refer to annotations while others do not, because all points of law in A.L.R. cases are digested but only the important ones are annotated. The publication of the Quick Indexes in compact, alphabetical form, subdivided into topics, facts and annotation titles, made case-finding much simpler and rendered the Digests largely obsolete although the A.L.R. Digest continues to be useful since there is no Quick Index to A.L.R.

ALTERNATIVE MORTGAGE INSTRUMENT. See G.P.M.

AMBULANCE CHASING. Term of derision describing the over-eager lawyer who follows ambulances to the scene of an accident in order to pass out his professional cards to obtain employment. Such direct solicitation violates the Canons of Ethics of the legal profession and may result in suspension or disbarment of a lawyer.

AMBULATORY WILL. Unless fixed by contract, a will may be changed by the testator at any time before his death. Thus, every will, unless fixed by contract, is said to be "ambulatory."

AMERICAN ACADEMY OF MATRIMONIAL LAWYERS. Organization of lawyers specializing in matrimonial and family law which seeks to elevate the standards and improve the practice and study of matrimonial law.

AMERICAN ARBITRATION ASSOCIATION (A.A.A.). Organization to foster the use of arbitration in settling disputes, composed of labor unions, civic groups, businesses, and individuals interested in arbitration. The A.A.A. publishes monthly, *Arbitration in the Schools, Labor Arbitration in Government,* and *Summary of Labor Arbitration Awards;* and publishes quarterly a *Digest of Court Decisions.*

AMERICAN ASSEMBLY. A public affairs forum, affiliated with Columbia University, founded in 1950 by former President Dwight D. Eisenhower when he was head of Columbia. It holds conferences for law, business, government and academic leaders at home and abroad and publishes books and reports.

AMERICAN ASSOCIATION FOR THE COMPARATIVE STUDY OF LAW. (A.A.C.S.L.). Established in 1951 to encourage an understanding of foreign legal systems. It is composed of several dozen American law schools and corporations, who sponsor research and publications in the field, including a quarterly periodical entitled *American Journal of Comparative Law.*

AMERICAN ASSOCIATION OF LAW LIBRARIES (A.A.L.L.). Founded in 1906. According to its constitution, A.A.L.L. "is established for educational and scientific purposes . . . to promote librarianship, to develop and increase the usefulness of law libraries, to cultivate the science of law librarianship and to foster a spirit of cooperation among the members of the profession." The Association was incorporated under the laws of the District of Columbia in 1939 and now has 13 regional geographic chapters, each of which has considerable autonomy in its direction and financial management. The Association is governed through an eleven-member board. Following debate at the Association's 1975 and 1976 conventions, an internal reorganization was approved under a new bylaw which provides for creation of new "Special Interest Sections" by the A.A.L.L. Executive Board. These sections initially will be project-oriented and should derive their activity from what are now several large committees. The Association has maintained a headquarters office in Chicago since 1965 that is responsible for the administra-

tion of routine Association business. Any person or institution interested in law libraries may become a member of the Association by complying with the provisions of the bylaws.

AMERICAN BAR ASSOCIATION (A.B.A.). A national organization of attorneys admitted to the bar in any state. The A.B.A. is the unofficial spokesman for all lawyers, since more than half of the 500,000 lawyers in the United States belong to it. The A.B.A. was founded in 1878, by 75 lawyers from New York, New England, and the South, under the leadership of Simeon E. Baldwin of Connecticut, who gathered in the elegant resort of Saratoga Springs to escape the summer heat, watch the horse races, and uphold the honor of the legal profession. Its publications include the monthly *American Bar Association Journal* and *American Bar News.* The governing body of the A.B.A. is its House of Delegates, which has representatives from all the states. In addition to playing an active role in law reform and continuing legal education, the A.B.A. is the sole accreditation agency for the approval of law schools, it acts as a clearing house for nominees to the federal courts, and it was the sponsor of the Canons of Professional Responsibility for lawyers and judges. In brief, the A.B.A. is the most powerful association of lawyers in the United States, if not the entire world.

AMERICAN BAR ASSOCIATION CENTER FOR PROFESSIONAL DISCIPLINE. See NATIONAL DISCIPLINE DATA BANK.

AMERICAN BAR FOUNDATION (A.B.F.). Research affiliate of the American Bar Association which has made comprehensive studies of class action suits, the criminal justice system, prepaid legal service plans, arbitration and dispute settlement, and delivery of legal services.

AMERICAN BLIND LAWYERS ASSOCIATION (A.B.L.A.). Established in 1969, it is a group of more than 100 American blind lawyers and law students. Its purpose is to aid the blind in the study and practice of law, including the production and dissemination of legal materials in braille or recorded form.

AMERICAN COLLEGE OF PROBATE COUNSEL. An international association of lawyers organized for the purpose of improving probate practices and procedures throughout the United States.

AMERICAN DIGEST SYSTEM. Covers all decisions published in all West reporters. It digests close to three million decisions and adds approximately thirty thousand more every year. The system is divided into nine multi-volume units, each of which covers the cases reported in the United States during a particular period of time: Century Digest (1658-1896), First Decennial (1896-1906), Second Decennial (1906-1916), Third Decennial (1916-1926), Fourth Decennial (1926-1936), Fifth Decennial (1936-1946), Sixth Decennial (1946-1956), Seventh Decennial (1956-1966) and General Digest, 4th Series (1966 to date). Each of the units is essentially independent of the other except they are tied together with the key number indexing scheme.

AMERICAN ENTERPRISE INSTITUTE FOR PUBLIC POLICY RESEARCH. An ultra-conservative non-profit organization headquartered in Washington, D.C., devoted to instructing the public in the benefits of capitalism. Among other things, it offers a professional base for ex-politicians in their adjustment to private life.

AMERICAN FEDERATION OF GOVERNMENT EMPLOYEES. See A.F.G.E.

AMERICAN FEDERATION OF MUSICIANS. See A.F.M.

AMERICAN FOREIGN SERVICE ASSOCIATION. An organization which functions as a trade union for the 10,000 Foreign Service employees and as a professional association for the 6,000 active and retired career officers. Among other activities to protect and promote the best interest of those who present and represent our foreign policy at home and abroad, it publishes the *Foreign Service Journal.*

AMERICAN HELSINKI WATCH COMMITTEE. A 40-member non-governmental monitoring unit for human rights in the United States. It was formed in New York City in 1979 with a grant from the Ford Foundation upon the recommendation of Arthur J. Goldberg, former Supreme Court Justice, American Ambassador to the United Nations and leader of the American delegation to the follow-up conference on the Helsinki Accords held in Belgrade in 1977, in which 35 nations agreed to guarantee freedom of thought, conscience, religion, speech, writing, travel and re-unification of families.

AMERICAN INDIAN MOVEMENT. See A.I.M.

AMERICAN INSTITUTE IN TAIWAN. Former members of the American Embassy in the Republic of China who, in a private civil capacity, represent and protect the American interests there since the break of diplomatic relations between the two countries upon the recognition of the People's Republic of China as the sole official Chinese government.

AMERICAN JOURNAL OF COMPARATIVE LAW. See AMERICAN ASSOCIATION FOR THE COMPARATIVE STUDY OF LAW.

ANCILLARY JURISDICTION DOCTRINE. Allows a federal court to hear a suit which is closely related to another claim in which the court has original jurisdiction. Federal courts typically have ancillary jurisdiction over third-party claims.

AMERICAN JURISPRUDENCE. A comprehensive legal encyclopedia containing expository statements of law, alphabetically arranged under 426 titles. It covers both substantive and procedural law. While *Corpus Juris Secundum* cites all reported decisions in support of its textual statement of the law, *American Jurisprudence* cites only selective decisions in its footnotes, but also gives citations to *American Law*

Reports, a sister publication. *American Jurisprudence* was first published in 1936, and it was kept current by pocket supplements. In 1962, the publishers of this encyclopedia created a complete new edition called *American Jurisprudence 2d* which is not yet finished.

AMERICAN LAW INSTITUTE (A.L.I.). Perhaps the one organization which has contributed the most to the continuing development and improvement of the substantive law. Founded in 1923, and composed of judges, law professors, and practitioners of national repute, the A.L.I. is probably best known for its *Restatements of Law* which have gained such recognition that they are considered the law in some jurisdictions. Before the first *Restatement of Law* in 1944, lawyers often had to find, read, and synthesize the decisions of myriad courts before an opinion could be rendered on a particular subject. The *Restatements* have considerably lessened this task. The A.L.I. also prepared the Model Penal Code, and, in conjunction with the National Conference of Commissioners on Uniform State Laws, drafted the Uniform Commercial Code.

AMERICAN LAW JOURNAL. The oldest American legal periodical. Strangely enough, it was started not by a lawyer but by a Professor of Rhetoric named John Elihu Hall at the University of Maryland in 1806.

AMERICAN LAW REPORTS. See A.L.R.

AMERICAN LAWYER. National bi-weekly newspaper started in 1978 with gossipy articles for lawyers about lawyers and the practice of law.

AMERICAN PARENTS COMMITTEE. A non-profit, nonpartisan public service organization which works for federal legislation on behalf of children. It also rates Congressmen based on how they voted on key children's issues.

AMERICAN SYSTEM. See CLAY, HENRY.

AMERICAN SELLING PRICE. A system, disliked by foreign manufacturers, by which the tariff paid on goods shipped to the United States is based not on the price of the imported merchandise as it comes into this country but rather on the prevailing price here for similar American-made merchandise.

AMERICANS FOR VOLUNTARY OBSERVANCE OF LAW. See A.V.O.L.

AMERICAN PARTY OF TEXAS v. WHITE (415 U.S. 767 (1974)). A Supreme Court case concerning ballot access barriers to independent candidates and small political parties. The Court concluded that the validity of qualifications for ballot positions depends on whether the qualifications are necessary to further compelling state interests.

AMERICA'S SOCIETY FOR DIVORCED MEN (A.S.D.M.). Advocate group for divorced men which helps its members deal with alimony, child support and custody, and provides referrals to attorneys adept at championing men in divorce proceedings.

A.M.I. See G.P.M.

AMICUS BRIEF. See AMICUS CURIAE.

AMICUS CURIAE (Latin—friend of the court). Individuals or groups who are not parties to litigation, but are nevertheless permitted to present their views to the court. The court exercises its discretion in determining whether to grant permission to participate Amicus Curiae or in fact to request the participation of an individual or group. Amicus representation is both most appropriate and most important when the issues before the court will affect the rights of persons other than those directly involved in the litigation and non-parties can offer valuable argument concerning the implications of a case. For example, the American Civil Liberties Union (A.C.L.U.) and the National Association for the Advancement of Colored People (N.A.A.C.P.) often submit Amicus Briefs to the Supreme Court in cases involving individual or civil rights. In some state courts, an Amicus Curiae acts as a permanent advisor to judges in juvenile, divorce or criminal cases. The federal government enjoys the right to participate as Amicus when a case before the Supreme Court concerns federal policies.

AMNESTY INTERNATIONAL (A.I.). A worldwide organization founded by Sean McBride, former Prime Minister of Ireland, headquartered in London, England, a provision in whose constitution states that "every person has the right freely to hold and to express his convictions and the obligation to extend a like freedom to others. The objects of Amnesty International shall be to secure throughout the world observance of the provisions of Universal Declaration of Human Rights." Basically, Amnesty opposes unjust imprisonment, torture and capital punishment. Founded in the shadow of the crimes committed during the Second World War, A.I. works for the release of so-called "prisoners of conscience"—men and women who have been imprisoned because of their race, religion or political beliefs, but who have never advocated the use of violence. To date, A.I. has been associated with the release of 11,000 of 17,000 prisoners aided since 1961. Amnesty International received the 1977 Nobel Peace Prize for these accomplishments in monitoring violations of human rights around the world.

AMORTIZATION TABLE. Shows the principal and interest required to repay a loan in equal payments. For example, mortgage payments made early during the life of the mortgage represent large payments of interest and relatively small payments against the principal. As the loan matures, however, interest payments decrease and payments of principal increase.

ANACONDA MORTGAGE. See MOTHER HUBBARD CLAUSE.

ANATOMICAL GIFTS ACTS. Laws in several states which regulate donating the body or parts of the body after death. Most Acts require that the physician certifying death shall not participate in procedures for removing or transplanting a part. The popular movie, *Coma,* which portrayed mercenary physicians who caused the premature death of their patients in order to market parts of their bodies, has chilled the popularity of such donations.

A.N.C. (African National Congress). A banned Black Nationalist political organization in South Africa, which advocates termination of the apartheid policies and practices of the government which protects White minority rule and makes the majority Blacks second-class citizens. Its leader, 60-year-old Nelson Mandela, has been in jail since 1963, serving a life sentence along with 350 others for subversion. To keep them docile, these political prisoners are denied access to radio, television, magazines and newspapers. *Spear of the Nation* is the sabotage arm of the A.N.C. in acts of violence against the Government.

ANCIENT DOCTRINE OF LIGHTS. Old English doctrine that the "owner" of a view possessed an easement for light and air across neighboring lots, which prevented his neighbors from erecting any structure that would interfere with his view. One did not "own" a view until a certain statutory period had elapsed, so spite fences were often erected for the express purpose of cutting off a neighbor's view, and thus insuring the right to erect future buildings on one's land. This rule is not in effect in the United States.

ANCIENT DOCUMENTS AFFECTING PROPERTY. See EXCEPTIONS TO HEARSAY RULE.

ANCILLARY TRUSTEE. The person who administers that portion of the settlor's property which is located outside the state of the settlor's domicile.

A.N.C.S.A. See NATIVE CLAIMS ACT OF 1971.

ANGKD LOEU. See ORGANIZATION ON HIGH.

ANIMUS ET FACTUS (Latin—intention and deed). The phrase describes those acts which are legally significant only when accompanied by a particular intention, such as the change of one's domiciliary state (to establish residence with the intention of remaining permanently).

ANNUAL CORPORATE REPORT. A formal financial statement required by the Securities and Exchange Commission of most major corporations. The yearly report is sent by the corporation to its shareholders identifying its assets, liabilities and earnings in addition to major new activities, future plans and an announcement of the annual stockholders' meeting.

ANNUITY BOND. A bond which has no maturity date so that it continues to accumulate interest.

ANNUITY POLICY. Provides that money invested will be repaid with interest at a future date in a series of periodic payments. Many individuals purchase such policies in anticipation of their retirement. Since annuity payments may continue for the duration of a person's life, the retiree who lives a long life has made a wise investment. On the other hand, the retiree who dies before he has had the opportunity to recoup the amount of money he invested has lost his gamble. Annuity payments receive tax advantages.

ANTARCTIC TREATY. Antarctica was given the status of No State's Land by the Washington International Treaty signed on October 1, 1959. It became effective in 1961. The terms of the Treaty, by prohibiting the acquisition of territory on the Antarctic continent by the signatories, for a period of at least thirty years, constitute a major exception to the international law concerning No State's Land. Referring to the Charter of the United Nations, the Treaty provides for an exclusively peaceful and scientific exploitation of the Antarctica, and forbids any military activity or bases. Moreover, as long as the Treaty is in effect, all existing claims to Antarctica are frozen and future claims prohibited.

ANTENUPTIAL CONTRACT. An agreement by which the parties to a marriage seek to vary their rights and duties before the marriage is solemnized. To be enforceable, such contracts must meet a much higher standard of fairness than business contracts because the parties are not considered to be dealing at arm's length. The court assumes that there is a relationship of confidence and trust between the parties, and thus it protects the party relinquishing rights. Most states require Antenuptial Contracts to be in writing. Contracts dealing with the distribution of property at death are generally upheld. Most states will not uphold a contract dealing with distribution of property upon divorce for fear that such agreements encourage divorce. Also, agreements dealing with waiver of support obligations and agreements dealing with sexual practices, agreements to raise a child in a particular religion or to send the child to a particular school have not been upheld. In short, courts have not favored Antenuptial Contracts. Such contracts have usually been of value generally to couples entering second and third marriages who wish to insure that upon their death their children by earlier marriages will inherit. Today Antenuptial Agreements are growing more popular, in part because women are less likely to be totally dependent upon their husbands.

ANTHONY, SUSAN B. Early twentieth-century suffragist whose image is on the new $1 coin, instead of the symbolic Miss Liberty, making her the first American woman to be so honored.

ANTICIPATORY BREACH. A repudiation of contractual duty before the time such duty must be performed.

ANTICIPATORY OFFENSE. See IN-CHOATE CRIME.

ANTI-DEFICIENCY ACT. The heart of the Anti-Deficiency Act, codified at 31 U.S.C. 665(a) (1976) provides that:

No officer or employee of the United States shall make or authorize an expenditure from or create or authorize an obligation under any appropriation or fund in excess of the amount available therein; nor shall any such officer or employee involve the Government in any contract or other obligation, for the payment of money for any purpose, in advance of appropriations made for such purpose, unless such contract or obligation is authorized by law.

The principal effect of the Act is to prevent federal government purchasing officers from contractually binding the United States before adequate funds have been made available pursuant to congressional appropriation.

ANTI-DUMPING LAWS. Federal trade legislation, first passed in 1921 and since amended, which makes it illegal for a foreign producer to sell his products in the United States at a price below the full cost of production which renders homemade American products uncompetitive. Foreign manufacturers dump their merchandise abroad for various reasons. One is to open a market. Another is to keep their plants in full operation during slack times and thus in effect export their unemployment to the United States. Whenever the Secretary of the Treasury determines that foreign merchandise is to be sold in the United States or elsewhere, he informs the United States International Trade Commission, which determines whether or not the sale will injure a United States industry. If the purchase price or exporter's sale price is less than the foreign market value, a "dumping" tax is levied in addition to other duties to bring the price of the product up to market value.

ANTI-FRAUD RULE. See RULE 10B-5.

ANTI-GAY. See GAY RIGHTS LAW.

ANTI-HEART BALM STATUTES. Legislation in a number of states to remedy abuses connected with breach of promise and other actions concerning the marital relationship. Such abuses were well illustrated in England by Charles Dickens, whose Mr. Pickwick was incarcerated in The Fleet, a debtor's prison, for failure to satisfy a judicial award for breach of promise to his housekeeper, Mrs. Bardell. The judgment had been rendered on the most outlandish of circumstantial testimony. The general pattern of Anti-Heart Balm

Statutes is either to abolish certain actions such as breach of promise to marry, alienation of affections, seduction and criminal conversation, or to impose safeguards for the defendant: e.g., a requirement of substantial corroboration of the plaintiff's testimony, limitation of the amount of damages which can be awarded, or reduction of the time period during which such actions can be brought.

ANTI-INJUNCTION ACT. A statutory prohibition, first enacted in 1793, against the issuance of injunctions by federal courts to stay proceedings pending in any state court. The Anti-Injunction Act, revised in 1948 and now codified as Section 2283 of the United States Code, reads: "A court of the United States may not grant an injunction to stay proceedings in a State Court except as expressly authorized by Act of Congress, or where necessary in aid of its jurisdiction, or to protect or effectuate its judgments." Despite obscure reasons for the adoption of the statute, it has played an important role in the federal system by preventing needless friction between federal and state courts. An express statutory exception was added in 1875, for cases where the bankruptcy laws authorized such an injunction. Until the 1940s, however, the Act's effectiveness was diminished by narrow interpretation and various judge-made exceptions to the rule. Recent cases, as well as the 1948 revision, have clarified the parameters of the Section 2283 rule and its exceptions to some degree, but it is still not well settled under what special circumstances a federal court may enjoin state court proceedings to prevent irreparable injury.

ANTI-JOHN LAW. Criminal punishment of fine and imprisonment on clients (Johns) of prostitutes.

ANTI-LAPSE STATUTES. Permit the heirs of a person who predeceases a testator to take the property which should have been inherited by the decedent. Such statutes were enacted in most states to protect grandchildren who under common law would be disinherited if a parent predeceased a grandparent.

ANTI-MERGER LAW. See CONGLOMERATE MERGER BILL.

ANTI-MISCEGENATION STATUTE. Prohibits intermarriage by members of different races. Although such statutes usually contemplate black-white couples, they often prohibit marriages between Caucasians and Orientals, American Indians, and Latinos. The rationales typically offered in defense of such statutes were genetic (to guard against inferior offspring) and religious (the Bible frowned upon interracial relationships). At one time or another, forty states have had these statutes in effect, with violators being subject to criminal prosecution resulting in imprisonment and fines. Not until 1967, in *Loving v. Virginia*, 386 U.S. 952 (1967), did the United States Supreme Court declare Anti-Miscegenation Laws unconstitutional.

ANTI-MISSIONARY LAW. Israeli law which proscribes inducing an Israeli to change his religion on penalty of a $3,200 fine and five years in prison. By official record, only 17 Israeli Jews were converted to Christianity from 1974 to 1976, though considerably more are suspected of joining the 80,000 Christians now living in Israel.

ANTI-NEPOTISM. See CLOSE RELATIVE RULE.

ANTI-PARASITE LAW. Soviet law which punishes persons who do not contribute to socially useful work. In 1963, for example, Joseph Broadsky was given a five-year term of "educative" labor for the crime of writing poetry.

ANTI-POVERTY ACT (Economic Opportunity Act of 1964). A federal act designed to correct the conditions, such as illiteracy and unemployment, which result in chronic poverty. To assist the poor in urban and rural areas, the Act authorized ten programs under the direction of the Office of Economic Opportunity. For example, the Job Corps was aimed at providing occupational training and experience for the poverty-stricken.

ANTIQUITIES ACT. A federal law that authorizes executive designation of historic landmarks, prehistoric structures and objects of scientific or historic interest situated upon land owned or controlled by the United States as national monuments.

ANTI-RED-LINERS. See RED-LINING.

ANTI-SCALPING ORDINANCE. Prohibits the sale of tickets to sporting events at a greater price than that advertised by the manager of the event. Such laws are of questionable validity and several state supreme courts have held them invalid on constitutional or public interest grounds.

ANTI-SKID ROW ORDINANCE. A zoning ordinance designed to maintain or improve the quality of a neighborhood by prohibiting certain businesses of the same type in one geographical area if such businesses tend to attract an undesirable quantity and quality of transients, adversely affect property values, increase crime, especially prostitution, and encourage residents and businesses to move elsewhere. Regulated uses in Anti-Skid Row statutes generally include adult theaters or bookstores.

ANTI-SNOB ZONING LAW (1969). Regulation in Massachusetts requiring towns and cities to permit construction of low and moderate income housing if it is needed by the residents of the region. The law mandates changing exclusionary zoning laws which prevent construction of needed low and moderate income housing.

ANTI-SUBSTITUTION LAWS. State laws that require the pharmacist to "dispense as written." They prohibit a pharmacist from substituting a different brand name drug for the one prescribed, or from substituting a generic equivalent in place of a drug prescribed by brand name, even if the substitute is therapeutically equivalent to the drug prescribed and less expensive. Drug reimbursement programs such as the Maximum Allowable Cost Program, which limit reimbursement to the lowest cost at which the drug is available, will be more effective when they override Anti-Substitution Laws.

ANTI-TRUST ENFORCEMENT ACT OF 1979. See PFIZER AMENDMENT.

A.N.Z.U.S. A treaty of security and mutual assistance signed at San Francisco on September 1, 1951, by Australia, New Zealand, and the United States. The organization includes a council of foreign ministers. Military representatives have met several times to implement the military cooperation provided for in the treaty. Since the creation of S.E.A.T.O., the role of A.N.Z.U.S. has decreased.

A.O. See ADMINISTRATIVE OFFICE OF THE UNITED STATES COURTS.

A.P.A. See ADMINISTRATIVE PROCEDURE ACT.

APARTHEID POLICY. The segregation and separation by race in South Africa of people in every aspect of human relations in favor of the numerically fewer Whites.

APODACA v. OREGON (406 U.S. 404 (1972)). A plurality opinion by the Supreme Court which upheld the constitutionality of a state nonunanimous jury verdict. Under the Oregon system sustained in *Apodaca,* the vote of at least ten out of twelve jurors is required for conviction in noncapital cases.

APPRAISAL RIGHTS. A remedy which allows minority stockholders to withdraw from a corporation when the corporation takes an extraordinary action, such as a merger, which is against their interests. If minority stockholders so desire, the corporation is required to repurchase minority stock at a price equivalent to its value prior to the extraordinary corporate action.

APPROPRIATE BARGAINING UNIT. The employee group which is empowered to bargain collectively with its employer. The National Labor Relations Board determines the appropriateness of the unit in every election proceeding. The principal criteria used are mutuality of interest, history of collective bargaining, desires of employees and extent of employee organization.

APRIL REVOLUTION. The coup in Afghanistan in April, 1978, which ousted President Mohammad Daud and brought a pro-Soviet administration headed by Noor Mohammad Taraki to power. In turn, President Taraki was ousted by Hafizullah Amin, former Prime Minister, who said his takeover marked the "beginning of a better socialist order." However, Amin was ousted and he and his family were assassinated on December 26, 1979, in a coup by Babrak Karmal, former Deputy Prime Minister, with the military assistance of the Soviets.

A PRIORI (Latin—from what goes before). A method of logic that allows one to deduce certain effects from an admitted fact or principle.

APTHEKER v. SECRETARY OF STATE (378 U.S. 500 (1964)). A Supreme Court case that invalidated a provision denying passports to Communist Party members on the ground that it violated the liberty guaranteed by the Fifth Amendment.

AQUINAS, THOMAS. Medieval Roman Catholic theologian who made it clear in his classic treatise on law and justice of his *Summa Theologica* that when laws or legal systems are unjust one is morally released from a duty to obey them.

ARAB ANTI-BOYCOTT LAW. A federal statute which took effect on June 22, 1977. Since the birth of Israel as a sovereign nation in 1948, the Arabs have refused to knowingly do business with firms that trade with Israel, and they will not accept products that obviously are of Israeli origin. For example, Coca-Cola, which has had a bottling plant in Israel since 1967, still can't sell its products in the rest of the Mideast or North Africa where the 21 countries of the Arab League are located. Under the new American law, U.S. firms no longer may promise the

Arabs that they will deal with neither the Israelis nor companies that trade with the Jewish state. Also, they may not tell the Arabs about their business ties to such blacklisted companies. In 1977 alone, Arab countries paid U.S. firms $8 billion to purchase such things as computers, heavy machinery and construction help. During the same period, U.S. exports to Israel remained constant at $1.5 billion. It remains to be seen what long range effect the Anti-Boycott law will have on Arab-American trade.

ARAB LEAGUE. See UNITED ARAB LEAGUE.

ARBITRARY AND CAPRICIOUS TEST. See STANDARD OF REVIEW.

ARBITRATION CLAUSE. In international law, a provision in a treaty providing for arbitration to settle disputes that may arise when subsequently interpreting an international treaty. It may also be used in private commercial contracts.

ARBITRATION PROCESS. The settlement of a dispute between two parties by a mutually acceptable third party who is given the authority to render a binding decision. A typical dispute may involve a disagreement between a company and a labor union which has resulted in a strike. A decision of award in this context is a solution, which both sides have agreed in advance to accept, and the agreement to be bound by such a decision is known as a submission, except in international law, where it is known as a compromise.

ARIFAT, YASIR. See P.L.O.

ARGUMENTATIVE QUESTION. See MISLEADING QUESTION.

ARGERSINGER v. HAMLIN. See PUBLIC DEFENDER.

ARMED CONFLICT. See LAW OF WAR.

ARMED FORCES OF NATIONAL LIBERATION FOR PUERTO RICO. See F.A.L.N.

ARMED SERVICES BOARD OF CONTRACT APPEALS (A.S.B.C.A.). This judicial-type administrative board hears and decides disputes arising under the "disputes" clause of Department of Defense, Army, Navy, and Air Force contracts. Although originally established on 1 May 1949, pursuant to Department of Defense Directive No. 5154.17 (March 1962), the Board began operations under its current charter, effective 1 May 1962. The A.S.B.C.A. is designated as the authorized representative of the Secretary of Defense, the Secretary of the Army, the Secretary of the Navy, and the Secretary of the Air Force. The Board considers and decides appeals by contractors from decisions of contracting officers or other authorities on disputed questions. Although appeals pursuant to the "disputes" clause are limited to disputes concerning questions of fact, the Board may in its discretion hear, consider, and decide those questions of law necessary for the complete resolution of the appeal.

ARMED SERVICES PROCUREMENT REGULATION. See DEFENSE ACQUISITION REGULATION.

ARM'S LENGTH TRANSACTION. An agreement reached by parties who are generally in equal bargaining positions. Contracts involving relatives or persons in positions of trust are not arm's length transactions.

ARMY INTELLIGENCE. See UNITED STATES INTELLIGENCE-GATHERING CENTERS.

ARRAIGNMENT PROCEEDING. After the grand jury or the prosecutor decides to indict or to press criminal charges which are filed in court, the defendant must appear in court for an Arraignment. Here the defendant is formally charged. Either immediately or within a reasonable period of time thereafter a plea of "not guilty," "guilty" or "nolo contendere" must be entered.

ARREST WARRANT. A legal command or order issued in the name of the government directing that a specific person be taken into custody for a specific offense against the government and ordering that person to be brought before a court of competent jurisdiction for trial.

ART ADVISORY PANEL (A.A.P.). A private group of 12 independent art experts (respected museum directors, curators, dealers, and art historians) which meets several times a year to appraise works of art valued at $20,000 or more which have been given as gifts for tax purposes. Although their opinions have no force of law, the government usually accepts them.

ARTICLE 15 PUNISHMENT. See NON-JUDICIAL PUNISHMENT.

ARTICLES OF INCORPORATION (Certificate of Incorporation). A document filed in a state office of the Secretary of State which begins the legal existence of a corporation. Its contents, and often official forms, are prescribed by general incorporation statutes. Requirements typical of those in most states can be found in the Model Business Corporation Act. These include: (a) The name of the corporation; (b) The period of duration (may be perpetual); (c) The corporate purpose; (d) The number of authorized shares, and if they are to have par value, the value of the shares; (e) If they are to be no par stock, a statement to that effect must be included; (f) If there are to be classes of shares, those classes must be described; (g) If any preemptive rights are to be given to shareholders, there must be an appropriate provision in the articles; (h) The number of the board of directors; and (i) The name and address of each incorporator.

ARTICLES OF PARTNERSHIP. An instrument by which a partnership is organized upon the terms and conditions provided.

ARTICLE 29A SESSION. A preliminary session of a trial by court martial conducted out of the presence of the court members (jurors). Such a session may be held only where the trial is presided over by a military judge.

It is an integral part of the proceedings and may be called by the military judge to hear motions raising defenses and objections; to rule on the admissibility of evidence; to determine the desires of the accused regarding his option to request trial before the military judge alone; to hold arraignment, receive pleas, and enter findings of guilty, if a guilty plea is accepted; and to dispose of any other interlocutory matter not amounting to a trial of the accused's guilt and which is inappropriate for consideration before the court members. While generally the Article 29A Session precedes the assembly of the court members, such sessions may be called by the military judge at any time during the trial when he determines that in the interest of justice the things to be discussed would be dealt with better outside the presence of the court members.

ARTIFICIAL INSEMINATION DONOR (A.I.D.). A male whose sperm is used to impregnate a woman who is not his lawful wife. This method of artificial insemination, by far the most common, is used where the husband is sterile, where there is a chance of transmitting a genetic defect, or if there is an Rh incompatability between the husband and wife. An A.I.D. assumes none of the legal rights or responsibilities of paternity. The offspring is legitimate if the mother was married and her husband consented to the pregnancy. The donor gives semen to a sperm bank, which can keep it indefinitely through freezing.

ARTIFICIAL INSEMINATION HUSBAND (A.I.H.). If a husband's semen is used alone or mixed with that of a donor in artificial insemination, the practice is referred to as Artificial Insemination Husband.

ARTS AND ARTIFACTS INDEMNITY ACT (1975). A federal law that authorizes the Federal Council on the Arts and Humanities to enter into indemnity agreements against loss or damage with any person, nonprofit agency, institution, or government to cover eligible items while on exhibition in the United States, elsewhere, when part of an exchange of exhibitions. Eligible items include works of art; manuscripts; and photographs, motion pictures, or audio and video tapes; which are (A) of educational, cultural, historical, or scientific value, and (B) the exhibition of which is certified by the Secretary of State or his designee as being in the national interest. The Act sets a $50 million indemnity ceiling for any single exhibition and limits the total dollar amount of indemnity agreements which can be in effect at any one time to $250 million. The indemnity agreements are backed by the full faith and credit of the United States. In the event of damage, loss or theft of any of the indemnified items, the Federal Council certifies the validity of the claim and requests Congress to appropriate money for payment.

A.S.A.P. (Alcohol Safety Action Program). Provides that those individuals who are guilty of driving while drunk but are first offenders are given a suspended sentence after their conviction if they agree to attend a special educational and medical course of treatment.

A.S.B.C.A. See ARMED SERVICES BOARD OF CONTRACT APPEAL.

A.S.D.M. See AMERICA'S SOCIETY OF DIVORCED MEN.

A.S.E.A.N. (Association of South East Asian Nations). Formed in Bangkok in 1967 by Indonesia, Malaysia, Singapore, Thailand and the Philippines in order to achieve regional economic integration and cooperation on common political and international issues as a safeguard against the domino theory that if the Communists gained control of Vietnam, they would eventually take over Laos and Cambodia and then the A.S.E.A.N. nations.

ASHBACKER DOCTRINE. An administrative law rule derived from *Ashbacker Radio Corp. v. F.C.C.*, 326 U.S. 327 (1945). Under the *Ashbacker* doctrine, when two mutually exclusive applications for a license are filed, the agency is required to hold a compara-

tive hearing to determine which applicant is better qualified. In *Ashbacker,* the radio stations applied for licenses to broadcast on the same frequency. The F.C.C. granted the application of one station, which in effect denied the application of the other. Thus, one hearing had to be held to consider both applications.

ASIAN-AFRICAN CONFERENCE OF BANDUNG (April 10, 1955). Attempt to affirm the sovereignty and independence of Asiatic and African communist countries against the great Western powers. The Conference did not succeed in creating strong institutions. It was, however, the occasion of reaffirming the principles of peaceful coexistence first elaborated by China in 1954. The Ten Principles of Bandung stressed peaceful coexistence, racial equality, and pacific settlement of disputes through arbitration. The Conference represents a decisive step in the political awareness of its member countries.

ASIAN DEVELOPMENT BANK. See A.D.B.

ASPORTATION OF PROPERTY. A carrying away of all portions of personal property, necessary to convict a defendant of larceny.

A.S.P.R. (Armed Services Procurement Regulation). In 1978 A.S.P.R. was redesignated the Defense Acquisition Regulation (D.A.R.).

ASSAY OFFICE. A division of the United States Mint, which is part of the Treasury Department, it is the country's only gold processing and refining plant. It refines one-half of the four million pounds of gold refined each year in the United States. It also serves as a storage center and holds about 55 million troy ounces of gold, or almost one-quarter of the nation's supply. Located in a fortress in Wall Street where it was built in 1930, the Office also has the responsibility for weighing and evaluating the gold that periodically moves in and out of government possession. For example, the United States might settle a trade account with a foreign nation by transferring some gold to that country. The gold bars would be assayed and stamped by the Assay Office and then shipped by plane or boat abroad. Or it could be sent a few blocks north to the Federal Reserve Bank of New York, which acts as a depository for a large part of the world's gold, storing in its basement piles of gold bars. If a foreign nation owes a debt to the United States to be settled in gold, the precious metal might be delivered to the Assay Office for evaluation before being sent to Fort Knox, Kentucky, where the government keeps a large amount of gold, or it might be kept at the Assay Office.

ASSEMBLY LINE LAW. The routine delivery of legal services to the public by para-professionals and law clerks, rather than by lawyers.

ASSESSED VALUATION FORMULA. Used to determine the value of property for tax purposes. For example, a city which assesses a $5 tax for every $100 of real estate figured at 10 percent of the fair market value, would levy a $500 tax on a $100,000 home.

$$(\$5 \times \frac{100,000}{100} \times .10)$$

ASSESSED VALUE. A value set on real estate by local governmental assessors for the purpose of determining property taxes. It is usually determined by taking a percentage of the property's market value.

ASSIGNED RISK. See F.A.I.R.

ASSIGNMENT OF EXPECTANCY. The transfer to another person of one's rights to an inheritance. Such agreements are recognized and enforced as valid contracts. If, however, the person who assigns the expectancy predeceases the source of the inheritance, or is disinherited, there is no inheritance and the assignment has no effect.

ASSISTANT PRESIDENT. See FIRST LADY.

ASSOCIATE ATTORNEY. Member of a law firm who has no partnership in the firm or corporation. It may also refer to an attorney hired to assist in the preparation and handling of a lawsuit.

ASSOCIATION FOR INTERCOLLEGIATE ATHLETICS FOR WOMEN. See TITLE IX OF THE EDUCATION AMENDMENTS OF 1972.

ASSOCIATION OF AMERICAN LAW SCHOOLS (A.A.L.S.). A group of law schools which describes its purpose as "the improvement of the legal profession through legal education." It is the law teachers' learned society and legal education's principle representative to the federal government and other national higher education and learned society organizations. The A.A.L.S. has its beginnings at a meeting held on August 29, 1900 at Saratoga Springs, New York. Thirty-two law schools became charter members of the Association. James B. Thayer was its first president. Professor Michael H. Cardozo of Cornell University Law School became the Association's first Executive Director and in the summer of 1963 established the Association's national office. After operating as an unincorporated association for 70 years, the Association was incorporated under the laws of the District of Columbia on February 2, 1971. Along with the American Bar Association (A.B.A.), A.A.L.S. is recognized as one of the two national accrediting agencies for law by the Council on Post Secondary Accreditation. The American Bar Association is recognized by the Commissioner of Education, Department of Health, Education, and Welfare as the "nationally recognized accrediting agency" for law. A.B.A. approval is the criterion used by most states to judge the quality of the legal education offered to qualify to take the bar examination. A.A.L.S. is literally an association of law schools; of the 163 A.B.A. approved law schools, 132 are A.A.L.S. members. After a school has graduated at least three annual classes it is eligible to apply for membership. Compliance with the rules of membership are determined through a three or four person inspection team. Recommendations for admission to membership are made by the executive committee, upon advice of the accreditation committee. Membership is attained by action of the house of representatives.

ASSOCIATION OF CONTINUING LEGAL EDUCATION ADMINISTRATORS. National association open to individuals from "any nonprofit educational or bar organization which operates a sustained program of continuing legal education and employs an administrator or director to conduct its educational activities." Its primary purpose is to foster exchange of information and ideas on continuing legal education.

ASSOCIATION OF SOUTH EAST ASIAN NATIONS. See A.S.E.A.N.

ASSOCIATION OF TRIAL LAWYERS OF AMERICA (A.T.L.A.). Established in 1948 as the National Association of Claimants' Compensation Attorneys (N.A.C.C.A.). Starting with nearly 700 members, the organization has grown to a 30,000-member bar association with national impact, and members in all fifty states, Puerto Rico, and Canada. The Association's objectives include promoting the administration of justice for the public good, encouraging brotherhood among the members of the bar, and improving the adversary system and trial by jury. Sponsored activities of A.T.L.A. include: (1) A Circuit Seminar Series, which offers two-day seminars each year in every judicial circuit of the United States on topics of special interest; (2) Basic Trial Advocacy Seminars which cover the fundamentals of sound courtroom strategy and effective execution; (3) National College of Advocacy which covers a continuing education and certification program, held annually in the East and West; (4) Educational counseling aids, which include videotapes, cassettes, and texts on all phases of trial advocacy; (5) *A.T.L.A. Law Reporter,* published ten times a year, which is a diverse and extensive case reference periodical; (6) *A.T.L.A. Law Journal,* originally known as the *N.A.C.C.A. Law Journal,* which offers in-depth analysis of legal trends and significant cases; (7) Tap The Exchange which provides valuable insights and information on thousands of products and medical procedures.

A.T.A.R.S. See C.A.S.

ATKINSON RULE. The levy of fines against professional football players who engage in excessive, unnecessary violence, especially against vulnerable wide receivers.

ATLANTIC INSTITUTE. An unofficial European-American group with headquarters in Paris and ties to foreign policy leaders in the nations of the North Atlantic Treaty Organization (N.A.T.O.). The director is normally a distinguished retired American diplomat. The Institute's standing is comparable to that of the prestigious Council on Foreign Relations in New York City, in its sponsorship of conferences, lectures and publications.

ATOMIC ENERGY COMMUNITY. See EUROPEAN ECONOMIC COMMUNITY.

ATTESTATION CLAUSE. The provision in a will in which the witnesses attest that the testator declared the document to be his or her will, signed it, and asked them to witness it.

ATTIC CODE. The first Greek codification of laws, which influenced the development of Roman law. Authored by Solon in the early 5th century B.C., it reflects a highly stratified, class-based society. The name of the code is derived from Attica, the area of Greece in which it was promulgated.

ATTORNEY-AT-LAW. An officer in a court of justice; the term Attorney as it is commonly used.

ATTORNEY - CLIENT PRIVILEGE. Protects from disclosure those confidential communications between an attorney, acting in his capacity as legal adviser, and his client. By encouraging the client to confide in his attorney, the privilege enhances the efficacy of the adversary process and facilitates the administration of justice. The nineteenth century English philosopher

Jeremy Bentham argued, however, that the privilege protects only the guilty since the innocent presumably have nothing to hide.

ATTORNEY DISBARMENT. A temporary or permanent revocation of the right to practice law for serious misconduct such as the commission of a felony. The American Bar Association's Standing Committee on Professional Discipline reported that 124 lawyers were disbarred by state disciplinary agencies in 1977. New York State had the most disbarments with 37. Virginia followed with 15, and California had 11. All other states disbarred 5 or fewer attorneys.

ATTORNEY GENERAL. The head of the Department of Justice, whose primary function is to represent in the courts the interests of the United States government. As a member of the Cabinet, he issues opinions and annual reports related to the workings of his office. His supervisory duties are broad, reaching to the United States attorneys and the United States marshals of the 94 federal judicial districts, the Director of the Federal Bureau of Investigation, the Commissioner for Immigration and Naturalization, the Director of the Bureau of Prisons, the Chairman of the Board of Parole, and the Pardon Attorney. Because of the hybrid character of the position, the Attorney General is said to have "three masters"—the President, the Congress, and the courts. The Constitution does not allude to an Attorney General. The office was created by the Judiciary Act of 1789. Thus, it ranks fourth in protocol behind the Secretaries of State, Defense, and the Treasury. George Washington appointed as the first Attorney General his personal attorney, Edmund Randolph of Virginia. Randolph received an annual salary of $1500, from which he had to pay his own rent and buy his own stamps and stationery. He had no assistants. Not until 1853 was the office of the Attorney General made a full-time position. In fact, the part-time nature of the job was emphasized to attract qualified individuals to the low-paying office, for until this time the Attorney General could continue private practice and the credentials of the office made one's private practice more prestigious. In 1870, the Office of the Attorney General became the Department of Justice. Each of the fifty states has an Attorney General with functions similar to the United States Attorney General but they are usually elected officials.

ATTORNEY GENERAL'S LIST. Initiated in 1947 as part of President Truman's loyalty program, the list contained the names of organizations which the Attorney General deemed to be subversive. Although the list had no legal consequence, it was considered in determining the loyalty of government employees. The Supreme Court ruled in *Joint Anti-Fascist Committee v. McGrath*, 341 U.S. 123 (1951) that before being included on the list, an organization had to be given notice and an opportunity to be heard. The list was abolished in 1974. By that time, most of the organizations whose names appeared on it were no longer in existence.

ATTORNEY-IN-FACT. A person, not necessarily a lawyer, to whom authority is given by another to act in his place. The authority to act as an Attorney-in-Fact is given by a power or letter of attorney.

ATTORNEY LIEN (Retaining Lien). An attorney's right to keep in his possession his client's documents or other property, which he has as a result of his professional duties to his client, until the general balance due him for his legal services is paid.

ATTORNEY OF THE DAY. Name given to the lawyer from the legal counsel division of the harassed office of the General Counsel of the E.E.O.C. (Equal Employment Opportunity Commission) who is assigned to answer inquiries from the irate public on the handling of the backlog of the hundreds of thousands of cases which are pending in the agency.

ATTRACTIVE NUISANCE DOCTRINE. See LEGAL FICTIONS.

AUDI ALTERAM PARTEN (Latin—in any dispute, hear the other side). A highly civilized principle of ancient Roman law that, in any dispute, both sides of the case should be heard. This concept is enshrined in the heart of the common law in the Western World and ignored in the Marxism-Leninism of the East.

AUDIENCE TEST (Ordinary Observer Test). Often invoked by courts of substantial similarity in the context of copyright infringement. Applying the "reasonable man" standard to copyright law, it requires a court to determine whether the average person would detect a common expression of ideas between two works without prolonged reflection and without the suggestion of others. The test dates from 1868 when it was employed in *Daly v. Palmer*, 6 F. Cas. 1132 (C.C.S.D.N.Y. 1868) (No. 3,552). That case compared two scenes in which a character was tied to railroad tracks, only to be released just before disaster struck. The action was nearly identical, though the dialogue differed. The Audience Test has been widely criticized. Some commentators contend that the spontaneous reactions of an ordinary individual ought to be used only as evidence that infringement has occurred, not to establish conclusively that a copyright has been violated. This criticism has led some courts to modify the Audience Test into a two-step inquiry. Initially, the works are compared to determine whether the defendant in fact copied the plaintiff's work. If that decision is affirmative, then the traditional Audience Test is invoked to inquire whether the copying was unlawful.

AUDIT TRIGGER. Any apparent excessive business or other expense claim on a tax return in a sensitive area such as travel or entertainment which will result in an audit of the taxpayer's entire return.

AUSTIN, JOHN. See LEGAL UTILITARIANISM.

AUTHORIZATION CARDS. Cards signed by employees designating a union to be the desired bargaining representative. Where a tally of the number of cards favoring a particular union indicates substantial support (usually more than thirty percent), a "showing of interest" is said to be established. This showing may be used to prove the existence of a "question of representation" as a basis for requesting a certification election for the union by the National Labor Relations Board. Alternatively, the showing of interest may be presented to the employer directly to demonstrate majority support and thereby induce the employer to bargain.

AUTHORIZED INVESTMENT TRUST. An investment or profit-oriented venture that is authorized by the trust arrangement itself, to be distinguished from an investment made at the option of the trust beneficiaries or the trust trustee. Investment trusts are usually used for estate planning as money can be removed from the trust settlor's estate and used to accumulate income which will later be distributed to his designated beneficiaries.

AUTHORIZING LEGISLATION. In the federal budget, legislation enacted by Congress which sets up or continues the legal operation of a federal program or agency indefinitely or for a specific period of time. Such legislation is a prerequisite for subsequent appropriations. It may limit the amount of the budget authority to be provided subsequently or may authorize the appropriation of such sums as may be necessary. The term is often used more narrowly to refer to annual dollar limits specified in authorizing legislation.

AUTOMATED TRAFFIC ADVISORY AND RESOLUTION SERVICE. See C.A.S.

AUTOMATIC PERFECTION. Refers to Purchase Money Security Interests in consumer goods. Under Article 9 of the Uniform Commercial Code (U.C.C.), such interests are automatically perfected and remain so without regard to debtor mobility. The rationale for this policy is that generally consumer goods are high-volume, low-priced items and it would be too burdensome to require retailers to file in order to perfect a security interest in each consumer purchase. Automatic Perfection, however, does not apply to motor vehicles required to be licensed under state law. Thus, if a retail dealer sells a mobile home, and if state law requires the mobile home to be registered, the dealer must file to perfect his security interest in this consumer good.

AUTOMOBILE GUEST STATUTES. In force in more than half the states, these laws provide that the driver of an automobile will not be held liable to a non-paying passenger for injuries resulting from mere negligence. But a driver may be liable for injuries caused by aggravated misconduct, such as gross negligence, wilful, wanton or reckless conduct, or action in disregard of the safety of others. Liability insurance companies lobbied strenuously for the enactment of these statutes. They argued that when a guest is injured, the driver is more eager to see the guest compensated than to see the truth revealed, often resulting in collusion between the guest and the host and eventually contributing to higher insurance rates. The theory behind the legislation is that one who receives a free ride may not be heard to demand the reasonable care of the driver not to injure him.

AUTOMOBILE INSURANCE. There are five different basic types. (1) Liability for bodily injury and property damage. Your responsibility for injuries to others or damage to their property. This coverage protects you against any lawsuits if you or anyone driving your car should happen to injure or kill anyone else or damage their property. In states where no-fault laws exist, if you negligently injure someone riding in another car, the expenses are paid by the company insuring that car, not by the firm insuring your car. (2) Medical payments. This coverage, unlike liability, is mainly designed to protect you and your family, no matter whether injured in your car, another car, or struck by a car. This coverage

also covers medical and funeral expenses for anyone hurt or killed getting in, getting out of, or riding in your automobile. (3) Uninsured-motorist coverage. This protects you and your passengers in case you are victims of an accident caused by an uninsured motorist. (4) Comprehensive. This is optional coverage of just about any kind of loss or damage to your car or its contents caused by fire, theft, vandalism, falling objects, tornadoes or collision with animals. Many policies specifically exempt such items as tape recorders or CB radios from comprehensive coverage. (5) Collision. Designed to cover the cost of repairs to your own car as a result of an accident. It is almost always written on a deductible basis, and the higher the deductible amount, the lower the premium.

AUTUMN HARVEST UPRISING. The beginning of the successful Communist revolution in China in 1927 which led to the defeat of nationalist General Chiang Kai-shek and his flight in 1949 to the Island of Taiwan in the South China Sea where he established the Republic of China (R.C.).

AVERY v. MIDLAND COUNTY (390 U.S. 474 (1968)). The first Supreme Court decision to apply the equal districting requirement to a unit of local government. The case involved a Texas county Commissioner's Court—an agency with "general governmental powers." Rejecting the argument that the Commissioner's Court was an administrative rather than a legislative body, the Court ruled that the Constitution allowed no substantial variation from equal population in drawing legislative districts.

A.V.O.L. (Americans for Voluntary Observance of Law). A sardonic concept coined by distinguished Harvard Economics Professor John Kenneth Galbraith as a travesty on former President Ford's unsuccessful recommended voluntary campaign against inflation entitled W.I.N. (Whip Inflation Now). President Carter later officially tried to do likewise with C.O.W.P.S. (Council on Wage and Price Stability). If

A.V.O.L. were expanded to its outermost limits, it would undoubtedly apply to such areas as voluntary tax collection and voluntary compliance with narcotics laws or securities regulations. Pure parody in an obvious take-off of A.W.O.L., the military offense of being absent without leave.

AWARD FEE. See COST-PLUS-AWARD FEE.

B

BABY BLUE. See BIG BLUE.

BABY BROKER LAWS. State statutes which seek to eliminate the practice of the sale of babies by making it a crime for strangers, including lawyers and doctors, to arrange for private adoptions. Only licensed private or public placement agencies may legally arrange for lawful adoptions.

BABY LIFT (Operation Baby Lift). An organized effort to evacuate South Vietnamese children during the final days of the Vietnamese War. As many as 2,000 children participated in Operation Baby Lift. Many were adopted by United States citizens, and the legality of numerous such adoptions was later disputed in the courts.

BABY MARKET. The national black market in which babies are sold to adoptive parents. Lawyers in the baby-selling market may instruct unwed mothers to lie concerning the whereabouts of the putative father or threaten them with the fear that they may have to go on public assistance if the baby is not adopted. Unwed mothers are often given paid vacations until the birth of the baby. The demand for adoptable children has risen so high that some unscrupulous persons advertise for women who are willing to become pregnant and then give their children up for adoption.

BABY WAGNER ACTS. State laws modelled on the Wagner Act, which was the original National Labor Relations Act.

BACHELOR OF LAWS. See J.D.

BACK BENCHER. A member of the British Parliament who does not simultaneously hold another government position and can be identified sitting in the rear of the legislative chamber.

BACKDOOR AUTHORITY (Backdoor Spending). In the federal budget, legislative authority for the obligation of funds outside the normal appropriation process. The most common forms of Backdoor Authority are borrowing authority (authority to spend debt receipts) and contract authority. Entitlement Authority is sometimes included as a form of Backdoor Authority since the enactment of a basic benefit legislation may effectively mandate the subsequent enactment of the appropriations to pay the statutory benefits. Section 401 of the Congressional Budget and Impoundment Control Act of 1974 specifies certain limits on the use of Backdoor Authority. Examples of programs that have Backdoor Authority are the Environmental Protection Agency's construction grant program and the Social Security trust funds.

BACKDOOR FINANCING. The technique used by government agencies of borrowing money directly from the treasury in order to avoid the procedures of congressional appropriation. The Reconstruction Finance Corporation, created in the 1930s, was the first agency authorized to obtain funds by this method.

BACKDOOR FOREIGN AID. Money given to a less developed country (L.D.C.) by an international organization supported by the United States after Congress has refused to make a direct grant of American financial aid. For example, in July 1978, the International Monetary Fund (I.M.F.) to which 131 nations belong, for which we supply 20 percent of its funds, made a 28 million dollar loan to Vietnam to enable the Southeast Communist nation to correct its adverse balance of payments (more imports than exports). Thus what the Third World cannot get from us directly they get from us indirectly and everyone is happy except the American taxpayer who once again is taken to the cleaners. See also A.I.D.

BACKDOOR SPENDING. See BACK-DOOR AUTHORITY.

BACK ROOM LAWYER. Term coined by basketball coach and TV commentator Al McGuire to refer to a problem player on a college team.

BACK-TO-BACK ESCROW (Double Escrow). An escrow arrangement intended to facilitate the sale of one property and the purchase of another property by the seller. Under a Back-to-Back Escrow the proceeds of the sale are applied to the subsequent purchase.

BACK-TRACKING (Bumping-Off). Practice of allowing workers with seniority to bump off junior workers when there are temporary or permanent layoffs in a business.

BACK-UP OFFER. An agreement by a third party to purchase property from a seller, who is under contract to sell to another, if the first buyer does not go through with the sale.

BACON, FRANCIS. English lawyer, philosopher and statesman who attended Cambridge University at the age of 12, and who attempted to reform all of science and philosophy. His conception of science and philosophy did not much influence scientists or philosophers until three centuries after his death, when his classification-of-nature proposals were embodied in the French Encyclopedia and his logical methodology prompted the formation of the Royal Society of London. Relatively unsuccessful as an attorney, Bacon sought political appointments. He proved very aggressive and used questionable tactics bordering on bribes to Queen Elizabeth. Finally, in 1604, King James named him to be King's Counsel; Bacon's friends had convinced James that Bacon's name had been inadvertently omitted from the list of officers Queen Elizabeth had directed to be reappointed after her reign. In fact, Bacon had never served the Queen. Bacon continued to ascend the political ladder with his appointment as Attorney-General, in which capacity he disdained independent courts. In 1621, Parliament found him guilty of bribery and corruption, removed him from office, and imprisoned and fined him. He received a full pardon in 1624. Two years later, he died of suffocation. He had purchased a hen and wanted to see if snow would preserve it as well as salt. He stuffed it with snow, became quite chilled in the process, and retired to a very damp room which was his undoing. Bacon has also been credited by some as the true author of certain plays attributed to Shakespeare.

BAD CONDUCT DISCHARGE (B.C.D.). A punitive separation from the armed forces, awarded to enlisted personnel as punishment by either a special or general court martial. It is designed as punishment for bad conduct rather than as punishment for serious offenses of either a civil or military nature. It is appropriate as punishment for an accused who has been convicted repeatedly of minor offenses and whose punitive separation from the armed forces appears to be necessary. Although it is less severe than a dishonorable discharge, it is a separation under other than honorable conditions. Imposition of such a discharge may result in denial of all benefits administered by the Veterans Administration as well as those administered by the military establishment.

BADGER GAME. The enticing of a wealthy person into a compromising position; often used to trap a man and a married woman into being "caught" by the husband, who then demands a money settlement from the male victim.

BADGES OF SERVITUDE. The Thirteenth Amendment to the Constitution of the United States prohibits slavery and involuntary servitude other than as punishment upon conviction of a crime. The Amendment has been interpreted by the Supreme Court of the United States, however, to mean more than just a ban on slavery. It forbids infliction of badges of servitude on account of race. This is a proscription of all incidents of slavery. The bar on involuntary servitude and the provision in section 2 of the Amendment that Congress has power to enforce the provisions of the Amendment have recently been used by the Court to approve of congressional acts designed to prohibit racial discrimination. The fact that the Thirteenth Amendment has no State Action Requirement has made it possible to regulate private behavior in a way not possible under the Fourteenth Amendment.

BAG MAN. A third party intermediary who obtains the money from the briber for delivery to the bribee. Unless the middle man is an innocent courier, which is most unlikely, he also is guilty of a criminal offense as are, of course, the other two culprits. So don't be tempted to make a fast buck because it may land you in the pokey—jail, that is.

BAIL BARGAINING. Negotiations between an accused and a prosecutor in a criminal case to reduce or eliminate bail in order to enable the accused to be released from jail before and during the forthcoming trial. The accused offers to give the prosecutor information about the particular crime and others in order to avoid the temporary imprisonment pending the trial.

BAIL BOND. Required to effect release of a defendant held in legal custody. If the defendant fails to appear for trial, the surety forfeits the amount of the bond.

BAILEY, FRANCIS LEE. Born in 1933, the Harvard-educated trial attorney will be remembered for the flamboyant, skillful advocacy that has made him a foremost criminal lawyer of the 1960s and 70s. Possessed of a quick wit, Bailey is known for his defenses of the "Boston Strangler", Patricia Hearst, and the My Lai massacre defendant, Captain Ernest Medina. He has espoused the use of the polygraph in criminal prosecution. In *Hearst,* he based the defense on the theory that an accused who has been subjected to brainwashing techniques cannot be held responsible for his actions.

BAIL JUMPER. One who fails to appear in court at the designated time as required by the conditions of his bail. Bail refers to the release of an accused from legal custody on condition that he submit himself to the court at a designated time and place. The Bail Jumper is not only subject to criminal penalties but forfeits any bail bond of money or property which had been posted to guarantee his appearance in court for trial.

BAIL OFFICIAL (Latin—baiulus: a porter). A minor quasi-police office official in the court; sometimes the term refers to an assistant sheriff. In feudal law, the bailiff was a high official, the steward or governor of a manor, with extensive administrative and judicial powers.

BAILEY v. DREXEL FURNITURE. See CHILD LABOR CASES.

BAIT-AND-SWITCH. Improper sales technique designed to lure customers to a place of business. Bait-and-Switch involves the advertisement of a low-priced product, which serves as the "bait." The "switch" occurs when the consumer inquires about the bargain and is informed that the low-priced model is out of stock or is in some way inferior to a more expensive, higher quality model. Drawn to the store by the advertisement, and usually in the frame of mind to buy, the consumer too often agrees to purchase an unnecessary item which is beyond his budget. This practice is common in the sale of televisions, sewing machines and other appliances but is illegal under current consumer laws.

BAKER v. CARR. See LEGISLATIVE REAPPORTIONMENT.

BAKKE RULING. See AFFIRMATIVE ACTION.

BALANCE OF PAYMENTS. A comparison of a country's imports with its exports which is said to be favorable when the former exceeds the latter and unfavorable when it is vice versa. An unfavorable Balance of Payments can have a severe adverse effect on a nation's economy and your pocketbook, as the United States has sadly witnessed in recent years as a result of the O.P.E.C. action in drastically increasing the price of oil which we consume so voraciously.

BALANCE OF TERROR. An equilibrium of offensive and defensive war arsenals, based on nuclear power, since World War II, which creates the fear of mutual annihilation in a total war. This reciprocal terror has led to outbidding in creating more and more efficient arsenals, up to the point where a sort of balance between sophisticated delivery systems for massively destructive powers on one side and increased retaliatory capability on the other side was reached. A deadlock which represents a significantly dissuasive effect to the use of total means of war, the Balance of Terror is also the starting point for mutual competition in armaments, the pursuit of which could only be stopped through international negotiations such as S.A.L.T.

BALANCE OF TRADE. See MERCHANDISE TRADE BALANCE.

BALANCING TEST. A technique, made prominent in many recent constitutional cases in the Supreme Court, by which individual interests are weighed against governmental or societal interests to determine the constitutionality of a given statute, ordinance or official action. Often the balancing technique is used to resolve thorny issues arising under the Due Process Clause of the Fourteenth Amendment. The concept of balancing interests, as opposed to more rigid applications of the law, has long been employed by courts, both overtly and Sub Rosa. The modern Supreme Court has begun to recognize balancing as an acceptable method of resolving difficult issues of individual rights and social or governmental prerogatives. Use of a Balancing Test necessarily involves a subjective analysis and implies a rejection of the "strict construction" technique of statutory interpretation.

BALDWIN, SIMEON E. See AMERICAN BAR ASSOCIATION.

BALKAN ALLIANCE. Created by the Treaties of Ankara on February 28, 1953, and of Bled on August 9, 1959, the Alliance includes Greece, Turkey and Yugoslavia. It represents an attempt to overcome the failure of the previous Balkan alliance signed by Greece, Turkey, Rumania and Yugoslavia on February 9, 1934. From the beginning, however, the new Balkan Alliance was characterized by an absence of solidarity among its members. Historical problems, disputes about Cyprus and Macedonia, and above all, the political opposition resulting from the membership of Turkey and Greece in N.A.T.O. prevented the effective functioning of the Balkan Alliance.

BALLOON CLAUSE. Found in mortgages, usually for property with a substantial purchase price. It is used to extend the duration of the mortgage so that the monthly installments will be lower, with a bulk sum being paid at maturity. The mechanics are similar to paying a down-payment after the installments have been paid. For example, if a parcel of land is priced at $120,000, a 5-year mortgage would require the purchaser to pay $2,000 per month, which would be onerous to all but the most wealthy buyers. A balloon clause would extend the mortgage to, say, 20 years; the purchaser then would only have to pay $500 per month for the first five years, with the balance, $90,000, payable thereafter in a lump sum, at which time a new loan could be negotiated.

BALTIMORE LAW CLUBS. Congenial dinner clubs for lawyers with colorful names such as Loophole Club, Wrangler's and Barrister's Round Table. While these clubs contribute to a beneficial exchange of information among members of the legal profession, they perpetrate the Old Boy Network which operates to exclude women and minority lawyers. One such club frankly admits that ladies are allowed only to attend a summer outing once a year!

BALTIMORE METHOD. A method of real estate appraisal which calculates the value of a corner lot as the total of the lots on each side of the property.

BAMBOO CURTAIN. A voluntary wall of isolation from the rest of the world imposed by the Communists on the mainland of China after their takeover in 1949 and not fully lifted until the normalization of relations with the United States in 1979.

BANANA REPUBLICS. Countries in Latin America whose largest income is from the sale of fruit to the United States and whose governments all too often are military dictatorships which specialize in a denial of human rights.

BANCO NACIONAL DE CUBA v. **SABBATINO** (376 U.S. 398 (1964)). See ACT OF STATE DOCTRINE.

BANK CERTIFICATES OF DEPOSIT. See BEARER BONDS.

BANK FAILURE. A bank's inability to pay out withdrawals demanded by depositors. The First National Bank of Attica, New York, represents the first failure of a National Bank. Because of injudicious practices and the failure of large debtors to honor their obligations, it was placed into receivership in 1865. Over 8,000 banks failed prior to 1929, and by the end of 1933 that figure had doubled. However, on June 16, 1933, Congress passed the Glass-Steagall Act establishing stricter regulation of banks and providing the first federal insurance of deposits. The banking reformers of the 1930s have made bank failures rare and have almost eliminated losses to depositors.

BANK FOR INTERNATIONAL SETTLEMENTS. See B.I.S.

BANKRUPTCY CODE OF 1978. A massive enactment by Congress which repeals the old Bankruptcy Act of 1898 and codifies an entirely new bankruptcy law which is to be known as Title 11 of the United States Code — Bankruptcy. This new law, which becomes effective on October 1, 1979, represents the first complete revision of the Bankruptcy Laws of the United States in 40 years. In addition, the legislation significantly modifies or affects other fields such as tax laws, securities laws, and many other laws encountered by an attorney in corporate practice. The new, upgraded bankruptcy court will be vested with complete jurisdiction to hear all matters arising in or related to a bankruptcy case; the distinction between summary and plenary jurisdiction is abolished. The status of bankruptcy judges is elevated and their tenure increased. The relationship of the bankruptcy judge to the administration of bankruptcy cases is changed and the functions of the Trustee in bankruptcy and other administrative personnel are enlarged. The new Bankruptcy Code substantially modernizes the substantive provisions of bankruptcy law. New sections set forth explicit rules concerning subjects such as use of collateral, issuance of certificates of indebtedness, and adequate protection of the interest of a secured creditor, which are not treated by the current statute. There are also new provisions governing setoff, executory contracts and leases, and compensation of attorneys and trustees. The traditional avoiding powers of a trustee in bankruptcy are altered significantly and new powers added. The new Code replaces present Chapters X, XI, and XII of the Bankruptcy Act with a completely new consolidated Chapter 11. All business reorganizations will operate under one chapter which combines the more favorable features of the three chapters of the old law with innovative substantive provisions designed to facilitate business reorganizations. For the first time, the Code establishes provisions assuring adequate disclosure when consents to plans are solicited. The interests of creditors are defined in explicit terms. The new consolidated reorganization chapter is responsive to many problems encountered under current law, including the well publicized "cram-down" section. An intricate new confirmation standard permits flexibility while protecting all creditors. The new Act makes the concept of the "fresh start" for individual debtors more meaningful. The ability of a creditor to extract from the debtor a legally binding reaffirmation of a discharged debt is substantially different under the new law. Exemptions are given more effect by allowing the debtor the opportunity to invalidate liens on certain exempt household goods. An explicit provision of the new Code also prohibits the government from discriminating against an individual debtor because of bankruptcy. This significant legislation is the product of many years of intensive study of bankruptcy laws and bankruptcy administration, commencing with the reports of the Brookings Commission in the late 1960s and of the congressionally-created Commission on the Bankruptcy Laws of the United States in the early 1970s. The new law represents the culmination of over four years of legislative effort during which hundreds of witnesses produced a record of more than 5,000 pages of testimony. The result is a voluminous, modern Bankruptcy Code that will have a wide-reaching effect on the business community in general, credit transactions in particular, and the problems of consumer insolvency.

BANKRUPTCY JUDGES. Appointed by the Chief Judges of each of the federal circuits, until March, 1984, when they will be nominated by the President, subject to Senate confirmation, for 14-year terms, at salaries of $53,-000, they preside over all bankruptcy cases with appeals from their decisions to United States district courts, unless both parties agree to appeal to the circuit courts.

BANKRUPTCY MILL. Any lawyer or organization which specializes in grinding out bankruptcy relief for its clientele at the expense of their creditors whose claims are wiped out.

BANKRUPTCY PROCEDURE (Italian—banca rotta: broken bench). Practice which originated in Italy whereby a trader who did not pay all of his debts, would find that his creditors had broken his work bench and hung it in his doorway as a warning to others that this man was a bankrupt. In this country Bankruptcy Procedure is controlled by statutory law and is an orderly method of liquidating the assets of an insolvent person in an equitable distribution to his creditors. Today, a debtor who cannot pay all of his bills has several options. He may get his creditors together and convince them to accept for full payment less than what is actually due: an "accord and satisfaction" if only one creditor was involved; or a "composition" if he were indebted to a number of people. Or the debtor could enter into a general assignment for the benefit of creditors by transferring all of his assets to a third party trustee with directions that the creditors be paid off as much as possible from this fund. The debtor may file a voluntary petition in bankruptcy as an admission of defeat and request to the court to administer his financial estate for him, or he may be dragged into court by his creditors, who can file an involuntary petition in bankruptcy against him. Involuntary petitions will only be granted under certain conditions and never against a farmer. A debtor may also choose to participate in a wage earner's plan (Chapter 13 Proceeding) which simplifies some of the Bankruptcy Procedures for those estates which are not too complicated. Once a debtor has gone through bankruptcy his debts are discharged and he may make a fresh start. Some debts, however, are said to be non-dischargeable, such as taxes and alimony. While there is no limit on the number of discharges a person may obtain in his lifetime, he must always wait at least six years after he has obtained one before he can obtain another.

BANK SECRECY ACT (Federal Currency and Foreign Transactions Reporting Act). A statute passed by Congress in 1970, largely through the sponsorship of Representative Wright Patman, who was Chairman of the House Banking and Currency Committee. The law is designed to stop the invisible flow of billions of dollars in criminal money through the nation's banking system. It is a crucial weapon in the fight against white collar crime and the laundering of money by gamblers, narcotics traffickers and international bribers. Anyone who transports, physically or through the mails, more than $5,000 into or out of the United States must report the transfer to the United States Customs Service. Banks and other financial institutions must report to the Internal Revenue Service detailed information on each unusual cash transaction over $10,000. United States taxpayers who have foreign bank accounts are required to file a report with the Treasury Department. Failure to comply with these reporting requirements gives rise to civil penalties and criminal prosecution.

BANNING OF PEOPLE. Decrees issued by the Minister of Justice of South Africa, which silence dissidents without jailing them. Kept under constant surveillance, victims are prohibited from taking part in political activities, from being quoted by newspapers, restricted to certain areas and prohibited from congregating with more than one person at a time. In South Africa there are several hundred of these "living dead," especially those who have criticized that country's policy of apartheid (forced separation of the races).

BANNING ORDERS. See BANNING OF PEOPLE.

BANNS PUBLICATION. After the Norman conquest and while the influence of Christianity grew in Great Britain, the power to regulate marriage was put in the hands of the Church. At the end of the twelfth century, the ecclesiastical requirement of "thrice publishing the Banns" for all Church weddings was imposed. The requirement was satisfied by publishing for three consecutive weeks in a Church bulletin the intention of the prospective bride and groom to marry. If any member of the community knew of any reason why they should not, he or she was expected to come forward and speak. The tradition is still carried on in many churches today.

BAREBOAT CHARTER. See DEMISE CHARTER.

BARE TRUST. See PASSIVE TRUST.

BAR EXAMINATION. The test of legal proficiency which one must complete successfully in order to be admitted to the bar to practice law. The term bar also refers to the partition or railing in a courtroom that separates the public from legal counsel involved in the case. Approximately 49,000 individuals attempted bar exams across the country in 1976; of these, about 10,000 were taking it for the second time or more. 1977 passing rates ranged from 100 percent in West Virginia to 25 percent in Mississippi. Leading states in terms of numbers of people taking the Bar Examination in 1976 included California, New York, Illinois, Texas, Pennsylvania, New Jersey, and Massachusetts in that order. Most states administer their respective exams in February and again in July. The exam usually consists of an essay portion on many subjects as well as an objective part covering core areas like contracts, torts, criminal law, constitutional law, real property, and evidence. Forty-three states now utilize a Multistate Bar Exam in which identical objective sections are standardized and administered, with each jurisdiction free to devise its own passing scales. Multistate exams have a general scope and are not geared to the law of any one state. Examinees must pay fees to take the exam, and many states offer review courses called coach classes for preparation. Some jurisdictions recognize reciprocity, so that an attorney who has been practicing for a set number of years in one state may request another state to waive the exam for him. Moreover, a few states honor a diploma privilege, whereby graduates of a state law school automatically may practice in that state without taking the exam. Most states condition the right to take their Bar Examinations on proving sound moral character or mental and physical ability to engage in active law practice. In 1977, for example, the Supreme Court of Arizona upheld an Arizona Bar Examiner's decision not to allow an applicant to take the Bar Examination because of his paranoid personality disorder. A few states will allow a person to study law in the lawyer's office and then take the Bar Examination as Abraham Lincoln did generations ago.

BARGAINING AGENCY FOR MEMBERS ONLY. A union which acts and bargains only for its own members in a place where non-union members are also employed.

BARGAINING ORDER. A directive from the National Labor Relations Board requiring an employer to recognize a union as a bargaining representative. Where an employer resists the directive, the N.L.R.B. may seek a Cease-and-Desist order against the employer or may take affirmative steps to remedy the situation.

BARGAINING TABLE. The place where labor and management meet to settle any disputes between them in order to avoid a strike.

BARGAINING UNIT. The group of employees formally recognized by an employer or officially designated by an authorized government agency, such as the National Labor Relations Board, as appropriate for representation by a union for purposes of collective bargaining.

BARRATRY OFFENSE. In criminal law, the offense of fomenting or stirring up law suits or quarrels. Recently barratry has been in the public notice because of charges that certain civil rights organizations sponsoring test cases were in effect practicing barratry. In admiralty law, barratry consists of an unlawful act or negligence by the masters of a vessel which is contrary to their duty to its owners, and which causes the owner's injury.

BARRETT v. UNITED STATES (423 U.S. 212 (1976)). A Supreme Court case upholding a provision of the Gun Control Act of 1968 which prohibited convicted felons from receiving firearms or ammunition which had been shipped in interstate commerce. The Court held the provision applicable to a purchaser's intrastate acquisition of a firearm that had been shipped interstate from the manufacturer to the distributor and then from the distributor to the dealer.

BARRISTER ORGANIZATIONS. See INNS OF COURT.

BARROWS v. JACKSON. See STATE ACTION.

BASE FEE. See COST-PLUS-AWARD FEE.

BASIC EDUCATIONAL OPPORTUNITY GRANTS. See FEDERAL COLLEGE-AID STATUTES.

BASIC MONEY SUPPLY (M-1 & M-2). M-1 consists of private demand, or checking account deposits plus cash in the public hands. M-2 consists of cash plus all private deposits except those large ones represented by certificates. The two measures represent funds readily available for spending. Thus, too fast a growth in the Basic Money Supply will produce inflation.

BASIC TRIAL ADVOCACY SEMINARS. See ASSOCIATION OF TRIAL LAWYERS OF AMERICA.

BASIS IN PROPERTY. A tax term which describes a taxpayer's original investment in property.

BASKET MONEY LOAN. A loan, such as a second mortgage, made under a so-called basket provision in the acts regulating banks and investment associations. Such provision allows a percentage of total assets to be placed in otherwise restricted investments.

BASQUE HOMELANDS AND LIBERTY. See E.T.A.

BASTARDY PROCEEDING. A method originating in 1576, called "An Act for Setting the Poor on Work" by which fathers could be forced to support their illegitimate children. The procedure commenced with the arrest of the defendant and included a preliminary hearing before a justice of the peace. Its chief purpose was not so much for the protection of the child as the relief of the parish from the burden of supporting the child. Today nearly all states have some statutory scheme compelling fathers to support their illegitimate children. While some states still retain the form of the old Bastardy Proceeding, it is now more frequently called a paternity suit or filiation proceeding.

BASTARDY STATUTE. A law which mandates that the reputed father of an illegitimate child can be incarcerated if he neglects or refuses to pay court-ordered support.

BASTILLE DAY. July 14th, the annual Independence Day of the French, celebrating the beginning of the French revolution with the storming of the prison in Paris named the Bastille, which was the symbol of the tyranny of the King.

BATES RULING. The United States Supreme Court ruling in *Bates v. State Bar of Arizona,* 434 U.S. 881 (1977), which struck down absolute bans against advertising by lawyers. A 1978 survey of a random sample of lawyers shows only 3 percent of them have advertised since the *Bates* Ruling, and 89 percent said they absolutely would not advertise.

BATTERED CHILD SYNDROME. A combination of physical and other signs indicating that a child's internal and/or external injuries are the result of intentional acts committed by a parent or caretaker. In some states, this term has been judicially recognized as an accepted medical diagnosis. This term is frequently misunderstood to be the only type of child abuse or neglect.

BATTERED HUSBAND. Men who suffer non-accidental physical or psychological injury inflicted upon them by their wives. It is estimated that about two million husbands in the United States suffer at least one serious attack a year from their mates. Such attacks range from kicks, bites or punches to murderous assaults with knives and other deadly weapons. The stricken husbands include helpless drunks and multiple amputees unable to defend themselves, as well as baffled he-man types, who fear that if they strike back

they may kill their wives or suffer social ostracism as a wife-beater. Some sociologists feel this is one of America's most underreported crimes because the victims are paralyzed with shame and guilt at having been beaten by the so-called weaker sex.

BATTERED PARENT. See PARENT ABUSE and GRANNY SLAMMING.

BATTERED SPOUSE. See BATTERED HUSBAND, BATTERED WIFE DEFENSE, SPOUSE ABUSE.

BATTERED WIFE DEFENSE (Murder By Installment). Defense raised in a trial against a battered wife for killing or otherwise striking back at her husband. Habitual wife-abuse has been termed "Murder by Installment" by defense lawyers who attempt to excuse a wife's violence against her husband under the rubric of self-defense. Several recent cases have used the Battered Wife Defense: e.g., a Michigan woman was acquitted by a jury for pouring gas around her sleeping husband and setting him afire; a South Dakota woman was acquitted for the stabbing death of her husband on the grounds of self-defense and defense of her unborn child when her husband battered her with a club; and in California a woman was acquitted of murdering her husband because he continually beat her. A 94-page *Handbook for Battered Women—How To Use The Law,* written in lay language, has been published as a guide through a complex legal system.

BATTLE ACT OF 1951. A federal law authorizing the President to cut aid to any Marshall Plan recipient that declined to cooperate with the economic ostracism of the Communist nations, following the June 1950 invasion of South Korea by North Korea. An existing embargo on strategic exports to Eastern Europe was tightened, and an even more restrictive embargo was placed on trade with China. Permanent committees were set up to coordinate the administration of the embargoes among the Western powers. While the American military action in Korea was eventually successful, the economic war was a failure. The success of the economic sanctions of the United States and others against Russia in 1980 after the Soviet rape of Afghanistan awaits the verdict of history.

BATTLE OF THE FORMS. At common law, the acceptance of a contract had to match the terms of the offer exactly. Often the result was a battle of forms between merchants, but this result was eliminated under the Uniform Commercial Code (U.C.C.). Under Article 2 of the U.C.C., an acceptance creates a valid contract if it is definite and reasonable although it states terms different from or additional to the terms of the offer. Where the agreement concerns consumers, the contract consists of the original terms and the new terms are considered a proposal to be accepted or rejected. Where the agreement is between merchants, the additional or different terms become part of the contract unless (1) the offer expressly precludes new terms, (2) the offeror objects within a reasonable time, or (3) the additional terms materially alter the agreement.

BAZELON, DAVID L. A great United States circuit judge appointed by President Truman who often disagreed with his fellow judge (and later Chief Justice under President Nixon) Warren Burger as to their respective philosophies of law. Judge Bazelon's approach to the great social issues of the age is best expressed by the following anecdote. A case in his court concerned a challenge to the laws requiring segregation in places of public accommodation in the nation's capital. The case caused a great commotion at the time and was heard by the entire court, rather than a panel of three judges. He remembered that his son, who was then not yet 10 years old, asked, "What do you need so many judges to decide that for?"

B.C.D. See BAD CONDUCT DISCHARGE.

BEADLE BUMBLE FUND. Founded by commentator James J. Kilpatrick, to rectify miscarriages of justice by paying fines or legal fees of persons who are "victims of idiotic law enforced idiotically." The Fund is named for the Dickens character in *Oliver Twist* who called the law "a ass, a idiot."

BEAGLE CHANNEL CASE. A dispute that has its origin in the confrontation between Chile and Argentina in the nineteenth century over control of Patagonia, the southernmost region of South America. In 1881, the issue was settled peacefully, with Argentina receiving most of the territory but Chile obtaining sole control of the Strait of Magellan. This left the islands for disposal. The island of Tierra del Fuego, which has proven to be rich in oil and gas, was divided, but the islands to the south of the Beagle Channel along the southern side of Tierra del Fuego were awarded to Chile. However, the course of the channel over the years has been a source of friction. This was finally submitted to arbitration, in 1972, by a board composed of judges of the World Court and, in 1977, the award, made in the name of Queen Elizabeth II of Britain, favored Chile. It was assigned possession of the three disputed islands of Nueva, Picton and Lennox, at the channel's Atlantic entrance. Although Chile has offered to limit its territorial waters around the islands to twelve miles, Argentina refuses to recognize the award. Extreme nationalists in both countries are making dangerous political and military issues over the controversy.

BEARER BONDS (No Name Bonds; Honor Bonds; Numbered Bonds; Bank Certificates of Deposit). Securities issued by a bank by number and not by name so that the bank does not have to report the interest payments to the Internal Revenue Service as it does for ordinary savings accounts. The result is that some owners of these securities may be tempted to engage in tax evasion by not reporting their interest payments as taxable income.

BECKET, THOMAS (Archbishop of Canterbury). Famed as a religious figure, he was nevertheless trained in the law and served as King Henry's chancellor. His appointment broke tradition of naming only Normans to high positions. Born in London in 1118, Becket often heard accounts of his parents' union. Gilbert, his father, was captured in the Holy Land and fell in love with his captor's daughter, Matilda. She helped him escape and followed him to London. Matilda only knew two English words—"Gilbert" and "London"—but she managed to find him and they married. Becket was responsible for the concept of mercenaries. In the War of Toulouse in 1159, he allowed men to pay others to fight for them rather than requiring personal military service of all males. Reluctantly, Becket accepted the archbishopry in 1162; he feared the switch from chancellor to archbishop would create tensions with King Henry. His fears materialized when Henry began instituting Church reforms such as subjecting clergymen to secular sentences rather than Church-proposed penalties for violations of the law. Becket's opposition to this charge culminated in his appeal to the Pope of a violation he committed in direct defiance of Henry's direction that only secular institutions be appealed to. Charged with treason in 1164, Becket escaped from prison in the middle of the night and sailed to the Pope's residence. From there, Becket continued in his capacity as archbishop and, motivated by revenge, excommunicated several of Henry's bishops. In 1170, Becket and Henry reconciled and the former returned to England. After a vituperative sermon delivered on Christmas, four of Henry's knights schemed to assassinate Becket. They did so on December 29th, despite attempts by monks to hide Becket in the cloisters. Two years after his death, Becket was canonized and, in 1221, his body was removed to a shrine. It remained there for several hundred years until King Henry VIII destroyed the shrine and burnt Becket's body as a "traitor to the throne."

BED OF JUSTICE. A medieval torture device used to obtain confessions of criminal responsibility. It was a bed with nails onto which the accused was pressed with heavy weights until a plea of guilty was extracted from the victim writhing in pain.

BEDROOM TAX. A one-time municipal assessment in the nature of an environmental excise tax imposed on land developers. It is based on the number of bedrooms in each private residence to be constructed.

BED WETTERS. Slang term for young liberal Congressional Democrats who panic easily when things don't go their way.

BELGRADE AGREEMENT. See HELSINKI ACCORD.

BELLIGERENT BLOCKADE. Strategy recognized by international law in which a belligerent country prevents access to the ports of the enemy during a state of war. One of the greatest Belligerent Blockade operations was the federal government's campaign to close Confederate ports to outside supplies during the Civil War.

BELLI, MELVIN MOURON. Melvin Belli, "King of Torts," was born in Sonora, California in 1907. He received his B.A. (1929) and LL.B. (1933) from the University of California at Berkeley and an honorable J.D. from the New England School of Law. Belli has pioneered many new approaches in tort law, especially in the presentation of evidence and the amount (usually large) of verdicts. His courtroom style is widely noted for its flamboyance. Belli is also a prolific author, having written a number of books on the law.

BELTWAY BANDITS. Nickname facetiously given to those few retired military officers whose offices as consultants to the federal government for high fees are located on the circumferential highway surrounding Washington, D.C.

BENCH BOOK. A manual of legal rules and principles which a judge brings to court for easy reference to aid in the proper disposition of any questions which arise in the course of a trial.

BENCH CONFERENCE (Sidebar Conference). A meeting between the judge and counsel out of the hearing of the jury and court reporter at which certain procedural matters are discussed. It is characterized by the judge saying: "Will counsel please approach the bench?" followed by a whispered conversation designed to avoid prejudicing the jury. While this is common practice in many jurisdictions, it has been held to be error in courts martial where a verbatim record of the entire proceedings is the only valid record of trial.

BENCHMARK SENTENCING. An innovative new voluntary program instituted in the Second Circuit in December, 1979 under the leadership of Chief Judge Irving R. Kaufman. The project offered a system of guidelines, called benchmarks, for federal trial judges to use in imposing criminal sentences. The benchmarks are recommendations of an appropriate range of time to be served by the defendants in typical criminal cases in the Second Circuit. A committee of judges in the Circuit formulated the benchmarks for 18 typical cases that sentencing judges can use as guidelines. A sentencing judge can measure the contemplated sentence against a benchmark, taking into account differences in the circumstances of the case. Judge Kaufman described the benchmark project as "an important new initiative." He said it sought to lessen sentencing disparities "without transgressing upon the traditional wide discretion of sentencing judges." Under the terms of the project, a sentencing judge who wants a defendant to serve a specific amount of time in prison should inform the Parole Commission of the time he expects the defendant to serve. But the judge is advised not to consider the mandatory time off that a defendant might get for good behavior. Typical cases cited as examples in the project included a stockbroker with no criminal record who used fraudulent statements to sell some stock. The maximum sentence could be five years, but the benchmark recommends three to six months in prison. The recommendation says: "Some incarceration required as a general deterrent." Another example involved someone with a criminal rec-

ord who helped move $100,000 of stolen merchandise from a hijacked truck. The maximum sentence could be five years, but the benchmark recommends two to three years in prison. "The offense is relatively serious, though not involving injury to person. Moderate incarceration indicated as a general and specific deterrent."

BENCH MEMO. The submission by a lawyer, usually upon the request of a trial judge, of a memorandum of law to support the position taken by the lawyer in a case.

BENCH TRIAL. The disposition of a criminal or civil case solely by a judge without the use of a jury.

BENCH WARRANT. A warrant issued by the court for the arrest or attachment of a person to compel his attendance before the court to answer a charge of contempt or to answer an indictment that has been filed against him. The Bench Warrant is usually issued in cases where a person fails to appear in court voluntarily to answer charges against him.

BENEFICIAL INTEREST (Equitable Interest). The right to income or principal of a trust fund. Under a trust arrangement, the legal title of property is held in trust by one person for the beneficiary.

BENEFIT-OF-BARGAIN RULE. Holds that a buyer who has been the victim of fraud is entitled to recover the difference between the actual value of the property and the value which was fraudulently attributed to it. This measure of damages thus allows the defrauded purchaser to recoup the benefit of his bargain.

BENEFITS-RECEIVED PRINCIPLE. A theory of taxation which suggests that taxes for government-supplied goods and services should be assessed in proportion to the benefit received by the taxpayer. The use of fuel taxes to fund highway construction illustrates this principle. In case of many services, such as national defense or government health research, however, it is impossible to measure the benefits. While the benefits-received principle brings the government into the market-place, it does not take into account the redistributive goals of the tax system.

B.E.N.E.L.U.X. A customs and economic union, consisting of Belgium, Luxembourg and Netherlands, created on October 21, 1943. In 1947, four permanent organs were established: a committee of ministers, a consultative joint committee, an arbitration body and a technical committee. Member states have developed successful international trade exchanges and have a common commercial policy. Dozens of commercial agreements have also been concluded with non-member countries.

BENIGN DISCRIMINATION. See AF-FIRMATIVE ACTION.

BENJAMIN, JUDAH PHILIP (1811-1884). An outstanding American and English attorney noted for his contribution to the development of English commercial law. Born to a poor Jewish family in North Carolina, Benjamin became a prominent lawyer and United States Senator. He declined a position on the United States Supreme Court in order to pursue an active political career. When the South seceded from the Union, Benjamin held several key posts in the Confederacy, including At-torney-General, Secretary of War and Secretary of State. He fled to England after the Civil War, where he published his *Treatise on the Law of Sale of Personal Property, with Reference to the American Decisions, to the French Code and Civil Law,* better known as *Benjamin on Sales,* which is still regarded as a classic of English law. He rose to prominence in the English Bar. Upon his retirement, the Bench and Bar gave an unprecedented dinner in his honor.

BENTHAM, JEREMY. English lawyer and philosopher, best known for his exposition of utilitarianism, i.e., the theory that right actions are those which are most useful for producing general welfare and happiness. Applying his theories to penal reform, Bentham ad-vocated requiring criminals to perform useful labor. Bentham was also the acknowledged leader of the philosophical radicals who espoused various reforms based on utilitarianism.

BENTON v. MARYLAND. See DOUBLE JEOPARDY.

B.E.O.G. See FEDERAL COLLEGE-AID STATUTES.

BERNE CONVENTION BACK DOOR. Because many countries are not parties to the Universal Copyright Convention, American citizens sometimes must resort to the protection of the Berne Convention "back door" for their copyrighted materials. While the United States is not a contracting Berne Union country, the terms of the agreement safeguard works in all of its signatory nations—regardless of the nationality of the creator—as long as the work is published first or within thirty days in a member country. The Convention was signed in Berne in 1886 and has been revised on numerous occasions, the last being in 1974. Sixty-five nations had contracted to the agreement as of January 1, 1976.

BERNHARD EXCEPTION. Exception to the Rule of Mutuality of Collateral Estoppel which rule prohibits a stranger to a former action from binding his adversary, who had been a party to the former action. *Bernhard v. Bank of America,* 122 P.2d 892 (1942), the case on which the Bernhard Exception is based, held that only three questions must be answered affirmatively for Collateral Estoppel to apply: (1) Is the issue in the present action identical to the issue decided in a former action? (2) Is the party against whom the issue is asserted a party or privy to the former action? (3) Was there a final judgment on the merits of the issue in the former action? By allowing a stranger to assert Collateral Estoppel, the Bernhard Exception has raised some problems. For example, suppose an airline is involved in an accident in which 100 passengers are injured. If the passengers do not consolidate their claims and if the first passenger to sue wins his action, the remaining 99 passengers may assert Collateral Estoppel against the airline and automatically win. The effect of the Bernhard Exception in such cases forces the airline to litigate each claim fully or face losing against all other claimants. Moreover, plaintiffs in such cases have a powerful incentive not to consolidate their claims, but rather to select a "sympathetic" plaintiff to bring the first suit.

BERNSTEIN EXCEPTION. An exception to the Act of State Doctrine. It holds that wherever the executive branch of the United States government expressly represents to a court that application of the Act of State Doctrine to the particular situation in issue would not advance the interests of American foreign policy, then the court should not apply the doctrine.

BEST EFFORTS CONTRACT. An agreement in which the law implies a promise by one of the parties to use best efforts in carrying out a promise. For example, if a manufacturer grants a retailer the exclusive right to sell its goods, the retailer presumptively promises to use his best efforts to promote their sale.

BEST EVIDENCE RULE. Actually, there is no rule requiring the best evidence obtainable to be produced at trial. The term, however, is sometimes used as a synonym for the original document rule. This rule requires the production of the original writing when proving its terms. Copies are admissible only if the original is unavailable through no serious fault of the party offering the evidence. The Rule is designed to insure the accuracy of evidence and to prevent fraud.

BEST'S RATINGS. Ratings of all major insurance companies published annually by the Alfred M. Best Company. Ratings of life insurance companies are found in *Best's Life Reports.* These ratings consider two factors which reflect financial stability: the results achieved by the company management, which are indicated as favorable, very

favorable, or most favorable; and the funds available to absorb adverse experience, which are rated as considerable, substantial, very substantial, or most substantial. Ratings of property and liability insurers are found in *Best's Insurance Reports,* which also include two ratings. The first is a policyholders' rating which reflects an opinion of the company's relative position in comparison with other companies, based on an analysis of these factors: profitability, economy of management, adequacy of reserves, and soundness of investments. From a consideration of these factors, companies are given a grade ranging from "A Plus" (excellent) to "C" (fair). The second rating is a financial rating which estimates a company's safety factor and is based solely on its financial resources. Ratings run from "AAAAA" for a net safety of $25 million or more, down to "CC" for a net safety factor of $250 thousand or less. Best's Ratings are useful to a prospective insured in selecting an insurance company. Care should be exercised when utilizing these ratings by checking prior ratings of the same company in order to detect downward trends.

BETH DIN. A religious rabbinical court which has the power to dissolve a Jewish marriage through the issuance of a divorce certificate called a Get.

BETTER RULE OF LAW. A doctrine which recognizes that courts faced with choice-of-law problems often follow what they deem to be the better rule. A court may not always select the law of its jurisdiction if such law is outdated.

BEYOND A REASONABLE DOUBT. See BURDEN OF PROOF.

B.F.P. (Bona Fide Purchaser). A purchaser for value in good faith who takes property without notice of any adverse claim. A B.F.P. must pay a valuable consideration, so that a person who acquires legal title to property as a gift is not a B.F.P. The laws of many states also protect B.F.P.s who purchase property which has been stolen.

BICAMERAL LEGISLATURE. A law-making body composed of two internal houses rather than one. The terms bicameral and unicameral originate from the Latin word camera, meaning chamber. Under the bicameral system, all proposed bills must pass both houses before they become law. The United States Congress and most state legislatures are bicameral. Only Nebraska has a unicameral, or one-house, legislature. The present bicameral scheme of the United States Congress reflects the Great Compromise reached by the Founding Fathers at the Philadelphia Convention of 1787. This agreement resolved the debate between proponents of representation based on state population and delegates who supported equal state representation regardless of size. Also called the Connecticut Compromise, it required that each state be represented equally in the Senate and proportionally (by population) in the House of Representatives. The compromise represented a victory for small states, permitting them to concede the necessity of a strong federal government. State legislatures, however, must apportion representatives to both houses on the basis of population. In the landmark 1964 case, *Reynolds v. Sims,* 379 U.S. 870 (1964), the Supreme Court rejected the "federal analogy" advanced by the state, arguing that "[l]egislators represent people, not trees or acres." It based its distinction between federal and state systems, on the sovereign nature of the states represented in the United States Senate.

BID CHOPPING. The practice of subcontractors, particularly in the construction industry, of voluntarily reducing their own bids under the low bid in order to get the subcontract from the general contractor. Because of the prevalence of Bid Chopping, prime contractors and subcontractors often do not expect to be legally bound by prices subcontractors submitted to prime contractors.

BID SHOPPING. A general contractor's use of the low bid already received to pressure subcontractors into submitting even lower bids. Bid Shopping is widespread in the construction industry, where prime contractors and subcontractors often do not regard themselves legally bound by prices submitted by subcontractors to prime contractors.

BIG BLUE (Baby Blue). Two separate but related Right of Privacy reports, so named because of their relative size and color, prepared by a special Federal Interagency Committee for President Carter in December of 1978. They are the result of a study of how to protect computerized personal records against misuse by government agencies and private companies. The Presidential decisions to be made based on them could affect the basic investigative powers of the police and prosecutors throughout the United States, the relationships between patients and doctors and the operations of the insurance and credit industries. Among the key issues and possible options for the President are the following: (1) What restrictions should be placed on the access of federal investigative agencies to personal records held by employers, doctors, the telephone company and other institutions? Federal law enforcement officials within the government have strongly lobbied for minimal controls, while the Privacy Commission recommended procedures to reduce federal access sharply. (2) Should the restrictions ultimately imposed on federal agencies be extended to include local and state law enforcement agencies? Police chiefs and district attorneys are expected to mount a potent lobbying effort against any move to limit their access to personal records. But failure to include such officials could make a promise of privacy an empty one. (3) Should federal restrictions limiting access to personal records be extended to cover insurance companies? Insurance regulation has long been left mostly to the states. But a federal law in this area would guarantee a uniform standard throughout the United States. (4) How much power should be granted an individual to examine and correct records about him held by various institutions? Many organizations are deeply concerned about the expense and administrative difficulty of opening their files to individual citizens. But without regular procedures to correct inaccuracies, great economic and other damage can be unjustly done to citizens.

BIG BULLY. See GUN BOAT DIPLOMACY.

BIGGS, JOHN, JR. Chief judge of the Third Circuit, from 1941 to 1965, who sat on 4,000 cases and wrote 1,500 opinions in his federal judgeship. Former Chief Justice Earl Warren called him a "one-man Ministry of Justice" because of his prodigious and successful efforts in law reform.

BIG SIX. The United States, Great Britain, West Germany, France, Japan and Saudi Arabia, who make the largest contributions to the deposits of the International Monetary Fund and thereby have control of the 21-member executive board of the international money-lending agency.

BIG STICK. See GUN BOAT DIPLOMACY.

BILATERAL CONTRACT. Consists of mutual promises so that each party is both a promisor and a promisee.

BILL OF ATTAINDER. A legislative act designed to punish a particular individual. The Bill of Attainder, which declares guilt and prescribes specific punishment without trial, is forbidden to both Congress and the state legislatures by Article I, sections nine and ten of the United States Constitution. The 1946 decision in *United States v. Lovett*, 328 U.S. 303 (1946), was the first case which held an act of Congress unconstitutional as a Bill of Attainder. The legislation had declared that three individuals were ineligible for continued employment by the government.

BILL OF RIGHTS. The first Ten Amendments to the Constitution of the United States. The Amendments were drafted by James Madison in response to pressures during the Constitutional Convention and the ratification

process for more clearly delineated personal and state rights. The Amendments were ratified in 1791 and include basic protection of free speech, free press and rights of due process of law. All state constitutions contain Bills of Rights, many with provisions similar or identical to those of the United States Constitution.

BILL 101. A controversial legislative proposal in the Provence of Quebec which made French the sole official language of the Provence in education, business and government as a major step in its drive to secede from the Federal Union of Canada and become a separate independent nation.

BIND OVER. To hold a defendant in custody pending the outcome of a criminal trial.

BIOLOGICAL-WARFARE CONVENTION OF 1972. An international agreement to which the United States is a party that prohibits the development, production and stockpiling of bacteriological and toxic weapons, and calls for the destruction of existing stocks of such weapons.

BIRCH ROD BELT. See CANING PRACTICE.

B.I.S. (Bank for International Settlements; Central Banks' Central Banker). A financial institution headquartered in Basel, Switzerland, which plays a key role in international monetary affairs. Among other things, it annually reviews the world's economy and makes recommendations that receive careful consideration within the European Common Market and in institutions such as the International Monetary Fund and the Organization for Economic Cooperation and Development.

BLACK AND WHITE. A police patrol car which is painted in those two colors.

BLACK BAG. See BOODLE BAG.

BLACK BAG JOB. F.B.I. slang for an investigation of questionable legality because it is conducted without a warrant, including illegal break-ins, unauthorized wiretaps and mail thefts, usually under the guise of national security but often perverted for political purposes. A Justice Department investigation resulted in the indictment of John J. Kearney, a retired F.B.I. special unit supervisor, in 1977. This was the first felony indictment in the Bureau's sixty-nine year history. The inquiry also ultimately resulted in the indictment of former F.B.I. Director Clarence Kelley.

BLACK BOOK. Prepared by the White House staff, the Black Book consists of questions which might be raised during a Presidential Press Conference and appropriate answers to be given by the President.

BLACK BOOK OF THE ADMIRALTY. Compiled during the reign of Edward III, it is the highest British authority in Admiralty matters. This book contains sea laws and miscellaneous directives, including the Rules of Oleron, on such matters as maritime torts, injuries, contracts, and Prize Jurisdiction, as well as crimes and offenses cognizable in Admiralty.

BLACK BOX. A sophisticated device aboard a commercial aircraft that automatically records a complete history of the speed, compass direction, altitude and engine power, which is invaluable as evidence to prove legal liability, if any, in the event of a fatal crash.

BLACK CAUCUS. Black members of the United States House of Representatives who consider themselves the political arm and spokesmen of the 25 million Black Americans.

BLACK FEDERAL JUDGES. The first Black man to be given a federal judicial appointment was Robert H. Terrell, who was named judge of the Municipal Court of the District of Columbia in 1910 by President Taft. Judge Terrell was reappointed to that position at four-year intervals by Presidents Wilson and Harding. Upon his death in 1925, he was succeeded by another Black man, James A. Cobb, who served for two terms from 1926 to 1934 by appointment of Presidents

Coolidge and Hoover. A third Black, Armond W. Scott, was later named to this same court by President Roosevelt and subsequently reappointed by Presidents Truman and Eisenhower. The first Black man to be given a lifetime federal judicial appointment was William Hastie, who was named to the United States District Court for the Virgin Islands by President Roosevelt in 1937. In 1949, Judge Hastie was elevated by President Truman to the United States Circuit Court of Appeals for the Third Circuit. Thurgood Marshall was appointed to the Supreme Court of the United States by President Johnson in 1967, after having served as Solicitor General, United States Judge for the Second Circuit, and Director of the N.A.A.C.P. Legal Defense and Education Fund.

BLACK, HUGO. An Associate Justice on the Supreme Court from 1937-71, he decided cases, against vested privilege and concentrated power in favor of the socially weak. Black took an absolutist position toward individual freedoms and felt that the literal language of the Bill of Rights should be adhered to strictly. This attitude was reflected in his view that the action of defamation constituted an unconstitutional threat to the absolute protection that all forms of speech should enjoy. In other words, one should be able to say or write anything about anyone without being sued. An introspective, demure personality, Black had an intense interest in history and civilization. He attended college and law school in Alabama, and was elected to the Senate in 1926. Black's early career was rocked when, immediately after his appointment to the bench, newspaper reporters revealed that he had once been a member of the Ku Klux Klan. In a nationwide radio address, Black calmed the public's fears by denying any present affiliation with the Klan and by affirming his commitment to racial tolerance.

BLACK MARIA. A police vehicle, formerly painted black, used to transport criminals and those accused of crime. Also called a paddy wagon, which probably derived from the fact that at one time many policemen were Irish (Paddy is slang for Irishman).

BLACK MARKET. Transactions conducted in violation of laws restricting price, supply or other trading conditions. Blackmarketeering is often associated with conditions of scarcity, such as during times of war. For instance, during World War II, one in every sixteen of the businesses selling gasoline in the United States was punished for Black Market rationing violations.

BLACK PAPER. A 71-page publication, released by the government of Cambodia (Kampuchea) documenting the take-over of its country by the Vietnamese in 1979, the first act of such aggression having taken place in 1971.

BLACKS AND THE LAW. The history of Black lawyers in America marks a pattern of gradual integration and sporadic acceptance of the Black attorney during the pre-Civil War era, ostracism and discrimination during Reconstruction, and a slow reintegration during the twentieth century. Although few facts are available about Black attorneys before the Civil War in America, Blacks have practiced before the American bar at least since 1848. A few Blacks achieved outstanding successes during the mid-1850s. For example, John Mercer Langston, the first Dean of Howard Law School, was born in 1829, read law in Glyria, Ohio, and was admitted to the Ohio Bar in 1854. After a political career devoted largely to developing the education of Blacks in the South, Langston was appointed the first dean of the newly formed Howard Law School, which opened in 1869 with six students. George Lewis Ruffin, born in 1834, became the first Black to attend Harvard Law School in 1868. He was an outstanding student, finishing his eighteen-months term in one year, and was elected to the Massachusetts legislature in 1870 and 1871. After a successful Boston law practice, Ruffin was appointed a judge of the Charlestown Municipal Court in 1878, becoming the first Black judge in the United States. He died in 1886. The advent of the post-Reconstruction era proved a setback for Black legal education. Even Howard Law School was closed down during 1876 and 1877. However, several Black attorneys achieved a success remarkable for the era in which they practiced. George White, a successful North Carolina lawyer, in 1886 became the last Black elected to Congress until 1928. James Cobb, an 1899 graduate of Howard, practiced successfully in the District of Columbia until 1926, when he was appointed to the D.C. Municipal Court. William Hart, an 1887 (LL.B.) and 1894 (LL.M.) graduate of Howard, was one of the first successful civil rights attorneys. In 1905, he won the case of *Hart v. State*, 60 A. 457 (1905), a significant victory for desegregation. During the 1920s and 1930s, Blacks again found an increasingly important place in legal education. Charles Houston, a Harvard graduate and an editor of the Harvard Law Review, became a famous civil rights attorney, and served as the first full-time legal counsel for the N.A.A.C.P. By 1940, there were about 1,925 Black attorneys in the United States, but Blacks continued to suffer low prestige and discrimination in the profession. During the 1950s, however, Black civil rights lawyers, including Robert Carter and Thurgood Marshall, came into their own. Civil rights cases provided a growing number of Black attorneys with a vehicle for long-deserved recognition of their talents. While subtle discrimination against Blacks continues into the 1970s, a marked trend has certainly begun toward a color-blind bar. More Blacks are entering law school than ever before, and they have received increasing acceptance by traditionally white law firms and businesses.

BLACK SASH. A private group of noble white women in South Africa who voluntarily try to help non-whites who have apartheid policy problems. The name is derived from the mourning sashes worn by the members in the 1950s when they rallied to oppose a law which would disenfranchise mixed-race voters.

BLACKSTONE, WILLIAM. Best known for his *Commentaries* on the law of England, he is one of the foremost British legal philosophers. Blackstone studied architecture at Oxford and was a proficient poet and annotator of Shakespeare prior to embarking on his legal career. Upon entering law school, he wrote *Farewell To A Muse*, in which he expressed his torment on giving up poetry and literature for the law. He did not enjoy much success initially in law and did not gain acclaim until he began delivering lectures on the law. These lectures served as the basis for his *Commentaries*, which he decided to publish himself in order to repress piratical book vendors from selling imperfect copies of his lectures. The first volume was published in 1765, and three more appeared in the next four years. The *Commentaries*, designed to make law attractive to students, are filled with classical allusions. Used by the American Colonists as the basis for their law, the *Commentaries* were disapproved of by Jefferson who feared that they might convert the young law students into Tories.

BLACK TUESDAY. October 29, 1929, the day of the great financial stock market crash which marks the end of the Golden Age of unbridled American capitalism. In the immortal words of the theatrical newspaper, *Variety*, "Wall Street lays an egg."

BLACK WEDNESDAY. June 7, 1978, the day the California citizens voted to roll back real estate taxes thereby putting politicians (who coined the term) on notice that big government and its powers would be curtailed once and for all.

BLAIR HOUSE. Built in Washington, D.C., in 1824 and furnished with rare Americana, this lovely former house of the Blairs of Kentucky is now owned by the federal government and is used as a guest house for visiting foreign dignitaries. Its most famous function was to serve as the site for the 1978 successful Egyptian-Israeli peace talks.

BLANKET AMNESTY. Forgiveness of criminal responsibility given to a group of offenders as a whole, such as draft-dodgers or workers engaged in a criminal strike, as an executive compassionate gesture of good will and healthy community relations.

BLANKET INJUNCTION. See DRAGNET RESTRAINTS.

BLANKET MORTGAGE. A mortgage secured by more than one piece of property. A common means of financing subdivisions, a Blanket Mortgage often contains a partial release provision, whereby the developer is released from the mortgage for each lot as it is sold.

BLEAK HOUSE. See DICKENS, CHARLES.

BLENDED TRUST. A trust for the benefit of a group or groups of people where no ascertainable individual is intended to have any separate rights apart from the others. In a Blended Trust arrangement, no member of the group has any alienable interest in the trust property, which is thus insulated from creditors. For this reason, courts will closely scrutinize Blended Trust arrangements where the group is a family, as such a situation may imply a fraud.

BLIND LAWYERS. There are roughly 500 to 1000 blind lawyers in this country. Some prominent blind lawyers include David Tatel, head of the office of civil rights in the Department of Health, Education and Welfare; Daniel Meador, Assistant Attorney General in charge of the Office for Improvements in the Administration of Justice; and Harold Krents, partner in Surrey, Karasik and Morse, a major international law firm. Krents' life story formed the basis of the broadway play and movie, *Butterflies Are Free*.

BLIND TRUST. A trust device created under federal law whereby assets are put into a trust and the beneficiaries are not furnished information concerning the administration of the trust. As there is no other enforcer of the trust, the trustee operates without restraint. Such a trust has not been worked into state law, and is used mainly by high government officials, to relinquish control of their personal wealth while they are in office.

BLOCK-BUSTING. Inducing homeowners to sell their property by spreading rumors about the prospective entry into the neighborhood of minorities. This reprehensible practice is prohibited by the Fair Housing Act. Speculators use Block-Busting to buy up houses cheaply and resell them at considerably higher prices to minority buyers.

BLUE BOOK. (1) A massive 1,300 page verbatim transcript of those parts of the Watergate tapes which were selected carefully by President Nixon for submission to the Judiciary Committee conducting the impeachment investigation in an unsuccessful attempt to conceal the President's criminal involvement, if not duplicity. The public was treated to a subsequent display of the Blue Book on TV with an accompanying plea for forebearance from the President, which was similar to his previously successful "Checkers Talk" when he ran for the Vice-Presidency. Checkers was the name of a dog given to his family as a gift and Nixon proclaimed proudly that he would not return it at the expense of the happiness of his family. (2) A collection of quotations and parables of Col. Mummar Qaddafi, fanatical leader of the Libyans, modeled after the Red Book of Premier Mao Tse-tung of China. It is also known as the Green Book. (3) A voluminous volume prepared by the staff of the Joint Tax Committee of Congress to explain to the public the terms of the complicated lawyer-drafted Revenue Act of 1978. (4) (A Uniform System of Citation). A small booklet which states elaborate rules for legal citation of authorities when writing briefs, memos, or law review articles. It states the official abbreviations to be used for all types of legal materials. The cover of the booklet is blue, hence the nickname. It was formerly known as the White Book, for the same reason.

BLUE BOX. A gadget which, when attached to a telephone, enables the cheat to make long distance telephone calls free of charge. A federal law makes it a criminal offense.

BLUE FLU. A mythical disease magically contracted simultaneously by public employees, such as the New Orleans police, who do not have the legal right to strike. Their failure to report for work on alleged medical disability at times inconvenient to the public is used as a potent weapon to obtain higher wages and increased fringe benefits.

BLUE LAWS (Lord's Day Laws; Sabbath Breaking Laws; Sunday Closing Laws; Sunday Trading Laws). Statutes which prohibit or regulate business and recreational activities on Sunday. Because the Puritans adopted the color blue as a symbol of opposition to the red emblem of the ruling British aristocracy, their rigid regulations for Sabbath observance were called Blue Laws. In 1961, the Supreme Court declared such laws constitutional, rejecting a claim that they established religion in violation of the First Amendment. While the theological dimensions of Blue Laws date from pagan worship on the "venerable day of the Sun," Emperor Constantine of Rome promulgated the first Civil Sunday Code in 321 A.D. Oliver Cromwell instituted far-reaching Sunday laws in seventeenth-century England. Originally religious mandates, Blue Laws thus became civil statutes. Virginia and the Plymouth Colony initiated Blue Laws in the United States in the 1600s. In Virginia, economic sanctions were imposed for the first violation of such laws, whipping for the second, and death for the third. The Plymouth Colony relied on the stocks as punishment. In 1656, Captain Kemble of Boston was put in the stocks for two hours because he kissed his wife on the steps of their house on the

Sabbath after returning from a three-year voyage. Even George Washington, shortly after his election to the Presidency, was stopped by a roadside guard because he was travelling by horseback on Sunday in violation of Connecticut's Blue Law. In the early part of this century, baseball could not be played in some states on Sunday. More lenient states restricted such amusements to people under age 14, postponed games until after 2 p.m., and prohibited them within certain distances of houses of worship. Today, many states still retain Blue Laws of varying degrees of severity.

BLUE RIBBON JURY (Special Jury). May be ordered by the court on the motion of either party in cases of great importance or unusual complexity. Such juries were used often at common law where the causes were too intricate to be decided by ordinary freeholders. Many states now provide for a Blue Ribbon Jury by statute in cases where the court determines that it is essential to a fair trial or where difficult technical issues require a special jury. Often, the Blue Ribbon Jury is used when an understanding of the facts in the case requires persons with certain skills or knowledge, as in a particular area of science or industry. Such juries are also used when the case consists of multiple defendants and issues and the trial will continue for several weeks, placing great demands on the jurors. Defendants often request the court to convene a special jury when the case has been in the public eye and the task of selecting impartial jurors under regular procedures is virtually impossible.

BLUE RIBBON LAW SCHOOLS (National Law Schools). The dozen alleged best law schools in the country. Their curricula is not geared to the law of the state in which the school is located and they do not concentrate entirely on enabling the graduates to pass the Bar Examination as is true for the so-called "trade" schools.

BLUE SKY LAWS. State statutes designed to protect the public from specu-lative and potentially devastating investment schemes. Blue Sky Laws are not pre-empted by the Federal Securities Act of 1933, and all states except Delaware have them today. They remain important regulatory laws because they cover some transactions exempt from the federal Act and also because many of them require more than the disclosure contemplated by the federal Act. Kansas is credited with passing the first Blue Sky Law in 1911. Although some commentators point out that Connecticut enacted the functional equivalent of a Blue Sky Law in 1903, the term probably originated in Kansas. Experts contend that because of the large number of Kansas farmers not versed in securities investments, it was possible for unscrupulous dealers to sell building lots in the blue sky itself. There are three basic types of Blue Sky Laws: those which protect against fraud; those which control registration of securities provisions, and those dealing with broker-dealer registration provisions. Lack of uniformity in these laws among states has caused complex conflict of laws problems. As a result, there is a trend to adopt the Uniform Securities Act which is acceptable to states with differing regulatory philosophies.

BLUE SLIP VETO. Rejection by one or two Senators of a nominee for the position of federal judge or United States Attorney. When the President appoints a federal judge or United States Attorney, the Senate Judiciary Committee sends Blue Slips to the Senators of the nominee's state. The slips ask each Senator whether he approves of the nomination. The Senate Judiciary Committee will not approve a nomination unless both Senators concur, thus giving a single Senator the power to veto a nomination. Senators of opposing parties respect each other's patronage arrangements. When neither Senator is of the President's party, the Senators usually defer to House members from their state.

BOARD FOR INTERNATIONAL BROADCASTING. An independent Federal agency responsible to the Presi-

55

dent and the Congress, consisting of five members appointed by the President by and with the advice of the Senate for a term of 3 years. Members are selected from among Americans distinguished in the fields of foreign policy or mass communications; no more than three members may be of the same political party. The Board's function is to oversee the operations of Radio Liberty, which broadcasts to the Union of Soviet Socialist Republics, and Radio Free Europe, which broadcasts to Poland, Romania, Czechoslovakia, Hungary, and Bulgaria.

BOARD OF CURATORS OF UNIVERSITY OF MISSOURI v. HOROWITZ. See DIRTY SMOCK CASE.

BOARD OF DIRECTORS. Manages a corporation by determining corporate policy and appointing officers to carry out such policies. The Board usually consists of at least three directors, elected by the shareholders, although many statutes presently allow fewer directors where there are only one or two shareholders. Some statutes state a maximum number of directors. In order to avoid deadlock, it is common to have an odd number of Directors on the Board.

BOARD OF IMMIGRATION APPEALS. The highest immigration administrative tribunal, charged with the interpretation and administration of the immigration laws. It is comprised of the Chairman and four members, who are appointed by the Attorney General. The Board has nationwide jurisdiction, and its rulings are the most important source of immigration administrative case law in the nation. Additionally, the board has the responsibility for carrying out the congressional mandate that the immigration laws be applied uniformly throughout the United States.

BOARD OF PATENT APPEALS. If an application for a patent privilege or any claims therein are rejected by the patent examiner, the applicant may appeal to this federal agency. The Board is under the auspices of the United States Patent Office and generally consists of three members selected from a group comprised of the commissioner, the assistant commissioners, and the examiners-in-chief.

BOARD OF PATENT INTERFERENCES. When the United States Patent Office institutes an Interference Procedure to determine which of two competing parties was the first inventor of a work, this board of three interference examiners reviews the evidence submitted and awards a patent privilege. Approximately 2 percent of the applications received by the Patent Office come before the board for review.

BOARD OF REVIEW. See COURT OF MILITARY REVIEW.

BOARDS OF CONTRACT APPEALS. Judicial-type administrative Boards which consider and decide appeals by government agency contractors from decisions of contracting officers or other government representatives.

BOAT PEOPLE. The Indo-Chinese who leave Southeast Asia by sea to join the 200,000 refugees already admitted to the United States and other nations since the fall of Saigon in April, 1975. Each month there are thousands of new refugees. The United States has been urged to accept these pitiful people in their flight to freedom in keeping with the spirit of the Statue of Liberty in New York Harbor: "Give me your tired, your poor, your huddled masses yearning to breathe free." Many Asian countries refuse to accept any of these refugees who are sent out to a certain death on the sea. Some ships violate the traditional law of the sea by refusing to take them on board in order to avoid difficulties with the port at which they will next land.

BODDIE v. CONNECTICUT, 401 U.S. 371 (1971). Supreme Court ruling which prohibits State Courts from refusing to grant a divorce solely because of inability of the parties to pay court fees.

BODY EXECUTION STATUTES. Allow a Sheriff to levy execution of a court judgment on the body of a debtor, thus empowering the Sheriff to imprison a debtor without any proof that he is able to pay his debts. Such statutes are unconstitutional unless they provide for hearings prior to incarceration to determine if the debtor was concealing assets in order to avoid paying the debt. Sheer inability to pay is not grounds for incarceration as it denies equal protection to poor people.

BOGOTA CONFERENCE (1948). Attended by all American countries, except Canada, in order to develop the Pan American Union. An attempt to create the structure of a regional organization under Article 51 of the U.N. Charter, it reinforces the principles of the Pan American Union by creating bases for the Organization of American States (O.A.S.). As defined by the Bogota Conference, its purposes are peace and security.

B.O.G.S.A.A.T. See KIDDIE KORPS.

BOILER PLATE. Standard formal legal language (legalese) used in motions, deeds, wills, pleadings, contracts, leases, closings and other formal documents. Boiler Plate may also be defined as excessive verbiage used in routine matters to cover every conceivable contingency. It is usually baffling to laymen, but has been accepted by courts for so long that lawyers have little incentive to simplify documents.

BOILER ROOM. A slang term for a noisy establishment which sells speculative stocks, often by phone, in violation of state and federal securities laws.

BOLIN, JANE. The first Black woman judge in the United States, having been appointed to the New York City Domestic Relations Court by Mayor Fiorello LaGuardia in 1939.

BOLLING v. SHARPE (347 U.S. 497 (1954)). A Supreme Court case decided the same day as *Brown v. Board of Education*. In this case, the Court held that racial discrimination in the District of Columbia public schools violated the due process clause of the Fifth Amendment.

BONA FIDE (Latin—in good faith, without fraud or deceit). A Bona Fide Possessor is one who possesses land or goods without knowledge of an adverse claim to title of the property.

BONA FIDE NEED RULE. In federal government contracting this Comptroller General-imposed rule states that the obligation of government funds is valid only to the extent the supplies or services contracted for are intended to serve a legitimate need of the fiscal year for which the appropriation was made.

BONA FIDE PURCHASER. See B.F.P.

B-1 VISA. See H-1 VISA.

BONN HIJACK AGREEMENT (1978). Toughest stand ever taken by seven major industrial nations to combat airline terrorism. The Agreement would cut off commercial airline service to or from any country that harbors airplane hijackers. This collective action should drastically reduce if not eliminate all future airplane hijacking since no nation could survive any such boycott of its air traffic.

BOODLE BAG (Black Bag). A packet of money in local foreign currency given to an American government V.I.P. visitor, usually $75 a day but more is available if requested, for "incidentals" even though all the expenses have already been taken care of. The money most frequently is drawn from funds owed by the host country to the United States in a foreign aid program.

BOODLING PRACTICE. A slang term used to describe legislative corruption.

BOOK ENTRY SECURITY. A transferable bond, not a certificate of indebtedness or bill, issued under the Second Liberty Bond Act, or a bond, note, certificate of indebtedness, bill debenture or similar obligation issued by any other agency of the United States government or by the Federal National Mortgage Association, the Tennessee Valley Authority or certain statutory banks, which is in the form of an entry on the records of a Federal Reserve Bank under certain banking or other federal regulations.

BOON-DOGGLING. A common expression for unproductive employment. The expression gained popularity during the Depression to describe many of the projects initiated by the Roosevelt Administration to stimulate the job market.

BOOTH, JOHN WILKES. After shooting President Lincoln on April 14, 1865, Booth fled through Maryland. He stopped at the home of Dr. Samuel Mudd, who set the broken leg of the assassin without knowing Booth's identity. Booth's flight ended at the farm of Richard Garrett near Bowling Green, Virginia, where he was surrounded by federal troops under the command of Secretary of War Edwin M. Stanton. The barn in which he was hiding was set ablaze, and the dead body of the actor found therein. Historians are largely undecided as to whether he was shot or committed suicide.

BOOTSTRAP SALE. In tax law, a sale to a charity or other buyer where the buyer pays for the property out of its profit without personal liability.

BOOT TRANSACTIONS. A tax term used to describe corporate reorganizations in which money or other property is received in addition to stock and securities. Originally, the term Boot referred to property which was given in an exchange to equalize the values of what was traded.

BORDER PATROL. See IMMIGRATION AND NATURALIZATION SERVICE.

BORMAN REPORT. Named after the former astronaut and chairman of a committee investigating Honor Code scandals at the United States Military Academy (West Point) in December, 1976, this investigation led to a drastic overhaul in many aspects of the operation of this institution.

BORROWING STATUTE. A state Statute which applies the Statute of Limitations of another jurisdiction to a suit in a court of the forum state. Under the common law, the forum state applies its own Statute of Limitations in all suits. Whether an action is barred thus depends on where the suit is brought. However, Borrowing Statutes achieve some uniformity, usually by adopting the Statute of Limitations of the jurisdiction in which a cause of action arose.

BOSTON BUCKLE. See DENVER BOOT.

BOTTLE BILLS. State laws designed to banish "throwaways" by requiring a small cash deposit on beer and soft drink containers to encourage their return to the retailer and thus reduce litter on the highways. The laws usually also ban the use of beverage cans with detachable flip-tops.

BOXCAR DISCOVERY. The type of discovery used by attorneys who wish to inquire into everything. The technique is so named because the mass of data requested is so great that the adverse party often feels compelled to transport it by boxcar. Under the broad rules of civil discovery, any information not otherwise privileged may be examined, so long as it is relevant to the subject matter of the action (Federal Rules of Civil Procedure, Rule 26(b)). Inquiry may thus be made not only of facts which bear on the case of the examining party, but also of information which relates to claims asserted by the adverse party.

BOYS IN BLUE. Slang for policemen who wear a uniform of that color.

BRACERO PROGRAM. An agreement between the United States and Mexico in effect between 1942 and 1964 which allowed unskilled Mexican laborers to come to work in the United States to alleviate the manpower shortage in the United States.

BRADWELL, MYRA. The first woman in the United States to seek official sanction to become an attorney. On August 2, 1869, she successfully completed her required legal studies meritoriously and filed her formal application for a license to practice law in Illinois. But the Supreme Court of

Illinois denied her petition on the technical ground that she was married, and this action was upheld by the United States Supreme Court in 1872, in the course of which Justice Joseph P. Bradley made the following statement: "The civil law, as well as nature herself, has always recognized a wide difference in the respective spheres and destinies of men and women. Man is, or should be, woman's protector and defender. The natural and proper timidity and delicacy which belongs to the female sex evidently unfits it for many of the occupations of civil life."

BRAIN TRUST. See FEDERAL CABINET.

BRANDEIS BRIEF. See BRANDEIS, LOUIS.

BRANDEIS, LOUIS. Appointed to the United States Supreme Court in 1916 and serving until 1939, he was hailed as a "liberal" Justice because he urged judicial restraint in overturning social welfare legislation. However, Brandeis felt that government should protect people against themselves and therefore supported legislation such as prohibition laws. To him, First Amendment freedoms deserved preferential treatment over economic liberties. Brandeis stressed empirical observation rather than reasoning from abstract principles; his oft-copied "Brandeis brief" enshrined the "living law" by forging legal principles out of masses of sociological, economic, and scientific studies. Later, his judicial opinions would be similarly suffused with statistical data. The son of German immigrants who settled in Kentucky, Brandeis entered Harvard Law School in 1875 at the age of 18. He felt uncomfortable there because he was a Southerner, a Jew, and had no college education. Upon graduation and prior to his service on the Court, he practiced law in Boston and gained a reputation as an economic reformer because of his numerous challenges of monopolies. He also was reputed to be quite austere. He shunned dancing, drinking, and other gaieties; he maintained short work days (to "keep his mind fresh"),

and always kept the heat in his office low to save money.

BRANDENBURG v. OHIO. See CLEAR AND PRESENT DANGER DOCTRINE.

BREAKING AND ENTERING. At common law, two major elements of burglary. Burglary, under the common law, was defined as breaking and entering a dwelling, at night, with the intent to commit a felony. "Breaking" referred only to uninvited entry, and did not necessarily require force or violence. Opening a closed door constituted breaking, as did entry of a servant into a forbidden section of the house. The "entering" element was satisfied by the slightest entry, such as a hand through a window. Today in most states, statutory criminal law supersedes the common law, and definitions of breaking and entering differ among the states.

BREAKING BULK. The act by a bailee of opening closed containers given to him by the bailor. Such act has legal significance in that it indicates when a bailee may be liable for larceny. If he does not break bulk, the bailee is considered in possession of the property. Although he may be guilty of embezzlement should he misappropriate the property, he cannot be guilty of larceny because larceny is a crime against possession. Once he breaks bulk, however, a bailee is no longer regarded as in possession of the property. Should he take the property with the intent of keeping it permanently, he is guilty of larceny.

BREATHALYZER TEST. Designed to determine whether a driver has been drinking alcohol. The Breathalyzer consists of a tube of chemical crystals through which the driver breathes. If he has been drinking, the alcohol on his breath causes the crystals to change color. The Breathalyzer Test is now given by British Bobbies and some law enforcement officers predict it will be widely used in the United States.

BRENT, MARGARET. The first woman to handle a law case for a client in

America. She was an English gentlewoman who reached the shores of Maryland in 1638. In her initial court appearance, armed with a power of attorney from one Fulke Brent, she sued for 3,000 pounds of tobacco due from one Marmaduke Snow. Thereafter, from 1642 to 1650, her name appears in records of the judicial and testamentary business of the Provincial Court no less than 124 times. The high point of her career was her appointment as the sole executrix of the estate of Governor Calvert of Maryland.

BRETTON WOODS CONFERENCE. (1944). Attended by representatives of 44 countries, the Conference was designed to create better international monetary and financial conditions for the post-war period. The goals of the Conference were (1) to promote international trade by reducing protectionist national measures, and (2) to restore world economic relations by a return to free convertibility of national currencies. To implement these goals, the Conference attempted to keep the various world currencies in stable relationship to one another, and to provide loans with which war-devastated countries could finance their reconstruction and future development. The Bretton Woods Agreement (1945) created two organizations: The International Monetary Fund (I.M.F.) and the World Bank (I.R.B.D.). Because of the decision of the United States on August 15, 1971 to stop the gold-convertibility of the dollar, and because of the international monetary crisis, the Bretton Woods System has been modified. Without renouncing the purposes of the Bretton Conference, the Jamaica Conference (1976) abandoned the Bretton Woods monetary system by abolishing the gold-standard system which constituted the basis of the I.M.F.

BREWER v. WILLIAMS (430 U.S. 387 (1977)). A Supreme Court case concerning the right to counsel. The Court held that the defendant had led a detective to the victim's body as a result of an interrogation that violated his Sixth Amendment right to assistance of counsel. Thus, the defendant's conviction was reversed.

BRIDGE LOAN (Bridge Mortgage; Gap Financing). Short-term financing paid in the interim until permanent financing of real estate has been obtained.

BRIEF IN FORMA PAUPERIS. Prepared in handwriting or typewriting in order to avoid the expense of printing. Courts often permit prisoners to submit such briefs.

BRINGING A GIFT INTO HOTCHPOT. A method by which the donee of an advancement can share in the distribution of the intestate estate by adding the amount of his gift to the estate, thus creating a "hotchpot." Once the gift has been "brought into hotchpot," the newly augmented estate is divided equally among the donee and the intestate successors. A donee will invoke this procedure if his Pro Rata share of the estate will exceed the amount of his advancement.

BRITISH BOBBY. Popular name for an English law-enforcement officer, coined by Prime Minister Sir Robert Peel, who established the first police force in London in 1829.

BRITISH OFFICIAL SECRETS ACT. A law first passed in England in 1911, during a spy scare period, which punishes through fine and imprisonment the publication of any military or civilian information which jeopardizes the national security. Section Two of the Act enables the government to jail anyone for publishing material which has not been officially released. Although Section Two is rarely used, it has been heavily criticized by the press for inhibiting "whistle blowers" and chilling journalistic probes into the government.

BROOKINGS INSTITUTE. A nonprofit think-tank engaged in research and education in the fields of economics, government, law, foreign policy and the social services. Founded in 1927 as a consolidation of the Institute for Government Research, the Institute of Economics and the Robert Brookings Graduate School of Economics and Government, the Institute is named after St. Louis businessman Robert Somers Brookings (1850-1932). It is supported largely by private funds and serves as a link between the academic community and public and private leaders dealing with issues of social and public policy.

BROWN v. BOARD OF EDUCATION (347 U.S. 483 (1954)). A United States Supreme Court case which held de jure segregation in public schools to be a violation of the 14th Amendment's Equal Protection Clause. Seventeen states had provided "separate but equal" community schools for Black and White children. The Supreme Court rejected the separate but equal argument, saying separate schools were inherently unequal because they caused Black students to feel inferior. The unanimous decision was such a serious one that Justice Jackson, who was in the hospital recovering from a heart attack, insisted on illustrating the Court's solidarity by coming to the Court for the announcement of the ruling. So sensitive were the issues that all writing between Justices about the decision was delivered personally, the only time such a practice was followed by the Warren Court. Chief Justice Warren intentionally wrote a short opinion for the Court because he wanted it to be publishable in its entirety in the daily press across the country. Reactions to *Brown* were vigorous. Over 100 Senators and Representatives signed a Southern Manifesto urging states to defy the ruling. President Eisenhower did not conceal his dissatisfaction and his close association with Chief Justice Warren was cooled considerably. Although *Brown* served as an impetus to strike down de jure segregation in other public facilities, southern states resisted the trend so vigorously that not until the passage of the 1964 Civil Rights Act and the spectre of federal action did desegregation begin on a broad scale.

BRUSSELS TREATY ORGANIZATION. Created on March 17, 1948, by the United Kingdom, France, Belgium, Netherlands, and Luxembourg, it was an organization of military defense and mutual assistance. One of its initial purposes was to prevent the possibility of new German aggression against Western Europe. It provided for a Council of Foreign Ministers, with a consultative role, a permanent commission, and a Supreme Allied Command. The political and military inadequacy of the Brussels Treaty Organization was corrected by the Atlantic Pact (N.A.T.O.) on April 4, 1949, and by the Council of Europe on May 5, 1949. In 1954, a series of agreements amending the Treaty created the Western European Union (W.E.U.).

BUBBLE CONCEPT. The Environmental Protection Agency's practice of considering a factory's pollution emission in the aggregate as though it were a bubble instead of separately gauging emission from each process within the factory, in order to determine any violation of federal law. Manufacturers prefer the Bubble Concept because it gives them more leeway in meeting statutory standards.

B.U.C.C.$. See DEBTORS ANONYMOUS.

BUCK v. BELL (274 U.S. 200 (1927)). A Supreme Court case that sustained a state law providing for the sterilization of mental defectives in installations. In an oft-quoted statement, Justice Holmes said that "Three generations of imbeciles are enough."

BUCKET SHOP. Fictitious stock exchange in which contracts are made for the purchase and sale of stocks with no intention of actually delivering the property bought or sold.

BUCKLEY AMENDMENT. A federal statute, which went into effect in 1975, whose purpose is to provide a student and his parents access to his school records and to limit dissemination of such records without consent. Since student records follow a person for life, they can influence his ability to get a job or even to obtain a loan. The Act is designed to assure that these records do not contain misinformation. Nevertheless, many institutions have balked at compliance with the Buckley Amendment and some have even destroyed student records to avoid disclosing the information they contain. The Buckley Amendment takes its name from Senator James Buckley of New York.

BUCKLEY 48. A group of federal civilian employees at the high-security Buckley Air National Guard Base outside Denver, Colorado, who were discharged after they had admitted to being infrequent smokers of marijuana. They were subsequently re-instituted when their lawyer proved that they were tricked by the government into making their statements as a voluntary part of an alleged investigation to unearth espionage.

BUCKLEY v. VALEO (424 U.S. 1 (1976)). A Supreme Court case that held unconstitutional the composition of the Federal Election Campaign Commission established by the Federal Election Campaign Act. The Act provided that a majority of the voting members of the Commission would be appointed by the President pro tempore of the Senate and the Speaker of the House. However, the Court held that congressional appointment of members violated the Appointment Clause of the Constitution because the Commission exercised non-legislative powers. Accordingly, Congress reestablished the Commission, providing that its membership would consist entirely of presidential appointees. The challengers also claimed that public financing of presidential election campaigns was contrary to the general welfare, but the Court ruled that Congress has power to regulate presidential elections and primaries.

BUDGET AND ACCOUNTING ACT OF 1921. See GENERAL ACCOUNTING OFFICE.

BUDGET AND CREDIT COUNSELING SERVICE OF THE COMMUNI- TY SERVICE SOCIETY. See DEBTORS ANONYMOUS.

BUDGET AUTHORITY. The authority provided by law to enter into obligations which will result in immediate or future outlays of government funds. Obligations are commitments of the Federal Budget Authority made by federal agencies during a given period which will require outlays of federal funds during the same or some future period.

BUENOS AIRES CONFERENCE (1967). Attended by the Foreign Ministers of the O.A.S., its purpose was to improve the structure of the O.A.S. The meeting of the chiefs of states at Punta del Este, which resulted from the Conference, set as a goal for the O.A.S. the establishment of a Latin-American Common Market by 1970, but this attempt has not as yet been successful.

BULK SALE ACTS. Statutes which are designed to prevent a secret sale of a debtor-merchant's goods in order to defraud his creditors. Such statutes require that creditors be notified of any sale of a debtor's stock.

BULLET PROOF. A legal document with no loopholes in it.

BULL PEN. A room in a large metropolitan law firm of the Wall Street type where new associates are housed together, securely isolated from contact with clients, to engage in researching and writing legal memoranda, until that happy day when they graduate into a room of their own complete with a private secretary.

BUMBLE BEES. See KILLER BEES.

BUMPERS AMENDMENT. A federal law proposed in 1980 which would alter the presumption of validity that attaches to a federal agency rule or regulation, and, in legal challenges, would require the federal government to prove the rule's validity by a preponderance of the evidence.

BUMPING-OFF. See BACK-TRACKING.

BUNCH OF GUYS SITTING AROUND A TABLE (B.O.G.S.A.A.T.). See KIDDIE KORPS.

BUNCO GAME. A scheme in which one person induces another, by a trick or play calculated to win his confidence, to play a game that he cannot win, such as a rigged lottery. In many states one who obtains property or money through a bunco game is guilty of larceny or a related criminal offense.

BURDEN OF PERSUASION. See BURDEN OF PROOF.

BURDEN OF PRODUCTION. See BURDEN OF PROOF.

BURDEN OF PROOF. Encompasses the obligations of presenting evidence (the Burden of Production) and of persuading the jury (the Burden of Persuasion). Both Burdens are generally placed on the same party in civil cases. The burdens are normally on the plaintiff, the party seeking to change the status quo. Since a criminal defendant is presumed to be innocent until proven guilty, the state must carry the Burden of Proof in a criminal trial. The party with the Burden of Persuasion must convince the jury that a certain proposition (e.g., that the defendant was negligent, that the defendant committed the robbery) is true in order to prevail at trial. The degree of conviction which the jury must have, however, varies with the type of court proceeding. In most civil suits, the jury must believe that it is more probable than not that the proposition at issue is true. To explain the degree of conviction required, a court will often instruct the jury that the party with the Burden of Persuasion must prove the critical proposition by a "preponderance of the evidence." The state must offer evidence sufficient to convince the jury "beyond a reasonable doubt" in a criminal trial. This standard is higher than that employed in civil litigation; yet, it does not imply that the jury must be convinced beyond any conceivable doubt. In a few civil actions (e.g., a claim of fraud), where

the plaintiff's contention is disfavored by the court since the jury is likely to be deceived, the plaintiff must prove his case by "clear and convincing proof." In such a case, the jury must be left with a degree of conviction between that required in a criminal case and in most civil suits. Whenever the jury is not convinced to the necessary degree, it must return a verdict against the party with the Burden of Persuasion. Before a court will allow a jury to decide whether a party has met the Burden of Persuasion, the court must determine whether the party has met his Burden of Production. This Burden is satisfied by producing enough evidence to allow a reasonable man to conclude that the proposition which the party seeks to prove is true. Unless a reasonable man could so conclude, a jury will not be allowed to do so. Rather, the judge will honor an opponent's motion challenging the "sufficiency of the evidence" and direct a verdict against the party with the Burden of Production. A party who satisfies his Burden of Production is said to have presented a "prima facie case" and is entitled to have his case submitted to the jury.

BUREAU OF INTELLIGENCE AND RESEARCH (Department of State). See UNITED STATES INTELLIGENCE-GATHERING CENTERS.

BUREAU OF LABOR STATISTICS. Federal agency best known for preparing the Cost-of-Living Index. The Bureau also functions to compile statistics and facts about the field of labor economics generally.

BUREAU OF MEDICAL DEVICES. See MEDICAL DEVICE AMENDMENTS TO FOOD, DRUG AND COSMETIC ACT.

BUREAU OF THE MINT. The Mint of the United States was established by Congress in 1792. The Bureau of the Mint was established by Congress in 1873. The functions of the Bureau are the production of coins, both domestic and foreign; the manufacture and sale of medals of a national character; the manufacture and sale of proof and uncirculated coin sets, Bicentennial coins and medals, and other numismatic items; and the custody, processing, and movement of bullion. The Mint disburses gold and silver for authorized purposes; directs the distribution of coins from the mints to the Federal Reserve Banks and branches; and compiles and analyzes general data of worldwide scope relative to gold, silver, and coins.

BURKE, HAROLD P. Oldest living active federal judge in the country (84 in 1980). He is senior in service, having been appointed by President Franklin D. Roosevelt in 1937, in Rochester, New York.

BURGER COURT. The Burger Court is also known as the Nixon Court since the Chief Justice, Warren Earl Burger, and three other members of the High Bench (Blackmun, Powell and Rehnquist) were all appointed by President Nixon. It differs from its predecessor, the Warren Court, in its protection of the institutions of government rather than the rights of individuals.

BURGLARY ATTEMPT. See BREAKING AND ENTERING.

BURGUNDIAN CODE. The Germanic law codified by Kings Gundogad and Sigismund in the late fifth and early sixth centuries. Although the Code covers Germanic law, it is written in Latin, reflecting the influence of the Roman Empire. The Code affords scholars the opportunity to compare the legal norms and institutions of a barbarian people with those of their more civilized neighbors, the Romans.

BURR, AARON. From March 30 to October 19, 1807, Aaron Burr stood trial in Richmond, Virginia, on a charge of treason against the United States. In a stormy trial, which involved political intrigue and scandal concerning then President Thomas Jefferson, Burr was acquitted on all charges. Chief Justice John Marshall, as a normal federal trial judge on the Richmond circuit, presided. The alleged overt act of treason was the assembling of a force in Virginia (now West Virginia) which was to create an independent nation from land recently acquired by the United States under the Louisiana Purchase. However, the plot never really matured. The force numbered less than 100 men. From the beginning the trial was very political with the Jeffersonian Democrats pitted against the Federalists. Even before the trial started, President Jefferson publicly branded Burr guilty of treason in a message to Congress. Although Burr was acquitted, his reputation was ruined. He lived in Europe for a while, then returned to the United States, where he lived quietly until his death on September 14, 1836.

BURROS AND HORSES ACT (1971). Congressional declaration that free roaming burros and horses should be protected from capture, branding, harassment or death. Under common law, wild animals are owned by the sovereign state in trust for the benefit of the people. Protection of burros and horses was so successful under this Act that the government recently initiated an adoption program (placement of the animals with private families) in order to cull the herds.

BURSTING BUBBLE THEORY. A principle of evidence which holds that a presumption vanishes with the introduction of evidence which supports a finding that the presumed fact does not exist. The Theory has been criticized on the ground that it makes presumptions appear too evanescent. Although some state courts still adhere to the Bursting Bubble Theory, it is rejected in the new Federal Rules of Evidence. Rule 301, dealing with presumptions in civil actions and proceedings, places upon the opposing party the burden of establishing the nonexistence of the presumed fact, once the party invoking the presumption establishes the basic facts giving rise to it.

BUSINESS CONDITIONS DIGEST. See CONSUMER BUYING EXPECTATIONS.

BUSINESS INSURANCE TRUST. A trust arrangement, consisting of life insurance policy contracts, created in connection with a business. The term is also applied to a trust arrangement created for the liquidation of business interests or business credit. Typically, these trusts are created to benefit corporate employees and to expedite the sound financial status of a corporation.

BUSINESS JUDGMENT RULE. Protects corporate management from liability for acts which are intra vires, performed with due care, and in accordance with their fiduciary duties. The purpose of the rule is to encourage creativity and independence in corporate management and to keep courts from having to second-guess decisions of corporate management. Management includes the board of directors, officers, and sometimes controlling shareholders.

BUSINESS RECORDS EXCEPTION. See SHOPBOOK RULE.

BUSINESS ROUNDTABLE. A major lobbying group for businesses.

BUSINESS TRANSFER PAYMENTS. Money paid by the business sector for which no goods or services are received in return. Thus, there is no offsetting contribution to the economy's productive process. Included are corporate gifts to nonprofit institutions, consumer bad debts, and personal injury payments by business to other persons other than employees. Estimates of unrecovered thefts of cash and capital assets and cash prizes are also included.

BUSINESS TRUST. See MASSACHUSETTS TRUST.

BUSINESS VISITOR STATUS VISA. See H-1 VISA.

BUY AMERICAN. (1) A basic tenet of public contracting by the federal government, enacted into law in 1933, which requires the government and its agencies to purchase American goods unless their cost is "unreasonable," in which case 6-12 percent was added to bids of foreign manufacturers who wished to do business with Uncle Sam. This "add-on" for foreigners bidding for defense contracts was raised to 50 percent in 1972 in order to protect a favorable American balance of payments status. (2) Laws enacted by some states which require state agencies to buy only domestic goods on which condition a public works contract is awarded on the agreement by the contractor to use only American-made materials. Such a statute was struck down by a California Court in *Bethlehem Steel Corp. v. Board of Commissioners of Department of W.C.P.,* 80 Cal. Rptr. 800 (1969), on the ground that any state statute which touches on foreign affairs is proscribed by the Constitution. Recently, however, the New Jersey Supreme Court held that the state's Buy American statute did not impermissibly interfere with the federal government's conduct of foreign affairs, nor was the statute held to conflict with the Commerce Clause. The New Jersey court held that the statute in question fitted a special exception to the General Agreement on Tariffs and Trade (G.A.T.T.), a multi-lateral international agreement that requires foreign products to be accorded no less favorable treatment under the law than that accorded domestic products. The important exemption concerns laws "governing the procurement by governmental agencies of products purchased for governmental purposes and not with a view to use in the production of goods for commercial sale."

BUY-BACKS. See GIVE-BACKS.

BUY-BACK SCAM. A fraudulent sale in which a dishonest seller defaults in his false promise to buy back a worthless product sold to a naive buyer.

BUZZO ACT (1959). California Vehicle Code law which proscribes throwing cigarettes, matches, or any other incendiary substance on the highway. Named for its sponsor, Paul Buzzo.

BY MARK. Practice of permitting persons, unable to sign their names to legal documents, to place some identification mark in lieu of a signature.

Generally there must be witnesses present to attest to documents signed By Mark.

BYRD MACHINE. An informal coterie of citizens in Virginia, who were of the same conservative political persuasion as Senator Harry E. Byrd, which ended in 1967. Under his strong and effective leadership, the Democratic Party reigned supreme in the state in both local and federal elections for several generations. The reward for absolute loyalty to its members was often an elective or appointive position. The votes of these grateful recipients, and their relatives and friends, were reflected in the ballot box. There was no proof or hint of any scandal during this period, however, because the officials were both honest and efficient in their work. Perhaps the greatest contribution of the Byrd Machine was fiscal responsibility and a strictly Pay-As-You-Go, no bonded indebtedness, balanced budget philosophy.

BYRNE, JANE. The victor of the mayoralty race in Chicago in 1979, Ms. Byrne was the first woman to be elected mayor of an American city.

C

C.A. See C. CASES.

C.A.A. (Citizens Against Abortion). A private non-profit group that seeks to make non-therapeutic abortions illegal.

C.A.B. (Civil Aeronautics Board). A federal agency which promotes and regulates the civil air transport industry, both within the United States and between the United States and foreign countries, in the interests of the foreign and domestic commerce of the United States, the postal service, and the national defense. The Board grants licenses to provide air transportation services, and approves or disapproves proposed rates and fares, as well as agreements and corporate relationships involving air carriers. The Board issues rules of general applicability and acts on individual applications. It is composed of a chairman and four other members, all of whom are appointed by the President with the advice and consent of the Senate.

CABELL, WILLIAM H. The first American to receive a law degree in the United States. After graduating from the College of William and Mary, Williamsburg, Virginia, in 1793, Cabell became one of the great early governors of Virginia.

CABOTAGE RIGHT. In aviation law, the right of an aircraft to take on passengers, mail and cargo in a foreign country and transport them for remuneration to points within the same country. This arrangement is usually under the exclusive control of the laws of the country involved or international accord.

C.A.I. (Confused Artificial Insemination). Variation of the artificial insemination process (A.I.D.) whereby the husband's semen is mixed with that of a third party donor. Although from a medical standpoint this method is no better than A.I.D., it affords some emotional satisfaction to the husband, who may feel like the biological parent.

CALENDAR WEDNESDAY. A House of Representatives rule whereby on Wednesdays bills in committee may be called up for consideration, with limited debate, by the full House. Calendar Wednesday is intended to allow controversial bills to reach the House membership, but it is frequently suspended by a two-thirds vote.

CALIFORNIA MOTOR TRANSPORT COMPANY v. TRUCKING UNLIMITED. See NOERR-PENNINGTON DOCTRINE.

CALIFORNIA TAX QUAKE. See PROPOSITION 13.

CALLEY CASE. The longest court martial trial (4½ months) in American history. William Calley, Jr., a 24-year-old baby-faced Army Lieutenant, was convicted in 1971 for having murdered 22 innocent unarmed Vietnamese civilians in 1968 in the village of My Lai. His unsuccessful defense was that he was merely following orders of his superior officers in the battle field and that he was an innocent scapegoat who was sacrificed to placate the protestors against the War. His life sentence was reduced to three years on appeal, and he was eventually paroled. His trial and conviction are a tragic symbol of the American dilemma in Vietnam.

CALVO CLAUSE. Named after Carlos Calvo, an Argentine jurist, the clause provides that a dispute arising out of a contract between a government and a foreigner shall not be subject to diplomatic intervention on the part of the foreign country. Typically inserted by Latin American countries, the Calvo Clause imposes upon the foreigner the obligation to rely solely upon local remedies. Most authorities in international law, however, consider that it does not deprive the foreign country of the right to intervene in order to protect its own citizens.

CAMBODIAN POLITBURO. See ORGANIZATION ON HIGH.

CAMP DAVID. United States presidential retreat located in the northwestern region of the state of Maryland on the 5,769-acre tract known as the Catoctin Mountain Park, authorized by congress in 1936.

CAMP DAVID SUMMIT. An historic meeting arranged by President Carter in September, 1978, at his presidential retreat in Maryland between President Anwar Sadat of Egypt and Prime Minister Menachem Begin of Israel which resulted in the signing of two documents to serve as the framework for the eventual termination of the 30-year-old Arab-Israeli War. A meeting held thereafter by four hard-line Arab countries (Syria, Algeria, South Yemen and Libya) and assorted Palestine Liberation Groups in Damascus to sabotage the Peace Plan was called the Steadfast Summit.

C. AND M. CLUB. See CHOWDER AND MARCHING CLUB.

CANINE WASTE LAW. An ordinance first passed by New York City in 1978, and since followed elsewhere, which requires dog and cat owners to clean up the droppings when their pets befoul the public streets. Violators are punished by heavy fines.

CANING PRACTICE. An Isle of Man practice of beating youthful offenders with a birch-twig whip. The Caning Practice is closely regulated: the whip may contain only four birch twigs, it can weigh no more than nine ounces, no more than six strokes can be administered, and a doctor must be present. Although the practice of administering the Caning to bare buttocks was abolished in 1970, the European Court of Human Rights has declared the practice an illegal form of degrading punishment.

CANNON SHOT RULE. See THREE-MILE LIMIT.

CANONICAL DISABILITIES. Rendered marriages voidable under ecclesiastical law. There were six disabilities: consanguinity, affinity, insanity, impotence, nonage, and a prior unvoided marriage. Proof of one or more of the disabilities entitled the wronged party to prevail in an Annulment Action, which permitted his or her remarriage without loss of standing in the church. Annulments occasionally were notoriously purchasable from the ecclesiastical authorities in the fourteenth and fifteenth centuries on the Continent and in England. It is curious, however, that the Reformation in England began as a result of Henry VIII's inability to secure an annulment on satisfactory proof of disability. He was probably the first person to obtain a divorce decree on the grounds of irreconcilable differences.

CANON LAW. The ecclesiastical code of a Christian church or denomination.

CANON LAW CODE. A five-book code containing 2,414 precepts, written in Latin, establishing standards for the Roman Catholic Church. Prior to the Code, Roman bishops decided cases and carried on the ecclesiastical government through correspondence. Laws were drafted in ecumenical councils. By the 12th century, however, confusion reigned: overlap and anachronisms made enforcement of ecclesiastical principles difficult. Gratian, an Italian monk, attempted to order all of the legislation and decrees that had accumulated through the ages. Additionally, the 19th ecumenical council, the Council of Trent, enacted many revised disciplinary measures during the period 1545-63. By then the printing press had been invented, thus enabling widespread distribution of the reformed rules. However, several centuries of lawmaking undermined the efforts of Gratian and the Council of Trent, moving Pope Pius X to initiate in 1904 the development of the Canon Code, a project that took over a dozen years to complete. Currently, the ecclesiastical law embodied in the Code is being recodified. The effort was initiated because of the spirit of reform generated by the Second Vatican Council of 1962-65 and is being supervised worldwide by a papal committee. In the United States, the Canon Law Society is responsible for recodification work, while thirteen similar commissions are working in other countries. All modifications must be approved by the Pope.

CANONS OF DESCENT. The seven common law principles of inheritance. The Canons Of Descent were the rules by which the property of persons dying intestate (without a will) were distributed. Most significantly, these rules ensured that the eldest son inherited all his father's land. This system of primogeniture embodied in the Canons helped sustain the feudal society of medieval England, and was not finally abolished until England's Administration of Estates Act of 1925.

CANONS OF THE CODE. One of three interrelated parts of the Code of Professional Responsibility. They express in general terms the standards of professional conduct expected of lawyers in their relationships with the public, with the legal system, and with the legal profession. The Canons embody the general concepts from which the Code's ethical considerations and disciplinary rules are derived.

CANTOR v. DETROIT EDISON. See PARKER v. BROWN DOCTRINE; NOERR-PENNINGTON DOCTRINE.

CAPIAS PROCESS. The process used in some states to arrest an individual on the basis of an indictment against him. It is basically the same process as if an arrest warrant has been issued upon complaint. In the prosecution for a misdemeanor, the court has discretion to issue a warrant or a summons. If a summons is executed and the accused fails to appear, the court may then issue a capias.

CAPITAL CONSUMPTION ALLOWANCES. Accounting charges which reflect estimates of wear and tear, obsolescence, destruction and accidental losses of physical capital. The three components which make up the Capital Consumption Allowance and figure in the National Income and Product Accounts are depreciation charges by businesses and nonprofit institutions, depreciation of owner-occupied dwellings, and accidental damage to fixed business capital. Allowances for depletion of natural resources are not included in Capital Consumption Allowances. Gross National Product minus Capital Consumption Allowances is referred to as Net National Product (N.N.P.).

CAPITAL DEPRECIATION. The decline in value of capital assets (assets of a permanent or fixed nature, goods and plants) over time, with use. The rate and amount of depreciation for tax purposes is calculated by a variety of different methods: e.g., straight line, sum of the digits, or declining balance, which often give quite different results.

CAPITAL SURPLUS. An account on the books of a corporation which reflects that part of the consideration received for stock which is above its par value. This can result not only from a sale but also from a reduction of the par value of the stock. Creating a Capital Surplus is desirable due to the restrictions which exist in many States against using funds other than surplus for the distribution of dividends or the expenditure by the corporation of its funds to repurchase its own shares. Thus, the existence of a Capital Surplus account gives a corporation a flexibility it could not have without it. Capital Surplus is distinguishable from Earned Surplus, which arises from the operation of the corporation's business.

CAPITALIZATION APPRAISAL. Valuating investment-real estate, such as apartment complexes or industrial sites, by determining its future earning potential. If any buildings are standing on the property, their annual net income is computed primarily by examining earnings derived from the buildings over a set period of years. This amount is then multiplied by the expected useful life of the property. Capitalization appraisal requires a considerable degree of expertise because of the need to convert future earning power into a present market value while taking into account expenses and making allowances for contingencies.

CAPITATION TAX. See POLL TAX.

CAPITOL HILL. Site of the American Congress. "Take it up with the Hill" means to confer with or clear it through the national legislature or its key members.

CAP LAWS. Local laws to curtail municipal extravagance and control taxes by limiting increases in spending to not more than an agreed-upon percentage (usually 5 percent) per year. A ceiling or cap is thus used to control run-away expenditures.

CAPTAIN'S MAST. See NON-JUDICIAL PUNISHMENT.

CAPTIVE INSURER. A subsidiary corporation originally formed to write insurance for the parent company or group only. As these insurers grew in experience (and in capital surplus) some began to accept risks from unrelated outside companies. This makes the Captive more of a full-fledged insurance company, with possibly important tax consequences. There are now at least 1,000 Captives, both individually and group owned, operating worldwide. Over a hundred have been formed in the last two years alone. Moreover, with costs continuing to escalate for full risk protection through conventional policy coverage, Captives are expanding both the volume and scope of their underwriting activities. At one time, a Captive was considered feasible only for the very large company or trade association, and the capital outlay required may still rule out a wholly-owned Captive for many companies. But many Captives are now being formed by groups and medium-sized firms. Many Captives today— about 700 of them—are based in Bermuda, where capitalization requirements are less stringent and investment and financial reporting rules more relaxed. American multinational companies that do not restrict their Captives to doing business with the parent company find Bermuda particularly advantageous, since income derived from overseas insurance operations is not taxable until the funds are repatriated. With the advent of the Captives, Bermuda has become a world insurance center, handling as much as $2 billion in premiums each year. Of this, as much as $500 million is outside business not related to the Captives' sponsors.

CARDOZO, BENJAMIN (1870-1938). Supreme Court Justice who succeeded Oliver Wendell Holmes to the bench. A supporter of judicial liberalism, Cardozo was concerned with the sociological implications of his decisions and was active in efforts to restate and simplify the law. Cardozo was a prominent attorney and Chief Justice of the New York Court of Appeals before President Hoover appointed him to the Supreme Court in 1932. His book, *The Nature of the Judicial Process*, is one of the American classics in jurisprudence.

CAREER CRIMINALS PROGRAM. Created to identify multiple offenders and to make sure their cases receive swift prosecution. Different localities select such violators on the basis of different criteria. For example, in

Washington, D.C., the focus is on individuals who commit crimes of violence while out on parole; Louisville selects those with two or more felony convictions or five arrests, and Detroit targets suspects with three convictions who are charged with rape, murder, or robbery. Cases involving career criminals are handled by a special district attorney whose case load is scaled down so that he can concentrate on these serious cases. The prosecutor tries to keep the suspect in jail by setting a high bail or no bail at all, avoids plea negotiation and seeks a prompt trial. In an effort to move the case along, the district attorney will frequently make his entire file open to the defense attorney, allowing full discovery of his case. Despite the open file system and the reticence about plea bargaining, conviction rates for career criminal programs are 94 percent compared to a national average of 73 percent. The program is also credited with reducing the time between apprehension and trial to about 60 days in some localities. Notwithstanding the apparent success of the program, funding by the Law Enforcement Assistance Administration, which was only $14 million over three years, is being phased out. Many cities are trying to continue on their own resources. Washington, D.C.'s version, Operation Doorstop, has been in operation since 1977 without the benefit of federal aid.

CAREY v. POPULATION SERVICES INTERNATIONAL (431 U.S. 678 (1977)). A Supreme Court decision that invalidated restrictions on the distribution and advertising of nonprescription contraceptives. A divided Court struck down provisions of the New York education law prohibiting the sale or distribution of contraceptives to minors under 16, the distribution of contraceptives to persons over 16 by anyone other than a licensed pharmacist, and the advertising or display of contraceptives.

CARIBBEAN ORGANIZATION. Economic and social development association established in 1960 by the United States, Britain, France, and the Netherlands, and originally composed of the Caribbean states of French Guinea, Guadeloupe and Martinique, Netherlands Antilles, Surinam, British Guiana, West Indies Federation, Puerto Rico, and the Virgin Islands. The Caribbean Organization's goals are to increase technical advisory groups, develop an inter-island transportation network, join in mutual promotion of tourism, and encourage educational exchange programs.

CAROLENE PRODUCTS FOOTNOTE. Footnote Four of Chief Justice Stone's opinion in *United States v. Carolene Products Co.*, 304 U.S. 144 (1938), which refers to "discrete and insular minorities" in American society, whom the Court must protect. The footnote signifies Court activism on behalf of fundamental rights and interests. Some commentators have said the footnote signifies the beginning of a new substantive due process concerned with personal rights.

CARROLL DOCTRINE. Derived from *Carroll Broadcasting Co. v. FCC*, 258 F.2d 440 (D.C. Cir. 1958), where the D.C. Circuit held that where the economic impact of new competition on an existing broadcast station might "damage or destroy service to an extent inconsistent with the public interest," the Federal Communications Commission (F.C.C.) must hold a hearing to determine whether to authorize competitive service. The Carroll Doctrine has typically been applied in broadcast cases to protect struggling U.H.F. television stations against competition from V.H.F. stations. This is part of the F.C.C. policy to promote U.H.F. television.

CARRY-BACK. A method of computing taxes whereby losses in one tax year are carried back to a previous year to offset a higher income for the earlier year. A Carry-Back is thus designed to average out taxable income for a specified period.

CARTER DOCTRINE. A tough anti-Russian policy presented in the 1980 State of the Union message. It provides that any attempt by a foreign country to gain control of the Persian Gulf region will be deemed an assault on the vital interests of the United States and will be repelled by military force if necessary.

CARTER REPORT. A study of graduate education which asked a national sample of faculty to rank the leading schools of Education, Law and Business. Recently revised, the study ranked top 10 law schools as follows: Harvard, Yale, Stanford, Michigan, Chicago, Berkeley, Columbia, Pennsylvania, Virginia, and U.C.L.A. These figures are suspect, however, in that only 51.9 percent of the surveys were completed. The low percentage of returns was probably due to an attempted boycott by law school deans who feared the uses to which such figures may be put.

C.A.S. (Collision Avoidance Systems). Programs created and administered by the Federal Aviation Administration to reduce airplane accidents.

CASE AT BAR. The judicial proceeding before the court.

CASE BOOK. Compilation of legal cases on a particular field or aspect of the law used for instruction in law schools.

CASH OPTION MERGER. Form of merger in which the shareholders of the subordinate corporation are given the option of exchanging their shares of stock for cash.

CASH OUT BUYER. When two people swap property of the same type for an identical price in which each has a profit, neither pays a capital gains tax. If one does not want the property of the other, he may sell to a third person who does want the property and that person in turn becomes a Cash Out Buyer to accommodate the seller who wants a tax-free trade.

CASH TAKE-OUT MERGER. See SINGER v. MAGNAVOX CO.

C.A.S.P.A.R. (Cambridge and Somerville Program for Alcoholism Rehabilitation). A program in Somerville, Massachusetts, sponsored by the N.I.

A.A.A. (National Institute on Alcohol Abuse and Alcoholism), to prevent, cure and control alcoholism in teenagers.

CASTRO, FIDEL. Lawyer and leader of the Communist guerillas who in 1959 overthrew Fulgencio Batista, the right-wing Cuban dictator. In 1961, revolutionary soldiers and militiamen crushed an American-backed anti-Castro invasion at the Bay of Pigs on the southern Cuban coast. Fearing direct American military intervention, Castro accepted a Soviet military presence on the island along with the Kremlin's economic aid, which amounts to $1 million a day. In the eyeball confrontation with the United States in 1962 after the Soviets placed missiles in Cuba, the weapons were withdrawn and World War III was postponed. Although Cuba's military activities in Africa since 1975 have alarmed the West, they have won prestige for Castro in many Third World countries, especially those with Left-wing governments. Cuban mercenaries working for the Russians also have shown Moscow that the Castro Government deserves aid. Despite the fact that Cuba is a satellite of Russia, Cuba is president of the non-aligned movement, which includes nearly two-thirds of the world's countries.

CATCH-ALL EXCEPTION. See HEARSAY EVIDENCE.

CAUSA MORTIS (Latin—on account of death). A Gift Causa Mortis or Donatio Causa Mortis is a gift of personal property occasioned by the donor's belief that his death is impending. It is made on condition that the donee survive the donor and that the donor not revoke the gift before death. The donor's recovery is often held to revoke the gift.

CAVEAT EMPTOR (Latin—let the buyer beware). The term signifies that the seller is giving no warranty for the goods sold, and that the risk of defects in the product or the title falls on the buyer. While this doctrine is as old as the common law, it may now be gradually giving way to its opposite, Caveat Venditor: let the seller beware. Courts and legislatures are increasingly discarding the common-law notion for the theory that a fair price implies a warranty. Caveat Emptor flourished in the laissez-faire economy of the nineteenth century and still characterizes many aspects of the free market today. The concept of Caveat Venditor reflects government recognition of the buyer's inability to protect himself in an increasingly complex technological society.

CAVEAT VENDITOR. See CAVEAT EMPTOR.

C.B. See C. CASES.

C-CASES. Label given to investigations of the National Labor Relations Board. If an employer is charged with unfair practices the case is labeled C.A., while union charges are labelled C.B.

C.C.C. See DEBTORS ANONYMOUS.

CELESTIAL KINGDOM (China). See LONG MARCH.

CEMETERY TRUST. A trust arrangement which has as its purpose the upkeep of a grave, burial plot, or cemetery. Typically, a small investment is made and the earnings are applied for maintenance. Often such trusts involve a group of people who pay into the trust in order to benefit deceased relative beneficiaries. Cemetery trusts are quite popular in Europe, particularly Italy and France.

CENTER FOR LAW AND EDUCATION. Funded by the Legal Services Corporation to support local Legal Services Offices throughout the United States, with special emphasis on the rights of students.

CENTER FOR LAW AND SOCIAL POLICY. Public interest institute staffed by experienced lawyers and law-student interns, which represents groups in the areas of environment, trade policy, consumer protection, women's rights, and health services for the poor and mentally ill.

CENTER FOR WOMEN POLICY STUDIES. A nonprofit organization funded by foundations and government grants. It aids organizational efforts of nonprofessional wage-earning women and serves as a clearing house for information on such legal topics as wife abuse and women's rights.

CENTER OF GRAVITY RULE. See PLACE OF MOST SIGNIFICANT RELATIONSHIP RULE.

CENTRAL BANKS' CENTRAL BANKER. See B.I.S.

CENTRAL CRIMINAL COURT. See OLD BAILEY.

CENTRAL INTELLIGENCE AGENCY. See C.I.A.

CENTRAL TREATY ORGANIZATION (C.E.N.T.O.). A regional organization for collective defense created by Iraq, Turkey, Pakistan, Iran, and the United Kingdom. Because of the hostility of the Arab League towards participation in a Western alliance, Iraq withdrew in 1959 from the Baghdad Pact. Consequently, the Baghdad Pact organization was moved to Ankara, renamed, and became C.E.N.T.O. on March 24, 1959. The security and self-defense system is based on an obligation. The organization provides for a Council, which holds regular meetings, an international secretariat, and four committees. The United States has the status of an observer and participates in the Military and Economic Committees of C.E.N.T.O.

CEREMONIAL MARRIAGE (Formal Marriage; Statutory Marriage). A union which meets certain statutory marital requirements. Though these requirements vary from state to state, they generally include obtaining a license, taking blood tests, and solemnizing the marriage.

CERTIFICATE OF TITLE. A document usually given to the buyer of real estate with the deed stating that title to the property is clear. It is usually prepared by a title company or attorney for the buyer.

CERTIFICATION MARK. Indicates to a potential purchaser that goods or services meet certain requirements or standards of someone other than the person marketing the goods or performing the services. Unlike a Trademark, a Certification Mark does not identify goods or services and distinguish them from those of others. Nor does a Certification Mark indicate that all goods or services in connection with which the Mark is used originate from the same entity. Generally it indicates only that the goods or services have been tested, inspected, examined, or otherwise checked according to the methods of the certifier and have been approved as meeting the standards which such certifier has adopted, promulgated, or established. A Certification Mark may serve as a Seal of Approval. Famous examples of this type of Certification Mark are the seals of the Good Housekeeping Bureau and the Underwriters' Laboratories. The certifier does not control the nature and quality of the goods or services, and he is not responsible legally for their nature or quality. A Certification Mark is a Seal of Guarantee when it is used to certify that the work or labor on goods or services was performed by members of a particular union or other organization. The guarantee function of the Certification Mark is much more evident than it is with respect to a Trademark or Service Mark. What is generally referred to as a Trademark guarantee is no more than the seller's announcement, implicit in the Trademark, and the buyer's expectation that goods or services bearing the same Mark will be of the same nature, quality, and characteristics.

CERTIFICATION OF AN ISSUE. A seldom-used procedure by which a Federal Court of Appeals or the United States Court of Claims may submit a specific question or proposition of law to the Supreme Court in a civil or criminal case. Certification is limited to "distinct and definite" questions of law, and the procedure must be triggered by the court, not the parties. The Supreme Court has declined to issue an opinion on every matter certified to it, with one exception. That exception occurred in 1964. A Federal Court of Appeals sitting En Banc was equally divided on the question of whether a state governor was entitled to a jury in an original contempt proceeding in that court. Another use of the certification technique has been in cases where federal appellate courts have certified difficult or unsettled questions of state law to the state supreme court. Several states have authorized such a procedure.

CERTIORARI GRANTED. The issuance of a discretionary writ by a superior court directing that an inferior court certify and return the record of a particular proceeding for review by the superior court for errors of law. Such extraordinary writs are issued only upon a showing of good cause and are available where no direct appeal is possible. Most cases reviewed by the Supreme Court result from the writ of certiorari. However, this Court has limited the issuance of such writs to cases which raise an issue of significant public interest or jurisprudential importance or conflict with controlling precedent. Where the Court refuses to issue the writ, the case is reported as Certiorari Denied.

CERTIORARI PETITION. See WRIT OF CERTIORARI.

CESTUI QUE (French—the one who). (1) Trust. A person for whose benefit a trust arrangement is created. A Cestui Que Trust enjoys the fruits of the trust property. (2) Use. A person for whose use and benefit land is granted to another, who holds the legal title. The Cestui Que Use, who receives the profits and benefits from the property, holds an equitable interest in the land. (3) Vie. A person whose life is the measure of the duration of a life estate. Thus, where *O* conveys Blackacre to *A* for the life of *B*, the Cestui Que Vie is *B*. When *B* dies, *A*'s estate terminates.

C.E.T.A. (Comprehensive Employment and Training Act). Founded in 1973 by the federal government as its main effort to fight unemployment, replacing the previous War on Poverty program. Unfortunately, it has been plagued by greed, nepotism, patronage, embezzlement and mismanagement so that much of its multi-billion-dollar annual payments to thousands of communities is diverted from the poor recipients it was designed to serve. The venality of the human species leaves much to be desired. There are four major titles to C.E.T.A. Title I provides funds for classroom and on-the-job training for unemployed, underemployed and economically disadvantaged persons. Title II provides public-service job funds (maximum salary, $10,000) to anyone who lives in a high unemployment area and who has been unemployed for 30 days. Title III gives funds to specific groups such as teenagers or migrant workers. Title IV provides the largest share of C.E.T.A. money to those who are unemployed at least 15 weeks and who had a previous year's income of below 70 percent of the federal government's minimum standard of living.

C.F.T.C. See COMMODITY FUTURES TRADING COMMISSION.

CHAIN OF CUSTODY. The persons who have possession of evidence from the time it is taken into custody by law enforcement officers to the time it is introduced at trial. Where the defendant is accused of narcotics possession, for example, the prosecution is required to establish a chain of custody for any narcotics used as evidence.

CHAIN OF TITLE. The record of successive conveyances of a particular piece of real property.

CHAIN VOTING. A system in which a voter (especially in a labor dispute) takes a blank ballot from the polling place, gives it to another to mark and a third person places it in the ballot box. This practice can be used by the unscrupulous to rig an election.

CHAMPERTY AGREEMENT. An arrangement whereby a third party to a law suit undertakes to carry on the suit at his own expense in considera-tion of receiving a part of the award if the suit is successful.

CHANCERY COURT. See COURT OF CHANCERY.

CHANGE ORDERS. Claim by a contractor for additional money above the bid-price submitted on a government contract. Change Orders can be authorized either because the owner of a building has changed the design or because the architect has omitted some necessary item from the blueprints. Contractors that specialize in government work often maximize profits by submitting a low bid and then trying to find as many Change Orders as possible. This practice, of course, produces vast cost overruns on many government projects.

CHANGES CLAUSE. A generally-required clause for federal government contracts authorizing a contracting officer to order certain modifications to a contract provided they are within the general scope of the contract.

CHAPEL MEETING. Colloquial term used in labor relations law which describes a meeting of composing-room employers in the printing industry.

CHAPLINSKY v. NEW HAMPSHIRE, 315 U.S. 568 (1942). A Supreme Court case which categorized obscenity, "fighting words" and libel as classes of speech outside the First Amendment. Justice Murphy wrote that such forms of expression are of such small social value that "any benefit that may be derived from them is clearly outweighed by the social interest in order and morality."

CHAPTER XIII PROCEEDING. A federal bankruptcy court action provided for by Chapter XIII of the Bankruptcy Act (whereby an insolvent debtor can obtain relief from the claims of his creditors without going through bankruptcy proceedings). In a Chapter XIII Proceeding, the debtor, who must be an individual deriving most of his income from wages and the like, formulates a Wage Earner Plan under which he agrees that a portion of his wages will be paid to a trustee and distributed among his creditors. The Wage Earner Plan, which may provide that the debtor pay less than he originally owed, must be approved by a majority of the debtor's creditors and confirmed by the bankruptcy court. At the completion of the terms of the Plan, the debtor is discharged of his debts. The advantage to the debtor of Chapter XIII Proceedings is that he retains his property, rather than giving it up in Bankruptcy Proceedings. Chapter XIII Proceedings may also benefit creditors, for their share of the debtor's future earnings may come to more than the small share they generally receive through Bankruptcy Proceedings.

CHARACTER DEFAMATION. A tort concerning invasions of the plaintiff's interest in his reputation. The tort consists of the publication to a third person of matter capable of a defamatory meaning which refers to the plaintiff and damages his reputation. Most courts will find liability where the matter merely tends to lower the reputation of the plaintiff, while others require that it subject him to hatred, contempt, scorn or ridicule. Defamation is concerned with reputation and so, if the defendant communicates privately with the plaintiff, recovery can not be had for any anger, sadness or humiliation because there has been no reputational effect.

CHARACTER DISORDER. Social maladjustment of long duration. Although the causes of the different subclasses (sexual deviations, alcoholism, drug addiction, and antisocial or delinquent behavior) are diverse, a common etiological element is social conflict, i.e., the inconsistent demands of peer group and authority figures. The most important of the character disorders is the antisocial reaction (once called psychopathic personality or sociopath). It is estimated that up to 80 percent of the prison population is plagued by this malady, which is characterized by self-defeating behavior, such as a criminal who habitually botches his attempted crimes in such a manner as indicating a desire to be apprehended,

self-contempt, and an unusual inability to learn from punishment. Hostility and aggression, which frequently accompany the condition, apparently result from insecurity in interpersonal relationships and unsuccessful social interactions. Lack of friends, employment, and direction result in a loss of self-esteem, leaving the psychopath with no place to turn. Charles Manson, product of a broken home, convicted of armed robbery at age fourteen, preferring incarceration to the outside world, presents a paradigm of Character Disorder. Individuals found to be suffering from Character Disorders are frequently treated under Defective Delinquent Statutes.

CHARACTER EVIDENCE. Evidence of a trait or disposition. Generally, Character Evidence is inadmissible at trial to show that a person acted in conformity with his disposition. However, a criminal defendant can present evidence of his or the victim's pertinent traits. For instance, a defendant accused of murder can introduce evidence of his peacefulness or, if he is claiming self-defense, of the victim's aggressive nature. If the defendant offers such evidence, the prosecution is then entitled to present character evidence in rebuttal. Furthermore, Character Evidence of a witness's propensity to lie is admissible to impeach a witness. In accordance with the general rule, evidence of other crimes or wrongs is not admissible to show that a defendant is likely to have committed a different crime. Such evidence, on the other hand, is admissible for other purposes. For example, if a defendant were charged with killing an eyewitness to one of his previous crimes, evidence of the earlier crime would be admissible to show the defendant's motive. If character is at issue in a particular case, Character Evidence is freely admissible. Thus, in an action for slander where the defendant claims truth as a defense, evidence of the plaintiff's character is admissible.

CHARGÉ D'AFFAIRES (French—one charged with affairs). A diplomatic officer, inferior in rank to an

CHARGING

Ambassador or Minister, who represents his nation in the absence of the Ambassador or Minister.

CHARGING DOCUMENT. A formal written accusation, filed in a court, alleging that a person has committed an offense. There are three types of charging documents: A Complaint is an accusation made by any person, but often by a prosecutor; an Information is an accusation made by a prosecutor; and an Indictment is an accusation made by a grand jury. The filing of a charging document in a court initiates criminal proceedings against the accused. Complaints, Informations and Indictments are sometimes collectively spoken of as Indictments. The term Charging Document covers all three types in order to eliminate ambiguity.

CHARGING LIEN. Grants an attorney an interest in the client's cause of action or claim which attaches and becomes enforceable when the client obtains judgment or verdict for money or something of value,

CHARITABLE TRUST. A trust arrangement created and sustained for the benefit of a legally-recognized charity. The difference between a Charitable Trust and a private trust arrangement is that, in the former, the trust beneficiaries are non-designated. Charitable Trusts can be traced to the Statute of Charitable Uses in 1601, during the reign of Queen Elizabeth. Scholars also point to 13th-Century England because conveyances of property for charitable purposes to the Franciscan friars occurred, since they could not own property due to their oaths of poverty.

CHARLES HUGHES & CO. v. S.E.C. See SHINGLE THEORY.

CHARTER BILL. A proposed federal law drafted by the Federal Bureau of Investigation (F.B.I), the Department of Justice and the staff of the Senate Judiciary Committee in 1979 to define the powers and the duties of the F.B.I.

CHARTERED LIFE UNDERWRITER. See C.L.U.

CHARTERED PROPERTY AND CASUALTY UNDERWRITER. See C.L.U.

CHARTER OF THE COMMON MARKET. See EUROPEAN ECONOMIC COMMUNITY.

CHARTER '77. A document signed by 800 intellectual dissidents in Czechoslavakia in 1977, urging the Government to respect human rights.

CHASE, SAMUEL. The only Justice of the Supreme Court, appointed by President Washington, ever to be indicted by the House of Representatives and tried by the Senate for "high crimes and misdemeanors," whatever that may mean. Aaron Burr, lawyer and third Vice-President, presided at the trial. John Randolph of Roanoke, Virginia, was the prosecutor, but Justice Chase was found not guilty on March 1, 1805, to the displeasure of his political adversary, Thomas Jefferson.

CHATTEL MORTGAGE. Where the debtor (mortgagor) agrees to give the creditor (mortgagee) a security interest (mortgage) on personal property which may be possessed by the lender in the event of a default. However, the mortgagor generally retains possession of the asset. Today the creditor must record his security interest or mortgage publicly in order to protect it against the claims of third parties.

CHECKERS TALK. See BLUE BOOK.

CHECK FRAUD. The issuance or passing of a check, draft, or money order that is legal as a formal document signed by a legal account holder but with the foreknowledge that the bank or depository will refuse to honor it because of insufficient funds or closed account. When the printed check is illegally created or signed by a person other than the legal account holder, the offense is forgery. Instances of Check Fraud are often called N.S.F. Checks, Non-Sufficient Funds Checks, Insufficient Funds, and Bad Checks.

CHECK KITING (Kiting Checks). A fraudulent system to build up, and ultimately withdraw in cash (or cashed checks), checking accounts in several banks at once. The "kiter" continually juggles his accounts using checks from one bank as deposits for others, all the while increasing the amounts and cashing checks locally. This scheme is illegal in many states, but enforcement is difficult as most kiters are transients.

CHECKOFF OF UNION DUES. A provision in a union contract authorizing the employer to deduct membership dues and service fees from an employee's pay check and pay them directly to the union. The provision does not in itself require anyone to join a union or maintain membership, and hence is usually used together with some more effective Union Security Clause. Such provisions are useful to the union in that they eliminate the burden in time and expense of collecting membership dues.

CHECKS AND BALANCES. A fundamental principle of the United States government providing for orderly diffusion of power among different organs of government. Theoretically, each governmental department exercises a check upon the acts of the others, so that the power enjoyed by the government as a whole is balanced among entities with different functions. Checks and Balances operate among the three branches of the federal government, between federal and state governments, and between the two houses of federal and state legislatures. A primary function of Checks and Balances is enforcement of the principle of separation of powers among the executive, judicial, and legislative branches of the federal government. For example, practices such as judicial review of congressional enactments and presidential and congressional vetoes, Congressional impeachment power, and Senate-approved presidential appointment of judges all serve to diffuse the powers of the federal government and to ensure that the same individuals cannot create, implement, and interpret the law at the same time.

CHESTER THE PARROT CASE. Illustrates the common-law rule that the owner of a wild animal has only a qualified property right; that is, if the animal escapes, it belongs to the next person who captures it. But if a domesticated animal (one subject to training and discipline) escapes, the owner retains a property right which supersedes that of a subsequent finder. When Chester the Parrot escaped from a Humane Society, the issue of whether he was a wild or domesticated animal arose. His captor wanted to retain the parrot while the Humane Society wanted him back. After keeping the parrot "under close scrutiny" during the trial, the judge concluded that Chester was indeed domesticated, and thus belonged to his original owners.

CHICAGO CONVENTION ON INTERNATIONAL CIVIL AVIATION (1944). Extended the Paris Convention on Aerial Navigation of 1919, which gives every state exclusive sovereignty over the airspace above its territory and territorial waters. The Chicago Convention reaffirms the principle that flight over the territorial airspace is thus under the discretionary power of the state. It also specifies that freedom of aerial traffic must be adjusted with state sovereignty.

CHICAGO EIGHT (David Dellinger, Rennie Davis, Tom Hayden, Abbie Hoffman, Jerry Rubin, Lee Weiner, John Froines and Bobby Seale). The Chicago Eight were all well-known Civil Rights activists during the 1960s except Weiner, a Ph.D. candidate in sociology at Northwestern University; and Froines, a professor of Chemistry at the University of Chicago. Commentators have viewed the prosecution of these defendants for actions taken protesting the 1968 Democratic National Convention as a crackdown on dissent generally. Judge Julius Hoffman tried the case and it was apparent from the outset that he had a personal bias either against the defendants and their lawyers or for the prosecution. Obviously negatively impressed with defense attorney Leonard Weinglass, 80-year-old Judge Hoffman addressed Weinglass variously as "Feinglass,"

"Weinrob," "Weinstein," "Feinstein," "Weinrus," "Weinberg," "Weinramer," and "Mr. What's Your Name," even though Weinglass actively tried the case for 20 weeks. In the course of the trial, Judge Hoffman ordered defendant Seale to be bound and gagged in the courtroom. When the charges were later dropped against Seale, the case became known as the Chicago Seven. Fortunately no judge has since had to resort to such draconian measures in order to control his courtroom. A conviction of five of the defendants was reversed on appeal on the grounds of the "demeanor of the judge," whose "deprecatory and often antagonistic attitude toward the defense was evident from the beginning."

CHICKEN HAWK. A pimp who procures young boys for homosexuals to engage in criminal sexual relations.

CHICKEN RUN. The departure of Whites, especially professionals, from Rhodesia and South Africa, in order to re-settle safely in other countries in anticipation of the violence that is expected precede the takeover of the government by the Blacks.

CHICKEN WAR. A dispute which took place from 1958 to 1963 between the United States and the European Economic Community, the subject of which was massive exports of U.S. poultry into Germany. The cause of the dispute arose when higher import fees were restored by the E.E.C. Customs Union, under its new agricultural program, thus jeopardizing the U.S. chicken exports. In reaction, the United States argued that the European Economic Community (E.E.C.) Customs Union distorted the Most-Favored Nation Principle of the G.A.T.T. Such customs unions are allowed by the G.A.T.T. under specific conditions, and it provides that the adjustments needed on the issues must be settled by negotiations. Negotiations were held on the poultry issue between the E.E.C. and the United States, and a G.A.T.T. panel rendered an advisory opinion evaluating the value of U.S. poultry exports to $26 million. Following an agreement, the United States then raised its bound rates affecting an equivalent number of imports from E.E.C. countries. The result of these customs restrictions on both parts was a substantial decline in U.S. poultry and other E.E.C. commodities trade.

CHILD ABUSE. An intentional act by a parent or child custodian which harms or threatens to harm a child's physical or mental health. All 50 states now have some sort of Child Abuse reporting law. These laws have varying provisions as to who must or may report, penalties for not reporting, and required agency action following the report. Physical Abuse is Child Abuse which results in physical injury, including fractures, burns, bruises, welts, cuts, and/or internal injuries. Physical abuse, which often occurs in the name of discipline or punishment, ranges from a slap of the hand to the use of objects such as straps, belts, or pipes. Psychological/Emotional Abuse is Child Abuse which results in impaired psychological growth and development. It frequently occurs as verbal abuse or excessive demands on a child's performance and results in a negative self-image on the part of the child and disturbed child behavior. It often does not involve physical abuse. Sexual Abuse is Child Abuse which results in any act of a sexual nature upon or with a child.

CHILD ABUSE CARELINE. A 24-hour, seven-day-a-week toll-free "Hot Line" telephone service which is used to report any suspected instance of Child Abuse.

CHILD ABUSE PREVENTION AND TREATMENT ACT (1974). Sponsored by then U.S. Senator Mondale, the Act established the National Center on Child Abuse and Neglect in the Children's Bureau of the Department of Health, Education and Welfare, and authorized annual appropriations of between $15 million and $25 million through fiscal year 1977. Congress has since extended the Act for several years. Actual appropriations have been less than authorized. The purpose of the

National Center is to conduct and compile research, provide an information clearinghouse, compile and publish training materials, provide technical assistance, investigate national incidence, and fund demonstration projects related to prevention, identification, and treatment of child abuse and neglect.

CHILD DIVORCE LAW. A statute proposed by the Swedish Commission on Children's Rights in 1979 that would enable children to sever legal ties with their natural parents through a divorce proceeding and establish a relationship of child-parent with strangers.

CHILD LABOR CASES. A series of Supreme Court cases reviewing federal prohibition of child labor. In the earlier cases, such as *Hammer v. Dagenhart,* 247 U.S. 251 (1918) and *Bailey v. Drexel Furniture,* 259 U.S. 20 (1922), the Court struck down congressional attempts to eliminate child labor. However, a 1941 decision, *United States v. Darby,* 312 U.S. 100 (1938), upheld the constitutionality of the Fair Labor Standards Act (1938), including the prohibition against child labor. *Darby,* dubbed the Fair Labor Standards Case, thus impliedly overruled *Hammer.*

CHILD PORNOGRAPHY. Using a child in pictures to depict erotic behavior intended to arouse sexual excitement or stimulation. There is a growing public pressure on legislatures to pass laws against these materials. The federal and some state governments are currently implementing special legislation to outlaw the sale of materials that portray children engaged in explicit sex acts. The constitutionality of these laws is, so far, untested. Child prostitution is a form of sexual exploitation in which a child is used in sexual relationships for monetary or other profitable purposes.

CHILDREN IN NEED OF SUPERVISION (C.H.I.N.S.). See STUBBORN CHILD LAW.

CHILDREN'S COURT. See JUVENILE COURT.

CHILDREN'S DEFENSE FUND. A non-profit organization formed in 1975 to provide legal counsel to children in need of such professional protection and representation and to protect their rights in general. Programs in which it is especially interested are: (1) Under child welfare, an increase in funds for services to prevent placement of children and to reunify them with their families, creation of a federal adoption subsidy program for hard-to-place children and provision for due-process protections for children. (2) Under child health, expansion of eligibility for the Medicaid program for the poor and increased coverage of health services. (3) Assuring the continuation, strengthening and expansion of the Head Start program for young children. (4) Reauthorization of the education aid program designed to help poor children and strengthening parents' involvement in it.

CHILDREN'S EXPRESS. A New York-based publication for youngsters which focuses on the plight of more than 100,000 children incarcerated in public institutions. Such children are often abused through unnecessary use of drugs, solitary confinement or unsanitary and brutal living conditions. The A.C.L.U. has been successful in obtaining their release or recovering damages for injuries sustained.

CHILDREN'S RIGHTS. Rights of children, as individuals, to the protection provided in the United States Constitution as well as to the care and protection necessary for normal growth and development. Children's rights are usually exercised through adult representatives and advocates. The extent to which a child's rights are protected varies according to each state's laws providing for the identification and treatment of child abuse and neglect. An unresolved issue is the conflict between children's rights and parents' rights. One of the most dramatic developments in the law, in the Seventies, was the sharp increase in the number of children suing their parents, guardians, third parties and the government.

In case after case, in both state and federal courts, children have been successfully asserting their claim to be given the rights of adults. Children who are sued are also winning more of their cases. Special organizations have been created to serve as counsel for children in court such as the Youth Law Center and Children's Defense Fund.

CHILDREN'S RIGHTS, INC. A national organization, headquartered in Washington, D.C., which serves as a clearinghouse and information center for parents whose children have been kidnapped in a custodial dispute.

CHILD STEALING (Child Snatching). One parent surreptitiously taking a child away from the other parent, who has legal custody of the victim. It is probably the most subtle and vicious form of child abuse. Approximately 100,000 violations take place a year, yet only a few states make the offense a crime. It is not a violation of the Federal Lindbergh Law, however, even if a state line is crossed, so the F.B.I. rarely helps the innocent parent to locate the child.

CHILLING EFFECT. The Supreme Court has held statutes to be unconstitutional because of the deterrent or chilling effect they might have on freedom of expression. Under the overbreadth doctrine, the Court has invalidated statutes because of the effect the statutes might have in discouraging non-litigants from engaging in expression that is actually protected under the First Amendment. The Court has expressed the fear that if an individual is uncertain as to whether his speech is actually protected, he may, out of fear, refrain from engaging in expression that is actually protected by the First Amendment.

CHINA TRIANGLE. The dilemma of the United States in wishing to recognize the People's Republic of China in Peking as the official government of the Chinese people, while, at the same time, maintaining treaty, military, economic and cultural ties with the third apex of the triangle, the Republic of China in Taipei where the Nationalists of China went in 1949, on the Island of Taiwan, when the Communists took over Mainland China.

CHINA WATCHER. Anyone who carefully observes every aspect of Chinese life and is qualified as an expert to report on and interpret the domestic and foreign policies of Peking.

CHINESE CARD. A lever effectively used by the United States to bring the Russians to heel whenever we think that they have been guilty of a serious violation of Detente. It consists of our playing footsie with the Chinese. Since the two major Communist giants have a paranoid fear of each other, the Soviets usually react positively to our action.

CHINESE INDIRECT BORROWING. See CROSS-DEPOSITING.

CHINESE OVERTIME. Calculated by dividing an employee's salary by the total number of hours he works, which results in a smaller rate of pay per hour for the greater number of overtime hours worked.

CHINESE WALL. (1) A term used in financial institutions with both trust and brokerage departments. A "Chinese Wall" is erected to prevent employees from using inside information gained in one department for the advantage of the other. (2) A condition in which a former government lawyer who agrees that in his subsequent private practice he will not participate in or discuss with any colleague any case in which he was substantially previously involved, while on the federal payroll, or share in any fee that the case generates for his firm. This is done by filing appropriate affidavits with the concerned federal agency.

C.H.I.N.S. (Children in Need of Supervision or Services). See STUBBORN CHILD LAW.

CHOICE OF LAW. Rules used by courts to determine which state law to apply when several states (1) Have an interest in a suit, (2) Have contacts with the plaintiff or defendant, or (3) Are the location of the act which gave rise to the suit. Aviation cases frequently involve choice of law problems due to the transitory nature of the industry. For example, in *Melville v. American Home Assurance Company*, 443 F. Supp. 1064 (1977), a beneficiary of a life insurance policy sued to recover the proceeds of the policy on one Jay Scott who was killed in a mysterious airplane crash in Delaware. Scott, a Delaware millionaire, had secretly squandered most of his family's wealth on, among other things, his secretary who was the beneficiary of the insurance policy. On the brink of exposure for his misdeeds, Scott died in a chartered light airplane which crashed into the airport after performing bizarre acrobatic maneuvers. The question on trial was whether Scott died accidentally, or as the result of suicide, which would have voided the policy. The insurance contract was made in New York, where the company had its main office. The plaintiff, Scott's secretary, was also a sometime resident of New York. If New York law were applied, the secretary would probably win, as New York law has a strong presumption against suicide. The opposite result would probably obtain if Delaware law were applied. New York law was ultimately applied and the secretary received her money, but the judge who had to decipher the complicated Choice of Law rules governing the case wrote a 106-page opinion in order to do so.

CHOWDER AND MARCHING CLUB. A group of young Republican Congressmen who meet weekly in each other's offices to discuss pending legislation, politics and other matters of mutual interest.

CHURNING AN ACCOUNT. Excessive trading by a stockbroker in an account in which he holds discretionary powers for the purpose of collecting a commission. Normally, the trading is viewed as excessive, either in relation to frequency of trade or volume of trades. Such excessive trading is prohibited by the Securities and Exchange Commission, which allows a defrauded trader to recover damages.

CHU RULE. A decision of the highest court in New York in a case requiring the automatic disbarment of any lawyer convicted of a federal felony. The punishment was mitigated in 1979 when the legislature passed a law providing for automatic suspension instead of automatic disbarment.

C.I.A. (Central Intelligence Agency). A federal agency directed by the President of the United States and the National Security Council. It advises the Council in matters concerning such intelligence activities of the government departments and agencies as relate to national security and it makes recommendations to the Council regarding the coordination of government intelligence activities which relate to the national security. In addition, the C.I.A. correlates and evaluates intelligence relating to the national security, and provides for the appropriate dissemination of such intelligence within the government. It produces and disseminates foreign intelligence relating to the national security, including foreign political, economic, scientific, technical, military, sociological, and geographic intelligence, to meet the needs of the President, the National Security Council, and other elements of the federal government. The C.I.A. also develops and conducts programs to collect political, economic, scientific, technical, military, geographic, and sociological information, not otherwise obtainable, relating to foreign intelligence in accordance with directives of the National Security Council. It collects and produces intelligence on the foreign aspects of international terrorist activities and traffic in narcotics, and conducts foreign counterintelligence activities outside the United States and, when in the United States, in coordination with the F.B.I., subject to the approval of the Attorney General. The Agency has no police, subpoena, or law-enforcement powers or internal security functions. In theory, it is just to operate overseas. For domestic federal law enforcement, see **F.B.I.** and **Secret Service.**

CICERO, MARCUS TULLIUS (106-43 B.C.). Great Roman orator, statesman, scholar, and lawyer. Born in Italy, Cicero received an excellent, eclectic early education, which included Stoicism, Epicureanism, and Platonism. His legal and political career took flight on the wings of a brilliant defense of the alleged murderer Sextus Roscius in 80 B.C. Later, his prosecution of the tyrannical Sicilian governor Gaius Verres earned him fame as the ablest orator in Rome. His yearning for politics was fulfilled when, in 63 B.C., he ascended to the consulship of Rome. When insurrection marred his tenure, and Cicero was criticized for his execution of Catiline, the leader of the revolt. A fifteen-month period of bitter exile followed before Cicero returned triumphantly to Rome. Disillusioned with the subsequent dictatorship of Caesar, he rejoiced in the assassination of the monarch, and thus came into irreconcilable conflict with Marc Antony. Angered by Cicero's speeches against him, Antony had the statesman slain on December 7, 43 B.C. Cicero was a prolific writer, many of whose works on oratory, history, and politics have greatly influenced succeeding generations. His political credo is based on the rule of law as executed by the aristocracy.

C.I.F. (Cost, Insurance, Freight). A commercial term used in overseas transactions to indicate that a price quotation includes the invoice price of the goods, plus insurance and freight to the named port of destination. When goods are shipped C.I.F., the buyer assumes the risk of loss in transit. The seller satisfies his obligations by procuring the necessary documents, such as the ocean bill of lading and the insurance policy, forwarding them to the buyer.

C.I.F. TERM (C. & F. Term). Indicates that the price includes the cost for goods, the cost for insurance, and the cost for freight to be shipped to the named destination.

CIGARETTE BOOTLEGGING. Transporting cigarettes illegally from Virginia, North Carolina and Kentucky, where they are manufactured and the tax is just a few cents a pack, across state lines. The cigarettes are then sold in other states in violation of law to evade taxes which are ten times as high. Approximately $500 million in unpaid taxes are lost annually in the states in which the cigarettes are ultimately sold without payment of the high local tax.

CIGARETTE RULE. First major substantive rule enacted by the F.T.C. Issued in June 1964, the Rule required a health-hazard warning on all cigarette advertisements and packages. After intense lobbying by the tobacco industry, which disputed the F.T.C.'s power to make substantive rules, Congress nullified the rule substituting a more limited disclosure requirement in 1965, and banning radio and television advertising in 1970. Eventually the rule, as originally issued by the F.T.C., was reinstated.

CIRCUIT BREAKERS. A means to prevent real estate taxes from exceeding a percentage of an individual's income. First enacted by Wisconsin in 1964, about 30 states now have some form of Circuit Breaker on property tax.

CIRCUIT COURT OF APPEALS ACT OF 1891. See EVARTS ACT OF 1891.

CIRCUIT JUSTICE FOR ADMINISTRATION. A new federal judiciary position recommended in 1978 by Chief Justice Warren E. Burger. The term "Circuit Justice" is now used by Supreme Court Justices when exercising individual responsibility over the federal judicial circuit to which they have been assigned. Chief Justice Burger said the suggested office would entail no judicial duties but would be purely administrative. He envisioned an experienced federal judge serving in the post, but he made no specific proposals on who would appoint the new administrator. The Federal Constitution makes no mention of the number of Supreme Court Justices. The number is set by federal law and has ranged from six to ten during the country's history.

CIRCUIT SEMINAR SERIES. See ASSOCIATION OF TRIAL LAWYERS OF AMERICA.

CIRCUMSTANTIAL EVIDENCE. Indirect evidence by which a fact to be proved may be inferred. For example, if a witness testifies to seeing the defendant running away from the scene of the crime carrying a gun, such testimony may be circumstantial evidence in a case where a murder victim has been shot.

C.I.T.E.S. See CONVENTION ON INTERNATIONAL TRADE IN ENDANGERED SPECIES.

CITIZEN-INFORMANT. A person who purports to be the victim or the witness of a crime. A Citizen-Informant is motivated by good citizenship and acts openly in aid of law enforcement, whereas informers are generally "stool pigeons" who are criminally involved and motivated by something other than good citizenship, namely, do-re-me. Courts have determined that the tests of reliability which are applied to mere informers do not necessarily have to be applied to every private citizen who aids the police.

CITIZEN'S ADVOCATE CENTER. Watchdog organization funded by the Ford Foundation to scrutinize government antipoverty programs for the benefit of the "poor people who depend on federal grant programs—and taxpayers who question the effectiveness of those programs."

CITIZENS AGAINST ABORTION. See C.A.A.

CITIZEN'S ARREST. An arrest made by a private citizen of a criminal caught in the act of a felon. Such an act is risky because the citizen is liable for damages if he arrests a person who turns out not to be a criminal. Only a police officer is protected if his mistake was based on reasonable grounds.

CITIZEN'S CHOICE. A nonprofit lobbying organization whose financial support is therefore not tax deductible. Founded in 1976, its purpose is to support free enterprise and stop the growth of the federal government. It publishes a monthly newsletter and participates in public opinion polls.

CITIZEN'S CRIME COMMISSIONS. Organizations formed by private citizens to serve as an independent watchdog to render reports on criminal problems and monitor the performance of official action by the police, the courts, prosecutors, and correction agencies.

CITIZEN'S LEAGUE ON CUSTODY AND KIDNAPPING. A non-profit organization, located in Smithtown, N.Y., which assists parents whose children have been kidnapped in a custodial dispute by providing a hot-line telephone service (516-724-8245) by checking official records such as Social Security numbers and driver registrations.

CIVIL ACTION. Having to do with a civil right or remedy as distinguished from a criminal action.

CIVIL AERONAUTICS BOARD. See C.A.B.

CIVIL COMMITMENT. Judicial proceeding in which a mentally ill person is confined in a psychiatric hospital for treatment of his illness. Such commitments are usually predicated on the patient's dangerousness to self, dangerousness to others, or need for care. The purpose of the hospitalization is therapeutic; therefore, continued incarceration is justified only if the individual is receiving psychiatric assistance. It is now recognized that an involuntarily committed patient has a right to treatment and the absence of treatment dictates that the patient must be released. Generally only the seriously ill, those suffering from psychotic disorders, are civilly committed. Less serious illnesses such as psychoneurotic disorders are usually handled on an out-patient basis. After the initial commitment hearing, the patient must receive a periodic review (usually every six months) to determine whether or not his condition merits continued hospitalization. The patient has the right to be represented by legal counsel at both the original and re-commitment hearings.

CIVIL CONTEMPT. (1) Refusal by a witness to testify either at a trial or before a grand jury. To compel his testimony, a judge may impose a jail sentence. Where a grand jury is concerned, however, the sentence may not exceed the term of the grand jury. (2) Refusal by a defendant to obey a lawful court order in an equity proceeding, such as an order to sign a deed in a specific performance case. To coerce his compliance, the defendant may be imprisoned until he obeys, or he may be ordered to pay a fine.

CIVIL DEATH. A legal fiction which applies usually upon conviction of a serious criminal offense. A criminal is said to suffer civil death when the state penalizes him by denying the right to vote, to run for public office, limiting the right to bring certain lawsuits, prohibiting suit on one's own contract, and dissolving marriage. Many recent critics have argued that these results, especially the latter, are inhumane. Civil Death, accordingly, serves no purpose in some jurisdictions.

CIVIL DISOBEDIENCE. Refusal to obey a law on the ground that the law is morally reprehensible. Civil Disobedience generally takes a passive form, such as refusing to pay taxes, to use racially segregated facilities, or to register for the draft. One of the United States' most celebrated practitioners of Civil Disobedience, Henry David Thoreau, wrote in 1848 that if the injustice of government "is of such a nature that it requires you to be the agent of injustice to another, then, I say, break the law. Let your life be a counter friction to stop the machine." Thoreau himself was jailed on his return from Walden Pond when he refused to pay taxes to the United States government, which sanctioned slavery and was at war with Mexico.

CIVILETTI, BENJAMIN R. First Attorney General of the United States to argue a case before the World Court on December 10, 1979, seeking the release of the 50 American hostages illegally detained by Iran in Teheran.

CIVIL INVESTIGATIVE DEMAND. An order by the Department of Justice compelling the production of books or records by anyone under investigation for potential violation of the antitrust laws. Such demand is issued only when civil prosecution is contemplated. If the primary intention of the Department is to bring criminal charges, it may convene a grand jury, which has subpoena powers to force production of necessary documents. However, it would be an abuse of the grand jury process to allow it to issue subpoenas for investigative purposes in civil actions. To increase the Department's effectiveness in pursuing civil actions, Congress passed the Antitrust Civil Process Act in 1973, enabling the Assistant United States Attorney General to issue Civil Investigative Demands when necessary to complete an investigation. The majority of investigations, however, proceed through informal interviews and questionnaires with the voluntary cooperation of the parties involved, so that Demands are issued in only few cases.

CIVIL LAW. (1) The legal system of a country which is based upon the Code Napoleon of France. (2) The body of rules regulating the rights of citizens between each other as distinguished from criminal law which prescribes the relationship between a citizen and a sovereign and provides for punishment for the violation of any of the commands of the sovereign.

CIVIL LIABILITY ACT. See DRAM SHOP LAWS.

CIVIL LIBERTIES. The rights protected from governmental infringement. They are guaranteed in the Constitutions of the United States and of the several states. Basic Civil Liberties include freedom of expression, due process of law, and rights to property. The government must generally prove a compelling purpose in order to justify restraints on Civil Liberties. For example, the government's interest in order and citizen protection may justify a prohibition on falsely yelling "Fire" in a crowded theater, but not on hissing or booing.

CIVIL RIGHTS. The rights guaranteed to all citizens, regardless of race, under the Constitution and laws of the United States. While Civil Liberties refer to rights specifically enumerated in the Bill of Rights, Civil Rights generally connote the free and equal exercise of rights and privileges by black citizens. Most specific Civil Rights guarantees appear in statutes rather than in the Constitution. The ratification of the Thirteenth Amendment in 1865, which forbade slavery and granted Congress power to enforce the prohibition, sparked passage of four Civil Rights Acts by Congress between 1866 and 1875. The 1875 Act, forbidding discrimination in public accommodations, was subsequently held unconstitutional in the Civil Rights Cases by a Supreme Court of the United States unprepared to confront the realities of full-scale integration. Only a few provisions of the original Civil Rights Acts remain in force today. Congress, deterred by the Supreme Court's rude treatment of its early statute, passed no new Civil Rights legislation for almost a century. The activist spirit of the 1960s, however, prompted the passage of four new Civil Rights Acts. The 1957 and 1960 Acts provide for enforcement of equal voting rights by court injunction and criminal penalties, and created the Civil Rights Division of the Department of Justice. The 1964 Act comprehensively outlaws discrimination in voter registration, public accommodations, schools, and employment, and provides several procedural remedies for persons aggrieved by discrimination. The 1968 Civil Rights Act prohibits discrimination in most housing sales or rentals.

CIVIL RIGHTS ACTS. See CIVIL RIGHTS.

CIVIL SERVICE ANTI-STRIKE LAW. See TAYLOR LAW.

CIVIL SERVICE COMMISSION (C.S.C.). A federal (and state) agency which administers a merit system of public employment. Initially, the Commission's job was largely restricted to recruiting and examining, but today it includes recruiting, examining, training, and promoting people on the basis of their knowledge and skills, regardless of their race, religion, sex, political influence, or other nonmerit factors. This group includes those who are, at least theoretically, hired and promoted on the basis of merit. It does not include military personnel, members of the judiciary, elected officials, or high-ranking appointees. The Civil Service Commission's role is to provide qualified people for government agencies and to make sure that the government provides an array of personnel services to applicants and employees. This explains why the Commission has often been called the "People's Agency" of government. It is the central personnel agency of the executive branch. Perhaps the reason for the name People's Agency is that it is so difficult to fire a Civil Service employee. In fiscal year 1976, for example, only 226 federal employees (in a total work force of 2.7 million) were fired for incompetence. This is equivalent to a private employer of 10,000 workers firing only one person for cause in an entire year. President Carter in 1978 recommended to Congress the first major overhaul in the Civil Service since it was created in 1883, in order to correct this and other defects in the system. Congress passed the law which now makes it easier to transfer or fire incompetents and to reward and promote the deserving. The Civil Service Commission has thus become the Office of Personnel Management.

CIVIL WAR AMENDMENTS. The Thirteenth, Fourteenth and Fifteenth Amendments to the Constitution of the United States which were enacted and ratified soon after the end of the Civil War. The basic aim of the Amendments was to protect the rights of Black Americans. The Thirteenth Amendment, ratified in 1865, prohibits slavery or any other form of involuntary servitude in the United States. The Fourteenth Amendment, ratified in 1868, prohibits any state from abridging the privileges and immunities of United States citizens, from denying due process of law, or from denying any person equal protection of the laws. The Fifteenth Amendment, ratified in 1870, prohibits the United States or any state from denying the right to vote to any citizen because of race, color or previous condition of servitude.

CLAIM-OF-RIGHT DOCTRINE. A principle of federal income taxation. Under this doctrine, if a taxpayer receives income under a claim of right and without restriction as to its disposition, he must report the income on his federal income tax return for the year of receipt, despite the fact that he may not be entitled to retain the income. The Claim of Right Doctrine is designed to relieve the I.R.S. of the burden of determining the legal merit of a taxpayer's claim. It is also based on the fact that the taxpayer controls the taxable property and derives benefit from such property.

CLARE REPORT. In 1975 the Advisory Committee on Proposed Rules for Admission to Practice of the Second Circuit, under the chairmanship of New York attorney Robert L. Clare, Jr., filed its report, now often referred to as the Clare Report. The Clare Committee had been appointed in January, 1974, to examine the quality of advocacy in the federal courts of the circuit and to make recommendations for improvement. The Committee found that a significant number of federal trial advocates showed a lack of proficiency directly attributable to a lack of legal training. The Committee recommended that, under the supervision of a three-person admissions committee, applicants to the United States district court would have to show, among other

requirements, that they had completed courses, either in law school or in a continuing legal education program, in five required subjects and either had participated in the preparation of four trials or had observed six trials. The required courses were evidence, civil procedure, including federal practice and procedure, criminal law and procedure, professional responsibility, and trial advocacy. The merits of the report of the Second Circuit Advisory Committee were the subject of considerable discussion and debate. The essence of the objections was that the Committee had not established an adequate factual basis in support of the need for the adoption of standards, that the requirement of certain courses would infringe upon the traditional role of law schools, and that the remedy would not be responsive to real problems. More significantly, even the supporters of the Clare proposal acknowledged the criticism that the adoption of higher standards by the courts of only one circuit might result in an undesirable "balkanization" of requirements, in derogation of the need for uniformity of standards for admission in all federal trial courts.

CLARK REPORT. A recommendation of an American Bar Association Committee chaired by retired Supreme Court Justice Tom C. Clark, in 1970, concerning the disciplining of lawyers engaged in unprofessional conduct which, unfortunately, has never been fully implemented despite its critical conclusion that "the prevailing attitude of lawyers toward discipline enforcement ranges from apathy to outright hostility. Disciplinary action is practically nonexistent in many jurisdictions; practices and procedures are antiquated, and many disciplinary agencies have little power to take effective steps against malefactors."

CLARKE'S LAW. An observation by science fiction writer Arthur C. Clarke that "the next great scientific advance will be the one which the most eminent scientist of our time has most recently declared impossible."

CLASS ACTIONS. Suits in which a class of persons is represented by one or more of its members. Such actions are permitted only when the class is large, although no specific number has been determined, in order to prevent inconvenience. Often class actions are test cases. Whereas individual suits may give rise to inconsistent judgments, a class action offers the benefit of a clear resolution of a particular issue. Such an action may be maintained, however, only when members of the class are concerned with common questions of law and fact.

CLASS GIFT. A gift that the donor intends to benefit a group or a class of persons. A typical class gift has some collective language such as "children," "issue," "heirs," "brothers and sisters," "nieces and nephews" or "grandchildren," that show "group-mindedness." The key feature in a class gift is the anticipated fluctuation in the number of donees.

CLASS GIFT RULE. An "all-or-nothing" construction of a class gift, applied where the gift is valid in part and invalid in part. The class gift fails under this construction if any part of the gift is invalid.

CLASSIFICATION CENTER. A functional unit within a correctional institution, or a separate facility which holds persons in custody for the purpose of determining to which correctional facility or program they should be committed. A sentenced adult, a delinquent or a status offender who has been the subject of a juvenile court disposition, may be held in a diagnosis or classification center to determine into which correctional institution he should be placed. The court may also place a person in a diagnosis or classification center to determine whether the sentence is appropriate. Adults may be held while a pre-sentence report is completed; juveniles, while a pre-disposition report is completed.

CLASSIFIED SERVICE (Competitive Service; Classified Civil Service). Jobs included in this civil service category are insulated from partisan politics in that those who occupy such positions cannot be removed as long as they perform efficiently and in accordance with set standards. Everyone charged with essentially equal responsibilities is to be graded and compensated according to the same schedule of considerations.

CLASS VOTING. Occurs where there is more than one class of shares authorized by the articles of incorporation. Generally each share of corporate stock has one vote. However, provision may be made for each class of shares to elect a certain number of directors. The articles must explicitly delineate the privileges and rights of each class. Class Voting is a means of assuring representation of each class on the board of directors.

CLAUSUM FREGIT (Latin—he broke the close). The term suggests that a person entered someone's land by breaking, literally or figuratively, a fence or imaginary boundary line. The common-law action of Trespass Quare Clausum Fregit (trespass wherefore he broke the close) was the remedy by which one collected damages for an unlawful entry by another on one's land.

CLAY, HENRY. Born in 1777, Clay was a legislative genius whose fifty-year career in public life included terms in the Kentucky State Legislature, the United States Senate, and the House of Representatives. An able Secretary of State under John Quincy Adams, Clay nonetheless failed five times to attain the nation's highest office. His outspoken stances on a variety of issues won enemies as well as friends, and the public soon tired of his candidacies. Yet the genteel Kentuckian distinguished himself by an unerring ability to orchestrate compromises among contending factions, and to enshrine those accords in law. The Tariff of 1833, whose provision for a gradual reduction in rates prevented South Carolina from "nullifying" the Tariff of 1832, and the Compromise of 1850, by which California was admitted to the Union, were largely the handiwork of "Prince Hal." But his most brilliant gem was the Missouri Compromise (1819-21) which persuaded Northern congressmen to support Missouri's admission to the Union despite a provision in the state constitution barring free Negroes from entering the state. The Compromise granted Missouri statehood, but stipulated that it could pass no laws in violation of the Federal Constitution. Clay's political philosophy finds expression in his *American System,* which called for the establishment of a Bank of America, a system of tariffs to protect industry, federally-funded internal improvements, and high expenditures for defense. Speaker of the House longer than any other nineteenth-century man, Clay died in Washington, D.C. at the age of 75.

CLEAN AIR ACT. A law passed by Congress in 1970 and revised in 1977 which requires all states to submit to the Environmental Protection Agency comprehensive air pollution abatement programs designed to produce compliance with federal air quality standards by 1982 or, in exceptional cases, by 1987. Failure to develop acceptable plans can bring sanctions such as the withholding of various lucrative federal subsidies or a refusal to license new industrial pollution sources.

CLEAN HANDS. Concept which provides that persons who seek equitable relief must not be guilty of any wrongdoing with respect to the claim asserted.

CLEAN-UP LAW. See CANINE WASTE LAW.

CLEAN WATERS ACT (1966). Federal legislation which authorizes funds for sewage treatment plants and provides financial incentives to states which improve the quality of their water.

CLEAR AND CONVINCING PROOF. See BURDEN OF PROOF.

CLEAR AND PRESENT DANGER DOCTRINE. In *Schenck v. United States,* 249 U.S. 47 (1919), Justice Holmes, writing for the Supreme Court, originated the theory that if words are used "in such circumstances and are of such a nature as to create a clear and present danger that they will bring about the substantive evils that Congress has a right to prevent," then the speaker can be punished for the words. Thus, under this Doctrine, the First Amendment does not protect speech that creates a clear and present danger of some act that Congress can forbid, such as rioting or insurrection. The Clear And Present Danger test has since been replaced by other standards. The current test in this area is the Brandenburg Incitement Standard, developed in *Brandenburg v. Ohio,* 395 U.S. 444 (1969). Under that standard, before speech can be regulated, the speaker must intend to incite immediate unlawful conduct and the circumstances must make it likely that illegal and violent conduct is imminent.

CLEARLY ERRONEOUS TEST. See STANDARD OF REVIEW.

CLEAR TITLE. Title to property which is free from any adverse encumbrance or burden involving any question of fact or law.

CLEAVAGE DOCTRINE. Rule of labor law that there must be a distinct separation between an outgoing union which was dominated by the company and the incoming independent union.

C.L.E.O. (Council on Legal Education Opportunity). A federally funded program instituted in 1968 to assist economically disadvantaged students to gain admission to an American Bar Association-approved law school. This is accomplished mainly through the cooperation of several law schools throughout the United States who conduct six-week summer educational institutes which are designed to enable the participants, who receive financial assistance, both to obtain admission to an accredited law school and thereafter to complete their legal studies successfully.

C.L.E.P.R. (Council on Legal Education for Professional Responsibility). Created in 1968 through a Ford Foundation grant. It provides financial assistance to law schools throughout the United States in order to promote clinical legal education and courses in professional responsibility.

CLERK OF THE COURT. Title used to denote an officer who keeps records, makes proclamations, or performs similar clerical tasks. In older legal texts the term "Clerk" (or Clericus) refers to a member of the clergy. The modern meaning derives from the fact that in the Middle Ages only the clergy were educated and capable of performing administrative tasks. Laymen were not entrusted with clerical duties until after the Renaissance when lay education became more generalized.

CLIENTS' SECURITY FUND. Programs in every state except North Carolina and Wisconsin (shame on them) subsized by lawyers to reimburse any client whose money has been stolen by a lawyer. Vermont, in 1959, was the first state to institute this beneficial public service, with the Colorado Bar Association and the Philadelphia Bar Association also establishing funds in that same year.

CLIFFORD TRUST. A legal device approved by the I.R.S. in 1939 and named after its creator, George B. Clifford, Jr., an imaginative taxpayer. Income generated from high bracket trust assets is transferred to low bracket individuals, such as college students, to finance their education. Such a trust must have the following characteristics: (1) The duration of the trust must be for the life of the beneficiary or for at least ten years and a day; (2) Its purpose must be other than fulfilling a legal obligation of the trustor; (3) It must be a bona fide trust, the trustor giving up domain over his property for the period of the trust. At the end of the trust period, the assets revert to the donor. Neat!

CLOSE CORPORATION. A corporation whose shares are sold only to a single person or a relatively small group of persons. There is no public trading or issue of the voting shares. Generally, the shareholders are actively involved in the management of the corporation. The great majority of business corporations take this form, because it allows for limited liability and tax advantages while retaining the simple and informal internal procedures of an individual proprietorship or partnership.

CLOSED CORPORATION. See CLOSE CORPORATION.

CLOSED DOOR INQUEST. A secret hearing held by a foreign country to which the public is not admitted. Its function is to determine whether individuals, who are not represented by a lawyer, have committed any crimes.

CLOSED MORTGAGE. A mortgage agreement whereby the buyer is penalized if he pays off the debt before its maturity.

CLOSED PANEL. Most common form of group legal plans. Under this arrangement, all legal services needed by those protected under the plan is provided by and restricted to designated attorneys.

CLOSED SHOP. An agreement between union and employer requiring that a prospective employee join the union as a condition of employment. Such agreements requiring union membership before hiring were legal under the original National Labor Relations Act as long as the union had majority support. However, this system led to situations in which unions controlled who was and was not hired. To correct these abuses the Taft-Hartley Act amended the National Labor Relations Act so that where a union was the exclusive bargaining agent for the unit, the union could negotiate for required union membership only after the employee was hired, and then membership is compelled only to the extent of paying dues and initiation fees.

CLOSELY HELD CORPORATION. See CLOSE CORPORATION.

CLOSE RELATIVE RULE (Anti-Nepotism Rule). Company rules which prohibit two or more close relatives, i.e., husband and wife, parent and child, from working in the same operational unit of the firm. Feminists have attacked such rules, because it is usually the wife who is fired while the husband retains his position with the company.

CLOSING ARGUMENT (Summation or Summing Up). Final statements by counsel at civil and criminal trials in which the attorneys attempt to summarize and interpret the evidence that has been presented in a manner which is most favorable to their respective clients. The attorney is engaged in the preparation of his closing argument from the initial interview with his client. The argument usually takes the form of a single, believable, and coherent theory of the case, based on the evidence introduced at trial. The summation itself is not evidence. Good tactics involve confronting the opponent's credible evidence and trying to mitigate its impact, allowing the jury to discover certain points through indirectness and analogy, avoiding overstatement and making the jury identify with the client. In addition, the attorney will usually thank the jury for contributing their time to the administration of justice.

CLOSING COSTS. Those incidental costs incurred by either a buyer or a seller in the sale of real estate such as loan fees or transfer taxes.

CLOSING STATEMENT. A listing of the debits and credits of the buyer and seller of real estate to determine the amount of the financial settlement between the two parties at the time title is transferred from the seller to the buyer.

CLOTURE RULES. See FILIBUSTER TACTIC.

CLOUD ON TITLE. A defect in the title to real property, which makes it unmarketable. Such defect may consist of a lien, or an encumbrance.

C.L.U. (Chartered Life Underwriter). A professional designation granted by the American College of Life Underwriters to insurance agents who successfully pass a series of rigorous examinations in the field of life insurance. Receipt of this designation indicates that the agent is sufficiently motivated to participate in a program of formal education and professional development in this particular area. The designation C.P.C.U. (Chartered Property and Casualty Underwriter) is granted by the American Institute for Property and Liability Underwriters to insurance agents demonstrating a similar degree of motivation, knowledge, and expertise in the area of property and casualty insurance. While these designations may be helpful to the average consumer in selecting an insurance agent, they say nothing about the integrity of the agent or about the calibre of services provided.

CLUB IN THE CLOSET. The weapon used by President Carter to encourage compliance with his voluntary anti-inflation wage and price control program. Any company seeking a procurement purchasing contract with the federal government in excess of $5 million would be barred from doing business with Uncle Sam if it violated the administration guidelines.

CLUB OF ROME. A group of lawyers, scientists, economists, educators, businessmen, and specialists in systems analysis from all over the world, led by Dr. Aurelio Peccei, an Italian industrialist who has held leading positions with both the Fiat and Olivetti Corporations, which seeks first to identify and then to solve world crises. For example, will human population ultimately grow so large that the earth's finite resources will be totally consumed and, if so, how near is the day of doom?

CLUB OF TEN. A mysterious group which, since 1972, has placed expensive advertisements promoting the political views of South Africa's apartheid government in leading newspapers in Western countries. The ads say the

Club consists of businessmen from South Africa and elsewhere, but statesmen and newsmen alike have suggested the Club is a front for the South African government.

CLUSTER ZONING. A modern concept in zoning, which regulates density for a large area, leaving it to the developer to arrange population within the area. In contrast, traditional zoning schemes generally treat similarly zoned property uniformly within a given area.

COAL AND STEEL COMMUNITY. See EUROPEAN ECONOMIC COMMUNITY.

COASTAL ZONE MANAGEMENT ACT. See C.Z.M.A.

COATTAIL PRINCIPLE. The theory that a candidate heading a party ticket is likely to attract votes for other candidates of his party on the same ballot. The coattail principle is shown by the tendency of people to vote a straight ticket consisting of candidates for different offices from the same party. When an unpopular candidate heads the ticket, a negative coattail principle results in split tickets.

COBBETT, WILLIAM. An early 19th Century pamphleteer and master of vituperation, the only person ever to be punished for libel both in the United States and in England.

CODE OF CONDUCT FOR LINERS. An international agreement sponsored by the United Nations, in 1974, to govern maritime transportation. The Code has not as yet come into existence largely because the developed countries have failed to ratify it.

CODE OF DETENTE. The unsuccessful American-Russian policy of togetherness negotiated in May, 1972, between Richard Nixon and Leonid Brezhnev in which the Russians got what they wanted (our recognition of their World War II conquest of independent East European nations such as Latvia, Estonia and Lithuania) and then reneged on their solemn agreement to recognize and protect human rights in their own country by persecuting and prosecuting such dissidents as Professor Yuri Orlov in 1978.

CODE OF FEDERAL REGULATIONS. The annual cumulation of executive agency regulations published in the daily *Federal Register*, combined with regulations issued previously that are still in effect. The Code thus serves as a convenient reference for the citizen desiring comprehensive information on federal regulations. Divided into 50 titles, each representing a broad subject area, individual volumes of the Code are revised at least once each calendar year and issued on a staggered quarterly basis. An alphabetical listing by agency of subtitle and chapter assignments in the Code is provided in the back of each volume under the heading "Finding Aids" and is accurate for the revision date of that volume.

CODE OF KING MAGNUS ERIKSSON. Promulgated in 1276 by King Magnus VI of Norway, the Code reformed the legal system common to both Norway and Iceland. Magnus, who reigned from 1263 until his death in 1280, was also known as Lagaboeter or Law-Mender because of the way in which he revised the laws of his realm.

CODE OF MAIMONIDES. A collection of fourteen books presenting the entire content of the rabbinic tradition. Maimonides took ten years to complete the Code, which chronicles the laws of Jewish life and observances and communicates in orderly fashion the oral law and rabbinical commentaries embodied in the Talmud, the most important work of religious principles of post-Biblical Judaism. Many Jews objected to the codification because they felt it was degrading to the religious spirit of Judaism. Although most of Maimonides' works were originally written in Arabic, the Code was written in Hebrew. Maimonides was also known as Moses ben Maimon and as Rambam, from the initials for Rabbi Moses ben Maimon. He was born in 1135 and lived most of his 69 years in Egypt. He enjoyed a great reputation as a philosopher, scholar, and physician, serving as the personal family doctor to Egyptian royalty.

CODE OF MENES. An Egyptian law enacted in 3,000 B.C. which decreed a monetary system based on gold and silver. For most of the 4,980 years since then, the important trading nations of the world have been on a bi-metallic monetary standard.

CODE OF PROFESSIONAL RESPONSIBILITY. Establishes standards of conduct for members of the legal profession. It contains nine Canons, expressing in general terms the conduct expected of lawyers in their relationships with the public. In addition, it indicates ethical considerations which represent objectives toward which every attorney should strive, and disciplinary rules which create mandatory guidelines for professional behavior. The Code was completed in 1971 under the leadership of Supreme Court Justice Lewis F. Powell. Since that time, most of the states have adopted the Code unchanged. Committees of the American Bar Association and of similar state organizations interpret the Code and publish their opinions.

CODE OF SECURITIES. See FEDERAL SECURITIES LAW CODE.

CODE OF THE WEST. A life style that originated in the Frontier Days, especially in Wyoming which proudly proclaims that it was the first government in the world to give women the right to vote and years before it even joined the Union. Its state motto today propiciously is Equality and its Code was tri-fold: "Treat every woman as your sister and never call a cowboy 'Mister' or ride a soreback horse." Simple but sweet.

CODES OF LAW. See ATTIC CODE, BURGUNDIAN CODE, FIELD CODE, HAMMURABI CODE, JUSTINIAN CODE, NAPOLEONIC CODE, TWELVE TABLES.

CO-DETERMINATION LAWS. Require mandatory shared decision-making between labor and management of business activities, particularly invest-ments and personnel policies. Co-determination legislation received its initial impetus in West Germany, under World War II United States occupational authorities. In Sweden, Co-determination laws require worker representation on most boards of companies with twenty-five or more employees, and require management to consult with labor before deciding on any important changes affecting working conditions.

CODICIL TO A WILL. A supplement to a will. A codicil may add to, delete from, or modify the terms of the original will. In the case of an attested will, the Codicil must be executed with the formalities of a will. Generally, alterations to a holographic will are self-executing.

C.O.E.T. (Crude Oil Equalization Tax). A device to raise domestic oil prices and reduce foreign oil imports in order to resolve the American energy crisis.

COGNOVIT CLAUSE (Latin—he has acknowledged). A contractual method of giving prior consent to judicial jurisdiction. The clause is included in a contract which later becomes the basis for a claim. It generally gives the plaintiff or his attorney the power to confess judgment for the defendant and it designates a party as agent for the defendant, upon whom Service of Process may be made. Because of the prior consent, a judgment against the defendant is valid despite the fact that the defendant never received direct notice. The Cognovit Clause is often found in adhesion contracts and perhaps that is why it is disfavored and even invalid in many states. Typically, it might be included in an installment contract for the purchase of a refrigerator. It would give the seller, upon the buyer's default, the power to go into court and confess judgment against the buyer for the amount of the default.

COHABITATION CONTRACT (Living Together Agreement). An agreement between two unmarried live-in lovers (homosexual or heterosexual) or other housemates dictating their legal rights and responsibilities during the existence of their relationship and after its termination.

COHAN RULE. Named after the Great Entertainer (George M.) who won the case, a taxpayer who does not have detailed records to document in full a claimed deduction, may be allowed a partial claim of deductions except for business, travel and entertainment expenses.

COINTEL-PRO. A former clandestine counter intelligence program by the Federal Bureau of Investigation (F.B.I.) to harass left-wing dissidents. This program is no longer in effect, and the F.B.I. now only conducts investigations when there have been charges of criminal misconduct.

COKER v. GEORGIA. See RAPE PUNISHMENT.

COKE, SIR EDWARD. Probably the greatest exponent of English common law as a judge, a barrister, a member of Parliament and an author, whose *Reports on the Law, Institutes on the Laws of England* and *Coke On Littleton* are scholarly classics. He served as Solicitor General and Attorney General to Elizabeth I and as Chief Justice to James I, whom he infuriated by quoting Bracton's famous maxim: "Rex non debet esse sub home, sed sub Deo et lege" (The King ought to be under no man but under God and the law). His battle against arbitrary royal power eventually resulted in imprisonment in the Tower of London for six months, but he nonetheless continued to be a staunch supporter of the Magna Charta. He championed the passage of the historic Petition of Right and Bill of Rights curbing the power of the throne. His early mastery of the Year Books (the compilation of the court decisions of early English common law) stood him in good stead throughout his professional career. In 1589 he won a clear-cut victory in court in what has become known as the Rule in Shelley's Case which is so complicated it plagues law students even to this day. A very great presence in the law indeed.

C.O.L.A. (Cost of Living Adjustment). Provision in a labor agreement which requires an increase in the wages of the employees to reflect a comparable increase in the cost of living caused by inflation, thereby giving rise to a never-ending upward spiral.

COLD BENCH. See HOT BENCH.

COLD WAR. Any non-military confrontation between the Western World (Europe and North America) and the East (China and the Soviets). It's better than bullets.

COLD WAR LAW. A federal law which seeks to prevent and control espionage by requiring anyone who is or has been affiliated with a foreign intelligence service to register with the Department of Justice. Failure to comply is a crime.

COLLAPSIBLE CORPORATION. A device whereby one or more individuals attempt to convert the profits from their participation in a project from ordinary income to long term capital gains. Typically, a group forms a corporation to construct a property. After that property is produced, but before a substantial amount of income from it is realized, the stock in the corporation is sold or the corporation is liquidated. On a sale, the taxpayers realize a long term capital gain if they have held the stock for over six months. If the corporation is liquidated, long term capital gain treatment of income realized results. By the use of the corporate form, the taxpayer has converted what would normally be ordinary income into capital gains. However, under section 341 of the Internal Revenue Code, if a corporation is deemed to be collapsible, the monies received upon liquidation or sale of stock will be treated as a dividend and taxed as ordinary income.

COLLATERAL ATTACK. Attempt to avoid the binding force of a judgment in a proceeding other than direct review via appeal, error, or certiorari. The challenge is mounted in an action other than that in which the judgment was rendered and such proceeding will have an independent purpose, although the overruling of the judgment may be essential for its success. The principal form of collateral attack is the prisoner's resort to Habeas Corpus, an action which questions the lawfulness of his incarceration. Generally, the attack must be premised on a glaring defect in the original proceeding, such as the state's failure to provide the defendant with counsel, if the prisoner is to successfully evade the effect of the judgment.

COLLATERAL ESTOPPEL (Issue Preclusion). An ancient common-law rule of procedure that permits a party who has won a lawsuit to rely on any findings which were made in the case in a second trial on the same issues. In a 1979 Supreme Court decision (*Parklane Hosiery v. Shore*, 47 U.S.L.W. 4079 (2d Cir. 1979)), this principle was expanded to apply to a new party plaintiff as long as it would not be unfair in the particular case. This prevents duplicative trials on issues that have already been resolved. This ruling will help to strengthen the power of regulatory agencies by encouraging companies to settle out of court because if they lose a case, private parties could thereafter sue them successfully based on any findings of an adverse nature against the companies which resulted from the litigation.

COLLATERAL HEIR. A person who, while not a lineal descendant of a deceased person, inherits property from him by virtue of sharing a common ancestor. For example brothers and nieces are Collateral Heirs, while grandchildren are not. Under current laws of intestacy as well as the common law's Canons of Descent, collateral heirs inherit only when the decedent has no lineal descendants.

COLLATERAL ORDERS DOCTRINE. The principle that a federal court order as to a purely collateral matter is immediately appealable, without regard to the status of the principal litigation. The scope of the Collateral Orders Doctrine remains unclear since its initial recognition in the United States Supreme Court in 1949, but it is generally thought that "final decisions" as to collateral issues do not come within the multiple-claim limitations of Rule 54(b) of the Federal Rules of Civil Procedure. Examples of cases involving Collateral Orders include a denial of a petition to proceed In Forma Pauperis, an order requiring plaintiff to post security for costs, and orders granting or refusing consolidation of actions. The usual reason for allowing immediate appeal of Collateral Orders is that the collateral rights asserted in an action are "too important to be denied review and too independent of the cause itself to require that appellate consideration be deferred until the whole case is adjudicated."

COLLATERAL SOURCES RULE. Allows the winner of a civil suit for damages to collect the full amount of damages without deducting benefits received from other sources. For example, a person injured in an automobile accident could collect damages for personal injuries even though his insurance company had already compensated him for his injuries. Although this rule is criticized for allowing a "double recovery," it is supported by the rationale that anyone prudent enough to insure against loss should not be penalized. Moreover, many insurance contracts have subrogation provisions which require the insured to refund any sums collected in a judgment which the insurer has previously paid.

COLLECTIVE BARGAINING. A procedure for determining wages, hours and other working conditions in which the employer or his representative meets with a certified representative of the employees. As contemplated by the National Labor Relations Act, this concept calls for good faith bargaining by both parties.

COLLECTIVE BARGAINING AREA. That geographical section or part of an industry in which workers are affected by one collective contract.

COLLECTIVE MARK. Used by the members of a cooperative, an association or other collective group or organization. There are three types of Collective Marks: (1) Trademarks used on goods; (2) Service Marks, used in the sale of services to identify the services of a group and distinguish them from the services of others; and (3) Membership Marks used to indicate ownership. An example of a Collective Mark is the "Quality Court" Mark, which is used by a group of independent motels. This type of Mark is owned and may be registered by the group or association, and it indicates to the public that members of the association rendered the services or made any goods bearing the Mark. If a Mark is adopted for the purpose of indicating membership in an established or organized group, it is called a Membership Mark. These Marks are not used on goods or services to identify and distinguish them from others. Rather, they simply indicate that the person displaying the Mark is a member of the organized group. Some examples of Membership Marks are lodge buttons of charitable organizations, Y.M.C.A. letterheads, and Greek letter society pins.

COLLEGE ASSISTANCE MIGRANT PROGRAM (C.A.M.P.). A federal program instituted in 1972 which subsidizes the cost of college for children of migrant (seasonal farm workers) families, thereby making the impossible dream come true.

COLLEGE OF CARDINALS. Despite its name, this is not an academic institution. It is a group of over one hundred advisers to the Roman Catholic Pope, all of whom are appointed by the Pope and whose main responsibility is to choose his successor. Those over 80 do not participate in this election nor do those who are In Pectore (Latin —in his heart), a term which applies to a Cardinal whose identification is not made public. Although the College has no legal status in the international community, it does exercise a powerful moral clout.

COLLEGE OF THE STATE JUDICIARY. Organized in 1963 as the National College of State Trial Judges. The college's primary objective is to improve the administration of justice through training and educating state judges to perform their duties more efficiently.

COLLISION AVOIDANCE SYSTEMS. See C.A.S.

COLLUSIVE CASES. See FEIGNED CASES.

COLOR BLINDNESS. A view advocated by some commentators that has not as yet been completely accepted by the Supreme Court of the United States that the United States Constitution requires all federal and state law to be strictly and uniformly applied without any consideration or exception based on race or ethnic origin.

COLOR OF TITLE. Title to real property which appears valid but which has a hidden defect.

COLUMBIAN CONNECTION. A billion-dollar network that smuggles pot (marijuana) and coke (cocaine) into the United States from Columbia, South America, making this backward country the drug capital of the world.

COME-BACK LAWS (Recidivist Statutes). Legislative provisions which provide for an additional punishment for criminals who have been previously convicted.

C.O.M.E.C.O.N. (Council for Mutual Economic Assistance; C.M.E.A.). Created in Moscow in January, 1949, to include the Soviet Union, Poland, Hungary, Rumania, Bulgaria, and Czechoslovakia. It is the response of Communist countries to the Marshall Plan and the European Economic Community (E.E.C.) to achieve greater economic co-operation among Communist nations. Its purpose was to surpass the most advanced capitalist countries as to G.N.P., industrial and agricultural production, and standard of living. C.O.M.E.C.O.N. required a unanimous vote to implement its decisions. Thus, it never succeeded in overcoming the reluctance of its members to give up part of their national sovereignty. This attitude prevented unification of their respective economic plans. During the Stalin era, C.O.M.E.C.O.N. was not active. On October 22, 1963, the International Bank for Economic Cooperation was created in Moscow to facilitate economic coordination and to increase the activities of the C.O.M.E.C.O.N. with third-world countries by creating a gold-convertible and transferable ruble. However, the fearlessness of Rumania in opposing the Soviet Union conception of the C.O.M.E.C.O.N. in 1962 has shown that Communist countries wanted their national economies to remain those of sovereign and independent countries.

COMMAND THEORY. See LEGAL POSITIVISM.

COMMERCE POWER. The power that the Congress possesses to regulate interstate commerce under Article 1, Section 8 of the Constitution. In *Gibbons v. Ogden,* 9 Wheat. 1 (1824), Chief Justice John Marshall gave an expansive interpretation to the commerce power but later cases, especially those of the Lochner Era, significantly hampered congressional power to regulate interstate commerce. After the Court-Packing Plan of President Franklin D. Roosevelt, the Supreme Court began to allow more congressional regulation to prohibit such undesirable practices as excessive hours, substandard wages and child labor. Now the power of Congress is almost unlimited in reaching matters that even tangentially affect interstate commerce.

COMMERCIAL SPEECH DOCTRINE. Holds that advertising or commercial speech does not enjoy the same First Amendment right of freedom from governmental control as political speech. The doctrine was based on the theory that when the First Amendment was drafted, the Founding Fathers were concerned only with speech that helped people to participate in representative democracy and that commercial advertising should not be so included. The Commercial Speech Doctrine was articulated by the United States Supreme Court in 1942 in the case of *Valentine v. Chrestensen,* 316 U.S. 52 (1942). But the doctrine proved difficult to apply and the Supreme Court limited its application. In *Virginia State Board of Pharmacy v. Virginia Citizens Consumer Council,* 423 U.S. 815 (1975), the Court finally rejected the Doctrine and held that even purely commercial advertising is entitled to First Amendment protection.

COMMERCIAL UNIT. Any unit of goods which is considered by commercial usage to be a single whole for the purpose of sale, the division of which will materially impair its character or market value and use. For example, a commercial unit may be a single article (a machine); a set of articles (suite of furniture); or a quantity (a carload or a gross).

COMMERCIAL WARRANTY OF GOOD TITLE. The doctrine which enables a person who accepts a forged instrument to recover from the wrongdoer.

COMMISSION AND COURT ON JUDICIAL CONDUCT AND DISABILITY. Using a procedure already applicable in almost every state, the Commission, proposed by Senator Nunn of Georgia, would screen complaints against federal judges, referring only the most serious allegations to an elaborate five-step judicial proceeding. All cases would be considered in secret to shield the judges from premature and unwarranted publicity. If found guilty, a judge would be subject to censure, removal or involuntary retirement. Supported by the American Bar Association, American Judicature Society and the Justice Department, Senator Nunn's bill was passed by the Senate in 1978, but was not considered by the House of Representatives. The legislation has been reintroduced in 1979. Of the thousands of federal judges who have served in the past 200 years, only 55 have been officially investigated by the Congress, only 9 have been impeached by the House of Representatives, and only 4 have been convicted by the Senate and removed from office.

COMMISSIONER OF INTERNAL REVENUE. See I.R.S.

COMMISSIONER OF PATENTS. See PATENT COMMISSIONER.

COMMISSION OF STATE SECURITY. See K.G.B.

COMMISSION OF THE EUROPEAN COMMUNITIES. See EUROPEAN ECONOMIC COMMUNITY.

COMMISSION ON A NATIONAL INSTITUTE OF JUSTICE. Created in 1972 to examine the feasibility of creating an independent public corporation to coordinate an expanded and accelerated program of research into the administration of justice. The proposed organization would perform functions for the legal profession comparable to those now provided for the medical and scientific communities through the National Institute of Health and the National Science Foundation.

COMMISSION ON CIVIL RIGHTS. A federal agency which has no enforcement authority, but submits findings of fact and recommendations to both the President and the Congress. More than 60 percent of the Commission's recommendations have been enacted, either by statute, Executive order, or regulation. The Commission evaluates the effectiveness of federal laws and government equal opportunity programs and also serves as a national clearinghouse for civil rights information.

COMMISSION ON HUMAN RIGHTS. A fact-finding agency of the U.N. established at the first meeting of the United Nations Economic and Social Council. Its mandate is to combat violations of fundamental freedoms and human rights. To accomplish this task, the Commission investigates cases which reveal consistent patterns of human rights violations. With the approval of the President of the Council and the Secretary General, it may call upon ad hoc working groups of specialists for assistance. In addition, it has created several sub-commissions, including the important Sub-Commission on Prevention of Discrimination and Protection of Minorities, which reports its findings to the Economic and Social Council.

COMMISSION ON JUDICIAL CONDUCT. See NUNN BILL.

COMMISSION ON JUDICIAL NOMINATIONS. A screening panel composed of non-partisan lay persons and members of the legal profession which examines candidates for judgeships and recommends those it approves to the incumbent executive Governor, or President, for appointment.

COMMISSION ON JUDICIAL PERFORMANCE. An agency found in every state except Washington whose function is to oversee judges in the exercise of the immense powers vested in them and to discipline or remove them if necessary.

COMMISSION ON REORGANIZATION OF THE EXECUTIVE BRANCH. See HOOVER COMMISSION.

COMMITTEE FOR THE SECURITY OF THE U.S.S.R. COUNCIL OF MINISTERS. See K.G.B.

COMMITTEE OF THE JUDICIAL CONFERENCE OF THE UNITED STATES TO CONSIDER STANDARDS FOR ADMISSION TO PRACTICE IN THE FEDERAL COURTS. See DEVITT COMMITTEE.

COMMITTEE OF THE WHOLE. A procedure used by the House of Representatives to expedite business by declaring the entire House a committee for the purpose of considering bills. The committee, whose full title is Committee of the Whole House on the State of the Union, suspends the formal House procedure normally used for floor debate.

COMMITTEE ON POLITICAL EDUCATION. See C.O.P.E.

COMMITTEE ON THE JUDICIARY.
A screening group to evaluate candidates for appointments to judgeships.

COMMITTEE REPORT. A formal report by a legislative committee to the House, Senate, or both, on a proposed law or other matter. The report is part of the legislative history and includes: a summary of the proposed law, recommendations as to its passage and amendments, relevant background information, a discussion and defense of its provisions, a detailed section-by-section analysis of the proposed law, a demonstration of the changes it makes in existing law, reports on the law from the administration, cost estimates, and dissenting views from members of the Committee.

COMMODITY FUTURES TRADING COMMISSION (C.F.T.C.). A federal agency which protects investors from sharp practices or fraud by brokers who deal in the purchase and sale of speculative securities known as commodity futures. The hot line for investors who have complaints against brokers is 800-227-4428.

COMMON CARRIER. An individual or firm which provides public transportation for either passengers or goods. Common Carriers are highly regulated, operating under an official franchise and charging rates which must be approved by a regulatory body. Once a Common Carrier is approved to offer a particular class of service, it must accept the business of all customers who fall within the class and must secure permission to discontinue the service.

COMMON CAUSE. A political action group formed in 1968 by former federal cabinet member John W. Gardner, who serves as Chairman. It has approximately 300,000 members and a staff of 100. It states its purpose to be "a national citizens' lobby dedicated to making government accountable to the citizens." It seeks the reordering of national priorities and the revitalization of the public process, so that political and governmental institutions will be responsible to the needs of the nation and its citizens.

COMMON LAW. The body of laws derived from judicial decisions rather than from statutory enactments, which developed in England and spread with British influence throughout the world. The common law is today in effect in Britain and the United States and most of the countries of the Commonwealth. Most Western countries not following the common law tradition trace the origins of their law to civil law of Rome. The major distinction between these two systems concerns the sources of law. The civil law consists primarily of legislative enactments or statutory law, while the common law is primarily judge-made, and is therefore found mostly in court decisions. Curiously, the term common law originally referred to law that was applicable throughout England—the King's law rather than that of local lords. Currently in the United States, however, it is customary to speak of the common law of each individual state. Beginning in the twelfth century in England, the King asserted jurisdiction over the resolution of disputes. At the same time, trial by ordeal, battle and compurgation were gradually superseded by jury trials and the doctrine of precedent arose. The decisions of the Royal Courts became precedents which bound future courts facing similar issues. In the event that no precedent on a particular issue existed, judges were allowed to formulate a rule based on their own sense of justice and fairness. Through this process of accretion, as courts faced new issues, they formulated rules and eventually a very broad body of law was developed in the reported decisions of the cases. When the early English settlers came to America, they brought with them the common law of England. Some states formally adopted the common law while others used common-law principles to decide cases but did not universally hold to English precedent. The common law grew in this country on a state-by-state basis such that the laws of the various states might differ from each other because of inaccurate knowledge of the English common law, a conscious decision to break with English precedent on a particular point or the development of a new rule to govern in situations that had never faced the English courts prior to Independence in 1776. Although decisions under the common law must bow to statutory and constitutional authority, the common law remains a vital force in American jurisprudence.

COMMON-LAW COPYRIGHT. Automatically, and without formalities, preserves for the originator or his successor in interest the right to reproduce a written, recorded, or artistic work prior to publication. It exists indefinitely until publication occurs, but publication is not simply the equivalent of putting a work into the public forum. Section 301 of the Copyright Act of 1976 in effect terminated Common-Law Copyright as of January 1, 1978. This federal pre-emption does not occur until a work is transcribed into a tangible medium of expression.

COMMON-LAW DOWER. An expectant or contingent interest held by the wife in lands owned by her husband during their marriage. This contingent right was called dower inchoate. After the husband's death the right ripened into dower consummate which granted to the widow a life estate in one third of the land which her husband owned during the marriage. Many states have abolished the concept of dower, by statute.

COMMON-LAW MARRIAGE. The present, mutual, unconditional consent of competent parties to become husband and wife with no license, no witness, no ceremony, no blood test, no publication of bans, and no writing. It is just as valid as a formal marriage in St. Patrick's Cathedral on Easter Sunday morning. It can be dissolved only by divorce. Although common-law marriage has been abolished in most states and changed in others, all states will recognize one validly entered into elsewhere. The children are legitimate.

COMMON MARKET. See EUROPEAN ECONOMIC COMMUNITY.

COMMON OCCUPANT. At common law, the first person to obtain possession of a life estate when the life tenant predeceased the person used as a measuring life. The common occupant was permitted to continue in possession until the death of the measuring life. Today, the life estate continues and passes to the heirs of the life tenant as personal property. Such heirs are known as special occupants.

COMMON-SITUS PICKETING. Picketing conducted by employees on property where employees of an uninvolved employer also work. Although such picketing can be carried out only on a common situs by employees in certain industries, such as shipping or construction, the activity conflicts with the general prohibition against secondary boycotts. The National Labor Relations Board allows such picketing where it complies with certain tests, but employs a different test in each of the shipping and construction industries. Both houses of Congress passed a bill broadening the permissible scope of Common-Situs Picketing in 1975, a bill strongly favored by organized labor. However, the bill was vetoed by President Ford.

COMMON STOCK. The shares of a corporation when only one class of shares is authorized. The holder of such stock has an interest in the corporation in proportion to the number of shares he holds out of the total number of shares issued. The nature of the shareholder's ownership interest is threefold. He has a proportionate interest in earnings of the corporation, in the net assets of the business, and in control of the corporation. Control is usually in the form of voting at shareholder's meetings to elect the Board of Directors who manage the corporation. Shareholders also have the inherent power to remove a director for good cause, subject to court review, to adopt, amend, or repeal corporate by-laws, and to ratify corporate action on extraordinary matters which are beyond the scope of ordinary management powers delegated to the Board of Directors.

COMMON TRUST FUND. A fund created by the combination of several individual trust funds in order to achieve a reduction in administrative costs and to allow greater diversity of investment.

COMMONWEALTH OF NATIONS. An economic and political association created under the British Empire authority and headed by the Queen. Its twenty-six members include three from Europe, five from Asia, two from Oceania, eleven from Africa, and five from the Western Hemisphere. The system is one of free and voluntary cooperation, on the basis of membership to the sterling block, trade preferences, financial, technical and military aid, as well as common institutions and languages. The Commonwealth's most remarkable feature is its flexibility; no formal treaties nor specific commitments exist among its members. The only permanent institution is a Secretariat.

COMMUNIST MANIFESTO. See MARXIAN THEORY.

COMMUNIST PARTY v. SUBVERSIVE ACTIVITIES CONTROL BOARD. See SUBVERSIVE ACTIVITIES CONTROL BOARD.

COMMUNITY ACTION FOR LEGAL SERVICES. A federally funded program for the poor, located in New York City, with 300 employees, including 160 lawyers. It receives about $10 million a year from the National Legal Services Corporation to operate 19 law offices in low-income neighborhoods in order to help some 40,000 clients each year with consumer complaints, divorce and foster-care cases, and other civil matters.

COMMUNITY ADVISORY BOARDS. See PUBLIC TELECOMMUNICATIONS ACT OF 1978.

COMMUNITY ASSISTANCE FUND. See EXIT TAX.

COMMUNITY COURT. See NEIGHBORHOOD COURT.

COMMUNITY HEALTH SERVICES LAW. A California law passed in 1969, consisting of a revision of the Short-Doyle Act of 1957 and the new Lanterman-Petris-Short Act (L.P.S.). The original Short-Doyle Act attempted to aid local communities in accepting responsibility for the care of their mentally ill. Under the Act, the state provided a 50 percent reimbursement of the cost of approved county mental health programs. As amended, the law makes community mental health centers mandatory in counties with 100,000 residents or more, but increases the state funding to 90 percent. The expenses of those county residents receiving inpatient care in the remaining state facilities are absorbed by the county. L.P.S. was intended to protect the rights of the mentally ill by eliminating indeterminate commitments and by setting stricter criteria for Involuntary Commitment. L.P.S. has been called the Magna Charta of the mentally ill, but there are indications that its operation falls short of expectations. Though inpatient populations in state hospitals are decreasing, a growing number of individuals with mental disorders are now handled through the criminal process. Tougher commitment standards may result in arrest, rather than hospitalization of disturbed individuals, for crimes such as public drunkenness, disorderly conduct, or malicious mischief. While recent trends in law enforcement have suggested diversion of minor offenders from the criminal system, L.P.S. has resulted in subjecting more mentally ill people to the criminal process. In addition to the criminalization of disordered behavior, some counties have elected to lease space in empty state facilities, thus defeating the community-oriented philosophy of the Act. Deinstitutionalization appears far more complex than just closing the doors of state hospitals.

COMMUNITY LAW (Community Re-Investment Act). Passed by Congress in 1977 to require federal regulatory agencies to encourage banks and other financial institutions to "meet the credit needs of their entire community, including low and moderate income neighborhoods." The Act contemplates evaluation of a bank's reinvestment performance in two contexts. First, routine bank examinations from now on will encompass a review of CRA compliance. Second, community reinvestment activity will be considered in deciding on every application for a deposit facility. Included in this enforcement scheme are applications for (1) new charters for national banks and federal savings and loan associations, (2) deposit insurance for newly chartered institutions, (3) branches and remote facilities that will accept deposits, (4) home office and branch relocations, and (5) mergers, consolidations, and acquisitions requiring approval under the Federal Deposit Insurance Act, Title IV of the National Housing Act, or the Bank Holding Company Act.

COMMUNITY MEDIATION CENTER. See NEIGHBORHOOD COURT.

COMMUNITY PROPERTY. Held in common by both husband and wife. Generally, such property is the result of the effort of either husband or wife during marriage. Community Property is recognized in a number of states, including California, Idaho, Louisiana, Nevada, New Mexico, Texas, and Washington and derives from civil law and not the common law.

COMMUNITY REINVESTMENT ACT. See COMMUNITY LAW.

COMMUNITY TRUST. A trust arrangement composed of donations by many people for educational, charitable and social purposes in a given area or community. Funds are distributed by a select group of citizens who act as a distribution committee. There is usually a community trust institution. Often such trust arrangements are called foundations. The first Community Trusts date back to the early seventeenth century in London, where wealthy landowners collected and invested to protect the value of real estate in their areas.

COMMUTED SENTENCE. The punishment of a convicted criminal which has been reduced from a greater to a lesser degree, as from life to 20 years.

COMPACT CLAUSE. The Constitutional provision which allows a state to "enter into any Agreement or Compact with another State" provided that Congress consents (Article I, Section 10, clause 3). The Supreme Court has held, however, that Congressional approval is not required where the interstate agreement does not increase state political power vis-à-vis the federal government. For example, in *United States Steel Corp. v. Multistate Tax Commission,* 434 U.S. 452 (1978), the Court held that a multistate tax compact was not an Agreement within the meaning of the Compact Clause because it did not expand the powers of the states.

COMPACT OF FREE ASSOCIATION (1980). An agreement between the United States and the U.S. Trust Territory of the Pacific Islands (Marshall Islands), granting limited independence to the central Pacific archipelago and assuring exclusive American military rights in the chain for at least 15 years. Establishing a unique political relationship, the accord grants the islanders all the attributes of sovereignty outside the defense and security sphere, including the right to enter into treaties with foreign states and to dispose of their resources, except that they will probably be unable to qualify for membership in the United Nations. This compact concludes four centuries of alien rule in the Marshall Islands by Spanish, German, Japanese and American occupiers.

COMPANIONATE MARRIAGE. See LINDSEY, BEN.

COMPANY UNION. A union all of whose members are employees of a single company. Where such unions are so dominated or supported by the company that they abridge employee rights under the National Labor Relations Act, they have been held illegal. Company unions flourished during the 1920s and early 1930s, when companies sought to stem the tide of unionization by taking initiative in establishing worker associations. By placing company officials in union offices and inducing workers to join the unions, the company effectively controlled the union and dictated its policies.

COMPARATIVE NEGLIGENCE. A doctrine adopted by statute in a minority of states to soften the impact of the common law's Contributory Negligence defense to Negligence suits. Such statutes, which are receiving considerable attention in many jurisdictions, are generally of two types: Pure and Partial Comparative Negligence. To understand how such laws work, imagine an automobile accident which was 80 percent *B*'s fault and 20 percent *A*'s fault, and in which each suffered $10,000 of injury. Under a Pure Comparative Negligence statute, *B* could recover $2,000 from *A*, and *A*, $8,000 from *B*. That is, each recovers in proportion to his innocence. Under Partial Comparative Negligence, however, *B* recovers nothing since his fault exceeded that of *A*. *A* could still recover $8,000. The Partial Comparative Negligence Statutes allow recovery only to the more innocent of the two parties.

COMPARATIVE RECTITUDE. The common law doctrine, codified by statute in some states, that, when both parties in a divorce suit are at fault, the court may grant a divorce to the party whose fault is the less serious. Judicial applications of the doctrine vary. Some courts specifically rely on Comparative Rectitude; others adopt its reasoning without expressly accepting it, and still others, in jurisdictions without a statute governing its use, accept or reject the doctrine according to the discretion of the presiding judge. Comparative Rectitude has allowed courts to grant divorce in situations where divorce would otherwise have been barred by the Recrimination Doctrine. With the development of No-Fault Divorce, Comparative Rectitude has lost some of its significance.

COMPARATIVE SURVEY OF FREEDOM. See FREEDOM HOUSE.

COMPARISON APPRAISAL. Assigning a value to property by comparing it to similar property whose current value is known. Allowances are made for the condition of the property to be appraised and any changes or improvements which might cause it to be worth more or less than the property whose value is known.

COMPELLING STATE INTEREST. See SUSPECT CLASSIFICATIONS.

COMPENSATION FOR VICTIMS OF VIOLENT CRIMES. A new state program which recognizes that tort actions often fail to compensate victims of violent crimes because the assailant is in jail or cannot be found. Many states have passed legislation allowing the state to indemnify needy victims. They have set up special funds, into which a part of each criminal fine is placed, to be distributed to victims on the basis of need. Other states take the money out of general state revenues. There is considerable difference of opinion on how effective such programs have been. However, they are a positive legislative response to the criticism that government is often more concerned about the criminal than the victim of violent crime.

COMPENSATORY DAMAGES. Money paid by a wrongdoer to his victim in compliance with a judgment at law. The core concept of damages is just compensation for the loss or injury sustained by the injured party so that he may be restored, as practically as possible, to the condition or position he was in prior to his injury. Thus, he is "made whole." Damages has been a vital feature of law since its origins. Before the Norman invasion of England (1066), the Anglo-Saxons used a system of Wergild, or man price, which fixed the atonement a slayer must pay the family of the dead man according to the rank and social position of the deceased. Today, Compensatory Damages will usually consist of two distinct elements: General Damages and Special Damages. These should be contrasted with Punitive Damages.

COMPETENCY TO STAND TRIAL.
Pre-trial judicial determination of an accused's ability to understand rationally and factually the proceedings against him and to aid his counsel in preparing a defense. The fact that one found incompetent to stand trial is never tried on the charges against him differentiates his status from the person who is found not guilty by reason of insanity. The focus of the competency inquiry is the accused's present mental condition rather than his state at the time of the offense which is crucial to the success of a psychiatric defense aimed at acquittal based on insanity. One does not beat the rap by being found incompetent to stand trial since he or she will be committed to a state hospital until sanity is restored, and then the prosecution may be resumed.

COMPETENT WITNESS. A person qualified to testify at trial. The common law barred anyone from testifying who had a pecuniary interest in the litigation, was the husband or wife of a party, had ever been convicted of an infamous crime, or did not believe that a Supreme Being would punish perjurers. Today, few remnants of these rules remain. But an attorney can still point to a witness's interest in the outcome of a case to discredit the witness in the eyes of the jury. No blanket rule disqualifies the insane or very young. But a witness must have personal knowledge or observation of the things about which he testifies. He must also remember the facts, and be able to narrate or explain them in a comprehensible way.

COMPETITIVE SEALED BIDDING.
Under the Model Procurement Code this term is used to describe the method of source selection known as formal advertising in federal government contracting.

COMPETITIVE SEALED PROPOSALS. Under the Model Procurement Code this term is used to describe the method of source selection known as competitive negotiation in federal government contracting.

COMPLAINT-MOBILE. A mobile van which tours San Francisco to advise dissatisfied consumers on the proper procedure for attaining relief. A new program designed to help people without clogging the courts, the Complaint-Mobile began with a grant from the Law Enforcement Assistance Administration and an old truck donated by United Parcel. It handled over 300 complaints the first year, ranging from false advertisements to faulty auto repairs. Funded by H.E.W., the Complaint-Mobile now includes a small claims court-educational project among its van services.

COMPLETION CONTRACT. See COST-PLUS-FIXED FEE.

COMPOSITE STATE. Under international law, a nation made up of independent sub-units. Examples of Composite States include: a personal union (two states with the same head of state, such as Great Britain and Hanover from 1714 till 1837); a confederation (a loosely connected grouping of sub-units which are of greater authority than the composite unit, such as Switzerland); and a federal union (a union of distinct sub-units with overlapping central authority, such as the United States).

COMPOSITION WITH CREDITORS.
An agreement between an insolvent debtor and two or more of his creditors, under which the creditors promise to discharge the debtor of his debts in return for partial payment. Such an agreement between the debtor and a single creditor would be called an Accord and Satisfaction. A Composition With Creditors is a contractual agreement between the parties, and does not bind any creditor not assenting to it. By contrast, a similar procedure established by the Federal Bankruptcy Act, the Chapter XI proceeding, provides for an agreement between a business debtor and his creditors which, if approved by a majority of the creditors and confirmed by a bankruptcy court, binds all duly notified creditors to its terms.

COMPOUNDING A CRIME. An agreement not to prosecute or inform on one who has committed a crime in exchange for money or other valuable consideration. Only the party receiving the consideration is liable for Compounding Crime; the original criminal giving the consideration is not guilty. Today, many states limit criminal liability to the compounding of felonies and some allow victims to accept settlements.

COMPOUND INTEREST. Interest paid on interest. Compound interest is earned when interest on a sum of money is added to the principal and additional interest is earned on the entire sum.

COMPREHENSIVE EMPLOYMENT AND TRAINING ACT. See C.E.T.A.

COMPROMISE AND SETTLEMENT. See ACCORD AND SATISFACTION.

COMPROMISE OF 1850. See CLAY, HENRY.

COMPROMISE STATUTES. Laws, adopted in about ten states, which allow the victim of a misdemeanor to bar the prosecution of the offender, by claiming that the offender has given satisfaction for the injury. These statutes change the common law rule that crimes, as offenses against the public, are punishable regardless of the victim's wishes.

COMPTROLLER OF THE CURRENCY. Created by Congress in 1863, as an integral part of the national banking system. The Comptroller, as the Administrator of national banks, is responsible for the execution of laws relating to national banks, and promulgates rules and regulations governing the operations of approximately 4,600 national and District of Columbia banks. Approval of the Comptroller is required for the organization of new national banks, conversion of state-chartered banks into national banks, consolidations or mergers of banks where the surviving institution is a national bank, and the establishment of branches by national banks. The Office of the Comptroller exercises general supervision over the operations of national banks, including trust activities and overseas operations. Each bank is examined periodically through a nationwide staff of approximately 2,000 bank examiners under the immediate supervision of 14 regional administrators. These examinations operate in the public interest by assisting the Comptroller in appraising the financial condition of the banks, the soundness of their operations, the quality of their management, and their compliance with laws, rules, and regulations.

COMPULSORY APPEARANCE. The participation of an individual in a judicial or other formal proceeding when he has been served with process.

COMPULSORY ARBITRATION. A procedure for settling labor disputes or grievances in which both parties agree to submit certain issues for decision by a mutually-approved third party and to be bound by that party's decision.

COMPULSORY COUNTER-CLAIM. See COUNTER-CLAIM.

COMPULSORY JOINDER. See JOINDER OF PARTIES.

COMPULSORY PROCESS. The constitutional right of a criminal defendant to have the court issue and serve a subpoena on any witness necessary for his defense. The right encompasses the responsibility of the court to compel the appearance of such individuals by warrant of arrest or attachment if they fail to obey or affirmatively act to evade the service of the subpoena. The defendant must give a reasonable opportunity to the court officer to effect service, and the officer must exert diligent efforts to serve the process or return it with a good explanation. The fact that the witness had left the country would be a sufficient reason for the failure to serve.

COMPUTER-ASSISTED LEGAL RESEARCH. An aid to quality legal research, utilizing a data-base of both statutory and decisional materials. Most systems now in use employ a full-text concept, whereby every word of a document is filed in the data-base. A search of filed materials is accomplished through a word-oriented approach. All materials of a particular type are scanned for a particular key word or phrase. In order to be effective, the selection of the key word or phrase must be made carefully if the retrieval of irrelevant materials is to be avoided. To aid in this selection, various advanced methods have been devised. Some systems currently in use include the government-sponsored system of F.L.I.T.E. (Federal Legal Information Through Electronics), operated by the Air Force, and J.U.R.I.S. (Justice Retrieval and Inquiry System), operated by the Department of Justice, along with the privately operated systems of Westlaw, sponsored by the West Publishing Company, and L.E.X.I.S., sponsored by Mead Data Central.

COMPUTER PUNCH CARD JUSTICE. See SENTENCING PROCEDURES.

C.O.M.S.A.T. (Communications Satellite Corporation). Established by the Communications Satellite Act (1962), C.O.M.S.A.T. consists of several hundred communications companies representing many nations.

CONCERTED ACTIVITIES. Combined action by employees, usually engaged in to improve conditions of employment. The right to engage in such activities is guaranteed under the National Labor Relations Act. To merit this protection, the acts must meet certain criteria which focus on whether the means and objectives of such activity are lawful. The general rule is that primary activity aimed at a party directly involved with the employees in question is lawful under federal statutes. Secondary activity, aimed at another employer or other uninvolved third party, is generally not lawful. Peaceful strikes, picketing and other self-organizing activities are protected by the N.L.R.B. and the courts. Activities which are often found to be unprotected include the Work Slow-Down, Sit-Down Strike, Wildcat Strike, trespass, violence, physical sabotage and refusal to obey rules.

CONCILIATION COURT. A non-judicial public facility which provides free professional counseling to married couples having serious domestic problems. Its purpose is to provide couples the opportunity to discuss their problems before reaching a final decision with respect to their marriage, to provide means for reconciliation of spouses and to attempt amicable settlement of domestic and family controversies. The purpose of counseling is to provide communication between the parties. Regardless of what the final outcome may be, most people feel better after they have used the counseling services. Other services provided are: (1) Premarital counseling to under-age individuals requiring court permission to get married; (2) Custody and/or visitation studies as ordered by the court; (3) Post-dissolution counseling, including counseling for visitation problems.

CONCLUSION OF FACT. A result reached by considering factual evidence.

CONCLUSION OF LAW. A result reached by applying a rule of law, rather than considering factual evidence.

CONCLUSIVE PRESUMPTION. Rules of decision which provide that where fact 1 is proved to exist, the law will assume fact 2 and will not allow evidence of its nonexistence. In *Vlandis v. Kline,* 412 U.S. 441 (1973), for example, a Connecticut statute provided that if a single student had a legal address outside the state during the year before his admission to the state university, he could not be considered a resident for tuition purposes. The Supreme Court held that when a presumption is not necessarily true in fact, an individual must be given an opportunity to rebut it. However, the Court is now retreating from the *Vlandis* position. Critics of the Conclusive Presumption doctrine have pointed out that Connecticut would be allowed to charge higher tuition rates to persons who had previously lived outside the state if it merely said so directly, so why not allow it to achieve the same result by means of a presumption?

CONCURRENT JURISDICTION. Jurisdiction exercised by two or more courts or administrative agencies at the same time over the same subject matter. Which court or agency actually exercises jurisdiction in such cases generally is determined by the claimant. Concurrent jurisdiction may be created by statute, such as where two courts within the same state are given authority to dispose of the same type of case. It may arise by operation of law, as where a tort occurs in one state but causes an injury in another state, thereby conferring jurisdiction in the courts of either state. Concurrent Jurisdiction may also exist between the courts of the federal judiciary and those of the various states.

CONCURRENT NEGLIGENCE. The independent negligent acts of two persons which contribute to the victim's injuries. Their acts are then held to be Concurrent even though they did not act in accordance with a common plan and each is held jointly and severally liable for all of the injuries caused. If a passenger is in a two-car collision, he may sue both drivers under a theory of concurrent negligence if the accident was the result of negligence on the part of each driver.

CONCURRENT SENTENCING. See SENTENCING PROCEDURES.

CONDEMNATION AWARD. The sum of money paid to a property owner whose land is taken for public use through the power of eminent domain. Such power is held by federal, state and local governments as well as by certain public corporations, such as railroads and utilities. Since the Fifth Amendment provides that private property shall not be taken for public use without "just compensation," condemnation awards are required by the Constitution. Generally, the property owner whose land is condemned is entitled to a jury determination of fair market value.

CONDEMNATION BLIGHT. A condition which often arises out of urban renewal projects which refers to the debilitating effect upon the value of property from a threatened imminent or potential condemnation.

CONDITIONAL GIFT TRUST. A trust arrangement which places some condition, precedent or subsequent, before a gift or benefit passes through the instrument. Historically, such a trust was either conditioned upon an offspring marrying a designated person or the birth of a son to carry on the family name. Today, such a Trust Arrangement usually delays receipt of a benefit until the beneficiary reaches a certain age or finishes school.

CONDITIONAL RELEASE. Allowing an incarcerated individual to leave confinement prior to the expiration of his term of commitment, on the condition that he fulfill certain obligations. In the criminal context, the term is synonymous with parole. The prisoner is released but he must report periodically to his probation officer, and usually refrain from use or possession of firearms, excessive consumption of alcoholic beverages, and association with known criminals. The term is also relevant to mental health law, where it refers to the practice of allowing the involuntarily committed psychiatric patients to go home as long as they take their medication, avoid use of alcoholic drinks and return to the hospital on an outpatient basis.

CONDITIONAL SALE. A legal device used to protect or to secure the seller's extension of credit to a buyer of personal property. The seller retains the security title until the particular asset sold is completely paid for.

CONDITION OF MERCHANTABILITY. A standard or regulation requiring that the goods be of a certain quality before being placed on the market to be sold. It should be noted, however, that regardless of how high the standard of quality may be, merchantable is not to be considered as a synonym for perfect.

CONDITION PRECEDENT. A condition which must be performed before a contract becomes binding or an estate will vest. For example, a buyer may agree to purchase a home on the condition that the seller provide a title free of encumbrances.

CONDITION SUBSEQUENT. An event or fact which discharges a pre-existing duty agreed upon by the parties to a contract. A Condition Subsequent generally refers to the happening of a future event, the occurrence of which defeats a previously existing contract. For example, an insurance company may be obligated to pay out for an accident, but this contractual obligation can be defeated by the beneficiary's failure to notify the insurance company of the accident.

CONDOMINIUM OWNERSHIP. Individual ownership of apartment units at various levels in large, multi-story buildings. Such a form of land development has become quite popular in urban areas because it has the advantages of permitting the apartment dweller to own his dwelling and to share proportionately in tax benefits, such as deduction of mortgage interest payments and real estate taxes. In actual practice, the co-operative apartment dweller generally has the right to occupy one apartment, and he must share in the expenses of operation of the common parts of the building. This is achieved by various devices including the corporation, the trust, and in some cases by conveyance of an undivided fee ownership in land and buildings with the right to occupy a particular portion. Though this term comes from the Roman law, its usage there was limited to a general description of joint or community ownership somewhat like co-tenancy in the United States. The concept of Strata Ownership was unknown to the civil law, but the practice of separate ownership of "flatted" buildings began several centuries ago in continental Europe. In Scotland, the practice was recognized by law and conveyancing problems were resolved at least by the early part of the eighteenth century. However, only recently have there been any major legal steps toward working out the myriad problems of large-scale co-operative ownership of dwellings in the United States. Enabling legislation has now been enacted or is under consideration in all of the states and, in 1961, Congress authorized the Federal Housing Authority to insure mortgages on condominium dwelling units.

CONDOMINIUM SOVEREIGNTY. The exercise of sovereignty over a particular territory and the persons living there conjointly by two or more countries. Though it is generally stated in international law that there can be only one full sovereign over a single territory at any given time, Condominium Sovereignty is the recognized exception. Examples of such condominia include the rule of the Sudan by Great Britain and Egypt in 1894 and the condominium of Austria and Prussia over Schleswig-Holstein from 1864 to 1866.

CONFINEMENT FACILITY. A correctional facility from which the inmates are not regularly permitted to depart each day unaccompanied. Correctional facilities are divided into three major groups: (1) Detention facilities and (2) Correctional institutions, both of which are Confinement Facilities, and (3) Community facilities. The distinguishing feature is behavioral, namely, whether or not the inmates can regularly leave each day without supervision.

CONFLICT OF INTEREST. Collision of the mutually exclusive obligations of one individual. If performance by a person of one duty causes or leads to the disregard of a different duty a Conflict of Interest is said to exist. An example would be an attorney trying to represent both the husband and the wife in a divorce proceeding. At some point his loyalty to one client may necessitate the performance of actions which breach his duty toward the other. The term may also be used to describe the conduct of an elected or appointed governmental agent who uses his position to his own personal benefit, i.e., he neglects to disqualify himself from voting on a matter in which he has a direct pecuniary interest.

CONFLICT OF LAWS. The body of jurisprudence to which a court refers in deciding whether to give effect to the law of another sovereignty. Conflict of Laws is significant in cases where the law of more than one jurisdiction may be applicable because of contacts between the parties or subject matter of the case and those jurisdictions. The rules of Conflict of Laws govern the Choice of Law according to the subject matter and other circumstances of the case. Although the laws of a sovereignty ordinarily have no independent force outside of the sovereign jurisdiction, and therefore need not be applied by foreign courts, they are often given force in accordance with principles of comity. The Full Faith and Credit clause of the United States Constitution requires states to accord recognition to the law of other states. The body of Conflict Law helps determine when such recognition is due. Foreign legal systems use the term Private International Law rather than Conflict of Laws.

CONFORMITY ACT. A federal statute passed in 1872, requiring procedure in federal courts to conform to the current procedure of the state in which the federal court is located. Until that time, an outmoded 1789 statute had required federal procedure to follow state procedure as it existed in 1789. For almost one hundred years federal procedure was one of "static conformity," unable to adopt changes in state procedure. The Conformity Act thus substituted a dynamic conformity to changing state procedure: in theory, a lawyer would have to master only one system of procedure for both state and federal courts. A number of problems and inconsistencies remained, however, ultimately leading to the adoption of the Federal Rules of Civil Procedure in 1938.

CONFRONTATION CLAUSE. That portion of the Sixth Amendment to the United States Constitution which provides that, "In all criminal prosecutions, the accused shall enjoy the right . . . to be confronted with the witnesses against him. . . ." The implications of this language are not entirely clear. At a minimum, the Confrontation Clause guarantees to the criminal defendant the right to be present at his trial and to be informed of the evidence which is introduced against him. The Supreme Court has interpreted the clause to guarantee the right to cross-examine witnesses and to bar the use of certain hearsay evidence.

CONFUCIANISM AND LEGALISM. Ancient Chinese doctrines of human nature and society which formed the building blocks of modern European jurisprudence. Confucianism emphasized the natural goodness of man. Law developed according to notions of propriety which existed in all people as a sort of tacit code of conduct. Legalism, on the contrary, either denied that man's nature was basically benevolent or disbelieved that it could ever prevail over pride, envy, and greed. Law, under the Legalist's view, should consist of positive rules imposed on people by governmental authority. Modern legal theory is actually a combination of these ancient doctrines: i.e., law is deemed necessary to maintain social order among people who lack innate goodness, but people deserve to be respected as individuals, at least for their potential to achieve the Confucianist ideal.

CONGLOMERATE MERGER BILL (S. 600; Anti-Merger Law; Small and Independent Business Protection Act of 1979). A law introduced into Congress in 1979 by Senator Edward M. Kennedy which would prohibit the merger of American companies with $2 billion or more in assets or sales and severely restrict mergers of somewhat smaller companies. It is aimed at so-called conglomerate mergers between companies in different lines of business. No showing of anticompetitive danger would be required to bar mergers involving firms with assets or sales of more than $2 billion. The proposed law thus assumes that big companies have inherent unfair advantages and that smaller is better if not more beautiful than bigger.

CONGRESSIONAL RECORD. A transcript of congressional proceedings and debates published by the United States government each day when either the House or Senate is in session. Actually the *Record* is not a very accurate transcript since Congressmen may revise the Record and insert additional unspoken statements. For example, the *Congressional Record* reported that Representative Hale Boggs addressed the House on October 18, 1976; unfortunately, he had disappeared in an Alaskan plane crash two days earlier. Although the publication rules were amended March 1, 1978 to require that unspoken insertions be marked by a "bullet," there is an exception for insertions the first sentence of which is spoken on the House or Senate floor. There is also an appendix in which a Congressman may include extensions of floor remarks, exhibits, or almost anything else that he wants in the *Record*.

CONGRESS OF RACIAL EQUALITY. See C.O.R.E.

CONGRESSIONAL RESOLUTION. A statement, especially a formal expression of opinion or will, adopted by vote in Congress.

CONGRESS OF VIENNA. An international conference hosted by Austria in 1814-15 which established the ground rules for relations between civilized nations in matters such as diplomatic immunity, extraterritorial rights and protocol. The last term is derived from the two Greek words protos, meaning "the first," and kolla, meaning "glue." An ancient Greek protokollon thus summed up briefly the accompanying official dispatch. It was glued on the top leaf of the papyrus. The idea of being "glued on first," or taking precedence, was thereby created. It survives today in modern diplomacy's word "protocol."

CONJUGAL FAMILY. See NUCLEAR FAMILY.

CONNALLY AMENDMENT (1946). Formal declaration by President Harry S. Truman announcing the United States' recognition of the jurisdiction of the International Court of Justice. With two-thirds of the Senators present concurring, Truman bound the United States to defer to the authority of that court in matters involving (a) the interpretation of a treaty; (b) any question of international law; (c) the existence of any fact which, if established, would constitute a breach of an international obligation; and (d) the nature or extent of the reparation to be made for the breach of an international obligation.

CONNECTICUT COMPROMISE. See BICAMERAL LEGISLATURE.

CONSANGUINITY RELATIONSHIPS. Blood ties which create a bar to marital and sexual relationship. For example, a wife cannot marry her son after the death of her husband and sexual intercourse between them constitutes the crime of incest. Every state has prohibitions based on Consanguinity which can either be horizontal (grandfather-son-granddaughter) or lateral (father-brother-daughter-niece).

CONSCIENCE FUND. Administered by the Treasury Department for Americans who want to ease guilt feelings. Money sent is accepted, recorded and acknowledged—with no questions asked and no danger of prosecution. Established in 1811, the Fund received its first contribution of $5 during the administration of President James Madison. Contributions rose after the Watergate scandal, then declined. Since its inception, the Fund has collected over three and a half million dollars, in contributions ranging from a few cents to several thousand dollars. Many of the contributions received by the Conscience Fund are accompanied by letters of explanation. One letter stated that the enclosed 16 cents was in payment for two eight-cent stamps used when the contributor was in the Navy. Another letter, along with $2,000, explained that the contributor, an employee at the Bureau of Engraving, was less than five feet—the minimum height for a printer's assistant. The $2,000 was the fine owed for perjury. The money received by the Conscience Fund is deposited in the Treasury's General Fund, which pays government expenses. Where possible, the Assistant Controller for Finance acknowledges receipt of the money in a letter which commends the contributor's desire to make restitution.

CONSCIENTIOUS OBJECTOR. A person who, for reasons of conscience, refuses to serve in the Armed Forces. The term has had this meaning since World War I, but prior to that time it referred to a person who objected to being vaccinated under the English Compulsory Vaccination Act (1898). The "conscience clause" in an Act of Parliament excused persons from meeting the requirements of the Act if their "conscientious scruples" were violated.

CONSCIOUS PARALLELISM. A technical term of antitrust law derived from the Supreme Court case of *Theatre Enterprises, Inc. v. Paramount Film Distributing*, 346 U.S. 537 (1954). The case held that the existence of an actual conspiracy to fix prices must be shown before there can be a violation of the Sherman Act. When there is a small number of sellers in a particular industry, each seller responds to his competitor's price and output decisions. The mere parallel business behavior of the firms, however, is not deemed a conspiracy to fix prices in violation of federal antitrust laws.

CONSECUTIVE SENTENCING. See SENTENCING PROCEDURES.

CONSENT DECREE. A device whereby certain equity cases may be settled by agreement of the parties. Consent Decrees are often used in antitrust suits when a defendant agrees to institute reforms acceptable to the government. Signed by the judge, a Consent Decree is enforced in the same manner as any other decree in equity.

CONSEQUENTIAL DAMAGES. Losses resulting from a breach of contract which could have been reasonably foreseen at the time of contract formation. To be liable for consequential damages, the defendant must have known or had reason to know about special circumstances which could give rise to consequential damages.

CONSOLIDATED GUIDANCE 9. Part of the Pentagon's budget process, under which the Defense Secretary reviews programs and issues long-range guidance to the military services in order to match Administration policy with the kind of hardware and weapons sought by the Army, Navy and Air Force. This particular 60-page memorandum, which was submitted to the White House, assesses Taiwan's military needs after the normalization of ties with China in 1979. The document stressed that the United States must continue military links to Taiwan and keep the island's forces from falling into disarray. Efforts to increase the sale of weapons to Taiwan have the support of ranking Defense and Administration officials, partly to assure Congress that the United States was not totally abandoning Taiwan.

CONSOLIDATED RAIL CORPORATION (C.O.N.R.A.I.L.). A government-created company which took over six bankrupt railroad lines with the help of a two billion dollar loan to pay the salaries of the 100,000 employees. The United States Railway Association was simultaneously and separately formed to monitor C.O.N.R.A.I.L. and to act as its banker.

CONSORTIUM VIOLATION. Deprivation of the rights and duties between marriage partners or between parent and child due to such illegal interferences in the relationship by a third party who becomes liable for damages. The concept of Consortium in marriage has historically included the husband's exclusive rights to his wife's services, aid, companionship, and sexual relations. With the advent of a greater recognition of women's rights, it includes the wife's rights to the same from her husband, with the addition of her traditional right to financial support. Some states now provide for a wife's duty to support her husband and his right to alimony upon divorce. An injury as a result of a tort which incapacitates a spouse or child for any of the aggregate of rights constituting Consortium can be grounds for recovery for loss of Consortium even though the interference in the relationship was not intentional.

CONSPIRACY OF SILENCE. In a suit against a professional, such as a lawyer or a doctor, or in a proceeding by the government to discipline a professional, his colleagues are reluctant to voluntarily appear to testify against him.

CONSPIRACY TO COMMIT CRIME. See CRIMINAL CONSPIRACY.

CONSTITUTIONAL CONVENTION. Called by the Founding Fathers to amend the Articles of Confederation, they drafted the Federal Constitution instead, Article 5 of which provides for two ways to amend it. The first is when two thirds of the Congress proposes an amendment which is then ratified by three fourths of the states. The second (which has never been used in American history) is when two thirds of the states pass a resolution asking the Congress to call a Constitutional Convention for the purpose of proposing an amendment. If the Congress passes the amendment, it becomes the law when it is ratified by three fourths of the states. The National Taxpayers Union claimed in January, 1979, that 20 states had proposed that Congress call a Constitutional Convention to require that there be a balanced federal budget.

CONSTITUTIONAL COURT. A federal court established pursuant to Article III of the Constitution. Article III specifies that the judges of such courts "shall hold their offices during good behavior, and shall, at stated times, receive for their services a compensation, which shall not be diminished during their continuance in office." The constitutionally-guaranteed tenure and compensation provisions seek to ensure the independence of the federal district courts, courts of appeals and the Supreme Court.

CONSTITUTIONAL PRIVILEGE. See NEW YORK TIMES STANDARD.

CONSTRUCTIVE ACCELERATION. In federal government contracting, this term refers to an explicit or implied requirement that a contractor complete contractually required performance by a date earlier than one to which he is entitled due to excusable delays. This is a recognized type of constructive change for which the contractor may be entitled to an equitable adjustment.

CONSTRUCTIVE BREAKING. See BREAKING AND ENTERING.

CONSTRUCTIVE CHANGE. In federal government contracting this term refers to an oral or written act or omission by a contracting officer or other government employee which has the same effect as a properly issued written change order pursuant to a contract changes clause.

CONSTRUCTIVE CONDITIONS. Terms of a contract that are neither expressed nor implied but are imposed by law. Generally, contractual conditions may be determined expressly by the terms of the contract or impliedly by the facts. Such determinations are a matter of interpretation. However, a Constructive Condition may be found in the absence of express or implied conditions when there arises a need for an equitable remedy.

CONSTRUCTIVE DESERTION. When one spouse violates marital obligations, such as by physical cruelty, the innocent victim may leave the home without being deemed a deserter and successfully sue the wrongdoer for support, custody of the children or a divorce.

CONSTRUCTIVE EVICTION. A doctrine which permits a tenant to terminate his lease without penalty under certain conditions. For example, if a landlord fails to provide heat or other basic services specified in the lease, the tenant may consider himself evicted and break his lease without being liable for damages.

CONSTRUCTIVE NOTICE. A presumption of law that holds a party responsible for knowing information which is a matter of record. Thus a buyer of real property is held to have constructive notice of all information recorded in the chain of title.

CONSTRUCTIVE SERVICE. Service of process other than by personal service. Generally Constructive Service consists of notification by mail or publication in a newspaper.

CONSTRUCTIVE TRUST. A trust arrangement imposed by a court of law as a means of promoting justice where a party fails to respect his obligations as a fiduciary. A Constructive Trust is distinguishable from an Express Trust in that it arises by operation of law and not at the initiation of an individual. Fraud is the essential catalyst behind a Constructive Trust. Thus, the historical underlying principle of a Constructive Trust is the equitable prevention of unjust enrichment which arises from fraud or the abuse of a confidential relationship.

CONSULT ACCOUNT TRUST. A trust arrangement in which the trustee is required to seek advice or agreement from a specified party prior to action concerning the trust property. Such a trust stems from the fear on the part of the settlor that the trustee is either dishonest or unable to make expert decisions concerning investments or distributions. Typically, where a parent sets up a trust arrangement for a child as beneficiary with the other parent as trustee, he may require the trustee parent to consult with an expert before investing the trust property in stocks or real estate. Such consultation must be documented according to state law, as may be the case.

CONSUMER CREDIT COUNSELING SERVICE. See DEBTORS ANONYMOUS.

CONSUMER PRICE INDEX (C.P.I.). An economic index prepared by the Bureau of Labor Statistics of the United States Department of Labor. It measures the change in the average prices of goods and services purchased by urban wage earners and clerical workers and their families. It is widely used as an indicator of changes in the cost of living, as a measure of inflation, and deflation if any, in the economy, and as a means for studying trends in prices of various goods and services. Many alimony and support agreements as well as wage contracts have an escalator clause for an increase geared to the Index.

CONSUMER PRODUCT SAFETY COMMISSION (C.P.S.C.). An independent five-member regulatory agency created by Congress in 1973 with authority over consumer products not regulated by other statutes such as the Food and Drug Act. C.P.S.C. is charged with developing and disseminating data on the cause and prevention of consumer product injuries, and promulgating and enforcing safety standards and laws of hazardous products. In pursuit of these goals the Commission has been empowered to seize hazardous products, conduct inspections and to require manufacturers to recall dangerous products. Authorized by the Consumer Product Safety Act of 1972, the Commission was originally hailed by Ralph Nader and other consumer advocates as a powerful watchdog, which would drastically reduce the 30,-000 deaths and 20 million injuries caused each year by unsafe products. Many critics say that the track record of the Commission has not lived up to its early high expectations either in setting rigid safety standards for manufacturers or informing the public of unsafe products.

CONSUMER PROTECTION AGENCY. A proposed federal agency for consumer advocacy. This agency would be authorized to help consumer groups represent themselves before governmental bodies deciding an issue of concern to consumers. It would not be empowered, however, to issue rules itself. On the national level, the Federal Trade Commission and the Consumer Product Safety Commission now handle a limited number of consumer complaints. The latter agency has a toll free number, 800-638-2666, one can call to find out whether a product has been found to be unsafe or to complain that a product is dangerous. Many states and localities also provide aid to disgruntled consumers. On the state level, the Attorney General's office often contains a bureau of consumer protection. The private sector has not turned a deaf ear to consumer complaints. Numerous big companies and trade and industry associations provide avenues an unhappy consumer can pursue. The United States Chamber of Commerce alone sponsors over a dozen consumer complaint centers.

CONTACT GROUP. The five Western nations (United States, Great Britain, Canada, France and West Germany) which banded together in 1978, under the sponsorship of the Security Council of the United Nations, with the various military nationalists to end the 11-year-old guerilla war as the first step in South West Africa in the creation of the sovereign nation of Namibia. It represented a major diplomatic defeat for Russia, which had supported the Marxist Southwest African People's Organization (S.W.A.P.O.). South Africa had ruled the territory under a League of Nations mandate for over half a century.

CONTACT VISIT. The legal right of prisoners awaiting trial (and other prisoners in some states) to have physical contact with visitors consistent with public decency and safety, such as kissing a wife or fondling a child.

CONTEMPORANEOUS OWNERSHIP. See DERIVATIVE SUIT.

CONTEMPT OF COURT. (1) Criminal. An act or words which tend to embarrass or obstruct a court in the administration of justice or which lessens the dignity of or respect for the court. Contempt of Court may be punished by a modest fine or brief imprisonment or both. It can be classified as either Direct or Constructive (Indirect). Direct Contempt is committed in the immediate view and presence of the court and is calculated to disrupt the orderly course of the judicial proceedings. Constructive Contempt is a matter not arising in the presence of the court but elsewhere which tends to defeat the orderly administration of justice. The difference factually is im-

portant legally since one is not entitled to Trial by Jury in Direct Contempt and if a severe sentence of punishment is to be imposed, the accused may be entitled to have his case heard by another judge. (2) Civil Contempt refers to the failure of a person to obey the lawful order of a court of chancery issued on behalf of another person. In that case the disrespect is directed toward the person in whose favor the order is issued and not the court. The court enforces its order by a heavy fine payable to the plaintiff or imprisonment of the defendant until such time as the prisoner decides to obey the order. He is thus said to carry the key to his freedom in his own pocket. (3) Legislative, Executive and Administrative Contempt. One may also be held liable for Criminal Contempt of the other three branches of government for wilful misbehavior in disruption of orderly proceedings but they do not have any power of civil contempt control. This strong weapon of coercion may be found only in the judiciary, each member of whom has had legal training and would presumably not abuse the awesome power of potential life imprisonment over a recalcitrant defendant.

CONTIGUOUS ZONE. A zone of the high seas contiguous to the territorial waters of a country, within which the coastal country may exercise its control. The country may not claim sovereignty beyond the territorial waters, but it may exercise jurisdiction as defined by the General Convention on the Territorial Sea and Contiguous Zone (1958). Such control is limited to: (1) "Preventing infringement of its customs, fiscal, immigration, or sanitary regulations within its territory or territorial sea, and (2) Punishing infringement of these regulations." The Contiguous Zone may not extend beyond twelve miles from the baseline from which the breadth of the territorial sea is measured. The Territorial Sea Convention of 1964 confirmed the concept of a Contiguous Zone.

CONTINENTAL CONGRESS. The group of delegates representing the thirteen original colonies. It first convened to protest unjust British practices and eventually constituted the first governing body of the new United States. The First Continental Congress of 1774 drafted the Declaration of Rights; The Second Continental Congress of 1775 adopted the Declaration of Independence and conducted the Revolutionary War. The Second Congress served as the national governing body until the adoption of the Articles of Confederation in 1781.

CONTINGENCY FEE CONTRACT. An agreement between a lawyer and the client that the lawyer receive no fee if the case is lost but a percentage of the award if the case is won. These contracts are illegal in England and in certain situations in the United States, such as criminal and divorce cases, as they are contrary to public policy. Most personal-injury cases are taken by lawyers for a percentage of the gross award, often one-third if the matter is settled before trial, perhaps 40 percent if a laborious trial is necessary. This creates a potential divergence of interest between lawyer and client. Since the potential additional reward for trial work may not be worthwhile, some attorneys encourage their clients to accept even an unreasonably low offer from an insurer. The worst aspect of a Contingent Fee contract is that the lawyer's percentage is on the gross award so that by the time the client pays all the cost of the litigation, the lawyer may earn a higher recovery than the client.

CONTINGENT BENEFICIARY. A trust beneficiary whose trust interest is conditioned upon the occurrence of a future event. If such a contingency does not take place, the interest does not vest. Such a device has historically been used to enable the trust settlor to condition his gift on certain occurrences, such as, "my son is to receive these monies held in trust commencing on his 30th birthday."

CONTINGENT REMAINDER. A remainder is contingent if at the time of creation the remaindermen are (a) unborn, (b) though born are unascer-

tained, (3) though born and ascertained, the remainder is subject to some condition precedent other than the natural expiration of a prior particular estate(s).

CONTINGENT TRUSTEE. A trustee whose appointment is contingent upon the actions or competence of an existing or upcoming trust trustee. Such an arrangement protects both the settlor and the beneficiary from a dishonest or incompetent trust trustee by making another trustee available to protect the trust.

CONTRACT ACCEPTANCE. An essential requirement to create a valid contract. At common law, an acceptance had to be absolute and unequivocal; had to meet the conditions of the offer; and in some instances, had to be communicated to the person who made the offer. For example, if Jane offered to sell her car to Bill if he paid cash in person, and Bill sent his secretary to pay Jane, there would be no contract. But if Jane sent her offer by mail and Bill replied by phone, a valid contract would probably exist as there was a reasonable means of Acceptance (unless, of course, Jane specified that Acceptance would only be valid if made in a certain way, e.g., in writing). Acceptance may also be inferred from behavior or even silence. If a newspaper was left at your door each day, and you take it and read it, you have technically accepted it by your behavior and are liable for its cost even if you did not order the paper. Acceptance by silence usually occurs where there has been a past history of dealings between businesses or individuals. For example, if Jane regularly ships cars to Bill who always pays for them and on one occasion Bill takes and retains a shipment, but fails to pay for them or notify Jane that he does not want them, an acceptance of the shipment may be inferred from Bill's silence plus the past course of dealings between Jane and Bill.

CONTRACT-BAR RULE. A policy of the National Labor Relations Board to dismiss petitions for certification elections where a properly executed collective bargaining agreement exists. The election is usually postponed until the contract is about to expire and the question as to the proper representative for the bargaining unit re-emerges. Exceptions to the rule are generally made only where the board finds circumstances in which an election would promote industrial stability.

CONTRACT CONSIDERATION. An essential requirement to create a valid contract. Consideration requires that something must be bargained for and exchanged in order to make a binding promise. Fundamental to the doctrine of consideration is the policy that exchange is beneficial. Some commentators question the value of requiring consideration. For example, "In consideration of your past thirty years of loyal service, we will pay you a pension of $300 per month." This promise is usually not enforceable because the consideration (thirty years of loyal service) was not exchanged for the pension. On the other hand, consideration serves the useful function of weeding out those promises the law will not enforce. Apparently no legal system has ever enforced all promises, and most systems strive to enforce only those promises which were undertaken solemnly and which are socially beneficial.

CONTRACT DISPUTES ACT OF 1978. A federal law which allows a contractor to appeal the decisions of government contracting officers with respect to all claims arising under the contract to either the Court of Claims or the appropriate agency administrative board. Decisions by these boards may be appealed by either party to the Court of Claims.

CONTRACTING OFFICER. That person who, in accordance with federal government departmental procedures, is currently designated as one having the authority to enter into and administer contracts and make determinations and findings with respect thereto. The term also includes the authorized representative of the Contracting Officer acting within the limits of his authority.

CONTRACT MODIFICATION. (1) A rule that requires the modification of agreements between parties be supported by consideration from each. The rule is enforceable under the Pre-Existing Duty Rule. However, the Uniform Commercial Code (U.C.C.) allows modification of a contract for the sale of goods, without consideration, under § 2-209(1). (2) As employed in federal government contracting, this term refers to any written alteration in the specification, delivery point, rate of delivery, contract period, price, quantity, or other provision of an existing contract, whether accomplished by unilateral action or by mutual action of the contracting parties.

CONTRACT OFFER. One of the three general requirements to create a valid Contract: i.e., offer, acceptance, and consideration. An offer is an expression of present intent to make a contract which is definite and certain in its terms and communicated to another, who then has the power or legally enforceable right to accept the offer and create a binding contract. If Jane says to Bill, "I am going to sell my car for $25," no offer has been made. Jane was merely stating her future intention, and not promising to sell her car to Bill. Similarly, an inquiry to make an offer is not an offer: Bill says to Jane, "Would you sell your car for $50?" Jane replies, "Couldn't sell it for less than $100." Jane again has not made an offer, but merely invited Bill to do so. In addition, ordinary advertisement is not an offer since no quantity is usually specified, and the law will not generally hold that the advertiser has committed himself to supplying unlimited quantities of an item.

CONTRIBUTORY NEGLIGENCE. A defense to a negligence suit. At common law, and in many states today, a plaintiff whose actions contributed to his injury will not be awarded damages. In some jurisdictions, for instance, if the injuries suffered in an automobile accident could have been avoided if the plaintiff had worn a seat belt, he is unable to collect damages, regardless of the negligence of the other driver. The harsh effects of common law Contributory Negligence have been mitigated somewhat by the doctrines of Comparative Negligence and Last Clear Chance.

CONTROLLED AIRSPACE. Airspace within specified dimensions designated as a continental control area, a control zone, or a transition area, in which air traffic control is exercised.

CONTROLLING SHAREHOLDERS. See FIDUCIARY DUTIES.

CONVENING AUTHORITY. An individual empowered to create (convene) a court martial for the trial of persons within a particular command. Such power is vested in the President, the Secretaries of the military departments, and the commanding officers of most substantial military units. The authority to convene a court martial includes the power not only to make the decision that a case should be tried, but also to detail the particular individuals to perform the various roles, such as military judge, trial counsel (prosecutor), defense counsel, and court members (jurors). The power of the Convening Authority vests in the office of the individual himself, so that proper succession to command by another relieves the incumbent of his power to act as convening authority. Likewise, the power of the Convening Authority is non-delegable and may be exercised only by the individual holding the particular office so empowered.

CONVENTIONAL MORTGAGE. A mortgage not guaranteed by the F.H.A. or the V.A. In a Conventional Mortgage, the loan is secured only by the property. Since they bear a higher risk than F.H.A. and V.A. insured loans, Conventional Mortgages generally have higher interest rates and larger down payment requirements.

CONVENTION BANNING MODIFICATION OF ENVIRONMENT OF 1977. An international agreement, to which the United States is a party, that prohibits military or any other hostile use of techniques to modify the environment. Although 32 other nations have signed it, the Senate has not as yet ratified it.

CONVENTION FOR THE SUPPRESSION OF THE TRAFFIC IN PERSONS AND OF THE EXPLOITATION OF THE PROSTITUTION OF OTHERS. Ratified by forty-two nations as of 1976, the Convention entered into force on July 25, 1951. It obligates parties to the Convention (1) to punish any person who keeps, manages, or otherwise finances a brothel, and (2) to stop the traffic in persons for prostitution.

CONVENTION OF CONSENT TO MARRIAGE, MINIMUM AGE FOR MARRIAGE AND REGISTRATION OF MARRIAGES. Ratified by twenty-eight countries as of 1976, the Convention entered into force on December 9, 1964. Nations party to this agreement bind themselves (1) to recognize the principle that no marriage should be entered into without the free and complete consent of the parties; (2) to enact legislation setting forth a minimum age for marriage, and (3) to register all marriages.

CONVENTION OF STANDARDS OF TRAINING, CERTIFICATION AND WATCHKEEPING FOR SEAFARERS. The first world international agreement by 72 nations, in July 1978, regulating and setting minimum requirements for seamen on all merchant ships over 200 tons gross on the High Seas. The pact is aimed at reducing accidents, 80 percent of which are caused by human error, in order to protect life and marine environment. It does so by prescribing the training and experience required for captains, officers and crew before licenses and certificates of employment are issued to them. The pact leaves to coastal countries however, the application of their own laws for ships navigating in "near" coastal waters.

CONVENTION OF THE NATIONALITY OF MARRIED WOMEN. Ratified by forty-seven countries as of 1976, the Convention had entered into force on

August 11, 1958. It provides that the nationality of a woman is not lost by marriage or the termination of marriage, although a woman may, of her own accord, choose to acquire the nationality of her husband through right or special privilege.

CONVENTION ON INTERNATIONAL TRADE IN ENDANGERED SPECIES (C.I.T.E.S.). A 1973 Treaty ratified by 50 countries, including the United States, to control the export and import of rare animals, birds, reptiles and plants. The protection of endangered species provoked a worldwide political battle with significant economic implications for industrial and developing countries alike in a multi-million dollars business. Of the roughly 13,200 mammal and bird species known to exist in the 17th century, more than 130 have become extinct including the passenger pigeon, Steller's Sea Cow and the West Indian Monk Seal. Today hundreds more are threatened by human exploitation such as crocodiles used in making shoes and handbags; leopards and cheetahs for coats, turtles for meat and shells, elephants for ivory, and exotic birds and monkeys for pets. Under the Convention, Treaty members have listed 982 species endangered, some of which should not be traded at all, and others which should be carefully controlled.

CONVENTION ON THE INTERNATIONAL RIGHT OF CORRECTION. Ratified by eleven countries as of 1976, the Convention had entered into force on August 24, 1962. It sets forth the notion of professional responsibility of information agencies and their correspondents to report fairly, without discrimination, and without distorting context. A nation party to this Convention which believes itself to be subjected to a foreign news report that is potentially injurious to its dignity or national prestige may give its version of events to the nation in which the report was disseminated. The nation in which the report was spread must then release the clarifying report provided by the offended nation and must transmit it to the individual originally responsible for the report.

CONVENTION ON THE NON-APPLICABILITY OF STATUTORY LIMITATIONS TO WAR CRIMES AGAINST HUMANITY. Ratified by twenty-one nations as of 1976, the Convention had entered into force on November 11, 1970. It provides that no statutory limitation or other cut-off date will apply to prevent prosecution of war crimes or other crimes against humanity (as defined in the charter of The Nuremberg International Military Tribunal), eviction by armed attack or military occupation, inhuman acts arising of apartheid policies, or genocide.

CONVENTION ON THE POLITICAL RIGHTS OF WOMEN. Ratified by seventy-nine countries as of 1976, the Convention had entered into force on July 7, 1954. The Convention specifies that women shall have the right to vote and serve in public office on terms equal to men and free from discrimination.

CONVENTION ON THE PREVENTION AND PUNISHMENT OF THE CRIME OF GENOCIDE. Ratified by eighty countries as of 1976, the Convention had entered into force on January 12, 1951. This Convention outlaws genocide under international law and obligates member nations to prevent this crime and punish it whenever it is committed. The Convention defines genocide as acts committed with the intent to destroy, wholly or in part, a national, ethnic, racial, or religious group. Genocidal acts include killing, serious injury to mind or body, intentional infliction of destructive conditions upon a group, imposition of birth control, and forcible transfer of children.

CONVENTION ON THE REDUCTION OF STATELESSNESS. Ratified by only six nations as of 1976, the Convention has not yet entered into force. Under this Convention, contracting parties agree to grant nationality to stateless persons (persons without a country) under specified circumstances. It

117

CONVENTION

also details conditions upon which nationality can be acquired or lost.

CONVENTION RELATING TO THE STATUS OF REFUGEES. Ratified by sixty-six countries as of 1976, the Convention had entered into force on April 22, 1954. This Convention regulates the treatment of refugees by nations which are party to it. A refugee, as defined in the Convention, is "outside the country of his nationality and is unable, or owing to such fear, is unwilling to avail himself of the protection of that country; or who, not having a nationality and being outside the country of his former habitual residence . . ., is unable or . . . unwilling to return to it." This Convention specifically addresses persons who are outside their country "as a result of events occurring before 1 January 1951 and owing to well-founded fear of being persecuted for reasons of race, religion, nationality, membership of a particular group or political opinions." Persons who are refugees as a result of events occurring after 1 January 1951 are accorded similar protection under the 1967 Protocol Relating to the Status of Refugees.

CONVENTION RELATING TO THE STATUS OF STATELESS PERSONS. Ratified by thirty countries as of 1976, the Convention had entered into force on June 6, 1960. It supplements the 1951 Convention on the Status of Refugees by providing regulation of the status of stateless persons not protected under the Refugee Convention. A stateless person is one "not considered as a national by any state under the operation of the state's law."

CONVERTIBLE SECURITY. A security which may be exchanged for another form of security, usually at the option of the holder. Convertible Securities are most typically debt securities or preferred stock which may be converted to common stock.

CONVEYANCE TAX. See TRANSFER TAX.

CONVICT LABOR LAW. Pursuant to the D.A.R. clause implementing this Act, codified at 18 U.S.C. 436, the government procurement contractor agrees not to employ any person undergoing sentence of imprisonment. The prohibition is inapplicable to purchases from Federal Prison Industries, Inc. and to persons on parole or probation.

COOLIDGE v. NEW HAMPSHIRE. See PLAIN VIEW DOCTRINE.

COOLIE OVERTIME. See CHINESE OVERTIME.

COOLING-OFF PERIOD. (1) The time within which a consumer has the right to cancel a sale, especially in situations of high pressure tactics such as the pitch door-to-door salesman. (2) In labor law, a provision of the Taft-Hartley Act, which allows the President to order strikers back to work for a limited period of time, usually 80 days, by means of an injunction against the strike issued by federal district court. However, the President may petition for an injunction only after he has reviewed the report of a special commission appointed to investigate the strike and its effects, and has determined that the national health and welfare are threatened.

COOLING THE CLIENT OUT. Deliberately lowering clients' expectations, so that they will be pleased with whatever settlement they eventually get, no matter how small. Lawyers who do a high-volume business in personal-injury cases are sometimes reluctant to go to trial and will "cool a client out" by persuading him to accept a lower settlement than might be attainable in a jury trial. The lawyer thus easily earns a large fee.

COOPERATIVE APARTMENTS. A type of legal ownership arrangement for apartments which is chiefly limited to a few urban centers such as New York or Chicago. Under the cooperative arrangement, title to the land and building is held by a single entity—usually a corporation. Each member of the cooperative must buy shares of stock based on the value of his or her apartment. The stock is accompanied by a proprie-

118

tary lease which gives the shareholder a right to occupy the apartment. The arrangement is distinguished by a higher degree of economic interdependence among the tenants than under the condominium form of ownership.

COOPERATIVE FARM CREDIT SYSTEM. Comprised of Federal Land Banks and Federal Land Bank Associations, Federal Intermediate Credit Banks and Production Credit Associations, and Banks for Cooperatives. Initially capitalized by the United States, the entire System is now owned by its users. The System is designed to provide adequate and dependable credit and closely related services to farmers, ranchers, producers or harvesters of aquatic products; persons engaged in providing on-the-farm services; rural homeowners; and associations of farmers, ranchers, or producers or harvesters of aquatic products or federations of such associations which operate on a cooperative basis and are engaged in marketing, processing, supply or business service functions for the benefit of their members.

COOPER REPORT OF 1970. See MEDICAL DEVICE AMENDMENTS TO FOOD, DRUG AND COSMETIC ACT.

COOPING OUT. Police officers on night duty who sleep in their cars on deserted streets instead of patrolling the area to which they have been assigned.

COORDINATED PROCUREMENT. The procedure by which a Department of Defense agency buys specified supplies or services for itself and other agencies within the Department.

COP A PLEA. See PLEA BARGAINING.

C.O.P.E. (Committee on Political Education). When it was illegal for unions to solicit contributions from members to be used for political purposes, they formed groups called Committees on Political Education which could lawfully raise money for this purpose. C.O.P.E. has become a powerful lobbyist organization which can success-

fully influence a majority of members in both houses of Congress. This power has been established by generous campaign contributions of money and services to "get out the vote," as well as extensive union newspaper and magazine coverage of political candidates.

COPELAND ANTI-KICKBACK. A Federal Act, codified at 18 U.S.C. 874, which forbids anyone from preventing an employee on a government construction contract from receiving his full wages.

COPYRIGHT ACT OF 1976. The first major revision of American copyright law since 1909. The Act, which went into effect on January 1, 1978, introduces several significant changes in prior copyright law. It eliminates common law copyright, except in limited circumstances. The duration of a statutory copyright for works created after January 1, 1978 is no longer fifty-six years, but extends for a period beginning with the date of creation of the work and terminating fifty years after the creator's death. For works created prior to January 1, 1978, the total length of protection is now seventy-five—rather than fifty-six—years, owing to a modification in the renewal period from twenty-eight to forty-seven years. Further, the Act protects pantomimes and choreographic works which had not been expressly included in American copyright law. Pertinent legislative history reveals that computer programs likewise now warrant protection. Other important revisions include the elimination of the Juke Box Exemption and the imposition of higher maximum limits on damage awards for copyright infringement.

COPYRIGHT HISTORY. Early civilization placed little emphasis on the protection of artistic property, although Martial, a Roman writer in the first century A.D., accused people of stealing his verses. He used the term "plagium," meaning kidnapping, to apply to such literary piracy. Hence, the roots of the word plaigarism. Not until the invention of the printing press in the fifteenth century made publishing lucrative did copyright law originate. The government of Venice encouraged printing by vesting certain authorship privileges. The Statute of Anne, passed in 1710 in England, represents the dominant influence in the first federal copyright law enacted in the United States in 1790. John Barry obtained the first copyright issued under this Act for "The Philadelphia Spelling Book, arranged upon a plan entirely new."

COPYRIGHT INFRINGEMENT. Use of a copyrighted work to reproduce a written, musical, or artistic work to prepare derivative works based on the copyrighted piece; to distribute copies of the work, to perform or show the work publicly for profit, or to publicly display copyrighted items. Using a copyrighted work is not an Infringement unless such use falls within one of these express rights. Hence, reading a novel or treatise in one's home or office, privately playing a musical composition, or even publicly engaging in these or similar activities without seeking profit would not constitute Copyright Infringement. The plaintiff in an infringement suit must prove his ownership of the copyright and the copying by the defendant. Some elements of ownership — originality, copyrightability, proper citizenship of the creator, and satisfaction of statutory requirements—may be proved merely by the possession of a copyright registration certificate. The certificate, plus evidence of sufficient copyright notice, constitutes prima facie evidence of ownership. However, copying is more difficult to prove since a plaintiff rarely will have direct evidence of copying and because copying can be accomplished by committing something to memory and subsequently recreating it. Consequently, a plaintiff frequently must rely on indirect evidence of copying to sustain his Infringement action. This indirect evidence generally consists of showing the defendant's access to the copyrighted work and substantial similarity between that work and the defendant's product. Access means the opportunity to copy rather than actual viewing of the copyrighted piece. The opportunity must be reasonable and not simply possible, so that, for example, the mere presence of the copyrighted work in the city in which the defendant lives would not by itself demonstrate access. Insofar as substantial similarity is concerned, various tests have been employed to attempt to resolve the troublesome determination of when similarity becomes substantial. Among the most widely accepted tests are the Abstractions Test, the Pattern Test, and the Audience or Ordinary Observer Test. If a plaintiff succeeds in proving access, copying, and their constituent elements, and the defendant can offer no sufficient defense, the plaintiff may seek to enjoin the infringing activity. Additionally, he may seek monetary damages to the extent of his actual loss plus an amount which represents the profits realized by the defendant from the illegal use of the copyrighted work.

COPYRIGHT NOTICE. One of the formalities necessary for statutory copyright protection. Such notice consists of the name of the owner of the copyright and the word "Copyright," the abbreviation "Copr." or the symbol ©. The encircled letter P is required in the case of a recording. Additionally, if the work is a printed, literary, dramatic, or musical work or a recording, copyright notice includes the year in which the copyright was obtained.

COPYRIGHT OFFICE. Established in 1897 within the Library of Congress, headed by the Register of Copyrights. The Office records over 400,000 copyrights annually. Originally, copyrights were under the auspices of the Department of State and, in 1859, they were transferred to the Department of the Interior under the supervision of the Commissioner of Patents. With this transfer of authority, submission of copies of a copyrighted work to the Library of Congress and to the Smithsonian Institution were no longer required. Submission to the Library of Congress alone was reinstituted in 1865. A comprehensive reform of intellectual property laws in 1870 included conferring on the Library of Congress the power to grant copyrights.

COPYRIGHT ROYALTY TRIBUNAL. Under the Copyright Act of 1976, the body responsible for reviewing and adjusting royalty rates, for overseeing payment of royalties to parties entitled to them, and in some circumstances for setting initial rates. Five members, appointed by the President with the Advice and Consent of the Senate, serve for staggered terms of seven years. The Tribunal, an independent agency of the legislative branch, receives administrative and financial support from the Library of Congress. The Tribunal must comply with the provisions of the Administrative Procedure Act, including publication of its procedures and methods of operation and notification in the Federal Register of its rate adjustments and royalty distributions. The United States Courts of Appeals retain exclusive jurisdiction for purposes of judicial review of Tribunal rulings, provided that appeals are brought within thirty days of the Tribunal's final decisions. Despite these controls, however, the creation of the Copyright Royalty Tribunal has raised important problems. To function smoothly it must obtain accurate information from copyright licensees, yet the Act does not suggest to what extent the Tribunal can compel detailed statements from licensees. Second, owners of small copyrights appear disadvantaged because of the high costs of seeking recourse to the Tribunal. Moreover, the breadth of the Tribunal's jurisdiction remains unsettled. While it can determine the size of one's royalty share, it is unclear whether it has the power to determine ownership of the share as is traditionally done in copyright infringement proceedings. If it lacks that power, there is no directive about what should be done with royalties pending judicial determination of ownership. The ambiguity concerning how to assess the amount of royalty distributions presents still another problem in that the Tribunal is given no firm guidelines on what costs to deduct from royalties before they are distributed.

CORAM NOBIS (Latin—before ourselves). A common-law Writ of Error, to obtain review of a case to correct an error in fact, directed to another arm of the same court as the reviewing court. In contrast, the writ of Coram Vobis ("before you") is directed from the reviewing court to the trial court.

C.O.R.E. (Congress of Racial Equality). A Civil Rights organization founded in 1942 by James Farmer and a group of students at the University of Chicago. C.O.R.E. is recognized as the developer of two famous and highly effective non-violent demonstration techniques: the Sit-In which was first utilized to protest segregationist policies at Chicago's Jack Spratt's Restaurant in 1943, and the Freedom Ride, which sought to carry out the Supreme Court's 1960 bus terminal integration edict. In addition, the organization was a motivating force behind the voting rights drive in Bogalusa, Louisiana during the high point of the Civil Rights movement. Farmer, who led 2,000 people in a Pilgrimage of Prayer to protest the Massive Resistance school closings in Virginia in 1959, stepped down as chairman of C.O.R.E. in 1966 and was later defeated in a bid for Congress by Shirley Chisolm, the nation's first black Congresswoman. The organization's peak membership of 200,000 became splintered on the question of Black Separatism and Black Nationalism. The Chicago Branch, now known as the National Black Liberation Alliance, is seeking links with African nations, encouraging investment of Black-American financial resources in Africa, the institution of dual citizenship status, and increased foreign aid for Africa.

CORFU CHANNEL CASE. A decision of the World Court in 1948 in which Albania has the dubious distinction of being the only country in the 50-year history of the Court to refuse to abide by the judgment of the Court in a contentious case.

CORPORATE BYLAWS. Rules and regulations enacted by a corporation to control and govern the actions, affairs, and concerns of the corporation, its shareholders, directors, and officers. Bylaws must be consistent with the Articles of Incorporation and any applicable statutory and constitutional provisions, but they need not be filed in any public office.

CORPORATE DEMOCRACY ACT OF 1980.
A new federal law, proposed by Ralph Nader and Professor John Kenneth Galbraith, among others including various religious, consumer, labor and environmental interests, to control the alleged growing abuse of power by big business. The alliance calls for legislation to set federal standards of behavior for large corporations. It would make corporations more accountable to shareholders, employees and consumers. The introduction to the proposed law says it would seek "to reform the internal governance structure of our largest corporations so that—consistent with a market economy—companies exercise their power and discretion in more democratic and accountable ways." Corporations with annual sales of $250 million or more would require an "independent" board of directors that includes no company employees, fuller disclosure about many corporate activities (such as foreign operations), and assurance that employees could report company misdeeds without losing their jobs.

CORPORATE OPPORTUNITY RULE.
See FIDUCIARY DUTIES.

CORPORATE POWERS.
The powers of a corporation are usually listed in modern statutes and typically include the power (1) to have a separate existence and to sue and be sued in the corporate name; (2) to acquire, hold, or convey property; (3) to contract; (4) to own stock in another corporation; (5) to use a seal, and (6) to have bylaws. Additionally, the corporation has an implied power to do all things that are reasonably necessary to the carrying out of the corporate purpose or powers. Corporations can be said to have almost every power a natural person would have for the carrying out of an authorized purpose.

CORPORATE PROFITS AFTER TAXES.
The earnings of United States corporations organized for profit after liability for federal and state taxes has been deducted.

CORPORATE PROFITS BEFORE TAXES.
The net earnings of corporations organized for profit measured before payment of federal and state profit taxes. They are, however, net of indirect business taxes. They are reported without deduction for depletion charges and exclusive of capital gains and losses and intercorporate dividends. Estimates of corporate profits before taxes for the National Income and Product Accounts are based on the annual tabulations of corporate income tax returns compiled by the Internal Revenue Service (I.R.S.) with several adjustments. Depletion allowances are included. Estimates are made of profits not reported to the I.R.S., but disclosable by audit. Intercorporate dividends and capital gains are deducted. Bad debt expenses are measured by actual losses, not additions to reserves, and the profit or loss of bankrupt firms includes the gains from unsatisfied debt. Oil-well drilling costs are capitalized, state income taxes are added, as are the profits of federally-sponsored lending agencies, and the costs of trading or issuing corporate securities are deducted. Income earned abroad is adjusted to equal the amount reported in the balance-of-payments statement. This procedure produces estimates of corporate profits in the business sector consistent with the other components of the income and product accounts. Corporate profit before taxes published in the National Income and Product Accounts are different conceptually from those reported by business firms to their shareholders. Profits reported to shareholders reflect accounting practices which vary from those in the National Income and Product Accounts—particularly in the treatment of depreciation charges, the use of reserve methods of accounting, and the recognition of earnings on foreign investments.

CORPORATE PURPOSE.
The statement, required by all jurisdictions to

be in the Articles of Incorporation, of the purposes for which the corporation has been formed. The stated purposes serve to limit the corporate powers. Thus, most corporations now state the purpose as broadly as possible or amend them later, if necessary. A majority of states permit incorporation "for any lawful business purpose."

CORPORATE REORGANIZATION UNDER BANKRUPTCY CODE OF 1978. The new Code of 1978 replaces present Chapters X, XI, and XII of the former Bankruptcy Act of 1898 with a completely new consolidated Chapter 11. All business reorganizations will operate under one chapter which combines the more favorable features of the three chapters of the former law with innovative substantive provisions designed to facilitate business reorganizations. For the first time, the Code establishes provisions assuring adequate disclosure when consents to plans are solicited. The interests of creditors are defined in explicit terms. The new consolidated reorganization chapter is responsive to many problems encountered under former law, including the well publicized "cram down" section. An intricate new confirmation standard permits flexibility while protecting all creditors.

CORPORATE TRUST. A trust arrangement in which a corporation is the trust settlor. Often such an arrangement is to secure corporate bond issues or employee benefit plans.

CORPORATE TRUSTEE. Generally a trust institution which serves as trust trustee. Interestingly, Corporate Trustees can also be much larger entities, such as the U.S. Government or a local town or large municipality. Also, in some states archbishops and other ecclesiastics are given the status of Corporate Trustee. Generally, it is required that a Corporate Trustee be qualified under the laws of the state where the trust is set up.

CORPORATION - BY - ESTOPPEL. Whenever it would be inequitable to allow the corporate existence of a busi-

ness to be denied by persons who have dealt with it as a corporation, or represented it as a corporation, those persons will be estopped to deny the incorporation of the association. Estoppel will not be found in every case in which holding out or reliance is found. Courts will rule on a case-by-case basis in this area, and the equities of each case will control.

CORPUS DELICTI (Latin—the body of the crime). The principle behind Corpus Delicti is that there must be proof that someone has indeed committed a criminal offense in order to convict a person accused of that offense. Thus, in most states, a defendant may not be convicted solely on the basis of his out-of-court confession; there must be some corroborating evidence of the Corpus Delicti. The term seems to get popularly confused with the idea of a "missing body." The misconception is understandable, for most cases involving Corpus Delicti issues are indeed "missing body" cases: homicide cases where no dead body can be produced so as to verify that there has been a death. Also common are cases where there is a dead body, but no evidence to suggest that a criminal agency caused the death. But Corpus Delicti is relevant to a wide variety of other crimes aside from homicide.

CORPUS JURIS (Latin—the body of the law). A comprehensive collection of law in book form. The Corpus Juris Civilis is the compilation of the Roman civil law published in the reign of Justinian. The Corpus Juris Canonici is the collection of the Canon Law of the Roman Catholic Church. Corpus Juris is also the name of an Anglo-American legal encyclopedia published by the West Publishing Company, whose purpose is to restate the entire body of American law based upon all reported cases from 1658 to 1931. This is a multivolume publication which includes procedural and substantive law. Corpus Juris has been superseded by Corpus Juris Secundum, which cites all reported federal and state cases decided since the publication of the corresponding titles in Corpus Juris. Where earlier cases are still valid, footnote references are given to the Corpus Juris page and note numbers which list them.

CORPUS JURIS CANONICI. See CANON LAW CODE.

CORPUS JURIS CIVILIS. See JUSTINIAN CODE.

CORPUS JURIS SECUNDUM. See CORPUS JURIS.

CORRECTIVE ADVERTISING. Remedial measure imposed by the Federal Trade Commission (F.T.C.) to offset the impact of prior false or deceptive advertisements. The remedy was originally suggested to the Commission by a public interest group known as S.O.U.P. (Students Opposing Unfair Practices) as the result of a Campbell Soup Company television ad in which marbles were placed at the bottom of a bowl of soup to make vegetables appear more prominent on the TV screen. The F.T.C. did not mandate corrective advertising in that case but did acknowledge its authority to require the remedy in the future. In 1971 the Commission persuaded the Continental Baking Company to devote 25 percent of its ads for one year to correct a prior claim that the Company's Profile Bread contained fewer calories than ordinary bread. (The bread did contain seven fewer calories per slice, but it was sliced thinner.) The ads revealed the true facts about the product but were not required to admit that the company had advertised deceptively. No significant reduction in sales of the bread were noted, consequently other advertisers have agreed to the practice in out-of-court settlements. Another example is the order to the Warner-Lambert Company, in 1978, to spend $10 million issuing the following public statement: "Contrary to prior advertising, Listerine will not help prevent colds or sore throats or lessen their severity." Refusal to comply with such an order will bar the Company from any future advertising of the product.

CORRESPONDENCE AUDIT. See TAX AUDIT.

CORROBORATING EVIDENCE. Supplementary evidence which confirms evidence already presented.

COST ACCOUNTING STANDARDS. Accounting principles issued by the Cost Accounting Standards Board, which apply to certain negotiated defense contracts. These principles, to be used by contractors in estimating, accumulating, and reporting costs, are designed to achieve uniformity and consistency in the cost accounting principles followed by defense contractors and subcontractors under defense contracts.

COST ACCOUNTING STANDARDS BOARD. This Board, created as an agent of Congress, by amendment to the Defense Production Act of 1950, is charged with the responsibility of promulgating cost accounting standards designed to achieve uniformity and consistency in the cost accounting principles followed by defense contractors and subcontractors under federal contracts.

COST CONTRACT. This is a cost-reimbursement government procurement contract, a type in which the contractor receives no profit. It is often used in research and development work, particularly with nonprofit organizations.

COST, INSURANCE, FREIGHT. See C.I.F.

COST OF LIVING ADJUSTMENT. See C.O.L.A.

COST OR PRICING DATA. That data required of prospective and current Department of Defense contractors pursuant to the Truth in Negotiations Act. As defined in the Defense Acquisition Regulation, such data "consists of all facts existing up to the time of agreement on price which prudent buyers and sellers would reasonably expect to have a significant effect on price negotiations."

COST-PLUS-AWARD-FEE. Two fees are provided under this cost-reimbursement government procurement contract.

In addition to allowable costs, the contractor is entitled to recover a "base fee" established prior to contract performance. He may also earn an "award fee" which is determined subjectively (and unilaterally) by the government based on the standard of performance in areas such as quality, timeliness, ingenuity, and cost effectiveness.

COST-PLUS-FIXED-FEE. Under this cost-reimbursement arrangement, the government procurement contractor is entitled to recover his allowable costs of performance plus a fixed amount of profit. D.A.R. allows use of two forms of this type contract—Completion and Term. The former is one in which the scope of work to be done is described as a clearly defined task or job with a definite goal or target expressed and with a specified end-product required. In the term arrangement, the scope of work to be done is described and obligates the contractor to devote a specified level of effort for a stated time.

COST-PLUS-INCENTIVE FEE. Similar to the Fixed-Price Incentive government procurement contract, this cost-reimbursement arrangement provides for the payment of a contractor's allowable costs with the profit adjusted according to the amount costs exceed or fall short of a target cost.

COST-PLUS-PERCENTAGE OF COST. Under this cost-reimbursement arrangement, a government procurement contractor is reimbursed his costs of performance and a fixed percentage of these costs as profit. This contracting method is statutorily prohibited for Department of Defense contracting.

COST PRINCIPLES. In federal government contracting, this term refers to the standards by which the allowability of a contractor's cost is determined. For Department of Defense procurement, such principles are found in Defense Acquisition Regulation Section XV.

COST-SHARING. This cost-reimbursement government procurement contract allows the contractor no profit and, in addition, requires him to absorb a portion of his costs. It is intended for use in research or development procurements where it can be demonstrated that the contractor will eventually reap substantial compensating commercial benefits.

COUNCIL FOR MUTUAL ECONOMIC AID. See C.O.M.E.C.O.N.

COUNCIL OF ECONOMIC ADVISERS. Established by the Employment Act of 1946, the Council consists of three men who assist the President in the preparation of his annual economic report to Congress and who make recommendations to the President to promote the economic well-being of the United States.

COUNCIL OF EUROPE. A Strasbourg-based organization created by the Treaty signed on May 5, 1949, among eighteen countries of democratic western Europe: West Germany, Ireland, Iceland, Italy, Luxembourg, Malta, Netherlands, Norway, the United Kingdom, Sweden, Switzerland, Turkey, France, Cyprus, Greece, Austria, Denmark and Belgium. The Council is designed to defend democratic ideals, and to protect human rights. It has only political and social, but not military, significance. Despite several attempts to promote the Council to the rank of an administrative center for all European institutions through the Eden Plan, which failed in 1952, it has not played any significant role in the integration of Europe. Perceived as a disappointing experience by those who saw in it the institutional basis for "The United States of Europe," the Council of Europe has nevertheless initiated more than sixty treaties which apply to a broad range of social and cultural questions. The most important conventions negotiated under its auspices were the remarkable Convention on Human Rights and Fundamental Freedoms, which came into force on September 3, 1953, and the European Social Charter.

COUNCIL OF STATE GOVERNMENTS. A Chicago-based organization formed by the states to serve as a clearinghouse for information and research on the improvement of state government administration. The Council encourages efficiency in the performance of state executive, legislative, and judicial functions, and promotes interstate, federal-state, and state-local cooperation. The Council consists of commissions of legislative and executive officers within each state. It also serves as secretariat for miscellaneous state organizations like the National Governors' Conference. Its monthly magazine is *State Government.*

COUNCIL ON ENVIRONMENTAL QUALITY. A federal Executive branch agency which advises the President and the Congress on environmental policy. One of its major projects is its Global 2000 Study, which is being conducted in collaboration with the State Department. The Study involves a nation-by-nation examination of populations, resources and environmental trends throughout the world and their implications for the United States.

COUNCIL ON FOREIGN RELATIONS (C.F.R.). A private organization founded in 1921 to study the international aspects of American political, economic and strategic problems. Political, business and academic experts act as advisors for the professional staff's research projects. The Council publishes a quarterly, *Foreign Affairs,* and the annual *American Foreign Relations,* as well as resarch on different aspects of United States foreign policy. The Council works with National Public Radio to produce interviews and discussion groups and annually awards eight to twelve grants through the International Affairs Fellowship Program for Advanced Research on International Relations.

COUNCIL ON LEGAL EDUCATION FOR PROFESSIONAL RESPONSIBILITY. See C.L.E.P.R.

COUNCIL ON LEGAL EDUCATION OPPORTUNITY. See C.L.E.O.

COUNCIL ON WAGE AND PRICE STABILITY. See A.V.O.L.

COUNSELOR-AT-LAW. In England the term refers to a barrister. In the United States the term varies in meaning in different states. In some states counselor and attorney are used interchangeably to designate any lawyer, while in others the term counselor is not used at all. In still others the term is used along with attorney to designate the full title of a member of the legal profession.

COUNTER-CLAIM. A claim for relief filed by the defendant to a lawsuit against the plaintiff. There are two types of counterclaims—permissive and compulsory. Pursuant to Rule 13(b) of the Federal Rules of Civil Procedure, a permissive counter-claim is not within the ancillary jurisdiction of a federal court and thus must meet jurisdictional requirements. In contrast, a compulsory counter-claim is considered ancillary to the main claim and pursuant to Rule 13(a) does not need to meet the jurisdictional action requirement.

COUNTER OFFER. A variation in a contract offer by the offeree, which constitutes a rejection of the offer. The common law holds that there can be no variances to the acceptance of an offer.

COUNTERVAILING DUTY. An additional duty imposed by the United States to match any subsidy that a foreign manufacturer has received from his own government on goods being imported into the United States, in order to protect American producers from unfair competition. The Trade Agreements Act of 1979 authorizes the Department of Commerce to impose a countervailing duty if the International Trade Commission also determines that an industry in the United States is materially injured or is threatened with material injury, or the establishment of an industry in the United States is materially retarded by reason of imports of the subsidized merchandise.

COUP D'ETAT (French—stroke of state). A quick, decisive overthrow of an existing government by a small group within the political or military system. Unlike a revolution, a coup d'etat involves no popular insurgency and does not necessarily generate massive changes in the political or social structure. Instigators of the coup usually execute their plan by killing or imprisoning existing leaders, occupying the government's power centers, and using mass media to gain popular acceptance of the new government.

COURSE OF DEALING. Sequence of previous business transactions between parties which will be recognized as having established a common basis for the general interpretation or understanding of similar or subsequent business conduct.

COURSE OF PERFORMANCE. Any sales contract that repeatedly allows either party the opportunity to perform with knowledge, regarding the nature of the performance, and with the chance to either object or accept such, will be recognized by law as a valid agreement.

COURT ADMINISTRATOR. Person designated either by statute or court rule to administer the business and records of courts. The professional service of this expert releases the judges to spend their entire time on what they do best, which is judging.

COURT DOCKET. (1) An abridged record of proceedings resulting in a judgment, containing the pleadings and other documents generally specified by statute. (2) A list of cases to be tried at a particular session or term of the court.

COURT EFFICIENCY. A characteristic so notably lacking in the American legal system that when an appellate court operates on schedule, it is a cause for celebration. In 1978 the United States Court of Appeals for the Second Circuit so celebrated in a special session attended by a galaxy of legal luminaries. President Carter congratulated the court for its "magnificent achievement." And all because the Second Circuit had no case backlog in a nation where, traditionally, the wheels of justice grind painfully slowly.

COURT EXECUTIVES. A corps of skilled executives established to alleviate the management functions of judges in federal and state courts.

COURT EXPERT. Judge's advisor used in cases where the technical nature of the remedy and presumed bias on the part of both parties' experts make necessary the appointment of a court expert. Often used in school desegregation cases, court experts have been criticized for meeting out of court with only one party and for developing remedies which go beyond the recommendations of either party and which have not benefited from examinaton and advocacy.

COURT MARTIAL. A military court, convened under authority of government, having power to try and punish offenses committed by members of the Armed Forces and other persons subject to military law. The name, which has almost universal application today, derives from the Marshal's court in England, which dates from the time when the Earl Marshal succeeded the Constable as commander of the English army. The Marshal had been second in command since the two officers were first appointed by William the Conqueror in 1066. In the United States, there are three types of courts martial; the summary court martial, the special court martial, and the general court martial. The summary court martial is intended to dispose of relatively minor offenses under a simplified form of procedure. It is composed of one commissioned officer who performs all the functions normally allocated to the judge, jury, prosecutor, and defense counsel. The jurisdiction of the summary court martial is limited to the trial of enlisted personnel, and it may only impose punishment not to exceed one month's confinement at hard labor, forfeiture of two-thirds of one month's pay, and reduction to the lowest enlisted grade. The special court martial is an intermediate trial court intended to try all manner of noncapital offenses made punishable by military law. It is composed of at least three commissioned officers who act as jurors in the case. In cases tried by special court martial, the government is represented by a prosecutor, who may or may not be a lawyer, known as the trial counsel, and the accused is represented by a defense counsel, who in most cases is a lawyer. The entire proceedings are, in nearly every case, presided over by a military judge. This court has jurisdiction to try any member of the Armed Forces, and it may adjudge punishment up to and including confinement at hard labor for six months, forfeiture of two-thirds pay per month for six months, reduction of enlisted personnel to the lowest grade, and discharge of enlisted personnel from the military service with a bad conduct discharge. The highest trial court in this three-tier structure is the general court martial. Organizationally, this court martial looks very much the same as the special court martial. It differs only in the number and qualifications of the personnel involved. In this case, the court or jury is composed of at least five commissioned officers, and both the government and the accused must be represented by lawyers. A military judge presides over the trial. The general court martial has jurisdiction to try any person subject to military law, including civilians. It may award any punishment, including death, not prohibited by military law. In this sense the general court martial is as close to a court of general jurisdiction as is known to military law.

COURT NOT OF RECORD. An inferior court or court of special or limited jurisdiction. The term is misleading in that most, if not all, courts not of record maintain some type of record of their judicial acts. It has come to negate the idea that the court so described is a court of general jurisdiction. Most such courts are designated as such by statute. In Virginia, for example, all courts below the jurisdictional level of the circuit courts, including the general district courts and the juvenile and domestic relations courts, are considered courts not of record.

COURT OF APPEALS FOR THE FEDERAL CIRCUIT. A proposal to streamline the federal administration of justice by consolidating the United States Court of Claims and the United States Court of Customs and Patent Appeals into a single court with a review of its decisions by the Supreme Court of the United States.

COURT OF CHANCERY. After the Norman Conquest of England in 1066, William the Conqueror established common law courts to hear disputes between his new subjects. These courts heard only limited types of cases, were very technical in their operation and could only award damages by way of relief to a successful party. If the loser did not pay, the sheriff would seize his property, sell it and pay the proceeds to the winner. Some of those whose cases could not be heard by the common law courts for relief for one reason or another would go to the chancellor who was the second most important person in the realm. If he thought justice had been denied, he would order the defendant to obey under threat of indefinite imprisonment until he changed his mind. By the 15th Century, he was getting so much business that he created a separate court of chancery to hear these extraordinary cases. We inherited this parallel system of common law courts and chancery courts sitting side by side. Most of our states have since combined both into a single judicial system. But the power of a judge to threaten a person who wilfully refused to obey a lawful order with potential life imprisonment, such as a man who can, but won't support his wife, ex-wife or children, is an awesome weapon which is used most effectively to obtain compliance.

COURT OF CLAIMS. See UNITED STATES COURT OF CLAIMS.

COURT OF EQUITY. See COURT OF CHANCERY.

COURT OF FIRST INSTANCE. The trial court; the first court to hear a particular case.

COURT OF GENERAL JURISDICTION. Normally a state trial court having broad judicial power to hear virtually all types of civil and criminal cases. In most State systems, such broad jurisdiction is typically vested in the local county or district courts, or in the superior court in larger metropolitan areas. These courts are generally authorized to consider any legal dispute, without regard to subject matter or amount in controversy, unless specialized local courts of limited jurisdiction have been specifically created to hear particular types of cases, such as family court or a small claims court. Most state courts are Courts of General Jurisdiction. Federal courts, however, cannot be courts of general jurisdiction, since they are empowered to hear only cases that are within the judicial power of the United States, as defined in the United States Constitution and entrusted to them by a congressional grant of jurisdiction.

COURT OF INQUIRY. A formal military adminstrative fact-finding body composed of at least three commissioned officers constituted to search out, develop, assemble, analyze, and record all available information relative to the matter under investigation. The Court of Inquiry is not a judicial body and its report is purely advisory in nature. Opinions, when expressed, do not amount to final determinations or legal judgment, and recommendations, when made, are not binding upon convening or reviewing authorities. Among the types of incidents which may be investigated by a Court of Inquiry are major aircraft accidents, explosions, ship collisions and groundings, loss of government funds or property, and serious security violations. The most notable Court of Inquiry investigation in recent years was that involving the seizure of the *U.S.S. Pueblo* in 1968 by the government of North Korea.

COURT OF LAST RESORT. The highest court which can try a particular case. Depending on the nature of the case, such court may not be the highest court of the jurisdiction and it may be the court of first instance.

COURT OF LIMITED JURISDICTION. A state or federal court which exercises judicial power only over limited types of cases or amounts in controversy. Such courts must be distinguished from court of general jurisdiction, which are presumed to have jurisdiction to hear all types of cases, unless a showing is made to the contrary. Examples of courts of limited jurisdiction in state systems are traffic courts, small claims courts, and family courts. All federal courts, on the other hand, are by definition courts of limited jurisdiction since they may hear only cases within the judicial power of the United States, as set out in the Constitution and entrusted to them by congressional grants cf jurisdiction. Even though all federal courts are of limited jurisdiction, some have broad judicial power over many subjects, such as the district courts, while others are specialized courts, such as the United States Court of Claims, the United States Tax Court, and the United States Customs Court.

COURT OF MILITARY APPEALS. See UNITED STATES COURT OF MILITARY APPEALS.

COURT OF MILITARY REVIEW (formerly known as Board of Review). An intermediate appellate court within the military justice system, established by each Judge Advocate General to review the record of certain trials by court martial. The judges of this court, who sit in one or more three-judge panels, may be civilians or commissioned officers, but they each must be a member of a bar of a federal court or of the highest court of a state. Unlike most appellate tribunals, this court has authority not only to determine the law of the case but also to judge the credibility of witnesses, resolve controverted question of fact, and consider the appropriateness of a sentence.

COURT OF RECORD. An imprecise term defining those superior courts of general jurisdiction which maintain a perpetual record of their proceedings and whose judgments import verity.

Most courts of record are designated as such by statute. This itself has added to the difficulty of inscribing a precise definition to the phrase. In Virginia, the circuit courts and Supreme Court are examples of courts of record.

COURT OF THE UNION. Proposed court which would be composed of the fifty chief justices of the states' supreme courts. The court of the union would have only one function: i.e., to decide whether or not a particular decision of the United States Supreme Court was unconstitutional. The proposed court could rule only when a case involved powers of the states or of the people, and an agreement of 26 justices would be needed to reverse a decision of the Supreme Court. In effect, the suggested court of the union is an attempt to change current state-federal relationships at the expense of federal government and thus is a modern counterpart of the court-packing plan of a generation ago.

COURT ON JUDICIARY. A special judicial disciplinary Court. Recently a New York State judge was disciplined by that state's court of the judiciary for rendering free legal advice, conferring with litigants and their lawyers in pending matrimonial matters and assisting in the preparation of property and support agreements activities which annoyed local attorneys. The court rested its opinion on a state constitutional ban against the practice of law by judges, as well as the Canons of Judicial Ethics which require judges to avoid impropriety or the appearance of impropriety.

COURT-PACKING PLAN. An attempt by President Franklin Roosevelt in 1937 to save New Deal legislation by appointing new justices to the Supreme Court of the United States. The Court, in a series of cases in the mid-1930s, had declared many New Deal programs unconstitutional, leading Roosevelt to propose fundamental changes in the tenure and appointment procedures for American judges. Under the proposal, judges who had attained age 70 and had served on the bench for at least ten years continuously or otherwise were given the option of resigning or retiring. For each judge who chose to continue serving, the President was given the power to appoint another judge, provided that no more than fifty judges were so appointed and that the appointments would not result in more than fifteen Justices sitting on the Supreme Court. The purported rationale for the Plan was to assure the vitality of the courts since, at the time, six Supreme Court Justices were older than 70. But the Senate Judiciary Committee rejected Roosevelt's scheme as an attempt to subjugate the independent judiciary to Presidential will. Although the President may have lost the battle, he won the war; the Supreme Court consistently sustained the constitutionality of New Deal legislation after the plan was turned down, leading to criticisms that there had been a "switch in time to save the Nine."

COURT REPORTER. A person who transcribes testimony and proceedings before a Court.

COURT STRUCTURE. There are two Court systems in the United States—state and federal. Federal courts generally try cases arising under federal Laws or cases between citizens of different states. The federal system has three levels of courts: the trial level or district court, the appeals level or circuit court, and the Supreme Court. There are also special federal Courts, such as tax and customs courts. State court systems vary among the states. Generally, there are superior trial courts, appeals courts, and a supreme court. In addition, there is usually an assortment of inferior courts. Inferior courts include city, municipal or county courts which hear misdemeanors, traffic offenses, and felony or civil cases, some of which may proceed for further action in a superior trial court. Other inferior courts may include special courts for juveniles, domestic relations, traffic or probate. To further complicate matters, an action may often be brought in either a federal district court or a state trial court, and an action arising in the state courts may eventually be appealed to the United States Supreme Court.

COURT TRUST. A trust coming under the supervision of a court of law, as where the court orders a trust set up to insure the just distribution or preservation of some asset.

COURT WATCHERS. Volunteer court observers acting on behalf of civil rights, church, or other groups to monitor the criminal justice system.

COVENANT NOT TO SUE. A promise not to sue made by a creditor. The promise may be permanent or limited. If it is permanent, the debtor will always have a defense and may counterclaim for damages resulting from the creditor's breach of the covenant. However, on the other hand if the promise is for a limited period of time, an affirmative defense may only be asserted for the violation of certain parts of the covenant.

COVENANT OF QUIET ENJOYMENT. An agreement included in a deed or lease which restricts the seller or landlord from interfering in the use of the property by the buyer or tenant. The covenant may be implied or expressed.

COVENANT OF SALT. Primitive people thousands of years ago settled disputes over a sacrificial meal in which salt was the preservative. Covenant of salt thus referred to an enduring bargain or a permanent settlement. In subsequent centuries the Romans coined the phrase "with a grain of salt" to refer to skepticism.

COVENANT OF SEISIN. Warranty by a seller of real property that he is the true owner and has the right to convey title to the property. The term seisin is derived from the Old English "seised," or "possessed," and comes from the ancient conveyancing practice of Livery of Seisin (delivery of possion) in which the seller would go on his land with the buyer and hand over a clod of dirt or twig from his property. This symbolic practice was discontinued as increasing numbers of Englishmen learned to read and write and written deeds replaced their picturesque counterparts.

COVENANTS RUNNING WITH THE LAND. Agreements which benefit or restrict successive owners of real estate. To burden the land, a covenant must "touch and concern the land." It must also be in writing, the original parties must have intended that it run with the land, and subsequent purchasers must have notice of the covenant.

COVERT ACTION INFORMATION BULLETIN. A periodical published in Washington, D.C., by Philip Agee, disgruntled former Central Intelligence Agency (C.I.A.) officer and its number one nemesis. The rag prints the names of C.I.A. agents stationed abroad and several have already been assassinated by this blowing of their cover. This is indeed a heavy price to pay for freedom of the press in so endangering our national security. Needless to say, he would be shot as a traitor if he were a Russian doing this to the K.G.B.

CO-VIVANTS. See LINDSEY, BEN.

C.O.W.P.S. See A.V.O.L.

COX, ARCHIBALD. See SATURDAY NIGHT MASSACRE; NIXON, RICHARD M.

C.P.I. See CONSUMER PRICE INDEX.

CRAIG v. BOREN (429 U.S. 190 (1976)). A Supreme Court case which dealt with the appropriate standard of scrutiny for gender-based classifications. At issue was an Oklahoma statute which set different minimum ages at which males and females could drink 3.2 beer. The Court adopted what has been called a "middle-tier" approach. Though gender-based classifications are not required to meet the strict scrutiny test, classifications by gender "must serve important governmental objectives and must be substantially related to achievement of those objectives."

131

CREASMAN PRESUMPTION. Arising in the state of Washington, this legal principle proclaims that when a man and woman live together, without being legally husband and wife, in the absence of some trust relationship, any property acquired during their cohabitation belongs to the person who has legal title to it. This result is contrary to that reached in the California case which involved movie actor Lee Marvin and which was won by the woman with whom he had been living.

CREATIVE FEDERALISM. A Lyndon Johnson Administration catch-phrase emphasizing joint decision-making by federal and state officials in planning and implementing intergovernmental programs. Creative Federalism encouraged direct consultation among federal, state, and local officials in carrying out federal programs as well as local responsibility for management through revenue sharing.

CREATIVE SENTENCING. Requiring convicted persons to do volunteer work in the community rather than pay a fine or go to jail. Recent examples include: a carpenter who was sentenced to build a wheelchair ramp at the home of a senior citizen; an educator, convicted of manslaughter, sentenced to lecure on the consequences of drinking while driving; and graffiti scrawlers sentenced to clean up their mess.

CREDIT CARD-CRIMES LAW. Statutes prohibiting fraudulent activities involving credit cards. Although the breadth of these statutes varies from state to state, the more modern ones prohibit the knowing use of another's credit card without his consent; the knowing use of an expired or revoked credit card; the knowing purchase of a credit card from one other than an authorized issuer; the sale of a credit card by one who knows that he is not an authorized issuer; and various other acts which damage or cheat the credit card system.

CREDIT CONTROL ACT OF 1969. A federal statute whose purpose is to control inflation by regulating extensions of credit. In 1980 the Act was invoked for the first time when President Carter, by Executive Order, authorized the Federal Reserve Board to exercise restraint on the growth of certain types of consumer credit extended by banks, credit card companies and certain investment funds. Consequently, the Federal Reserve Board implemented the following regulations: (1) a voluntary Special Credit Restraint Program, applied to all domestic commercial banks, bank holding companies, business credit extended by finance companies, and credit extended to U.S. residents by the U.S. agencies and branches of foreign banks; (2) an increase from 8 to 10 percent in the marginal reserve requirement on the managed liabilities of large banks; (3) a special deposit requirement of 10 percent on increases in the managed liabilities of large non-member banks; (4) a special deposit requirement of 15 percent on increases in the total assets of money market mutual funds above the level as of March 14; and (5) a special deposit requirement of 15 percent for all lenders on increases in certain types of consumer credit, including credit cards, check credit overdraft plans, unsecured personal loans and secured credit where the proceeds are not used to finance the collateral.

CREDIT LIFE. A form of insurance not required by law but used as a rip-off by many sellers of cars and appliances who charge the buyer an exhorbitant premium for a policy to pay off the unpaid balance of an installment contract purchase upon the death of the buyer.

CREDITOR BENEFICIARY. See THIRD PARTY BENEFICIARY.

CREDITORS FOR NECESSARIES. While the proceeds of a spendthrift trust generally cannot be touched by the creditors of its beneficiary, an exception to this rule is in some cases made for creditors who have supplied necessary goods and services to the beneficiary. Usually, the supply of goods or services must have been made with consent of the trustee, although in situations when such consent could not be obtained, medical emergencies, for example, this requirement may be relaxed.

CREDIT UNION. Not a labor organization but rather a cooperative savings and loan association operating under supervision of federal or state law.

CRIMES AGAINST NATURE. Crimes involving unnatural sex acts. Although limited at common law to sodomy and bestiality, statutes have broadened the range of prohibited acts. Although charges are seldom brought against consenting adults, many states still maintain such criminal prohibitions and do occasionally press charges.

CRIMINAL ARREST. The act whereby a person is taken into custody in order to answer for a penal offense. A criminal arrest may be accomplished in any of the following ways: (1) Physical restraint; submission on the part of the arrested person, coupled with intent to arrest or deprive of freedom; (2) The use of weapons by a police officer in such a way as to restrict freedom of movement; or, (3) Statements and actions of the officer indicating a person is not free to move about as he desires.

CRIMINAL ATTEMPT. Conduct which is part of a criminal act, performed with the intent to commit such an act, but which does not consummate the crime. The crucial question is how close the defendant must come to committing the crime. The older view was that the defendant must have performed the last act necessary to commit the crime, such as actually pulling the trigger. The general view today is that the defendant need only have engaged in conduct constituting a "material factor" in causing the prohibited result. However, such conduct must be strongly corroborative of a criminal intent, such as lying in wait or searching for the victim, unlawful entry of the building where commission of the crime is contemplated, or enticing the victim to go to where the crime is contemplated.

CRIMINAL CONSPIRACY. An agreement by two or more parties to achieve a prohibited result. Although the Model Penal Code requires that the prohibited objective itself be a crime, the common law and many state statutes permit conspiracy convictions if the objective was immoral, dangerous to health, or a perversion of justice, such as stacking a jury. Thus in England a defendant was convicted for conspiring to distribute a "prostitute directory" even though the distribution of such a directory was not criminal. At common law the crime of conspiracy was complete when the parties intentionally agreed to engage in prohibited conduct. Today, many statutes require an Overt Act in furtherance of the conspiracy as a manifestation of an intent to carry out the plan. Under the Pinkerton Rule (*Pinkerton v. United States*, 328 U.S. 640 (1946)) one is liable for all crimes committed by a co-conspirator in furtherance of the conspiracy. Thus, if *A* and *B* conspire to rob *C*, and *B* kills *C*, then *A* could be prosecuted for murder. Many states require that the additional crime be a "natural and probable consequence" of the original conspiracy so that *A* would not be guilty of *C's* murder if the conspiracy was to steal hub caps rather than to rob. Many States incorporate this doctrine in statutes codifying Accomplice Liability as well as in codifications of Conspiracy. Today, most States allow conviction and cumulative sentences for both the substantive offense and the conspiracy to commit it. Thus, if *A* and *B* conspire to rob *C* and do so, they can be convicted of both robbery and conspiracy to commit robbery, and can be consecutively sentenced. The rationale behind the rule is that conspiracies involve a greater threat to the public than the achievement of the offenses involved and so demand greater punishment. The Model Penal Code rejects this rationale and prohibits a double conviction. In 1925, Judge Learned Hand called Conspiracy "the darling of the modern prosecutor's nursery," and in many ways this statement seems true. There are at least four advantages to the government in bringing a conspiracy charge. First the doctrines of Conspiracy are vague, particularly as to non-criminal objectives of a conspiracy and as to what constitutes an agreement. Second, hearsay evidence is admissible under the Co-Conspirator Exception. Third, since conspiracy convictions are usually based upon Circumstantial Evidence, evidence only remotely relevant is admitted to prove the conspiracy. Lastly, co-conspirators may be required to accept a joint trial. Some defendants may "gang up" or "point fingers" at others, and the admission of confusing and conflicting testimony may induce jurors to follow the "birds of a feather" theory.

CRIMINAL CONTEMPT. See CONTEMPT OF COURT.

CRIMINAL CONVERSATION. Strictly, another name for adultery. The use of the term conversation as a synonym for sexual intercourse dates back to the sixteenth century, and its use in a legal sense may be traced to the seventeenth. At common law, an action for criminal conversation was available only to a husband though in the states which retain the action today, a wife may also sue. The reasoning behind the original double standard was that a husband's infidelity did not commit his wife to the support of his illegitimate child, whereas similar conduct on her part could do so for him. Such conduct might also cast doubt on the legitimacy of his own children. Further, a husband was deemed to have a property interest in his wife's person. An action for criminal conversation requires proof of adulterous relations. It is not usually an adequate defense that husband and wife were not living together, that it was the defendant rather than the spouse who initiated relations, or that the plaintiff was himself incapable of sexual relations. Damages are awarded for mental anguish, loss of consortium, and embarrassment. In special circumstances where malicious intent is involved, punitive damages are sometimes awarded. Heart balm statutes have recently abolished the action for criminal conversation in a number of states, and may mark a trend towards its eventual complete abolition.

CRIMINAL HOMICIDE. Killing that is not authorized or excused by law. Forms of criminal homicide include murder and voluntary manslaughter.

CRIMINAL JUSTICE AGENCY. Makes recommendations concerning matters such as bail and release of defendants awaiting court appearances. Financed by state and federal funds, the Agency interviews the accused between the time of arrest and arraignment. A Criminal Justice Agency is typically found in large cities like New York.

CRIMINAL JUSTICE SYSTEM. Includes the police, prosecution and defense, the judiciary, and all phases of the correction system insofar as society is involved in dealing with those who violate our criminal laws.

CRIMINAL LAW. The area of the law concerned with protecting the public interests through the punishment of crime. Actions are initiated by a prosecutor (i.e., United States Attorney, State District Attorney) as representatives of the public. The offender may be punished by fine, imprisonment, death, the loss of certain rights, or a combination thereof. However, the victim is not compensated. Criminal law should thus be distinguished from civil law, where suit is brought by an injured party for monetary damages, injunctive relief, specific performance or some other remedy. Conduct, such as assault, battery, homicide and antitrust violations, may give rise to both criminal and civil liability.

CRIMINAL LAW REPORTER. A weekly publication concerning current developments in criminal law distributed by the Bureau of National Affairs. Individual issues are stored in a loose-leaf binder which is divided into four sections. The first, "Summary and Analysis" contains synopses of new developments and their ramifications. The second, "Courts and Legislatures," provides digests of important court decisions, legislative actions and reports and proposals. The third, "Text," contains the full text of all United States Supreme Court opinions in criminal cases. The last, "Supreme Court Proceedings," provides summaries of court orders, summaries of recently filed cases, and special articles on the Supreme Court's work.

CRIMINAL NEGLIGENCE. Conduct which creates an unreasonable risk of harm to persons or property. Generally, the risk created must be greater than that required for ordinary civil negligence. As in the case of homicides caused by automobiles, liability may be imposed for ordinary negligence. Although a few courts require that the defendant actually perceive the risk, most utilize an objective standard and impose liability if the defendant, as a reasonable man, should have perceived it. The Model Penal Code imposes liability for certain crimes if the defendant has a negligent state of mind. The Code requires the creation of a risk greater than that required for ordinary negligence. Additionally, the accused must not have perceived the risk. Such a perception would make his state of mind one of "recklessness" rather than "negligence."

CRIMINAL OFFENSE. Conduct which is prohibited by law and punished by the government through a court proceeding brought by a prosecuting attorney. Every criminal offense has two elements: an act or failure to act when legally required (Actus Reus) and a certain state of mind or culpability (Mens Rea). A criminal offense has not occurred unless both elements are present. For example, first degree murder involves an intentional killing. The killing is the act and the intent to do so is the state of mind. Without such an intent there has not been a first-degree murder, although there may have been a less serious homicide such as manslaughter or negligent homicide. Even if both elements are present, a

defendant may be exonerated if he successfully raises an affirmative defense such as self-defense or insanity. There are two types of crimes: felonious offenses and misdemeanors. Felonious offenses are more serious and are punishable by death or imprisonment in a state penitentiary, whereas misdemeanors are punishable only by fine or imprisonment in a local jail.

CRIMINAL RESPONSIBILITY. See DURHAM TEST; M'NAGHTEN TEST; MODEL PENAL CODE TEST.

CRIMINAL SOLICITATION. Inciting, counselling or inducing another to commit a crime with the intent that such other person actually commit it. The crime of solicitation is complete when the defendant invites another to commit a crime, regardless of whether the crime is actually committed or the invitation even accepted. However, under the Model Penal Code, voluntary renunciation is an affirmative defense if the defendant persuades the other person not to commit the crime. Although most states punish only solicitation to serious felonies, and punish solicitation less severely than the offense solicited, the Model Penal Code punishes solicitation to any crime, except murder, with the same severity as the crime solicited.

CRISIS TEAM. See SPECIAL CO-ORDINATION COMMITTEE.

CROMWELL, THOMAS (Earl of Essex). Like many legally-trained men in fifteenth- and sixteenth-century Europe, he gained religious, not legal, recognition in the court of Henry VIII. He became prominent in his early life because of his adeptness in foreign languages and affairs. His comraderie with the King provided him with a wealthy living, but Cromwell never forgot his working-class upbringing. He distributed bread, milk, and drink at the gates of his house twice a day to over 200 poor people. Cromwell is best remembered for the ecclesiastical agitation he instigated. After King Henry split with the

Pope and the Catholic church, he named Cromwell vicar-general. In that capacity, Cromwell initiated the dissolution of monasteries in England and promoted ballads and books ridiculing the Pope. He fueled the Reformation by requiring the Lord's Prayer and the Ten Commandments to be taught in English instead of Latin. To prevent erroneous versions of the Bible, Cromwell obtained a patent which prohibited the printing of English editions of the Bible except by people deputized by him. Among the civil reforms instituted by Cromwell was the use of county-wide birth, marriage, and death registries. Cromwell's Reformationist zeal ultimately alienated him from the King. He recommended that Henry marry Anne of Cleves because he felt it would be good to have a Protestant queen on the throne. Henry went ahead with the marriage even though he did not like Anne. As their marital problems escalated, the King charged Cromwell with heresy and beheaded him on July 28, 1540.

CROOKED CREEK, COLORADO, CADAVER CASE. Classic 1892 case illustrating an exception to the Hearsay Rule of evidence which allows evidence as to state of mind. In the Crooked Creek case, an insurance company was trying to establish the identity of a cadaver found in Crooked Creek, Colorado. The issue was whether or not the cadaver was an insured of the company or another man named Walters. The court allowed into evidence letters Walters had written regarding his intentions to go to Crooked Creek.

CROSS CLAIM. An action brought by a defendant in a law suit against a plaintiff, or codefendant or both. Generally the purpose of a cross claim is to bring a new matter to aid the defendant. A cross claim is permitted when it involves the same matter as the original claim.

CROSS DEFAULT CLAUSES. Provisions inserted in each of several loans made by a bank to the same borrower which provide that if there is a default in one of the loans, then all of the loans are in default. The chain reaction to this situation can have devastating adverse consequences to the debtor.

CROSS-DEPOSITING. The first major financial deviation of Communist China from its previous policy of self-reliance. In an effort to finance foreign investment, foreign banks are allowed to deposit currency in the Communist Bank of China at an interest rate fixed by Peking. Begun in 1978, this cooperation with the capitalistic world is sponsoring billions of dollars of industrial development in sophisticated technology in China. The reason for the drastic reversal of policy is their paranoid fear of Russia.

CROSS-LICENSING. The practice of two or more business competitors pooling complementary patents to promote the development of new products and to avoid the possibility of litigation. Control of the patents is usually assigned to a separate corporation which disburses the royalty payments to the members of the pool. Such arrangements are legal and necessary, and they violate the antitrust laws only when used to create monopolies, fix prices, or otherwise restrain interstate commerce.

CROSS-PICKETING. Picketing by two or more rival unions, each claiming to represent the employees of the business concern being picketed.

CRUDE OIL EQUALIZATION TAX. See C.O.E.T.

CRUELTY TO CHILDREN STATUTES. See PERSONS IN NEED OF SUPERVISION (P.I.N.S.).

CRY-BABY CLAUSE. A provision in a contract that excuses a party from compliance with the agreement voluntarily entered into by paying a forfeiture fee.

C.S.C. See CIVIL SERVICE COMMISSION.

C-3. Tax exempt classification for non-profit educational, church and social-issue groups. Under a recent I.R.S. ruling, such groups may lose their tax privileges if they use tax-deductible contributions for political activities. However, organizations which report candidates' views on a broad range of issues and which imply no approval of one candidate over another, are not affected by the new ruling.

CULTIVATED INFORMANT PROGRAM. Instituted by the Internal Revenue Service in the 1930s to investigate the financial affairs of gangsters like Al Capone, who was jailed for income tax evasion. Certain people were paid periodically for information regularly provided to the I.R.S. As much as $800,000 a year has been paid to 2,000 regular informants but the sum dropped to $9,000 in 1976 largely as a result of criticism of the practice by the G.A.O.

CULTURAL AFFAIRS OFFICERS. See INTERNATIONAL COMMUNICATION AGENCY.

CULTURAL IMPERIALISM. See NEW WORLD INFORMATION ORDER.

CULTURAL REVOLUTION. See LONG MARCH.

CULTURAL SOVEREIGNTY. See NEW WORLD INFORMATION ORDER.

CUM CLAVE (Latin—with a key). The practice of the Roman Catholic Church since the 13th century to lock its Cardinals in the Sistine Chapel of the Vatican after the death of a Pope until such time as they elect his successor. The period of time between the death of a Pope and the election of his successor is called a Papal Interregnum.

CUMULATIVE PREFERRED STOCK. See PREFERRED STOCK.

CUMULATIVE SENTENCING. See SENTENCING PROCEDURES.

CUMULATIVE VOTING. A method of electing a corporate board of directors whereby each shareholder may multiply the number of shares he owns by the number of directors to be elected to determine the number of votes he may cast. He may then cast all his votes for a single candidate, or allot them among several candidates. The purpose of cumulative voting is to assure minority representation on the board of directors. However, this purpose can be defeated by decreasing the size of the board or reducing the number of vacancies to be filled.

CUNO ENGINEERING CORP. v. AUTOMATIC DEVICES CORP. See FLASH OF GENIUS TEST.

CURE NOTICE. In Department of Defense contracting, this written notice to the contractor is issued by the contracting officer pursuant to the contract disputes clause when there is a failure to perform relating to other than timeliness. The notice specifies the defect and allows at least ten days in which to remedy the defect.

CURIA ROMANA. The Civil Service which aids the Pope in the government of the Roman Catholic Church.

CUSTODIAL INFERENCE. A crime under some state statutes which is committed whenever a relative of a minor child, without lawful authority, holds or intends to hold such a child permanently or for a protracted period, or takes or entices such a child from his lawful custodian.

CUSTODIAL PARENT. The parent who is granted custody of the minor children in a divorce action.

CUSTODY VIGILANTE. A slang term describing a person who undertakes child snatching for pay. Some self-styled custody vigilantes say they work not only for money, but also out of concern for the rights of divorced parents denied visitation rights or parents whose children (adult, as well as minor) have become involved with far-out religious sects.

CUSTOMARY INTERNATIONAL LAW. That body of international law based on the customs and usages of civilized nations. Since no world government exists to draw up international laws in the same way national governments do, international tribunals often look to the several practices of nations and declare that these are international laws if the practice is so widespread as to constitute a custom. The role of custom in international law was addressed by the Supreme Court of the United States in two classic decisions in 1900: The Paquete Habana Case and The Lola Case. In these two cases the court noted an "ancient usage" among civilized nations of exempting fishing vessels from capture as prizes of war and declared that this custom had ripened into a rule of international law. Other sources of international law besides custom are treaties, general principles of law recognized by civilized nations, judicial decisions, and the writings of publicists.

CUSTOMARY LAW. Those practices and beliefs which have been carried on since time immemorial and finally officially recognized by the sovereign as the legal basis for the enforcement of rights and responsibilities.

CUSTOMS APPEALS COURT. See UNITED STATES COURT OF CUSTOMS AND PATENT APPEALS.

CUSTOMS COURT. See UNITED STATES CUSTOMS COURT.

CY-PRES DOCTRINE (Latin—as nearly as possible). The judicial attempt to carry out as nearly as possible a testator's intention when the exact terms of a trust or will cannot be given effect.

C.Z.M.A. (Coastal Zone Management Act). A federal program launched in 1972 by Congress to encourage each state to design a legal system to protect coastal land and water resources and which reconciled or mediated between conflicting needs for the same coastal areas.

D

DADDY GRABBERS. State Child Support Enforcement Agencies which locate runaway fathers and threaten them with imprisonment if they fail to contribute financially to the support of their children.

DAISY CHAIN. See PROJECT X.

DAMNUM ABSQUE INJURIA (Latin —damage without injury). A legal principle that says not all harm gives rise to a cause of action by an injured party.

DANGEROUS SPECIAL OFFENDER STATUTE. A federal law enacted in 1970 which allows judges to sentence repeat or dangerous felons for up to twenty-five years for an offense which generally receives a lesser sentence. Generally, a defendant is subject to this enhanced sentencing if he either: (1) has been convicted of two previous offenses punishable by imprisonment for more than one year, and has actually been imprisoned for at least one conviction; (2) commits a felony as part of a pattern of conduct which constitutes a substantial part of his income and in which he manifests special skill; or (3) commits a felony in furtherance of a conspiracy which he organizes, directs, or finances. The statute appears aimed at repeat offenders, professional criminals, and organized crime. "Dangerous" does not require that the defendant pose a hazard to the physical security of individuals or society; he need only be "dangerous" in the sense that a longer sentence is needed to protect society from his criminal, albeit nonviolent, conduct.

DANNY THE RED. Nickname for Daniel Cohn-Bendit, fiery left-wing youthful leader of the 1968 French student uprisings which resulted in a complete and long due overhaul of the entire educational system throughout the country, for the success of which he was rewarded by being exiled from France for 10 years.

D.A.R. See DEFENSE ACQUISITION REGULATION.

DARE, VIRGINIA. See NATURAL BORN CITIZEN.

DARROW, CLARENCE SEWARD. A philosopher of compelling skepticism, a social reformer of genius, Clarence Darrow championed the cause of society's downtrodden as no lawyer had before, and as few have since. The son of an Ohio furniture maker, Darrow had a year of law school at the University of Michigan, then read law on his own until his admission to the Ohio Bar in 1878. He practiced in several small Ohio towns before going to Chicago in 1887 to begin the first important stage of his legal career. The young counsel for the Chicago and North Western Railway left his position in 1894 to defend the striking Eugene V. Debs and the American Railway Union against charges of violating an injunction and conspiring to obstruct interstate commerce. The *Debs* case launched his career as a labor lawyer, although he fell from grace with labor seventeen years later as counsel for the McNamara brothers. When the two labor leaders pleaded guilty to the charge of murder, the unions denounced Darrow for having misled them as to the guilt of the brothers. Soon thereafter, Darrow himself was indicted on two counts of conspiracy to suborn perjury. Though never convicted, Darrow returned to Chicago in 1913, his career in shambles. His labor clientele lost, Darrow turned to criminal law. As defense counsel in the Loeb-Leopold murder trial, he marshalled psychiatric evidence to show that the adolescent defendants had been temporarily insane, and won a commutation of the death sentence. But all roads led to Tennessee and the famous Scopes trial. Tennessee could not, argued Darrow, pass a law forbidding the teaching of evolution in its public schools. The trial culminated in a courtroom confrontation with William Jennings Bryan, whose literal interpretations of the Bible lost their persuasiveness under Darrow's withering attack. Darrow's deep compassion for other human beings made him a compelling advocate. The cornerstone of his theory of criminality was that social and economic forces had made pawns of his clients, depriving them of free agency. This determination lent a melancholy hue to Darrow's life—at age 75, he wrote, "If I have been charitable in

my judgments of my fellow man . . . if I have done my best to truly understand him, I know why I have taken this course—I could not help it."

DARTMOUTH COLLEGE v. WOODWARD (17 U.S. 517 (1819)). A classic case decided by the United States Supreme Court in 1819. The case struck down New Hampshire legislation which attempted to modify the college's 1769 Royal Charter as a violation of the contract clause, Article 1, section 10 of the United States Constitution. The opinion comprises 197 pages in the *United States Reports*.

DAVIS-BACON ACT. A federal law codified at 40 U.S.C. 276(a), as implemented by the D.A.R. clause, which was passed by Congress in 1931, at the depths of the Depression, at a time when there was no unemployment compensation, minimum wage or welfare. Fearful of cut-throat competition for federal construction jobs, the national legislators enacted a short and simple law which said that contractors on federal projects must pay "prevailing" wages for "projects of a character similar to the contract work in the city, town, village or other civil subdivision." Covered contracts are those in excess of $2,000 involving "construction, alteration or repair (including painting and decorating) on public buildings or public works within the United States. Serious disputes have persisted over what is "prevailing" and what is "similar," and today the Davis-Bacon Act is an even bigger headache than ever before because construction contributes more than any other industry to the Gross National Product. After studying the law for a decade, the General Accounting Office concluded that it has boosted construction costs by 5-15 percent, which is inflationary, to say the least, in the light of the many safeguards labor has today which were not available a generation ago. The sponsors of the legislation were strange bedfellows even though both were Republicans. Bacon was Boston-born, a Harvard Law School graduate and a New York banker. Davis emigrated from Wales to

Pittsburgh in 1881, went to work as a puddler in a steel mill as an 11-year-old boy, and moved up so brilliantly in the Iron, Steel & Tin Workers Union that President Harding named him Secretary of Labor in 1921. Coolidge and Hoover reappointed him, and Davis went to the Senate in 1930.

DAVIS, JEFFERSON. West Point graduate, Congressman and Senator from Mississippi, Secretary of War and sole President of the Confederacy during the Civil War. Acquitted of treason, he died in New Orleans at the age of 81 in 1889. His American citizenship was restored posthumously by President Carter in 1978.

DAY OF THE COVENANT. The annual Thanksgiving Holiday in South Africa commemorating the December 16, 1838 battle in which 470 White Afrikaner farmers defeated 15,000 Black Zulu warriors. Believing this victory to have resulted from a special covenant with God, the Dutch Reformed Church and the government joined forces to establish their apartheid policy thereby creating the last remaining Protestant theocracy, and a bigoted one at that in its denial of human rights.

D.B.A. (Doing Business As). Identifies a fictitious business name.

D.C.A.B. (Department of Commerce Appeals Board). See BOARDS OF CONTRACT APPEALS.

D.D. See DISHONORABLE DIS-CHARGE.

DEACCESSIONING CASES. Suits brought against museum trustees for selling off items in a museum's collection. "Deaccessioning," an euphemism for selling off art, is fairly commonplace because it allows the museum to update collections, eliminate duplications, reduce storage costs, and restrict the scope of collections in order to concentrate on particular aspects or genres. However, problems arise for example, when donors, who have purchased a work for the museum, often at the museum's request, find the item on the auction block. A famous Deaccession-

ing Case is the sale of 50 Impressionist and Expressionist paintings by the New York Metropolitan Museum; a sale in violation of the donor's posthumous wishes, for a comparatively low price, and conducted in order to purchase *one* work of dubious value by a contemporary American sculptor. This scandal led to an investigation by the New York State Attorney General of Deaccessioning practices.

DEAD DROP. A secret cache where one spy can deposit information to be picked up by another.

DEAD HAND CONTROL (Restraint on Alienation). Control of property, usually real estate, by someone who gives or sells the property to another and who imposes restrictions on enjoyment of the property which extend beyond his lifetime. Various attempts have been made to limit Dead Hand Control because it ties up property and tends to make it less marketable. One such attempt is the ancient Rule Against Perpetuities which requires an estate to vest, if at all, no later than 21 years after some life in being. Substantially in effect in most States, this Rule has been described by one scholar, who spent his lifetime making sense of it, as a "technicality-ridden legal nightmare."

DEAD-HEADING. Practice of the transportation industry to provide a free ride to the crew when moving empty vehicles to a particular destination.

DEAD MAN STATUTE. Prevents an interested party from testifying about a communication on transactions with a decedent in a civil suit involving the decedent's representative. The Statute is designed to prevent perjury. Absent such a law, one party to a communication could testify though the other party could not respond. At common law, no person with an interest in the outcome of a suit could testify. While this broad rule of disqualification was abolished in most jurisdictions in the United States at the end of the nineteenth century, vestiges of the rule are still embodied in Dead Man Statutes.

DEAD RENT. A mining term which describes the fixed amount paid for a mine or a quarry, in addition to royalty payments.

DEAD SOULS. An old Russian practice of keeping the names of dead serfs on the tax records. A variation called ghosting is currently used in the West when a person adds the names of non-existent people to payrolls or welfare lists and privately pockets the money.

DEAD TIME. A period of time when an employee cannot work because of a malfunction in the business, such as a delay in the delivery of raw materials or any equipment breakdown. Generally, employees are paid at a full rate for Dead Time.

DEAF ATTORNEYS. According to the National Center for Law and the Deaf, there are only three deaf attorneys in this country. One such attorney, Lowell Myers, a successful tax lawyer with Sears and Roebuck, has written *The Law and the Deaf* which illustrates some of the issues confronting deaf people under our legal system. For example, some deaf people have been denied the right to adopt children, the deaf are often more prone to be victims of violent crimes, and some deaf people have been committed to mental institutions under the mistaken belief that they were mentally incompetent rather than deaf.

DEAN, JOHN W., III. Disbarred lawyer who had served as Counsel to President Nixon. His Congressional Watergate testimony was the key to the future resignation of the President on August 9, 1974 and he himself went to jail for his criminal involvement in Watergate.

DEATH ON THE HIGH SEAS ACT (D.O.H.S.A.) (1920). A federal statute which, for the first time in maritime law, provided a cause of action for wrongful death occurring on the high seas beyond the territorial waters of the United States and its possessions. Such an action may be brought within the admiralty jurisdiction of the United States District Courts, in favor of the decedent's immediate family. Death

may be caused by wrongful act, neglect, or default, but it must occur on the high seas beyond a marine league from the shores of the United States or its territories. A marine league is a nautical measurement equal to approximately three nautical miles. Although contributory negligence is not a bar to recovery under the Act, the court must consider such negligence and reduce the recovery accordingly. The Act has also been extended by the courts to aircraft accidents in the airspace over the high seas.

DEATH ROW. Name given to that part of a prison where criminals awaiting capital punishment are housed.

DEATH SENTENCE. Clause in the Public Utility Act of 1935 which provides that holding companies in the public utility industry must reorganize to form individual integrated systems of operating companies. A matter of bitter controversy in the early days of the New Deal, the constitutionality of the clause was upheld by the Supreme Court in 1946.

DEATH TAX. See INHERITANCE TAX.

DE-BARMENT. In federal government contracting, this term refers to the disqualification of a contractor to receive a solicitation for or actual award of a contract for a specified period.

DE BONIS ASPORTATIS (Latin—carrying away of property). The common law action to recover damages for the taking of the plaintiff's personal property is called Trespass De Bonis Asportatis.

DEBS CASE (In re Debs, 158 U.S. 564 (1895)). A Supreme Court decision which upheld the authority of the federal government to secure injunctive relief where a strike interferes with government interest. An injunction had been obtained in the 1894 Pullman Strike on the ground that the strike interfered with the movement of mail and goods in interstate commerce. When Eugene Debs, the leader of the strikers refused to obey an injunction, he was fined and imprisoned. When Debs lost his appeal to the Supreme Court, organized labor pressured Congress for a statute restricting court actions in labor disputes.

DEBTORS ANONYMOUS. Organizations for people who owe money, located all over the country, similar in operation to Alcoholics Anonymous and Gamblers Anonymous. They are broadly represented by two different types. (1) B.U.C.C.S. (Budget and Counseling Service of the Community Service Society). This organization, which does not charge any fees, advises its clientele of their rights against their creditors, including the filing of a Bankruptcy Petition or a Wage Earner's Plan. Critics say they are too friendly to the debtors, if not a Bankruptcy Mill. (2) C.C.C. (Consumer Credit Counseling Service). It provides debtors with three basic services: (a) Credit Counseling; (b) Budget Counseling; and (c) Debt Management. Small fees are charged only for the third category of assistance. Critics say they are just a glorified collection agency for creditors. C.C.C. was founded by Bess Myerson, former New York City Consumer Affairs Commissioner and TV personality, in 1973.

DEBT SECURITIES. Create a debtor-creditor relationship between a corporation and the securities holder. They are thus high priority securities. A corporation must pay interest due on debt securities before it can pay dividends on equity securities. Debt securities usually involve the corporation's promise to pay the principal amount owed at a stated maturity date, anywhere from 30 days to 100 years, together with interest while the debt is outstanding. The interest on a Debt Security is regarded as an expense and is tax deductible, whereas dividend payments are not tax deductible. A Debt Security is a convertible security if the holder has the option of converting it to another form of security, generally common stock. Convertible Debt Securities combine the safety of creditor status with the possibility for speculative profits.

DECERTIFICATION ELECTION. A vote initiated by employees to remove the previously certified union from its position. Such votes are taken when employees believe that the certified union no longer represents a majority of the employees or when the employees believe an employer has unofficially recognized a rival union.

DECLARATION OF INDEPENDENCE. Written largely by Thomas Jefferson and adopted July 4, 1776, by the Second Continental Congress in Philadelphia's Pennsylvania State House (now Independence Hall), the document is an attempt to justify to the American people and the world why the colonies separated from Great Britain. It has five parts: the preamble; a statement of underlying political theories, such as "All men are created equal," influenced heavily by Aristotle, Cicero, Coke, Hooker, Locke, and Milton; a series of eighteen charges against King George III, the longest section and patterned after the 1689 English Bill of Rights; a general description of prior attempts to secure redress which had failed; and an assertion of independent status. The Declaration had a significant impact outside the United States, spurring revolutionaries in France and Simon Bolivar and Jose de San Martin during Hispanic revolutions. The Second Continental Congress convened in May 1775 after Great Britain refused to rescind coercive taxes and after the fights at Lexington and Concord. The delegates explicitly disavowed intent to separate, but altered their positions when the British remained intransigent. Thus, North Carolina, followed by Rhode Island on May 4, declared their independence. Richard Henry Lee of Virginia proposed a resolution for independence, but debate was postponed till July 1 after South Carolina and the middle colonies refused to support it. Nevertheless, on June 11, a drafting committee was appointed, consisting of Thomas Jefferson, John Adams, Benjamin Franklin, Roger Sherman, and Robert Livingston. Jefferson, at age 33 and in Congress for only one month, wrote the draft. A preliminary vote showed nine colonies favoring independence, two (South Carolina and Pennsylvania) against, Delaware divided, and New York abstaining. On the final vote, South Carolina and Pennsylvania switched, and Caesar Rodney, Delaware's third delegate, arrived after a day-long journey to cast the vote to break his state's tie. Thus, the Declaration passed 12-9, with New York still abstaining. John Hancock of Massachusetts, President of the Congress, signed the document first. His signature was intentionally large so that "[King] George can see it without his spectacles." Printing originally on a broadside and distributed to all of the states, the Declaration was publicly proclaimed on July 8 in Philadelphia, ratified by New York the next day, and printed on parchment the following week. Fifty-seven signatures ultimately were affixed—those of fifty-six delegates and Charles Thomson, the congressional secretary.

DECLARATORY JUDGMENT. A judicial decree which states the rights of the parties in an already completed transaction, or in an already existing situation. Declaratory Judgments cannot be used as a means of obtaining legal advice from the court concerning contemplated action.

DEED OF TRUST. A three-party instrument used instead of a mortgage to convey real estate as security for a debt. The Deed of Trust conveys legal title to the property to a trustee who is generally chosen by the lender while the homeowner retains an equitable interest in the property. The practical difference between a Deed of Trust and a mortgage is that foreclosure procedures for default are generally simpler under a Deed of Trust.

DEEMED DISTRIBUTIONS. A taxable stock dividend in which no stock is actually received by a shareholder. A distribution is deemed with respect to a shareholder whose interest in the assets of the distributing corporation is increased.

DEEMED SPOUSE. A putative spouse who is entitled to Social Security benefits.

DEEP POCKET. A term used by lawyers to apply to a client (usually a corporation) with seemingly limitless financial resources to fight a case, whether it wins or loses, while ensuring lucrative gain to the lawyer for professional services rendered.

DE FACTO (Latin—in fact). Characterizes a state of affairs which must be accepted as existing but which may lack legal validity. A de facto government is one which is in actual possession of power but which may have come into power unlawfully.

DE FACTO CORPORATION. A business entity which has failed to comply with requirements for incorporation, but which, nevertheless, is recognized as a corporation for most purposes. Traditionally, de facto status was achieved when the following elements were shown: the presence of a statute under which the corporation might have been properly incorporated; a good faith attempt to comply with that statute, and exercise of the corporate privileges. A product of judicial decision, the doctrine is designed to insure the security of business dealings with corporations.

DE FACTO DISCRIMINATION. Racial discrimination is referred to as De Facto when it exists in fact but not by reason of present law. An example is a neighborhood which is all white because developers and homeowners have refused to sell homes to Black customers.

DE FACTO SPECIALIZATION. Specialization in fact, but not sanctioned by law, of lawyers in certain fields, such as bankruptcy, antitrust, or taxation. As of 1976, 7 states have approved some form of specialization which would identify qualified lawyers in a particular specialty. In addition, 28 states are studying the regulation of legal specialties, while 3 states have rejected the concept, and 12 states have no plan to study De Facto

Specialization. The fact that few lawyers advertise exacerbates the problem of finding a qualified specialist. One of the major problems confronting those who would regulate specialization is the popular egalitarian theory that all lawyers are equal. Supporters of specialization point out that not all lawyers are equal in ability—a fact which should be admitted openly to the users of legal services.

DEFAULT JUDGMENT. Results when a party to a lawsuit fails to appear in court, and judgment is given to the party who does appear. Generally in a Default Judgment, a judge will not give a party more than what he requests in his pleading, which prompts most litigants to ask for as much as possible.

DEFECTIVE DELINQUENT STATUTES. See CHARACTER DISORDER.

DEFECT NOTIFICATION. A statutory requirement imposed by the National Traffic and Motor Vehicle Safety Act of 1966 that compels the manufacturer of motor vehicles or automotive equipment to give written notice of any defect in such vehicles or equipment which relates to motor vehicle safety. This notice must be given to the purchaser within a reasonable time after the manufacturer discovers the defect, and it must describe clearly and specifically the defect as well as its consequences.

DEFENSE ACQUISITION CIRCULARS. See DEFENSE ACQUISITION REGULATION.

DEFENSE ACQUISITION REGULATION (D.A.R.). Effective March 8, 1978, the Armed Services Procurement Regulation (A.S.P.R.) has been redesignated the Defense Acquisition Regulation (1978). The Regulation is issued by the Department of Defense pursuant to authority granted by 10 U.S.C. 2202 (1976). It is updated from time to time by Defense Acquisition Circulars in accordance with procedures described in Department of Defense Directive No. 5000.35, Defense Acquisition Regulatory System, para. D.2 (8

March 1978). It is found in Title 32 of the Code of Federal Regulations, Subtitle A, Chapter 1. The D.A.R. prescribes rules and sets forth policy governing Department of Defense acquisition of supplies and services by contract and the performance, termination, and settlement of the awarded contracts.

DEFENSE INTELLIGENCE. AGENCY. See UNITED STATES INTELLIGENCE-GATHERING CENTERS.

DEFENSIVE PAYMENT. See INTERNATIONAL CORPORATE BRIBERY.

DEFERRED MOTHERHOOD TAX PLAN. A proposal by Marjorie Tifford of Maryland to remedy the problem of unwed teenage motherhood. It would involve yearly federal cash payments to all single girls, ages 14 to 21, who pass a physical showing they are not pregnant and have not given birth. For example, a 14-year-old would receive $100, a 15-year-old $200, etc., up to $800 for the 21-year-old. These would be universal payments, including all income levels. A special annual tax deduction of at least $500 per child for parents of girls between ages 14 and 21 would apply to all who qualify for the cash payment. This idea is a reaction to our present welfare system, which seems to reward teenage motherhood with welfare benefits while ignoring more responsible teenagers. A conservative estimate of the cost to society of an unwed teenage mother with one child is as follows: $5,000 per year in Aid to Families with Dependent Children payments and benefits; $15,000 per year in supportive services, such as the welfare system, for a total of $20,000. In contrast, the minimum cost of the deferred motherhood plan, which would span 8 years, is $3,600 in cash payments, plus the tax deductions for the parents.

DEFINED BENEFIT KEOGH PLAN. Allows a taxpayer to defer the income tax on a maximum of $10,800 of earned income a year. The contributions are based on actuarial calculations beginning with a defined retirement objective. To determine the annual contribution on which tax will be deferred, an actuary includes such factors as age, income, the interest earned and the size of the capital fund needed to guarantee the retirement income. Here are examples of annual retirement income starting at age 65 and maximum deposits on which 1978 taxes could have been deferred:

Age	Deposit on Which 1978 Taxes were Deferred	Annual Retirement Income
40	$10,800	$47,875
45	10,500	32,000
50	10,500	20,475
55	10,600	11,650

The above figures are based on a maximum present earnings level of $50,000. (They are estimates only. The figures are determined by an actuary.) As in a "regular" Keogh, both the annual deposits and the earned interest are tax-deferred until retirement, when one is likely to be in a lower tax bracket. In some cases, one may be able to begin withdrawals as early as age 59-1/2, but, in all cases, one must begin by age 70-1/2. Unlike a "regular" Keogh plan, in the Defined Benefit plan, each year an actuary calculates the necessary information to determine that year's deposit on which tax will be deferred. The actuarial cost is borne by the Keogh participant. How would one pay for the increased deposit? Depending upon one's tax bracket, part if not most, of the funds could come from the dollars one saves because of the increased tax deduction. Another benefit is that installment payments to a named beneficiary, other than the participant's estate, paid at the death of the participant are exempt from federal estate taxes.

DEFINITE QUANTITY CONTRACT. As its name suggests, this type of contract provides for a definite quantity of specified supplies or for the performance of specified services for a fixed period, with deliveries or performance pursuant to later orders.

DE JURE (Latin—of right). Describes a state of affairs characterized by rightness and legitimacy. A De Jure government is thus one which has rightful title to power but which may lack actual possession of such power.

DE JURE CORPORATION. A corporation recognized by law. Where there has been sufficiently full compliance with all statutory conditions required for incorporation, such incorporation is generally immunized from both quo warranto and collateral attack on the basis of defect in incorporation. Failure to comply with a statutory provision which is directory in nature will not always deny a corporation De Jure status.

DE JURE DISCRIMINATION. Racial discrimination which exists because of a law. An example would be a statute which forbids Whites and Blacks from attending the same schools.

DELANEY CLAUSE. A federal law which forbids the use of any food additive shown to cause cancer. This clause has led to the Food and Drug Administration's ban on saccharin, even though it is a weak carcinogen.

DELAWARE v. PROUSE. See RANDOM OR SPOT CHECK.

DELAY OF WORK CLAUSE. In Department of Defense contracting, this clause requires that a contractor be compensated for all government-caused delays of all or any part of the contract work. The compensation is to provide no allowance for profit.

DELEGATION DOCTRINE. The legal theory restricting the amount of legislative power which the Congress can grant to executive agencies. Since the constitutional system of separation of powers rests the primary responsibility for lawmaking on the Congress, there are questions concerning the extent to which that power may be delegated to the executive branch. In the first case to consider the issue, *The Brig Aurora v. United States,* 11 U.S. 382 (1813), the Supreme Court upheld a delegation of authority to the President when a specific contingency occurs. In an 1892 case, the Court said that the principle that Congress cannot delegate legislative power is universally recognized as "vital to the integrity and maintenance of the system of government ordained by the Constitution." Only on a few occasions, however, has legislation been held invalid due to excessive delegation. It now seems that the Court has adopted the position that since the Congress cannot be expected to foresee exactly what actions an agency should take, Congress must be allowed broad flexibility in telling an agency what to do. An example of this flexibility may be seen in the original Federal Trade Commission Act which instructed the Commission to prevent the use of "unfair methods of competition" without specifying the meaning of that broad term.

DELEGATUS NON POTEST DELEGARE (Latin—delegated power may not be further delegated). Principle that discretionary delegated power may not be further delegated, unless there is special power of substitution express or implied. This principle is often invoked against schools or governmental subdivisions. For example, a board of education cannot lawfully delegate to others, or even to one or more of its members, the exercise of any discretionary power given it by law.

DE MINIMUS NON CURAT LEX (Latin—the law does not concern itself with trifles). This maxim embodies the principle that generally courts will not take notice of trivial matters, such as a fraction of a cent or a fraction of a day, or where a small error or transgression is involved. Notwithstanding this idea, it should be noted that courts of equity will seldom fail to grant some remedy for the violation of a legal right, such as an invasion of property.

DEMISE CHARTER (Bareboat Charter). A contractual arrangement whereby the charterer leases an entire vessel for a period of time. During this period, the charterer mans and operates the vessel with his own personnel and becomes in effect the owner Pro Hac Vice with all the rights, duties and responsibilities inherent in ownership of a leasehold interest. This form of charter arrangement may be useful where a charterer is temporarily short of vessel tonnage and the benefits of temporary ownership outweigh the heavy responsibilities he assumes. In recent years, Demise Charter has been a device for getting the United States government into the shipping industry, either through the demise of government-owned vessels to private companies or, in time of war or national emergency, through demise of privately owned vessels to the government.

DEMOCRACY IN AMERICA. The impressions of Alexis de Tocqueville, an observant young French aristocrat who toured the United States in 1831. Tocqueville's insights were deepened by the sense of perspective which he brought to the American scene. For example, a chapter of his book is devoted to the predominance of "applied" over "pure" scientific research in nineteenth-century America. He sees this phenomenon as unique to a democracy where, not theory, but hard practical results are of the highest importance. It was Tocqueville's fate to have arrived in America during the Presidency of Andrew Jackson (1828-1836). A rugged individualist and anti-intellectual, Jackson soon marked the whole administration with his brand of rough-and-ready (but often mediocre) political philosophy. Tocqueville thought of the signers of the Declaration of Independence when he reflected, "This race of men is disappearing . . . [w]ith them is lost the tradition of cultivated manners. The people become educated, knowledge extends, a middling ability becomes common. Outstanding talents and great characters are more rare. Society is less brilliant and more prosperous."

DEMOCRACY WALL. A public bulletin board on a main street in Peking on which the Chinese may occasionally post a complaint against the government as the only form of their expression of free speech.

DEMOCRATIC SOCIALISM. An economic system which represents a compromise between capitalism and communism. Although a private sector of the economy may continue, for the most part essential industries and services are controlled by the government. The extent of such regulation is determined by a democratic political process, hence the name. In Britain and the Scandinavian countries, for example, where Democratic Socialism has taken hold, all people are assured of receiving adequate health services.

DEMONSTRATIVE EVIDENCE. Real evidence, consisting of things such as a gun or chart, which the jury can observe. The testimony of a witness, on the other hand, supplies the jury with the observations of another. Since "seeing is believing," demonstrative evidence may be quite convincing.

DEMONSTRATIVE LEGACY. A gift intended to be paid from a particular source, but if this source is insufficient to satisfy the legacy, the legacy then is taken out of the general assets of the estate.

DEMOSTHENES (384-322 B.C.). Great Athenian orator and jurist. It is said that the young Demosthenes perfected his speaking voice by practicing his speeches with pebbles in his mouth. The practice would be invaluable to him later, when he would argue political issues in the law courts which served as forums for such debates. The lynchpin of Demosthenes' political views was his concern to persuade Athenians to arm themselves against Macedon, the burgeoning city-state to the north. When the Macedonian warrior Philip II sent an army eastward, threatening Athens' grain supply, Demosthenes delivered his famous speeches vilifying the Macedonian ruler and calling on Athenians to resist him. By 324, both Philip and his son Alexander the Great had defeated the Athenians in battle, and Demosthenes fled the city. When Alexander's successor, Antipater, sent messengers demanding that Demosthenes be surrendered to them, the orator committed suicide.

DÉNIED BOARDING COMPENSATION. See AIRLINE BUMPING.

DENNIS CASE. See SMITH ACT.

DE NOVO (Latin—anew; again; a second time). A Trial De Novo is a new trial of a case, where the entire case will be re-tried as if it had not previously been tried. A Trial De Novo, also known as Venire Facias Des Novo, can be ordered by an appellate court for error in the record of the trial below. In many states, there is an automatic right of Trial De Novo on appeal from the decision of a trial court not of record. An intermediate court will re-try such a case, without reference to the proceedings or decision in the lower trial court.

DE NOVO TEST. See STANDARD OF REVIEW.

DENTAL TECHNICIAN LAW. See DENTURIST LAW.

DENTURIST LAW (Dental Technician Law). A statute passed in 1978, to become effective July 1, 1980, which makes Oregon become the first state to allow non-dentists to fit and sell dentures directly to patients. The law was strongly supported by senior citizens, who are disgusted with the astronomical increase in cost of medical and dental care. For example, it is estimated that a denturist can supply one with dentures at a cost of $250-$300, compared with a price of $600-$2,000 by a dentist.

DENVER BOOT (Boston Buckle). Invented in France and first used in Denver in the United States, hence the name. It is a bright yellow contraption that is clamped on the right front wheel of a car, making it impossible to drive the car. The police place the device on cars owned by people who have not paid their traffic tickets. In Boston, use of the Buckle has proven to be a very effective collection technique in that it has produced an average of $180 per car in unpaid fines. In addition to the inconvenience and embarrassment to the victim, anyone who attempts to remove the device from the car commits a felony for which the punishment is a maximum of 10 years in jail.

DEPARTMENT OF DEFENSE INTELLIGENCE AGENCY. See UNITED STATES INTELLIGENCE-GATHERING CENTERS.

DEPARTMENT OF EDUCATION. The thirteenth unit of the Presidential Cabinet, created in 1979, when the Congress transferred to it most of the education programs formerly in the Department of Health, Education and Welfare (H.E.W.) and simultaneously changed the latter's official name to Health and Human Services (H.H.S.).

DEPARTMENT OF ENERGY. See D.O.E.

DEPENDENT RELATIVE REVOCATION RULE. Relief granted for revocation of a will conditioned upon the existence of facts as the testator believed them to be. Courts may grant relief for mistakes of law—where the Rule against Perpetuities voids a provision in a revoking will or where, upon the mistaken belief that a prior will is revived by revocation of the revoking will, a testator revokes a subsequent will.

DEPLETION ALLOWANCE. A tax deduction allowed for a wasting asset, such as coal or gas reserves, which is consumed. Under the provisions of the Internal Revenue Code, Depletion Allowances may be calculated either on a percentage basis of gross income from the specific asset or on a per-unit-of-production basis.

DEPOSITION PROCEDURE. A procedure which varies, depending on who is being deposed and whether depositions are oral or written. Any party without the aid of a court may depose any person, whether or not a party to a suit. If the deponent is a party, he is required to attend the deposition upon receipt of notice; a non-party may be compelled to attend by subpoena. Oral depositions are taken under oath. As at trial, there is examination and cross-examination. Generally, testimony is recorded by a stenographer and no transcription is made. If the deponent declines to answer certain questions, a court order may be obtained directing him to answer. When written depositions are used, written questions are served on all persons. Cross and re-cross questions may also be served. Questions are then answered orally under oath and the answers are recorded as for oral depositions. At trial, depositions are subject to the rules of evidence. They may be used for impeachment purposes.

DEREGULATION ACT OF 1978. A federal law which will gradually reduce the power of the Civil Aeronautics Board (C.A.B.) to fix airline routes and rates, so that by 1983 there will be complete deregulation and the C.A.B. itself will be abolished by 1985. This was the first time in recent decades that an entire industry was deregulated by law and the concept may rapidly spread to other fields.

DERIVATIVE ACTION. An action brought by a shareholder to assert a legal right of the corporation. The shareholder's suit is "derived" from the corporation's claim and the shareholder sues as a "representative" of the corporation and a class or classes of similarly situated shareholders. Under the majority rule, the shareholder must own the shares at the time of his suit, but this is not required for a suit in a federal court to stop a corporate insider's short-swing trading profits under the Securities Exchange Act. The shareholder must also exhaust the intra-corporate remedies; that is, he must make a demand to the directors to sue, except where such a demand is futile. He must make a similar demand on the shareholders where a mere majority could ratify the alleged wrong, except where futile. Where ratification must be unanimous, the American rule is that a demand is necessary wherever a majority of the shareholders are not wrongdoers. Such requirements may place great financial burdens on the plaintiff. Some states even go so far as to require that the shareholder post security for expenses, for the corporation's legal fees, to show good faith and to prevent blackmail or fraud.

DERIVATIVE EVIDENCE. See FRUIT OF THE POISONOUS TREE.

DERIVATIVE WORK. A dramatization, translation, arrangement, or other significant adaptation of a work in the public domain or a copyrighted work, produced with the consent of the copyright owner. A derivative work is itself subject to copyright. Since there can be few, if any, purely original concepts in literature, the arts or science, a work is derivative only when it borrows in large part from other sources.

DESCRIPTIVE TERMS. In trademark law, such terms describe products and do not perform the essential trademark function of identifying the source of products or services. The term "bouncy," for example, describes a basketball, and does not signify the source of the product or distinguish the basketballs of one manufacturer from those of another. Descriptive terms are not technical trademarks and therefore are not subject to legal protection unless they have attained secondary meaning. Whether a word is descriptive or not depends upon the article to which it is applied. A word which is fanciful for one article may be descriptive when applied to another. For instance, the word "Health" in the phrase "Health Fishing Rods," is fanciful and deserves trademark protection because it is not descriptive of fishing rods. On the other hand, the word "Health" in the phrase "Health Diet Pills" is undeserving of protection because it describes a weight-reducing product.

DESIGNATION PLAN. A program, such as that first adopted by New Mexico, which allows lawyers to proclaim that they are specialists in an area of the law if they can prove that 60 percent or more of their practice in the past five years has been in that field.

DESTINATION CONTRACTS. Term used by commercial lawyers which refers to those agreements or contracts which require that the seller be responsible for the shipment of goods to specific points of delivery.

DETENTION CENTER. A government facility which provides temporary care in a physically restricting environment for juveniles in custody pending court disposition.

DETENTION HEARING. A court hearing to determine whether a child should be kept away from his parents until a full trial of neglect, abuse, or delinquency allegations can take place. Detention hearings must usually be held within 24 hours of the filing of a detention request.

DETENTION REQUEST. A document filed by a probation officer, social worker, or prosecutor with the clerk of a juvenile or family court, asking that a detention hearing be held and that the child be detained until the hearing has taken place. Detention requests must usually be filed within 48 hours of the time protective custody of the child begins.

DETERMINATE SENTENCING. System of fixed, predetermined sentences for given offenses adopted by several states, including Illinois, Maine, California, and Indiana, as a replacement for traditional discretionary release by parole authorities. Under an Indeterminate Sentencing Plan, a convicted individual might receive a sentence of two to ten years, the duration of his actual incarceration to be determined by an evaluation of his progress toward rehabilitation done by prison and parole authorities. One danger of indeterminate sentencing is illustrated by the case of Soledad Brother George Jackson who spent eleven years in prison for a gas station holdup which netted only $70. Associates of Jackson claimed that his refusal to tone down his political militancy was viewed as a failure to cooperate with rehabilitation efforts. By contrast, under Determinate Sentencing the judge imposes an exact penalty—for example, 2 years—which the legislature deemed appropriate for a given offense. That term could be shortened only by good time credits, a day off for each day of infraction-free prison life. Some critics claim that the good time provision only transfers discretion from the qualified prison officials and parole officers down to the least-educated and lowest-paid members of the corrections department guards. An additional criticism is that the inability of judges and parole boards to act mercifully in a given case will increase the pressure on the accused to engage in plea bargaining.

DETERMINATIONS AND FINDINGS (D.&F.). This term refers to written determinations and supporting findings which justify the use of the authority to enter into government procurement contracts by negotiation, make advance payments under negotiated contracts, determine the type of contract to be used, or waive a requirement for submission of cost or pricing data and certification thereof.

DE TOCQUEVILLE, ALEXIS. See DEMOCRACY IN AMERICA.

DETRIMENTAL RELIANCE DOCTRINE. See ESTOPPEL DOCTRINE.

DEVELOPMENTAL JOURNALISM. See NEW WORLD INFORMATION ORDER.

DEVIL'S ADVOCATE. An individual who champions the worse cause for the sake of argument or for the purpose of discovering the whole truth. Attorneys in our adversarial legal system must often play the devil's advocate. The term is derived from the Catholic Church. The Devil's Advocate is an official of the Congregation of Rites, whose duty is to point out flaws in the character of a person who is to be canonized as a saint, or to discover defects in the evidence upon which the canonization is based.

DEVITT COMMITTEE REPORT. A 24-member committee of distinguished judges, lawyers and professors, appointed by Chief Justice Warren Burger in 1978 pursuant to a resolution of the Judicial Conference of the United States and chaired by Judge Edward J. Devitt, to consider uniform qualifications for admission to practice in the federal courts.

Its 10 recommendations were as follows:

1. Minimum uniform standards of competency for attorneys in federal trial courts should be implemented by uniform district court rules providing for an examination in federal practice subjects, and four trial experiences, at least two of which must involve participation in actual trials.

2. Attorneys admitted to the federal bar before the effective date of the adoption of the new standards should not have to satisfy the examination requirement.

3. Each district should adopt these standards as implemented in a uniform rule and create a District Committee on Admission.

4. A performance review system should be instituted in each district to assist in improving the performances of attorneys practicing in that district, and a District Performance Review committee should be created in each district.

5. District courts should adopt a student practice rule to provide second- and third-year law students an opportunity to participate, under close supervision, in the preparation and trial of actual cases.

6. Law schools, with the support of the bench and bar, should make available to students the opportunity to take trial practice courses and to engage in supervised simulated trials.

7. District courts, in cooperation with bar associations and law schools, should periodically sponsor seminars on federal practice subjects and improvement of trial skills.

8. A Standing Committee on Admission to Practice of the Judicial Conference should be created to oversee the development and implementation of uniform national standards.

9. A Committee on Admission to Practice of the Judicial Conference should study developments in testing methods for determining trial skills, the need for continuing qualification of all members of the Bar and the feasibility of sponsoring programs for continuing legal education, particularly with respect to knowledge and developments affecting federal practice, procedure and trial advocacy.

10. The American Bar Association's Code of Professional Responsibility should be examined with a view toward giving more particular and specific guidance to standards for trial advocates.

DEVLIN, BERNADETTE. See LADY ASTOR.

DICKENS, CHARLES. Literary giant famous for his dislike of lawyers and the legal system generally. Although it has been said that Dickens was once a lawyer himself, actually his contacts with the legal profession stem largely from his early work as an office boy in several law firms, and later as a reporter of proceedings in Parliament. Dickens also participated in five law suits against a publisher who had pirated his *Christmas Carol*. As a novelist, Dickens effected more law reform in England in the 19th century than anyone else. His books, such as *Bleak House*, published in 1853, poked such fun at the legal profession that it was forced to take corrective action. His fictitious law suit of Jarndyce v. Jarndyce, for example, is settled only after the lawyers' fees have consumed the entire estate. Vitriolic but effective.

DIEF THE CHIEF. John G. Diefenbacker, country lawyer and progressive conservative Prime Minister of Canda from 1957 to 1963.

DIFFERENTIAL DUTY. See PREFERENTIAL DUTY.

DIFFERING SITE CONDITIONS CLAUSE. In Department of Defense contracting, this clause entitles a contractor to an equitable adjustment when he encounters physical conditions at a construction site materially different from those indicated by the contract or ordinarily encountered.

DIFFUSION THEORY. The doctrine that the burden for any tax is ultimately placed on the consumer in the form of higher prices.

DIGITUS IMPUDICUS (Latin—lewd finger). An upraised middle finger as a sign of arrogant defiance. As an insulting affront, the digital uplift was first used in the fourth century B.C. by the Greek cynic Diogenes against the great orator Demosthenes. It shortly thereafter became the standard reply of a defeated or disgraced gladiator who had been given a thumbs-down verdict of death by Roman Emperor Nero. Among others, it has lately been used by former Vice-President Nelson Rockefeller, tennis star Jimmy Connors, Prince Philip, Prince Charles and Princess Anne of British Royalty. In England the gesture is called a Harvey Smith, after the famed equestrian of the same name who aimed it regularly at horse show judges to whom he had taken a dislike. A Connecticut judge ruled in 1978 that its use could not give rise to a conviction for criminal obscenity since the imperial gesture is intended to arouse anger and not sexual desire.

DILLARD, HARDY CROSS. Distinguished international law expert and former professor of law at the University of Virginia, who was appointed to the World Court by President Nixon in 1971. Upon the expiration of his nine-year term in 1980, he was succeeded by Professor Richard Baxter of Harvard Law School, who was appointed by President Carter.

DILLON ROUND. See TOKYO ROUND.

DILLON'S RULE. A doctrine which limits the power of local government. Expounded by Judge John F. Dillon, an authority on municipal corporations, the rule provides that a local government can exercise only those powers which are granted by the Constitution and laws of the state. Some state constitutions favor local government by providing that the powers of municipalities are to be liberally construed. A growing trend toward home rule for local government has limited Dillon's principle.

DIMICK v. SCHIEDT. See REMITTITUR DOCTRINE.

D.I.N.A. (National Intelligence Directorate). The dreaded secret police in Chile who have the dubious honor of violating more human rights than any other similar group. The agency was abolished in 1977 after it had, among other things, assassinated the former Chilean Ambassador to the United States, Orlando Letelier in Washington, D.C.

DIPLOMA PRIVILEGE. See BAR EXAMINATION.

DIPLOMATIC IMMUNITY. An exception to the principle of international law under which a sovereign state has supreme jurisdiction over its territory and all persons therein. Diplomats are exempt from national and local jurisdictions of the country to which they are accredited. Such immunity applies to civil and criminal fields as well, and includes freedom from prosecution and arrest, and from searches and seizures. The staff and household of diplomats may also be protected. Immunity may be granted them by treaty, and United Nations personnel also enjoy a special status provided by agreement. Immunity does not, however, allow a diplomat to violate the laws of the country to which he is delegated. Sanctions for wrongful conduct may range from a request made by the host country to the foreign government for recalling the diplomat, or waiving his immunity, to extreme cases where a diplomat may be declared Persona Non Grata, and be subject to expulsion. There are 20,000 persons in Washington, D.C., who enjoy Diplomatic Immunity and 6,000 in New York City, the headquarters of the United Nations, the largest number of any country in the world. Despite the fact that the United States had the most generous Diplomatic Immunity Law of any country in the world, it was grossly abused by foreigners living here. Accordingly, Congress in 1978 not only drastically reduced the number of those stationed at each Embassy or Consolate who would be given this privileged status, but also subjected them to being liable for certain crimes such as parking violations and additionally required all foreign embassy officials and employees, including the Ambassador, to carry liability insurance if they operate "any motor vehicle, vessel or aircraft" in the United States.

DIPLOMATIC LANGUAGE. The language of diplomacy that assures mutual certainty of meaning and understanding. Latin was the language of diplomacy until the 17th-century because it was the universal discourse among educated men. Latin was replaced by French which was spoken by educated persons and upper-class students all over the world, and was considered a precise language. Not until 1919, at the Versailles Peace Conference, did English gain equal status with French as the language of diplomacy. In 1945, the United Nations, beginning with its Charter, extended diplomatic authenticity to Chinese, Russian and Spanish.

DIRECT ACTION STATUTE. A state statute which permits an injured party to sue the liability insurer of a tortfeasor, without first having obtained a judgment against the tortfeasor. Such a statute allows an injured party to seek recovery without getting personal jurisdiction over the tortfeasor. These statutes usually provide a remedy if the contract of insurance was made in the state or if the injury occurred there. However, some forums have refused to recognize claims against insurers under the Direct Action Statutes of other states.

DIRECT ATTACK. A challenge to a judgment within the same action, such as an appeal.

DIRECTED VERDICT. A verdict ordered by a judge, despite the presence of a jury. If a judge determines that there is no question for the jury to decide, he may withdraw the case from the jury and direct a verdict. Any party may request a directed verdict after the opposition has presented all its evidence.

DIRECTORY OF INDUSTRY ATTORNEYS. A reference book which provides the telephone numbers of the top officers and legal department staff of the nation's major corporations. Over 750 companies are included.

DIRECTORY OF KEY GOVERNMENT PERSONNEL. Published by Hill and Knowlton and distributed free of charge, this reference book gives the name, address, title and telephone number the important government officials. It is an ideal guide for a lawyer to locate the appropriate person to help the attorney serve his client.

DIRECT TAXES. Taxes demanded of a person who, it is intended, should actually pay. Indirect taxes are demanded of one person in the expectation that he will pass their expense on to another. The question of directness of the income tax was a matter of some concern to the Supreme Court for a number of years. The Constitution provides that direct taxes must be "Apportioned Among the Several States" according to their respective populations, that is, the tax to be collected must be distributed among the states in such a way that the most heavily populated state makes the largest contribution while the state with the least number of citizens, and hence the least representatives in Congress, pays the smallest portion of the tax. This seems quite equitable until we realize that the size of a state's population has little bearing on per capita income. Until 1894 it had been held that the only direct taxes in the constitutional sense, that is, the only taxes subject to the requirement of apportionment, were

property taxes and poll taxes, the latter taxes being payable by a citizen in a flat fixed sum, usually for the privilege of voting. Under this interpretation, a number of analytically direct taxes which had not been apportioned were upheld, among them the first income tax in this country, enacted in 1861. Three decades later, however, this ruling was discarded and the Supreme Court declared that if an income tax was to be levied, the Constitution would have to be amended. This, needless to say, was promptly done in the Sixteenth Amendment.

DIRTY INDUSTRY. Any manufacturing concern or commercial activity which pollutes the environment and is subject to civil and criminal sanctions for failure to comply with federal and state protection standards.

DIRTY THIRTY. See KILLER BEES.

DISCHARGE BY NOVATION. An agreement among three parties which substitutes a new party for one of the parties in a previous contract. As between the original parties to the contract, their obligations are discharged. The novation becomes a new contract.

DISCHARGE OF DEBT. The release of a person's legal obligation to pay his debts, granted by a bankruptcy court. A person adjudged to be bankrupt is granted a Discharge unless certain grounds for opposition are present. Such grounds include fraudulent or immoral actions by the bankrupt party, such as concealing his assets, or a prior Discharge of Debts, obtained within six years of the filing of the debtor's current Voluntary or Involuntary Petition in Bankruptcy. A Discharge will not release the debtor from certain Non-Dischargeable Debts, such as taxes, alimony and child support, wages owed to employees, and debts "not duly scheduled," or reported, by the bankrupt during bankruptcy proceedings. When the debtor is a corporation undergoing a Corporate Reorganization pursuant to a Chapter X Proceeding, or an individual debtor participating in a Wage Earner's Plan pursuant to a Chapter

XIII Proceeding, he is granted a Discharge after completion of a repayment program.

DISCHARGE RULE. A legislative procedure whereby bills not reported out of committee within a particular period of time are subject to discharge for consideration by the full legislature. The Discharge Rule is designed to curtail the power of minority members who may kill new bills by refusing to report them out of committee.

DISCLAIMER CLAUSE. Used to exclude or limit a seller's warranties. Thus, a Disclaimer Clause serves as a seller's defense against a Breach of Warranty suit.

DISCRETE AND INSULAR MINORITIES. See AFFIRMATIVE ACTION.

DISCRETIONARY TRUST. A trust arrangement in which the trustee distributes income or principal as he deems best. Discretionary Trusts are quite popular in family estate planning.

DISCRIMINATORY DUTY. See PREFERENTIAL DUTY.

DISENFRANCHISED VOTER. A person whose voting privilege has been revoked. Disenfranchisement may occur when a person loses his citizenship, is convicted of certain crimes (generally felonies), or fails to reregister to vote. Temporary disenfranchisement may also occur when a person changes domicile.

DISGUISED ALIMONY. See EQUITABLE REMEDY.

DISHONORABLE DISCHARGE (D.D.). A punitive separation from the Armed Forces, awarded as punishment to noncommissioned warrant officers and enlisted personnel by a general court martial. It is the most severe form of punitive separation and is reserved for individuals who should be separated under conditions of dishonor, after having been convicted of offenses usually recognized by the civil law as felonies, or of offenses of a military nature requiring severe punishment. Imposition of a Dishonorable Discharge generally results in the denial of all benefits administered by the Veterans Administration as well as those administered by the military establishment.

DISMISSAL WITHOUT PREJUDICE. Refers to a case which has been dismissed but which may be brought again. Generally, such dismissal results when (1) the court orders dismissal for improper venue or lack of jurisdiction; (2) the plaintiff voluntarily dismisses the case before the defendant has filed an answer or motion for summary judgment; (3) all parties agree the suit should be dismissed; or (4) a party has not been joined in the action. If a claim has previously been voluntarily dismissed, a second voluntary dismissal is likely to be with prejudice.

DISMISSAL WITH PREJUDICE. Generally, when a court dismisses a lawsuit, such dismissal is with prejudice. The result is that the suit cannot be brought again in any court, as if there had been a trial on the merits.

DISORDERLY CONDUCT. A broadly defined criminal offense, used to proscribe all types of unacceptable behavior. The offense is often defined as behaving in a riotous or disorderly manner in any street, public place, school or place of worship.

DISPARAGEMENT OF GOODS (Trade Libel). False or misleading statements about the quality of a competitor's goods, designed to discourage consumers from buying such goods. The question of what type of intent the disparager must have before being held liable is still not settled.

DISPARATE SENTENCING. See SENTENCING PROCEDURES.

DISPLACED HOMEMAKER. An individual 35 years old or older who has worked in the home providing unpaid household services for family members, who is not gainfully employed, and who has become displaced from her position as homemaker due to divorce or widowhood. Various states are now creating service programs to help displaced homemakers become financially secure.

DISPLACED HOMEMAKERS CENTERS. See ALLIANCE FOR DISPLACED HOMEMAKERS.

DISPOSITIVE PROVISIONS. The clause or directive language in a trust agreement or will which relates to the manner in which the property is to be distributed among the beneficiaries.

DISPUTES CLAUSE. The federal government contract clause which prescribes the administrative procedure by which disputes arising under a contract are resolved. Generally, a decision on the dispute is rendered by a contracting officer. This decision may be appealed by the contractor to the appropriate board of contract appeals.

DISTRICT OF COLUMBIA COURTS. In 1970, the District of Columbia Court Reorganization Act ended the system of combining federal and local jurisdiction in the courts of the District. After a brief transition period, federal jurisdiction is to be exclusively vested in the United States District Court for the District of Columbia, with appeals to the United States Circuit Court of Appeals for the District of Columbia. Local jurisdiction was transferred to two local courts: the superior court, which is the new trial court of general jurisdiction, and the District of Columbia Court of Appeals, the highest local court, whose judgments are in turn reviewable by the United States Supreme Court as if they were rendered by a state supreme court.

DIVERSION LAWS. State procedures which place first-time drug offenders on probation for a period of time during which they are lectured on the dangers arising from the use of drugs. If no further offenses occur during this period, the charges are dropped and the record is sealed.

DIVERSITY OF CITIZENSHIP (Diversity Jurisdiction). The condition which exists when the parties to a lawsuit are citizens of different states. Article III, section 2 of the Constitution grants the federal district courts jurisdiction of such cases. By federal stat-ute, the district courts have concurrent jurisdiction of cases in which there is diversity of citizenship and the amount in controversy exceeds $10,000. If such a case is brought in state court, a defendant not a resident of the forum state has a federal statutory right of removal by which the case can be removed to the federal district court for the district in which the state court is located. Note that in a case with multiple parties, there is a requirement of complete diversity: all of the parties on one side must be of different state citizenship from all of the parties on the other side.

DIVIDED CUSTODY. An arrangement whereby custody of the child after divorce is divided between the parents. The danger for the child is that shuttling between parents may cause confusion and insecurity. The advantage for the child is that he or she will know both parents. While historically it has been more common to give the mother custody and the father visitation rights, the modern trend may be leading to divided custody because the mother is no longer presumed to be the best parent.

DIVINE RIGHT OF KINGS. The doctrine that the right to rule is given by God. It is the law of God and of nature that authority is transmitted to a ruler from his ancestors, whom God appointed to rule. Active resistance to the King was a sin because the Sovereign was not accountable to the governed — only to God.

DIVISIBLE DIVORCE. The doctrine that a divorce which is valid to end a marriage will be invalid as to any adjudication of support or property rights unless the court has personal jurisdiction over the defendant in the action. The term "divisible" derives from the fact that one part of the divorce is valid and one part is invalid. The financial and property-division aspects of a divorce decree are considered to be In Personam Judgments. Without In Personam jurisdiction over the defendant spouse, those elements of the decree are not entitled to Full Faith and Credit, though the decree of dissolution is valid and entitled to recognition. For example, if *H* leaves *W* in New York and gets a divorce in Nevada, which decree denies *W* alimony, although the divorce is effective in New York, *W* may sue *H* for alimony in New York because the Nevada court lacked personal jurisdiction over *W* at all times. The Nevada divorce is a divisible divorce, one part of which is valid and one part of which is invalid.

DIVORCE A MENSA ET THORO (Latin—from bed and board). The physical separation of spouses for cause. This remedy, retained in only a very few American jurisdictions, is inherited from ecclesiastical jurisprudence. As in its ancient form, such a decree does not end the economic duties of marriage and it does not free either party to remarry. The parties are divorced for some purposes and still married for others—an awkward social position. The remedy was based on the belief that marriage was a sacrament of the church, indissoluble by man. Therefore, the law could order the parties apart, but the marriage itself could not be dissolved.

DIVORCE A VINCULO MATRI- MONII (Latin—from the bond of marriage). The type of divorce most common in America today. It completely destroys the marriage contract freeing both parties from marital obligations and allowing them to remarry. The A Vinculo or Absolute Divorce was made possible by the Protestant reformers who rejected the belief that marriage was a sacrament which could not be ended by man. Martin Luther was the first to treat divorce as a temporal matter. However, because marriage was central to his social philosophy, Luther was willing to grant an absolute divorce only in cases of adultery and malicious desertion. Still, only the innocent party was free to remarry. After the Reformation of 1560 in Scotland, adultery and desertion as grounds for absolute divorce were incorporated into Scottish law. In America the grounds for allowing an Absolute Divorce vary from state to state. Most states, however, allow

Absolute Divorce on the grounds of adultery, desertion, physical and mental cruelty and insanity. Many states now also recognize No Fault grounds for divorce.

DIVORCE CLINIC. A do-it-yourself divorce business that provides services for persons who desire to represent themselves in marital dissolution proceedings. Such businesses have been held to violate state statutes which forbid the encouragement of divorce as well as statutes which regulate persons who undertake to give legal advice.

DIVORCED MOTHERS. This is a national problem of increasing propor- tions. Women heading families have tripled in numbers since 1960, yet many of these families live in poverty. About 40 percent of divorced mothers receive no financial aid from their husbands after the first year, and their median income was about $6,800 in 1978. Many divorced mothers are living in poverty because women still receive less pay than men, the child support system works poorly, and many employers are unwilling to hire divorced mothers because they may require time off to tend to family responsibilities.

DIVORCE KIT. See DO-IT-YOUR- SELF DIVORCE LAW.

DIVORCE MILL. Any lawyer or state whose practice and policy are both aimed at easy dissolution of a marriage.

D. NOTICES. A guide list on national security information, both civil and military. that every British editor keeps on his desk. It is prepared by a committee of government, military, press and broadcast leaders. If any of this information is made public, the editors can be fined and imprisoned.

DOCTOR OF LAW. See J.D.

DOCTOR - PATIENT PRIVILEGE. Shields from disclosure any information which a physician obtains by examining and communicating with his patient. The privilege is designed to promote sound health by assuring the patient that he can reveal his innermost secrets to a doctor and obtain medical services without fear of public disclosure. Unknown to the common law, the privilege was first established by an 1828 New York statute and is now recognized in a majority of the states.

DOCTOR v. HUGHES. See WORTHIER TITLE DOCTRINE.

DOCTRINE OF MERGER. See RULE IN SHELLEY'S CASE.

DOCTRINE OF PARAMOUNTCY. The unique legal relationship, similar to a Protectorate, between Great Britain and the Princely States of India, which continued from the middle of the nineteenth century to the independence of India in the middle of the twentieth century.

DOCTRINE OF WORTHIER TITLE. An English common-law rule, applied to the following inter vivos transfer: To *A* for life, and upon *A*'s death to my heirs at law. Application of the doctrine resulted in granting *A* a life estate and the grantor a reversion in fee simple. The remainder in the grantor's heirs was not recognized. The majority of the states now treat the doctrine as a rule of construction based on presumed intent. A modern trend rejects the doctrine as either a rule of law or a rule of construction.

D.O.E. (Department of Energy). Created by President Carter on October 1, 1977, as the first new Cabinet-level bureaucracy in over a decade. It absorbed the previous functions of the Federal Power Commission, the Federal Energy Administration, the Energy Research and Development Administration and a dozen smaller federal bureaus, all of which ceased to exist separately. With an annual budget of several billion dollars and a staff of 20,000 employees, it is one of the largest and most important of all federal agencies.

DOE v. COMMONWEALTH'S ATTORNEY (425 U.S. 901 (1976)). A Supreme Court case that summarily affirmed the dismissal of a challenge by male homosexuals to Virginia's sodomy law. The lower court concluded that homosexual acts are "obviously no portion of marriage, home or family life" and thus may be prohibited even when committed (in private) by consenting adults.

D.O.H.S.A. See DEATH ON THE HIGH SEAS ACT.

DOING BUSINESS. One test of minimal contacts necessary to meet the "fair play and substantial justice" requirements in the exercise of personal jurisdiction over a foreign corporation. *McGee v. International Life Insurance Co.*, 355 U.S. 220 (1957) is among the most liberal interpretations of the Doing Business test. There, the defendant insurance company, a Texas domiciliary, assumed the obligations of another insurance company which had issued a policy to a California resident. Although the defendant company conducted no business in California, other than accepting payments from the California policy-holder, California was able to exercise jurisdiction over the company on Doing Business grounds.

DOING BUSINESS AS. See D.B.A.

DO-IT-YOURSELF DIVORCE LAW (No-Hard-Feelings Divorce Law). First enacted by California in 1978 as one of its many liberal innovations in family law, this statute permits childless couples with limited property who have been married less than two years to obtain a divorce for $50 without the services of a lawyer and without going to court.

DO-IT-YOURSELF LAW. The use of self-help books on subjects such as wills, trusts, contracts and bankruptcy. For readers who wish to avoid paying legal fees, these books contain blank forms and instructions on how to complete them. *Divorce Yourself*, for instance, is a $90 kit published by Susan Rabiner in New York. Some states prohibit the publication and distribution of such materials on the grounds that the author is engaged in the practice of law without a license to do so.

DOMBROWSKI DOCTRINE. Deriving from *Dombrowski v. Pfister*, 380 U.S.

479 (1965), this Doctrine attempts to set out the special circumstances in which a federal court may impose the extraordinary remedy of an injunction against a state court proceeding. Generally, such injunctions are forbidden by the Anti-Injunction Act, the Abstention Doctrines, and the notion of equity that federal courts will not interfere with a state's good faith enforcement of its criminal laws. In *Dombrowski,* the Supreme Court held that the plaintiffs were entitled to an injunction to prevent state officers from prosecuting them or threatening to prosecute them under a state law that was so vague and broad that it interfered unconstitutionally with First Amendment rights. The Doctrine articulated by the court seemed to include situations where state law arguably was an unconstitutional curb on First Amendment rights, or where such state law was enforced in a bad faith manner to create a chilling effect on the exercise of First Amendment rights. Since *Dombrowski,* there have been hundreds of cases in the lower federal courts in which litigants have sought to claim the benefits of the doctrine, yet its exact meaning and application remain uncertain.

DOMESDAY BOOK (Doomsday Book). In 1086, under the auspices of William the Conqueror, this survey was compiled to determine the holdings of the crown, to list economic resources for taxation, and to conduct a census. Written in Latin, the two volumes (one is an abridged version) take their title from "domesday," meaning day of judgment, here, in the economic or legal sense. William felt they were necessary because, after the Norman Conquest, he rewarded the faithful with land, thus causing a great change in ownership. The country was divided into districts called "hundreds," each hundred being represented by a 12-man jury that provided information under oath to royal officers. This information included such details as the number of livestock in the district, the amount of arable land, and the number of forests. In addition, descriptions of the towns, customs, and histories were re-corded. Interestingly, London was omitted from the Book. Today, the Book is in the London public record office; it is still used occasionally to trace the title of landowners in real estate transactions.

DOMESTIC CORPORATION. A corporate entity organized under the laws of the particular state. It is subject to In Personam jurisdiction in that state, as well as states where the corporation is doing business, has its principal office, and has minimum contacts. In federal statutes, the term means a corporation organized under the laws of the United States.

DOMESTIC RELATIONS COURT (Family Court). A state court with limited jurisdiction over domestic relations matters, usually including questions of marital status, alimony, divorce, and child custody. These courts are normally found in larger cities, where trial courts of general juirsdiction cannot bear the burden of hearing all domestic relations problems. In some states, the domestic relations courts have been combined with the juvenile court to form family courts, which often make extensive use of specialized counseling, correctional and probation services.

DOMESTIC VIOLENCE AND MATRIMONIAL PROCEEDINGS ACT OF 1976. A law enacted in Great Britain which authorizes restraining orders in spouse abuse cases. The statute provides for orders enjoining the defendant spouse from further offensive conduct and for orders excluding the defendant from the marital home. The English statute goes further than most similar legislation enacted or under consideration in the United States in that it attaches explicit arrest powers to the injunction. A British constable may arrest without warrant a person who he has reasonable cause to believe has violated the provisions of the injunction. This power of arrest is an important aid to the battered spouse, who generally must swear out a warrant for the offender's arrest.

DOMESTIC VIOLENCE ASSISTANCE ACT OF 1978. A proposed federal bill which was rejected by the House of Representatives. The defeat of the measure surprised many Americans. However, many members of the House seem to view domestic violence as a state and local problem, rather than a federal one, while others were concerned about the financial effects of the bill. The Act would have authorized appropriations totaling $125 million over the next five years and would have been established in the Office of the Secretary of the Department of Health, Education and Welfare (H.E.W.) or the Office on Domestic Violence to co-ordinate federal programs and serve as a clearinghouse for information. The Act also would have established a twelve-member Council on Domestic Violence, which would have been responsible for awarding grants to communities to establish and maintain shelter for victims and provide services such as counseling, employment assistance, and legal services.

DOMICILIARY TRUSTEE. A trustee of that portion of the settlor's property which has its situs in the state of his domicile. A domiciliary trustee thus has obvious added responsibilities, especially where the trust property involves land or tangible property which requires close supervision.

DOMINANT CONTACTS RULE. See PLACE OF MOST SIGNIFICANT RELATIONSHIP RULE.

DOMINO THEORY. See A.S.E.A.N.

DONATIO CAUSA MORTIS. See CAUSA MORTIS.

DONEE BENEFICIARY. See THIRD PARTY BENEFICIARY.

DO NOTHING LEGISLATURE. A term of derision used by the press or a Chief Executive to characterize a legislature which has failed to pass laws sponsored by the Chief Executive.

DOOMSDAY CLOCK. A picture which first appeared on the cover of the Bulletin of Atomic Scientists magazine in 1947 to reflect impending nuclear dis-aster. In 1947 the clock was set at 7 minutes to midnight. Based upon international conditions, the time is changed. For example, in 1953 the clock was moved to within 2 minutes of midnight when both the United States and the Soviet Union developed the hydrogen bomb. In 1972, when the Strategic Arms Limitation Treaty (S.A.L.T.) talks led to the first nuclear arms control agreement between the two superpowers the clock was moved back to 12 minutes before doomsday time. In 1974 because of the lack of S.A.L.T. progress and the detonation of a nuclear device by India, the clock advanced to 9 minutes before doomsday. With the invasion of Afghanistan by Russia in December of 1979, it was set at 5 minutes before midnight.

DOOMSDAY MACHINE. A telephone code, changed daily, which is carried by a military aide of the President in a black briefcase. The aide is never more than several feet away from the President who would use the gadget to give an order to respond immediately to a surprise nuclear attack by an enemy.

DOORWAY SEARCH CASE. Decision in *United States v. Santana,* 427 U.S. 38 (1976), that a police officer does not have to obtain a warrant to search a suspect standing in the doorway of a home, so long as the officer has probable cause for arrest. According to the Court a doorway is considered a public place where one need not have any expectation of privacy.

DORMANT ROUTE CASE. The award in November, 1978, by the Civil Aeronautics Board of 248 routes to 22 different airlines, parcelling out then unflown routes to airlines that said they wanted to serve them.

D.O.T.C.A.B. See BOARDS OF CONTRACT APPEALS.

DOUBLE BUNKING. A practice upheld as constitutional by the Supreme Court of the United States, in May of 1979, which consists of housing two prisoners of the same sex in the same cell.

DOUBLE CUTOUT. The use of two dummy recipients to transfer funds secretly, especially on an international level, in order to make secret investments.

DOUBLE DIPPER. A person who takes early retirement from the Armed Forces and then works as a civilian for the federal government. It is perfectly legal to take a military pension as well as the second salary. Tens of thousands do it every year. Some double dippers even have a higher take-home pay than the Cabinet member in whose department they work. Forty receive a total income higher than the salary of the Vice-President.

DOUBLE JEOPARDY. A second prosecution for the same offense or multiple punishments for the same offense. Double jeopardy is prohibited by the Fifth Amendment to the Constitution of the United States, which provides that no person shall "be subject for the same offense to be twice put in jeopardy of life or limb." In 1969, in *North Carolina v. Pearce,* 395 U.S. 711 (1969), the Supreme Court of the United States explained that the Fifth Amendment protected a defendant from double jeopardy whether he had been convicted or acquitted at his first prosecution. That same year, in *Benton v. Maryland,* 395 U.S. 784 (1969), the Court extended the double jeopardy prohibition to the states through the Due Process Clause of the Fourteenth Amendment.

DOUBLE NATIONALITY. Articles 3 to 6 of the Hague Convention of 1930 on the Conflict of Nationality Laws attempt to reduce problems arising from Double Nationality. Such status may result from birth in the territory of a country other than the one of which the parents are nationals, or from the acquisition by a woman of her foreign husband's nationality at the time of marriage. Article 5 of the Convention provides that within a third country a person of double nationality shall be treated as if he only had one nationality. Such country shall recognize exclusively either (1) the nationality of the country of habitual residence, or

(2) the nationality of the country with which the person has the closest connections. Conflicts of allegiance are most frequently resolved by treaties, which tend to confer a right of option on the person concerned, especially when he is a minor. Moreover, the Declaration on the Elimination of Discrimination Against Women of 1967 reduces problems of double nationality for married women.

DOUBLE NICKEL. Colorful Citizens Band Radio (C.B.) terminology for the 55 miles-per-hour speed limit.

DOUGLAS, WILLIAM O. Supreme Court Justice who served longer than any other Justice. Justice Douglas was appointed to the Court in 1939 by President Roosevelt and retired after suffering a stroke in 1975. A leading Court liberal, Douglas strongly advocated human rights and was considered a possible presidential contender in 1948, although he expressed no desire for the office. Douglas taught in the law schools at Columbia and Yale and was a member of the Securities Exchange Commission where he initiated sweeping reforms before joining the Court. Described by his colleagues as generous, extraordinarily competent and creative, a lone eagle, and a great teacher as well as a great jurist, Douglas' outlook is exemplified by his statement: "I think the heart of America is sound. I think the conscience of America is bright. I think the future of America is great." Justice Douglas died in 1980.

DOWER INCHOATE. See COMMON LAW DOWER.

DOWN ZONING. A change in the zoning clasification from a higher valued commercial use to a lower valued residential or conservation use.

DRACONIAN LAWS. Statutes imposing harsh penalties. The term derives from Draco, seventh century B.C. Athenian lawgiver, who drafted one of the earliest written legal codes. For most crimes Draco prescribed the death penalty.

DRAFT DODGER (Draft Evader; Draft Avoider). Persons who dodge subscription into military service during a war. During the Vietnam War, Draft Evaders included the half-million deserters and others who broke the law in order to escape from or protest that War. Another eight million became Draft Avoiders—those who complied with the law but escaped military service on one technicality or another. An example of a Draft Evader is an American who went to live in Canada or Sweden rather than serve in the military. An example of a Draft Avoider is a movie star who received a hardship deferment because of his dependent mother who relied on his $200,000 salary for support. By contrast, more than two million Americans were in military service in Vietnam. Over one million of these were in combat; fifty thousand died, and several hundred thousand were wounded.

DRAGNET CLAUSE. See MOTHER HUBBARD CLAUSE.

DRAGNET RESTRAINTS. In labor disputes, court orders which prohibit almost any action taken by workers to prolong the dispute.

DRAM SHOP LAWS. Impose liability upon liquor store and tavern owners and their employees for injury, loss of family support, and damage to property suffered by third parties. Generally, this liability is based on the fact that a tavern owner served liquor to an intoxicated person or minor, and that the person so served subsequently caused harm to a third person. Enacted in about half the states, the laws vary from state to state. Some impose virtually absolute liability for the violation of the Dram Shop laws.

DRED SCOTT DECISION (*Dred Scott v. Sanford*, 60 U.S. 393 (1857)). A Supreme Court case, in 1857, which struck down the Missouri Compromise, declared slaves to be property with no rights as citizens and thereby laid the foundation for the Civil War.

DREYFUS AFFAIR. Disgraceful persecution by a conspiracy of French Generals, of Dreyfus, a Jewish officer in the French army. Dreyfus was convicted of treason in 1894. The fact that Dreyfus was innocent was well-known to the government, but by convicting a Jew, the government was relieved of the embarrassing prospect of prosecuting the real culprits which included the Chief of Intelligence. Anti-semitism plus public esteem for the Army prevented Dreyfus' exoneration, even in the face of overwhelming evidence of his innocence. Dreyfus was finally vindicated in 1906 and made an officer of the Legion of Honour.

DRINAN BILL (Press Protection Act of 1978). Proposed legislation which would require that a hearing be held before a search warrant could be issued, unless the person being searched was suspected of committing a crime. The Bill is designed to counteract the chilling effect on the press of the Supreme Court's decision in *Zurcher v. Stanford Daily*, 436 U.S. 547 (1978). The *Zurcher* decision gave police officers the power to search private documents and papers of individuals who are in no way implicated in a crime. Reporters believe the decision will inhibit confidential sources because their identity could be revealed by a police search.

DRIVING WHILE INTOXICATED. See D.W.I.

DROIT DES GENS (French—the right of people). The term refers to the concept more widely known as international law.

DROPOUT FATHER. A divorced father who fails to keep up his previous income level on which a support order was based. If the standard is potential rather than actual earnings, then there must be a finding that the father is failing to exercise his capacity to earn in disregard of his parental obligation.

DR. RIBICOFF'S FRIENDLY NEIGHBORHOOD TAX REPAIR SHOP. Named after the Chairman of the Senate Finance Committee International Trade Subcommittee, this group once a year gives any individual or group a hearing of five minutes duration on why a given tariff should be raised, lowered, suspended, modified or instituted. A perfect illustration of special interest pleading.

DRUG COURIER PROFILE. Loosely formulated list of characteristics used by the Drug Enforcement Agency (D.E.A.) to indicate "suspicious" persons. These characteristics include: (1) use of small currency for ticket purchases; (2) travel to and from major drug import centers, especially for short periods of time; (3) absence of luggage or use of empty suitcases; (4) nervousness and (5) use of an alias. D.E.A. agents claim that the presence of a number of these traits suggests that a person may be carrying contraband drugs. However, in *United States v. McCaleb*, 423 F.2d 413 (1977), the Sixth Circuit determined that the profile is not sufficient, in and of itself, to constitute probable cause for the purposes of a legal arrest.

DRUG LAG. See KEFAUVER-HARRIS AMENDMENT.

DRUMHEAD COURT MARTIAL. Historical form of military court assembled for the summary treatment of offenders, usually during a military operation. It derives its name from the practice of the "court's" asembly around an upturned drum for a table.

DRUNK DRIVING. See D.W.I.

DRY CELL. See KEEPLOCK SENTENCING.

DRY TRUSTS. See PASSIVE TRUST.

DUAL NATIONALITY. Simultaneous citizenship by an individual in two or more countries.

DUCES TECUM. See SUBPOENA DUCES TECUM.

DUEL IN THE DARK. The colloquial term for a trial prior to the reform in civil procedure which allowed lawyers to use broad discovery techniques. Before this reform, a trial placed a premium on lawyers' ability to think on their feet in response to unexpected surprise witnesses and evidence. A modern trial is more designed to be effective in its search for the truth.

DUE-ON-SALE CLAUSE (Accelerator Clause). A provision in a mortgage or secured loan agreement which states that the balance of the secured debt becomes due immediately when the property is sold.

DUE PROCESS. The right to due process is guaranteed to individual citizens by the Fifth and Fourteenth Amendments to the Federal Constitution. As now used, the term refers to the rights of an individual to a fair trial and to be free from certain forms of government intrusion.

DUKE POWER CO. v. CAROLINA ENVIRONMENTAL STUDY GROUP, INC. See NUCLEAR DISASTER CASE.

DURAND LINE. The hotly disputed northwest boundary near the Khyber Pass between Afghanistan and Pakistan, established by British Sir Mortimer Durand in the late nineteenth century.

DURHAM TEST. A test for determining criminal responsibility enunciated by Judge Bazelon of the D.C. Circuit in 1954. The test holds that an accused is not criminally responsible if his unlawful act is the product of a mental disease or defect. The Durham Test was praised for its elimination of the right or wrong dichotomy and the cognitive preoccupation of the earlier M'Naghten Test. The new rule implies that the mental disease itself, and not such products as cognitive or volitional impairment, was the excusing factor. As a result, critics suggested that the sole inquiry at trial was the presence or absence of a mental disease or defect, and that in testifying on this ultimate issue the psychiatrist was usurping a jury function. If applied literally, the Test was extremely broad, including virtually all offenders. The Durham Test was hailed as humanitarian by some members of the psychiatric profession and Judge Bazelon was awarded a certificate of commendation by the American Psychiatric Association. But the Test has proved unworkable and has recently been rejected. Crucial application problems centered on the definitions of "disease," "disorder," "defect," and especially "product." There was speculation that even tension headaches would exculpate an individual under the Durham Test.

DUTCH AUCTION. An auction sale where goods are offered at a high initial price and then at successively lower prices until they are sold.

DUTY TO WARN. Duty imposed by some states on therapists to warn of dangers emanating from their patients' mental illness. In 1975, a California court held a University hospital civilly liable for the murder of a young girl by a released mental patient. The patient had threatened to kill the girl, yet his therapists did not disclose this information because disclosure would have breached the confidentiality of patient-therapist communications essential to effective psychiatry.

D.W.I. (Driving While Intoxicated; Drunk Driving). The crime of operating a motor vehicle while under the influence of alcohol. Conviction can result in loss of license, incarceration and fine. European laws are much more severe in their punishment for this criminal offense with many European countries providing for mandatory imprisonment.

DYING DECLARATION. See HEARSAY RULE.

DYNAMITE CHARGE. See ALLEN INSTRUCTION.

E

E.A.E.C. (European Atomic Energy Community; E.U.R.A.T.O.M.). Created in 1957, E.A.E.C. is one of the three European communities. Its primary purpose is to stimulate the rapid growth of nuclear industries in order to improve the standard of living in member states. The purpose of E.U.R.

A.T.O.M. is (1) to develop research and provide for a diffusion of technical knowledge; (2) to establish uniform security norms and supervise their application; (3) to facilitate investments; (4) to provide for regular and equitable supply of nuclear ore and combustibles; (5) to guarantee, by appropriate controls, that nuclear matters are not used for improper purposes; and (6) to create a common market for specialized matters and equipment. E.A.E.C., E.E.C. (European Economic Community) and E.C.S.C. (European Coal and Steel Community) are collectively known as the Common Market.

EARL OF ESSEX. See CROMWELL, THOMAS.

EARNED INCOME CREDIT (E.I.C.). A reduction in tax liability rather than a deduction from taxable income, which is available to taxpayers under certain conditions. (1) You must have maintained a household in the United States; (2) This household had to be the principal home for you and at least one of your children who was less than 19 years old or a full-time student, or your child who is 19 or older and disabled and is entitled to be claimed as a dependent; (3) The Earned Income Credit is 10 percent of the first $4,000 of earned income, for a maximum of $400. However, the maximum credit must be reduced by 10 percent of the amount by which adjusted gross income or earned income, whichever is larger, exceeds $4,000. In other words, you cannot claim the E.I.C. when income reaches $8,000.

EARNED SURPLUS. The balance of corporate net profits, gains, income, and losses, computed from the date of incorporation, which have not been distributed to shareholders as dividends or transferred to stated capital or capital surplus. Earned surplus, commonly referred to as retained earnings, is to be distinguished from capital surplus since it arises from profits realized during the conduct of the business.

EARNEST MONEY. Advance payment of part of the purchase price to bind a contract for real property.

163

EARTH DAY. See SOLAR RESEARCH INSTITUTE.

EASEMENT APPURTENANT. Attached to real property so that it benefits the owner of such property. Typically such an easement consists of access to a highway or street from one piece of property across the property of another.

EAST-WEST CONFLICT. The ideological split between the Communist nations of the East and the capitalist nations of the West.

E.C.A. (Economic Commission for Africa). A specialized agency of the Organization of African Unity (O.A.U.) which is also under United Nations (U.N.) auspices, designed to improve the financial viability of Africa.

ECCLESIASTICAL LAW. The code of conduct governing the religious rites, beliefs and practices of any organized church.

E.C.H.R. See EUROPEAN COURT OF HUMAN RIGHTS.

ECONOMIC AND SOCIAL COUNSEL. (E.C.O.S.O.C.) The United Nations organ responsible for economic and social programs. Its functions include making or initiating studies, reports, and recommendations on international economic, social, cultural, educational, health, and related matters; promoting respect for, and observance of, human rights and fundamental freedoms for all; calling international conferences and preparing draft conventions for submission to the General Assembly on matters within its competence; negotiating agreements with the specialized agencies and defining their relationship with the United Nations; coordinating the activities of the specialized agencies; and consulting with non-governmental organizations concerned with matters within its competence. The Council consists of 54 members of the United Nations elected by the General Assembly for 3-year terms; 18 are elected each year.

ECONOMIC COMMISSION FOR AFRICA. See E.C.A.

ECONOMIC COMMUNITY OF WEST AFRICAN STATES. See E.C.O.W.A.S.

ECONOMIC DEVELOPMENT ADMINISTRATION. See E.D.A.

ECONOMIC DIVORCE. Refers to the division of property between the spouses when a legal dissolution of a marriage occurs. This is perhaps the most critical aspect of a divorce. The distribution of marital assets and the flow of support money from one spouse to another affects the well-being of any children born of the marriage, the future life-style of both spouses and their subsequent families and, ultimately, the self-respect and autonomy of the divorced parties. It is essential that the legal system provide equitable and efficient means whereby the parties to a broken marriage may not only have their marriage dissolved, but may have their economic lives disentangled as well. Most states have conferred some power upon their divorce courts to adjudicate personal and real property rights between divorcing spouses. Only three states (Virginia, Mississippi and South Carolina) do not allow their divorce courts jurisdiction over property rights.

ECONOMIC ESCAPEES. See POLITICAL REFUGEES.

ECONOMIC OPPORTUNITY ACT OF 1964. A federal act intended to further the War on Poverty by helping the poor become self-sufficient.

ECONOMIC SANCTIONS. Means of enforcing international obligations by economic and financial pressure. Examples would be the ineffective United Nations boycott of chrome directed at Rhodesia for its apartheid policies or the similar unsuccessful unilateral boycott of Cuba by the United States.

ECONOMIC STRIKE. Work stoppage designed to effect economic objectives, e.g., higher wages. "No Contract, No Work" would be an example of placard legend in an economic strike.

E.C.O.W.A.S. (Economic Community of West African States). An association of 16 West African countries which banded together in 1975 in order to constitute an economic common market by the year 1993 including the elimination of customs and tariff duties, free movement of workers and convertibility of currencies. Meanwhile, they cooperate in other respects such as recognizing existing borders as being definitive and agreeing not to attack each other.

E.C.S. See EUROPEAN CURRENCY SYSTEM.

E.C.S.C. See EUROPEAN COAL AND STEEL COMMUNITY.

E.C.U. See EUROPEAN CURRENCY SYSTEM.

E.D.A. (Economic Development Administration). A successful business loan program of the United States Department of Commerce. It was instituted in 1965 as a lender of last resort in areas of low income and high unemployment, especially for minorities, companies hurt by foreign imports and public works such as roads, sewers and community development.

EDEN PLAN. See COUNCIL OF EUROPE.

E.D.F. (European Development Fund). An organization created by several European countries in order to coordinate their financial and technical assistance to Less Developed Countries (L.D.C.s).

EDGE BANKS. The sobriquet for financial institutions engaging in international banking operations. The name derives from the Edge Act (1919), a federal law which permitted the federal incorporation of such banks.

EDUCATIONAL COUNSELING AIDS. See ASSOCIATION OF TRIAL LAWYERS OF AMERICA.

EDUCATIONAL RIGHTS AND PRIVACY ACT OF 1976. A federal law which prohibits schools from showing student records to outsiders without prior written parental permission which can be tough on a parent (usually a father) when the other spouse has been granted legal custody of a child.

EDUCATIONAL TRUST. A trust arrangement set up to provide funds for educational purposes. Often grandparents design such trusts for the benefit of grandchildren.

EDUCATION OF ALL HANDICAPPED CHILDREN ACT. A federal law passed by Congress in 1975, which became effective in 1977. It requires every school system in the United States to provide individualized education by September of 1978 to the 3-1/2 million children with physical, mental or emotional handicaps who previously had been ignored by the public educational system. Any school which does not fully comply forfeits all federal support.

EDUCATION VOUCHERS. Education tax money that parents could choose to spend on the private or public school of their choice. Proponents of the vouchers, including two law professors from the University of California at Berkeley, believe that such vouchers would increase competition among the various public schools as well as competition between private and public school systems to improve their programs. Opponents of Educational Vouchers point to the potential for increasing, rather than decreasing, racial segregation in schools.

E.E.C. See EUROPEAN ECONOMIC COMMUNITY.

E.E.O.C. (Equal Employment Opportunity Commission). A federal agency whose purpose is to end discrimination based on race, color, religion, sex, or national origin in hiring, promoting, firing, wages, testing, training, apprenticeship, and all other conditions of employment. The E.E.O.C. also promotes voluntary action programs by employers, unions, and community organizations to make equal employment opportunity an actuality. Its main defect is a chronic backlog of more than 100,000 cases to process despite its $77 million budget and 2,500 employees.

E.E.Z. (Exclusive Economic Zone). The recent establishment of a 200-mile Exclusive Economic Zone, a significant new development in Ocean law, gives coastal nations resource jurisdiction over an area approximately the size of the earth's present land.

E.F.T.A. See OUTER SEVEN.

E.I.C. See EARNED INCOME CREDIT.

EICHMANN TRIAL. Adolf Eichmann, former chief of the Nazi organization entrusted with the so-called "final solution of the Jewish question," was tried before an Israeli court in 1961, found guilty of war crimes and hanged. The Eichmann trial is of particular interest to the legal profession because it raises serious questions which challenge the legality of the trial under commonly accepted rules of international and criminal law. Eichmann was kidnapped from Argentina in order to stand trial in Israel, was tried for crimes committed outside the jurisdiction of Israel, and was tried under a retroactive law. Despite its questionable legality, the Eichmann Trial served to reaffirm the principle that responsibility for crimes against humanity should lie with those who commit the crimes, and strengthened the proposition that blind obedience to authority is no defense to the commission of heinous crimes such as genocide.

EIGHT-A CONTRACTS (8-A Contracts). A federal program to enable minority groups to win procurement orders from Uncle Sam by making special S.B.A. grants to companies which are at least 51 percent owned and operated by members of minorities. In order to permit them to compete with big companies in procurement orders, the S.B.A. makes up for the difference between the price the federal government is willing to pay for goods or services and the production cost, plus margin, of the small businessman.

EIGHTEEN-B (18-B) **LAWYERS.** Named after Article 18-B of the County Law of New York State which provides for the appointment and reimbursement of lawyers for indigents in criminal cases who are not already represented by the Legal Aid Society. The fees are $15 an hour for time spent in court, $10 an hour for other time and a maximum of $1,500 per case, all of which is paid by public funds.

EIGHTH SISTER. See SEVEN SISTERS.

E.I.S. See ENVIRONMENTAL IMPACT STATEMENT.

EISENHOWER DOCTRINE. A joint congressional anti-Soviet resolution signed into law by President Dwight D. Eisenhower in 1957. It stated that the United States regarded the Middle East as vital to its national interest and, if requested, would use armed forces to assist any Middle Eastern nation in resisting foreign intervention.

EJUSDEM GENERIS (Latin—of the same kind). A rule of construction which provides that if general words in an instrument follow words with a specific meaning, such general words are not to be given their broadest possible meaning, but are to be confined to things of the same kind or class as those specifically mentioned, except where a contrary intention of the parties is shown to exist. For example, if a statute refers initially to the operation of trucks over a particular tonnage, a subsequent reference in the same statute to motor vehicles is to be construed to refer only to trucks over the previously specified tonnage and not to all motor vehicles.

ELECTORAL COLLEGE. The complex process which determines the outcome of national elections for President and Vice-President. Before the presidential election, each political party in each state chooses a partisan slate of electors equal to the number of the state's representatives in both houses of Congress. During the presidential election, the party whose candidate receives a plurality of the state's popular votes sends its slate to the Electoral College, held in the state capital. The candidates receiving a majority of electoral votes (270) are elected President and Vice-President. Because the electoral vote often does not accurately reflect the popular vote, three popular-vote losers—Adams in 1824, Hayes in 1876, and Harrison in 1888 — became electoral-vote winners and were elected as minority Presidents. The obvious inequities of the Electoral College system prompted several distinguished critics to advocate its abolition.

ELECTRONIC SURVEILLANCE COURTS. In October, 1978, Congress established a special federal court to consider and then grant or deny applications for electronic surveillance within the United States in foreign counter-intelligence (F.C.I.) cases. These applications would be first filed with one of the senior United States district judges; and, when review is sought from a denial, appeal could be made to a special review court of three federal judges, with a final review possible on writ of certiorari to the United States Supreme Court.

ELEEMOSYNARY TRUST. See CHARITABLE TRUST.

ELEMENTARY AND SECONDARY EDUCATION ACT OF 1965. The first major federal assistance program for education, providing aid for both public and parochial schools. This groundbreaking statute set the stage for continued federal assistance for education. Its passage was a victory for politicians and educators who claimed that federal aid to education did not signal federal control of local schools.

EL FATAH. See P.L.O.

ELIZABETHAN POOR LAW. See RELATIVE RESPONSIBILITY STATUTES.

ELKINS ACT (1903). A federal statute which forbids interstate carriers from offering secret rebates or discriminatory concessions to shippers.

ELKINS v. UNITED STATES. See SILVER PLATTER DOCTRINE.

EMANCIPATED MINOR. See UN-EMANCIPATED MINOR.

EMBARGO ACT OF 1807. A federal statute promulgated by President Thomas Jefferson which, with similar legislation passed by Congress the following year, forbade the further legal importation of slaves.

EMERGENCY CUSTODY. The ability of a law enforcement officer, pursuant to a criminal code, to take temporary custody of a child who is in immediate danger and place him in the control of a child protective service. A custody hearing must usually be held within 48 hours of such action.

EMERGENCY GOVERNMENT. Term coined by Senator Frank Church and the Special Committee on National Emergencies and Delegated Emergency Powers, to describe vast presidential powers triggered by 470 emergency statutes. Many of the statutes were hastily considered, provide for no review by Congress, and often have no means for terminating their use, even though most are designated "temporary" laws. A typical example is the 1861 Feed and Forage Act, passed to enable the cavalry to feed their horses when Congress was not in session, and used by Defense Secretary Melvin Laird to defend paying American troops in Cambodia, even though Congress had decided to cut off funding for such troops.

EMERGENCY HOSPITALIZATION. Designed to provide immediate care to an individual suffering from acute mental illness. Therefore, procedural safeguards which ordinarily protect the individual's liberty are suspended. In most states no judicial approval is required for Emergency Hospitalization, merely certification by one or more physicians that the patient needs to be confined. Typically the patient is taken to the emergency room of a general hospital or, absent room facilities, to a local jail. Emergency Hospitalization is not intended to replace the regular commitment process. It can effect hospitalization for only a limited period of time, ranging from twenty-four hours to thirty days. However, many states allow further retention of the patient for a longer term at the end of the statutory emergency period without resort to the usual commitment process.

EMERGENCY PROVISION. That provision in a trust arrangement which empowers the trustee to pay or apply trust income or principal to meet certain situations that might arise during the life of a beneficiary such as accident or illness. Equally, such a provision will often include maintenance allowances, as well as providing for a wide variety of circumstances that the trust settlor has the good judgment to anticipate.

EMERGENCY SPECIAL SESSIONS. See GENERAL ASSEMBLY.

E.M.I. See EXTRA-MILITARY INSTRUCTION.

EMINENT DOMAIN. The power of a government to take private property for public purposes upon payment of just compensation to the owner.

EMOTIONAL DISTRESS. Usually an intentional tort in which a person acts in an extreme and outrageous manner, causing severe emotional distress or mental anguish in another. Typical examples are bullying tactics used by bill collectors or landlords.

EMPLOYEES TRUST. A trust arrangement established by a corporate employer for the benefit or remuneration of its employees. Employees Trusts constitute insurance trusts, stock option trusts, stock bonus trusts, pension trusts and many related arrangements.

EMPLOYEE THEFT. Accounts for more inflationary waste than shoplifting. In 1978, a management-engineering firm estimated that for every dollar spent in a supermarket, it costs fifteen cents to cover employee theft. While supermarket shoplifting only averages $6 per theft, employee theft averages $50 per transaction. Generally an employee will under-ring or void items for friends and relatives, which re-duces the likelihood of being caught. Ex-employees or presently-employed workers also account for approximately 20 percent of all supermarket robberies.

EMPLOYMENT RETIREMENT INCOME SECURITY ACT. See E.R.I.S.A.

E.M.S. See EUROPEAN CURRENCY SYSTEM.

EN BANC (French—on the bench). The consideration of a case by a full circuit court of appeals, rather than by a single judge or a three-judge panel. The advantage of an en banc hearing is that it avoids formal conflicts of interest within a circuit and promotes finality of decision in important appeals cases. By statute, a majority of circuit judges in active service in a circuit may order a hearing or rehearing of a case before the entire court. Use of an en banc procedure has become more frequent since its approval by the United States Supreme Court in 1943. The procedure itself is described in Rule 35 of the Federal Rules of Appellate Procedure. It is also used by state courts.

ENCUMBRANCE TO PROPERTY. Binding claim or liability attached to real property. Encumbrances are generally liens which affect the title to the property or restrictions which affect the physical use of property, such as easements or encroachments.

ENDANGERED SPECIES ACT OF 1973. Empowers the Secretary of the Interior to declare a species of plant, animal, bird, or fish to be endangered. Once a species has been identified as endangered all federal agencies must refrain from actions which may jeopardize the continued existence of the endangered species. Interpreting this Act to apply to agency actions already undertaken, the Supreme Court in *T.V.A. v. Hill*, 437 U.S. 153 (1978), ordered construction of the $100 million Tellico Dam, which was 75 percent completed, to cease, lest the endangered snail darter (a fish) be jeopardized. An amendment to the Act also prohibits interstate sale of scrimshaw as of 1980. "Scrimshaw" refers to jewelry or other objects fashioned of whalebone or teeth that are carved or otherwise decorated. Critics of this amendment believe that a legitimate folk art form is being eliminated from the market, and that sale of antique scrimshaw does not endanger modern whales.

END USE STATEMENT. A provision in an international contract that the foreign party will not use the American goods or services for military purposes.

ENERGY MOBILIZATION BOARD. A three-member federal agency created by congress in 1979 to fix binding timetables for action by federal, state and local energy officials to expedite the development of energy projects such as refineries and pipelines by cutting through red tape and roadblocks of every type.

ENERGY PETROLEUM ALLOCATION ACT. A law passed by congress in 1973 which gave the Department of Energy (D.O.E.) the power to direct the distribution of gasoline supplies to the nation's 12,000 wholesalers and 225,000 retailers, whenever shortages occur. The country is divided into five areas known as Petroleum Administration for Defense Districts (P.A.D.D.s). Late each month, all the oil companies estimate approximately how much fuel they will have available for sale in each region in the coming month. From this total supply, they subtract 5 percent to be set aside and distributed at the discretion of state authorities to alleviate local crises. They then subtract the amount they will require to supply all the needs of top priority customers like the military and farmers. The rest is divided among retail gas stations throughout the nation.

ENERGY SECURITY CORPORATION. An organization outside the federal government created by congress in 1979 to use independent business judgment in order to encourage the creation of alternative energy sources to oil in order to replace two and one-half million barrels of imported oil per day by 1990. The corporation will issue up to $5 billion in energy bonds, in small denominations, so that average Americans can invest directly in America's energy security.

ENERGY SECURITY TRUST FUND. A program created by congress in 1979 consisting of billions of dollars (arising from a tax on oil company profits) to be spent by the federal government annually in order to reduce American dependence on foreign oil.

ENERGY TAX ACT OF 1978. Instead of four major new energy taxes proposed by President Carter's National Energy Plan, this new federal law contains only a scaled-down version of the original gas-guzzler tax. It also provides a tax credit for installing household insulation and other energy-saving measures and an additional ten percent investment tax credit for expenditures on new energy technologies.

ENGEL'S LAW. The doctrine that the standard of living of a particular group may be measured by determining the percentage of income spent for food. The underlying theory is that low income groups spend a larger proportion of their income on food.

ENGLISH BARRISTER. An English lawyer who renders legal advice to solicitors and conducts cases in the higher Courts. Barristers are divided into two ranks: Junior barristers and Queen's counsel (Q.C.). The latter are referred to colloquially as "Silks," from the fact that they are entitled to wear a silk gown which distinguishes their elite status. In spite of the barrister's attractive social status, his income is relatively low—undoubtedly a factor in the declining number of practising barristers in England.

ENGLISH SOLICITOR. An English lawyer who handles the office work of a case. A solicitor gives legal advice, prepares legal documents, and handles the day-to-day legal work. He may not appear before a court, and must appoint a barrister to appear for him if his client's case must go to court.

ENOCH ARDEN STATUTE. When a person is missing for a set number of years, this statute permits the presumption of death to permit the surviving spouse to remarry, the family to receive insurance payments, or any other legal consequence of death. The periods vary among the states, ranging from two years to seven years, with five years being quite common. The statute is named after the protagonist of a Tennyson poem, who returned home after a ten-year absence due to a shipwreck to find his wife married to another man.

ENTITLEMENT AUTHORITY. In the federal budget, legislation that requires the payment of benefits or entitlements to any person or government meeting the requirements established by such law. Mandatory entitlements include social security benefits and veterans' pensions. Section 401 of the Congressional Budget and Impoundment Control Act of 1974 restricts the enactment of new entitlement authority.

ENTITLEMENTS PROGRAM. Established by President Ford in 1974 to equalize the burdens of rising oil import prices between refineries that depend on expensive foreign oil and those with supplies of low-cost domestic petroleum. The complex program works this way: For every barrel of domestic crude that a refinery processes, the company must make a payment into an entitlement pool. The payment raises the price of each barrel of domestic oil halfway up to the cost of more expensive foreign crude. At the same time, any refinery that imports costlier foreign crude gets to withdraw an equal amount from the pool. For example, a refinery that buys domestic oil for $9.45 a barrel would pay $2.50 to the fund; a refinery that imports foreign oil for $14.55 would then collect that $2.50.

ENTITY THEORY (Fiction Theory). A theory of ecclesiastical law based on the concept of the corporation as a fictitious person, or a separate juristic entity, thus making it incapable of committing torts and crimes requiring human intent.

ENTRAPMENT DEFENSE. A claim by the defendant that the intent to commit the crime, not merely the opportunity to commit it, originated with law enforcement officers. The prosecution may defeat this defense by showing that the defendant was predisposed to commit the crime.

ENTRUSTMENT AGREEMENT. Consent by parents transferring their child to a licensed private adoption agency or welfare board to enable the child to become adopted by strangers and severing their legal relationship as parents.

ENTRY INTO FORCE (Enter Into Force). The process by which a treaty or other international agreement takes effect. This phrase, a technical term in international law, indicates the date at which an agreement is binding on those who sign it, as opposed to when it is prepared. A treaty may state that it is not binding until a particular date or until a specified number of nations sign or otherwise ratify it and thereby become party to it. The treaty enters into force at the point where the conditions it sets forth are met. In some cases, years pass between the time a multinational treaty is drawn up and the date the requisite number of nations sign it and allow it to enter into force.

EN VENTRE SA MERE TRUST. (French—in mother's womb.) A trust arrangement to benefit a child in gestation. Traditionally, such trusts were used by European aristocratic families to divest interests such as estates in land in favor of an expected child of noble background.

ENVIRONMENTAL IMPACT STATEMENT (E.I.S.; IMPACT STATEMENT; I.S.). A document which must be prepared by a federal agency proposing any major action that will affect the environment, including its social and aesthetic aspects. First required by the National Environmental Policy Act (1969), Impact Statements are designed to encourage the agency's consideration of environmental factors in its decision-making, and to provide the President and Congress with an adequate basis to review and perhaps to redirect the agency's action in light of its effect on the environment. The procedures for the preparation of Impact Statements established by the Council on Environmental Quality also provide for participation of private citizens, at public hearings considering a draft Impact Statement, before preparation of the final statement. A number of states require state and local agencies to prepare reports similar to the Federal Impact Statements.

ENVIRONMENTAL PROTECTION AGENCY. See E.P.A.

E-1 OR E-2 VISA. See H-1 VISA.

E.P.A. (Environmental Protection Agency). A federal agency whose purpose is to protect and enhance our environment. In co-operation with state and local governments, the agency mounts a co-ordinated attack on environmental pollution in the areas of air, water, solid waste pesticides, noise, and radiation.

E PLURIBUS UNUM (Latin—one out of many; i.e., one formed out of many). The motto on the Great Seal of the United States, and on many United States coins. The motto was chosen for the Continental Congress in 1776 by John Adams, Benjamin Franklin, and Thomas Jefferson. It was then later incorporated into the Great Seal, designed in 1782.

EPPERSON v. ARKANSAS. See MONKEY TRIAL.

EQUAL ACCESS TO JUSTICE ACT. A federal law proposed in 1979 by Senator Comenici, Republican of New Mexico, which would award both administrative and court litigation costs to the prevailing party in a lawsuit with a government agency.

EQUAL CREDIT OPPORTUNITY ACT (1976). A federal statute which makes it unlawful for any creditor to discriminate against a credit applicant on the basis of race, color, religion, national origin, sex, marital status or age, or because an applicant derives income from a public assistance program. Within a reasonable period of time after receiving an application for credit, generally thirty days, a creditor is required to notify an applicant of action on the credit application. Further, each applicant against whom adverse action is taken is entitled to a statement of reasons for such action from the creditor. Any creditor who fails to comply with the Act is liable for actual and punitive damages.

EQUAL DIGNITY RULE. A rule of agency law, whereby the authority given to an agent is entitled to as much dignity as the principal contract. Thus, if an agent is authorized to sell land on behalf of a principal, the authorization must be in writing because the agreement for the sale of real property must be in writing.

EQUAL EMPLOYMENT OPPORTUNITY COMMISSION. See E.E.O.C.

EQUAL RIGHTS AMENDMENT. See E.R.A.

EQUAL TIME RULE. The requirement that broadcasters who permit any legally qualified candidate for any poiltical office to use a broadcasting station must afford equal opportunities to all other such candidates for the same office. Appearances by candidates on documentary programs, interviews or bona fide new reports do not however give rise to equal time rule requirements. The Carter-Ford debates of 1976 proceeded under this exception and the fact is that the rule has fallen into disfavor recently. The Kennedy-Nixon debates of 1960 were carried pursuant to a congressionally enacted exemption to the rule.

EQUIPMENT TRUST. A trust which finances the acquisition of heavy equipment. Such modern business financing arrangements are quite popular, especially in the transportation industry.

EQUITABLE ADJUSTMENT. In federal government contracting, this term describes the adjustment in contract price to which a contractor, or the government, is entitlted as a result of changed work pursuant to a change order under the Changes Clause, constructive change or, under certain conditions, other contract clauses.

EQUITABLE ADOPTION (Adoption by Estoppel). Recognition of a parent-child legal relationship despite some defect in the adoption proceeding.

EQUITABLE INTEREST. See BENEFICIAL INTEREST.

EQUITABLE OWNERSHIP. In a trust arrangement, the trust beneficiary is said to have Equitable Ownership of the trust property, whereas the Trustee holds legal or actual ownership. For example, where a trust arrangement involves $100,000 invested for the benefit of X, who receives quarterly distributions of income earned thereon, the trust trustee really owns the funds legally, and if a problem of priority arises, the trust beneficiary must initiate action as an Equitable Owner to secure what is legally not "really" his. Historically, the trust beneficiary was said to have an equitable trust title, which indicated a right to the benefits of the trust arrangement enforceable in a court of equity.

EQUITABLE REMEDY IN NONMARITAL COHABITATION. (Disguised Alimony; Palimony; Severance Pay). A new principle of family law just announced by Judge Arthur K. Marshall of California in the Lee Marvin case in 1979. The court ruled that when a woman who has lived with a man cannot prove the existence of an express contract, oral or written, or implied contract, to share his assets after they separate, she is entitled to a fixed sum of money in order to have the economic means to re-educate herself and to learn new employable skills or to polish her former skills in order to support herself. In this case, Michelle Triola was awarded $104,000 which was a payment equal to the higest sum she had ever earned ($1,000 a week as a singer) for a period of two years. If the parties had been legally married, the award would have been called Rehabilitative Alimony.

EQUITY COURT. See COURT OF CHANCERY.

EQUITY OF REDEMPTION. The power of a homeowner mortgagor who is behind in his payments to avoid forfeiture of his property by going to a court of chancery. If, within a reasonable time after the due date, payment of all past principal and interest is made to the bank mortgagee, title to the land will be returned to the homeowner. Any attempt by a Simon Legree to include in the original contract a waiver of the Equity of Redemption power (called a Clog on the Equity of Redemption) is declared void on the grounds of public policy.

EQUITY RECEIVERSHIP. See UMBRELLA RECEIVERSHIP.

EQUITY SHARES. Corporate shares of any class which have a right to unlimited dividends. Unlike Debt Securities, such shares do not have a right to interest. The distinction between Debt Securities and Equity Shares is sometimes difficult to draw, but factors which indicate that shares are equity include (1) a right to vote, (2) participation in corporate profits, and (3) an undetermined date for payments by the corporation in return for the sum contributed. One who holds Equity Shares in a corporation is an owner of the corporation, as opposed to the debtor-creditor relationship created between the holder of Debt Securities and the corporation. The holder of Equity Shares may not compete with creditors of the corporation.

E.R.A. (Equal Rights Amendment). The proposed 27th Amendment to the Federal Constitution which will become the law if ratified by three fourths of the states (38 out of 50) on or before 1982 which is seven years from the date Congress first passed the law. Of the 35 states which have already ratified the Amendment, three (Idaho, Nebraska and Tennessee) have since attempted to rescind their approval. Some commentators say that this change of heart is unconstitutional. The proposal is the essence of simplicity in its brief dynamic statement: "Equality of rights under the Law shall not be denied or abridged by the United States or any State on account of sex." Contrary to the popular belief of some, the E.R.A. will not affect rights of privacy, personal relationships or private contracts. It will not break up families, disrupt Social Security, cause women to be drafted, prescribe coed toilets, legalize homosexual marriages, permit abortion on demand, or force housewives to take paying jobs. On the other hand, E.R.A. may help to remedy the bleak situation for women in jobs, pay, and housing. According to a 1978 U.S. Civil Rights Commission report, women have failed to make any significant strides toward economic and social equity with white men since 1960. Women still earn just half that which white males earn and college-educated women generally earn less than men with high school diplomas.

ERIE DOCTRINE. Derived from *Erie R.R. Co. v. Thompkins*, 304 U.S. 64 (1938), the Erie Doctrine holds that in diversity actions a federal court must apply state substantive judicial, as well as statutory, law. The Erie Doctrine upholds fundamental principles of separation of powers and attempts to prevent forum shopping by reducing the differences in outcome of cases brought in state and federal courts.

E.R.I.S.A. (Employee Retirement Income Security Act). A complicated law passed by Congress in 1974, designed to protect the rights of employees in employer pension plans in which they participate. It was promulgated as a result of vast previous misuse of pension funds and poor management of pension plans. Since the problem was national in nature, the law applies throughout the entire country and supersedes state laws. Strict rules are established for the administration of the pension plans and heavy penalties are provided for violators. As a direct result of this law to benefit employees, its cost and red tape eliminated 7,000 private pension plans in small businesses during the first year of its application.

ERITREAN (PEOPLES) LIBERATION FRONT. Military guerilla rebels in the Northeast of Ethiopia who have been fighting to secede by force since 1961. They were slowed down after the overthrow and death of Emperor Haile Sellassie when the Rusians supplied the government with one million dollars worth of arms in 1978 and the Cubans sent 20,000 mercenary troops to crush the 40,000 secessionists. Since the Province of Eritrea is Ethiopia's only access to the Red Sea, the establishment of Russian naval bases on this crucial international waterway and ensuing control of the Suez Canal is an ominous development for the West.

ERRORS AND OMISSIONS INSURANCE. Protects against liability for misquoting, misrepresenting or erroneously editing the work of an artist. It is available for motion pictures as well as for television.

ESCALATOR CLAUSE. Allows for an increase in rent, alimony, child support or mortgage payments in the event certain specified events occur. The increase may be determined at will or may be a pre-set amount. Examples of the contingencies which may activate an escalator clause are sharp rises in the cost of living caused by inflation and unexpected increases in the value of the property. The Consumer Price Index is often used as a guide for any adjustment in payment.

ESCALATOR MORTGAGE (Interest Adjustment Clause Mortgage). A real estate loan which calls for adjustment of the interest rate after a certain period, usually three or four years. The adjustment may be linked to an index. It has wide use in Wisconsin and other Midwest states.

ESCAPE CLAUSE. Found in contract of sale for real estate. Such a clause protects a prospective buyer who is unsure of his ability to obtain a mortgage with which to finance the purchase. If he cannot secure suitable financing, the escape clause releases him from his obligations under the contract. Clauses of this type most often are used in connection with applications for mortgages from the Veterans' Administration or the Federal Housing Administration.

ESCHEAT DOCTRINE. Provides that real property reverts to the state if the property owner dies intestate and has no heirs. State laws regarding escheats allow several (in some cases as high as twenty) years for heirs to come forward and claim their inheritance, and usually provide that money realized on escheated property be paid to some charitable fund maintained by the state.

ESCOBEDO v. ILLINOIS (378 U.S. 478 (1964)). The defendant, a murder suspect, while being interrogated at the police station, requested to consult his attorney. Although his attorney was present at the station, the defendant's request was denied. During the interrogation, the defendant, when confronted with an accomplice's statement that he (the defendant) was guilty, retorted, "I didn't shoot Manuel, you did it." The prosecution sought to use this seemingly exculpatory statement to show knowledge. The Supreme Court held that the statement was illegally obtained in violation of the defendant's Sixth Amendment right to counsel, and thus inadmissible. The Court further held that when an investigation has become focused on an accused, he may refuse interrogation in the absence of his attorney.

ESCROW AGREEMENT (French—escroue: a strip of parchment or bond or writing). An agreement whereby money, securities, instruments or live property is given by one person to a third party to hold "in escrow" until the occurrence of a certain event. A landlord places a tenant's security deposit "in escrow" at a bank to be returned to the tenant upon expiration of the lease and return of the premises in an undamaged condition; another example would be the purchase price for the sale of a home, customarily placed "in escrow" to be delivered to the vendor upon the final closing of the deal.

ESCROW FUNDS. Money given to a third party to hold until all conditions in an agreement are fulfilled.

ESQUIRE TITLE (Esq.). Courtesy title after a lawyer's name, derived from a word for shieldbearer or squire. To language purists, the masculine term should only be used in connection with male lawyers; however, others point out that the title has come to mean simply an indication of courtesy, which should naturally be extended to female as well as male lawyers.

ESTATE BY THE ENTIRETY. See TENANCY BY THE ENTIRETY.

ESTATE FOR YEARS. A tenancy for a specified period of time.

ESTATE IN COMMON. See TENANCY IN COMMON.

ESTATE PLANNING. Arranging one's affairs in an orderly business-like fashion to enable your executor to distribute your earthly goods as quickly and as inexpensively as possible. And just as important, to reduce or eliminate the inheritance tax bite to Uncle Sam and the states as well. Remember the mess Howard Hughes left and profit accordingly by taking action now while you're still young. It will more than pay for the price of this book! And if you try to do it yourself to save a few dollars, your estate will pay some lawyer enough to send a child through college in order to unscramble affairs. A word to the wise . . .

ESTATE TAX. A tax imposed by the federal government on the testamentary transfer of property. The tax applies to transfers made at death through a decedent's probate estate, either under a will, or by operation of the Law of Intestate Succession. Additionally, the tax applies to other transfers which may have taken place before death but which are not considered complete until death. First enacted in 1916, the estate tax was designed to decrease the concentration of wealth. The statutory scheme underwent sweeping revision under the Tax

Reform Act of 1976. Some states also have an estate tax.

ESTATES IN LAND. Possessory interests in real property. Such estates may be presently possessory or they may become possessory in the future. Thus, a fee simple is an estate in land, but a nonpossessory interest, such as a license, is not.

ESTOPPEL DOCTRINE. An equitable remedy applied to a promise or misrepresentation of fact which causes detrimental reliance by the other party. Frequently, there is a need to enforce certain promises even in the absence of consideration; therefore, the Law has adopted this doctrine as a remedial device to protect the party who has justifiably relied to his detriment.

E.T.A. Acronym for Basque Homelands and Liberty, a terrorist guerrilla group in the four northwestern provinces of Spain (Guipuzcoa, Vizcaya, Alava and Navarra) which are populated by Basques who seek greater local autonomy in government, if not complete separation from Spain in the creation of an independent state.

ETHICAL CONSIDERATIONS OF THE CODE. One of three interrelated parts of the Code of Professional Responsibility. Aspirational in character and representative of the objectives toward which all lawyers should strive, the Ethical Considerations constitute a body of principles upon which a lawyer can rely for guidance in many situations. Violation of an Ethical Consideration by a lawyer does not give rise to any disciplinary action or punishment.

ETHICS IN GOVERNMENT ACT OF 1978. See FEDERAL ETHICS LAW.

ET SEQ. (Latin—and the following). An abbreviation of the Latin phrase "et sequentia." Used to refer to following pages in a citation or reference, as in "p. 356, et seq."

ET UX. (Latin—and wife). An abbreviation of the Latin phrase "et uxor."

Commonly used to denote legal action involving a man and wife together, as in naming parties in a case, John Doe v. Richard Roe, et ux., or in describing a conveyance, Joe Jones et ux.

ET VIR (Latin—and husband). Commonly used to denote legal action involving a wife and husband together, as in naming parties in a case, "John Doe v. James Roe, Et Vir," or in describing a conveyance, "Jessica Jones Et Vir."

EUCLIDEAN ZONING (Area Zoning). The most common land-use regulatory scheme under which the area to be zoned is divided into geometric regions. Each region is then limited to a specified land use, such as residential or commercial.

EUROPEAN COAL AND STEEL COMMUNITY (E.C.S.C. Treaty). Signed in Paris on April 18th, 1951 and entered into force on July 23, 1952, by six European nations for the purpose of contributing to economic expansion of the signatory nations through the establishment of a common market in coal and steel. The original member nations—Belgium, France, Italy, Luxembourg, the Netherlands, and West Germany—later signed the treaty establishing the European Economic Community which, together with the E.C.S.C. treaty and the treaty establishing the European Economic Atomic Energy Commission, forms the basis of what is now commonly known as the Common Market. One goal of the nations establishing the E.C.S.C. was to avoid the threat of war by sharing the coal and steel resources of Europe.

EUROPEAN CONVENTION ON HUMAN RIGHTS AND FUNDAMENTAL FREEDOMS. Negotiated in 1950 under the auspices of the Council of Europe, the Convention defines the rights and freedoms of individuals within the member nations. Articles 9 to 11 provide that "every one has the right of thought, religion, expression, peaceful assembly and association." Its most important organ, the European Commission of Human Rights, consists of a national of each contracting party. The Commission hears complaints by any person, non-governmental organization or group of individuals which claims to be the victim of a human rights violation by one of the member nations. The dispute may be resolved by a Committee of Ministers. If the case is brought by the Commission or by a nation, it is resolved by the European Court of Human Rights. When a violation of the Convention is disclosed, the Committee or the Court prescribes a period during which the nation concerned must take the remedial measures required by the Committee of Ministers. The relatively small number of cases heard by the Committee or the Court should not diminish the value of the Convention, for it serves an important ideological function.

EUROPEAN COUNCIL. See EUROPEAN ECONOMIC COMMUNITY.

EUROPEAN COURT OF HUMAN RIGHTS (E.C.H.R.). Roughly comparable to the United States Supreme Court, the E.C.H.R. was established by fifteen European countries to insure that their governments observe citizens' basic civil rights. The Court emphases out-of-court settlement or redress rather than full-scale litigation.

EUROPEAN COURT OF JUSTICE. See EUROPEAN ECONOMIC COMMUNITY.

EUROPEAN CURRENCY SYSTEM (E.C.S.) (European Monetary System (E.M.S.); European Currency Unit (E.C.U.)). A new currency plan for eight of the Common Market countries (Italy, France, West Germany, Belgium, Luxembourg, Denmark, Ireland and the Netherlands), which became effective in March, 1979. It is designed to stabilize the values of the currencies of the seven countries in relation to each other. This will be accomplished through a $33 billion fund from which members can borrow to defend fixed exchange rates between their currencies, which in future will fluctuate no more than 2.25 percent of each other on either side. Each member will contrib-

ute 20 percent of its gold and dollar reserves and an equivalent amount of national currency into the new credit fund. Members will also use their gold reserves as backing for a new monetary unit, known as the European Currency Unit (E.C.U.), in which they plan to settle among themselves debts incurred defending their new fixed exchange rates. Europe hopes that this gold-backed currency unit would in time evolve into a new international reserve currency similar to and rivaling the dollar. Moreover, its emergence could mean that gold would once again play a central role. Great Britain may join the E.C.S. at a later date. The first E.C.U. was a French coin minted by Louis IX seven centuries ago. The creation of the E.C.U. is a strong step forward in the formation of a United States of Europe.

EUROPEAN CURRENCY UNIT. See EUROPEAN CURRENCY SYSTEM.

EUROPEAN DEFENSE COMMUNITY (E.D.C.). A proposal by the Treaty of Paris of May 27, 1952 to integrate the military forces of six European countries within the framework of N.A.T.O. The Treaty provided that any aggression against a member would be considered aggression against each member of the E.D.C. The goals of E.D.C., however, have not been realized because of France's refusal to ratify the project. The failure of the E.D.C. was caused by a fear of German rearmament, and the deep hostility of the French Gaullist Party against a supranational defense organization. Consequently, N.A.T.O. treaties were modified to limit German rearmament.

EUROPEAN DEVELOPMENT FUND. See E.D.F.

EUROPEAN ECONOMIC COMMUNITY (E.E.C.; Common Market). Fulfilling the dream of Charlemagne for a United States of Europe (Europa), this is an association of countries seeking "a continuous and balanced expansion" of Europe's economy to foster political stability and, eventually, unity by eliminating customs duties among members and setting up common transport, agricultural and external trade policies. It was established on January 1, 1958, by the Treaty of Rome (the Charter of the E.E.C.), signed on March 25, 1957, by Belgium, France, West Germany, Luxembourg, Italy and the Netherlands. It had been preceded by a Coal and Steel Community in 1951. An Atomic Energy Community was also created along with the E.E.C. Great Britain, Denmark and Ireland became members in 1973. An agreement for eventual membership was signed first with Greece in 1962, which will become the tenth full-fledged member on January 1, 1981. A similar agreement was signed with Turkey, in 1964, for its eventual admission. Spain and Portugal are also actively seeking membership. The European Council of the E.E.C. decides on major policies and is formed by the heads of state, who meet three times a year. Two other main bodies based in Brussels are the Commission of the European Communities and the Council of Ministers. France, West Germany, Italy, and Britain have 10 votes each on the Council. Belgium and the Netherlands have 5 votes, Denmark and Ireland 3, and Luxembourg 2. The Commission carries out policies laid down by the Council and makes recommendations. The European Parliament supervises these three communities and has the power to dismiss its executives. It meets seven or eight times a year in Strasbourg, France. The first direct elections for the Parliament were held in June, 1979. There is also a European Court of Justice in Luxembourg, which settles disputes within the Community.

EUROPEAN FREE TRADE ASSOCIATION (E.F.T.A.). Created by the Convention of Stockholm of May 3, 1960, at the initiative of the United Kingdom. It included Austria, Denmark, Norway, Portugal, the United Kingdom, Sweden, Switzerland, and Finland, countries threatened by the European Economic Community (E.E.C.). Its purpose was to create a zone of free exchange between its members for a period of eight years in order to create a larger market. Its organs were a Permanent Secretary in Geneva, and a Council of Ministers. Since the entry of the United Kingdom and Denmark into the Euorpean Communities, the situation of E.F.T.A. has been modified; its members have signed cooperation and exchange treaties with the E.E.C. The result of these treaties will be to grant E.F.T.A. members the same treatment as the United Kingdom and Denmark in their relations with the E.E.C.

EUROPEAN INVESTMENT BANK. An international nonprofit investment bank based in Luxembourg, created by the European Economic Community (E.E.C.) Treaty of 1957. Its purpose is to contribute to the balanced and steady development of the Common Market. The Bank grants loans to facilitate the financing of projects in the less-developed regions of the Community. It also finances projects of common interest to several member nations, which exceed their financing capacity.

EUROPEAN MONETARY SYSTEM. See EUROPEAN CURRENCY SYSTEM.

EUROPEAN PARLIAMENT. See EUROPEAN ECONOMIC COMMUNITY.

EUROPEAN PAYMENTS UNION (E.P.U.). Created in July, 1950, by the Organization For European Economic Cooperation (O.E.E.C.), it is a financial clearinghouse through which members settle their multilateral payments on a monthly basis. The Bank for International Settlement, at Basle, provided for enforcement of E.P.U. multilateral agreements, and settled the balance in credits or debits of each country in gold and credits. In 1958, the E.P.U. was replaced by the E.M.A. (European Monetary Agreement).

EVARTS ACT OF 1891 (Circuit Court of Appeals Act of 1891). Reshaped the federal judiciary, creating federal circuit courts of appeal. Earlier circuit courts had no appointed members but consisted of Supreme Court and district court judges who "rode circuit." Though the 1891 law retained both the district and circuit courts as Courts of Original Jurisdiction, it abolished the appellate jurisdiction of the circuit courts. Instead, circuit courts of appeal were interposed between the Supreme Court on the one hand and the circuit and district courts on the other hand. The Act also created a third circuit judgeship in each circuit, to be filled by a district judge. The long-standing scandal of district judges sitting in review of their own judgments was thus eliminated. Finally, the Act sharply delimited the right of review by the Supreme Court. It introduced the principle of discretionary Supreme Court review by writ of certiorari, which had the effect of making final most decisions of the circuit courts of appeals. In certain important cases, the Act provided for direct review by the Supreme Court. Other cases were to be appealed to the circuit courts of appeals.

EVERSON RULE *(Everson v. Board of Education,* 330 U.S. 1 (1947)). Supreme Court case in 1947 which forbade the use of public funds for religious schools; however, public aid which primarily benefited the student, rather than the school, was allowed. For example, state supported bus service to parochial schools and loaning of state textbooks to parochial school children is not considered state aid to parochial schools. The *Everson* decision was grounded in fundamental concepts of religious liberty articulated in essays written by Thomas Jefferson and James Madison, excerpts of which were attached to the *Everson* opinion.

EX AEQUO ET BONO (Latin—from the fair and the good). A principle of international law analogous to "equity" or "justice." The Statute of the International Court of Justice permits the court-wide discretion to decide cases on this principle without regard to technical legal rights, if the parties agree to submit to the jurisdiction of the court. The phrase, derived from civil law, is mentioned in Blackstone's *Commentaries* as a type of equity or

conscience. The power of the court to decide cases on principles ex aequo et bono at times has been thought to depend on whether the dispute is of a legal or non-legal nature.

EX CATHEDRA (Latin—from the chair). An authoritative pronouncement. The Supreme Court is said to speak ex cathedra on matters within its jurisdiction. The phrase is derived from Roman Catholic doctrine. The Pope, head of the Roman Catholic Church, is said to speak "ex cathedra" or from the "chair of Peter" when he claims to speak as the successor of Peter on Earth and as the Vicar of Christ.

EXCEPTIONS TO HEARSAY RULE. (1) Reported testimony: Depositions or transcripts of testimony given by a witness at some prior hearing or trial which were under oath and afforded an opportuinty for cross-examination. (2) Admissions: Any extrajudicial statement or conduct by a party to the present litigation which is inconsistent with or contrary to his present position. (3) Confessions: Direct acknowledgment of criminal guilt by an accused admitting all elements of the crime. (4) Declarations against interest: Hearsay statement admissible into evidence if (a) the person who made the statement is not a party to the action and is now unavailable and (b) if a reasonable person would not have made the statement unless it was true and sufficiently "against his interest" when spoken. (5) Dying declaration: Admissible declarations of the victim regarding the cause or circumstances of his impending death. The declaration must be that of the victim while believing that his death was imminent. (6) Excited utterance: Admissible statements by any participant or observer made at the time of some occurrence which was startling enough to produce shock and excitement in the observer. (7) Declarations of present sense impressions: Perceptions of an event or condition (even though not exciting) which describe or explain that event or condition. (8) Declaration of physical condition (state of body cases): Spontaneous statements made at a specified time are admissible to prove the physical condition of a person at that time which is in issue. (9) Declarations of mental condition (state of mind cases): Declarations made under circumstances indicating apparent sincerity as to the state of mind at the time in question are admissible whenever a person's state of mind at a particular time is itself in issue. (10) Business records (Parties' shopbook doctrine): Business records made in the course of a regularly conducted business activity are admissible where the sources of information and the method and time of preparation indicates their trustworthiness. (11) Official records: Statements and documents of public officials prepared in the performance of their official duties. There must be a duty to record the facts involved. (12) Judgment: A certified copy of a judgment from any court of record is admissible to prove that such judgment has been entered. But a criminal conviction is not admissible in any civil suit. (13) Declarations concerning family history (Pedigree): Entries in family bibles or other ancient writings, reputation in family, judgments, church records or out-of-court declarations by family members may be relied on to prove various births, deaths, marriages, etc. which establish a relationship whenever family relationships are in issue. (14) Reputation evidence: The following different types of reputation evidence are generally admissible: family reputation in re pedigree; community reputation in re pedigree; community reputation in re character; community reputation in re land boundary-line disputes; community reputation in re matters of general history. (15) Ancient documents affecting property: Admissible declarations contained in ancient deeds, mortgages, wills or other property-disposing documents as evidence of the facts recited therein. Such recitals must be relevant to the purpose of the writing and subsequent dealings with the property must have been consistent with the facts recited. (16) Learned treatises: An expert witness can refer to the contents of accepted texts and treatises in his field

when stating the matters upon which he has relied on in forming his expert opinion. However, as a rule, statements from books or treatises are inadmissible hearsay. (17) Catchall exception: Allows in other kinds of hearsay which meet the same standards of "necessity" and "trustworthiness" as required for the above exceptions created by the Federal Rules of Evidence. In addition to the above, the Federal Rules and other statutes provide various other exceptions.

EXCEPTO PLURIUM CONCUBENTIUM (Latin—exception for sleeping with more than one). Doctrine whereby if the mother of an illegitimate child had sexual relations with a man or men other than the defendant at about the time the child was conceived, the defendant cannot be found to be the father in a paternity suit. The child's mother has the burden of proof in bastardy, and she has not sustained it where evidence shows that any one of several men could have been the child's father. The position of the defendant is more difficult because evidence of intercourse can only be admitted when limited to the period of conception; and if the mother denies it, the question will go to the jury, which more often than not finds the defendant is the father.

EXCITED UTTERANCE. See EXCEPTIONS TO HEARSAY RULE.

EXCLUSIONARY CLAUSE. A legal remedy that serves as a restrictive mechanism where there is a breach of contract between buyer and seller. For example, a buyer may claim that there has been a breach of warranty while the seller asserts that there was a Disclaimer Clause which precludes such a claim. An exclusionary clause may restrict the claims for damages that may be asserted by one or both of the parties involved.

EXCLUSIONARY RULE. Evidence seized illegally may not be used in a criminal trial.

EXCLUSIONARY ZONING. Term used to describe local land use measures designed to bar access of minority groups to suburban areas by raising the cost of housing beyond the reach of most low-income families. This purpose is accomplished by the adoption of minimum lot and building size requirements, restrictions on multiple dwelling units, limits on the permissible number of bedrooms per unit, etc. On the federal level, exclusionary zoning has withstood constitutional challenges based on the due process and equal protection clauses of the Fourteenth Amendment. In a landmark case (*Village of Arlington Heights v. Metropolitan Housing Development Corp.*, 429 U.S. 252 (1977)), the Supreme Court has held that a state's refusal to change its zoning restrictions was unconstitutional only if motivated by an intent to discriminate—the mere "racially disproportionate impact" of an ordinance does not, then, sound its death knell. Such a conservative trend, if continued, bodes ill not only for low-income families, but for innovative local developers who espouse a general relaxation of the land-use restrictions.

EXCLUSIVE AGENCY LISTING. See LISTING ARRANGEMENTS.

EXCLUSIVE BARGAINING AGENCY (Sole Bargaining). The right of a union, when appropriately designated to represent the bargaining unit by private agreement or, with the approval of the appropriate governmental agency, to be the sole negotiator for all employees, including the non-union members. Such acceptance by the employer is called Union Recognition.

EXCLUSIVE BARGAINING AGENT. The representative group selected by employees to conduct their collective bargaining. Such representation manifests a bedrock principle of American labor law—majoritarian control. The policy supporting this principle centers on the concern that plural representation would be divisive and undermine industrial stability. The theory holds that pluralism invites the employer to bestow favors so as to promote inter-union rivalry and abrogate representational rights of employees.

EXCLUSIVE JURISDICTION. The jurisdiction possessed by a court or administrative agency to the exclusion of all other courts or agencies. Generally based upon the subject matter of a particular case, such jurisdiction is normally granted by statute and limits the disposition of a case to a particular grade of court or particular agency, although Exclusive Jurisdiction may be vested in a single tribunal. For example, the district courts of the United States have Exclusive Jurisdiction in most admiralty cases, thus precluding the exercise of jurisdiction by state courts.

EXCLUSIVE RIGHT TO SELL. See LISTING ARRANGEMENTS.

EX CONTRACTU (Latin—out of contract). An action in contract.

EXCULPATION CLAUSE. A provision in a contract, usually a lease, which limits the liability of one party to the value of the asset which is the subject matter of the agreement.

EXCULPATORY PROVISION. The clause or language in a trust instrument which seeks to insulate the trustee from liability for a breach of his duties. Such clauses have historically been disfavored as an escape clause by trust settlors.

EX DELICTO (Latin—out of wrong). An action in tort.

EXECUTIVE ADVISORY COMMITTEE ON SENTENCING. See MORGENTHAU REPORT OF 1979.

EXECUTIVE CONTEMPT. See CONTEMPT OF COURT.

EXECUTIVE OCCUPATIONAL DISEASE. The Illinois Supreme Court has ruled that the widow of an executive who suffered a heart attack from the emotional and mental pressures of his job could recover death benefits under the Workmen's Compensation Act. The court ruled that the job did not have to be the sole cause of the decedent's heart attack, but only had to be a causative factor in the injury, which is a common malady among executives.

EXECUTIVE ORDER. A rule or regulation with the effect of law, issued by the executive branch of federal or state governments. Federal executive orders are generally issued by the President himself. They serve to implement statutes, treaties, and Constitutional provisions. The ambitious reader may find samples of executive orders in the *Federal Register*, where they are required to be published under the Administrative Procedure Act of 1946. Although the Constitution does not explicitly grant law-making powers to the Executive, the President has traditionally promulgated rules and regulations concerning all areas of domestic and foreign affairs. The power to issue such orders is derived from the general Executive power and from the President's duty to see to the faithful execution of laws enacted by Congress. Executive orders have made a substantial impact in the civil rights area by prohibiting discrimination in government employment, in federally-assisted housing, and in other areas of federal involvement.

EXECUTIVE ORDER NO. 10988. Order issued by President John F. Kennedy, in 1962, which first recognized the right of federal employees to bargain with management. The order, however, was limited to Executive Department employees and was narrow in the scope of bargaining it authorized. Employees covered by the order were given the right to organize into appropriate units for the limited purpose of formulating personnel policies which affected their daily working environment. For example, wages were outside the scope of bargaining permissible and the historic ban on striking was not lifted. This order was supplanted and somewhat expanded by President Nixon's Executive Order 11491 in 1969.

EXECUTIVE ORDER NO. 11490. A little known federal law of 1976 that gives the President dictatorial powers in the event of a national emergency, as he determines, subject to review by Congress in six months. This includes wage, price, currency, food and other controls of every type. Frightening but true.

EXECUTIVE PRIVILEGE. The power of the President of the United States to protect the confidentiality of communications within the Executive Branch of Government if disclosure would adversely affect the public interest, the national security, or the orderly functioning of government. The concept originated in 1791 when the House of Representatives requested the Secretary of War to produce documents concerning a disastrous military expedition against the Wabash Indians in Ohio. President Washington consulted with his Cabinet members, and according to notes taken by Thomas Jefferson, then Secretary of State, the Cabinet agreed that a President had the Privilege to withhold certain secret information. The Constitution is silent on the question of Executive Privilege. At best, the President can claim an implied power under Article II, Section 3, requiring him to "take care that the laws be faithfully executed." Nor has there been a determination as to whether it is a personal privilege, or if others can claim it on the President's behalf, such as the 500 members of his White House staff. From 1792 to the early 1950s the question only arose 27 times, but the dispute has intensified in recent years. Since 1954 the Executive Privilege has been claimed at least 59 times, and the prospect is for the issue to arise frequently in the future unless reasonable procedures are developed.

EXECUTIVE COMMISSION. The agency of the Common Market which enforces its antitrust rules. Under Common Market law, the Commission can fine companies up to 5 percent of their annual turnover. In 1979, it imposed a 10-million-dollar fine, almost a quarter of all the fines the Commission had imposed in the last 10 years, on Pioneer Electronic Europe of Antwerp, Belgium, the Common Market subsidiary of the Tokyo-based company, and on the parent's German, French and British distributors. Announcing the fine at its Brussels headquarters, the Commission said the alleged market-rigging scheme constituted serious interference with free trade among the Common Market members and violated Article 85 of the Treaty of Rome, which created the European Economic Community. The decision may be appealed to the Common Market European Court of Justice which sits in Luxembourg.

EXECUTORY INTEREST. Any future interest that will become a present interest, if at all, in someone other than the transferor or his successors, which is not a remainder. (1) Springing executory interest is one that divests only an interest left in the grantor or his successors. (2) A shifting executory interest is one that divests only an interest left in someone other than the grantor or his successors.

EXEMPLARY DAMAGES. See PUNITIVE DAMAGES.

EXHAUSTION OF ADMINISTRATIVE REMEDIES. An administrative law rule regarding judicial review. Generally, courts decline to review the decision of an administrative agency until the plaintiff exhausts all administrative avenues for relief.

EXHAUSTION OF REMEDIES. A doctrine of almost universal application which requires that where a remedy is provided by an administrative agency, such remedy must be pursued through final determination before the courts will act in the matter. The doctrine is based on the presumption that an administrative agency, if given the chance to act on issues within its competence, will reach the correct result. Imposed on the courts as a product of judicial self-restraint, the doctrine determines the stage at which a person may secure judicial review of administrative action.

EXIM BANK (Export-Import Bank of the United States). A federal agency which facilitates and aids in financing exports of U.S. goods and services. Exim Bank has implemented a variety of programs to meet the needs of the United States exporting community, according to the size of the transaction.

These programs take the form of direct lending or the issuance of guarantees and insurance, so that exporters and private banks can extend appropriate financing without taking undue risks. Exim Bank's direct lending program is limited to larger sales of United States products and services around the world. The guarantees, insurance, and discount programs have been designed to assist exporters in smaller sales of products and services.

EXIT TAX. A law found in a few states in the Northeast and Midwest which applies to any business that leaves its present location. In general, it requires firms with more than 100 employees to give a two-year notice if they plan to move, either elsewhere in the state or outside. Employees who lose their jobs would receive a severance payment of a week's wages times the number of years worked. The employer must also file an Economic Impact Statement and make a payment of 10 percent of the annual wages of these unemployed workers to a Community Assistance Fund.

EX OFFICIO (Latin—by nature of office). A position held by virtue of election or appointment to another related position. For example, a person elected governor becomes, Ex Officio, a member of several state commissions and boards.

EX PARTE (Latin—from one side). Usually refers to an application to a court by or for one party, without notice to the adverse party. A court may hold an Ex Parte proceeding, or issue an Ex Parte order or injunction. In cases of necessity, an Ex Parte deposition may be ordered. In all these cases, the adverse party does not receive notice. In another sense, Ex Parte refers to an application in a judicial proceeding by one not a party to the proceeding, but with a special interest therein. A communication, outside of official proceedings, with the judge in a proceeding by the attorney for one side without notice to, or the presence of, the attorney for the adverse side, is commonly known as an Ex Parte Contact. The

Code of Professional Responsibility of the American Bar Association prohibits attorneys from making such contacts. In agency law, Ex Parte Contacts are interactions between agency decision-makers, and individuals or groups outside the agency, concerning subjects to be decided by the agency on the basis of an on-the-record administrative procedure. These external influences and extra-record communications defeat the twin purposes of the procedure—to provide a fair hearing before an impartial tribunal and to make all considerations relevant to the decision available for public scrutiny so that affected parties, the courts, Congress and the executive can discern the basis on which the agency acts. The prohibition of Ex Parte Contacts is generally applicable to adjudications. However, such contacts are also impermissible in rule-making procedures which have adjudicative functions, e.g., a general policy determination which affects one or two private concerns more directly. For example, in *Sangamon Valley Television Corp. v. United States*, 358 U.S. 49 (1958), the problem arose in the context of a proposed rule-making that would have peculiarly benefitted Signal Hill, a licensee of channel 36 in St. Louis. Since Signal Hill had made frequent personal contacts with Federal Communications Commission (F.C.C.) staff, had taken several Commissioners to lunch and had sent them turkeys as Christmas presents, the court of appeals vacated the F.C.C.'s order holding, "Whatever the proceeding may be called, it involved not only allocation of TV channels among communities, but also resolution of conflicting private claims to a valuable privilege, and that basic fairness requires such a proceeding to be carried on in the open."

EXPEDITING ACT OF 1903. A statute intended to provide speedy determination of actions brought by the United States under the Antitrust Laws or the Interstate Commerce Act. After its passage in 1903, the Expediting Act subsequently was extended to cover actions under the common carrier sections of the Federal Communications Act. Essentially, the Act has two main features. First, upon certification by the Attorney General that a case is of general public importance, a special three-judge district court hears the case at the earliest possible date. Secondly, an appeal from the final judgment of the special district court lies only to the Supreme Court. The two aspects of the Act are independent. Even if a case has not been certified by the Attorney General and decision is made by a single district judge, direct review by the Supreme Court is available.

EXPERT WITNESS. One who has specialized knowledge or skill not in the possession of the average juror. To qualify as an expert, a witness need not have a formal degree. Training or experience alone can qualify a person as an expert. Unlike ordinary witnesses, an expert is allowed to voice an opinion or answer a hypothetical question. He cannot be forced to testify as is the case for an ordinary witness.

EXPORT-IMPORT BANK OF THE UNITED STATES. See EXIM BANK.

EXPORTS OF GOODS AND SERVICES. Often referred to as Merchandise Exports, valued at their F.A.S. (Free Alongside Ship) price. As such, they include all costs incurred up to the point of loading the goods on the vessel at the domestic port. Exports of services include items such as ocean and air fares paid to United States carriers, insurance, profits earned by United States business firms operating abroad, and earnings received from other United States-owned public and private assets located abroad.

EX POST FACTO LAW. A retroactive law designed to impose criminal penalties for acts that were not illegal when they were performed. Article I, sections 9 and 10 of the United States Constitution prohibit both state and federal governments from passing Ex Post Facto laws. These provisions have also been interpreted to forbid both retroactive increases in penalties for existing crimes and retroactive changes in evidentiary rules that could facilitate conviction. Ex Post Facto changes which favor the accused, however, are permitted under the Constitution. The Ex Post Facto Doctrine does not apply to civil cases.

EXPRESS TRUST. A trust arrangement which is set out either orally or in writing in which the terms and conditions of the trust arrangement are specifically described. The Express Trust is the most widely-used trust arrangement today.

EX REL. (Latin—in behalf of). Indicates the complaining party in a criminal action.

EXTENDER CLAUSE. Gives a real estate broker a grace period, usually six months, beyond the expiration date of his contract in order to assure that he will receive his commission. Such a clause presumes that the broker already has begun negotiating a sale prior to the date on which his contract is due to end.

EXTRADITION DE FACTO. The deportation of undesirable aliens, especially those deportations of a political nature.

EXTRA-MILITARY INSTRUCTION (E.M.I.). Additional tasks assigned by a superior to military personnel to correct behavioral or performance deficiencies. E.M.I. may not be assigned as punishment, but it may have to be performed outside of normal duty hours. However, the E.M.I. assigned must serve some valid training purpose, and it must reasonably relate to the deficiency to be corrected. As an example, suppose an individual is assigned the responsibility of locking a particular space each evening and he repeatedly neglects to do so. Such conduct may exhibit either a lack of knowledge or lack of self-discipline. Where the deficiency is lack of knowledge, requiring the individual to spend several hours in the evening reading and reviewing security regulations should meet the prerequisites of E.M.I. But where the deficiency is lack of self-discipline, shortcomings of personality and character are generally the cause and may be corrected only by the assignment of tasks designed to get at the root of the problem. In this example, it may not be unreasonable to assign several hours of close-order drill where the instant obedience of commands would develop the strength of self-discipline.

EXTRAORDINARY WRITS. Mandatory orders issued by a court which are intended to make available certain types of relief not obtainable in an ordinary law or equity action. Such writs are considered collateral to the regular judicial process and are not available as a substitute for appeal in the normal course. The most common of these prerogative writs are habeas corpus, mandamus, prohibition, certiorari, and the writ of error coram nobis.

EXTRA-TERRITORIAL PROCESS. Service of process on a defendant who is physically outside the state in which the forum court is located. Under the law of many states, extraterritorial process is accomplished under so-called Long-Arm Statutes, subject to the limitations of the Due Process Clause of the Fourteenth Amendment. Extraterritorial federal process exists under the Federal Interpleader Act which authorizes nationwide service of process, and under the Federal Rules of Civil Procedure which authorize out-of-state service of process on third-party defendants, and certain additional parties, who are in the United States and within 100 miles of the federal district court hearing the action.

EXTRINSIC EVIDENCE. Evidence which is not contained in the agreement at issue. In litigation concernng contracts, extrinsic evidence is generally inadmissible.

F

F.A.A. See FEDERAL AVIATION ADMINISTRATION.

FABER'S LAW. "If there isn't a law, there will be."

FABIAN SOCIALISM. An economic theory which declares that the socialist state can be brought about by evolution, rather than revolution, and that compromise can replace class struggle. The term derives from the Fabian Society, organized in England around the turn of the century.

FACTOR'S LIEN. A legal mechanism asserted to secure the loans against inventories already acquired. It makes no difference whether the inventory consists of manufactured goods or raw materials. Generally, the lien has to be in writing.

FACULTY APPOINTMENTS REGISTER. On the payment of the fee of $30 a person interested in a full-time faculty position or a full-time professional staff position with a law school may register that interest by completing a structured one-page résumé. Those résumés are duplicated and distributed to the law schools, who use them as a basis for recruiting additions to the faculty. The registrants receive, without additional cost, a copy of the Placement Bulletin. Supplementing this service is the register for faculty who wish to consider invitations as visiting faculty during the coming school year, the register of full-time faculty members who will retire from teaching at the end of the current school year, and the register of those foreign law teachers who wish to consider invitations to be a visiting member of a United States law faculty. The information gathered for these three registers is distributed in the form of a memorandum to the deans of law schools.

F.A.I.R. (Fair Access to Insurance Requirements Program). A special program designed to rehabilitate inner-city areas by providing essential property insurance in depressed areas where commercial insurers will not write policies. It operates like private insurance but is established through state legislation and monitored by the federal government. Ironically, a General Accounting Office study reports that the program has encouraged massive fraudulent schemes of arson for profit.

FAIR CREDIT REPORTING LAW. A federal statute enacted in 1970 which represents the first federal regulation of the vast consumer reporting industry. It covers all credit bureaus, investigative reporting companies, detective and collection agencies, lenders' exchanges, and computerized information reporting companies. The purpose of this Act is to insure that consumer reporting activities are conducted in a manner that is fair and equitable to the affected consumer, protecting his right to privacy against the informational demands of others. The consumer is given several important new rights, including notice of reporting activities, access to information contained in consumer reports, and the right to correct erroneous information that may have been the basis for a denial of credit, insurance, or employment.

FAIR DEAL. Phrase coined by President Harry F. Truman in his 1949 State of the Union address, intended to refer to the web of domestic policies he had championed since 1945. Truman considered his proposals extensions of the social reform initiated by Franklin D. Roosevelt—his request for a full employment law embodied the notion that providing jobs for all those willing and able to work assured "maximum opportunity under the American system of responsible freedom." Before the advent of the Korean War diverted interest from domestic reform, Truman had asked Congress for legislation on housing, aid to education, atomic energy, minimum wages, social security, and fair employment practices. The first fruits of Truman's labor appeared in 1946, when Congress passed the Employment Act of that year. Later, the passing of the Social Security Act of 1950 extended the benefits of that legislation to approximately 10,000,000 more people. Finally, in an amendment to the Fair Labor Standards Act of 1938, Congress responded to Truman's minimum wage plea, raising the wage from 40 to 75 cents per hour.

FAIR DEBT COLLECTION PRACTICES ACT. A federal law passed in

1978 and enforced by the Federal Trade Commission (F.T.C.). It covers only debts relating to personal, family and household expenses and does not apply to banks, creditors acting on their own, or their attorneys. It prevents professional debt collectors from using the following unpleasant practices: (1) Harassment by threatening violence or calling between 9 p.m. and 8 a.m.; (2) Publishing lists of purported "deadbeats"; (3) Using obscene language; (4) Repeatedly calling about a debt or calling at work if an employer disapproves; (5) Making false statements when collecting a debt, such as falsely implying that the debt collector represents a government agency or is an attorney; (6) Using unfair methods in trying to collect a debt, including asking for more money than is owed, calling a consumer collect or depositing a postdated check before the date on the check; (7) Informing anyone else that a consumer owes money; (8) Putting anything on an envelope that identifies the writer as a debt collector; (9) Repeatedly telephoning the consumer; (10) Advertising the debt; (11) Giving false credit information about the consumer to anyone else; or (12) From threatening harm to a consumer, his property or reputation, and from threatening to arrest the debtor or to seize, garnish or attach property unless it is legal and the collector intends to do so. Within five days after the collector makes contact with a consumer about a debt, the consumer has the right to a written notice from the collector explaining exactly how much is owed and to whom and what the debtor can do to challenge the debt if he thinks it is not accurate. In addition, the law provides that a debt collector must stop communicating with a purported debtor if the debtor notifies the collector that he wants no further communication. Aggrieved consumers may bring civil suits in state or federal courts within one year of the date of the violation for actual damages sustained. According to the Federal Trade Commission, which is responsible for administering the law, the debt collector may also be liable for up to $1,000 in additional damages, court costs, and attorney's fees. The statute permits Class Actions under which the debt collector may be liable for up to $500,000 in additional damages.

FAIR HOUSING FOR CHILDREN COALITION. A Los Angeles-based group which combats restrictions against renting apartments to people with children. The "Adults Only" policy has been adopted by an increasing number of landlords, particularly in areas like San Francisco and Los Angeles, which have a low vacancy rate. Such restrictions suit older couples who have raised their children, young swingers, and landlords seeking to reduce maintenance costs. Several cities, however, including San Francisco now prohibit apartment owners from refusing to rent to families with children.

FAIR LABOR STANDARDS CASE. See CHILD LABOR CASES.

FAIRNESS DOCTRINE. The requirement that radio and television broadcasters provide fair coverage for both sides of public issues. While the Equal Time Rule is essentially reactionary, e.g., obligations arise only when the station first elects to grant one candidate air time, the Fairness Doctrine places an affirmative duty on the station to present all sides of controversial issues. Exact parity is not required so long as the issue is treated fairly over the course of a reasonable time. Outside commentary need be aired only where necessary to ensure balance and fairness. However, in the event that there is an attack on the honesty, character, or integrity of an organization or individual on a given station, the "Personal Attack-Political Editorializing" rules require the broadcaster to provide the person or group attacked with a reasonable opportunity to respond. Under these circumstances substantially equal time must be given.

FAIR PACKAGING AND LABELING ACT. A federal statute passed in 1966 which requires that packages and labels permanently show: 1) the name and place of business of the manufacturer, packer, or distributor; 2) the net quantity of contents in a uniform location on the front of the label; and 3) the quantity of contents in units of measure specified by the Act. The Act enables consumers to obtain accurate information as to the quantity of the contents of the packages and thus facilitates value comparisons. The Act applies to "consumer commodities," which include a drug, food, device, or cosmetic within the Federal Food, Drug and Cosmetic Act. It also applies to any product which is 1) distributed through retail agencies; 2) is used by individuals for personal care or in the performance of services normally rendered within the household; and 3) is consumed or expended in use. The Federal Trade Commission has jurisdiction over all consumer commodities except that the Department of Health, Education and Welfare enforces the provisions concerning foods, drugs, devices, and cosmetics.

FAIR SHARE. A taxpayers' revolt organization found in various states which seeks to tax private homes at substantially lower rates than commercial and industrial property. It also promotes the enactment of a Circuit Breaker law which would rebate up to $500 a year on any residential property tax that exceeds 8 percent of the individual's taxable income.

FAIR TRADE LAWS. State statutes which allow a seller of labeled commodities to establish a maximum or a minimum resale price, which cannot be varied by the wholesaler or distributor. Fair Trade Laws were first enacted in the early 1930s at the request of retail trade associations. Such groups were often dominated by small retail merchants, who faced stiff competition from the larger, more efficient chain stores and self-service supermarkets. For many years these laws were exempted from the antitrust prohibitions by the Miller-Tydings Act. But, in 1975, after a period of high inflation, Congress strengthened the antitrust legislation by repealing that Act. Today, Fair Trade Laws are barred by both the Sherman and Clayton Acts.

FAIR USE. A use of a copyrighted work which does not constitute Copyright Infringement. At common law, most courts define Fair Use as an "insubstantial" taking. However, the term is also used to mean a taking which would be an infringement but for the circumstances. Generally, at common law, three types of taking are considered to be Fair Use: (1) Notes taken from a copyrighted work for the private use of the reader; (2) Quotations from a work used as part of a critical essay or response to the work and reasonably necessary for that purpose; and (3) Copyrighted material which is included incidentally in a documentary or commentary as part of the atmosphere without any special gain accruing to the user as a result of the inclusion. Section 107 of the Copyright Act, which took effect on January 1, 1978, states that four factors should be considered in order to determine whether the use made of a work is a Fair Use: (1) The purpose and character of the use, including whether such use is of a commercial nature or is for nonprofit educational purposes; (2) The nature of the copyrighted work; (3) The amount and the substantiality of the portion used in relation to the copyrighted work as a whole; and (4) The effect of the use upon the potential market for a value of the copyrighted work.

FAIR VALUE. The price at which goods produced abroad are sold abroad. If the exporter sells them at a lower price in the United States, an additional import duty may be imposed to protect American manufacturers from this unfair competition.

F.A.L.N. The initials represent the Spanish words for Armed Forces of National Liberation for Puerto Rico. It is a miniscule but dangerous underground terrorist group supported and financed by Communist Cuba which destroys buildings owned by multinational corporations in the United

States and Puerto Rico. It seeks to establish Puerto Rico as a separate sovereign in place of its present special relationship with the United States despite the fact that in the last election where the question was raised more than 99 percent of the Puerto Ricans voted to keep the status quo.

FALSE ARREST. See FALSE IMPRISONMENT.

FALSE CASE. See FEIGNED CASE.

FALSE CLAIMS ACT. As originally enacted in 1863, this federal law provided for both criminal and civil penalties for the making of any false statements with regard to any matter within the jurisdiction of any department or agency and the making of false claims to any department or agency. At present there are three criminal provisions relating to false claims and statements: False Claims, 18 U.S.C. 287; False Statements, 18 U.S.C. 1001; and Conspiracy to Obtain Payment or Allowance of false claims, 18 U.S.C. 286. In addition, civil liability for the making of false claims is provided by 31 U.S.C. 231 which imposes a forfeiture of $2,000, and, in addition, "double the amount of damages which the United States may have sustained by reason of doing or committing such act. . . ."

FALSE IMPRISONMENT. A tort consisting of an intentional act by the defendant which causes the confinement of the plaintiff against his will. Sometimes referred to as False Arrest, the tort protects from restraint of movement. Imprisonment need not consist of iron bars and stone walls and indeed no physical barriers at all are necessary. It is enough that the defendant threaten sufficient force to intimidate the plaintiff into obeying his orders.

FALSE PRETENSES. Using an intentionally false statement to obtain title to the personal property of another.

FALSUS IN UNO, FALSUS IN OMNIBUS (Latin—false in one, false in all). A maxim relating to the weight of evidence. It means that where a witness is proven to have deliberately testified falsely on a material issue, the jury is entitled to disregard or discount his testimony on all other issues.

FAMILY CONFIDENTIALITY. A few states protect parents and children by allowing them to refuse to testify against each other in court as to information they obtained in the family relationship. The Supreme Court of the United States has not yet passed on the legality of this new concept.

FAMILY CORPORATION. See CLOSE CORPORATION.

FAMILY COURT. A specialized court with limited jurisdiction over all matters pertaining to the family, including domestic relations and juveniles. In states where it exists, the family court has usually taken over the functions of both the domestic relations court and the juvenile court. Family courts normally make extensive use of family counseling services, screening services for juvenile offenders and juvenile correctional centers.

FAMILY EDUCATIONAL RIGHTS AND PRIVACY ACT. See BUCKLEY AMENDMENT.

FAMILY JEWELS. A sick joke designation given by the C.I.A. to a 693-page secret list prepared in 1973 of 700 different major activities of the C.I.A. which were direct violations of law or at least questionable activities such as attempts to assassinate world leaders (Castro of Cuba, Lumumba of the Congo and Trujillo of the Dominican Republic); surveillance and bugging of journalists; opening of mail of citizens; experiments on individuals without their knowledge including mind-control drugs; and other serious unsavory tid-bits. The anti-war movement and similar dissident but innocent citizen groups were particular victims of these illegal practices.

FAMILY PURPOSE DOCTRINE. A rule of Vicarious Liability, holding the owner of an automobile liable for its negligent operation by members of his household who use the car with his permission. This Doctrine, recognized in many states, is regarded as a step toward Permissive Use Legislation, which would hold a car owner liable for damages caused by anyone using his car with his permission.

FANNIE MAE (Federal National Mortgage Association). The nation's largest provider of housing finance, which made a net profit of $165 million dollars in 1977. Fannie Mae raises billions of dollars annually from private sources and then buys real estate mortgages from banks and other lenders, thus enabling them to lend even more money. For its first 26 years it was a Government Agency, but in 1968 Congress converted it into a private profit-oriented company answerable to its individual and institutional stockholders. Of its 15 directors, 5 are appointed by the President of the United States and 10 are elected by its stockholders. Its shares are traded on the New York Stock Exchange and it can borrow money at the low rates enjoyed by government agencies. Fannie Mae is the largest single supplier of mortgage money in the country.

F.A.O. (Food and Agricultural Organization). A specialized agency of the U.N., created in 1945, headquartered in Rome, Italy, and composed of 136 member countries. Its purpose is "raising the levels of nutrition and standards of living of the peoples under their respective jurisdictions, securing improvements in the efficiency of the production and distribution of all food and agricultural products, bettering the condition of rural populations, and thus contributing toward an expanding world economy."

FARBER CASE (1978). A Supreme Court case which holds that neither the United States Constitution nor a state law protects newspaper reporters and their sources from refusing to give information demanded by a defendant in a criminal trial.

FARCE OR MOCKERY TEST. Used to determine whether counsel for a defendant in a criminal prosecution has rendered effective assistance as is required by the Sixth Amendment's Right to Counsel. When such assistance has been challenged as inadequate, courts have traditionally asked whether the alleged inadequacy turned the trial into a farce or mockery so as to deprive the defendant of his rights. Recently, many courts have abandoned the Farce or Mockery test. In its place, they have substituted an inquiry which scrutinizes counsel's performance against that of the average practitioner.

FARM CREDIT ADMINISTRATION. A federal agency responsible for the supervision, examination, and coordination of the borrower-owned banks and associations that comprise the Cooperative Farm Credit System. Such institutions include the Federal Land Banks which make long term loans on farm or rural real estate through local Federal Land Bank associations; the Federal Intermediate Credit Banks which provide short and intermediate term loan funds to production credit associations and other institutions financing farmers, ranchers, rural homeowners, owners of farm-related businesses, and commercial fishermen; and the banks for cooperatives which make loans of all kinds to agricultural and aquatic cooperatives. The loan funds provided borrowers by these institutions are obtained primarily through the sale of securities to investors in the nation's capital markets.

FARMING OUT (Brokering). The practice whereby a lawyer gives a case to another lawyer, usually a specialist who does all the work, for a Forwarding Fee. An efficient if not an unethical way to make money.

F.A.S. (Free Alongside). Mercantile symbol, which is standardized by legislation. F.A.S. means the seller is obliged, at his own expense and risk, to deliver the goods alongside a ship at port.

FAUCHILLE THEORY. A principle adopted by the Institute of International Law in 1906, which declares that airspace is free, subject only to the rights of Nations required in the interests of their self-protection.

F.B.I. (Federal Bureau of Investigation). The principal investigative arm of the United States Department of Justice, charged with gathering and reporting facts, locating witnesses, and compiling evidence in matters in which the Federal Government is, or may be, a party in interest. The F.B.I. does not express opinions concerning the guilt or innocence of subjects of its investigations, nor does it otherwise assume the role of accuser, prosecutor, jury, or judge. The Federal Bureau of Investigation was established in 1908 by the Attorney General who directed that Department of Justice investigations be handled by a group of special investigators. The F.B.I. is charged with investigating all violations of federal laws with the exception of those which have been assigned by legislative enactment or otherwise to some other federal agency. The F.B.I.'s jurisdiction includes a wide range of responsibilities in the criminal, civil, and security fields. Among these are espionage, sabotage, and other domestic security matters; kidnapping; extortion; bank robbery; interstate transportation of stolen property; civil rights matters, interstate gambling violations; fraud against the government; and assault or killing the President or a federal officer. Fines and recoveries in F.B.I. investigated cases are often larger than its annual budget. Cooperative services of the F.B.I. for other duly authorized law enforcement agencies include fingerprint identification, laboratory services, police training, and the National Crime Information Center. Upon the death of Director J. Edgar Hoover, women were allowed for the first time to become F.B.I. agents. Dozens joined, and one has already been killed in the line of duty (Sheila Regan, in 1974, at Dulles Airport).

F.B.I. IDENTIFICATION RECORD. See RAP SHEET.

F.C.C. See FEDERAL COMMUNICATIONS COMMISSION.

F.C.M.A. See FISHERY CONSERVATION AND MANAGEMENT ACT.

F.C.S.C. (Foreign Claims Settlement Commission). An executive agency of the federal government which hears all claims against a foreign country, determines their validity and amount, and then certifies them to the State Department, which distributes the prenegotiated lump sum settlement with the foreign country in pro-rata shares to the claimants.

F.C.Z. See FISHERY CONSERVATION AND MANAGEMENT ACT.

F.D.A. (Food and Drug Administration). A federal agency whose activities are directed toward protecting the health of the nation against impure and unsafe foods, drugs and cosmetics. This administrative agency was created by the Food and Drug Act of 1906, which authorized the government to bring enforcement proceedings against individuals violating the proscription against the marketing of adulterated or misbranded products. The Food, Drug, and Cosmetic Act of 1938 provided three different methods of handling violations: (1) seizure of the offending product; (2) injunction against its manufacture or shipment; and (3) criminal prosecution. Seizure is the F.D.A.'s favorite sanction, but the action has such deleterious effects that most violators settle before the action is completed. Injunction is appropriate where the process under scrutiny has not resulted in the introduction of offending goods into commerce, or where the goods cannot be located. The remedy is somewhat unusual since judges are reticent about shutting down an entire business. The criminal sanction involves the imposition of strict liability, but prosecution is rarely sought absent criminal knowledge. United States Attorneys, not F.D.A. personnel, must initiate criminal proceedings. The 1938 and 1962 Amendments were significant in their emphasis on premarketing review of the safety (1938) and effectiveness (1962) of new drugs. While the definitions of both "new" and "drug" are complex, and the procedure for having a new drug approved is quite detailed, the basic inquiry is whether the new substance's therapeutic benefits outweigh its potential risks—particularly any adverse side effects.

F.D.I.C. (Federal Deposit Insurance Corporation). A federal organization sponsored by Congress which protects bank depositors up to $40,000 when a bank becomes insolvent. It is similar to S.I.P.C. which protects investors up to $100,000 when a brokerage firm goes bankrupt.

FEATHERBEDDING PRACTICE. A derogatory term applied to an employee or union working rule which allegedly limits output or requires the employment of unnecessary employees, thereby creating "soft"—hence the notion of featherbed—or unnecessary jobs. The term may also refer to a fee levied by a union upon an employer for services which are not actually performed. The reverse of Featherbedding, when practiced by management, is a Stretchout Program which requires employees to operate more machines or assume additional duties without a corresponding increase in compensation, or a Speedup Program, which forces employees to increase their efforts and production without receiving any additional earnings. This is frequently accomplished by cutting the piecework rate.

F.E.C. (Federal Election Commission). A federal agency which seeks to obtain compliance with the Federal Election Campaign Act Amendments, including the federal campaign disclosure requirements, contribution and expenditure limitations, and public financing of presidential nominating conventions and elections. The Commission receives campaign reports, makes rules and regulations subject to review by Congress, maintains indexes of reports filed and not filed, makes special and regular reports to Congress and the President, and serves as a national clearinghouse for information on the administration of elections. The Commission has the power to issue Advisory Opinions, conduct audits and investigations, subpoena witnesses and information, and initiate civil proceedings. The Commission reports to the President and to each House of Congress no later than March 31 of each year. Each report contains a detailed statement of the activities of the Commission, together with recommendations for legislative or other actions that it considers appropriate.

F.E.C.A.A. See FEDERAL ELECTION CAMPAIGN ACT AMENDMENTS OF 1976.

FEDERAL AVIATION ADMINISTRATION (F.A.A.). Formerly the Federal Aviation Agency, the F.A.A. became a part of the Department of Transportation in 1967 as a result of the Department of Transportation Act. The Federal Aviation Administration is now charged with regulating air commerce to foster aviation safety; promoting civil aviation and a national system of airports; achieving efficient use of navigable airspace; and developing and operating a common system of air traffic control and air navigation for both civilian and military aircraft. The Administrator issues and enforces rules, regulations, and minimum standards relating to the manufacture, operation, and maintenance of aircraft as well as the rating and certification of airmen and airports. The Administration provides a system for the registration of an aircraft's nationality, its engines, propellers, and appliances as well as a system for recording aircraft ownership. In addition, the F.A.A. conducts research and development activities, and maintains electronic aids to air navigation.

FEDERAL BUREAU OF INVESTIGATION. See F.B.I.

FEDERAL CABINET. A creation of custom and tradition dating back to George Washington's administration, it functions at the pleasure of the President. Its purpose is to advise the President upon any subject on which he requests information, pursuant to Article II, section 2, of the Constitution. The Cabinet is composed of the heads of the eleven executive departments—the Secretaries of Agriculture, Commerce,

Defense, Health, Education, and Welfare, Housing and Urban Development, Interior, Labor, State, Transportation, and Treasury, and the Attorney General—and certain other executive branch officials to whom the President accords Cabinet rank. The Vice President participates in all Cabinet meetings and, from time to time, other individuals are invited to participate in discussions of particular subjects. A Secretary to the Cabinet is designated to provide for the orderly handling and follow-up of matters brought before the Cabinet. The term "Brain Trust" was coined by columnist Raymond Moley to refer to the unofficial advisers of President Franklin D. Roosevelt (who were not members of his Cabinet) during the early years of his New Deal.

FEDERAL CASE. Federal courts usually hear cases that are more important than those heard in state courts. The slang expression "Don't make a federal case out of it," therefore means don't exaggerate or attempt to make something more serious than it really is. In other words, it is the same as "Don't make a mountain out of a molehill."

FEDERAL CIVIL JUSTICE REFORM LAW OF 1979. A proposal by President Carter for a major reform of the federal judiciary to improve the administration of justice, especially for the less affluent, in six major respects: (1) Eliminate the federal district courts' obligation to hear civil cases in which the parties are residents of different states (known as Diversity of Citizenship) and thereby shifting to state courts these disputes, which make up nearly a quarter of federal court calendars. (2) Eliminate the requirement that the Supreme Court accept for review cases involving state court decisions as to the Federal Constitutionality of statutes. Actually, the Court frequently sidesteps such mandatory review by asserting "lack of jurisdiction" or "lack of a substantial Federal question." (3) Authorize the use of existing Law Enforcement Assistance Administration funds to help states

and localities establish and operate agencies to resolve minor disputes involving neighbors, tenants, customers and family members, thereby keeping them out of the courts. (4) Permit federal magistrates, rather than judges, to hear misdemeanor criminal cases and certain relatively simple civil cases, thus reducing the work loads of judges and giving litigants faster and less expensive relief. (5) Permit federal district courts to lighten their case loads by ordering arbitration of damage suits involving less than $100,000 and no claim for relief other than money. (6) (a) Merge the United States Court of Claims and the United States Court of Customs and Patent Appeals into a new court; (b) require the loser in a civil suit to pay the winner interest on a judgment; and (c) improve judicial administration in the federal courts generally.

FEDERAL COLLEGE-AID STATUTES. In addition to Social Security benefits, there are six major federal programs which contribute billions of dollars annually to college expenses for the 11 million Americans who have graduated from high school. Information on any of them may be obtained by calling toll free 800-638-6700. The programs are as follows: (1) Middle Income Student Assistance. (M.I.S.A.). Federal grants to students from families whose incomes are as high as $25,-000 a year. Even more important, the new 1978 law broadens the federal student lending program so that any family, regardless of income, can qualify for low-interest loans with special repayment provisions. (2) Basic Educational Opportunity Grants. (B.E.O.G.). The money goes directly to the student and the grant can be as high as $1,800 or half the total cost of going to college yearly, whichever is less. Family income determines eligibility. (3) Supplemental Educational Opportunity Grants. (S.E.O.G.). Individual stipends can be as much as $1,500 a year. (4) College Work-Study. (C.W.S.). Students are employed to work part-time for the University and are paid by the federal government. (5) National Direct Student Loans. (N.D.S.L.). Federal loan money administered through the colleges. (6) Guaranteed Students Loans. (G.S.L.). This enables a student to borrow up to $2,500 a year, or a total of $7,500 as an undergraduate. Interest is federally subsidized while the student is in school; repayment starts 9 to 12 months after leaving school, with interest at a rate of 7 percent. To get the basic grants you have to apply through the federal government, U.S. Office of Education, Seventh and D Streets, S.W., Washington, D.C. 20202, and mark the envelope, "Attention: B.E.O.G." To get a guaranteed student loan, you go to your local bank or lending institution. The other three programs are available through campus financial-aid offices. So, in the words of Bill Shakespeare, "look to it!"

FEDERAL COMMON LAW. That body of law which is applied by a federal court whenever it is free to decide the substantive rule of decision in a case. Such a situation arises when the Constitution, a valid act of Congress, or a state law is not explicit or is inapplicable as to the rule of decision. Even where the Constitution or federal statutes generally cover the issue in controversy, a federal court is said to make federal common law when it specifically fills in the gaps or interstices left open by federal statutory regulation or the Constitution. The Erie Doctrine, emanating from *Erie R.R. Co. v. Tompkins*, 304 U.S. 64 (1938), sharply limited the ability of federal courts to make law by requiring them to resort to state law as the rule of decision in most diversity of citizenship cases. Where two states are in dispute, however, it may be unsuitable to apply the law of one state and a federal court is free to fashion its own rule, assuming both the Constitution and federal statutes are silent on the issue. The same rule applies when a significant federal question arises, and it is unclear whether state or federal law controls. Finally, even where a federal court makes federal common law, it may look to a variety of sources for the content of the new federal rule: it may incorporate or "borrow" a particular state's rule as its own, or it may fashion an entirely new, independent federal rule.

FEDERAL COMMUNICATIONS COMMISSION (F.C.C.). An independent agency of the federal government created in 1934 to regulate radio, television, broadcast, cable and wire communications. Successor to the Federal Radio Commission, the F.C.C. has jurisdiction over AM and FM radio, VAF and UHF and cable television and private business and citizens radio services. In the course of these duties the Commission assigns frequencies and issues broadcast licenses in accordance with its statutory mandate to serve the "public interest, convenience and necessity." The F.C.C. is comprised of seven commissioners appointed by the President with the approval of the Senate.

FEDERAL CONTRACT COMPLIANCE OFFICE. A subdivision of the Department of Labor, charged with supervising the efforts of government contractors and subcontractors to eliminate discrimination in employment.

FEDERAL COUNCIL ON ENVIRONMENTAL QUALITY. See COUNCIL ON ENVIRONMENTAL QUALITY.

FEDERAL COUNCIL ON THE ARTS AND HUMANITIES. See ARTS AND ARTIFACTS INDEMNITY ACT.

FEDERAL COURT DIRECTORY. A reference book that features the telephone numbers of all U.S. judges and clerks of court. Also included are the names and telephone numbers of all U.S. attorneys and the counties within each federal district.

FEDERAL COURTS IMPROVEMENT ACT OF 1979. Comprehensive legislation to reform and restructure the entire federal judiciary introduced into Congress by Senator Edward M. Kennedy on March 15, 1979. In addition to proposals announced by President Carter, the bill contains provisions that would: (1) create a special United States Court of Tax Appeals; (2) establish new procedures for disciplining federal judges; (3) revise the present composition of Circuit Councils; (4) make retirement rules for federal judges more flexible; (5) allow the temporary assignment of justices or judges to other offices within the judicial branch; and (6) permit certain federal appeals on interlocutory issues prior to the completion of a case in the district court.

FEDERAL CURRENCY AND FOREIGN TRANSACTIONS REPORTING ACT. See BANK SECRECY ACT.

FEDERAL DIPLOMATIC IMMUNITY ACT OF 1790. See DIPLOMATIC IMMUNITY.

FEDERAL ELECTION CAMPAIGN ACT AMENDMENTS OF 1976. (F.E.C.A.A.). Regulates candidates and activities of those who come into contact with candidates for federal office. Regulations cover: (1) organization of political committees, including committees which are not authorized by a candidate; (2) filing of financial and other reports; (3) limitations on contributions; and (4) political advertising. The Federal Election Campaign Act Amendments of 1976 augment Federal Election Campaign Acts of 1972 and 1974. The 1972 Act limited the amount of money which could be spent for broadcast advertising and set the total amount which could be spent in any campaign according to the number of eligible voters. It also established reporting procedures, regulated political contributions by labor unions and corporations, and limited the amount which individual candidates and their immediate families could contribute to their own campaigns. The political contribution scandals growing out of the 1972 campaign led to the enactment of more sweeping regulations in 1974. The 1974 Act provided for complete public financing of presidential election campaigns as well as the creation of a special regulatory commission to enforce both the 1972 and 1974 laws. The Act provides $20 million for each major party candidate and allows other candidates to receive a proportion of that amount based on their percentage of the vote in primaries. The Act also provides for a one-dollar voluntary check-off on personal income tax returns to raise political campaign subsidies.

FEDERAL EMERGENCY MANAGEMENT AGENCY. See F.E.M.A.

FEDERAL EMPLOYERS' LIABILITY ACT (F.E.L.A.). Originally enacted in 1906 prior to the rise of workmen's compensation schemes, this Act governs the liability of railroads for injuries suffered by their employees. The United States Supreme Court quickly expressed its disfavor with the Act in the Employers' Liability Cases of 1908, holding the Act unconstitutional as exceeding the power of Congress. Following these decisions, Congress limited the coverage of the Act to make it acceptable to the Court and repassed the legislation. Further amendments in 1939 made the present Act very much like its 1906 predecessor which was declared invalid. The effect of F.E.L.A. is to codify the common law of negligence. Its importance, however, lies in the sometimes subtle deviations from the common law which were intended to increase the availability of compensation to the employee for workplace accidents. This result is achieved in several ways: (1) the railroad no longer enjoys the protection of the common law Assumption of Risk defense; (2) a showing of contributory negligence will not bar recovery, and (3) the worker is required to show less evidence of negligence than under the common law. F.E.L.A. has probably increased the amount of litigation in this area with some dispute remaining as to how advantageous the Act is for railway workers. The Jones Act of 1915 and the Merchant Marine Act of 1920 apply essentially the same provisions to seamen.

FEDERAL ETHICS LAW. Legislation passed in 1978 which requires public financial disclosures from the top 14,000 federal government officials, including the President, Vice-President, members of Congress and the Supreme Court. The law marks the first time any across-the-board ethics standard has been applied to all three branches of government. It requires a public accounting of the financial standing of senior level officials. The disclosure is designed to show potential conflicts of interest. An official must show sources of income and gifts and list assets and liabilities and other positions held. The system combines privacy and disclosure. For example, while an official must name individuals or firms to which a debt is owed, the size of the liability might be identified as "between $10,000 and $50,000." It also created an Office of Government Ethics for the Executive Branch to handle complaints or questions. The director would be a presidential appointee whose nomination would require Senate confirmation.

FEDERAL HOME LOAN MORT-GAGE CORPORATION (F.H.L.M.C.; Freddy Mac). See FREDDY MAC.

FEDERAL HOUSING ADMINISTRA-TION (F.H.A.). A government agency, created in 1934, that insures against loss on housing loans by requiring the borrower to pay an insurance premium. This system has increased the ability of many people to purchase homes because insured mortgages entail smaller down payments and provide longer repayment periods. Moreover, F.H.A. programs have improved the quality of homes in that the agency will not protect a lender unless the home meets certain minimum construction standards. The importance of F.H.A. loans for the moderate-income buyer has decreased somewhat due to availability of low down-payment conventional home loans.

FEDERAL INFORMATION CEN-TERS (F.I.C.). Created by President Lyndon B. Johnson in 1965 and located throughout the United States, these offices answer questions by citizens in person, by mail or over the telephone concerning any legal or other problem which a citizen may have with the federal government.

FEDERAL INTERPLEADER ACT. A federal statute designed to protect a stakeholder from inconsistent and multiple obligations. Generally, the Act is invoked when a common fund or thing is claimed by several persons and the stakeholder is indifferent as to which person acquires the disputed stake. The Interpleader Act was passed in response to a case in which an insurance company was forced by inconsistent adjudications to pay the same fund to two beneficiaries, only one of whom should have collected. Interpleader is also provided for under the Federal Rules of Civil Procedure, Rule 22; however, the statutory Interpleader allows greater flexibility in subject-matter and personal jurisdiction.

FEDERALIST PAPERS. A collection of essays, under the pseudonym Publius, written soon after the 1787 Federal Constitutional Convention. While the essays were originally written as campaign propaganda urging ratification of the new Constitution by the state of New York, later generations of scholars have viewed the *Federalist Papers* as the authoritative commentary on the meaning of the Constitution. The bulk of the 85 essays were written by Alexander Hamilton and James Madison with John Jay contributing at least five.

FEDERAL JUDICIAL CENTER. The research arm of the federal judiciary. Created in 1967, the Center is run by a Board, whose chairman is the Chief Justice of the Supreme Court, and its day-to-day affairs are managed by a Director. The Center is under the immediate direction of the Judicial Conference of the United States. The Center is designed (1) to conduct and stimulate "research and study of the operation of the federal courts"; (2) to make recommendations to the Judicial Conference for improvements in the administration and management of the federal courts; (3) to develop and conduct programs of continuing legal education for judges and other court personnel; and (4) to provide research, staff and planning assistance to the Judicial Conference and its committees. The success of the Center is largely due to its first Director, retired Supreme Court Justice Tom C. Clark.

FEDERAL LAND BANKS. See CO-OPERATIVE FARM CREDIT SYSTEM; FARM CREDIT ADMINISTRATION.

FEDERAL LAW ENFORCEMENT TRAINING CENTER. A federal inter-agency training center serving twenty-nine federal law enforcement agencies representing ten executive departments. The Center conducts law enforcement training for the special agents and police officers from the participating agencies, and provides the necessary facilities, equipment, and support for the accomplishment of that training. The Center also provides training on a space-available basis to the law enforcement personnel of an additional fifteen federal agencies to qualified civilian personnel from military agencies, and to the training personnel of various state and local law enforcement agencies. The recruit courses and other training for more than one agency are conducted by the Center's Criminal Investigator Training Division and Police Training Division. The Special Training Division provides firearms, driver, and physical training for both the recruit and advanced programs.

FEDERAL LAWYERS. As of 1978 there were approximately 20,000 federally employed lawyers. The Department of Defense employs the most lawyers, 5,247, while the Justice Department employs 3,608 lawyers. Other smaller staffs of lawyers work for various agencies throughout the government.

FEDERAL LEGAL INFORMATION THROUGH ELECTRONICS. See COMPUTER-ASSISTED LEGAL RESEARCH.

FEDERAL MAGISTRATE. An appointed federal official who conducts the administration of minor and preliminary legal matters in the federal district courts. The system of federal magistrates was created by the Federal Magistrates Act of 1968 and came into full operation after a brief transition pe-

riod. Magistrates are appointed by the federal district judges, in such numbers as the Judicial Conference of the U.S. may determine for each court. They may be full- or part-time. Essentially, they carry out the responsibilities formerly assigned to U.S. Commissioners, such as issuing warrants, conducting probable cause and other preliminary hearings in criminal cases and trying "minor offenses" under 18 U.S.C. § 3401. Most importantly, they may also be assigned additional duties as needed by the district court, including service as special masters in civil actions, assistance to the district judges in the conduct of pre-trial or discovery proceedings, and preliminary review of requests for postconviction relief such as Habeas Corpus.

FEDERAL MAGISTRATES ACT. See FEDERAL MAGISTRATE.

FEDERAL MARITIME COMMISSION. See F.M.C.

FEDERAL MARITIME LIEN ACT. A federal law enacted in 1910 to balance the conflicting interests of shipowners and materialmen who provide goods and services to vessels in United States ports. Prior to 1910, maritime law was inconsistent regarding the rights of materialmen to establish a lien upon a vessel, as each coastal state had its own Maritime Lien Act. Further, the jurisdiction of the Federal Admiralty Courts was in doubt, except where the vessel was not in its homeport at the time the lien was sought. The Federal Maritime Lien Act corrected this situation by providing that any person who, on order of the owner or his authorized agent, furnishes repairs, supplies, towage, use of dry dock or marine railway, or other necessaries, to any vessel, has a maritime lien on that vessel, enforceable by a suit In Rem in the Admiralty Courts of the United States. The Act supersedes all state statutes which purport to create such a cause of action.

FEDERAL MEDIATION AND CONCILIATION SERVICE (F.M.C.S.). An independent federal agency created by the Labor-Management Relations Act of 1947 (the Taft-Hartley Labor Act) for the purpose of minimizing interruptions in interstate commerce which result from labor disputes, except for those involving railroads and airlines. The F.M.C.S. has no power to intervene or to participate in any collective bargaining relationship, except in the event of a strike or threatened action that involves public safety. Even in the latter case, it may only make recommendations which either or both of the parties are free to reject. Normally the F.M.C.S. goes into operation only when its services are requested by both of the parties or when its proffered services are jointly accepted by the parties. In no case may it do more than act as an "honest broker" who attempts to smooth the road to agreement between the parties. It does not itself become a principal party to the bargaining. Though the F.M.C.S. is not an arbitration board, and has no authority to arbitrate and employs no arbitrators, it does regard arbitration as one of the major methods for settling disputes. It thus may suggest arbitration and it may suggest arbitrators to the parties. If accepted, however, these arbitrators have no relationship to F.M.C.S.

FEDERAL OFFICE OF JUVENILE JUSTICE AND DELINQUENCY PREVENTION. Created by Congress in 1974 and located within the Department of Justice, this agency grants millions of dollars to states and cities each year to keep minor juvenile criminals or non-offenders such as abused or neglected youngsters out of jail and place them instead in foster homes and group homes.

FEDERAL PARENT LOCATOR. Located in the nation's capital, this is a computer system that uses the Social Security, Internal Revenue and military records to trace absentee parents throughout the country. It was first introduced in 1976 under an addition to the Social Security Act. Other provisions of the law require all states to establish child support units with parent locator computers, authorized the Internal Revenue Service to make collections in some cases and permits wages and benefits of federal employees to be garnisheed for child support payments. Failure of parents to obey court child support orders costs taxpayers $8 billion a year in welfare benefits.

FEDERAL PROCUREMENT POLICY. Set in 1974 by an agency called the Office of Federal Procurement Policy, these are 39 requirements the government applies to anyone who wants to enter the $100 billion-a-year business with the government. They include socioeconomic goals such as buying American products, especially in areas of high unemployment, dealing with small businesses and minority groups and using only equal opportunity employers.

FEDERAL PROCUREMENT REGULATIONS (F.P.R.). These regulations apply to the acquisition of supplies and services by United States government civilian agencies. They are issued by the General Services Administration, under authority of the Federal Property and Administrative Services Act and appear in Volume 41 of the *Code of Federal Regulations*. The Federal Procurement Regulations are similar to the Defense Acquisition Regulations.

FEDERAL PUBLIC DEFENDER ORGANIZATIONS. See ADMINISTRATIVE OFFICE OF THE UNITED STATES COURTS.

FEDERAL QUESTION. A jurisdictional requirement which must be satisfied to confer original jurisdiction on a federal court. Even though the Constitution provides that federal courts may be given jurisdiction over cases "arising under" the Constitution, laws and treaties of the United States, it was not until 1875 that Congress gave the federal courts general original jurisdiction over such cases. Until that time, litigants were forced to look to state tribunals in the first instance for vindication of federally-protected rights, subject to limited review by the

United States Supreme Court. The 1875 statute contains substantially the same language as the Constitution. The key inquiry to this day remains the scope of the phrase "arising under." Generally, to have Federal Question jurisdiction, rather than Diversity of Citizenship jurisdiction, there must be a substantial claim founded "directly" upon federal law. Such federal law may include the Constitution, a statute of the United States, a federal administrative regulation, or a treaty. Even though the jurisdictional amount requirement ostensibly applies to Federal Question cases in federal courts, a series of particular federal statutes grants jurisdiction without regard to the amount in controversy in virtually all the areas that would otherwise fall under the general Federal Question statute.

FEDERAL REGISTER. Published daily by the federal government, the *Register* makes available to the public federal agency regulations and other legal documents of the executive branch. The *Register* includes government requirements in such fields as environmental protection, consumer product safety, food and drug standards, and occupational health and safety. Perhaps more importantly, the *Federal Register* includes proposed changes in regulated areas. Citizens or groups are invited to participate in the consideration of the proposed regulation by submitting written data, views, or arguments, and sometimes by oral presentations. The publication of proposed rules and notices of public meetings affords citizens a significant opportunity to be informed of and participate in the workings of their government. The Office of the *Federal Register* conducts regularly scheduled educational workshops in Washington, D.C., open to the general public and federal agency personnel on how to use the *Federal Register*. These sessions cover the following areas: a brief history of the *Federal Register*; the differences between legislation and regulations; an introduction to the finding aids of the Office of the *Federal Register*; the rela-tionship between the *Federal Register* and the *Code of Federal Regulations*; and the important elements of a typical *Federal Register* document.

FEDERAL RESERVE SYSTEM. Established by President Wilson in 1913 to create a favorable economic climate by regulating credit conditions to counteract inflationary and deflationary trends. The Federal Reserve System controls the flow of money to its twelve Reserve Banks and all nationally chartered banks, which must join the Federal Reserve. It also regulates the economy through the open market by buying or selling securities. Theoretically, when securities are bought, more money is fed into the market place to stimulate the economy, and the reverse is true when securities are sold.

FEDERAL RULES FOR THE TRIAL OF MINOR OFFENSES BEFORE UNITED STATES MAGISTRATES. Instructions for procedures to be followed in minor or petty offenses if the accused consents to being tried before a magistrate rather than in the district court.

FEDERAL RULES OF APPELLATE PROCEDURE. Procedures regarding the steps necessary to bring an appeal in the federal courts. The Rules, originally adopted in 1967 by the Supreme Court, deal with matters such as Habeas Corpus, appeals from the tax court and appeals from the district courts.

FEDERAL RULES OF CIVIL PROCEDURE. Uniform Rules which govern procedure in federal courts in civil cases. The struggle for Federal Rules of Civil Procedure was initiated in 1911 by the American Bar Association, which for 20 years proposed that Congress give the courts the power to make such rules. It was not until 1934, however, that the Supreme Court was given rule-making powers by Congress via the Enabling Act (28 U.S.C. 2072). After several years of proposals and drafts, the new Federal Rules were adopted by the Supreme Court in late 1937, and became effective the following year. The

Federal Rules of Civil Procedure essentially streamlined federal procedure and merged law and equity. They provide a uniform procedure for federal courts that is "flexible, simple, clean and efficient." Many of the states have revised their own procedure along the lines of the Federal Rules, and the general reaction to the Rules has been positive. Significant amendments to the Rules were adopted in 1961, 1963, and 1966.

FEDERAL RULES OF CRIMINAL PROCEDURE. A set of instructions, originally adopted by the Supreme Court in 1944, for the federal courts in criminal cases. The Rules specify the procedures to be followed during the course of a criminal proceeding, from search, arrest and arraignment, through final judgment, and also deal with matters such as bail and the appointment of counsel.

FEDERAL SECURITIES LAW CODE. A monumental research and drafting project in progress since 1970 under the aegis of the American Law Institute and with the active encouragement of the American Bar Association. It is directed by Professor Louis Loss of Harvard Law School, author of the Blue Sky Laws in effect in 35 states, with the assistance of a team of experts. When passed by Congress, the Code would reconcile the six basic securities laws enacted by the national legislature between 1933 and 1940, clarify the confusing and contradictory judicial decisions in the area, and reflect the modern developments in the world of finance. It would make fundamental changes in the powers of the regulators and impose new and different compliance requirements on those subject to the new Code.

FEDERAL SUPPLY SERVICE AGENCY. An agency of the General Services Administration (G.S.A.) set up to purchase commonly-used supplies on a federal government-wide basis.

FEDERAL SUPPLY SERVICE CONTRACTS. The contracts by which the

Federal Supply Service Agency (an agency of the General Services Administration) arranges to purchase commonly-used supplies on a federal government-wide basis.

FEDERAL TORT CLAIMS ACT (1946). Legislation which waived the federal government's immunity from suit in tort. The Act makes the United States liable for the negligent or wrongful acts or omissions of federal employees acting within the scope of their employment "in the same manner and to the same extent as a private individual under like circumstances." This language, however, becomes somewhat misleading considering the exceptions embodied in the Act. One exception exempts the government from liability for "any claim arising out of assault, battery, false imprisonment, false arrest, malicious prosecution, abuse of process, libel, slander, misrepresentation, deceit or interference with contract rights." Another provision exempts the government from liability for any "discretionary" act or function. While courts vary somewhat in their interpretation of the latter provision, it is generally considered to preclude liability for decisions made at the planning or policy level. Under this definition, for example, it is discretionary to establish a post office at a particular location, but not discretionary to negligently fail to construct handrails.

FEDERAL TRADE COMMISSION (F.T.C.). An independent regulatory agency created by the 1914 Federal Trade Commission Act to prevent unfair methods of competition. More recently, the Commission's jurisdiction has been expanded to encompass unfair and deceptive acts or practices in or affecting interstate commerce. This extension has allowed the Commission to investigate instances of ghetto fraud and deceptive advertising not explicitly covered under its original mandate. The F.T.C.'s investigative, rule-making and adjudicatory powers are directed by five commissioners appointed by the President with Senate approval.

FEDERAL TRADE COMMISSION IMPROVEMENT ACT. See MAGNUSON-MOSS WARRANTY ACT.

FEDERAL TRIANGLE. (1) The nine square blocks of handsome federal government buildings in the nation's capital lying between Pennsylvania Avenue and Constitution Avenue in the form of a physical triangle. (2) A conceptual triangle composed of (a) federal government workers in the Executive branch who have formed powerful (b) federal employee unions which successfully lobby for substantial increases in salary and fringe benefits with (c) members of Congress who react sympathetically to their requests in a self-serving wish to be re-elected. A very cozy relationship indeed which we poor taxpayers foolishly subsidize annually.

FEDERATION OF WOMEN LAWYERS' JUDICIAL SCREENING PANEL. A panel of women lawyers started in February, 1979, at a national meeting of women lawyers in Washington, D.C., and which has headquarters in New York City. This panel serves the important function of screening candidates to the federal bench. This is the first time any group other than the American Bar Association has been formally included in the judicial evaluation process of the Senate Judiciary Committee and made a formal part of the confirmation record. The panel receives the names of the candidates from the Department of Justice at the same time the names go to the American Bar Association. The Panel investigates and interviews these candidates on the basis of whether they "possess and have demonstrated a commitment to equal justice under law"—Executive Orders 12059 and 12097 promulgated by President Carter in connection with the legislation authorizing the appointment of new federal judges. The Panel seeks nominees that have demonstrated by concrete action their commitment to equal justice. The candidates are rated on a five-grade scale: "exceptional commitment," "affirmative commitment," "adequate commitment," "no significant action demonstrating commitment," and "opposition to equal justice."

FEE ARBITRATION. First established in Massachusetts in 1974, Fee Arbitration Boards head and settle fee disputes between lawyers and clients. They also decide cases between attorneys (over the division of fees) as well as between lawyers and doctors, stenographers and expert witnesses over disputes arising out of a professional relationship other than attorney-client.

FEE ARBITRATION BOARD. See FEE ARBITRATION.

FEEDING THE POLAR BEAR CHOCOLATES. A Chinese expression for any attempt to appease the Russians.

FEE SIMPLE. Absolute ownership. Property held in Fee Simple is free of any condition, limitation or restriction.

FEE SIMPLE DETERMINABLE. A fee simple which automatically terminates upon the happening of a contingency or stated event.

FEE SPLITTING. An act by which fees obtained for legal services are split or divided between lawyers or non-lawyers who participated in the resolution of the legal matter. Under the Code of Professional Responsibility, fee splitting is not permitted between a lawyer and a non-lawyer. And only with complete disclosure and consent by the client, may a lawyer split his fees with another lawyer outside his law firm.

FEE TAIL. At common law, an estate in land created by the use of the phrase, "To *A* and the heirs of his body." As the magic phrase suggests, the fee tail was intended to keep property within a given family. The possessor of the fee tail could not freely alienate it, nor could he devise it to whomever he chose, only to his lineal heirs. If there was a failure of lineal heirs in any generation, the property would revert to the original grantor or his estate. Today, in most jurisdictions the fee tail has been abolished and entailed land may be conveyed in fee simple.

FEE TAIL SPECIAL. At common law, an estate in land which can be inherited only by lineals of a particular marriage.

FEIGNED CASE (Fictitious Suit, Feigned Action). A suit based upon a pretended right, brought by a plaintiff who has no true cause of action. Such a suit is instituted for the purpose of obtaining a judicial opinion without having an actual or existing controversy between the parties. In most instances, the courts dispose only of actual controversies and refuse to consider feigned cases. Feigned cases differ from false cases in that the words of the pleadings in the former are true, whereas in the latter they are false.

FEINBERG LAWS. A series of laws enacted in the early 1950s in New York and other states, directing the State Board of Regents (e.g. in New York) to enforce a state statute which required the dismissal of public school teachers who advocated that the U.S. government should be overthrown by force or violence, or who belonged to any organization so advocating. New York's Feinberg Law was upheld as constitutional by the Supreme Court in 1952, but in 1967 the Court overturned its earlier decision, holding substantial portions of New York's Feinberg Law (as well as some later amendments) invalid.

F.E.L.A. See FEDERAL EMPLOYERS' LIABILITY ACT.

FELONIOUS ASSAULT. See AGGRAVATED ASSAULT.

FELONIOUS OFFENSE. A serious crime, as distinguished from a minor offense known as a misdemeanor. Although some states statutorily label each crime as a felonious offense or misdemeanor, others classify crimes as felonies according to (1) the place of imprisonment, whether in a state prison or penitentiary, or (2) the maximum possible length of imprisonment. In most states, the maximum possible penalty determines whether a crime is a felony, not the sentence actually imposed or served. Felonious offenses are usually punishable by imprisonment for terms longer than one year. A convicted felon may lose privileges not lost by a misdemeanant, such as the right

147—Mod. Legal Glossary (8388K) hs
to hold office, to vote, to sit on a jury, or to practice as an attorney. However, some states deprive a person of these rights if convicted of a crime involving Moral Turpitude, notwithstanding its classification as a misdemeanor.

FELONY MURDER. The doctrine which states that murder includes any killing, however accidental, which occurs during the commission of a felony. The rule originated in England at a time when most felonies themselves were punishable by death. Today, when many felonies have the lesser penalties of a fine or several years' imprisonment, the traditional Felony Murder rule seems unduly harsh to many legal scholars. A number of states have modified the rule, and England has abolished it. Many states have limited the doctrine to those felonies which are "dangerous to life." However, these states are split as to the proper test of determining whether a felony is "dangerous to life." Some use a subjective test based upon the defendant's particular manner of committing the felony, whereas others use an objective test based upon the general nature of the felony itself. Most states classify a Felony Murder as Murder in the First Degree if the homicide occurs during one of the most serious felonies, such as robbery, rape, arson or kidnapping. Otherwise it is Murder in the Second Degree. The requirement that the felony be the proximate cause of the homicide has raised some difficult analytical problems. For example, suppose that A and B rob X and Y, and that Y fires a gun intending to kill A, but kills X instead. Are A and B guilty of Felony Murder? If Y killed A, would B be guilty of Felony Murder? The traditional answers are affirmative although there are some modern decisions contra. Clearly, the defendant's conduct was the cause in fact of the homicide, but some courts are reluctant to punish a fortuity. However, California, the leading state in narrowing the breadth of Felony Murder, has made clear that A and B would be liable for murder if they initiated the use of deadly force.

F.E.M.A. (Federal Emergency Management Agency). A federal agency established by President Carter in 1979 after the nuclear energy power plant disaster at Three Mile Island in Pennsylvania, to deal with nuclear and natural disasters in addition to terrorist attacks.

FEMME COVERT (Latin—covered woman or married woman). Under English law, not only was the legal capacity of a Femme Covert greatly reduced but her competence to exercise private rights was nearly totally suspended during coverture. The married woman was considered Sub Virga (under the rod of her husband). Consequently, this antiquated conception resulted in complete control by the husband over the wife's realty. Under case law and statutes today, nearly all the married woman's disabilities have been removed.

FEMME SOLE (Latin—single or unmarried woman). A single woman with legal capacity slightly less than that of a man. Although under English law she was excluded from public functions, a single woman was considered nearly wholly competent to exercise private rights.

F.H.A. See FEDERAL HOUSING ADMINISTRATION.

F.H.L.M.C. See FREDDY MAC.

F.I.C. See FEDERAL INFORMATION CENTERS.

FICTION THEORY. See ENTITY THEORY.

FIDELITY INSURANCE. Protects an employer against financial loss due to the dishonesty of an employee. Such insurance uses a fidelity bond, whereby any person holding a position of trust is covered.

FIDUCIARY DUTIES. (A) The legally enforceable duties which a corporate management owes to its shareholders. There are several classes of fiduciary duties. (1) Fiduciaries are forbidden to compete with their corporation by disclosing corporate trade secrets, by using their corporation's funds, facilities, or personnel for their own business, or by using their position to unfair advantage; (2) They cannot divert to themselves opportunities in which the corporation has any right, interest, or expectancy; this is called the Corporate Opportunity Rule. However, if, after full disclosure of all relevant facts to a corporation, its board of directors impartially rejects its "opportunity," the opportunity ceases to exist in the eyes of the law; (3) A fiduciary cannot have any interests conflicting with his corporation. The Unfairness Test is usually applied here: Would an independent corporate fiduciary in an arm's length bargain (that is, a fair and openly disclosed bargain) legally bind his corporation to such a transaction?; (4) Fiduciaries cannot use "inside" information to make profits—usually called Insider Trading—to the detriment of any shareholders; (5) Corporate fiduciaries must exercise their unbiased judgment in the best interest of the corporation as a whole; they cannot favor one intracorporate group over another, as to do so would be to create "fraud or oppression on the minority." This rule relates especially to controlling shareholders, or to those persons who own enough shares in a corporation to influence its decisions. Hence, where shareholder consent to corporate matters other than the election of directors is required, such controlling shareholders will be held to fiduciary standards. In a large corporation, 5 percent ownership would probably qualify a person or group as a controlling shareholder; (6) Finally, if a controlling shareholder decides to sell his control or power in a corporation, he is held to fiduciary standards of good faith and full disclosure of all relevant facts on the theory that control is a corporate asset in which all shareholders have equal interest. The leading *Perlman Case*, 219 F.2d 173 (1955) held that the burden of proof was always on the fiduciaries to show the fairness of their dealings. (B) Duties arising out of a trust relationship, such as those owed by a trustee to a beneficiary, an attorney to a client or a parent to his child.

FIELD AUDIT. See TAX AUDIT.

FIELD CODE. The product of a mid-nineteenth century movement to simplify American Civil Procedure. It bears the name of its drafter, David Dudley Field, an American law reformer, scholar, and practitioner in New York. The Code had three purposes: (1) the substitution of a single action, the Civil Action, for all common law forms of action; (2) the use of equitable rules of pleading, parties, and judgments instead of technical common law rules; and (3) the consolidation of legal and equitable procedure. New York, in 1848, was the first state to adopt these reforms. California soon followed, largely owing to the advocacy of Field's brother, Stephen. Among Field's other reforms were Codes for Criminal Procedure, penal offenses, civil wrongs, and political conduct. However, none of these gained the acclaim and widespread use that the Civil Procedure Code enjoyed. Most of the American states now follow the Field Code as the basis for their civil litigation, especially in the West since the early pioneers who left the East usually carried a copy of the Code with them to serve as a guide in the absence of any other law books.

FIELD, STEPHEN. During his tenure as an Associate Justice of the United States Supreme Court in the post-Civil War era (1863-97), he became identified as a protector of private property rights against government interference. Field's visibility in the late 19th century was illustrative of the rise of associate justices generally; no longer did the Court primarily reflect the personality and legal bent of its Chief Justice. While Field served on the Court, it was preoccupied with resolving disputes under the 13th, 14th and 15th Amendments. Field was the son of a New England minister, and received his legal training as an apprentice with his brother, David Dudley Field, who promulgated the Field Code. He left his brother's employ to search for gold in California, and later served in the California legislature, on the California Supreme Court, and on the Ninth Circuit Court of Appeals. His career was marked by political animosity and volatileness. After a disagreement with Grover Cleveland, Field remained true to his word never to enter the White House while Cleveland was still President. Moreover, while sitting on the Ninth Circuit, Field had ruled against a Mrs. Terry in a suit involving her prior marriage. Both she and Mr. Terry threatened Field's life. In 1889, on a train from San Francisco to Los Angeles, Field encountered the Terrys, who had just been released from imprisonment for the threats they had made. In the dining car one morning, Mr. Terry accosted Field and struck him on the side of the face. Field's bodyguard, believing Terry had drawn a knife, shot Terry and killed him. In the meantime, Mrs. Terry arrived in the dining car carrying a briefcase with a gun inside (presumably intended for Field). Mrs. Terry filed a murder complaint against Field and his bodyguard. Field was arrested but was released shortly thereafter.

FIERI FACIAS (Latin—that you cause to be made). The ordinary writ of execution for the seizure and sale of personal property in satisfaction of a judgment rendered against a debtor. The writ issues to a sheriff, who causes the goods of the debtor to be sold and collects the amount of the judgment from the proceeds of sale. After he has levied on the debtor's property, the sheriff returns the writ, endorsed Fieri Feci which means, "I have caused it to be made." A writ of Fieri Facias De Bonis Testatoris is a writ of execution against the executor of an estate for a judgment debt of his testator, to be satisfied from property in the estate. If the judgment cannot be executed because the executor has wasted the assets of the estate, the creditor can cause a writ of Fieri Facias De Bonis Proprias to be issued, which will order the sheriff to seize and sell the executor's personal property to satisfy the judgment against the testator.

FIFTH AMENDMENT. See TAKE THE FIFTH.

FIGHTING JUDGE. Nickname given to cocky George C. Wallace, a former inferior court judge and bantam-weight boxer, who used his inaugural address as Governor of Alabama in 1962 to proclaim "Segregation now! Segregation tomorrow! Segregation forever!" in his unsuccessful act of defiance to Washington on the inevitable forthcoming lawful integration of the races in the educational system in his home state. Although Wallace was an unsuccessful presidential candidate four times, he served as Governor of Alabama longer than any other person in the history of the state.

FIGHTING WORDS. See CHAPLINSKY v. NEW HAMPSHIRE.

FILE WRAPPER ESTOPPEL. A File Wrapper is the full written record of a patent application contained in the file of the United States Patent Office. File Wrapper Estoppel occurs when a patentee attempts to secure benefits of his invention which he has previously disclaimed or the nonexistence of which he has conceded during the prosecution of his application. For example, File Wrapper Estoppel might be invoked as a defense in an infringement suit where a patentee previously narrowed the scope of a claim in response to a rejection of that claim by a Patent Examiner and subsequently asserts a claim broader than the narrowed claim to support his infringement action.

FILIATION ORDER. A judicial or other official acknowledgement that a man is the natural parent of a given child, which is required in some states as a condition to the support of the child or inheritance of the child from the father.

FILIBUSTER TACTIC. A prolonged discussion of a proposed bill in the Senate to prevent a vote. It is an attempt by a minority to wear down the majority forces, so that they will abandon a bill in order to move on to other business. Senator Strom Thurmond of South Carolina holds the record for a one-man filibuster, speaking for 24 hours and 18 minutes in opposition to the 1957 Civil Rights Act. However, in February of 1979 on a 78-16 vote, the Senate placed new curbs on the filibuster by limiting the amount of time the Senate can be stymied by opponents of legislation after a motion to cut off debate has been approved. It still will require the vote of 60 senators to end a filibuster and each Senator will be allocated one hour after that. However, the new rules set a limit of 100 hours for debate, amendments, roll call votes and other time-delaying tactics after cloture has been approved. Once that 100 hours is up, the Senate must vote on the legislation. The word filibuster is derived from the Dutch "vrij buit" (free booty) or "vlieboot" (flyboat) and originally denoted the plundering activities of buccaneers who stripped treasure ships returning from the New World. In the period between the Mexican War and the Civil War, a filibuster was an individual who conducted irregular military expeditions in order to expand American influence abroad. One such filibuster was William Walker of Tennessee, who raided Nicaragua in the mid-19th century and caused himself to be named President of that country.

FILIUS NULLIUS (Latin—child of no one). An illegitimate child; a bastard; a person born out of lawful wedlock; an outlaw without rights at common law. Fortunately, other states are following the lead of Arizona in abolishing the concept by ruling that every child is the lawful offspring of its natural or biological parents, whether they were married or not at the time of the child's birth. This is compassionate because children are not bastards, their parents are. In some cities, such as the nation's capital, more than 50 percent of the children are born to parents who were not legally married to each other. So the law of Arizona should become the law of the land.

FINAL JUDGMENT RULE. The long-standing policy of the federal courts that permits appeals only from a final decision of a lower court. The general purpose of the rule is to prevent delay in litigation resulting from Interlocutory Appeals. The final judgment policy, first announced in the Judiciary Act of 1789, is embodied today in the most recent Judicial Code. Though the precise meaning of "final" is not settled, leading cases suggest a final decision ends the litigation on the merits, leaving nothing for the court to do but execute the judgment. In certain cases, however, a party's rights may be damaged irreparably if prompt review of particular issues were unavailable. Some issues are so readily separable from the rest of the case that no advantage is gained in postponing their review. Under these circumstances, certain statutory provisions permit Interlocutory Review. There also are a variety of court-made rules by which particular orders are treated as "final" and appealable as such.

FINAL SOLUTION. The name given by Hitler to his program of genocide against the Jews to preserve the racial purity of the Germans, through the attempted annihilation of the victims by the millions in the gas chambers was in violation of every moral and legal norm of any civilized society.

FINANCIAL INSTITUTIONS REGULATORY AND INTEREST RATE CONTROL ACT OF 1978. A federal consumer-privacy law that requires (1) governmental agencies to notify individuals of the intent to summon their records from banks and other institutions, after which notification, the individual has up to 14 days to challenge the agency; and (2) banks and other financial institutions to send each customer in a blanket mailing a statement of his rights of recourse to the agency's request for records.

FINANCIAL RESPONSIBILITY LAWS. Intended to induce motorists to carry adequate automobile liability insurance. The laws require that under specified circumstances the motorist must show evidence of financial responsibility following an accident. A valid automobile liability insurance policy with a specified minimum limit is the most common evidence of financial responsibility although the laws permit the deposit of cash or bond to satisfy the requirements. The inability of a motorist to meet the requirements of the financial responsibility laws results in the suspension of his driver's license and automobile registration.

FINDER'S FEE. An amount of money given to an individual who helps bring about a business transaction, such as a corporate merger or a real estate deal.

FINDING A LAWYER. Some of the best methods are: (1) asking friends who have had similar legal problems; (2) checking the Martindale-Hubbell Law Directory in the public library. This directory gives brief biographical sketches of many lawyers, describes the type of practice they engage in, and for some, rates their legal ability, ethical standards and professional reliability; (3) checking the yellow pages of the phone book under attorneys, particularly noting whether or not a Lawyer Referral Service exists in your area. Such services, operated by local bar associations, often allow a limited consultation with an attorney at minimal or no charge; (4) reading lawyer advertising; and (5) asking a social service or counseling agency for a referral. Some counseling agencies, such as those which deal with marital problems, often compile lists of attorneys who handle family law cases. Once you have tentatively selected a lawyer, the American Bar Association (A.B.A.) suggests that you ask him about his experience with your kind of case and do not hesitate to discuss fees. If the lawyer works on a contingency fee basis (the lawyer is paid only if he recovers money for you), find out if the fee is a percentage of the gross award, or the net award after other costs are deducted.

FINK BREAKER. See STRIKE BREAKER.

FIREMEN'S RULE. A legal principle that negligence of a person in causing a fire is not a basis for liability to a professional fireman who is injured while fighting the fire.

FIRM-FIXED PRICE. Under this Fixed-Price contract, the government procurement contractor is paid a fixed price for specified performance. As the contractor's cost experience is not relevant to determining his compensation, his profit and loss depends entirely on the ability to control costs.

FIRM FIXED-PRICE ARRANGEMENT. See FIXED-PRICE REDETERMINATION.

FIRM FIXED-PRICE LEVEL OF EFFORT TERM. This Fixed-Price government procurement contracting method describes the scope of work in general terms, usually calling for investigation or study in a specific research and development area. It obligates the contractor to devote a specified level of effort over a stated time for a fixed dollar amount.

FIRM OFFER RULE. According to section 2-205 of the Uniform Commercial Code, the power of the offeror to withdraw a firm offer can and will be limited if the offeree had reason to rely on the firmness of the offer. Unlike the common law of contracts, which allows the offeror more flexibility in withdrawing his offer at any point as long as no consideration was received, the U.C.C. is more restrictive.

FIRST BRIGADE. A proposed military elitest mobile strike force trained in anti-terrorist, anti-hijacking and anti-kidnapping techniques. As a result of the Iranian hostage seizure, the Brigade was proposed in 1979 by Republican Senator Howard H. Baker, Jr.

FIRST DEGREE MURDER. See MURDER IN THE FIRST DEGREE.

FIRST DEVELOPMENT DECADE. See SECOND DEVELOPMENT DECADE.

FIRST JUDICIARY ACT. See JUDICIARY ACT OF 1789.

FIRST LADY. The wife of an American President. If she is a forceful person who has an impact on the decision-making of her husband, such as Eleanor Roosevelt or Rosalynn Carter, she is called an Assistant President. Indeed, for the year that sickness totally immobilized President Wilson, his wife ran the country in his place.

FIRST MONDAY IN OCTOBER. Named after the first day of the annual new term of the Supreme Court of the United States, this play, written by Jerome Lawrence and Robert E. Lee in 1978, is about the first woman ever appointed to the high bench.

FIRST OFFENDER TREATMENT PROGRAM. Allows those convicted of certain misdemeanors (taking soft drugs, shoplifting, drunk driving or committing sexual offenses), who have not had a prior criminal record, to be given a suspended sentence if they voluntarily participate in a medical or educational program designed to cure their particular problems.

FIRST PEACE PROCLAMATION. The ancient Jewish people first presented the world with the vision of eternal peace, of universal disarmament, and of abolishing the teaching and learning of war. Two of their Prophets, Yeshayahu Ben-Amotz [Isaiah] and Micha Hamorashti [Micah], having foreseen the spiritual unity of man under God—with His word coming forth from Jerusalem—gave the nations of the world the following vision expressed in identical Biblical terms:

"And they shall beat their swords into plowshares and their spears into pruning hooks. Nation shall not lift up sword against nation: neither shall they learn war anymore."

FIRST PEACE TREATY. Concluded 3,000 years ago between Egyptian Ramses the Great and Hattusilis, Prince of the Hittites, who reciprocally resolved to establish "Good Peace and Good Brotherhood."

FIRST WORLD (Free World). Generally refers to the capitalist nations of the West, many of which are political democracies.

FISCAL DRAG. Increasingly higher rates of inflation which push taxpayers into higher tax brackets thereby reducing their real net income.

FISHERY CONSERVATION AND MANAGEMENT ACT OF 1976 (F.C.M.A.). A federal law passed in 1976 which gave the United States the authority (1) to assess more accurately the conditions of the fish stocks within 200 miles of the U.S. shores which contain 20 percent of the estimated world's fish resources, and (2) to take measures to rebuild fish stocks to the point where they could supply the greatest harvestable yield without danger of depletion. The U.S. obligations, under F.C.M.A. and Governing International Fishing Agreements (G.I.F.A.) were (1) to use the best scientific data available as the basis for setting fishing limits, and (2) to aim for optimum yield from fisheries in order to avoid wasting vital food resources and (3) to provide benefits in food production and recreational opportunities. This meant that the true size of the allowable catch had to be determined using the latest scientific methods, and that available fish resources could not be withheld for the purpose of gaining an economic advantage over foreign fishermen. Given these assurances, the nations which traditionally fished the international waters off the U.S. coasts then signed Governing International Fishing Agreements (G.I.F.A.) with the United States and these were approved by Congress. G.I.F.A. provided for recognition of U.S. fishery conservation and management authority in the 200-mile Fishery Conservation Zone (F.C.Z.) in return for agreements by the United States to permit signatory nations to fish for the surplus. The United States also agreed in G.I.R.A. that fisheries would be managed for optimum utilization of fishery resources. In addition, the United States promised that it

would take into account "the need to minimize economic dislocation in cases where vessels have habitually fished for living resources over which the United States exercises fishery management authority."

FISHERY CONSERVATION AND MANAGEMENT ACT OF 1977. A federal law which established a 200-mile offshore limit consisting of a 2-¼ million square mile area, limiting the rights of foreigners to fish in American waters.

FISHING EXPEDITION. See BOXCAR DISCOVERY.

FITZGERALD, A. ERNEST. An Air Force civilian employee who has become the nation's best known Whistle-Blower. In 1970, after he revealed to a congressional committee that cost overruns on the C5-A, the Air Force's mammoth jet cargo plane, could total as much as $2 billion, Fitzgerald was fired. After a lengthy and expensive appeal to the Civil Service Commission, he was returned to the payroll, but deprived of most of his former responsibilities.

FIXED-PRICE INCENTIVE. Under this fixed-price government procurement contract, there is included a provision for adjustment of profit and establishment of a final contract price by a formula based on the relationship which final negotiated total cost bears to total target costs. There must be included in the contract provisions a ceiling price which requires contract performance at a maximum amount of compensation.

FIXED-PRICE REDETERMINA-TION. The Defense Acquisition Regulation offers two of this type of Government Procurement Fixed-Priced Arrangement: Prospective Price Redetermination at a stated time or times during performance, and Retroactive Price Redetermination after completion. The former calls for a Firm Fixed-Priced Arrangement during the initial phase of contract performance and for a Prospective Price Redetermination either upward or downward at stated intervals during later performance.

FIXED-PRICE WITH ECONOMIC PRICE ADJUSTMENT. Under this Fixed-Price Arrangement, certain specific cost elements are identified. The government procurement contract price varies according to increases or decreases experienced by the contractor with respect to these elements, usually material costs or labor rates.

FIXED SENTENCING. See SENTENCING PROCEDURES.

F.J.C. See FEDERAL JUDICIAL CENTER.

FLAG OF CONVENIENCE. The arbitrary registration of a ship in a foreign country, such as Liberia or Panama, where the owner does not have a legal residence nor do any business. The purpose is to avoid paying taxes or to take advantage of a low wage scale for the crew or to evade compliance with strict safety requirements.

FLAG SALUTE CASES. A group of cases which generally involved Jehovah's Witnesses, who claimed that flag-saluting requirements violated their religion. In 1940, the Supreme Court in *Minersville School District v. Gobitis,* 310 U.S. 586 (1940) held that schools could require the Flag Salute as a means of achieving a feeling of national unity. However, *West Virginia State Board of Education v. Barnette,* 319 U.S. 624 (1943) overturned *Gobitis* and is still good law. In that case, Flag-Saluting requirements were held to invade rights protected by the First Amendment. The difference in result may be attributed to a feeling by the Court that there was less need for patriotic fervor in 1943 after the Battle of Midway which ensured that the Allies would win World War II.

FLASH OF GENIUS TEST. In a 1941 case, *Cuno Engineering Corp. v. Automatic Devices Corp.,* 313 U.S. 553, the Supreme Court stated that an item was not patentable, notwithstanding its usefulness, unless it revealed "the flash of creative genius" rather than mere mechanical skill. While the test received considerable application in the decade following the decision, it was criticized with equal fervor. The Patent Act of 1952 eliminated the test. Patentability is no longer based on the manner in which an invention was made.

FLAST v. COHEN. See TAXPAYER SUIT.

FLEET MARRIAGES. See LORD HARDWICKE'S ACT.

FLEXIBLE PAYMENT MORTGAGE. A real estate loan in which the monthly payments are set low enough to cover just the interest payments for a period, say, of five years. Thereafter, the payments are increased so that they amortize the mortgage for the full period of the loan.

FLICKER TEST. The traditional standard used to determine abandonment for parental rights termination. As long as a parent indicated a "flicker of interest," abandonment was not established as a matter of law. The Flicker Test is still used in many jurisdictions though it is being replaced with a new Insubstantial Contact Standard, which makes it easier to find abandonment for parental rights termination.

FLIP TOP LAW. Effective January 1, 1979, California became the first state to ban the manufacture or sale of beverages in cans that were opened by disposable metal tabs which constituted dangerous items of litter.

F.L.I.T.E. See COMPUTER-ASSISTED LEGAL RESEARCH.

FLOATER POLICY. A type of insurance which provides coverage of easily movable property, wherever it may be located. It is often used in commercial transactions to cover goods in transit which cannot be covered by specific insurance because of the rapid change in the property's location. A Floater Policy is intended as supplemental insurance and becomes effective only when specific insurance ceases to cover the risk.

FLOATING LIEN (Cross-Collateral Clause; Add-On Clause). A security interest which continues to exist not only in the presently existing collateral of a buyer, but also in collateral which is subsequently acquired. For example, W buys a sofa from X who uses it as collateral to secure W's installment loan for the sofa. W subsequently purchases a stereo and a washing machine from X. All three items purchased from X will be used as collateral for any existing debt owed X on the original installment agreement. This practice has been condemned as unconscionable by some courts because it may result in an unreasonable forfeiture. In the example above, W's default on any payment on the sofa may result in repossession of the sofa, the stereo, and the washing machine. On the other hand, such clauses may be necessary when rapid depreciation of goods necessitates additional collateral. Moreover, the best collateral may be that which the seller sold the buyer because the seller is in a better position to resell the goods and he is more certain of their market value.

FLOATING RATE NOTE. See F. R. N.

FLOATING SUPERMARKETS. European ships that sail just beyond their Territorial Waters so that their citizens may legally buy from bonded warehouses local and imported luxury goods at greatly reduced prices and bring them back into their home country tax free and duty free on the return trip.

FLOATING ZONES. The result of land-use regulation based on a comprehensive zoning plan. Under this technique, each landowner asks for a zoning classification for his property. This classification is then applied to the land in conformity with a region-wide comprehensive plan. This type of zoning yields results analogous to spot zoning.

FLY AMERICAN. The official United States policy which requires every passenger to use an American airline when the trip is paid for by federal funds.

FLY COP. See SHOO-FLY COP.

FLYING PICKETS. See SOCIAL CONTRACT.

FLYING UNIVERSITIES. Underground lectures sponsored in Poland by 58 professors and writers who founded the Society for Academic Causes in January, 1978. They are so named because the classes are moved from place to place by the participants to avoid arrest. It is a response to the Human Rights program of President Carter since Russia controls the Polish Universities. Should this movement for Freedom of Speech and Press which we take for granted in America spread to the rest of the Communist East Europe or to the U.S.S.R. itself, it could spell real trouble for the Soviets.

F.M.C. (Federal Maritime Commission). A federal agency which regulates the waterborne foreign and domestic offshore commerce of the United States, assures that United States international trade is open to all nations on fair and equitable terms, and guards against unauthorized monopoly in the waterborne commerce of the United States. These objectives are accomplished through maintaining surveillance over steamship conferences and common carriers by water; assuring that only the rates on file with the Commission are charged; approving agreements between persons subject to the Shipping Act; guaranteeing equal treatment to shippers and carriers by terminal operators, freight forwarders, and other persons subject to the shipping statutes; and ensuring that adequate levels of financial responsibility are maintained for indemnification of passengers or oil spill cleanup.

F.M.C.S. See FEDERAL MEDIATION and CONCILIATION SERVICE.

F.O.B. (Free on Board). A commercial term which indicates when the risk of lost or damaged goods passes from the seller to the buyer. If the sales contract provides "F.O.B. seller's factory," the buyer bears the risk of loss during transit. The seller completes his performance under the contract when he delivers the goods to the carrier. Under this provision, the contract price does

F.O.I.A.

not include freight charges. Where the contract provides "F.O.B. point of destination," the seller bears the risk of loss during transit and his obligations under the contract are satisfied only upon delivery of the goods to the destination indicated. The price quoted for the goods under such a provision generally includes freight charges.

F.O.I.A. See FREEDOM OF INFORMATION ACT.

FOOD AND AGRICULTURAL ORGANIZATION. See F.A.O.

FOOD CHOKING LAW. First promulgated by New York City in March, 1978 and since followed elsewhere in an attempt to reduce the 5,000 deaths each year of people who choke to death while eating. It requires restaurants to publish pictures of the Heimlick technique, named after the Xavier University of Cincinnati doctor who perfected it. It consists of placing one's arms around a victim's waist, making a fist and pressing with an upward motion between the navel and rib cage, thereby forcing air up the windpipe to disgorge the food particle.

FOOD STAMP ACT (1964). Established a program, administered by the Department of Agriculture through state welfare agencies, whereby households may purchase food stamps in the amount they generally spend for foods. The food coupons have a higher monetary value than the money required for their purchase, thus enabling participants to buy more food than could be bought without the stamps.

FOOL'S TEST. The standard used by the Federal Trade Commission to determine if advertising is deceptive. It seems that the Commission believes the vast majority of people are so credulous that it does not need to show that a reasonable person was deceived to classify an advertisement as deceptive. It need show only that a fool would be deceived.

FORCED HEIRSHIP. Found only in Louisiana which follows French civil law, this legal principle prevents a parent from disinheriting a child. In the other 49 States, though parents can disinherit their children, they usually must have cause to do so.

FORCED REPORTING STATUTE. Laws which place an affirmative duty on selected groups to report information to specified authorities. The laws are usually enforced by fines and prison sentences for those who fail to report. They are most widely used by states to require health care professionals, social workers and teachers to report suspected cases of child abuse and abuse of aged or incapacitated adults. These statutes usually provide immunity for persons not covered by the act who report suspected cases from criminal or civil prosecution if the information proves to be unfounded. Several states are now expanding these statutes to cover cases of suspected spouse abuse.

FORCE MAJEURE (VIS MAJOR) (French—superior or irresistible force). A higher or irresistible force. Force Majeure, as well as the similar Act of God, may cause a supervening impossibility which may justify the discharge of a contractual or legal duty. Unlike an Act of God, Force Majeure may result from the actions of human agencies, such as governmental intervention resulting from the necessities of war.

FORCIBLE ENTRY. At common law a landlord could enter the apartment of a defaulting tenant and use reasonable force to evict the tenant. While this rule is no longer in force in a majority of states, many leases include provisions reserving the right of entry. Some states hold these provisions void, favoring judicial process rather than self-help remedies.

FORD, GERALD. Attorney and only American to be personally appointed, and not elected by the people, as Vice-President of the United States, by a sitting President, Richard M. Nixon, in December, 1973, after the resignation of Spiro Agnew in October, 1973, who pled nolo contendere to charges of federal tax evasion in plea bargaining. This is the only instance in the United States in which a judge (Walter Hoffman) agreed before the plea was entered to the punishment of a fine, rather than a jail sentence, which had been agreed upon between the United States Attorney prosecutor and defense counsel. The reason given by Judge Hoffman was the fact that the President was also under criminal investigation and the prospect of both the President and Vice-President being in jail had momentous implications on the domestic and international scene too grave even to contemplate.

FOREIGN AFFAIRS. (1) The diplomatic relationships of one country with another. (2) The prestigious and highly influential periodical sponsored by the Council on Foreign Relations which publishes articles by leading private and public officials on current crucial issues of world significance.

FOREIGN AGENT'S REGISTRATION ACT. A federal law that requires the registration of a paid agent of a foreign government or foreign company doing business in the United States. The maximum penalty for violating the Registration Law is five years in prison and a $10,000 fine, but criminal prosecutions usually occur only when a person conceals a relationship with a foreign government.

FOREIGN CLAIMS SETTLEMENT COMMISSION OF THE UNITED STATES. A federal agency which determines claims of United States nationals against foreign governments for losses and injuries sustained by them, pursuant to programs which may be authorized under its law. Commission funds are obtained from international settlements, liquidation of foreign assets in this country by the Departments of Justice or Treasury, and at times from Congress.

FOREIGN CORPORATION. A corporate entity organized under the laws of another state. Such a corporation may still be subject to In Personam jurisdiction in a state other than that of its incorporation if it is doing business, has its principal office, or has minimum contacts in that state. In federal statutes, the term means a corporation organized outside the United States.

FOREIGN COUNTER-INTELLIGENCE. See ELECTRONIC SURVEILLANCE COURTS.

FOREIGN EXCHANGE HOLDINGS. See FOREIGN EXCHANGE MARKETS.

FOREIGN EXCHANGE MARKETS. Markets in which the monies of different countries are legally exchanged. Rates of exchange are the prices of currencies quoted in terms of other currencies. As with other organized markets, transactions are either "spot" (for prompt settlement) or "future" (contracted for settlement at a stated future date). The financial instruments exchanged are all current, that is, money in the form of notes and coins, or bank deposits denominated in different currencies, or near-money in such forms as bank drafts and bills of exchange. Foreign Exchange holdings, sometimes referred to as "Foreign Exchange," are holdings of current or liquid claims denominated in the currency of another country.

FOREIGN INTELLIGENCE SURVEILLANCE ACT OF 1978. A federal law which required for the first time (1) a judicial warrant for most electronic surveillance conducted in the United States for foreign intelligence and (2) evidence of criminal activity before a court can issue a warrant for electronic surveillance of an American citizen.

FOREIGN OIL TAX CREDIT. American oil companies which pay royalties to foreign producers are allowed to charge off such expenses as a credit against any taxes that they owe to Uncle Sam. This costs the American taxpayers more than one billion dollars a year.

FOREIGN PAY-OFF LAW. A federal law passed by Congress in 1977. It requires American companies, including their foreign subsidiaries, to maintain accurate books and records in such reasonable detail as will prevent foreign corporate bribery. Corporate management must maintain systems of accounting controls to insure that no funds are spent to corrupt foreign government officials. The law makes it a crime, punishable by a fine of $1 million per violation, for a corporation to bribe a foreign government official. Payoffs to foreign government officials by American corporations became a national scandal during the mid-seventies. Over 350 firms subject to the jurisdiction of the Securities and Exchange Commission admitted they had made payments amounting to three-fourths of a billion dollars to foreign government officials to increase business. The United States is the only country in the world that makes it a crime to bribe a foreign official, so American companies are losing a lot of business to other less ethical competitors.

FOREIGN POLICY. Prestigious quarterly periodical sponsored by the Carnegie Endowment for International Peace which publishes articles on foreign affairs by distinguished leaders in the field.

FOREIGN POLICY ASSOCIATION. Founded in 1918 as a nonpartisan nonmembership educational organization to stimulate greater interest by citizens in international relations. It sponsors the Great Decisions discussions on National Public Radio for more than five million listeners, publishes books and pamphlets on foreign policy issues for over one million readers and arranges dozens of conferences annually on world affairs.

FOREIGN SERVICE. A federal agency composed of career State Department personnel who serve overseas. To a great extent the future of our country depends on the relations we have with other countries, and those relations are conducted principally by the United States Foreign Service. Our representatives at one hundred and thirty-five Embassies, ten Missions, sixty-seven Consulates General, forty-eight Consulates, one Special Office, one Branch Office, and twelve Consular Agencies throughout the world report to the State Department on the multitude of foreign developments which have a bearing on the welfare and security of the American people. These trained representatives provide the President and the Secretary of State with much of the raw material from which foreign policy is made and with the recommendations which help shape it. The Ambassador is the personal representative of the President abroad and reports to the President through the Secretary of State. Ambassadors have full responsibility for implementing the United States foreign policy by any and all government personnel within their country of assignment, except those under military commands. Their responsibilities include negotiating agreements between the United States and the host country, explaining and disseminating official government policy, and maintaining cordial relations with that country's government and people.

FOREIGN SERVICE JOURNAL. See AMERICAN FOREIGN SERVICE ASSOCIATION.

FORENSIC HYPNOSIS. The practice of using hypnosis as a tool to fight crime. In the past decade Forensic Hypnosis has grown increasingly popular with law-enforcement agencies, and its supporters contend that it soon will be as commonplace as the polygraph or the breathalyzer. Often police call in a professional hypnotist, but more police officers are learning the technique themselves. The new Forensic Hypnotists claim that "information yield" increases by as much as 80 percent when the victims of a crime, or witnesses to it, succumb to hypnotic suggestion. In one case, a kidnap victim, unable to recall the appearance of her assailants, was put under hypnosis and offered a vivid description, leading to the criminal's apprehension. Hypnosis has figured in police work on several pronounced cases including the Hillside Strangling murders in Los Angeles and the 1976 kidnapping of a busload of children in Chowchilla, California. Israeli police use this technique in their search for terrorists. Critics of Forensic Hypnosis charge that it is a form of totalitarian mind-manipulation. They warn that well-meaning law enforcement officers, eager to solve a case, may suggest "memories" that would help bring about a conviction. Despite such criticism, the Law Enforcement Hypnosis Institute, Inc., in Los Angeles predicts it will be a standard tool in criminal investigations within the next ten years.

FORMAL ADVERTISING. This term refers to a statutory procedure for government procurement contract acquisition of supplies or services which involves the issuance of invitations for bids, submission of firm closed bids, public opening of bids at a specified time and place, and award to the lowest responsive and responsible bidder.

FORMULA CLAUSE. The provision or language in a trust arrangement which enables the trust trustee to ascertain the federal estate-tax value of the involved trust property. Essentially, this is a question of value for tax assessment purposes and not one of trust law. Such clauses are utilized pursuant to the Internal Revenue Act of 1954.

FORNICATION LAWS. Laws which proscribe sexual intercourse between unmarried persons. If one of the persons is married, the offense is generally termed adultery for the married person and, in some states, adultery is charged to both of the persons if only the woman is married.

FORUM NON CONVENIENS (Latin —not convenient to the forum) (Inconvenient jurisdiction). A common law doctrine borrowed from Scotland, by which a court in its discretion may decline to exercise its jurisdiction in a matter on the ground that the interests of the parties and the public would best be served if the plaintiff brought suit in another more convenient forum. The grant of Forum Non Conveniens is dependent on the avail-

ability of an appropriate alternative forum. Some factors to be considered in exercising the discretion are the inconvenience to the defendant in defending the suit in the present forum; whether the law that will be applied in an alternative forum will be less favorable to the plaintiff; the inconvenience to the plaintiff in having to bring suit in an alternative forum; the relative availability of witnesses and evidence in the forums, and whether present forum will have to apply foreign law in the suit. Courts often place conditions on the grant of Forum Non Conveniens to insure that the defendant will submit to a suit in the alternative forum.

FORUM SHOPPING. The practice of choosing the most favorable place in which to bring a suit. Where a plaintiff has a choice of where to bring suit, such as between federal or state court, or the courts of different states, he may "shop" for the forum that is likely to provide him with the most favorable result. Forum Shoppers take into account the substantive law as well as the procedural rules that a particular forum would apply in the action.

FORWARD FUNDING. See ADVANCE APPROPRIATION.

FOSTER CHILD. See FOSTER PARENTS.

FOSTER PARENTS. "Quasi" parents, not related by blood, but who perform the duties of a parent to the child of another couple. In the typical situation, foster parents rear, educate, and care for their foster child with the same love and attention they would extend to their own child.

FOUNDATION FOR RESPONSIBLE EFFORTS FOR EX-OFFENDERS. See F.R.E.E.

FOUNDING FATHER. A name coined by President Warren G. Harding for George Washington, first President of the United States. The "Founding Fathers" are the signers of the American Declaration of Independence.

213

FOUR FREEDOMS. Articulated by President Franklin D. Roosevelt in a speech in 1941, in response to the excesses of Fascism and Nazism before and during World War II. They are Freedom of Speech, Freedom of Religion, Freedom from Want, and Freedom from Fear.

FOUR HORSEMEN. The ultraconservative Associate Justices of the Supreme Court who declared as unconstitutional many of the New Deal programs of Democratic President Franklin Roosevelt. The four Justices were George Sutherland, Willis Van Devanter, Pierce Butler and James McReynolds. All four were appointed to the Court by Republican Presidents before the Depression and disagreed with what they considered to be the New Deal's interference with private property rights. The Horsemen preferred the tradition of laissez-faire economics and severe limits on the power of the national government.

FOUR MODERNIZATIONS. See LONG MARCH.

FOUR MODERNIZATIONS PLAN. A development program devised by Deputy Prime Minister Ten Hsido-ping of the People's Republic of China in 1979 that calls for the updating of Chinese agriculture, industry, technology and armaments which will bring the Chinese up to the level of modern industrialized nations by the year 2000.

FOUR-MONTH RULE. A rule of commercial law which applies to security interests under Article 9 of the Uniform Commercial Code which require action to perfect. The Rule holds that such collateral perfected in one state remains perfected for four months if moved to another state. If the interest is to remain perfected, however, the secured party must file in the second state before the four-month period expires. If the four months expires, the secured party is unprotected against purchasers during this period.

FOURTH BRANCH OF GOVERNMENT. See ADMINISTRATIVE LAW.

FOURTH WORLD. The 45 poorest countries in the world whose per capita income is under $300 per year.

F.P.R. See FEDERAL PROCUREMENT REGULATIONS.

FRANKFURTER, FELIX. Nominated to the Supreme Court by Franklin Roosevelt in 1939, he retired from that position in 1962. Frankfurter's background was largely responsible for his belief that the elite should use their status to assure participation by the majority in economic, political, and educational matters. A very energetic jurist who thrived on controversy for its own sake, Frankfurter grew up on New York's lower east side, the son of German Jewish immigrants. He graduated from Harvard Law School in 1906 and was a Professor of Law there at the time of his appointment to the Supreme Court. His law clerks were known as "Felix Frankfurters" and they all went on to successful careers of their own in the law.

FRANKING PRIVILEGE. Allows Congressmen and other government officials to send material through the mail without cost by substituting their signature for postage. Designed to enable Congressmen to keep their constituents informed, the Franking Privilege has often been abused. The Federal Election Campaign Act of 1974 prohibited the use of franked mail to solicit campaign funds.

FRANK, JEROME. Appointed by Franklin Roosevelt to the Second Circuit Court of Appeals in 1941, he served in that capacity until his death in 1957. Frank was one of the founders of the school of "realist" jurisprudence. As such, he emphasized that judges were human and that therefore judicial decision-making essentially reflected their subjective preferences and values. Judging relied on idiosyncracies and intuition, according to Frank, and jurists were being disingenuous when they tried to give the impression of being depersonalized and systematic. His most significant contribution was his psychoanalytic theory of the judicial function. This theory held that judging was an attempt to find legal principles to supply rationalizations for judges' predetermined conclusions. Frank felt that if judges were candid about their biases, adjudication would benefit because they would not feel compelled to strive for specious consistency and uniformity at the expense of all else. This iconoclastic jurist was also an accomplished author whose books reflect an enduring devotion to legal philosophy. Among his important works are *Law and the Modern Mind* (1930), *If Men Were Angels* (1942), *Fate and Freedom* (1945), *Courts on Trial* (1949) and *Not Guilty* (published posthumously, 1957).

FRAUD IN THE FACTUM (Fraud in the Execution). Fraud with respect to the character or content of a writing by one party, which causes the other party to assent to the agreement. Thus, if *X* is reasonably led to believe by *Y* that he is leasing his house to *Y* whereas he is actually deeding it over to *Y*, this is fraud in the factum.

FRAUD IN THE INDUCEMENT. A fraud with respect to the inducement of a person to sign an instrument, as in *X* selling *B* a car, having told him that the mileage is 25,000 whereas actually it is 125,000. The false claim of low mileage, if knowingly made, is fraud in the inducement if it induces *B*, in reasonable reliance thereon, to sign the purchase agreement.

FRAUDULENT MISREPRESENTATION. A tort consisting of a knowing misrepresentation of present fact by the defendant made with the intent to induce the plaintiff's reliance which results in damages to the plaintiff. The cause of action dates back as far as 1201 and is to be distinguished from the contract action of warranty which involves strict liability. Thus if a seller warrants that his product will last ten years and it does not, he will be liable for damages despite his belief that it would. But if the seller of a house says it is not termite infested and so believes it, he will not be liable for Fraudulent Misrepresentation even if the house turns out to be infested.

FREDDY MAC (F.H.L.M.C.; Federal Home Loan Mortgage Corporation). Created in 1970 to supplement the secondary mortgage market activities of Fannie Mae and Ginny Mae. Freddy Mac principally buys conventional mortgages, pools them, and then sells bonds which are secured by the mortgages.

F.R.E.E. (Foundation for Responsible Efforts for Ex-Offenders). A private organization prophetically founded by Attorney Herbert Fineman, former Speaker of the House of Representatives of Pennsylvania, in 1977, to obtain jobs for criminals on probation or parole. Ironically, Mr. Fineman was sentenced to jail in Philadelphia in 1978 after he was convicted of extortion.

FREEDOM HOUSE. A New York-based private organization formed during World War II to monitor human rights around the world. Each year it publishes an annual survey of each country in the world. Its 1978 report stated that only one-third of the population of the world live in countries that can be thought of as being free but conditions have improved for the better since President Carter's campaign for human rights everywhere.

FREEDOM OF INFORMATION ACT (F.O.I.A.). Governs disclosures of information by Federal Administrative Agencies. Amending Section 3 of the Administrative Procedure Act (A.P.A.) in 1966, the F.O.I.A. was intended to limit agency discretion by making the A.P.A. a full disclosure law. Among the provisions of the F.O.I.A. are that substantive rules and general policies be published in the *Federal Register,* that the public have access to staff manuals, opinions, orders, and policy statements, and that certain identifiable records be available for inspection. Perhaps the drafters of the F.O.I.A. were mindful of the assertion by James Madison that "[a] popular Government without popular information or the means of acquiring it is but a Prologue to a Farce or a Tragedy; or perhaps both." But legislators were not committed to unlimited disclosure. The F.O.I.A. contains nine exemptions. Materials exempted from disclosure include national defense and foreign relations secrets, personnel rules and practices, trade secrets, certain interagency memoranda, investigatory files and banking records. The federal courts are split regarding the issue of Reverse-F.O.I.A.—whether the Act confers a right to enjoin disclosure on the supplier of the information.

FREEDOM OF PRESS. Protected by the First Amendment to the United States Constitution which provides that "Congress shall make no Law . . . abridging the Freedom . . . of the Press." It is generally conceded that this guarantee of a free press encompasses at least as much liberty for the media as the Freedom of Speech provision does for the private individual. Some scholars have argued that the Free Press guarantee must include additional freedoms or merely be a redundancy since publishing would in their view be protected as free speech absent the press provision. The additional freedom generally put forward is a right of access to news sources in some general sense. The argument here is that the press is the custodian of the "people's right to know" and that to fulfill that role the media might have a right to gather information not available to an individual citizen. The opposing argument is that the Free Press guarantee merely extends the right of free speech to the printed word. One need only compare President Carter's human rights campaign with the contrary Russian practice to appreciate our good fortune in living in a free and open society.

FREEDOM OF SPEECH. Protected by the First Amendment of the United States Constitution which provides that "Congress shall make no Law . . . abridging the Freedom of Speech." In attempting to determine exactly what is and what is not protected under the Amendment, most scholars have made an attempt to determine what limita-tions, if any, were intended by the constitutional framers. Arguments have been made that the major or only purpose of the Amendment was to prohibit prior restraints. Others have argued that the framers were very much concerned with the problem of seditious libel. Some commentators have maintained that the major purpose of the Amendment is the protection of the political process and that the "core concern" of the Amendment, therefore, is so-called "Political Speech." The Political Speech rationale was first put forward by Alexander Meiklejohn and stands for the notion that speech on public issues, speech involving "self-government" is what the Amendment was designed to protect. When first enunciated by Meiklejohn, the Political Speech rationale was expansive in that it argued for protection in certain areas that had not yet been recognized by the Supreme Court. Now that the Court has expanded the scope of the Amendment, it is generally conceded that the Political Speech rationale would not offer protection in some areas that are now protected to some degree. Another view of the First Amendment is that it is especially concerned with the rights of the individual to self-development and self-actualization. Under this rationale, speech that does not contribute in any way to the political process would still be protected because of the desire to encourage individuals to think and express themselves on all topics. The other major view of the First Amendment is that it protects all speech. This absolutist view of the First Amendment has been presented most consistently and eloquently by the late Supreme Court Justice Hugo L. Black who argued that the clear language of the First Amendment provided that all speech, including obscenity and defamation, are given absolute protection against government repression. Thus, in effect, Justice Black advocated the abolition of civil and criminal libel and slander. He would allow anyone to say anything about anyone else no matter how vicious, or damaging.

FREEDOM RIDERS. Blacks and Whites who courageously violated the segregation laws of the South in a peaceful assertion of their civil rights, subsequently vindicated by the Supreme Court after they had been subjected to physical violence, arrest, imprisonment and all sorts of abuse.

FREEDOM SHARES. The popular name given to United States savings notes. First issued in 1967, they mature in 4-½ years. Notes purchased after June 1, 1968 earn 4.74 percent annual interest payable on maturity.

FREEDOMS OF THE AIR. International rights in air transport, including: (1) Freedom of innocent transit; (2) Freedom of technical stop; (3) Freedom to take traffic from the homeland out to other countries; (4) Freedom to take traffic from other countries back to the homeland; and, to a limited extent; (5) Freedom to pick up and discharge traffic between points en route. Such freedoms grew out of the developing law of commercial entry by air and were reciprocally granted to signatories of the "United States Document" presented at the Convention on International Civil Aviation of December 7, 1944 (The Chicago Convention). The Freedoms of the Air are analogous to the Freedom of the High Seas which the Dutch philosopher Grotius championed in a parallel controversy in the 17th century.

FREE EXERCISE CLAUSE. The clause in the First Amendment of the Constitution which provides that "Congress shall make no Law . . . prohibiting the free exercise" of religion. In most Free Exercise cases, religious convictions are raised as defenses to state legislation. Illustrative of free exercise cases is *Wisconsin v. Yoder*, 406 U.S. 205 (1972), where adherents of the Amish faith successfully refused to comply with compulsory education laws because of an alleged conflict with their religious tenets.

FREEHOLD ESTATE. An estate created by the ceremony called feoffment with livery of seisin which signifies physical dominion over land. The fee simple, fee tail or fee simple conditional and the life estate are the only freehold estates.

FREE ON BOARD. See F.O.B.

FREE TRADE ZONE. An area set aside by a Sovereign where goods may be imported, exported, manufactured or trans-shipped free of customs duties and taxes in order to stimulate the local economy.

FREE WORLD. See FIRST WORLD.

FREEZE OUT MERGER. See SHORT MERGER; SINGER v. MAGNAVOX CO.

FRESH START. Applied to a debtor who has undergone a discharge from his prior indebtedness by the action of the Federal Bankruptcy Act and is permitted to start afresh. Not all debts, however, are dischargeable in bankruptcy. Section 523 of the Bankruptcy Reform Act of 1978 provides nine classes of debts for which the debtor is still liable even after a bankruptcy proceeding. These include (1) past due taxes, (2) credit obtained through actual fraud, (3) debts which the debtor failed to acknowledge during the bankruptcy case, (4) debts owed due to embezzlement or larceny, (5) alimony and child support, (6) money owed because of an intentional or willful tort, (7) fines and other government penalties, (8) government financed educational loans and (9) debts in which discharge was waived in a prior proceeding. An important limitation of the action of the fresh start is that an individual can file a petition in bankruptcy only every six years. The term is also applicable to section 1023(h) of the Internal Revenue Code. Under this provision, also known as the Stepped-Up Basis Rule, an adjustment is allowed on the basis of any asset owned by a decedent on December 31, 1976. The transferee of such property computes his basis from the December 31, 1976 value rather than the decedent's basis. Thus, the transferee is said to have a Fresh Start from the December 1, 1976 value. He receives an asset with a Stepped-Up Basis.

FREUND v. UNITED STATES. See GENERAL SCOPE OF THE CONTRACT.

FRIDAY NIGHT MASSACRE. That evening on January 12, 1979, when former Congresswoman Bella Abzug from New York was dismissed by President Carter from her position as the non-paid Chairperson of the National Advisory Committee for Women. The co-chairperson and a majority of the Committee promptly resigned in protest.

FRIENDLY SUITS. See COLLUSIVE CASES.

FRIENDS OF FREE CHINA. A lobby formed in 1954 to promote the interests of non-Communist China (the Republic of China on the island of Taiwan) in the United States. For example, in 1979, after the American recognition of Communist China (the People's Republic of China on the Mainland of Asia), to keep their property in Washington, D.C. from falling into the hands of the Communists, the Nationalist Chinese sold their American Embassy Building to Friends of Free China for a nominal $20.

FRINGE BENEFITS. Any tax free gratuity given by an employer to an employee such as a waiver of tuition to a college professor for his children, airline tickets to airline workers, use of vacation facilities at no cost, complementary luncheon meals, and gratuitous health policies.

FRIVOLOUS SUITS. Suits brought which are so groundless that one can infer that the lawyer knew, either at the beginning or at some later point, that no action existed and having learned that nonetheless proceeded with the case. Generally brought for harassment purposes, the lawyer may be disciplined professionally or sued for damages for the Tort of Abuse of Process or Malicious Prosecution.

F.R.N. (Floating Rate Note). A loan obligation whose interest is not fixed but fluctuates periodically to correspond to the rise or fall in interest rates as determined by an agreed upon base, such as the prime rate charged by major banks to their best customers.

FROLIC AND DETOUR. A term used in cases involving vehicle accidents of employees. The issue is whether the employee was pursuing the employer's business, in which case the employer is liable for unintentional torts committed by the employee. Generally, a small departure from business activities is considered "detour" and held to be within the scope of employment. In contrast, a significant departure is a "frolic," and beyond the scope of employment. Where a trip serves two purposes—one business and the other personal—courts often hold the activity within the scope of employment if any substantial business purpose is served.

F.R.O.L.I.N.A.T. (National Liberation Front of Chad). A revolutionary group of Arab Muslims under the leadership of Goukouni Oueiddi in the North of Chad who have been fighting the government and Black Christians in the South of Chad since the country obtained its independence from France in 1964. They seek either secession or the overthrow of the government and are supported by Libya which is its neighbor to the North. The French Foreign Legion was unsuccessful in its two efforts to crush the rebels in 1968 and 1971. Noah's Ark is said to have landed in Chad, which is ironic since the lonely land has been so ravaged by drought in recent years that it is the poorest country in the entire world community of 150 nations.

FRONT FOOT. A piece of property one hundred feet deep and one foot wide. The term derives from the old practice of purchasing the Front Foot of property and then owning all the property behind it.

FRONTIERO v. RICHARDSON (411 U.S. 677 (1973)). A U.S. Supreme Court case which held that differential treatment of military servicewomen and servicemen with respect to dependent benefits violated the Due Process Clause of the Fifth Amendment. The case appeared to open the door for greater scrutiny of sex-based classifications since four Justices, Brennan, Douglas, White and Marshall, found gender to be a suspect classification.

FRONT LINE STATES. The African nations (Angola, Zambia, Tanzania, Mozambique and Botswana) that collaborated with the Western Group (United States, West Germany, France, Canada and Great Britain), under United Nations auspices, to negotiate with the various nationalistic groups in Southwest Africa, as a major step in the creation of the new independent sovereign nation of Namibia.

FROZEN ASSETS. Funds and property of persons seized by a foreign country in which they are located, such as the $76 million of Chinese holdings confiscated by the United States at the start of the Korean War in 1950 and the $197 million of American interests taken by the People's Republic of China.

FRUIT OF THE POISONOUS TREE (Derivative Evidence; Secondary Evidence). Evidence obtained as a result of an unconstitutional search and seizure, or as the result of a confession elicited in derogation of the suspect's right to counsel or to remain silent. Under the Exclusionary Rule, the primary evidence (the seized goods or the confession) were not admissible at trial. In *Nardone v. United States,* 308 U.S. 338 (1939), the illegal police activity was labeled the poisonous tree, and the derivative evidence its fruit. Recent Supreme Court decisions have allowed the fruit to be depoisoned if the evidence would have been inevitably discovered, if an independent source of the evidence could be proved, or if the causal chain between the illegal act and the evidence secured is sufficiently remote or attenuated.

FUGAM FECIT (Latin—he has made flight; he has fled). In old English law, Fugam Fecit meant that a person in-dicted for felony or treason had fled, and that his personal property would forfeit absolutely the Crown, along with the profits of his real property until such time as he should be acquitted or pardoned.

FULL EMPLOYMENT BALANCE. An estimate of the amount at which federal revenues would equal federal expenditures if the economy were operating at current price levels. Changes in the Full-Employment Balance from period to period are generally considered to be more significant indicators than the absolute value for indicating the extent of fiscal restraint or stimulus. The methodology generally employed in calculations of the Full-Employment Balance can be summarized in four steps: (1) Real Gross National Product (G.N.P.) is estimated on the basis of potential full-employment growth, and converted to current dollars using the actual rate of price change; (2) Full-employment income is divided into various tax bases, such as personal income and corporate profits; (3) Effective tax rates under present laws are computed for each tax base, and full-employment revenues derived; and (4) Full-employment expenditures are calculated by subtracting from actual expenditures the difference between actual and estimated full-employment levels of unemployment compensation.

FULL EMPLOYMENT LAW. See HUMPHREY-HAWKINS LAW OF 1978.

FULL FAITH AND CREDIT. The requirement that the courts of each state honor the judgments and laws of sister states. Article 4, section 1 of the U.S. Constitution says "Full Faith and Credit shall be given in each state to the public acts, records, and judicial proceedings of every other state." The clause, which does not apply to criminal proceedings, is an important unifying force under a federal system. Thus, if *A* sues *B* on a $10,000 debt in a New York court and prevails, *A* may use his New York judgment in an enforcement proceeding in California. Similarly should *A* lose the New York suit, he could not then go to a different state and try again. Full faith and credit requires that a final judgment be honored elsewhere.

FUNDAMENTAL RIGHTS AND INTERESTS. In determining what areas were appropriate for strict scrutiny under the Equal Protection Clause, the Supreme Court under Chief Justice Earl Warren looked for two characteristics: the presence of suspect classifications, or an impact on a fundamental right or interest. Voting, criminal appeals and the right of interstate travel have been the most important fundamental rights and interests designated but commentators have suggested that the analysis used under this rubric could also be applied in other areas such as welfare benefits, municipal services and school financing. The use of the concept of fundamental rights and interests has been criticized by some as a new form of Substantive Due Process because it has limited legislative choices in the name of rights that lack clear support in the text of the Constitution or in precedent.

FUNDED INSURANCE TRUSTS. Generally insurance trusts which have cash, securities and life insurance policies as their main trust property. Such assets are expected to produce sufficient income to pay premiums and other changes on or assessed against policies involved therein. Such trust arrangements can be quite profitable.

FUNGIBLE GOODS. Goods like grain or other produce in which all units are identical and freely interchangeable.

FUNK MONEY. See HOT MONEY.

FURMAN v. GEORGIA (408 U.S. 238 (1972)). A Supreme Court case which struck down the Georgia statutes providing for the death penalty for murder and rape and the Texas statute providing for capital punishment for rape. The question presented was whether death in these cases constitutes cruel and unusual punishment in violation of the Eighth and Fourteenth Amendments. The majority feared that jury discretion could lead to discriminatory and disproportionate use of the death sentence.

FUTURE INTEREST. A potential ownership which cannot be enjoyed until some future time. For example, Father gives to Son all his property, but if Daughter marries Protege then half the property is hers. Daughter has a Future Interest in the property contingent on her marrying Protege. If she marries someone else or no one, then she has lost her Future Interest.

FUZZ BUSTER. An automobile radio detection device which enables a driver to avoid being caught in a police (Fuzz) speed trap. Its use has been outlawed in a number of states.

G

GAG ORDER. A judicial restriction in a court case, prohibiting lawyers, parties to the case, witnesses, or jurors from making any statement outside the courtroom relating to the formal court proceedings. These court orders, generally imposed by the judge for the duration of the court proceedings, have been sharply attacked by the press as unconstitutional restraints on its right of free speech. Hence the characterization "gag order."

GAG RULE. A legislative Rule that limits the time available for debate or consideration of a proposed bill or resolution. A Gag Rule generally sets an arbitrary time limit below that provided by the legislative chamber's regular rules. A Gag Rule should not be confused with a Gag Order, a judicial prohibition of publicity about an ongoing trial.

GALLOPING RATE. See CHINESE OVERTIME.

GANDHI, MOHANDAS K. The gentle martyred leader of the independence of his native India from England. After having studied law in London for three years, he returned home to practice in 1891. His first case as a barrister in court was a shambles since he was nervously tongue tied and had to flee in disgrace. He then spent 20 years as a lawyer in South Africa where the reading of Tolstoy's *The Kingdom of God is Within You,* led him to develop the tactics of Satyagraha, a non-violent resistance, in his fight to end discrimination against his fellow Indians. Martin Luther King was later inspired to use the same strategy successfully in the American South. It should be realized, of course, that this Christ-like philosophy would be effective only in a civilized Democracy. To try it elsewhere could lead to a brutal slaughter. Gandhi is the modern Folk Hero of the youth of the world who practice his vegetarian life style, with no desire to acquire material goods, in a return-to-the-land and rejection of the industrial complex. Although Sir Winston Churchill, who had the unpleasant task of presiding over the dismantling of the British Empire, contemptuously and unfairly called him a "one time Inner Temple lawyer, now seditious fakir," Gandhi's concept of the role of an attorney is sweetly expressed in his autobiography as follows: "My joy was boundless. I had learned the true practice of law. I had learned to find out the better side of human nature and to enter men's hearts. I realized that the true function of a lawyer was to unite parties and never to put them asunder. The lesson was so indelibly burnt into me that a large part of my time during the twenty years of my practice as a lawyer was occupied in bringing about private compromises of hundreds of cases. I lost nothing thereby—not even money, certainly not my soul."

GANG OF FOUR. The four radical leaders of China, including the widow of Chairman Mao Tse-tung, who tried to seize power after the leader's death but were jailed instead when Hua Kuofeng replaced Mao as the first Communist Chinese Ruler.

GANNETT CARD. A wallet-size card, prepared by the Gannett News Company, which equips newsstaffers with a prepared plea for a hearing on any move to close a courtroom to the press or the public. This card also includes a reminder of the people's First Amendment rights to a free and unfettered press. During the trial of a pornography king in Rome, Georgia, in 1979, for example, the judge suddenly ordered the doors of justice shut on the public and their free press while he heard the testimony of a key witness. Reporter Neil Craig of Station WXIA-TV, the Gannett television station in Atlanta, immediately objected. He read into the record a statement of protest from the Gannett card. The next morning, WXIA-TV sent its legal counsel from Atlanta to Rome by helicopter to back Craig's protest. But before this attorney arrived, the judge reversed his decision and reopened the courtroom doors. The quick use of the Gannett Card by reporters, coupled with the capable support of local counsel, has thus kept courtroom doors open to reporters in 11 of 15 cases in five months following the 1979 Supreme Court decision in *Gannett v. DePasquale,* which allowed courtroom doors to be closed in certain cases.

G.A.O. See GENERAL ACCOUNTING OFFICE.

G.A.O. (Government Accounting Office) HOT LINE. A toll-free telephone number (633-6987) for callers in Washington, D.C.; (800) 424-5454 (for callers elsewhere) that allows citizens to tattle anonymously on bureaucratic fraud and waste. In 1979, the first year of operation, nearly 7,500 allegations of wrongdoing were reported to the General Accounting Office, the investigative arm of Congress, which followed up on forty percent of the calls. Among investigations that paid off were: (1) A University of Wisconsin professor, who had financed a Colorado ski trip with $900 in federal research funds and repaid that sum plus a $4,000 fine; and (2) an Energy Department employee who had padded an expense account by $360 and suffered a $1,700 reduction in annual pay.

G.A.P. (Groups of the Armed Proletariat). Left-wing terrorist band in Spain which specializes in assassination of high-ranking government officials and military officers.

GAP FINANCING. See BRIDGE LOAN.

GARCIA AMENDMENT. See P.A.C.E.

GARDNER, ERLE STANLEY. Lawyer and creator of Perry Mason (played by Raymond Burr on TV) whose 96 courtroom dramas have sold over 200 million copies since 1942.

GARNISHMENT PROCEEDING. The payment by an employer of a statutory share of an employee's wages to a creditor of the employee until the debt is paid in full.

GASHOUSE GANG. See KILLER BEES.

G.A.T.T. (General Agreement on Tariffs and Trade). Signed in 1947, G.A.T.T. now has eighty-three contracting parties and sixteen associate members, including the United States, most Western countries, and six communist countries: Cuba, Czechoslovakia, Poland, Yugoslavia, Rumania and Hungary. G.A.T.T. tries to promote the reduction of tariffs and of other barriers to international trade, and to eliminate discriminatory treatment and restrictive policies. Based on an unconditional Most Favored Nation clause, the Agreement includes rules for tariff negotiations and tariff schedules, and rules governing international trade. The principle of the clause has been challenged by some developing countries. However, since it favors the most efficient country, it is still in effect. Conferences are held regularly to implement G.A.T.T. policies. The Kennedy Round, for instance, was held from 1964 to 1967, and resulted in a drastic reduction of United States and European Economic Community tariffs, and the Tokyo Round was started in 1973.

GAY LAWYERS. As of 1977 the National Gay Task Force listed eight lawyer or law student gay caucuses in the United States. No studies have been done to indicate how many gay lawyers there are in this country, but the Kinsey report estimates that 10 percent of the general population is homosexual, a figure which presumably applies as well to lawyers. Although the American Bar Association and the Model Penal Code recommend removal of criminal sanctions against private sexual conduct between consenting adults, only nineteen states have done so. Consequently, most gay lawyers do not publicly profess their sexual preferences.

GAY RIGHTS LAW. Any legislation passed at the municipal, state or federal level outlawing discrimination against homosexuals or lesbians in areas such as employment and housing. People who oppose such laws are called anti-gays.

GENERAL ACCOUNTING OFFICE (G.A.O.). A federal agency which is composed of the Comptroller General of the United States and other high government officials. Its basic purposes as the federal watch-dog are to assist the Congress in carrying out its legislative responsibilities, consistent with its role as an independent nonpolitical agency; to carry out legal, accounting, auditing, and claims settlement functions with respect to federal government programs and operations as assigned by the Congress; and to make recommendations designed to provide for more efficient and effective government operations.

GENERAL AGREEMENT ON TARIFFS AND TRADE. See G.A.T.T.

GENERAL ASSEMBLY. Composed of countries that are members of the U.N. (United Nations). Its functions are to discuss any matter within the Charter of the U.N. and to make recommendations; to approve and apportion the budget among member countries; to call the attention of the Security Council to situations likely to endanger international peace; to initiate studies; and to receive and consider reports from other organs of the U.N. Under the Uniting for Peace Resolution (1950), if the Security Council fails to act on an apparent threat to peace because of lack of unanimity of its five permanent members, the Assembly may take up the matter itself within 24 hours and may recommend use of force when necessary to maintain or restore peace. The General Assembly has held five such Emergency Special Sessions to date.

GENERAL ASSIGNMENT FOR THE BENEFIT OF CREDITORS. A forerunner to the Bankruptcy procedures now available under the Federal Bankruptcy Act. A General Assignment for the Benefit of Creditors is still available under the laws of most states. Under such a procedure, an insolvent debtor transfers all his assets to a trustee. With the proceeds of the sale of the assets, the trustee satisfies as many creditors' claims as possible. For the debtor, the primary attraction of a general assignment is that he avoids the stigma of being formally labeled a bankrupt. The imprecision of the statutes regulating this procedure in many states, is a drawback to this procedure, especially from the point of view of creditors.

GENERAL DAMAGES. Damages which the law deems to be inherent in the injury itself. Thus, if a pedestrian were to be run down by a careless automobile driver, he might suffer a broken leg and hip, along with great pain. When the pedestrian sues the driver for negligence, he will ask the court to award him general damages consisting of pain and suffering (past, present and future) and compensation for the physical consequences of the accident. This latter compensation is directed toward any disfigurement, such as loss of limb or unsightly scars, or disability, such as paralysis or loss of sight, suffered by the pedestrian. Also recoverable are loss of earnings and medical expenses.

GENERAL ELECTRIC v. GILBERT. See PREGNANCY DISCRIMINATION ACT.

GENERAL GUARDIANSHIP. The relationship between an adult called the guardian and someone who is legally incompetent (such as an unemancipated minor child or someone suffering from a mental or physical handicap) who is called the ward. There are various kinds of guardianships: (1) Guardian of the estate. One who is responsible for the care, management, protection and investment of the ward's property. The guardian does not have title, either legal or equitable, to the property of the ward. The term guardian of the property is synonymous with guardian of the estate. Parents are not automatically guardians of the estate of their children. They must apply to a court to be appointed for this purpose. (2) Natural guardian. (Guardian of the person). A child's biological parent. (3) Guardian ad litem. (Latin —to the litigation). One appointed by the court to represent the ward in litigation. The term prochein Ami (French —next friend) for the ward's representative was traditionally used when the ward was a plaintiff, while the guardian ad litem represented the defendant ward. This distinction is no longer made in most jurisdictions, and the term guardian ad litem is commonly used, regardless of the position of the ward in the lawsuit. The role of the guardian ad litem is to arrive at independent determinations of what is best for the ward and to protect the ward's interest in the litigation. While the guardian ad litem is usually authorized to receive payment of a judgment on behalf of the ward, he or she may not make a binding settlement of the case without court approval. (4) A guardian by estoppel is a quasi-guardian in that someone assumes to act as a guardian for another without authority to do so. The person so acting is estopped from denying that he or she is not a guardian in order to avoid responsibility for performance of duties with respect to the ward's property. A person who assumes, without authority, to manage a child's property is held liable for violation of any fiduciary duties which the proper guardian is bound to observe. Liability may even be imposed for any loss in investment even though there was no negligence and no liability would have been imposed if the person had been a lawful guardian. In other words, don't monkey around with someone else's money. (5) Guardianship in socage. This and similar types of guardianship based on inheritance of title to land and title of royal rank stemming from feudalism at early common law are no longer used today.

GENERAL INTENT CRIMES. See SPECIFIC INTENT CRIMES.

GENERAL LEGACY. A gift of personal property which the testator intends to be satisfied from the general assets of the estate.

GENERAL PARTNERSHIPS. See REAL ESTATE SYNDICATE.

GENERAL POWER EXERCISABLE BY DEED OR WILL. See POWER OF APPOINTMENT.

GENERAL SCOPE OF THE CONTRACT. This term refers to the nature and amount of performance reasonably contemplated by contracting parties at the time of contract formation. These words were defined by the Supreme Court in *Freund v. United States*, 260 U.S. 60 (1922), as that work which "should be regarded as fairly and reasonably within the contemplation of the parties when the contract was entered into."

GENERAL STRIKE. A concerted refusal by a substantial proportion of the working community of a city or a nation to continue their normal activities until certain conditions are attained. It has been used very effectively by European and Latin American workers for political purposes.

GENERAL TESTAMENTARY POWER. See POWER OF APPOINTMENT.

GENERAL TRADE RULES. See WORLD TRADE PACT.

GENERAL VERDICT. A jury decision in favor of either plaintiff or defendant. A general verdict does not discuss the specific issues of law or fact in the case.

GENERAL VERDICT WITH INTERROGATORIES. A general verdict accompanied by jury answers to specific factual questions posed by the judge. In effect, the general verdict with interrogatories is a cross between a general verdict and a special verdict. It enables the judge to review the factual basis of the jury decision as a check on the reasonableness of the verdict.

GENERATION-SKIPPING TRANSFER TAX. A provision of the Federal Estate Tax System which was enacted by the Tax Reform Act of 1976. It is now found at sections 2601-2622 in the Internal Revenue Code. The tax was designed to close a loophole in the old system which allowed a doner to avoid tax for several generations by the creation of successive life estates. In closing the loophole, the increased complexity of the tax laws has probably benefited lawyers more than it has taxpayers.

GENERIC EXCEPTION DOCTRINE. Provides that the exclusive right to use a trademark is lost if the mark ceases to be distinctive. If the purchasing public understands the mark to mean a kind of goods, then the trademark rights are lost. For example, if people begin to call all jeans "Levi's," the "Levi" trademark has lost its trade distinctiveness and no longer refers to its original owner. When a trademark like "Levi's" becomes successful, competitors often attempt to deprive it of its value and reduce it to a generic word available to use by all. Section 45 of the Lanham Act, the Federal Trademark statute, states that abandonment of a trademark includes its transition from a distinctive trademark into a generic word if that development was caused or aggravated by acts of commission or omission on the part of the trademark owner. Recently, courts have begun to consider affirmative steps taken by the owner to preserve his Trademark to be as important as public opinion about the word. It has been said that once a Trademark is introduced and the article to which it refers established, the Trademark owner assumes the risk that his distinctive word may degenerate into a common word. If a Trademark is to have value, it must be well known, but if it becomes too well known, it may become generic and therefore worthless. Courts have recognized this irony and hold that a Trademark has changed character only if there is conclusive evidence. If courts did not take notice of this fact, most valuable Trademarks would soon become common property. Ever since Trademarks have been widely advertised, the courts have bent over backwards to create an equity in favor of the advertiser.

GENERIC GEOGRAPHIC NAMES. Product names which are so commonplace that they are no longer associated with their geographic area of origin; e.g., Danish pastry, Venetian blinds, Swiss cheese. Problems arise when the public understanding of Generic Geographical Names changes; for example, in the 1960 British Champagne Case, a British Court held that "champagne" does not mean a type of wine, but rather that wine produced in the Champagne district of France. A few years later another British Court found that Sherry no longer meant the Sherry district of Spain, but was instead, a type of wine.

GENEVA CONVENTION OF 1948. Ratified or adhered to by thirty-seven nations as of 1976, the Convention addresses international recognition of aircraft rights. The Convention was designed to encourage investors to make financial assistance toward the purchase of new aircraft by recognizing property rights in the air on an international basis. Accordingly, the property rights in aircraft crossing national boundaries are protected.

GENEVA CONVENTION ON FISHING AND CONSERVATION OF THE LIVING RESOURCES OF THE HIGH SEAS. Signed in 1958, it allows coastal countries to establish conservation zones on the high seas adjacent to their territorial waters. The purpose of such a zone is to protect natural resources and fisheries' activities of coastal countries. It is usually a reaction against over-fishing coastal countries, by establishing conservation systems on resources which are in fact generally more oriented towards protection of their nationals and prevention of fishing by foreigners than towards conservation based on appropriate scientific findings. Conservation zones created by the United States and Britain extend to twelve miles. In 1952, Chile, Peru and Ecuador extended their conservation zones to two hundred miles. The provisions of the Convention which condemn discrimination against foreign fishermen by establishing scientifically unjustified conservation zones are frequently disregarded.

GENEVA CONVENTION ON THE CONTINENTAL SHELF. Signed at Geneva on April 29, 1958, it attempts to solve claims to the seabed and subsoil of the open sea. Article 1 of the Convention defines the continental shelf as "the seabed and subsoil of the submarine areas adjacent to the coast, but outside the area of the territorial sea, to a depth of two hundred metres, or beyond that limit, to where the depth of the superjacent waters admits the exploitation of the natural resources of the said areas." Under the Convention, the coastal country exercises over the continental shelf sovereign rights for the purpose of exploring and exploiting its natural resources. Such exploitation by the coastal country must not impair freedom of the open sea, nor create unjustifiable interference with other countries' navigation, fishing, or laying of submarine cables or pipelines on the continental shelf. The coastal country has an exclusive and unrestrictable right to exploit the natural resources of its continental shelf, including sedentary fisheries. Finally, the Convention provides that where the continental shelf is adjacent to the territories of more than one country, the boundary of the continental shelf shall be determined, absent an agreement among the parties, by the line equidistant from the base lines from which the breadth of the territorial sea of each country is measured.

GENEVA CONVENTION ON THE HIGH SEAS. Signed on August 23, 1958, it confirms and codifies the freedom of the seas principle, accepted as a rule of international law since the nineteenth century. The underlying conception is that because the oceans can never be possessed by occupation, no country can claim sovereignty over them. High seas are defined as all parts of the world's waters which are not included within territorial or interior waters of a country. As provided by the Convention, "no country may validly purport to subject any part of them to its sovereignty." All countries have equal rights to engage in commerce, navigation, fishing, laying of submarine cables and pipelines, and overflight in the high seas. Complete freedom of the high seas is, however, limited by the obligation of Maritime Flags. Jurisdiction for collisions on the high seas of ships of different nationalities has not been resolved by the Convention, and each country applies its own test for claiming jurisdiction. However, penal or disciplinary proceedings against a ship's crew may be enforced only by the authorities of the flag's country or of the country of which the accused is a national.

GENEVA DISARMAMENT CONFERENCE. The main international disarmament negotiating body since 1963.

GENEVA SPACE BROADCASTING CONFERENCE. A multi-nation meeting in Switzerland, in 1977, to attempt to allocate by law the relay stations of satellites in outer space and to control the beaming of uncontrolled propaganda from spacecraft into radios and television sets by one nation to another. The less developed countries are especially fearful of this imperialism of the mind.

GENEVA WAR CONVENTIONS. See LAW OF WAR.

GENOCIDE CONVENTION. A Pact, drafted in 1948, which has been ratified by 83 countries, as a response to the murder of six million Jews by the Nazis. It obligates ratifying governments to punish those who act against or attempt to destroy a national, ethnic, religious or racial group. Although every President since Truman has recommended American ratification, conservative members of the Senate have refused to act. Indeed, of the 19 international

treaties on human rights that would be legally binding, the United States has ratified only the five least controversial, including those that outlaw slavery, protect refugees and promote the political rights of women. When he visited the United Nations in October 1977, President Carter signed two 11-year-old covenants designed to translate the eloquent but non-binding phrases of the declaration of human rights into legal instruments. (1) The covenant on civil and political rights requires governments to protect freedom of religion, thought and peaceful assembly, to prevent arbitrary arrest and torture, to guarantee fair trial and voting rights. (2) The Convention on Economic and Social Rights commits governments to progressively promote such goals as the right to work, to an adequate living standard and to education and health care.

GENTLEMEN'S AGREEMENT. (1) In American history, an agreement between the United States and Japan in 1907 providing that Japan would stop the emigration of laborers to the United States and the United States would stop discriminating against the Japanese. In 1924 Congress banned immigration from Japan, terminating the agreement. (2) In business, a gentleman's agreement is an informal agreement based not on written contract, but the word of the parties. Because no record exists, such agreements are preferred where the subject matter is of questionable legality.

GEOGRAPHIC TERM. Refers to or describes the place of origin of a product or the situs of a business. Manufacturers and merchants are free to use words that geographically describe their businesses. Nevertheless, there are exceptions to this general rule. If a geographic term has attained secondary meaning, or if it lacks geographical significance or meaning in association with particular products or services, then it may be protected under trademark law.

GEORGE JUNIOR REPUBLIC. An official institutional care center for troubled adolescents formed in New York in 1873 which successfully operates on a self-government basis.

GEORGIA MAFIA. An inner circle of powerful advisors to President Jimmy Carter, in and out of government, from his home state, headed by the White House Chief of Staff, Hamilton Jordan, and including former Attorney-General Griffin Bell and Press Secretary Jody Powell.

GERRYMANDERED DISTRICTS. Practice of a political party in power which arbitrarily changes the physical boundaries of voting districts so that the opposition will win as few legislative seats as possible. It has also been defined more broadly as any political manipulation to gain an unfair advantage. According to historian John Fiske, the term was derived as follows: Massachusetts Governor Gerry arbitrarily formed certain towns into an odd shaped district. One day, Gilbert Stuart, the painter, walked into the office of Benjamin Russell, an editor and ardent opponent of Governor Gerry. Above Russell's desk was a map of the state with an outline of the recently formed and arbitrary district. Stuart penciled a head, wings and claws to the outline of the dragonlike contour and exclaimed, "that will do for a salamander." Growled Russell promptly, "Better say a Gerrymander."

GERSTEIN HEARING *(Gerstein v. Pugh,* 419 U.S. 815 (1975)). A constitutionally required hearing held within twenty-four hours after an arrest without a warrant or indictment. The purpose is to determine whether there is probable cause to detain the defendant since probable cause is necessary to obtain an arrest warrant. Note that this is a lesser standard than that at the subsequent preliminary hearing, which is whether there is probable cause to believe that an offense has been committed and that the defendant is responsible. A Gerstein Hearing is non-adversarial and conducted by a judicial officer. The basic objectives are preventing the detention of persons without reasonable grounds and informing judicial officials that the defendant

is being held. Many states combine the Gerstein Hearing with the Initial Appearance so bail is then set and an attorney appointed.

GERTZ v. ROBERT WELCH, INC., 418 U.S. 323 (1974). A landmark Supreme Court decision on defamation. Mr. Justice Powell's majority opinion holds that, unless the defendant has shown a "reckless disregard for the truth" or has published material which he knows to be false, a state court plaintiff may recover only special damages for defamation. Included within the ambit of permissible recoveries are damages for humiliation, mental anguish and suffering, and damage to reputation in the community. It is unclear whether the holding was meant to apply to cases not involving the publishing and broadcasting media.

GIBBONS v. OGDEN. See COMMERCE POWER.

G.I. BILL (Servicemen's Readjustment Act) (1944). A federal law which provides assistance for veterans of World War II and subsequent conflicts. Under the G.I. Bill, allowances are available to veterans who are unemployed or attending school. In addition, the Bill provides for guaranteed loans to veterans purchasing homes or businesses.

GIDEON v. WAINWRIGHT. See PUBLIC DEFENDER.

GIFT CAUSA MORTIS. See CAUSA MORTIS.

GIFT OVER. See LIMITATION OVER.

GIFT TAX. A tax imposed by the federal government, on the transfer of property by Inter Vivos gift. As the result of a 1924 dispute between Andrew M. Mellon, Secretary of the Treasury and Representative John Nance Garner, the tax was enacted to supplement the estate tax. Wealthy persons had evaded the 1916 estate tax system by transferring their wealth before death. Still applicable under the law in some states, it was abolished by the Tax Reform Act of 1976.

GIFT TRANSACTIONS. See GRATUITOUS ASSIGNMENTS.

GINNIE MAE. (Government National Mortgage Association.) A division of the Department of Housing and Urban Development (H.U.D.) designed to administer special H.U.D. programs and work with Fannie Mae in purchasing government-subsidized loans, such as F.H.A. and V.A. loans. If Ginnie Mae did not agree to purchase these low-yield loans, lenders would be reluctant to make such loans to low and moderate income buyers.

GIORDENELLO v. UNITED STATES (357 U.S. 480 (1958)). In this case the defendant was convicted of the unlawful purchase of narcotics on the basis of evidence seized pursuant to a search incident to a lawful arrest. The defendant appealed on the ground that his arrest was unlawful; the Supreme Court agreed and reversed the conviction. The Court held that an arrest warrant which merely recites the complaint is insufficient and that a warrant must contain a factual basis for a finding of probable cause and affirmative allegation that the source of the information has personal knowledge. It should be noted that the decision was based on the requirements of the Federal Rules of Criminal Procedure and not on the Constitution.

GIVE-BACKS. Management demands in collective bargaining negotiations that the employees return some of the fringe benefits won in previous years as a condition to the granting of new concessions.

GLASS-STEAGALL ACT. See BANK FAILURE.

GLOBAL 2000 STUDY. See COUNCIL ON ENVIRONMENTAL QUALITY.

G.N.P. See GROSS NATIONAL PRODUCT.

GODDESS JUSTITIA (Goddess of Justice). Roman Goddess who personifies Justice and the legal profession generally. In one hand Justitia holds scales to weigh the evidence, and in the other, a sword to enforce her decision. Her eyes are usually closed or blindfolded for impartiality. Some legal scholars have argued that the blindfold is misplaced as a symbol of impartiality, and that Justitia's maidenly form symbolizes her purity. Placing a blindfold over Justitia's eyes appears to have begun in Germany in 1494 to ridicule and criticize the ignorance of courts, but the derisive meaning of the blindfold changed after a few decades.

GOING BY THE BOOK. See SLOW DOWN.

GOLDBERG RESERVATION. Action taken by Arthur Goldberg, our Ambassador to the United Nations in August, 1965, recognizing our right to withhold our financial contribution to any United Nations project which was contrary either to our national interest or to our commitment under the United Nations Charter.

GOLDBERG v. KELLY (1970). A Supreme Court decision frequently cited as the cornerstone of the "due process revolution." The case held that a state could not cut off welfare payments without first giving the recipient the right to a formal hearing. From it flowed a series of subsequent Supreme Court rulings limiting the power of the federal and state governments to deal unilaterally or arbitrarily with the rights of individuals.

GOLD CLAUSE. Clause in contracts requiring a debtor to repay a loan in gold dollars the same weight and fineness as those loaned to him. The Gold Clause was used frequently after the Civil War when costs of the war effort forced the government to issue "Greenbacks"—dollars that were not convertible to gold. Greenbacks precipitated a 24 percent inflation rate in 1862, and in a brief period the dollar had declined to one-third its former value. Congress forbade the use of Gold Clauses in 1933, an action that was upheld by the Supreme Court in the Gold Clause Cases of 1935.

GOLDEN FLEECE AWARD. A sarcastic honor without remuneration frequently bestowed by Senator William Proxmire upon any recipient of a federal grant for research on a silly and wasteful project, such as "Why do people try to escape from prison," "Love life of the red carpenter ant," or "Why do animals gnash their teeth." When the Senator was sued by an irate donee, a Michigan judge dismissed the case on the ground of legislative immunity, but this decision was reversed by the Supreme Court.

GOLD ROOM. Room in London's Rothschild bank where five representatives of gold-dealing firms meet daily to fix the gold price for that day's business. The fixed price is flashed all over the world and serves as a guideline for other dealers. There is no strict regulatory body like the American Security Exchange Commission to monitor price-fixing in the Gold Room.

GOOD FAITH BARGAINING. The duty imposed on both union and employer by the National Labor Relations Act (N.L.R.A.) to make a sincere effort to reach agreement in their negotiations. Neither party is compelled to make concessions, but must do more than go through the motions. Courts look to external manifestations of subjective intent to find whether bargaining was in good faith. The policy on which the requirement is based is protection of weak unions from being "talked to death" by a powerful employer.

GOOD FAITH RULE. Requires that the consideration received by a corporation, in exchange for the issuance of shares, have a market value which the Board of Directors in good faith believes is at least equal to the par value of the stock at the time of issuance. The Good Faith Rule is now the majority rule largely because it recognizes the difficulty in valuing property and services. Though the True Value Rule has been adopted by only a minority of courts, excessive valuation is still considered an indicium of fraud.

GOOD OFFICES. Services rendered as a mediator, especially as between belligerent nations or in international disputes.

GOOD SAMARITAN LAW. (1) State or city legislation which reimburses innocent third parties who are injured in the course of aiding people in trouble, especially victims of crimes. If the volunteers, who are so named after the Biblical characters of the same bent, are killed, then substantial financial benefits are given to their survivors. (2) Laws, adopted by a substantial number of states following the California example of 1959, which exempt physicians from negligence liability when they render emergency aid. As a general rule, the common law imposes no duty to aid a stranger in an emergency. However, the law has traditionally imposed the duty of due care upon one rendering aid in an emergency situation. This has created an anomalous situation in which physicians who witness an accident may ignore seriously injured persons without incurring the disfavor of the law. But if physicians attempt to assist victims, they will be held liable for any damages arising from defects in their services. Good Samaritan statutes are designed to encourage physicians to assist others in need of immediate aid by removing the fear of potential tort liability.

GOOD TIME CREDIT. Time deducted from a prison term for good behavior. Many states allow an inmate's sentence to be shortened one month for every month served without violation of any prison rule or regulation. This credit may be revoked upon bad behavior or restored at the discretion of prison officials. Such credits usually do not have the effect of reducing the period of time a prisoner must serve before becoming eligible for parole. Other credits may be earned by participating in vocational education, by "extraordinary service," such as donating blood or preventing an escape, or by other methods provided by statute.

GOOD TIME LOSS. The deprivation of "good time" earned by a prisoner. *Wolff v. McDonnell,* 418 U.S. 539 (1974), held that such loss must meet the minimum requirements of procedural due process, including written notice of charges, a hearing at which the prisoner may present evidence in his own behalf, and a written statement explaining the evidence relied on for the decision. In addition, if the prisoner is illiterate or the issue complicated, the prisoner must be allowed to receive aid from other prisoners or staff members.

GOON SQUADS. Workers who plan and execute violence during labor disputes.

GOOSE LIST. Potential buyers of fraudulent or dishonest goods or services.

G.O.P. (Grand Old Party). Identification of the Republican Party (Political Organization) formed in 1854 in the turmoil over the slavery issue.

GOSS CASE (*Goss v. Lopez,* 419 U.S. 565 (1975)). Under a 1975 Supreme Court ruling, school officials suspending a student for 10 days or less must tell the student what rule has been broken and give the student a copy of the rule. If the student denies the offense, the officials must explain why they believe the rule has been broken. The student must then have a chance to give his or her version of what has happened. The court ruling involved brief suspensions only; the court mentioned that longer suspensions or expulsions might require more formal procedures, but it did not spell them out. Nothing in the Supreme Court action or the law protects students from properly imposed suspensions. In addition, a student whose conduct is dangerous to other persons or who continually threatens to disrupt school, may be suspended immediately; a hearing according to the rules set down by the Court must be held as soon as possible after the suspension.

GOULASH COMMUNISM. Keeping retail stores well stocked with consumer goods as much as possible to keep the population docile in a Communist country.

GOULDEN, JOSEPH. Author of *The Million Dollar Lawyers, The Super Lawyers* and other modern scurrilous stories about the American legal profession.

GOVERNING INTERNATIONAL FISHING AGREEMENTS. See FISHERY CONSERVATION AND MANAGEMENT ACT.

GOVERNMENT BY CRONY. The American practice of appointing friends of victorious politicans to positions in the government. The term originated with Harold L. Ickes, a Cabinet member under Franklin D. Roosevelt. Ickes voiced his opposition to government by crony when he resigned in 1946 from the Cabinet of Harry S. Truman.

GOVERNMENT LAW CENTER. A legal research institute established by Albany Law School in 1979 (and since established elsewhere at other law schools) which assists municipalities and states to solve their major legal problems.

GOVERNMENT LAW FIRM. The staff of the federal or state office of the Attorney General.

GOVERNMENT MANUAL. A directory published by the federal government which lists the names and titles of the top officials in each of four branches of government (Judicial, Executive, Legislative and Administrative) together with a brief history and description of the jurisdiction of the particular department or agency.

GOVERNMENT NATIONAL MORTGAGE ASSOCIATION. See GINNIE MAE.

G.P.M. (Graduated Payment Mortgage; A.M.I. (Alternative Mortgage Instrument)). A house financing method growing in popularity which is aimed at younger home buyers or moderate income families. It allows a person to buy a house with lower monthly payments which increase each year in anticipation of future higher salaries of the borrower. In other words, the future larger monthly mortgage payments will be matched by future larger salary checks.

GRADUATED LEASE. Provides for increases in rent at certain intervals to cover increases in expenses.

GRADUATED PAYMENT MORT-GAGE. See G.P.M.

GRAIN OF SALT. See COVENANT OF SALT.

GRANDCHILD EXCLUSION. An exception to the General Skipping Tax which enables a transferor to place assets in trust for the benefit of his children. Upon the child's death such assets may be passed on to the transferor's grandchildren without taxing the child's estate. The Grandchild Exclusion exempts up to $250,000 from the generation skipping tax from the child's estate if the property passes to the grandchildren in such a manner that the property will vest in the grandchild's estate for federal and state tax purposes. However, the assets that escape the Generation Skipping Tax are taxed in the grandchild's estate.

GRANDFATHER CLAUSE. A provision in a regulatory statute which exempts from its requirements those already engaged in the regulated business or activity. Also, a provision in the constitution of certain southern states which exempts descendants of persons voting before 1867 or descendants of persons serving in the United States or Confederate military during wartime from property or literacy restrictions on suffrage.

GRAND JURY. Grand juries derive their existence from the Fifth Amendment to the Constitution. Traditionally grand juries have great freedom in investigating criminal law violations: i.e., no judge presides, the grand jury may compel the production of evidence and the questioning of witnesses, and its operation is unrestrained by the technical rules of evidence and procedure governing criminal trials. Generally, a prosecutor calls the wit-

nesses and conducts the questioning, and prosecutors have often been criticized for exerting too much power in the grand jury process. As early as 1931, the Wickersham Committee criticized grand juries for merely rubber-stamping the prosecutor's allegations. The A.B.A. has proposed several changes to the grand jury process in order to make it more fair to witnesses; such changes include: advising witnesses of their right to counsel, allowing counsel to be present, and permitting witnesses to testify in their own behalf.

GRAND OLD PARTY. See G.O.P.

GRANNY SLAMMING. A popular term for the social phenomenon of parent abuse. When elderly men and women live with their grandchildren, they are often as physically, financially and emotionally dependent upon them as children are on their parents. They are, therefore, subject to the same sort of battering which takes place in other family relationships.

GRANTOR-GRANTEE INDEX. Public records in a courthouse which relate to a particular property under the names of the successive grantors or grantees of the property. The Index is used by lawyers when doing a title search.

G.R.A.P.O. (October 1 Anti-Fascist Revolutionary Group). A left-wing Maoist underground terrorist guerilla group in Spain which specializes in the assassination of high-ranking government and army officials in similar fashion to the despicable acts of the proletarian armed group which has a like purpose and ideology.

GRATUITOUS ASSIGNMENTS. Gift transactions which require no consideration on the part of the recipient. To be valid, generally there must be a donative intent, actual or constructive delivery, and acceptance of the gift.

GRAYING THE BUDGET. That amount of the federal budget which is allocated annually to the support of senior citizens. It was 24 percent or

$112 billion in 1978. Actuarial experts predict that the figure will rise in 5 years to 40 percent or $635 billion. The reason for the sharp increase is that the life expectancy of Americans is growing longer each year. In 1978, 24 million Americans or 11 percent of the population were over 65. The Department of Health, Education and Welfare believes that in two more generations the figures will be 55 million or 18 percent of the population. This has frightening implications for the viability of the Social Security System. In 1940 there were 9 active workers contributing to the System to support each retired person. In 1978 the ratio was reduced to 6 to 1. In 50 years it will be down to 3 to 1. How can a shrinking base of workers continue to support an increasing number of retirees? We may be harboring a self-destructive time bomb with little, if anything, that can be done about it.

GRAY-MAIL. A threat by a criminal defendant, in a sensitive national security case, to disclose government secrets as part of his defense if the government proceeds with the prosecution of his case.

GRAY PANTHERS. A national organization of elderly people who lobby actively at the local, state and national levels to protect and advance their legal rights.

GRAY'S INN. See INNS OF COURT.

GREASE PAYMENT. See INTERNATIONAL CORPORATE BRIBERY.

GREAT AND GENERAL COURT. The General Assembly of the colony, or state, of Massachusetts begun and held at Boston, in Suffolk County, on Wednesday the 28th of May, 1777, being the last Wednesday in the month. Today, the words "General Court" still refer to the Massachusetts legislature consisting of two branches, a Senate and House of Representatives, that convenes every year on the last Wednesday in May.

GREAT COMMONER. See BRYAN, WILLIAM JENNINGS.

GREAT COMPROMISE. See BICAMERAL LEGISLATURE.

GREAT DISSENTER. See HOLMES, OLIVER WENDELL.

GREAT GAME. Coined by Rudyard Kipling to describe the century-old battle between Russia and Great Britain to control Afghanistan. The power struggle was finally won by the Soviets in May, 1978, when they established an overwhelming military and political influence in Kabul following a coup in which hundreds of the Afghan leaders were killed. The following year the Soviets strengthened their victory by sending Russian soldiers into Afghanistan. The end of this long duel which had been conducted by espionage, diplomacy and intrigue between the East and the West has frightening implications concerning the preservation of world peace.

GREAT HELMSMAN. See LONG MARCH.

GREAT LAKES RULES OF THE ROAD. See RULES OF THE ROAD.

GREAT LEAP FORWARD. See LONG MARCH.

GREAT LEAP OUTWARD. See LONG MARCH.

GREAT SOCIETY. The name coined by President Lyndon B. Johnson to describe his political programs.

GREAT TOMATO WAR. The economic struggle between Mexican and Florida vegetable and fruit growers, who compete for the lucrative market of Americans seeking fresh produce in the wintertime.

GREENBACK DOLLARS. Issued by the United States Treasury in 1862 as a temporary currency to finance the Civil War. Of the $450 million in Greenbacks issued, it is estimated that $300 million are still technically in circulation.

GREEN BOOK. (1) A master file of photographs and fingerprints of known terrorists compiled by West Germany and distributed free to the police of all nations to enable them to arrest any terrorists seeking to enter their countries. (2) A directory of all federal, state, county and city government agencies and officials by name and address.

GREEN CARD. Named after its original color and still so called even though it has been printed in red, white and blue since 1965. This is a highly prized and difficult to obtain legal federal document. Millions apply annually but only a select few obtain them which enables the fortunate recipients to live in the United States indefinitely. They are only granted to aliens who have (1) close relatives living here; (2) specialized skills which are needed here or (3) a minimum of $40,000 to invest here.

GREEN PEACE. A foundation headquartered in California which protects the environment and endangered species. The foundation has successfully challenged killers of whales and baby seals on the open seas.

GRESHAM'S LAW. Expounded by Sir Thomas Gresham, a sixteenth-century English financier, this law states that if two currencies with the same nominal value but with different intrinsic values are circulated during the same period of time, people will hoard the currency with the higher intrinsic value. The result of such hoarding is that the good currency will eventually disappear from circulation.

GRETNA GREEN MARRIAGES. Ceremonies performed in the village of Gretna Green, Scotland, which did not require such customary formalities as posting of banns or getting a license. After 1753, when England abolished fleet marriages, many young couples eloped to the Scottish town just across the border. Thus, Gretna Green Marriages are said to be performed in any jurisdiction where couples can marry quickly.

GREY MARKET ADOPTION RACKET. Independently arranged adoption, usually by doctors and lawyers for handsome fees which unfortunately is illegal in only a few states. Generally an attorney secures an illegitimate newborn infant through personal contact with a doctor, often in another state. After the birth of the child, the attorney obtains the mother's consent to adoption, the adoptive parents take physical custody of the child, and adoption procedures are completed. The attorney usually charges a single fee for his professional services and pays for the mother's childbirth expenses.

GRIFFIN v. CALIFORNIA (380 U.S. 609 (1965)). See TAKE THE FIFTH.

GRISWOLD v. CONNECTICUT (381 U.S. 479 (1965)). An important case decided by the Supreme Court, holding that a Connecticut statute prohibiting the use of contraceptive devices by married couples was unconstitutional. The Court relied on the First and Fourth Amendments to the Constitution in determining that a state does not have a right to invade marital privacy, a constitutionally protected freedom. In his majority opinion, Mr. Justice Douglas delivered the famous lines: "would we allow the police to search the sacred precincts of marital bedrooms for telltale signs of the use of contraceptives? The very idea is repulsive to the notions of privacy surrounding the marital relationship."

GROSS NATIONAL PRODUCT (G.N.P.). The market value of the output of goods and services produced by the Nation's economy. G.N.P. is a "gross" measure because no deduction is made to reflect the wearing out of machinery and other capital assets used in production. Net National Product (N.N.P.) is G.N.P. minus Capital Consumption Allowances.

GROSS NEGLIGENCE. The failure to exercise even slight care. Originating in Roman law, this concept has taken root in several areas of American law, but it is often said to be the source of more confusion than clarification. Part of that confusion arises from the difficulties inherent in defining the term.

Some courts have suggested that it involves the failure to exercise even that care which a careless person would use, while others describe the concept in terms of wilful misconduct or recklessness. When applied, however, it is not clear how these definitions differ from that of ordinary negligence. British Baron Rolfe once characterized gross negligence as being the equivalent of ordinary negligence "with the addition of a vituperative epithet." The concept enjoys current vitality in only two major views of the law. The driver/host of an automobile will often not be held liable for injuries to his guest in the absence of Gross Negligence and neither will the bailee of property for the benefit of its bailor.

GROTIUS, HUGO (1583-1645). A leading Dutch legal scholar, known as the father of Western International law as a result of his definitive treatise entitled *De jure belli ac pacis* (Latin for *The Law of War and Peace*), published in the seventeenth century.

GROUND LEASE. Provides for a long-term rental of undeveloped land, on which the tenant agrees to construct a building which becomes the property of the landowner when the lease expires. Generally, by the end of the lease period, the tenant has been able to recover the cost of the building through depreciation.

GROUND RENT. The amount of money paid for the use of undeveloped land.

GROUP OF SEVENTY-SEVEN (77). The over-100 less developed countries (L.D.C.s) which disagree with the other nations participating in the Law of the Sea Conferences who have bonded together in a common stand to seek a new international economic order in the exploitation and use of the world maritime resources.

GROUP OF THIRTY (30). Formed in 1979 and financed by the Rockefeller Foundation under leadership of H. J. Witteveen, former managing director of the International Monetary Fund, this is an informal organization of experts which meets regularly in an attempt to solve the problems, legal and otherwise, of the international economic system. The first meeting was held in Bermuda in February, 1979. The agenda consisted of a study of the various aspects of the floating rate system, including the effect of technology, which has created the 24-hour market; the integration of international and domestic money markets; the emergence of New York as a center of foreign exchange activity; and the changing behavior of corporations.

GROUPS OF THE ARMED PROLETARIAT. See G.A.P.

G.S.B.C.A. See BOARDS OF CONTRACT APPEALS.

G.S.L. See FEDERAL COLLEGE-AID STATUTES.

GUAM DOCTRINE. See NIXON DOCTRINE.

GUARANTEE CLAUSE. The first clause of Article IV, Section 4 of the Constitution of the United States provides that "the United States shall guarantee to every State in this Union a republican form of government." In this clause the term "the United States" means the government of the United States, especially the Congress and the President. The Supreme Court has held that what is "a republican form of government" is a "political question" to be resolved by the Congress and the President, acting within their own spheres of responsibility. Congress may approve the government of a new state by admitting it into the union or by seating the Representatives and Senators from that state. The President may show his approval by furnishing military assistance to a state when he is authorized to do so. The Supreme Court has consistently refused to adjudicate claims brought under the guarantee clause, holding that the clause is nonjusticiable. This position was reiterated in *Baker v. Carr*, 369 U.S. 186 (1962), the classic "one man, one vote" case.

GUARANTEED ANNUAL INCOME (Negative Income Tax). Long espoused by leading economists, including distinguished University of Chicago Professor of Economics Milton Friedman, as a simple and effective way to bring the very poor up to a minimum income level. Ideally, such a system could be administered through the Internal Revenue Service, and the swollen federal and state welfare bureaucracy could be dismantled. In theory, since the poor could keep most of any additional income they earned for themselves, they would work hard and pull themselves up by their bootstraps, in the great American tradition. Every Administration since Lyndon Johnson's has proposed such a Negative Income Tax plan, including the Carter Administration. And behind much of the effort, under both Presidents Johnson and Nixon, was Daniel Patrick Moynihan, the former Harvard professor who has held posts as an Assistant Secretary of Labor, White House counselor, Ambassador to India, Ambassador to the United Nations, and is now a Senator from New York.

GUARANTEED SALES PLAN. Agreement between a broker and a seller of a home that the broker will buy the home if it does not sell within a certain period. Brokers generally charge one to two percent of the selling price for this service.

GUARANTEED STUDENT LOANS. See FEDERAL COLLEGE-AID STATUTES.

GUARDHOUSE LAWYER. A soldier under arrest in the guardhouse who proclaims that he is an expert on military law.

GUARDIAN AD LITEM. See GENERAL GUARDIANSHIP.

GUARDIAN BY ESTOPPEL. See GUARDIAN DE SON TORT.

GUARDIAN DE SON TORT (Latin —of his wrong). A person who acts as a guardian without valid authority. This person is also called a "guardian by estoppel" or a "quasi guardian."

GUARDIAN IN SOCAGE. See GENERAL GUARDIANSHIP.

GUARDIAN OF THE ESTATE. See GENERAL GUARDIANSHIP.

GUATAMALA PROTOCOL. See WARSAW CONVENTION.

GUEST STATUTES. See AUTOMOBILE GUEST STATUTES.

GUILTY AS CHARGED. A finding, by a judge or jury, that the defendant was criminally responsible for the charged offenses. Such a finding imports that the defendant caused the results while possessing the required Mens Rea and without mitigating circumstances such as self-defense or insanity.

GULF OF TONKIN RESOLUTION. An attack on a United States naval vessel off the coast of North Vietnam in the China Sea in 1968 which President Lyndon B. Johnson used as the excuse to send American combat troops to Vietnam in the absence of any declaration of war as required by the Constitution.

GUN BOAT DIPLOMACY. An ostentatious display of military power in order to blackmail another country into action favored by the bully. The greatest American proponent of this extortion was Theodore Roosevelt who advocated the carrying of a "big stick" as a warning to others. For example, he successfully so threatened Columbia in the creation of the Panama Canal. In fact, he was even proud of his nickname of Big Bully.

GUN CONTROL. Legislative attempts to cool an American love affair with guns. Since 1900 guns have killed or injured more people than the sum of American casualties in every war from the Revolution to Vietnam. Approximately 20,000 people are shot to death every year and some 200,000 are wounded, yet resistance to gun control legislation is fierce. Two arguments are frequently used to attack gun control: (1) Individuals should be allowed to have guns to defend their homes against intruders; and (2) A ban on the sale or manufacture of handguns would discriminate against sportsmen. Supporters of gun control legislation point to studies which show that more homeowners are killed by gun accidents in a one-year period than are killed by robbers or burglars in a four-year period. Supporters also contend that sportsmen would not be affected by gun control legislation which only seeks to ban the sale and manufacture of handguns, which are generally unsuitable in sporting use.

H

HABEAS CORPUS (Latin—you have the body). Codified by Charles II in 1679, the Writ of Habeas Corpus is historically famous as the remedy for deliverance from illegal confinement. The writ, more specifically known by the fancy name of Habeas Corpus Ad Faciendum, Subjuciendum Et Recipiendum, is directed to a person detaining another, ordering him to produce the body of the prisoner along with information as to the date and reason for his arrest and detention and to do, submit to, and receive whatever the court issuing the writ shall order. The provision for Habeas Corpus originated in the early common law courts in England and has retained its historical significance in American courts. Its use was first authorized in the federal courts in the First Judiciary Act and was then greatly expanded by the Habeas Corpus Act of 1867, which authorized federal courts to grant the writ "In all cases where any person may be restrained of his or her liberty in violation of the Constitution, or any treaty or law of the United States." Subsequent statutory codifications added important procedural limitations. Today, the writ of Habeas Corpus is used primarily as an extraordinary post-conviction remedy for federal or state prisoners who claim a federal constitutional or statutory defect in their convictions. It can also serve as a mechanism for a constitutional attack upon official claims

of power to detain, or to provide judicial review of agency or administrative decisions resulting in detention. Habeas Corpus further performs certain traditional functions in connection with criminal charges: testing the sufficiency of cause of a complaint for commitment or removal, the denial of bail, the legality of interstate rendition or extradition to a foreign country, or the conditions of confinement. It is important to remember that the writ of Habeas Corpus is not an instrument for redetermining the merits of a case but rather a limited device to test the legality of detention or confinement under constitutional or statutory guarantees. The present federal Habeas Corpus statute vests authority to grant the writ in the Supreme Court and in the federal district courts, as well as in any single Supreme Court Justice or circuit court of appeals judge. In addition, most of the States have their own Habeas Corpus statutes, but the vast majority of those seeking the writ go to Federal Court for vindication of their federal constitutional or statutory rights. Federal Habeas Corpus procedure is broadly governed by the Federal Rules of Civil Procedure, subject to specific provisions in the federal laws, such as the Habeas Corpus statutes themselves. In cases where a state prisoner seeks a federal writ of Habeas Corpus to challenge his conviction, the Supreme Court has developed a doctrine of exhaustion of state remedies, which must be satisfied before a Habeas application will be entertained. More recently, the Burger Court, in *Stone v. Powell*, 428 U.S. 465 (1976) and other cases, has begun to close the doors of the federal courts to state prisoners seeking to challenge their convictions, leaving the state courts as their only alternative. Finally, it should be noted that this is a civil and not a criminal proceeding and thus can be used in private cases such as custody disputes.

HABITUAL CRIMINAL STATUTES (Habitual Offender Statutes). State statutes which provide for an increased sentence upon the third conviction of certain felonies. In many states, habitual criminals are subject to life imprisonment without possibility of parole.

HACKING THE PIE. What happens at a year-end meeting of partners when they divide a law firm's profits.

HAGUE CONFERENCE ON PRIVATE INTERNATIONAL LAW. An international body concerned with conflicts of laws and procedural problems that arise in the course of international transactions. Prior to 1951, the Hague Conference met on an ad hoc basis. In October 1951, the Conference became a full-fledged international organization, with a permanent secretariat and scheduled plenary sessions, at which drafts of proposed uniform laws and conventions, prepared by special commissions are considered and revised and then recommended to governments for adoption. The United States adhered to the statute of the Hague Conference in 1964.

HAGUE CONVENTION ON HIJACKING. An international agreement which outlines jurisdiction for prosecuting hijackers and imposes an obligation on nations which are parties to the convention to prosecute or extradite hijackers.

HAGUE PEACE CONFERENCES. See THE HAGUE PEACE CONFERENCES.

HAGUE RULES. See HAMBURG RULES.

HAKEM SHARE. A Persian term which can be translated into Judge of Religious Court, Governor of Religious Law or Executive Authority of Religious Law. In any event, it was the title and position which Ayatollah Sadegh Khalkhali gave himself in 1979 as head of the infamous Islamic Revolutionary Court after the coup in Iran by Ayatollah Ruholla Khomeini, which ousted Shah Mohammad Reza Pahlavi from his 2,500-year-old Peacock Throne.

HALF A LOAF. A Judge who tries to give something to both parties in a lawsuit.

HALFWAY HOUSE. A detention or treatment center utilized in the rehabilitation of prisoners, juveniles, or other institutionalized persons, utilizing community resources in its rehabilitation effort. The centers are usually small, residential, and located in a city or town. Persons involved in the programs participate in the daily life of the community, either working or going to school. Halfway houses usually have very minimal security provisions. The halfway house stands literally "halfway" between the community and the institution, and many serve persons who are released from an institution, as well as those received directly from a court.

HALLOWEEN MASSACRE. (1) Name given to the most massive single important firing and shifting of high-ranking government officials in American history on November 2, 1975, when President Ford dismissed William Colby as Director of the C.I.A., James Schlesinger as Secretary of Defense, Henry Kissinger as National Security Assistant to the President, and Vice-President Nelson Rockefeller as his running-mate on the 1976 G.O.P. ticket. The name derives from the fact that President Ford made his decision the last day of October (Halloween), although he did not make a public announcement for two days. (2) The discharge or premature retirement on the day of that holiday in 1977 by the C.I.A. of 800 of its veteran agents as part of an efficiency campaign. The newly appointed Director of the C.I.A., Admiral Stansfield Turner, justified his hatchet-man action on the grounds that (a) The Agency was overstaffed because of the Vietnam War, (b) Technical means were replacing the traditional cloak-and-dagger operation and (c) The decks had to be cleared for younger men coming up from the ranks. Many critics attribute our setbacks in countries such as Iran, Ethiopia and Afghanistan, to this massive house-cleaning operation.

H.A.L.T. (Help Abolish Legal Tyranny). An organization formed in Washington, D.C., in 1978, by private citizens and industry groups to stir up public support for curtailing the fast growth of litigation in the United States.

HAMBURG RULES. A new set of legal principles for the allocation of shipment risks between carriers and shippers proposed by the 1978 United Nations Convention on the Carriage of Goods by Sea to replace the Hague Rules established in 1924 in the International Convention for the Unification of Certain Rules Relating to Bills of Lading.

HAMILTON, ALEXANDER (1757-1804). An American lawyer and revolutionary statesman who was primarily responsible for the ratification of the United States Constitution and the establishment of a strong central government. He was the first Secretary of the Treasury and instituted sound fiscal policies to establish the credit of the United States at home and abroad. As the leader and most eloquent spokesman of the Federalist party, he was the political and personal enemy of Thomas Jefferson, leader of the Democratic-Republican party. However, during the 1800 presidential election, he supported Jefferson to insure the defeat of Aaron Burr, whom he considered to be the worse of the two. Hamilton is remembered more for his duel with Aaron Burr, which resulted in Hamilton's death and thus the abrupt end of his career.

HAMMER v. DAGENHART. See CHILD LABOR CASES.

HAMMURABI CODE. The first attempt to codify laws and societal norms. It probably dates from around the eighteenth century B.C. when the Babylonian emperor, Hammurabi, attempted to compile all of the imperial ordinances of his realm. Now housed in the Louvre Museum in Paris, the Code includes a poetic prologue celebrating Hammurabi's justice and greatness and expresses his desire to preserve his accomplishments for posterity. Most of the 282 laws are stated in the conditional; only five are direct prohibitions. The laws are organized according to subject matter, such as offenses against the admin-

istration of justice, property regulations, offenses against the person, tenets governing marriage and family life, agricultural specifications, and rules applicable to commercial transactions. The Code also offers insights into the structure of Babylonian society. It establishes three social classes: slaves, propertied men, and an intermediate group roughly comparable to a middle class. The rights of women are surprisingly liberal, with some women allowed to own property and all entitled to divorce their husbands. Less progressive are the provisions for Trial by Ordeal and for Retaliatory Punishment.

HANCOCK, JOHN. The largest, most defiant and most prominent signature on the Declaration of Independence. The courage of the gentleman from Massachusetts is highlighted when one realizes his act was treason for which the British could hang him. To place one's John Hancock today is to place one's signature to a document. Another expression of signing a paper is to put your John Henry to it. Henry was the legendary hero of cowboy folklore whose strength was so great he could outdrive a steam drill with his hammer and steel in laying railroad ties.

HAND, AUGUSTUS NOBLE (1869-1954). Born in Elizabethtown, New York, the son of a prominent local lawyer, Hand served for forty years on the federal bench: first as United States District Judge for the Southern District of New York (1914-1927), then as Judge for the Second Circuit Court of Appeals (1927-1954). Having received a superb education at Phillips Exeter and Harvard, Hand excelled at Harvard Law School, where he was an editor of the Law Review. When, in 1914, President Wilson appointed him to the federal district bench, Hand was an experienced practitioner whose legal career had been largely spent in the service of his uncle's firm—Hand, Bonney and Jones. Although not so renowned as his cousin B. Learned Hand (with whom he sat on the district bench), Augustus sculpted circumspect, well-reasoned opinions which have been selected for law school casebooks. So impressed by Hand's soundness was Justice Robert Jackson that the High Court jurist once advised his colleagues, "Quote B. [Learned], but follow Gus." His legal expertise extended to fields as diverse as admiralty and administrative law, and his constitutional opinion in *United States v. Kauten*, 133 F.2d 703 (2nd Cir. 1943) (holding that Congress could limit exemption from military service to those having strictly religious objections) may have marked the apogee of his attainment. Reserved and dignified, Hand had a grave mien which belied a good humor he revealed only in private moments. When he died in 1954, Charles E. Clark, then Chief Judge of the Second Circuit Court of Appeals, reflected that

> the touchstone of his life seems, indeed to be that passage from Thomas Carlyle's *Past and Present* which he was fond of quoting, and which concludes:
>
> Here is all fulness
> Ye brave, to reward you;
> Work, and despair not.

HAND, LEARNED (1872-1961). One of the most influential jurists of the twentieth century, he served for fifteen years as a federal judge for the Southern District of New York and for thirty-seven years on the Second Circuit Court of Appeals (1923-61). Prior to his appointment to the judiciary in 1909, Hand, the son and grandson of judges, practiced law in Albany, New York and in New York City. Unlike most of his contemporaries, Hand enjoyed a long life, and this longevity had a marked effect on his legal philosophy. When he died in 1961 at the age of 89, Hand had experienced the post-World War II social and technological boom in the United States. Consequently, he became increasingly aware of the judge's changing role in the American law-making process. Hand frequently questioned the degree to which a judge was "free" in rendering decisions. In this regard, he felt it nearly impossible for judges to make rulings solely on the basis of precedent and judicial tradition; judges could not ignore the fact that they were human beings and American citizens as well. Despite his stature as a jurist, Hand never reached the Supreme Court. William Howard Taft twice blocked Hand's nomination to the Court because Hand had supported Teddy Roosevelt in the 1912 presidential election against Taft. Geographical considerations twice prevented him from being nominated. Fellow New Yorkers Benjamin Cardozo and Charles Evans Hughes were appointed at times when Hand was also in contention. In 1942, Franklin Roosevelt decided to nominate 70-year-old Hand, but reconsidered after realizing the implications for the Court Packing Plan. Roosevelt had premised that plan on the principle that Supreme Court justices lost their vitality as they grew older, and he felt Hand's nomination would make the plan vulnerable to political attack.

HANDICAPPED MAINSTREAMING. A gradual integration, by judicial decision and legislative fiat, of the 6 million physically, emotionally and mentally handicapped children in the United States into the educational system which had previously been reserved exclusively for the non-handicapped.

HANGING JUDGE. The name given to Roy Bean who liberally imposed capital punishment on those convicted of the slightest offense in his nineteenth-century court in the Wild West.

HANSON v. DENKLA RULE. A due process rule which requires that a defendant avail himself of state law in order to come within that state's power of personal jurisdiction. The most recent case on this point, *Shaffer v. Heitner*, 429 U.S. 813 (1977), adds 2 requirements to the purposely availing test: (1) fair play and substantial justice, generally defined as contacts with the state relevant to the cause of action; and (2) a constitutionally valid statute which asserts personal jurisdiction over the defendant.

HARD ESPIONAGE. Theft by spies of military and diplomatic secrets as distinguished from soft espionage which is the theft of business and trade secrets.

HARE PLAN. A method of proportional representation which has been adopted in a number of American municipalities. Under the Plan, a vote quota is established, and every candidate who obtains the required number of votes is elected. The Plan further provides for a transfer of votes, so that surplus votes cast for winning candidates and the votes cast for candidates who fail to meet the quota are transferred according to voter preference. While the Hare Plan is designed to reflect voter preferences accurately, it is often difficult for legislative bodies elected under a proportional representation system to reach a consensus.

HARMLESS ERROR. An inconsequential mistake committed by a trial court. Since such an error will not affect the outcome of a trial, it will not prompt an appellate court to reverse or modify a judgment. An error which probably influenced a verdict is not harmless. Even an error which results in a violation of a defendant's constitutional rights may be harmless. The prosecution, however, must convince the appellate court that the error was harmless beyond a reasonable doubt.

HARPER v. VIRGINIA BOARD OF ELECTIONS (383 U.S. 663 (1966)). A United States Supreme Court decision declaring unconstitutional the imposition of poll taxes on voters in federal elections. Poll taxes were held to discriminate among voters on the basis of wealth, in violation of the Equal Protection Clause. The Court held that the state may proscribe reasonable restrictions on voter qualifications, such as age or residency, but that a tax on the privilege to vote has no rational relation to a voter's ability to participate intelligently in the electoral process.

HARTER ACT (1893). A federal law which sought to balance the conflicting interests of ocean carriers and shippers regarding liability for the lost or damaged goods shipped in maritime commerce. The Act makes it unlawful for any Ocean Bill of Lading to contain a provision relieving a vessel or its owner from liability for loss or damage arising from negligence, fault, or failure in proper loading, stowage, custody, care, or proper delivery of the cargo or lessening the obligation of the carrier to properly equip and man the vessel or make it seaworthy. This provision provides shippers with protection against exculpatory clauses long held by the courts of the United States to be contrary to public policy. The Act also protects the interests of ocean carriers by relieving such carriers of liability for damage or loss resulting from faults or error in navigation or in the management of the vessel provided the carrier exercises due diligence to make the vessel in all respects seaworthy. The latter provision relieves the vessel owner of liability for the negligence of those he puts in charge of the vessel.

HART, H.L.A. Professor of Jurisprudence at Oxford University, and considered by many the leading contemporary legal philosopher. Perhaps Hart's most famous work is *The Concept of Law*, in which he attempts to determine what is "law." Hart initiated a revised version of legal positivism. His position was that traditional positivism, in its emphasis on law as rules and commands, was tantamount to saying a gunman's orders were "law" and that the Nazi regime was legitimate. He would impose on legal rules a minimum content of natural law, taking into consideration such normative concepts as human vulnerability and approximate equality.

HART-SCOTT-RODINO ANTI-TRUST IMPROVEMENTS ACT OF 1976. A federal law that empowers State Attorneys General to seek damages in behalf of all citizens of their jurisdictions when it is impractical for individual consumers to litigate claims of price-fixing violations involving small amounts such as a nickel on a loaf of bread.

HATCH ACT. A federal law passed in 1939 which bans the more than 2 million federal civil servants from active roles in partisan political campaigns. It prohibits them from collecting funds, managing campaigns or running for office as Democrats or Republicans. Many attempts to modify or repeal the law in the past have been defeated, including a veto by President Ford of a law passed by Congress.

HAUPTMANN/LINDBERGH CASE. Highly publicized kidnapping of Charles Lindbergh's infant son, resulting in the conviction and execution of German immigrant, Bruno Richard Hauptmann in 1936. Hauptmann demanded and received $50,000 ransom but the child was murdered anyway, inciting public anger in a frenzied search for the kidnapper. It was estimated that the government spent $1.5 million investigating the crime and the bill for the trial alone amounted to more than 130,000 depression-era dollars.

HAVANA CONVENTION ON INTERNATIONAL TRADE (November 21, 1947 to March 24, 1948). Promoted by the U.N. Economic and Social Council (E.C.O.S.O.C.) to foster the expansion of international commerce. However, the International Trade Organization (I.T.O.), which it created, failed because participating countries finally refused to approve it. Nevertheless, these countries passed the General Agreement on Tariffs and Trade (G.A.T.T.). It was not until 1964 that the U.N. created an international commercial organization, the United Nations Conference on Trade and Development (U.N.C.T.A.D.).

HEAD AND MASTER LAW. A carryover from the Napoleonic Code which governs civil proceedings in Louisiana, the only state in the Union to use the French law. Although it refers only to community property jointly owned by husband and wife, that is, property acquired by earnings after the marriage, the husband alone is given absolute dominion over such property. Only he alone can borrow money on it and control the income without the wife's consent, even if the wife is the sole worker in the family. It was not until 1978 that

a federal judge finally declared the law unconstitutional as a violation of the equal rights clause of the 14th Amendment to the Federal Constitution. Feminists had just cause to celebrate this long overdue victory.

HEALTH AND HUMAN SERVICES (H.H.S.). See DEPARTMENT OF EDUCATION.

HEALTH MAINTENANCE ORGANIZATION. See H.M.O.

HEARING EXAMINER. See ADMINISTRATIVE LAW JUDGE.

HEARSAY RULE. Bars the receipt into evidence of oral or written statements made by someone who is not testifying. Codified by Federal Rule of Evidence 801, the Rule operates only if the statement is offered to prove the fact it asserts. For example, if a witness testifies that his wife said she heard two shots, the testimony is objectionable as Hearsay if it is offered to prove that there were, in fact, two shots. But, the testimony would be admissible if it were offered to prove that the witness' wife spoke English. Hearsay Evidence is excluded because it is considered unreliable. The person whose statement is reported is not under oath and is not subject to safeguards, such as cross-examination, which seek to insure the accuracy of evidence. Furthermore, the credibility of the person whose statement is reported cannot be assessed for the jury cannot observe his demeanor. The Hearsay Rule was a late development of the common law. Its acceptance was fueled by the manifest injustice of using hearsay at political trials. Sir Walter Raleigh, for instance, was convicted of conspiracy to commit treason on the basis of hearsay, which Raleigh was able to show was later recanted. The Hearsay Rule is subject to numerous exceptions which reflect the acute necessity for using, and the reliability of, a particular type of hearsay.

HEART BALM SUITS. Term which applies to any one of the four "romantic love" civil actions of Breach of Promise, Criminal Conversation, Alienation of

Affections or Seduction. The poetic name "Heart Balm" refers to a financial soothing of the pocketbook of a victim in compensation for an unfortunate affaire de coeur. Breach of Promise is an action in contract whereas the latter three are in tort. A male or female may qualify as a plaintiff in the first three but only a female (or her legal guardian) may sue for seduction. In other words, a man may be seduced factually but not legally. Legally, seduction is sexual relations by a man with a woman of previous chaste character under a false promise that he will later marry her. Criminal Conversation, despite its name, is a civil action brought against one who has had sexual intercourse with the plaintiff's spouse. It was originally an action available only to a husband because it was based to a large extent on the premise that the husband might be required to support his wife's illegitimate offspring as a result of the third party's act. Now it is probably based on the doctrine of Consortium, i.e., that a spouse is entitled to exclusive comfort, affection and sexual relations with the other spouse; and the action can now be brought by a wife in a number of states. Alienation of Affections stems from an eighteenth-century English case which was originally brought against one who has caused another's spouse to leave the family home. This action also could at first be brought only by a husband, but since the time of the Married Women's Acts a century ago, it has been generally considered as available to the wife as well. Proof of sexual intercourse is not ordinarily necessary to such an action. In recent years there has been a movement toward enlarging the action of Alienation of Affections to permit children of the marriage to bring suit against one who has disrupted the home by causing either parent to leave. The Greeks, of course, were directly involved in the most famous Alienation of Affections controversy, the Trojan War. The first Breach of Promise suit for the loss of romantic love in America apparently was conducted at Jordan's Point, about 30 miles down the James River from Richmond, Virginia, in 1623. A minister, the Rev. Mr. Granville Pooley, had wooed a widow, Cecily Jordan. According to witnesses, they repeated together the marriage vow informally as an engagement pact, drank from a single cup, and kissed. Mrs. Jordan elicited from the minister a promise not to announce the engagement publicly, but he did so anyway. Enraged, she decided to marry somebody else. The minister sued her for Breach of Promise, and the case went before the Governor's court which did not have to make a decision in the matter, for the minister's eye soon fell upon another woman and he forgot all about Mrs. Jordan. The court warned her to watch her step in the future, however, and dismissed the case.

HEART LAW. Originally enacted in 1970 in New York City as a temporary measure, it provides that policemen and firemen may retire at three-quarters pay if they develop a heart ailment during their term of employment. Unlike a corresponding state law, the city law does not require that an incident be associated with the heart disease or that the ailment be directly caused by the job. In 1977 the Heart Law cost New York City more than twenty million dollars. The law was criticized by New York City's Mayor as "outrageous and a ripoff." It is estimated that under the standards of the police and firemen's pension systems, fifty-five percent of the uniformed officers with at least thirty years of City service could retire under the provisions of the Heart Law. A number of other cities have similar laws.

HEAT OF PASSION. See VOLUNTARY MANSLAUGHTER.

HELMS UNITED NATIONS AMENDMENT. Named after its sponsor, the Republican Senator from North Carolina, this federal law of 1978 stopped funds for the U.N. dues of the United States from being used for Third World technical assistance on the grounds that all foreign aid should be voluntary.

HELP ABOLISH LEGAL TYRANNY. See H.A.L.T.

HELPLESS PERIL. See LAST CLEAR CHANCE.

HELP THROUGH INDUSTRY RETRAINING AND EMPLOYMENT. See H.I.R.E.

HELP UNDO SEXUAL HYPOCRISY. See H.U.S.H.

HELSINKI ACCORD. An agreement among the United States, Russia and 33 other countries reached in Helsinki, Finland, in 1975. It ratified the territorial expansionist conquests of Russia in Europe after World War II, denounced the use of force to settle international or internal disputes, committed the signers to a variety of measures to protect the human rights of their citizens and provided for a meeting in Belgrade, Yugoslavia in 1978 to assess what had been done to implement these commitments. At the Belgrade meeting, which ended in March, 1978, platitudes were exchanged to facilitate trade among the member countries and to reduce the danger of surprise attacks. The parties agreed to meet again in Madrid, Spain, in 1980. So much for Detente.

HELSINKI GROUP. A band of brave dissident Russian intellectuals who attempted to monitor Soviet compliance with the Human Rights Agreement in the Helsinki Accord. They were convicted of the crime of anti-Soviet agitation and sentenced to long terms of imprisonment in forced labor camps and exile. Among these courageous martyrs to freedom were Anatoli Scharansky, Andrei Sakhdrov, Yuri Orlov, Alexander Ginsburg, Anatoli Filator, and Victoras Pyatkus.

HENRY, JOHN. See HANCOCK, JOHN.

HENRY, PATRICK. Virginia lawyer most known for his call to arms at the second revolutionary convention in Virginia in 1775. A failure as a shopkeeper and farmer, Henry turned to law. As a revolutionary, politico, and lawyer Henry met with success. He was elected Governor of Virginia in 1776, and twice re-elected; was among those responsible for the adoption of the Bill of Rights; and was offered the positions of Secretary of State and then Chief Justice, which he declined.

H.H.S. See DEPARTMENT OF EDUCATION.

H.H.S. HOT LINE. A national toll free telephone number, 800-638-0742, which enables a patient to obtain a second opinion from a qualified surgeon on whether or not surgery is a necessary medical procedure for the condition from which the person is in need of medical treatment.

HICKENLOOPER AMENDMENTS. Amendments to the Foreign Assistance Act enabling the President to suspend assistance to the government of any country to which the United States is providing foreign aid if that country repudiates or nullifies contracts with or imposes discriminatory taxes on or nationalizes or expropriates property which is owned 50 percent or more by American citizens.

HICKMAN v. TAYLOR (328 U.S. 876 (1946)). The Supreme Court case upon which Federal Rules of Civil Procedure, Rule 26(b)(3), was based. The basic issue in *Hickman v. Taylor* was the extent to which an adverse party may discover materials collected by an attorney in preparation for litigation. With the exception of the attorney's mental impressions or legal theories, an adverse party may discover trial preparation materials if he has substantial need of them and is unable to obtain the materials without undue hardship. Rule 33(b) limits to some extent the protections provided by *Hickman v. Taylor* in Rule 26(b)(3).

HIDDEN JUDICIARY. See ADMINISTRATIVE LAW JUDGE.

HIDDEN POWER ELITE. See INVISIBLE GOVERNMENT.

HIGH CITADEL. A book published in 1978 by Joel Geliginan of the Northwestern University law faculty which describes what the author calls the pernicious influence of Harvard Law

School for over 100 years on the other 160 law schools in the country. Geliginan recommends a complete overhaul of American legal education to emphasize new training for public service.

HIGH NOON PROVISION. A proposal of Senator Edward M. Kennedy in 1980 that the President and Congress be required to evaluate the need for every federal regulatory agency every ten years.

HIGHWAY BEAUTIFICATION ACT OF 1965. See LADY BIRD'S BILL.

HILL-BURTON ACT. A federal law passed in 1944 which requires private hospitals that receive federal grants for construction or expansion of their facilities to provide free medical care to the poor for a period of 20 years after the completion of the facility.

HIPPOCRATIC OATH. A sentimental and ceremonial statement of ethical standards for doctors governing their relationships with patients and the profession, which is part of the graduate rite of some medical schools, created by the father of medicine, Hippocrates, who was born in Greece in 479 B.C. and died there in 399 B.C. It has no legal status and there are no penalties for violating it, which is done regularly. For example, it bars all abortions. On the other hand, it would allow fee-splitting, which most modern doctors regard as unethical if not illegal. Its most dramatic tenet is "Physician, do no harm."

HIRABAYASKI v. UNITED STATES. See SUSPECT CLASSIFICATIONS.

H.I.R.E. (Help Through Industry Retraining and Employment). A program sponsored by private employers with federal funds to place Veterans, especially those who served in Vietnam, in permanent full-time jobs.

HIRED GUN. (1) A disparaging term for a lawyer coined two thousand years ago by the Roman philosopher Seneca, especially one who goes all out to accomplish the desired goals of the client regardless of moral consequences. (2) An Expert Witness who wrongfully shades his testimony to favor the person who pays his exorbitant fee.

HIRING HALL. A union-operated headquarters from which requests for jobs are filled. The Hall functions as a job security device for industries in which seniority with any single employer cannot practically be used to determine job rights. Hiring Halls are typically found in industries where work is unpredictable and of short duration—construction, maritime and longshore are examples. The agreement establishing the Hall usually specifies whether the employer must take his employees from the Hall or whether he may get them through other sources. The Joint Hiring Hall is one operated by both the union and the employer. A Preferential Hiring Hall is one in which first referrals are granted to union members.

HISS - NIXON - CHAMBERS CASE. Alger Hiss, a Boston Brahmin, and once a protegé of Felix Frankfurter, adviser to President Roosevelt at Yalta, Clerk to Supreme Court Justice Oliver Wendell Holmes, former high-ranking State Department official and President of the Carnegie Endowment for International Peace, was accused of being a Communist spy in 1948 by then California Congressman Richard Nixon and ex-Communist undercover agent, *Time* magazine writer, Whittaker Chambers. He was convicted of perjury in 1950 and served 44 months in jail. In 1975, years after his release from prison, Alger Hiss became the first person ever re-admitted to the practice of law in Massachusetts after a major criminal conviction. Many American liberals say he is the equivalent of the Frenchman Dreyfus in having been wrongfully convicted.

HISTORIC PRESERVATION ZONING. In its strictest form, zoning that forbids private owners of historical buildings from altering the structure without approval of a local preservation committee. Some legal analysts equate this type of zoning with a taking of private property by the government—an act which would require compensating the owner for his loss.

HIT-AND-RUN. A crime in which the passenger or driver of an automobile leaves the scene of an accident in which he was involved and another person was injured. The individual who leaves fails to render assistance, give his name, address, license and registration numbers, or report the accident to the police.

HIT MAN. A person whose profession is the killing of any designated victim for an agreed-upon fixed fee.

H.L.A. TEST. Developed in the 1960s in the course of organ transplant research, the H.L.A. test is now gaining acceptance as a reliable scientific means of determining paternity. The test focuses on the antigens (genetic substances that stimulate the production of antibodies by the white blood cells) of the newborn as well as those of the mother and alleged father. Every child inherits two antigens from each parent, and the chances of the two unrelated persons possessing identical antigens is approximately one in a thousand. Now recognized as evidence of paternity in the courts of eleven states, the H.L.A. test has a proven accuracy rate of 90 percent in a study of 1,000 paternity disputes. Whereas the traditional method of comparing blood types of child, mother, and supposed father can be employed only to disprove parentage, the H.L.A. test has been used to negate paternity as well as to affirmatively identify the father.

H.M.O. (Health Maintenance Organization). A pre-paid medical plan, subsidized in part by the federal government, which emphasizes preventive medicine. Subscribers pay a monthly fee which entitles them to prescribed medical services free or for a small fee. Advocates claim that an H.M.O. provides cheaper and better medical care to its members than other medical programs.

HOBBES, THOMAS. A seventeenth-century legal philosopher, Hobbes de-veloped his theory of legal obligation in 1651, described in part in *The Leviathan*. Hobbes wrote during a period beset by civil war, which explains in part his view of the social contract which obligated citizen but not sovereign and granted virtually unlimited legal power to the latter. The Leviathan, or mortal god, was an individual or council in whom all power was to be concentrated in order to protect the populace from invasion by foreigners and from self-inflicted harms. The Leviathan ascended to power in one of two ways—by natural force, similar to the way a father controls his children, and by covenant, as when men agree among themselves to submit to authority. He could never be punished by his subjects, could never breach the covenant between himself and them, and had exclusive executive, legislative, and judicial powers. The Leviathan's sovereignty could not be transferred. To the charge that this theory of obligation subjected people to despotic rule, Hobbes countered that the miseries accompanying civil war or a masterless society were much worse.

HOBBY PROTECTION ACT (1973). The first federal statute to protect collectors of political and numismatic items. Under the Act, any imitation political item manufactured in, or imported into the United States for commercial distribution must conspicuously state the year of its manufacture. Further, any imitation numismatic then manufactured in, or imported into the United States for commercial purposes must be marked "Copy." The Act provides for enforcement by both private individuals and the Federal Trade Commission.

HOHFELDIAN PLAINTIFF. A traditional plaintiff who sues in his own personal and proprietary capacity, in contrast to one who sues as a representative of the public interest as in a Private Attorney General Suit. The distinction between Hohfeldian and non-Hohfeldian plaintiffs derives from W. Hohfeld's treatise *Fundamental Legal Conceptions* (1923), and has been discussed in a few Supreme Court cases with respect to the issue of Standing to Litigate.

HOLD AND TREAT LAWS. Involuntary detention of persons reasonably suspected of having a venereal disease. Such laws have been held constitutional if the person detained is held for a limited time and receives proper medical diagnosis and treatment. Such laws have been justified in order to bring venereal disease under control.

HOLD-HARMLESS AGREEMENT. As its name indicates, this agreement provides that one party will not hold the other liable. For example, a buyer who purchases real estate from a broker threatened with a lawsuit may demand a Hold-Harmless Agreement from the broker to assure that the buyer is not liable for damages.

HOLDER IN DUE COURSE DOCTRINE. Common-law rule which originated in the ancient case of *Miller v. Race* (1758) stating that anyone accepting in good faith a note or negotiable instrument can enforce the note against its maker. In other words, a note is as good as money in the hands of a Holder In Due Course. The Federal Trade Commission (F.T.C.) has disallowed this doctrine in modern consumer credit transactions due to fraudulent practices of some creditors. For example, if Allied Roofing sells Homeowner a defective roof on credit, and then sells the credit agreement to Finance Company, under the old rule, Finance Company becomes a Holder In Due Course. As a Holder In Due Course, Finance Company can enforce the debt against Homeowner even though he may have legitimate grievances with Allied Roofing. The F.T.C. ruling thereby assures the consumer that a transfer of his debt will not jeopardize his rights.

HOLDING COMPANY. Any company which owns enough stock in one or more corporations to dictate their policies or materially influence their managements. It is a concept similar to that of a parent corporation, but the term "parent" contemplates ownership of the stock of only one subsidiary corporation. A subsidiary is a corporation whose stock is controlled by another to an extent sufficient to make it the instrumentality of the other. A "pure" holding company is organized for the sole purpose of holding the controlling interest in one or more other corporations. Some of the reasons for the formation of holding companies are: (1) to limit risk to the assets of the subsidiary rather than the assets of the entire enterprise; (2) to reduce tax by splitting income into smaller units each of which is in a lower tax bracket; and (3) to avoid subjecting the holding company to the jurisdiction of a foreign state.

HOLLYWOOD TEN (10). The ten movie film writers who were accused of Communist Party membership and radical behavior by the House of Representatives Committee on Un-American Activities in 1947. Because of their refusal to answer questions, they were imprisoned for contempt and blacklisted by Hollywood. They were all eventually released from jail and re-instated by Hollywood, but their punishment represents a dark period of civil liberty persecution in our national history.

HOLMES, OLIVER WENDELL, JR. (1841-1935). Great legal scholar and jurist, Holmes was known as The Great Dissenter because of his frequent dissenting opinions as a Supreme Court Justice. During the thirty years Holmes served as a Supreme Court Justice, he gained a worldwide reputation for eloquent and forceful legal opinions. It is said that Holmes always wrote his opinions standing up, so as to prevent excess verbiage. One of Holmes' fundamental tenets was that if a man was to do anything of importance, then he should do it before he was forty. His major book, *The Common Law*, hailed as an epoch for law and learning, was published just five days before his fortieth birthday. As a young man, Holmes was advised by his father that "A lawyer can't be a great man," but the son was to prove his father wrong. Holmes once commented that as a legal scholar "you gain the secret isolated joy of the thinker, who knows that, a hundred years after he is dead and forgotten, men who have never heard of him will be moving to the measure of his thought. . . ."

HOLOGRAPHIC WILL. A will written and signed entirely by the testator with his own hand. Although a holograph does not automatically eliminate the necessity for the formal execution, by statute in nineteen states holographic wills are valid without formal attestation by witnesses. The handwritten character of the will is considered a guarantee of its genuineness. Any non-handwritten or self-typewritten matter in the will which the testator intended as a part of his will renders the will invalid. Holographic wills require the same testamentary capacity and testamentary intent as ordinary wills, but a holographic will may be informal. A letter has often been held sufficient. Statutes in some jurisdictions require that holographic wills be wholly dated in the testator's hand. Although a correct date is not required, if the date is incomplete, i.e., March 1976, or if it is illegible, the will is invalid. All holographic will statutes require that the will be signed by the testator, but he need not sign his full name. Initials, abbreviations of the first name, even "mother" or other familiar terms have been found sufficient.

HOLY SEE. The papacy, the position of leadership of the Roman Catholic Church. Upon the death of a Pope, the See is declared vacant (Sede Vacante) and must be filled by the election of a new Pope by those members of the College of Cardinals who have not then reached their 80th birthday.

HOMEMAKER RETIREMENT BILL. A proposed federal act which would allow a homemaker to provide for his or her own retirement through an Individual Retirement Account (I.R.A.). Under present law, only persons with earned income may own such account.

It is estimated that 30-50 million homemakers are approaching retirement age with no insured earnings to provide for financial needs in later years. Opponents of the measure fear that it would create an immediate financial loss since I.R.A.s are tax deductible. However, supporters stress the long range benefits of the bill. Homemaker I.R.A.s would provide an alternative to Social Security by which a person could prepare for his or her own retirement.

HOLY WAR (Jihad). A military action by Moslems to convert heathens by force and violence to Islam.

HOME RULE. A theory of government whereby localities are permitted to manage their own affairs. Whereas cities are generally established by the granting of a charter by the state legislature, under home rule an elected commission drafts a charter which is then approved by the voters. By allowing local government to resolve its own problems as long as the state's constitution and laws are not violated, the principle of home rule encourages greater citizen participation in the democratic process.

HOMESTEAD ACT. See PUBLIC DOMAIN.

HOMESTEAD TRUST. A trust arrangement to protect the land and building occupied by an owner and his family. Such trust arrangements might include investments for maintenance and expansion, tax funds, insurance coverage, etc. Presently, most states protect homesteads by statute against certain creditors, and the Homestead Trust is a sound device which provides additional protection to families.

HOME WARRANTIES. Insurance policies offered by brokerage firms to protect a home buyer from certain defects in his home for a specified period. Home warranties often enhance the buyer's position with a lender, because the lender is assured that the buyer will not be financially burdened with major home repairs during the early years of the mortgage.

HOMOSEXUAL

HOMOSEXUAL MARRIAGE. Marriage between members of the same sex. Some states ban homosexual marriage outright, while others fail to define "marriage." State courts which have heard the issue have found that forbidding homosexual marriage is not unconstitutionally discriminatory, even when the state has enacted an Equal Rights Amendment.

H-1 VISA. Permits temporary nonimmigrant permission to "an alien having a residence in a foreign country which he has no intention of abandoning, who is of distinguished merit and ability, and who is coming temporarily to the United States to perform services of an exceptional nature requiring such merit and ability. It offers several advantages over other working visas. In contrast with the H-2 (Temporary Worker) visa, H-1 eligibility does not depend on whether or not the job can be done by unemployed Americans on the local market; nor does it matter whether the salary offered would reduce American wages. Unlike the requirements for the much used L-1 (Intra-Company Transferee) visa, there is no need to show that the applicant worked for the international organization abroad for the last year. And while the E-1 (Treaty Trader) and E-2 (Investor) visas are often more convenient than is generally recognized, they simply do not work in the absence of an appropriate treaty of commerce. In the special situations where a B-1 (Business Visitor Status) visa contemplates employment, the alien is prohibited compensation from an American source, and the use of this status is otherwise limited. On the other hand, the H-1 applicant is faced with a formidable array of procedures established by regulation, operation instruction and practice including petition requirements and special arrangements for entertainers.

HONEY TRAP. An espionage term for catching someone in a compromising sexual situation and then threatening to blackmail the innocent victim unless the party agrees to become a spy.

HONOR BONDS. See BEARER BONDS.

HOOVER COMMISSION. Commission on reorganization of the executive branch. Appointed in 1947 to study the federal executive branch, the Commission consisted of twelve persons appointed by the President, the House and the Senate, and headed by former President Herbert Hoover. The Commission made several hundred recommendations, most of which have been adopted, to assure greater efficiency in the executive branch and to extend the President's power. In 1953 a second Hoover Commission was appointed to determine which federal activities should be terminated.

HOPSCOTCH LEASING. The subrenting of commercial property from a lessee of the property.

HORIZONTAL MERGER. The union of business entities engaged in the same business.

HORN BOOK. Basic legal textbook usually written by the top scholars in each field of law. In the sixteenth century, the Horn Book was a common teaching device in which a leaf of paper was protected by a thin translucent piece of horn mounted on a tablet of wood.

HOSTILE WITNESS. A witness who is antagonistic toward the party that calls upon him to testify, and who may thus be cross-examined by that party.

HOT BENCH. An appellate court, such as the New York Court of Appeals, in which judges read the record and briefs of counsel before hearing oral argument. Prior to oral argument in a Warm Bench, judges read a summary prepared by their legal staff. In contrast, judges in a Cold Bench hear a case without having read either briefs or a summary.

HOT BLOOD (Sudden Passion). Refers to the emotional state of a defendant at the time of his crime (such as a husband who kills the paramour

248

of his wife upon discovering them in the act of adultery) which reduces the nature of his crime from murder to manslaughter.

HOT CARGO CLAUSE. An agreement which requires that an employer not do business with any person with whom the union has a disagreement. The Teamsters Union often wrote such clauses into their contracts with truckers. Where a manufacturing plant was being struck, the Teamsters refused to handle the plant's goods in their trucks. These agreements and strikes to enforce them are illegal under the National Labor Relations Act.

HOT GOODS. (1) Contraband, smuggled, or recently stolen articles, usually sold to or disposed of by a person known as a fence, or, (2) in labor law, manufactured products shipped in interstate commerce by an employer who did not pay his employees at least the wage required by the Federal Minimum Wage and Hour Law.

HOT-LINE AGREEMENT OF 1963. An international Agreement that establishes a direct communications link between Washington and Moscow for use in emergency situations. The Supplemental 1971 Accord provides for a similar satellite communications system.

HOT MONEY (Funk Money). Short-term capital lured to one country from another to take advantage of temporarily higher interest rates there, or funds taken out of a country deemed unstable for one reason or another and invested abroad for security purposes.

HOT OIL. Refers to crude oil illegally taken from a producing well in excess of allowables (the number of barrels which may be taken per day or month from a given producing property, as fixed by a conservation commission or other state regulatory body); it may also refer to crude oil pumped from beneath the land of another through such methods as Slant Drilling or Whipstocking.

HOT PURSUIT. Has several meanings, depending on the context. As applied domestically, it refers to any criminal fleeing from arrest after committing a crime enabling the pursuing law-enforcement officer to cross over into another jurisdiction to make a valid arrest, which could not have otherwise been legally effectuated. Hot pursuit also occurs when the suspected criminal is being pursued within a jurisdiction immediately after a crime—within this context, some deviations from the Constitutional "Search and Seizure" rules are allowed because of necessity.

HOT SHEET. See MARINE SAFETY INFORMATION SYSTEM.

HOT SPOTTING. Annual selective re-appraisal of real estate for tax purposes.

HOUSE ARREST. A judicial experiment created by California, in 1979, to save the taxpayers money after Proposition 13. Instead of being sent to jail, non-violent non-addicted criminals are required to stay at home for one year except to go to work, receive medical care or do necessary personal errands. They must report twice daily to probation officers and are subject to spot checks at home. If the program works, it may revolutionize the entire criminal justice system throughout the nation.

HOUSE LAWYER. See KEPT LAWYER.

HOUSE OF COMMONS. See HOUSE OF LORDS.

HOUSE OF DELEGATES. See AMERICAN BAR ASSOCIATION.

HOUSE OF LORDS. The non-elective upper House of the British bi-cameral legislature made up of the peerage and high-ranking members of the clergy. The real power of the government rests in the elective lower House of Commons. Both constitute the Parliament.

HOUSTON & TEXAS CENTRAL RY. CO. v. UNITED STATES. See SHREVEPORT RATE CASE.

HOYLE'S LAW. Rules governing card games first promulgated, in 1742, in a book by a British barrister entitled *A Short Treatise on the Game of Whist.*

HUFSTEDLER, SHIRLEY M. Appointed to the Ninth Circuit Court of Appeals by President Johnson in 1969 (the highest judicial post held by a woman in the United States), in 1979 she was named the first Secretary of Education by President Carter in the newly created Cabinet position. Many predict she will one day become the first female member of the Supreme Court.

HUGHES, CHARLES EVANS. Republican Governor of New York in the early 20th Century who nonetheless sponsored progressive liberal measures such as minimum wage and child labor laws and a commission to regulate utilities. Appointed to the Supreme Court in 1910, Hughes left the Court in 1913 to run unsuccessfully for the Presidency against Woodrow Wilson. After serving as Secretary of State and Judge on the Permanent Court of International Justice, Hughes became Chief Justice of the Supreme Court in an appointment by Republican President Herbert Hoover. He presided over the Supreme Court from 1930 to 1941 in what was perhaps its stormiest period in the history of the Court, including the constitutional crisis posed by President Franklin Roosevelt's controversial but unsuccessful Court Packing Plan.

HUGHES-RYAN AMENDMENT. A federal Law passed in 1974 which bars the C.I.A. from any covert action unless the President expressly determines that it is necessary for national security and reports his findings to Congress.

HULETT, ALTA M. The first woman admitted to practice law in the United States. She thereafter inspired confidence in her clients as well as her colleagues and was a successful member of her profession until her untimely death in 1877.

HUMAN BEAST. See WAGNER, GUSTAV FRANZ.

HUMAN CANNONBALL CASE. Supreme Court decision that a television station violated Zachini's (The Human Cannonball) right of publicity when it broadcast his entire 15-second performance. Although the media is protected by the First Amendment, the Court drew the line at broadcasting an entire act without the performer's consent, because it poses a substantial threat to the economic value of the performance.

HUMAN FREEDOM CENTER. A private organization founded in 1978 in California (where else?) to help ex-members from off-beat cult groups, such as People's Temple, Synanon and Hare Krishna, in their difficult adjustment in rejoining a normal society. These poor brain-washed refugees apparently have a tough time in obtaining even the bare minimum physical necessities of life to say nothing of a job or human companionship.

HUMANITARIAN DOCTRINE. See LAST CLEAR CHANCE.

HUMAN LEUCOCYTE ANTIGEN TEST. See H.L.A. TEST.

HUMAN RIGHTS. Values we Americans all-too-often take for granted, which regrettably are non-existent in much of the Communist and Fascist world, such as those which are expressly guaranteed in our Declaration of Independence and Constitution and vigorously enforced in our Courts, including "Life, liberty and the Pursuit of Happiness;" "Freedom of Religion, Speech and Press;" and "Due Process of Law."

HUMPHREY-HAWKINS LAW OF 1978 (Full Employment Law). A memorial to the late great liberal Senator from Minnesota, Hubert Humphrey, which laid the foundation for a major change in the role of government in our society by requiring the President, for the first time, to establish annually a comprehensive set of national economic goals and then incorporating, in each year's budget, the policies and programs necessary to implement and achieve those goals. A private group known as the Initiative Committee for National Economic Planning did most of the groundwork for the passage of this significant new law. The law also legislated other ambitious goals (unemployment down to 4 percent by 1983, inflation down to 3 percent by 1983 and zero by 1988) but initiated no programs, leaving it up to the President and Congress to determine how to achieve the goals.

HUMPHREY'S EXECUTOR v. UNITED STATES (295 U.S. 602 (1935)). A case before the Supreme Court in which the Court held that the President may not remove a Federal Trade Commissioner from his position except for inefficiency, neglect of duty or malfeasance in office. In a previous case the Court had held that the President could remove, at his pleasure, a postmaster. The difference between the two cases lay in the fact that the Congress had established the F.T.C. as an independent agency whereas the Post Office was always considered to be wholly a part of the executive branch. *Humphrey's Executor* is important in establishing the principle that so-called independent agencies can, at least in some respects, be insulated from the powerful influence of the Executive branch.

HUNG JURY. A jury which cannot agree upon any verdict because they are hopelessly divided. In most states when a hung jury exists, a new trial must be granted.

HUNTING LICENSE. A document issued by a Bishop of the Episcopal Church which will enable a person whose marriage has been dissolved by a civil court to re-marry in the future within the Church.

HUSBAND-WIFE PRIVILEGE. Designed to promote family harmony, the privilege prevents the prosecution in a criminal trial from calling the defendant's spouse as a witness without the consent of the defendant. Once justified by the fiction of the husband and wife as one person, the privilege is the last remnant of a broad common law rule which barred a party's spouse from testifying for or against the party in a criminal or civil suit. In most states, the privilege can even be asserted by a defendant who marries specifically to prevent another from testifying against him.

H.U.S.H. (Help Undo Sexual Hypocrisy). A lobbying group organized by an Atlanitc City madam which has been highly unsuccessful in its attempts to legalize prostitution. The practice of the world's oldest profession is illegal in every state except Nevada.

HYDE AMENDMENT. Enacted September 30, 1976, as part of the Labor-H.E.W. Appropriations Act for fiscal year 1977. The controversial law prohibits Medicaid reimbursement for abortions to women in all cases unless the woman's life would be endangered by continuing her pregnancy. Several cases immediately challenged the constitutionality of the law, and not until August 1977 did the Amendment become effective. It is likely that the requirements a Medicaid mother must fulfill before receiving abortion funding will be substantially broadened in the future. In 1980, a federal court in New York held the Amendment unconstitutional.

I

I.A.A.C. (Civil Aviation Administration of China). The National Airline of Communist China which is so austere in its lack of creature comforts that the acronym for its name is said to represent the hysterical and anguished cackle of the passengers who vow never to fly again with this airline.

I.A.D.B. (Inter-American Development Bank). Headquartered in Washington, D.C., it is a Multilateral International Organization created in 1959 by nineteen Latin American Republics and the United States with subsequent member countries from other continents. Its purpose is to promote the economic development of Latin American countries individually and collectively.

I.A.E.A. (International Atomic Energy Agency). A Multilateral International Organization created in 1956 with over one hundred member countries including the United States, which seeks to enlarge the contribution of atomic energy to peace, health, and prosperity throughout the world. It ensures, through the international safeguards system, that its assistance is not used to further any military purpose.

I.A.T.A. (International Air Transport Association). Headquartered in both Geneva and Montreal, this organization is composed of 109 different airlines flying the flags of eighty-five different nations. Its main function is to serve as a cartel to fix the fares on all the routes flown by the member airlines in order to eliminate individual cut-throat competition. Violators pay heavy fines to the Association. Whenever members are unable to agree upon a fare, an Open Rate period results, during which any fare may be charged. Freddie Laker, whose small, independent British company Laker Airways, does not belong to I.A.T.A., became the first David ever to attack the flying Goliath Association successfully. When Laker instituted his no-frill, no-reservation flights between London and New York in 1977 at half the price set by I.A.T.A., other airlines were forced to reduce their fares to compete with him. Freddie has become the darling of all the poor people who want to join the jet set.

I.B.C.A. (Department of Interior Board of Contract Appeals). See BOARDS OF CONTRACT APPEALS.

I.C.A. See INTERNATIONAL COMMUNICATION AGENCY.

I.C.A.O. (International Civil Aviation Organization). A specialized Agency of the U.N. headquartered in Canada and composed of over one hundred member countries. Created in 1944, I.C.A.O. develops principles and techniques of international air navigation to foster planning and development of international air transport, so as to insure the safe and orderly growth of international civil aviation; to encourage the design and operation of planes for peaceful purposes; and to meet the needs of the peoples of the world for safe, regular, efficient, and economical air transport.

I.C.C. (International Chamber of Commerce). A private organization founded in 1919 and based in Paris. It represents business interests from more than ninety countries in all parts of the world. The I.C.C. plays a leading role in gathering and publishing information on international commerce, including "Incoterms" and "Documentary Credit Operations." The International Arbitration Center was created under its auspices. The I.C.C. Rules of Conciliation and Arbitration are followed worldwide, and its jurisprudence has played a decisive role in promoting the development of international commercial arbitration.

I.C.C. (Interstate Commerce Commission). The oldest of the independent Federal Administrative Agencies, established in 1887. The I.C.C. assures that the carriers it regulates will provide the public with rates and services that are fair and reasonable. It controls interstate surface transportation, including trains, trucks, buses, inland waterway and coastal shipping, freight forwarders, oil pipelines, and express companies. The regulatory laws vary with the type of transportation. However, they generally involve certification of carriers, rates, adequacy of service, purchases, and mergers.

I.C.E.R.R. See INTERSTATE CONGRESS FOR EQUAL RIGHTS AND RESPONSIBILITIES.

I.C.R.C. See LAW OF WAR; RED CROSS.

I.D.A. (International Development Association). An affiliate of the World Bank that makes subsidized loans to lesser-developed countries (LDCs).

I.D.C.A. See INTERNATIONAL DEVELOPMENT CO-OPERATION ADMINISTRATION.

I.F.B. See INVITATION FOR BIDS.

IGNORANCE OF THE LAW. See MISTAKE OF FACT; MISTAKE OF LAW.

I.I.s. See ILLEGAL IMMIGRANTS.

ILLEGAL ALIEN. See WET BACK.

ILLEGAL CORPORATE BEHAVIOR.
A detailed analysis by the Legal Enforcement Assistance Administration (L.E.A.A.) in 1980 of the legal record of the country's 582 largest publicly-owned corporations in the mid-1970s, which revealed that during one brief two-year period more than 60 percent of the corporations were accused of violating a federal law. The allegations included serious crimes such as fraudulent securities practices, income tax fraud, financial manipulations, advertising misrepresentation, anticompetitive practices, air and water pollution, food and drug law violations and the payment of illegal kickbacks, rebates and bribes. "Corporate crime costs run into the billions of dollars," the report notes, although precise figures are difficult to obtain. Estimates range from a Senate subcommittee's $200 billion to the Justice Department's approximation of $10 billion to $20 billion. "Few members of corporate management ever go to prison, even if convicted," the L.E.A.A. report states. Among those incarcerated, the longest prison terms were six-month sentences imposed on two executives. Three others were sentenced to 60, 45 and 30 days in prison. The average sentence for the remaining executives was exactly nine days. "Ordinary" criminals invariably lose their jobs after being convicted, but the L.E.A.A. study found that 12 of 21 executives convicted of making illegal campaign contributions remained in their original corporate positions a year later, while two others were retained as "consultants." Only seven retired, resigned or were dismissed from their jobs. The typical penalty against corporations in such cases is a requirement that its officers sign a Consent Agreement, a harmless legal document in which the company promises not to commit the crime in question in the future, but it is not required to admit to violating the law in the past.

ILLEGAL IMMIGRANTS (I.I.s). The thousands of Chinese who escape to Hong Kong each month from the Communist life style which is not their cup of tea.

ILLINOIS BRICK LEGISLATION.
See PFIZER AMENDMENT.

ILLUSORY PROMISE. Appears valid, but in fact is not. Such a promise voids a contract.

I.L.O. (International Labor Organization). Headquartered in Geneva, Switzerland and established as a specialized agency associated with the U.N. by the Treaty of Versailles in 1919 as part of the League of Nations. The United States joined this autonomous intergovernmental agency in 1934 and is now one of 132 member countries which finance its operations. Governments, workers, and employers share in making the decisions and shaping its policies. This tripartite representation gives the I.L.O. its balance and much of its strength, distinguishing it from all other international agencies. The purpose of the I.L.O. is to improve labor conditions, raise living standards, and promote economic and social stability as the foundation for lasting peace throughout the world. An annual I.L.O. Conference developed an international labor code that covers such questions as employment, freedom of association, hours of work, migration for employment, protection of women and young workers, prevention of industrial accidents, workmen's compensation, conditions of seamen, social security and other labor problems. Standards were developed as guidelines, and no country is obligated to adopt, accept, or ratify them.

I.M.F. (International Monetary Fund). A U.N. Agency created in 1946 and headquartered in Washington, D.C. Its 126 members include practically all member states of the U.N., except communist states. Working like a bank, the I.M.F. promotes international monetary cooperation, facilitates the expansion and balanced growth of international trade, and promotes exchange stability. It also assists in the establishment of a multilateral system of payments for current transactions among members and extends short-term credit. At the Stockholm Conference of 1968 the Group of Ten gave the I.M.F. the responsibility for Special Drawing

Rights (S.D.R.s), a new kind of international currency created to relieve the problems of international liquidity. The S.D.R.s were originally related to gold and based on a system of monetary stability. Their value was defined by units referring to 16 currencies, each of which accounted for more than 1 percent of the world trade. As of 1977, there were over nine million S.D.R.s in existence. To foster the interconvertibility of every currency, each member was to maintain a fixed value of its currency relative to gold and to other currencies. The weakness of the "paper-gold" system of the S.D.R.s, however, appeared in August 1971 with the abandonment by the United States of the gold standard.

IMMIGRATION AND NATIONALITY ACT (McCarran-Walter Act). A federal law passed by Congress in 1952 over President Harry S. Truman's veto which reflected the most bitter phase of the cold war between the Soviet Union and the West as well as the conservatism of its authors, Senator Pat McCarran of Nevada and Representative Francis E. Walter of Pennsylvania. Though amended several times since 1952, it limited the number of refugees admitted under regular immigration procedures.

IMMIGRATION AND NATURALIZATION SERVICE. A federal agency which is responsible for administering the immigration and naturalization laws relating to the admission, exclusion, deportation, and naturalization of aliens. Specifically, the Service inspects aliens to determine their admissibility into the United States; adjudicates requests of aliens for benefits under the law; guards against illegal entry into the United States; investigates, apprehends, and removes aliens in this country in violation of the law; and examines alien applicants wishing to become citizens. Through offices in the United States and in other areas around the world, the Service provides information and counsel to those seeking United States citizenship. Wherever possible, the Service, in conjunction with public schools in this country, provides textbooks and other instructional services to those wishing naturalization. Through numerous enforcement activities, such as the Border Patrol, the Service protects the national security of the United States and the welfare of those legally residing here. In addition to citizenship and immediately related matters, the Service, in cooperation with other federal, state, and local law enforcement agencies, works to stem the inflow of illegal drugs.

IMMOVABLE PROPERTY. A Conflict of Laws term referring to land and things so attached or related to land as to be considered part of it. When property is immovable, the Law of the Situs of Property is the law applied to all questions concerning the property.

IMMUNITY FROM PROSECUTION. See TRANSACTIONAL IMMUNITY.

IMPACT AID. Millions of dollars paid by the federal government to local school systems to relieve the burden placed on them to educate children of federal employees who work at neighboring tax-exempt federal installations such as military bases.

IMPACT STATEMENT. See ENVIRONMENTAL IMPACT STATEMENT.

IMPAIRMENT OF DECISION-MAKING CAPACITY. An incapacitating condition resulting from mental illness that will, in some states, provide a basis for Civil Commitment. The crucial inquiry is whether the patient is capable of making a responsible but not necessarily a "wise" decision regarding hospitalization. The state decides for the patient, who, because of illness, cannot decide for himself. There is concern that this basis of commitment may be only a surrogate for the patient's willingness to accept moral, legal, or social norms. For example, a fifty-year-old woman who leaves her husband to live with a sixteen-year-old boy, and who quits her job in search of "inner peace," may be deemed to have poor insight or judgment. She may be declared

254

unable to make a responsible decision about hospitalization because she sees no evidence of mental abnormality in her actions.

IMPEACH A WITNESS. To cast doubt on the reliability of a person testifying at trial. Common impeachment techniques include confronting a witness with prior inconsistent statements he has made, showing that the witness lacks the ability to observe or remember, and proving that the witness is biased or has a reputation for dishonesty. One cannot impeach one's own witness in most states. By calling a person to the stand, one has vouched for his veracity in the eyes of the law.

IMPEACHMENT TRIALS. Under the United States Constitution, Impeachment Trials are initiated by the House of Representatives and tried by the Senate for "Treason, Bribery, or other High Crimes and Misdemeanors." Only twelve such trials have been held to date: i.e., Supreme Court Justice Samuel Chase in 1804; President Andrew Johnson in 1868, Secretary of War, General Belknap in 1876; Senator Blount in 1799; and eight federal court judges. Of the cases that were tried, only four resulted in removal from office and those were all federal court judges. Many of the impeachment trials, however, were primarily political inquisitions brought with little or no evidence of actual misconduct in office. This was particularly true of the Johnson trial which took place during the hysteria of the post-Civil War Reconstruction period.

IMPERATIVE THEORY OF LAW. See LEGAL POSITIVISM.

IMPERIALISM OF THE MIND. See GENEVA SPACE BROADCASTING CONFERENCE.

IMPERIAL JUDICIARY (Judicial Activism). A condition that exists when judges legislate, make policy, and even administer the law, thereby preempting all the roles of the other branches of government. An Imperial Presidency, by contrast, is a dictorial Chief Execu-

tive who seeks to exercise dictatorial control over the other branches of government.

IMPERIAL WIZARD. See KU KLUX KLAN.

IMPLEADER RULE. Permits a defendant to bring into a lawsuit a person who may be liable to him for the plaintiff's claim against him. Under the Impleader Rule, the defendant to the original suit becomes the third-party plaintiff. The new person brought into the case is the third-party defendant. The defendant may deny liability to the plaintiff and also contend that if he is liable then the third party is liable to him. The defendant, however, may not deny his own liability and assert only the liability of the third-party. The third-party may deny liability to the defendant, and also raise any defense against the plaintiff which the defendant may raise.

IMPLIED CONSENT ACTS. State statutes which imply the consent of a driver to a chemical test of his blood, breath or urine to determine its blood alcohol content. In the District of Columbia, for instance, a police officer may order an intoxication test if he suspects a driver is intoxicated and the driver has either been involved in a traffic accident, or is arrested for a traffic violation.

IMPLIED PROMISE. See INFERRED PROMISE.

IMPLIED TRUST. A trust arrangement created by judicial order or by operation of law. For example, an Implied Trust may be created when a trust beneficiary is being cheated, or a trust arrangement fails to have legal effect because of some technicality, resulting in a frustration of the trust settlor's donative intent.

IMPLIED WARRANTY OF MERCHANTABILITY. A warranty, arising by operation of law in most states, which guarantees that the goods sold are fit for the ordinary purpose for which they are intended. Under such a warranty, the goods do not have to be of the best quality, merely of average grade. Although it is possible for a seller to disclaim all implied warranties, the disclaimer, if printed, must be in conspicuous type.

IMPORTED LITIGATION. Bringing a lawsuit to a state which has little if anything to do with the matter in dispute.

IMPOUNDMENT OF FUNDS. Power of the President to impound funds Congress has appropriated to finance an Act. While the President cannot impound funds simply because he disapproves of enacted legislation, he can do so for fiscal reasons. For example in the fiscal years 1973 and 1974, Congress voted to spend sums considerably in excess of the budgetary ceiling, while at the same time admonishing President Nixon to control inflation. Nixon responded, as other Presidents have done in this situation, by impounding funds to control spending.

IMPUTED INCOME. Non-cash income which results from labor on one's behalf or from the ownership of property. For example, a person does not pay rent in his own house, or report as income the value of his labor when he paints his own house. Housewives render the largest amount of imputed income as they perform services without pay to their families. Imputed income is not taxed.

INACTIVE TRUST. A trust arrangement whereby the trustee merely holds title to the trust property and does not dispose or distribute assets to the trust beneficiary. These trust arrangements are used to divest property from the settlor's estate for estate planning and tax reasons, but have limited applications today.

INATTENTIVE PERIL. See LAST CLEAR CHANCE.

IN BANC. See EN BANC.

IN CAMERA (Latin—arched or vaulted roof or chamber). In the secrecy of the judge's chamber, rather than in open court. Often, if the judge feels that certain evidence or conversation at trial may be prejudicial to a party, he may order an In Camera conference or inspection of the evidence so as not to unduly influence the jury.

INCHOATE CRIMES. Committed in preparation for other crimes. Soliciting another person to commit a felony, attempting to commit a felony or conspiring to commit a felony are all inchoate crimes. Such crimes are complete when the solicitation, attempt or conspiracy is complete, whether or not the principal crime is actually carried out. Generally, attempt and solicitation merge into the completed crime so that the defendant may not be charged with the crime and with the attempt or solicitation of such crime. In many jurisdictions, however, conspiracy remains a separate offense so that a person may be charged with conspiring to commit a specific crime and with actually committing the crime.

INCIDENTAL BENEFICIARY. A person who has no real interest in a trust, and who cannot enforce the rights of a trust beneficiary, but who benefits only incidentally from the creation of a trust.

INCOME AVERAGING. A method of computing income taxes which is designed to benefit taxpayers whose taxable income fluctuates widely from year to year. The income averaging provisions now in the Federal Tax Code permit a taxpayer whose taxable income in a year is substantially increased over his average taxable income in the preceding four years to be taxed at lower graduated rates on the increase.

INCOME BENEFICIARY (Immediate Trust Beneficiary). Recipient of trust income. For example, a trust arrangement might designate X to receive the income of an investment in stocks but not the actual stocks themselves. Here the trustee is obliged to pay over such income as accruals from the dividends and other growth of the stock but not title to the principal, corpus or trust property.

INCOME TAX AMENDMENT (1913). The Sixteenth Amendment which permits Congress to collect taxes on incomes without apportioning them among the states according to population.

INCOMPETENT TO STAND TRIAL. A term which describes the mental condition of a defendant at the time of trial, not at the time he allegedly committed the crime. Thus, it is not a defense to the criminal charge. The trial judge has a duty to determine if the accused has a reasonable understanding of the charges and proceedings and if he can consult with his attorney. A defendant who is found to be incompetent may be sent for a brief period of time to a mental hospital for treatment. If he regains his competency, he may proceed to trial. If prolonged hospitalization is required, civil commitment proceedings must take place.

INCORPORATED PARTNERSHIP. See CLOSE CORPORATION.

INCORPORATION CONTROVERSY. Concerns which rights possessed by an individual as against the federal government also exist as rights against the states because of the Fourteenth Amendment. Associate Justice Hugo L. Black argued that the Fourteenth Amendment, taken as a whole, incorporated all the Bill of Rights guarantees and made them applicable to the states. The traditional approach of the Supreme Court, however, has been that the due process clause of the Fourteenth Amendment incorporated only those rights essential to "fundamental principles of liberty and justice" and "essential to a fair trial." This view has been most eloquently and consistently put forth by Justices Cardozo, Frankfurter and Harlan. Although the Court has selectively incorporated almost all of the guarantees of the Bill of Rights, there has never been a majority ready to accept the total incorporation theory of Justice Black.

INCORRIGIBLE CHILD. Defined by such states as Vermont, Mississippi, Pennsylvania and Colorado as a child who is incapable of being managed and who exhibits a continual pattern of disobedience of parental communications. When reformation is impossible by present parental control, the child is deemed "incorrigible" and the power of the state becomes involved.

IN-CO-TERMS (International Commercial Terms). Definitions of the most important commercial terms used in international trade, published by the I.C.C. (International Chamber of Commerce) in 1923, 1936 and in 1953. They follow the most common meanings used in practice. They are considered the first step of an autonomous law of international commerce. The In-co-terms of 1953 define the following seven commercial terms, which are often used in commercial sales: alongside the quay; free on train; F.A.S.; F.O.B.; C. & F.; C.A.F.; freight or carriage paid to . . .; ex-ship; and clear on the quay. By referring to one of the Incoterms, the parties to a contract make plain their obligations. The I.C.C. has also published uniform definitions and rules for credit operations.

INCRESCITUR DOCTRINE. See REMITTITUR DOCTRINE.

INDEFEASIBLE TRUST PROPERTY. Real estate trust property the title to which cannot be void. Such property is so strongly controlled that no possibility exists that a contest will arise as to its title. For obvious reasons, trust property that is indefeasible is very desirable as it yields unusual certainty to trust settlors.

INDEFINITE DELIVERY CONTRACT. In federal government contracting, this contractual arrangement provides for the furnishing, within stated limits, of specific supplies or services, during a specified contract period, with deliveries of performance pursuant to later orders.

INDEPENDENT SOURCE RULE. Admission of illegally obtained evidence into a trial if knowledge of its existence is also obtained from a source independent of police illegality.

INDETERMINATE SENTENCE. A sentence of imprisonment imposed by a court or statute on one convicted of a crime which has no fixed length but rather a minimum and maximum length. Thus, a criminal might be sentenced to "10 to 20 years" for armed robbery. After serving the minimum length of time, the prisoner may be eligible for release. His eligibility would be determined by a parole board or a similar administrative body. The use of the indeterminate sentence, which has replaced the fixed sentence in most states, envisions that some prisoners will be sufficiently reformed for release at an earlier time than other prisoners convicted of the same offense. The practice is not as popular or as widely used as it once was.

INDEX LIBRORUM PROHIBITORUM (The Index) (Latin—index of prohibited books). A censored list of books instituted in 1559 and not abolished until 1966 which Roman Catholics could not read, without special permission, under threat of excommunication. Descartes, Cervantes, Pascal, Voltaire, Swift and Stendhal among others were some of the proscribed authors over the centuries.

INDEX OF NET BUSINESS FORMATION. Measures the net number of new businesses formed each month. It is compiled from data on new business incorporations, number of business failures, and confidential data on telephones installed. The data on new business incorporations represent approximately the number of corporations to which charters were issued under the general business incorporation laws of the various states. The statistics include new businesses which are incorporated, existing businesses which have changed from a noncorporate to a corporate form, existing corporations which have been given certificates of authority to operate in another state, and transfers of existing corporations to new states. Also included are cases in which the promotion of a projected corporation was not completed and the charter, though issued, was never exercised.

INDEX TO LEGAL PERIODICALS. An alphabetical listing by author and topic of the articles published in many American legal journals and substantially all British periodicals. Published since 1908 by the W. H. Wilson Company, in cooperation with the American Association of Law Libraries, the current numbers of the multi-volumed series are published monthly, except September; they are cumulated semiannually, annually, and for three-year periods. Since 1961, the index has been divided into three sections: (1) subject and author index, (2) table of cases commented upon, and (3) book review index.

INDIAN CHILD WELFARE ACT. A federal law passed by Congress in 1978 at the urging of American Indian leaders, church groups and child welfare experts which allows Indian Tribal Courts to apply Indian Tribal Law in the settlement of custody disputes involving Indian children. In too many cases Indian parents had been oppressed by bureaucracy which declared them unfit to raise their children because their homes did not have a minimum of 14,000 square feet of space, or running water, or indoor plumbing or enough windows, etc. At any given time, one-third of all Indian children had been taken from their parents and placed in foster homes or put up for adoption. Indians may be the poorest ethnic group in the United States, but their simplistic life style has much to be admired by our sophisticated society. This humanitarian legislation was long overdue.

INDIAN CLAIMS COMMISSION. A federal agency which hears and determines claims against the United States on behalf of any Indian tribe, band, or other identifiable group of American Indians residing within the United States.

INDIAN NON-INTERCOURSE ACT. A federal law passed in 1790 which provided, as each State joined the Union, that no land sales between whites and Indians were valid unless approved by Congress. The law was largely ignored until the 1970's, but many Indian tribes are now claiming ownership of millions of acres of land in various states, including one-fourth of all of Maine.

INDIAN TRIBAL LAW COURT (Tribal Court). A general term which includes three types of American Indian Courts, the most common of which is the Tribal Court, based on a Tribal Code of Law adopted in accordance with the Indian Reorganization Act. Such courts ordinarily are competent to adjudicate civil cases but are limited in criminal cases to minor offenses with a maximum of 6 months in jail and a $500 fine by the Indian Civil Rights Act of 1968. These courts vary widely from tribe to tribe in organization and adjudicative authority, and many tribes do not have courts but rely on the state court system. The Traditional Court, another type of Indian court, is concerned only with tribal customs and traditions and does not adhere to a codified law. The third type of tribal court is the Court of Federal Regulations (C.F.R. Court), which operates under a federal codification originating from the Indian Service. There are 19 Courts of Federal Regulations, 18 Traditional Courts and 51 Tribal Courts currently operating.

INDIRECT BORROWING. See CROSS DEPOSITING.

INDIRECT TAX. See DIRECT TAXES.

INDISCRIMINATE CHECK. See RANDOM OR SPOT CHECK.

INDISPENSABLE PARTY. See JOINDER OF PARTIES.

INDIVIDUAL RETIREMENT ACT (I.R.A.). Permits an individual to deduct up to 15 percent of his earned income as a contribution to a Personal Retirement Plan or Account. The I.R.A. was created by the 1974 Pension Reform Act to allow an employee or a self-employed person who is not an active participant in any other qualified pension, profit-sharing, stock bonus, or annuity plans to set up his own individual retirement account. There are three basic types of plans available to an individual: (1) an individual retirement account plan, (2) an individual retirement annuity plan, and (3) a retirement bond plan. Any amount paid or distributed from an Individual Retirement Account or other option must be included in gross income of the taxpayer. The distribution does not qualify for long-term capital gains treatment.

INDUSTRIAL COURT. A specialized judicial body, not found in the United States, which settles disputes between employers and employees.

INDUSTRIAL PIRACY. See TRADE SECRET.

INDUSTRIAL UNION. A labor organization that represents all or most of the employees, both skilled and unskilled, in a given industry or in a particular company or enterprise. Soon after the A.F.L. convention in 1935 where the general problem of unskilled labor was discussed, several unions broke away and formed the Committee for Industrial Organization (C.I.O.). Two of these unions were the United Mine Workers (U.M.W.) led by John L. Lewis, and the powerful International Ladies' Garment Workers' Union (I.L.G.W.U.), although the latter rejoined the A.F.L. in 1940. Shortly after the formation of the C.I.O., as a federation of autonomous national unions, it was joined by the International Union of United Auto Workers, the United Rubber Workers and numerous other unions. In December, 1955, the A.F.L. and the C.I.O. patched up the differences which had arisen between them over the years and formed a new and powerful central labor organization known as the A.F.L.-C.I.O., and representing 16 million workers of 85 percent of the membership then claimed by all unions in the United States. The first president of the new organization was George Meany, former head of the A.F.L., and the first vice-president was Walter Reuther, former head and only president of the C.I.O. It is reported, however, that the new arrangement has never been completely successful, and both groups still engage in bitter jurisdictional disputes.

INDUSTRIAL WORKERS OF THE WORLD (I.W.W. Wobblies). Turn of the century labor union committed to achieving supremacy of the worker in society by extra-legal methods.

INEFFECTIVE ASSISTANCE OF COUNSEL. Term used when the representation provided by an attorney is of such inferior quality that a defendant's Sixth Amendment right to counsel is violated. Obviously, assistance is not ineffective merely because the defendant lost. The quality of the assistance must have been so inferior that the attorney was grossly negligent in fulfilling his duties. Ineffective assistance has become a very popular ground for attacking conviction on Habeas Corpus since the Supreme Court has recently closed the federal courts to Habeas Corpus petitions grounded on the Fourth or Fifth Amendment where there was an adequate opportunity to present the claim in state courts.

INFAMOUS CRIMES. Offenses which under the United States Constitution, as well as under some state constitutions, require prosecution by grand jury indictment. Today most states equate infamous crimes with felonious offenses. Thus the punishment, usually imprisonment in a penitentiary, determines whether a crime is infamous. However, some states classify a crime as infamous according to the nature of the crime itself, thus equating infamous with Malum In Se. In a number of states, a person convicted of an infamous crime is subject to disbarment or disenfranchisement and may be prohibited from testifying as a witness. This term generally refers to felonies as well as such crimes as bribery, perjury and forgery. At common law, however, only crimes involving falsehood were classified as infamous.

INFERRED PROMISES (Implied Promise). The communication of a promise by way of silence or conduct. Contrary to general belief, a promise need not be communicated solely by word. For example, if one's silence or conduct justifiably allows another to infer from such actions that an acceptance to an offer has been made, then it may be recognized as a valid acceptance. However, there are some instances, like the acceptance of a counteroffer, when silence will not be recognized as an acceptance. Thus, whether there is justifiable inference based upon conduct or silence, will ultimately depend upon the individual case and circumstances.

INFLUENCE PEDDLING. Selling the power of a political, administrative, or other influential position for money or other favors. Most common among politicians and government employees, influence peddling occurs when a person agrees to vote a certain way or otherwise influence decisionmaking so as to benefit the person or political or corporate entity offering the favor.

IN FORMA PAUPERIS (Latin—in the character of a poor person). Characterizes the permission of a court for a poor person to proceed with his cause of action or appeal without incurring the normal expenses.

INFORMATIONAL PICKETING. Picketing done not for the purpose of economic coercion, but rather for the enlightenment of the public. Protesters carrying signs describing the harsh treatment of migrant workers by grape growers would be engaging in informational picketing.

INFORMED CONSENT. A legal doctrine which requires the physician to inform the patient of the risks involved in any treatment or any alternative methods of treatment. The law does, however, recognize two necessary exceptions to the requirement of informed consent. One is the situation of emergencies where prompt treatment is essential and the patient is unconscious or otherwise incapable of granting consent. The other involves the physician's therapeutic privilege to withhold information from his patient when the physician reasonably concludes that full disclosure would not be in the patient's best interests.

INGRAHAM v. WRIGHT. See SCHOOL SPANKING CASE.

IN HAEC VERBA (Latin—in these words). A writing quoted verbatim in another document is said to be In Haec Verba.

INHERENT POWER. A power claimed by a branch of the government, not because the power is explicitly granted by the Constitution, but because it is deemed necessary to the execution of the agency's duties. Inherent power is most often claimed by the Executive branch because of the vast responsibility of that branch and the broad, non-specific powers of the Executive outlined in Article II of the Constitution. An example is the Presidential power to make war, derived from his position as Commander-in-Chief of the Armed Forces. Truman's seizure of the steel industry during the Korean War was held not to be within the inherent power of the Executive.

INHERITANCE TAX. A tax imposed by the states on the receipt of wealth from a decedent. Generally, the tax is computed on the basis of the closeness of kinship with the decedent: the closer the kinship, the lower the tax rate. An inheritance tax is in addition to the federal estate tax. Both illustrate clearly that death and taxes are inevitable.

IN-HOUSE COUNSEL. A lawyer who offers his legal services solely to an employer instead of engaging in the private practice of law.

INITIATIVE COMMITTEE FOR NATIONAL ECONOMIC PLANNING. See HUMPHREY-HAWKINS LAW OF 1978.

INJUNCTIVE RELIEF. A form of equitable relief whereby a court prohibits a defendant from performing a particular act.

INJURY-IN-FACT TEST. Limits court access under the judicial review provi-

sions of the Administrative Procedure Act to those who have suffered harm as a result of the administrative action in question. In *Sierra Club v. Morton,* 405 U.S. 727 (1972), a conservationist group sought review of a United States Forest Service decision to allow the development of a large commercial recreation project adjacent to Sequoia National Park. The club charged that the project would "impair the enjoyment of the park for future generations." However, the Supreme Court held that the "mere special interest" of those "who seek to do no more than vindicate their own value preferences through the judicial process" did not provide standing to sue. The injury-in-fact test requires more than an injury to a cognizable interest. It demands that the party seeking review be himself among the injured. The Club members arguably could have attained standing by alleging that they liked to camp in the area in question and that the proposed development would have a negative impact on that activity.

INLAND RULES OF THE ROAD. See RULES OF THE ROAD.

IN LOCO PARENTIS (Latin—in the place of a parent). Description of a private person or Government official who has taken the position of a parent with reference to a child, though not the parent, thereby assuming the rights, duties and responsibilities of the child's lawful parents.

IN NEED OF SUPERVISION. See P.I.N.S.

INNER CIRCLE OF ADVOCATES. A private group of less than 100 American plaintiff-trial lawyers founded in 1972. New members are added by invitation only if the lawyer has won a 1 million dollar judgment for a client in a personal injury case and meets the other requirements for eligibility, such as experience, integrity and professional standing. The organization conducts annual educational meetings.

INNER TEMPLE. See INNS OF COURT.

INNOCENT PASSAGE. A principle of international law which gives merchant ships the right to travel through the territorial waters of another country. Under this principle a country may forbid foreign military vessels from passing through the waters adjacent to its coastline, but it must allow civilian shipping with non-military or "innocent" purposes. Innocent passage applies to a ship whose presence in territorial waters is caused by a superior force, particularly in situations involving distress. The classic case of innocent passage before the International Court of Justice was the *Corfu Channel* case in which the court based this right on certain well-recognized principles of international law, including the principle of free maritime communication, elementary considerations of humanity, and every country's obligation not to allow its territory to be used for acts contrary to the rights of other countries. Some countries argue that the passage of certain types of vessels, such as warships, are inherently non-innocent and that "innocence" may depend on the flag, cargo, or destination of a vessel. Under the Convention on the Territorial Sea and Continuous Shelf of April 27, 1958, neither aircraft nor submerged submarines have a right of innocent passage.

INNS OF COURT. Professional organizations for English barristers (the attorneys who argue cases before England's highest Courts). The four extant Inns, dating from the time of Edward I in the late thirteenth century, are Lincoln's, Gray's, the Inner Temple, and the Middle Temple. Originally serving a dual role as educational institutions and living quarters, they were formed by barristers and law students who together rented hotels or inns. The Inns enjoyed their golden age in the mid-fifteenth and early sixteenth centuries. However, three developments led to their decline. Many people not intending to become barristers began attending school at the Inns, because universities were under ecclesiastical influence. Furthermore, the invention of the printing press made it easier to study by book than exclusively by "readings" (lectures) and "moots" (mock arguments). Finally, it became increasingly more difficult to retain instructors since they were not paid and had to take time off from private practice to teach. Nonetheless the Inns are very much alive today.

IN PECTORE. See COLLEGE OF CARDINALS.

IN PERSONAM. A court action against or involving the person; opposed to In Rem, against the thing. Thus, In Personam Jurisdiction (Personal Jurisdiction) is jurisdiction over the defendant; an Action In Personam is one against a particular person; and a Judgment In Personam is rendered against a particular person.

INQUIRY NOTICE. Circumstances which lead one to believe that a third party has rights to property. The law imposes a duty to inquire if one suspects a conflict in the ownership of property.

INQUIRY PANEL. An adjunct to lawyer discipline committees, the Panel reviews investigation by committee members or staff to determine if formal disciplinary action should be brought against a lawyer charged with misconduct.

IN RE GAULT. See YOUTH RIGHTS CASE.

IN REM JURISDICTION. Judicial jurisdiction over a thing, as opposed to a person. In Rem jurisdiction is asserted in an action brought directly against property or to enforce a right in property. To acquire In Rem jurisdiction, it is necessary that the property, typically real estate, be within the physical limits of the court's jurisdiction, and that some form of notice, generally by publication, be given to all persons who might have an interest in the property. The court's decree will then determine the rights in the property as against all the world.

INSANE DELUSION. A false belief which is the product of a diseased mind.

In the law of wills, an Insane Delusion does not invalidate the will unless the delusion affects the disposition of property under the will. The characteristic which distinguishes an Insane Delusion from other mistaken beliefs is that it is not a product of reason but of the imagination. It is not a mistake of fact induced by deception, fraud, insufficient evidence, or erroneous reasoning, but rather the spontaneous conception of a perverted imagination having no basis whatever in reason or evidence. Although mere eccentricities, prejudices or unusual religious beliefs, such as a belief in witches, do not in themselves constitute Insane Delusions, they are of evidentiary value in determining whether Testamentary Capacity exists.

INSANITY PLEAS. See M'NAGHTEN TEST; DURHAM TEST; IRRESISTIBLE IMPULSE TEST.

INSECURITY CLAUSE. A contractual provision allowing creditors to accelerate the maturity of the entire debt. This clause may cause unfavorable consequences for any debtor whose creditor is immoral or unfair.

INSIDER PRIVILEGES. Free overdrafts, low-interest rate loans and other preferential treatment given by the 15,000 banks in the country to bank directors, officers and major stockholders. Such privileges forced former Budget Director Burt Lance out of office. These unethical practices are unfair to the public and customers of the banks, but they are neither illegal nor criminal.

INSIDER TRADING. Trading in corporate securities by directors, officers, or controlling shareholders. By virtue of their position in the corporate power structure, these persons have special access to information which materially affects the value of the shares being sold and which is not known to the other party. The use of such information had been a subject of concern long before the enactment of the Securities Exchange Act of 1934. In 1909 the United States Supreme Court developed the Special Facts Rule, which imposed a duty to disclose material inside information only where extraordinary or "special" facts exist. The Special Facts Rule was chiefly applicable to personal exchanges and not to the exchange of over-the-counter securities. However, the promulgation of Rule 10B-5 of the Securities Exchange Commission has gone well beyond the Special Facts Rule in prohibiting the use of inside information for the benefit of directors, officers, and controlling shareholders to the detriment of the public securities holders.

I.N.S.L.A.W. (Institute for Law and Social Research). Provides computer-assisted analysis for statistics in any realm of the law such as the Criminal Justice System. For example, New York City makes approximately 240,000 arrests a year, yet in more than one-half of the cases the prosecutor drops the charges against the accused.

INSPECTOR GENERAL OFFICES. Positions created by Congress in 1978 in a dozen federal departments and agencies giving them control over internal auditing staffs. The job of these offices is to investigate and audit programs in their departments and agencies. The legislation insulates the Inspectors General from interference by agency heads and requires them to report to Congress twice a year on abuses they uncover in order to control widespread indifference, inefficiency and fraud in how the taxpayers' dollars are spent. The savings from the program will amount to millions of dollars each year. The law was triggered by the actions of the General Services Administration in 1978, which is said to have been the greatest kickback scandal in American history.

INSTALLMENT PAYMENTS TRUST. A trust arrangement whereby the trustee is directed to make equal periodic payments of income to the designated trust beneficiary or beneficiaries; a typical Installment Payment Trust would call for quarterly distributions to trust beneficiaries. Two traditional reasons for this type of trust arrangement exist: (1) to promote frugality on the part of trust beneficiaries; and (2) to encourage the distribution of income as it is earned for accounting reasons.

INSTANCE JURISDICTION. The general jurisdiction of admiralty courts to adjudicate disputes and claims, both civil and criminal, of a maritime nature which arise out of commerce and navigation upon the sea. As regards property captured in time of war, see Prize Jurisdiction.

INSTITUTE FOR LAW AND SOCIAL RESEARCH. A Washington-based organization which conducted a study of arrest and conviction records in Washington, D.C. from 1974-1976 under a grant from the Law Enforcement Assistance Administration (L.E.A.A.) The results, which were comparable to findings in Los Angeles, San Diego, Baltimore, Detroit and Chicago, indicated that only about 33 percent of those individuals arrested by the police were ever brought to trial. While police were making an increasing number of arrests, the apprehensions did not lead to a proportionate increase in convictions. Partially responsible for the discrepancy is the emphasis placed on arrests as criteria for promotion in many police departments. In fact, the study stated that 31 percent of D.C. policemen who made arrests in a given year saw none of those arrests turn into convictions. The report suggests encouragement of better arrests, full warning of rights, and recorded witness verification, as remedies for the problem.

INSTITUTE FOR TECHNOLOGICAL CO-OPERATION. See INTERNATIONAL DEVELOPMENT CO-OPERATION ADMINISTRATION.

INSTITUTE OF JUDICIAL ADMINISTRATION—AMERICAN BAR ASSOCIATION JUVENILE JUSTICE STANDARDS. See JUVENILE JUSTICE STANDARDS.

INSTITUTE OF WOMEN TODAY. A national non-profit organization headquartered in Chicago and founded in 1974 by a Roman Catholic Nun, Sister Margaret Ellen Traxler, who serves as the Director. This network of women volunteers from every religious denomination services the personal needs of that quarter of the 400,000 prisoners around the country who are women.

INSTITUTIONAL CHILD ABUSE AND NEGLECT. Either (1) abuse and neglect as a result of social or institutional policies, practices, or conditions —the widespread practice of detaining children in adult jails is one example, or (2) child abuse and neglect committed by an employee of a public or private institution against a child in that institution.

INSTITUTIONAL REVIEW BOARDS (I.R.B.s). Organizations established in compliance with the requirements of H.E.W. under the National Research Act to assure that all research conducted or sponsored by institutions receiving H.E.W. funds involving human beings meet federal standards that conform to basic ethical and legal principles.

INSUBSTANTIAL CONTACT. See FLICKER TEST.

INSURABLE INTEREST. A basic principle of insurance law which requires that before a person may be insured against a particular risk, he must have an interest in the object insured such that, if the peril occurs, he will be damaged. The owner of property has an insurable interest in that property. A person has an insurable interest in his own life and in the life of close relatives, such as the interest of a parent in a child. As regards the interest in property, it must exist at the time of the loss. Because of historical developments, the insurable interest in a life need exist only at the inception of the contract.

INSURANCE COMPANY RATINGS. See BEST'S RATINGS.

INSURANCE ENDORSEMENT. See INSURANCE RIDER.

INSURANCE FREE TRADE ZONE LAW. A New York law that should have the long-range effect of helping to put this country's business-insurance marketplace on an equal competitive footing with many foreign locations traditionally regarded as world centers of the industry. Under the legislation, effective September 1, 1978, specially licensed insurers in the state are now able to write primary policies on large corporate risks—contracts with an annual premium of $100,000 or more—without the need for prior state approval of rates and policy provisions. However, the state will require such insurers to maintain at least twice the capital surplus normally required and will oversee their operations. In effect, the State of New York thus becomes a free trade zone for insurance, the first of its kind in the United States, where large-scale buyers and sellers of insurance can do business swiftly and conveniently, unhampered by legalistic restrictions. As such, the free trade zone will provide a more productive environment for insurance transactions—one that is responsive to the sophisticated risk management needs of business today. Moreover, the advantages of the New York free-trade zone also apply to policies covering unusual or unprecedented risks, including those with premiums far under $100,000. They include such diverse exposures as insurrections, catfish farms, animal rides, ear piercing and new drugs. With its free-trade zone New York seems to be creating an American version of Lloyd's of London. The world's largest single insurance market, Lloyd's is known for its exceptionally broad range of insurance coverage, including both very large and highly unusual risks. The parallel with Lloyd's will also be heightened with the opening in 1979 of the New York Insurance Exchange, which will allow individual investors and others to participate in the underwriting of both primary and reinsurance risks.

INSURANCE RIDER (Insurance Endorsement). A modification to a basic insurance policy. A rider makes it possible to alter a basic contract in a variety of ways to fit the needs of an individual insured. Riders are typically used to increase or decrease coverage, change the premium, make a correction, waive a condition, or change a beneficiary.

INTAKE UNIT. A government agency or agency subunit which receives juvenile referrals from police, other government agencies, private agencies, or persons, and screens them, resulting in closing of the case, referral to care of supervision, or filing of a petition in juvenile court. The intake function can be assigned to individual personnel as in many probation departments, or to a special subunit within a probation agency, or can be performed by an agency that has no other primary function. It usually operates under the authority of a juvenile court. If its personnel, who are usually probation officers, exercise judicial authority, then their decisions are considered equivalent to juvenile court decisions.

INTANGIBLE PROPERTY. Such things as stock certificates, bonds, promissory notes, contracts and franchises.

INTEGRATED WILL. A will comprising two or more separately executed instruments, intended by the testator together to constitute his will. A will comprising several sheets of paper, but executed in only one place, may also be referred to as an integrated will.

INTELLIGENCE IDENTITIES PROTECTION ACT. A proposed federal law, authored by the Central Intelligence Agency and rejected by Congress in 1979, which would have made it illegal for any person who has had access to information that identifies undercover intelligence personnel to disclose such information. The proposed statute also would have made it a felony for anyone else to do so with the "intent to impair or impede the foreign intelligence activities of the United States."

INTELLIGENCE OVERSIGHT BOARD. See I.O.B.

INTENTIONAL MISREPRESENTATION. See FRAUDULENT MISREPRESENTATION.

INTENTIONAL TORTS. Distinguished from negligent torts and strict liability torts in that the wrongdoer must have known, or at least been substantially certain, that an injury would result. Recognizing merely a risk of harmful result, however, leads only to negligence. Thus, to run down a plaintiff one did not see is negligence. To run over one's wife intentionally is a battery, which is an intentional tort and a crime. Other intentional torts include assault, false imprisonment, trespass, malicious prosecution, libel and slander. The damages awarded for negligent torts compensate the victim for injuries he actually suffered, but plaintiffs may receive punitive damages in addition to compensatory damages when they are the victims of an intentional tort. The law recognizes the difference between accidents and acts of malice. As Oliver Wendell Holmes once said, "Even a dog distinguishes between being stumbled over and being kicked."

INTENT TO KILL. See MALICE AFORETHOUGHT; MURDER TWO.

INTER-AMERICAN COURT OF HUMAN RIGHTS. A seven-judge judicial tribunal established in 1979 under the Inter-American Convention on Human Rights, which has not yet been ratified by the United States. The Convention came into force in July, 1978, after it had been ratified by the required number of 11 governments. The seven members of the Court, who were elected by the General Assembly of the Organization of American States (O.A.S.), are: César Ordóñez Quintero of Columbia, Rodolfo Piza Escalante of Costa Rica, Miguel Rafael Urquia of El Salvador, Carlos Roberto Reina Idiáquez of Honduras, Huntley E. Monroe of Jamaica, Máximo Cisneros Sánchez of Peru, and the American, University of Texas law professor Thomas Buergenthal. The Court began its inaugural session in July, 1979, at San Jose, Costa Rica, its permanent seat.

INTER-AMERICAN DEVELOPMENT BANK. See I.A.D.B.

INTER-AMERICAN TREATY OF RECIPROCAL ASSISTANCE. See RIO TREATY.

INTERDEPARTMENTAL PROCUREMENT. In Department of Defense procurement, this term refers to the acquisition of supplies and services by the military departments from or through other federal government agencies. The General Services Administration (G.S.A.) is a prime source for commonly-used supply items acquired in this manner. Specifically, within G.S.A., the Federal Supply Service Agency is set up to purchase on a government-wide basis. This agency enters into federal supply schedule contracts with industry for the furnishing of supplies. In turn, other agencies of the federal government then place delivery orders directly with contractors pursuant to these contract terms.

INTERDICTED PERSONS. Alcoholics against whom court orders have been issued forbidding them from buying, possessing or drinking alcoholic beverages under a threat of imprisonment for a maximum of one year for each and every violation.

INTEREST ADJUSTMENT CLAUSE MORTGAGE. See ESCALATOR MORTGAGE.

INTERFERENCE PROCEDURE. Conducted by the Patent Office when two or more applicants for a patent claim inventorship of the same subject matter. The purpose of the procedure is to determine priority between the competing inventors as only one patent can be issued. Interference procedures may also be instituted when there is an application on an already-existing patent, as long as the application is filed within one year of the granting of the patent. During the procedure, the parties present evidence concerning the conception of the invention and its reduction to practice. The Board of Patent Interferences issues an award of priority which the losing party may appeal to the United States Court of Customs and Patent Appeals or as a result of which he may file a civil suit in a federal district court against the winning party.

INTERGOVERNMENTAL MARITIME CONSULTATIVE ORGANIZATION. See CONVENTION OF STANDARDS OF TRAINING, CERTIFICATION AND WATCHKEEPING FOR SEAFARERS.

INTERLOCKING DIRECTORATES. Two or more corporations which have directors or officers in common. Issues of a breach of the fiduciary duty against directors' conflict of interest arise where the corporations having interlocking directorates make contracts with each other. The majority view of such contracts is that they are voidable by the courts if the terms of the contract are found by the court to be unfair. All such contracts will be subjected to close scrutiny by the courts. Some jurisdictions put the burden of proof on the corporations to show the fairness of the contract. Critics of the majority rule point out the inherent subjectivity of any finding whether a contract is fair or not.

INTERLOCUTORY APPEAL. An appeal of a specific order to a state or federal court of appeals prior to the rendering of a final judgment in the entire action. Interlocutory review in federal courts is governed by 28 U.S.C. § 1292(b). In general, federal courts may review: (1) Interlocutory orders relating to the issuance of an injunction; (2) Interlocutory orders concerning receiverships or other disposals of property; (3) Interlocutory decrees determining the rights and liabilities of the parties to admiralty cases in which appeals from final decrees are allowed; (4) Judgments in civil actions for patent infringement that are final except for accounting; and (5) Judgments, orders, or decrees in bankruptcy, either interlocutory or final.

INTERLOCUTORY ORDER. An order issued by a court, after the commencement of a judicial proceeding and before its termination, which relates only to some question of law or to some matter of practice collateral to the primary issue in the case. Such an order settles the rights of the parties as they relate to that collateral issue but does not touch the merits of the action. An order that the pleadings of the plaintiff be made more definite and certain is an Interlocutory Order.

INTERNAL REVENUE BULLETIN. See TAX RULING.

INTERNAL REVENUE CODE (I.R.C.). Codifies all federal tax provisions. Enacted in 1954, the Code brought together for the first time all the laws on more than fifty different federal taxes. Like all tax laws, the Code originated in the Ways and Means Committee of the House of Representatives, progressed through a series of House and Senate hearings, and was ultimately signed by the President. The rules and procedures embodied in the I.R.C. are often complex. Albert Einstein remarked that the federal income tax was the hardest thing in the world to understand and allegedly asserted that the tax return required not a mathematician but a philosopher. One of the earliest attempts by the federal government to raise revenue from internal sources was the 1791 tax on carriages and distilled spirits proposed by Alexander Hamilton. This tax led to the Whiskey Rebellion in western Pennsylvania in 1794. The first year's net receipts from this tax were approximately $250,000, compared to an estimated $297.5 billion acquired by the federal government in 1976. Throughout American history, various taxes on certain goods were levied in wartime and repealed shortly thereafter. Not until the Sixteenth Amendment was passed in 1913 did Congress have the right to tax income. Prior to that time, such taxes were held to be unconstitutional as direct taxes not apportioned among the states.

INTERNAL REVENUE SERVICE. See I.R.S.

INTERNAL REVENUE SERVICE PROBLEM RESOLUTION OFFICER. See P.R.O.

INTERNAL SECURITY ACT. See Mc-CARRAN ACT.

INTERNAL SECURITY DIVISION. A former Justice Department agency, used from 1970-1973 to intimidate New Left opponents to the Nixon administration. The harassment tool was the grand jury, an institution once designed to protect the innocent from over-zealous prosecutors. During its period of operation the Internal Security Division was responsible for approximately 100 grand jury inquiries directed at the activities of radicals including Abbie Hoffman, the Berrigan Brothers, and Daniel Ellsberg. While few convictions resulted, several witnesses were ultimately jailed for refusing to answer questions.

INTERNATIONAL AGRICULTURE ADVISORY COUNCIL. See WORLD TRADE PACT.

INTERNATIONAL AIR TRANSPORT ASSOCIATION. See I.A.T.A.

INTERNATIONAL ANTI-COUNTER-FEITING COALITION. A private group formed in 1978 by American business interests to control the annual multi-million dollar counterfeiting of goods made in Asia but sold in the United States under brand names. Under a new federal law which the group sponsored, customs officials are empowered to seize goods that are questioned and give the importer the opportunity to show that they are not bogus. In cases where the importer takes the position that the goods are genuine, the trademark owner must post a bond and prove the products are indeed fakes. If the merchandise is finally proven to be phony, it can be turned over to the government for its own use, given to a charitable institution, or auctioned off after one year.

INTERNATIONAL ATOMIC ENERGY AGENCY. See NUCLEAR NON-PROLIFERATION ACT OF 1978.

INTERNATIONAL BAR ASSOCIATION. Formed in 1946 to ensure better cooperation and improvement in the services of national bar associations in all countries, to provide opportunities for individual lawyers to make personal contacts through organizing conferences and by sharing expertise to contribute to the solution of common international legal problems, and to contribute to the establishment and maintenance of the rule of law throughout the world.

INTERNATIONAL BASELINE (Bay Closing Line). A line that separates the internal waters of a country, over which it has absolute control, from the adjacent sea, in which other nations have certain rights, particularly as regards fishing. Since a country has greater control over its internal waters, it becomes significant to determine at which point an area in a large bay ceases to be internal. The normal baseline is simply the low water tide mark, although the question that has arisen in international law is whether the baseline should uniformly follow the coast at a specified length from the shore or, in case of large bays, jump from one outermost point of land to the next. The classic case on this point is the *Fisheries* case, in which Norway claimed huge portions of water as internal by drawing baselines between outer points of land 24 miles apart. This relates to Norway's unique, bay-riddled coastline. The International Court of Justice held that this was permissible in Norway's case, in light of historical and geographic circumstances, but in all other cases baselines could not exceed 24 miles in length.

INTERNATIONAL CIVIL AVIATION ORGANIZATION. See I.C.A.O.

INTERNATIONAL COCOA AGREEMENT. Under the sponsorship of the United Nations, this is an association of cocoa-growing countries and cocoa-consumer countries to control the price of the commodity through export quotas and stock-piling facilities, established in 1975, to which the United States does not belong.

INTERNATIONAL COFFEE AGREEMENT (1962). Multi-national pact entered into by 54 nations (of which the

United States is one) whose avowed goal is to enhance co-operation between importing and exporting nations on the coffee market. The agreement aims at assuring equilibrium between production and consumption, minimizing the effect of price and supply fluctuations, promoting fair labor practices, and encouraging the consumption of coffee.

INTERNATIONAL COMITY. An act of courtesy in the international legal community. International comity often leads nations to bind themselves to rules they are not under any obligation to accept under international law. Rules of International Comity are considered by those accepting them as legally binding, not because of any international law rule, but out of courtesy.

INTERNATIONAL COMMISSION OF JURISTS. A group of eminent international legal scholars dedicated to focusing international attention upon violations of fundamental human rights. Limited by its charter to a membership of forty, the Commission presides over thirty-three national sections, whose job it is to maintain liaison with the legal profession and to keep the Commission posted on national developments. Though the Commission is powerless to call a nation to trial, it has achieved a reputation as an efficient fact-finding team, having conducted intensive investigations of the political situations in Hungary, Tibet, Cuba, and South Africa.

INTERNATIONAL COMMITTEE OF THE RED CROSS. See LAW OF WAR; RED CROSS.

INTERNATIONAL COMMUNICATION AGENCY (I.C.A.). The first large scale Agency (8,500 employees) to be created by President Carter, on April 1, 1978. It absorbed the functions of the former United States Information Agency whose motto had been "Telling America's Story Abroad," the Voice of America and the 236 Cultural Affairs Officers of the Department of State. The new mission of I.C.A. is "To listen as well as to speak." John Edward Reinhardt, first director of I.C.A., prefers a quotation of 19th Century American author Oliver Wendell Holmes (father of the Supreme Court Justice of the same name) "Man's mind, once stretched by a new idea, never regains its original dimensions." The purpose of I.C.A. is to inform other countries about the United States and to supervise our cultural exchanges with them. It is expressly forbidden to disseminate information for domestic consumption. Voice of America will continue to explain our foreign policy and American Society to listeners abroad in 36 different languages. The separate Board for International Broadcasting will continue to supervise (1) Radio Free Europe which was formed by the C.I.A. in 1950 and broadcasts in six languages to five Communist East European countries and (2) Radio Liberty which was also formed by the C.I.A. in 1963 and broadcasts in 16 languages to the Soviet Union. Both of these are located in Munich, Germany, and were divorced from the C.I.A. in 1971. They try to avoid agitation and propaganda and concentrate instead on giving listeners information about their own countries which is unavailable to them as a result of Russian censorship. The success of their efforts is demonstrated by the $100 million a year the U.S.S.R. spends in an attempt to jam their transmissions. It is also the world's leading broadcaster with a total of 2,000 hours a week in 80 different languages from three separate sets of networks. Some critics question the unnecessary timing of the creation of I.C.A. on April Fool's Day and many foreigners already think that I.C.A. and C.I.A. are one and the same.

INTERNATIONAL CONVENTION FOR THE UNIFICATION OF CERTAIN RULES RELATING TO BILLS OF LADING. See HAMBURG RULES.

INTERNATIONAL CORPORATE BRIBERY. An illegal payment by an American corporation to a foreign official. It takes many forms such as: (1) Aggressive payment. One designed to solicit new business. (2) Defensive payment. One designed to protect a vested business interest. (3) Grease payment. One designed to cut through bureaucratic red tape. It has many names such as Tea Money in Asia, Dash in Africa, Pots de Vin in Europe, Baksheesh in the Middle East, La Mordita in Latin America and Mattabiche in Zaire.

INTERNATIONAL COURT OF JUSTICE (The Hague Court; I.C.J.; The World Court). An international tribunal which decides questions of international law arising out of disputes between Nations. The Court, the principal judicial organ of the United Nations, was established by articles 7 and 92-96 of the U.N. Charter, which entered into force in 1945. It was intended to replace the dormant Permanent Court of International Justice (P.C.I.J.) established in 1921 by the Assembly of the now-defunct League of Nations (Article 92 of the U.N. Charter makes evident the significant continuity between the P.C.I.J. and the present court). The Statute of the I.C.J., annexed to the U.N. Charter provides that the Court be composed of fifteen judges (no two of whom may be nationals of the same state) who serve nine-year terms. The Court sits in the Hague, Netherlands, and accordingly is sometimes referred to simply as the Hague Court. The U.N. Charter and the Statute of the I.C.J. reflect two fundamental principles of classical international law: First, that only nations and not individuals may be parties to litigation before the I.C.J. (the sole "subjects" of international law are nations, under the classical view). Second, both the charter and the statute base the jurisdiction of the Court upon the consent of the nations involved; only when the parties to a controversy agree to accept the decision of the Court does it have the power to decide the case. The requirement of voluntary co-operation of litigants limits somewhat the effectiveness of the Court; and no decision of the Court has ever been enforced by the U.N. against any nation.

INTERNATIONAL COVENANT ON ECONOMIC, SOCIAL AND CULTURAL RIGHTS. Ratified by thirty-seven countries as of 1976, the Covenant entered into force on January 3, 1976. Member states are required under its terms to move by all appropriate means —particularly the adoption of legislation—toward full implementation of economic cultural rights, including the right to safe, just and favorable working conditions, to participation in strikes, to social security, to union protection, to adequate standards of living, to physical and mental health, to education, to participation in cultural life, and to enjoyment of the benefits of science. Parties to this Covenant agreed to submit periodic reports of progress in these areas to the United Nations Economic and Social Council through the Secretary General of the U.N.

INTERNATIONAL COVENANT ON CIVIL AND POLITICAL RIGHTS. Ratified by thirty-five countries as of 1976, the Covenant entered into force on March 23, 1976. Member states to the Covenant are required to undertake measures to ensure their citizens the right to a fair trial, to freedom of thought, to freedom of science, to freedom of religion, to freedom of expression, to freedom of association, to equal protection of the law, to privacy, to family, to freedom of movement, to compensation for wrongful arrest or imprisonment, and to the prohibition of propaganda for war. These measures are guaranteed to citizens of member nations without regard to race, color, language, sex, religion, political persuasion, opinion, national or social origin, property, birth, or status. This Covenant established a Human Rights Committee to which implementation reports concerning compliance with the Covenant are directed. Member states may, by separate declaration, recognize in the committee the authority to receive and deliberate on complaints by member nations that other member nations are not living up to the obligations of the Covenant. To date, however, only three such declarations have been made.

INTERNATIONAL COVENANT ON THE ELIMINATION OF ALL FORMS OF RACIAL DISCRIMINATION. Ratified by eighty-nine countries as of 1976, the Convention entered into force on January 4, 1969. It requires member countries to end racial discrimination by any person, group, or organization. Under the terms of Article 14 of the Convention, which is not yet in force, a Committee on the elimination of racial discrimination can examine complaints among parties to the Covenant and facilitate conciliation of disputes.

INTERNATIONAL CONVENTION ON THE SUPPRESSION AND PUNISHMENT OF THE CRIME OF APARTHEID. Ratified by only eighteen nations as of 1976, the Convention has not yet entered into force. This Convention outlaws apartheid under international law as a crime against humanity. Apartheid is defined as "inhuman acts committed for the purpose of establishing and maintaining domination by one racial group of persons over any other racial group of persons and systematically oppressing them." Acts of apartheid include: denial of the right to life and liberty of person; wilful imposition of destructive living conditions calculated to physically destroy a particular group in whole or in part; measures designed to exclude specific racial or other groups from participating in the political, social, economic, or cultural aspects of a nation; exploitation of the labor of a racial group or groups; and any measure intended to divide a population by race.

INTERNATIONAL CONVENTION FOR SAFETY OF LIFE AT SEA. See RULES OF THE ROAD.

INTERNATIONAL CRIMINAL POLICE ORGANIZATION. See I.N.T.E.R.P.O.L.

INTERNATIONAL DAIRY PRODUCTS COUNCIL. See WORLD TRADE PACT.

INTERNATIONAL DEVELOPMENT ASSOCIATION. See I.D.A.

INTERNATIONAL DEVELOPMENT CO-OPERATION ADMINISTRATION (I.D.C.A.). An independent federal agency created by President Carter in 1979 upon the suggestion of the late Senator Hubert Humphrey of Minnesota to consolidate and coordinate in one place all the United States foreign assistance programs formerly scattered throughout various federal departments such as the Agency for International Development and the Overseas Private Investment Corporation. Included in the action was the creation of an Institute For Technological Co-operation (I.T.C.) to support research and technological innovation that could reduce obstacles to economic development.

INTERNATIONAL DISASTER INSTITUTE (I.D.I.). A London-based group established in 1978 to facilitate adequate emergency relief for disaster victims. The Institute plans to publish a scholarly journal and hold seminars on disaster aid. Typical of the blunders I.D.I. hopes to remedy are such incidents as a consignment of evening gowns sent to war-torn Biafra, laxatives sent to Burmese diarrhea sufferers, and huge supplies of pork sent to starving Muslims who are forbidden by their religion to eat pork.

INTERNATIONAL ENERGY AGENCY (I.E.A.). Created in 1974 in response to the Arab reduction of the world supply of oil, the I.E.A. is an autonomous body within the framework of the Organization for Economic Cooperation and Development (O.E.C.D.). The governing board of the I.E.A. implements policies to develop common levels of crisis self-sufficiency in oil supply, and provides for the distribution of oil in emergencies.

INTERNATIONAL FINANCIAL ASSOCIATION. See WORLD BANK.

INTERNATIONAL HUMANITARIAN LAWS OF 1978. The two new legal instruments which supplement the four Geneva Conventions of 1949 for the protection of war victims, namely, the two

"Protocols additional to the Geneva Conventions" which came into effect on December 7, 1978. Protocol I relating to international armed conflicts has been signed by 62 countries and Protocol II relating to non-international armed conflicts has been signed by 58 nations. On the entry into force of the additional Protocols, the International Committee of the Red Cross launched an appeal to the governments of the Conventions asking them to ratify the two texts. By doing so, they would show the world how important they feel it is that humanitarian rules be better observed on the battlefield. They thus would conform to the desire of the nations to see basic guarantees for humanity being universally accepted. These Protocols, which take into account the realities of numerous conflicts since the Second World War, were negotiated in Geneva between 1974 and 1977 at a diplomatic conference convened by the Swiss government. They reaffirm and develop considerably the rules for the protection of war victims, and especially of civilians. While, for example, the Fourth Geneva Convention protects civilians against the arbitrary power of the enemy or of the occupying authority, Protocol I extends the rules of humanitarian law to the protection of civilians against the effects of hostilities. It also extends the category of prisoners of war to include henceforward both members of the regular armed forces and, under certain conditions, non-uniformed guerrillas, and it improves the safety of recognized civilian medical units, transports and their personnel, by giving protection similar to that hitherto reserved for military medical personnel and units. Protocol II supplements and develops substantially the rules to be observed in non-international armed conflicts.

INTERNATIONAL INSTITUTE FOR THE UNIFICATION OF PRIVATE LAW (U.N.I.D.R.O.I.T.). More commonly called the Rome Institute, it drafts and proposes uniform substantive laws on an international basis. It was established as a result of a decision made by the Council of the League of Nations in 1924 and for a time it op-erated as a special agency of the League of Nations. In 1940 it was constituted as an intergovernmental organization, with organic status. The United States adhered to the Statute of the International Institute in 1964.

INTERNATIONAL LABOR ORGANIZATION. See I.L.O.

INTERNATIONAL LEAGUE OF THE RIGHTS OF MAN. Human rights group working in conjunction with the United Nations. The League protests political repression both to the Secretary-General of the U.N. and to the particular countries involved. Never does the League hesitate to "harass" those countries which are insensitive to its policies, and its pleas for clemency have probably been a factor in the commutations of the death sentences of political prisoners.

INTERNATIONAL MEAT COUNCIL. See WORLD TRADE PACT.

INTERNATIONAL MINIMUM STANDARD. The lowest level of accepted treatment of foreign nationals which is required of sovereign nations under customary international law.

INTERNATIONAL MONETARY FUND. See I.M.F.

INTERNATIONAL ORGANIZATION OF CONSUMER UNIONS. A coalition of over 180 consumer groups from both developed and less developed countries. The I.O.C.U. has represented the views of consumers before the United Nations as well as other international bodies on such issues as food standards. At its eighth Congress, attended by nearly 200 representatives, the I.O.C.U. identified inflation as the single most serious consumer problem and called for reform of the International Air Transport Association cartel.

INTERNATIONAL PERSONALITY. The status of a nation or other entity with rights and duties under international law. Typically, a nation obtains an International Personality when it is officially recognized by other countries.

INTERNATIONAL PROTOCOL. See CONGRESS OF VIENNA.

INTERNATIONAL RECOGNITION. An official political act whereby one country declares a particular government of another to be the lawful authority with which it will deal. The term applies to a number of situations which raise the question of who represents the legitimate power of a nation. Such situations include the emergence of a new state, the dismemberment of a nation through civil war, the extinction of a nation by conquest, or changes of government by violation or unconstitutional means. In each instance, a new government asserts a claim of power over territory and people, which foreign States accept or reject.

INTERNATIONAL RULES OF THE ROAD. See RULES OF THE ROAD.

INTERNATIONAL SHOE CO. v. WASHINGTON. See MINIMUM CONTACTS.

INTERNATIONAL STANDARD BOOK NUMBER. See I.S.B.N.

INTERNATIONAL SUGAR AGREEMENT. Multi-national pact entered into in London in 1958. The goals of the Agreement are both specific and general. On the one hand, the Pact purports to provide adequate returns for sugar-producing countries, thus maintaining the purchasing power of nations whose economies are largely dependent upon the production or export of sugar. On the other hand, the Agreement seeks to further international cooperation regarding world sugar problems, and to improve the living conditions of sugar consumers worldwide.

INTERNATIONAL SURVEY ACT OF 1976. A federal law which authorized the United States Department of Agriculture to examine the feasibility of a system to monitor the foreign ownership of land, especially farms, in the United States. The first such study of the 3,000 counties in the country has been made in Rappahannock County, Virginia which hopefully will serve as the prototype for other similar studies.

Although presently there are no reliable statistics, foreign investment in American land was estimated at $800 million for 1977. Big spenders from abroad make it difficult for Americans to purchase land and are driving up taxes. In response to this problem, seven states have laws against nonresident aliens owning land—New Hampshire, Connecticut, Kentucky, Indiana, Mississippi, Nebraska, and Oklahoma. Thirteen other states limit this sort of ownership, as do many foreign countries. Citizens of West Germany and the O.P.E.C. nations are most often mentioned as foreign landowners, but buyers also come from France, Taiwan, Canada and Latin America. Some have acquired United States land because they consider it one of the cheapest commodities in the world. Others, afraid their own countries will turn Communist, believe their descendants may prefer to live in the United States.

INTERNATIONAL TELECOMMUNICATION UNION. See I.T.U.

INTERNATIONAL TIN COUNCIL (I.T.C.). A worldwide cartel composed of 27 countries (seven producers of tin and 22 consumers) which consults regularly to fix the price at which tin is sold on the international market. The United States is the largest consumer and Malaysia is the largest producer.

INTERNATIONAL TRADE CODES. See WORLD TRADE PACT.

INTERNATIONAL TRADE COMMISSION (I.T.C.). An independent federal agency which has broad powers of investigation relating to the customs laws of the United States and foreign countries. It is concerned with all factors affecting competition between articles manufactured in the United States and imported articles. The I.T.C. is required to make available to the President and to the Committee on Ways and Means of the House of Representatives and to the Committee on Finance of the Senate, whenever requested, all information at its command, and is directed to make such investigations and reports as may be requested by the

President or Congress. The Commission advises the President as to the probable economic effects of proposed modifications of duties. The Commission also advises the President with respect to every article which may be considered for preferential removal of the duty on imports from designated developing countries. In order to carry out its responsibilities, the Commission engages in extensive research, conducts specialized studies, and maintains a high degree of expertise in all matters relating to the commercial and international trade policies of the United States.

INTERNATIONAL UNION. A labor organization claiming jurisdiction or membership outside the continental limits of the United States.

I.N.T.E.R.P.O.L. (International Criminal Police Organization). Contrary to popular opinion, this is not an international police force. It is a private organization to which law enforcement agencies of over 100 countries, including the United States, belong in cooperating to arrest criminals and control drugs across international borders. Founded in 1924, its headquarters are in Paris. Since we do not have a national police force, our relationship with I.N.T.E.R.P.O.L. is through the Treasury Department.

INTERPRETIVE RULES. Rules or statements issued by an agency to advise the public of the agency's construction of the statutes and rules which it administers. These interpretations are ordinarily of an advisory character, indicating merely the agency's present belief concerning the meaning of applicable statutory language. They are not binding upon those affected, for, if there is disagreement with the agency's view, the question may be presented for determination by a court. In contrast to legislative rules, interpretive rules are not made pursuant to a Congressional delegation of lawmaking power and courts are free to substitute their judgment as to the content of such rules. However, courts frequently give considerable weight to the views of the agency, sometimes giving the rules the force of law. A particular Interpretive Rule will have increased authoritative effect where the agency promulgating it has special expertise, where a subsequent statute has incorporated the interpretation, or where the interpretation has a long history of application.

IN TERROREM CLAUSE. A condition in a gift or devise which states that if the recipient takes, or fails to take a specific action, he will forfeit the gift. This type of condition subsequent may be in restraint of marriage in a gift or devise. In Terrorem clauses are generally void when they transfer personal property and contain no limitation over. The presence of a limitation over validates the clause because it signifies an intent other than mere intimidation. It shows an intent to donate to the beneficiary of the limitation. However, American courts have generally upheld the use of all manner of In Terrorem Clauses in wills, whether they deal with real or personal property and whether or not they contain a limitation over. A commonly encountered example is the no-contest provision in a will, which typically prevents a legatee from retaining a devise, or grants him one dollar, in the event he contests or attacks the will.

INTERROGATORIES TO PARTIES. Written questions to be answered under oath served by one party to a suit on another party. Under the Federal Rules of Civil Procedure, a defendant need not answer interrogatories until 45 days after the complaint has been served, but other parties must answer within 30 days. Furthermore, a party answering interrogatories has a duty to search his files for the requested information. Alternatively, he may permit the party who served the interrogatories to examine and copy his records.

INTERSTATE COMMERCE COMMISSION. See I.C.C.

INTERSTATE CONGRESS FOR EQUAL RIGHTS AND RESPONSIBILITIES (I.C.E.R.R.). An organization formed in 1976 as a white backlash to fight the increasing recognition of civil and property rights being awarded to American Indians.

INTER VIVOS (Latin—between living persons). The term describes something made during a person's lifetime, such as a trust or a gift.

INTOXICATION AS DEFENSE. Refers to the exculpation of a defendant on the ground that he was intoxicated when committing the crime. He is excused if he became intoxicated involuntarily and, as a result, did not know what he was doing. "Involuntary" means either that the accused was tricked or forced to consume the intoxicant or that he did so inadvertently. Generally, voluntary intoxication is a defense to crimes requiring either proof of a specific Mens Rea (i.e., assault with intent to commit rape) or proof of premeditation, if the intoxication is so severe as to deprive the defendant of the ability to mentally form such an intent or premeditation.

INTRA-COMPANY TRANSFEREE VISA. See H-1 VISA.

INTRA-SPOUSAL IMMUNITY. A doctrine followed in a dwindling majority of states, either by statute or judicial decision, whereby a husband or wife may not sue his or her spouse for an intentional tort. In other words, if a woman is beaten by a stranger, she may sue him for medical bills, lost wages during time missed from work due to her injuries, and pain and suffering. If, however, her husband beats her, she may not sue him in tort for the same losses. This doctrine derives from the common-law theory that at marriage a husband and wife become one person in the eyes of the law, and a person may not sue himself. Most courts that retain the doctrine explain it on the grounds that allowing such suits would disrupt and destroy the peace and harmony of the marital home. The doctrine has come under heavy attack during the last few years by people seeking ways to aid battered spouses. Dean Prosser sums up much of the criticism of the

doctrine in his famous essay on tort law as follows:

> Not allowing intraspousal tort suits is on the bald theory that after a husband has beaten his wife [or vice versa, he might have added], there is a state of peace and harmony left to be disturbed; that if she is sufficiently injured or angry to sue him for it she will be soothed and deterred by reprisals by denying her the legal remedy. If this reasoning appeals to the reader, let him by all means adopt it.

INVENTORY VALUATION ADJUSTMENT. Applied to book profits—profits before taxes—in order to exclude the gains or losses due to differences between the replacement cost of goods taken out of inventory and their recorded acquisition cost. Such an adjustment is necessary because many business firms do not keep their books in terms of current market prices, but rather at original cost or some other basis. This adjustment is required to prevent overstatement or understatement of earned profits in periods of changing prices. Generally, this item carries a minus sign during periods when prices of goods carried in inventory are rising, and a plus sign when inventory prices are falling.

INVERSE CONDEMNATION. Compensation to a property owner by a government whose action has reduced the value of the land.

INVERSE ZONING. A zoning scheme which seeks to disperse rather than concentrate particular types of establishments. For example, the Adult Entertainment Code in some American cities includes an ordinance designed to regulate the geographical placement of "adult" book stores and motion picture theatres. The Supreme Court has upheld such an application of inverse zoning.

INVESTIGATORY FIELD STOP. The temporary detention of a suspected criminal by law enforcement officers at the place where they find him. As its name suggests, the purpose of an Investigatory Field Stop is to permit the officers to investigate further to determine whether or not there is sufficient basis for an arrest. Under such cases as *Adams v. Williams,* 407 U.S. 143 (1972) and *Terry v. Ohio,* 392 U.S. 1 (1968), the officers may detain suspected criminals in an Investigatory Field Stop without a warrant and without probable cause.

INVESTMENT ADVISERS ACT OF 1940. A federal law which requires that persons who engage for compensation in the business of advising others about security transactions must register with the Securities and Exchange Commission (S.E.C.). The Act prohibits certain types of fee arrangements and fraudulent or deceitful investment practices, and requires disclosure of any adverse interests the advisers may have in transactions executed for clients. It also authorizes the S.E.C. to issue rules proscribing acts and practices which may operate as a fraud or deceit upon investors.

INVESTMENT COMPANY ACT OF 1940. A federal law which provides for the registration with the Securities and Exchange Commission (S.E.C.) of Investment Companies. To protect investors, the Act authorizes the S.E.C. to regulate sales and management fees, composition of boards of directors and capital structure. Also, various transactions of investment companies, including transactions with affiliated interests, are prohibited unless the S.E.C. first determines that such transactions are fair to security holders. Under the Act, the S.E.C. may institute court action to enjoin the consummation of unfair merger plans and other reorganization devices. It also may impose administrative sanctions against investment company managements for violations of the Act and other federal securities laws. In addition, it may file court actions to enjoin management officials from breaches of fiduciary duty involving personal misconduct and may disqualify such officials from office.

INVESTMENT CREDITS. Permit a taxpayer to deduct from his tax liability a percentage of the cost of the depreciable personal property he purchased or constructed. To be eligible for the credit, the property must have a useful life of at least three years and must be used in a trade or business. The credit was first enacted in 1962 to bolster a lagging economy by stimulating purchases of new machinery and equipment. Since then it has been an effective instrument of fiscal policy.

INVESTMENT TAX CREDIT BONUS. A federal law which allows an employer to qualify for a bonus 1.5 percent on the ten percent investment tax credit by contributing to employee stock ownership plans. To encourage more businesses to contribute to these plans, Congress decided in 1978 to continue until 1983 the additional point of investment credit to corporations that contribute an amount equal to the point of credit to the plan. The maximum tax credit in this case is 11 percent, and the plan must meet the standards of the Tax Reduction Act of 1975. A business is eligible for an additional one-half percent of investment credit when a sum equal to that contributed by the business is contributed by an employee. This plan brings the maximum credit to 11.5 percent. Employee stock ownership plans allow employees to own shares in their employer's corporation in proportion to their relative salaries.

INVESTMENT TRUST. A form of business organization that usually is involved in investing its available capital in securities. The organization then utilizes its earnings from such investments to lower operating costs and similar expenses and debts, and, in the event additional funds remain, distribute the same to company stockholders in the form of cash dividends and performance bonuses.

INVISIBLE EMPIRE. See KU KLUX KLAN.

INVISIBLE GOVERNMENT (Hidden Power Elite; Shadow Lawmakers). The more than 13,000 people who staff the committees and offices of members of Congress. Because no Congressman can absorb all the technical information demanded of him, staff experts have become a necessity. Most staffers are under 40, well paid, and reflect the political leanings of their employers. The growing number of staff members has been criticized for actually increasing the work load. According to Parkinson's Law: work expands to fill the man-hours available for it.

INVISIBLE HAND. The influence of special-interest groups and lobbyists, many of whom are lawyers, who know how to draft legislation and often do so for legislators, both local and national.

INVITATION FOR BIDS (I.F.B.). This term refers to the assembly of required documents (whether attached or incorporated by reference) furnished prospective bidders for the purpose of bidding on formally advertised government procurement contracts. It is a solicitation package designed to furnish prospective bidders all the information necessary to allow submission of a firm bid.

INVITEE CLASS. A class of guests to whom a landowner owes the highest duty of care. An invitee is one who comes on the land by express or implied invitation for some purpose related to the interests of the landowner or occupier. For example, garbage collectors, paperboys, business visitors, and shoppers in a store are all invitees. By contrast, a social guest in one's home is classified a licensee, and the landowner owes a lesser duty of care to such guests.

IN VITRO FERTILIZATION. See TEST-TUBE BABY.

INVOLUNTARY COMMITMENT. See CIVIL COMMITMENT.

INVOLUNTARY MANSLAUGHTER (Negligent Homicide). An unintentional killing committed while engaged in either an unlawful act or a lawful act conducted in a manner which constitutes criminal negligence. The former is known as misdemeanor manslaughter and provides liability for any accidental homicide occurring while engaged in any unlawful, Mal in Se conduct. Some states have modified or dropped the Mal in Se requirement. Thus, if *A* assaults *B*, causing *B* to suffer a heart attack, then *A* is guilty of involuntary manslaughter. If the accused's conduct constitutes a felony, then he may be guilty of felony murder. Unintentional homicides also constitute involuntary manslaughter if the defendant's conduct, though lawful, was performed in a criminally negligent manner. An example would be conducting blasting operations without adequately searching the area for bystanders. A higher degree of negligence than that required in tort law generally has been required for a conviction.

INVOLUNTARY PETITION IN BANKRUPTCY. A petition filed in bankruptcy court, in which one or more creditors request that their debtor be adjudged bankrupt. If the bankrupt has fewer than twelve creditors, a single creditor may file an involuntary petition; if there are more than twelve creditors, at least three of them must join in the petition. The petition must state the size and nature of the debts owed, names of the petitioning creditors, and allegations that the debtor is insolvent and has committed one of the six Acts of Bankruptcy in the preceding four months. A debtor may contest the involuntary petition at an adjudication hearing in bankruptcy court. An involuntary petition in bankruptcy may not be filed against certain classes of debtors, including farmers, banks, and insurance companies. The process has been simplified for petitions filed after October 1, 1979.

I.O.B. (Intelligence Oversight Board). A group of three persons charged with the sole responsibility of detecting and reporting directly to the President of the United States on any wrongdoing by the various Federal Intelligence Agencies, such as the C.I.A. and the F.B.I.

I.O.C.U. See INTERNATIONAL OR-GANIZATION OF CONSUMER UN-IONS.

I.R.A. See INDIVIDUAL RETIRE-MENT ACT.

I.R.A. (Irish Republican Army). A highly organized underground private military organization, which for generations has engaged in the use of force and violence against the British in order to obtain the complete independence of Ireland.

I.R.B.s. See INSTITUTIONAL RE-VIEW BOARDS.

I.R.C. See INTERNAL REVENUE CODE.

IRISH MAFIA. A small but powerful inner circle of advisors to President John F. Kennedy who were of Irish descent.

IRISH REPUBLICAN ARMY. See I.R.A.

IRON CLAD OATH. See YELLOW-DOG CONTRACT.

IRON CURTAIN. Term coined by Sir Winston Churchill in a speech delivered in Fulton, Missouri on March 5, 1946 to describe the deliberate policy of Russia in isolating herself from the rest of Europe, particularly with respect to suppression of human rights.

IRON CURTAIN ACTS. Laws which require that property willed to an alien living in a Communist country to be held by the state where the will was probated. Such Acts are often justified on the premise that the alien will not have the benefit or use of the property while living in a Communist country.

IRON LAW OF WAGES. Theory of German socialist, Ferdinand Lassalle, that wages will never exceed the bare minimum necessary for a subsistence level of living.

IRON LADY. See THATCHER, MAR-GARET.

IRON TRIANGLE. A term coined by Political Science Professor James Thurber of American University. It applies to a powerful if not an unholy alliance of (1) "middle" federal government administrators; (2) members of key Congressional subcommittees; and (3) lobbyists. They bound together to thwart the attempts of the President or the Congress to reduce the appropriations to the private groups the triangle represents or wishes to protect.

IRREBUTTABLE PRESUMPTION. See CONCLUSIVE PRESUMP-TIONS.

IRRECONCILABLE DIFFERENCES. Grounds for divorce in many states. The requirements when seeking a divorce on this basis typically are (1) a finding by a court that the marriage is irretrievably broken, and (2) the parties have lived separate and apart for a certain period, usually 6 months to 1 year. This basis for divorce is quite popular because it facilitates divorce without guilt or fault where the parties desire termination of their formal relationship. The term is synonymous with irretrievable breakdown, or irremediable breakdown, the terminology used in some jurisdictions.

IRRESISTIBLE IMPULSE TEST. An insanity test, often combined with the M'Naghten Test, which entitles the defendant to an acquittal if his mental illness led him to be overcome by an uncontrollable desire to commit the crime. The absence of criminal responsibility is predicated on the defendant's loss of free will, self control, and choice as to his actions. Narrowly construed, the defense is available only where the loss of control was unexpected, sudden, and spontaneous.

IRREVOCABLE TRUST. A trust arrangement which cannot be voided by the trust settlor unless the trust beneficiary consents. An Irrevocable Trust provides certainty to both the parties to the trust and the general public.

I.R.S. (Internal Revenue Service). Created by Congress in 1862, the I.R.S. is responsible for administering and enforcing the Internal Revenue Laws, except those relating to alcohol, tobacco, firearms, and explosives. The I.R.S.

mission is to encourage and achieve the highest possible degree of voluntary compliance with the tax laws and regulations and to conduct itself so as to warrant the highest degree of public confidence in the integrity and efficiency of the Service. Basic I.R.S. activities include providing taxpayer service and education; determination, assessment, and collection of internal revenue taxes; determination of pension plan qualifications and exempt organization status; and preparation and issuance of rulings and regulations to supplement the provisions of the Internal Revenue Code. The source of most revenues collected is the individual income tax, social insurance, and retirement taxes, with other major sources being corporate, excise, estate, and gift taxes. The United States is unique in the world in that there is voluntary good faith payment by more than 99 percent of its taxpayers on all taxes which are due.

I.R.S. OMBUDSMAN. A new position created in January, 1980, for the purpose of resolving the thousands of complaints voiced each year by the 130 million American taxpayers. The first person appointed to the post, with the rank of Assistant to the Commissioner of Revenue, was a 20-year career veteran of the I.R.S., Harold M. Browning, who will direct the Problem Resolution Program (P.R.P.).

ISAACS, RUFUS (1860-1934). Prominent English lawyer, politician and judge who served as Attorney-General, Ambassador to the United States and Viceroy of India. He participated in many of the famous cases of his day, including the prosecution of financier Whitaker Wright. Although Isaacs himself was accused of using his position as Attorney-General to further his financial interests, the House of Commons found him innocent. In 1926, on his return from India, he became a Marquess, the highest rank of nobility given a Jew.

I.S.B.N. (International Standard Book Number). Identifies one title or edition of a title from one specific publisher and is unique to that edition. It is used primarily for ordering publications and has no copyright significance. The I.S.B.N. applies mainly to books although it may be used for a variety of published or recorded works. It is generally found on the back of the title page. The I.S.B.N. consists of ten digits preceded by the letters I.S.B.N. Each number is separated by hyphens into four parts: the group identifier, which specifies the national or geographic grouping of publishers (zero stands for the United States and other English-speaking countries); the publisher's prefix; the title identifier; and the check digit. The need for an international numbering system was first discussed in 1966, and a process was introduced in the United Kingdom one year later. Today, the system is administered internationally in Berlin. The group in the United States is headquartered at the Standard Book Numbering Agency in New York City.

ISLAMIC BOMB. A nuclear weapon built surreptitiously by Pakistan, in 1979, on the grounds that Muslims needed such a weapon to match those possessed by the Christians (United States, France and Great Britain) and the Jews (Israel).

ISLAMIC LAW (Sharia). In Muslim society, a comprehensive legal system based on the divine will of Allah, as interpreted from reasoning by analogy. There are four major schools of Islamic law: Hunafi, Maliki, Shafii, and Hanbali. When the four schools agree, the rule is considered an expression of Allah's will; when the four schools disagree, the different rules are all ratified as probable definitions of Allah's will. Islamic law originally dominated all aspects of Muslim culture. However, it became impractical in some areas, such as commerce, where the prohibition against any form of interest was commercially unfeasible. Islamic law still governs, to a large extent, marriage and divorce rules. For example, under Islamic law a Muslim may have up to four wives concurrently, and the husband has an unrestricted power to divorce his wife at will, "talaq." Some

Muslim countries, such as Tunisia, have abolished both the practices of polygamy and talaq, and have claimed the right to interpret Islamic law in light of modern conditions.

ISLAMIC REVOLUTIONARY COURTS. Judicial bodies established by the Ayatollah Ruhollah Khomeini government in Iran in 1979 to punish the former leaders of the regime of the overthrown Shah by trying and executing an accused on the same day of the trial without the use of judges or lawyers. This is known as a summary death sentence because there is no appeal of any sort.

ISLE OF YOUTH. A special "school" 100 miles south of Havana attended by thousands of children from the Third World who return to their home land after they have been "educated" by the Cubans.

ISRAELI KNESSET. The Parliament or Legislative Branch of the Israeli government.

ISRAEL NATIONALITY LAW. See THE LAW OF RETURN.

ISSUE PRECLUSION. See COLLATERAL ESTOPPEL.

ITALIAN COMMUNIST PARTY. See P.C.I.

I.T.C. See INTERNATIONAL TIN COUNCIL; INTERNATIONAL TRADE COMMISSION.

ITEM VETO. See RIDER PROVISION.

ITEM VETO POWER. The ability possessed by some state Governors and municipal officials, but not the American President, to veto or strike out specific items in proposed legislation instead of being forced to approve the law in its entirety. Item veto power would substantially curtail, if not eliminate entirely, the vicious Pork Barrel system.

I.T.U. (International Telecommunications Union). A specialized agency of the U.N., located in Geneva, Switzerland, with 152 members. It originated from the International Telegraph Union established in 1865 and the International Radio-Telegraph Union established in 1906. The present International Telecommunication Union resulted from a merger in 1932 into one convention of provisions pertaining to radio, telegraph, and telephone. The purpose of the I.T.U. is to maintain and extend international cooperation for the most efficient and economical systems of telecommunications possible throughout the world through regulations governing the international use of telegraph, telephone, and radio services, and through technical and scientific studies designed to improve the means of communication.

I WON'T WORK. See I.W.W.

I.W.T. See WAR CRIMES.

I.W.W. (Industrial Workers of the World). The first national industry-wide Union formed in the United States in 1905 which disintegrated after World War I to be eventually replaced by the Congress of Industrial Organizations (C.I.O.). Its members were called Wobblies and a facetious translation of I.W.W. was "I Won't Work."

J

JACKSON, ROBERT. Served as United States Attorney General, Supreme Court Justice and World War II Allied War Crimes Prosecutor (Germany), despite his not having graduated from an accredited law school.

JACKSON-VANIK AMENDMENT. Congressional legislation named after its sponsors which made trade concessions to the Soviets in the naive hope that Russia would ease its uncivilized policy against emigration of Jews to Israel. However, the Russians did not change their policy.

J.A.G. Seee JUDGE ADVOCATE GENERAL.

JAILHOUSE LAWYER. A prisoner who is not a lawyer but has trained himself to do research in the law. On behalf of himself and other prisoners, he prepares legal documents which are submitted to judges. Many jailhouse lawyers are so capable that they obtain freedom for themselves and their "clients." Although they are in violation of the law by giving legal advice without a license, judges wink at their practice.

JANE DOE/JOHN DOE. See RICHARD ROE.

JAPANESE FORMULA. A solution reached between Japan and the Republic of China (Taiwan) when they officially broke diplomatic relations with each other in 1972 but wished to maintain their close commercial and cultural ties. They simply created what they called an Interchange Association, housed in their former Embassy buildings and staffed by career foreign service personnel "on special leave of absence." As a practical matter, it would appear that the only change is to refer to the person in charge as Mr. Director instead of Mr. Ambassador. This clever and typically Oriental ploy was used by the United States in its relationship with Taiwan, after its recognition of the People's Republic of China (the Communist Mainland), in 1979, as the sole legal representative of the Chinese people.

JAPAN, INC. A deliberate government-industrial alliance by which Japan was able to build its post-World War II commercial empire so successfully and at the expense of Uncle Sam. It is based on an intricate system of tariffs, impact quotas, tax breaks, excessively high corporate debt structure supported by banks, subsidies with a large measure of red tape, some dumping and a lifetime employment policy. The overall result is a highly favorable balance of trade in which their exports constantly exceed their imports.

JARNDYCE v. JARNDYCE. See DICKENS, CHARLES.

JAW BONING. Informal but heavy pressure by the federal government on labor and management to limit wage and price increases to reasonable levels under a threat of a government intervention if the voluntary efforts prove unsuccessful.

JAWORSKI, LEON. See SATURDAY NIGHT MASSACRE.

JAY, JOHN. The first Chief Justice of the Supreme Court, serving from 1789 to 1795. Jay played a crucial role in the ratification of the Constitution when he helped James Madison and Alexander Hamilton write the essays, now known as the *Federalist Papers,* that helped sway New York and several other states in favor of the Constitution. The most famous Supreme Court case Jay decided, *Chisholm v. Georgia* (1793), provoked such an outrage, at its allowance of the suit of one state by the citizens of another, that the Eleventh Amendment to the Federal Constitution was passed to nullify its holding. Jay took leave of the Court in 1794 to negotiate a treaty with Great Britain concerning the Northwest Territory, and returned in 1795 to find himself elected Governor of New York. As Governor, he led in the abolition of slavery and revision of the State's penal code. In 1800, John Adams nominated Jay to be Chief Justice of the Supreme Court a second time; although Congress confirmed the nomination, Jay declined, electing instead to enter a long retirement.

JAY WALKERS. Pedestrians who cross a street at an angle instead of straight across at the corner or who walk when the traffic light does not so permit, with the risk of a modest fine if they are caught in the act.

J.D. (Abbreviation for Juris Doctor (Doctor of Law) or Jurum Doctor (Doctor of Laws)). The initial degree granted in the study of law, and a prerequisite for admission to the bar in most states. It is academically equivalent to the LL.B. (Bachelor of Laws), and increasingly replacing that degree at United States law schools, so that every lawyer may also be a "doctor." Since most American law schools require a college degree for admission, it was ridiculous after three years of graduate study to award the successful candidate another Bachelor's degree.

JEFFERSON'S EMBARGO ACT. See EMBARGO ACT OF 1807.

JEFFERSON, THOMAS. Lawyer, scientist, musician, author, ecologist, politician, educator, inventor, statesman, architect, linguist and farmer. Third President of the United States, he also gained fame as the drafter of the Declaration of Independence. His political accomplishments included the elimination of primogeniture and the safeguarding of religious freedom in Virginia while Governor of that state, and the Louisiana Purchase and the Embargo Act while President. He lost his first bid for the Presidency to John Adams and was forced to preside over the Senate. In that capacity, he compiled the *Manual of Parliamentary Practice,* the forerunner of *Robert's Rules of Order.* Founder of the University of Virginia, Jefferson designed the grounds, planned the curriculum, and served as its first Rector. In addition, he devoted a great deal of time to his home, Monticello. There he kept meteorological records, classified fossils, and experimented with new seeds he had smuggled out of Italy. For a man of such intellect and abilities, Jefferson shunned public life. During his term as Governor, British troops overran Virginia, and he became the subject of a legislative inquiry because of the state's military unpreparedness. The ordeal caused him to retreat from public office, and only the death of his first wife motivated him to return.

JENCKS ACT. A federal law that allows a defendant to obtain from the government the out-of-court statements by a witness who has testified for the prosecution at a criminal trial in a federal court. The Statute codifies a Supreme Court decision which was designed to insure that a defendant was not convicted on the basis of untrustworthy testimony. The Act is significant because in a criminal proceeding, unlike a civil proceeding, few discovery devices generally are available to the defendant.

JEOPARDY ASSESSMENT. An Internal Revenue Service (I.R.S.) tax collection device that permits the federal government to freeze a taxpayer's savings, wages, and property. It is employed if an I.R.S. agent believes that delay in tax payment is likely to jeopardize eventual collection of the tax due. Although the taxpayer can protest in a court of law, until the suit is settled the disputed assets remain frozen. This extraordinary power was granted by Congress to enable the I.R.S. to reach assets of gangsters and drug traffickers, but it is used occasionally against the ordinary taxpayer.

JESSEL, SIR GEORGE (1824-1883). A great English judge who served as President of the Court of Appeal. He was known particularly for his clarity of mind and prompt, precise decisions. His self-confidence was reflected in his characteristic expression, "I may be wrong, and sometimes am, but I never have any doubts." Such confidence was deserved for there were few appeals in his court. In fact, the most telling criticism directed at Jessel was that he understood the heart of a case so swiftly that counsel did not have time to conclude their arguments. Jessel was the first Jew to sit on the judicial bench, to be sworn as a regular member of the Privy Council, and to participate in the executive government of England.

JESSUP INTERNATIONAL LAW MOOT COURT COMPETITION. Founded in 1961 and named after the former American member of the International Court of Justice. It seeks to strengthen and improve legal education in the United States through the sponsorship of an annual trial competition among law students on a current international law problem.

JESUS ON TRIAL. As recounted in Luke (Lk. 22.63-23.24), the trial of Jesus unfolded in four stages. Shortly after his arrival in Jerusalem, Jesus found himself surrounded by a crowd, composed largely of the scribes and chief priests of the community. After they had "led him away to their council," they asked him whether he was the Son of God. To this he replied, "You say that I am." (Lk. 22.70) He was thereupon taken to Pontius Pilate who, despite the false accusations of the scribes and chief priests, noted that there was no proof that Jesus had committed any crime. The third stage of the trial began when Pilate, told that Jesus was from Galilee, sent the prisoner to Herod. Herod questioned Jesus, received no answers, and returned him to Pilate. His sentiments unchanged, Pilate proposed to free Jesus in accordance with the custom requiring the release of one prisoner during the Passover festival. The enraged crowd exhorted him instead to pardon one Barrabas, who had been arrested for insurrection and murder. Pilate relented, surrendering Jesus to the angry mob. The "charges" brought against the accused can only be inferred from the invective heaped upon Jesus during the four stages of his "trial." Before Pilate, for example, the scribes and chief priests accused him of "perverting our nation, and forbidding us to give tribute to Caesar, and saying that he himself is Christ a king." (Lk. 23.2) The first two of these charges were false; the third, however, has some support. When asked by Pilate whether he was King of the Jews, Jesus responded, "You have said so" (Lk. 23.3) (interpreted by some authorities as meaning, "You are correct in saying so."

JEWISH GETT. A divorce under Rabbinical law which a man may obtain without his wife's consent, but not vice versa.

JIM CROW LAWS. Statutes which illegally enforce racial segregation. The term originated with a nineteenth-century blackface comedian named Thomas D. Rice, who sang in his act about "Jumping Jim Crow."

JIMMY CARTER CONFERENCE. See CAMP DAVID SUMMIT.

JIMMY HIGGINS. A slang labor term which describes a rank-and-file union member who works conscientiously for the union.

J.N.O.V. (Judgment Notwithstanding the Verdict). An order by a judge that sets aside the verdict reached by a jury. The test for a J.N.O.V. is not whether the judge agrees with the jury's verdict, but whether the jury could reasonably have reached such a verdict based on the evidence presented at the trial. Under the Federal Rules of Civil Procedure, a party must move at the close of all the evidence and prior to the verdict for a directed verdict in order to preserve the right to move for a J.N.O.V. Where a court reserves decision on the motion for a directed verdict, the losing party must move for J.N.O.V. after the verdict, except where the court has set a hearing on the reserved directed verdict motion. A motion for J.N.O.V. must be made between the verdict and ten days after judgment and is generally made along with a motion for a new trial in the alternative.

JOAN OF ARC. Captured in 1430 by the Duke of Burgundy, Joan was delivered into the hands of the Bishop of Beauvais for trial. Seventy charges were brought against her, including that, in claiming to adhere to the direct commands of God, she had denounced the sovereignty of the church. She was unsuccessful in arguing that her duty to God did not preclude recognition of the infallibility of the church. Imprisoned and enjoined to recant, Joan refused. The Bishop then decided to turn her over to the secular authority for execution, but changed his mind when the maid of Orleans agreed to sign a sort of abjuration. She was returned to prison, where she declared that St. Catherine and St. Margaret had disapproved of the abjuration. Convinced that Joan had reverted to her old intransigent ways, the Bishop transferred her to secular authorities for execution. After the burning of Joan on May 30, 1431, the executioner claimed that he found her heart intact amid the ashes.

JOHN BIRCH SOCIETY. An ultra-reactionary private political organization which is anti-liberal, anti-United Nations and anti-Communist. It was formed by a patriotic retired manufacturer named Robert Welch on December 9, 1958 and has approximately 100,000 members throughout the country. The Society is named after an American military intelligence officer who was killed in China nine days after the end of World War II, thus becoming the first casualty of the Cold War.

JOHN BROWN. An abolitionist who used extra-legal methods to free slaves prior to the Civil War. Brown was accused of brutally murdering five prominent slaveholders whom he singled out for bloody reprisals in Kansas. Rewards for his capture were offered by the President of the United States, and Brown was taken prisoner by Col. Robert E. Lee after leading an uprising in Harper's Ferry, Virginia. He was convicted by a Virginia jury of treason and hanged to death in 1859.

JOHN LAW. See ANTI-JOHN LAW.

JOINDER OF PARTIES. A procedural device used where more than one party asserts or contests a claim arising out of the same transaction or event. Joinder may be permitted even where the parties seek different relief. Separate judgments may be entered with respect to the individual parties. A court may order compulsory joinder where it determines that a judgment rendered in a person's absence will be prejudicial to him or to those persons who are already parties. If a court concludes that compulsory joinder is equitable but not feasible, the suit may be dismissed. The party needed for the trial but who cannot be joined is called an indispensable party.

JOINT AND SURVIVORSHIP TRUST. During the term of the trust arrangement while both a husband and a wife are alive, they are considered joint beneficiaries. At the death of either party, the share of the dead spouse passes to the survivor, who becomes the sole and only remaining beneficiary. Hence the term "Joint and Survivorship."

JOINT CHILD CUSTODY. An arrangement in which the natural mother and natural father have joint control in the care, upbringing and education of the child and an equal voice in decisions pertaining to health, religious training, vacations and the choice of schools.

JOINT HIRING HALL. See HIRING HALL.

JOINT STOCK ASSOCIATION. An unincorporated business enterprise having written articles of association and capital stock, divided into transferable shares. Although the company is treated as an entity for certain purposes, the shareholders are personally liable for the obligations of the association. It is usually managed by a board of directors and officers, who are agents of the shareholders.

JOINT TENANCY. Ownership of real property by two or more persons who each possess an undivided interest with survivorship. The advantage of such a scheme is that if any joint tenant dies, the property automatically goes to the surviving joint tenants.

JOINT VENTURE. A partnership, usually formed to carry out a specific business venture, and dissolving upon its completion. No formality is required for its formation. Parties to a joint venture owe fiduciary duties to each other, and such parties are subject to unlimited liability. Joint ventures may be formed by two or more corporations, and the enterprise itself can be incorporated, resulting in what is called a Joint Venture Corporation.

JOINT VENTURE CORPORATION. See JOINT VENTURE.

JOINT WILL. One will validly executed to dispose of the assets of two or more persons.

JONES ACT. A federal law that prohibits foreign-controlled companies from owning ships engaged in interstate commerce. A company is considered to be foreign-controlled if 25 percent or more of its shares are owned by non-Americans. Because it is difficult at times to determine the percentage of foreign-owned shares, the Act provides an alternative yardstick: A company is not deemed to be foreign-controlled if at least 90 percent of the registered addresses of stockholders are in the United States.

JONES-COSTIGAN SUGAR ACT OF 1934. A federal statute and its successor, the Sugar Act of 1948, which expired in 1974, but was revived by President Carter in 1977, which subsidizes American growers of sugar with payments to protect them from lower-priced imported sugar, the amount of which is strictly limited, at the expense of the American consumers. Congressman Harold D. Cooley, powerful former Chairman of the House Agricultural Committee, which regulated this complex area, was called the Sugar King. The taxation of sugar for revenue purposes in 1789 was one of the first laws passed by the infant Republic.

JONES v. MAYER CO. (392 U.S. 409 (1968)). Supreme Court case which prohibits all racial discrimination without exception, in the sale or rental of real estate. This case is significant in that certain exceptions to the prohibition against racial discrimination were granted under the Federal Fair Housing Act of 1968. For example, the owner of a single family dwelling who did not use the services of a broker, or engage in discriminatory advertising could discriminate in the sale of his home, and the "Mrs. Murphy Exception" allowed landlords of owner-occupied small apartment buildings to discriminate. According to the Supreme Court, these exceptions are not enforceable.

JOURNALIST'S PRIVILEGE (Shield Law). Entitles a newsman to refuse to disclose the identity of his source of information on the ground that the information was received in confidence. The privilege is designed to insure that news sources will not be deterred from providing vital information to the media. While not resting on the Constitution or the common law, the privilege is recognized by legislation in about half the states. It was first established in 1896 by a Maryland statute passed in response to the public furor over the jailing for contempt of a Baltimore *Sun* reporter who refused to reveal how he learned of secret grand jury proceedings.

JOYNER'S GUIDE. A subject index to the federal government, privately published by Nelson Joyner and Associates, a consulting firm in Reston, Virginia, which provides detailed information about doing business at home and abroad and which agency can be of assistance to you. It is an ideal quick access for a lawyer to obtain the background information to better service his clients.

JOY RIDING. (Unauthorized Car Use). Borrowing the vehicle of another temporarily, without permission, with the intent to abandon it or return it to the owner. While not so serious as stealing, it is still a criminal offense which is committed most often by teenagers off on a spree.

JUDAIC LAW (Rabbinical Law). The Code of the Jews respecting their religious beliefs, rites and practices.

JUDGE ADVOCATE GENERAL (J. A.G.). The senior legal officer of each of the Armed Forces. The term refers, severally, to the Judge Advocates General of the Army, Navy and Air Force. Each service J.A.G. acts as legal advisor to his service secretary and performs the various functions required by law. A military lawyer also is known as a J.A.G. officer.

JUDGE PRO TEM. See JUSTICE, INC.

JUDGES BILL OF 1925. A landmark federal act drafted by a committee of Supreme Court Justices. Its purpose was to reduce the burden on the Supreme Court in two ways. First, it sharply narrowed the scope of Supreme Court review as a matter of right from both state appellate courts and United States Circuit Courts of Appeals, replacing it with expanded discretionary review by Writ of Certiorari. In addition, direct review of United States District Court decisions was eliminated, except in limited classes of cases of particular importance and urgency.

With the passage of the Judges Bill, the structure of the federal judiciary acquired the basic form which it retains to this day.

JUDGE SHOPPING. Trying to have your case docketed so that it will be heard by a judge who might be disposed to decide in your favor.

JUDGMENT NOTWITHSTANDING THE VERDICT. See J.N.O.V.

JUDGMENT-PROOF. Defendant or potential defendant in a civil trial who would be unable to pay a judgment for damages if it were rendered against him. Whether or not a defendant is judgment-proof is often crucial in deciding who to sue when a plaintiff has a choice of several defendants.

JUDICIAL ACTIVISM. A philosophy of judicial decision-making holding that a judge should use his position to promote desirable social goals. Its opponents favor self-restraint on the part of judges, expecting them to defer to the legislature and executive, which are more directly accountable to the electorate. The play between these two philosophies is particularly apparent in the workings of the Supreme Court, whose decisions often reflect broad policy questions. Judicial activism does not necessarily imply either liberal or conservative political thinking. Activism by the Supreme Court struck down much of the New Deal reform legislation in the 1930s as well as finding a constitutional right to abortion in the 1970s.

JUDICIAL ASSISTANCE TREATY. An agreement between Switzerland and the United States in which the former agrees to reveal information or turn over funds in its otherwise secret anonymous numbered bank accounts if the latter could show that the money had been originally illegally deposited in Switzerland.

JUDICIAL CODE OF 1948. The third and most recent revision and recodification of the federal law governing the organization and operation of the federal judiciary. The Code was an attempt to bring together in an easily accessible format those statutes having continued validity in the field; to add new provisions where needed; to eliminate obsolete legislation; and to integrate the new Rules of Civil and Criminal Procedure. In passing the Judicial Code of 1948, Congress enacted one single code and repealed all prior statutes, thus limiting the task of researching the law for the federal judiciary. Among the many improvements effected by the Code are those directed toward the efficient administration of the federal judiciary; the establishment of a federal judicial district and circuit within the District of Columbia; a revision of the statutory provisions relating to habeas corpus; a statutory recognition of the Writ of Error Coram Nobis in the case of federal prisoners; a provision authorizing a change of venue in civil actions on the ground of Forum Non Conveniens; and a revision of the procedures for removal of actions from state to federal courts. The Judicial Code appears in Title 28 of the United States Code.

JUDICIAL CONDUCT COMMISSION. State tribunals which admonish or punish judges who violate the Judicial Canons of Ethics.

JUDICIAL CONFERENCE OF THE UNITED STATES. An administrative and policy-making branch of the federal judiciary. In 1922, in response to the need for more informed and coordinated administration of justice, Congress passed an act providing for an annual Judicial Conference to make a comprehensive survey of the condition and business of the federal courts and to prepare plans for transferring judges according to workload requirements. The conference was comprised of the senior circuit judges of each circuit under the direction of the Chief Justice of the Supreme Court. On this foundation, Congress in 1939 created the Administrative Office of the United States Courts to assist the Judicial Conference in the direction and administration of the judicial system. The 1939 Act was modified in part by the Judicial Code of 1948, which officially named the body the Judicial Conference of the United States and directed it to submit an annual report to Congress. In addition, the Code provided for the creation of a Judicial Council within each circuit as well as a large number of standing committees to assist the entire Conference. In 1967, the Conference acquired a research arm in the Federal Judicial Center, whose task it was to produce long-range studies and provide research assistance to help the Conference make recommendations to Congress. Among its various duties, the Judicial Conference studies the Supreme Court's rules of procedures. It also organizes various committees and councils on sentencing in order to achieve uniformity in sentencing procedures. Finally, it also oversees the administration of justice within each circuit.

JUDICIAL COUNCILS. See JUDICIAL CONFERENCE OF THE UNITED STATES.

JUDICIAL EVALUATION. See JUDICIAL REPORT CARDS.

JUDICIAL IMMUNITY. Protects judges from being sued for damages for acts done in their official capacity even when they act maliciously, exceed their authority or commit grave procedural errors. The Supreme Court upheld the doctrine of Judicial Immunity in a 1978 case of a young woman who sued an Indiana judge issuing an order to have her sterilized. The judge had no authority to make such an order, but acted anyway on the basis of the mother's opinion that her daughter was slightly retarded and promiscuous. Upholding the principle of Judicial Immunity, the Court found that the doctrine was particularly necessary in controversial cases so that a judge may act without fear of suit.

JUDICIAL LEGISLATION. Judge-made law as distinguished from law made by legislators (statutes), executives (orders) and administrators (rulings and regulations).

JUDICIAL NOTICE. A process whereby a judge, without requiring a party to introduce evidence, accepts a particular fact as true. A judge will judicially notice an indisputable fact—one which is a matter of common knowledge or subject to authoritative verification—in order to shorten and simplify a trial. For instance, a judge would not require that a party formally present evidence to prove that April Fool's Day took place on a Saturday in 1978, since this fact could be conclusively determined by reference to a competent almanac. The term is also used to describe the making of factual assumptions by a court in the course of interpreting a statute, applying a common-law doctrine, or deciding a constitutional question. For instance, the Supreme Court in *Brown v. Board of Education,* 347 U.S. 483 (1954), judicially noticed that segregated school facilities, even if they are identical, generate a feeling of inferiority among minority students. Finally, the term refers to a court's independent determination of the law to be applied in a given case.

JUDICIAL OFFICER. Any person exercising judicial powers in a court of law. There are two types of judicial officers: judge and subjudicial officer. The latter type includes those probation officers who exercise judicial powers. A judge is distinguished from a subjudicial officer in that the decision of a judge in criminal or juvenile cases is not subject to De Novo review and may only be reviewed by a judge of a higher court; whereas the decision of a subjudicial officer is always subject to De Novo review by a judge, sometimes by a judge at the same court level.

JUDICIAL PANEL ON MULTIDISTRICT LITIGATION. Created in 1968 and consisting of seven federal judges, it is authorized to temporarily transfer to a single district, for co-ordinated or consolidated pretrial proceedings, civil actions pending in different districts which involve one or more common questions of fact.

JUDICIAL PERFORMANCE COMMISSION. A state administrative agency designed to assure judicial integrity and accountability. California first established such an agency in 1960, and some forty states have since followed its lead. The agency investigates state court judges when it receives complaints of bias, senility, incompetence, dishonesty, and even tardiness in delivering opinions. It may censure the judge or ask him to resign. Most courts have followed its recommendations. For example, in 1977, the California Commission (in an unprecedented action) effected the removal of a state Supreme Court judge for senility. Many Commissions are also empowered to withhold the salaries of judges who delay the issuance of opinions past a stated time period, usually ninety days.

JUDICIAL REPORT CARDS (Judicial Evaluation). Periodic monitoring of the performance of state judges through public polls or reports of lawyers, which are used to determine whether judges should be re-appointed or re-elected.

JUDICIAL REVIEW. The function of courts in determining the constitutionality of legislative and executive or administrative acts. Any court may declare an act of a legislative or executive branch of government unconstitutional, subject to appear to a court of last resort, which is the highest state court when determining validity under a state constitution, or the Supreme Court of the United States for federal constitutional questions. The United States Constitution neither expressly grants nor denies the power of Judicial Review to the Supreme Court. However, John Marshall, second Chief Justice, asserted the Court's right of Judicial Review in *Marbury v. Madison*, 5 U.S. 87 (1803), and the power has gone virtually unquestioned since that time. Only in recent years has this uniquely American concept been made a part of the Legal Systems of other countries.

JUDICIAL SCREENING. The procedures governing the evaluation of the qualifications of prospective state judges. Judicial screening may be practiced both by local and state officials and by local and state Bar Associations.

While procedures vary widely, screening generally involves gathering information about the candidate's education, experience, integrity, and temperament; obtaining references from adversary attorneys and other disinterested parties; and conducting rigorous personal interviews to evaluate the candidate's performance under pressure.

JUDICIAL TENURE COMMISSION. See NUNN BILL.

JUDICIARY ACT OF 1789 (First Judiciary Act). A landmark Act, creating and organizing the federal judicial system. Article III of the Constitution empowers Congress to form a federal judiciary, and the first Congress swiftly exercised this power. Many members of Congress had also taken part in framing the Constitution, so that the Act is seen as weighty evidence of the Framers' intent. The most important effect of the Act was to create a single Supreme Court and two sets of lower federal courts, divided into district courts and circuit courts. Judges were to be appointed for the Supreme Court and the district courts, but not for the circuit courts. Instead, the circuit courts were to hold two sessions each year at each district within the circuit. The circuit court was to be comprised of two Supreme Court Justices and the district judge for that district. The Act further set out the areas of original and appellate jurisdiction for each level of federal courts. Other features of the First Judiciary Act included the device of a Removal Action from state to federal courts, and the circuit riding duties of the Supreme Court Justices. Finally, Section 34 of the Act, known as the Rules of Decision Act, provided that, except as otherwise required by federal law, "the Laws of the several States" should be regarded as the rules of decision in trials at Common Law in Federal Courts in cases where they applied. This section of the Act was subsequently to become one of the foundations of the Erie Doctrine.

JUMPING JUVENILE (Junior Accumulator; Junior Estate Creator). A life insurance policy designed specially for a child. It provides a basic amount of coverage, in increments of $1,000, during the early years of life. This coverage automatically increases by some multiple of the basic amount (generally five times) when the child reaches age 21, without a change in premium. Such a policy guarantees the insurability of the child even if he becomes medically uninsurable prior to his twenty-first birthday.

JUNIOR ACCUMULATOR. See JUMPING JUVENILE.

JUNIOR BARRISTER. See ENGLISH BARRISTER.

JUNIOR ESTATE CREATOR. See JUMPING JUVENILE.

JUNIOR MORTGAGE. See SECOND MORTGAGE.

J.U.R.I.S. See COMPUTER-ASSISTED LEGAL RESEARCH.

JURISDICTION IN PERSONAM. See PERSONAL JURISDICTION.

JURISDICTIONAL STRIKE. A work stoppage resulting from a jurisdictional dispute, which is a conflict between two or more unions or groups of employees.

JURIS DOCTOR. See J.D.

JURUM DOCTOR. See J.D.

JURY INSTRUCTIONS. The final charges made to the jury by the court prior to the submission of the case to the jury. The instructions provide the jury with the law to be applied in the case and explain what each side must prove in order to merit judgment in its favor. These instructions ordinarily constitute the only assistance and guidance which the court may give the jury in its deliberations. In the absence of a statute or rule so providing, the court need not deliver written instructions to the jury. In such a situation, it is left to the court's discretion whether to deliver oral or written instructions. All parties in a case may submit a list of proposed jury instructions to the court. An erroneous instruction may be grounds for reversal of a verdict upon appeal. Model Jury Instructors are sponsored or approved by an official body, such as the Supreme Court of a state.

JURY NULLIFICATION. Acquittal of a defendant, even though the evidence shows that he actually committed the acts alleged, because the jury does not feel that his conduct should draw criminal sanctions. Because judges seldom instruct juries of their right to acquit on this ground, many jurors may be unaware of this prerogative. It is perhaps the greatest protection in a Democracy against a Dictatorship.

JURY POLL. An inquiry as to whether jurors did in fact vote in accordance with the announced result.

JURY VERDICT. See GENERAL VERDICT; SPECIAL VERDICT.

JUS COGENS (Latin—compelling law). A rule or norm accepted and recognized by the international legal community. A treaty permitting piracy, for example, or one reestablishing slavery clearly would violate Jus Cogens.

JUS IN BELLO (Latin—law in war). Those laws governing the conduct of war.

JUS SANGUINIS (Latin—law of the place of one's descent or blood). The principle that nationality by birth is decided on the basis of parentage.

JUS SOLI (Latin—law of the place of one's birth). The principle that nationality by birth is determined on the basis of the territory in which the birth took place.

JUST DESERT See POETIC JUSTICE.

JUS TERTII. The right(s) of a third party.

JUSTICE, INC. A proposal by entrepreneurial New York lawyer Carl Person to establish a profit-making private judicial system as an alternative to the government monopoly on justice. To cure the delay and high cost in having a civil case tried in a state or federal court, which could be as long as several years where there is a heavy docket, he would establish a National Private

Court (N.P.C.). The litigants would pay all the costs of having their case tried by lawyers or retired judges without a jury. A few states by statute already permit this practice. The name of the person who is appointed to decide the case is Judge Pro Tem. His decision is enforced the same way as that of a "real" judge.

JUSTICE OF THE PEACE. A judicial officer often with jurisdiction to try minor civil and criminal cases, issue search warrants and perform marriage services. Frequently an elected office, its holders are often criticized for their lack of legal knowledge since most states do not require a law degree. Further, many Justices of the Peace are paid through fees, which brings their independent judgment into question. The office was first established in England in 1360 extending royal authority to local government. Members of the gentry held the office, which at that time enjoyed wide administrative authority and jurisdiction over most crimes. The proceedings in a justice's court are typically informal and a record is not compiled. A common feature of these courts is that Trial De Novo, or retrial, may be had in a higher state court of general jurisdiction, with a right of appeal of the trial court's judgment to an intermediate court of appeals or to the state's court of last resort. In the last few decades, there has been an increasing tendency to replace the Justice of the Peace with state district or county courts of somewhat broader jurisdiction. In many larger cities, municipal courts were established to handle minor civil and criminal matters. Some populous locations even have traffic courts, police courts, or magistrate's courts to deal with specialized cases. Where Justices of the Peace have not been supplanted by county or municipal courts, or by one of the specialized courts, they continue to exercise petty civil and criminal jurisdiction, principally in rural areas.

JUSTICE RETRIEVAL AND INQUIRY SYSTEM. See COMPUTER-ASSISTED LEGAL RESEARCH.

JUSTICIABLE ISSUE. Term of art applied to a federal court's determination that a particular matter is proper for judicial resolution. Derived from the "case or controversy" requirement of Article III of the Constitution, the term involves two distinct considerations. First, the court must assure that the case is posed in the proper adversary context, with parties of diverse interests to bring the facts of the case to light and enable the court to resolve the issue. Second, justiciability recognizes the role of the judiciary as one of three separate branches of government, and the court must take care not to intrude into the business of other branches of the government.

JUSTINIAN CODE (Corpus Juris Civilis: Latin—the body of civil law). Perhaps the most famous of the early Law Codes, promulgated by Emperor Justinian I of Rome in approximately 534 A.D. It was an attempt to remedy the chaotic state of Roman law which had developed over the preceding centuries. The Code consists of four main divisions: (1) imperial constitutions and ordinances; (2) writings of jurists; (3) institutes or outlines of classical law and procedure; and (4) novel or new constitutions issued by Justinian. The Code was abandoned in the ninth century when Leo the Wise introduced a new legal system. Though it resurfaced in the eleventh century, it was no longer practically useful.

JUVENILE AWARENESS PROGRAM (Scared Straight). A successful program begun by New Jersey in 1976 and since followed elsewhere. It was created and is run by "lifers" (convicts serving life sentences), and is run this way: Twice a day, five days a week, a dozen or so juvenile delinquents are given a tour of the maximum-security penitentiary and then are submitted to three hours of shock treatment during which the lifers deliberately try to frighten them with the prospect of their likely futures. The young people who attend these sessions are not occasional pranksters. They have long records of breaking-and-entering, selling drugs, assault with a deadly weapon, auto theft, arson, murder and rape. They have been sent to the program by judges, social workers, police officers and even parents in a last-ditch attempt to help their children. The lifers hurl obscenities; they provide the harrowing details of sexual abuses that are inflicted on young men in prison. A description of a prison killing becomes a chance for the lifers to emotionally maul the group; a personal recollection by one of the convicts of his own juvenile exploits turns into a verbal browbeating. More than 10,000 young people have been through the sessions since the program first started in 1976—and a considerable number of them have been and remain "Scared Straight." Since juvenile offenses represent more than half the crimes committed each year, this is a most important crime prevention program.

JUVENILE COURT (Children's Court). A state court having limited jurisdiction over matters of juvenile delinquency or neglect. Some states have separate juvenile or children's courts while in others juvenile matters are handled by the lower state courts of general jurisdiction, such as the county or district courts, or by specialized branches of the police court or municipal court. In still other states, special courts known as family courts have been created to handle both juvenile and domestic relations problems. A judge presiding in juvenile court usually follows informal procedures, and often makes extensive use of auxiliary services, such as social welfare workers and probation officers. The court's object is to help the child become a better citizen, but in serious cases the judge may sentence a juvenile offender to a term in a reformatory. Juvenile courts ordinarily have no jury.

JUVENILE COURT PROCEDURE. There are three basic steps of procedure for actions against persons under the age of majority: (1) intake and detention hearings, where an intake officer decides whether or not the case should go into the juvenile court system; (2) adjudicatory hearing, which closely resembles a criminal trial proceeding; (3) dispositional hearing, where the juvenile judge decides what action to take regarding the juvenile. During the dispositional hearing, an attorney may choose to act as a substitute parent (Guardian Ad Litem) and present his own opinion as well as his client's opinion as to what may be in the best interest of the juvenile. Justification for abandoning an advocacy role during the dispositional hearing seems to be based on the premise that services provided by the court are beneficial to the juvenile, and should not be resisted. Unfortunately, social data do not support this premise, and some commentators have maintained that anything less than an advocacy role violates the attorney's Code of Professional Responsibility.

JUVENILE DELINQUENT. A child under the age of eighteen who is characterized by unsocial behavior such as violence, truancy, and incorrigibility. Because of the age of the offender and the desirable social goal of teaching young citizens how to lead productive and enjoyable lives, the juvenile delinquent in America has special status. The juvenile courts, which have jurisdiction over these children and exist in one form or another in every state, emphasize clinical attention and rehabilitation of the juvenile delinquent in lieu of criminal punishment.

JUVENILE JUSTICE AND DELINQUENCY PREVENTION ACT OF 1974. Establishes standards for the treatment of juvenile offenders and attempts to prevent commingling of juveniles and adult criminals. Two key provisions of the Act provide: (1) that status offenders, children who break laws which only apply to juveniles, should be placed only in home-like shelter facilities where counseling is available; and (2) that all juveniles should never be housed with adult offenders. A study finished in 1978 revealed little success in meeting the standards of the Act. Of 47,000 juveniles detained in 1975 only 2,322 were in group homes or shelters.

JUVENILE JUSTICE STANDARDS. An eight-year-old project sponsored by the American Bar Association and the Institute of Judicial Administration which was completed in 1979, in 21 volumes, with controversial recommendations to all the states on how misbehaving minors should be treated by courts. The standards represent a return to the old-fashioned ideas of fairness, objectivity and personal responsibility with a sharp rejection of the century-old reform concept of the juvenile court as an arm of the child welfare agencies, presided over by a paternalistic but all-powerful judge unrestrained by indeterminate sentences or due process of the law on the right of the defendants.

JUVENILE RECORD. An official record containing, at a minimum, summary information pertaining to an identified juvenile concerning juvenile court proceedings, and, if applicable, detention and correctional processes. This term is the generic name for the type of record which is typically the subject of a statutory provision permitting or requiring sealing by court order when the juvenile reaches a certain age.

K

KANGAROO COURT. A sham proceeding, usually in a prison, where the inmates punish someone who violated their rules of behavior. It probably originated in Australia, habitat of the jumping mammal, which was used by the British as a penal colony. It connotes any type of unfair proceeding, such as a trial arising out of a speed-trap, where one is the victim of strict enforcement of a law he unwittingly violates.

KATKO v. BRINEY. See SPRING GREEN CASES.

KAUFMAN COMMISSION. A special Commission of lawyers, judges and professors appointed by the Chief Judge of the Second Circuit in 1977 to reduce or eliminate the tremendous cost incurred in pre-trial discovery under the Federal Rules of Civil Procedure. The proposed change would recommend that a party could serve on an adversary "a list of subject matters as to which he desires production"; the list to be "as brief and concise as the issues allow." In response, the other party would be required to give the location of "all files relating to those subject matters" and give the names of persons familiar with the filing system. The party seeking discovery could then inspect those files after allowing its adversary "a reasonable opportunity" to weed out "privileged, proprietary or other confidential material." Any differences on what is properly confidential would be decided by the judge. The Commission states that acceptance of its proposal would drastically reduce the delay and cost which now infect pre-trial discovery.

K.C. See KING'S COUNSEL.

KEEPLOCK SENTENCING (Padlock Sentencing). A method of punishing a prisoner by confining him to his cell for twenty-three to twenty-four hours a day. The inmate is not allowed to work or participate in other daily routines, is denied contact with other prisoners, and has limited access to showers and physical activities. Other forms of punishment by segregation and confinement include a maximum security cellblock and solitary confinement, usually in a "strip" or "dry" cell, with no sink or toilet. Keeplock or Padlock Sentencing is the least severe form of punitive segregation since the prisoner is confined to his own cell and has access to his personal belongings.

KEFAUVER-HARRIS AMENDMENT. An amendment in 1962 to the Federal Drug Law, prompted by the thalidomide drug tragedy which resulted in the birth of thousands of deformed babies. Aimed at consumer protection, it requires manufacturers to prove the efficacy and safety of a drug by a series of animal and human experiments before a new drug can be made and sold to the public. It therefore can now take up to 10 years and cost millions of dollars to develop and test a new drug before marketing. This tends to discourage development of drugs for rare conditions with a corresponding slowdown in the introduction into medical practice of new drugs in what is known as a Drug Lag, to improve present therapeutic regimens and to discover therapies where none currently exist. It also leads to a long delay in licensing in this country of drugs that were approved for use in Canada, England, Sweden and other countries where less stringent pre-marketing tests are required.

KELLEY v. JOHNSON (425 U.S. 238 (1976)). A Supreme Court decision that upheld a local regulation concerning the length and style of a policeman's hair. Speaking for the Court, Justice Rehnquist emphasized that the claimant was a policeman. Noting that most police forces were uniformed, he explained that similarity in appearance "may be based on a desire to make police officers readily recognizable to the members of the public, or a desire for the esprit de corps which such similarity is felt to inculcate within the police force itself."

KELLOGG-BRIAND PACT (General Treaty for the Renunciation of War as an Instrument of National Policy; Pact of Paris). A multilateral international treaty signed in Paris on August 27, 1928, and ratified by almost all countries, including the United States, which condemns recourse to war for the solution of international controversies. Inspired by the League of Nations peacekeeping system, it was drawn up by United States Secretary of State Frank B. Kellogg and French Foreign Minister Aristide Briand. Many states have concluded that the Pact does not prevent them from protecting their fundamental rights, and they have attached reservations to their ratification. The United States, for instance, declared that its right of self-defense was not impaired by the Pact, and that it was not prevented from enforcing the Monroe Doctrine. Those reservations largely nullified the Pact's general condemnation of war, since belligerents could easily avoid charges of violating the Pact by claiming self-defense. Although criticized for its imprecision, the Pact did outlaw war except when specifically justified by international law, and it has been relied upon by international tribunals after World War II.

KEMENY COMMISSION. A group of distinguished citizens headed by the President of Dartmouth College and appointed by President Carter to report on the future of nuclear energy after the Three Mile Island nuclear plant disaster in Pennsylvania in March of 1979.

KEMP-ROTH BILL. A proposal introduced into Congress by a Republican Representative from New York and a Republican Senator from Delaware which would provide an average income-tax cut of 33 percent over three years to stimulate the economy. The theory is that taxes have already gone so high that they discourage initiative and productivity and a dramatic cut will unleash so much economic activity that more, not less, tax revenue will come in to the government.

KENNEDY, ROBERT F. Lawyer, former Attorney General of the United States and United States Senator from New York who was assassinated on June 6, 1968, in the Ambassador Hotel in Los Angeles, while campaigning for the American Presidency, five years after his brother, President John F. Kennedy, was assassinated in Dallas, Texas.

KENNEDY ROUND. See TOKYO ROUND.

KENT, JAMES. A Professor of Law at Columbia University who became Chancellor (Head of the Court of Chancery) of New York in 1814. His *Commentaries on American Law* is one of the great American law books.

KENT'S COMMENTARIES. See KENT, JAMES.

KEOGH PLANS. Named for the Brooklyn Congressman who sponsored the legislation in 1962, Keogh Plans enable self-employed Americans to defer taxes on part of their earnings until they retire. Under the terms of the original law, participants could contribute a percent of their incomes, up to a maximum of $2,500 a year. At that time, however, only 50 percent of this amount would be tax deductible. With passage of E.R.I.S.A., the limits went to 15 percent and $7,500, respectively, 100 percent of which is tax deductible. Keogh contributions are not only tax deferred but also tax sheltered. The law applies to all self-employed individuals who derive income for themselves by selling goods or services. Owners of and partners in any unincorporated business also qualify for the Keogh Plan, regardless of whether their proprietorships have employees. Salaried individuals who earn additional income from freelance activities can set up Keogh Plans as well. Thus, the law extends to corporate accountants who prepare individual tax returns, university professors who also serve as consultants, teachers who do tutoring outside the classroom and others who earn additional money in their spare time. There is a special provision for those netting less than $5,000 in self-employed income. They may contribute up to $750 or 100 percent of their annual earnings, whichever is less. If, then, an individual made just $600 from additional activities in one year, he could only contribute $600—not $750—to the Keogh Plan. If a person contributes more than the law allows to a Keogh account, the Internal Revenue Service (I.R.S.) may assess a penalty of 6 percent, plus interest, on the excess. In addition, the agency will disallow that portion of the tax deduction. An employer with at least one employee in a Keogh Plan can make additional contributions (over and above the 15 percent limit) to his own account of up to 10 percent, with a maximum of $2,500 a year. While such additional contributions are not tax deductible, the returns they earn are not taxable until the fund is distributed. An employer adding to his account in this way is not required to do so for employees. Employees, however, are al-lowed to make their own extra contributions to Keogh Plans; the ceilings are the same—10 percent of earned income, with a top of $2,500 annually. Contributions are not tax deductible, but, again, any returns that are earned are not taxable until distribution. Worth noting is the fact that employees' interests are vested. Their accounts—the full amount of contributions, plus accumulated returns—become payable upon termination of employment for any reason. In case of death, the account is transferred to a designated beneficiary, or to the estate if no one has been named.

KEPT LAWYER (Corporate or In-House Lawyer). Derogatory term used in the 1920s when corporate lawyers were viewed with some disdain. It was assumed that the corporation controlled a lawyer's conscience by controlling his paycheck, thus threatening the independence of the legal profession. As the business world became more and more complex and corporations found they needed more and continuous legal help, corporate lawyers were gradually accepted as a legitimate branch of the legal profession.

KEY MAN INSURANCE. Life insurance taken out by a small company on the key executives of the firm. Such insurance is often required by lenders when a small company depends heavily on a key man.

KEY MAN SYSTEM. Method of jury selection in which the jury commissioner chooses prospective jurors from the community. This system has been under attack recently on the ground that it fosters systematic racial exclusion, and the Supreme Court has scrutinized such systems for discrimination.

KEY NUMBER SYSTEM. West Publishing Company's system which indexes significant points of law in all reported appellate decisions. The most comprehensive index to case law, the system has 420 major legal topics and thousands of sub-topics, with the entire field of law divided into seven main divisions: persons, property, contracts, torts, crimes, remedies, and government. The 420 topics are arranged alphabetically from "Abandonment" to "Zoning." West created "squibs" or abstracts for every significant point of law discussed in the cases appearing in the West Reporters. Each squib is assigned a topic name and key number which identified its subject matter within the system. The legal researcher may bring together all headnotes with the same topic and key number, and thereby be aided in finding the answer to the particular legal problem at hand.

K.G.B. (Committee for State Security of the U.S.S.R. Council of Ministers). The Soviet counterpart of the Central Intelligence Agency (C.I.A.), responsible for espionage activities. The K.G.B., unlike the C.I.A., is also responsible for detection of domestic political and economic sabotage. In addition, the K.G.B. provides security for government and party leaders, and maintains special prisons.

KHMER ROUGE. The Red Communists of Cambodia.

KICK BACK. Forced return of part of one's wages as a condition for procuring or retaining employment. Also applied in contract negotiations, a kick back may involve a secret rebate of part of a purchase price by the seller to the buyer or to the one who influences the sale.

KIDDIE KORPS. A group of relatively young and inexperienced men and women, all-too-often from Georgia, who were given key government positions by domestic affairs adviser Stuart Eizenstat whose main qualification for appointment to their high positions was their help in getting President Carter elected. Their inability to reach accord on tough decisions and then implement them has given rise to the derisive term B.O.G.S.A.A.T. (Bunch of Guys Sitting Around a Table). Those who have the most direct access to and impact on the White House are called the "Georgia Mafia."

KIDDIE PORN BILL. A federal criminal law, also adopted by several states, passed in 1977 to prohibit the use of minors in hard-core or obscene pornographic films and pictures by punishing the promoters with fines or imprisonment.

KILLER BEES. The 12 Texas State Senators who wore lapel "bee" pins when they fled the state in May, 1979 (presumably for Mexico, to avoid their capture and arrest by the Texas Rangers on the order of the Lt. Governor to be returned to the state legislature in order to create a quorum) to kill the bill that would establish an early state Presidential Primary favorable to the state's conservative Democrats and to enhance the chances of John B. Connally, a Republican Presidential candidate. The sting of the dozen liberal legislators was sufficient to paralyze the legislature. Queen bees are the wives of the missing legislators. The Texas Rangers are the bumble bees, and the loyal Senators (conservative Democrats and Republicans) who stayed home are, of course, the worker bees. Other colorful liberal legislators in the history of the Texas legislature have been known as the Gashouse Gang, who committed heresy by recommending a tax on natural gas, and the Dirty Thirty.

KING EDWARD VIII. The only British monarch in recorded history to abdicate the throne voluntarily, in 1936, after less than a year of occupancy (others died or were assassinated). He left to marry Wallis Warfield Simpson, a 38-year-old American divorced socialite who had set her cap for him and, in her successful quest, caused him to give up the throne. His mother, Queen Mary, put it simply when she said, "To give up all of this for that!"

KING OF TORTS. See BELLI, MELVIN MOURON.

KING'S COUNSEL (K.C. or Queen's Counsel, Q.C.). A few select barristers (court lawyers as distinguished from office lawyers who are called solicitors) who are honored by the Monarch in Great Britain and Commonwealth countries in their appointment to serve as counsel for the Crown. They also try private cases and the formal listing of the title after their names gives them great professional prestige.

KING'S EVIDENCE. See QUEEN'S EVIDENCE.

KING'S RANSOM. See RANSOM PAYMENT.

KING v. SMITH. See MAN IN THE HOUSE RULE.

KITCHEN CABINET. An informal cabinet, generally consisting of close friends of the President, which advises the President on issues of national importance. The term was derived from the group which advised President Andrew Jackson and which is rumored to have met in the White House kitchen.

KITE FINANCING. The unlawful practice of issuing a check in excess of deposits, then making up the difference by depositing another check, also in excess of deposits, but drawn on another bank. Like kite flying, such financing is borne aloft by air and destined for a rapid descent.

K.K.K. See KU KLUX KLAN.

K.K.K. LAW. See KU KLUX KLAN ACT.

KLAXON DOCTRINE. A Conflict of Laws doctrine which provides that, in hearing an action not governed by federal law which requires a choice between the laws of two or more states in order to determine the applicable law, a federal district court must apply the Conflict of Laws rules of the state in which it is situated. This rule was propounded by the United States Supreme Court in *Klaxon Co. v. Stentor Elec. Mfg. Co.*, 313 U.S. 487 (1941). For example, if Jones, a resident of state *A*, has an accident in state *B* with Smith, a resident of state *C*, and sues Smith in the federal district court of *B*, then that court must apply the Conflict of Laws rules of state *B* in order to determine if the applicable substantive law is that of *A*, *B*, or *C*.

KNAPP COMMISSION REPORT. A two-year study on police corruption in New York City (1970-72) headed by Whitman Knapp.

KNEE CAPPING. Shooting the legs of businessmen and politicians, a technique used by the Italian Communist terrorist group called the Red Brigade and other urban guerillas.

KNIGHTS OF LABOR. The first large-scale American union, organized in 1869, which reached the height of its power in the 1880s. It was later replaced by the A.F.L. at the turn of the century.

KNOCK - AND - ANNOUNCE RULE. Requires police officers who enter private premises for the purpose of conducting a search to give prior notice. The Rule dates back to a 17th century English case which held that before the sheriff could make a forced entry to execute the king's process, he ought to make known the purpose of his visit and request that the door be opened. In many states, specific Knock-and-Announce Statutes prohibit a police officer from making a forced entry to execute a search warrant unless he has first announced his identity and purpose and had been denied admittance. In addition to both the common law and statutory enactments of the Rule it has been held that the Rule is constitutionally mandated by the Fourth Amendment's prohibition against unreasonable searches and seizures.

KNOCKING UP. The British system of Members of Parliament engaging in a door-to-door election polling process.

KNOCKOFF DESIGN. A copyright infringement in the toy industry. Under American copyright law, stuffed animals are considered sculpture and designs for such toys are protected as artistic creations. Manufacturers that produce animals very similar to copyrighted creatures may be sued for infringement. Because sales of stuffed toys reached nearly $200 million in 1976, suits alleging knockoff designs have become particularly lucrative for successful plaintiffs and have increased markedly in recent years.

KNOCK ON THE DOOR. An unannounced visit, usually at night, either by a social worker checking on a family adopting a child to ascertain their normal life style, or by a government official to determine whether an unmarried female welfare recipient with children has a man living with her and should forfeit her support.

KNOW-NOTHING POLITICS. Political activities which reflect fears and prejudices rather than reasoned analysis. The expression derives from the Know-Nothing Party, a secret nineteenth century conservative group which espoused isolationist anti-Catholic policy. In recent politics, the McCarthy Era has been called an example of Know-Nothing Politics.

KORAMATSU v. UNITED STATES. See SUSPECT CLASSIFICATIONS.

KU KLUX KLAN (K.K.K.). Organized in the South during the Reconstruction period and originally composed of reputable persons who joined to fight injustices under the rule of Northern "carpetbaggers," the Klan degenerated into a racist group committed to terrorizing Blacks. In 1871, Klan activities were revealed in a federal court trial of several prominent Klan members. It was shown that many Blacks entitled to vote were prevented from doing so by Klan members who made raids to their homes during the night and beat or murdered them. The jury, the majority of whom were Black, showed remarkable impartiality and proved that Black citizens were capable of acting justly and reasonably, even though some of their white neighbors were not.

KU KLUX KLAN ACT (K.K.K. Law; Section 1985 Law). A federal statute passed by Congress in the Reconstruction Era of 1871 (and named after the bigoted secret white-sheeted society) which provided for civil and criminal penalties for those who conspire to deprive anyone "of equal privileges and immunities under the Law." Although the criminal sanctions were removed in 1882, the law is still an effective modern legal weapon in civil rights cases.

KUTAK COMMITTEE. A group of lawyers under the leadership of an Oklahoma lawyer charged with the responsibility of promulgating a revised version of the American Bar Association Code of Professional Responsibility.

L

LABOR CONSPIRACY. Early labor law concept that workers who organized themselves were violating laws against criminal conspiracy.

LABOR-MANAGEMENT REPORTING ACT OF 1959. See LANDRUM-GRIFFIN ACT.

LABOR UNION HISTORY. The first American Labor Unions were groups of carpenters, shoemakers, printers and other craftsmen who formed separate organizations in Philadelphia, New York and Boston to resist wage reductions. These organizations were usually short-lived. The first recorded meeting of representatives of labor and management to engage in collective bargaining involved the Philadelphia shoemakers and their employers in 1799. In 1741 the New York bakers are said to have stopped work to enforce their demands, although this action was directed more against the local government, but the first authentic strike was called in 1786 by the Philadelphia printers who provided benefits in support of fellow workers. These early labor activities were largely scattered and short lived. The economy was still largely agrarian, and it was not until the growth of large industry following the Civil War with its countless numbers of new workers that the so-called American Labor Movement began and labor unions began to be a factor in American life and culture. As unions began to grow they were resisted at every turn by employers who wished to keep wages low, by the federal courts and state courts which believed that they violated the "right of free contract" and due process of law, and by the people who believed that all Unionists were Communists, Socialists, and anarchists. It is not surprising that some unions originated as secret societies such as the Molly Maguires which became strong in the anthracitic coal regions of Pennsylvania and which used terroristic methods against employers and strikebreakers. Probably the worst year in the history of American Unionism occurred in the great railway strike of 1877 involving all railways east of the Mississippi. This was the first recorded instance of the use of federal troops in a labor dispute, and during the strike, which was marked by violence and property damage, more than 100 persons were reported killed and 200 injured. In subsequent years conditions improved slowly until about 1932 when numerous remedial labor law provisions were passed and put into effect. By 1938, most of the great battles of the labor movement had been won, and the unions, once the underdogs, had become so powerful that by 1947 Congress found it necessary to pass the Taft-Hartley Act to regulate them. By the early 1960s it appeared that the great surge for "organized labor" of the 1930s and '40s and '50s had slowed to a standstill. Although the total United States work force had risen by 5,000,000 between 1955 and 1961, A.F.L.-C.I.O. membership dropped in that period from 13,500,000 to 13,300,000. The cause is difficult to determine. Corruption, though limited, has had a shaking effect. Wages were high enough that workers would hesitate to champion a strike in most industries. The new industries in the southern states carefully kept their pay above union wage scales to dampen attempts at organization. And in some industries, automation or the use of new automatic machines reduced the number of workers. But none of these factors, probably, is as responsible for the membership decline as the fact that so many of the old goals have been achieved and so many of the old fighters are gone. As one union official has put it, "And this is where our big problem lies—in apathy."

LACHES DOCTRINE (French—to neglect or postpone). Failure to state a claim or assert a right may bar legal enforcement of the claim in equity if there has been undue delay prejudicing the party against whom the claim is brought. For example, if neighbor *X* erects a home which encroaches five feet on neighbor *Y*'s property, and neighbor *Y* sits back and watches the construction, knowing that it encroaches on his land, the Laches Doctrine may bar the assertion of his claim after the house is built. It is comparable to the Statute of Limitations for Actions at Law.

LA COSA NOSTRA. See NATIONAL CRIMINAL CONSPIRACY.

LADY ASTOR (Nancy Langhorne). The first woman member of the British Parliament (The "Men's Club") in 1919. Born in Virginia, her constituency included the port from which the good ship Mayflower set sail from England for America centuries ago. The youngest woman ever to sit in the British Parliament was the tempestuous representative of Northern Ireland's Roman Catholics, Bernadette Devlin, in 1969. Among other things, she thereafter had a child out of wedlock and refused to identify the father.

LADY BIRD'S BILL (Highway Beautification Act of 1965). A federal law named by President Lyndon Johnson after his wife since it was one of her pet projects. It was designed in part to eliminate unsightly billboards along 43,000 miles of federally funded interstate highway. It prohibited "outdoor advertising signs" within 660 feet of the road and restricted them to land zoned for commercial use. Existing signs that didn't comply with the new law were to be pulled down. So far, 88,000 offending road signs have been removed—but 208,000 others remain. Some states (Missouri and New Jersey) have not removed a single sign to date. Others such as Georgia have even built new signs so the law has not been a smashing success.

LADY IN WAITING. See THATCH-ER, MARGARET.

LAFAYETTE v. LOUISIANA POWER AND LIGHT CO. See PARKER v. BROWN DOCTRINE.

LAFFER CURVE. Right-wing financial advisor to Ronald Reagan and Professor of Economics at the University of Southern California, Arthur B. Laffer has concocted a theory expressed by a bullet-shaped curve which states that tax cuts can result in larger revenue to the government. The Kemp-Roth Bill, which would cut income taxes by as much as 33 percent, is based on Laffer's theory that a sharp cut in taxes will produce a rush of economic activity that will produce more income and consequently more revenue to the government. Critics of the Kemp-Roth Bill point out that this is just a theory and that economics is far from a certain science, while supporters contend that even if the government does have less revenue, limiting government receipts may go a long way toward limiting government spending.

LAKE v. CAMERON. See LEAST RESTRICTIVE ALTERNATIVE.

LAKESIDE v. OREGON (1978). See TAKE THE FIFTH.

LAME DUCK AMENDMENT (Twentieth Federal Constitutional Amendment of 1933). Designed to increase government efficiency by allowing the new Presidential and Congressional terms to begin earlier. The Amendment provides that the President and Vice-President will assume office on January 20, and that a new Congress will convene on January 3. Prior to the Amendment, the President did not assume official duties until March 4, and the new Congress did not convene until December of the year after it had been elected. Such delays created the Lame Duck problem where the government is being run by politicians who have not won re-election and who thus do not represent the will of the people. The Amendment enables a newly-elected President and Congress to develop new programs quickly.

LAME DUCKS. Legislators who continue to represent their constituents after their defeat at the polls until such time as their successors are officially sworn into office to replace them.

LAND CONTRACT. A method of selling real property which is financed by the owner who retains legal title until all payments of principal and interest have been completed.

LAND GRANT COLLEGE ACT OF 1862. See MORRILL ACT.

LANDIS, KENENSAW MOUNTAIN (Baseball Judge). A United States federal district judge who was named the first Commissioner of American Baseball in 1920 after the Chicago White Sox gambling scandal.

LAND LEASEBACK. A transfer in which a real estate developer sells unimproved land to an investor, who then leases it back to the developer on a long-term basis, thereby enabling the developer to obtain any required financing.

LANDLORD DUTY TO PREVENT CRIME. Although a landlord is not an insurer of his tenants' security, several courts have imposed a duty on landlords to take reasonable precautions against crime. A New Jersey landlord, for instance, was fined $6,100—the cost of stolen jewelry from tenants who had repeatedly complained about a malfunctioning lock on their apartment door.

LANDLORD'S SECURITY DEPOSIT LAWS. Laws which require landlords to make a security deposit just as their tenants must do, in order to guarantee that essential repairs will be made. Currently in force in some New Jersey cities, a state-wide Landlord Security Deposit Law is being considered in Massachusetts.

LANDMARK CASE. See LEADING CASE.

LANDMARK LEGISLATION. Laws which impose restrictions on historical landmarks, even when such are owned by individuals. The Supreme Court recently upheld New York City's Landmark Legislation, refusing to allow the Penn Central Transportation Company to build a 53-story office building above Grand Central Terminal because the tower would significantly alter the terminal's status as a historical landmark.

LANDRUM-GRIFFIN ACT (The Labor-Management Reporting Act of 1959). A federal statute passed in the wake of revelations of trade-union dishonesty. The Act requires all unions to file annual reports with the Labor Department. It also prohibits persons convicted of embezzlement, bribery, extortion and murder from holding union office for five years after conviction or imprisonment. In addition, the Act guarantees equal rights to all union members, provides safeguards against improper disciplinary action against union members, and requires election of national union members at least every five years and of local union officers each three years by secret ballot.

LAND TRUST. Usually an association having unincorporated status which holds real property in trust. Generally, a Land Trust places title to the real estate in trustees for the benefit of the members who are given land trust certificates.

LANGDELL, CHRISTOPHER COLUMBUS. The Dean of Harvard Law School who in the latter part of the 19th Century transformed Harvard into the first modern American law school. Langdell extended classwork from 18 months to three years and originated a first-year curriculum still used to this day (Property, Torts, Procedure, Contracts, Criminal Law). He was the first dean to hire career law professors—rather than part-time practitioners and and judges—to serve as the core of his faculty. Rigorous examinations and the college-degree admission requirement were initiated. Now-familiar institutions —the Law Review, elective courses, Moot Court, the Law School Alumni Association—were created or shaped to their present form by Langdell. Most celebrated was his transformation of the method of law school teaching from the study of general principles in textbooks called Horn Books to the study of actual law cases guided by the "Socratic" questioning of law professors. In the 70 years after Langdell stepped down as dean, the Harvard Law School "model" of legal education has been emulated by virtually every American law school. This "case" technique of teaching has been followed by other educational programs such as Business Administration.

LANGHORNE, NANCY. See LADY ASTOR.

LANTERMAN-PETRIS-SHORT ACT. See COMMUNITY HEALTH SERVICES LAW.

LAPSE OF TRUST. The failure of a trust to take effect, generally due to the death of a beneficiary during the life of the settlor. Absent provisions for such an occurrence in the trust agreement, the trust property passes back to the estate of the trust settlor since the purpose of the trust arrangement has become frustrated. To prevent such a result, most settlors insert a clause designation a subsequent beneficiary.

LAPSE STATUTES. See ANTI-LAPSE STATUTES.

LARCENY BY TRICK. A crime in which possession of property is obtained by misrepresentation. Thus, although the victim consents to the thief's taking possession of the property, the consent is invalid. If the thief intends to deprive the victim of his property permanently, the taking constitutes larceny.

LAST CLEAR CHANCE. A tort doctrine which allows a plaintiff to recover damages, despite his contributory negligence, if the defendant could have averted the accident at the last minute. To illustrate: *A* is a motorist, and *B* an inebriated pedestrian lying asleep in the middle of the road. *A* has ample time to see *B* and does see him. *A* carelessly drives over *B*'s outstretched form. Legally, *B*'s negligence in lying in the middle of the road contributed to his being run over, but this fact is not necessarily fatal to *B*'s case, for *A* had a last clear chance to avoid the accident.

LAST EVENT RULE. A choice of law rule that provides that the place of wrong in a tort suit is the state in which the plaintiff was injured. The Rule is invoked in cases where the defendant's negligent act occurred in one state and the plaintiff's injury in another. To determine the applicable law, the court must establish which state is the place of wrong. The state of injury is chosen on the theory that the plaintiff sues the defendant not for a negligent act, but for the harm caused by such an act.

LATENT DEFECTS. A seller is obliged to inform a buyer of hidden defects on his property which a reasonable inspection would not disclose. Failure to disclose may be grounds for rescission of the contract of sale.

LATERAN TREATY. Signed in Rome on February 11, 1929 between Italy and the Roman Catholic Church, the Treaty created the Vatican City. In addition to a financial agreement, and to a Concordat governing the relations between the Holy See and Italy, the Treaty provides for the juridical status of the Holy See and gives it full international competence. Italy, by legally giving up part of its territory in Rome, recognized the full ownership, and sovereign authority of the Holy See over the Vatican. Containing one hundred acres and seven hundred citizens, the Vatican is the government with international duties and rights. The state has diplomatic relations with other states, it can be a member of international organizations within the limits of its pacific mission, and can in any event always exert its spiritual powers. The Treaty affirms the permanent neutrality and inviolability of the Vatican.

LATIN IN LAW. Although attempts have been made to simplify legal language as early as the 1833 best seller, *Pocket Lawyer,* many in the legal profession support the continued use of Latin phrases for the consistency and certainty it brings. Some Latin phrases have become commonplace, such as "versus," "prima facie," "alias," and "bona fide," while others might lose something in the translation. Habeas Corpus, for example, was once translated by Charles Dickens as "you have the carcass."

LATRINE LAWYER. A self-proclaimed authority on military law.

LAUNDERED MONEY. An illicit payment of money into a foreign bank account, in order to "clean it up" in the hope that it will not be traced by law enforcement officers.

LAUNDRY LIST. Any valid combination of legal requirements. For example, a judge might grant a suspended sentence to a defendant who would be on probation and told not to leave the city without permission, to attend Alcoholics Anonymous, to be home by midnight each evening, not to drive a car, etc.

LAW ASSISTANT. A career judicial aide, as in New York. He exercises tremendous power in an efficient administration of justice by recommending settlements or ruling on motions in behalf of the judge for whom he works.

LAW CLERK. Assistant to a judge or Supreme Court justice who is generally a recent law school graduate. Clerkships are usually much sought-after positions among law school graduates and the higher the court in the appellate chain, the higher the prestige attached to a clerkship.

LAW DAY. International Labor Day is celebrated as a holiday annually on May first by Communist and Socialist Workers around the world. It is called May Day. Perhaps in retaliation, under the leadership of the American Bar Association, President Dwight D. Eisenhower announced the first American Law Day on May 1, 1958. It has since been so proclaimed by every President to date as a permanent fixture in our life style. National and state bar associations conduct 50,000 different programs annually on May first in which five million participants advocate the

Rule of Law in the preservation of liberty and promotion of justice.

LAW ENFORCEMENT ASSISTANCE ADMINISTRATION (L.E.A.A.). A federal agency that assists state and local governments in strengthening and improving Law Enforcement and criminal justice. Projects funded by L.E.A.A., which exceed several billion dollars a year, concern court administration, organized crime, white collar crime, public corruption, disorders and terrorism, the rehabilitation of offenders, victim assistance, and the implementation of criminal justice standards and goals.

LAW ENFORCEMENT INTELLIGENCE UNIT (L.E.I.U.). A fraternity of intelligence officers from 225 state and local police departments that gathers and exchanges information, founded in the fifties in California as a tax-exempt charitable organization and therefore not subject to public disclosure laws. Part of its financing originally came from the federal government but it now operates with state and local funds. The unit is rarely mentioned in the press and is unknown to most citizens.

LAW FACTORY. A slang expression for a major law firm whose staff and workload continue to increase at a spectacular rate. In 1963 there were only about ten law firms in the United States which employed more than one hundred lawyers. Today approximately sixty firms are that large, and eleven consist of more than two hundred lawyers. Since 1963, many of the large New York firms have doubled or tripled in size.

LAW FIRM ADMINISTRATOR. Non-lawyers who manage the offices of law firms. The trend to larger firms with as many as fifty or more lawyers, and the increasing value of professional legal time has stimulated the advent of professional Law Firm Administrators, who often possess M.B.A. degrees in management.

LAW FIRM ROLES. One firm describes the various roles as: finders, those who generate business; minders, those who maintain the business generated by the finders; grinders, those who do the actual work; and binders, those who do good work in the community, join various clubs, lecture, attend meetings and enhance the image of the firm generally.

LAW GHOST. Colloquial term for a lawyer who prepares criminal cases for trial, but never appears in court.

L.A.W. INC. See LAY ADVOCATES AT WORK.

LAWLESS CASE. First case ruled on by the European Court of Human Rights, in 1960, which affirmed the right of an international tribunal to hear a complaint of an individual against his own government for a denial of civil rights. Lawless, an alleged member of the Irish Republican Army, was detained without trial by the Irish government. Although the court ruled against Lawless, the importance of the decision is that a citizen's complaint was aired before the court, and the Irish government acknowledged the competence of an international court to decide the case.

LAW OF RETURN. An Israeli law that grants every Jew the right to come ("aliyah") to Israel as an Oleh ("Jewish immigrant"). Under the Israel Nationality Law every Oleh automatically is granted Israeli nationality upon entering the country.

LAW OF ARMED CONFLICT. See LAW OF WAR.

LAW OFFICER. See MILITARY JUDGE.

LAW OFFICE STUDY. A few states such as California, Mississippi, Vermont, Virginia and Washington permit a person to take the Bar Examination after having studied with a lawyer in his office for a minimum period without having graduated from a law school. A few other states such as Maine, New York, Texas and Wyoming permit an applicant to take the Bar Examination without a law degree after having taken some courses in a law school and studying for the balance of the required time in a lawyer's office.

LAWMAKER LOOPHOLES. The elected representatives' practice of adopting important federal or state legislation which applies to everyone but themselves. For example, Congress has exempted itself from numerous laws over the years, including the Civil Rights Act of 1964, Social Security, Freedom of Information, the Equal Opportunity Act, Labor Relations and Occupational Health and Safety Regulations. The New York State Legislature also has exempted itself from various laws, among them the Freedom of Information Law, which enables voters to scrutinize the finances of every government agency in New York, except the State Legislature.

LAW OF THE CASE. The principle that a final judgment of an appellate court will, unless properly set aside, bind the parties at all subsequent stages of the litigation. Enshrined within this principle is the idea that, once a case has been remanded, both the trial court and any subsequent court of appeal shall adhere to the interpretations of the law rendered by the original appellate court.

LAW OF THE JUNGLE. A breakdown of civilization and disappearance of due process in which a "dog-eat-dog" or "every man for himself" policy prevails.

LAW OF THE SEA CONFERENCE. A series of international meetings conducted since 1973 under the sponsorship of the United Nations with representatives from 162 countries. Its purpose is a complete rewriting of the international rules governing the use and exploitation of the planet's nonterritorial waters. It now has before it in draft form a 365-article Law Of The Sea Treaty, affecting the $18 billion-a-year worldwide fishing industry, the rights of maritime powers to free transit of the oceans, explorations for offshore oil and seabed minerals, and the regulation of commercial navigation, pollution and scientific research.

LAW OF THE SEA TREATY. See LAW OF THE SEA CONFERENCE.

LAW OF WAR. An outgrowth of centuries of warfare among nations from which the rules and customs governing the conduct of armed hostilities have developed. It has two branches. The first consists of the four 1949 Geneva Conventions protecting the wounded, sick and shipwrecked prisoners of war and civilians in the hands of an enemy. The International Committee of the Red Cross (I.C.R.C.) had nurtured these Conventions since 1864 when the first Wounded and Sick Convention was adopted. The present Conventions have been signed by 145 countries including the United States. The second branch covers the rules regulating methods and means of warfare. They were last codified in the Hague Conventions of 1907. There was a wide spread recognition in recent years that they were badly in need of updating. In 1949, the United Nations were reluctant to undertake such a project in the belief "that was having been outlawed, the regulation of its conduct has ceased to be relevant." In 1968 the United Nations Conference on Human Rights, meeting in the shadow of Vietnam, decided that updating the Law of War was a suitable project for United Nations attention. In response, the I.C.R.C. undertook a project to update and clarify the four Geneva Conventions as well as to modernize the law dealing with methods and means of warfare. These instruments were to supplement, but not amend, the 1949 Geneva Convention. With the aid of several conferences of government and Red Cross experts, the I.C.R.C. drafted two protocols, the first on international armed conflict and the second on internal armed conflict. These formed the single negotiating texts for a Diplomatic Conference convened by the Swiss government in 1974. After four yearly sessions in Geneva attended by 135 countries, the Conference adopted two protocols to the 1949 Geneva Conventions on June 10, 1977. By January 15, 1979, 64 countries had signed or acceded to Protocol I. All N.A.T.O. countries have signed the protocols. The other signers included a representative number of European, Latin American, African and Asian countries. Greece,

Cyprus, the Philippines and Vietnam signed Protocol I, but declined to sign Protocol II. It is expected that the two Protocols will be submitted to the United States Senate for its advice and consent to ratification sometime in 1980. It is likely that during the Senate's consideration, there will be more public attention than the Protocols have had so far.

LAW POLL. Surveys sponsored by the American Bar Association on current important issues of interest to the public in general and the legal profession in particular. Its findings are published in the *American Bar Association Journal.*

LAW REVIEW. Publication of American law schools. Each issue of a Law Review will typically contain two or three principal or leading articles of about twenty-five pages dealing with a subject of current or historical interest, usually written by well-known law teachers, lawyers or judges. In addition, the Law Review will contain two or three "comments" on current legal problems and five or six "case notes." The comments and case notes are usually prepared by law students under the supervision of the faculty. They summarize, analyze and criticize current judicial opinions. There is complete freedom of expression in the American Law Reviews. They are valuable research tools, but probably their most important function is to improve the quality of the work of the reviewing courts by subjecting their opinions to continuing scrutiny and analysis. It would not be an exaggeration to say that the outstanding feature of American legal education which distinguishes it from the systems of every other country in the world is this concept of a distinguished law magazine edited, sponsored, and published by law students. In fact, law is the only profession in which the learned journals are published by students.

LAW REVIEW DIGEST. See LEGAL PERIODICAL DIGEST.

LAW SCHOOL ADMISSION COUNCIL (L.S.A.C.). An association of law schools organized to facilitate the admissions process. According to its charter of incorporation, the Council's purposes are "to construct, administer, and report scores for tests for admission to law school; to conduct educational research; and to provide services to law schools and the educational community." As the number of applicants has increased, causing law school admissions to become more competitive and complex, so has the range of Council activities expanded to enable all those involved in the process—law schools, applicants and undergraduate institutions—to deal effectively with it. Services and publications are now provided through the Council to assist each of these "client" groups.

LAW SCHOOL ADMISSION TEST. See L.S.A.T.

LAW STORE. Designed to make legal services accessible to the public, this California legal emporium enables consumers to pay $9.95 to consult by telephone with an attorney. For additional fees, customers can purchase telephone advice and preparation of forms for wills, step-parent adoptions, name changes and divorce. The participating attorneys are from Group Legal Services, founded in 1973, which offers legal consultations by telephone for annual fees ranging from $35 to $60. Though many lawyers criticize this concept of a Law Store, other members of the Bar view such a development as inevitable.

LAW STUDENT INTERNSHIP PROGRAM. Awards academic course credit to law students who engage in professional activity in courts, legal aid clinics, prosecutors' offices and similar services, under the supervision of a law professor.

LAWSUIT STOCK. Proposed method of financing lawsuits by selling shares of stock in the potential lawsuit recovery. At least one lawyer has attempted to finance a lawsuit in this manner. Carl Person of New York, offered $5 shares in a $100,000 suit and has registered his offering with the Securities Exchange Commission. Although a New York court has ruled that no law stands in the way of selling interests in a lawsuit, Person has found no buyers for his Lawsuit Stock.

LAW TWENTY-TWO (22). A statute enacted by Puerto Rico in 1976 which allows the police to stop people arriving to the Island from the mainland United States and search their possessions without a search warrant, thereby creating a de facto international border. Some authorities state the law is an unconstitutional violation of the Fourth Amendment and the Supreme Court so held in 1979.

LAWYER REFERRAL SERVICES. A system of matching up of people who have legal problems with lawyers who are willing to take referred clients. It is a partial solution to the problem of those people, mainly middle-class, who neither qualify for free legal assistance, nor can afford to retain a regular attorney to handle their personal or business affairs, and do not know where to go for help when they need legal advice. There are currently more than 270 such services nationwide and at least 25 in New York City. By making a toll free telephone call, someone in need of help can make an appointment with a qualified local attorney for a half-hour consultation at a fixed nominal fee. Neither the lawyer nor the client is under any obligation to continue the relationship after the initial consultation. In Virginia, for example, in 1977 the local Lawyer Referral Service received 15,589 calls from persons seeking help and referred 8,600 of them to participating lawyers for a half-hour consultation. Approximately 1,500 lawyers, or roughly 20 percent of the practicing bar in Virginia, enrolled in the program in 1977 and processed 7,000 inquiries from the public. The fee paid by the Virginia lawyer to participate in the program was $15 a year and the fee paid by the client for the initial half-hour consultation was likewise $15.

LAWYERS' COMMITTEE FOR CIVIL RIGHTS UNDER LAW. Founded in 1963 at the request of President John F. Kennedy in order to involve the leadership of the American legal profession in the Civil Rights Movement, which was then sweeping the South. After a meeting at the White House, a group of prominent lawyers, including past Presidents of the American Bar Association and former Attorneys General of the United States, formed the Committee and set up offices in Washington, D.C. and Jackson, Mississippi. They then raised funds from the legal community to staff these offices with full-time lawyers. However, substantial voluntary representation by lawyers constituted the core of the efforts of the Committee, as it still does. The Lawyers' Committee now has full-time staff lawyers in its national office in Washington, D.C. and in major cities across the country, complemented by a growing voluntary involvement of the bar. The Committee participates in hundreds of civil rights cases throughout the country each year.

LAWYERS COMMITTEE FOR INTERNATIONAL HUMAN RIGHTS. A group of 1,600 young lawyers formed in 1975 in New York who volunteer their professional services to monitor and redress violations of human rights around the world.

LAWYER'S DREAM. Just enough law to keep all the loopholes in place.

LAWYER'S HISTORY. History shaped to sustain points in a lawyer's brief before a court.

LAWYER SOLICITATION. Although Lawyers have the right to advertise, traditionally the profession does not allow its members to solicit clients the way bankers or stockbrokers do. The ban on solicitation apparently originated in England, where English barristers did not want to compete with each other and act as "ordinary tradesmen." Recently the prohibition against solicitation has come under fire by lawyers in this country who believe it violates their First Amendment right of free speech. Ralph Nader's Public Citizens Inc. and the National Resource Center for Consumers of Legal Services, two groups seeking reform of the legal system, maintain that an outright ban on solicitation does not distinguish between helpful and harmful solicitations. An example of the former, according to these groups, is the case of South Carolina attorney, Edna Smith, who offered by letter to represent a welfare mother, sterilized after her third child by a doctor who refused to deliver the baby if she didn't agree to the procedure. Smith was reprimanded by her State Bar Association for solicitation, however, the Supreme Court of the United States held in 1978, that prohibitions against solicitation do not apply to public interest lawyers such as Ms. Smith.

LAWYERS' PECKING ORDER. A recent study of 777 Chicago lawyers revealed a definite Pecking Order. Big business lawyers were seen as most prestigious while those who dealt with individual clients—family, poverty, divorce, landlord-tenant relations, and consumer law—were viewed at the bottom of the social-prestige scale. Criminal lawyers, labor, environmental and civil rights advocates fell somewhere in the middle. Civil rights advocates, while not particularly "prestigious," were considered the most ethical of all lawyer groups.

LAWYERS' RELIEF BILL. A tongue-in-cheek reference to E.R.I.S.A., a law passed by Congress that is so complex and ambiguous, it will support thousands of lawyers for generations to come.

LAWYERS REPORTS ANNOTATED. See L.R.A.

LAWYER'S SYNDROME. A term coined by psychologists to describe an attorney's difficulty in solving his own personal emotional problems. It is supposed to be caused by an educational training of an intellectual and analytical nature. We lawyers like to reduce everything to neat packages with logical solutions to clear issues based on objective facts. An inability to do so, especially in marriage, where the other partner may be concerned more with "feelings" whereas we are prone to deal with "relevance," may lead to an injury to if not a breakdown of the relationship.

LAY ADVOCATES AT WORK (L.A.W. INC.). A private organization started by a Maine widow after she had paid $50,000 in legal fees to four different law firms, who nonetheless failed to settle her deceased husband's estate. It assists those who have complaints against lawyers in filing their grievance with the appropriate state bar disciplinary authorities.

LAY ASSESSORS (Peoples' Assessors). Two Russian non-lawyers who sit with a judge to perform a role similar to an American jury but with more control and power in the disposition of the case. They are thus really law judges.

L.D.C. (Less-Developed Country; Under-Developed Country; Third World Country). Those nations in Asia, Africa and South America whose economic and educational standards are substantially lower than the nations of Europe and North America from whom they receive Foreign Aid financial assistance in order to increase their G.N.P. (Gross National Product) and thereby raise their standard of living.

L.D.F. (Legal Defense and Educational Fund). Originally part of the N.A.A.C.P. in 1939, but now independent, and formerly under the direction of incumbent Justice of the Supreme Court Thurgood Marshall, this is a group of lawyers which has a high rate of success in serving as counsel in hundreds of civil rights cases involving employment, education, housing and prisons.

L.E.A.A. See LAW ENFORCEMENT ASSISTANCE ADMINISTRATION.

LEAD COUNSEL. The lawyer selected by the other attorneys in a complex case, each of whom represents a different client, when the attorneys want one of themselves to speak for all of them on a matter of common mutual interest.

LEADING CASE (Landmark Decision). An important judicial decision which is so sound in its reasoning and result that it has become a legal landmark and is frequently cited and relied upon by other courts.

LEADING QUESTION. Suggests a desired answer to the witness. For instance, "It was cold that morning, wasn't it?" is leading, whereas "Was it cold that morning?" is not. Since a party's own witnesses are more likely to be susceptible to suggestion than the witnesses called by the opposing party, leading questions are generally allowed during cross-examination but not during direct examination. If, however, the witness undergoing direct examination is a hostile witness, leading questions are allowed.

LEADING THE WITNESS. See LEADING QUESTION.

LEAGUE OF NATIONS (1919-1947). Inspired by President Wilson, the League of Nations represents the first attempt to found an international political institution with worldwide authority. A result of the First World War, it aspired to restore and maintain peace throughout the world through international cooperation. Located in Geneva, the League included (1) a Council, which played a predominant role, (2) an Assembly, and (3) a Permanent Secretariat. None of these organs was empowered with a supranational authority, as the member countries refused to surrender part of their national sovereignty. The only power of the League was to submit recommendations, which had no binding powers upon its members. Thus the League could not prevent World War II. The first political obstacle encountered by the League of Nations was the refusal by the United States Senate to ratify the Treaty of Versailles, and its decision to sign a separate Peace Treaty with Germany. The United States thus never joined the League of Nations, and her absence undermined from the start the organization's chances of success. The withdrawal of Germany, Japan, and Italy, and the expulsion of the Soviet Union were preludes to World War II. The principles on which the League was constructed did not allow it to function efficiently. Only certain types of war were condemned, and there was no absolute interdiction denying the members resort to war. The members were not obliged to submit their disputes to the pacific settlement procedure of the League. They had the option of referring their cases either to an international tribunal or to the Council, but in most instances did not agree to do so. In any event, the Council's power was only one of recommendation, counting on the members' goodwill and cooperation. The whole procedure for pacific settlement was weak. The covenant provided for mutual assistance if the members resorted to war in violation of the covenant, but there was no obligation to take military sanctions. The Council could also recommend economic sanctions, but as Emperor Haile Sellassie prophesied when the League failed to act against Mussolini when Italy invaded Ethiopia in 1935, the League was doomed to die. The League of Nations, however, helped solve small conflicts and participated in the reconstruction of Austria and Hungary. The most important achievement of the League was the creation in 1920 of the Permanent Court of International Justice, which was construed under its auspices. It also sponsored the Kellogg-Briand Pact in 1928. The League of Nations finally had a decisive psychological impact; it showed the possibility and the need for an international organization and set a framework for it.

LEAGUE OF WOMEN VOTERS. Public service organization organized in 1920 as an outgrowth of the National American Woman Suffrage Association. Founded to educate American women in the intelligent use of the ballot, the League has since broadened its scope to deal with the full range of legal, political, economic and social issues. In 1974 the League first voted to accept males as full members. It distributes information on candidates and issues, campaigns to increase registration and voting, and offers courses in politics. Though the League does not support or oppose candidates or political parties, it does study local, state and national political issues and takes positions if there is a consensus among the membership. It now has more than 100,000 members.

LEAST RESTRICTIVE ALTERNATIVE. A constitutional principle requiring that a legal curtailment of individual rights be executed in a manner which affords the highest deference to individual liberties consistent with the legitimate state objective. From the perspective of mental health law, the term is synonymous with outpatient and intermediate care facilities. Implementation of this ideal has been hindered by the reluctance of local communities to accept responsibility for those individuals previously warehoused in state institutions. The high cost of mental health care is at least partially responsible. In *Lake v. Cameron*, 364 F.2d 657 (1966), where a senile but non-dangerous woman was sent to St. Elizabeth's Hospital, the court held that the state had the responsibility to search out alternative courses of treatment and that a transfer of the burden to the patient is both unfair and inefficient.

LEE TAI-YOUNG. See MYONGDONG DECLARATION.

LEE v. SMITH. See S.S.I.

LEFT-HANDED MARRIAGE. See MORGANATIC MARRIAGE.

LEGAL ACTION CENTER. A public-interest law firm with a major commitment to opening up opportunities for employment to persons suffering from discrimination by reason of a history of drug abuse.

LEGAL ADVICE CENTER. An individual or group of lawyers who try to do privately what an organized Bar Association Lawyer Referral Service can do better, in screening inquiries by members of the public on whether or not they have a legal problem and if so who could handle it professionally and at what cost.

LEGAL AFFAIRS MANUAL. In the fall of 1976, the Law School Admission Council and the Association of American Law Schools (A.A.L.S.) joined in publishing the Legal Affairs Manual. It contains a checklist of the impact of federal statutes and regulations on the operations of law schools, memoranda analyzing the impact of particular statutes and regulations on law schools and suggesting the ways in which these schools might respond, the pertinent federal statutes and regulations, and a litigation bulletin summarizing state and federal cases of particular interest to legal education. The Manual and its supplements are distributed without cost to schools that are members of the Law School Admission Council, which includes all A.A.L.S. member schools. The annual subscription rate for others is $50 for the original binder and $25 for up-dated service.

LEGAL AID ON WHEELS (Older American Legal Action Center; O.A. L.A.C.). An innovative program just launched in Dallas, Texas, which is a law office in a mobile van. It visits senior citizens in nursing houses in order to make legal advice available to shut-ins, especially in the field of estate planning, domestic relations and consumer fraud.

LEGAL AMERICAN CENTER. Opened in early December, 1978, this is the first law office in the country to open in a basement of a department store dispensing legal advice at advertised "rock bottom prices" seven days a week.

LEGAL ASSISTANCE TREATY. An agreement between Switzerland and the United States executed on January 23, 1977, whereby the former agreed to send all records and money in its private secret bank accounts to the latter upon proof that the accounts had been established from the proceeds of criminal activity such as prostitution, gambling or narcotics violations.

LEGAL CLINICS. Cut-rate legal firms which offer lower prices to middle class consumers by advertising to produce a high volume of business and by using standarized forms for routine legal services. A study conducted by the University of Miami School of Law contends that such Legal Clinics do not necessarily sacrifice quality of service for quantity of business.

LEGAL COMMON TRUST FUND. A Common Trust arrangement which invests wholly in property according to the laws of a given state where the Common Trust is administered. Usually this term describes trust funds which exist in states that have statutory or judicially approved lists for trust investment. Such lists regulate trustees in their investment authority when the trust arrangement itself is silent on this issue.

LEGAL COMPUTER TECHNOLOGY. The use of modern electronic data processing equipment in litigation support, document preparation, billing, legal research and information retrieval to make the practice of law more efficient.

LEGAL DEFENSE AND EDUCATION FUND. See L.D.F.

LEGAL EMBEZZLEMENT. The payment to union officials of full salaries by each of the several different unions they represent. Such practice, which resulted in individual salaries as high as $350,-000 in 1976, is not prohibited by federal labor law.

LEGAL FEATHERBEDDING. Any excess or abuse in the legal system whether in padded fees, delayed access to justice, light sentencing or unnecessary red tape and bureaucracy. The term was first coined nationally by President Carter in his devastating attack on the legal profession in a speech he delivered in Los Angeles on May 4, 1978.

LEGAL FEE ARBITRATION BOARD. First established in 1974 in Massachusetts and since adopted elsewhere, it is an arbitration procedure by lawyers who hear disputes between clients and their counsel over the size of the fee charged. Factors used to calculate a reasonable fee when no prior agreement was made between the parties at the beginning of the case include the difficulty of the case, the number and length of conferences, the number of court appearances, the amount of research required, the amount of money at stake, and the expertise and experience of the lawyer.

LEGAL FICTIONS. Used in law to reconcile a legal result with some premise or postulate about behavior. For example, a recipient of a gift is presumed to have accepted it even though he was totally unaware a gift had been given him. This legal fiction reconciles the legal principle that title to property cannot pass without a person's consent, with the behavioral premise that most people want to accept gifts. Another example is the Attractive Nuisance Doctrine which holds a landowner responsible for injuries to trespassing children when they are "attracted" to his land by some object such as a deserted house. The legal fiction is that the landowner "invited" the children onto his land by maintaining an attractive nuisance. This fiction is necessary to protect children, for ordinarily landowners are under no responsibility to trespassers unless they are invited onto the land.

LEGAL GIMMICK. Any devious but legal solution to a client's problem.

LEGAL GOLD. The highly lucrative practice of law in Washington, D.C., to service the ever-proliferating number of complex laws and regulations spawned by the federal government each year. More and more law firms from all over the country and some from abroad are opening branch offices in the nation's capitol.

LEGAL GOOD HOUSEKEEPING SEAL OF APPROVAL. Sardonic reference to the vast power of the A.B.A. to grant or deny accreditation to a law school.

LEGAL GUILT. Based on a factual determination that a defendant committed the offense with which he is charged, together with strict adherence to the procedural and substantive safeguards guaranteed by law to one accused of crime. Failure of any one of these elements will result in a determination of legal innocence.

LEGAL HEADHUNTER. A private individual or firm which serves as an employment placement agency for a fee, to recommend experienced and specialized lawyers to firms or corporations in search of suitable professional legal counsel.

LEGAL LIST. State-approved investments in which certain banks and insurance companies are allowed to invest without being held liable if the investment decreases in value. In some states a fiduciary can invest only in investments on the list. Because of the fiduciary responsibility owed by the investor, these lists are limited to high-grade securities posing minimal risks.

LEGAL MALPRACTICE. The failure of an attorney in the discharge of his duties to his client to use that degree of professional skill and diligence used by other attorneys in similar circumstance in which event the attorney can be disciplined professionally or held personally liable for any loss sustained by the client.

LEGAL PERIODICAL DIGEST *(Law Review Digest).* A bi-monthly periodical of the American Bar Association that publishes detailed abstracts of articles concerning the law from diverse legal publications. The *Digest,* which emphasizes the practical aspects of law practice, also contains an index of other articles not abstracted. It is indexed bi-monthly by subject and cumulated annually.

LEGAL PERSONA. Persona was the name of a mask worn by an actor in ancient Greek drama to signify the role that he played. Legal persona is the myth that lawyers have certain special characteristics that set them above and apart as a group. Law school professors, for example, love to say that they are training their students to "think like a lawyer" or to "speak like a lawyer," which of course is conceited nonsense.

LEGAL POLLUTION. The dark side of the American legal system when it is characterized by expensive fees, inadequate representation, protracted litigation, incompetent judges, corrupt jurors, delayed justice or any other abuse by the rich and powerful at the expense of the poor and weak.

LEGAL POSITIVISM (Command Theory; Imperative Theory of Law). Emphasizes that law is a set of positive rules that people must follow and that courts must uphold. No discretion exists to refuse to adhere to these rules. Laws are expressions by one person that another person should or should not engage in some act, accompanied by a threat of punishment likely to follow disobedience. A rule is a law if it is general and, secondly, if it is promulgated by a person or group who receives habitual obedience from most of society.

LEGAL REALISM. A school of jurisprudence which emerged in the 1930s. Its major spokesman in the United States was Karl Llewellyn. Legal realism is based on several tenets, the first and most important being that law is a judicially-created mechanism, a product of human decision-making and personality and, therefore, necessarily fluctuates. Additionally, realists believe law is a means to social ends and not an end in itself. A third principle holds that society fluctuates faster than the law and, consequently, the law must be re-examined constantly to determine if it fulfills the social purpose it purports to serve. Lastly, realists stress the distinction between what law is and what it ought to be. Observers must concentrate on what courts are doing, not on what they ought to be doing; jurists must apply the law as it is, not as they believe it ought to be. According to realists, the conclusion to be drawn from all of these principles is that it is nearly impossible to predict accurately what courts will do and that traditional legal rules are illusory.

LEGAL RETRIBUTIVISM. A philosophy of punishment. Its central tenet is that criminals should suffer sanctions equal to and no greater than the measure of their crime. This concept derives from the Biblical teaching that one who causes harm must give an "eye for an eye. . . ." The Code of Hammurabi incorporated retributivism. Immanuel Kant represents the archetype of modern retributivism. He argued that only those who have voluntarily and knowingly violated legal rules can be punished, that the degree of punishment should match the offense, and that an evil-for-evil scheme is morally permissible, if not mandatory, and needs no further justification. Retributivism often is attacked as allowing "savage" punishment. In an historical context, however, it must be seen as a humanizing gain over unlimited retaliation.

LEGAL RUNNERS. Generally, hospital employees or jail workers who are paid to send cases to a lawyer. This practice is condemned by the legal profession because it involves solicitation of clients, and because lawyers are not permitted to split their fees with non-lawyers.

LEGAL SERVICES CORPORATION (L.S.C.). Chartered by Congress in 1974 to provide financial support for organizations which help the needy obtain legal services. The Corporation's predecessor, the Office of Legal Services (O.L.S.), was formed in 1965 and quickly drew criticism from conservatives for its involvement in busing, draft resistance, and abortion cases. In response, Congress abolished the O.L.S. and created the L.S.C., with regulations prohibiting the use of L.S.C. funds for such controversial purposes. Despite these regulations, however, the L.S.C. has financed liberal causes, such as the suit by the Passamaquoddy and Penobscot Indians to reclaim two thirds of the state of Maine. It supports hundreds of legal service programs throughout the country and is governed by an 11 member Board appointed by the President.

LEGAL SERVICES FOR CHILDREN. A San Francisco legal clinic opened in 1975 to provide free legal services for juvenile offenders who frequently have lost contact with their families. The clinic is funded by a local foundation and is comprised of 3 attorneys and 3 paralegals. The legal goal is often locating an alternative to reform school, a task which the clinic's orientation toward personal attention accomplishes more effectively than their overworked counterparts in traditional legal aid societies.

LEGAL SINOLOGIST. An American lawyer who speaks Chinese and specializes in the Chinese legal system. In 1979, only a dozen attorneys were so qualified and with the new policy of normalization between the two superpowers, thousands of others are desperately needed.

LEGAL SUPERMARKETS. See LEGAL CLINICS.

LEGAL TENDER. Any exchange medium required by law to be accepted as payment for a debt. Article I, section 10 of the United States Constitution grants the federal government sovereign power to determine the nature of legal tender. The Supreme Court in 1871 upheld congressional power to issue paper money as legal tender as a substitute for gold or silver coin.

LEGAL TENDER CASES. A series of Supreme Court cases dealing with the constitutionality of the Legal Tender Act of 1862. The Act authorized the government to issue $150 million in notes, "greenbacks," which were not backed by either silver or gold. The Act was declared unconstitutional in 1870, but in the following year the Court reversed itself, upholding the Act's validity as a constitutional means of borrowing money.

LEGAL TIMES OF WASHINGTON. A national weekly newspaper published in Washington, D.C., beginning in 1978, containing recent legal information of interest to lawyers, especially on the maze of federal regulations.

LEGAL UTILITARIANISM. According to this school of legal philosophy, punishment can be justified only as a deterrent or reforming influence upon individuals and society. Sanctions should be only as severe as necessary to deter the specific crime and to reform the character of the actual criminal. The theory proceeds on the principle that law ought to maximize the greatest good for the greatest number of people. Consequently, punishment, which is itself an evil, ought to be levied only insofar as it prevents some greater evil. It serves no purpose where it is groundless, inefficacious, too expensive, or needless. Jeremy Bentham and John Austin are the two most prominent legal utilitarians.

LEGISLATIVE CONTEMPT. See CONTEMPT OF COURT.

LEGISLATIVE COURT. A court created not under Article III of the Constitution but by Congress in the exercise of its general legislative powers under Article I of the Constitution. Legislative courts, not empowered to hear cases of a "judicial" nature, are confined to matters which are largely administrative or executive in nature. Moreover, judges on a legislative court are not protected by the Constitutional provisions concerning tenure for good behavior and assurance against diminution of compensation while in office, as are their brethren on Constitutional courts. It was originally thought that all territorial courts of the United States, District of Columbia courts, and certain other courts, such as the court of claims, were beyond the judicial power of the United States and thus could be only legislative courts. This status occasionally caused confusion, especially where judges on legislative courts were assigned to hear and decide cases on constitutional matters. Recent decisions and legislation, however, have broadened the scope of Constitutional courts so that the only remaining legislative courts are the United States Tax Court and courts in territories of the United States.

LEGISLATIVE DAY. The politician's way of measuring time. A legislative day may actually span several calendar days; it begins with a formal call to order and ends with a formal adjournment. Recesses called at the end of each calendar day permit legislators to organize their time as the rest of us do.

LEGISLATIVE EXPULSION. The power of a legislative chamber to expel a member for misconduct. Article I, section 5 of the United States Constitution grants each chamber of the Congress the power to expel a member by a two-thirds vote. Most state constitutions contain similar provisions. Grounds for expulsion include moral turpitude, disloyalty, and unbecoming conduct. Because popular sentiment provides a generally effective check on unseemly behavior, legislatures rarely invoke the expulsion sanction.

LEGISLATIVE HISTORY. The written record created when a legislature passes a law. It may be used by a court in interpreting the law to ascertain or detail the intent of the legislature if the Act is ambiguous or lacking in detail. For federal laws, the legislative history is listed in the Slip Law and consists of the House, Senate and Joint Committee Reports if any, and the House and Senate floor debates on the law. The history often contains the only available complete explanation of the meaning and intent of the law.

LEGISLATIVE IMMUNITY. Protects a legislator from being held liable civilly or criminally for any statement or action made in an official capacity on or off the floor of the legislature.

LEGISLATIVE POWERS. The lawmaking authority granted to a legislature and specifically granted to Congress by Article I, section 1 of the United States Constitution including the powers to collect taxes, regulate interstate commerce, declare war, raise military forces, borrow and coin money, and create patents and copyrights. Congress also creates the administrative agencies through which the Executive branch implements congressional statutes.

LEGISLATIVE RE-APPORTIONMENT (One Man—One Vote). Response to population growth or other change within a political entity to insure equal political representation. The failure of many states to respond to the increase in population from 1900-1960 resulted in gross malapportionment of representatives among voters. Reliance on outdated census reports and use of geographic and economic apportionment schemes often gave rural counties as many representatives in the state legislature as the more populous urban districts. The practical effect was to give some voters more voting "weight" through their greater representation in the Legislature. As recently as 1962, in *Baker v. Carr*, 369 U.S. 186 (1962), the Supreme Court had refused to review apportionment schemes, contending they were not justiciable matters. In 1964, the "one man—one vote" concept was articulated in *Reynolds v. Sims*, 377 U.S. 533 (1964), which invalidated an Alabama apportionment system on Equal Protection grounds. Population was to be the determinative factor in apportioning representatives, and states were to create districting schemes which gave the same number of representatives to equal numbers of constituents.

LEGISLATIVE RULES. Administrative enactments made pursuant to a grant of law-making power by the Congress. Legislative Rules have the same force as statutes as long as they are constitutional, are adequately grounded in statutory authority, and have been developed in accordance with proper procedures. Judicial review is confined to monitoring these requirements and may not concern the content of the Rules. The nature of issues involved in Legislative Rules suggests a compromise of competing values based on social and economic facts not susceptible to detailed proof in a judicial proceeding. Examples of Legislative Rules are the Federal Trade Commission's edict that gasoline stations post octane rating numbers on gas pumps, and the Department of Transportation mandate that all passenger cars manufactured for sale in this country after January 1, 1969, be factory equipped with front seat head restraints which meet specific federal standards.

LEGISLATIVE VETO. A practice that allows the Congress or some part of it (one House or even one committee, depending on how the veto clause is worded in the bill under consideration) to block a federal executive or agency action within a specified time period, usually sixty or ninety working days. Not cast as a statute, the veto needs neither the signature of the President nor, if it is a one house veto, the concurrence of the other chamber. Such a provision appears hundreds of times in hundreds of pieces of legislation now on the books covering such diverse matters as Federal Election Commission Regulations, international arms sales, Office of Education rule-making and most executive reorganizations. The Legislative Veto turns a chamber of Congress, or the relevant committee, into a political court of last resort. President Carter has denounced the practice as an "infringement on the executive's constitutional duty to faithfully execute the laws."

LEGITIMATION STATUTE. See ACKNOWLEDGMENT OF CHILD.

L.E.I.U. See LAW ENFORCEMENT INTELLIGENCE UNIT.

LESS DEVELOPED COUNTRY. See L.D.C.

LESTER RULE. A tax regulation under which an ex-wife pays the income tax on the gross amount paid to her by her former husband for her support and that of her children. If she wishes to pay the income tax solely on the amount for her own support, this must be expressly separated out by the alimony decree of the court or the contractual provision of the property settlement.

LETTER CONTRACT. In federal government contracting, this written preliminary contractual arrangement authorizes immediate commencement of performance pending negotiation of a definitive contract.

LETTER OF ADMINISTRATION. A certificate issued by a court certifying that the named administrator is authorized to administer an estate.

LETTER RULING. See TAX RULING.

LETTERS ROGATORY. A formal written communication by one court to a court in another jurisdiction, requesting that the testimony of a witness residing in the foreign jurisdiction be taken upon interrogatories which accompany the request. The testimony is taken in the foreign jurisdiction and forwarded to the requesting court. This discovery technique is applicable to interstate and international lawsuits.

LETTERS TESTAMENTARY. Issued by a probate court, empowering an executor to administer an estate.

LEVELLERS MOVEMENT. Dissenters in 17th-century England who were fined and imprisoned for their "radical" beliefs of decentralization of government, power to the House of Commons rather than to the King, and equality before the law. The name "Levellers" was coined by their opponents who feared the movement intended to level men's estates.

LEVERAGE BUY-OUT. The sale of substantially all the assets of a company for cash to a privately-held corporation often composed of shareholder/managers of the former public firm. The private company finances the acquisition largely with borrowed funds, the payment of which is secured by the newly-acquired assets. The private company enters into the transaction with the intention of continuing in the same line of business and usually under the same name of the former public company. Typically, the private company employs the managers of the liquidating public company under long-term employment contracts.

LEVERAGE CONTRACT. A lay-away arrangement through which investors make regular payments toward the ultimate purchase of gold, silver, diamonds and other valuable items strictly regulated by the Commodity Futures Trading Commission.

LEVIATHAN'S SOVEREIGNTY. See HOBBES, THOMAS.

LEX FORI (Latin—law of the forum). The law of the jurisdiction in which a court sits. At common law, the Lex Fori where the suit is brought is the law applicable to all matters concerning remedy, rather than the law concerning substantive rights. Thus, Lex Fori is a Choice of Law principle designed to simplify the ascertainment of the applicable law and to allow the forum to use familiar and customary procedures and forms.

LEXIMATIC SERVICE. A computerized system of document control created in 1973 to replace manual document management in litigation in order to streamline the administration of trial court justice.

L.E.X.I.S. See COMPUTER-ASSISTED LEGAL RESEARCH.

LEX SITUS (Lex Rei sitae) (Latin—law of the locality of the thing). A Choice of Law principle which provides that any litigation concerning real property must be governed by the law of the jurisdiction where the property is situated. Thus, if Able, a domiciliary of state X, dies intestate, leaving property in state Y, the courts in state X will apply the intestate succession laws of state Y in the determination of the distribution of the property in state Y.

L.H.C.A. See LONGSHOREMEN'S AND HARBOR WORKERS' COMPENSATION ACT.

LIBEL AND SLANDER. The twin torts which constitute character defamation. Libel is defamation appearing in a written or printed form while slander is usually oral. The distinction, however, is not based so much on the written/oral dichotomy as it is on the permanence of the communication. Thus photographs, statutes and motion pictures constitute libel. Gestures, on the other hand, are slander. Because libel's permanence is thought to make it more serious, courts will presume damages. For slander, however, the plaintiffs must generally prove actual damages before they will be entitled to recover.

LIBERTY BELL. One of the greatest symbols of freedom in the United States. Ordered in 1752 by the Pennsylvania provincial council for the golden jubilee of Penn's Charter of Privileges of 1701 and cast in England, it cracked when it was tested shortly after its arrival and was immediately successfully recast in Philadelphia from the same metal. The Bell weighs about 2,080 pounds and had only a $300 price tag on it when it came from England. On the Bell is this appropriate inscription, taken from the Old Testament: "Proclaim Liberty throughout the land unto all the inhabitants thereof." The Bell was rung in 1776 when the Declaration of Independence was signed, and on each successive anniversary until July 8, 1835, when it cracked while being rung during the funeral of John Marshall, the second Chief Justice of the Supreme Court of the United States. In 1839 the Bell became known as the Liberty Bell, a name given it by Abolitionists. Before that time it had been called the Old State House Bell, the Bell of the Revolution or Old Independence. Although the Liberty Bell is no longer rung, it has been sounded on a number of special occasions. On June 6, 1944, for example, when the Allied forces successfully landed in France, the city fathers in Philadelphia struck the bell. Sound equipment broadcast the tone to all parts of the nation.

L.I.B.O.R. (London Interbank Offered Rate). The rate of interest charged by one bank in London which makes a loan to another bank in London. It in effect is the "prime" rate for interest in the international financial world.

LIBRARY OF CONGRESS. Established under the federal law approved April 24, 1800, appropriating $5,000 "for the purchase of such books as may be necessary for the use of Congress." The Library's scope of responsibility has since been widened by subsequent legislation. The Librarian, appointed by the President with the advice and consent of the Senate, directs the Library. Thomas Jefferson sold his personal library to the government to start its Library since he needed the money to stave off bankruptcy. Supported mainly by the appropriations of Congress, the Library also has the use of the income from funds received from foundations and other private sources and administered by the Library of Congress Trust Fund Board; it has the use also of gifts of money presented for direct application. Under the law, the Library's first responsibility is service to Congress. One department, the Congressional Research Service, functions exclusively for the legislative branch of the government. As the Library has developed, its range of service has come to include the entire governmental establishment in all its branches and the public at large, so that it has become a national library for the United States. Since 1870, the Library has been responsible for the business of copyrighting, which is now carried on through the Copyright Office. Works subject to copyrighting and copyright renewal include books, periodicals, dramatic and musical compositions, maps, works of art and reproductions of a work of art, photographs, prints, or labels used for articles of merchandise, motion pictures, and sound recordings.

LIBSON SHOPS DOCTRINE. A tax rule concerning the carry-over of net operating losses where business enterprises have merged. Enunciated by the Supreme Court in the 1957 *Libson Shops* Case, 353 U.S. 382 (1957), this doctrine holds that the net operating losses of one merger party carry over to the surviving corporation only to the extent that income is earned after the merger by the business enterprise that suffered the loss. The *Libson Shops* principle was expanded by the courts to require a continuity of ownership as well as a continuity of business enterprise. The vitality of the *Libson Shops* Doctrine is now uncertain. Though the 1954 Code limited the principle, the Internal Revenue Service continues to apply it to disallow certain net operating loss carry-overs. The Service has announced it will rely on the *Libson Shops* Doctrine in any case involving a net operating loss carry-over where there has been less than a 50 percent shift in the benefits of the net operating loss carry-over. But the determination of what constitutes a shift in benefits will be accomplished on a case-by-case basis.

LIE DETECTOR. See POLYGRAPH TESTIMONY.

LIFE BENEFICIARY. See LIFE TRUST BENEFICIARY and TRUST BENEFICIARY.

LIFEBLOOD OF ADMINISTRATIVE PROCESS. Informal discretionary action. Despite the fact that formal adjudication, rule-making and judicial review represent the core of modern American administrative law, informal agency action, which is not reviewed, is responsible for the vast bulk of the effects of the administrative process. The description of lifeblood of administrative process was conceived by the Attorney General's Committee on Administrative Procedure in 1941. Among the activities aptly denoted as informal are investigating, prosecuting, negotiating, settling, advising, threatening, recommending and supervising.

LIFE ESTATE. An estate in land whose duration is determined by the life or lives of one or more persons. If property is given "To X for life," a life estate is created measured by the life of X.

LIFE ESTATE "PUR AUTRE VIE" (French—by another life). A life estate whose duration is determined by the life of a person other than the life tenant. If property is given "To X for the life of Y," the life estate of X will terminate when Y dies.

LIFE TENANT. The person who possesses a life estate.

LIFE TRUST BENEFICIARY (Life Beneficiary). A trust beneficiary entitled to receive trust benefits as long as he lives. However, he cannot assign, bequeath or otherwise dispose of his interest. Such an interest in a trust arrangement can either be for the life of the trust beneficiary or for the life of some other person designated by the trust settlor.

LIMITATION OF COST CLAUSE. This required clause for all Department of Defense cost-reimbursement contracts limits the government's legal obligation to the estimated cost of contract performance and allows a contractor to stop performance when available funds have been expended. It also requires the contractor to notify the contracting officer when performance costs approach the estimated cost of performance.

LIMITATION OVER (Gift Over). An estate or interest in property, generally real property, which is created by a deed or will and which arises upon the termination of the interest first granted by the instrument. Such termination is provided for or contemplated in the deed or will and the limitation over specifies the subsequent disposition of the property. Thus, if O grants a life estate to X, with the remainder interest in A, that remainder is a limitation over.

LIMITED LIABILITY. The liability of each corporate associate, for obligations arising from the common business enterprise, is normally limited to his agreed contribution to the capital of the corporation. No matter how large a debt the corporation may incur, the shareholders may not be required to go into their own pockets to meet it. In return for this rare privilege, most states require the shareholders to contribute a stipulated fund permanently to the enterprise. This fund is to protect corporate creditors by creating an excess of assets over liabilities in case of subsequent corporate failure. This protective money fund is called capital stock and may not be deliberately reduced.

LIMITED PARTNERSHIP. A partnership formed under a limited partnership statute and consisting of one or more general partners and one or more limited partners. A limited partner differs from a general partner in the following respects: (1) He enjoys limited liability; (2) He does not participate in the control of the business; (3) He may not contribute services to the business although he may contribute money; and (4) He has priority upon liquidation over general partners in the net assets of the firm. Such partnerships must be created according to the formalities required by the limited partnership statute. These generally include the filing of a limited partnership certificate which states the name of the business, the nature of the business, the names of all partners and their contributions, and other relevant information. Some states, such as New York, require publication of this certificate. Substantial compliance in good faith with the statute is all that is required to form a valid limited partnership. In forming a limited partnership, one should not include the name of a limited partner in the firm name or else he will lose his limited liability.

LIMITED TERM MARRIAGES. Alternative form of marriage suggested by law reformers which would last a specified term, such as three years, and could be renewed for specified periods or an indefinite term. If the marriage partners did not want to continue their relationship beyond its expiration date, they could simply separate. In 1971, a bill proposing a three-year limited term marriage was introduced unsuccessfully in the Maryland general assembly.

LIMITED-TEST-BAN TREATY OF 1963. An international agreement, to which the United States is a party, that prohibits the tests of nuclear weapons in the atmosphere, in outer space and underwater. Two nuclear world powers, France and China, were not among the 103 signatories so they are free to experiment at will (which they in fact do).

LINCOLN'S INN. See INNS OF COURT.

LINDBERGH LAW. See RANSOM PAYMENT.

LINDSEY, BEN. A lawyer who wrote a book entitled *Companionate Marriage*, in 1929, about the cohabitation relationship in lieu of a legal marriage of so many young people today, which has various names such as live-in lover, temporary living arrangement, covivants.

LINE LAW. The other line moves faster. This applies to all lines—in banks, supermarkets, toll booths, customs and so on. And don't try to change lines. The other line—the one you were in originally—will then move more quickly. By Barbara Ettore in *Harper's Magazine*, August 1974.

LINE-UP. A pre-trial procedure in which a witness is shown a group of persons and asked to identify the one who committed the crime. If judicial proceedings have been initiated, the defendant has the right to counsel at a line-up to assure that the line-up is not overly suggestive.

LISTING ARRANGEMENTS. Determine the rights between a seller of real estate and his real estate broker. An Open Listing gives the seller the right to employ any number of brokers or to sell the property himself without the aid of a broker. An Exclusive Agency Listing still retains the right of the seller to sell the property himself, but also gives only one broker the authority to act as the seller's agent. An Exclusive Right to Sell Agreement voids the seller's right to sell the property himself and gives that right to one broker. A Multiple Listing Agreement is similar to an Exclusive Right to Sell Agreement. However, all brokers who belong to the multiple listing organization also have a right to sell the property. Finally, a Net Listing gives the seller a net amount for the property, but allows the broker to list the property for a higher price and keep the difference between the two prices as his commission. To prevent fraud, many states outlaw Net Listings.

LITCHFIELD LAW SCHOOL. A money-making institute to train lawyers started in 1784 in Litchfield, Connecticut, by Tapping Reeve. It was wrongly proclaimed by some as the first law school in the United States. However, this honor belongs to the College of William and Mary in Virginia, which created the first Chair of Law in 1779, first occupied by George Wythe. Litchfield terminated its operation in 1833 when the bulk of legal training was assumed increasingly by colleges and universities.

LITERARY EXECUTOR. Appointed to handle the productions of a writer, composer or artist after his death. William Shakespeare failed to appoint such an executor in his will, and some scholars cite this failure as proof that Shakespeare did not, after all, write the many works attributed to him.

LITTLE PEACE. See LONG MARCH FORWARD.

LITTLE STATE DEPARTMENT. A small but powerful group of foreign affairs specialists in the Office of the Assistant Secretary for International Security Affairs of the Department of Defense in the nation's capitol.

LITTLE WANDERER'S RULE. A principle of family law first enunciated (but since abandoned) by the Massachusetts Supreme Court which stipulated that the state could intervene and remove a child from the custody of its family on the basis of the best interest of the child even in the absence of any finding of parental unfitness.

LITTORAL RIGHTS. Allow the owner of property at the seashore to use the water bordering his property.

LITVINOFF ASSIGNMENT. In a series of letters between President Franklin Roosevelt and Maxim Litvinoff, the People's Commissar for Foreign Affairs of the Soviet Union, the Russians agreed on November 16, 1933, to release all their claims against the United States government and citizens and to assign those claims to the United States.

"LIVE FREE OR DIE" CASE. The case concerning a Jehovah's Witness who objected to the state of New Hampshire's motto on his license plates and was arrested three times for covering it with tape. The Supreme Court of the United States found that a state could not compel an individual to espouse an ideological message with which he disagrees, and allowed the dissenter to cover the motto. Other Justices on the Court, however, felt that precedent might have been set to allow defacing of currency by those who object to the motto, "In God We Trust." And one Justice even suggested that instead of defacing his license plates, the plaintiff should buy a bumper sticker proclaiming his disagreement with the motto.

LIVE-IN CIRCUIT JUDGE. A judge who lives where he maintains his chambers. Under the existing system, circuit judges are required to live within their circuit, but they may locate their chambers wherever they wish. Traditionally, they have located their main chambers in the communities where they resided when they were appointed. This practice developed in the nineteenth century when circuit judges, instead of sitting in one place, were circuit riders, holding court with district judges. Although they no longer ride the circuit, many judges still live away from the principal location of their courts. Critics claim that having live-in circuit judges is more efficient than permitting judges to live at a distance from their chambers.

LIVE-IN LOVER. See COHABITATION CONTRACT.

LIVERY OF SEIZEN (Old French—livrer: to hand over, allot or deliver; and saisine: ownership of land or chattels). In medieval Europe, before the written deed came into general use, property ownership was transferred in a ceremony called "Livery of Seizin." Under the eyes of witnesses, the grantor handed the grantee a branch or twig, a clod of earth, a key or other object symbolic of the particular property to be transferred. The glaring flaw in this system was that the only record of the transaction was the perishable memory of the witnesses. Today, we put our faith in the more permanent and formal recorded deed. And to assure that title to the property in question is as stated, owners now can have the protection of title insurance.

LIVING IN SIN FOR TAX PURPOSES. An automatic tax deduction of $3,200 is available to a married couple. Two people cohabiting who are not married can file separate tax returns and claim an automatic deduction of $2,200 each. Uncle Sam thus encourages immorality.

LIVING SEPARATE AND APART. Statutory divorce provision in most states which requires spouses to live completely separate for a period, usually extending several years. The statute most often requires that the couple abstain from cohabitation and customary marital relations, but it is not limited to mere abstention from sexual intercourse. Because the requirement of living separate and apart is a condition to be met before a divorce decree will be granted in most jurisdictions, it is important that couples contemplating divorce pay close attention to the particular requirements in their states.

LIVING TOGETHER AGREEMENT. See COHABITATION CONTRACT.

LIVING TRUST. An express trust arrangement which comes into being on the initiative of the settlor during his lifetime and thus is to be distinguished from a testamentary trust which is created at the death of the trust settlor through a will.

LIVING WILL. A document directed to one's relatives, physician, lawyer and clergyman, requesting that they not artificially prolong the life of the signer by heroic medical procedures in the event of a terminal disease or injury. It should be executed by a person still in good health, and should be witnessed by two adults. It should contain an affirmation of the signer's belief in euthanasia, a legal release of physician and family from liability, and a clear expression of the circumstances in which the signer wishes to refuse medical treatment. After its execution, the document should be easily accessible to the signer, his family, and his physician. It should not be locked away or hidden, because one of its purposes is facilitating discussion of attitudes toward death and dying. While the validity of a Living Will has never been tested in a court case, legal experts agree that its provisions will probably be binding if the signer's intent is clear. A typical Living Will states:

> "If the time comes when I can no longer take part in decisions for my own future, let this statement stand as a testament of my wishes. If there is no reasonable expectation of my recovery from physical or mental disability I request that I be allowed to die and not be kept alive by artificial means or heroic measures. Death is as much a reality as birth, growth, and old age, and it is the one certainty. I do not fear death as much as I fear the indignity of deterioration, dependency and hopeless pain. I ask that drugs be mercifully administered to me for terminal suffering even if they hasten the moment of death."

LL.B. See J.D.

LLEWELLYN, KARL. See LEGAL REALISM.

LLOYD'S OF LONDON. The oldest and most famous insurance institution in the world. In existence as early as 1688, Lloyd's is not an insurance company, but an organization of over 8,500 individual underwriters who engage in the insurance business at that location under the supervision of a governing committee. The individual members of Lloyd's do not assume all of any one risk but spread the risk among several underwriters within the organization. Should the particular event occur, the various underwriters become individually liable, but only in the amount for which they subscribe. Lloyd's is licensed to do business directly only in two states, Illinois and Kentucky. Premiums on policies written in the United States are paid into Lloyd's American Trust Fund, which affords special protection to American policy-holders. Lloyd's is widely recognized for the unusual and often bizarre risks its members insure against. Its reputation over the years has resulted in an annual premium volume of approximately one billion dollars.

LOBBYING ACT (1946). An early congressional attempt to control special interest groups. The Act provided for registration of lobbyists and reports in the *Congressional Record* of their activities. Although the law specified penalties for noncompliance, no congressional agency is charged with its enforcement, and violations have been widespread.

LOCAL ACTION. A damage suit for trespass upon or harm done to land. Such suit must be tried at the situs of the land. The rule, often criticized as having no utility, is a product of the historical role of English jurors as witnesses, not fact finders. The jury in England was originally expected to testify in a case from personal knowledge. Therefore, all cases had to be tried near the situs of the property or occurrence in question, so that an informed jury could be found.

LOCHNER ERA. A term derived from the case of *Lochner v. New York,* 198 U.S. 45 (1905), which describes the period in the early twentieth century in which the Supreme Court invalidated many laws on the grounds of Substantive Due Process. The Court especially disapproved of legislative regulation of working conditions, labor relations and entry into business.

LOCK OUT. The refusal by management to give its employees work when such work is available. The use of lock out techniques is not per se illegal under the National Labor Relations Act— management's intent determines the permissibility of its techniques. Thus, if the lock out is designed to discourage membership in unions, it is in violation of sections 8(a)(1) and (3) of the Act. A breach of section 8(a)(2) is established where the employer's intent is to force a favored union on employees. Finally, a lock out perpetrated in order to shirk the duty to bargain contravenes section 8(a)(5) of the Act.

LOCKWOOD, BELVA ANN (1830-1917). The first woman admitted to practice before the Supreme Court of the United States. She had to fight for this right as she had at each earlier step in her career. Widowed in her twenties, she first supported herself and her daughter by teaching school in New York. She later moved to Washington, D.C., to open her own school. When she decided to train as a lawyer, one law school rejected her with the excuse that a woman's presence in the classroom would distract her classmates. The new National University Law School accepted her, but refused to graduate her until she wrote a letter to President Grant, an Ex Officio member of the school's board, "demanding" that she be given her degree. Although she was admitted into the District of Columbia Bar, the Supreme Court would not permit her to practice before it for reasons of "custom." Undaunted, Lockwood won passage by Congress of a bill allowing women membership in the Supreme Court bar in 1872, and a year later she sponsored to the Supreme Court bar its first southern Black man, Samuel P. Lowery. Lockwood fought throughout her life for women's rights and world peace, and in 1884 was nominated by a feminist convention to be the first woman candidate for President.

LOCUS SIGILLI (Latin—place of seal). Used in some legal documents, generally with the abbreviation "L.S." placed at the signature line. This formalism is a holdover from the days when all contracts and formal documents were sealed with wax.

LOCUS TEST (Last Event Rule). Under Article 9 of the Uniform Commercial Code (U.C.C.), perfection requirements in a multistate transaction are governed by the law of the jurisdiction where the collateral is when the last event occurs which is needed to perfect.

LOGAN ACT. A response to the action by one Dr. George Logan, who traveled to Paris in 1799 to speak with French government officials in an attempt to improve relations between America and France. Congress, resenting such action, passed the Logan Act, giving the government a monopoly on international negotiations. The statute makes it a crime for any citizen without authority of the United States to communicate with a foreign government intending either (1) to influence that government with respect to a controversy with the United States or (2) to defeat the measures of the United States. There never has been a conviction or even a trial under the Logan Act. Only one indictment has ever been returned, and that was in 1803 against Francis Flournoy, a Kentucky farmer, for an article he wrote in the *Frankfort Guardian of Freedom* in which he advocated a separate western nation allied to France in what became the Louisiana Territory. The subsequent Louisiana Purchase by Thomas Jefferson mooted the controversy.

LOG ROLLING. The legislative embodiment of the free enterprise system, whereby legislators trade votes in order to obtain support for pet bills or resolutions. Typically, one legislator will agree to support an appropriation favorable to another's home district in exchange for a similar promise to vote for a bill benefiting his own constituents. The term derives from the era when the American West was being settled and the pioneers helped one another to roll heavy logs in order to clear the land.

LOME CONVENTION (1975). Provides for association agreements between the European Economic Community (E.E.C.) and forty-six countries from Africa, the Caribbean and the Pacific Islands (the A.C.P. countries). The Lome Convention supersedes the Yaounde Conventions, and provides for an association based on reciprocal nondiscrimination and on the Most Favored Nation clause. It also provides for financial aid for A.C.P. development and for joint A.C.P.-E.E.C. institutions.

LONDON FIVE. The five financial experts who have fixed the international price of gold by announcing the rate at meetings held twice each weekday in the London office of Rothschild & Sons.

LONDON INTERBANK OFFERED RATE. See L.I.B.O.R.

L-1 VISA. See H-1 VISA.

LONG ARM STATUTE. State laws designed to exercise personal jurisdiction over a defendant who is not a resident of the state. Thus the statute permits the "Long Arm" of the state to reach outside the state and bring a defendant to court. Illinois was the first state to pass a comprehensive Long Arm Statute in 1955, and many states have followed suit, particularly in obtaining jurisdiction over out-of-state motorists who are involved in traffic offenses within the state.

LONGEST TRIALS. (1) World. A lawsuit filed in Poona, India in 1205 which was finally settled in 1966. (2) American—Completed. The El Paso Natural Gas antitrust divestiture case that ended in 1972 after 15 years of litigation. (3) American—Incomplete. The I.B.M. antitrust case that was filed by Attorney General Ramsey Clark on January 17, 1969, the last working day of President Johnson's Administration. Former Attorney General Nicholas B. Katzenbach of the Administration of President Kennedy is the defense counsel for I.B.M. The case was still going strong when this book went to press 10 years after it was started.

LONGEST WALK. A coast-to-coast march to Washington, D.C. in July 1978, by 500 participants representing 80 American Indian Tribes from all over the United States to protest laws which restricted their Constitutional rights. It was symbolic of the forced marches they involuntarily made to degrading reservations in the nineteenth century to our everlasting shame.

LONG MARCH FORWARD (Great Leap Outward; Four Modernizations). The Long March in the Celestial Kingdom was a 6,000-mile retreat of the Chinese Communists from the coast into the hills under the leadership of

Mao Tse-tung (Great Helmsman) in the generation-long Civil War. They regrouped to defeat the Chinese Nationalists (Kuomintang) in 1949 under the leadership of Chiang Kai-shek whose followers then flew to the Island of Taiwan to establish a new Republic of China. And so ended Sun Yat-sen's Republic of China. The People's Republic of China then came into existence, whose first Premier was Mao Tse-tung, and followed a conservative xenophobic policy of national self-reliance and independence from outside sources for two generations. Upon his death, Vice Premier Ten Hsido-p'ing (an Underground alias which means Little Peace in Chinese—his real name was Kan-Tse-kao), seized power in his capacity of Vice Chairman of the Communist Party and Army Chief of Staff. In 1979, with the resumption of full diplomatic relations with the United States, the P.R.C. embarked on a new Long March Forward with the rest of the world in order to achieve a state of relative modernity and become a world economic and military power by the year 2000. Since the population of China (one billion) is one fourth of that for the entire world, the import of this new Open Door policy of reciprocal exchange of business and culture in the cause of international peace and prosperity is earthshaking. Hopefully, it will be more successful than the Great Leap Forward in 1958-60 whose ridiculous farm-yard industry program under Mao left China in a state of severe famine and economic depression, or Mao's disastrous Cultural Revolution a decade later whose vendetta against complacency and bureaucracy dislocated every institution in Chinese life, especially in law and education.

LONGSHOREMEN'S AND HARBOR WORKERS' COMPENSATION ACT (L.H.C.A.). A federal law enacted in 1927 and substantially revised in 1972, which provides a scheme of workmen's compensation for persons employed to load and unload vessels (longshoremen) or to build or repair vessels (harbor workers). To be eligible, longshoremen and harbor workers must be engaged in maritime employment upon the navigable waters of the United States. The Act resulted from a declaration of the Supreme Court that state Workmen's Compensation Laws, as applied to maritime employment, were an unconstitutional intrusion into the admiralty jurisdiction of the United States. L.H.C.A., which is administered by the Secretary of Labor, establishes a set schedule of benefits to be paid by an employer to employee for death or any disability occurring while in maritime employment, including accidental injuries, occupational diseases and infections, and willful acts of third parties directed against an employee because of his employment. Liability of the employer under the Act is not limited by the contributory negligence of the employee. The Act establishes a system of regional deputy commissioners to whom all claims for compensation must be submitted. The commissioners are charged with the responsibility of adjudicating claims and ordering awards of compensation where appropriate. The Act also establishes an appeals procedure. In addition to a monetary award, an employer must furnish an injured employee without charge such medical services as are deemed necessary for the proper treatment of his injury. In order to secure the provision of this and other benefits under the Act, the employer is required to maintain adequate insurance coverage or provide evidence of his ability to self-insure. Failure of an employer to properly secure the payment of claims under the Act is a misdemeanor punishable by a fine of not more than $1,000, or by imprisonment for not more than one year, or both.

LOOKING AT LAW SCHOOL. A student guide from the Society of American Law Teachers, which attempts to reveal the mysteries of law school to prospective law students. Each of the traditional first-year courses is discussed by law professors, and advice is provided on those subjects which generally instill fear and trembling in the first-year student: legal writing and law examinations.

LOOP-HOLE. Any opening in a law, especially in the field of taxation, and usually of a technical nature, which one may use to one's advantage. Litigants love lawyers who locate loop holes.

LORD CHANCELLOR (Lord High Chancellor). A British officer of state who presides over the House of Lords in both its legislative and judicial capacities. This person is the highest ranking judicial officer in England and is usually a leading member of the Cabinet. Judicial appointments are made on his advice.

LORD CHIEF JUSTICE. The highest judicial officer in Great Britain and other common law countries.

LORD ELDON. See SCOTT, JOHN.

LORD HARDWICKE'S ACT. A British statute, passed in 1753 which required that a legally valid marriage must meet licensing requirements, must be announced by publication of banns, and must be celebrated in a church ceremony. It had as its principal motive the prevention of fraudulent unions as "fleet marriages," performed informally by clergymen incarcerated in the Fleet Prison. It governed marriage in England, but left the old rule allowing informal marriage intact in Scotland, Ireland and America, where the legal apparatus for formal licensing was not yet in operation.

LORD MANSFIELD. See MURRAY, WILLIAM.

LORD MANSFIELD'S RULE. A rule of evidence and family law which is applied to exclude testimony as to facts that would bastardize a child. Neither the wife nor the husband can testify to the impossibility of sexual access during the time when the child could have been conceived. The rule was named after Lord Mansfield who said in 1777 that husband and wife "shall not be permitted to say after marriage that they had no connection and therefore that the offspring is spurious."

LORD OF MISRULE. A person chosen to preside over the games and festivities in British royal homes at Christmas.

LORD OF THE RING. Harvard Law School graduate and Wall Street lawyer Robert Arum whose company, called Top Rank, controls most of the leading professional prize fighters in a multi-million-dollar business.

LORD'S DAY LAWS. See BLUE LAWS.

LORD VERULAM. See BACON, FRANCIS.

LOSS LEADER SALE. A sale advertising certain goods at prices below cost which attracts customers to the store. Although the store loses money on the "leader" items, it usually can make up the loss by selling other goods to the increased number of customers. Sales below cost are not generally considered to be an unfair sales practice, unless it can be shown that the sale is conducted purposely to entice customers away from a competitor and into stores where other goods are deliberately marked up. In such instances, sales designed to injure a competitor are outlawed by statute in many states.

LOSS, LOUIS. See FEDERAL SECURITIES LAW CODE.

LOSS OF CONSORTIUM. A cause of action in tort by one spouse against a tortfeasor whose actions result in physical injury or incapacity of the other spouse. Where the injury is to the wife, the husband recovers loss of services, society and sexual relations. Where the injury is to the husband, the wife originally had no cause of action because the common law never recognized any right on the part of a wife to the services of her husband. Several states now allow the wife to bring the action.

LOST JUDGE. New York Supreme Court Justice Joseph F. Crater had dinner in a restaurant in New York City on August 6, 1930, entered a taxi and has not been seen since then. He left a wife, a $25,000 salary and a substantial bank account to become a legend among the tens of thousands who disappear from the Big Apple each year never to be heard from again.

L.O.S. TRIBUNAL. A proposed international court composed of 21 members representing the major legal systems of the world which would adjudicate disputes arising under the Law of the Sea Treaties. If a dispute involves deep seabed mining, the parties would submit the disagreement to the Sea-Bed Disputes Chamber (S.D.C.) of the L.O.S.

LOVING v. VIRGINIA (388 U.S. 1 (1967)). A Supreme Court decision invalidating a Virginia statute prohibiting marriage between persons solely on the basis of race. At the time of the decision, sixteen states imposed penalties for miscegenation, based on the notion of White supremacy. Recognizing that marriage is one of society's fundamental freedoms, the Court held that proscription of racial intermarriages was violative of the due process clause and the equal protection clause of the Fourteenth Amendment to the United States Constitution.

LOWERY, SAMUEL P. See LOCKWOOD, BELVA ANN.

LOW PAR. Stock which has a par value set at an amount which is substantially less than the price at which the stock is originally issued. The difference between the par value and the value received is placed in the capital surplus account which is more subject to the discretion of management than the capital account. When par value stock is issued, all proceeds go to the capital account. Thus low par provides more flexibility for the corporation's management. Additionally, corporate management is protected against liability for the issuance of stock in return for property which a court, under either the True Value or Good Faith Rule, finds to be worth less than the par value of the stock.

LOYALTY OATHS. See COLD WAR.

LOYOLA BAILOUT. A provision in the 1969 federal tax law, inserted by Louisiana Senator Russell Long and Louisiana Congressman Hale Boggs, exempting from income tax the profits from the New Orleans radio and television stations owned by Loyola University, thereby giving such stations a competitive advantage over other media operators.

L.P.S. See COMMUNITY HEALTH SERVICES LAW.

L.R.A. (Lawyers Reports Annotated). An early series of annotated reports of significant court decisions, published between 1888 and 1918. During its existence, the L.R.A. competed with three other annotated case reporters until all were merged in 1918 into the current A.L.R. series. The L.R.A. was similar in most respects to today's A.L.R. system, except that federal cases were not included and the annotations were not so detailed. Accompanying the L.R.A. was a conventional digest, a complete index, and an L.R.A. green book with later case citations. The L.R.A. series is still useful today for searching significant cases reported during the period of its existence.

L.S. See LOCUS SIGILLI.

L.S.A.C. See LAW SCHOOL ADMISSION COUNCIL.

L.S.A.S. (Law School Admission Services). Administered by Educational Testing Service (E.T.S.), a nonprofit corporation in Princeton, New Jersey, for the Law School Admission Council (L.S.A.C.), a nonprofit corporation consisting of one representative from each law school accredited by either the American Bar Association or the Association of American Law Schools. The two principal services are the Law School Admission Test (L.S.A.T.) and the Law School Data Assembly Service (L.S.D.A.S.). The Council also sponsors publication of the Prelaw Handbook and, with other graduate school advisory bodies, the Graduate and Professional School Financial Aid Service (G.A.P.S.F.A.S.), which provides a standardized form for financial assistance and passes information on to interested graduate schools, including law schools. Every accredited American law school requires applicants to take the L.S.A.T. which is designed to measure certain mental capabilities important in the study of law. The test covers a broad range of disciplines and gives no advantage to candidates with a particular discipline. The questions yielding the L.S.A.T. score are designed to measure the capacity to read, understand, and reason logically using a variety of verbal and quantitative material. The questions in the writing ability sections of the test are designed to measure skill in using standard written English to express ideas clearly, precisely and fluently. The L.S.D.A.S. helps law schools compare their applicants' undergraduate records fairly and quickly. For schools that require the service, the L.S.D.A.S. produces for each applicant a report containing L.S.A.T. results and a summary of undergraduate transcripts and sends copies of this report and the transcripts to each law school designated by the applicant to receive them. Central processing of transcripts eliminates the need for applicants to send separate transcripts to multiple institutions.

L.S.A.T. (Law School Admission Test). See L.S.A.S.

L.S.C. See LEGAL SERVICES CORPORATION.

LUCIDO, JOHN. Brash barrister who, in 1978, unsuccessfully sued his Wall Street law firm (Cravath, Swaine & Moore), claiming that he had not been made a partner, in general because of his Catholic religion, because he was Italian in particular, and to some extent because he didn't go to an Ivy League law school.

LUXURY TAX. Imposed on articles or services considered nonessential to a reasonable standard of living. Current examples include taxes on alcohol, tobacco, furs, jewelry, entertainment and candy. Luxury taxes may be established for revenue-generating purposes or, as in time of war, to discourage the pro-

duction of goods not related to the national emergency.

LYNCH LAW. The practice of punishing alleged offenders after a summary proceeding has been conducted by a self-appointed court with no legal authority. The common practice was to tar and feather or flog the victim, but the term has now come to apply more narrowly to punishment by death. The origin of the term is unclear. Historians often assert that it derives from the proceedings of Charles Lynch, a Justice of the Peace in Virginia after whom the City of Lynchburg was named. Lynch illegally fined and imprisoned suspected Tories during the latter part of the eighteenth century. Little evidence exists, however, which associates the types of acts involved in Lynch Law with his brand of justice. The term may have originated in Lynche's Creek in South Carolina, a meeting place for vigilantes who harassed the Tories in that area.

LYONS LAW (Residency Law). Named after its sponsor, James Lyons, Bronx Borough President, this legislation by New York City was enacted in 1937 and has since been followed by a number of other cities and counties throughout the country. With jobs scarce because of the Depression, the policy behind the law was "Hometown jobs for Hometown folks." A city employee was required to live within the city or be discharged from employment. In a test case brought by Philadelphia in 1976, the Supreme Court upheld the constitutionality of the practice.

LYONS v. GRETHER. See WHITE CANE ACT.

M

MACKEY v. NATIONAL FOOTBALL LEAGUE. See ROZELLE RULE.

MADISON AVENUE ATTORNEYS. Lawyers whose offices are usually located on Madison Avenue in uptown New York City who work for law firms specializing in advertising matters, or those who work for ad agencies, or those employed by the ad departments of large corporations throughout the country.

MADISON, JAMES. The fourth President of the United States, he led a varied political life. Early in his career, Madison was active in religious causes, attacking persecution of the Baptists and drafting an article on religious liberty in the Virginia Declaration of Rights which assured free exercise of religion rather than mere toleration of minority religions. On the national level, Madison was the youngest member of the Continental Congress. Along with Alexander Hamilton and John Jay, he wrote 29 of the Federalist Papers, which sought to illustrate that the Constitution achieved the proper balance of state-federal power. Madison believed that power was better in a large republic than in many small entities because the former divides people into too many interests to permit the rise of an oppressive majority. Madison held a variety of other positions. He was elected to a county revolutionary committee but was denied re-election because he refused to treat voters to alcoholic drinks. He served as Secretary of State under Thomas Jefferson and was instrumental in securing the Louisiana Purchase. During his tenure, he dismissed the British foreign minister for using foul language, leading the Briton to ridicule Madison's 5'6" height and to call him "obstinate as a mule." Upon retiring from the Presidency, he was appointed Rector of the University of Virginia.

MAGGIE MAE (Mortgage Guaranty Insurance Corporation; M.G.I.C.). Secondary mortgage market for conventional mortgages which is the first private market of its kind, and performs (as its name implies) similar functions as do Ginnie Mae, Fannie Mae, and Freddy Mac.

MAGHREB STATES. A phrase used in international law to denote Algeria, Libya, Morocco, and Tunisia. The close relations among these countries is evidenced by the establishment of a permanent consultative committee for these countries for the harmonization of their economic development plans and an industrial studies center.

MAGISTRATE'S COURT. A state court of limited jurisdiction over minor criminal offenses, similar to a municipal court or a police court. While in most states a magistrate's court handles only minor criminal matters, in some locations it may also have jurisdiction over petty civil cases, such as traffic violations or small claims. Magistrate's courts are usually found in cities, having usurped the jurisdiction of the Justice of the Peace. The judicial officer presiding over a magistrate's court is usually called a magistrate. In many of the larger metropolitan areas, this type of minor criminal court may be known as a police court.

MAGNA CARTA (Latin—great charter). On Monday, the fifteenth day of June, 1215, John, King of England, met the barons "in the meadow which is called Runnymede between Windsor and Staines." There the barons made demands which the King accepted. The demands were written down in the Latin script by one of the clerks in the Royal Chancery. When accepted, they became the Great Charter. Many copies were made, and to each was affixed the Great Seal of the Realm. They were sent to castles and cathedrals throughout the land. To this day one can see in the British Museum the copy that was sent to Dover Castle and in the cathedrals at Lincoln and at Salisbury the copies that were sent there. This Great Charter dealt with grievances of the time in a practical way. It gave legal redress for the wrongs of a feudal age. But Magna Carta's effect on succeeding generations has been due not so much to the specific remedies which it provided as to the language in which it was couched. Here are set down the guarantees of freedom under the law. "No free man shall be taken, imprisoned, disseised, outlawed, banished, or in any way destroyed, nor will We proceed against or prosecute him except by the lawful judgment of his peers and by the law of the land." Immediately following in the Charter is the guarantee of impartial administration of justice: "To no one will We sell, to none will We deny or delay, right or justice." Those words have echoed down the centuries. When the colonists crossed the seas from England and settled in Virginia, they took with them the principles of freedom under law set forth in the Great Charter. The Constitution of the United States and the Bill of Rights are direct legal descendants of the Great Charter.

MAGNA CHARTA. See MAGNA CARTA.

MAGNIFICENT 13. See RED BERETS.

MAGNUSON-MOSS WARRANTY ACT (Federal Trade Commission Improvement Act). A federal law enacted in 1975 which makes warranties in the sale of goods easier for the buyer to understand and compare; and improves competition in the marketing of consumer goods, to prevent deception and to encourage the informal settlement of disputes between buyer and seller.

MAILBOX RULE. Provides that when a contract is accepted by mail or similar means, the acceptance is effective when a properly addressed and stamped reply is posted. An offeror, however, can stipulate that acceptance of his offer is effective only upon receipt. The Mailbox Rule does not apply to option contracts. Acceptance of an option is not effective until received.

MAIL FRAUD. A federal offense which includes devising any scheme to defraud a person by means of false or fraudulent representations, with the specific intent to use the mail to carry out some essential step of the plan. The mailing need not be between the perpetrator and the victim. The offense is punishable by a fine of up to $1,000 and/or five years imprisonment. In the most celebrated Mail Fraud trial of the 1970s Governor Marvin Mandel of Maryland was found guilty of using the mail in a scheme to corrupt the honest administration of government. The Governor was said to have used the mail in providing inside information to friends and former business associates. A federal court held that the Governor had deprived the state and its citizens of certain intangible rights such as the right to honest government and the right to faithful and loyal service.

MAIL ORDER DIVORCE. The dissolution of a marriage by mailing papers to another state or foreign country which purports to issue a decree ending the relationship of husband and wife. It is a futile procedure which no state recognizes if the proceeding is contested.

MAINTENANCE AND CURE. Money an injured or sick member of a crew of a vessel is entitled to recover from a shipowner to cover the cost of lodging, food and medical care.

MAINTENANCE OF MEMBERSHIP CLAUSE. A provision in a union contract which requires workers to remain union members for the duration of the contract.

MAINTENANCE TRUST. See SUPPORT TRUSTS.

MAJORITY STOCKHOLDERS. Those stockholders of a corporation sufficient in number to control the actions and policies of a corporation. A majority stockholder is subject to the same fiduciary duties as a director since he has the power to choose and control the directors. They have the duty to protect the interests of the minority stockholders.

MAJOR VIOLATOR PROGRAM. An effective criminal justice enforcement system for large cities sponsored by the Law Enforcement Assistance Administration. It is designed to identify hard-core criminals and bring them to trial as soon as possible. The conviction rate for multiple offenders is high, and they are given long prison terms to protect society by getting them off the streets.

MALICE AFORETHOUGHT. The state of mind which must be present for a homicide to constitute murder. Malice aforethought is an imprecise term which has grown over the years to include four different types of Mens Rea. These are intent-to-kill, intent-to-do serious bodily injury, felony murder, and depraved heart murder. Originally malice aforethought meant an intent to kill accompanied by premeditation, but its meaning has expanded to include an intent to kill without premeditation. Today the presence or absence of premeditation can determine the applicable degree of murder. Malice aforethought has also come to refer to homicides where the defendant, though lacking an intent to kill, did intend to cause serious bodily injury. Such injury generally refers to a grievous injury approaching death. An example is an assailant who repeatedly strikes his victim, intending to "break his skull," but causing death instead. The third type of murder has become known as depraved heart murder, and refers to killings resulting from extremely negligent conduct. An example is a construction worker who kills someone by carelessly tossing lumber from the roof of a building onto the street. Here, malice aforethought requires no intent to injure at all. Malice aforethought may also refer to a killing, albeit unintentional, which occurs during the commission of a felony. Here too, malice aforethought requires neither premeditation nor an intent to injure. Courts have distinguished between a premeditated intent to kill and the other forms of malice aforethought by referring to "express malice" and "implied malice." Thus many statutes define murder as "an unlawful killing with malice aforethought, express or implied."

MALICIOUS HOOLIGANISM. The favorite crime for which a person is convicted by the Russians for any criticism of the paradise of communism.

MALICIOUS PROSECUTION. A tort consisting of the wrongful institution of criminal proceedings by one private person against another private person. The person wrongfully prosecuted may sue to recover for damage to his reputation, interference with his personal integrity, and the expense incurred in defending himself against the criminal charge. His success in such a suit will depend on his ability to prove that the defendant maliciously instituted criminal proceedings, that the proceedings found the plaintiff not guilty, that the defendant lacked probable cause and was motivated by an improper purpose.

MALLORY v. UNITED STATES. See McNABB-MALLORY RULE.

MALUM IN SE (Latin—wrong in itself). Describes crimes which are inherently dangerous or immoral, as distinguished from Malum Prohibitum offenses, which are prohibited by statute but are not inherently wrong. This distinction is a difficult one and is based on several factors. Generally common law crimes are considered Malum in Se, as are crimes which require a Mens Rea element or involve moral turpitude—a description problematic in itself. Courts have held that battery, larceny and murder are Mala in Se while holding that speeding, selling liquor, and hunting without permission are Mala Prohibitum. Courts have differed as to the classification of driving while intoxicated. The classification of a crime may be important in several circumstances. For example, one may be liable under misdemeanor manslaughter for an unintentional killing if he is engaged in conduct which is Malum in Se. The classification is also important as to whether a conviction warrants disbarment of an attorney or impeachment of a witness.

MALUM PROHIBITUM. See MALUM IN SE.

MAMMY WAGONS. See MARKET MAMMIES.

MANDAMUS WRIT. See WRIT OF MANDAMUS.

MANDATED REPORTERS (Mandatory Reporters). Persons designated by state statutes who are legally liable for not reporting suspected cases of child abuse and neglect to the mandated agency. The persons so designated vary according to state law, but they are primarily professionals, such as pediatricians, nurses, school personnel, and social workers, who have frequent contact with children and families.

MANDATORY INJUNCTION. A judicial order requiring a person to perform a positive act.

MANDATORY SENTENCING. See SENTENCING PROCEDURES.

MANDATORY TRUST ORDERS. Obligatory language contained in a trust arrangement which clarifies certain orders to be obeyed by the trustee. The purpose of such an order is to remove from the trustee the power to make certain decisions.

MANDELA, NELSON. See A.N.C.

MAN IN THE HOUSE RULE (Substitute Father). A presumption, once employed by some states, that any male who dwelled in the same home as a potential A.F.D.C. recipient was a "parent" under § 406 (a) of the Social Security Act, and therefore his income could be deemed available to support the family unit. The Supreme Court rejected such a Rule in Alabama in *King v. Smith,* 392 U.S. 309 (1968), holding that in determining "need" the state may only take into account resources that are in fact available to the family. The state interest in morality can be dealt with only through rehabilitative measures, not in any way that would punish dependent children who are the intended beneficiaries of the A.F.D.C. program.

MANN ACT. See WHITE SLAVERY.

MANSFIELD, ARABELLA (1846-1911). The first woman admitted to a state Bar in the United States. At the time Mansfield passed her law examination with high honors and applied for admission to the Illinois Bar in 1869, the laws of the State of Illinois, like most states, restricted membership in the Bar to men. Fortunately, the liberal local Judge, Judge Francis Springer, had a flexible enough legal mind to interpret "men" and "male" to include women as well, and Mansfield was admitted. She never practiced, but instead pursued a long career as administrator and teacher at DePauw College in Iowa.

MANUAL FOR COURTS MARTIAL (M.C.M.). A Presidential directive, issued pursuant to authority granted by the Uniform Code of Military Justice, prescribing the procedure to be used, the applicable rules of evidence, and the punishments which may be imposed in trials by Court Martial. In granting the President such authority, Congress explicitly stated that he shall, so far as possible, apply the principles of law and the rules of evidence generally recognized in the trial of criminal cases in the United States District Courts. Last issued in its current revised edition in 1969, the M.C.M. has become an indispensable tool in the operation of the military justice system.

M.A.P. (Multiple Aiming Points). Hiding nuclear ballistic missiles in large fields containing decoy empty holes or moving them around to confuse the Russians if they attempt to destroy the United States in a massive pre-emptive first attack. A variation of the old carnival shell game—now you see it, now you don't. The Russians would be confused because their spy satellites could not tell which silos contained the live missiles. This program was one of the main hangups in S.A.L.T. II.

M.A.P. (Mutual Aid Pact). Formed in 1958 with the express approval of the Civil Aeronautics Board (C.A.B.), this is a group of 15 airlines companies. It assesses members on an annual basis and when one of them is on strike, it is paid half of its normal operating expenses. Since the striking workers receive unemployment compensation as well as payments from the Union Strike Fund for not working, the only ones who suffer during a strike are the public. In 1978 the striking Northwest Airline pilots, incidentally, received $85,-000 a year for less than 40 hours a week of work. And they wanted a raise of $11,000. Not bad, if you can get it. Other public utilities such as railroads have similar financial agreements with respect to strikes.

MARBURY v. MADISON (5 U.S. 87 (1803)). A Supreme Court case which stands for the proposition that the Court can declare an act of Congress affecting the role of the federal judiciary unconstitutional. Chief Justice John Marshall, speaking for the Court, held that § 13 of the Judiciary Act of 1789 was unconstitutional because it proposed to alter the jurisdiction of the Supreme Court as set forth in Article III, § 2 of the Constitution. Marshall stated that an act repugnant to the Constitution is void and that it is the express role of the Supreme Court to say what the Constitution means. And thus was the concept of judicial review created for the first time in Western Civilization.

MARIJUANA MEDICAL RESEARCH AND PRACTICE PROGRAM. First established by law in New Mexico in 1978, to allow a patient, upon a prescription from his doctor, to obtain free from the federal government at a state pharmacy, marijuana to be used to alleviate the pain, nausea, and other deleterious side effects following chemotherapy for the treatment of cancer and glaucoma.

MARINE SAFETY INFORMATION SYSTEM (Rouges List). A computerized hot sheet maintained by the United States Coast Guard since 1977 on errant shipping that can provide an instant printout on a ship's history of inspections, safety violations and accidents. Thousands of ships are inspected each year and, in 50 percent of the cases, citations are issued for problems in operation or maintenance of the vessels.

MARIN, LUIS MUNOZ. The grand old man of Puerto Rican politics who led the Island from its 50 years of American Colonial status into an independent Commonwealth in special association with the United States in 1958 when he became the first locally-elected Governor. At the age of 80 he was still active in the practice of law, and in the welfare and affairs of the Island, in 1980.

MARITAL COMMUNICATIONS PRIVILEGE. Protects confidential communications of a married couple from disclosure in either a criminal or civil suit. A derivative of the notion that a husband and wife are one being, the privilege is presently justified as protecting the privacy of the marital relationship. Unlike the husband-wife privilege, which can be asserted only during marriage, the marital communications privilege survives divorce.

MARITAL DEDUCTION. A provision of the federal estate and gift tax laws, exempting a portion of a person's estate passing to his or her spouse from taxation. Under the marital deduction, up to the greater of $250,000 or 50 percent of the adjusted gross estate which passes to the spouse from the deceased spouse's estate is deducted from the adjusted gross estate and is not taxed.

MARITAL PENALTY. See MARRIAGE PENALTY.

MARITAL RAPE. Several states, such as Oregon, Iowa, Delaware and New Jersey, have changed the common law by passing legislation which makes it a crime for a man to injure his wife or woman with whom he is living by forcing her to have sexual relations against her will.

MARITAL SHARE (Indefeasible Share). A share of a decedent's estate which goes to the surviving spouse and cannot be changed or defeated by any condition. Most state statutory systems prohibit a decedent from cutting off a surviving spouse's share of the estate. Although state statutory systems vary, the usual scheme provides that the surviving spouse can elect against the decedent's will and take a share of the estate even if the decedent's will states otherwise.

MARITIME FLAG. Every ship on the high seas must sail under the maritime flag of a country. This practice is inspired by the need to protect order and safety on the high seas. Ships on the high seas are subject to the jurisdiction of their flag country and must comply with safety regulations enacted by such sovereign. Nations are free to determine the conditions under which they allow a ship to fly its flag. Panama and Liberia have mainly been known for granting "flags of convenience" to ships with little or no link with such countries. Foreign companies use a flag of convenience to take advantage of low wage scales and lax safety requirements. Since World War II, the right to a maritime flag extends to every country, and nations without a seacoast have the same rights as nations with a seacoast.

MARITIME LAW (Admiralty Law). That body of law governing the business of carrying goods and passengers by water. It includes these rules, concepts, and legal practices which deal with the shipping industry, though its scope does not cover the whole reach of the industry's legal concerns. Typically, maritime law deals with contracts for the carriage of goods and the chartering of vessels, collisions of vessels, injuries to and death of seamen and passengers, and salvage. It does not deal with contracts for the building and sale of vessels and injuries occurring on artificial islands, such as drilling rigs. Maritime law began in antiquity when man first took to the sea for transportation. Although sea commerce nearly died out during the Dark Ages, it regained its momentum with the rise of the great Italian city-states about 1000 A.D. As the shipping industry continued to grow and prosper, maritime law attracted the attention of European legal scholars. Their treatises and commentaries systemized this area of the law for the first time and imprinted it indelibly with the mark of civil law, its most notable characteristic being the virtual absence of trial by jury. While maritime law began as a body of international law, when the great nations of Europe appeared, it quickly came to be assimilated into national law.

MARKETABLE TITLE. Title to real property that is free from encumbrances.

MARKET MAMMIES. The successful feminine traders of West Africa who transport goods and passengers across the borders of numerous countries in their colorfully decorated "mammy wagons," cheerfully ignoring customs and immigration officers. Even those who are illiterate are experts in marketing and foreign currency conversion. Many modern African leaders were educated by the profits of these industrious relatives who remain the backbone of many economies today.

MARRIAGE BROKER. One who arranges, for a fee, the identification of persons suitable to become husband and wife. Such contracts, although wide-spread, are usually not enforced in law since they are deemed to be contrary to public policy.

MARRIAGE CONTRACT. The relationship into which a man and woman enter upon the solemnization of the marriage. The idea of marriage as a civil contract stems from the rejection of the sacramental character attributed to it during the middle ages. It differs from traditional contracts between parties in that the terms of the contract are specified by the state and are, for the most part, non-negotiable by the contracting parties. One commentator has observed:

> The marriage contract is unlike most contracts. Its provisions are unwritten, its penalties are unspecified, and the terms of the contract are typically unknown to the contracting parties. Prospective spouses are neither informed of the terms of the contract nor are they allowed any options about these terms. In fact, one wonders how many men and women would agree to the marriage contract if they were given the opportunity to read it and to consider the rights and obligations to which they were committing themselves.

MARRIAGE IN JEST. The law of marriages is similar to the law of contracts in requiring that an intention to make such an agreement be expressed by the parties before the terms become binding. If, however, the expressed intentions were manifested in the context of an obvious joke, then no contract or marriage. Consequently, when in a context plainly showing that both parties intended that the act be nothing more than a joke, then the marriage is susceptible to an annulment action by suit of either party. Yet, there is law which maintains that if a consummation has taken place it will not be annulled. The supporting rationale is that regardless of the joking context, a valid marriage must have been intended since some of the consequences of the normal marriage occurred.

MARRIAGE PENALTY. Internal Revenue Code provisions that work to the disadvantage of married individuals. Before 1948, income was taxed without regard to marital status. Under this scheme, married couples who lived in community property states were able to split their income on a 50-50 basis, thereby enjoying lower tax rates than those of married couples in non-community property states. The Revenue Act of 1948 eliminated this disparity by allowing all married couples to file joint returns. Because the 1948 amendment disadvantaged single taxpayers, the Tax Reform Act of 1969 was passed. The 1969 Act, however, works to the disadvantage of married taxpayers, particularly those who earn comparable incomes. The court of claims, upholding the 1969 Act in *Mapes v. United States*, asserted that a legislature is entitled to make reforms on a piecemeal basis, and solve one inequity at a time. In other words, married taxpayers may be burdened now, but single taxpayers had better watch out for the next amendment.

MARRIAGE UNDER DURESS. A voidable marriage that results when one or both parties have been forced to marry by physical or mental abuse. Generally, duress involves the use of physical force or a threat against the prospective spouse. Duress may be exercised by someone other than the defendant spouse, who may even be unaware of its use. Unlike seduction, duress involves violent persuasion.

MARRIED NAMES. Although a number of states permit married women to retain their maiden names after marriage, other states, such as Rhode Island, have rejected such forward-looking measures. In such states the only remedy for a woman who wishes to keep her name is to petition the probate court to change it.

MARRIED WOMEN'S PROPERTY ACTS. Legislation enacted during the nineteenth century to improve the lot of married women and to attempt to provide equality between the spouses. Under the common law, the husband and wife were considered one person and that person was the husband. The statutes basically allow a married woman to acquire property, to sue and be sued without joining her husband, to recover damages alone for all civil injuries, to enter into contracts and incur liabilities on her own, to use and possess her own earnings, to obtain by descent, gift, or purchase, real and personal property in her own right, etc. While these Acts removed some of the legal impediments of married women, many still remain which will be abolished if the Equal Rights Amendment is ratified.

MARSH v. ALABAMA. See STATE ACTION.

MARSHALL, JOHN. Widely regarded as the greatest Chief Justice of the United States, even though he only had two months of legal education at the College of William and Mary in Williamsburg, Virginia. A political enemy of Thomas Jefferson, his most important opinion was probably *Marbury v. Madison*, 5 U.S. 87 (1803), which established the principle of Judicial Review, that the Supreme Court could declare null and void those laws of Congress which were in conflict with the Federal Constitution.

MARSHALL, THOMAS R. Former Vice-President of the United States best known for his infamous remark, "What this country needs is a good five-cent cigar," because Mrs. Woodrow Wilson preferred to serve as Acting President of the United States during the long terminal illness of her husband. This travesty led to the adoption of the Twenty-Fifth Amendment to the Constitution, which provides specific procedures for the removal of a president who is unable to discharge his duties.

MARSHALL, THURGOOD. See BLACK FEDERAL JUDGES.

MARTIAL LAW. A temporary military regime which controls a civilian population during emergencies. Martial law supersedes civilian law, and normal civil rights may be suspended by its invocation. The President's power to declare martial law, while not specifically granted by the Constitution, is implied from his enumerated powers over matters of national security. State governors have similar discretion to employ state militia during crises. However, martial law cannot co-exist with civilian law; if civil courts operate during emergencies, the military cannot violate civil rights in the name of martial law.

MARTINDALE-HUBBELL LAW DIRECTORY. Named after the two gentlemen who created it, this is a seven-volume standard reference and research text which has served the legal profession well for over 100 years. It supplies up-to-date detailed information on more than 400,000 lawyers throughout the United States and the world and attempts to rate one third of them as to areas of specialization and competence. In addition, it provides a digest on the laws of the 50 States, the Commonwealth of Puerto Rico, American possessions and foreign countries. It is the only law list book which has been granted a certificate of compliance by the American Bar Association.

MARTIN v. HUNTER'S LESSEE, 14 U.S. 141 (1816). A Supreme Court case which held that the Court has the power to review state court judgments resting on interpretations of federal law. The Court rejected the Virginia Supreme Court's ruling that section 25 of the Judiciary Act of 1789 was unconstitutional. Section 25 provided for Supreme Court review of final decisions of the highest state courts rejecting claims based on federal law. The decision thus ensured that the Supreme Court would be the final judicial arbiter of Federal Constitutional and statutory questions.

MARXIAN THEORY. Economic, social and political theories espoused by German reformer Karl Marx which invoke the inevitable decline of capitalism and eventual evolution to a classless society. Ironically, Marx was born to a substantial middle class family and was supported, while writing the *Communist Manifesto*, by his well-to-do associate, Friedrich Engels. Marxian theory forms the basis for Russian and Chinese Communism as well as many non-Communist socialist countries.

MARXISM-LENINISM. The legal system of a Communist country. Karl Marx died in 1883, before his theories of socialistic economics and the doctrines of history based on materialistic forces presented in his classic book, *Das Kapital,* could be put into action. This was first done successfully by Vladimir Lenin, a lawyer, in Russia in 1917 with the assassination of the Tsar and the abolition of capitalism in its alleged exploitation of labor.

MARY CARTER AGREEMENTS. Contracts by which one co-defendant secretly agrees with the plaintiff that if such co-defendant will proceed with his defense, his own liability will decrease proportionally by increasing the liability of other co-defendants. Named after a Florida case involving the Mary Carter Paint Company, such agreements pose serious ethical problems.

MASSACHUSETTS BALLOT (Office-Block Ballot). Lists the candidates for each office under the title of the office. Used in almost half the States, this type of ballot focuses attention on individual candidates and encourages people to split their vote.

MASSACHUSETTS TRUST. A type of business enterprise named in Massachusetts in 1830 where the assets are conveyed or transferred to a board of trustees which manages the business. Today, the device is used extensively in developing land subdivisions for sale and marketing and managing oil and gas leases. An important characteristic of this type of business operation is that the beneficiaries are really partners; thus, the Massachusetts Trust is not really a trust in the strict sense at all.

MASSIAH v. UNITED STATES (377 U.S. 201 (1964)). In this Supreme Court case the defendant, who had already been indicted, was interviewed by an informant in a car. Unknown to the defendant, the car was "bugged" and the police recorded an admission that he made during the conversation. The Court held that the admission had been illegally obtained because the defendant's Sixth Amendment right to counsel had been denied. The case stands for the proposition that an indicted defendant may not be interrogated without the assistance of counsel.

MASSIVE RESISTANCE. A phrase coined by United States Senator Harry Flood Byrd, Sr., of Virginia, in 1956. The phrase became the battle cry of Virginians and, later, other Southerners who wanted to fight even token compliance with the Supreme Court decision to end racial segregation in public education. In 1956, Senator Byrd's forces in the Virginia General Assembly, led by Mills E. Godwin, Jr. and whipped to a near hysteria by the editor of the Richmond *News Leader,* James J. Kilpatrick, Jr., moved to halt the integration of Virginia's public schools. In a special summer session in 1956, the General Assembly passed several laws which required Virginia's governor to close any public schools ordered to integrate by the federal courts. In 1958 public schools in several counties and cities were closed. In 1959, after the Navy threatened to pull the fleet out of Norfolk and business leaders became wary of moving to Virginia because of the lack of public education,

Governor J. Lindsay Almond, Jr. reversed his own Massive Resistance stance and fought the Byrd machine, of which he had been a loyal part, to end the plan. Governor Almond won by a vote of 20 to 19, ending Massive Resistance in Virginia.

MASTER OF THE COURT. Appointed by a judge to act as a fact finder, a referee, an auditor, an examiner, a commissioner, or an assessor to render special assistance in a particular case. The appointment of a master, to be made only in exceptional circumstances, may be useful to relieve court congestion or to expedite complex cases and unusually long trials. These advantages, however, must be weighed against the deprivation of a litigant's traditional right to have his case passed upon by a court or jury in the first instance. The use of masters in federal courts is described in Rule 53 of the Federal Rules of Civil Procedure. Each United States District Court may appoint one or more standing masters for its district; the court may also appoint special masters for individual cases or issues. In a jury case, the master's findings are read to the jury as mere evidence, which the jury is free to disregard. In a non-jury situation, however, the report of the master must be accepted by the court as findings of fact unless the judge determines they are clearly erroneous.

MASTER OF THE ROLLS. Chief Judge of the Civil Court of Appeal in England. Since few cases go to the House of Lords, the Master of the Rolls is influential in shaping English law. The current Master of the Rolls is Lord Denning, who reminded the Attorney-General of England, "Be you ever so high, the Law is above you."

MATCHING ACCEPTANCE RULE. See BATTLE OF THE FORMS.

MATERIAL BREACH OF CONTRACT. The failure of one party to perform according to an agreement. A material breach gives the other party the power to cancel the contract and to sue for damages. If the breach of prom-

McCARRAN

ise was based upon a constructive condition, the aggrieved party may still treat the condition as a material breach. Absent a material breach, the aggrieved party has the right to sue for partial breach, but may not cancel the contract.

MATERIAL EVIDENCE. Evidence relating to an issue which the law deems important to the deciding of a case and which is raised by the pleadings. For instance, in a suit to recover damages for injuries caused by a defectively manufactured product, evidence showing that the maker was not negligent would be immaterial since a manufacturer is, in most states, strictly liable for damage caused by his defective goods. Material evidence should not be confused with relevant evidence.

MATHEMATICAL EVIDENCE. Generally, the introduction of probability, statistics and mathematics, as evidence at trial. In the controversial case of *People v. Collins*, 66 Cal. Rptr. 497 (1968), the California Supreme Court overturned a conviction based on such evidence, holding that on the record of that case "the defendant should not have had his guilt determined by the odds." While the court did not totally foreclose the use of probabilities at trial, it voiced its dissatisfaction with the techniques used in this case. It held that mathematical odds are not admissible as evidence to identify a defendant in a criminal proceeding when the odds are based on estimates, whose validity has not been shown.

MAXIMUM ALLOWABLE COST PROGRAM (M.A.C.). A federal program which limits reimbursement for prescription drugs under the Medicare and Medicaid programs and Public Health Service projects to the lowest cost at which the drug is generally available.

MAXIMUM JOHN. A nickname given to the United States District Judge John Sirica as a result of the heavy fines and long jail sentences he gave to those who were convicted of Watergate crimes.

MAXI-TAX. The highest federal income tax rate for personal service income, which is 50 percent.

M.B.F.R. (Mutual and Balanced Force Reductions). A counterpart to S.A.L.T. in the eternal quest for East-West Detente. It is an attempt to negotiate a reduction in the military forces and equipment that N.A.T.O. and the Warsaw Pact have poised against each other in Central Europe, triggered to start World War III. Formal talks to so save Western Civilization first began in Vienna in 1973 and they seem to be getting nowhere fast.

M.C.A. (Monetary Compensation Amounts). Common Market payments which subsidize agricultural exports from strong currency countries such as Germany while preventing farmers in weak currency countries such as Italy from gaining an unfair price advantage. The program is designed to protect the system's single farm price policy from fluctuations in national currency values.

McCARRAN ACT (Internal Security Act). Federal legislation passed in 1950, over President Harry S. Truman's veto, which was aimed at deterring Communist subversion. The Act was named for its chief sponsor, Nevada Senator Patrick A. McCarran, known for his promotion of several McCarthy-era immigration control and red-scare measures, as well as legislation benefiting producers of, and encouraging the use of, domestic silver. The Act created the Subversive Activities Control Board, which could, on motion by the Attorney General, require any organization found to be Communist to register with the Justice Department and to reveal information about its funding and members. In addition, the Act made it a felony to contribute substantially to the establishment of a totalitarian regime in the United States, and it authorized the President, in time of emergency, to arrest and detain persons suspected of being spies or saboteurs. Neither the Presidential power nor the prosecution for the new felony was ever exercised. The Act was amended in 1968 to eliminate the registration requirement, though a list of organizations found to be Communist could still be maintained.

McCARRAN-WALTER ACT. See IMMIGRATION AND NATIONALITY ACT.

McCULLOCH v. MARYLAND (17 U.S. 315 (1819)). A Supreme Court decision which ruled that the government of the United States derives certain implied powers from the Constitution of the United States. Chief Justice John Marshall, upholding the constitutionality of the Congressional charter of the Second Bank of the United States, held that the "necessary and proper" clause of Article I, section 8 is the basis for this implied power. Marshall stated, "Let the end be legitimate, let it be within the scope of the Constitution, and all means which are appropriate, which are plainly adapted to that end, which are not prohibited, but consist with the letter and spirit of the Constitution are constitutional."

McDOUGAL-LASSWELL JURISPRUDENCE. Comprehensive new theories about law, designed to make use of the findings of modern physical and social science brought to the enterprise of international law by Myres S. McDougal and Harold D. Lasswell. McDougal was the former Sterling Professor of Law at Yale University and former President of the American Society of International Law. Lasswell, also of Yale, was the Phelps Professor of Law and Political Science and has been McDougal's distinguished colleague in intellectual endeavors for over thirty years. These two theorists apply an emerging, policy-oriented jurisprudence to important contemporary problems in world order. The framework of this inquiry has accented the reconstruction of international law. McDougal and Lasswell have authored several books individually and with others, and co-authored the invaluable works *Studies in World Public Order and Law* and *Public Order In Space.*

M.C.M. See MANUAL FOR COURTS MARTIAL.

McNABB-MALLORY RULE. Rule 5 (A) of the Federal Rules of Criminal Procedure states that a person arrested without a warrant or under a warrant issued upon a Bill of Complaint shall be taken before a committing magistrate "without unnecessary delay." In *McNabb v. United States,* 318 U.S. 332 (1943), the Supreme Court held that incriminating statements made by a person during a period of unlawful detention between arrest and appearance before a magistrate could not be used against him at trial. The Court reaffirmed this ruling in *Mallory v. United States,* 354 U.S. 499 (1957), stating that while the duty to bring arrested persons before a committing magistrate "without unnecessary delay" did not call for "mechanical or automatic obedience," it allowed "arresting officers little more leeway than the interval between arrest and the ordinary administrative steps required to bring a suspect . . . before the nearest available magistrate." The McNabb-Mallory Rule is, of course, an exercise of the Court's "supervision of the administration of criminal justice in the Federal Courts" and presumably not binding on the states.

MEASURING LIFE. The person used to determine (1) the duration of a life estate, or (2) the time within which a trust must vest to satisfy the Rule Against Perpetuities.

MECHANICS LIEN. Created by state law to secure or guarantee payment for services which improve, repair, or maintain real property. The lien can be enforced through court-ordered foreclosure and sale of the property to pay off the lien.

MERIT SYSTEM PRODUCTION BOARD. A federal agency created under the Civil Service Reform Act of 1979 to protect whistle-blowers within the government from reprisals. The Board was established because of the Nixon Administration's punishment of Pentagon analyst A. Ernest Fitzgerald in 1970 after he told Congress about a $2-billion cost overrun in weapons contracts.

MEDAL OF THE JUST. Heroism award by Jerusalem's Historical Institute of Yad Vachern which honors persons who saved the lives of Jews during the Nazi occupation of Europe.

MEDIATION DISPUTE CENTER. See NEIGHBORHOOD COURT.

MEDICAL CERTIFICATION. A non-judicial commitment procedure for the mentally ill. Certificates signed by one or more physicians, stating that they have examined the patient and that he meets the statutory criteria for commitment, authorize the hospital to accept and retain the patient. The judge verifies only the signatures and qualifications of the physicians.

MEDICAL DEVICE AMENDMENTS TO FOOD, DRUG AND COSMETIC ACT. A federal law passed in 1976 which became effective on December 18, 1978, creating a Bureau of Medical Devices within the Food and Drug Administration with control over 5,000 products ranging from simple toothbrushes and eyeglasses to complicated pacemakers and kidney dialysis systems. Every manufacturer of such products must now (1) conduct at least two independent studies on the safety and effectiveness of prescribed devices; (2) keep records, audits and quality control statements; and (3) submit to unannounced, on-site inspections.

MEDICARE PROGRAM (Title XVIII). A nationwide health insurance program for people aged 65 and over, for people eligible for Social Security disability payments for over two years, and for certain workers and their dependents who need kidney transplants or dialysis. Health insurance protection is available to insured persons without regard to income. Monies from payroll taxes and premiums from beneficiaries are deposited in special trust funds for use in meeting the expenses incurred by the insured. The program became effective on July 1, 1966.

MEMBERSHIP CORPORATIONS. A term loosely used as a synonym for non-profit corporations. Often these organizations are characterized by the absence of stock. They do not distribute gains or profits to their members on invested capital, but provide a convenient method of organizing such entities as country clubs, where the activity involves ownership of property and engaging in some incidental business.

MEMOIRS v. MASSACHUSETTS. See REDEEMING SOCIAL VALUE TEST.

MENOMINEE LEGAL DEFENSE-OFFENSE COMMITTEE. Organization headed by lawyer Phyllis Girouard to provide legal services at nominal or no expense to the Menominee Indian tribe. The group has been active in civil rights litigation, as well as in promoting tribal, rather than state, legal remedies. For example, under the traditional Indian system, a couple wanting a divorce merely appears before the tribal elders who married them, rather than hiring a White lawyer to take the case to state court.

MENS REA (Latin—guilty mind). The criminal culpability which, when accompanied by a criminal act, constitutes a crime. Mens Rea refers to any state of mind required for a crime. Thus, crimes punishing objective fault, like strict liability crimes, do not have a Mens Rea element. Traditionally, there have been two types of Mens Rea. General Mens Rea refers to the intentional performance of a criminal act where the accused intentionally, knowingly, willfully or recklessly performs an act. In a broader sense, he has an evil mind. Specific Mens Rea refers to an intent to do a further act or to cause additional consequences. For example, in the crime of assault with intent to commit murder, both a general intent to commit the assault and a specific intent to kill must be shown. Additionally, crimes of attempt, such as attempted murder, require that a specific intent to kill be shown. Note that a specific intent to kill is not required for the crime of murder itself. Modern codes, such as the Model Penal Code, often do not use specific intent and general intent, because the terms have various meanings.

MENTAL HEALTH LAW. A developing field of jurisprudence concerned with the due process rights and civil liberties of mentally ill individuals who are involuntarily committed to state psychiatric hospitals. Commitment standards, the patient's right to treatment or right to refuse treatment, and the right to payment of the patient-worker are among the questions addressed. This body of law is predicated on the recognition that involuntary civil commitment results in the same deprivation of freedom as criminal incarceration and hence demands comparable procedural oversight. Similarly, the conditions of confinement must be in accordance with written guidelines designed to reflect the therapeutic justification for civil commitment. On the criminal side, the two key issues of mental health law concern the defendant's competency to stand trial and the availability of psychiatric defenses to the crime charged.

MENU BILLS. City ordinances which make punishable by a heavy fine any misleading statement in a restaurant menu. Samples of violations would include: (1) Farmer's Choice. Farm-fresh eggs; creamery butter; hearty Colombian java; stacks of extra crisp toast with rasher of Canadian bacon (ninety-two percent egg white; 7 percent whey with calcium and sodium caseinates; lecithin and vegetable mono- and diglycerides; cellulose; zanthan gums; artificial colors; aluminum sulfate; ferric orthoposphate; zinc sulfate; calcium pantothenate; last night's reheated coffee; slightly scorched day-old bread; 1 slice sandwich ham); (2) The Fish You Eat Today Slept Last Night in Chesapeake Bay (frozen fish from Japan).

M.E.O.W. (Moral Equivalent of War). Name of speech and message to Congress by President Carter in May of 1977 in which he warned the nation of the forthcoming energy crisis and urged the passage of the laws he deemed necessary to protect the interests of the people.

MERCEDARIAN ORDER. See RANSOM PAYMENT.

MERCHANDISE TRADE BALANCE. Measures the difference between the value of United States goods exported to other countries and foreign goods imported into this country. The trade balance is generally regarded as "favorable" when exports exceed imports, resulting in a trade surplus, and "unfavorable" when imports exceed exports, resulting in a trade deficit.

MERCY KILLING (Euthanasia). Causing the death of a critically ill person by some affirmative action or by withdrawing life-sustaining treatment or medication. Considered by many to be a humane act of mercy, such an act is still legally murder. Doctors, however, are rarely, if ever, convicted for murder or manslaughter for having withheld treatment in order to end suffering. Also, juries are usually lenient with relatives who end the suffering of a family member.

MERE CHARRING RULE. A common law rule to determine when arson has been committed. Under this rule, if a fire causes any damage to the structural material of another's dwelling, a person who maliciously set the fire is guilty of arson. Mere charring is sufficient to meet the requirements of arson.

MERE EVIDENCE RULE. Limitation on the seizure powers of law enforcement officials. Formulated during a period when the Fourth Amendment to the United States Constitution was viewed as protecting property interests, the rule prohibited the police from seizing evidence which did not consist of contraband or fruits of a crime. Now that the Fourth Amendment is seen as protecting privacy and not property, the rule has been discarded.

MERGER-IN-LAW. Term used to describe the effect of a former judgment rendered in favor of the plaintiff. From the moment the judgment is handed down, the cause of action which was the subject of the judgment, together with any item thereof, is extinguished. The plaintiff's claim has been "merged" with the judgment, and may not later be relitigated. The plaintiff's only recourse is to proceedings for the enforcement of the judgment, such as execution.

MERGER RULE. See RULE OF MERGER.

MESSIAH COMPLEX. An unfortunate tendency on the part of some judges to play the role of God after they don their black robes.

M.E.T. (Multiple Employer Benefit Trust). A pre-paid legal services plan. Generally, pre-paid legal services are provided either by insurance companies, which must meet stringent surplus and capital requirements, or by M.E.T.s, which do not have to meet such requirements. Recently, a number of M.E.T.s have failed, leaving the consumer no recourse; consequently, the United States Department of Labor has taken the position that M.E.T.s are not exempt from state regulation, and several states are now requiring that providers of pre-paid legal services stand behind the fiscal responsibility of the plan.

METES AND BOUNDS. A system of measurement used to determine boundaries for real property. Metes are measures in feet while bounds describe direction in degrees.

"ME TOO" SYSTEM. Department of Defense (D.O.D.) practice where any shipper of household goods who would meet the lowest rate already bid could share equally in the total shipments. This system gave no incentive for one shipper to underbid another shipper and profits under the "me too" system were twice those considered reasonable by the Interstate Commerce Commission. When the D.O.D. abandoned this system in some areas, costs were reduced by as much as 34 million dollars. The Freight Forwarders Association, of course, is actively fighting to retain this system.

METRIC CONVERSION ACT OF 1975. A federal law which created the United States Metric Board to assist those who voluntarily wished to convert to the Metric System (based on

10 and multiples of 10) followed in most of the world. Since the cost of total conversion would be in excess of 100 billion dollars, the voluntary conversion has been at a snail's pace, apart from the pharmaceutical and beverage industries and General Motors.

METRIC UNION. A permanent association created by the Treaty of the Meter in 1875, which adopted the Metric System of weights and measures. This system was created in 1789 by French scientists, and was subsequently adopted by most countries of the world. The United States became a member of the Metric Union in 1785, under the influence of Thomas Jefferson. Since then, however, and despite numerous governmental and congressional attempts to induce its use, the Metric System has not yet entered into effect in the American way of measuring. Although many more apply this system, 39 countries are permanent members of the Treaty of the Meter, and take part in its activities; the organization of the Treaty includes (1) the International Bureau of Weights and Measures, which is responsible for the development and the maintenance of the Metric System, and (2) the General Conference of Weights and Measures, composed of representatives of the member nations, which is the central governing body. The Conference meets once every six years.

M.F.N. See MOST FAVORED NATION STATUS.

MEXICAN CURSE. "May your life be filled with lawyers."

M.G.I.C. (Mortgage Guaranty Insurance Corporation). A private company formed in 1957 by a Milwaukee lawyer named Max H. Karl which successfully competes with the Federal Housing Administration in insuring private home mortgage loans.

MICHIGAN v. FORD MOTOR COMPANY. The first criminal case of reckless homicide against an automobile company, based on the faulty design of a gas tank on a Pinto car. Three girls were killed when their Pinto exploded in flames after being hit by another car. The court held that the automobile manufacturer was not liable for their deaths.

MIDDLE EAST PEACE ACCORD. See CAMP DAVID SUMMIT.

MIDDLE INCOME STUDENT ASSISTANCE ACT (M.I.S.A.A.). Passed by Congress in 1978 to become effective in the fall of 1979, this was the first federal law in American history to provide financial support grants to college and vocational students in families whose annual income did not exceed $26,000. An estimated 1.5 million students took advantage of this program for middle income families in the first year of its application.

MIDDLE TEMPLE. See INNS OF COURT.

MIDNIGHT APPOINTMENTS. A legal practice by elected officials in their waning days of office to name their cronies to plush government jobs. A related practice is the granting of midnight pardons. For example, Governor Ray Blanton of Tennessee pardoned hundreds of hardened criminals on his way out of office.

MIDNIGHT EXPRESS. Prison lingo for escape of an inmate.

MIDNIGHT JUDGES ACT (Circuit Court Act of 1801). Passed by the Federalist Congress during the dying days of the Adams Administration, only four days prior to the election of Thomas Jefferson. The Act reorganized the federal judiciary by eliminating the circuit riding duties of the Justices of the Supreme Court and authorizing the appointment of sixteen new circuit court judges, so that each circuit court would consist of three judges. As expected, Adams promptly appointed federalists to the newly created posts, hastily nominating his midnight judges during the last two weeks of his term. The incoming Jeffersonians felt the Act was merely a device of the defeated Federalists to maintain control of the federal judiciary. The new administration quickly repealed the Act in 1802, es-

sentially reestablishing the old circuit court system, with Supreme Court Justices and district judges once again sitting on the circuit court benches. The short-lived Act was repealed while the famous case of *Marbury v. Madison,* 5 U.S. 87 (1803) was still pending in the Supreme Court, so the Act's constitutionality was never directly tested. Modern commentators have observed that the Midnight Judges Act "combined thoughtful concern for the federal judiciary with selfish concern for the Federalist party."

MIDNIGHT MERGERS. Secretive corporate mergers, recently outlawed by Federal Trade Commission (F.T.C.) pre-merger notification rules promulgated under the Hart-Scott-Rodino Antitrust Improvements Act (1976). The rules, which became effective in 1978, require persons contemplating an acquisition to notify the F.T.C. and the Justice Department thirty days before consummation of the merger. In the case of tenders, the agencies must be notified within fifteen days. After evaluating the transaction, the agencies are empowered to seek preliminary injunctions in federal district court and to obtain $10,000-a-day penalties for each day a person is in violation of the Act.

MIKADO KOSHO OF JAPAN. An oriental leader who in 457 B.C. arrested and beheaded the leaders of an association formed to settle the estates of wealthy subjects. In the view of the sovereign, the persons who offered to provide such services did not have the qualifications or conscience essential to such a confidence and trust. This is the earliest reported instance of a governmental sanction being imposed for the unauthorized practice of law.

MILITARY CLAIMS ACT. A federal law, first enacted by Congress in 1943, authorizing the various federal military departments to settle and pay claims against the United States for the loss or damage to real or personal property or for personal injury or death, either caused by military personnel or civilian employees of the military departments while acting within the scope of their employment or otherwise incident to noncombat activities of the military departments. Included within the scope of the Act are claims arising out of the use or occupancy of real property, whether under a lease, express or implied, or otherwise; criminal acts resulting in the loss or damage of registered or insured mail while in the possession of the armed forces; and loss or damage to personal property leased to the United States. Noncombat activities which may give rise to a claim under the Act are those which are peculiarly military in nature and have little parallel in the civilian community, such as maneuvers and special exercises; practice firing of heavy guns; practice bombing; naval exhibitions; operation of missiles, aircraft, and antiaircraft equipment; sonic booms; use by the military of instrumentalities having latent mechanical defects not traceable to negligent acts or omissions; explosions of ammunition; movement of combat vehicles or other vehicles designed especially for military use; and the use and occupancy of real estate. The secretaries of the military departments or the respective Judge Advocates General are authorized to settle claims not in excess of $25,000. If a meritorious claim in excess of $25,000 and cognizable under this Act is submitted, the first $25,000 may be paid, with the remainder reported to Congress for consideration. Claims covered by the Foreign Claims Act and the Federal Torts Claim Act may not be paid under the Military Claims Act.

MILITARY CLAUSE. A provision in a lease that enables a member of the Armed Forces who is transferred to another location to break the lease without being liable in damages to the lessor.

MILITARY JUDGE (Formerly known as Law Officer). A commissioned officer of the armed forces, who presides over all open sessions of the court martial to which he or she is assigned. The term first became recognized in military law with the passage of the Military Justice Act of 1968. Assigned to all general courts martial and most special courts martial, the military judge must be a member of the bar of a federal court or of the highest court of a state and be certified as qualified for duty as a military judge by the Judge Advocate General of the armed force of which he or she is a member. In creating this role, Congress intended to raise the military judge to the level of judges of the United States District Courts.

MILITARY JUSTICE ACT OF 1968. Legislation which created an independent military judiciary outside the pressures and controls of base commanders. Among other things, the Act required competent legal counsel and judges in many areas where they had not been previously required, gave military judges powers similar to those of civilian judges, allowed an accused his freedom pending appeal, and prohibited a general court martial consisting of a single judge from deciding a case in which the death penalty could be imposed. When President Johnson signed the Act, he noted that it had brought military personnel a long way from the "drumhead justice of Valley Forge" by giving them first-class justice in addition to the other first-class services provided by the armed forces.

MILITARY LAW. The comprehensive body of law regulating the military establishment. Developing historically from two distinct bodies of law, naval law and the law of land armies, military law has come to encompass the full panoply of matters affecting the operation and maintenance of the armed forces, including discipline, military and civil crimes, administrative law matters, international law and relations, claims against the government, admiralty law, procurement of military property, and the law of war. Military law in the United States is based on the various statutes enacted by Congress pursuant to authority granted by the Constitution. Military law provides the rules by which a military society is to function, both internally and externally.

MILITARY PERSONNEL AND CI-VILIAN EMPLOYEES' CLAIMS ACT. A federal law enacted by Congress in 1964 which permits the secretaries of the military departments and the heads of federal agencies or their designees to settle and pay claims for damage to and loss of personal property of military personnel and civilian employees of the federal government, including employees of the government of the District of Columbia. The damage or loss must be incident to the service, but it need not have occurred during the actual performance of the claimant's official duties. The possession of the property damaged or lost must be reasonable, useful, or proper under the circumstances. The statutory limit on each claim is $15,000.

MILLER v. CALIFORNIA (413 U.S. 15 (1973)). A Supreme Court case that changed the definition of obscenity from "utterly without redeeming social value" to "no redeeming social value," and imposed local community standards rather than national standards for pornography. This decision generally gives censors wider scope in prohibiting artistic and literary works. The Georgia Supreme Court was one of the first to act in response to the *Miller* decision, when it found the R-rated movie *Carnal Knowledge* obscene. However, the Georgia decision was overturned by the Supreme Court of the United States, which found *Carnal Knowledge* not "patently offensive," as required under Miller.

MILLER v. RACE. See HOLDER IN DUE COURSE DOCTRINE.

MILLIONAIRES' CLUB. The United States Senate, one fourth of whose members own assets in excess of one million dollars each.

MILLION DOLLAR LAWYERS. See GOULDEN, JOSEPH.

MINERSVILLE SCHOOL DIST. v. GOBITIS. See FLAG SALUTE CASES.

MINI-MISSIONS. Small-staffed diplomatic representations in countries deemed less important than others.

MINIMUM CONTACTS. The shorthand statement of a test of personal jurisdiction established by the Supreme Court in the case of *International Shoe Co. v. Washington,* 326 U.S. 310 (1945). Under this test, a state court may acquire personal jurisdiction over a nonresident who does not receive service of process within the forum state. The state can satisfy the due process requirements of the United States Constitution if the non-resident has minimum contacts with the forum state, such that the exercise of the forum's jurisdiction does not offend traditional notions of fair play and substantial justice. Accordingly, personal jurisdiction has been based on such factors as the defendant's presence, domicile or residence in the state, an act in the state, an act out of state with an effect in the state, business transacted in the state, or the ownership or possession of property in the state. Many states now have long-arm statutes to facilitate their exercise of jurisdiction on these theories.

MINIMUM FEE SCHEDULES. Suggested minimum fees lawyers should charge their clients, generally set by a local or state bar association. Minimum fee schedules have been successfully attacked as violating the Sherman Anti-Trust Act in several courts, including the Supreme Court.

MINIMUM MARKUP LAW. A statute requiring retailers or wholesalers to sell their merchandise at cost plus an additional minimum amount. Thirty-four states enacted such legislation during the 1930s and much of it has survived. Some of the statutes specify a fixed percentage which must be added to cost while others require a markup which will cover operating costs. Although this legislation is criticized as being anti-competitive and fostering inefficiency, its defenders claim it is necessary to protect against price-cutting.

MINIMUM TAX. A special levy to guarantee that wealthy people, especially those with tax shelters, are no longer able to avoid paying any tax at all on their large incomes.

MINI-TRIAL. See PRE-TRIAL DIS-COVERY.

MINORITY PRESIDENT. See ELEC-TORAL COLLEGE.

MINOR'S INSTITUTES. A four-volume learned treatise on American law written by Professor John B. Minor of the University of Virginia School of Law during his 50-year-old teaching career (1845-1895). Chief Justice Waite said he would rather have been the author of this scholarly tome than Chief Justice of the United States. Praise indeed!

MIRANDA WARNINGS. Issued by a police officer prior to interrogating an individual who has been taken into custody. They are intended to protect the privilege against self-incrimination and the right to counsel. The warnings are based on the decision of the Supreme Court in *Miranda v. Arizona*, 384 U.S. 436 (1966). The Court held that in a criminal trial the prosecution may not use statements, incriminating or otherwise, made by a person who has been taken into custody, unless it demonstrates the use of procedural safeguards which protect the privilege against self-incrimination. The warnings are:

1. You have the right to remain silent.
2. Anything you say can and will be used against you in a court of law.
3. You have the right to talk to a lawyer and have him present with you while you are being questioned.
4. If you cannot afford to hire a lawyer one will be appointed to represent you before any questioning if you wish one.

After these rights have been explained, if the individual indicates in any way before or during questioning that he wishes to remain silent, the interrogation must cease. If the interrogation continues without the presence of a lawyer and a statement is taken, a heavy burden rests on the government to show that the person knowingly and intelligently waived his privilege against self-incrimination and his right to retained or appointed counsel. An express statement that the individual is willing to make a statement and does not want an attorney, followed closely by a statement, could be a waiver. The Court stated that a valid waiver would not be presumed simply from the silence of the individual after being warned or from the fact that a confession was in fact eventually obtained.

MIRROR IMAGE RULE. See BATTLE OF THE FORMS.

M.I.S.A. See FEDERAL COLLEGE-AID STATUTES.

M.I.S.A.A. See MIDDLE INCOME STUDENT ASSISTANCE ACT.

MISCARRIAGE OF JUSTICE. Whenever a friend or relative or member of a cause you believe in is sent to jail.

MISDEMEANOR MANSLAUGHTER. A form of involuntary manslaughter. As the name suggests, the killing occurs during the commission of a misdemeanor. Generally, the misdemeanor must be Malum In Se, involving conduct that is inherently wrong, though some courts hold that any misdemeanor is sufficient. If the misdemeanor is not malum in se, however, the death must be a foreseeable result of the commission of the manslaughter.

MISLEADING QUESTION (Argumentative Question). Assumes as true a fact which is not established. At trial, for example, an attorney may not ask a witness, "Where did you dispose of the murder weapon?" Such a question is misleading in that it tricks the witness into admitting possession of the murder weapon.

MISPRISION OF FELONY. Failure to prevent or reveal the commission of a felony. At common law, both misprision of felony and compounding a crime were misdemeanors. Compounding a crime, however, consists of accepting valuable consideration in exchange for a promise to conceal the identity or whereabouts of a criminal or to prevent his prosecution. Today most jurisdictions hold that a person may be guilty of compounding a crime even if the original crime was a misdemeanor.

MISPRISION OF TREASON. Failure to prevent or reveal an act of treason.

MISSOURI COMPROMISE. An interstate pact which banned slavery in the United States territories during the 1850s. In the Dred Scott Decision, which many commentators view as the spark which started the Civil War, the Supreme Court held the Compromise unconstitutional.

MISSOURI PLAN. Method of selecting state court judges, first adopted by Missouri in 1940, designed to stop control of judicial appointments by political machines and to permit popular judgment of state court judges' records. Under the plan, the state Governor selects judges from a list of three nominees who are named by a commission composed of the state supreme court justice, three lawyers elected by the bar, and three laymen appointed by the Governor. In the trial courts the judges serve for six years, and in the appellate courts for twelve years. The judges then run against their records without opposition, and only a majority vote is needed for re-election. Proponents of this sensible plan feel it removes judges from the unseemly task of campaigning for office while retaining some measure of accountability to the electorate.

MISTAKE OF LAW OR FACT. Ignorance of particular laws or factual circumstances by an individual who engages in criminal acts. The distinction between a mistake of law and a mistake of fact is often strained, but is crucial in states which hold that a mistake of fact excuses criminal acts, while a mistake of law does not. Bigamous marriage is a good example. If A marries C after obtaining an invalid divorce from B, is his erroneous belief that the divorce was valid a mistake of fact or law? The answer could logically go either way, but most courts have held that it is a mistake of law. The success of a mistake defense depends on the applicable state of mind. If the required mental state is "knowing," then A is excused; but if, as in most states, no Mens Rea is required, then A is not excused. The modern trend is not to differentiate between mistakes of fact or Law Per Se, but rather to excuse any mistake which negatives the existence of a necessary Mens Rea element. For example, the crime of larceny requires an intent to steal. If A takes B's coat, erroneously believing that it is his own, then there is no intent to steal and A is excused. However, if A takes B's coat, knowing that it belongs to B, but not knowing that his conduct is prohibited, A is not excused since he intended to deprive B of his property. In other words, knowledge that the law prohibits such conduct is not a necessary Mens Rea element. If A found the coat and publicized his finding in the newspaper for five days before keeping it, A would be excused if he thought that he had gained legal title by advertising for five days even though the law actually required advertisement for ten days. A's mistake was one of a collateral law and negatives his intent to steal. Many states require that the accused's mistake be reasonable. The mistake must be one which a reasonable man could make. Additionally, many states disallow mistake as a defense if the accused's conduct was morally wrong. For example, an accused generally will not be excused from the crime of statutory rape on the ground that he thought that the victim was over the age of consent.

MITCHELL, JOHN. Attorney-General of President Nixon, who became the highest American government official to be convicted of a felony and sent to jail. After spending a year and a half in prison, he was released on January 19th, 1979, the last of the 25 Watergate criminals who had been jailed.

MITCHELL-LAMA LAW. A 1956 New York law which stimulated the growth of middle-income co-operative apartments by the use of long-term, low-interest loans and property tax abatement.

M'NAGHTEN TEST. Used in the overwhelming majority of states to determine whether criminal conduct should be excused by reason of insanity. The test originated in mid-nineteenth century England in the *M'Naghten* case, where Daniel M'Naghten, believing that Sir Robert Peel was leading a conspiracy to kill him, killed Edward Drummond, whom he mistook for Peel. In deciding whether M'Naghten's delusions should excuse him, the Queen's Bench developed the test which survives today. Basically, the M'Naghten Test excuses a defendant if (1) he was laboring under a defect of reason, from a mental disease and (2) at the time of the crime he did not know the nature and quality of the act or that it was wrong. Although parts of the test are vague, such as "mental disease," "know the nature and quality of the act," and "wrong," there has been little explanatory case law. The jury is usually given a recital of the rule with little explanation. Critics of the M'Naghten Test, who feel that it is outdated, argue that the science of psychiatry now recognizes that the power of reason is only one facet of man's personality and should not be the sole determinant of legal insanity. Thus about half of the states using the M'Naghten Test supplement it with the Irresistible Impulse Test, and a few states have rejected the M'Naghten Test in favor of the Product Test. The Model Penal Code has adopted a "substantial capacity" test which is basically a refinement of the combined M'Naghten and Irresistible Impulse tests, but which requires a substantial rather than a total lack of the capacity to distinguish right from wrong.

MOBILE BRIGADES. See ORGANIZATION ON HIGH.

MODEL PENAL CODE. A Model Criminal Code drafted by the American Law Institute, parts of which are now being adopted in an increasing number of states. One of its main innovations is the coordination between acts and states of mind. It abandons the amorphous Mens Rea terms previously used and replaces them with four states of mind — Purpose, Knowledge, Recklessness and Negligence. Additionally, it clarifies the confusion created when the Actus Reus of a crime involves several physical elements. For example, the crime of murder has two physical elements—a physical act such as pulling a trigger and a result, death. Does the required state of mind apply to the act, the result or both? The Model Penal Code solves this problem by dividing crimes into as many as three physical elements—an act, circumstances, and a result, each with an accompanying Mens Rea requirement. For example, the Model Penal Code defines the crime of reckless burning or exploding basically as follows: "[To] purposely start a fire ... and thereby recklessly place another person in danger of death or bodily injury." The act is starting a fire and the accompanying State of Mind is purposely; the result is placing another person in danger of death and the accompanying state of mind is recklessly. Thus, each of the two physical elements has a specified state of mind.

MODEL PENAL CODE TEST. A modern standard for determining criminal responsibility. It recognizes the mind as a unified entity in which gradations are inevitable. The test holds that a person is not responsible for criminal conduct if at the time of such conduct, as a result of mental disease or defect, he lacks substantial capacity either to appreciate the criminality or wrongfulness of his conduct, or to conform his conduct to the requirements of the law. As used in this test, the terms "mental disease or defect" exclude an abnormality manifested only by repeated criminal or otherwise antisocial conduct. Such exclusions have been construed as eliminating certain character disorders. Generally, the test is intended to incorporate a volitional element which would not require total impairment. This standard has been adopted by the federal courts and a growing minority of states.

MODEL PROCUREMENT CODE (M.P.C.). The Model Procurement

Code is a 1978 product of the American Bar Association's Coordinating Committee on a Procurement Code for state and local governments. The Code, which in many respects represents an abbreviated version of the Defense Acquisition Regulations (D.A.R.), is offered as a reasonably short statute designed to be implemented by regulations developed by the enacting jurisdictions. Like D.A.R., the Model Code addresses selection of contractors, contract performance, termination, and settlement.

MODEL STATE CONSTITUTION. A proposal for state constitutional reform drafted by the National Municipal League. The Model features a strong executive branch, a unicameral legislature, a uniform court system and a Bill of Rights. It also includes modern techniques of financial and personnel management. The Model appears skeletal compared with most state constitutions, which contain numerous random restrictions on the residual powers delegated to the states by the United States Constitution.

MODERN BOSTON TEA PARTY. A project sponsored by the American Conservative Union to continue the Taxpayers' Rebellion exemplified by Proposition 13. Disgruntled taxpayers are encouraged to send tea bags to their state and federal officials as a message that the over-taxed citizen has had enough.

MODIFIED UNION SHOP. See UNION SHOP.

MODUS OPERANDI (Latin-manner of operating). Used by police agencies to discover a suspect, the term describes the character of an individual and the manner in which he commits a criminal act.

MODUS VIVENDI (Latin—manner of living). A temporary arrangement pending the final resolution of a dispute.

MOLLY MAGUIRES. Secret organization of Irish miners in Pennsylvania who participated in a bitter strike against coal owners when they cut wages and failed to improve miserable working conditions. The Molly Maguires were blamed for a campaign of terror, altogether it was later revealed that the coal operators were responsible for some of the violence. Nevertheless, ten Molly Maguires were hanged and fourteen others imprisoned during the labor dispute. Their name comes from a widow who once led a group to intimidate Irish landlords.

MONDALE MAFIA. A small but powerful inner circle of federal government officials who served as advisors to Vice-President Walter Mondale, especially in the realm of foreign affairs.

M-ONE (M-1). See BASIC MONEY SUPPLY.

MONETARY COMPENSATION AMOUNTS. See M.C.A.

MONKEY TRIAL (Scopes Trial). A 1927 mockery of a trial in which John Scopes, a public school teacher, challenged Tennessee's Anti-Evolution Law, which prohibited teaching any theories of creation other than a literal interpretation of the Bible. The Law was sponsored by the great orator and religious Fundamentalist, William Jennings Bryan, who defended it against Scopes and his attorney, Clarence Darrow. Darrow, an equally great orator, devoted his life to defending the underprivileged and offered his services free of charge to Scopes. The courtroom in Dayton, Tennessee, was so packed with Fundamentalists that the timbers of the floor threatened to give way, and the proceedings were moved to the courthouse lawn where it took on the air of a revival, the spectators shouting "Hallelujah" and "Amen" when Bryan scored a point. Obviously, Scopes was unable to get an impartial hearing; he was duly pronounced guilty, but the decision was later reversed by the Tennessee Supreme Court. More recently, in *Epperson v. Arkansas*, 393 U.S. 97 (1968), the United States Supreme Court invalidated an Arkansas statute that prohibited the teaching of evolution.

MONROE DOCTRINE. Promulgated by President James Monroe in 1823 and hailed as one of the most fundamental documents in American foreign policy, the Doctrine attempted to limit European influence in the Western Hemisphere. Hailed as sheer folly by its opponents given the embryonic state of the American armed forces at that time, it was spurred by two developments—the dispute with Russia over the Pacific northwest coast and European intervention in newly-independent former Spanish colonies in the Americas. The Doctrine lay dormant until the 1840s, when it was invoked against Great Britain and France over United States acquisition of Texas and against Great Britain regarding activities in Oregon. The Roosevelt Corollary, proposed by Theodore Roosevelt in the early 20th century, extended the Doctrine to allow affirmative, offensive intervention by the United States in other nations in the hemisphere. Interestingly, the League of Nations charter stipulated that it would not abrogate "regional understandings," a direct attempt to accommodate the Monroe Doctrine.

MONROE, JAMES. Best known for his adeptness in foreign affairs, his opposition to ratification of the Constitution vaulted him to national prominence. Prior to assuming the Presidency, Monroe had been a protégé of Thomas Jefferson and had been appointed by George Washington as envoy to France. He was recalled eventually because of his indiscretions. Having gone to France to obtain navigation rights to the Mississippi River, he ended up negotiating for the Louisiana Purchase. Monroe's other achievements in foreign relations include diplomatic posts in Spain and London and service as Secretary of State under James Madison. As President, he fashioned the Monroe Doctrine to preempt intervention by European powers in the Western Hemisphere. He also assembled one of the strongest cabinets in American history, and was responsible for the first Harbor Act in 1823 and the Survey Act of 1824; the latter entailed a comprehensive economic and social plan for the future.

MONROE v. PAPE. See 1983 SUITS.

MONRONEY AMENDMENT. A change in the Federal Wage System Law which provides that federal wages can be based on private sector wages outside the local area if there are no comparable jobs within the area.

MONTESQUIEU. See THE SPIRIT OF THE LAWS.

MONTEVIDEO TREATY. Signed on February 18, 1960, by Argentina, Brazil, Chile, Colombia, Equador, Mexico, Peru, Paraguay, and Uruguay. The Treaty created the L.A.F.T.A. (Latin-American Free Trade Area). Based in Montevideo, L.A.F.T.A. provides for a free exchange program among its members and unifies customs and commercial regulations with regard to third countries. The long-term goal of the Treaty is to reach a Common Market on the Euopean model.

MONTREAL AGREEMENT. An international aviation agreement, which took effect in 1973, intended to suppress unlawful acts against the safety of civil aviation. Meeting in Montreal, Canada, the major foreign powers agreed to impose severe penalties upon any person guilty of endangering the safety of an aircraft. The offenses proscribed include performing an act of violence against a person on board an aircraft which is likely to endanger the safety of the passengers, destroying or damaging the aircraft, or placing or threatening to place a bomb on any aircraft. Such offenses are also made extraditable, and the Montreal Agreement serves as a legal basis for extradition in lieu of an extradition treaty. The Agreement also provides for efforts to prevent such crimes.

MONTREAL PROTOCOL. See WARSAW CONVENTION.

MOORE, JOHN BASSETT. The first American member of the original World Court (Permanent Court of International Justice) created by the League of Nations after World War I.

MOORE v. CITY OF EAST CLEVELAND (431 U.S. 494 (1977)). A Supreme Court case which invalidated a zoning ordinance that limited occupancy of a dwelling unit to members of a single family. Because her two grandsons lived with her, Mrs. Moore was convicted of violating the statute. Despite the city's contention that the constitutional right to live together as a family was limited to the nuclear family, consisting of a couple and its dependent children, Justice Powell's plurality opinion held that this right included extended family relationships as well. Noting that when the government "intrudes on choices concerning family living arrangements, this Court must examine carefully the importance of the governmental interests advanced and the extent to which they are served by the challenged regulation," Justice Powell found only a tenuous relation between the ordinance and the city's articulated interest in preventing overcrowding and minimizing traffic and parking congestion.

MOOT CASE. The principle that a court will refuse to decide a controversy once the matter has been otherwise satisfactorily resolved. The doctrine is a result of the Constitution's Article III requirement that there be a "case or controversy" before a federal court can decide the matter. In criminal cases, the Supreme Court has had particular difficulty in determining whether the case is moot after the defendant has served his sentence and has been released. The court initially held such a case moot, but more recently has gone forward with such cases, acknowledging that a criminal conviction often entails adverse collateral legal consequences even after the person is released. In a few cases, the Mootness Doctrine has been employed by the Supreme Court as a device to avoid deciding difficult cases, as in its 1974 reverse discrimination decision of *De-Funis v. Odegaard*, 418 U.S. 903 (1974), where a law student challenging his law school's preferential admissions policy for minority applicants had been admitted and was about to graduate when the case came before the Supreme Court.

MOOT COURT. Law school training exercise in which two-member teams compete against each other, testing their skills at appellate advocacy. The teams progress through several rounds of competition arguing alternate sides of a hypothetical case, often based on an issue of contemporary interest. Winners are selected on the basis of their oral presentation and the quality of their written briefs. Federal and state judges often hear the final two rounds.

MOOTNESS DOCTRINE. See MOOT CASE.

MORAL EQUIVALENT OF WAR. See M.E.O.W.

MORAL RIGHTS DOCTRINE. Principle which protects an artist in the product of his creation. Picasso, for example, could sue anyone who changes, without his consent, one of his paintings even though the work had been sold. While the Moral Rights Doctrine is well recognized on the European Continent, the United States does not grant protection to such rights.

MORAL TURPITUDE. Any conduct which is contrary to principles of honesty, justice, or good morals. The term is normally applied to a type of conduct which is due particular opprobrium. Commission of a crime which involves moral turpitude is generally considered more serious than other crimes.

MORATORIUM DAY. November 16, 1969, on which occasion students around the nation wore black armbands to school to protest against the American involvement in the war in Vietnam. Several students at a high school in Iowa who were suspended were vindicated when they took their case all the way to the Supreme Court. In the famous decision, *Tinker v. Des Moines*, 393 U.S. 503 (1969), Justice Fortas wrote that students do not "shed their constitutional rights at the schoolhouse gate."

MORE, SIR THOMAS. A lawyer appointed to the chancery court by King Henry VIII and remembered for his confrontations with the King over the latter's divorce. His appointment was unusual because he was a layman, the first person to be appointed Chancellor of England who was not a Roman Catholic Cardinal. He resigned as Chancellor when King Henry VIII sought his approval of the monarch's divorce and subsequent marriage to Anne Boleyn. When he refused to take an oath asserting the validity of Henry's divorce and second marriage, More was imprisoned and deprived of his property. He refused another oath which proclaimed Henry to be the head of the Church of England. Convicted of treason July 1, 1535, More was beheaded five days later. One account relates that when he put his head on the block, he asked the executioner to put his beard aside because "it had committed no treason."

MORGANATIC MARRIAGE (Morganic Marriage). A marriage in which the wife and the children are not legally entitled to the husband's property or hereditary positions. The phrase is derived from the Latin term matrimonium ad morganaticam, meaning literally marriage with morning-gift. The morning-gift is usually a dower provided the wife at the ceremony as her sole expectation from her husband's wealth. The term is usually applied to a marriage in which a husband of high rank takes a wife of an inferior status such as a commoner. It is also known as a Left-Handed Marriage, in which the husband offers the wife his left hand during the ceremony instead of his right to emphasize the disparity in rank.

MORGAN HEARSAY. Nonassertive conduct which is offered at trial as an assertion. For example, if a doctor treats a patient for a particular disease, the doctor's conduct might be offered as proof that the patient was in fact suffering from the disease. At common law, nonassertive conduct was deemed to be hearsay. Under modern law and the Federal Rules of Evidence, nonassertive conduct is not hearsay on the ground that it is not likely the actor intended to deceive other people.

MORGENTHAU PLAN. A proposal of the Secretary of the Treasury, Henry Morgenthau, Jr., who advocated stripping Germany of all industrial potential after World War II so that it could never again start a war. His recommendation was rejected even before the Western allies decided that West Germany was needed militarily to offset the Soviet threat.

MORGENTHAU REPORT OF 1979. Named after the Chairman (New York District Attorney Robert M. Morgenthau), this is a study of sentencing procedures submitted to Governor Hugh Carey of New York by a distinguished 15-member committee of judges, lawyers and professors. Recommending the abolition of the Parole Board, the Report stated that the present system of sentencing criminals was erratic, unpredictable and inconsistent, resembling a lottery. The Committee proposal would allow the state legislature to retain its role of setting maximum terms but a new nine-member commission would establish sentencing guidelines. The commission would be appointed by the Governor, the legislature and judges. The commission would compute the sentence based on the severity of the crime and the criminal record, if any, of the offender.

MORNING HOUR. The time which Congress traditionally sets aside at the start of each working day for the consideration of routine matters, such as the presentation of committee reports or the introduction of new bills. During this time, Congressmen may address a wide variety of issues. In the Senate, the Morning Hour generally is a two-hour period, whereas the House, which conducts ordinary business in a Committee of the Whole, rarely uses the Morning Hour.

MORRILL ACT (Land-Grant Act of 1862). Provided grants of land to the states to fund colleges for the study of agriculture and mechanics. Many of the Land Grant Colleges later developed into major universities, such as Purdue in Indiana.

MORRIS, NORVAL. Dean of the University of Chicago School of Law who withdrew his nomination as Director of the L.E.A.A. The National Rifle Association opposed his appointment because of his recommendation of a tough gun-licensing law, and various conservative groups opposed the appointment because of his stand on no criminal punishment for victimless crimes, such as gambling and public intoxication.

MORRISSEY v. BREWER. See PAROLE REVOCATION PROCEDURE.

MORTGAGE ASSUMPTION. An agreement whereby the purchaser of real property assumes personal liability for an existing mortgage on the property. Generally, a buyer wants to assume a mortgage (1) when interest rates have gone up, or (2) when he wants to avoid having to provide a down payment large enough to repay the amount due on the existing mortgage.

MORTGAGE GUARANTY INSURANCE CORPORATION. See M.G.I.C.

MORTGAGE INNOVATIONS. Five major non-standard mortgage plans currently under consideration by lenders and lender-regulators. Only two of the plans respond directly to the needs of borrowers: (1) The graduated payment plan makes it easier for people who have never owned a home to buy one. Under this plan, monthly rates start out lower, but get bigger later. The length or term of the loan and the interest rate remain unchanged. (2) The reverse annuity mortgage plan helps people who own homes free and clear, usually older, retired people, to go on living in them. Under this plan, the homeowner takes out a loan secured by the equity in his home. The loan is used to purchase an annuity which provides a monthly income. Sale of the home pays off the loan. The other three plans are variations of the variable rate mortgage in which the interest rate moves up and down as changes occur in the money market. In 1976, three-quarters of all mortgages offered by California savings and loan institutions were of the variable rate type. Such loans benefit lenders by preventing repayment of mortgages at obsolately low interest rates at times when inflation or tight credit policies send interest rates soaring.

MORTMAIN STATUTES. A series of English statutes restricting the conveyance of lands to religious and charitable organizations. The statutes have their antecedents in the Magna Carta. The first Mortmain Statute was enacted in 1279, during the reign of Edward I, and prohibited any sales or gifts of land to religious houses without consent of the mesne lord or king. Commentators have ascribed the statutes to a desire to constrict the growth and power one. Under this plan, monthly rates first Mortmain statute was enacted in of the religious orders. By invalidating any transfer of property made to a religious organization within a specified period prior to a person's death, these statutes avert undue influence.

M.O.S.T. See P.R.I.D.E.

MOST FAVORED NATION (M.F.N.). A term that dates back to an agreement signed in Geneva in 1947 by 23 of the world's major non-Communist countries, known as the General Agreement on Tariffs and Trade (G.A.T.T.). One of its most important provisions was the Most Favored Nation principle which states that the signers of the G.A.T.T. agreement must extend to one another any tariff concession given to any other member country. American trade law sets tariff rates on thousands of individual products. In general, rates for nations enjoying M.F.N. status are substantially lower than for nations that do not. For example, since the People's Republic of China was not a signatory to the G.A.T.T. agreement, it did not qualify as a Most Favored Nation. Communist Chinese goods thus were subject to far higher duties than goods sent to the United States by most of this country's other trading partners. Recently, however, M.F.N. status was extended to the People's Republic of China.

MOST MIS-LABELLED PRODUCT. Derogatory title given by reformers to wine produced in the United States and labelled according to the Bureau of Alcohol, Tobacco, and Firearms regulations. Some problems of wine-labelling include: (1) Wine having a prestigious designation such as "Napa Valley" may contain only 75 percent of grapes produced in that region; (2) A label marked "made by" does not necessarily mean the wine was made by a particular winery; and (3) A wine can bear the name of its most expensive grape even though it contains as little as 51 percent of that grape.

MOTHER HUBBARD CLAUSE (Dragnet Clause). A slang expression for a provision in a mortgage which states that the mortgage secures all debts which the mortgagor may owe the mortgagee. Such a mortgage, often called an Anaconda Mortgage because of its tendency to entangle the mortgagor in debt, is generally frowned upon by the courts.

MOTHERING FUNCTION. See NURTURING PARENT.

MOTHER SHIP. A large vessel owned and operated by organized criminal syndicates which makes a surreptitious rendezvous with smaller boats on the high seas to unload drugs for illegal entry into the United States.

MOTION TO STRIKE. A defense motion which may be made when a pleading is scandalous, immaterial or redundant. Under the Federal Rules of Civil Procedure, a motion to strike must be made before a defendant files a responsive pleading or within 20 days if no responsive pleading is filed.

MOTLEY MANDATE. A decision by United States District Judge Constance Baker Motley that women sportswriters have the right to ply their trade in the locker rooms of professional male athletes. The wives of the jocks will undoubtedly disagree with the lady judge who decided that journalist chicks have the legal right to interview their husbands in the shower.

MOTOR VEHICLE EXCEPTION. See AUTOMATIC PERFECTION.

MOUTH-PIECE. A slang term meaning a criminal lawyer. It derives from the fact that the lawyer does the talking for the criminal defendant.

M.O.V.E. A back-to-nature anarchist group that seeks to overthrow the establishment.

MOVEMENT FOR LEGITIMATE SELF-DEFENSE. See SPRING GUN CASES.

MPC. See MODEL PROCUREMENT CODE.

MR. MURPHY CLAUSE. A provision in the Federal Civil Rights Act of 1968 that eliminated discrimination in housing, which exempted from its application small landlords who rented rooms or apartments in the building in which they personally lived.

MRS. MURPHY EXCEPTION. See JONES v. MAYER.

M-TWO (M-2). See BASIC MONEY SUPPLY.

MUGGER'S EXPRESS. See RED BERETS.

MULTIPLANT BARGAINING. Collective bargaining between a company and the union representing workers in more than one of its plants.

MULTIPLE EMPLOYER BENEFIT TRUST. See M.E.T.

MULTIPLE FILER. An individual who bilks Uncle Sam out of money through refunds by filing more than one tax return. Although it is a crime, thousands do it each year with over 100 million dollars being paid to them illegally. Ironically, 19 percent of those caught are prisoners who regularly file such returns postage free and do not pay any tax on their "earnings" while they are in jail.

MULTIPLE LISTING. See LISTING ARRANGEMENTS.

MULTI-STATE BAR EXAMINATION. A national bar exam prepared and graded under the direction of the National Conference of Bar Examiners.

It tests general knowledge in areas such as criminal law and procedure, torts, constitutional law, contracts and property. The examination is given in thirty-five states.

MULTI-STATE TORT. A wrongful act which occurs in more than one state, causing damage to the same person. The chief examples are invasion of privacy and libel, because these torts may become multistate simply by publishing the same material in different states. In theory, the injured party may sue for damages in each state in which a tortious publication took place, under the tort laws of the respective states. The Uniform Single Publication Act, adopted in some states, gives a plaintiff one cause of action founded upon any single publication, and judgment in that action in any jurisdiction bars any further actions as between those two litigants for that publication.

MULTI-YEAR PROCUREMENT. The policy of awarding contracts on a term of several years. In the Spring of 1978, G.A.O. (General Accounting Office) urged Congress to enact laws authorizing federal agencies to issue procurements on a multi-year basis. G.A.O. cited several advantages to the policy including cost-saving features, the fact that the quality of performance would be improved, and the probability that competition for the original contract would be increased.

MUNICIPAL CORPORATION. A Public Corporation such as a city, town, or village, established by an act of the legislature consisting of the inhabitants of a designated area for the purpose of local self-government. Municipal Corporations are invested with the powers necessary to achieve that purpose, including a limited capacity to own and hold property.

MUNICIPAL COURT. A local court of limited jurisdiction established in many cities to handle minor civil and criminal controversies. Its territorial authority is usually limited to the boundaries of a particular city or community. Munici-pal courts generally deal with traffic cases, the enforcement of city ordinances, small claims, and misdemeanors. In some cities, municipal courts dispose only of minor civil matters. Petty criminal offenses, such as infractions or misdemeanors, are relegated to a police court. Since municipal courts are not normally courts of record, in most states litigants can usually obtain a completely new trial of their case, called Trial De Novo, before a state district or county court, which is a court of general jurisdiction.

MURDER BY INSTALLMENT. See BATTERED WIFE DEFENSE.

MURDER IN THE FIRST DEGREE. See MURDER ONE.

MURDER IN THE SECOND DEGREE. See MURDER TWO.

MURDER ONE. The most depraved form of homicide, generally defined as the killing of another human being with malice aforethought. The elements of Murder One are defined by statute in the various states. Most jurisdictions include the elements of an intent to kill with deliberation and premeditation, or during the commission of certain dangerous felonies such as rape or arson. Some legal commentators have criticized the emphasis on premeditation in view of the recent phenomena of senseless, spur-of-the-moment killings which are surely as reprehensible as those which are carefully planned, yet are often punished less severely.

MURDER TWO. Originally developed by the Quakers of Pennsylvania to mitigate the death penalty used for all those convicted of murder. The Quakers classified murder into two degrees, reserving the death penalty only for deliberate and premeditated murders, which became known as Murder One. Some states have as many as five classifications of murder, while most have two or three. Murder Two and other lesser homicides usually involve some mitigating circumstances such as the diminished capacity of a murderer to appreciate his act, due to intoxication.

MURPHY'S LAW. Named after Captain Edward Murphy, an Air Force development engineer: "If anything can go wrong, it will."

MURRAY, WILLIAM (EARL OF MANSFIELD). Lord Chief Justice of the King's Bench from 1756-88, he often is called the founder of commercial jurisprudence. He exerted much influence during his term. Under him, the Court handed down only two nonunanimous decisions in 32 years, and only two of his decisions were reversed on appeal. Lord Mansfield held liberal viewpoints, especially concerning religious tolerance. Among his landmark decisions were ones declaring that a slave became free upon being brought to Britain and that witnesses not of the Christian faith could be sworn according to their own religion. He espoused the principle that one should never prosecute where there was any risk of failure. Born in Scotland in 1704 or 1705, Mansfield intended to pursue a career in the Church. He switched to law, however, and though he struggled to finance his education, he immediately enjoyed a good reputation. Mansfield often practiced his oratory in front of a mirror, with Alexander Pope, a famous English poet, acting as his "coach." His opponents charged that, because of his Scottish heritage, he relied too heavily on the civil law.

MUSLIM BROTHERHOOD. A terrorist organization formed in Egypt, in 1928, for the purpose of imposing a strict legal Islamic order in the 33 Muslim countries in the world.

MUSLIM JIHAD. A Holy War against the infidels such as Jews and Christians which is recommended by Mohammed in the Koran to convert the entire world to Islam through the use of the flaming sword. And they almost succeeded in the eighth century, as you see if you look at a map of their Empire at its peak, which included the Middle East, North Africa, South Asia and Southern Europe.

MUTINY ON THE HIGH SEAS. A revolt against constituted authority on any ship at sea, it is usually a conspiracy, though not necessarily premeditated. Mutiny differs from sedition, which is a revolt against the government itself rather than its officers. The death sentence was mandatory for mutiny in the early nineteenth century. Perhaps the most famous mutiny occurred on the English ship *Bounty* in 1789. The *Bounty* was returning from the British West Indies where it had delivered some Tahitian plants when Fletcher Christian, the third in command, led a mutiny against Captain Bligh. Bligh and nineteen sympathizers were put in an open boat. They sailed 4,000 miles to safety. Three of the mutineers were executed, and ten others (including Christian) and their Polynesian wives settled on Pitcairn Island, where descendants live today. A mutiny in the United States in 1842 resulted in the hanging of midshipman Philip Spencer, son of Secretary of War John Canfield Spencer. During World War I, the Russian, Austrian, and German navies all mutinied. The latter resulted in the sinking of the German battle fleet.

MUTUAL AID PACT. See M.A.P.

MUTUAL BALANCED FORCE REDUCTION. See M.B.F.R.

MUTUAL FUNDS. An investment company whose primary business is to invest shareholders' money in securities and manage these investments for a fee. Funds for investment are obtained through the sale of shares to investors. The money received from the investors, less sales cost, is combined and invested as though it were a single account. Each shareholder participates in net income and capital appreciation in proportion to the number of shares owned. The securities owned by the fund are known as its portfolio. There are various kinds of mutual funds, generally categorized by the types of investments they make.

MUTUALITY OF COLLATERAL ESTOPPEL. See BERNHARD EXCEPTION.

MUTUAL WILLS. Wills with reciprocal provisions made by two individuals to dispose of their property in consideration of each other.

MYERSON, BESS. See DEBTORS ANONYMOUS.

MYONGDONG DECLARATION. A statement signed by leading citizens calling for the restoration of human rights, civil liberties and democracy in South Korea in 1977. One of the signers was Lee Tai-Young, the first woman lawyer in that East Asian country. She was convicted of anti-government activity and suspended from the practice of law for 10 years.

N

N.A.A.C.A. See A.T.L.A.

N.A.A.C.P. v. BUTTON. See PRE-PAID LEGAL SERVICE PLAN.

N.A.B.E. (National Association of Bar Executives). Founded in 1953, the Association was previously known as the National Conference of Bar Secretaries and the National Conference of Bar Executives. The group, whose general purpose is to stimulate activities of Bar Associations, has an estimated membership of 16,500 and conducts semi-annual meetings with the American Bar Association (A.B.A.). Membership is open to any executive of a Bar Association or organization of lawyers whose purpose relates to the bench or the bar. A publication, *Nabe News,* is issued semiannually.

N.A.C.C. See NATIONAL ASSOCIATION OF COUNSEL FOR CHILDREN.

NADER'S RAIDERS. A group of consumer advocates, consisting primarily of students and young lawyers led by Ralph Nader. The Raiders have led the fight for consumer legislation to improve product safety, advertising and labeling, and availability of credit. To enforce such regulations, the group has often taken to the courts.

N.A.E.O.A. See NATIVE AMERICAN EQUAL OPPORTUNITY ACT.

NAKED TRUST. See PASSIVE TRUST.

NAMED-PERIL INSURANCE. See ALL-RISK INSURANCE.

NAME LAW. Under Title IV of the Educational Amendments of 1972, prospective students or employees may not be asked by federally-assisted schools for their marital status, including questions as to their maiden or former name. However, applicants can be asked to state any name by which they may have been identified in academic or employment records.

NAPOLEONIC CODE. One of the most significant modern codes, enacted in 1804 and named after Napoleon I, who brought the drafting to completion. This Code differs from earlier endeavors in that it was not merely a restatement or compilation of existing law, but was meant to supersede prior law. Also, whereas other codifications had relied on custom and monarchical power, the Napoleonic Code was the first to be premised solely on rationality. Inconsistencies, overlap, and general confusion of French laws necessitated the development of a comprehensive Code. The mixture of Roman law in South France, feudal law in the North, and the impact of the Church on domestic relations law moved Voltaire to remark that a traveler changed laws as often as he changed horses. After the French Revolution, the need for codification became even more apparent: a new political order surfaced, the secular power of the Church declined, and a sense of national unity developed. In this environment the Napoleonic Code took form. Its thirty-six statutes and 2,281 articles were divided into three books, covering the Law of Persons, the Law of Things, and the Law of Acquiring Rights. Its drafters believed that, because it relied solely on human reason, the Code could stand as the only source of law, unlike its counterparts in common law jurisdictions. Louisiana is the only American state to adhere to the civil law concept embodied in the Napoleonic Code. A number of European, Asian and South

American countries base their legal system on this civil law approach as distinguished from the common law of England.

N.A.R.A.L. See RIGHT TO LIFERS.

NARDONE v. UNITED STATES. See FRUIT OF THE POISONOUS TREE.

N.A.S.A. (National Aeronautics and Space Administration). A federal agency established by the National Aeronautics and Space Act of 1958 to carry out the policy of Congress that activities in space should be devoted to peaceful purposes for the benefit of all mankind. The principal statutory functions of N.A.S.A. are to conduct research on problems of flight within and outside the Earth's atmosphere and to develop and operate aeronautical and space vehicles. N.A.S.A. arranges for the most effective utilization of the scientific and engineering resources of the United States with other nations engaged in aeronautical and space activities for peaceful purposes and provides for the widest practicable and appropriate dissemination of information concerning N.A.S.A.'s activities and their results.

N.A.S.A.B.C.A. (National Aeronautics & Space Administration Board of Contract Appeals). See BOARD OF CONTRACT APPEALS.

N.A.S.H. (National Association for Smoking and Health). An organization formed to protect the legal rights of persons who wish to smoke, which, in 1978, sued A.S.H. (Action on Smoking and Health), an organization to protect the legal rights of non-smokers, for trademark infringement, unfair competition and common law deceit. The case went up in flames.

NATIONAL ABORTION RIGHTS ACTION LEAGUE (N.A.R.A.L.). See RIGHT TO LIFERS.

NATIONAL ACADEMY OF SCIENCES. A private organization, established by Congress in 1863, responsible for carrying out government research in the fields of science and art. Based in the nation's capital, the Academy numbers among its most noteworthy achievements the drawing up of instructions for the government's Arctic expedition in 1871. In 1916, the Academy established the National Research Council as a subagency. Originally organized to promote war-related research, the Council has become a leader of all forms of research in both the pure and applied sciences; in 1950, it merged with the Academy to form the National Academy of Sciences—National Research Council. Both the National Academy of Engineering and the Institute of Medicine have been established under the aegis of the parent academy.

NATIONAL ACADEMY PEACE COMMISSION. An organization created by Congress in 1978 under the chairmanship of Professor James Laue of the University of Missouri whose mission is to establish a Federal Government Peace Academy similar to the Military Service Academies at West Point and Annapolis. This notion was first suggested by President George Washington in 1783 when he proposed the formation of "a proper Peace Establishment."

NATIONAL AERONAUTICS AND SPACE ADMINISTRATION. See N.A.S.A.

NATIONAL AIR QUALITY COMMISSION. A 13-member panel of legislators, public officials and representatives of environmental, labor, business and other groups, created by Congress in 1977, to recommend to Congress any desired changes in the Clean Air Act.

NATIONAL ASSOCIATION FOR LAW PLACEMENT. An organization established in 1971 to meet the placement problems of law students and employers. The need for such an Association arose from the discrepancy between the increasing numbers of students graduating from law schools and the relatively stable market for new lawyers.

NATIONAL ASSOCIATION FOR SMOKING AND HEALTH. See N.A.S.H.

NATIONAL ASSOCIATION OF BAR EXECUTIVES. See N.A.B.E.

NATIONAL ASSOCIATION OF CLAIMANTS' COMPENSATION ATTORNEYS. See ASSOCIATION OF TRIAL LAWYERS OF AMERICA.

NATIONAL ASSOCIATION OF COUNSEL FOR CHILDREN (N.A.C.C.). An organization whose purpose is to provide self-training and education for attorneys, guardians ad litem, and others who act as advocates on behalf of children. The N.A.C.C. supports the regulation of legal professionals and others who represent children in judicial proceedings to assure that such representation is adequate.

NATIONAL BAR ASSOCIATION (N.B.A.). Composed mostly of Black members of the Bench and Bar. With over 4,000 members, the N.B.A. seeks to encourage judicial reforms, promote fellowship, and stimulate interest in the study of law.

NATIONAL CENTER FOR STATE COURTS. Founded in 1971 with the active support of Chief Justice Warren Burger, the National Center is dedicated to assisting state courts in their modernization efforts. The Center is headquartered on the campus of the College of William and Mary in Williamsburg, Virginia, and has regional offices in San Francisco, St. Paul, Atlanta, Boston and Norman (Oklahoma) as well as a Washington office which serves as a liaison with federal agencies. The Center boasts a professional staff of fifty, including experts in law, court administration, data processing, communications, management, behavioral sciences, public administration, legal education and research, library science, and empirical research. The staff, believed to be the largest group of professionals working exclusively in the area of court improvement, uses electronic data processing and videotape to assist the court-reform effort. While the Center has received some government financing in the past, it is moving toward decreased dependence on federal funding.

NATIONAL CENTER ON CHILD ABUSE AND NEGLECT. A federally funded program to identify, prevent and treat both victims and offenders of emotional, physical and sexual child abuse.

NATIONAL COLLEGE OF ADVOCACY. See ASSOCIATION OF TRIAL LAWYERS OF AMERICA.

NATIONAL COLLEGE OF THE STATE JUDICIARY (National Judicial College). Established in 1963 as an activity of the American Bar Association to provide for judicial education. Justice Tom C. Clark played an integral role in the formation and development of the National College, now located in Reno, Nevada. The College has trained over 6,000 state judges and is the primary training facility for trial judges.

NATIONAL COMMISSION FOR THE REVIEW OF ANTI-TRUST LAWS AND PROCEDURES. A group of experts appointed by President Carter in 1978 to make recommendations to him on how to (1) expedite the settlement and trial of complex anti-trust cases and (2) increase competition in the economy. Some antitrust cases, such as the I.B.M. litigation which began in 1969, is still going strong and has already cost millions in lawyers' fees, drag on for decades.

NATIONAL COMMITMENTS RESOLUTION. A law promulgated by the Senate in 1969 calling upon the President not to commit troops or money to foreign countries without the express approval of Congress.

NATIONAL CONFERENCE OF BAR PRESIDENTS. An unincorporated voluntary association of presidents and other Bar Association officers. While the National Conference is wholly independent of the American Bar Association, it works closely with that organization and its various sections and committees. Its purposes are to provide a forum for the mutual interchange of ideas, to stimulate the work of Bar Associations in general, and to develop a cordial relationship and spirit of unity and common understanding between the Bar Associations of the nation and the several states for the benefit of the public and the profession. The Conference also secures a closer coordination of state bar activities of states with the American Bar Association.

NATIONAL CONFERENCE OF COMMISSIONERS ON UNIFORM STATE LAWS. An organization established in 1889 to promote uniformity in state laws on all subjects where uniformity is deemed desirable and practical. The National Conference has drafted and recommended dozens of laws such as the Uniform Probate Code, the Uniform Class Actions Act, the Uniform Comparative Negligence Act, and, in cooperation with the American Law Institute, the Uniform Commercial Code.

NATIONAL COURT OF STATE APPEALS. A new court proposed by Chief Justice James Duke Cameron of the Arizona Supreme Court. It would be composed of nine judges appointed by the President pursuant to Article III of the United States Constitution with exclusive original appellate jurisdiction to review all state court decisions, both civil and criminal, in which federal questions are raised. It would consider not only direct appeals from the state's highest court, but it also would have exclusive original jurisdiction over all collateral attacks on state court decisions. Not only would it be a discretionary court, but it also would be a court of entry to the United States Supreme Court in that certiorari could be taken to the Supreme Court from its decisions in certain instances.

NATIONAL CRIME INFORMATION CENTER. A computer operated by the F.B.I. in Washington, D.C., which enables local law enforcement officers to secure immediately criminal records of suspected felons.

NATIONAL CRIME PANEL SURVEY REPORTS. Criminal victimization surveys conducted for the Law Enforcement Assistance Administration (L.E.A.A.) by the United States Bureau of the Census, which gauge the extent to which persons aged twelve and over, households, and businesses have been victims of certain types of crime, and describe the nature of the criminal incidents and their victims.

NATIONAL CRIMINAL CONSPIRACY. For generations the concept of an organization known as the Mafia or La Cosa Nostra ("this is our thing") has existed in American folklore and the public testimony of criminals. In May, 1979, however, for the first time, the Attorney General of New Jersey, in an indictment of eight alleged members of the Vito Genovese organized crime family, set out to prove the existence of such a National Criminal Conspiracy. According to the indictment, the defendants and their alleged co-conspirators "knowingly, willfully and unlawfully did conspire, confederate and agree to gather and with each other to enter into a continuous relationship of affiliation with a secret nationwide criminal organization . . . for the purpose of promoting and facilitating the commission of crimes, committing repeated and varied crimes in order to make money and in order to aid, support and perpetuate the secret nationwide criminal organization . . . and to accomplish the objectives of the conspiracy, the defendants and their associates plotted to engage in loan-sharking at interest rates up to 4 percent a week and 50 percent a year, run bookmaking operations, extort money from drug dealers, commit armed robbery and kill various individuals.

NATIONAL CRIMINAL JUSTICE REFERENCE SERVICE. See N.C.J.R.S.

NATIONAL DEVELOPMENT BANK. A proposed federal agency which would underwrite businesses in economically depressed areas in the United States as the World Bank and similar international institutions do for less developed countries.

NATIONAL DIRECT STUDENT LOANS. See FEDERAL COLLEGE-AID STATUTES.

NATIONAL DISCIPLINE DATA BANK. Created in 1968 by the American Bar Association Center for Professional Discipline, this is the use of computer tapes by the 50 American states to coordinate lawyer discipline throughout the country. It is thus virtually impossible for an attorney who has been disciplined in one state to apply for admission elsewhere without being called to answer for past transgressions. Latest figures from the Bank reveal that 124 lawyers were disbarred in 1977, 47 resigned with charges pending, 27 were suspended for other reasons, and 74 received public Discipline less severe than suspension. New York led in disbarments with 37, while Virginia had 15 and California 11. No other state had more than five. The total number of public Discipline actions reported was 503, compared to 614 in 1976, 573 in 1975, and 419 in 1974. Since there are over 400,000 lawyers in the country, the above figures do not speak so much for the integrity of the Bar as they do for the failure of the authorities to enforce vigorously high standards of professional conduct.

NATIONAL DIVORCE CENTER. A proposed institute which would study the causes of marital breakdown. The Center would have a comprehensive data bank, a research element, education and publication programs, as well as a legal studies division. Statistics and information would be compiled and analyzed in an effort to formulate public policy concerning the rapidly rising divorce rate in America.

NATIONAL ENDOWMENT FOR THE ARTS. A federal agency created in 1965 which donates millions of dollars each year to hundreds of private and government organizations in every field of the arts throughout the country.

NATIONAL ENERGY CONSERVATION POLICY ACT OF 1978. Aimed at achieving greater energy efficiency in homes and businesses, this new federal law, which is part of President Carter's National Energy Plan, contains special provisions for conservation and the use of solar energy in govern-ment buildings as well as mandatory energy efficiency standards for the manufacturers of household appliances.

NATIONAL ENERGY PLAN. See ENERGY TAX ACT OF 1978; NATIONAL ENERGY CONSERVATION POLICY ACT OF 1978; NATURAL GAS POLICY ACT OF 1978; POWER PLANT AND INDUSTRIAL FUEL USE ACT OF 1978; PUBLIC UTILITY REGULATORY POLICIES ACT OF 1978.

NATIONAL ENVIRONMENTAL POLICY ACT. See N.E.P.A.

NATIONAL INCOME. Represents aggregate earnings which arise from the current production of goods and services. Earnings are recorded in the forms in which they are received, inclusive of taxes on those earnings. Such earnings consist of compensation of employees, the profits of corporate and unincorporated enterprises, net interest, and the rental income of persons. Because of the manner in which the National Income and Product Accounts are organized, National Income is restricted to the earnings of the private sector of the economy plus wages and salaries earned by government employees.

NATIONAL INSTITUTE FOR TRIAL ADVOCACY. Created in 1971 by the American Bar Association, Association of Trial Lawyers of America and the American College of Trial Lawyers, to improve teaching techniques in the field of advocacy.

NATIONAL INTELLIGENCE DIRECTORATE. See D.I.N.A.

NATIONAL INTERCOLLEGIATE ATHLETIC ASSOCIATION. See TITLE IX.

NATIONALITY OF MARRIED WOMEN. A problem of double nationality arising from the traditional principle that a woman marrying someone not of her own nationality acquires her husband's nationality, but also retains her nationality according to the law of the country of which she is a national. Articles 8 to 11 of the Hague Convention of 1930 on the Conflict of Nationality Laws enable women under certain conditions to retain their premarital nationality. The resulting convention on the Nationality of Married Women provided that marriage should have no automatic effect on the woman's nationality, while including a provision for facilitating the voluntary acquisition by the woman of her husband's nationality. Finally, Article 5 of the U.N. General Assembly Declaration on the elimination of Discrimination against Women, adopted in 1967, declares, "Women shall have the same rights as men to acquire, change or retain their nationality. Marriage to an alien shall not automatically affect the nationality of the wife, either by rendering her stateless, or by forcing upon her the nationality of the husband."

NATIONAL JUDICIAL COLLEGE. See NATIONAL COLLEGE OF THE STATE JUDICIARY.

NATIONAL LABOR RELATIONS BOARD. See N.L.R.B.

NATIONAL LAW JOURNAL. A national weekly newspaper first published in New York in 1978 with articles and information on the law of interest to members of the legal profession.

NATIONAL LAW SCHOOL. See BLUE RIBBON LAW SCHOOLS.

NATIONAL LAWYERS GUILD (N.L.G.). An organization of 6,000 liberal American lawyers formed in 1937 in response to the conservative American Bar Association, which was allegedly fighting the New Deal, excluding Blacks from membership and opposing the labor movement. Describing itself as "the indispensable legal arm of the American Left," its charter states that it is "an association dedicated to the need for basic change in the structure of our political and economic system."

NATIONAL LIBERATION FRONT OF CHAD. See F.R.O.L.I.N.A.T.

NATIONAL MEDIATION BOARD (N.M.B.). An independent federal agency established in 1934 by amendments to the Railway Labor Act of 1926 for the purpose of avoiding and minimizing interruptions of important interstate commerce on railways and airlines due to labor disputes. The N.M.B. superseded the previous United States Board of Mediation established in 1926. The Act provides for jurisdiction of three general classes of controversy: (a) Representation disputes: disagreements arising among employees as to who will represent them in collective bargaining with the employer (if necessary, N.M.B. can conduct secret ballot elections and determine the representative); (b) Major disputes: disagreements between the railway or airline companies (the latter since a 1936 amendment to the Act) and their employees to make or revise collective bargaining agreements, and the Act contains notice provisions similar to those for the F.M.C.S.; and (c) Minor disputes: disagreements between the railway or airlines and their employees to interpret or apply agreements already existing. If it becomes obvious that mediation is failing in a particular case, the N.M.B. has authority under the statute to induce the parties to submit to arbitration which may be arranged by the N.M.B. itself. Minor disputes in the railroad realm are usually brought before the National Railroad Adjustment Board which was created by the 1934 Act to hear and, if necessary, decide issues involving interpretation of collective bargaining contracts. The 1936 amendment to the Act provides that when the N.M.B. deems necessary, the airlines may also have an "adjustment board" for minor disputes, but this practice has not as yet been established.

NATIONAL MUSIC PUBLISHERS. See N.M.P.A.

NATIONAL ORDER OF THE PATRONS OF HUSBANDRY (The Grange). Former secret society of farmers established in 1867 to improve rural life and influence legislation favorable to farmers and ranchers.

NATIONAL ORGANIZATION FOR THE REFORM OF MARIJUANA LAWS. See N.O.R.M.L.

NATIONAL ORGANIZATION OF BAR COUNSELS. A group of local bar association officials who are responsible throughout the country for the disciplining of lawyers engaged in unprofessional conduct.

NATIONAL PARKS ACCESS ACT OF 1978. A federal law which provides $10 million over the next three years to subsidize low-cost public transportation to a number of national parks, including the "urban national recreation areas" created in the 1970s at the doorsteps of three of the nation's most densely populated regions. This is the first time that Congress has ever provided funds on such a scale to help make parks accessible to people without cars.

NATIONAL PRIVATE COURT. See JUSTICE, INC.

NATIONAL RAIL PASSENGER CORPORATION. Operator of Amtrak, whose 6,000 federally paid government employees run the railroads on rail lines which are privately owned.

NATIONAL RAILROAD ADJUSTMENT BOARD. See NATIONAL MEDIATION BOARD.

NATIONAL RECONNAISSANCE OFFICE. See UNITED STATES INTELLIGENCE-GATHERING CENTERS.

NATIONAL REPORTER SYSTEM. Founded by the West Publishing Company in 1887, the National Reporter System publishes the opinions of state and federal trial and appellate courts. It consists of thirteen units: four federal units (Supreme Court Reporter, Federal Reporter, Federal Supplement and Federal Rules Decisions); two state units (California Reporter and New York Supplement); and seven state-regional units (Atlantic, Pacific, North Eastern, South Eastern, North Western, South Western and Southern). The System is tied together by the key number indexing scheme in which every case is given a headnote and key number reference to the American Digest System. The National Reporter System has significantly simplified the task of legal research in the United States.

NATIONAL RIGHT TO WORK LEGAL DEFENSE FUND. Founded by two prominent TV commentators, William F. Buckley, Jr. and M. Stanton Evans, who resisted being forced to join a union, the American Federation of Television and Radio Artists (A.T.F.R.A.) and pay dues in order to hold their jobs in the broadcasting industry. After winning their legal battle, they created this organization to help other workers of similar views in other fields.

NATIONAL SECURITY AGENCY. See UNITED STATES INTELLIGENCE-GATHERING CENTERS.

NATIONAL SECURITY COUNCIL. Principal advisors to the President on foreign policy, who are privy to top-secret information flowing to the President from the C.I.A.

NATIONAL SOCIALIST PARTY OF AMERICA (N.S.P.A.). A small group of 1,000 Americans who are fanatic Nazis. A few dozen Nazis wanted to march in Skoki, Illinois, a suburb of Chicago, where 40,000 Jews including 4,000 survivors of World War II concentration camps lived. An appellate court in 1978 upheld their constitutional right to parade on the grounds that "if these civil rights of freedom of speech, expression and assembly are to remain vital for all, they must protect those whose ideas society quite justifiably rejects and despises." Ironically, the A.C.L.U. which won this case as counsel for the Chicago Nazis lost 15 percent of its membership and $500,000 in annual dues for defending this unpopular cause. The case thus caused a serious split in the ranks of libertarians.

NATIONAL STREET LAW INSTITUTE. Created by a Law Enforcement Assistance Administration grant in 1975, this organization was the outgrowth of a program instituted by a law student (Edward O'Brien) and his professor (Jason Newman) at Georgetown University. It sponsors lectures by law students to high school students, prison inmates and similar community groups on "street law," which deals with subjects of value to citizens in their daily lives, such as car warranties and rental contracts.

NATIONAL STUDENT MARKETING CASE. See N.S.M. CASE.

NATIONAL SUPREMACY. A basic principle of constitutional law holding that actions of the federal government are supreme over those of the states. The source of the principle is Article IV of the Constitution, which provides that the Constitution, national treaties, and acts of Congress shall be the supreme law of the land. Because state as well as federal officials are required by Article IV to swear to uphold the Constitution, state actions which conflict with federal laws are superseded by the Supremacy Clause. A recent application of the principle occurred in 1959 in the case of *Cooper v. Aaron*, 358 U.S. 1 (1959). The Governor of Arkansas claimed not to be bound by the Supreme Court's *Brown v. Board of Education* decision, 347 U.S. 483 (1954), and refused to permit desegregation of Arkansas schools. The Supreme Court held that the Governor's oath of office requiring him to uphold the Constitution encompassed both the letter of the Constitution and its interpretation by the Supreme Court.

NATIONAL TAX LIMITATION COMMITTEE. A private organization which recommends a constitutional Amendment to impose rigid limits on the growth of federal spending.

NATIONAL TAXPAYERS UNION. A private organization that lobbies for a balanced federal budget by calling for a constitutional Convention to consider an Amendment to that effect. Two-thirds of the required number of 34 states have already so petitioned Congress to conduct a convention.

NATIONAL TELECOMMUNICATIONS AND INFORMATION ADMINISTRATION. Created in March, 1978, as a branch of the Department of Commerce, to absorb the functions of the replaced White House Office of Telecommunications Policy dealing with cable television, satellites, computers and other electronic innovations.

NATIONAL TRANSPORTATION SAFETY BOARD. See N.T.S.B.

NATIONAL URBAN LEAGUE. An interracial organization formed to secure the legal rights of equal opportunity for Blacks in education, employment, housing, health, and welfare. The League was founded in 1910 in New York City by George Edmund Haynes and Ruth Standish Baldwin. Its forerunners included the National League for the Protection of Colored Women and the Committee for Improving the Industrial Conditions for Negroes in New York. The League promotes social service efforts among Blacks and emphasizes scholarly investigation as a basis for conservative racial reform. Approximately 100 local chapters, aided by the United Fund, exist throughout the United States.

NATIONAL URBAN RECREATION STUDY OF 1978. The first federal examination of recreation systems, by the Department of Interior, in the Nation's highly populated regions. It describes the disaster areas that many of America's recreation areas have become, and it is in part responsible for government recognition that such facilities are an essential part of urban life and that federal financing is crucial if they are not to be abandoned to vandals or made useless by overuse. Massive national funding thereafter took place as a result of the Study.

NATIVE AMERICAN EQUAL OPPORTUNITY ACT (N.A.E.O.A.). Drastic and controversial proposed federal legislation which would cancel all government treaties with American Indians.

NATIVE CLAIMS ACT OF 1971 (Alaska Native Claims Settlement Act; A.N.C.S.A.). A federal law that gave 65,000 native Eskimos and Indians 44 million acres of land in Alaska worth more than one billion dollars.

N.A.T.O. (North Atlantic Treaty Organization; Atlantic Pact or O.T.A.N.). A military and political organization created by a treaty signed on April 4, 1949, by twelve Western European and Northern American countries to oppose the expansionist policy of the Soviet Union. N.A.T.O. was formed in response to the 1948 blockage of Berlin. The members agreed to mutual assistance and solidarity in case of aggression against N.A.T.O. countries, and to optional consultations about security questions. A Permanent Council of Chiefs of Armies conducts and supervises the various regional military organizations. The withdrawal of France from most of the military organizations of N.A.T.O. and the creation of the Warsaw Pact in 1955 have weakened N.A.T.O.'s basic principles. Some European states perceive the overwhelming American supremacy in N.A.T.O., together with some contradictory United States foreign policies, as an obstacle to N.A.T.O.'s success.

NATURAL-BORN CITIZEN. A person whose citizenship derives from the nation where he or she was born. Under Article II, Section 1 of the Constitution, only natural-born citizens are eligible to serve as President. Virginia Dare could be called the first natural-born English person in the United States. Born in 1587 on Roanoke Island, Virginia (now North Carolina), she was the first child of English parents born in the New World. "Naturalized" citizens are those who accept voluntarily a nationality other than the one of their birth. Strict laws and regulations govern naturalization.

NATURAL DEATH LAW. See RIGHT-TO-DIE LAW.

NATURAL GAS POLICY ACT OF 1978. The most controversial part of President Carter's National Energy Plan, this new federal law changes the method of pricing new domestic natural gas in interstate and intrastate markets. Many different price categories for natural gas could result.

NATURAL GUARDIAN. See GENERAL GUARDIANSHIP.

NATURAL INSTINCTS RULE. Dog owners, according to a New York Court, are not liable for the amorous adventures of their pets, but can be held liable for property damage caused by their dogs trespassing on another's land. The distinction lies in the Natural Instincts Rule. Sexual prowess is excusable as a natural instinct, but physical property damage is not!

NATURAL LAW. A concept espoused by Plato, Cicero, Thomas Jefferson and our first Chief Justice (John Jay), among many others, that law arises out of unchangeable and immutable truths that govern all human conduct and relationships.

NATURAL RESOURCES DEFENSE COUNCIL. One of the country's oldest and most effective environmental public-interest law firms. With a legal and scientific staff of minimal size but maximum quality, the Council has been supported since its founding in 1969 not only by some 75 foundations but also by thousands of individual Americans increasingly alarmed by the growing threat of irretrievable damage to the world's environmental life-support system. Its primary purpose is to ensure the protection of ecological values through negotiation when possible, and litigation only when necessary.

NATURAL RIGHTS. See NATURAL LAW.

NAVAL LAW. See MILITARY LAW.

NAVIGATION SAFETY REGULATIONS. Rules established by the United States Coast Guard in 1977 requiring all ships over 1,600 tons entering American waters to carry radar, a gyrocompass, depthfinders and current coastal charts, designed mainly to prevent oil spills. All equipment is checked each time a vessel re-enters the United States. Eight million gallons of oil are carried to American ports each day and there are millions of gallons of oil spillage each year.

N.B. (Latin—nota bene: note well). An abbreviation, used frequently in legal briefs, memoranda or law texts.

N.C.B.L. COMMUNITY COLLEGE OF LAW (National Conference of Black Lawyers Community College of Law). Newly established, yet unaccredited, law school to train practical lawyers for Chicago's Black community. The Community College was founded in part as a memorium to Fred Hampton, controversial Black Panther leader, who was shot in a police raid on his apartment in 1969.

N.C.J.R.S. (National Criminal Justice Reference Service). An information clearinghouse and reference service available to the federal judiciary. The types of services offered the federal judges and their supporting personnel are as follows: (1) A professional staff of reference specialists, knowledgeable in specific subject areas such as courts, corrections and sentencing, who respond to inquiries using a 37,000 document data base; (2) Free microfiche copies of many documents in the N.C.J.R.S. collection available upon request, as well as paper copies of selected documents; (3) A document loan program making the entire N.C.J.R.S. collection available to other libraries when public or organizational libraries submit an interlibrary loan form; (4) A reading room and reference library maintained in downtown Washington, D.C., that provides access to the N.C.J.R.S. collection and many basic sources of information; (5) A selective notification of information service through which N.C.J.R.S. mails a monthly journal announcing publications and meetings to those who register for it.

N.D.S.L. See FEDERAL COLLEGE-AID STATUTES.

NECESSARY AND PROPER CLAUSE. That part of Article I, Section 8 of the Constitution which empowers the Congress to make all laws necessary and proper to carry out such powers as borrowing money, declaring war and regulating interstate commerce. The scope of the Necessary and Proper Clause has been delineated in a number of Supreme Court decisions.

NEED FOR CARE OR TREATMENT. Grounds for civil commitment in some jurisdictions, rooted in the belief of treatment personnel that the patient in question will not take his prescribed medicine unless he is hospitalized. Disregarding medication presumably increases the risk that the person will not be able to function in the community. The standard incorporates the concept that mentally ill individuals suffer from defective judgmental capacity. Inasmuch as the evaluation rests on observations made by hospital staff, it usually is brought up at a recommitment hearing, required as part of periodic review procedures, as opposed to the initial commitments. An analogous category which does serve as the basis for an individual's original involuntary hospitalization is Substantially Unable to Care for Oneself. Critics of this ground for commitment suggest that it can be used against sane people who maintain unusual but harmless lifestyles. For example, an early 1960's case in Florida resulted in a commitment for the "hippie-type" behavior of an unemployed college dropout. The elderly may also be kept in psychiatric hospitals because they need some supervision and no less restrictive alternative is available. The absence of a category of this sort arguably results in many mentally deficient individuals being processed through the criminal system on charges of disorderly conduct or malicious mischief.

NEEDLE-IN-A-HAYSTACK LITIGATION. Phrase used by Supreme Court Justice Rehnquist to describe routine and uninteresting litigation in federal trial courts, such as appeals of social security claimants from decisions of the Secretary of Health, Education and Welfare.

NE EXEAT (Latin—let him not leave). A writ forbidding a person from leaving the jurisdiction of the court, the state, or the country. Although the right to travel was guaranteed as early as the Magna Carta (1215), many English monarchs placed restraints on the foreign travels of Englishmen through the use of the writ, Ne Exeat Regno (let him not depart from the kingdom).

N.E.F. See NOISE EXPOSURE FORECAST.

NEGATIVE INCOME TAX. See GUARANTEED ANNUAL INCOME; EARNED INCOME CREDIT.

NEGLIGENT HOMICIDE. See INVOLUNTARY MANSLAUGHTER.

NEGLIGENT MISINFORMATION. Tort of negligently giving out false information which causes physical, emotional or economic harm to another. For example, a New York hospital which had two patients by the same name, negligently informed the wrong family of the death of one of the patients. The mistake was not discovered until after funeral arrangements had been made and the body was displayed for viewing in a funeral home. Claimants against the hospital were able to recover both the funeral expenses and damages for extreme emotional anxiety caused by the hospital's negligence.

NEGOTIATED PROCUREMENT. This term refers to a federal statutory procedure for acquisition of supplies or services by which the contracting agency and government procurement contractors, after submission of contractors' proposals, bargain with respect to price and technical requirements. Proposals are submitted pursuant to a Request for Proposals and are not publicly disclosed. A contract award is made to the contractor whose final proposal is most advantageous to the contracting agency.

NEIGHBORHOOD COURT (Neighborhood Justice Center). An informal and unofficial means of settling disputes between neighbors, parents and children, roommates, spouses, friends or landlords and tenants. It differs from a small claims court, which can only award a sum of money to the winner.

A volunteer mediator, usually one's peer, without legal training, hears both parties without lawyers and settles the case in a friendly fashion for a small fee. The disputants save time, money and emotional strain. The parties agree beforehand to abide by the decision. Three such organizations were created in 1978, in Atlanta, Kansas City and Los Angeles with a grant of $200,000 each from the Law Enforcement Assistance Administration. Former Attorney General Griffin Bell said that their purpose was to provide "an avenue to Justice for many persons now shut out of the legal system" and to help to unclog court dockets. If the experiment proves successful, it is expected that the concept will spread rapidly throughout the entire country. Each pilot Center consists of an office in the community to which people can go with a wide variety of problems. The Center will provide mediation or arbitration services, through a panel of members of the community trained in these skills, for those disputes in which both parties agree to have the matter resolved in this manner. Where such a means of resolution is inappropriate or not agreed to, the Center will refer the parties to the agency or court best suited to deal with this problem.

NEMO EST HAERES VIVENTES (Latin—no one is an heir to the living).

N.E.P.A. (National Environmental Policy Act). Landmark legislation which requires a systematic consideration of the environmental impact of all major federal activities. Under the Act passed in 1969, federal agencies must file a written analysis of the environmental impact of a proposed action, together with a discussion of any adverse environmental effects which cannot be avoided should the proposal be implemented. The Environmental Impact Statement must also discuss the alternatives for the proposed action, and any irreversible or irretrievable commitment of resources must be specified. N.E.P.A. does not mandate necessarily pro-environment decisions. Rather the Act's purpose is to ensure that environmental factors have been included in the decisional calculus.

NET ASSETS. Assets minus liabilities equal net assets. In corporate accounting, net assets will be equivalent to the sum of the stated capital, capital surplus, and earned surplus. Net current assets, or working capital, represent the excess of current assets over current liabilities. Where there is no such excess and current liabilities exceed current assets, a corporation is technically insolvent.

NET CORPORATE PROFITS. Gross earings of a corporation minus operating expenses equal net profits. Such profits may be measured either annually or from the time of incorporation. Certain statutes will allow the payment of dividends only from net profits or net earnings without any further qualification. Some courts have interpreted these statutes as meaning dividends may be paid only from earned surplus. Others allow the payment of dividends out of profits from the current year even though there is a cumulative deficit in the surplus account.

NET INTEREST. Measures the excess of interest payments made by the domestic business sector over its interest receipts, plus net interest received from abroad. Interest paid by one business firm to another business firm is a transaction within the business sector and has no effect on the net interest payments or receipts of the sector. The same is true of interest payments within other sectors—as from one individual to another, or one government agency to another.

NET LISTING. See LISTING ARRANGEMENTS.

NET NATIONAL PRODUCT. See GROSS NATIONAL PRODUCT.

NEVER-NEVER PLAN. The British slang expression for buying something on an installment basis. (You *never* finish making your payments.)

NEW DEAL. Term first used in 1932 by President Franklin D. Roosevelt to describe his plan for relief, recovery, and reform, implemented between 1933 and 1939. The New Deal unfolded in two phases: the "First" New Deal (1933-1935), which aimed at recovery, and the "Second" (1935-1939), whose objective was reform. During the former phase, Roosevelt proposed measures designed to produce price rises which he hoped would redound to the benefit of employees through increased wages. Thus, the Agricultural Adjustment Act (A.A.A.) provided for subsidies to farmers who would limit the production of certain commodities, thus forcing prices up. On the heels of the A.A.A. came the National Industrial Recovery Act (N.I.R.A.), designed to assure collective bargaining and minimum wages, and to provide new employment through programs of public construction organized by the Public Works Administration. Two subsequent measures —the Tennessee Valley Authority Act and the Federal Securities Act—were harbingers of reform. The latter stipulated that each issuer of securities account both to the F.T.C. and to the potential buyer for the financial condition of his business; the former established a corporation vested with the authority to enhance economic development over a seven-state area. The second, or reform phase of the New Deal, sought to increase the purchasing power of the people through projects designed to produce jobs (Works Progress Administration, Rural Electrification Administration, National Youth Administration). Finally, the Federal Securities Act of 1935 kicked off an unemployment plan financed by taxes on the payrolls of employers. Though the A.A.A. and the N.I.R.A. were subsequently found unconstitutional, Roosevelt weathered the storm when, during his second term, Congress enacted acceptable substitutes, such as the Fair Labor Standards Act which set minimum wage, maximum hour requirements and forbade child labor. Though such Second New Deal policies received support in the Northeast, Roosevelt felt compelled to soft-peddle further domestic reform to preserve favor in the South. As war approached, national unity would become his foremost concern, as "Dr. New Deal" gave way to "Dr. Win-the-War."

NEW FEDERALISM. A political philosophy that attempts to synthesize the best of both centralized and decentralized governmental functions. Richard Nixon popularized the term in a national speech in 1969. Revenue sharing, with its centralized decision-making and local administration, is a good example of the kind of program New Federalism espouses.

NEW FOUNDATION. The theme of President Carter's Administration of peace and prosperity for the world in general and the United States in particular.

NEW FRONTIER. The name given to the administration of President John F. Kennedy, 1960-1963.

NEW HAMPSHIRE TEST. See DURHAM TEST.

NEW INTERNATIONAL ECONOMIC ORDER (N.I.E.O.). A redistribution of global wealth and power among industrial and non-industrial nations. Proposed by the countries of the third world, the New International Economic Order was formally adopted in 1977 by the United Nations as a worldwide objective.

NEW LEFT. A liberal political and social movement which appeared during the 1960s, flourished in the early 1970s, and was comprised largely of college students, the New Left fed the cultural revolution challenging traditional American values concerning sex, drugs and dress codes. Politically, the movement opposed the so-called military-industrial complex in general and the Vietnam War in particular and stressed the importance of ecology. The New Left is to be distinguished from the Old Left, which espoused Communist and Socialist ideas, primarily by its political disorganization and ideological concern with individuality.

NEW LONG MARCH. See LONG MARCH FORWARD.

NEWSMAN'S PRIVILEGE. See JOURNALIST'S PRIVILEGE.

NEW YORK INSURANCE EXCHANGE. See INSURANCE FREE TRADE ZONE LAW.

NEW YORK LAW JOURNAL. Established in 1888, it is the oldest of all the legal newspapers in the country. Its pages contain judicial opinions, legal notices, articles on the law and other information of interest to the legal profession. It is thus a unique legal chronicle for the state of New York.

NEW YORK TIMES CO. v. UNITED STATES (403 U.S. 713 (1971)). This case, along with its companion case, *United States v. The Washington Post Co.*, 403 U.S. 713, allowed American newspapers to continue publishing The Pentagon Papers in 1971. The Court turned a deaf ear to the government's argument of national security as unconstitutional prior restraint. The classified study, *History of U.S. Decision-Making Process on the Viet Nam Policy*, told of high-level deliberations involving the United States' role in the Viet-Nam conflict. In 1972 *The New York Times* received a Pulitzer Prize for its Pentagon Papers project.

NEW YORK TIMES STANDARD (Constitutional Privilege). A qualified privilege growing out of the Supreme Court case, *New York Times v. Sullivan*, 376 U.S. 254 (1964). This standard provides that no one shall be held liable for defamatory remarks about a public official unless the remarks were made with malice. In the *New York Times* case, the Supreme Court defined "malice" as "knowledge of falsity or reckless disregard of the truth." The case concerned a paid advertisement in *The New York Times* which criticized police conduct in racial disturbances in Montgomery, Alabama. Montgomery Police Commissioner Sullivan sued the *Times* under the theory that he personally was libeled and an Alabama jury awarded him $500,000 in damages. The Supreme Court reversed, holding that the First Amendment protected comments concerning public officials. The Constitution favors free discussion of issues of public concern and "right conclusions are more likely to be gathered out of a multitude of tongues, than through any kind of authoritative selection."

NEXUS ANALYSIS. See STATE ACTION REQUIREMENT.

N.I.A.A. See TITLE IX.

NIAGARA MOVEMENT. One of the first American civil rights protest groups composed of Black elite. The brilliant and eccentric Black leader, Dr. William E. B. Du Bois, founded the Niagara Movement, which was named for the location of its first meeting in 1905.

NICHOLS v. UNIVERSAL PICTURES CO. See ABSTRACTIONS TEST.

N.I.E.O. See NEW INTERNATIONAL ECONOMIC ORDER.

N.I.J. (National Institute of Justice). A proposed federal agency which would include five offices and would consolidate many Department of Justice activities. Major units would be (1) a Bureau of Justice Statistics, to include current Law Enforcement Assistance Administration (L.E.A.A.) statistical functions and others to include civil and criminal judicial statistics, both state and federal; (2) an Office of State and Local Assistance, to distribute block grants to the states, but with less stress on criminal justice planning; (3) a Justice Research and Development Institute, basically for applied research, in the belief that "research and action activities need to be routinely linked . . . so that . . . appropriate action program needs affect research priorities" and vice versa; and Offices of (4) Community Anti-Crime and (5) Juvenile Justice. Chief Justice Warren Burger suggested as early as 1972 before the American Law Institute that Congress might create the N.I.J. to be national in scope and not in the exclusive control of judges and lawyers. The N.I.J. would give technical assistance, on a consulting basis with the National Center for State Courts, on problems facing the state courts. In November, 1977, Attorney General Griffin Bell recommended to President Carter that the N.I.J. be created to replace the L.E.A.A., headed by a Director appointed by the President serving at a salary level comparable to the F.B.I. Director.

NIMBLE DIVIDENDS. Dividends paid according to a statutory authorization out of net profits for the current or preceding fiscal year, even though there is a cumulative deficit in the capital surplus account. The term "nimble" suggests that the directors must be "nimble" to declare dividends out of the net profits within a prescribed period, usually the current or preceding fiscal year. A growing number of states allow the payment of such dividends despite the resultant impairment of stated capital.

1983 SUITS. Suits brought under Section 1983 of the Civil Rights Act of 1871, which gives a cause of action to individuals deprived of federal constitutional or statutory rights by persons acting under color of the law "of any State or territory." Such suits have most often been brought against individual state officials, especially police officers, who have allegedly violated the plaintiff's constitutional rights. The availability of a 1983 suit in federal court against state officers was first recognized by the Supreme Court in the celebrated case of *Monroe v. Pape,* 365 U.S. 167 (1961), where thirteen Chicago policemen allegedly invaded and searched the plaintiff's home and illegally arrested and detained him. Under the *Monroe* decision, 1983 suits do not impose liability on state governments, cities or counties, but only on individual state officials. In succeeding cases, the Court has developed a series of qualified or absolute immunities for prosecutors, judges, grand jurors and certain policemen which has substantially narrowed the scope of liability in a 1983 action.

NINETEENTH AMENDMENT (1920). Prohibits the states from abridging a citizen's right to vote on account of sex. The Amendment was the result of the

Suffragette Movement of the late nineteenth and early twentieth centuries.

NINETY-DAY TAX LETTER. Notice to a taxpayer of a tax deficiency which must be issued by the Commissioner of Internal Revenue. The taxpayer is given ninety days from the date of the notice of the deficiency to file a petition with the tax court for a re-determination of deficiency. No assessment of a defiiency or levy, or any other collection proceeding, can begin until the notice has been mailed and ninety days have expired.

NISI PRIUS (Latin—first unless). Courts for the original trial of issues of fact, as distinguished from appellate courts. The term originally described a case arising in the Courts of Westminster to be tried by a jury.

NITROGLYCERIN CHARGE. See ALLEN INSTRUCTION.

NIXON COURT. See BURGER COURT.

NIXON DOCTRINE (Guam Doctrine). Proposed by President Richard Nixon on Guam Island in 1969, this policy limits American involvement in the internal affairs and military struggles of foreign countries. The Nixon Doctrine emphasized that each nation must be primarily responsible for its own defense though American aid was not altogether ruled out. The Doctrine represented a reaction against the increasing commitment of American armed forces abroad.

NIXON, RICHARD M. Wall Street lawyer and 37th President of the United States; the only President voluntarily to resign from office—on August 9th, 1974, while under consideration by the House of Representatives for impeachment on grounds arising out of the Watergate scandal. He was subsequently pardoned by Gerald Ford, the man he appointed to succeed him as President. By resigning, Nixon ensured the payment of his pension and other government fringe benefits amounting to hundreds of thousands of dollars annually, which would have been for-feited if he had been impeached. And, of course, he has made millions of dollars from T.V. and book royalties arising from his revelations of his betrayal of the public trust. Indeed, Special Prosecutor Archibald Cox is the only Watergate luminary who has not engaged in commercial exploitation of his professional involvement in the greatest scandal of the history of our nation.

NIXON-SAMPSON AGREEMENT. See NIXON v. GENERAL SERVICES.

NIXON v. ADMINISTRATOR OF GENERAL SERVICES (433 U.S. 425 (1977)). In this case concerning President Richard M. Nixon, the Court rejected constitutional challenge to the Presidential Recordings and Materials Preservation Act of 1974. Adopted four months after Nixon resigned under the threat of impeachment, the Act directed the Administrator of General Services to take custody of Nixon's materials and to promulgate regulations for archivists to screen the materials, for Nixon to reclaim personal materials, and for the public to have access to the materials retained by the government. The Act responded to the Nixon-Sampson Agreement, an agreement announced the day President Gerald Ford pardoned Nixon, which allowed Nixon to withdraw papers after three years and to destroy tape recordings. Finding that the problems of public access were not ripe for review, the Court upheld the custody and screening provisions of the Act. Thus, the Court rejected the argument that the Act violated separation of powers, presidential privilege, First Amendment Rights, privacy interests, and the constitutional prohibition against bills of attainder.

N.J.P. See NON-JUDICIAL PUNISHMENT.

N.L.G. See NATIONAL LAWYERS GUILD.

N.L.R.B. (National Labor Relations Board). An independent federal administrative agency which administers the nation's laws relating to labor relations. The N.L.R.B. is vested with the power to safeguard employees' rights to organize, to determine through elections whether workers want unions as their bargaining representatives, and to prevent and remedy unfair labor practices. The National Labor Relations Act of 1935 (Wagner Act), as amended by the acts of 1947 (Taft-Hartley Act) and 1959 (Landrum-Griffin Act), affirms the right of employees to organize and to bargain collectively through representatives of their own choosing or to refrain from such activities. The Act prohibits certain unfair labor practices by employers and labor organizations or their agents. It also authorizes the N.L.R.B. to designate appropriate units for collective bargaining and to conduct secret ballot elections to determine whether employers desire representation by a labor organization.

N.M.P.A. (National Music Publishers Association). Founded in 1917, it was called the Music Publishers Protective Association until 1966. The need for the organization arose in the 1880s when the popular music publishing business responded to the high demand for piano sheet music, and songs, for the first time in history, which could be popularized by constant repetition. The objectives of the Association are to promote, protect, and encourage the art of music and song writing. The organization is unique in that it is an association of a copyright industry.

NO ACTION LETTERS. Advisory opinions provided by the Security Exchange Commission (S.E.C.). Securities issuers may present proposals to the S.E.C. for informal advice, and pursuant to section 551(2)(2) of the Administrative Procedure Act, statements of policy and interpretation which have been adopted by the agency, and not published in the *Federal Register,* must be made available. If the staff approves the proposal, a No Action Letter is sent to the issuer and published. Opinions of this sort are not technically binding, but the Commission generally follows them.

NO-BAIL COMPACT. An agreement among New England states that allows an out-of-state motorist who is given a ticket for speeding to post bond in the amount of the fine, which is forfeited if the accused does not appear in court for the trial.

NOBLE EXPERIMENT (Prohibition). The enactment of the 18th Amendment to the Federal Constitution in 1919 at the instigation of the Women's Christian Temperance Union (W.C.T.U.) and similar lobbying groups which prohibited the manufacture, sale, possession and use of alcoholic beverages. So many Americans openly and covertly violated the law that it became unenforceable and was finally repealed by the 21st Amendment in 1933.

NO-COMMENT RULES. Court rules restricting a lawyer's comments on pending criminal cases if such comment would seriously interfere with a fair trial.

NO CONTEST. See NOLO CONTENDERE.

NO-CONTEST PROVISION. A clause in a will which provides that if anyone contests the will, the contestant shall be disinherited completely or given merely a nominal bequest. State laws vary as to the validity of such provisions, often requiring a gift over.

NOERR-PENNINGTON DOCTRINE. Derived from the Supreme Court decisions in *Eastern R.R. Presidents Conference v. Noerr Motor Freight, Inc.,* 365 U.S. 127 (1961), and *United Mine Workers v. Pennington,* 381 U.S. 657 (1965), this doctrine holds that joint efforts to induce enactment or enforcement of laws do not constitute a violation of the antitrust statutes. *Noerr* involved a campaign by a group of railroads to persuade legislative and executive branches of state governments to take action injurious to truckers, who were competitors of the railroads for long-haul freight business. Despite the fact that the railroads' motive in seeking governmental action was to reduce competition from the trucking industry, the Court held that lobbying **did**

not violate the Sherman Act. Lobbying, concluded the Court, provides government with the information essential to its ability to make informed policy judgments. Additionally, to restrict petitioning would threaten rights guaranteed by the First Amendment. Four years later, in *United Mine Workers v. Pennington,* the Court held that concerted efforts to influence executive actions also are not violative of the Sherman Act, even though they include conduct that can be termed unethical, such as deception and misrepresentation. In *Pennington,* the Court held that the *Noerr* doctrine protected the mine workers' alleged efforts to influence the Secretary of Labor and other government officials to establish a high minimum wage for employees of contractors selling coal to the Tennessee Valley Authority. More recently, in *California Motor Transport Company v. Trucking Unlimited,* 404 U.S. 508 (1972), the Court extended the *Noerr-Pennington* doctrine to attempts to influence administrative agencies. That case involved administrative hearings for motor carriers before the California Public Utilities Commission and the Interstate Commerce Commission.

NO-FAULT DIVORCE. First created by statute in California in 1969 and since followed by most states, to reflect the new loose marital life-styles of the late 1960s and early 1970s, this legislation allowed a marriage which had been dissolved in fact to be dissolved in law unilaterally by either party over the objection of the other. All that was required was to live apart for a prescribed period of time, usually one year. It can create problems for a wife, especially in those states which do not allow alimony, who suffers the double emotional shock of the severance of the family tie and a difficult entry into the job market when her old skills have become rusty.

NO-FAULT INSURANCE. Legislative plans enacted in a number of states which permit re-imbursement for automobile accidents to be made independently of any determination of fault.

Although commonly called No-Fault plans, they are more accurately described as Self-Insurance. The Department of Transportation, interested in the development of such plans, has supported the drafting of the Uniform Motor Vehicle Accident Reparations Act. At present no-fault legislation in the states varies considerably. Despite their differences, No-Fault plans share two features. First, that an insured motorist who suffers an injury from an automobile accident receives compensation from his own insurer regardless of legal fault. Second, tort liability is abolished at least to the extent of the benefits received. Most plans, however, apply conventional tort principles in cases of serious injury. No-Fault insurance is designed to afford prompt recovery for out-of-pocket expenses and increased flexibility in avoiding duplicate coverage. In return the motorist gives up the chance to collect for such non-out-of-pocket damages as pain and suffering and to receive a windfall at the hands of a sympathetic jury.

NO-GROWTH ZONING. Communities which freeze population at present levels through zoning ordinances. Municipalities have the power to create zoning laws which promote the general welfare by controlling growth, but highly restrictive No-Growth Zoning is an unconstitutional restriction on the freedom to travel, which also includes the right to enter and live in a state or municipality.

NO-HARD-FEELING DIVORCE. See DO IT YOURSELF DIVORCE LAW.

NOISE EXPOSURE FORECAST (N.E.F.). A technique raised to anticipate the effect of aircraft noise on people at various distances from an airport. The N.E.F. technique takes into account such factors as the frequency of aircraft movements as well as the size of the aircraft and flight profile.

NOISE ZONING. A land-use scheme designed to restrict activities involving high noise levels to certain areas. Such zoning maintains lower noise levels in suburban and residential areas.

NOLLE PROS. See NOLLE PROSEQUI.

NOLLE PROSEQUI (Nolle Pros) (Latin—I do not wish to prosecute). A formal entry upon the record by the Prosecutor in a criminal trial or a plaintiff in a civil action declaring that he will not prosecute the case further. The entry can apply to some of the defendants, some of the counts in the indictment, or the entire action.

NOLO CONTENDERE (Latin—I do not wish to contend). A plea made by a defendant in response to a criminal charge, which has the same effect as a plea of guilty in that particular proceeding, but which cannot be used as an admission in a subsequent civil proceeding. However, it is considered an admission of guilt in a later proceeding to revoke a license (i.e., disbarment) or in a sentencing proceeding under a Habitual Offender Statute. Additionally, a plea of Nolo Contendere to a prior charge generally may be used to impeach a witness. The court has discretion to reject the plea, and some states allow the plea only when the charge is a misdemeanor. Probably, the most famous recent use of the plea was in 1973 when then-Vice President Spiro Agnew pleaded Nolo Contendere to income tax evasion rather than face a forthcoming verdict of guilt on bribery charges. He agreed to pay a heavy fine in order not to risk a long prison sentence if the case had gone to trial.

NO-MARRIAGE RULE. A discriminatory rule, formerly commonplace among airlines, to fire stewardesses when they married, but to retain stewards regardless of marital status. In 1971 a federal circuit court found this practice violated Title VII of the Civil Rights Act of 1964, because the airlines failed to explain why marriage should affect a stewardess' ability to meet the requirements of the job, while not impairing the capabilities of stewards.

NOMINAL CONSIDERATION. A Rule of Law stating that any consideration, regardless of adequacy or amount, is sufficient contractual consideration. Thus the amount of one dollar has been recognized as fulfilling the necessary consideration requirement of a valid contract, providing that a bargain was in fact made. Where there is in fact no bargain, but merely an attempt to make a gratuitous promise binding, nominal consideration may be unenforceable.

NOMINAL CONTRACTUAL DAMAGES. A symbolic sum of money, generally a dollar or less, awarded in a Breach of Contract action when the aggrieved party has suffered no damage. It presumably allows the recipient to feel vindicated for that which was wrong.

NON-ALIGNED NATIONS. See THIRD WORLD.

NO-NAME BONDS. See BEARER BONDS.

NON COMPOS MENTIS (Latin—not of sound mind). A general term embracing all types of insanity and mental derangement. However, it is used most often to describe a mental condition approaching near-total incompetency.

NON CURAT LEX. See DE MINIMIS NON CURAT LEX.

NON-CUSTODIAL PARENT. The parent who is not granted custody of the minor children in a divorce action. Many courts have recognized that a non-custodial parent has a fundamental right to the companionship of his or her child. Therefore, visitation rights cannot be denied without a showing that the parent's activities may tend to impair the emotional or physical health of the child.

NON-DELEGABLE CONTRACTUAL DUTIES. A duty of performance that cannot be transferred to another when the performance of the obligor would be considerably and materially altered.

NON-DELEGATION DOCTRINE. Holds that the legislature may not transfer responsibility for preferential judgments to an administrative body. Despite the Supreme Court's ruling in *United States v. Shreveport Grain and*

Elevator Company, 287 U.S. 77 (1932), that the legislative power of Congress cannot be delegated, such delegation to administrative agencies has long been recognized as vital to the implementation of legislative power. Congressional delegations to public authorities have been held invalid on only two occasions, *Panama Refining Co. v. Ryan*, 293 U.S. 388 (1935) and *Schechter Poultry Corp. v. United States*, 295 U.S. 495 (1935). The original retreat from the doctrine was based on the notion that administrators could issue rules to fill gaps in laws without actually usurping the legislative function. Later, the Court recognized the legitimacy of delegation as long as adequate standards were provided to control administrative action. However, the acceptance of such vague standards as "just and reasonable," "public convenience, interest or necessity," and "unfair methods of competition" indicate that the Non-Delegation Doctrine does not prevent delegation of power to make law, nor does it assure meaningful legislative standards.

NON-DISCHARGEABLE DEBTS. Debts which may not be discharged through bankruptcy proceedings. Such debts include most tax liabilities, liabilities for property obtained through false pretenses, tort liabilities for willful and malicious injuries, alimony and support obligations, and debts not duly scheduled, that is, debts not properly listed on the schedules of debts the bankrupt must file during bankruptcy proceedings.

NON-EQUITY PARTNER. See PARTICIPATING ASSOCIATE.

NON-FREEHOLD ESTATE. See ESTATE FOR YEARS.

NON-JUDICIAL PUNISHMENT (N.J.P.). Punishment imposed by a commanding officer in the armed forces upon personnel of his unit for minor violations of the Uniform Code of Military Justice (U.C.M.J.). The term has come to encompass not only the particular punishment imposed, but also the proceedings leading to its imposition. While the punishment is imposed in a summary fashion without the intervention of a court martial, it is specifically sanctioned by the U.C.M.J. which, along with the Manual for Courts Martial and other service directives, provides for basic procedural and substantive safeguards of the rights of service personnel. Non-judicial punishment finds its historical roots in ancient Athens, which recognized, as a matter of military necessity, the need to punish summarily disciplinary infractions. The evolution of the practice has been painful and often tragic, so that today the procedures followed by the Armed Forces of the United States bear little or no resemblance of those of ancient Athens. Gone are the old days when a commanding officer could impose a severe punishment, including death, in a manner so summary that the accused had no right to a hearing, much less to a defense. The pendulum has swung now to the other extreme in that the full panoply of rights guaranteed service personnel in the United States has turned non-judicial punishment, when it is available at all, into a mini-court martial. Some commentators have said that the over-protective attitude of the armed forces has dealt a fatal self-inflicted blow to one of the most important tools of discipline available to military commanders. Non-judicial punishment is known in the Navy as Captain's Mast; in the Marine Corps as Office Hours; and in the Army and Air Force as Article 15 Punishment.

NON-MOLESTATION CLAUSE. Customarily found in separation agreements by which both parties agree not to molest or interfere with each other. The husband typically asserts the wife's violation of the clause as a defense to his liability for support payments though the cases hold the violation is not a defense. A violation of the clause may give the husband a remedy in damages, the amount being fixed by the degree of violation. If the wife's violations of the agreement are more serious than the non-molestation clause or more closely related to important marital rights, the husband's payment for his support may be erased.

NON-PROFIT FOUNDATIONS. Organizations which distribute private wealth for public purposes. The earliest foundations date back to Greek and Roman times when they existed as religious organizations to honor deities. Among the earliest American Foundations were those organized by Benjamin Franklin in 1791 to aid "young married artificers of good character" and by James Smithson in 1846 which established the Smithsonian Institution. Subsequently aided by the growth of huge personal fortunes following America's industrial development and the encouragement of favorable tax treatment, foundations have become major contributors to endeavors in education, international activities, health, welfare, the humanities and religion.

NON-RESIDENTIAL FIXED INVESTMENT. Includes capital expenditures by the business sector and non-profit institutions for (1) new and replacement construction, such as buildings, stores, and warehouses and (2) producers' durable equipment, such as machinery, office equipment, and motor vehicles. Estimates for Non-residential Fixed Investment are based on the Bureau of Economic Analysis (B.E.A.) surveys of plant and equipment expenditures by the business sector and on other information such as the sales of producers' durable goods and the value of construction. Adjustments must be made on the basis of other estimates to include investment in agriculture and other businesses not covered by the B.E.A. surveys.

NON-VOTING STOCK. See VOTING RIGHTS.

NO PAR. Refers to stock issued without a nominal or par value required by law. No par stock must be authorized by statute. A majority of jurisdictions presently allow the use of No Par stock, which may be issued at any price which is satisfactory to the Board of Directors. Consideration received for the stock may be allocated between surplus and stated capital at the discretion of the Board. Critics of no par stock point out that it makes impossible the determination of the minimum stated capital of a corporation, which it is required by either the Articles of Incorporation or by statute to keep intact. As a result, it is difficult to enforce the liabilities of Directors for improper diversion of minimum stated capital. In addition, no par stock makes it difficult to determine the amount a particular shareholder is bound to pay for his stock.

N.O.R.M.L. (National Organization for the Reform of Marijuana Laws). A private organization which lobbies for the decriminalization and legalization of marijuana at both the federal and state levels. It has been successful in eleven states, including parts of the country such as Alaska and Oregon.

NORTH CAROLINA v. PEARCE. See DOUBLE JEOPARDY.

NO SEARCH RULE. After the Supreme Court upheld a surprise police search of the student newspaper at Stanford University, the Carter Administration introduced a Bill in Congress in 1978 which would protect from a search or seizure the work product of journalists, authors or others preparing for publication, plus any other documentary material they have gathered. The proposed legislation would include two exceptions permitting unannounced searches: where there was "imminent danger" to life or serious bodily injury and where the target was a "suspect in the crime for which the evidence is sought." Under the proposal, such items as notes, tapes, photographs, videotapes, negatives, films, interview files and drafts would be protected from review or seizure by police. The new law would require that criminal investigators at all governmental levels use subpoenas duces tecum instead of search warrants when they want to see material gathered for publication by reporters, free-lance writers, scholars and publishers. There is a crucial difference between the two. A subpoena specifies just what documents are wanted, demands that they be produced and allows time to contest the demand in court. A search warrant, by contrast, lets the law authorities appear without any warning and rummage at will.

NO SHOW. See AIRLINE BUMPING.

NORTHERN COUNCIL. Created in 1952, the Northern Council is a union of Denmark, Norway, Sweden, and Iceland, which Finland joined in 1955. The Council provides for informal contacts, at parliamentary and ministerial levels, but plays merely an advisory role.

NORTHERN IRELAND PROVISIONAL IRISH REPUBLICAN ARMY. See I.R.A.

NORTH-SOUTH CONFLICT. A term that has gained prominence in the 1970s to describe the international conflict between industrial nations and underdeveloped nations—the "haves" and "have nots."

NO-SOLICITATION RULE. Prohibits organized labor activities in certain areas. Some courts have upheld such rules in non-profit hospitals. Other courts have held that No-Solicitation Rules violate the Taft-Hartley Act.

NO-STRIKE CLAUSE. A provision in a labor contract whereby the union promises not to strike for the term of the contract, usually in return for the employer's promise not to lock out workers and to submit union grievances to arbitration. Such provisions create a procedure for the peaceable settlement of contract disputes. These clauses grew in popularity in the 1920s and 30s as the federal government endeavored to prevent federal courts from using injunctions to stop unions from peaceful striking, assembling and publicizing facts concerning a labor dispute.

NOTA BENE. See N.B.

NOTARY PUBLIC. A citizen of high moral character and integrity appointed by a public official to perform notarial acts for a small fee in connection with written and oral agreements. During the Roman period, the notarius was a public official who committed agreements to writing and affixed the parties' seals. Notaries were vital functionaries because of the widespread lack of writing skills. Today the notary may perform acts of a non-legal and ministerial nature, and the powers may vary from state to state. In general, however, the official duties and powers of a notary are limited to determining that the parties to a written agreement are the parties they claim to be, obtaining the acknowledgment that the parties are aware of the contents of the agreement, affixing a seal to prevent subsequent alteration of the document, and keeping an official record of the act of notarization. A notary public must take an oath and give a bond pledging the faithful performance of his or her duties. The beneficiary of the bond is the person who suffers as a result of the perpetration of misdeed by the notary. In civil law countries notaries are lawyers who specialize in real estate and probate matters.

NOTICE OF ALIBI STATUTE. A law enacted in many states which requires the defendant to notify the prosecution of an intent to raise an alibi defense at trial. The defendant must inform the prosecution of the place he claims to have been and of any witness he plans to call to support him. The purpose of the statute is to allow the prosecution time to prepare an effective case rebutting the alibi. The Supreme Court has held that these statutes are constitutional as long as the defendant has a reciprocal right to be notified of the prosecution's rebuttal witnesses.

NOTICE OF INTENT TO SUE. A prerequisite to a hearing of certain civil cases. For example, the Age Discrimination in Employment Act requires the offended party to give such notice to his or her employer within 180 days of the alleged discriminatory act. Questions may arise as to when the discriminatory act actually occurred. Where unequivocal notice of termination and the employee's last day of work coincide, the alleged unlawful act will be deemed to have occurred on that date, notwithstanding the employee's continued reception of benefits through a later date. Notice of Intent to Sue is also required by many state laws before a citizen may sue a municipality over performance of a non-governmental function. Local laws should be checked to determine the relevant deadlines and starting dates.

NOTICE PLEADING. The type of pleading required by the Federal Rules of Civil Procedure, so-called because its purpose is to give general notice of the suit, not specific details of law or fact.

NOVATION AGREEMENT. See DISCHARGE BY NOVATION.

NO-WORK, NO-PAY STATUTE. A little known federal law passed by Congress in 1856 and rarely, if ever, enforced. It provides that Senators and Representatives forfeit their pay for each day of work that is missed unless a satisfactory excuse is provided. The amount of money taxpayers would save each year if the legislators were docked their salaries as required by the statute is in excess of one million dollars.

N.P.C. See JUSTICE, INC.

N.R.C. See NUCLEAR REGULATORY COMMISSION.

N.S.A. (National Security Agency). Created by President Harry S. Truman in 1952 and located in a closely-guarded nine-story building in Fort Meade, Maryland, 23 miles northeast of Washington, D.C. Its 20,000 employees engage in two major missions. The first is to gather all possible intelligence about foreign military forces, political developments and economic conditions in nations around the world by such means as long-distance listening devices and satellites. The N.S.A.'s sources of intelligence are extremely broad and include radar signals given off by Soviet test missiles, routine radio traffic at important airports, and telexed orders from foreign buyers of such American goods as computers, bulldozers and oil-drilling equipment. The data the N.S.A.

collects are then sorted by computer and passed on to the C.I.A. and other United States official users. The second responsibility of N.S.A. is to protect sensitive American domestic communications from intrusion by foreign powers.

N.S.M. CASE (National Student Marketing Case). This complex suit, involving actions by both private parties and the Securities and Exchange Commission, grew out of a financial and accounting fraud by certain officers of the National Student Marketing Corporation (N.S.M.). It was held that in negotiating a merger with Interstate National Corporation (Interstate), officers of N.S.M. failed to disclose material financial information, either to the Interstate shareholders or to the purchasers of the N.S.M. stock sold by the Interstate principals following the merger. The concealed information reflected that N.S.M. had suffered a net loss during the preceding nine-month period, rather than the profit which the company had claimed. As the District Court for the District of Columbia noted, "In a merger transaction . . . accurate financial information is necessary in order for a shareholder fairly to be able to vote." In fact, the proxy materials which were sent to the Interstate shareholders in connection with the proposed merger advised them of the importance of N.S.M.'s financial statements. The proxy materials also contained copies of the proposed Merger Agreement, which not only represented and warranted that the financial statements of N.S.M. were accurate and truthful but, in addition, required a "comfort letter" from N.S.M.'s independent accountants to the effect that they had no reason to believe that the unaudited interim financial statements for the relevant period were not prepared in accordance with generally accepted accounting principles or that any material adjustments were necessary to present accurately the results of N.S.M.'s operations. These provisions effectively assured the Interstate shareholders that the financial statements would be accurate. The comfort letter requirement provided an extra measure of assurance. However, when the unsigned comfort letter was received at the merger closing, it indicated that certain adjustments were necessary. Nevertheless, after receiving assurances concerning the accuracy of the financial statements from counsel for N.S.M., the Interstate representatives opted to proceed with the merger. In holding that this action constituted a violation of the securities laws, the court concluded, "Although it is arguable whether a better business decision under the circumstances was to proceed with the merger, the antifraud provisions prohibited such a course of action when a material misrepresentation or omission has occurred, regardless of the business justification for closing the merger." Additionally, it was held that some of the attorneys and accountants involved in the merger were guilty of violating the securities laws because despite knowledge that the N.S.M. financial statements were incorrect, they allowed the merger to proceed. To avoid this type of problem, many firms have adopted such procedures as the Two-Partner Rule, which requires an attorney to get a second opinion within the firm before certain actions are taken.

N.T.S.B. (National Transportation Safety Board). An independent federal administrative agency which seeks to assure that all types of transportation in the United States are conducted safely. The Board investigates accidents and makes recommendations to government agencies, the transportation industry, and others on safety measures and practices. The Board also regulates the procedures for reporting accidents and promotes the safe transport of hazardous materials by government and private industry.

NUCLEAR-ACCIDENTS PACT OF 1971. An international agreement that provides for safeguards by Russia and the United States against the accidental detonation or the unintended launching of nuclear weapons.

NUCLEAR DISASTER CASE (1978). A Supreme Court decision upholding the validity of the Price-Anderson Act. The Act is designed to protect the public and encourage the development of the nuclear energy industry. To achieve these goals, the Act imposes a $560 million limitation on liability for nuclear accidents resulting from the operation of a federally licensed private nuclear power plant and requires those persons indemnified under the Act to waive all legal defenses in the event of a substantial nuclear accident. The case involved a suit by an environmental organization, a labor union, and a number of individuals against *Duke Power Company,* a public utility constructing nuclear power plants in North and South Carolina. The district court held that the Act violated the due process clause of the Fifth Amendment because the amount of recovery is not rationally related to the potential losses and that the Act encouraged irresponsibility in matters of safety and environmental protection. Furthermore, the district court held the principles of equal protection were violated in that victims of a nuclear accident were forced to bear the burden of injury, whereas society as a whole benefits from the development of nuclear power. In reversing the district court, the Supreme Court in *Duke Power Co. v. Carolina Environmental Study Group, Inc.,* 438 U.S. 59 (1978), emphasized the importance of nuclear power development and the Act's assurance that Congress would take appropriate steps to protect the public.

NUCLEAR FAMILY (Conjugal Family). A social group consisting of parents and their children, in the narrowest sense.

NUCLEAR NONPROLIFERATION TREATY OF 1968. An international agreement, to which the United States is a party, that is designed to prevent the spread of nuclear weapons, the pact commits non-nuclear countries to refrain from developing nuclear weapons and commits the nuclear-power countries to reduce their armaments.

NUCLEAR NONPROLIFERATION ACT OF 1978. A federal law which severely restricts the supply of nuclear fuels to foreign countries in an attempt to exploit the atom for the generation of electric power and other peaceful pursuits and not for warlike activities. It requires all nations with whom we deal to comply fully with all International Atomic Energy Agency (I.A.E.A.) safeguards.

NUCLEAR REGULATORY COMMISSION (N.R.C.). A five-member Board appointed by the President to license the erection and supervise the safe operation of nuclear energy plants. Its incompetent operation was revealed by the nuclear accident in 1979 at the Three Mile Island nuclear plant in Pennsylvania.

NUDUM PACTUM (Latin—naked promise). A voluntary promise without legally sufficient consideration. A Nudum Pactum may be based on mere good will or natural affection. Because the consideration is legally insufficient, a valid contract cannot be formed. Under a Nudum Pactum, a mere promise exists between the parties.

NUISANCE ABATEMENT. A self-help doctrine of ancient origin permitting the entry upon another person's property in order to stop a nuisance. Under this doctrine a person may be allowed to cut off branches of overhanging trees or to move a car from a space where it is illegally parked. However, most courts have required that the property owner be notified of the nuisance before self-help is employed. In no case may one do damage disproportionate to the harm suffered. Thus, one may not cut down his neighbor's overhanging tree, although he may top off the offending branches.

NUISANCE TAX. A tax which, after administration costs are deducted, does not yield enough return to justify the inconvenience it causes.

NUKE-IN. A 1979 anti-nuclear energy rally held in Washington, D.C. The 75,000 demonstrators at the nuke-in expressed the nationwide concern over nuclear safety that followed the reactor accident at Three Mile Island. Given an audience with President Jimmy Carter, the leaders of the anti-nuclear movement have probably seized on a major political issue of the 1980s.

NUMBERED BONDS. See BEARER BONDS.

NUNC PRO TUNC (Latin—now for then). Applies to acts done now which should have been done at some earlier time. Such Nunc Pro Tunc acts are given retroactive effect as if done at the regular time.

NUNCUPATIVE WILL (Oral Will). A majority of states statutorily allow such wills of personalty but only Georgia allows oral wills to dispose of real property. The statutes usually require that the will be uttered while the testator is "in the last illness" and some require that it be made at the testator's home or in the place where he dies. As with other wills, testamentary intent is necessary and the testator must intend that the words he utters shall operate as his will. The mere giving of instructions for a written will or dictating a letter, which when written the testator intends to be his will, does not result in a nuncupative will. Two or three witnesses to an oral will must be present at the same time, in contrast to the usual rule as to witnesses to written wills. Since witnesses to oral wills must testify to the terms of the will as well as its execution, it is important that all witnesses testify to the same transaction. Some statutes limit the amount of personal property which may pass by oral wills. Personal property over the fixed limit can pass only by a written will. Most statutes require that the oral testimony be reduced to writing and probated within a limited period (usually six months). Due to the problems of proof surrounding oral wills, it is not surprising that the courts have declared that nuncupative wills should be disfavored.

NUNN BILL. A proposed federal law to establish a Commission and Court on Judicial Conduct and Disability. It was suggested by the Democratic Senator from Georgia in 1973 but rejected by Congress each year since that date. The legislation would create a disciplinary mechanism for federal judges in a three-stage approach. All complaints would first go to a Judicial Tenure Commission, consisting of judicial representatives from each federal circuit. If a complaint were found to have merit, it would be forwarded to the circuit where the judge involved sits for further processing. A formal hearing may then be scheduled before the Judicial Conference of the United States, which would have total disciplinary authority, including removal from the bench. Proponents see it as a viable alternative to the present cumbersome impeachment process, the only way federal judges can now be removed. They insist that the benefits would be substantial without any impairment of judicial independence. The proposal would establish a system for removing judges physically unable—for reasons of age or disability —to continue on the bench. Impeachment and conviction of federal judges have been rare. There have only been nine impeachment attempts and only four convictions in the past two centuries, the last of which was in 1936. Several states have established similar procedures for the discipline and removal of state judges such as the New York Commission on Judicial Conduct which have worked well in practice.

NURTURING PARENT (Mothering Function). A new phrase used by lawyers and courts to describe the parent in a custody contest who is more involved with the child. More and more courts are looking at a child custody dispute as an analysis of the best interest of the child and are ceasing to rely on an arbitrary presumption in favor of mothers.

NUTS AND BOLTS DECISION. President Carter's commitment to a free trade policy which overrode the metal fastener industry's demand for trade restrictions on imported nuts, bolts, and large screws. Imports currently account for $300 million in sales, and almost 50 percent of domestic consumption of nuts, bolts, and large screws.

O

O.A.L.A.C. See LEGAL AID ON WHEELS.

O.A.P.E.C. (Organization of Arab Petroleum Exporting Countries). An international cartel of Arab oil-exporting nations which attempts arbitrarily to restrict the production and raise the price of petroleum to suit their own political views and financial gain.

O.A.R. (Offender Aid and Restoration). First organized in Charlottesville, Virginia, by Jay Worrall, this is primarily a volunteer organization. With more than 20 chapters in eight states, most programs include (1) a one-to-one prisoner-volunteer program to help offenders work their way back into community life; (2) a bail-bond program to help accused persons get out of jail quickly and return to families and jobs; and (3) an employment program to help prisoners on work release and ex-offenders find jobs.

O.A.S. (Organization of American States). An American regional organization created by the Bogota Conference of 1948. The O.A.S. took over the Pan American Union structure and incorporated the Rio Treaty within its charter. Its purposes are cooperation, collective security, pacific settlement of disputes, and economic, social and cultural relationships between its members. Membership is open to all American states. Cuba, however, was expelled in 1962. The O.A.S. structure provides for: (1) the Inter-American Conference, a supreme organ which meets every five years; (2) a Meeting of Consultation of Foreign Ministers, and an Advisory Defense Committee; (3) a Council of diplomatic envoys; (4) the Pan American Union, which now has the role of a general secretariat; (5) specialized conferences, and (6) specialized organizations. In 1961, the Charter of Punta del Este created the Alliance for Progress, which favored greater economic activities among O.A.S. members. It also provided for a framework for the $20 billion given by President Kennedy on behalf of the United States to Latin-American countries.

O.A.U. See ORGANIZATION OF AFRICAN UNITY.

OBITER DICTUM. According to a journal of the same name, Obiter Dictum is a "gratuitous opinion, an individual impertinence, which, whether it be wise or foolish, right or wrong, bindeth none—not even the lips that utter it." Obiter dictum, more commonly known by the plural, dicta, generally refers to those portions of a court opinion which are not essential to resolving the issue or issues of a case. Separating dicta from the essential holding of a case is the bane of most law students' existence.

O.C.A. (Office of Court Administration). State agencies involved in the efficient operation of the judicial system whose experts in their respective fields enable the judges to spend their time in judging and not on administrative matters in which they are not qualified.

OCCUPATIONAL SAFETY AND HEALTH ACT. See O.S.H.A.

OCCUPATIONAL SAFETY AND HEALTH REVIEW COMMISSION. See O.S.H.R.C.

OCEAN ALLIANCE. A voluntary association of Western, Middle Eastern and Asian nations in a security system, proposed by Ray C. Cline, executive director of studies at the Center for Strategic and International Studies at Georgetown University. The Ocean Alliance would be formed to defend the freedom of the seas and protect territory and people for mutual security and commercial benefits. The core of the proposed Alliance would be the United States, Canada, West Germany, France, Britain, Italy, Israel, Japan, Taiwan and Australia. To these he would add Mexico, Spain, Iran, Turkey, Egypt, Saudi Arabia, Indonesia, Singapore, South Korea, Brazil, South Africa, Nigeria and New Zealand. Criticism is centered on two aspects of Mr. Cline's plan. One is that such an Alliance, although its members' combined economic, military and political power would far exceed that of the Soviet Union and its allies, would be too unwieldy for effective crisis management. The second is that the American people are not attuned to grandiose plans of this type. Such policies, the critics say, suggest empire building to Americans, who favor short-term pragmatic policies.

OCEAN BILL OF LADING. Sets forth the contractual terms for the carriage of goods in maritime commerce and serves as an acknowledgment that a carrier has received the goods for shipment. Since an Ocean Bill of Lading is usually negotiable, it also controls the actual possession of the goods. Thus it is considered indispensable in financing the worldwide movement of commodities and merchandise.

OCEAN DUMPING ACT. The popular name of the Federal Marine Protection Research and Sanctuaries Act of 1972, which attempts to restrict the harm done to the marine environment by the dumping of waste into the ocean. The statute creates a permit system regulating the dumping of material into ocean waters. The E.P.A. administers the permit system, and also designates certain offshore areas as suitable dumping sites, and others as sanctuaries, whose ecological value precludes any dumping.

OCEAN THERMAL ENERGY CONVERSION. See O.T.E.C.

OCTOBER 1 ANTI-FASCIST REVOLUTIONARY GROUP. See G.R.A.P.O.

ODOMETER LAW. A regulation, issued by the Department of Transportation, which makes it a federal crime punishable by heavy fine and imprisonment to tamper with a mileage meter. The law is aimed primarily at the unscrupulous automobile dealer who sets the odometer back before selling a car in an attempt to defraud the prospective purchaser. If a buyer can prove he was so deceived, he can recover $1,000 in damages from the seller without any proof of injury. In spite of this law, it is estimated that American Consumers lose $1 billion dollars a year from sales in violation of the Odometer Law. Some schemes involve titling a car in a state which does not have a mileage statement, thus allowing for eventual hard-to-trace Odometer rollbacks.

O.E.C.D. (Organization for Economic Co-Operation and Development). Headquartered in Paris, France, the O.E.C.D. is an international intergovernmental organization, successor to the Organization for European Economic Co-operation (O.E.E.C.) created in 1948, to implement the Marshall Plan for European recovery. The constituent Convention of the O.E.C.D. was signed by eighteen European countries, Canada, and the United States, on December 14, 1960, and was ratified by the required number of national parliaments by September 30, 1961. Since that date Japan, Finland, Australia, and New Zealand have become full members of the Organization, bringing the total of member countries to twenty-four. Yugoslavia participates in certain O.E.C.D. activities. The Convention specifies that the Organization shall promote policies designed to promote economic development, improve trade and raise the standard of living in member as well as non-member countries.

O.E.E.C. (Organization for European Economic Co-Operation). An international organization of European nations created in 1948 to administer United States financial aid under the Marshall Plan. The long-term goal of the O.E.E.C. was to achieve a solid European economy through economic co-operation among the nations of Europe. The O.E.E.C. was replaced in 1961 by the Organization for Economic Co-operation and Development. (O.E.C.D.).

OF COUNSEL. An attorney who has a continuing close and regular relationship of consultation with another lawyer or law firm.

OFF-BROADWAY BOOKING AGREEMENT. Similar to a Four Walls Booking Agreement, except that the theater owner furnishes the theater lighted, heated, and air-conditioned. The producer is prohibited from engaging any non-performing, non-creative personnel in the theater without the express consent of the theater owner.

OFFENDER AID AND RESTORATION. See O.A.R.

OFFERING CIRCULAR. Prospectus-like document required by Securities and Exchange Regulation A (S.E.C. Rules 251-62) to be submitted by a certain class of offerors of securities to their respective offerees. Responding to the problems posed by the onerous burdens of the registration requirements of the Securities Act of 1933, the draftsmen of Regulation A have provided for a simplified form of registration for securities whose value does not exceed $300,000 ("small-issues" securities). Such issues may now be offered for sale as soon as certain requirements are met by the offeror. Among these is the stipulation that an offering circular be submitted wherever the value of the securities in question exceeds $50,000. The circular is essentially an abbreviated prospectus whose purpose is the same: to provide a description of the offeror's business and financial status.

OFFICE AUDIT. See TAX AUDIT.

OFFICE HOURS. See NON-JUDICIAL PUNISHMENT.

OFFICE OF COURT ADMINISTRATION. See O.C.A.

OFFICE OF FEDERAL PROCUREMENT POLICY. See FEDERAL PROCUREMENT POLICY.

OFFICE OF GOVERNMENT ETHICS. See FEDERAL ETHICS LAW.

OFFICE OF HUMAN RIGHTS AND HUMANITARIAN AFFAIRS. State Department agency which, among other things, monitors human rights in foreign countries and has the power to approve commercial deals between United States manufacturers and foreign dealers in countries that have violated human rights. An example of the far-reaching effects of this office is the Steel Groin Protectors Case. The Office of Human Rights delayed a $411 shipment of steel groin protectors and helmets for Indonesian riot police even though Indonesia sells the United States 9 percent of all our imported oil. Delay of the shipment was eventually overruled after press disclosure of the absurdity of the case.

OFFICE OF LEGAL SERVICES. See LEGAL SERVICES CORPORATION.

OFFICE OF NAVAL INTELLIGENCE. See UNITED STATES INTELLIGENCE-GATHERING CENTERS.

OFFICE OF PERSONNEL MANAGEMENT. See CIVIL SERVICE COMMISSION.

OFFICIAL GAZETTE. The official journal relating to patents and trademarks. Published weekly since 1872 by the Patent Office, it includes abstracts of patents granted on that day, selected decisions rendered by the Patent Office and by the courts, notices of pending suits, and general information such as changes in rules.

OFFICIAL SECRETS ACT. See BRITISH OFFICIAL SECRETS ACT.

OFF-THE-BOOKS INCOME. Money paid for goods and services which is not reported on the books of an employer, so that his employee avoids paying income and social security taxes. The employee often works at a reduced rate to induce the employer to engage in this illegal activity. When individuals who are self-employed, such as free lance writers and artists, fail to report part of their earnings, the unreported portion is also known as off-the-books income. It is difficult to estimate how extensive this practice is. However, some economists say that unemployment figures are overstated since the poor, the middle income and the well-

to-do all earn more than statistics indicate.

OFF-TRACK BETTING. See O.T.B.

OKUN'S LAW. Created by Arthur Okun, economic adviser to President Lyndon Johnson, this principle was developed in the early 1960s to express the relationship between economic growth and reductions in unemployment. The theory was designed to help the government spur the economy without inviting new inflation. It was discarded as unworkable in the late 1970s.

OLD BAILEY. An ancient historic criminal court of London, England, formerly adjoining notorious Newgate Prison which was demolished in 1903. The central criminal court now stands upon this site, which is still called Old Bailey. Old Bailey was one of the baileys of early London, meaning the open space between a fortification's inner and outer walls. The surviving judges of Charles I were tried in Old Bailey after the Restoration of 1660, as well as Lord William Russell in 1683, Jack Sheppard in 1724, Jonathan Perceval in 1812, and the Cato Street conspirators in 1820.

OLD-BOY NETWORK. See BALTIMORE LAW CLUBS.

OLDER AMERICAN LEGAL ACTION CENTER. See LEGAL AID ON WHEELS.

OLD LEFT. See NEW LEFT.

O.L.S. See LEGAL SERVICES CORPORATION.

OMEGA SEVEN. An anti-Castro Cuban group that gets its jollies from planting bombs to blow up people and buildings in New York City and other metropolitan areas.

OMERTA OATH. See WITNESS SECURITY PROGRAM.

OMNIBUS CRIME CONTROL AND SAFE STREETS ACT OF 1968. A law enacted to assist state and local governments in reducing the incidence of crime and improving the quality and coordination of law enforcement. The

Act provides financial assistance to state and local law enforcement for educational and training programs and for controlling riots and combatting organized crime. In addition, federal controls are established over interstate and foreign commerce in firearms. Restrictions are placed on mail order sales, sales to juveniles, transportation of firearms into a state where such firearms are unlawful, and interstate transportation of stolen firearms. Although the original Act excluded rifles and shotguns, subsequent amendments have abolished the exemption. The Act also requires that importers, manufacturers and dealers be federally licensed, and record their transactions. Finally, the Act prohibits wiretapping and surveillance by persons other than law-enforcement officials acting pursuant to a court order. There are, of course, narrow exceptions, such as Presidential acts in the interest of national security. Violators are subject to civil actions for damages as well as criminal penalties.

OMNIBUS JUDGESHIP BILL OF 1978. Created 152 additional federal district and appellate court judgeships, thereby giving President Carter more power (through his nomination of candidates subject to Senate confirmation) over the federal judiciary than any other President in our history.

OMNIBUS PARKS LAW OF 1978. A federal law which funds a five-year, $725-million program to help cities to restore their parks and recreation facilities. This was not only the largest amount of federal money ever to be spent on urban parks but also the first such federal aid to be directly extended to cities.

ONE FREE BITE RULE. Popular misconception that every well-behaved dog is entitled to one free bite before the dog's master is liable to the bitee. A more accurate statement of an animal-owner's responsibility is that an owner must act as a reasonable person in discovering the propensities of his pet to injure others, and must take reasonable precautions to prevent such injuries.

ONE HOUSE VETO. The power of either House of Congress to disapprove of any exercise of authority which it lawfully delegated to another branch of government. Such a reservation of veto power, a feature of nearly 200 pieces of recent federal legislation, has been attacked frequently as an unconstitutional infringement on the separation of powers principle, requiring all legislation to be passed by both Houses of Congress. The constitutionality of the one-house veto, however, has never been squarely decided by the Supreme Court of the United States.

ONE "L." Novel by Scott Turow describing the intellectual rigors of student life in Harvard Law School but equally applicable to most American law schools.

ONE-MAN CORPORATION. See CLOSE CORPORATION.

ONE-TWENTY (1-20). A form issued by an Admissions Office of a University to a foreign student which certifies that the student has been accepted by the University, is fluent in English and is financially able to pay his tuition. The certificate is then submitted by the student to the local American Embassy of the country where he lives which issues a visa to the student for admission to the United States.

O.P.E.C. (Organization of Petroleum Exporting Countries). A cartel composed of the 13 major oil-producing countries in the world, mostly Arab, which control the production of, and fix the price at which they will uniformly market, their product.

OPEN CITY. Any area which belligerent nations agree shall be spared from damage by any of the warring parties.

OPEN DOOR POLICY. See LONG MARCH FORWARD.

OPEN-END INVESTMENT TRUST. A trust arrangement whereby the trustee is authorized under the terms of the trust to make investments to enhance trust property in stocks and securities, which were not part of the trust property at the inception of the trust arrangement. Such a trust arrangement offers the trustee wide latitude in promoting trust growth.

OPEN-END MORTGAGE. A mortgage which provides that the remaining unpaid amount of the loan can be increased by mutual agreement of the parties, not to exceed the original amount of the loan.

OPEN-END OFFENSE. Treated either as a misdemeanor or a felony, depending on the sentence imposed. The Supreme Court of Arizona recently ruled that a defendant found guilty of such an offense may be placed on probation for a longer period than the maximum sentence for a misdemeanor and still have the offense regarded as a misdemeanor after probation was completed.

OPENING THE DOOR (Opening The Floodgates). A rationale used by courts to justify denying a new remedy or limiting a cause of action. For example, if a child sued his father for damages arising from the fact of his illegitimate birth, a court may use this argument to deny recovery, on the ground that other children dissatisfied with the circumstances of their births may also use this argument, thus opening the floodgates to numerous frivolous suits.

OPENING THE FLOODGATES. See OPENING THE DOOR.

OPEN LISTING. See LISTING ARRANGEMENTS.

OPEN MARKET COMMITTEE. A 12-person federal group that meets 10 times a year to set the national monetary policy.

OPEN MARRIAGE. An agreement between a husband and wife which permits either to engage in sexual relations with third parties.

OPEN MORTGAGE. May be paid off without penalty prior to the maturity date. The term Open Mortgage may also refer to an overdue mortgage that may be foreclosed at any time.

OPEN-PANEL PLAN. Group legal services plan, analogous to Blue Cross health care, which allows the member of the group to visit the lawyer of his choice, the fee being paid by the group plan. In contrast, a Closed Panel Plan is one in which participation in the plan guarantees the payment of legal fees only if the member consults one of a team of lawyers specifically designated by the group. Labor unions have recently become interested in group legal plans, favoring the Closed Panel as a money saver. However, the American Bar Association has fought strongly to allow only Open Panel plans to protect the attorneys involved from Conflicts of Interest. The Open Panel also usually results in higher fees for a larger number of lawyers.

OPEN-PRICE TERM. Section of the Uniform Commercial Code (§ 2-305) which allows the buyer and seller the right to negotiate price at a date subsequent to concluding a contract for sale. Open Price Terms are often used in inflationary periods.

OPEN SHOP. A hiring policy by an employer to employ both union and non-union workers. The term is occasionally used in a derogatory sense by unionists, expressing their belief that such policies are motivated by an anti-union bias.

OPEN SKIES. A key United States proposal to the 1944 Chicago conference which established the International Civil Aviation Organization, a branch of the United Nations. That proposal would have multilaterally opened world air commerce to the air carriers of the ratifying nations with a minimum of restrictions. Then, as now, however, the sovereign rights of other nations and particularly their specific political, social and often economic objectives in light of their sizes and resources led generally to the firmest of resistance.

OPEN-SPACE EASEMENT (Scenic Easement; Conservation Easement). A voluntary restriction on the use of private property which is adjacent to or near public land to protect and preserve the character of the private property to conform with the nature of the public property which is usually a park or a wildlife habitat. Tax benefits are granted to encourage people to create such Easements on their land in the public interest of maintaining our natural resources in their primitive beauty.

OPERATION ALIAS. See ALIAS OPERATION.

OPERATION BABY LIFT. See BABY LIFT.

OPERATION BOOTSTRAP (1) (Fomento: Spanish—fuel, encouragement, or support). Project initiated in 1942 and administered by the Economic Development Administration in which the United States Government encouraged industries to locate their operations in Puerto Rico. Incentives such as temporary exemptions from corporate income taxes and tax exemptions for dividends or profit distributions paid to Puerto Rican residents led to the addition of thousands of new industries. As a result of this industrial influx, considerable increases were made in investment capital and new jobs. (2) Self-help, nonprofit operation instituted by Low Smith and Robert Hall in Watts after the riots of 1965. The goal of the program was to get local residents to discover the creative potential within the community. The operation did not accept any federal money. Rather, it approached businesses and education centers for training and money when either resource was needed. Included in Operation Bootstrap projects were a job training center, a printing center and Shindana Toys—the manufacturers of "Baby Nancy," a black doll. Shindana stimulated the Mattel Toy Company, the country's largest toy manufacturer, to contribute extensive administrative and marketing training to the Operation in 1970.

OPERATION CONDOR. A multi-million dollar annual payment in cash and equipment by the State Department to the Mexican police to reduce the sale and transportation of illegal drugs into the United States. Unfortunately, the Mexican police are notorious for their use of torture and other violations of human rights in their treatment of suspects and prisoners, so we are in the uncomfortable position of indirectly sanctioning such practices.

OPERATION DOORSTEP. See CAREER CRIMINALS PROGRAM.

OPERATION FRONTLOAD. A massive but largely unsuccessful undercover operation by the F.B.I., in 1979, to gain access to construction companies with ties to the mob of organized crime in New York City and elsewhere.

OPERATION LEPRECHAUN. A despicable project of the Internal Revenue Service which was happily abandoned in 1975. It involved informants who were paid to spy on the affairs and habits of prominent public officials in Florida.

OPERATION STOPGAP. A program of the United States Drug Enforcement Administration (D.E.A.) which uses information supplied by Navy Ocean Surveillance satellites to control the illegal smuggling of marijuana into the country. The data supplied by the satellites is fed into computers at a central control center which then reports to the D.E.A. The Coast Guard in turn intercepts the carrier ships on the high seas before they reach United States waters.

O.P.I.C. (Overseas Private Investment Corporation). A federal agency which assists United States investors in making profitable investments in about eighty developing countries. It encourages investment projects that will help the social and economic development of these countries. At the same time it helps the balance of payments through the profits returned to this country, as well as the jobs and exports created. O.P.I.C. offers investors assistance in finding investment opportunities, insurance to protect their investments, and loans and loan guaranties to help finance their projects. By reducing or eliminating the risks for investors and providing financing and assistance not otherwise available, O.P.I.C. helps ease the social, political, and economic problems that can make investment opportunities in the developing areas less attractive than in advanced countries. At the same time, it is reducing the need for government-to-government lending programs by involving the private sector in establishing capital-generating capacity and industrial capacity in developing countries. O.P.I.C. insures investors against the political risks of expropriation, inconvertibility of local currency holdings, and damage from war, revolution, or insurrection. It also offers a special insurance policy to construction and service firms seeking contracts in developing countries. Since O.P.I.C. programs are available only for a new facility, expansion or modernization of an existing plant, or new inputs of technology or services, the investments it covers are more likely to produce significantly new benefits for host countries.

OPINION OF TITLE. A document by a person competent in researching real estate titles, usually an attorney, stating that he has exercised care in examining the title and offering his opinion as to the status of the title. An opinion of title does not guarantee the title.

OPPORTUNITY TRUST. Standardized trust agreement which allows trust administrators to reduce costs of administration by handling substantially more accounts. A client using an opportunity trust can create a trust merely by checking a series of boxes that fit his estate planning needs. Generally, trust departments focus primarily on the wealthy (minimum trust assets of $250,000), who comprise only one half of one percent of the population. Opportunity trusts make it economically feasible for trust departments to offer their services to a broader percentage of the population.

OPTIONAL PROTOCOL TO THE INTERNATIONAL COVENANT ON CIVIL AND POLITICAL RIGHTS. Ratified by twelve countries as of 1976, the optional protocol entered into force on March 23, 1976. Ratification of this Protocol binds the ratifying nation to accept the authority of the Human Rights Committee set forth in the international covenant on civil and political rights. The authority of the Human Rights Committee is the power to "receive and consider communications from individuals subject to its jurisdiction who claim to be victims of a violation by that State Party of any of the rights set forth in the Covenant." The committee can then require the country against whom the complaint is received to submit to the Committee a written explanation.

ORBITAL TRANSPORT UND RAKETEN AG. See O.T.R.A.G.

ORDER BILL. Any negotiable Bill of Lading. Such Bill will be considered negotiable when the goods are destined to be delivered to the order of "any" person who may be named in the bill. An Order Bill thus differs from a Straight Bill which is non-negotiable and requires that the delivery be made to a specified person.

ORDER OF ACCOUNTING. A court order for the submission of a record indicating the transactions which involve the trust property. Commonly, such a legal action is brought by a trust beneficiary who is in doubt of either the honesty or ability of the trust. Such a judicial order stems historically from the fear that one in charge of money or property will not honor the wishes and orders of its owner.

ORDER OF THE COIF. The scholastic honorary society of legal education, comparable to Phi Beta Kappa in college. It is composed of the top 10 percent of each graduating law class. In medieval England, judges wore a close fitting hood covering all but their face as a required mark of their station. This hood was called a Coif, and collectively judges became known as the Order of the Coif. To honor the intellectual elite of the legal profession, Northwestern University Law School established the first American Order of the Coif in 1907. More than 50 outstanding law schools now have local Chapters.

ORDER OF THE TEMPLE. See TRIAL OF THE TEMPLARS.

ORDINARY WITNESS. One who knows something about a trial and can be forced to testify, contrary to the rights of expert witnesses who do not have to testify if they do not wish to do so.

ORGANIZATIONAL MEETING. Completion of the organization of a corporation occurs at an organizational meeting. The majority of states having statutory requirements for these meetings require the presence only of those persons who have signed the articles of incorporation. Other states simply require a meeting of the board of directors. At the meeting, the articles of incorporation are formally accepted and entered into the minutes. Also approved are the by-laws, the corporate seal, any preincorporation agreements, and other formalities. It is common practice for the corporation's attorney to complete a formal record of a meeting although one was never held.

ORGANIZATION FOR ECONOMIC CO-OPERATION AND DEVELOPMENT. See O.E.C.D.

ORGANIZATION OF AFRICAN UNITY (O.A.U.). Created on May 25, 1963, at Addis-Ababa, Ethiopia, the purpose of the O.A.U. is to further co-operation between African countries on all political, social, military, economical, scientific and cultural matters. Its organization, however, lacks the strong supra-national element necessary to implement any of these goals. O.A.U's principal institutions are: an Assembly of Heads of State, which holds annual meetings, a Council of Ministers, a General Secretariat based in Addis-Ababa, and specialized commissions. The O.A.U. mostly devotes itself to political actions against any form of colonialism. Its Charter emphasizes "the total emancipation of the African territories which are still dependent." The elimination of apartheid is of primary importance to the O.A.U.

The O.A.U. also represents an attempt to solve on the African level the frontier disputes arising on its continent. A conciliation committee was set on November 18, 1963, in a futile attempt to solve the dispute between Algeria and Morocco. Now a Commission of Mediation, Conciliation and Arbitration for the peaceful settlement of African disputes has been created in order to avoid submitting such disputes to the U.N. Security Council. The agreement reached by this Commission, in July of 1964 at Cairo, provided for a conciliation committee composed of twenty-one members elected by the Assembly.

ORGANIZATION OF AMERICAN STATES. See O.A.S.

ORGANIZATION OF ARAB PETROLEUM EXPORTING COUNTRIES. See O.A.P.E.C.

ORGANIZATION OF PETROLEUM EXPORTING COUNTRIES. See O.P.E.C.

ORGANIZATION ON HIGH (Angka Loeu). The shadowy members of the Cambodian Politburo, which governs the nation under the leadership of Premier Pol Pot, most of whom are young Marxists who were trained in Paris. They have engaged in a genocide unparalleled in recorded history. One million of their population of seven million in Cambodia (now known as Democratic Kampuchea) have already been assassinated in a bloody attempt to build the perfect communist society. The rest are conscripted to do manual labor in mobile brigades where they work 17 hours a day without pay from the government. And what has the United Nations done about this holocaust? Nothing.

ORGANIZED CRIME STRIKE FORCES. Special sections of the United States Department of Justice, whose purpose is to ferret out organized criminal activity and develop evidence against it. The Forces oversee administration of the federal criminal statutes relating to gambling, extortion, alcoholic beverages, infiltration of legitimate business by organized criminal elements and similar laws. In strike forces, federal prosecutors join with investigative agents from the Federal Bureau of Investigation (F.B.I.), the Drug Enforcement Administration, and the Immigration and Naturalization Service of the Department of Justice, the Internal Revenue Service (I.R.S.), the Secret Service, the United States Customs Service, and the Bureau of Alcohol, Tobacco, and Firearms of the Treasury Department, the United States Postal Service, and the Department of Labor. Some Strike Forces also include representatives of the United States Marshalls Service, and the Securities and Exchange Commission. They also cooperate with state and local police units. Most of the strike forces operate out of the 10 largest cities in the United States.

ORIENTAL MESSAGE. An international delay in the manufacture or delivery of goods meant to indicate the procrastinator's displeasure to the other contracting party.

ORIGINAL DOCUMENT RULE. See BEST EVIDENCE RULE.

ORIGINAL JURISDICTION. That jurisdiction of a court which permits it to take cognizance of a matter at its inception, to try the case and to pass judgment. Generally speaking, it is the jurisdiction conferred on a trial court, as distinguished from the jurisdiction conferred on an appellate court, to review the actions of an inferior court. A particular court may have both original and appellate jurisdiction. The Supreme Court exercises both kinds of jurisdiction. It has original jurisdiction in all cases affecting ambassadors, other public ministers and consuls and cases in which a state is a party. In all other cases coming before the Court, it has appellate jurisdiction.

ORPHAN'S DEDUCTION. See ORPHAN'S EXCLUSION.

ORPHAN'S EXCLUSION (Orphan's Deduction). The Tax Reform Act of 1976 modified the federal estate tax so that the decedent's estate receives a deduction equal to $5000 times the number of years the child is under age 21 at the date of the deceased parent's death.

OSBORN, JOHN HAY, JR. Former law professor and lawyer, successful author of modern novels such as *The Paper Chase,* an exposé of Harvard Law School and *The Associate,* a take-off on a Wall Street law firm.

O.S.C.A.R. (On Line System of Computer Assisted Research). See V.A.L.I.D.

O.S.H.A. (Occupational Safety and Health Act of 1970). Requires safe and healthful working conditions for virtually every employee in the United States. The law directs the Secretary of Labor to set and enforce safety and health standards for all businesses affecting interstate commerce. The only employers exempted are the federal, state and local governments, but special provisions require standards for them. The Labor Department makes inspections and issues citations, and an independent Occupational Safety and Health Review Commission performs the adjudicatory functions.

O.S.H.R.C. (Occupational Safety and Health Review Commission). An independent federal administrative agency concerned with providing safe and healthful working conditions for both the employer and the employee. It decides cases forwarded to it by the Department of Labor when disagreements arise over the results of safety and health inspections performed by the Department. See also O.S.H.A.

OSWALD, LEE HARVEY. See WARREN COMMISSION REPORT.

O.T.B. (Off-Track Betting). A professional pari-mutuel horse-racing wagering operation which is legal in some states which then share in the profits of the enterprise.

O.T.E.C. (Ocean Thermal Energy Conversion). A source of power created by the contrast of warm surface water with cold water moving upwards from the ocean depths whose development and utilization may be the solution to the economic war against Western Civilization which is being waged by O.P.E.C. Two different systems exist for the conversion of this potential into electricity. The first is the "open-cycle" system. In this technique, warm sea water is exposed to a vacuum and brought to a boil. Steam from the water drives the turbine, which in turn generates electricity. The used steam is fed into pipes, cooled and expelled as pure condensed water; the pure water, a by-product of the energy-making process, could be piped into dry areas. The second method is the "closed-cycle" process. In this system, sun-warmed surface water heats a low-boiling substance like ammonia. The vapor from the low-boiling ammonia is driven into a turbine, which creates electricity as it spins. The steam from the ammonia is then piped through the cold water brought up from the depths, condensing the ammonia and recycling it. This second method is rather like the conventional oil-fed generating plants with the oil substituting for the ammonia.

O.T.R.A.G. (Orbital Transport Und Raketen AG). A West German private company which is testing its design for low cost poor man's rockets capable of launching satellites. Third World countries would then be able to afford their own military reconnaissance and communication devices in outer space. The experimental site is a 50,000 square mile area (half the size of West Germany) in the middle of Africa where the company has leased the land from Zaire until the year 2000. This secret base in which the company exercises virtual extraterritorial sovereignty has been given various labels such as a C.I.A. cover, an international tax shelter and an underhand dodge to enable West Germany to build military rockets in violation of treaty restrictions.

OTTO THE TERRIBLE. Term of derision given to former powerful Louisiana Congressman, Otto Passman, for his sharply expressed opinions in his violent official opposition to foreign aid. But his parsimony did not extend to himself, and he was indicted in 1978 for having accepted substantial and numerous bribes from Koreagate Tongsun Park.

OUTER SEVEN (E.F.T.A.). A group of seven European countries, including Austria, Denmark, Norway, Portugal, Sweden, Switzerland, and the United Kingdom, which was formed in 1959 in response to the Common Market. Within a decade the group had achieved its goal of establishing a policy of free trade among its members.

OUTER SPACE TREATY. Adopted by the U.N. General Assembly in 1966, it confirms a previous declaration of the United Nations, which stated that international law, including the Charter of the U.N., applies to outer space and celestial bodies. It states that no country can exert jurisdiction nor appropriation over outer space, and that it must be free for exploration and use by all countries, on the basis of equality and in accordance with international law. Based on the recognition of "common interest of mankind in furthering the peaceful use of Outer Space," the Treaty provides that (1) countries conducting activities in outer space bear international responsibility for their acts, (2) countries are liable for any damage on earth, in the airspace or in outer space caused by objects they launch into outer space, (3) countries retain jurisdiction over objects and personnel launched in outer space, (4) outer space exploration must be made under principles of co-operation, and (5) in case of accident all countries have a duty of assistance to astronauts and must return space objects, wherever they may land, to the country to which they belong. The two main problems involved by the Treaty related to the definition of "peaceful use" and of "outer space," no consensus having been reached on these matters.

OUTPUT CONTRACT. An agreement to buy the entire amount of merchandise produced by a given company. Though such an agreement fails to specify a precise quantity, it is a valid contract because the law implies that a reasonable quantity will be produced.

OUTRAGEOUS SPOUSE SUITS. Although, under the common law, one spouse cannot bring a negligence suit against the other spouse (as for an injury caused by an auto accident), a Maryland court has agreed to hear such cases when one of the spouses has acted outrageously. The decision was based on a case where the husband of a separated couple pointed a high-powered rifle at his wife while she was driving. He forced her off the road, beat and molested her and threatened further violence if she went through with plans to divorce him. Speaking for the court, Judge Smith wrote that: "We can conceive of no sound public policy in the latter half of the 20th century which would prevent one spouse from recovering from another for the outrageous conduct here alleged."

OVAL OFFICE. So named because of its shape, the official room in the White House where the American President spends his working day.

OVERBREADTH DOCTRINE. See CHILLING EFFECT.

OVERSEAS PRIVATE INVESTMENT CORPORATION. See O.P.I.C.

O.W.L.S. (Organized Workers of Legal Services). First union for lawyers in the United States, certified by the National Labor Relations Board in June, 1978. The new national organization will consist of Legal Aid lawyers and para-legal workers who provide legal services for the poor. One of the purposes of the organization is to bring wage increases which may encourage more lawyers to stay in the field of legal aid which currently pays about $14,000 per year.

OWN MOTION. See SUA SPONTE.

OYEZ OYEZ (French—hear ye, hear ye). Commonly used by bailiffs to command the attention of all present to the business of the court and to rise when the judge enters the court room. It is misunderstood by many to be the English words, "Oh yes, oh yes."

P

P.A. See PARTICIPATING ASSOCIATE.

P.A.C.E. (Professional, Administrative Career Exam). A federal government test designed as the first step to meaningful federal careers for junior level executives and professionals. Minority groups have long contended that the examination is so structured that it discriminates against them. As a result, Congress adopted the Garcia Amendment, which directs the government to strengthen and improve its hiring of minorities. The impact of the government's new personnel policies began in 1980 when the P.A.C.E. examination was no longer given for 2,800 positions in the Social Security Administration, which is a substantial portion of the total P.A.C.E.-based federal hirings of 8,000 people a year. To insure a large selection of minority employees interviews, work experience, community involvement and school performance will be substituted for the written examinations. Other federal departments and agencies are expected to follow suit, either by abandoning P.A.C.E. examinations or modifying them. Critics charge that the new policy means the end of the merit system in the government and in many instances will result in reverse discrimination against whites. But in 1980, the Office of Personnel Management began to delegate to the individual federal departments and agencies full authority for examining and recruiting for most of the better-paying jobs.

PACIFIC BLOCKADE. A naval operation designed to cut off access to and from a foreign port in an attempt to compel the territorial sovereign to redress certain wrongs. It is a form of reprisal short of war. The Blockade does not necessarily involve the taking or withholding of property although it does prevent use of port facilities and flag vessels. Generally in international law the Pacific Blockade is not applicable to the flag vessels of neutral nations engaged in commerce with the blockaded nation. The most spectacular Blockade of modern times was established by Russia around West Berlin in 1948. The United States broke the blockade with a massive airlift which the Russians could not effectively challenge without shooting down American planes.

PACIFIC LEGAL FOUNDATION. A non-profit, self-styled public interest law firm headquartered in California which specializes in cases for the protection of property rights and against big government.

P.A.C.s (Political Action Committees). Separate groups or organizations formed by corporations and private fund raisers to collect money and solicit political funds from employees and stockholders in accordance with the regulations of the Federal Election Campaign Act of 1971 up to a maximum of $5,000 per candidate.

PACTA SUNT SERVANDA (Latin—treaties are to be obeyed). Principle of international law which states that a nation is obligated to observe the treaties it enters into. According to Article 26 of the Vienna Convention of the Law of Treaties, a nation must perform its obligations "in good faith" and not "with utmost fidelity" as sometimes argued under customary international law.

PADDLING CASE. See SCHOOL SPANKING CASE.

P.A.D.D.s. See EMERGENCY PETROLEUM ALLOCATION ACT.

PADDY WAGON. See BLACK MARIA.

PADLOCK SENTENCING. See KEEPLOCK SENTENCING.

PAID-IN-SURPLUS. See CAPITAL SURPLUS.

PAIN AND SUFFERING. An element of damages for which recovery is allowed in an action for personal injuries. While the term pain resists adequate definition, it can be distinguished from suffering which courts have considered the recognition of possible danger resulting from the sensation of pain. Although juries and judges daily make awards for pain and suffering, the theoretical justifications are troublesome. It is impossible to determine how many dollars a plaintiff should receive for undergoing X amount of pain and suffering because dollars and pain are not equivalents.

PALACE OF PEACE. Ornate home of the World Court in The Hague, Holland, built in 1903 with funds contributed by the American industrialist, Andrew Carnegie.

PALESTINE LIBERATION FRONT. See P.L.O.

PALESTINE LIBERATION ORGANIZATION. See P.L.O.

PALMING OFF. See PASSING OFF.

PAN AFRICAN FORCE. Military troops of African Nations on duty in Zaire under the sponsorship and with the support of West Germany, France, Great Britain, Belgium and the United States, to counteract the influence of Cuban and Russian soldiers scattered all over Africa on mischievous missions.

PANAMA REFINING CO. v. RYAN. See NON-DELEGATION DOCTRINE.

PAN AMERICAN UNION. Originally conceived of by Simon Bolivar, the liberator of South America, the Pan American Union was a single assembly in which all the nations in America were to be represented. Formally created in 1910, the Pan American Union grew out of the Commercial Bureau of The American Republics and was replaced ultimately by the Organization of American States.

PANCHA SHILA. See PEACEFUL CO-EXISTENCE.

PANIC SELLING. Rapid turnover of property when a neighborhood has a drastic influx of non-white residents. A town in New Jersey sought to restrain panic selling by prohibiting "house-for-sale" signs, but the Supreme Court of the United States held that such an ordinance is unconstitutional as a violation of freedom of speech.

PAO-WEI. The secret police force of the People's Republic of China.

PAPAL CONCLAVE. The method by which the Pope, the leader of the Roman Catholic Church, is selected. When one Pope dies the See is declared vacant (Sede Vacante) and preparations are made for the election of a new Pope. The Pope is elected by those members of the College of Cardinals who have not, at the time of the Conclave, reached their 80th birthday. Those Cardinals eligible to vote (called Cardinal Electors) are sealed into the Sistine Chapel until they reach a decision. Initially a candidate (papabile) could only be elected by a two-thirds plus one vote of the Electors but under reforms mandated by Paul VI the Conclave could elect to reduce the required majority to a simple majority after six days of balloting. In a deadlock, the Electors could delegate their power of selection to a committee of nine to fifteen Cardinals. Votes are taken four times daily in the Conclave —twice in the morning and twice in the evening. Twice a day, after each pair of ballots, the ballots are burned in a chimney to tell the world outside the progress of the Conclave. White smoke signifies a new Pope has been selected. Black smoke signals no decision. After the white smoke has appeared a senior Cardinal Deacon steps onto the balcony at St. Peter's Basilica and announces in Latin: "Nuntio vobis gaudium magnum. Habemus papam!" ("I announce to you a great joy. We have a Pope!") The Cardinal then announces the new Pope and his chosen name. Shortly thereafter the newly elected Pope appears on the balcony to greet the world.

PAPAL COURT. See ROTA COURT.

PAPAL ENCLAVE. See SACRED COLLEGE OF CARDINALS.

PAPAL INFALLIBILITY. Roman Catholic doctrine holds that Divine Grace prevents the teaching of error in matters of faith and morals. The Pope makes an infallible declaration when (1) the matter discussed concerns Christian faith and morals, (2) the Pope states clearly that he is making a solemn and irrevocable statement, (3) the Pope addresses himself to the whole Church, and (4) he makes it clear that his declaration binds the conscience of all the faithful. The dogma of Papal Infallibility was proclaimed by Pope Pius IX.

PAPAL INTERREGNUM. See CUM CLAVE.

PAPER CHASE. Novel by John Osborn subsequently converted into a movie and TV show describing academic and social student life in Harvard Law School but equally applicable to most American law schools.

PAPER WARS (Papering a Case). Trying to drown the other side in a law suit in motions, interrogatories, depositions, pleading, cross-claims and countersuits; exploiting every procedural and technical nook, cranny and nuance in order to avoid or delay a hearing of the trial on the merits. This improper procedure is often used to great effect in complex antitrust cases. It has aptly been called a "Brobdingnagian procedural imbroglio."

PARA-LEGAL. An individual, usually the graduate of a para-legal studies program, working as a legal assistant under the supervision of a licensed member of the legal profession. Para-legals, used widely in the legal profession, perform many of the non-advocacy functions of the law office. Para-legals conduct client interviews, do legal research, draft documents pertaining to divorces, wills, and incorporation, process workmen's compensation claims, and perform many other duties which do not involve advocacy, case analysis, or strategy planning. Para-legals may even make routine court appearances, such as in default divorces and trial-setting conferences.

PARASTATAL BODIES. Government-owned economic development enterprises in the Third World.

PARANOID SCHIZOPHRENIA. Psychotic disorder characterized by disturbances in thought, mood and behavior. The condition is most often indicated by the presence of persecutory or grandiose delusions or excessive religiosity. Victims assign all initiative and motives for their behavior to outside forces. Once externalized, these deviant impulses and actions can be accepted without a concurrent assumption of responsibility for their origin. Paranoid schizophrenia is a recurring illness and is difficult to treat. Since the patient may be prone to strike out against his imagined pursuers he is likely to be considered dangerous to others and therefore a candidate for Involuntary Commitment. The delusional basis of this malady makes it a workable psychiatric defense to criminal responsibility.

PARENS PATRIAE SUIT (Latin— parent of the country). A suit brought in federal court by a state acting as the representative of all its citizens. Such suits are uncommon, however, and must be distinguished from cases where a state sues in its proprietary capacity or on behalf of a few individual complainants. Several Parens Patriae cases have involved one state seeking to abate a nuisance that exists in another state but produces noxious consequences in the first state. Such suits have been carefully limited so as to not open the door to duplicate recoveries by both individual plaintiffs and a state.

PARENT ABUSE. Non-accidental physical or psychological injury inflicted upon parents, usually elderly parents, by their children.

PARENTAL ABUSE LAW. On July 1, 1979, Sweden became the first country in the world to make it a crime for a parent to spank or humiliate a child, despite the recommendation on the use of the rod found in the Old Testament of the Bible, the Eddas, mythological works in poetry and prose collected in the 13th century, and the warning of Odin, the Norse god of war and wisdom in the Havamal, an ancient north-country collection of Talmudic-style admonition and Confucian-style advice, that "He who goes without corporal punishment will go lawless and die without honor."

PARENTAL DELINQUENCY. The failure of parents to maintain proper control and discipline of their children. Delinquent parents may be held liable in some states in damages for acts of vandalism committed by their children or punished criminally for failure to control their delinquent offspring.

PARENTAL MALPRACTICE. King Lear aptly said it centuries ago, according to Shakespeare, "How sharper than a serpent's tooth to have a thankless child." But it wasn't until April, 1978, that the first case for parental malpractice was brought in the United States when 25-year-old Tom Hansen sued his parents Richard and Shirley Hansen for damages in the sum of $350,000 on the grounds that he will require psychiatric care for the rest of his life as a result of their failure to provide psychological support to him at a critical stage of his life. Even Socrates' sharp-tongued wife Xanthippe never gave him such a hard time as Tom is giving his parents.

PARENT LOCATOR SERVICE. A program established in 1975 by the Office of Child Support Enforcement, Department of Health, Education and Welfare, (H.E.W.), to ascertain the whereabouts of a parent in order to enforce that parent's duty to support a child. The program is designed to keep children off welfare rolls by forcing parents to honor their duty of support. The service utilizes programs set up within every state and reciprocal agreements among states to locate a parent. If the states are unable to locate a person, then the Department's resources are utilized. The whereabouts of a parent can be transmitted to any authorized person, including agents of states having approved plans, the court which issues the support order, and the resident parent of the child.

PARENTS AND STUDENT SAVINGS. See P.A.S.S.

PARENTS ANONYMOUS. A national private organization dedicated to assistance to parents whose children were victims of child abuse.

PARENTS' RIGHTS. Include the right to custody and supervision of their children, including the parents' rights to make decisions about their children's health care. This right, in addition to the parents' right of privacy, makes investigations into suspected child abuse and neglect cases difficult. Beyond the obvious problem of taking a child out of a home where he is in danger, there is the problem of parents who because of religious or philosophical belief refuse medical treatment that may save a child's life. In such cases, courts often act as Parens Patriae and order the treatment over the parent's objections.

PARI DELICTO (Latin—in equal fault). Along with the Doctrine of Unclean Hands, the rationale bars recovery in suits in equity where the plaintiff shared equally in the wrongdoing. For example, courts dismiss private actions for antitrust violations when the plaintiff either participated in the alleged antitrust practice, or violated another antitrust law. The Supreme Court has now severely limited, and possibly eliminated, these doctrines. Emphasizing the deterrent aspects of the antitrust law, the Court held in a 1968 case that they served to insure the constant threat of private actions against anyone contemplating anticompetitive practices. This reasoning highlights the unique role of treble damages in antitrust suits. Such damages are aimed primarily at punishing the offender, rather than compensating the injured party.

PARITY GRID. See E.M.S.

PARKER v. BROWN DOCTRINE. A state action doctrine derived from the Supreme Court decision in *Parker v. Brown,* 317 U.S. 341 (1943). This doctrine holds that state laws can immunize conduct that otherwise would violate the antitrust statutes. *Parker* involved a challenge to the California Agricultural Pro-Rate Act, which au-

thorized the State Director of Agriculture and a publicly appointed Commission to adopt marketing programs regulating the production and sale of agricultural products—in contravention of federal antitrust laws. However, in a series of recent decisions, the Supreme Court has redefined, and in some measure, restricted *Parker* immunity. For example, the Court has held that to qualify for *Parker* immunity, the state action must further an important state policy and this compliance with the state policy must be mandatory. Thus, in *Goldfarb v. Virginia State Bar,* 421 U.S. 773 (1975), the Court struck down a minimum fee schedule for lawyers published by a local bar association and enforced by the state bar. The following year, this ruling was reaffirmed in *Cantor v. Detroit Edison,* 428 U.S. 579 (1976). That case concerned the activities of Detroit Edison, which for many years had provided light bulbs and electric service to its customers for a single rate. When the State of Michigan began regulating the electric utility industry, it approved a tariff submitted by Detroit Edison covering the light bulb program. The Court invalidated the tariff on the ground that the *Parker* doctrine was limited to official action taken by state officials. More recently, in *Lafayette v. Louisiana Power and Light Co.,* 435 U.S. 389 (1978), the Court refused to extend the state action exemption of *Parker* to municipalities.

PARK-INS. A nationwide demonstration by independent truckers in 1979 against the high cost of diesel fuel. Truck drivers shut down major truck stops for periods of twenty-four hours or less in order to disrupt the trucking industry. Their efforts were intended to produce empty shelves in supermarkets and thereby gain public support for their protest.

PARKINSON'S LAW. Thesis of useless proliferation of bureaucracy: work expands so as to fill the time available for its completion. Parkinson's Law, popularized by C. Northcote Parkinson over 20 years ago, was based on insights Parkinson gained from committee work and service in the army during World War II. Another of Parkinson's theories is that the amount of deliberation a committee gives a budget item varies inversely with the amount of money involved.

PARKS, ROSA. The black woman who helped to set in motion the civil rights movement by her refusal in 1955 to give up her bus seat to a white man in Montgomery, Alabama.

PAROLE AUTHORITY. The unwritten powers of certain government officials to take emergency action without having to wait for the customary legislative process to be completed. For example, at the request of the State Department, the Attorney General of the United States used his Parole Authority to permit the emergency entry into the United States of 170,000 Hungarian refugees in 1956, 500,000 Cubans in the 1960s and 172,000 Vietnamese refugees in 1975.

PAROLE BOARD. A committee of private citizens which determines when an inmate may be released from prison on parole and when parole may be revoked because of violations by the inmate. Members are usually appointed by the governor without special consideration for their knowledge of corrections. Parole Boards are generally allowed to develop their own methods of obtaining information about inmates —from prison records, police officers, or prison officials—and are given wide discretion in their decision-making. The hearings are short and simple, in relative secrecy, and the prospective parolee has few statutory rights before the Parole Board. In many states he has no right to counsel or even to make a personal appearance. The Parole Board has complete autonomy in revoking parole for violations of parole conditions. The parolee does, however, have the right to a pre-revocation hearing with adequate notice and the opportunity to call witnesses on his behalf.

PAROLE COMMISSION. Consists of nine members, appointed by the President with the Advice and Consent of the Senate. The Commission has sole authority to grant, modify, or revoke paroles of all federal prisoners and is responsible for the supervision of parolees and prisoners released upon the expiration of their sentences with allowances for statutory good time. In addition the Commission may determine the date of parole eligibility of the prisoner, and discharge parolees from supervision. The Commission also determines in accordance with the provisions of the Labor-Management Reporting and Disclosure Act of 1959, whether the service as officials in the field of organized labor of persons convicted of certain crimes is contrary to the purposes of that Act. Likewise, under the Employment Retirement Income and Security Act of 1974, the Commission determines whether or not such persons may provide services to, or be employed by, employment benefit plans. States have Parole Commissions which perform functions similar to those of the Federal Agency.

PAROLE REVOCATION PROCEDURE. Consists of an informal preliminary probable cause hearing and a revocation hearing. *Morrissey v. Brewer*, 408 U.S. 471 (1972) held that the parolee is entitled to written notice of the charge, the right to present evidence and to confront his accuser, provided that the accuser is not subject to risk of harm.

PARTIAL VERDICT. In criminal law, a verdict whereby the defendant is found to be guilty for only a portion of the accusation against him and innocent as to the remainder of the accusation.

PARTICIPATING ASSOCIATE (P.A.: Special Partner; Non-Equity Partner). A lawyer in a law firm who is promoted from receiving a straight salary into sharing a percentage of the firm's net profit but has no vote in determining firm policy and no ownership interest in the firm.

PARTY GIVER CASE (1978). A California Supreme Court decision which holds that private hosts may be liable for resulting damages when they negligently serve intoxicating beverages to guests. California thus joins a small but growing number of states, including New York, Iowa and Oregon, where a generous host may be held liable for excessive drinking by his guests.

PAR VALUE. A nominal dollar value attributed by law to a share of stock. This value also represents the amount of money the purchaser of the stock is deemed to have contributed to the corporation. It does not necessarily equal the actual value of the stock. It is illegal to issue shares at a price which is below par value. The rigidity of the par value system has led to the increasing use by corporations of no par stock which may be issued at any price satisfactory to the directors or stockholders at that time. Once a par value has been adopted, it can be changed only by an amendment of the Articles of Incorporation.

P.A.S.S. (Parents and Students Savings Plan). A pet project of Governor Carey of New York in 1978 and since adopted elsewhere. It basically is a tax sheltered savings account in which parents, regardless of the size of their income, can put up to $750 per child per year in a special fund free of state tax for future college, with taxes to be paid in the future within five years of completion of college.

PASS ALONGS. Increases in rent which a landlord may impose above any increase allowed in a rent-controlled building where the landlord can prove that the regular allowed increase is not sufficient to cover the landlord's expenses on items such as labor costs and capital expenditures.

PASSING OFF (Palming Off). The sale of the goods of one manufacturer or vendor as if they were the goods of another. The law prohibits this practice, for it will not allow manufacturers to "reap where they have not sown" by beguiling the public into buying their wares.

PASSIVE RESISTANCE. A form of protest characterized by the simple refusal to comply with some lawful demand without active or violent opposition. One of the most successful famous implementors of this strategy was Mahatma Gandhi.

PASSIVE TRUST (Bare Trust; Dry Trust; Naked Trust). A Trust arrangement in which the trustee has little or no active duties to perform with respect to his fiduciary position vis-à-vis the trust property, trust settlor or the trust beneficiaries.

PASS LAWS. Statutes and regulations in South Africa which determine who is a pure white and then discriminate against all others in every aspect of life such as employment, housing, right to marry, use of public transportation and recreation facilities.

PASSPORT DOCUMENT (French—passer: to pass; port: port). Originally applied to governmental permission to enter or leave a harbor, passport is defined today in the United States Code as "any travel document issued by competent authority showing the bearer's origin, identity and nationality if any, which is valid for the entry of the bearer into a foreign country." The first United States statute governing passports was enacted in 1856, and it forbade their issuance by any one in this country other than the Secretary of State. The basic regulation of passports now in effect derives from a 1938 Executive Order of President Franklin D. Roosevelt, though there have been some later presidential proclamations such as that in 1953 which requires a passport for travel to and from the United States. Passports may be denied for several reasons such as lack of United States citizenship, attempt to avoid legal sanctions (e.g., a passport would not be issued to a draft dodger) or inability of the United States government to protect the applicant in the area where he intends to travel. Restrictions have been placed in American passports at various times with respect to such countries as travel in Communist China, the U.S.S.R., Albania, and Bulgaria.

PATENTABILITY CONDITIONS. The most significant conditions for patentability are inventorship, novelty, utility, unobviousness, and reduction to practice. Inventorship refers to the requirement that, generally, only the inventor or, in the event of death or incapacity, his legal representative, has standing to seek a patent. In many foreign countries, one who introduces the subject matter of the patent into the country may apply for a patent. Because the patent privilege is designed to recognize an individual's own inventive abilities, the law deems it paramount that the subject matter be new. Novelty has been a condition common to all patent regulations in the common law system beginning with the English Statute of Monopolies in 1623, and later incorporated into the first United States Patent Act of 1790 and its successors. The utility requirement means that the invention must be operative and useful. The utility requirement may be justified further because Article 1, section 8 of the Constitution gives Congress the power to "promote the progress of science and the useful arts." Unobviousness refers to inventive quality and was not a condition for patentability until 1952. Differences in subject matter must be such that the changes would not have been apparent to a person having ordinary skill in the art involved. Finally, requiring reduction to practice contemplates completion of an inventive act. Patent law refuses to protect mere theory or intellectual conception.

PATENT AND TRADEMARK OFFICE (P.T.O.). Established by Congress "to promote the progress of . . . the useful arts" under Article 1, section 8, of the Federal Constitution. The P.T.O. examines applications for three kinds of Patent Privileges: Patents (issued for three and one-half, seven, or fourteen years), Plant Patents (issued for 17 years), and Utility Patents (issued for 17 years). The more than 70,000 patents which are issued an-nually provide inventors with exclusive rights to the results of their creative efforts. The patent system is intended to give incentive to invent, to invest in research and development, to commercialize new technology, and to make public inventions that otherwise would be kept secret. About 30,000 Trademarks are registered each year and 7,000 renewed. Trademarks, registered for twenty years with renewal rights, are examined by the P.T.O. for compliance with various statutory requirements to prevent unfair competition and consumer deception. In addition to the examination of patent and trademark applications, issuance of patents, and registration of trademarks, the P.T.O. sells printed copies of issued documents, records and indexes documents transferring ownership, maintains a scientific library and search files containing over twenty million documents, including United States and foreign patents and United States Trademarks, provides search rooms for the public to research their applications; hears and decides appeals from prospective inventors and trademark applicants; participates in legal proceedings involving the issue of patents or trademark registrations; helps represent the United States in international efforts to cooperate on patent and trademark policy; compiles the Official Gazettes—a weekly list of all patents and trademarks issued by the P.T.O.; and maintains a roster of grants and attorneys qualified to practice before the P.T.O.

PATENT APPEALS COURT. See UNITED STATES COURT OF CUSTOMS AND PATENT APPEALS.

PATENT APPLICATION. Consists of a petition and oath, a specification, and a drawing where possible, and must be accompanied by a filing fee. Only the inventor or his legal representative may apply for a patent. The petition is little more than a legal formalism, requesting that a patent be granted to the applicant. The oath must be taken before a notary public and requires the applicant to swear to his belief that he is the first inventor. Generally, the oath, like the petition, follows a form prescribed by the Patent Office. Several elements comprise the specification: the title of the invention, a brief summary of the invention, a detailed description, and a listing of the claim or claims sought. A drawing must be included with the application, except where a process or a composition of matter is involved. Working models of the invention were required in the past, but are no longer necessary except upon specific request by the Patent Office. Approximately 110,000 patent applications are filed annually, and over 70,000 patents are awarded.

PATENT APPLIED FOR. See PATENT PENDING.

PATENT COMMISSIONER. As the head of the Patent Office, the Commissioner prescribes rules, subject to approval by the Secretary of Commerce, for the conduct of patent proceedings, adjudicates issues brought before him by petition, and performs general administrative functions. The first person to perform these duties was Dr. William Thornton, designer of the United States Capitol. He was appointed in 1802 by then Secretary of State James Madison to head the Patent Office, a division of the State Department. Legend has it that Thornton threw himself across the mouth of a British cannon to prevent the invaders from destroying the Office and its models and drawings during their destruction of government buildings in Washington at the height of the War of 1812. Although Thornton did save the structure and its contents, it was by less dramatic persuasion.

PATENT EXAMINER. The person who determines whether the patent application meets statutory requirements and whether a patent should be granted. Examiners refer interfering applications to the Board of Patent Interferences. The Examiners dispose of applications assigned to them in the order in which they are filed. After completing his review of an application, the Examiner notifies the applicant of his decision by mailing an action to the applicant's attorney. The Examiner must include reasons for the rejection of any claim, so that the applicant may evaluate the propriety of challenging the Examiner's ruling. If the applicant properly challenges an adverse decision, the Examiner reconsiders the application and issues a final ruling, again specifically outlining the underlying reasons. Approximately one-half of the employees of the Patent Office are Examiners.

PATENT HISTORY. There were no legal safeguards in antiquity for inventions because manual labor was thought to be beneath the dignity of a true thinker and because such labor was performed by slaves. Patent law had its origins in the government's attempts to entice laborers to Renaissance Italy through the use of exclusive manufacturing privileges. But it was the English Statute of Monopolies of 1623 which served as the direct model for American experiments in patent law. Legislative efforts in the United States culminated with the passage of the first Federal Patent Statute in 1790. Samuel Hopkins received the first patent under the 1790 Patent Act for his process of making pot and pearl ashes.

PATENT INFRINGEMENT. Patent infringement involves the unauthorized manufacture, sale, or use of an invention protected by the patent privilege or the active inducement of such manufacture, sale, or use. The federal courts, which have exclusive jurisdiction over patent infringement cases, prohibit the unauthorized activity and award damages to the plaintiff. The defendant may contest the validity of the plaintiff's patent or, alternatively, contend that the activity in which he engaged did not constitute an infringement.

PATENT MARKING. Consists of the word patent and an appropriate patent number on a patented item. Failure to so mark an item prevents the inventor from recovering damages in an infringement suit, unless the infringer had actual knowledge of the patent. Patent marking of an item which is not patented is a punishable violation of the law.

PATENT PENDING (Patent Applied For). Phrase which serves as public notification that an application for a patent has been filed in the United States Patent Office. The phrase has no legal effect and does not entitle the applicant to the protections afforded by the patent privilege. False use of these terms is against the law.

PATENT PRACTITIONERS. Patent attorneys are specialists in the field of patent law, are registered with the Patent Office and are licensed to practice law in some jurisdiction in the United States. Patent agents are also registered with the Patent Office and perform many of the same duties as a patent attorney, but are not attorneys-at-law. Both types of patent practitioners must be competent in science and patent law.

PATENT PRIVILEGE. Exclusive property rights conferred by the government on an inventor so that other people cannot manufacture, sell, or employ his invention. The privilege is granted to reward the inventor for the knowledge, skill, and labor required to develop his invention. Processes, machines, items of manufacture, compositions of matter, or any improvement thereof may be protected by the patent privilege subject to certain patentability conditions. Generally the duration of the privilege is seventeen years, and the rights associated with it extend throughout the United States and its territories and possessions. The term of a patent can be extended in exceptional circumstances by acts of Congress.

PATENT THICKET. The utilization by a patent owner of some patents but not others, or a failure to license others for the purpose of obtaining or maintaining an illegal monopoly.

PATERNITY SUIT. A legal action to charge a father with a limited duty to support his illegitimate child. A number of state statutes allow the court to confer legitimate status on the child in the paternity proceeding or award inheritance rights in addition to support. Absent a paternity statute, the common-law rule of Filius Nullius (son of no body) denies the child the right to be supported by its father. The evidence admissible to prove paternity includes scientific blood-grouping tests, exhibition of the child to make a comparison of his appearance with the defendant, declarations by deceased members of the family as to paternity, and admissions or acknowledgments of paternity by the father.

PATIENT DUMPING. The crass and scandalous dismissal by states of elderly patients from mental institutions into inadequately equipped boarding and nursing homes supported by federally funded welfare programs for the aged for the sole purpose of saving money for the states. It costs a state approximately $21,000 a year to maintain a patient in a mental institution in contrast to the $2,000 a year provided annually by the Federal Supplemental Security Income program to support an aged, indigent person in a boarding house.

PATIENT'S BILL OF RIGHTS. Prepared by the American Hospital Association, and adopted by the New York City Department of Health. The Bill of Rights states that: (1) The patient has the right to considerate and respectful care. (2) The patient has the right to obtain from his physician complete current information concerning his diagnosis, treatment, and prognosis in terms the patient can be reasonably expected to understand. When it is not medically advisable to give such information to the patient, the information should be made available to an appropriate person in his behalf. He has the right to know by name the physician responsible for coordinating his care. (3) The patient has the right to receive from his physician information necessary to give informed consent prior to the start of any procedure and/or treatment. Except in emergencies, such information for informed consent should include but not necessarily be limited to the specific procedure and/or treatment, the medically significant risks involved, and the probable duration of incapacitation. Where medically significant alternatives for care or treatment exist, or when the patient requests information concerning medical alternatives, the patient has the right to such information. The patient also has the right to know the name of the person responsible for the procedures and/or treatment. (4) The patient has the right to refuse treatment to the extent permitted by law, and to be informed of the medical consequences of his action. (5) The patient has the right to every consideration of his privacy concerning his own medical care program. Case discussion, consultation, examination, and treatment are confidential and should be conducted discreetly. Those not directly involved in his care must have the permission of the patient to be present. (6) The patient has the right to expect that all communications and records pertaining to his care should be treated as confidential. (7) The patient has the right to expect that within its capacity a hospital must make reasonable response to the request of a patient for services. The hospital must provide evaluation, service, and/or referral as indicated by the urgency of the case. When medically permissible a patient may be transferred to another facility only after he has received complete information and explanation concerning the needs for and alternatives to such a transfer. The institution to which the patient is to be transferred must first have accepted the patient for transfer. (8) The patient has the right to obtain information as to any relationship of his hospital to other health care and educational institutions insofar as his care is concerned. The patient has the right to obtain information as to the existence of any professional relationships among individuals, by name, who are treating him. (9) The patient has the right to be advised if the hospital proposes to engage in or perform human experimentation affecting his care or treatment. The patient has the right to refuse to participate in such research projects. (10) The patient has the right to expect reasonable continuity of care. He has the right to know in advance what appointment times and physicians are available and where. The patient has the right to expect that the hospital will provide a mechanism whereby he is informed by his physician or a delegate of the physician of the patient's continuing health care requirements following discharge. (11) The patient has the right to examine and receive an explanation of his bill regardless of source of payment. (12) The patient has the right to know what hospital rules and regulations apply to his conduct as a patient.

PATRIOTIC FRONT. Black native guerrilla groups in Rhodesia who use force and violence to overthrow the white-controlled government which denies them the right to participate in the political process to control their own destiny.

PATTERN TEST. Among the tests devised to show substantial similarity for purposes of proving copyright infringement. It is designed to determine when, in the process of dissecting a work into its component parts, its creator has copied too closely the expression of an idea in the protected work. "Pattern" refers to characters as well as events and dialogue. "Romeo and Juliet" and "West Side Story" are often used to exemplify the Pattern Test as it applies to artistic works: both plays involve two warring factions; a boy and a girl from opposite groups meet at a dance; they fall in love; one is told erroneously that the other has died; the "survivor" dies as a result of the mistaken information. Insofar as non-artistic pieces are concerned, unless specific factual descriptions are copied, the Pattern Test would lead to a conclusion of no infringement. Thus, a cookbook which includes the same recipes using the same ingredients as an earlier, copyrighted book does not violate the copyright as long as it does not detail recipes in the same manner.

PAULINE PRIVILEGE. Allows an annulment action in Roman Catholic Canon Law for marriages between two unbaptized persons, even if consummated, where one is subsequently baptized and the other refuses to continue normal cohabitation.

PAUL v. DAVIS (424 U.S. 693 (1976)). A Supreme Court case holding that a person's reputation was not within the constitutional protection afforded by the Fourteenth Amendment. The case involved a newspaper photographer whose name and photograph were included in a policy flyer listing "active shoplifters," which was distributed to local merchants. Though Paul had been arrested for shoplifting, charges against him were dismissed. Despite his claim that the label of "shoplifter" had injured his reputation and would harm his employment opportunities, the Court concluded that "reputation alone, apart from some more tangible interests such as employment," was neither liberty nor property within the meaning of the due process clause.

PAYROLL TAX. A tax liability imposed on an employer or employee, related to the amount of the company payroll or individual pay, the revenues from which are used to finance a specific benefit. The Social Security tax is an example of such a tax.

P.C.I. (Communist Party in Italy). The largest political Communist party in a Western Democracy, which admits that when it gains complete control of the Italian government (which seems likely), its loyalty will be to the Soviets and not to N.A.T.O., of which Italy is a member. This would of course be a serious threat to our national security.

P.C.O. See PROCUREMENT CONTRACTING OFFICER.

PEACE ACADEMY. See NATIONAL ACADEMY PEACE COMMISSION.

PEACE AND FRIENDSHIP TREATY. A ten-year international agreement of close relationship signed in 1978 between the world's most populous nation (Communist China) and the Asian economic powerhouse (Japan), to the great consternation of Russia. It restores full economic, cultural and diplomatic relations between Tokyo and Peking for the first time since Japan invaded China in 1931, thus ending the technical state of war between them.

PEACE BOND (Recognizance to Keep the Peace). A quasi-criminal action based not just on a defendant's past wrongdoing, but also on what he might do in the future. The Peace Bond is basically a conditional fine—much like a bond. Once the condition is satisfied, the payor-defendant is entitled to reimbursement. This procedure has the advantages of a suspended sentence, without the stigma of a conviction for a violent crime. The Peace Bond has, in some areas, proven to be an effective procedure for dealing with domestic violence. This effectiveness can be attributed in part to the notice given an aggressor that the authorities are keeping him or her under surveillance and that society disapproved of the conduct. There have been serious constitutional questions raised about the Peace Bond procedure, which may explain why it is used in so few jurisdictions.

PEACE CORPS. On creating the Peace Corps in 1961, the Congress declared that the Corps was to promote world peace and friendship; to help the peoples of other countries in meeting their needs for trained manpower; to help promote a better understanding of the American people on the part of the peoples served; and to promote a better understanding of other peoples on the part of the American people. To fulfill that mandate, men and women from all ages and walks of life are trained over a 9-14 week period in the appropriate local language, the technical skills necessary for the particular job, and the cross-cultural skills needed when approaching a society with traditions and attitudes different from their own. They are then placed overseas in countries whose needs are critical, and who request volunteers to aid in their economic and social development. Volunteers serve for a period of 2 years, work in the communities to which they are sent, and live among the people they are helping. Beyond the immediate demands of their jobs, they are expected to become involved in community life and to demonstrate, through their voluntary service, that people can be an essential impetus for development. Thousands of volunteers have served in 65 countries throughout Latin America, Africa, the Near East, Asia, and the Pacific. Their services vary widely, according to talent and to host country needs. These volunteers work primarily in the areas of agriculture and rural development, health and education. Programs coordinate efforts to match the skills and community-level approach of the volunteers with the resources of host country agencies and other international organizations. An auxiliary effort within the Peace Corps is the Peace Corps Partnership, which provides opportunities for elementary, junior and senior high schools, civic groups, and neighborhood and youth organizations in the United States to meet a specific need of an overseas community by sponsoring the construction of a school, clinic, or community facility recommended by a Peace Corps volunteer. Cross-cultural exchange is a major element in Partnership projects. The Peace Corps also serves as the sponsor for United States citizens who serve in the similar United Nations Volunteer Program.

PEACE CORPS PARTNERSHIP. See PEACE CORPS.

PEACEFUL CO-EXISTENCE. Concept coined by Premier Khruschev at the 20th Soviet Party Congress in Moscow in 1956 proclaiming that wars between capitalism and communism were no longer an inevitability. It has previously been used as part of the term "Pancha Shila" in the Sino-Indian Agreement of 1954 to cover the five principles of mutual respect for territorial integrity and sovereignty, mutual nonaggression, noninterference in each other's internal affairs, equality and mutual benefit, and peaceful co-existence.

PEACE WOMEN. Two women, Mairead Corrigan and Betty Williams, who started a social movement in Northern Ireland in 1976 designed to end the murderous confrontation in the undeclared war between Catholics and Protestants, for which they were awarded the Nobel Peace Prize in 1977. Tragically, their efforts resulted in failure and the chaos continues in that "Land of Terrible Beauty."

PEEPING TOM. When the Lord of Coventry imposed what his wife thought were exorbitant taxes on his subjects, his wife, Lady Godiva, complained so much that he agreed to reduce them if she rode naked on horseback through the city. She made her famous bareback ride on a white horse, and the only male who peeked through the shutters was Tom, the town tailor, who was struck blind for his impudence. Today the criminal offense of Peeping Tom applies to anyone who secretly looks into the window of another from a public street with salacious intent.

PEER GROUP COURT. See NEIGHBORHOOD COURT.

PEER REVIEW. Proposals to institutionalize periodic examinations of lawyers by fellow lawyers in order to determine whether or not professional malpractice has been committed or grounds exist for disciplinary action to suspend or revoke the license to practice.

PEKING CARD. Any ploy in the courtship of capitalistic Japan by Communist China in its Cold War confrontation with Communist Russia.

PENDENTE LITE (Latin—pending the suit). Denotes some legal action taken or remedy allowed while litigation is pending and is generally subject to the final outcome of the suit.

PENDENT JURISDICTION DOCTRINE. Allows a claim based on state law to be brought in federal court when such claim is joined with a claim over which the federal court has original jurisdiction. The federal court determines whether the federal and state claims are so linked that they should be adjudicated in one proceeding.

PENDENT PARTIES. The plaintiff and defendant in a lawsuit with pendent jurisdiction, the modern foundation for such labels was established in *United Mine Workers v. Gibbs*, 383 U.S. 715 (1966). Pendent jurisdiction enables a federal court to exercise power over a claim based on state law when both the state and federal claims are between the same parties and the claims are related enough so that the plaintiff would be expected to raise them in one proceeding. The rationales underlying pendent parties include economy of resources, fairness to litigants, the prevention of relitigation and overlapping litigation, and to assure the plaintiff of a federal forum. The federal courts' power to hear pendent claims emanates from Article III, Section 2 of the Constitution, which authorizes federal courts to hear cases "arising under . . . the Laws of the United States." This language, it is said, includes state claims closely connected to federal ones.

PENDLETON ACT. A century old federal law which prohibits the solicitation of campaign funds on government property. There has only been one prosecution under the statute in the past 70 years.

PEN REGISTER. Device used by police in surveillance activities which records the outgoing numbers dialed on a particular phone, but does not monitor the contents of a call.

PENSION TRUST. A trust arrangement which is usually established and maintained by a corporate employer for the benefit of corporate employees. A Pension Trust can be termed a fringe benefit to the extent it may either require or not require employee contributions. A vast majority of pension trusts serve retired or injured employees and these are widely present today.

PENTAGON CLUB. A small group of high-ranking military officers and civilian Department of Defense personnel who pack a powerful amount of clout in national and international affairs.

PENTAGON PAPERS CASE. See *NEW YORK TIMES CO. v UNITED STATES*.

PENTAGON PULPIT PROGRAM. For years religious speakers were allowed to conduct services on the public concourse of the Pentagon Building, the American Military Complex just outside of Washington, D.C. A federal court reversed the conviction of a defendant who had disrupted one such service in 1977 on the grounds that this practice violated the American Constitutional principle of separation of church and state. The Pentagon Pulpit Program was first allowed by federal law during the presidency of Franklin D. Roosevelt.

PENTAGON TAX DRAIN. The tax burden imposed on major metropolitan areas by the military budget.

PENTECOSTAL SEVEN. Seven Russians who fought their way into the American Embassy in Moscow in 1978 to seek refuge in the basement while protesting the refusal of the Soviets to allow them to emigrate in order to practice their Christian faith which they were barred from doing in Russia.

PEOPLE'S AGENCY. See CIVIL SERVICE COMMISSION.

PEOPLE'S ASSESSORS (Lay Assessors). Two non-lawyer citizens who sit with a single judge (and can therefore outvote the law-trained professional) in court trials in Communist countries. They have the power to decide questions of law as well as of fact.

PEOPLE'S COURT. A trial bench, especially for criminal cases, in a communist country, composed of non-lawyers who are often illiterate peasants. The court may be convened on the spot, such as at the arrest of a thief in a marketplace. It may also impose summary punishment, including capital punishment, at the scene of the crime. Our system may not be as speedy, but which would you prefer if you were an accused criminal?

PEOPLE'S LAW SCHOOL (P.L.S.). A private group in California that provides free legal education in order to help people understand and improve the American legal system. It also refers individuals with legal problems for professional assistance.

PEOPLE'S LAWYER. Affectionate nickname given to New York Attorney General Louis J. Lefkowitz as a result of his leadership in the protection of individual rights in general and the consumer protection movement in particular.

PEOPLE'S REVOLUTIONARY COMMANDOS. A leftist underground guerrilla group which bombs innocent people in their advocacy of complete independence for Puerto Rico.

PEOPLE v. COLLINS. See MATHEMATICAL EVIDENCE.

PEPPERCORN PAYMENT. Payment of some nominal amount in exchange for a contractual obligation of some value, derived from the medieval practice of paying in peppercorns for rent of land. The Peppercorn Doctrine is used in contract law to justify enforcing a contractual obligation even when the consideration given seems grossly disproportionate to the goods or services received. Such contracts are generally enforced so long as the parties did in fact bargain for the exchange.

PER CAPITA (Latin—by heads). A method of dividing an intestate estate by which equal shares are given to all persons who stand in equal degree to the decedent. The following example illustrates per capita distribution:

ESTATE OF GRANDPARENT—$100,000
2 CHILDREN
CHILD ONE—$50,000   CHILD TWO—$50,000
$33,333 $33,333 $33,333
ONE GRANDCHILD   TWO GRANDCHILDREN

Under per capita distribution each grandchild receives an equal share of the grandparent's estate. No reference is made to the per stirpes right of representation.

PER CURIAM (Latin—by the court). An opinion written by the whole court, or sometimes the chief justice, rather than by any one judge.

PEREMPTORY CHALLENGE. Allows an attorney to reject a certain number of prospective jurors without stating a cause for rejection.

PERFECT TENDER RULE. U.C.C. § 2-601 requires the seller to make a perfect tender. If he fails to do so, the buyer has an absolute right of rejection. He can reject either the whole shipment or part, or he can accept the defective goods and sue for damages later. The rationale for the Perfect Tender Rule is that this is the result most parties would bargain for. The Rule minimizes the costs of breach through providing certainty in the allocation of rights between the parties. The Code thus changes the common law doctrine of Substantial Performance, which required only that the seller perform "substantially" rather than "perfectly." The drafters of the U.C.C. felt that the Substantial Performance Doctrine injected uncertainty into post-breach negotiations.

PERFORMING RIGHTS SOCIETIES. Evolved as a collective means of safeguarding the performing rights of individual composers and publishers. Affording copyright protection to musical compositions is quite difficult, because such works are performed so widely and in so many variations. The societies act as agents for individual artists, licensing small or non-dramatic performing rights in the musical works created by its members. The members themselves retain the power to license grand or dramatic performing rights in their musical pieces. One of the most significant Performing Rights Societies is the American Society of Composers, Authors, and Publishers (A.S.C.A.P.). Founded in 1914 largely through the efforts of Victor Herbert, the Irish-American composer known for his operettas, A.S.C.A.P. collects fees from individuals or businesses who want to perform, for profit, works of its members. The fees are then divided between the publisher and writer.

PERLMAN CASE. See FIDUCIARY DUTIES.

PERMISSION-TO-MARRY STATUTE. A law requiring a support-obligated non-custodial parent to show his child is not likely to become a public charge if the parent remarries. The Supreme Court, in the case of *Zablocki v. Redhail*, 434 U.S. 374 (1978), has recently held such statutes unconstitutional.

PERMISSIVE COUNTER-CLAIM. See COUNTER-CLAIM.

PERMISSIVE JOINDER. See JOINDER OF PARTIES.

PER SE (Latin—by itself). Refers to words or acts which are distinguishable in some legal context without reference to words or acts not directly under examination. In an action for defamation, words may be Per Se libelous where only one meaning may be attached and that meaning is opprobrious.

PER SE VIOLATIONS. Acts which are by themselves, with no further showing required, considered to be unreasonable restraints of trade under the Sherman Act (1890). The courts have banned certain types of activities, such as price fixing, tying arrangements, and customer or territorial restrictions because they are anticompetitive. The Per Se violations may be seen as the complement to the Rule of Reason, in that while they form a separate category for case disposition, they do not constitute a separate analytical framework.

PERSONAL ATTACK RULE. Federal Communications Commission Rule that if during a presentation of views on a controversial issue of public importance, a station broadcasts an attack on the personal character, integrity or honesty of an identifiable person, the station should provide the person with notification of the attack and an opportunity to respond.

PERSONAL CONSUMPTION EXPENDITURES. Reflect the market value of goods and services purchased by individuals and nonprofit institutions or acquired by them as income in kind. The rental value of owner-occupied dwellings is included, but not the purchases of dwellings. Purchases are recorded at cost to consumers, including excise or sales taxes, and in full at the time of purchase whether made with cash or on credit. The nonprofit institutions included are those rendering services principally to individuals.

PERSONAL INCOME. The income received by all individuals in the economy from all sources. It is made up of wage and salary disbursements, proprietors' income, rental income of persons, dividends, personal interest income, and the difference between transfer payments and personal contributions for social insurance.

PERSONAL JURISDICTION. Authority of a court to adjudicate a dispute between the parties before it, based on the relationship of the party and the forum state. Personal jurisdiction permits imposition of a personal obligation on the defendant. If the obligation is to pay money damages, the defendant's assets, beyond those which may have been the subject matter of the suit, may be seized. If the obligation is in the form of an injunction, enforcement may result through contempt proceedings. However, if the court merely exercises In Rem Jurisdiction, enforcement of a defendant's obligation to pay damages may not extend to his personal assets beyond those invested in the subject matter of the adjudication.

PERSONAL PROPERTY (Chattel). Generally, anything subject to ownership which is not real property. This includes all interests in things temporary, non-local or movable, and lease-interests in land. Personal property may also consist of intangibles, such as contract rights, stocks, patents, etc.

PERSONAL RECOGNIZANCE. The release of an arrested person who has no previous criminal record—without his having to post any bail—merely upon his promise to appear for trial.

PERSONAL REPRESENTATIVE. An executor who manages a decedent's estate. If the testator fails to appoint a personal representative in his or her will, the court will appoint one.

PERSONA NON GRATA (Latin—an unwelcome person). A diplomatic representative who is declared unacceptable to the receiving nation and whose recall home is desired.

PERSONS IN NEED OF SUPERVISION (P.I.N.S.) Minors subject to control by the state for committing violations such as school truancy or parental disobedience.

PER STIRPES (Latin—by roots or stocks). By representation. A method of dividing an estate whereby a class or group of distributees take that share which their deceased ancestor would have taken had he survived the intestate. The following example illustrates Per Stirpes distribution:

ESTATE OF GRANDPARENT—$100,000

2 CHILDREN

CHILD ONE—$50,000   CHILD TWO—$50,000

ONE GRANDCHILD—$50,000

$25,000 $25,000

TWO GRANDCHILDREN

Under Per Stirpes distribution, the children of child two get $25,000 apiece while the child of child one gets $50,-000.

PESKIND'S LAW. The legal doctrine which encourages secured creditors to use every means available to protect their interest if and when they may have doubts regarding the perfection of such. For example, one method that could be used to assure perfection would be to procure insurance. Another method would be to make sure that all documents are correct, completed, and filed.

PETIT JURY. The ordinary jury of twelve (or fewer) persons which decides the facts in a civil or criminal case. "Petit" is used to distinguish this jury from the grand jury.

PETRINE THEORY. This term is sometimes used to describe the Roman Catholic position that the Pope, the head of the Church, is the direct spiritual heir to the leadership of the Church entrusted to the apostle Peter by Jesus Christ. The Catholic view is that Peter became the first Pope by direct appointment by Christ and that each of his successors, whether it be Linus, whom Peter himself chose to succeed him, or later Popes elected by the faithful or Popes elected by the modern method of Papal Conclave, becomes automatically the Vicar of Christ on earth after his selection. The theory relies in part on a conversation between Jesus and Peter reported in the 16th Chapter of the Gospel of Matthew. Jesus had asked who his disciples considered him to be and Peter had replied "Thou art the Christ, the Son of the living God." Jesus then blessed Simon Peter and said "Thou art Peter, and upon this rock I will build my church; and the gates of hell shall not prevail against it. And I will give unto thee the keys of the kingdom of heaven; and whatsoever thou shalt bind on earth shall be bound in heaven; and whatsoever thou shalt loose on earth shall be loosed in heaven."

PETROLEUM ADMINISTRATION FOR DEFENSE DISTRICTS. See EMERGENCY PETROLEUM ALLOCATION ACT.

PFIZER AMENDMENT (Anti-Trust Enforcement Act of 1979; Illinois Brick Legislation). A Congressional proposal to overrule the 1977 Supreme Court of the United States in the *Illinois Brick* case in order to restore the legal standing of consumers to bring civil price-fixing cases against a business even if the consumers did not buy directly from the accused company. The law would also overrule the 1978 Supreme Court of the United States in the *Pfizer* case which held that foreign governments could sue American companies under the Clayton Act.

PHANTOM STOCK PLAN. A corporate scheme for compensating management-level employees which serves as an alternative to stock option plans. Under a Phantom Stock Plan, the employee receives no actual stock, but cash in amounts equal to the earnings and market value appreciation of a particular block of the corporation's stock. Under many of these plans, the company retains some control over the employee's access to the income, a feature not available with stock options. If the employee falls into disfavor, the corporation may, subject to statutory restrictions, terminate the plan's benefits. However, the employee does not run the risk under these plans of a drop in the market price of the stock, since he has no investment to lose. Some courts have struck these plans down for the reason that they bear no reasonable relation to the value of the services being compensated through the plan.

PHAROAH'S FIFTH. See TAXATION, ART OF.

PHILADELPHIA LAWYER. A particularly skillful attorney. The term originated in the 1735 case of John Peter Zenger, who was accused of seditious libel for publishing articles critical of the British governor of New York. Zenger's lawyers were debarred when they questioned the right of the presiding judge, an appointee of the governor, to hear the case. They were replaced by Andrew Hamilton, an attorney from Philadelphia, who won the case against high odds. Hamilton admitted that his client had published the articles, yet persuaded the jury that the criticisms in the articles were valid. The case stands as a landmark in the area of Freedom of the Press.

PHILADELPHIA NUN EXEMPTION. A federal law, repealed in 1969, which had granted members of religious orders exemption from paying any income tax upon compliance with certain conditions. It was first applied to a Roman Catholic nun in Philadelphia, the City of Brotherly Love.

PHILOSOPHICAL RADICALS. See BENTHAM, JEREMY.

PHOENIX PROGRAM. The C.I.A.-sponsored program of violence and torture which resulted in the surrender of 17,000 Viet Cong during the Vietnamese War, the capture of 28,000 and the assassination of 21,000 more. This became one of the symbols of resistance to the War by younger Americans and eventually led to the discrediting and weakening of the C.I.A.

PILGRIM POPE. Roman Catholic Pope Paul VI who logged more miles than any of the previous 261 Pontiffs in his travels around the globe as a space age apostle in his unsuccessful efforts to bring peace to the world.

PILOT RULES FOR INLAND WATERS. See RULES OF THE ROAD.

PILOT RULES FOR THE GREAT LAKES. See RULES OF THE ROAD.

PILOT RULES FOR WESTERN RIVERS. See RULES OF THE ROAD.

PINCUS, WILLIAM. The founder of clinical legal education which is sweeping throughout the law school world—even at Harvard. For over 200 years, law was the only profession in the United States in which a student learned the practical aspects of his future career after graduation and largely at the expense of his clients. Pincus persuaded the Ford Foundation to provide the money to create the Council on Legal Education for Professional Responsibility (C.L.E.P.R.) and became its first President in 1968. This organization has since brought about the greatest change in the curriculum of American law schools in the past century in that the teaching of practical skills is no longer the subject of ridicule and neglect. Bravo, Brother Pincus!

PINKERTON RULE. Renders co-conspirators liable for all crimes committed in furtherance of a Criminal Conspiracy. The rule gained prominence in the case of *Pinkerton v. United States*, 328 U.S. 640 (1946), where the defendant was convicted of tax evasion offenses committed by his brother while the defendant was in prison. The Supreme Court upheld the conviction on the ground that the defendant was involved in a continuing conspiracy to evade payment of taxes and was thus liable for specific crimes committed in furtherance of the conspiracy. Although the Court implied that the crime must be a foreseeable consequence of the conspiracy, many courts have not applied this limitation. There has been increased opposition to the Pinkerton Rule in recent years, and most states now require a greater degree of complicity than is required by the Pinkerton Rule.

P.I.N.S. See PERSONS IN NEED OF SUPERVISION.

PINS AND NEEDLES ACT. Tax regulations covering campaign organizers, political contributors, lobbyists, and the politicians themselves. The name is derived from the thorny and sensitive area the Act seeks to govern.

PLACEMENT BULLETIN. In the fall of 1976 the Association of American Law Schools established the Placement Bulletin. This Bulletin, published six times a year, carries the listing of openings for law teaching positions at accredited law schools, other law schools and other schools and colleges within the universities. It is distributed without charge to deans and placement directors at law schools.

PLACE OF MOST SIGNIFICANT RELATIONSHIP RULE (Center of Gravity Rule; Dominant Contacts). A modern Choice of Law rule that selects as the applicable law the law of the place which had the Most Significant Relationship, or Dominant Contacts, with the transaction or part of the transaction at issue in a suit. This test is criticized as lacking any objective standard to govern its application and as simply allowing a court to weigh policies and governmental interests in deciding which law to choose. Framing the issue as a quest for the Most Significant Relationship also fails to identify the underlying considerations to be identified in making the Choice of Law and thus offers courts little guidance.

PLACE OF WRONG RULE (Place Of Impact Rule). State Choice of Law Rule that requires the forum to use the law of the jurisdiction in which the injury or harm took place. Suppose Baker and Jones, both domiciled in state *C* have an automobile accident in state *X*. When Baker sues Jones in the courts of state *C*, if the court follows the Place of Wrong Rule, the law that will be applicable to the accident will be that of state *X*.

PLAIN LANGUAGE LAW. This legislation will warm the hearts of non-lawyers. It provides that non-technical language must be used in residential leases and other contracts under $50,000 when a consumer is a party, and when the money, property or service is mainly for personal, family or household uses. Any business that does not make a good faith effort to write such contracts in a clear and coherent manner, using common words, is liable in damages to a maximum of $10,000. In 1977 New York became the first state to pass such a revolutionary law, which went into effect in 1978. The father of this great idea was Alan M. Siegel of New York City, who has helped over 100 companies to simplify their legal documents. Here is a sample of the new loan form he prepared for Citibank:

> To protect you if I default on this or any other debt to you, I give you what is known as a security interest in my [ ] Motor Vehicle, [ ] Stocks, [ ] Bonds, [ ] Savings, [ ] Other account and any other accounts or securities of mine coming into your possession.

This understandable document replaced a long technical form which had so much legalese that even a Philadelphia lawyer would have had a tough time to decipher it. Most of the legal mumbo jumbo was eliminated by the exclusion of "boiler plate." On November 18, 1977, President Carter issued an Executive order which recommended that all federal regulations be written in language "as simple and as clear as possible in order not to impose unnecessary burdens on the public or the economy."

PLAIN LANGUAGE MOVEMENT. Efforts by the legal profession to write comprehensible documents devoid of excess verbiage, such as "whereas," "herein," and "aforesaid." The problem with many of these lawyerlike words, apart from arousing the indignity of most laymen, is that they invoke a false sense of precision. For instance, "whereas" could mean "the fact is," "because," or "in spite of the fact." "Aforesaid" and "herein" share the problem of ambiguity; e.g., does "aforesaid" refer to that which is immediately before it, or to everything which has gone before, or only to the preceding paragraph? If the antecedent is uncertain, "aforesaid" and "herein" add nothing but an illusion of certainty, while if the antecedent is certain, there is no need for the modifying terms. Legal language also uses unnecessary doubled words: "null and void," "mutually covenant and agree," "fit and proper," and the tendency, according to one commentator, of stuffing "too many thoughts into overlong periods."

PLAIN VIEW DOCTRINE. Allows a police officer to seize an object that is contraband or evidence if (1) he is lawfully on the premises where the object to be seized is located and (2) the object's discovery is inadvertent. These two tests were set forth by the Supreme Court in *Coolidge v. New Hampshire*, 403 U.S. 443 (1971).

PLANNED PARENTHOOD OF CENTRAL MISSOURI v. DANFORTH (428 U.S. 52 (1976)). A Supreme Court case involving a Missouri statute that regulated abortion. The Court invalidated a provision requiring an unmarried woman under 18 to obtain the consent of a parent in order to obtain an abortion in most circumstances. As Justice Blackmun explained, the Constitution did not allow the state to give a third party "an absolute, and possibly arbitrary veto over the decision of the physician and his patient to terminate the patient's pregnancy." The Court also held unconstitutional a provision that required a married woman to obtain her husband's written consent to an abortion. Because the state cannot proscribe abortion during the first trimester of pregnancy, said Justice Blackmun, the state cannot delegate the authority to do so. Also found unconstitutional was Missouri's prohibition against saline amniocentesis as an abortion method and the requirement that the physician preserve the life and health of the fetus, regardless of the stage of pregnancy. The Court found only two of the challenged provisions constitutional: one requiring that physicians and hospitals maintain records; the other defining viability as "that stage of fetal development when the life of the unborn child may be continued indefinitely outside the womb by natural or artificial life-supportive systems."

PLANT PATENT. A patent privilege extended to individuals who create new plants by means such as grafting. Plants were not originally protected by the patent privilege because legislators thought that the development of new varieties of plants was no different from the discovery of a new mineral. Since 1930, however, a distinction has been recognized: Minerals are created wholly by nature and should be deemed the property of the individual on whose land they are found, while a plant developed by asexual reproduction and cultivation is a man-made, protectible entity. A plant patent cannot be issued for the discovery of a new plant in nature nor for plants which are propagated asexually by the same part of the plant that is used for food.

PLEA BARGAINING (Cop a Plea). Attempt by a criminal defendant to get a lighter sentence by pleading guilty to a lesser included offense of the crime charged in exchange for the prosecutor's promise that the more serious offense will not be brought up at trial. The defendant may also plead guilty as a quid pro quo for the prosecutor's recommendation of a light sentence which is called plea sentencing. The judge is not involved in the plea negotiations and according to most authorities, he is not bound by the deal. Recent reform efforts have focused on this fact and have attempted to add more certainty to the process. As a practical matter a judge usually goes along with the deal. Plea bargaining clearly conserves judicial resources, but critics charge it creates an irresistible pressure on defendants to waive their constitutional right to trial. For example, if a person is charged with assault with intent to commit murder, he may be allowed to cop a plea of guilty to simple assault. The former is a serious felony. The latter is only a misdemeanor. If the defendant is unlikely to arouse jury sympathy and he has limited financial resources, he may figure his best bet, despite being innocent, is to plead to the lesser offense (presuming he will get a minimal sentence or probation), to avoid the possibility of a very severe sentence if convicted at the end of an expensive trial. Some authorities claim more than 90 percent of all criminal cases are disposed of through plea bargaining or plea sentencing so that if they were eliminated or restricted the entire judicial process would come to a complete standstill.

PLEADINGS IN A CASE. The documents, such as the plaintiff's complaint, the defendant's answer, and the plaintiff's reply, which set forth the facts of the case and the issues to be decided.

P.L.E.N. (Public Leadership Education Network). A network of five women's colleges (Carlow in Pennsylvania; Goucher in Maryland; Spellman, the oldest black women's college in the country, in Georgia; Stephens in Missouri; and Wells in New York) and two resource groups (the National Women's Education Fund and the Center for the American Woman and Politics) established in 1978 by lawyer Frances Tarlton Farenthold of Texas.

The project, funded by the Carnegie Corporation, is intended to educate women about politics. Each college has its own program, for academic credit or not, limited to the campus or open to the community, but all programs encourage young women to consider public life as a career.

PLESSY v. FERGUSON (163 U.S. 537 (1896)). A Supreme Court case (later overruled in *Brown v. Board of Education*, 347 U.S. 483 (1954)), which sustained a Louisiana statute requiring "equal but separate accommodations" for black and white railroad passengers. The Court held that the object of the Fourteenth Amendment was "undoubtedly to enforce the absolute equality of the two races before the law" but that "Laws permitting, and even requiring, their separation in places where they are liable to be brought into contact . . . have been . . . recognized as within the competency of the state legislatures in the exercise of their police power." Justice John Marshall Harlan dissented in *Plessy* with the classic statement that "[o]ur Constitution is color-blind."

P.L.F. See P.L.O.

P. L. I. See PRACTICING LAW INSTITUTE.

P.L.O. (Palestine Liberation Organization). An Arab terrorist guerrilla group dedicated to the destruction of Israel. It is divided into splinter factions such as the El Fatah (headed by the infamous Yasser Arafat who once addressed the United Nations with a pistol in his belt), and the Palestine Liberation Front (P.L.F.), which often fight with each other.

P.L.S. See PEOPLES LAW SCHOOL.

PLUMBERS OPERATION. An executive directive promising immunity from criminal prosecution to government officials who have committed violations of law.

PLURAL NATIONALITY. Status of an individual who is a citizen of more than one country.

PLURIES SUMMONS. A third or subsequent summons issued when the first two summonses have not been served.

P.M. See PUSH MONEY.

P.M.I. See PRIVATE MORTGAGE INSURANCE.

P.M.I.C. (Presidential Management Improvement Council). A panel created by President Carter in 1979, headed by the Federal Director of the Budget, composed of business, labor and academic leaders to seek ways to improve the efficiency and productivity of the federal bureaucracy.

POCKET VETO. A device whereby the President can veto a Congressional bill merely by keeping it "in his pocket," or perhaps less elegantly, by sitting on it. During the ongoing term of a legislative session, a bill will become law after submission to the President if he does not sign it or actively veto it within ten days. If Congress adjourns during the ten-day period, however, all unsigned bills are automatically "pocket-vetoed." It is thus a Presidential cop-out. In the 1929 pocket veto case, the Supreme Court held that pocket vetos were not limited to the end of a session but could also be used at any time that Congress has temporarily adjourned, as for Christmas break, and no arrangements have been made to receive Presidential messages. It is now standard practice to have an officer of the House available to receive Presidential vetos during intrasession adjournments to prevent "surprise" pocket vetos.

P.O.D. (Payable on Death). The naming of the recipient of a bank account to whom the remaining balance is paid upon the death of the depositor.

POETIC JUSTICE (Just Desert). To get what is coming to you in a retaliatory spiteful sense. In New England they call it come-uppance.

POLAR BEAR. Identification of Russia by the People's Republic of China as a term of derision for the Soviet's aggressive policy of expansionism which the paranoid Chinese call hegemony.

POLICE COURT. A local court, found in many larger cities, having limited jurisdiction over minor criminal, and in some states, civil matters. In some locations, this type of court may be known as a magistrate's court or a municipal court. In some cities appeals from the police court go to the municipal court, while in others an appeal goes directly to the state district or county court of general jurisdiction. In addition to minor criminal offenses, many police courts also dispose of traffic violations and other minor infractions.

POLICE CUSTODY. See EMERGENCY CUSTODY.

POLICE LAWYERS. Lawyers who work with police departments to help their officers correct various legal problems such as improper searches, poorly drafted warrants, and general procedural problems. There are approximately 320 such police lawyer units in the United States, mostly in municipal police departments.

POLICEMEN'S BILL OF RIGHTS. Laws which establish procedures to hear complaints by law-enforcement officers and grant relief in appropriate cases, including collective bargaining on salaries, pensions, terms of employment and fringe benefits.

POLICE POWER. The authority of the state to regulate health, safety, welfare, and sometimes morality. Theoretically at least, the police power is reserved to the states under the Constitution. However, the federal government has recently assumed an increasingly activist role in regulating health and welfare through Congressional exercise of the power to regulate interstate commerce.

POLICE STATE. Any government that uses torture, imprisonment and non-violent tactics of suppression to deny its citizens the full enjoyment of their civil and human rights which all too often are hypocritically and theoretically protected by law.

POLISARIO FRONT. A guerilla group waging an undeclared war against both Morocco and Mauritania in Northern Africa in order to establish an independent nation of Western Sahara.

POLITICAL ACTION COMMITTEES. See P.A.C.s.

POLITICAL ASYLUM. See POLITICAL REFUGEES.

POLITICAL PRISONER. A person who, in being prosecuted, convicted and jailed for having committed some alleged crime, is being persecuted for his political or anti-government beliefs. It does not include those who are imprisoned unjustly apart from their political stand as dissidents to the government.

POLITICAL QUESTION DOCTRINE. Holds that federal courts will not adjudicate political questions on the ground that such issues are non-justiciable and must be resolved by another branch of government. The main application of the Political Question Doctrine has been to questions of international and domestic law that immediately concern the political or military interaction of the United States government with foreign governments. For example, it was held in several cases that the courts could not pass on the legality of American involvement in Vietnam. Another specific area where the Political Question Doctrine has been controversial is in cases concerning legislative or congressional apportionment claimed to cause inequality of voting power. In most of these latter cases, the Supreme Court has found the issue justiciable, and not a Political Question.

POLITICAL REFUGEES. Foreign citizens who may legally enter the United States, under a theory of political or territorial asylum, and qualify for American citizenship, having fled from their native land, usually as "boat people," in fear of persecution by imprisonment, torture or death for their active opposition to the government of their home country, such as Cuba or Vietnam. When the Attorney General of the United States makes this decision unilaterally instead of pursuant to normal immigration procedures, it is called parole authority. Political refugees are to be distinguished from economic escapees who flee from their home country, such as Mexico or Haiti, because they cannot survive on a mere subsistence level, who are refused admission to the United States and are summarily returned (at our expense) to the country from which they came, in a procedure known as refoulement.

POLL TAX (Capitation Tax) (Middle English—polle: a head). A uniform tax levied on each individual "per head." In the United States the term has become synonymous with a tax on voting. The 24th Amendment to the United States Constitution, ratified in 1964, outlawed Poll Taxes as prerequisites to voting in national elections. Shortly thereafter in *Harper v. Virginia Board of Elections,* 383 U.S. 663 (1966), the Supreme Court declared Virginia's one dollar Poll Tax unconstitutional, thus outlawing state poll taxes as well. Historically, the poll tax was a requirement for voting in all states after the adoption of the Constitution in 1787. While poll taxes were eliminated in most northern states, upper class coalitions in the southern states used these taxes, particularly during the Reconstruction Era, to limit the franchise for low income groups by making qualifications to vote more burdensome. In states which retained poll taxes, voter registration and participation ranked well behind national averages.

POLL THE JURY. When the court asks each member of the jury (1) after they have reached a verdict, whether each of them agreed to it or (2) when the jurors are unable to agree on a verdict, whether there is any chance of their so agreeing if they are given more time to deliberate.

POLLUTER PAYS PRINCIPLE. The theory that industries which pollute environmental resources should pay for their use. Such payment may be in the form of taxes or licenses.

POLL WATCHER. Assigned by a political party to watch election activities at a polling place to be certain that regulations are followed.

POLYGRAPH TESTIMONY. The results of a lie-detector examination which are generally not accepted into evidence under the theory that the scientific principle on which it rests is not sufficiently established to have gained general acceptance in its field. This rationale, laid down in a 1923 case, is now often the subject of heated dispute. Advocates of the polygraph claim that it can achieve up to 90 percent accuracy under the use of expert examiners and that evidence of this importance ought not be excluded at trial. Many remain unconvinced, questioning the expert ability of most examiners, while others are unenthusiastic about what they consider to be trial by machine. At present, most courts only admit lie detector evidence by the express agreement of both parties.

PONT NEUF (French—new bridge). A subversive pamphlet issued in violation of law attacking the French government distributed on the bridge of the same name, which was built across the Seine River in Paris in 1578.

PONZI SCHEME. An illegal swindle named after Charles Ponzi, a crook from Boston. In 1920 he raised millions of dollars from gullible investors by promising to pay 50 percent interest in 45 days. Early investors received their interest from the principal of future investors but the pyramid eventually collapses when future investors are not forthcoming. Human greed is such that several Ponzi schemes are going on throughout the country at any given time.

POOPER-SCOOPER LAW. See CANINE WASTE LAW.

POOR MAN'S ROCKETS. See O.T.R.A.G.

PORK-BARREL LEGISLATION. Enactments by a legislature which provide appropriations for local projects not justified in the national interest, but of particular advantage to the locality in which the project will be placed. Appropriations for local highways, water projects and construction are common examples. Pork-barrelling is closely related to log-rolling, an agreement by one legislator to support another's pet legislation not for its value but in return for similar support for legislation in which the first is interested.

PORK BENCH. The practice of United States Senators to consider the appointment of federal judges to be a matter of patronage.

PORTAL-TO-PORTAL PAY. Compensation paid to an employee for time spent in traveling to and from a plant or mine entrance to the working site.

PORT SAFETY AND TANKER SAFETY ACT OF 1978. A federal law that prescribes a variety of new standards for tanker construction and requires a number of new, stringent tanker-inspection and crew-training programs. For example, new tankers must have double bottoms (which make oil spills in the event of grounding less likely) and improved navigation and safety equipment. Many of the new features are expensive, but under intense public pressure in the light of the many oil spills desecrating the environment, the industry has accepted the most important ones.

POSSE COMITATUS (Latin—power of the county). The power of a sheriff or any other law enforcement official to temporarily enlist the aid of a certain portion of the civilian population for assistance in keeping the peace or pursuing and arresting a felon.

POSSIBILTY OF REVERTER. The future interest a transferor retains when he transfers an estate with a special limitation attached.

POST-INDICTMENT LINEUP. Pretrial procedure where a witness attempts to identify a suspect from a group of people. The procedure cannot be unduly suggestive. For instance, a Black suspect cannot be placed in a lineup with only Whites. Because unduly suggestive lineups may prejudice a later trial identification, the indicted suspect has a right to have an attorney present as an observer. There is no right to counsel, however, at a pre-indictment lineup.

POTENTIAL G.N.P. An estimate of how much a nation's economy can produce with relatively full utilization of its productive resources and existing technology. The concept allows for some margin of unused resources due to population shifts, transition between jobs, and incomplete utilization of inefficient productive facilities. The accepted level of utilization of resources may vary from one country to another. In the United States at the present time an unemployment rate of about four percent or slightly less is generally regarded as consistent with full employment of resources, and an average annual increase of four percent or slightly more in the real G.N.P. is considered a reasonable rate of potential growth.

POT-GATE. Term coined by the news media to describe a drug scandal precipitated when President Carter's drug abuse advisor allegedly violated a drug abuse law. Pot-Gate stimulated rumors of drug use by high government officials, including the assertion by an investigative reporter that 60 to 75 members of the House and 5 members of the Senate smoke marijuana regularly. In view of the fact that millions of Americans smoke marijuana, these charges may seem innocuous, but not for the numbers of pot-smokers who are spending time in jail for their use of the drug.

POTOMAC FEVER. A disease to which lawyers are particularly susceptible. It strikes politicians or attorneys who come to Washington, D.C., on the Potomac River, after a change of administration. They are so taken by the peaks of power or the social and diplomatic intrigue of the Nation's Capital that when their temporary tour of duty is over, they find some other job to keep them in town.

POUR-OVER CLAUSE (Spill-Over Trust). Provision in a trust arrangement which provides for the transfer of funds or property from one trust arrangement to another upon the occurrence of specified events. An example is a clause which directs the transfer of funds from one trust to another at such time as the trust property increases in value beyond a particular amount.

POUR-OVER WILL. Directs that certain assets of the decedent be added into or "poured over" an existing trust. Such an estate planning device offers the testator flexibility as well as savings on taxes and estate administration.

POWELL v. McCORMACK (395 U.S. 486 (1969)). A Supreme Court case which reversed a decision by the House of Representatives refusing to seat Adam Clayton Powell for alleged improprieties. The Court held that the House was limited in its exercise of Article I, section 5 powers to judging the qualifications of membership expressly set forth in Article I, section 2 of the Constitution: namely that a member shall be twenty-five years of age, shall have been a citizen of the United States for seven years and shall be a resident of the state in which he was elected. Thus, a Congressman could be elected while in jail or could serve while imprisoned.

POWER IN TRUST. See MANDATORY TRUST ORDERS.

POWER OF APPOINTMENT. An authority conferred by a will or other proper instrument upon a person to determine who is to receive property or the income thereof after the termination of varied interests.

POWER OF SALE CLAUSE. Empowers a trustee to sell trust assets and reinvest the cash proceeds, or otherwise dispose of them, pursuant to the desire of the trust settlor as evidenced in the trust arrangement.

POWER OF TERMINATION. See RIGHT OF ENTRY.

POWER PLANT AND INDUSTRIAL FUEL USE ACT OF 1978. By establishing a policy to expand the use of coal for new electric power plants, Congress expects this new federal law, which is part of President Carter's National Energy Plan, to reduce oil imports.

PRACTICE BROKERS. Intermediaries who sell the practice of a retiring lawyer to another lawyer or law firm. Sale of client loyalties may be ethically improper because it could violate confidentiality of client files, and recommendation of a successor may be based on the financial interest of the retiring lawyer rather than the best interests of his clients.

PRACTICING LAW INSTITUTE (P.L.I.). Founded in 1933, the Institute seeks to strengthen the legal system of the United States by sponsoring hundreds of seminars and publications of a practical nature on recent developments in the law.

P.R.C. (People's Republic of China; Mainland China; Communist China). The Asian Chinese nation of 800 million Chinese, in contrast to the capitalistic Republic of China (R.C.; Nationalist China) of 17 million Chinese on the Island of Taiwan (Formosa) in the South China Sea where they settled down in 1949 after being driven from the mainland of China by the Communists.

PRE-DELINQUENCY PROGRAM. Designed to identify children who are likely to become delinquents. Such detection programs have been established in a number of states, including Hawaii, Pennsylvania, Virginia, California, Oklahoma, New York and Maryland. They are often in conflict, however, with the Buckley Amendment concerning privacy of school records.

PRE-DISPOSITION REPORT. The document resulting from an investigation undertaken by a probation agency or other designated authority, which has been requested by a juvenile court. The Report concerns the past behavior, family background and personality of a juvenile who has been adjudicated a delinquent, a status offender, or a dependent; and is used to assist the court in determining the most appropriate disposition.

PRE-EMPTIVE RIGHT DOCTRINE. Allows a corporate stockholder to purchase a sufficient number of subsequently issued shares to preserve his current proportional ownership of the corporation. Such a right may be guaranteed by the Articles of Incorporation or by state law. Preemptive rights developed as early as 1807 when the closely-held Corporation was developing. The rationale was that the existing stockholders were the owners of the corporation and should be allowed to continue such ownership in the same proportion, to the extent of the transfer of shares already in existence. The application of the Preemptive Right Doctrine is relatively simple when there is but one class of common stock outstanding. However, it becomes more difficult as new classes of shares are created, each with variable rights with respect to voting, participation in dividends and assets upon dissolution. Where such variations exist the problem of how to preserve the particular proportionate interest may be impossible. These situations are most commonly encountered with a publicly-held corporation but are rare in the context of a closely-held corporation. An issuance of shares is subject to Preemptive Rights where the present proportionate interests of the shareholders as to corporate assets, dividends or voting are to be diluted. There are, however, judicial exceptions to the existence of preemptive rights in these cases. Exceptions have been made, for example, where shares have been issued in payment for a debt or in exchange for property, or in the case of a merger or consolidation. Where there is an issuance of stock subject to a presumptive right, the issuing corporation must give the existing stockholders reasonable notice and sufficient time to allow for arrangement of payment for the shares. The delay caused by this requirement may defeat the purpose of the new issuance, that is, to obtain financing with a minimum cost in terms of time and money. By placing the corporation in this disadvantageous situation, the Doctrine may eventually work to the detriment of the shareholder whose rights are protected to a large extent by the enforcement of the fiduciary duty of the Directors not to issue shares to themselves or others for the purpose of changing voting control. Perhaps as a result, most jurisdictions authorize the elimination of preemptive rights by amendment of the Articles of Incorporation.

PRE-EXISTING DUTY RULE. When a person promises to do, or refrain from doing, that which he is legally obligated to do, or refrain from doing, the promise is unenforceable for lack of consideration. For example, a law officer who has a duty to apprehend a criminal cannot collect a reward for doing so.

PREFERENTIAL DUTY. A customs duty which varies generally according to the source of the goods being taxed.

PREFERENTIAL HIRING HALL. See HIRING HALL.

PREFERRED CREDITORS. (1) Creditors whose claims are paid from the bankruptcy estate before those of General Creditors, in an order established by the Federal Bankruptcy Act. First paid are the expenses of administering the bankruptcy estate itself, including fees for the trustee in bankruptcy; then claims for wages owed the bankrupt's former employees. The claims of these preferred creditors take precedence over holders of tax liens and landlord's liens. The third class of claims given priority status are the costs of creditors who had to revoke an arrangement or a Wage Earner's Plan which the bankrupt did not fulfill. Taxes are the fourth class of preferred claims, and the fifth class includes both debts entitled to priority under other federal statutes—the most important of these confers priority status to debts owed to the United

States—and landlord's liens when given priority by state law. Only after these priority claims are paid are the general creditors entitled to their share of the bankruptcy estate. (2) Creditors paid within four months prior to bankruptcy who must repay the trustee and file claims as mere general creditors.

PREFERRED POSITION. In several opinions the Supreme Court has used language indicating that certain freedoms, notably Freedom of Speech, have preferred positions, meaning that they are of special concern to the Court. Justice Frankfurter attacked the notion of preferred freedoms, stating that it put forth the idea that "any law touching communication is infected with presumptive invalidity."

PREFERRED STOCK. A class of corporate shares which is entitled to priority over common stock in either the distribution of dividends or distribution of net assets upon liquidation of the corporation, or both. The dividends, however, are subject to an upper limit. If two or more classes of preferred stock are authorized, they are usually titled first preferred, second preferred, and so forth, to indicate relative priorities. There are five types of dividend preferences: (1) Cumulative, under which all past unpaid dividends must be fully paid before any dividends may be distributed on stock having subordinate dividend rights; (2) Non-cumulative, under which past unpaid dividends do not need to be paid prior to a dividend distribution on other stock as long as the current dividend is paid; (3) Cumulative to the extent earned, under which unpaid dividends accumulate during past fiscal periods only to the extent there were then funds legally available to pay them; (4) Participating, under which the preferred stock, whether cumulative or non-cumulative, share in further dividends with another class or classes of shares as defined by the Articles of Incorporation; (5) Non-participating, under which the preferred stock receives no dividends beyond the dividend preference. The recent trend has been to replace participating preferred stock with non-participating convertible securities. In general, preferred stock has no voting rights except for matters of fundamental changes affecting preferred stock. If there is a failure to pay dividends for a specified period, the right to elect directors may be given.

PREGNANCY DISCRIMINATION ACT OF 1978. A federal statute which requires employers to treat pregnancy the same as any other medical condition so far as any employee benefit program is concerned, thereby overruling the case, *General Electric Company v. Gilbert*, 429 U.S. 125 (1976), which had held to the contrary.

PREGNANCY PAY. Proposed legislation which would make discrimination because of pregnancy equivalent to discrimination because of sex, under Title VII of the Civil Rights Act of 1964. The bill does not mandate pregnancy pay for all pregnant workers, but requires that if compensation is made for elective surgery, or disabilities resulting from voluntary activities such as sports, then compensation should also be given for pregnancy disability. At issue in this legislation is whether or not the loss of earnings which comes from having a baby should be borne by the mother, as it currently is, or be covered by disability-compensation plans as a proper cost of doing business.

PREGNANT MARINE RULE. In 1976 a United States Court of Appeals struck down the rule that a pregnant Marine would be automatically and permanently discharged from military service. While the court acknowledged that the Marine Corps had an important interest in maintaining the mobility and combat readiness of its troops, it also noted that Marines were not discharged for other temporary disabilities. Reprimanding the Marines for their Victorian attitudes about pregnancy, the court stated the pregnant Marines were probably capable of working for the several weeks prior to giving birth and possibly for years afterward.

PREGNANT PATIENT'S BILL OF RIGHTS. Drafted by the Committee on Patient's Rights of New York City, this Bill of Rights recognizes that the pregnant patient has the right to participate in decisions involving her well-being and that of her unborn child, unless there is a clearcut medical emergency that prevents her participation.

PRE-HIRE AGREEMENT (Members Only Contract). An agreement between an employer and a labor union covering employees not yet hired. These agreements, valid only in the building and construction industry, enable employers to measure labor costs when submitting bids and to guarantee a ready supply of skilled employees. Negotiated before a union establishes its majority status, pre-hire agreements are not enforceable if a union fails to achieve such status.

PREJUDICIAL ERROR. A mistake of law made by a trial court that is prejudicial to a party in a suit. Prejudicial error is grounds for reversal by an appellate court whereas, generally, reversal will not lie if the trial court commits harmless error—one that is not prejudicial.

PRE-LAW HANDBOOK. A publication of the Law School Admission Council and the Association of American Law Schools. It contains general information on the legal profession and law schools for those interested in the study of law and a description of the program of each American Bar Association (A.B.A.) approved law school and the admissions profile for the most recently admitted class for the great majority of these schools. It may be purchased at most college bookstores or by mail from Educational Testing Service in Princeton, New Jersey.

PRELIMINARY HEARING. A hearing held within a reasonably short time after an arrest to determine whether a crime has in fact been committed and whether there is probable cause to believe that the accused committed it. If probable cause is found, then depending on the state, the accused is either

416

bound over for a grand jury or bound over for trial, and bail is set. A preliminary hearing is required to protect persons from being tried on unsupported charges. However, such a hearing is not required if a grand jury has issued an indictment or if the crime charged is a misdemeanor.

PRELIMINARY OFFENSE. See INCHOATE CRIME.

PREMEDITATED MURDER. See MALICE AFORETHOUGHT.

PREMIER POL POT. See ORGANIZATION ON HIGH.

PREPAID LEGAL SERVICE PLAN. Provision of legal advice to the members of a particular union or organization by virtue of their affiliation with the group in question. The Plan may be supported wholly by the employer as a fringe benefit, or funded by contributions from group members. The Plans are designed to make legal services more readily available to members of middle income class ($5-$15,000). Several hundred are in effect throughout the country. In *United Transportation Union v. State Bar of Michigan*, 401 U.S. 576 (1971), the Supreme Court recognized the right of consumer groups to seek legal services for their members. The decision followed *N.A.A.C.P. v. Button*, 371 U.S. 415 (1963), which vindicated the concept of group legal action in the civil rights context. The right to collective activity, however, was seen as a hollow one absent a means of enabling members of the organization to meet the cost of legal representation. The A.B.A. Code of Professional Responsibility has been amended to allow Open Panel Plans (similar to Blue Cross medical care, in that the client may choose any lawyer) and resistance to Closed Panel Plans (one lawyer or law firm serves all the clients) is breaking down. Union participation was sanctioned by a 1973 amendment to the Taft-Hartley Act which allowed unions to bargain for prepaid legal plans. In addition, the Internal Revenue Code now exempts prepaid legal plans for designation as income for tax purposes. For example, under a 1978 U.A.W.-Chrysler agreement, 120,000 hourly workers and 40,000 retirees will get prepaid legal service, from a staff of 100 lawyers plus contract arrangements with non-staff lawyers, for such problems as traffic violations, social security claims, divorces, misdemeanors, wills, and immigration matters. It's by far the largest plan to date and the first to be approved by the Internal Revenue Service since the Tax Reform Act of 1976 made most prepaid legal plans tax-exempt. Finally, the Pension Reform Act prohibits Bar Associations from interfering with Prepaid Legal Plans negotiated by unions. We may soon have Prepaid Legal Service Plans as widely in use as Prepaid Medical Services because the rich can afford lawyers, the poor get free legal advice and the rest of us in the middle are in need of help.

PREPONDERANCE OF THE EVIDENCE. See BURDEN OF PROOF.

PRESCRIBED SEX. Psychiatrists who prescribe sex between themselves and their patients as part of a "therapeutic" treatment. A New York Court upheld a malpractice suit against a psychiatrist who prescribed sex, finding it an act of coercion by a person in a position of overpowering influence and trust.

PRESENT BENEFICIARY. See IMMEDIATE TRUST BENEFICIARY; INCOME BENEFICIARY.

PRE-SENTENCE REPORT. The document resulting from an investigation undertaken by a probation agency or other designated authority, at the request of a criminal court. The Report concerns the past behavior, family circumstances, and personality of a person who has been convicted of a crime, and is used to assist the court in determining the most appropriate sentence.

PRESIDENTIAL MANAGEMENT IMPROVEMENT COUNCIL. See P.M.I.C.

PRESIDENTIAL PARDON POWER. Granted to the President by Article II, section 2, of the Constitution and used most dramatically by President Ford in pardoning former President Nixon. The pardon power was originally designed as another check in the system of checks and balances. The framers of the Constitution, however, foresaw that the power may be abused, and included an exception to the pardon power for impeachment. Unfortunately, they did not foresee a President resigning from office in order to avoid the exception clause which would have prevented a pardon.

PRESIDENTIAL TREATY TERMINATION. The constitutional power of the President unilaterally, without Congressional approval, to abrogate a Treaty between the United States and a foreign country. The first American to do so was President James Madison who abolished a commercial pact with Holland in 1815. Abraham Lincoln later did so with Canada (Rush-Bagot Agreement of 1817); William McKinley with Switzerland (1850 Convention of Friendship); Franklin Roosevelt at least five times; Lyndon B. Johnson once, and President Carter with the Mutual Defense Treaty of 1955 with the Republic of China, which he terminated in 1978 when he recognized the People's Republic of China. This action was the first time the power was ever used with respect to a military alliance.

PRESIDENT PRO TEMPORE (Latin —president for a time). The temporary presiding officer of any organization. For example, the presiding officer of the Senate in the temporary absence of the Vice-President, who is the traditional presiding officer of the Senate. The President Pro Tempore is elected by the Senate. He is fourth in line for the Presidency of the United States, succeeding to the office on the death or disability of the President, Vice-President, and Speaker of the House.

PRESIDENTS WHO WERE LAWYERS. Although twenty-five of the thirty-nine men who have served as President of the United States have passed the Bar and practiced law, only six Presidents attended law school. The rest read law and passed the Bar. John

Adams, the second President of the United States, was the first lawyer to serve as President, but it was 1877 before the United States had a law school-educated President, Rutherford B. Hayes, the first law school graduate elected President and the fourteenth attorney elected President, who graduated from Harvard Law School in 1845. The other Presidents who were law school graduates are: William H. Taft (Cincinnati Law School, 1880); Woodrow Wilson (University of Virginia School of Law, 1881); Franklin D. Roosevelt (attended Columbia Law School and passed the bar in 1907); Richard M. Nixon (Duke University School of Law, 1937); and Gerald R. Ford (Yale Law School, 1941). The other Presidents who read law and passed the bar are Thomas Jefferson, James Madison, James Monroe, John Quincy Adams, Andrew Jackson, Martin Van Buren, John Tyler, James K. Polk, Millard Fillmore, Franklin Pierce, James Buchanan, Abraham Lincoln, James Garfield, Grover Cleveland, Benjamin Harrison, William McKinley, Warren Harding, and Calvin Coolidge.

PRESUMED INTENT. A permissible inference that the accused intended the consequences of his act. Since mens rea is difficult to prove, the law allows the inference from the act itself. Thus, if *A* points a gun at *B*, pulls the trigger and kills him, the trier of fact may decide that *A* intended to kill. However, the inference is not mandatory and may be rejected. For example, it may be shown that *A* thought that the gun was not loaded and that he intended only to scare *B*. *A* will be punished, nevertheless, but the degree of the homicide will be less.

PRESUMPTION OF INNOCENCE. A convenient shorthand phrase for the fact that the burden of proof in a criminal trial rests with the prosecution. While not technically a presumption, the phrase does have the salutary effect of reminding the jury not to draw any inferences adverse to the defendant merely on the basis of the defendant's arrest and prosecution.

PRESUMPTIVE SENTENCING. See SENTENCING PROCEDURES.

PRE-TERMITTED HEIR. A person, usually a child of the decedent, who would have shared in the estate of the decedent, had the decedent died intestate, but who is not named in the will left by the decedent. Because society regards disinheritance as an extreme and unnatural act, statutes in most states provide that a child omitted from his parent's will may take his intestate share of his parent's estate where it can be shown that the omission was unintentional.

PRE-TERMITTTED HEIR STATUTE. This statute provides that when a child or other descendant is unintentionally omitted from a will, he is entitled to take his intestate share. His claim is defeated only by a statement in the will that disinheritance was intended.

PRE-TRIAL CONFERENCE. First adopted by the federal courts in 1938 in the form of Rule 16 of the Federal Rules of Civil Procedure. Since that time most states have added some form of pre-trial practice to their civil litigation systems. The federal rule permits the court, at its discretion, to direct the attorneys for the parties to appear before it for a conference to consider the simplification of the issues, amendments to the pleadings, admissions of fact and documents, the number of expert witnesses, reference to a master, and "such other matters as may aid in the disposition of the action." Rule 16 further provides that the court shall make an order reciting the action taken at the conference and that the order will control the subsequent course of the action. The chief academic proponent of the pre-trial conference was Professor Sunderland, who in 1937 predicted that pre-trial examination of cases by judges and attorneys at informal hearings "might do much to restore the confidence of the public litigation as a desirable method of settling disputes." Today there is substantial agreement, however, that the pre-trial conference mechanism has not lived up to early expectations.

PRE-TRIAL DISCOVERY (Mini-Trial). One party to a lawsuit is given access to the evidence in the possession of the opponent in order to deliberate the issues to be decided at the forthcoming trial. It is designed to eliminate trial by ambush in which one party holds back his evidence in an attempt to overwhelm the opponent in court.

PRE-TRIAL SERVICES AGENCY. An adjunct to a state Supreme Court system, which determines when unconvicted criminal defendants deemed good risks may be released on their own recognizance or be required to pay a refundable deposit. Under the old system, bail bondsmen could post a bond and charge a fee equal to ten percent of the bail set by the court. The bondsmen, who had arrest authority, were responsible for the defendants' appearance for trial. A person who could not raise the bail bondsman's fee stayed in jail. Now, a defendant may be released on his own recognizance if he has lived in the state a long time and has strong community ties. Or, he may be released after depositing ten percent of the bail with the court. In some intances the defendant can sign an unsecured signature bond. After all court appearances are completed, the defendant's money is refunded, except for a one percent fee for administrative costs. A defendant is interviewed by a representative of the Pre-Trial Services Agency within a few hours of his arrest and rated on a 22-point system based on such factors as the severity of the crime, whether it is a first offense, community ties, family ties and employment. Defendants considerd low risks are released on their own recognizance. Those considered moderate can be released after paying the ten percent fee. Some who are considered high risks may prove themselves worthy of release through such other programs as the work-release program, in which they go to work by day and return to jail at night.

PREVENTION OF TERRORISM ACT. A despicable law passed by the British in 1974. The Act permits the arrest of an alleged terrorist in Northern Ireland, his detention without charges for seven days and his subsequent conviction and imprisonment by a judge presiding secretly without a jury where the sole evidence is usually the confession of the beaten accused.

PREVENTIVE DETENTION. (1) A controversial method of protecting society from potentially dangerous persons by denying them release on pretrial bail. Although the Eighth Amendment protects only against excessive bail, federal courts and state constitutions have established the right to bail for all criminal defendants except those charged with a crime punishable by death. Preventive detention, designed to prevent suspected criminals from committing crimes while on pre-trial release, runs counter to this right to bail. Although adopted by several States and the District of Columbia, the practice has been attacked on the grounds that the defendant is punished before conviction and that he is denied the chance to properly prepare his case for trial. (2) Preventive detention also refers to the arrest and imprisonment of a person without trial in order to protect a community from an expected crime. A common practice in a number of countries, it is unconstitutional in the United States to hold a person without any prospect for a trial.

PREVENTIVE LAW. Arranging one's personal, financial, business and social affairs so as to minimize or avoid completely any run-in with the law.

PRICE-ANDERSON ACT (1957). A federal law that limits liability for any single nuclear accident to 560 million dollars. The Supreme Court of the United States upheld the constitutionality of the legislation in June, 1978, accepting that argument of private industry that they could not afford to continue doing A-Plant business without a ceiling on the potentially vast liability for a nuclear catastrophe.

PRICE DISCRIMINATION. A decision to set a price that bears a relation to factors other than actual costs of production or delivery. In some situations the discrimination entails selling to one buyer at a given price and refusing to sell to someone else at any price. Either practice is prohibited by the Robinson-Patman Price Discrimination Act. As used in the Clayton Act, the term refers to allowing certain customers to secure longer options, lower prices or longer periods in which to take delivery. If the discrimination decreases competition or tends to create a monopoly in any line of commerce, the Act requires the seller to charge uniform prices to competing purchasers.

P.R.I.D.E. (Productivity and Responsibility Will Increase Development and Employment). A successful voluntary program instituted by the construction industry in St. Louis in 1972 to encourage and promote peaceful and productive labor-management relations. Other cities have similar programs under different names, such as M.O.S.T. (Management and Organized Labor Striving Together) in Columbus, Ohio.

PRIDE'S PURGE. See RUMP PARLIAMENT.

PRIEST-PENITENT PRIVILEGE. Protects the confidential communications between a priest, clergyman, or rabbi and his penitent from disclosure. The privilege is designed to insure that those in need of spiritual aid or comfort will not be deterred by the risk of betrayal. A New York court first sanctioned the use of the privilege in 1813 by not requiring a Catholic priest to disclose the identity of a person who gave him stolen goods to return. The privilege is not recognized uniformly throughout the country.

PRIMA FACIE CASE. See BURDEN OF PROOF.

PRIMA LINEA. See REVOLUTIONARY JUSTICE.

PRIMARY BENEFICIARY. See IMMEDIATE TRUST BENEFICIARY; INCOME BENEFICIARY.

PRIME MINISTER. The elective head of the government and leader of the

Cabinet as Chief Executive in Great Britain and other common law countries.

PRIME RATE. The rate of interest charged by the major American banks for their most credit-worthy corporate customers which in turn determines the interest rate charged by all banks to all customers.

PRINCIPAL IN THE FIRST DEGREE. The actual perpetrator of a criminal act. Such a person engages in conduct which causes a criminal result. Included are persons who perpetrate crimes through innocent human agents, such as one who induces an unknowing child to poison the food of another.

PRINCIPAL IN THE SECOND DEGREE. One who counsels, encourages or assists in the commission of a criminal act and who is present at its commission. Such assistance is commonly known as aiding and abetting. A principal in the second degree differs from an Accessory Before the Fact in that he is actually present when the crime is committed. His presence includes assistance at the time of the crime even if at some distance. A look-out man, stationed a block away from the scene of the crime, is a Principal in the Second Degree. Modern codes, such as the Model Penal Code, deal with Principals in the Second Degree through a general provision on Accomplice Liability.

PRINCIPAL REGISTER. Governs trademark protection within the United States. It provides constructive notice of the registrant's claim of ownership of the trademark. The Principal Register was created by provision of the Lanham Act (1946), the Federal Trademark Statute.

PRINCIPAL TRUST BENEFICIARY. See ULTIMATE TRUST BENEFICIARY.

PRIOR RESTRAINT. Repression of free speech by preventing the distribution of ideas through injunction or submission to a censorship board before publication. The concept has encountered great hostility from the United States Supreme Court in its rulings on free speech.

PRISONERS LEGAL SERVICES. Non-profit corporations established in various states with funds provided by the Law Enforcement Assistance Administration. As its name implies, the organization provides lawyers at no cost to inmates who require their professional services.

PRIVACY ACT OF 1974. A federal act which grants individuals access to personal information about them contained in federal records. The act reasserts the federal fundamental right to privacy, derived from the Constitution of the United States, and provides a series of basic safeguards for the individual to prevent the misuse of personal information by the federal government. The Privacy Act requires the agencies to adopt regulations that list and describe routine transfers of their personal records and to establish procedures for access to and amendment of such records. The act further provides for civil remedies for the individual whose records are kept or used in contravention of the requirements of the act. Virtually all agencies of the federal government have issued regulations implementing the Privacy Act. These regulations generally inform the public how to determine if a system of records contains pertinent personal information, how to gain access to such records, how to request amendment of such records, and how to appeal an adverse agency determination on such a request. The Office of the Federal Register publishes an annual compilation which includes descriptions of all the systems of records maintained by each agency of the federal government, the categories of individuals about whom each record system is maintained, and the agency rules and procedures whereby an individual may obtain further information. The compilation is available at many public libraries or may be purchased from the Superintendent of Documents, Government Printing Office, Washington, D.C. 20402.

PRIVATE ATTORNEYS GENERAL. Citizens who sue in behalf of themselves and others, usually in a Class Action and especially in a case relating to ecology, to protect the rights of the public. The Supreme Court of the United States discourages such lawsuits by not making the guilty defendant pay the large attorney fees of the successful plaintiff and by requiring that the individual who sues show some direct personal injury in order to go to trial on the merits of the case.

PRIVATE BILLS. Federal and state legislation directed at specific matters or individuals, rather than general policies and problems. The Congress considers thousands of such Bills each year most of which fall into one of the following categories: Immigration and naturalization bills in favor of specific individuals; claims against the government that do not fit into existing judicial or administrative processes; and bills assigning title to lands. Approximately one third of the legislation passed by Congress is in the form of Private Bills which many feel contribute to legislative inefficiency and require the legislature to perform an essentially judicial function to which it is unsuited. During the early nineteenth century, private bills were even used extensively to obtain divorces because many states made no other provision for dissolution of a marriage.

PRIVATE EYE. A private detective. The phrase was coined from the Pinkerton Detective Agency trademark of an open eye.

PRIVATE MORTGAGE INSURANCE (P.M.I.). The payment of a fee by the mortgage lender for protection against any loss which might be sustained in the event of a default by the mortgagor on any payment on the loan.

PRIVATE NUISANCE. A tort consisting of the unreasonable, non-trespassory invasion of a person's interest in the use or enjoyment of his property. The action for nuisance arose at least as early as the thirteenth century in England, where it was defined to cover invasions of the plaintiff's land due to conduct wholly on the land of the defendant. In 1705 an English judge, in deciding a case where sewage from the defendant's privy flowed into his neighbor's cellar, stated, "He was bound of common right to keep his well so his filth would not damnify his neighbor." Today liability for nuisance can rest on intentional interference, negligence or strict liability.

PRIVATE PLACEMENT. Securities sold to a limited number of persons in such a manner as to be exempted from the requirement of registration under the Securities Act of 1933. An offering will be deemed a Private Placement as opposed to a Public Offering if (a) the securities are purchased by no more than 35 persons; (b) there is no general advertising of the issue; (c) the securities are offered only to sophisticated buyers who are able to understand and to bear the risks of the investment and have the services of a knowledgeable representative; (d) each prospective buyer has access to the kind of information available on a registration statement; and (e) the issuer takes steps to protect against subsequent resales that violate rules covering resales. Even if the offering meets these criteria, it may still be construed as a Public Offering if it is found to be a part of a scheme to evade the registration provisions of the Securities Act of 1933.

PRIVATE TRUST. A trust arrangement which is not public in operation as is a charitable trust, for example. The Private Trust is typically in the form of a parent or spouse settlor and child or spouse as beneficiary.

PRIVILEGED COMMUNICATIONS. Information obtained from a special relationship which cannot be disclosed in a trial over the objection of the holder of the privilege. Such privileges include the attorney-client privilege, the priest-penitent privilege, the physician-patient privilege, the journalist privilege, and the marital communications privilege. While such communications may be of undoubted relevance in resolving a lawsuit, they are not exposed in order to protect relationships and institutions which society deems to be important.

PRIVILEGES AND IMMUNITIES. Certain rights guaranteed to citizens by the United States Constitution. Article IV, section 2 states that, "The citizens of each state shall be entitled to all Privileges and Immunities of citizens in the several States," and the Fourteenth Amendment contains a clause providing that, "No State shall make or enforce any Law which shall abridge the Privileges and Immunities of citizens of the United States." Neither provision has received complete interpretation by the Supreme Court, but the former is considered to mean that a state may not deny to the citizen of another state certain rights which it accords to its own citizens, such as the right to own property or the right to the protection of the law. The Fourteenth Amendment protects from state interference certain rights of United States citizens which inhere to them by virtue of their national citizenship, such as access to national officials, the right to travel, and the right to engage in interstate and international commerce.

PRIVITY OF CONTRACT. Only those in "privity" can sue on a contract. Privity generally applies to those who exchanged the promise in question, and to those who were intended to benefit from the contract.

PRIVY COUNCIL. An exclusive group of 350 men and women appointed by the British Sovereign to act as Honorary Advisers to the Crown.

PRIZE JURISDICTION. The jurisdiction of admiralty courts to determine the lawfulness of the capture of property at sea in time of war. Such courts may subject prizes to condemnation and sale if the seizure is determined to be lawful under international law, or they may restore the prize to the rightful owner if the seizure is unlawful.

P.R.O. (Problem Resolution Officer). An employee of the Internal Revenue Service who assists taxpayers with difficulties such as finding a missing refund check or arranging time payments for tax bills. A P.R.O. can be reached by calling the nearest regional taxpayer information office, toll free, which number can be obtained from your local telephone directory.

PROBABLE CAUSE. Refers to an arresting officer's belief that an offense has been committed or is being committed and that the arrested person is the guilty party. In 1925 the Supreme Court in *Carroll v. United States*, 267 U.S. 132 (1925), held that probable cause exists where the facts and circumstances of which the officer had reasonably trustworthy information are sufficient to warrant a man of reasonable caution to believe that an offense has been or is being committed. The Court further explained this standard in *Brinegar v. United States*, 338 U.S. 160 (1949), where it emphasized that probabilities are the factual and practical considerations of everyday life on which reasonable and prudent men, not legal technicians, act.

PROBATION AGENCY. A correctional agency whose principal functions are juvenile intake, the supervision of adults and juveniles placed on probation status, and the investigation of adults or juveniles for the purpose of preparing presentence or predisposition reports to assist the court in determining the proper sentence or juvenile court disposition. Probation agencies are classified as correctional agencies because their chief functions include the supervision of adjudicated juveniles or convicted adults. However, probation agencies organized at local levels of government usually operate under the authority of a court, and juvenile probation officers are often considered judicial officers. Adult and juvenile probation agencies are often separate governmental units. In many states a single state agency performs both probation and parole supervision functions for adults, but juvenile probation functions are typically local and supervised by a juvenile court. A probation agency's concern with adults is usually limited to those convicted of an offense. Its discretionary powers regarding juveniles are much greater, in that it usually administers the intake unit that can decide to close a case at intake, to take other actions that preclude or defer the intervention of the juvenile court, or to file a petition asking the court to assume jurisdiction over the juvenile. The juvenile concern is also broad in that the intake function and subsequent supervision and care authority may apply to dependent juveniles, especially those in custody pending court disposition.

PRO BONO LEGAL ASSISTANCE (Latin—for the good). Legal service rendered on a "no-charge" basis, viewed as a public service by members of the legal profession.

PROCEDURAL DUE PROCESS. The right of an individual to be free from certain kinds of government intrusion or to be protected in certain areas if he is accused of a crime. Procedural due process rights include the right to be free from unreasonable searches and seizures; the right to a speedy and public trial by an impartial jury; the right to be informed of the nature and cause of an allegation of criminal conduct; and the right to the assistance of counsel when accused of a criminal offense. Most of these rights are enumerated in the Bill of Rights.

PROCHEIN AMI (French—next friend). A term of technical legal procedure. An infant cannot, as a matter of law, sue someone else in his own name to vindicate his rights. Therefore, the action must be brought by his next friend. The next friend will appear as a plaintiff in his own right to represent the interests of the infant.

PROCUREMENT APPEALS BOARD. Under the Model Procurement Code this term refers to the administrative board enacting jurisdictions it may establish to hear and decide contract disputes.

PROCUREMENT AUTOMATED SOURCE SYSTEM (P.A.S.S.). A new method employed by the Small Business Administration to make it easier for small enterprises to get federal business. It makes available to federal procurement officials the names and capabilities of small companies that can carry out federal contracts. The goal is to have 150,000 such companies registered by 1981.

PROCUREMENT CONTRACTING OFFICER (P.C.O.). In federal government contracting this term refers to a contracting officer at a purchasing office.

PROCUREMENT OFFICER. Under the Model Procurement Code this term refers to that person authorized by a governmental body, in accordance with prescribed procedures, to enter into and administer contracts and to make determinations and findings with respect thereto. This definition corresponds to that accorded a contracting officer in federal government contracting.

PROCURING AGENT. A defense used in a criminal drug case to defeat a prosecution for the sale of a controlled substance. For example, if *A* purchases heroin from *S*, takes possession of the drug, and gives it to *B* in return for the amount of money *A* paid *S* for the drug, *A* may not be found guilty of the sale of heroin to *B* if *A* convinces the jury that *B* had engaged him to make the purchase from *S* on *B*'s behalf.

PRODUCTS LIABILITY. Deals with the seller's liability for defects in the product supplied which result in physical harm to a person or his property. The theoretical underpinnings of this liability are several, some arising from the law of tort and others springing from contract law. At early common law the concept of privity of contract restricted liability in this area. A manufacturer or supplier could only be held liable to persons who actually purchased the product from him. Thus if one purchased contaminated food and served it to his guests, those guests who got ill could not sue the manufacturer as they were not in privity. Gradually courts began to eliminate the privity requirement—first with respect to food and more recently with any inherently dangerous product. Where privity is not required, courts have held manufacturers and suppliers to a duty of due care — essentially a negligence standard—toward users, consumers and even bystanders. Courts have now in some instances gone beyond even the negligence standard. Many are moving toward strict liability or liability without fault. This theory would allow recovery for injuries sustained by almost anyone when a manufacturer or supplier allows a defective product to enter the stream of commerce. A term virtually unknown to the legal profession a generation ago, Products Liability is an umbrella today under which one finds various legal theories of negligence, breach or warranty and strict liability. The volume of litigation in this area is as great as the variety and complexity of products common to the home and business.

PRODUCT TEST (Durham Test). A test, adopted in only a few states, for determining whether criminal conduct should be excused by reason of insanity. It provides that one is excused if his conduct is the product or result of a mental disease. Although it was adopted to ameliorate what was viewed as the harshness of the M'Naghten Test, its vagueness has precipitated a barrage of criticism. Influenced by the writings of Dr. Isaac Ray, New Hampshire first adopted the Product Test in 1871. Ray contended that insanity was established by many diagnostic symptoms, which should be evaluated in each particular case. The District of Columbia adopted the rule in 1954, but in 1972, after much confusion and criticism, it switched to the Model Penal Code's Substantial Capacity Test.

PROFESSIONAL ADMINISTRATIVE CAREER EXAM. See P.A.C.E.

PROFESSIONAL LIABILITY REPORTER. A malpractice law magazine which covers cases of national significance involving alleged misdeeds of lawyers, doctors, engineers, accountants, architects, and others.

PROFESSIONAL MALPRACTICE. Holding a doctor, lawyer, dentist, architect, engineer or any other type of professional, civilly or criminally liable for any injury committed through the commission of a tort such as negligence in the discharge of a professional duty.

PROFESSIONAL STANDARD REVIEW ORGANIZATIONS. See P.S.R.O.

PROFIT-SHARING TRUST. A trust arrangement which, in its most common form, allows employees of a company to share in corporate profits according to their respective positions. Such trust arrangements are popular because they are believed to promote a feeling of heightened morale and ambition on the part of employees.

PRO FORMA (Latin—as a matter of form). A person named to a lawsuit simply pro forma does not become a party to the action.

PROGRAM 245. See SECTION 245.

PROGRESSIVE POLITICS. A turn of the century theory that championed the urban working class and challenged those with economic privilege. It was practiced disastrously by 31-year-old Dennis Kucinich in Cleveland in 1978 when the brash anti-establishment politician was the youngest mayor ever elected for a major city. He brought the municipality to the brink of bankruptcy in his extreme populism.

PROGRESSIVE TAX. A revenue system which taxes a higher percentage of income as income rises. Under a progressive tax system, a person earning $5,000 may be taxed one percent, or $50, while a person earning $50,000 may be taxed fifty percent, or $25,000. The United States Internal Revenue Code is one example of a progressive tax. This concept is the opposite of a regressive tax, which imposes a lower percentage of tax on the rich than it does on the poor.

PRO HAC VICE (Latin—for this turn). Permits a lawyer who is not admitted to practice in a state to appear only for a particular case before the court upon proof that the applicant has been admitted to practice in another state.

PROHIBITION AMENDMENT OF 1919. See VOLSTEAD ACT.

PROJECT HAVEN. A highly touted but largely unsuccessful ten-year-old probe by the Internal Revenue Service and the Department of Justice into the use of offshore tax havens by wealthy Americans seeking to evade tax payments.

PROJECT MATCH. A federal project which uses computers to match employees on the federal payroll with a list of welfare recipients in order to discover names which appear on both lists. Conducted by the Department of Health, Education and Welfare, the Project has uncovered thousands of federal employees who are defrauding the welfare system by receiving payments to which they are not entitled. H.E.W. officials insist that the program is vital to preserving the integrity of the welfare system, but Project Match has been denounced by civil libertarians as an invasion of privacy reminiscent of George Orwell's novel, *1984*.

PROJECT X. A major investigation of a leading American oil company in 1978 by the Department of Justice which was concerned about illegal price manipulations. In 1973 the federal government established a two-tier price structure in order to encourage oil exploration as part of the solution to the energy crisis. Oil from old wells could be sold at $5.34 a barrel whereas oil from new wells could bear a price tag of $11.87 a barrel. Apparently, hundreds of thousands of barrels of old oil have been sold as new resulting in illegal profits of billions of dollars. The paper work shuffling involved in this type of conspiracy is called a Daisy Chain.

PROLETARIAN ARMED GROUP. See G.R.A.P.O.

P.R.O.M.I.S. (Prosecutors Management Information System). An agency which assists criminal prosecutors to com-

puterize their record-keeping systems and manage their personnel and resources more efficiently. For the first time, all of the myriad details of the criminal justice system are easily retrievable for analysis and examination. For example, of the 100,000 felony arrests in New York City each year, only 3,000 go to trial. The other 97,000 are dismissed or disposed of through plea bargaining. The average time actually served in prison by those convicted is only 26 months.

PROMISSORY ESTOPPEL. See ESTOPPEL DOCTRINE.

PROPERTY TAX. May include a levy on all property: real, personal, tangible and intangible; although most frequently levied on real estate. Prior to World War II, property taxes ranked first in productivity among tax sources used by federal, state, and local governments. In recent years, however, personal income taxes have exceeded property taxes by a wide margin, and corporate income taxes have been well above property taxes. In colonial days, property taxes were levied on slaves, carriages, watches, clocks, money, land and houses. Values for such items were frequently determined by arbitrary classifications: e.g., houses were valued according to the number of doors, windows or chimneys they had.

PROPORTIONAL TAX. See REGRESSIVE TAX.

PROPOSITION THIRTEEN (13). The name of the law on the ballot of the election in California on June 6, 1978, in which annual local real estate taxes were limited to a ceiling of not more than 1 percent of the appraised fair market value in 1976. It was the first successful taxpayers' revolt since the Boston Tea Party. Sponsored by businessmen Howard Jarvis and Paul Gann, it resulted in a reduction of 60 percent in tax for all property owners. The California tax quake caused repercussions throughout the land.

PROSECUTORIAL DISCRETION. The absolute and unlimited right of the prosecutor to determine whether or not to prosecute an accused. This discretion exists even if a grand jury has already returned an indictment. The purpose is to allow the prosecutor the freedom to decide the allocation of available resources. There is no way any one can make a prosecutor bring a suspect to trial. The only remedy for any abuse is to vote the official out of office at the next election.

PROSECUTORS MANAGEMENT INFORMATION SYSTEM. See P.R.O.M.I.S.

PROSPECTIVE PRICE REDETERMINATION. See FIXED-PRICE REDETERMINATION.

PROTECTION FROM ABUSE ACT. A statute which authorizes the use of restraining orders in spouse abuse cases. The complainant can, upon a showing of good cause at a hearing at which the defendant spouse is not present, be granted an order restraining the defendant spouse from further abusive conduct. In some states the court has explicit authority to exclude the offending spouse from the marital home, even if the defendant is the sole or joint owner or the lessee of the residence. Temporary custody and visitation rights can often be settled by the court at these hearings. The defendant is entitled to a hearing on the merits in such cases within a short time, usually ten days, at which the complaining spouse must prove the allegation by a preponderance of the evidence. Some state statutes give courts jurisdiction over both spouses and persons living as spouses, expanding the remedy to include couples who are not legally married. These provisions are considered to be an innovative and helpful response to the problem of spouse abuse. One criticism has been that while many of these programs provide that the offending spouse can be excluded from the marital home, most do not provide that temporary support orders may be issued at the initial proceeding. A spouse without financial support may be deterred from pursuing this remedy.

PROTECTIVE JURISDICTION. Theory of federal court jurisdiction which suggests that Congress, in any area where it has the constitutional power to prescribe federal rules of decision may enact a jurisdictional statute which would provide a federal forum for the application of state substantive law. In this manner, federal court jurisdiction would be broadened to cover cases involving only state-created rights without offending the definition of federal jurisdiction in Article III of the Constitution. A federal court would be able to resolve a case arising under the "laws of the United States" even where there existed no federal right or remedy, since the mere congressional grant of jurisdiction would be construed as part of the "laws of the United States." The concept of protective federal jurisdiction has not been squarely faced by the Supreme Court, but the few cases that discuss the issue suggest that it intrudes upon the accepted understanding of Article III as a jurisdictional limitation on the federal courts.

PROTECTIVE PRINCIPLE. Permits a sovereign country to enact criminal laws punishing the conduct of aliens in a foreign territory when such conduct threatens the security of the country or the operation of its governmental functions. Illustrative of such crimes are counterfeiting and terrorism.

PROTOCOL OF AMENDMENT TO THE WARSAW CONVENTION OF 1929. Adopted at a diplomatic conference at The Hague in 1955, the Protocol revises the Warsaw Convention, which regulates and limits the liability of commercial air carriers. The Protocol, which entered into force as between the ratifying states on August 1, 1962, received one hundred ratifications by 1976.

PROXIMATE CAUSE (Legal Cause). An element of an action for negligence which looks to the question of how far the defendant's liability extends for the consequences of his actions. The proximate cause requirement of a negligence action can be satisfied only if the following question is answered affirmatively: Did the defendant owe a duty to protect the plaintiff against the event which in fact occurred? Proximate cause, therefore, does not really refer to cause at all, but rather to the extent of liability. One of the most hotly and frequently debated tort cases concerns this issue. In *Palsgraf v. Long Island Railroad Co.*, 248 N.Y. 339 (1928), the railroad's conductors, helping a passenger board a train, knocked a package from the passenger's arms. The package, which contained fireworks, fell to the ground and exploded. The force of the explosion knocked over some scales which fell on the plaintiff, causing injury. The majority of the court held that there was no liability because there was no negligence toward the plaintiff. It defined negligence in terms of the relation between the parties and said that there could be no liability where there was no foreseeability of harm to the person actually injured. Since the conductors could not anticipate harm to Mrs. Palsgraf resulting from their efforts to assist the passenger, the railroad could not be held negligent. The dissenting judges, whose view is followed in a majority of the states, felt that in helping the passenger, the conductors owed a duty of care to anyone who might be injured as a result of their conduct. The dissent was willing to conclude that Mrs. Palsgraf's injuries were proximately caused by the negligent acts.

PROXY MARRIAGE. A marriage which is contracted or celebrated by agents or representatives of one or both of the parties. These absentee marriages may be classified either as valid ceremonial marriages provided there is compliance with the statutes or valid common law marriages provided such marriages are recognized in the jurisdiction. This type of marriage is more common in wartime since it enables servicemen to marry while they are away. There is a strong public policy in favor of proxy marriages under these circumstances since they often are entered into for the purpose of legitimizing children.

PROXY STATEMENT. An authorization, usually in writing, given by a person such as a stockholder to another party to exercise the voting rights of his stock. Although it is an agency relationship, revocable at any time under normal circumstances, it is somewhat unusual in that generally the agent solicits the principal (stockholder) to establish the agency relation. A written proxy statement, containing all information relevant to the choice, must either precede or accompany the solicitation. The contents of this Statement are thoroughly regulated by section 14 of the Securities Exchange Act of 1934. These are known as the S.E.C. proxy rules, and they forbid false or misleading statements or omissions during proxy solicitation and provide other regulations for the process.

PRUDENT MAN RULE. A rule of investment which provides that investment should be made with regard to expected income as well as the safety of the capital invested. As applied to trust investments, this rule was first set out by the Supreme Judicial Court of Massachusetts in the famous case of *Harvard College v. Amory*, 9 Pick. 446 (1830). The rule requires that a trustee exercise sound discretion and judgment in the performance of his fiduciary responsibilities. Further, this rule requires a trustee to act as a reasonably prudent man would in investing and disposing of assets and to avoid unreasonable speculation.

P.S.R.O. (Professional Standards Review Organizations). A network of physician panels throughout the United States to monitor the quality of medical care received by patients covered by Medicaid, Medicare and Maternal and Child Health Programs. It was established by a federal law in 1972. No other profession, including law, is subjected to such strict federal scrutiny.

PSYCHIATRIC DEFENSE. Response to criminal charges that admits factual guilt for the offense but denies criminal responsibility due to the perpetrator's mental aberration. To be found not guilty by reason of insanity, the defendant must meet the standard set out by one of three appropriate tests: (1) The M'Naghten Rule; (2) The A.L.I.-Model Penal Code test; or (3) The Durham Test. Under some circumstances the defense will lead to immediate release from custody. However, in most states an acquittal on psychiatric grounds will result in a prompt civil commitment of the defendant to a state hospital for the criminally insane. Inasmuch as such facilities are likely to be just as restrictive as prisons and perhaps even more depressing, psychiatric defenses are employed in only the most serious cases, frequently where the death penalty or life imprisonment is possible. As far as diagnostic categories are concerned, a psychotic disorder, paranoid schizophrenia, or a dissociative state must usually be alleged if a psychiatric defense is to be successful. While sufficient to qualify one as a defective delinquent, character disorders generally do not merit acquittals on the basis of insanity.

PSYCHOLOGICAL POLITICS. The Communist use of political trials not for the punishment of crime but rather for the administration of bureaucratic terror. They are thus more like perverse morality plays than democratic courtroom proceedings. Franz Kafka expressed it well in his novel *The Trial:* "There can be no doubt that behind all the actions of this Court of Justice, that is to say in my case, behind my arrest and today's interrogation, there is a great organization at work." Naked fear is thus the rule of law in Russia.

PSYCHOTIC DISORDER. Severe mental illness which is generally the basis for a psychiatric defense as an involuntary commitment. Psychotic disorder is characterized by grossly impaired reality testing. Included in the class are schizophrenic reactions, manic depressive reactions, and paranoid reactions. Psychotic individuals suffer serious disruption of their cognitive and emotional processes. While a psychoneurotic disorder can be treated on an outpatient basis, a psychosis is most effectively attended to in a residential facility. The diagnosis is most frequently applied to disturbed individuals in the low socio-economic class.

P.T.O. See PATENT AND TRADEMARK OFFICE.

PUBLIC ADVOCATE. First established in New Jersey, this is a program of government lawyers who bring civil law suits to protect the public interest in every field of human relationships.

PUBLICATION OF BANNS. See BANNS PUBLICATION.

PUBLICATION 17. See TAX BIBLE.

PUBLIC CITIZEN. A Ralph Nader organization which keeps tabs on members of Congress and publishes ratings on how each one voted on major issues.

PUBLIC CONTRACT. Governmental instrument used for the benefit of the general public. A contract made by the government will generally help to improve the welfare of its citizens. For example, inhabitants of a city benefit from an agreement to build such structures as fire houses or post offices. However, individual citizens have no legal rights regarding the enforcement of the governmental contract.

PUBLIC CORPORATION. One created by the state for public purposes only, to serve as an agency of the state. It is usually granted limited political powers, such as legislation, regulation, or taxation. Examples are municipal corporations, villages, and towns. Whether a particular corporation is public or private is determined by reference to the terms of its charter and the laws under which it was organized. Certain corporations are privately owned yet have been given powers of a public nature such as the power of eminent domain so that they can render services for the public's benefit. These are known as quasi-public corporations.

PUBLIC DEBT. The total indebtedness of a country or a government, including interest. A country's public debt equals the total debts of all its governmental units. When the government's expenditures exceed its revenue during a fiscal year, the deficit is added to the public debt. The practice of "pump priming" or deficit spending, has regrettably become an economic fixture of federal revenue planning. We have strayed from Ben Franklin's sage advice. "Earn 10 shillings and spend one equals happiness. Earn 10 shillings and spend 11 equals disaster."

PUBLIC DEFENDER. An attorney, employed by the government, who represents indigent criminal defendants at trial. Some public defenders work for private organizations, such as Legal Aid Societies, which have contracted with a governmental unit to provide representation for poor defendants. The role of the public defender is particularly significant in light of the fact that 65 percent of all felonies and 47 percent of all misdemeanors (excluding traffic violations) involve defendants who cannot afford to retain private counsel. In 1963, the Supreme Court ruled that defense services must be provided by States for the poor in felony cases where there is a likelihood of incarceration. This case, *Gideon v. Wainwright*, 372 U.S. 335 (1963) was extended nine years later in *Argersinger v. Hamlin*, 407 U.S. 25 (1972), which established a constitutional right to counsel for any criminal defendant who may be imprisoned for a misdemeanor. Presently, there are approximately 3,000 full-time public defenders in the United States. It has been estimated that in order to comply with the mandates of *Gideon* and *Argersinger*, 15,000 to 20,000 additional public defenders must be hired. Increased budgets also must be implemented. State and local governments currently spend up to seven times more money on prosecution than they allocate to indigent defense.

PUBLIC DOMAIN. (1) The public lands owned by the government. The public domain includes national parks, national forests, Indian reservations, and grazing lands. In the Homestead Act of 1862, when the public domain was considerably larger than it is today, Congress offered 160 acres of land to any homesteader willing to pay a ten-dollar registration fee and live on the land for five years. (2) Any monopoly, such as a copyright or patent, which has expired so that the property right now belongs to all the people.

PUBLIC EMPLOYEES FAIR EMPLOYMENT ACT. See TAYLOR LAW.

PUBLIC FUNCTION ANALYSIS. See STATE ACTION REQUIREMENT.

PUBLIC HEALTH SERVICE. A federal agency whose duty is to promote and assure the highest level of health attainable for every individual and family in America, and to develop cooperation in health projects with other nations. The major functions of the Service are to stimulate and assist states and communities with the development of local health resources and to further development of education for the health professions. It also assists with improvement of the delivery of health services to all Americans and conducts research. The Public Health Service protects the health of the nation against impure and unsafe foods, drugs and cosmetics, and communicable disease.

PUBLIC INTEREST LAW. Efforts to provide legal services to those unable to pay for them or otherwise unable to obtain them. Public interest lawyers represent clients in routine legal affairs and also work toward policy-centered law reform. The term public interest law dates from the mid-1960s when it referred mainly to civil rights and poverty law. Now, however, additional areas of concern include environmental issues, consumerism, and medical and tax reforms. At least five distinct programs are included under the generic term Public Interest Law: (1) Legal Aid Societies, which had their origins in New York City in 1876 when the German Society of New York provided legal services for recently-arrived immigrants. Today there are Legal Aid Offices throughout the United States with full-time staffs; (2) The American Civil Liberties Union, formed in 1916 by a group of prominent citizens as a lobbying force to guard against the violations of First Amendment rights apt to occur during the heat of World War I, continues to take up the cause of freedoms of speech, religion, and association; (3) Begun in the early 1930s, the Legal Defense and Education Fund of the National Association for the Advancement of Colored People (N.A.A.C.P.) used litigation to obtain specific social objectives, a mechanism upon which it still relies; (4) The Legal Services Corporation is an endeavor in public interest law. It uses federal money administered to a corporation which, in turn, allocates funds to local, regional, and State legal assistance foundations; (5) The Lawyers' Committee for Civil Rights Under Law is a national organization that encourages voluntary commitments of time from law firms and other attorneys in the private sector to handle Public Interest cases.

PUBLIC LEADERSHIP EDUCATION NETWORK. See P.L.E.N.

PUBLIC NUISANCE. Almost any type of interference with rights held by the public in common. It is a catch-all criminal offense which has been held to include such conduct as the obstruction of a highway, running a public gaming house, and indecent exposure. Nuisance of the public variety is to be distinguished from private nuisance, which involves interference with private land rights.

PUBLIC OFFERING. Occurs when there is a sale of securities to the public in a way that does not qualify it for an exemption as a private offering under Section 4(2) of the Securities Act of 1933. The issuer of the stock will then have to file a registration statement with the Securities and Exchange Commission (S.E.C.) which assures adequate disclosure of all necessary information to purchasers.

PUBLIC SAFETY OFFICER'S BENE-FITS ACT OF 1976. A federal law, administered by the Law Enforcement Assistance Administration which grants substantial financial aid to families of law-enforcement officers killed in the line of duty.

PUBLIC TELECOMMUNICATIONS ACT OF 1978. In addition to federal funding of 600 million dollars for non-commercial television and radio for a three-year period, this law required the recipients of such financial support to (1) conduct all of their policy-making meetings in the open; (2) place their annual audits in a public file; (3) provide access to independent producers; (4) encourage public participation through Community Advisory Boards; and (5) be in compliance with the Equal Employment Opportunity requirements. The only meetings that may be closed to the public are those involving contract negotiations and matters of utmost confidentiality, such as those concerning personnel changes.

PUBLIC TRUST. See PRIVATE TRUST.

PUBLIC UTILITY HOLDING COMPANY ACT OF 1935. A federal law which provides for regulation by the Securities and Exchange Commission (S.E.C.) of the purchase and sale of securities and assets by companies in electric and gas utility holding company systems, their intra-system transactions and service and management arrangements. In addition to limiting holding companies to a single coordinated utility system, it requires simplification of complex corporate and capital structures and elimination of unfair distribution of voting power among holders of system securities. The issuance and sale of securities by holding companies and their subsidiaries, unless exempt, must meet statutory standards, namely: that the new security is reasonably adapted to the security structure and earning power of the issuer; that the proposed financing is necessary and appropriate to the economical and efficient operation of the company's business; that the consideration received, and fees, commissions, and other remuneration paid, are fair; and that the terms and conditions of the sale are not detrimental to investors, consumers, or the public. The purchase and sale of utility properties and other assets may not violate rules, regulations, or orders of the Commission regarding the consideration to be received, maintenance of competitive conditions, fees and commissions, accounts, disclosure of interest, and similar matters. In passing upon proposals for reorganization, merger, or consolidation, the Commission must be satisfied that the objectives of the Act generally are complied with and that the terms of the proposal are fair and equitable to security holders.

PUBLIC UTILITY REGULATORY POLICIES ACT OF 1978. A major feature of this new federal law, which is part of President Carter's National Energy Plan, calls on state regulatory agencies to consider alternative rate structures to force more energy conservation. The Secretary of Energy is empowered to intervene in state regulatory hearings and may participate in any legal appeal of a state's decision.

PUBLIC WELFARE OFFENSES. See STRICT LIABILITY.

PUBLIC WORKS EMPLOYMENT ACT. A federal law that requires 10 percent of federal programs to be awarded to private businesses which are at least one half owned by members of minority groups, composed of Blacks, Orientals, Indians, Eskimos, Aleuts or those who speak Spanish. Thousands of government contracts involving billions of dollars are at stake. In its concept of reverse discrimination, it is for "hard hat" employment what the *Bakke* case is for admission to graduate professional schools.

PULLMAN DOCTRINE. See ABSTENTION DOCTRINES.

PUMP PRIMING. See PUBLIC DEBT.

PUNITIVE DAMAGES (Smart Money; Exemplary Damages). Money award-ed to the plaintiff in a tort suit in excess of the amount which would be required to fully compensate him for his injuries. As their name suggests, these damages are intended to punish the defendant and to deter him from repeating his act and dissuade others from following his original example. To the extent that punitive damages have as their goals retribution and deterrence, rather than compensation, they are more characteristic of the criminal law than they are of the law of tort. Because of their special character, such damages are awarded only when the wrongdoer has acted maliciously or with a cavalier disregard for the consequences of his actions. Thus, mere negligence will not give rise to punitive damages. However, they are not uncommon in actions for assault and battery, libel and slander, deceit, seduction and alienation of affection. Punitive damages are designed to teach defendants a lesson by hitting them hard in their pocketbook, so that they will be encouraged not to do the wrongful act again. It also serves as a lesson to others. The amount awarded by the trial court will not be reduced on appeal unless there was such an abuse of discretion by the trial court as to shock the conscience of the appellate court. The highest award ever made in the United States for punitive damages was for 125 million dollars (but subsequently reduced) against the Ford Motor Company in 1978 for an accident caused by a poorly designed Pinto car.

PURCHASE MONEY RESULTING TRUST. A judicially-imposed trust which arises where a transfer of property is made to one person and the price is paid by another.

PUSH MONEY (P.M.; SPIFF). Payments given by wholesalers to retail salesmen to promote particular brands of merchandise. Usually made without the knowledge of the retail store, such push money probably is seldom reported for income tax purposes.

PUTATIVE FATHER (Latin—putare: to consider or think). The biological or natural father of a child born out of wedlock.

PUTATIVE MARRIAGE. A matrimonial union, recognized as lawful in a few western states, which has been solemnized in due form and good faith on the part of one or both of the parties, but which is by reason of some legal infirmity either void or voidable. The parties involved in such a marriage are each called putative spouses.

Q

Q.C. See KING'S COUNSEL.

QUALIFIED IMMUNITY. See ABSOLUTE IMMUNITY.

QUALIFIED TRUST. A trust arrangement which qualifies under the I.R.S. Code of 1954 and accordingly provides certain tax advantages to employers who established them. Essentially, a Qualified Trust must be for the exclusive benefit of employees or their designated beneficiaries in order for the employer-settlor to take advantage of the favorable tax consequences.

QUARANTINE LAW. (1) At common law, a period of 40 days, during which a widow may occupy the manor house of her deceased husband, while waiting for dower to be assigned to her. (2) In constitutional law, the right of police power assumed by the state, to prevent entry into a state of goods likely to be harmful. Similar quarantines apply against persons suffering from contagious diseases. (3) In maritime law, the period during which a vessel may be detained before disembarking passengers or unloading goods to determine whether there is any danger of infectious disease.

QUASH AN INDICTMENT. To invalidate an indictment.

QUASI CONTRACT (Latin—quasi ex contractus: as if there were a contract). A non-contractual obligation which is treated as if it were a contract. Quasi contracts may be implied in fact or by law. For example, if a homeowner calls

an exterminator to service his home, an obligation is implied in fact to pay for the service. If a doctor renders necessary medical care to a child abused by his parents, an obligation may be placed by law on the parents to the doctor.

QUASI GUARDIAN. See GUARDIAN DE SON TORT.

QUASI-IN-REM. An action or proceeding which is not strictly In Rem, against a thing, but rather is brought against a person, in order to determine the rights, as between the parties, to a particular thing.

QUASI-IN-REM JURISDICTION. Judicial jurisdiction which is not In Rem jurisdiction in the strict sense. The object of the action is to determine rights to, or interests in, property which is subject to the jurisdiction of the court. However, the rights to the property are adjudicated only as between specified parties. For example, Able may bring a tort action against Baker in the courts of state X by causing the court to make a judicial attachment of Baker's bank account located in state X, and if Able prevails on the merits of his tort claim, he will be entitled to collect the amount of the judgment out of the attached bank account. The Supreme Court in *Shaffer v. Heitner*, 433 U.S. 186 (1977), cast doubt on the use of Quasi-In-Rem jurisdiction to obtain personal jurisdiction over a defendant when the property upon which jurisdiction is based is unrelated to the cause of action. *Shaffer* requires that actions brought under Quasi-In-Rem jurisdiction must meet the minimal contacts test, consonant with fair play and substantial justice, set down by the Supreme Court in *International Shoe Co. v. State of Washington*, 326 U.S. 310 (1945).

QUEEN BEES. See KILLER BEES.

QUEEN CAROLINE'S RULE. A rule of evidence concerning the impeachment of a witness by a prior inconsistent statement. Where the statement was written, it had to be shown to the witness before he could be cross-examined about it. The Federal Rules of Evidence have eliminated this procedure.

QUEEN'S COUNSEL. See KING'S COUNSEL.

QUEEN'S EVIDENCE. Witnesses and other proof submitted in court by the Crown in Great Britain which, of course, is called King's Evidence if the reigning monarch is a male.

QUIA TIMET (Latin—because he fears or apprehends). An antiquated term used in equity pleading and procedure. It names a bill in equity which is filed by a party who fears some future injury to his rights or interest. This bill is one of the forerunners to the modern declaratory judgment action.

QUICKIE STRIKE. A brief work stoppage called without advance notice, usually in reaction to some employer practice resented by employees or the local union. Such strikes usually are unauthorized by the national or international union. The strikes represent minority pressure on the employer to deal with a group other than the exclusive bargaining agent. As such, the strike is unprotected by the National Labor Relations Act and may be redressed by the employer through dismissal or other discipline.

QUID PRO QUO (Latin — this for that). Colloquially, "You scratch my back, I'll scratch yours." A bargaining tactic frequently used by politicians, diplomats, union officials and attorneys. Generally not considered proper form for judges, however.

QUIET MEAL RULE. A tax rule which allows a taxpayer to deduct the cost of entertaining business associates at breakfast, lunch or dinner even if the only purpose of such meals is general goodwill and there is no actual discussion of business at all. However, the food and beverages must be served under conditions conducive to a business discussion. The quiet meal requirement is not met where there are major distractions, such as at nightclubs, sporting events, large cocktail parties or social gatherings. But the dining room of a country club where there are no major distractions can be the setting for a quiet meal.

QUIET TITLE SUIT. See SUIT TO QUIET TITLE.

QUI TAM (Latin—who as well). A little-used legal action. It can be brought only under a criminal statute which provides that the penalty for the crime shall also be recoverable in a civil action brought by a private person, part of the penalty going to the person who brings the action and the rest to the state. The person bringing the action is said to sue for himself as well as for the state.

QUITCLAIM DEED. Used in transfers of title to real estate where the transferor does not guarantee anything about the condition of the property, nor does he warrant his title. Trustees, executors, and others similarly in fiduciary capacities often give quitclaim deeds.

QUORUM REQUIREMENT. When the number of directors or shareholders required in order to conduct business either by statute, Articles of Incorporation, or Bylaws are present at a meeting, a quorum is established. A majority of the whole usually constitutes a quorum. Greater than normal Quorum requirements are objected to as being inconsistent with majority rule and as enhancing the possibility of deadlock. They allow, for instance, any minority shareholder with sufficiently large holdings, in effect, to veto any action by refusing to attend the meeting. A growing number of states, however, now authorize by statute the adoption of greater than normal quorum requirements.

QUOTIENT VERDICT. A money verdict in civil suits determined by: (1) each juror writing a sum he wishes to award; (2) adding all the sums; (3) dividing by the number of jurors.

R

RAAB AFFAIR. Medical student, Henry Raab, was expelled from the

University of Maryland Medical School ten days before his graduation and has been fighting 25 years for his degree. Raab was allegedly expelled in 1954 for psychiatric symptoms, yet the psychiatrist who examined him maintained there was nothing at all wrong. Raab contends that he was expelled for being a misfit. He was a foreign student at a time when there were few such students in American medical schools; he transgressed the school's dress code by wearing sandals to a final exam and failing to wear a tie while dissecting a cadaver on a hot summer's day; and he had a tendency to challenge his professor's views. One educator commented that Raab would have had no problems at all if he had been enrolled in the sixties rather than the fifties. Raab's latest approach is a suit against the University seeking a court order to obtain his degree.

RACIAL QUOTAS. See AFFIRMATIVE ACTION.

RACKETEER INFLUENCED AND CORRUPT ORGANIZATIONS LAW. See R.I.C.O.

RADAR. See V.A.S.C.A.R.

RADIO FREE EUROPE. See INTERNATIONAL COMMUNICATION AGENCY.

RADIO LIBERTY. See INTERNATIONAL COMMUNICATION AGENCY.

RAILWAY LABOR ACT (1926). Created the National Mediation Board to mediate disputes in the railroad industry. The Act endorsed collective bargaining as a means of avoiding disruptive labor problems in the important public transportation sector. The Act also expressed a national interest in protecting the organizational rights of employees. In 1936, an amendment expanded its coverage to airlines.

RAIN MAKER. A partner of a large law firm whose major if not sole role is to attract new clients to the firm, frequently as a result of previous government experience. Among the most

famous was Richard Nixon, who managed to attract the Pepsi-Cola account to his New York law firm partly because as Vice President in 1959 he steered Nikita Khrushchev to the Pepsi kiosk in Moscow as photographers clicked away. Rainmakers can come up dry, however, such as ex-Attorney General Ramsey Clark who did so much free Pro Bono work that he lost money for his former New York firm.

RALPH NADER PUBLIC CITIZEN, INC. An organization established in 1971 by Ralph Nader to raise money for consumer advocacy. Prior to the formation of Public Citizen, Nader funded his lobbying and reform activities largely through personal appearances and contributions by foundations. He devised Public Citizen as a means of going directly to the public for funds, hoping to free himself from reliance on the "Establishment" money of the foundations. Nader compiled approximately 200,000 names which he obtained from magazine mailing lists and solicited these people for small donations. In its first four months, the corporation collected $100,000. In order to qualify for tax-exempt status, Nader set up a board of trustees, thus severing the group from his public personality. His sister, two university professors, and a Canadian attorney comprised the board. Nader himself became managing trustee. One of Public Citizen's foremost contributors quipped that, if for no other reason, the group was worthwhile because it provided the ubiquitous Nader with the money for "an office, a telephone, and someone to answer it."

R.A.M. (Reverse Annuity Mortgage). A lending device which enables an older person to borrow money using the increased value of his home as security. Some of these plans do not require repayment of the loan until the death of the homeowner. Others provide monthly payments for a fixed term and require repayment or refinancing at the end of that time. For example, a homeowner gets a 10-year loan of $32,000 from a lender at 9 percent interest. He or she receives $165.36 a month for 10 years, tax free, since the money is advanced as a loan. When the loan is repaid, the borrower may take a deduction for interest of $12,156 in computing federal income tax.

RANDOLPH, EDMUND (1753-1813). The first Attorney General of Virginia, the first Attorney General of the United States, Secretary of State, and representative for Virginia at the Constitutional Convention in Philadelphia. He also was private counsel for George Washington, assumed Thomas Jefferson's practice of law when Jefferson entered politics, and was counsel for Aaron Burr in Burr's famous trial for treason.

RANDOM AUDIT (Spot Audit). Periodic unannounced checking of a lawyer's finances to determine whether a client's money is securely kept in a safe and separate account. Regrettably, only a few states (Delaware, Iowa, New Jersey and Washington) so protect clients in their trust accounts.

RANDOM OR SPOT CHECK (Indiscriminate Check). The police may not constitutionally stop a motorist at random to check his license and registration under the guise of improving highway safety unless there is some reason to believe that the motorist is violating the law. *Delaware v. Prouse*, 99 S.Ct. 1391 (1979). It is permissible, however, for the police to follow this practice systematically for all motorists in what is known as a roadblock check.

RAND REPORT. A definitive and impartial study conducted in 1978 by the "Think Tank" in Santa Monica, California, in the field of medical malpractice with recommendations on solutions to the many problems which exist.

RANSOM PAYMENT. Given for the redemption of captured persons or property. Ever since man realized the commercial potential in holding his prisoners hostage instead of killing them, ransom has been a profitable adjunct of warfare. For example, when Richard the Lion-Hearted of England was captured in Vienna while disguised as a woman, the knights of England contributed $4 each toward his ransom. To raise the rest of the $500,000 ransom, the English government levied what is said to have been the first tax on movable property. Late in the Hundred Years War, the French paid $2.5 million to free King John from the British. The sum was so large it had to be paid on the installment plan. A King's ransom is thus known as any large amount of money. More recently, the death of Charles Lindbergh's son, who was kidnapped for ransom in 1932, led Congress to enact the Lindbergh Law which provides for capital punishment for those convicted of carrying a ransom victim across state lines. And in 1962, Fidel Castro became the first head of state in the twentieth century to exact ransom for prisoners of war. Castro exchanged 1,163 prisoners from the Bay of Pigs invasion, 5,000 of their relatives, and 35 other Americans for approximately $503 million contributed by American private citizens and corporations. Another recent twist in the art of ransom is the practice of Free World/Communist spy swapping. A dramatic illustration of this form of ransom was the exchange of American U-2 pilot, Francis Powers, for Colonel Rudolph Abel, the master Russian espionage agent, in 1961. Interestingly enough, it was James Donovan, a New York attorney appointed to represent Abel, who suggested that his client not be given capital punishment if convicted, since his life might have future ransom-value. Donovan also negotiated the Cuban ransom exchange a year later. Donovan's activities were said to be inspired in part by the Mercedarian Order, officially known as the Glorious, Royal and Military Order of Our Lady of Mercy or Ransom, an organization founded in the thirteenth century by a group of Spanish noblemen to seek the release of Christians who were being held by the Moors.

RAP BROWN LAW. Federal amendment to the Civil Rights Act of 1968 which imposes a maximum sentence of five years imprisonment or a $10,000 fine for crossing state lines with the intent to cause a riot. The Law is named for the 1960s civil rights leader, H. Rap Brown, chairman of the Student Nonviolent Coordinating Committee, and present immediately before or during race riots in Tampa, Cincinnati, and Atlanta.

RAPE ASSAULT CENTER. An agency, composed of a specially trained professional staff, usually located at a hospital, which offers legal counsel, emotional comfort and other guidance to victims of sex crimes. It preserves clinical evidence for use in any forthcoming trial and both assists and protects the victim in her participation in the legal proceedings.

RAPE PUNISHMENT. In *Coker v. Georgia,* 433 U.S. 584 (1977), the Supreme Court concluded that the death penalty in rape cases is cruel and unusual punishment. The decision was a victory for Coker, who had been fighting a 14-year battle for his life. Surprisingly enough, the decision is also a victory for women. Women's groups filed Amicus Curiae briefs supporting Coker's position because many juries have often been willing to let rapists go if they are forced to give a death sentence. Also, the severe penalty is an incentive for a rapist to kill the victim, who is usually his best witness.

RAPE SHIELD LAWS. Statutes passed in most of the states which control or prohibit the use of evidence relating to the chastity of the victim of a sexual assault.

RAPE VICTIM PRIVACY PROTECTION LAWS. These are statutes which have been enacted by the federal government and more than one-half of the states. They typically provide that in any case in which an accused is charged with rape or with assault with intent to commit rape, no court shall admit into evidence either testimony concerning the reputation in the community of an alleged victim with respect to sexual conduct or an opinion by a witness concerning the past sexual behavior of an alleged victim. These laws represent

a welcome departure from the previous 200-year-old view expressed by British Lord Chief Justice Hale, who said that rape was "an accusation easily to be made and hard to be proved, and harder to be defended by the party accused, though ever so innocent."

RAPID CHARGE PROCESSING SYSTEM. A procedure adopted by E.E.O.C. to avoid lengthy investigation processes and to eliminate the current case backlog in over 100,000 employment discrimination cases based on race, color, religion, sex, national origin, age or physical handicap.

RAPID DEPLOYMENT FORCE (R.D.F.) An American military group created in 1980, in which the Marines are the core. The mission of the new force is to swing into areas in the Third World, including the developing nations of Asia, the Middle East, Africa, and Latin America, to support a threatened friendly government or to protect vital American interests, such as oil. The pivot is a fleet of 15 or 16 new ships, each at a cost of $120 million, positioned in flotillas of five in ports from which they could sail on short notice.

RAP SHEET. A list of convictions and, sometimes, arrests employed by federal, state or local law-enforcement officers for use in investigation, prosecution and sentencing of criminal offenders.

RAT BREAKER. See STRIKE BREAKER.

RATCHET JAWING. Use of obscene language on citizens band radios. It is a federal penal offense.

RATIO DECIDENDI (Latin—reason for deciding). The legal principle or ground which determines the judgment of a court in a particular case.

R.C. See P.R.C.

R.C.C.L.S. See RESOURCE CENTER FOR CONSUMERS OF LEGAL SERVICES.

R.D.C. (Running Down Clause). In marine insurance policies, a clause which covers tort liability of the insured ship to a third party, similar to auto liability insurance.

READING OF THE LAW. Legal apprenticeship whereby a student, in lieu of attending law school, studies law under the direction of a court-approved member of the practicing bar. Although graduation from an accredited law school is a prerequisite to admission to the bar in most states today, law school attendance was not required in the past. Many famous lawyers including Patrick Henry, Daniel Webster, Abraham Lincoln, Stephen Douglas and Clarence Darrow acquired their legal education by reading of the law.

READING THE RIOT ACT. In England, an official command for rioters to disperse, derived from the practice of the Crown to send out a magistrate to a rioting crowd and read a proclamation warning them of the Riot Act. Thus the warning became known, inaccurately, as "reading the Riot Act."

REAL ESTATE INVESTMENT ACT. See REAL ESTATE INVESTMENT TRUST.

REAL ESTATE INVESTMENT TRUST (R.E.I.T.). Type of mutual fund organization involving 100 or more investors who buy shares in a trust to purchase, develop, or sell real estate. If the R.E.I.T. distributes 90 percent of its income to the shareholders, it does not have to pay any corporate income tax, and after the property is sold any profits are also distributed to the shareholders as capital gains, which are taxed lower than ordinary income. Real Estate Trusts are regulated by the Real Estate Investment Act of 1960.

REAL ESTATE SETTLEMENT PROCEDURES ACT. See R.E.S.P.A.

REAL ESTATE SYNDICATE. A partnership that deals with real property, designed to allow small investors to pool their funds with other small investors and buy into a project they could not otherwise purchase. Such syndicates are generally organized as general or limited partnerships. A general partnership is one in which all partners share equally in managerial decisions, profits and losses; while a limited partnership has two tiers of partners—general partners who are responsible for the overall operation, and limited partners who have limited managerial responsibility and share in the profits and losses only to the extent of their investment.

REAL EVIDENCE. Appeals to the sense impressions of the trier of fact. Such evidence, for example, might include clothing worn by a murder victim or objects found at the scene of the crime. Demonstrative evidence is real evidence which is prepared for trial purposes, such as a drawing.

REAL PARTY IN INTEREST. The party whose right is being enforced. This party is usually, but not necessarily, the person who will ultimately benefit from a successful lawsuit. For example, in a suit to enforce a claim of one who has died, the deceased's representative (executor/administrator), and not the beneficiary of the estate, is the Real Party In Interest.

REAL-POLITIK. From the German term which means practical or realistic politics, including the use or threatened use of force by one nation against another to reach a desired goal or relationship.

REAL PROPERTY. Generally, land and things erected, affixed or growing upon it. This includes all interests therein which rise to the status of a freehold interest. Real property is often judicially and legislatively defined as "lands, tenements, and hereditaments."

REAL WAGE INSURANCE. A tax relief proposal of President Carter for employees whose wage increase does not exceed their voluntary anti-inflation wage guideline of 7 percent, if inflation exceeds the 7 percent figure.

REASONABLE MAN. The standard of conduct against which actions are measured to determine liability for negligence. One commentator has noted that in all the voluminous literature which bears upon this branch of the law, no mention is made of a reasonable woman.

REASONABLE PRICE. Term that allows courts to determine what the parties intended during the negotiation of a contract if there is misunderstanding about price. For example, should a price discrepancy arise when the two parties have negotiated beforehand, the courts may decide to use evidence of prior dealings to determine what should be used as a reasonable price.

REBUS SIC STANTIBUS (Latin—in these circumstances). A doctrine which provides for revision or termination of international treaties in case of vital change in circumstances. This doctrine may lead to unilateral denunciations of treaties, which explains the current divisions among various international authorities about the validity of the doctrine. The main problem relates to the definition of "vital change of circumstances"; a majority of authors consider that this should be interpreted with regard to the interests of the signatory states. Although never formally applied by an international court, the doctrine has been frequently invoked, mainly by Russia, against the Treaty of Paris of 1856, and by Germany, against the Treaty of Versailles of 1919. The League of Nations Covenant and the U.N. Charter include provisions applicable to optional revision of treaties, and more and more states voluntarily include the clause Rebus Sic Stantibus in their treaties.

RECALL TECHNIQUE. Used by witnesses who do not want to answer a question, but also want to avoid refusing to answer by invoking the Fifth Amendment. One of the most famous users of the Recall Technique was Jimmy Hoffa, Teamster's Union president, who was indicted on a series of charges ranging from jury tampering to corruption and mismanagement of Union funds. By claiming that he cannot recall an event, a witness only risks perjury if his opponent can prove that he did in fact recall the matter. Since human memory is fallible, it is unlikely that many attorneys would attempt to prove perjury in a Recall statement.

RECEIVER IN BANKRUPTCY. A person appointed by a bankruptcy court to take charge temporarily of the property of a person who has filed a voluntary petition in bankruptcy or is the subject of an involuntary petition in bankruptcy. Once a debtor is adjudged as bankrupt, a trustee in bankruptcy will be appointed to administer the bankrupt's property, which becomes the bankruptcy estate. Until then, however, the receiver acts to preserve the property.

RECIDIVIST STATUTES. See COME BACK LAWS.

RECIPROCAL ADMISSION. Agreements between one or more states that passage of a Bar Examination and subsequent admission to practice in one state will trigger the admission to practice in the other state upon timely application, usually after a practice of several years, and vice versa. This type of practice is recognized in only a limited number of states.

RECLAMATION PETITION. A petition filed in bankruptcy court, in which the petitioner claims that property belonging to him has been included in the bankruptcy estate, and requesting that it be returned to him. Property may be reclaimed if it is held by the bankrupt in trust or acquired by the bankrupt through fraud. If the petitioner proves his claim, but the property has been sold, the petitioner is entitled to the proceeds of the sale.

RECOGNITIONAL PICKETING. Picketing aimed at applying economic pressure on employees who are reluctant to join the union and on employers who refuse to recognize and bargain with the union. The pickets usually bar deliveries to and from the business picketed and they discourage patronage by customers. At common law, recognitional picketing was vulnerable to court injunctions because this activity was too far removed from the central union purpose of improving wages and working conditions. Such picketing is generally recognized today, but the National Labor Relations Act severely restricts it where the employer is currently recognizing another union, or where a valid election has been held within the preceding twelve months.

RECOGNIZANCE TO KEEP THE PEACE. See PEACE BOND.

RECRIMINATION IN DIVORCE. The judicial practice of refusing to grant a divorce where both parties are guilty of a marital offense. The historical basis for this doctrine stems from such equity maxims as "One who seeks equity must do equity" and "One must come to equity with clean hands." Today, No-Fault Divorce provisions in many states have reduced the necessity to establish guilt in order to obtain a divorce, and thus Recrimination In Divorce is on the way out.

RED BERETS (Magnificent 13). A self-appointed group of private citizen vigilantes without any official law-enforcement powers who patrol the subways of New York City, especially the Mugger's Express which runs from Woodlawn in the Bronx to Atlantic Avenue in Brooklyn, in an attempt to prevent crime.

RED BOOK. A collection of quotations and parables of Premier Mao Tse-tung extolling communism, which was revered by the Chinese during the life of their leader but fell into disuse upon his death.

RED BOOK DIRECTORY. Published annually by the American Bar Association, this volume contains the names and addresses of the more than 200,000 members of the Association, plus the names and addresses of all the Association's directors, officers, officials and section and committee chairpersons.

RED BRIGADES. See REVOLUTIONARY JUSTICE.

RED CROSS. An international relief organization, headquartered in Geneva, Switzerland, which has sponsored numerous treaties to protect human rights. It was established in the nineteenth century by a young Swiss citizen, Henry Durant, after he saw the wounded and dying strewn around the battlefield of Solferino, in Northern Italy. Since then the Red Cross has saved millions of lives. Today the International Committee of the Red Cross (I.C.R.C.) is particularly concerned with the fact that modern warfare may cause greater loss of life and injury amongst civilians—especially among children—than in the combatants' ranks. Some people have observed that it is less dangerous to don a uniform and carry arms than to continue to perform one's everyday tasks. A Swedish delegate at the 1977 Diplomatic Conference on the Development of International Humanitarian Law quoted the following figures in support of this position: in the First World War, the number of civilian casualties was 15 percent of the total death toll, in the Second World War, it was 50 percent, and in the Korean and Viet Nam Wars, this proportion rose to 60 and 70 percent, respectively.

RED CROSS LAWS. International treaties, such as the Geneva Convention of 1949, which provide humanitarian treatment for those subject to armed warfare, including prisoners of war, civilians and guerillas. The International Red Cross Society, based in Geneva, Switzerland, takes an active role in sponsoring and supervising such treaties.

REDEEMING SOCIAL VALUE TEST. Promulgated in 1966 by the Supreme Court to determine whether material was obscene. In *Memoirs v. Massachusetts*, 383 U.S. 413 (1966), the Court held the government could regulate the distribution of prurient material which affronted contemporary community standards relating to sexual matters if such material lacked redeeming social value. The Social Value Test proved difficult to apply, however, and in 1973, in *Miller v. California*, 413 U.S. 15 (1973), the Court revised the test for obscenity and explicitly rejected the Social Value Test of the *Memoirs* case.

RED HERRING PROSPECTUS. A preliminary prospectus which can be used to disseminate information before a final prospectus and related registration statement approved by the Securities and Exchange Commission become effective. It is so named because the prospectus must carry a special warning, printed in red ink, stating that the related registration statement has not yet become effective, that the information is subject to correction, and that the prospectus is not to be considered as an offer to sell to the public.

RED-LINING. The practice of refusing to issue fire, liability and other forms of property insurance on a building in an inner-city area, regardless of its physical condition, because the insurance company deems the ghetto neighborhood too risky. The term also describes geographical discrimination by banks in their money-lending policies. The term is derived from the alleged practice of drawing a red line on a map, figuratively if not literally, to surround the area which is the basis of the discrimination. This practice is often connected with racial discrimination because insurance companies and banks usually Red-Line neighborhoods which become racially mixed. The Federal Insurance Agency and the Department of Housing and Urban Development have held hearings to evidence their serious concern about Red-Lining, and federal and state laws ban the practice. The refusal of shortsighted or bigoted money lenders and insurance companies to do business with residents of depressed or decaying urban areas ensures the continuing decline of such areas. Green-Liners or Anti-Red-Liners are concerned citizens who fight the discriminatory practice in an attempt to encourage investment in blighted ghettos.

RED MASS. A traditional religious ceremony, celebrated in many Roman Catholic churches and attended by members of the bench and bar of all religious faiths at the opening of the judicial year in various countries throughout the world. Its purpose is to invoke God's blessing and guidance in the administration of Justice. The Red Mass was introduced in this country in the city of Washington in the 1920s and has been observed annually in October of each year, prior to the annual convening of the Supreme Court of the United States. It is now celebrated in many of our large cities. In Boston, where it has been carried on since 1941, under the sponsorship of the Boston College Law School, it has probably reached its greatest development. The precise origin of the Red Mass is obscured by its antiquity. The tradition goes back many centuries in Rome, Paris and London. From time immemorial it has officially opened the judicial year of the Roman Catholic Ecclesiastical Court called the Sacred Roman Rota. During the reign of Louis IX, Saint Louis of France, La Sainte Chapelle was designated as the proper setting for the service. This magnificent edifice was used but once during the year, and then only for the Red Mass. The custom in England began in the early Middle Ages and, even during crises such as World War II, English judges and lawyers of all religious faiths annually attended the Red Mass in Westminster Cathedral.

RED SQUARE. See WHITE HOUSE.

RED TAPE. Bureaucracy running rampant. For example, 87 different federal agencies regulate American business. The 4,400 different forms which must be completed and filed consume 143 million hours of executive and clerical time each year. In addition, the thousands of new restrictive regulations which are issued annually exceed 70,000 pages of print in the *Federal Register*. The only ones who profit from this unholy mess, obviously, are lawyers.

REDWOOD EMPLOYMENT PROTECTION PROGRAM. See R.E.P.P.

REED-BULLWINKLE ACTS OF 1948. A federal law which granted antitrust immunity to the trucking industry, thereby enabling these carriers to get together and fix freight rates.

REFUGEE ACT OF 1979. A proposed federal law which recognizes global chaos as a permanent phenomenon, and deals with the inevitable human tragedies on an orderly basis by providing for a normal annual admission to the United States of at least 50,000 refugees. The President also would be allowed to determine the number of special admissions necessary on humanitarian grounds.

REFUGEES INTERNATIONAL. A Tokyo-based organization created in 1979 to provide emergency relief in the form of food and housing until permanent homes can be found for the hundreds of thousands of innocent victims who are forced to leave their native land each year.

REGISTRATION STATEMENT. Document which an issuer of securities must file before conducting a full-fledged selling campaign pursuant to the Securities Act of 1933. (15 U.S.CA. §§ 77a-77aa (1933)). Unless expressly exempted under the Act, securities may not be offered or sold through the mails or through instrumentalities of foreign or interstate commerce until a 20-day "waiting period" after filing has elapsed. This bar applies not only to the issuing corporation, but also to underwriters for, and persons in control of, the corporation. When the securities are sold, a prospectus (containing some of the data in the filed statement) must be provided to each purchasor. Finally, the Act requires that the statement contain certain kinds of data, of which the following are illustrative: the names of the officers of the issuing business, its character, size, history and financial structure, underwriters' commissions, pending or threatened litigation, etc. In this regard, the purpose of the Act is to place upon the issuer the lightest possible burden consistent with disclosure of essential facts.

REGRESSIVE TAX. Ratio of tax liability to income. If income declines as tax increases, it is a regressive tax. Sales tax is often referred to as regressive because lower income families spend proportionately greater amounts of their income than higher income families, and thus pay proportionately greater sales taxes. In contrast, a progressive tax is one which takes a greater percent-

age of income as income rises, and in a proportional tax, the ratio between tax and income remains constant.

REGULATION M. A law passed by the Federal Reserve Board which regulates the domestic American money supply by requiring an American bank to keep a reserve of 4 percent on foreign funds loaned to customers in the United States.

REGULATION Z. Federal Truth in Lending Act of 1969 requirement of strict disclosure of the true annual percentage rate in credit transactions.

REHABILITATION ACT OF 1973. Intended to protect 50 million Americans, this federal law proclaims that no otherwise qualified handicapped individual shall, solely by reason of his handicap, be excluded from participation in, be denied the benefits of, or otherwise be subjected to discrimination under any program or activity receiving federal financial assistance.

REHABILITATIVE ALIMONY. See EQUITABLE REMEDY.

R.E.I.T. See REAL ESTATE INVESTMENT TRUST.

REJECTED COUNSEL. Coined by columnist William Safire, the term describes the White House staffer whose job is to go into the Oval Office in times of crisis and declare, "Mr. President—do the popular thing! Take the easy way!" The President then can say, "Some of my advisers have suggested that I do what is politically popular. I have rejected such counsel. . . ."

RELATIVELY LEAST DEVELOPED COUNTRIES (R.L.D.C.s). Those countries designated by the United Nations General Assembly in 1971 as meeting three criteria: per capita incomes of $100 or less in 1968; manufacturing shares in the Gross National Product of 10 percent or less in 1968, and literacy rates of 20 percent or less. Approximately thirty countries qualify as R.L.D.C.s.

RELATIVE RESPONSIBILITY STATUTES. Impose support duties on relatives based on the common law obligations of husbands to support their wives and parents to support their children. They originated with the Elizabethan Poor Law in 1601, providing that the father, grandfather, mother, grandmother and children of every old, blind, lame, impotent or poor person should maintain every such poor person according to the note assessed by a Justice of the Peace. The statutes today imposing support duties fall into two broad categories: those imposing general duties to support indigent persons upon named relatives; and those imposing a duty to pay to the state the cost of maintaining indigent persons being cared for in state institutions. The most significant aspect of these statutes is that they provide support duties outside the nuclear family.

RELEASE ON OWN RECOGNIZANCE. See R.O.R.

RELEVANT EVIDENCE. Evidence having a tendency to make the existence of a material fact more probable or less probable than it would be without the evidence. For example, if one driver sued another for damages caused by the latter's alleged failure to stop at a red light, evidence that the defendant's car was blue would be irrelevant, whereas evidence that the defendant was color blind would be highly relevant. No foolproof test can be applied to decide whether evidence is relevant. Rather, a judge must rely upon logic and experience in making the determination. Evidence which is relevant is ordinarily admissible at trial while irrelevant evidence is inadmissible. But, even relevant evidence may be inadmissible if its value is substantially outweighed by the chance that it may prejudice or confuse the jury, or if its admission would result in an undue waste of time. Relevant evidence which is excluded for such a reason is often said to be legally irrelevant while logically relevant.

REMAINDER INTEREST. A future interest that will become a present estate (if ever), in a person other than the grantor or his successors, immed-iately upon, and no sooner than, the natural expiration of a prior particular estate created by the same instrument.

REMAINDERPERSON. One who is entitled to the remainder interest in an estate in land.

REMAINDER VESTED SUBJECT TO TOTAL DEFEASANCE. A remainder interest given to one person that would go to another person upon the occurrence of a stated condition.

REMITTITUR DOCTRINE (Latin—it is sent back). Conditional order in which a plaintiff must agree to a specified reduction in damages awarded him, on penalty of retrial. Remittitur is generally ordered when a judge finds the jury verdict excessive, but wishes to avoid ordering a new trial. Similarly, Additur or Increscitur (add to or increase) may be ordered when damages are excessively inadequate. Additur was found in *Dimick v. Schiedt*, 293 U.S. 474 (1935), to be a violation of the Seventh Amendment, and therefore is not allowed in federal courts.

REMOTE CHECKING. An improper if not illegal practice by stock brokers and other firms of paying their customers located East of the Mississippi River with checks drawn on West coast banks and paying those located West of the Mississippi with checks drawn on East coast banks. The reason for this diverting diversion of course, is to prolong the use by a firm of a customer's funds.

REMOTE DISBURSEMENT. See REMOTE CHECKING.

REMOVAL OF ACTIONS. A procedure by which a defendant in a state court case can transfer the case to an appropriate United States District Court. The right to remove a case from state to federal court is statutory. The first provision for the right goes as far back as the Federal Judiciary Act of 1789, and the present removal statute is codified in 28 U.S.C. § 1441. There are two ways of removing a case from state to federal courts: first, by review in the United States Supreme Court after the state courts have made their final judgment; second, by transfer from a state court to a lower federal court for trial in the first instance. Since the first method is limited by the Supreme Court's discretionary review powers, the second is the more common way of getting into a federal court. In general, the removal procedure is available only in cases which originally might have been brought in a federal court. Assuming the proper jurisdictional requirements for federal court are met, a defendant can remove a case where the plaintiff's claim is based on federal law, but neither party can remove a case where federal law is set up as a defense to a non-federal claim by the plaintiff.

RENEGOTIATION BOARD. A watchdog federal agency which seeks the elimination of excessive profits on defense and space contracts and related subcontracts. This is accomplished through informal and non-adversary proceedings before the Board and its regional boards. Contractors not agreeing with Board determinations may petition the court of claims for redetermination. For years the military-industrial complex, for obvious reasons, has tried to put the Board out of business and finally succeeded in 1979.

RENT COLLECTORS. Hoodlums who engage in murder and mayhem in the illegal pursuit of the narcotics trade.

RENVOI DOCTRINE (French—reference back). The practice of referring to the law of another jurisdiction, including its Conflict of Law rules, which may refer the court in turn back to the law of the forum state. Renvoi may cause an infinite cross-reference between the laws of two jurisdictions. Most forum states avoid the problem by referring only to the substantive law of the other state and not to its conflicts rules. The problem with this solution is that results which often depend on selection of forum are not uniform.

REOPENING CLAUSE. A stipulation stating the time or circumstances under which negotiations on wages or other issues can be requested, prior to the ex-piration of the collective bargaining agreement.

REORGANIZATION ACT OF 1977. A law passed by Congress to enable President Carter to fulfill his campaign promise to make government more efficient by consolidating or combining agencies performing related functions. The first implementation was to re-align the Executive Office in the White House. The second was to create a new semi-independent organization called the International Communication Agency (I.C.A.) which took over the activities of the United States Information Agency and the Bureau of Educational and Cultural Affairs of the State Department.

REPLEVIN ACTION. An action to recover personal property which is wrongfully held by the defendant.

REPLY LETTER DOCTRINE (Solicited Reply Doctrine). A rule of evidence which permits a document to be authenticated when the proponent shows it was written in response to a communication sent to the author. A form of the reply letter doctrine is used to authenticate telephone conversations. If the proponent shows that he dialed the number of a particular person or entity and that he recognized the voice of the person answering the phone, or if the person answering identified himself as the individual or entity in question, the conversation will be admitted into evidence.

R.E.P.P. (Redwood Employment Protection Program). The most lavish financial dislocation program in American history. As a result of the addition of 48,000 acres of land to the Redwood National Park, and a cessation of all commercial activities, President Carter signed a law on March 27, 1978 which gave 1,500 loggers and mill workers an average annual salary for up to 5 years, at taxpayer's expense, while they looked for other jobs.

REPUBLICATION BY CODICIL. A will is republished and revalidated as of the date upon which a codicil is executed.

REPUBLICAN PARTY. See G.O.P.

REPUTATION EVIDENCE. See HEARSAY RULE.

REQUEST FOR PROPOSALS (R.F.P.). This term refers to the assembly of required documents (whether attached or inccrporated by reference) furnished prospective government procurement offerors for the purpose of submitting a proposal for the award of a negotiated contract. It is a solicitation package designed to furnish prospective offerors all information necessary to submit a proposal which will serve as the basis for negotiations. However, when the R.F.P. so states, the contracting agency reserves the right to award a contract based on initial offers received without any written or oral discussions with the offerors.

REQUEST FOR QUOTATIONS (R.F.Q.). This term refers to a solicitation package used in negotiated government contract procurement. Because it is a request only for information (quotes), responses thereto are not offers that the contracting agency may accept without some confirmation or discussion with offerors.

REQUIREMENTS CONTRACT. This type of contract provides for the satisfaction of all actual purchase requirements of specific supplies or services during a specified contract period.

RESALE PRICE MAINTENANCE. A contractual agreement between a seller, usually a manufacturer, and a buyer, usually a retailer, which establishes either a maximum or a minimum price for which the buyer can resell the product. For many years, the Miller-Tydings Act exempted from antitrust prohibitions such agreements for commodities bearing the names of their producer or distributor if resale price agreements were allowed by the state of sale. Many large national corporations, taking advantage of Fair Trade Laws were able to maintain high prices for their products. Such laws were banned in 1975 when Congress repealed the Miller-Tydings Act, and Resale

Price Maintenance Agreements are now considered Per Se violations of the Sherman (1890) and Clayton Acts (1914). The only remaining exception is where there is valid consignment of goods for resale to a genuine agent acting for the manufacturer.

RESCUE PACKAGES. Federal financial bailouts in the form of loan guarantees. For example, rescue packages were given to New York City in 1975 and 1978 ($1.65 billion) and the Chrysler Corporation in 1979 ($1.5 billion), conditioned on concessions made by the respective employees, unions and banks.

RESIDENCY LAW. See LYONS LAW.

RESIDUARY CLAUSE. The language in a trust arrangement which serves to dispose of whatever remains with respect to trust property after expenses, taxes and other trust distributions have been satisfied.

RESIDUARY LEGACY. A gift of the remaining estate after claims against the estate and specific, general or demonstrative legacies have been satisfied.

RESIDUARY LEGATEE. A person who receives the residue of an estate.

RESIDUARY TRUST. A trust arrangement which has as its principal trust property that which is left in the estate of a deceased settlor after expenses of administration are paid and distributions under the will are made.

RES IPSA LOQUITUR (Latin—the thing speaks for itself). A doctrine of tort law which allows the plaintiff to rely on circumstantial evidence to raise an inference of negligence. If he cannot come forward with proof of negligence, the plaintiff may avoid a directed verdict for the defendant by showing that (1) the injury in question generally results from negligence, and (2) the defendant was in sole control of the instrumentality which caused the injury. Although Res Ipsa establishes a Prima Facie case for negligence, the jury may still find for the defendant.

RES JUDICATA (Latin—the thing has been adjudicated). A common-law rule

445

which states that a final judgment in an action precludes the parties from any subsequent litigation on the same claim. Upon judgment for the plaintiff, the entire claim or cause of action which was the subject of the suit is said to merge in the judgment, extinguishing any further litigation of the claim. Similarly, judgment for the defendant is said to bar any subsequent suit on the same claim. The effect of merger and bar was often harsh at common law because the strict rules of pleading forced the plaintiff to select one form of action or theory of recovery, to the exclusion of all others. An improvident choice of form which led to defeat in court would forever bar the plaintiff from recovery. Modern pleading rules, such as in the Federal Rules of Civil Procedure, have ameliorated this problem by allowing liberal joinder of claims and theories in one action. Another aspect of res judicata is collateral estoppel. Under this principle, any issue in a suit which has been previously litigated in another suit by the same parties, and which the court or jury necessarily determined, is precluded from relitigation. The prior determination is res judicata in the subsequent suit; the parties are estopped from raising it anew. The principles of res judicata apply only as between the same parties and those in privity with them, except in those jurisdictions which follow the Bernhard Exception.

RESOURCE CENTER FOR CON-SUMERS OF LEGAL SERVICES. Founded in 1975, the Center is a foundation-funded coalition of the legal profession and its consumers, particularly labor unions. It seeks to improve the practice of law by reducing the cost and upgrading the quality of legal services. Its focus is largely on prepaid legal service plans.

RESOURCE CONSERVATION AND RECOVERY ACT. A federal law which places "cradle-to-grave" controls over the generation, transport, disposal and subsequent monitoring of hazardous wastes. Administrative Rules proposed in December, 1978, would require all producers of hazardous wastes to provide full information about the nature of the substances and keep track of the materials on a permanent basis. They would also require the disposal of the wastes by permit and only at a "secure site." The sites, designed to prescribed standards, would have to be monitored after disposal to insure their continued security. The Administrator of the Environmental Protection Agency said that the regulations, if promulgated, would cost industry a total of $750 million a year for full compliance. The federal, state and local governments would also have to spend an additional $30 million annually to administer and monitor the program.

R.E.S.P.A. (Real Estate Settlement Procedures Act of 1974). Enacted to prevent certain abuses such as kickbacks in the sale of real estate and to give home buyers more information about settlement costs. Regulation X of this Act requires lenders to provide borrowers with a good-faith estimate of closing costs at the time of the loan application.

RESPONSIBLE CONTRACTOR. In federal government contracting, to be eligible for contract award, a contractor, in general, must be responsible and submit a responsive (see Responsive Contractor) offer. The Defense Acquisition Regulation specified, for example, that a responsible contractor is one who has or can obtain "adequate financial resources;" is "able to comply with the required or proposed delivery schedule;" has "a satisfactory record of performance" and "integrity;" and is "otherwise qualified and eligible to receive an award under applicable laws and regulations. . . ."

RESPONSIVE CONTRACTOR. In federal government contracting, to be eligible for contract award, a contractor, in general, must be responsible and submit a responsive offer. The Defense Acquisition Regulation specifies, for example, that a responsive bid is one which complies in all material respects with the invitation for bids so that, both as to the method and timeliness of submission and as to the substance of any resulting contract, all bidders may stand on an equal footing.

RESTATEMENT OF LAW. A codification by scholars of the common law in a particular field, such as torts, property or contracts. The Restatements are often cited by Courts as authority for particular rulings.

RESTRAINT ON ALIENATION. See DEAD HAND CONTROL.

RESTRICTIVE COVENANTS. Private agreements which limit the use and enjoyment of real property, generally for the benefit of the community at large. Common restrictive covenants include prohibitions against use of property for commerce in residential areas, and minimum requirements for the size and style of a home in a particular neighborhood. Restrictive covenants differ from zoning ordinances in that the former are private agreements while the latter are public laws.

RESULTING TRUST. A trust arrangement brought about by law due to certain actions by parties in a financial or fiduciary relationship. Hence the intentions of the parties are irrelevant. A Resulting Trust may exist when the settlor of a private trust names a trustee but fails to name specific beneficiaries. Here the trust fails and the trust property is said to revert back to the settlor or to his successors.

RETAINED EARNINGS. See EARNED SURPLUS.

RETAINING LIEN. See ATTORNEY LIEN.

RETIRED SENIOR VOLUNTEER PROGRAM. See R.S.V.P.

RETURN-TO-WORK ORDER. A threat by a judge to hold a union or workers on strike in contempt of court, subject to fine and imprisonment, for refusal to return to work, when they are acting in violation of law.

REVENUE RULING. See TAX RULING.

REVERSE ALIMONY. Support payments by a woman to her former husband which may legally be imposed in all states.

REVERSE ANNUITY MORTGAGE. See R.A.M.

REVERSE DISCRIMINATION. See AFFIRMATIVE ACTION.

REVERSE F.O.I.A. Litigation brought to prevent federal agencies from disclosing documents under the Freedom of Information Act (F.O.I.A.). Until recently the focus of F.O.I.A. litigation has been, almost without exception, to compel the government to disclose information. Reverse F.O.I.A. cases, however, are brought by private individuals or corporations to prevent disclosure of confidential information which they have supplied to the government. For example, Company X may wish to obtain from the Federal Trade Commission financial data supplied by Company Y. Company Y, interested in protecting its competitive position, may sue the agency to prevent disclosure. The drafters of the F.O.I.A. did not include provisions to prevent disclosure, and the validity of Reverse F.O.I.A. actions has not as yet been tested in the Supreme Court.

REVERSE INCORPORATION. The proposition that any right possessed by an individual as against a state by virtue of the Constitution of the United States, is also possessed by that individual as against the government of the United States by virtue of the Fifth and Fourteenth Amendments.

REVERSE REVOLVING DOOR. The practice of private attorneys, particularly those in Washington, D.C., of going to work for the federal government. A proposed amendment to Canon 9 of the Code of Professional Responsibility would prohibit a new government attorney from handling matters involving a party who was a client of his former employer during his last year in private practice.

REVERSE SPLIT. Reduces the number of outstanding shares in a corporation. A reverse split is designed to increase the value of each share. In a reverse split, the recalled shares become treasury stock.

REVERSION OF AN ESTATE. Any future interest left in a transferor or his successor.

REVISED UNIFORM RECIPROCAL ENFORCEMENT OF SUPPORT ACT. See R.U.R.E.S.A.

REVOCABLE TRUST ARRANGE-MENT. A trust arrangement in which the trust settlor has reserved the right to terminate the trust arrangement as he sees fit, or to designate another party as having the same authority.

REVOLVING DOOR. (1) Used to describe criminals who are sent right back to jail for committing another crime soon after their release from prison. (2) What Washington lawyers go through as they pass back and forth between private practice and government. In 1978 Congress passed a new law which provides that for two years after leaving office, former high-ranking federal bureaucrats may not "aid, assist, counsel, advise or aid in representing" anyone on any governmental matter that they had responsibility for in office. And for one year, those ex-officials can have virtually no contact with their former agencies at all. Penalties range up to a $10,000 fine and two years in prison, and the ex-bureaucrat and his new employer can be blacklisted from further dealings with the government.

REVOLVING DOOR CRIMINAL PROSECUTIONS. Periodic punishment of criminals who commit victimless crimes such as prostitution, gambling or public drunkenness. The accused pay their fines and are back in court the following week.

REYNOLDS v. SIMS. See LEGISLATIVE REAPPORTIONMENT.

R.F.P. See REQUEST FOR PROPOSALS.

R.F.Q. See REQUESTS FOR QUOTATIONS.

RICHARD ROE (JANE DOE; JOHN DOE). A fictitious name used in legal documents since the fourteenth century, often to protect the name of an actual witness. More recently, the name has been used typically to protect the identity of a defendant in a lawsuit.

RICHARDSON, ELLIOT. Harvard-educated Boston lawyer who has held more different high-level governmental positions than any previous American: Secretary of the Departments of Commerce, of Defense and of Health, Education and Welfare; Attorney-General; Director of The Central Intelligence Agency; Ambassador to the United Kingdom; and Ambassador-at-Large in charge of the Seventh Law of the Sea Conference in Geneva in 1978. Rather than obey President Nixon's order to discharge Watergate Special Prosecutor Archibald Cox, Richardson resigned as Attorney General.

RICHARD III SOCIETY. An informal association of 2,000 (including 650 Americans) who think that the last Yorkist King of England, who was killed and succeeded by Henry VII, was a Tudor conspiracy victim of the Big Lie technique at the hand of Shakespeare, contending that Shakespeare libelously wrote that Richard III was a liar, a cheat and a murderer who usurped the Crown of Great Britain, they seek to vindicate Richard's good name and restore him to his proper role in history.

R.I.C.O. (Racketeer Influenced and Corrupt Organization's Law). An obscure 1970 federal statute, originally designed to combat organized crime and rarely used until 1975. It has become a leading tool for prosecutions against businessmen, doctors, labor union leaders, government officials and others charged with white-collar crimes. It has significantly expanded federal law-enforcement powers. The wider use of the law is part of a move by federal prosecutors away from the traditional, narrow definition of "organized crime" toward a broader designation that takes account as well of crooked business executives and other white-collar offenders. The statute broadly prohibits "Racketeering Activities" which it defines as at least two violations of any of thirty-two separate types of federal or state crimes. The law also prohibits any person from using the proceeds of racketeering activity in any enterprise or organization and subjects illegal gains to possible forfeiture.

RIDER PROVISION. A law which is unlikely to be passed and is consequently attached to a more popular bill on which it can "ride" through the legislature. Such provisions are often attached to appropriation measures. Almost all the state governors can defeat rider provisions by exercising their item veto power. The President does not have such a veto power although many constitutional amendments have been introduced to give him one.

RIGHT OF ENTRY. The future interest a transferor retains in real property when he attaches a condition subsequent to the transfer.

RIGHT ON RED. Municipal ordinances which allow drivers to turn right in intersections when they come to a red light, if they come to a full stop and the road is clear, in order to expedite the free flow of traffic.

RIGHT TO CONFRONTATION. Guaranteed by the Sixth Amendment to the United States Constitution, which states that "In all criminal prosecutions, the accused shall enjoy the right . . . to be confronted with the witnesses against him." Like the Hearsay Rule, though not co-extensive with it, the Right to Confrontation insures the accuracy of the trial process by subjecting prosecution witnesses to cross-examination by the defendant and the critical eye of the jury. The Right to Confrontation, however, is not an absolute. Thus, a disorderly defendant may be excluded from the courtroom.

RIGHT TO COUNSEL. Guaranteed by the Sixth Amendment to the United States Constitution, which provides that "in all criminal prosecutions, the ac-

cused shall enjoy the right . . . to have the Assistance of Counsel for his defense." If the defendant faced with a possible jail term cannot afford an attorney, the state must provide him with one. An indigent defendant may be required, however, to reimburse the state for the cost of his defense if he later becomes financially able to pay. The Right to Counsel is triggered by the initiation of adversary judicial proceedings against a defendant. Before such proceedings are commenced, no right to an attorney obtains. For instance, one who is subject to questioning by a grand jury or an investigation by the police has no Sixth Amendment Right To Counsel. Once the criminal prosecution has begun, however, the accused has a Right To Counsel during every critical stage of the proceeding. A "critical stage" is a stage where the absence of counsel might prejudice the defendant. The appointment of counsel must be more than a formality. Unless counsel provides "effective" assistance, the Sixth Amendment guarantee is not satisfied.

RIGHT-TO-DIE LAW (Natural Death Law). First enacted by California in 1977, and later adopted by a dozen other states, this legislation allows a person to fill out a "Directive to Physicians," which becomes valid when signed by two adult witnesses. The form provides that if the person ever suffers from an incurable disease or injury, diagnosed as terminal by at least two physicians, the patient's life will not be artificially prolonged by medical procedures or equipment. Some critics of the law claim that it will open the door to legalized mercy killings. The California Medical Association reported that more than 100,000 Right-To-Die forms were distributed in 1977. A sampling of 100 doctors who had ordered 11,000 forms revealed they had actually been used in only 67 cases in 1977.

RIGHT-TO-KILL (Excuse to Kill). Name given by courts to the successful defense asserted by a battered wife (or girl friend), in a criminal trial, who killed her husband (or boy friend) after having been the victim of years of physical and emotional abuse, on the grounds of self-defense or temporary insanity.

RIGHT-TO-LIFE AMENDMENTS. Proposed amendments to the Constitution which would overrule the 1973 Supreme Court decision in *Roe v. Wade*, 402 U.S. 941 (1973), which held that a woman has the unlimited constitutional right to an abortion during the first trimester of her pregnancy. The proposals, which have not been well received by Congress, are typified by the following: "With respect to the Right Of Life guaranteed in this Constitution, every human being, subject to the jurisdiction of the United States, or of any State, shall be deemed, from the moment of fertilization, to be a person and entitled to the Right To Life." Opposed to the Right-To-Lifers is the National Abortion Rights Action League (N.A.R.A.L.), which engages in pro-choice activities. N.A.R.A.L. represents those who believe women must have a right to choose whether or not to bear a child, yet emphasize that abortion should only be used as a last resort contraceptive measure.

RIGHT TO PAYMENT OF PATIENT-WORKER. According to the 1966 amendments to the Fair Labor Standard Act as interpreted in *Souder v. Brennan*, 367 F. Supp. 808 (1973), if an institution derives any consequential economic benefit from the work, patient-workers must be paid the minimum wage or an amount commensurate with that paid non-patient-workers. Under a Work Activities Center Certificate, the hospital may pay as low as 25 percent of the minimum wage if such a center provides work activities only for patients whose impairment is so severe as to render their productive capacity inconsequential. While vindication of this right has resulted in an economic benefit for some patients, patient positions at other institutions were simply eliminated due to a lack of funds, thereby depriving the patient of some way to pass the time and a chance to make a little money.

RIGHT TO REFUSE TREATMENT (Right Against Treatment). Privilege of an involuntarily committed mental patient to avoid certain forms of treatment. Generally, hospital administrators and doctors have the legal authority and responsibility to treat a patient in what they consider to be an appropriate manner. However, they are limited by the possibility that the prescribed treatment may harm the individual patient, such as allergic reaction to a drug, that the particular treatment may have irreversible side-effects, or that the patient may have religious or ethical considerations concerning a type of therapy. Patients have a legal right to refuse coercive techniques such as electroshock therapy (E.C.T.) and aversive conditioning, as well as experimental techniques such as psychosurgery, where electronic probes are inserted into particular areas of the brain associated with a given type of functioning. A more complicated and as yet undecided question concerns the use of psychotropic medications, particularly Thorazine. While the drug is somewhat effective in its anti-psychotic purpose, it is subject to abuse by staff as a chemical control device. Under its influence patients can become drowsy, lethargic, and confused. Serious neurological side effects can also result. Since the size of dosage controls the drug's effect, and since appropriate amounts differ from patient to patient, the courts have been reluctant to second guess therapists by giving patients the right to reject this form of treatment.

RIGHT-TO-WORK LAWS. State statutes which make unlawful labor-management agreements that require membership or non-membership in a union as a condition of obtaining or retaining employment. These statutes were first enacted by Arkansas and Florida in 1944 and thereafter by other state legislatures, primarily in the South and Midwest. Right-To-Work Laws seem to be designed not only to protect the employees' freedom of choice but also to attract new business with the lower wage scales resulting from the absence of unions.

RING OF THE FISHERMAN. The Papal Seal of the Roman Catholic Church which is used to validate official documents. It is destroyed immediately on the death of the Pope to prevent forgeries.

RIOT INSURANCE. Passed after the wave of urban riots and disorders in 1968, this federal program provides for the government to share with private insurers the cost of coverage in high-risk areas.

RIO TREATY (1947) (The Inter-American Treaty of Reciprocal Assistance). A mutual defense agreement among twenty-one American republics. With the growth of Cuba's communist government, the Rio Treaty has recently assumed new significance. The United States has led a campaign to make internal revolution a concern of all Rio Treaty countries.

RIPARIAN RIGHTS. The privileges of owners of real property on the banks of water.

RIPENESS DOCTRINE. A principle which allows a federal court, notably the Supreme Court, to refuse to entertain a suit on the grounds that the case is not yet ripe for judicial consideration, and thus no present case or controversy exists to support the exercise of federal jurisdiction. The Ripeness Doctrine is closely allied with the notion of justiciability, and has been applied principally in cases where a declaratory judgment of the rights and liabilities of the parties has been requested. Although there are few cases on ripeness, two general criteria determine whether a case is ripe for review: first, whether the issues presented are appropriate for judicial consideration, and, second, what the hardship to the parties will be if judicial review is denied.

RISK DISCLOSURE STATEMENT. A document which must be signed by an investor and deposited with a broker before they may legally engage in the purchase and sale of speculative securities known as commodity futures. Sample language in this publication would include the following: (1) You may sustain a total loss of the initial funds and any additional funds that you may deposit with your broker; (2) Under certain market conditions, you may find it difficult or impossible to liquidate a position; (3) This brief statement cannot, of course, disclose all the risks.

R.L.D.C.s. See RELATIVELY LEAST DEVELOPED COUNTRIES.

ROADBLOCK CHECK. See RANDOM OR SPOT CHECK.

ROAD LAW. When traffic halts on a four-lane superhighway, cars in the other lanes move while those in your lane stay glued to the road. By Alfred Sheinwold, in *The New York Post*, March 8, 1972.

ROADLESS AREA REVIEW AND EVALUATION. A report submitted by the Secretary of Agriculture to the President in January, 1978, identifying the 62 million acres of potential wilderness in the 187 million acres in the national forests within each of the 50 states, except Hawaii, and then recommending which sections should be kept forever wild; which should be put to regular national forest uses—including timber cutting, oil development, livestock grazing, mining and recreation—and which should be given further study.

ROBERT'S RULES OF ORDER. Originally the *Pocket Manual of Rules of Order for Deliberative Assemblies* by then Major (later General) Henry M. Robert, the publisher shortened the title when it was first printed in 1876. The Rules basically are an adaptation of the Rules of Practice used by the House of Representatives and were intended to be used by the average society or organization. Major Robert was an engineering officer in the army. While on leave in 1863 to recover from tropical fever, he became interested in procedure when asked to preside over meetings. He and his wife later moved to San Francisco, where he joined numerous organizations and felt the need for uniform rules to replace the regional rules that new settlers in San Francisco had brought with them. He did not compile a comprehensive volume, however, until a severe winter stranded him in Milwaukee, making engineering work impossible. Robert's predecessors date to Germanic tribes who met to make "bye-laws" for their villages. Such meetings were called "moots" and were carried over into Anglo-Saxon England. By the late 16th century, Parliamentary procedure had evolved. The colonists adopted similar procedures in their state legislature, ultimately leading to Thomas Jefferson's codification of the first procedural manual while he was Vice-President presiding over the Senate.

ROCKEFELLER DRUG LAW. A tough anti-narcotic statute enacted in 1973 by New York and upheld as constitutional by the Supreme Court which commands a mandatory life imprisonment for first-felony offenders of the New York drug laws.

ROE v. WADE (402 U.S. 941 (1973)). A landmark 7 to 2 decision of the United States Supreme Court, which struck down as unconstitutional state criminal laws prohibiting abortion. The Court stated that laws which except from criminality only abortions aimed at saving the life of the mother are violative of the Due Process Clause of the Fourteenth Amendment and an unwarranted invasion of a woman's constitutional right of privacy, which it found to include her decision to terminate her pregnancy. However, the Court held that this right was not absolute so as to entitle a woman to terminate her pregnancy at whatever time, in whatever way, and for whatever reason she chooses, but that the state has a legitimate interest in protecting both the pregnant woman's health and the potentiality of human life. The state may justify its regulation when it has a compelling interest. In addressing this point, the Court further stated that the compelling point as regards the mother's health is at approximately the end of the first trimester (three months) of the pregnancy. Thus, the state may not interfere prior to this point with a decision made by a patient and her physician to terminate a pregnancy. After this point, the state may regulate the abortion procedure as it relates to the health of the pregnant woman, such as the qualifications of those performing abortions and the facilities in which the procedure may be performed. As regards the state's interest in the potentiality of human life, the Court held that the compelling point is at viability, when the fetus is capable of sustaining full life outside the womb. At this point, approximately six months, the state may prohibit abortion except when necessary to protect the life or health of the mother. The decision in *Roe v. Wade* has had a profound effect upon the incidence of abortion in the United States and has served as the impetus for the Right-To-Life and the Anti-Abortion Movements.

ROGATIO TESTIUM (Latin—a witness in Roman law). The request by a person making a non-cupative will that a person bear witness to the will. The Rogatio Testium is an absolute requirement for the admission to probate of a nuncupative will. No particular form or words need be used, but the testator must convey his desire that those present bear witness to his will.

ROGOVIN REPORT (1980). A report submitted to the Nuclear Regulatory Commission (N.R.C.) on the accident at the Three Mile Island reactor in Pennsylvania. It concluded that the N.R.C. as currently organized is incapable of managing an adequate nuclear safety program to ensure the public health and safety. It was prepared at the request of the Regulatory Commission by an independent investigative team headed by Mitchell Rogovin, a Washington lawyer.

ROLL-BACKS. See GIVE-BACKS.

ROLL OF ATTORNEYS. Upon admission to practice law, a lawyer's name is inscribed upon the state's Roll of Attorneys. This roll, usually maintained by the clerk of the state's highest court, establishes the record that a lawyer is licensed to practice law within the state.

ROLLOVER CONTRIBUTIONS. Intended to serve the needs of those who leave jobs where they have accrued tax-sheltered retirement benefits and sign on with employers that do not offer retirement plans. As a rule, they receive one-time payments in settlement of their vested interests. Normally, these sums would be immediately subject to taxation at ordinary-income rates. But under the rollover provisions of I.R.A. law, such individuals can continue their tax deferral by putting all the money they receive into an Individual Retirement Account. While there are no limits on the amounts that can be rolled over into new accounts, you have to make the rollover contribution within 60 days of the time you receive your lump-sum settlement. The rollover contribution also must represent the entire amount received from the retirement plan, minus any funds you may have contributed to the plan on your own over the years. A rollover contribution cannot be made to an existing I.R.A. and rollovers between two I.R.A.s may be made only once every three years. The Internal Revenue Service subjects excessive I.R.A. contributions to an excise tax of 6 percent annually.

ROLLOVER PLAN. A method of allowing an employee who has received a sum of money from an employer from a pension or profit-sharing program paid for by an employer to invest the money and to postpone the payment of any income tax until the employee actually receives the money.

ROMAN CURIA. See CURIA ROMANA.

ROMAN LAW. See JUSTINIAN CODE.

ROME CONVENTION OF 1952. Convention which addresses damages caused to persons by foreign airplanes. The Convention adopts the principle of absolute liability on the party operating an airplane, provides for compulsory recognition and execution of foreign judgments and limits the compensation that can be awarded to an injured party. The Convention was ratified by twenty-seven countries as of 1976.

R.O.R. (Release On Own Recognizance). Pre-trial release of a criminal defendant without bail, merely on his own promise to reappear for trial.

ROSCOE POUND AMERICAN TRIAL LAWYERS FOUNDATION. Founded in 1956 and named in honor of the late great dean of Harvard Law School, the Lawyers Foundation conducts research and supports members of the bar who seek to improve the adversary process. It also cooperates with the Department of Justice in the distribution of law-enforcement educational materials.

ROSENBERG CASE. In 1953 Julius Rosenberg and his wife Ethel were executed after having been convicted of Conspiracy to Commit Treason. Some critics say that they were the first martyrs of American Fascism and victims of the policies of Senator Joseph McCarthy and the Cold War. The only American civilians ever executed for espionage, the Rosenberg's execution had been stayed three times to permit appeals, all of which were unsuccessful. Mrs. Rosenberg's brother testified that his sister and brother-in-law recruited him to steal information on atomic bomb secrets while he was an Army sergeant. Other evidence alleged that the Rosenbergs turned over such information to the Soviet vice consul. In June, 1978, the Department of Justice agreed to pay the Rosenberg sons $195,000 in legal fees incurred in their lengthy dispute with the federal government in their attempt to prove the innocence of their parents.

ROSSELL SNAP-BACK EFFECT. See WHITE FLIGHT.

ROTA COURT (Latin—wheel or circle). Oldest religious Court in which the Pope of the Roman Catholic Church exercises his sovereign power under canon law. The Court derives its name from the round table (rota) at which the judges sit. An international tribunal, the Rota consists of ten judges or Auditores, all of whom are priests with doctorate degrees in canon and civil law, appointed by the Pope. The presiding officer is the Rotal Dean. Only those whose names are inscribed on the Roll of Rotal Advocates may argue cases before the Rota. Admission to the Roll requires a doctorate degree in canon law, successful completion of a three-year course in rotal law, and a final examination conducted by the Rota itself. The Rota is governed by precedent and its first published volume of decisions dates from 1374. When Henry VIII wished to dissolve his marriage to Catharine of Aragon in order to marry Anne Boleyn, the Rota rejected his plea on the ground that even the King was subject to its law.

ROTTEN BOROUGH. An election district which has fewer voters than any other district, and hence, each inhabitant's vote in a rotten borough has greater weight than his fellow citizens' votes in other districts.

ROUGES LIST. See MARINE SAFETY INFORMATION SYSTEM.

R.O.W.S. (Relocation Out Of Washington Study). Pentagon study of decentralization, to move many programs and offices from the Washington, D.C. area to other areas of the country. The decentralization movement is based, in part, on the feeling that too many federal jobs, cushioned from economic reality by the guaranteed federal payroll, insulate Washington, D.C. from the rest of the nation's economic problems.

ROYAL COMMISSION. A group of government officials and lay experts appointed by the Crown to make an investigative study of an important current issue and make a report with recommendations for implementation. An example is the Wolfenden Report (1957) which dealt with changes in the sex laws. Ten years after publication of the Wolfenden Report, Parliament repealed all laws proscribing homosexual acts between consenting adults—except members of the merchant-marine onboard ship.

ROZELLE RULE. Named after Pete Rozelle, the National Football League Commissioner. It states that once a pro-

fessional player has been signed by one team, no other team may sign that player without compensating the original team. This process begins with the player draft which allows each League club to select prospective players. Once a player is drafted, no other club may negotiate with him without the consent of the selecting team. If the two clubs cannot agree on a player's status, the Commissioner resolves the issue. The Rule was articulated in a 1976 federal case, *Mackey v. National Football League*, 543 F.2d 606 (8th Cir. 1976).

R.S.V.P. (Retired Senior Volunteer Program). A federal agency whose purpose is to create a variety of meaningful volunteer service opportunities so that persons of retirement age may participate more fully in the life of their communities. R.S.V.P. projects are planned, organized, and operated at the local level. They are developed under the auspices of an established organization able to generate local financial support. Although Volunteers must be at least 60 years of age, and must serve on a regular basis, there are no income or educational requirements. R.S.V.P.s perform every kind of service according to preferences and needs, working in a variety of settings, including courts, schools, parks, libraries and museums, day-care centers, hospitals, nursing homes, economic development agencies, and other community service outlets.

RUBBER CHECK. A check which bounces. Because of insufficient funds, the check is returned to the payee, who is out of pocket.

RUBY, JACK. See WARREN COMMISSION REPORT.

RUCKELSHAUS, WILLIAM. See SATURDAY NIGHT MASSACRE.

RULE AGAINST PERPETUITIES. See DEAD HAND CONTROL.

RULE IN SHELLEY'S CASE. Ancient technical rule from English common law which addresses the situation in which land is left "To *A* for life, and on *A*'s death to his heirs at law." The application of the Rule did not recognize the remainder interest in *A*'s heirs, but granted to *A* a fee simple in merging *A*'s life estate with the remainder in fee. The Rule in Shelley's Case has been rejected in most jurisdictions, which now handle the above conveyance by granting *A*'s heirs a contingent remainder and a reversion to the transferor.

RULE NISI (Latin—rule to show cause). A court order to show cause why a particular relief should not be granted.

RULE OF ADMINISTRATIVE CONVENIENCE. In a class gift case, when a member of the class can demand ascertainment of his share, the class closes as a matter of administrative efficiency.

RULE OF DESTRUCTABILITY OF CONTINGENT REMAINDERS. A remainder will be destroyed unless it vests at or before the termination of all estates prior to it in possession.

RULE OF 80. A proposal of the Federal Courts Improvement Act of 1979 to allow the retirement or senior status to be effectuated in any case where the age of a federal judge, when added to his years of continuous service, adds up to 80 or more. The current law requires that in order for a federal judge to retire or assume senior status, he or she must be at least 70 years of age and have served a minimum of ten years as a federal judge. The service requirement is retained in the proposal.

RULE OF FOUR. An informal working rule in the Supreme Court requiring the votes of only four of the nine Justices to grant a writ of certiorari or to hear an appeal. Under this practice, if four Justices find that a question of general importance is raised in a case, certiorari is granted or an appeal considered, despite the contrary views of the other five members of the court. The Rule of Four has been a well-settled policy since the expansion of discretionary review in the Judges Bill of 1925.

RULE OF LAW. A principle of American democracy, inherited from the English common law, emphasizing the supremacy of the legal system over the discretionary power of public officials; popularly characterized a government of law and not of men. Generally invoked to shield private parties from arbitrary official actions.

RULE OF MERGER (Merger Rule). A criminal law rule designed to prevent double jeopardy. Under a rule of merger, a lesser offense is merged into a more serious offense. Thus, a defendant may not be convicted for both offenses nor retried for one offense if acquitted on the other.

RULE OF REASON. The standard by which activities are judged in determining whether or not the Sherman Act (1890) has been violated. Section One of that Act reads: "Every contract, combination in the form of trust or otherwise, or conspiracy in restraint of trade or commerce . . . is hereby declared illegal. . . ." If literally applied, Section One would bar almost every business arrangement concerning trade or commerce. Thus, the Supreme Court has read a Rule of Reason into the Act, adopting as its base the common law meaning of the term Restraint of Trade. Only those contracts or agreements which harm the public interest by unduly restricting competition are banned. The Rule received its classic formulation in *Standard Oil Co. of New Jersey v. United States,* 221 U.S. 1 (1911), in which the great Standard Oil trust was partially disassembled. It is important to note that the test does not allow restraints that are reasonable in the sense that the public is somehow better off because of the anti-competitive conduct, but allows only behavior which does not unduly hamper the competitive process. Under this reading, a covenant not to compete made by the seller of a business to a buyer, would not be deemed an unreasonable restraint of trade, but an agreement among competitors to fix the price of their product, no matter how fair, would violate the Sherman Act.

RULES COMMITTEE. A standing committee of the House of Representatives with power to enact special rules for the consideration of particular bills. Because the Rules Committee serves as a channeling device for other committee bills, its members have great discretion and awesome power in deciding which bills actually reach the House floor for consideration.

RULES OF DECISION ACT (Section 34 of the Federal Judiciary Act of 1789). Provides that "the Laws of the several States, except where the Constitution, treaties or Statutes of the United States shall otherwise provide, shall be regarded as Rules of Decision in trials at Common Law in the Courts of the United States in cases where they apply." The statute has remained basically unchanged to this day, yet few issues in the field of federal jurisprudence have been more difficult than determining the meaning of this law. The principal question has been whether state court decisions are "Laws of the several States" within the meaning of the statute, and thus of controlling effect in diversity of citizenship cases in the federal courts. The first attempt at an answer was in *Swift v. Tyson*, 41 U.S. 1 (1842), where the Supreme Court found in the negative, and held that federal courts in diversity cases were free to make their own rules of federal law. However, the Court reversed itself in *Erie R.R. Co. v. Tompkins*, 304 U.S. 64 (1938). The Erie Doctrine holds that in most such cases, the federal courts are bound to apply state and not federal law.

RULES OF THE ROAD. Govern the safety and navigation of vessels, with primary emphasis upon the prevention of collisions. Rules of the Road have the force and effect of law, and their violation may be punished as a crime. There are several sets of regulations which comprise the Rules of the Road. In 1960, the United States, along with other leading maritime nations, ratified the International Convention for Safety of Life at Sea. This Convention constitutes a basic code of maritime law and was subsequently adopted by the legislative bodies of the ratifying nations as the Regulations for Preventing Collisions at Sea. These regulations have come to be known as the International Rules of the Road. The purpose of the International Rules was to establish a uniform system of regulations which would be obligatory throughout the world. As adopted by Congress through enabling legislation, observance of the International Rules of the Road is required of all vessels of the United States, both public and private, upon the high seas and in connected waters navigable by seagoing vessels, except where navigation on such waters is regulated by special rules. Excepted by the United States from the general application of the International Rules of the Road are vessels navigating the harbors, rivers, and other inland waters of the United States. To these, special rules promulgated by the Coast Guard apply. Included within this special group are the Pilot Rules for the Great Lakes, also known as the Great Lakes Rules of the Road, applicable to navigation upon the Great Lakes and their connecting and tributary waters as far east as Montreal; the Pilot Rules for Western Rivers, also known as the Western Rivers Rules of the Road, applicable to navigation upon the Red River of the North, the Mississippi River and its tributaries above the Huey P. Long Bridge, and that part of the Atchafalaya River above its junction with the Palquemine-Morgan City alternate waterway; and the Pilot Rules for Inland Waters, also known as the Inland Rules of the Road, applicable to navigation upon all other harbors, rivers, and inland waters of the United States.

RULE 10B-5 (Anti-Fraud Rule). Prohibits any person, directly or indirectly, from engaging in any manipulative or deceptive device or contrivance, including any type of fraud or deceit, in connection with the purpose or sale of any security, whether listed or not on any securities exchange, in interstate commerce, through the national securities exchange, through the mails or by the use of any means or instrumentality of interstate commerce. Violations create a civil liability and any harmed person may sue for damages in the appropriate federal court. Rule 10B-5 was promulgated under section 10(b) of the Securities Exchange Act of 1934 and was initially called Rule X-10B-5.

RUMP PARLIAMENT. The remnant of Parliament after the expulsion of the majority of its members by the army of Oliver Cromwell under the command of Colonel Thomas Pride in 1648 (Pride's Purge), which occurred during the Second Civil War of England. The High Court of Justice, set up by the Rump Parliament, tried and convicted King Charles I for treason. After beheading Charles I on January 30, 1649, the Rump Parliament set up the republic known as the Commonwealth, which was governed by the Rump Parliament without the House of Lords and by an Executive Council of State. This Parliament was forcibly dissolved by Cromwell on April 20, 1653 for opposing certain demands of the army. It was reinstated twice thereafter, but only for brief periods of time. The Restoration of Charles II in 1660 ended the Rump Parliament forever.

RUNAWAY SHOP. An anti-union tactic by an employer involving a transfer or threat to transfer a plant to another location to demonstrate economic power over employees. The tactic was generally held to be an unfair labor practice by the National Labor Relations Board prior to 1965. However, the Supreme Court's decision in *Textile Workers Union v. Darlington Co.*, 380 U.S. 263 (1965), severely limited the N.L.R.B.'s discretion to enjoin the use of the tactic by requiring a specific showing that the employer purposely designed the plant shutdown to chill unionism.

RUNNING-DOWN CLAUSE. See R.D.C.

RUNNING UP THE METER (Churning). Legal research and motions that have marginal, if any, relevance or no usefulness at all but add to billable hours resulting in a high unearned fee to be paid by the client.

R.U.R.E.S.A. (Revised Uniform Reciprocal Enforcement of Support Act). A law found in every state to protect an abandoned spouse, who is usually a mother. The victim at no cost has the local prosecutor sue the runaway. If a case for non-support is proven, the runaway spouse in the other state must pay the support money to the local court clerk where he lives. It is then forwarded to the other court clerk, who in turn pays the abandoned spouse. The catch, of course, is to locate the runaway.

RUSSIAN CARD. The ability of the capitalistic Republic of China on Taiwan to blackmail the United States and the Communist People's Republic of China, separately or jointly, by threatening to have closer military, economic and cultural ties with the U.S.S.R.

RUSSIAN REFUSENIKS. Soviet Jews, especially scientists, seeking to immigrate to Israel who are unmercifully harassed when they are denied permission to leave the Communist Paradise on the excuse that their work involved state secrets, which is a gross violation of the Helsinki Agreement Russian guarantee of the protection of human rights.

RUSTICATION POLICY. Unpopular mandatory program of the People's Republic of China (Mainland Communist China) from 1963-1978 to force every urban high school graduate to leave the cities and settle down in rural areas. Those who refused to leave or returned from the countryside were treated as criminals and denied indispensable privileges such as ration cards.

RUTLEDGE, JOHN. The man who almost became Chief Justice of the United States. Nominated by President John Adams, he presided over two cases in the Supreme Court before being rejected for the post by the Senate in a vote of 14 to 10. The adverse action was probably based on an incendiary speech he had made against a treaty with Great Britain, which had been negotiated by John Jay, the outgoing and first Chief Justice. Rutledge had been a judge in South Carolina and he subsequently retired as a recluse there until his death in 1800. An interesting footnote is that Rutledge was one of the original Justices appointed to the Supreme Court in 1789 by President Washington, but he resigned in 1791 before the Court had heard its first case.

S

S.A. (French—Société Anonyme). A corporation under civil law.

SABBATH BREAKING LAWS. See BLUE LAWS.

SACCO-VANZETTI CASE. Two Italian anarchist immigrants, the shoe maker, Nicola Sacco, and the fish peddler, Bartolomeo Vanzetti, were charged with the murder of a paymaster and guard in Massachusetts in 1920. Despite their plea of innocence, both were executed on January 31, 1928. The case became an international cause célèbre. Some critics say it was a travesty of American Justice. Professor Felix Frankfurter of Harvard Law School, subsequently Justice of the Supreme Court of the United States, claimed that they had not had a fair trial. Many citizens felt Sacco and Vanzetti were persecuted for their alien political beliefs.

SACRED COLLEGE OF CARDINALS. The 100 or more highest-ranking governing members (Cardinals) of the Roman Catholic Church who are appointed by the Pope and in turn choose his successor in the oldest election in the world in a secret ceremony known as a Papal Enclave.

SACRED ROMAN ROTA. See ROTA COURT.

SACRED ROTA. A religious Canon Law court of last resort in Rome which has the power to dissolve a Roman Catholic marriage. Of the 205 cases heard in 1978, from the 750 million Catholics in the world, 139 annulments were granted and 66 were denied.

SAFE HARBOR RULE. A ship has the legal right to enter the territory of a foreign country freely when it is necessary for the safety of the vessel or persons aboard and to leave the territory without hindrance once the conditions that have made the entry necessary have ceased to exist.

SAFE HOUSE. A refuge where a spy or refugee can be hidden from arrest.

SAFE PLACE STATUTES. State laws which require public agencies such as schools to provide employees with a safe place to work, and the public in general, a safe place to frequent.

SAFETY BOOK SLOWDOWN. Illegal action by workers who comply in overly strict fashion with all safety precautions to force an employer to meet their labor demands.

SAGEBRUSH REBELLION. A movement in the late seventies under the leadership of the Governors of Utah and Nevada to develop the thousands of acres owned by the federal government and to reduce, if not eliminate, the control exercised by Washington, D.C. over western land.

SAHEL CLUB. An association of the eight Northwest African countries located in or near the Sahara Desert which have been cursed by drought in recent years. They have banded together to coordinate the receipt of foreign aid to enable them to survive as viable sovereign nations. Their Gross National Product (G.N.P.), Per Capita Income (P.C.I.), and life expectancy are the lowest in the world. Their infant mortality and illiteracy rates are the highest in the world. There are 27 million Sahelians from 45 ethnic groups living in the eight countries of the Cape Verde Islands, Chad, Gambia, Mali, Mauritania, Niger, Senegal and Upper Volta.

SAINT IVO HÉLORY (1253-1303). A priest and a lawyer, he retired from secular life to devote his efforts to works of charity. To offer legal aid to the poor, he founded "con fraternities" which spread over France, Belgium, Brazil and Rome. He was canonized in 1347. His cult spread rapidly in Britanny, and he is the second Patron Saint of Britanny, Patron of Lawyers and Patron of the University of Nantes.

SAINT-SIMON SOCIETY. French followers of Claude Henri de Rouvroy Comte de Saint-Simon (1760-1825) who believed private property was the root of all evil. The Saint-Simonians wanted the state to be the sole inheritor of all property because they felt that through the laws of inheritance, the wealth of society went to those incompetent to use it for societal good.

S.A.L.T. See SOCIETY OF AMERICAN LAW TEACHERS.

S.A.L.T. (Strategic Arms Limitation Talks). The series of conferences, known as S.A.L.T. I, between the U.S.A. and the U.S.S.R. which culminated in 1972 in a Treaty limiting defensive strategic arms and an interim accord on offensive arms. The interim accord limited long-range missiles, allowed the United States to have 1,710 land-based and submarine missile launchers, and the Soviet Union to have 2,360. The accord, which excluded bombers, expired October 3, 1977, but both sides said they would abide by its provisions pending negotiation of the new Treaty. The 1972 Treaty on defensive systems allowed each side 200 antimissile launchers. The pact was amended in 1974 to cut the number to 100 each. A second round of strategic arms limitation talks (S.A.L.T. II) was concluded in 1979 after 7 years of negotiation. A third round of strategic arms limitation talks (S.A.L.T. III) began in 1979 and presumably will go on for years. But hopefully a nuclear holocaust will be avoided as long as negotiations and agreements continue to take place.

SAME SEX MARRIAGE. See HOMOSEXUAL MARRIAGE.

SANDER v. BRENNAN. See RIGHT TO PAYMENT OF PATIENT-WORKER.

SANGAMON VALLEY TELEVISION CORP. v. UNITED STATES. See EX PARTE CONTRACT.

SATURDAY NIGHT MASSACRE. The events of Saturday, October 20, 1973, which led to the resignation of Elliot Richardson, Attorney General of the United States and Deputy William Ruckelshaus when they refused to obey President Nixon who had ordered them to fire Harvard Law School Professor Archibald Cox, who was the Special Prosecutor in the Watergate investigation. Cox had been assured a free hand in his role which President Nixon sought to curtail in order to save his career. Cox was eventually fired by Solicitor General Robert Bork, a Yale Law School Professor, and replaced by Leon Jaworski, a Houston, Texas lawyer and former President of the American Bar Association. Jaworski performed so well he was subsequently appointed Special Prosecutor in the Korean bribery scandal.

SATURDAY NIGHT SPECIAL. (1) A .25 caliber hand gun manufactured by the Italian Company named Baretta. It was popularized as the favorite weapon of the fictional James Bond, Secret Agent 007 and is the type that was used to kill Robert Kennedy. It is condemned by gun control advocates because of its widespread use in crime, but the National Rifle Association lobby has successfully convinced Congress not to outlaw its manufacture, sale or possession. Some states strictly regulate its purchase, use, possession and sale; however, it is estimated that there are 50 million such hand guns in the United States today. (2) Takeover offer by one company to another which puts tremendous pressure on management to accept the offer. The technique is dubbed "Saturday Night Special" because it is like putting a gun to the company's head.

SAVE-OUR-BUCKS TASK FORCE. An informal alliance of federal legislators headed by Republican Senator William V. Roth of Delaware, which tries annually to effectuate substantial savings of billions of dollars in our astronomical national budget by cutting out as much waste as possible.

S.B.A. (Small Business Administration). A federal agency whose purpose is to assist small business concerns. It ensures that they receive a fair proportion of government purchases, contracts and sales. The S.B.A. makes loans to small businesses, state and local development companies, and the victims of floods or other catastrophes, or of certain types of economic injury. It licenses, regulates, and makes loans to small business investment companies and guarantees surety bonds for small contractors. In addition, it improves the management skills of small business owners, potential owners, and managers and conducts studies of the economic environment.

SCALES CASE (*Scales v. United States*, 367 U.S. 203 (1961)). Supreme Court case which held that the third section of the Smith Act, making it a crime to be an active member of a political party advocating violent overthrow of the government, was constitutional.

SCARBOROUGH WARNING. A rough kind of justice in which punishment is meted out and questions are asked later. The term derives from the town of Scarborough, in Yorkshire, where traditionally criminals caught in the act were hanged without trial.

SCARED STRAIGHT. See JUVENILE AWARENESS PROGRAM.

S.C.C. See SPECIAL COORDINATION COMMITTEE.

SCHECHTER POULTRY CORPORATION v. UNITED STATES. See SICK CHICKEN CASE.

SCHENCK v. UNITED STATES. See CLEAR AND PRESENT DANGER.

SCHOOL BUSING. The transportation of elementary and high school children in public schools to institutions located a distance from their homes to achieve racial integration with respect to minority groups.

SCHOOL DESEGREGATION CASE. See BROWN v. BOARD OF EDUCATION.

SCHOOL SPANKING CASE (*Ingraham v. Wright*, 430 U.S. 651, (1977)). A Supreme Court decision which upheld the right of a Florida school district to administer corporal punishment to students without imposition of prior adminstratve safeguards. The Court concluded that the Eighth Amendment's Cruel and Unusual Punishments Clause protects only those persons convicted of crimes. The Court said that available civil and criminal sanctions for abuses protected against unjustified use of paddling. An arguable conclusion, to say the least.

SCHOOL SUSPENSION. See GOSS CASE.

SCIENCE EASEMENT. See OPEN SPACE EASEMENT.

SCIENTER REQUIREMENT. Guilty knowledge on the part of the defendant, which renders him liable for his conduct. For example, scienter exists in fraud cases when the defendant has knowledge of certain facts which he has a duty to guard against or disclose, and he fails to do so.

S.C.M. v. XEROX (70 F.R.D. 508 (D.C. Conn 1978)). The longest and most expensive trial in the history of the federal judiciary, an anti-trust suit for 1.52 billion dollars. It began on June 20, 1977 and did not end until July 11, 1978 when it took Judge Jon Newman one hour to read the verdict of the jury which had deliberated 27 days. More than 200 lawyers from eight law firms in six cities ran up legal bills in excess of $60 million dollars. A good time was had by all except the defendant, who lost the case.

SCOFFLAW. An individual who arrogantly thumbs his nose at the establishment. The most frequent offender is someone who contemptuously does not pay his traffic ticket fines. The record is said to be held by a Connecticut woman who was reported by the *New York Times* to have received 599 summonses in a three-year period totaling $21,925 in fines. The term was coined during the Prohibition Era by two Massachusetts residents who entered a contest to invent a word that described people who violated the Prohibition laws.

SCOOP LAWS. See CANINE WASTE LAW.

SCOPES TRIAL. See MONKEY TRIAL.

S.C.O.R.E. (Service Corps Of Retired Executives). A group of retired business and law experts, under the sponsorship of S.B.A. (Small Business Administration), who offer free professional guidance to those operating or seeking to start a business.

SCOTCH VERDICT (Not Proven). Found only in Scotland and other civil law countries. In the United States a jury can reach a verdict only of guilty or not guilty in a criminal case. In a Scotch Verdict, although the jury believes the defendant to be guilty, it acquits him because the prosecution has not proven its case beyond a reasonable doubt.

SCOTTISH NATIONAL PARTY. See S.N.P.

SCOTT, JOHN (EARL OF ELDON). One of the great Lord Chancellors of England in the late eighteenth and early nineteenth centuries, he was known for his deliberateness and even-handedness. His opponents, however, accused him of unnecessary delay in the disposition of cases. The Earl was born in 1751. Much of his early life is recorded in an anecdotal book he wrote for the amusement of his grandchildren in which he includes tales of floggings as a schoolboy. As a young man, Lord Eldon was found guilty of running away with a banker's daughter and, consequently, he had to relinquish his Oxford fellowship and a position in the Church. He turned to law and studied diligently, rising daily at 4 a.m. and putting wet towels on his head in order to stay awake at night. Nevertheless, he did not enjoy much success in his early years of practice; he earned only one-half guinea in his first year. Lord Eldon gained much political power during his service and often escaped

assassination attempts. Spurred by disagreements with his peers regarding Catholicism, he resigned in 1827. He died eleven years later.

SCREENING PANEL. See COMMISSION ON JUDICIAL NOMINATIONS.

SCRIBES SOCIETY. An organization of lawyers formed in 1953 to improve legal writing. It is the result of a suggestion of the late Chief Justice of New Jersey, Arthur Vanderbilt, who was the former dean of N.Y.U. Law School and past president of the American Bar Association. The first meeting of this informal association was held at the Harvard Club in Boston on August 23, 1953, and its members currently constitute some of the leading lawyers throughout the country.

S.D.C. See L.O.S. TRIBUNAL.

S.D.R.s. See SPECIAL DRAWING RIGHTS.

SEA BED DISPUTES CHAMBER. See L.O.S. TRIBUNAL.

SEABED TREATY OF 1971. An international agreement, to which the United States is a party, that bans the positioning of nuclear or other weapons of mass destruction on the seabed beyond the 12-mile limit.

S.E.A.L. (Sea, Air and Land Platoon). A special elitist Naval military group trained to combat terrorists who attack Americans abroad.

SEA, LAND AND AIR PLATOON. See S.E.A.L.

SEA LAWYER. A sailor, or anyone else for that matter, with an argumentative nature, whose volubility as a know-it-all on law and every other subject is exceeded only by his ignorance.

SEALED CONTRACT. A formal contract which requires no consideration. In early common law, sealed contracts were surrounded by impressive ceremony; however, as times changed, the ceremony was largely abandoned and the word "Seal" or "L.S." was substituted for an actual seal. Today, the Uniform Commercial Code and many states have declared use of a seal inoperative. In states which still allow sealed contracts, formalities generally include: (1) a sufficient writing; (2) a seal, and (3) delivery of the contract.

SEAL OF APPROVAL. See CERTIFICATION MARK.

SEAL OF GUARANTEE. See CERTIFICATION MARK.

SEAT BELT DEFENSE. In a personal injury suit resulting from a car accident, a defendant can use the seat belt defense to show that an injured person failed to exercise due care in preventing or mitigating injuries because he failed to wear a seat belt. The seat belt defense was probably first used in a New York Court in 1975 when an injured person who broke her leg after being thrown from her car, would not have been injured had she worn seat belts.

S.E.A.T.O. (South East Asia Treaty Organization). Created by the Treaty of Manila on September 8, 1954, among Australia, France, New Zealand, Pakistan, the Philippines, Burma, the United Kingdom, and the United States. Organized, in the same mode as N.A.T.O., against communist expansion, its purpose is to provide for collective defense of South East Asia. S.E.A.T.O. is composed of (1) a Council of Ministers, who act unanimously, (2) a Permanent Council, and (3) three Committees of military, economic, and political experts.

S.E.C. (Securities and Exchange Commission). An independent federal agency which provides the fullest possible disclosure to investors and protects them against malpractices in the securities and financial markets. The Securities Act of 1933 requires issuers of securities making public offerings of securities in interstate commerce or through the mails, directly or by others on their behalf, to file with the Commission registration statements containing financial and other pertinent data about the issuer and the securities offered. The Act exempts from registration government securities, nonpublic offerings, and intrastate offerings, as well as certain offerings not exceeding $500,000. A registration statement may be refused or suspended after a public hearing if it contains material misstatements or omissions. Registration of securities does not imply that the Commission finds the registration disclosures to be accurate. It does not insure investors against loss, but serves rather to provide information upon which investors may make an informed and realistic evaluation of the worth of the securities. Persons responsible for filing false information with the Commission subject themselves to the risk of fine or imprisonment or both. Persons connected with the public offering may be liable in damages to purchasers of the securities if the disclosures in the registration statement and prospectus are materially defective. Also, the Act contains antifraud provisions which apply generally to the sale of securities, whether or not registered.

SECONDARY BOYCOTT. Pressure applied by a union or other group, usually in the form of strikes, picketing, organized refusals to patronize, or other coercion, on parties uninvolved in the immediate dispute, for the purpose of having the uninvolved parties withhold business or otherwise bring pressure on the opposing primary party. The term boycott is taken from the name of an Irish nobleman of the 11th Century who was subjected to such pressure to force him to change his land reform policies. The use of Secondary Boycotts by unions to force recognition is sharply circumscribed by the National Labor Relations Act.

SECONDARY EVIDENCE. See FRUIT OF THE POISONOUS TREE.

SECONDARY ISSUES. An informal Wall Street term of no legal significance for the shares of stock in a company that is off the beaten path because it may be little known or not widely traded, with the result that it is not widely followed by security analysts.

SECONDARY MEANING. A geographically or otherwise descriptive word or phrase which, through continued use, has come in the consumer's mind to be associated with the product of a particular manufacturer. At common law, when a word had acquired a secondary meaning it was given protection under trademark law. Under the Lanham Act (1946), now the basic Federal Trademark statute, descriptive, geographic and surname marks and terms can be registered if they become distinctive of the applicant's goods. For example, the word "Bud" for beer has taken on a secondary meaning, so that when people ask for a "Bud," they mean only that beer produced by Anheuser-Busch, Inc. Similarly, the word "Coke" for a soft drink has taken on a secondary meaning so that when someone asks for a "Coke," they mean only that soft drink produced by the Coca-Cola Company.

SECONDARY MORTGAGE MARKET. A marketplace where investors can buy and sell mortgages as easily as they can buy and sell stocks and bonds. It has proved to be a growing source of new funds for mortgage lenders. Until recently, the secondary mortgage market was primarily the work of three government agencies commonly called Ginny Mae, Fannie Mae, and Freddy Mac. These agencies bought mortgages as a means to supply more funds to mortgage lenders. In the past few years, major brokerage houses on Wall Street have entered the secondary mortgage market by actively broadening the base of investors willing to buy mortgages through their own sales and trading efforts.

SECONDARY SEARCH. A person arrested on one charge, such as customs violation, may thereafter be searched and evidence discovered on the commission of a second charge, such as illegal possession of drugs, which may then be seized and used as the basis for a conviction on the second offense.

SECONDARY STRIKE. A work stoppage which has spread to an enterprise which has been furnishing goods to the business where a strike has been in effect. This differs from a sympathy strike in that a relationship exists between the employers involved in the original and secondary strikes. However, this distinction is not always recognized and it is frequently referred to as a type of Sympathy Strike.

SECOND CLASS CITIZENS. Americans who do not enjoy the full benefits and privileges of citizenship. For example: (1) Puerto Ricans may vote in a Presidential election only if they live in the continental United States; (2) Children born overseas of one American parent, in order to retain their United States citizenship, must live continually in the United States for two years between the ages of 14 and 28, or the alien parent must be naturalized before the child is 18; (3) Children of American parents who are born outside the United States and acquire dual nationality at birth, can be automatically and involuntarily stripped of their U.S. citizenship if they live for three consecutive years in the foreign country of which they also are citizens after reaching the age of 22; (4) A U.S. citizen married to an alien spouse and residing overseas, in order to be able to transmit U.S. citizenship to his children, must have lived in the United States for at least 10 years, at least five of which were after attaining the age of 14.

SECOND COLLISION LIABILITY. Liability of car manufacturers for injuries caused by design defects which enhance the possibility of injury to the occupants when an initial collision propels the occupant through or out of the vehicle. For example, sharp objects such as gear shift knobs or rearview mirrors may increase injuries when a driver is propelled into them, but such objects were not the cause of the initial collision.

SECOND DEVELOPMENT DECADE. A United Nations program which seeks to continue in the 1970s economic and social goals for under-developed countries established during the First Development Decade of the 1960s. For the Second Decade, however, the annual G.N.P. rate has been increased from five percent to six percent.

SECOND LOOK DOCTRINE. See WAIT AND SEE DOCTRINE.

SECOND MORTGAGE (Junior Mortgage). A loan on real property which is subordinate to the first mortgage and usually has a higher mortgage rate of interest for a shorter period of time.

SECOND MOST IMPORTANT PERSON IN THE UNITED STATES. A select advisor upon whom an individual President would most rely as a confidant. In recent years such advisors would include Rosalynn Carter, Henry Kissinger, Dean Rusk, Robert Kennedy, John Foster Dulles, Clark Clifford, Sherman Adams and Harry Hopkins.

SECOND WORLD. Refers to the Communist countries under the influence of Russia.

SECRETARY OF THE INTERIOR. The Presidential Cabinet member in charge of the preservation, development and use of the nation's natural resources. In other countries, the Minister of Interior is the government official in charge of the police and secret security forces.

SECRET SERVICE. Federal agents authorized to detect and arrest any person committing an offense against the laws of the United States relating to coins, currency, and other obligations, and securities of the United States and of foreign governments; to detect and arrest any person violating any of the provisions of sections 508, 509 and 871 of Title 18 of the United States Code; to execute warrants issued under the authority of the United States; to carry firearms; and to perform such other functions and duties as are authorized by law. In addition, subject to the direction of the Secretary of the Treasury, the United States Secret Service is authorized to protect the person of the President of the United States, the members of his immediate family, the President-elect, the Vice President or other officer next in the order of succession to the Office of President, the immediate family of the Vice President, the Vice-President-elect, major Presidential and Vice-Presidential candidates, former Presidents and their wives during his lifetime, widows of former Presidents until their death or remarriage, and minor children of a former President until they reach age 16, and visiting heads of a foreign state or foreign government. The Secret Service predates the F.B.I. by more than five decades, and for many years it was the country's only general investigative agency. Because it was the only such agency available, its agents were borrowed for various purposes over the years, such as investigating the Teapot Dome Scandals, the Ku Klux Klan, illegal importation of the fruit fly, and an attempted theft of the remains of Abraham Lincoln.

SECRET SEVEN. Of a total of 47 federal agencies, these are the ones found by Common Cause in 1978 to be the most serious violators of the Federal Sunshine Law which requires all federal agency meetings to be open to the public. They are the (1) Export-Import Bank; (2) National Labor Relations Board; (3) Occupational Safety and Health Review Commission; (4) United States Parole Commission; (5) Federal Reserve Board; (6) Commodity Futures Trading Commission and (7) the Federal Home Loan Bank Board.

SECTION 1985 LAW. See KU KLUX KLAN LAW.

SECTION 245 (Program 245). The number of a federal law passed in 1975 in which the government insures graduated mortgage payment loans up to a maximum of $60,000 to enable young people to buy a home now without having to wait until they earn salaries sufficient to meet the usual mortgage payments. In other words, small payments are made at the beginning of the loan and large payments are made at the end.

SECURITIES ACT OF 1933. See S.E.C.

SECURITIES AND EXCHANGE COMMISSION. See S.E.C.

SECURITIES CODE. See FEDERAL SECURITIES LAW CODE.

SECURITIES EXCHANGE ACT. See S.E.C.

SECURITIES INVESTOR PROTECTION CORPORATION. See S.I.P.C.

SECURITIES INVESTOR PROTECTION LAW. See S.I.P.C.

SECURITY COUNCIL. United Nations organization responsible for maintenance of international peace and security. The Security Council consists of 15 members, five of which are permanent members—the People's Republic of China, France, the Union of Soviet Socialist Republics, the United Kingdom, and the United States of America. The Security Council also elects the Judges of the International Court of Justice, and makes a recommendation to the General Assembly on the appointment of the U.N. Secretary General.

SECURITY FOR EXPENSES. See DERIVATIVE SUIT.

SEDITIOUS LIBEL. A common-law crime consisting of written attacks on the government or governmental agents. It is generally conceded that at least one purpose of the First Amendment provisions in the United States for Freedom of Speech and Freedom of Press was to abolish the common law of seditious libel.

SELDEN SOCIETY. Founded in 1887, it consists of over 1,500 lawyers and historians who sponsor publications and lectures on the history of English law.

SELECTIVE SERVICE SYSTEM. A method of conscripting adult males for involuntary military service in the Armed Forces of a nation as opposed to depending upon a purely voluntary program of enlistment.

SELF-INCRIMINATION. Prohibited by the Fifth Amendment of the United States Constitution, which states that no person "shall be compelled in any criminal case to be a witness against himself." To insure this right, the Supreme Court of the United States has held, as one of the famous Miranda warnings, that an arrested person must be informed of his right to remain silent. An individual can waive this right, but such a waiver must be made "voluntarily, knowingly and intelligently."

SEMI-SUPREME COURT. A new court proposed by Chief Justice Warren Burger to hear appeals from the Federal Circuit Courts of Appeals in order to reduce the case load of the overburdened Supreme Court.

SENATE BILL ONE. See S-1.

SENATORIAL COURTESY. In an awesome display of the Separation of Powers concept, this is an unofficial and informal but highly effective practice of United States Senators to vote for an issue of local importance to one of their members, especially in the choice of federal judges. Thus, if the President nominates a person for a federal judgeship who does not have the personal approval of the Senator from that state, the Senate will zap the nominee under their constitutional advice and consent power.

SENIOR CITIZENS ANTI-CRIME NETWORK. Organizations formed throughout the country, especially in large cities, financed by the federal government to protect the aged from crimes, by the formation of private street patrols and the monitoring of criminal trials in the courts.

SENTENCING COUNCIL. A group of lawyers, prison officials and members of the public who recommend the appropriate sentence of punishment for a convicted criminal, taking into consideration all the relevant factors such as age, prior record, use of a deadly weapon, nature of offense, method of commission and the applicable aggravating or mitigating circumstances, in order to achieve a more fair and uniform system of sentencing.

SENTENCING PROCEDURES. In criminal cases: (1) a Fixed or Mandatory Sentencing Procedure is one where the convicted defendant receives the exact penalty specified by a statute, such as 10 years for robbery; (2) a Presumptive Sentencing Procedure is one where a normal sentence is specified for a convicted criminal, but it may vary from individual to individual dependent upon his particular background in the light of established guidelines which some critics refer to as Computer Punch Card Justice; (3) an Accumulative or Cumulative or Consecutive Sentencing Procedure is one where there are two or more separate punishments which the convicted defendant must serve, one after the completion of the other; (4) a Concurrent Sentencing Procedure is one where there are two or more separate punishments which the convicted defendant may serve simultaneously rather than successively; (5) a Disparate Sentencing Procedure is one where a convicted defendant may be given a substantially higher or lower punishment than another who has committed the same crime; (6) an Alternative Sentencing Procedure is where a judge requires the defendant to perform a useful public service in lieu of a fine or imprisonment.

SENTENCING TO COMMUNITY SERVICE. See CREATIVE SENTENCING.

SEPARATE BUT EQUAL. See BROWN v. BOARD OF EDUCATION.

SEPARATE MAINTENANCE. A civil remedy for non-support. Separate Maintenance is a statutory suit for support of the wife, which contemplates the parties living apart but not divorced. The action will result in a decree which orders the husband to support the wife. The effect of reconciliation, in a number of states, terminates the husband's obligations under the decree. In addition to awarding support to the wife in a separate maintenance suit, the court has the authority to require support for the children.

SEPARATION AGREEMENT. A contract between the husband and wife which states that they shall live separately and be free from mutual interference. These agreements usually provide the terms by which the property should be divided and the amount of support to be paid to the wife. Separation agreements are said to be valid if they do not intend to induce divorce or separation, and thus they usually are executed when a couple is already separated. The agreement is evidence of a legal separation, which many states require before a suit for divorce can be maintained.

SEPARATION OF FUNCTIONS. Safeguard to fairness and integrity of decisionmaking imposed by the Administrative Procedure Act. A single employee who is engaged in investigative or prosecuting functions for an agency is precluded from participation or recommendation in the decision of that case or a factually related case. Determination of applications for initial licenses, and proceedings involving the validity or application of rates, facilities, or practices of public utilities or carriers, are not included. Separation of functions is best described as internal separation. While the agency itself may engage in the tripartite powers of legislation, enforcement, and interpretation, different individuals within the agency must perform the Separate Functions. Recent commentators have called for a total removal of judicial functions from at least the most prosecutorial agencies like the N.L.R.B. and the F.C.C. However, the courts have rejected the idea that a combination of judging with prosecution or investigation violates the procedural due process rights of the party in question. For example, the Social Security Administration maintains an inquisitorial procedure in which the Administrative Law Judge supervises the production of evidence and then decides the outcome of welfare cases. The Supreme Court in *Richardson v. Perales*, 402 U.S. 389 (1971), rejected a Procedural Due Process objection to this procedure, holding: "Neither are we persuaded by the advocate-judge-multiple hat suggestion. It assumes too much and would bring down too many procedures designed, and working well, for a government structure of great and growing complexity."

SEPARATION OF JURY. When one or more members of the jury are separated from the other jurors or from the supervision of the court. The permissibility of separation varies among the states, but many prohibit it once the jury commences deliberations. If an unpermitted separation does occur, the judge may declare a mistrial.

SEQUEL RIGHTS. Allow publications, motion pictures, and television programs to use characters from previous works. Generally, a work need not be a continuation of the story line of its predecessor in order to qualify as a sequel.

SEQUESTRATION OF WITNESSES. The right to exclude all witnesses except the defendant from the courtroom while other witnesses are testifying. This right exists to insure that one witness for a party does not adjust his or her story to the testimony of other witnesses. Not only does it exist at trial, but the parties may ask the judge to prohibit the witnesses from discussing the case among themselves even outside the courtroom and before the trial begins.

S.E.R.I. See SOLAR ENERGY RESEARCH INSTITUTE.

SERVICE CONTRACT ACT. A federal law which requires covered service contractors to pay the minimum wages, provide certain fringe benefits or the equivalent payment, to notify employees of the foregoing, and to insure that the contract is not performed under hazardous or unsanitary conditions.

SERVICE CORPS OF RETIRED EXECUTIVES. See S.C.O.R.E.

SERVICE MARK. Unique mark used in the sale of services to identify the services of a group and to distinguish those services from the services of oth-

ers. For example, "Johnny Carson" identifies both the comedian and the entertainment services he renders, thus the name "Johnny Carson" can be registered as a service mark.

SET-ASIDES. A federal requirement that 10 percent of all contracts awarded under public works programs—totaling billions of dollars—go to minority business enterprises.

SEVEN DIRTY WORDS CASE. Supreme Court ruling in 1978, that a radio station had overstepped the bounds of decency when it broadcast an explicit recording by George Carlin which included seven well-known "dirty words." In a dissenting opinion Justice Brennan observed that under the Court's rationale both Chaucer and the Bible could be banned from the air. A later Federal Communications Commission interpretation of the ruling qualified the ban on explicit language: occasional use of expletives aired late at night is acceptable.

SEVEN SISTERS. Seven major oil companies (British Petroleum, Texaco, Shell, Exxon, Standard Oil of California, Gulf and Mobil) which work closely together to control and dominate the international exploration, production, transportation, refining and marketing of the non-Communist world's oil. A French company (Compagnie Française des Pétroles) which often collaborates with them, is called the Eighth Sister.

SEVERANCE PAY. See EQUITABLE REMEDY.

SEWER SERVICE. A slang expression referring to the failure of a process server to serve notice on a defendant being sued for nonpayment of a debt. The term derives from the practice of process servers of actually throwing the notice down the sewer to avoid having to carry out their mission. Several jurisdictions are taking steps to ensure that a defendant is in fact served. In New York, for example, attorneys often must send additional notice of suit by first-class mail to the defendant at his last known address. If such notice is returned, it must be re-mailed to the defendant's place of employment or any other known address. Since the mailing is designed to check the integrity of the process service which the attorneys employ, the attorney himself, not his secretary, must mail the additional notice. Attorneys must write on the envelope "personal and confidential" and must not indicate on the envelope that the letter is from an attorney or that it concerns an alleged debt.

SEXUAL DISCRIMINATION. See E.R.A.; TITLE IX OF THE EDUCATION AMENDMENTS OF 1972; AFFIRMATIVE ACTION.

SEXUAL TRIAL TACTICS. Term coined by Jill Volner, an attorney for the prosecution of various Watergate crimes, to describe tactics used by opposing lawyers to discredit female attorneys in front of the jury. Such tactics may include referring to an opposing attorney as "young lady" or exhibiting "gentlemanly" courtesies with great flourishes, such as helping an attorney to the bench or commenting on her perfume. Such tactics are designed to destroy the jury's confidence in a female attorney by portraying her as an untrustworthy, frivolous young girl.

SHACKING UP. A nautical term which refers to a man and woman living together without being married.

SHADOW JURY. Members of the public recruited by social scientists to sit in court and hear a case. The purpose of a shadow jury is to give insights into the workings of the real jury in the case. Shadow jurors usually hear the same evidence, retire when the real jury retires, and record their deliberations for future analysis. Studies determine how evidence was perceived and interpreted, how arguments influence jurors, and how jurors are influenced by sympathy for the accused and by their own conceptions of justice and equity.

SHADOW LAWMAKERS. See INVISIBLE GOVERNMENT.

SHADOW MINISTRY (Shadow Cabinet). The English practice of assigning members of the opposition party to "Shadow" or watch over the activities of Government Ministers. By becoming experts in particular areas, Shadow Ministers can criticize effectively the work of government officials. Because of their expertise, Shadow Ministers are likely to become Government Ministers when the opposition comes to power.

SHADOW PRESIDENTS. Top aides to the Chief Executive. Recent Shadow Presidents such as Clark Gifford, Sherman Adams, Ted Sorenson and H. R. Haldeman have wielded great power in their advisory roles.

SHAFFER v. HEITNER. See QUASI-IN-REM JURISDICTION.

SHAM CONTRACT. An agreement in which the recited nominal consideration has in fact not been paid.

SHANGHAI COMMUNIQUÉ. An historic agreement signed between the United States and the People's Republic of China (Mainland Communist China) on February 27, 1972, during the eight-day visit by President Richard M. Nixon, which not only called for progress toward normalization between the two great powers but also outlined the differences between the two countries on the Taiwan issue. The United States acknowledged in the Communiqué that Taiwan was part of one China and called for the peaceful settlement of the dispute by the Chinese people themselves. It also affirmed "the ultimate objective of the withdrawal of all United States forces and military installations from Taiwan." The Chinese restated their traditional position on Taiwan in the Communiqué, namely that "Taiwan is the crucial question obstructing the normalization of relations between China and the United States." It added that the "liberation of Taiwan is China's internal affair in which no other country has the right to interfere." The Communiqué was fulfilled on December 15, 1977, when both countries agreed to establish full diplomatic relations on January 1, 1979 with an exchange of ambassadors on March 1, 1979 and an official visit to the United States by Deputy Prime Minister Teng Hsaio-ping on January 29, 1979.

SHANGHAI LAW. An unwritten law of the sea that a sailor discharged by a captain in the course of a voyage was entitled to be paid his fare back to the home port from which the ship had sailed.

SHARE CERTIFICATES. Documents which serve as proof of the shareholder's interest or ownership in a corporation, and are usually denoted by the shorter terms "stock," "share," or "security." Issuance of share certificates is usually required by statutes which regulate both their form and content. Each share certificate must list such essentials as the fact that the corporation is organized under the laws of the state, the name of the person to whom it is issued, what class such share is in, the number of shares in such class, the value of the share, and any special rules regarding such stock.

SHARE DIVIDEND. See STOCK DIVIDEND.

SHARED MONOPOLY. An antitrust term which refers to an oligopoly. An oligopoly exists when there are so few firms producing a particular product that they have the ability to manipulate the market price and output of the product even though there is no active collusion going on among the firms.

SHAREHOLDER APPROVAL. A vote of the shareholders is necessary to make certain fundamental changes in a corporation. Typically, these changes include dissolution, mergers and consolidations, Bylaw changes, amendments of the Articles of Incorporation, and sale, lease, or exchange of assets. In some cases, approval by the Board of Directors may also be necessary.

SHAREHOLDER PROPOSAL RULE. An S.E.C. requirement of 1942 that when a corporation solicited proxies there be disclosure of the fact that some shareholders planned to introduce a resolution at the annual meeting, plus the opportunity to vote yea or nay on the resolution via the company's own form of proxy. Almost immediately, difficulties arose and in 1945 the Commission issued a release expressing the view of the Director of the Division of Corporation Finance that not all shareholder resolutions had to be included in the proxy statement because not all shareholder resolutions were appropriate for inclusion under a rule based upon "Shareholder Democracy." Those proposals which the management would not be required to include were basically of two types. First, the shareholder's proposal had to pertain to the business of the corporation and could not be "of a general political, social or economic nature." This was to preclude referenda on such matters as whether the income tax should be repealed. Secondly, the shareholder's proposal had to be a proper subject for action by the security holders. Thus, the proposal has to be one as to which the shareholders as a group can properly concern themselves under corporation law. For example, if under the corporation laws of a state only the Board of Directors is empowered to amend the bylaws, a shareholder resolution attempting to amend the corporation's bylaws would not be a proper subject for shareholder action. On the other hand, a resolution recommending to the Board that it take action itself to amend the bylaws would pass muster as a proper matter for action by the stockholders.

SHAREHOLDER'S SUIT. See DERIVATIVE ACTION.

SHARE OPTION. See STOCK OPTION.

SHARE WARRANTS. See STOCK OPTION.

SHARP SHOOTER. A lawyer who aims at and is most effective in discovering loopholes in a legal document, drawn by another lawyer, to the advantage of his client.

SHAW, LEMUEL. As Chief Justice of
the Supreme Court of Massachusetts
from 1830-60, he was noted for his judicial activism in the extent to which
he upheld governmental infringement
on private property rights. During
Shaw's tenure, the Massachusetts legislature passed numerous laws which, in
the decades immediately preceding his
appointment, would have been struck
down because of their adverse effect on
established landowners. His opinions
in this area were seen as triumphs for
aspiring entrepreneurs and as fostering
"public well-being." Tending to de-
emphasize precedents, Shaw relied heavily on a "common sense" approach to
deciding cases and construed legal principles in terms of contemporary com-
munal values rather than static doctrines. Consequently, he is remembered
for his ability to mold existing doctrines
to the needs of an expanding society.
Shaw served as a Federalist in the
Massachusetts state legislature 1811-15,
1820-22, and 1829-30. There he met
Daniel Webster, who was influential in
persuading him to accept the Chief
Justiceship. Shaw dominated the Court:
he received unanimous approval from
his fellow justices on 47 out of 50 Constitutional Law decisions he authored,
and he wrote only one dissent in his
thirty years on the bench.

SHELLEY v. KRAEMER. See STATE
ACTION.

SHELTERED WORKSHOP. An organization designed to provide employment
for handicapped persons who are unable to work in competitive industry.
Such organizations receive certain exemptions with respect to taxes and other
regulations such as those imposed by
the minimum wage and hour law.

SHELTER HOME. A facility established to receive on a temporary basis
victims of spouse abuse or child
abuse. Because spouse and child abuse
are problems which resist settlement
through traditional criminal and civil
remedies, many experts have encouraged the establishment of facilities to
which the battered spouse and battered
child can retreat for refuge from further abuse, and where they can receive
care, counseling and rehabilitation. The
Shelter Home concept is not new. In
1973 Great Britain opened its first Shelter for abused women and their children in a dilapidated four-bedroom
house. Soon after it opened, there were
thirty-four women and children bedded
down on mattresses spread wall to wall.
Today in England there are more than
seventy government-supported Shelters
and Homes for battered women and
their children. The demand for such a
government program in the United
States is growing. In the last few years
the popular press has promoted the
idea and several states including Maryland, California, Florida, New Jersey
and New York are working on legislation to establish such Shelters. Thus
far, however, the only functioning Shelter Homes in the United States are
private, some of which receive federal,
state, and local governmental funds.
Typical of the established Shelters in
America is Haven House in Los Angeles, California. Founded in 1964 and
funded by California's Alcoholism Fund
and Los Angeles County revenue-shar-
ing funds, Haven House has served more
than 800 women. The usual live-in period is twenty to twenty-five days, during which time psychological and employment counseling, as well as food,
shelter and emotional support, are available.

SHENEFIELD REPORT. A voluminous
report named after the Assistant Attorney General for Anti-Trust who chaired
the 22-member commission and submitted the results of their study to the
White House in 1979. It recommends
the first substantial changes in the Sherman Act since it was passed by Congress in 1890. Specific proposals of the
Report include: (1) Changing the Federal Rules of Civil Procedure to allow
judges to control big antitrust cases. A
maximum of two years would be allowed
for the pretrial phase of such cases, and
judges would be encouraged to focus
issues and to limit the submission of
documents. Early in such cases, companies would be required to exchange
market information defining relevant

markets that currently can be gained only through protracted litigation. (2) Amending the Clayton Antitrust Act to require companies that lost antitrust cases to pay interest on damages from the date a complaint was served, rather than from the date of final judgment. This change would provide an incentive for companies to avoid delaying these cases. The draft report also urges judges to consider other financial sanctions to discourage foot-dragging in antitrust litigation. (3) Amending the Clayton Act to make clear that where the government has won an antitrust case, courts can rule that further argument isn't needed on the previously argued issues in subsequent private antitrust suits. (4) Developing a Manual to guide judges in decisions on sale of assets and other structural changes ordered in big antitrust cases. The Report urges that this Manual be prepared by a task force drawn from the Justice Department's Antitrust Division, the F.T.C., the S.E.C. and the I.R.S. The manual's purpose would be to encourage often-reluctant judges to consider structural changes in major cases. (5) Eliminating, after a brief transition period, regulation by the Interstate Commerce Commission of entry, rates and mergers in the trucking industry. In addition, the Report recommends that "substantial steps should be taken to deregulate railroads." (6) Repealing the existing antitrust exemption for the insurance industry and substituting a "narrowly drawn" exemption for "a limited number of essential collective activities." In addition, the Report urges state insurance regulators to "place maximum reliance on competition." (7) Limiting the scope of certain aspects of existing antitrust exemptions for agriculture cooperatives, ocean-shipping conference agreements and export associations.

SHERIFF OFFICER (Old English—Shire-Revee: Governor of the Shire). Generally an elected officer of a county who exercises police powers not within the jurisdiction of the organized police force of an incorporated city. The Sheriff is responsible for executing writs issued by the courts, particularly those levying execution on property and selling it to satisfy a court judgment. Sheriffs are generally bonded and are personally liable for all erroneous seizures of property or other unauthorized acts.

SHERIFF'S JURY (Sheriff's Panel). A wealthy men's private club established in New York City in 1684 and shockingly not abolished until 1979. Its members were divided into three groups of 150 each. They met occasionally to hear competency matters but were otherwise exempted from regular jury duty. Each elitist member paid annual dues of $150, used largely for lavish parties for each other.

SHIELD LAWS. Legislation passed in more than one-half of the states to protect newspaper and other news media reporters from being imprisoned, fined or sued if they failed to reveal the source of their information. It thereby placed them on a pedestal of immunity shared by lawyers, doctors and clergymen. In 1978, a *New York Times* reporter named Myron Farber was sent to jail in New Jersey, despite the fact that New Jersey had a Shield Law, when he failed to give information in a criminal trial in which Dr. Mario Jascalevich was accused of having murdered a patient. The court in sending Farber to jail held that the law had to yield to the Sixth Amendment to the Federal Constitution which guarantees a defendant the right to a fair trial.

SHIFTING EXECUTORY INTEREST. See EXECUTORY INTEREST.

SHINGLE THEORY. A broker who represents himself or "hangs out his shingle" as an expert and gives advice to his customers on securities transactions will be deemed to have committed a fraud under both the Securities Act of 1933 and the Securities Exchange Act of 1934 if he does business with customers without disclosing his possible conflicts of interest or other relevant information. The theory originated in the case of *Charles Hughes & Co. v. S.E.C.*, 139 F.2d 434 (2nd Cir. 1943), where a broker sold securities to unsophisticated clients at up to 40 percent over their market value without disclosing that fact.

SHIPMENT CONTRACT. Term used by commercial lawyers which refers to any contract that requires the seller to send goods to the buyer but fails to request that the delivery be made to a particular destination. Consequently, risk of loss generally passes to the buyer at the point of shipment; unlike Destination Contracts.

SHOO-FLY COP (Fly Cop). A slang expression that refers to a law enforcement officer who spies on fellow officers. The expression derives from the Civil War ditty, "Shoo Fly, Don't Bother Me."

SHOPBOOK RULE. A rule of evidence which allows a merchant doing business on account to use his books as proof that a defendant owes him money. The Rule, which developed from an early English custom, has been justified on the ground of necessity. At common law in the eighteenth and early nineteenth centuries, interested parties were barred from testifying in their own behalf. To establish legitimate debts, merchants needed to introduce their books into evidence. If the merchant kept a clerk, some jurisdictions did not apply the Shopbook Rule on the theory that the clerk could testify to the debt. Other jurisdictions have required various guarantees as to the reliability of the books, such as an oath by the merchant or testimony by other people regarding the accuracy of his accounts, inspection by the court to see if the books are fair, or proof that the goods, or at least some of them, were actually delivered. The Shopbook Rule, which is an exception to the rule prohibiting Hearsay Evidence, is now codified in Rules 803(6) and (7) of the new Federal Rules of Evidence.

SHOPPING MALL CASES. Challenges to restrictions in shopping center leases which forbid the entry of discount stores or which reserve to certain "anchor" stores the right to approve entry of other stores into the mall. Such "right of approval" clauses have been widely discontinued as probable anti-trust violations.

SHOP STEWARD. An officer of a labor union, whose duty is to keep a record of all non-union people on works where he is employed and present their names at the branch meeting. It is also his duty to notify every non-union worker to report at such meeting and attempt to persuade such person to join the organization.

SHORT DOYLE ACT. See COMMUNITY HEALTH SERVICES LAW.

SHORT MERGER (Freeze Out Merger). Some statutes provide that where a corporation owns at least ninety percent of the outstanding shares of each class of another corporation it may merge that corporation into itself without approval of the shareholders of either corporation. The minority shareholders may be entitled only to a cash payment for the fair market value of their shares instead of shares in the surviving corporation. The purpose of the short merger may be solely to eliminate the minority shareholders.

SHORT SWING TRANSACTION. A purchase and sale, or sale and purchase, of securities by the same person within a six-month period. Such transactions are regulated by the Securities Exchange Act when they occur in the context of Insider Trading. Section 16 of the Act prohibits Short Swing profits. Thus, any officer, director, or beneficial owner of more than ten percent of any class of stock in a corporation cannot buy and sell, or sell and buy, any stock of his corporation within six months after he has purchased its stock. If he does so, the corporation may sue and "recapture" the Short Swing profits. If it fails to sue diligently, any shareholder may sue within two years.

SHOTGUN INSTRUCTION. See ALLEN INSTRUCTION.

SHOW CAUSE. An order by a judge to a party to appear in court and explain to the satisfaction of the judge that there has been no intentional violation of a previous mandate of the judge as to what the party was directed to do. Failure to so satisfy the judge will result in the party being held in contempt of court for which the party may be fined or imprisoned or both.

SHOW TRIALS. Degrading judicial proceedings during the 1930s under the dictator Joseph Stalin for the public excoriation of high-level Communist figures who had fallen from grace. After they had been tortured and brainwashed, they "confessed" to heinous and improbable crimes against the state. In its 50-year-old history, no Soviet court has ever acquitted a defendant accused of having committed a political crime. And no wonder. They are held in jail incommunicado. The trial is not open. They have no access to the charges against them. They cannot introduce witnesses or evidence in their own defense. Their lawyer is appointed by the government and not one of their own choice. There is no appeal. Arthur Koestler gives a graphic picture of this corruption of the law in *Darkness At Noon.*

SHOW-UP. A pre-trial procedure in which a witness confronts a suspect in order to identify him as the person who committed the crime. As in a line-up, the defendant has the right to counsel at a show-up only if judicial proceedings in the case have begun.

SHREVEPORT RATE CASE (*Houston & Texas Central Ry. Co. v. United States,* 238 U.S. 617 (1914)). A Supreme Court case which held that it is within Congress' commerce power to regulate intrastate railroad rates which discriminate against interstate railroad traffic. The *Shreveport* decision is one of few cases giving a fairly broad reading to the commerce power in the first part of the twentieth century.

SHYSTER LAWYER. Dishonest person who carries out business, particularly legal business, in a devious manner. Although "shyster" can refer to any businessman, the term most frequently modifies "lawyer."

SICK CHICKEN CASE. In *Schechter Poultry Corporation v. United States,* 295 U.S. 495 (1935), the Supreme Court struck down the National Industrial Recovery Act of 1933 (the N.I.R.A.), an important piece of New Deal legislation. The N.I.R.A. authorized the President to promulgate "codes of fair competition" for a trade or industry upon application by a trade association. Although the N.I.R.A. was not designed to continue for much longer, the President was deeply concerned about the fate of more permanent New Deal legislation. The *Schechter* case concerned a conviction for violating the minimum wage, maximum hour and trade practices provisions of the Code of Fair Competition for the Live Poultry Industry of the Metropolitan Area in and about the City of New York and for selling an "unfit chicken." Schechter owned a slaughterhouse which sold only to local dealers. The Supreme Court reversed the conviction, holding that Schecter's activities did not "directly affect interstate commerce" and thus were not reachable by the Congress under its Commerce Clause powers. The Court has since held that Congress has extremely wide powers under the Commerce Clause.

SICK DOCTORS' LAWS. State statutes which temporarily suspend doctors who are alcoholics or drug addicts from the practice of medicine. The doctors are subjected to medical treatment in lieu of the harsh penalty of having their licenses to practice medicine revoked. This compassionate legislation is designed to salvage and rehabilitate innocent victims of a stressful profession, instead of barring them permanently from the practice of medicine.

SICK OUT. A labor tactic in which substantial numbers of employees fail to report to work during a labor dispute on the grounds of sickness. Miraculously, when the employer grants an increase in wages or fringe benefits, they all become well spontaneously and promptly return to work.

SIDEBAR CONFERENCE. See BENCH CONFERENCE.

SIERRA CLUB v. MORTON. See INJURY-IN-FACT TEST.

SIGNALS INTELLIGENCE ACT. A federal law which makes it a crime to publish classified information obtained through electronic eavesdropping. A reporter who publishes such classified information may face a sentence as long as 10 years, and a fine as much as $10,000 or both.

SILVER PLATTER DOCTRINE. Evidence that is illegally seized by state law enforcement officials is admissible in federal criminal trials. The doctrine was created in *United States v. Lustig*, 338 U.S. 74 (1949), resting on the notion that so long as federal authorities were not involved in the illegal conduct, it was senseless to enforce the deterrence-based exclusionary rule on them. *Lustig* was overruled, and the Silver Platter Doctrine rejected, in *Elkins v. United States*, 364 U.S. 206 (1960), which held that all illegally-seized evidence was inadmissible, regardless of who performed the illegal search. The decision was based on the judicial integrity rationale, that the dignity of the court system was compromised by the introduction of tainted evidence. The doctrine made a comeback of sorts in *United States v. Janis*, 428 U.S. 433 (1976), a Supreme Court case which held that evidence obtained illegally by state police could be used against the victim of the search in a civil proceeding for collection of taxes. The court, focusing on the deterrence rationale of the exclusionary rule, found that exclusion of the evidence from state and federal criminal proceedings was punishment enough.

SILVER SHIRTS. A World War II fascist organization headed by Hitler-adherent William Dudley Pelley, who was convicted of sedition as a result of a treasonable speech.

SIMPLE INSURANCE TRUST. A trust arrangement which is composed entirely or partially of life insurance policies or contracts for the same.

SIMULATED LAW FIRM (S.L.F.). A law school teaching device which simulates an actual law firm. The Simulated Law Firm includes a managing partner (law professor), a senior partner (one or two practicing attorneys), and associates (sixteen second-year law students). The student associates handle simulated cases from the initial client interview through the trial and closing of the file. Because no real clients are involved, students are free to make independent decisions, and follow through on those decisions, even though the "client" may lose. Knowledge of the law is developed by library research and consultation with the senior partners at weekly law firm meetings, rather than by the traditional case method and Socratic questioning. In addition, the simulated experience allows students to tackle ethical issues and to develop lawyering skills, two aspects of legal education often overlooked in the traditional classroom. The S.L.F. was first offered by the State University of New York at Buffalo Law School.

SINE QUA NON (Latin—without which it is not). An indispensable requisite or condition. Mutual consideration, for example, is the Sine Qua Non of a valid contract.

SINGER v. MAGNAVOX CO. (380 A.2d 969 (Del. 1977)). A landmark case decided by the Delaware Supreme Court concerning the law of corporations. The court held that no Delaware corporation may conduct a merger solely to eliminate minority shareholders. As part of a merger with the North American Phillips Corporation in September, 1974, the Magnavox Board of Directors gave notice to its minority shareholders that they were to be given $9.00 cash for each of their shares then worth a book value of $10.16. By this action the minority shareholders would have no further interest in the corporation. Such an action is called a Cash Take-Out Merger or a Freeze-Out Merger. By receiving a cash payment which is less than book value, minority shareholders are taken out of continued participation in the corporation. The

Delaware Supreme Court, ruling that such an action was a per se breach of the fiduciary duty owed to the minority shareholders by the majority, enjoined the proposed Cash Take-Out Merger.

SINGLAUBED. Military-ese which has turned former General Singlaub's name into a verb. "Singlaubed" generally means being fired for speaking out on a sensitive political issue. General Singlaub was fired by President Carter when he repeatedly criticized his Commander-in-Chief's foreign policy decisions.

SINGLE BUSINESS TAX. See VALUE ADDED TAX.

SINGLE INTEREST GROUPS. See SPECIAL (SINGLE) INTEREST GROUPS.

SING SING. The name of a small town in New York state where a prison with a reputation for brutality was located. The townspeople were so embarrassed by this identity that they changed the name of their village to Ossining, but the name of the prison and its reputation have survived intact. Since Ossining is located on the Hudson River north of New York City, the underworld slang expression for a person confined in prison there or elsewhere is Up The River.

SINKING FUND DEBENTURES. Notes or bonds which require that funds be held in escrow in order that the debentures may be redeemed.

S.I.P.C. (Securities Investor Protection Corporation). Formed by federal law in 1970, this organization protects investors from any loss sustained when a securities broker or stock dealer goes bankrupt.

SIRICA, JOHN. See MAXIMUM JOHN.

SIT-DOWN STRIKE. A voluntary cessation of work by employees who unlawfully refuse to leave the premises of the employer until their demands are met.

SIT IN. Employees who refuse to leave the premises of an employer in a labor dispute or citizens who occupy a public building to protest against the policies of the establishment.

SIXTEENTH AMENDMENT. The infamous law passed in 1913 which created the federal income tax. Ouch!

SIXTH MONTH RULE. Requires a jury trial where a judge imposes a sentence larger than six months for criminal contempt. Regarding separate incidents of contempt, a defendant may receive separate sentences totalling longer than six months if they are imposed during the trial. If they are imposed after the trial, however, then the Sixth Month Rule applies.

SIXTY (60) POINTS. Policies agreed upon and announced by China's leaders encouraging peasants and their families to profit from their private plots, to develop income by catching fish, raising ducks, and similar activities, and to sell this private output at rural fairs or markets. This has aroused some opposition as there are those who argue this will lead to individual wealth, and this is not the socialism basic to communist ideals. They feel that a serious gap will develop between rich and poor, and this will cause unrest.

SKI LAW. Legislation first passed by Vermont in early 1978 and since followed elsewhere to protect owners and operators of ski resorts from being successfully sued for accidents on the slopes. The law proclaims skiing to be a hazardous sport in which skiers assume "obvious and necessary risks."

SKIPPING BOUNDS. An adolescent who runs away from an institution of incarceration.

SLANT DRILLING. See HOT OIL.

S.L.F. See SIMULATED LAW FIRM.

SLIGHT EVIDENCE RULE. A doctrine created by the federal case of *Tomplain v. United States*, 282 U.S. 886 (1930), which proclaimed that once a criminal conspiracy is conclusively established, other defendants may be found guilty of having participated in it on the basis of slight evidence (whatever that may be), which has remained good law despite criticism by commentators.

SLIP LAWS. Pamphlet prints of federal and private laws, issued a few days after Congress passes the legislation. Public laws, which are later bound as part of the statutes volume, carry statutes page numbers, sidenotes and citations, a guide to legislative history, and related Presidential statements.

SLOW DOWN (Work-To-Rule). An effective device used by labor to obtain concessions from management. Instead of going on strike, the employees pursue a deliberate policy of "going by the book" in the discharge of their duties. For example, a policeman gives a ticket for each and every traffic offense or an air traffic controller rigidly adheres to each and every safety precaution.

SLOVIK SYNDROME. The imposition of a criminal sentence upon an accused under the mistaken assumption that it will never be carried out. Named after World War II Private Eddie Slovik, the only American soldier executed for desertion since 1864. The presiding officer of the nine-member General Court Martial Tribunal which imposed the capital punishment sentence on Slovik erroneously expected it to be reduced at one of the many stages of appeal.

SLUM LORD. A landlord who does not keep the premises in a state of good repair.

SMALL AND INDEPENDENT BUSINESS PROTECTION ACT OF 1979. See CONGLOMERATE MERGER BILL.

SMALL BUSINESS ADMINISTRATION. See S.B.A.

SMALL BUSINESS INVESTMENT ACT (1958). Seeks to foster organization of investment companies which might furnish equity capital to small businesses.

SMALL CLAIMS COURT. A local court having limited jurisdiction over minor civil claims, usually up to $500. Small Claims Courts normally are found in larger cities and towns. In many locations, the court having jurisdiction over such minor civil cases may be known as a municipal court or, less commonly, as a police court or magistrate's court. A Small Claims Court generally is not a court of record, and a litigant may usually obtain a completely new trial in a state district or county court of general jurisdiction. Small Claims Courts are used to handle such things as landlord-tenant conflicts and business-consumer disputes over goods and services. The atmosphere is informal; you present your own case to a judge. You usually do not need a lawyer and, in some areas, may be prohibited from using one. There is also no jury. A limited study by the New York Public Interest Research Group of judgments awarded in one borough of New York City found that over 43 percent of the individuals who had won their cases never collected. A collection provision is included in the "Model Consumer Justice Act" proposed by the Chamber of Commerce of the United States which has called for a complete overhaul of Small Claims Courts.

SMALL PURCHASE. In federal government contracting this term refers to procurements whose aggregate amount does not exceed $10,000. In Department of Defense contracting such purchases must be accomplished pursuant to negotiation.

SMART MONEY. See PUNITIVE DAMAGES.

SMITH ACT (Alien Registration Act of 1940). Provisions of the Act make it a crime to (1) "advocate overthrowing any government in the United States by force or violence"; to (2) "organize or help to organize" any group that advocates overthrowing the government; and to (3) belong to any such group "knowing the purposes thereof." The Smith Act was invoked against Communist leaders for the first time in 1948, and the constitutionality of the first provision of the Act was upheld in the case of *Dennis v. United States,* 341 U.S. 494 (1951), when the Supreme Court sustained the conviction of eleven top-ranking Communist leaders.

SMITH, MARGARET CHASE. The first serious woman candidate for the American presidency. The United States Senator from Maine was defeated by Senator Barry Goldwater in the Republican Primary of 1964.

SMITH v. ORGANIZATION OF FOSTER FAMILIES FOR EQUALITY AND REFORM (O.F.F.E.R.) (429 U.S. 883 (1977)). United States Supreme Court decision validating New York statutory procedures for the removal of children from foster homes. The challenged statute, the New York Social Service Law, provides that the state may remove a child from a foster family subject to the latter's right to invoke two state procedures: a conference with the Social Services Department and (pursuant to a decision against the foster home) a full adversary appeal before that Department. Arguing that the foster family had a protected "liberty interest," O.F.F.E.R. contended that an adversary hearing should be held automatically before a child could be removed. Citing *Mathews v. Eldridge*, 424 U.S. 319 (1976), the Court held that, even granting the "liberty interest" of the foster family, the state procedures were not constitutionally defective.

SMOG SCOFFLAW. A Californian who buys and registers his car in another state in order to avoid compliance with California's tough auto emission standards law. The California statute is stricter than the federal law applicable in the other 49 states.

SMOKING PISTOL. Direct evidence and proof positive that the accused has committed a crime. For example, the June 23rd, 1972 Watergate tape in which President Nixon asked his Chief of Staff H. R. Haldeman to have the C.I.A. limit the F.B.I. investigation for political reasons, thereby committing the crimes of conspiracy and obstruction of justice.

SMOOT-HAWLEY TARIFF ACT OF 1930. Trade protectionist law designed originally to shield farmers and a few industries from foreign competition, but to which eventually were attached 1,250 amendments protecting most American industries. As a result of the Act, tariffs were raised 53 percent, and industrial exports declined 73 percent. The Act was proposed to combat unemployment, yet the loss of foreign trade engendered by the Act eliminated more jobs, closed factories, and prolonged the Depression.

SNITCH BOUNTY. Name given to money received by a tax ferret.

S.N.P. (Scottish National Party). A political organization which seeks greater local autonomy for Scotland, if not complete secession from Great Britain.

S.N.U.P.P.S. (Standardized Nuclear Unit Power Plant Syndicate). Cooperative agreement among a group of utility companies to make group purchases of standardized nuclear power plant facilities. S.N.U.P.P.S. was created largely to save regulatory compliance costs by standardizing nuclear plants so that only one hearing would be necessary, rather than separate compliance hearings for each plant.

SOCIAL CONTRACT. Named after the famous book of Rousseau, this was an agreement made by the trade unions with the English government, in 1975, that they would hold down their wage demands in return for increased government benefits. For four years it successfully reduced the rate of inflation from 25 percent to 8 percent but the truce was destroyed by the successful strike of 80,000 truck drivers in early 1979 which had a devastating impact, especially through the hit-and-run tactics of "flying pickets" who raced from one spot to another to harass the deliveries by nonunion drivers.

SOCIOLOGICAL JURISPRUDENCE. Roscoe Pound espoused this jurisprudential theory based partly on nineteenth century German social interest theory. Sociological jurisprudence views the law not as a series of rules promulgated in the abstract, but as an attempt to compromise conflicting individual rights by turning to social interests. These social interests include the following general security: institutions such as marriage and religion; politics; economics; morality; conservation of social resources; protection of dependents and defectives; progress; aesthetics; and individual life.

SOCIAL SECURITY. A Federal program enacted by the Federal Social Security Act (42 U.S.C.A. § 301 et seq., 9A F.C.A. title 42, § 301 et seq.) designed to create a public assistance fund by levying taxes on employers and employees. The eleven titles of the Act provide for old-age assistance, unemployment insurance, and survivors' insurance benefits. The Act further establishes financial grants to be poured into state funds for child welfare services, aid to dependent children, public health work, services for crippled children, and aid to the blind. State Social Security statutes parallel the federal one, and the states' eligibility for federal funds under the Act is made contingent upon approval of the state statute by Federal Social Security officers. Among the most important of the state statutes are enactments which provide compensation for workers disabled by non-occupational injuries, who are ineligible for workmen's compensation or unemployment benefits.

SOCIAL SECURITY ADMINISTRATION (S.S.A.). The administration within H.E.W. which manages the Social Security program, including the Medicare Program which is the responsibility of the S.S.A.'s Bureau of Health Insurance. Since S.S.A. is not under the direction of H.E.W.'s Assistant Secretary for Health, the Medicare Program is administered separately from the Department's other health programs.

SOCIAL WAGE. Those benefits paid by a government to its citizens, such as food stamps, welfare, unemployment insurance, disability benefits, pensions, etc.

SOCIETY FOR ACADEMIC COURSES. See FLYING UNIVERSITIES.

SOCIETY FOR PHILOSOPHY AND PUBLIC AFFAIRS. See S.P.P.A.

SOCIETY OF AMERICAN LAW TEACHERS (S.A.L.T.). An organization whose members consist of persons who are teaching or have taught students for credit given by law schools. The Society encourages developments in legal education which include attention to legal ethics and the public responsibilities of the profession that will make curriculum, programs, and forms of instruction more responsive to social needs. It makes studies and, where appropriate, issues public statements, participates in litigation, and gives testimony on matters of professional concern, such as the proposed new Federal Penal Code and proposed amendments to the United States Constitution. The Society expresses opinions on judicial appointments and appointments to other governmental positions bearing on the administration of justice as well as on issues of academic freedom and fair treatment of minorities and violation of academic freedom directed against law teachers.

SOCRATES' TRIAL. (c. 470-399 B.C.). Socrates was a Greek philosopher and moralist who used inductive statements, arguments or words as a way of discovering the truth. The "Socratic method," an inquiry consisting of a series of questions designed to elicit a clear and concise understanding of a subject, originated with Socrates. He left no writings; thus, all knowledge of his work and life comes from secondary sources, most notably Plato. At the age of seventy, he was convicted of "impiety" and was condemned to drink a fatal cup of hemlock. Charged with disrespect of the state religion and corrupting youth, Socrates essentially stood trial for asking embarrassing questions of important people. Characterized as a shyster lawyer by the right-wing playwright Aristophenes, Socrates suffered from "bad press" at the time of his trial. Some of his embarrassing questions seem wholly innocuous today; for example, he questioned the efficiency of 501-man juries (defended by the government as insuring impartiality). Believing that the only real harm that can befall a person is his own decision to become a worse human being, Socrates defended his right to ask questions regardless of where the inquiry may lead. He was convicted by a 280 to 221 vote of the jury and sentenced to death. The trial, which took place in 399 B.C. stands today as testimony to the importance of free speech and the duty to obey one's conscience.

SOFT ESPIONAGE. See HARD ESPIONAGE.

SOLDIERING WORKERS. Workers who deliberately perform less than ordinary performance standards.

SOLDIERS' AND SAILORS' CIVIL RELIEF ACT. A federal law, enacted by Congress in 1918 and extensively revised in 1940, which provides for the temporary suspension of enforcement of civil liabilities against military personnel on active duty, when the opportunity and capacity of such persons to perform their obligations is materially impaired by reason of their being in the military service. The Act provides that a default judgment in a civil action may not be entered by any court unless the plaintiff first files an affidavit setting forth the fact that the defendant is not in the Armed Forces. If such an affidavit is not or cannot be filed, the court must appoint an attorney to represent and protect the interests of the defendant before a default judgment may be entered. The Act also provides that a stay in the proceedings of any civil action will be granted upon application of any service member, unless it appears to the court that his ability to prosecute or to defend the case is not materially affected by reason of military service. As regards installment contracts, mortgages, trust deeds, and other secured obligations, this provision only applies to obligations incurred prior to entry into military service. In addition to relief from liabilities imposed through civil litigation, the Act provides extensive protection from double taxation of service personnel. By declaring that a serviceman's residence for tax purposes is not affected by military assignment, the Act reserves the right of taxing his military income and personal property to the domiciliary state. This applies also to the taxation of motor vehicles, including registration and licensing. However, if such personal property tax is not paid to the domiciliary state, the host state may levy its tax thereon.

SOLDIERS' AND SAILORS' WILLS. Testamentary bequests by soldiers in actual military service and sailors at sea in tidal waters. This type of will was used at least as early as the times of Caesar's military victories. Such wills may be oral or written. If they are oral, usually only one witness is necessary. In most States, these wills are excepted from the Statute of Frauds, so that verbal wills or unattested written wills are capable of passing personalty. The valid will of a soldier or sailor remains in effect even after he has returned to another occupation. Unlike other nuncupative wills, the testator need not die from the perceived peril. Because of this fact, the privilege of making such a will may be a dubious one. What an ex-G.I. said, or is said to have said, to a barmaid in an English pub during World War II might govern the disposition of his estate many years later if he has not revoked his Soldier's Will. In order to avoid the claim that they had made an informal Soldier's or Sailor's Will which was unrevoked at their death, ex-service people may be well advised to execute a formal will.

SOLICITED REPLY DOCTRINE. See REPLY LETTER DOCTRINE.

SOLICITOR GENERAL. The official in the Department of Justice immediately below the Attorney General. The Solicitor General decides which cases the federal government will appeal, supervises all matters before the Supreme Court in which the federal government is involved, controls appellate preparation, and argues the most important cases before the Court. In Great Britain, the Solicitor General likewise ranks below the Attorney General and is the law officer responsible for all litigation of the Crown. The British Solicitor General is a politician as well as a legal practitioner and he usually is a member of the House of Commons.

SOLICITOR OF LABOR. A lawyer in the United States Department of Labor, responsible for all the legal activities of the Department and its legislative program. He also serves as legal adviser to the Secretary and other officials of the Department. The Solicitor, through a subordinary staff of attorneys in Washington and 16 field offices, directs a broad-scale litigation effort pertaining to the many statutes administered by the Department of Labor, including institution and prosecution of Civil Court actions under the Fair Labor Standards Act, as amended, and the trial of cases under the Longshoremen's and Harbor Workers' Compensation Act, Employee Retirement Income Security Act of 1974, and the Farm Labor Contractor Registration Act. Attorneys also represent the Department in administrative hearings under various statutes, including the Occupational Safety and Health Act. The litigation is conducted independently under an agreement and delegation of authority from the Department of Justice. Litigation under several other acts is carried out in cooperation with the Department of Justice. Appellate litigation is conducted by attorneys in the national headquarters, whereas the large majority of litigation under various statutes is carried out by attorneys under the direction of the regional solicitors and attorneys who are the legal advisers to the Department officials in the field.

SOLOMONIC COMPROMISE. An agreement which splits down the middle the differences of both sides. The term alludes to the Biblical judgment of Solomon who determined the true mother of a disputed child by proposing to split the child in two.

S-1 (Senate Bill One; S-1437). A congressional bill introduced in 1975, which completely revises the Federal Criminal Code. Though S-1 was rejected by Congress, a similar bill, S-1437, was approved by the Senate in early 1978. If it is approved by the House of Repre-

sentatives, a comprehensive and coherent criminal code will replace the confusing, archaic and sometimes contradictory statutes accumulated during the past two centuries. S-1437 utilizes the Model Penal Code's innovations in classifying states of mind. It recognizes four possible states of mind for each element of an offense—intent, knowledge, recklessness, and negligence. Probably the most controversial aspect of the bill is its elimination of broad judicial discretion in sentencing. Presently, punishment for a crime such as rape may be anything from a suspended sentence to death. Under S-1437 the maximum sentence cannot exceed the minimum by more than 25 percent, and the judge must explain any departure from the guidelines. Additionally, parole would be phased out, save in extraordinary circumstances, and time off for good behavior could not exceed ten percent of the sentence, rather than the present one-third. Thus, S-1437 departs from the prevailing philosophy of institutional rehabilitation and replaces it with one of deterrence. Congressional disagreement focuses on the substance of the proposed criminal and sentencing provisions, not on the concept of a uniform code. It seems likely that some version of S-1437 will eventually pass. S-1437 is a compromise between the bill's sponsor, Senator Edward M. Kennedy (D-Mass.) and the late Senator John L. McClellan (D-Ark.) and represents an unusual coalition between liberals and conservatives.

S-1437. See S-1.

SOOT TAX. A fine imposed on individuals and business entities who pollute the atmosphere. First proposed by Professor William Nordhaus of Yale University in 1980, the effectiveness of such a tax remains to be seen.

SOPHISTICATED INVESTOR. A person with a net worth in excess of $100,000 who is experienced in the world of finance. One seeking to raise money may contact up to a maximum of 35 such people without having to file an offering circular or registration statement with the Securities and Exchange Commission.

SOUTHERN CALIFORNIA CENTER FOR LAW AND THE DEAF. Formed in California in 1978 by four lawyers who charge no fees and are supported by the Greater Los Angeles Council on Deafness, this is the first organization in the United States to dedicate itself exclusively to solving the legal problems of deaf people. The magnitude and importance of their work may be gleaned from the fact that California alone has two million deaf people.

SOUTHERN MANIFESTO. See BROWN v. BOARD OF EDUCATION.

SOUTHWEST AFRICA PEOPLE'S ORGANIZATION. See S.W.A.P.O.

SOUTHWESTERN LEGAL FOUNDATION. Founded in 1947 at Southern Methodist University Law School under the sponsorship of Robert Story, former President of the American Bar Association. Its purpose is to conduct research in international law and relations through seminars and institutes, especially for lawyers from abroad. It also publishes books and pamphlets on international law and foreign business transactions.

SOVIET BLOC COUNTRY. Any nation under Russian control and domination.

SOVIET IMPERIALISM. The death of capitalism and the expansion of communism throughout the world under Russian domination. As Premier Krushchev arrogantly shouted to the American Ambassador at the United Nations "We will bury you." This secret desire for world conquest was revealed by Peter the Great centuries ago when he beseeched Mother Russia in his last will and testament to seek warm water ports. And they have followed his advice to obtain naval bases in the Mediterranean, the Red Sea, the Persian Gulf, the Indian Ocean and the South Atlantic. Eastern Europe has fallen into their camp and Marxism-Leninism also prevails in Asia (Afghanistan, China and Vietnam), Africa (Ethiopia and Angola), South America (Guyana) and the Caribbean (Cuba and Jamaica).

S.P.A.C.E. (Special Admissions and Curriculum Experiments). An affirmative action program first instituted by Dean Peter J. Liocouris of Temple Law School in response to the reverse discrimination problems raised in the *Bakke* case. Under this plan one-fourth of the entering class each year consists of disadvantaged students, regardless of color or ethnic background, who show exceptional promise. Although they are not given any special remedial help, these students must meet the same academic standards as others. The Temple experiment may be both legally and politically more defensible than other more rigid programs. It has been praised as "affirmative action at its democratic best" because it achieves desirable social goals without granting special privileges to some groups.

SPACE OBJECTS CONVENTION ON INTERNATIONAL LIABILITY. An agreement signed in 1972 by 53 countries, including the United States, which prescribes orderly procedures for the recovery of damages for any injury to persons or property from space objects falling to earth. In the case of the United States, a claim must be fully documented and supported, filed with N.A.S.A. under the Federal Tort Claims Act or through N.A.S.A. as a private bill in Congress if the claim exceeded $5,000.

SPANISH CONSPIRACY. An abortive attempt in 1787 by American Commander-In-Chief of the Army, General James Wilkinson (who euphemistically called himself the Washington of the West), to obtain Spanish support in a plot to detach the Western states from the rest of the country and join them to the Louisiana Territory, either under the Spanish Crown or as a neutral Nation. America was plagued in its early years by a number of such wild ill-starred schemes to dismember it.

SPANISH CORTES. The bicameral legislative Parliament of Spain which was elected by popular ballot only after the death of Generalissimo Franco.

SPANISH SCHOOL OF INTERNATIONAL LAW. Founded by Vitória in the late fifteenth and early sixteenth century, the Spanish School became the center of international law learning when Spain rose to international prominence. The Spanish School continued the tradition of the Italian School of international law by insisting on the universal validity of international law. In the noted work *De Inde,* Vitória first extended the scope of international law by arguing—against the pleasure of his king—that international law applied not only to Christian states but to all nations, including the Indian civilization in America.

SPANO v. NEW YORK (360 U.S. 315 (1959)). An important criminal law case where the defendant, after being indicted for murder in the first degree, was interrogated continuously for eight hours during the night. After the defendant's repeated refusals to answer on the advice of the attorney, the police brought in Officer Bruno, a "childhood friend" of the defendant, who falsely told him that he (Bruno) was in danger of being fired because of the defendant's refusal to confess. Bruno then mentioned how disastrous the loss of his job would be to his family. Finally, the defendant confessed and was later convicted. The Supreme Court reversed the conviction on the ground that the defendant's Fourteenth Amendment rights had been violated. The Court stated that even if the confession were reliable, the techniques used by the police were so distasteful so as to violate the Constitution.

SPEAR OF THE NATION. See A.N.C.

SPECIAL APPEARANCE. An appearance by a party in a lawsuit for the specific purpose of contesting the jurisdiction or venue of the court. Under the Federal Rules of Civil Procedure, one may not make a Special Appearance, as questions of jurisdiction and venue, if timely raised, are preserved for appeal. Where the court asserts Quasi-In-Rem jurisdiction, however, one who defends his property may not be subject to In Personam jurisdiction.

SPECIAL CAUCUSES. Members of Congress who band together to promote a common cause. They include the following: (1) Black Caucus. Wants a shift of at least 11 billion dollars in planned military spending into domestic assistance for people. (2) Blue Collar Caucus. Advocates curbs on imports to protect jobs. (3) Congresswomen's Caucus. Recommends changes in the Social Security Law to benefit women, more hiring and promotion of women in federal employment. (4) Congressional Clearinghouse. Members are informed of the impact on state and local governments of pending legislation. (5) Democratic Study Group. Provides the liberal point of view for members on issues coming up on Capitol Hill. (6) Environmental Study Conference. Maintains background information on all energy and environmental proposals. (7) Great Lakes Senators. Fights any proposal to reduce federal funds for environmental protection in the Great Lakes area. (8) Hispanic Caucus. Seeks specific programs to aid Hispanics. (9) New England Congressional Caucus. Fights to hold down fuel costs in the area by opposing higher oil-import fees. (10) Northeast-Midwest Economic Advancement Coalition. Tries to head off the closing of any more military bases in the regions, monitoring and opposing any tax changes that operate against the nation's older cities. (11) Peace Through Law. Works for peace-promoting treaties, including a new arms pact with the Soviets. (12) Port Caucus. Concentrates on keeping the financing of port operating, dredging and maintenance costs where it now is: in Washington. (13) Rural Caucus. Urges a review of all rural-aid programs to make sure they work to stimulate the private economy. (14) Steel Caucus. Demands more protection from imports of steel. (15) Suburban Caucus. Requests specific programs for the suburbs.

SPECIAL COORDINATION COMMITTEE (S.C.C.; Crisis Team). A subgroup of the National Security Council (N.S.C.) created by President Carter in 1977 as an advisory guide under the Chairmanship of the National Security Adviser (N.S.A.), which meets daily during international emergencies such as the seizure of American hostages at the Iranian Embassy on November 4, 1979.

SPECIAL COURTS OF THE UNITED STATES. In addition to the United States Supreme Court, the United States Courts of Appeals, and the United States District Courts, there have been created by the Congress, from time to time, special courts to deal with particular types of cases. Appeals from the decisions of these courts may ultimately be reviewed in the Supreme Court. There have been created two courts for the District of Columbia: the Superior Court for the District of Columbia and the District of Columbia Court of Appeals. The Economic Stabilization Act Amendments of 1971 created a special court known as the Temporary Emergency Court of Appeals of the United States. The court has exclusive jurisdiction of all appeals from the district courts of the United States in cases and controversies arising under the Economic Stabilization Laws, and consists of eight district and circuit judges appointed by the Chief Justice. The court has been in operation since February 1972, and its principal location is at the United States Courthouse in the District of Columbia. The court operates under its own rules and the Federal Rules of Appellate Procedure.

SPECIAL DAMAGES. Specific losses and expenses which the plaintiff suffers as a result of an injury and for which he may receive compensation from the defendant. If, for instance, Pedestrian is injured in an accident caused by Driver's negligence, he is entitled not only to general damages, but also to compensation for medical bills, lost wages and business profits and any other out-of-pocket expenses that would not have been incurred but for the accident. In his claim for special damages Pedestrian may ask not only for amounts already incurred, but also for those expenses which he proves he probably will incur in the future. Special damages are one element of compensatory damages.

SPECIAL DRAWING RIGHTS. See I.M.F.

SPECIAL FACTS RULE. Imposes a fiduciary duty upon the directors or officers of a corporation who trade its shares. The Rule requires that where there are special facts, such directors or officers must reveal any information which was not disclosed to the public. Recently, this Rule has been expanded and has tended to merge with the rule which held that there was always a fiduciary duty to disclose inside information of fact. This Rule is also buttressed by Rule 10B-5 of the Securities Exchange Commission.

SPECIAL (SINGLE) INTEREST GROUPS. Legislators or lobbyists who protect and promote the welfare of a few at the expense of the larger public weal.

SPECIAL JURY. See BLUE RIBBON JURY.

SPECIAL MASTER. See MASTER OF THE COURT.

SPECIAL OCCUPANTS. See COMMON OCCUPANT.

SPECIAL PARTNER. See PARTICIPATING ASSOCIATE.

SPECIAL POWER. See POWER OF APPOINTMENT.

SPECIAL PROSECUTOR. A private lawyer (usually employed and paid by the family of the victim) to assist the official state prosecutor in a criminal case in an attempt to ensure the conviction of the accused. Revenge is undoubtedly a moving factor.

SPECIAL REVIEW COURT. See ELECTRONIC SURVEILLANCE COURTS.

SPECIAL VERDICT. A jury verdict in which the jury answers specific factual questions posed by the judge. After the jury has determined issues of fact, the judge applies the law to the facts.

SPECIAL WEAPONS AND TACTICS. See S.W.A.T.

SPECIFIC INTENT CRIMES. Require that defendant have a specific objective while performing the criminal act. For example, generally, in order to commit larceny, a person must intend to permanently deprive another person of his property when the property is taken. If the thief intends to borrow the property and return it later, he does not have the requisite intent for larceny. Furthermore, certain defenses, such as voluntary intoxication, may be used only with respect to Specific Intent Crimes. The theory is that an offender who is drunk cannot formulate the Specific Intent needed to constitute the crime. Thus one may defend against a charge of larceny on the ground of voluntary intoxication, but such defense would not be available against General Intent Crimes like rape or arson.

SPECIFIC LEGACY. A gift of property which can be distinguished from other property within the testator's estate with reasonable certainty.

SPECIFIC PERFORMANCE. When money damages would be inadequate compensation for a breach of contract, the promisor is compelled to perform specifically that which he promised to do. Specific performance is often ordered for land sales; or in the case of sales of goods, whenever the goods are unique and could not be purchased elsewhere.

SPECIFIC TARIFF. See AD VALOREM.

SPEED TRAP. See KANGAROO COURT.

SPEED-UP PROGRAM. See FEATHERBEDDING PRACTICE.

SPEEDY TRIAL ACT OF 1974. A federal statute that creates mandatory "30-10-60" time limits in all federal criminal trials. It requires that an indictment be filed against a defendant within 30 days of the arrest, that arraignment take place within 10 days of indictment and that trial commence within 60 days if no plea-bargaining agreement is reached. The law also provides that sanctions will be imposed by the court if a defendant is not brought to trial within the time limits specified by the Act. The sanctions will generally take the form of dismissal of the charges, although the judge can do so "without prejudice," allowing re-prosecution. A growing chorus of judges, prosecutors, law-enforcement officials and defense attorneys have spoken out against the Act on the grounds that the law forces government attorneys to drop prosecutions, places heavy burdens on defense lawyers and has pushed the civil case backlog in many districts to an all-time high.

SPENDTHRIFT CLAUSE. Under this provision in a trust arrangement, the trust beneficiary is restricted from transferring his right to future payments of trust income or capital and his creditors are unable to reach the trust interest in attempting to satisfy their claims. In England and in some American states, such clauses are void as creating an unlawful restraint on alienation. Most American states allow such clauses, and where they are prohibited, the remainder of the trust absent the clause, will be judicially enforced.

SPENDTHRIFT TRUST. A trust arrangement containing a spendthrift clause.

SPERM BANK. See A.I.D.

SPEVACK v. KLEIN (1967). See TAKE THE FIFTH.

SPIELBERG DOCTRINE. A policy of the National Labor Relations Board to defer under certain circumstances to arbitration decisions previously made where the decision effectively disposes of the Unfair Labor Practice or representation problem at issue. In exercising its discretion not to disturb the earlier award, the Board generally must find that the decision by the arbitrator was arrived at through fair and regular proceedings and that it is consonant with the policies and aims of the National Labor Relations Act. This doctrine had its source in the case of *Spielberg Manufacturing Co.*, 112 N.L.R.B. 1080 (1955).

SPILLOVER TRUST. See POUR-OVER CLAUSE.

SPIN-OFF. Bonus shares which a stockholder may receive as the result of a corporate merger. For example, if *X* Incorporated merges with *Y* Company, *X* stockholders may receive *Y* shares in addition to their *X* shares.

SPIRITUAL COLONIALISM. See NEW WORLD INFORMATION ORDER.

SPITE FENCES. See ANCIENT DOCTRINE OF LIGHTS.

SPLIT CHILD CUSTODY. Where there are several children and custody of one or more is given to one natural parent and custody of others is given to the other natural parent.

SPLIT-DOLLAR PLAN. An arrangement between an employee and his employer whereby both agree to share the premium cost of an insurance policy on the life of the employee. The employer agrees to pay that portion of the annual premium equal to the increase in the cash value of the policy. The employee pays the remainder. Each year the contribution of the employer increases and that of the employee decreases.

SPLIT TICKET. See STRAIGHT TICKET.

SPOT AUDIT. See RANDOM AUDIT.

SPOT CHECK. See RANDOM OR SPOT CHECK.

SPOT MARKET. The price paid for a commodity on a fluctuating daily basis, which is usually higher than the fixed price negotiated in a long-term contract.

SPOT ZONING. A zoning ordinance directed at a particular piece of property and which puts such property in a different zoning classification from surrounding property.

SPOUSAL SUPPORT. A new concept to replace alimony payments. Whereas alimony is money paid by a man to support his ex-wife, spousal support recognizes reciprocal financial obligations between husband and wife. If a male is unable to get a job and his ex-wife has money, she must share her largess with him.

SPOUSE ABUSE. Intentional physical or psychological injury inflicted on either husband or wife by his or her marital partner.

S.P.P.A. (Society for Philosophy and Public Affairs). Founded in 1969 by a small group of professional philosophers in order, as they put it, "to overcome the detachment of philosophy from concrete social issues." It has since become a national body and has organized symposiums in which its members have tackled contemporary problems like preferential hiring, genocide, abortion and civil disobedience. The formation of the S.P.P.A. has encouraged the development of political philosophy into a minor industry, issuing a torrent of distinctions, theories, ideologies and suggestions for reorienting the aims of government.

SPRAYING TRUST. See SPRINKLING TRUST.

SPRING EXECUTORY INTEREST. See EXECUTORY INTEREST.

SPRING-GUN CASES. A group of recent cases which state that the use of spring guns to protect unoccupied property is illegal. Generally, the courts have deemed the use of such device out of proportion to the petty thievery committed by burglars and have thus enforced the common-law doctrine that booby-trapped weapons which are used to fire at intruders on empty premises are excessively violent. In a 1971 Iowa case, *Katko v. Briney*, 183 N.W.2d 657 (1971), the State Supreme Court upheld an award of $30,000 in damages to a would-be thief who broke into an abandoned farmhouse. In France the Movement for Legitimate Self-Defense seeks a broader legal definition of legitimate self-defense to allow citizens to defend property the way they choose.

SPRINKLING TRUST. A trust arrangement in which the income or trust property is distributed among the named trust beneficiaries by the trustee at his discretion. Because such trusts leave great decisional power with the trustee as to who will receive how much, they have become increasingly unpopular in recent decades, especially because lawyers are reluctant to employ a device which may engender family discord. The colloquial term derives from the decision of a New York Court which referred to a trustee's authority "freely to sprinkle the income" as if the trustees "were playing a hose" among the members of the trustor's family. Such provisions allow a testator to achieve flexibility in the distribution of his estate, to protect against the creditors of beneficiaries, and to reduce taxes.

SQUARE DEAL (1901-1908). Term made popular during the Presidency of Theodore Roosevelt (1901-1908) embodying the philosophy of austerity held by "the Rough Rider." The Square Deal enshrined Roosevelt's ideas on the primacy of good citizenship, the dignity of labor, and the importance of honestly-earned wealth and Christian morality.

SQUATTER'S RIGHTS. See ADVERSE POSSESSION.

S.S.A. See SOCIAL SECURITY ADMINISTRATION.

S.S.I. (Supplemental Security Income). A federal program designed to aid aged, disabled, and blind persons who are unable to support themselves because of their physical condition. According to *Lee v. Smith*, 387 N.Y.S.2d 952 (1977), a state may not arbitrarily deny public assistance to recipients of S.S.I. when such public funds are available to other state residents.

S. 600. See CONGLOMERATE MERGER BILL.

STALKING HORSE. A political candidate who is not serious about running, but who tests voter response for the benefit of another candidate. The expression derives from the practice of hunters using their horses as cover when moving in for the kill. In recent years, the widespread use of opinion polls has limited the need for the Stalking Horse technique in political contest.

STAMP ACT. On March 22, 1765, Great Britain imposed a tax on the American colonies, requiring stamps on most legal documents and commercial papers. This "taxation without representation" initiated rumblings among colonists to revolt. The tax was repealed in March, 1766, on the ground that it was unenforceable.

STANDARDIZED ARREST ABBREVIATIONS. A manual used by the F.B.I. and police agencies to standardize notations made on an identification record. Examples include: A & B—Assault and Battery, B of P—Breach of Peace, A to K—Assault to Kill.

STANDARDIZED NUCLEAR UNIT POWER PLANT SYNDICATE. See S.N.U.P.P.S.

STANDARD OF REVIEW. The standard used by a court to review the decision of a jury, a lower court, or Review includes the following: (1) Arbitrary and Capricious Test—the ordinary standard applied by a reviewing court in evaluating the decisions of an administrator or trial judge. Under this test, the decision will be set aside only if it shows an abuse of discretion; (2) Substantial Evidence Test—the ordinary standard applied by a court to a jury verdict. Under this standard, the verdict will be upheld if it is supported by substantial evidence allowing a reasonable person to reach the same verdict as the jury. In administrative law, the Substantial Evidence Test is a more stringent Standard of Review than the Arbitrary or Capricious Test. Generally, the Substantial Evidence Test is applied only to agency decisions based on a formal written record. (3) The Clearly Erroneous Test applied to factfinding by a judge; (4) De Novo Test—a rarely used test available to appellate courts where the trial verdict was based on a paper record. In that case, the appellate court may make its own findings of fact.

STANDARD OIL CO. OF NEW JERSEY v. UNITED STATES. See RULES OF DECISION ACT.

STANDARDS AND GUIDELINES FOR THE MERIT SELECTION OF UNITED STATES DISTRICT JUDGES. An Executive Order signed by President Carter on November 8, 1978 which provides an entirely new approach to the Federal Judiciary as follows: (1) Whenever a vacancy occurs in a district court of the United States, the President shall nominate as district judge to fill that vacancy a person whose character, experience, ability, and commitment to equal justice under law qualifies that person to serve in the federal judiciary. (2) The Attorney General shall assist the President by recommending to the President persons to be considered for appointment who are qualified to be district judges and by evaluating potential nominees. The Attorney General shall receive recommendations of such persons from any person, commission or organization. (3) The use of commissions to notify the public of vacancies and to make recommendations for district judges is encouraged. The Attorney General shall make public the suggested guidelines for such commissions. (4) Before making recommendations, the Attorney General shall consider whether: Public notice of the vacancy has been given and an affirmative effort has been made, in the case of each vacancy, to identify qualified candidates, including women and members of minority groups; the selection process was fair and reasonable; those recommended meet the standards for evaluating proposed nominees. (5) In evaluating proposed nominees, consideration will be given to reports of Department of Justice investigations and all other relevant information concerning potential nominees and their qualifications. The standards to be used in determining whether a person is qualified to serve as a district judge are whether that person: (6) Is a citizen of the United States, is a member of a bar of a state, territory, possession or the District of Columbia, and is in good standing in every bar in which that person is a member. (7) Possesses, and has a reputation for integrity, good character, and common sense. (8) Is, and has a reputation for being, fair, experienced, even-tempered and free of biases against any class of citizens or any religious or racial group. (9) Is of sound physical and mental health. (10) Possesses and has demonstrated commitment to equal justice under law. (11) Possesses and has demonstrated outstanding legal ability and competence, as evidenced by substantial legal experience, ability to deal with complex legal problems, aptitude for legal scholarship and writing, and familiarity with courts and their processes. (12) Has the ability and the willingness to manage complicated pretrial and trial proceedings, including the ability to weigh conflicting testimony and make factual determinations, and to communicate skillfully with jurors and witnesses.

STANDING MASTER. See MASTER OF THE COURT.

STANDING TO LITIGATE (Standing to Sue). A doctrine developed in both state and federal courts requiring that all parties seeking relief to have some legally-protected interest in the outcome of the controversy. This stake in the outcome of a dispute may take one of two forms—either as a personal or proprietary interest in relief, or as a sufficiently appropriate representative of other interested persons. The law of standing in federal courts comprises a narrow line of cases, almost exclusively concerned with such public law issues as the constitutionality of statutes and review of administrative or other government action. Generally, the person bringing suit must show that he has been harmed by the alleged wrong, or that the question is of such a public nature that he should be granted standing to litigate as a concerned, although not injured, citizen. A related concept of standing is the general principle that even where one has suffered an injury of the sort required to give him standing, he may not, save in exceptional cases, assert the rights of another injured person. In addition, a defendant cannot claim a statute is unconstitutional in some of its reaches if the statute is constitutional as applied to him. In recent decisions the Supreme Court has gradually broadened its notion of who has standing to litigate in federal courts, permitting greater numbers of cases "in the public interest."

STANFORD DAILY NEWSPAPER CASE. See NO SEARCH RULE.

STANLEY v. GEORGIA. Landmark 1969 United States Supreme Court case which held that the knowing possession of obscene matter could not be made a crime due to the First Amendment freedom of speech clause and the Fourteenth Amendment due process clause. Thus, the mere possession of pornography by an individual cannot constitute a crime.

STAR CHAMBER. Equity courts did not have trial by jury. Some British monarchs, especially Henry VIII, abused the chancery process by having those who had fallen in royal disfavor tried by the Chancellor for alleged crimes they had not committed but for which they were invariably held guilty. One of the conditions to the restoration of Charles II to the throne was that equity courts would give up their criminal jurisdiction. The room in which the abuses had taken place had stars painted on the ceiling, hence the name. Now a Star Chamber proceeding means a "stacked" trial in which the accused will most certainly be found guilty.

STARE DECISIS (Latin—to abide by decided cases). The principle that courts should abide by precedent in deciding future cases, unless it is shown that a prior decision was based upon a misapplication or misunderstanding of the law.

STATE ACTION REQUIREMENT. The rights of Americans detailed in the Constitution of the United States exist as rights as against government and not as rights as against individuals. Therefore, a person usually must demonstrate some form of "State Action" before he can successfully maintain an action based on a deprivation of his rights. For example, although the government of the United States or individual states cannot forbid an individual from publishing and selling a newspaper, there is no constitutional proscription of an *individual* using his own economic or personal influence to retard a newspaper's availability or success. The most obvious form of State Action is the case where the state itself unequivocally acts as a government to deprive someone of his constitutional rights. For example, it is clearly State Action when a state legislature enacts a statute forbidding newspapers from being published in the state. State Action has been found, however, in cases in which the state does not act entirely on its own in areas of proscribed conduct. State Action cases where the state is not the principal actor fall into two categories, public function and nexus. The public function analysis strand of State Action applies to cases in which a private entity has such power in an area that it rises to the level of operating as a government. This strand of State Action analysis was developed in *Marsh v. Alabama*, 326 U.S. 501 (1946). In that case State Action was found to be present because a private corporation owned the entire town and the only difference between the "company town" and a public municipality was the ownership. If a "company town" similar to the one in the *Marsh* case prohibited the publishing of newspapers that would likely constitute State Action under the public function analysis. The other method of establishing State Action is by the nexus analysis. In this approach State Action is found where the private entity and the government are so interconnected that the acts of the private entity become the acts of the government. Under the nexus approach State Action has been found where a private entity initiated court action to enforce a racially restrictive housing covenant, as in *Shelley v. Kraemer*, 334 U.S. 1 (1948), and where a private entity engages in racial discrimination on premises leased from the government. In the newspaper example, there would be State Action if an individual sought a writ of injunction to enjoin the publication of a newspaper. It must be understood that the State Action requirement is an initial hurdle. After State Action is found, the substantive violation must still be shown.

STATED CAPITAL. An item in corporate accounting which consists of the total of all shares with par value that have been issued, the consideration received for all no par value stock that has been issued, except that portion of the consideration which was allocated to capital surplus, and other amounts transferred to stated capital from issue of shares or as a share dividend. From this amount must be subtracted all reductions made pursuant to statute. Where solely par value stock is used, stated capital will equal the par value of each share times the number of outstanding shares. Corporations are usually subject to state statutory minimum capital requirements; most states require a corporation to have from $300 to $1,000 capital before commencing business. Many jurisdictions prohibit the impairment of stated capital by the payment of dividends. Dividends usually may be paid only from capital surplus.

STATE GOVERNMENT DIRECTORY. A reference book which provides the telephone numbers of the top officials in the executive, judicial and legislative branches in the fifty states.

STATEHOOD ACT OF 1958. The admission of Alaska as the 49th state in the Union.

STATE JURISDICTION. Under international law, the right of a state or nation to subject persons, places, or things to its own Rule of Law. The existence of the right to jurisdiction in a state does not necessarily mean that the state has legislated the authority to assume or enforce that jurisdiction. However, the phrase state jurisdiction can refer to five different types of jurisdiction under international law: (1) objective territoriality—jurisdiction over conduct occurring in or having direct effect in a state's territory or contiguous zones; (2) nationality—jurisdiction over nationals of the state wherever they are; (3) passive personality—jurisdiction over aliens outside the state whose actions affect a national of the state; (4) protective jurisdiction—the right to control extra-territorial alien activity which affects the national interest; and (5) universal jurisdiction—concurrent jurisdiction exercised by all states over certain activities, such as piracy.

STATE OF MIND. The mental part of a crime. The requirement that criminal culpability or Mens Rea be present for liability is expressed in the Latin maxim, actus non facit reum nisi mens sit rea (an act does not make one guilty unless his mind is guilty). Crimes differ in the degree of culpability required, and can be divided into three categories. Some require subjective fault in that to some extent the accused knew or intended that his conduct would result in harm. Traditionally these crimes have been designated by terms such as "wilfully," "wantonly," "with intent to," "with knowledge that," "fraudulently," "feloniously" and "recklessly." Other crimes require objective fault in that the defendant should have known that his conduct would result in harm. These crimes employ terms such as "negligently," "with criminal negligence," and "carelessly." Finally, crimes which require no fault are known as Strict Liability Crimes. Such crimes include the sale of liquor to a minor. The sale alone constitutes the crime. The imposition of Strict Liability, which seems inconsistent with the concept of criminal fault, is the subject of much debate among legal scholars today. Modern criminal codes, such as the Model Penal Code, divide subjective fault into three categories—"intentional" ("purposeful" under the Model Penal Code), "knowing" and "reckless." "Intentional" means that the accused acted with the purpose of causing a forbidden result, while "knowing" means that the accused was practically certain that his act would cause a forbidden result. "Reckless" means that the accused acted with conscious disregard of a substantial risk that his conduct would cause a forbidden result. For example, assume that *A*, while driving his car, sees *B* crossing the street and kills him. If *A* wants to kill *B*, then his state of mind is "intentional." If *A* does not want to kill *B*, but in attempting to escape a pursuing policeman, does not slow down, and is substantially certain that *B*'s death will result, then *A*'s state of mind is "knowing." If *A* does not want to kill *B*, and thinks that *B* may escape injury, but still realizes there is a substantial risk that *B* will not, then *A*'s state of mind is "reckless." The applicable state of mind determines the crime, if any, of which the defendant is guilty. Under the Model Penal Code, both intentional homicide and knowing homicide constitute murder, whereas a reckless homicide is the lesser crime of criminal manslaughter. Note that although both intentional and knowing homicides are murder, there are other offenses where the presence of intent versus knowledge results in different crimes. An example is the crime of arson which under the Penal Code requires an intent to damage a building. A knowing state of mind is insufficient. If in the preceding hypothetical *A* did not see *B* because *A* failed to keep a proper lookout, *A* may be guilty of negligent homicide, also called involuntary manslaughter. This crime punishes objective fault in that although *A* did not consciously disregard the risk of killing *B*, he nevertheless drove his car in a manner which posed a high risk of harm to others. Obviously state of mind is impossible to prove with certainty. Absent a confession it is usually proven by circumstantial evidence and the doctrine of Presumed Intent.

STATE OF THE JUDICIARY. A practice instituted by Warren E. Burger to have the Chief Justice render a yearly report on the judiciary to the American public at the annual meeting of the American Bar Association.

STATE RESEARCH BUREAU. The infamous prison in the capital of Uganda where the mad dictator-president-for-life Idi Amin brutally butchered several hundred thousand innocent victims in gross violation of every basic concept of due process of law before he was blessedly deposed in 1979.

STATE SUCCESSION. The international law doctrine under which a state or nation succeeds another as the legitimate authority in the same territory and is bound by all of the obligations of the state it succeeded.

STATUS OFFENDER. A minor who has not committed a crime but only a minor infraction such as running away from an unfavorable family situation or being truant from school, for which he is subject to confinement in a public institution.

STATUS SUITS. Generally suits involving such matters as divorce and adoption. The suits are so named because the court determines the status of the parties.

STATUTE OF FRAUDS. Requires that the contractual terms of an agreement be in writing in order to be legally valid and enforceable. Early in the history of contract law many oral promises resulted in charges of perjury. Therefore, in 1677 the English Parliament enacted a law to prevent fraud and perjury. There is legislation now in all the states which requires writing in numerous business transactions and contracts. The statute covers such areas as contracts for the sale of goods, contracts for the sale of land, contracts in consideration of marriage, contracts not to be performed within one year, contracts of executors and administrators, and contracts to answer for the debts of another.

STATUTE OF LIMITATIONS. Any law which fixes the time within which parties must take judicial action to enforce rights. Enacted to prevent the pressing of stale claims, these statutes encourage parties to seek judicial relief while the matter is still fresh in order to minimize the problems of proof caused by lost evidence or faulty memory. Those statutes apply both in civil and criminal law.

STATUTE OF USES (1536). An English statute which opened the way for the development of the law of modern trust arrangements. During this period there were substantial burdens attached to the ownership of land. To escape this, a landed gentry "enfeoffed" or transferred legal title to another person, but retained the "use" of his land. The Statute of Uses merged the legal title and the equitable title, or use, that aristocrats had been separating for generations. Thus, the Statute of Uses "killed the use" and forced those in beneficial possession to assume the legal responsibilities of ownership. However, the Statute of Uses did not have its intended effect because courts failed to convert all equitable interests into legal interests, as the statute was enacted to do. The remaining equitable interests which did not take legal effect formed the basis of the modern trust.

STATUTES AT LARGE. See UNITED STATES STATUTES AT LARGE.

STATUTORY COPYRIGHT. Protection afforded by federal statute to written, recorded or artistic work. The Copyright Act of 1976 embodies the current provisions of Statutory Copyright. To enjoy Statutory Copyright, an inventor must comply with certain formalities. Failure to do so may result in discharging the work into the public realm. The necessary formalities include providing Copyright Notice, observing domestic manufacturing provisions in connection with books and periodicals, and registering and depositing the work with the Copyright Office.

STATUTORY DOWER. A right of dower of all land seized by the husband during coverture as prescribed by law.

STATUTORY RAPE. Unlawful carnal knowledge by a male of a female under the age of consent. Generally the age of consent is 16 to 18. As long as the female is under the age set by statute, the male is guilty of Statutory Rape whether or not she consents. The theory is that the female is not old enough to give effective consent to sexual intercourse. And the male is guilty even if he thinks the girl is over the age of consent and even if she thinks she is or tells him that she is.

STATUTORY SHARE. The portion of a deceased spouse's estate—typically one-third if there are children, one-half if there are not—to which a surviving spouse is entitled by statute. Most states provide for a Statutory Share, replacing the common law rights of dower and courtesy which entitle the surviving spouse to a life estate in some portion of the deceased spouse's real property. A spouse can take his or her Statutory Share regardless of the terms of the deceased's will. However, in most states the surviving spouse must choose to either take the Statutory Share or accept the portion of the estate passing to him or her under the terms of the will.

STAY OF EXECUTION. A postponement, generally allowing the defendant an opportunity to seek relief from his criminal sentence.

STEADFAST SUMMIT. See CAMP DAVID SUMMIT.

STEAM GENERATION JUMPERS (Sponges). Unskilled, short-term employees who expose themselves to quick doses of high radiation for high pay, often for only minutes of work. Chosen for their small size, which enables them to crawl through the 18-inch-wide passageways of mammoth steel nuclear reactor pressure vessels, they may do no more than turn a bolt. But, in a workplace giving off as many as 25 rems an hour of radiation, it must be done in seconds. Radiation workers are limited by federal regulations of the Nuclear Regulatory Commission

(N.R.C.) to three rems of exposure per calendar quarter, which members of a plant's permanent staff would absorb quickly in doing a nuclear plant's "dirty work." So temporary workers take the rems, which are measures of cell-damaging radiation absorbed by the body. The measure is most often expressed in thousandths, or millirems. The use of Steam Generation Jumpers is contrary to the policy of the A.L.A.R.A. (As Low As Reasonably Achievable) established by the N.R.C. in 1960. In 1979, the N.R.C. amended its record-keeping regulations to require all nuclear licensees to obtain and to take account of the cumulative radiation doses of transient workers before exposing them to any more radioactivity in order to protect their health from these hazards.

STEEL GROIN PROTECTORS CASE. See OFFICE OF HUMAN RIGHTS AND HUMANITARIAN AFFAIRS.

STEEL SEIZURE CASE. See YOUNGSTOWN SHEET AND TUBE CO. v. SAWYER.

STEEPLE EXEMPTION. Concern of religious leaders that the government will limit church tax exemptions to activities carried on in the church building itself.

STEPPED-UP BASIS. See FRESH START.

STEP-RATE MORTGAGE. See GRADUATED PAYMENT MORTGAGE.

STING OPERATION. The nickname, popularized by the 1973 movie, "The Sting," for a confidence scheme. The Law Enforcement Assistance Administration reports that there have been over 100 federally-assisted sting operations in 47 cities with the cooperation of local police departments, which recovered a total of $250 million in stolen goods and made over 10,000 arrests. In 1976 undercover law enforcement officers from the District of Columbia Police Department purchased and sold goods which allegedly had been stolen. Over 100 people were arrested and convicted, and, in 1980, the F.B.I. conducted a sting operation (Abscam) in which congressmen and senators were accused of accepting bribes.

STOCK BONUS TRUST. A trust arrangement which enables corporate employees to share in the fruits of their work. By distributing its own stock to employees, a corporation obtains the obvious benefit of greater investment capital and enhanced business morale. Stock Bonus Trusts are popular in the middle and upper echelons of corporate America.

STOCK CERTIFICATES. See SHARE CERTIFICATES.

STOCK DIVIDEND. A distribution to the existing shareholders of additional shares of stock by the corporation without any new consideration. As a result of the stock dividend, the par value of each share remains unchanged, but the total number of shares and, therefore, the capital stock of the corporation are increased. Stock dividends are used either to retain profits in the corporation while giving the shareholders some evidence of the profit, or to give a dividend where cash dividends are not allowed. For instance, statute or common law may prohibit the distribution of cash dividends from cash surpluses derived solely from re-valuation of present assets, but will permit stock dividends under such circumstances. The only legal requirements for stock dividends are that there be a sufficient number of unissued shares and a sufficient surplus to be capitalized by the stock dividend. If there are not enough unissued shares to cover the stock dividend, it will be necessary to increase the number of authorized shares, an action normally requiring shareholder approval. There are tax advantages to stock dividends. They are not taxable to the shareholder when received because there has been no distribution of assets. If the stock is later sold, the gain realized from the stock dividend will be taxed as a capital gain, while cash dividends are taxed as ordinary income.

STOCKHOLDER'S SUIT. See DERIVATIVE SUIT.

STOCKHOLM SYNDROME. A psychiatric term for political prisoners who eventually sympathize with the views of their captors. It was first observed in Stockholm, Sweden, in a bank robbery in 1973.

STOCK OPTION. A right in the holder to purchase a specified number of shares at a stated price within a limited time period. The right is issued by the corporation, usually to an officer or employee to compensate him for past services and to provide him with a continuing incentive. Stock options are often traded over the counter and are evidenced by share warrants. They must be supported by adequate consideration and be authorized by law. Preemptive rights must also be observed where applicable.

STOCK SPLIT. Where one share is split into a larger number of shares. The par value of the stock is divided and the number of shares is correspondingly increased. The purpose of a stock split is usually to lower the price of the one hundred share lot, the normal unit of trading, and, therefore, increase the marketability of the stock. This requires board of director action, and often shareholder approval when the Articles of Incorporation must be amended in order to change the par value of the stock on the number of authorized shares to be increased.

STONE, HARLAN FISKE. Former dean of Columbia Law School and Attorney General of the United States who succeeded Charles Evans Hughes as Chief Justice of the United States in 1941. With his handsome beard and paternal demeanor, Stone was the perfect model of a Chief Justice.

STONE v. POWELL. See HABEAS CORPUS.

STOP AND FRISK. Under certain circumstances a police officer may stop and frisk an individual without a search warrant. A stop and frisk cannot be as extensive as a full search, however. According to *Terry v. Ohio*, 392 U.S. 1 (1968), the classic case in this area, a police officer may stop an individual he reasonably expects has committed a crime and conduct a preliminary and cursory frisk to check for weapons if he reasonably believes that his safety or the safety of others is in danger. The right to frisk does not arise automatically from the stopping, however. The officer may frisk only "where nothing in the initial stages of the encounter serves to dispel his reasonable fear for his own or others' safety."

STOPPAGE IN TRANSITU (Latin —Stop in transit). The right of an unpaid venor of goods sold upon credit to stop their progress and retake them while they are in the possession of a carrier on the discovery of the insolvency of the buyer or vendee. The vendor has the right to stop the transit of such goods until they are delivered to the buyer or until active or constructive possession is taken by the buyer.

STOP THE CLOCK. A device used by deliberation bodies such as state legislatures or those engaged in collective bargaining where there is a deadline approaching and the task under consideration is not consummated. The participants physically stop an official clock from running so that they may claim later to have completed the chore within the appointed hour.

STOP-WORK ORDER CLAUSE. In Department of Defense contracting, this clause requires that a contractor be compensated for all government-directed delays of all or any part of the contract work. The compensation allowed is to be in the nature of an equitable adjustment.

STOREFRONT LAW. Legal aid clinics or lawyers who provide professional services to middle class or low income clients at low fees. Since they are usually conveniently located in suburban shopping centers or neighborhood stores, they have a lower overhead than traditional law firms. Jacoby and Meyers, of Los Angeles, California, which claims to be the first such operation, has served more than 20,000 clients since it began in 1972. This revolutionary practice of law will probably mushroom now that the Supreme Court of the United States has struck down the ban against advertising by lawyers.

STORY, JOSEPH. A Justice of the Supreme Court who simultaneously served as a Professor of Law at Harvard (1829) where he reorganized the curriculum and revitalized the School. His lectures were later published as a book entitled *Commentaries on the Law*, which is one of the great works of American legal scholarship.

STRAIGHT BILL. Any bill of lading that is considered non-negotiable. Generally such bills will explicitly state that the goods are specifically destined to a particular person.

STRAIGHT LINE DEPRECIATION. The standard rate of depreciation for real property established by the United States Treasury Department.

STRAIGHT TICKET. The practice of voting for all candidates of one party on a single ballot. Often used by voters with a general ideological preference who have inadequate information about the actual qualifications of particular candidates. This practice contrasts with split-ticket voting, or voting for candidates from each political party on a single ballot.

STRATA OWNERSHIP. See CONDOMINIUM OWNERSHIP.

STRATEGIC ARMS LIMITATION TREATY. See S.A.L.T.

STRAUSS, ROBERT S. See WORLD TRADE PACT.

STREET LAW. See NATIONAL STREET LAW INSTITUTE.

STRETCH-OUT PROGRAM. See FEATHERBEDDING PRACTICE.

STRICT LIABILITY. Liability without fault which applies to certain lesser criminal offenses and to some torts. Traffic infractions exemplify the application of strict liability in the criminal law. Generally, for instance, the government is not required to prove that a driver knew he was exceeding the speed limit in order to obtain a conviction. On the other hand, guilty knowledge is required to prove murder. Early tort law was not so much concerned with fault. As one English judge said in 1681, "In all civil acts the law doth not so much regard the intent of the actor, as the loss and damage of the party suffering." With the development of actions for negligence in the nineteenth century, however, fault became more of a legal factor. In this context fault is not considered the equivalent of moral blame, but rather the failure to live up to an expected level of conduct. Recently, strict liability has begun to receive more attention and is now the accepted standard in the areas of extra-hazardous activities and products liability. The imposition of strict liability is frequently justified because of the risk of harm, the difficulty of proving fault, and the high number of violations.

STRIKE BENEFITS. Payments made by a union to its members who are on strike.

STRIKE BREAKER. An employee who accepts employment or continues to work in a place where a strike is in process. A goon is any person employed by management or labor for the purpose of using force or violence to terrorize the opposing party in a labor dispute. Striking members of a maritime union are said to be "on the beach."

STRIKE FUND. A sum of money allocated by a union to defray expenses of a work stoppage, which may include benefits to members on strike, publicity costs and legal fees.

STRIKE NOTICE. The formal notification of an impending work stoppage presented by a Union to an employer or to the appropriate government agency, should this be so required by law.

STRIKE VOTE. Held by the members of a union to determine whether or not a work stoppage should be called.

STRIP CELL. See KEEPLOCK SENTENCING.

STRIP FRISK SEARCH. A degrading and dehumanizing but regrettably legal practice by prison guards, policemen and customs officials compelling a person to remove all clothing and submit to a close visual inspection including body cavities in a search for contraband.

STUBBORN CHILD LAW. Legislation which permits the state to commit a child to a state institution even though no crime has been committed for serious misbehavior such as truancy, running away, drug addiction, consensual sexual behavior, ungovernability or serious disobedience. Such minors are called status offenders, C.H.I.N.S. (Children in Need of Supervision), or P.I.N.S. (Persons in Need of Services).

STUCHKA, P. I. The first Soviet writer (Lenin's Commissar of Justice) to deal with international law in his treatise entitled *The Role of Law and the Revolutionary State*, published in 1921.

STUDENT RECORDS. See BUCKLEY AMENDMENT.

SUA SPONTE (Latin—of his own will). An action by a judge on his own motion and without the application of either party is said to be Sua Sponte.

SUBCHAPTER S CORPORATIONS. Subchapter S of the Internal Revenue Code was enacted in 1958 in order to minimize the effect of federal income taxes on businessmen's choices of the form of business organization in which they conduct their businesses, and to permit the incorporation and operation of certain small businesses without the incidence of income taxation at both the corporate and shareholder levels. One of the most common uses of the Subchapter S election is in a family owned or controlled corporation. The Subchapter S rules allow corporations engaged in active trades or businesses an election to be treated for income tax purposes in a manner similar to that accorded partnerships. Where an eligible corporation elects under the Subchapter S provisions, the income or loss (except for certain capital gains) is not taxed to the corporation, but each shareholder reports a share of the corporation's income or loss each year in proportion to his share of the corporation's total stock. An election under Subchapter S is made by, and requires the consent of all shareholders. It may be terminated either voluntarily or involuntarily in certain circumstances. In order to be eligible for Subchapter S treatment, the stock ownership of the corporation must meet certain qualifications. First, it must be a corporation with only one issued and outstanding class of stock. Under prior law the corporation was required to have fewer shareholders, all of whom were individuals or estates and none of whom were trusts or nonresident aliens. Under the Tax Reform Act of 1976, the number of shareholders in a Subchapter S corporation was raised to fifteen after the corporation had been an electing Subchapter S corporation for five taxable years.

SUBJECT MATTER JURISDICTION. The jurisdiction of a court over the subject matter of a controversy; the power to decide cases of a general type or class. Within the federal and state judicial systems, some courts have limited jurisdiction in that they may hear only certain types of claims, or cases involving certain amounts of money. For example, a family court is not competent to hear criminal cases; it has no subject matter jurisdiction over crimes. Or, a municipal court may be limited to hearing cases involving less than a certain amount of money.

SUBJECT TO MORTGAGE. A provision in a mortgage agreement which means that a buyer assuming an existing mortgage assumes no personal liability if he defaults on the mortgage payments.

SUB JUDICE (Latin—under consideration). Refers to a matter which is before the court or before a judge for determination; under judicial consideration.

SUBORNATION OF PERJURY. At common law, the crime of inducing another person to commit perjury.

SUBPOENA DUCES TECUM (Latin—produce the writing under penalty). A form of process whereby a court commands the presence of a person and instructs him to bring with him documents or other evidence in his possession. It is the usual method of compelling the presence of documentary evidence in a witness's possession.

SUBSEQUENT REMEDIAL MEASURES. Identifies testimony generally held inadmissible to prove negligence or culpable conduct. Thus, if a visitor to *X*'s home fell on his staircase, the fact that, after the fall, *X* had a new handrail installed could not be introduced at a trial to prove that the original handrail was defective. Two reasons for this rule are frequently cited. First, that evidence of a subsequent repair is of little logical assistance in determining whether the original condition was the result of negligence. Second, that if the evidence were admitted, people would be unwilling to take precautions following an accident.

SUBSERVIENT TENEMENT. The estate in land which is subject to an easement.

SUBSIDIZED ADOPTION. Payments made by a state to adoptive parents to cover the cost of medical care required by the adopted child to enable the adoptive parents to adopt the child which they otherwise could not have afforded to do in the absence of the subsidy.

SUBSTANTIAL EVIDENCE TEST. See STANDARD OF REVIEW.

SUBSTANTIAL PERFORMANCE DOCTRINE. See PERFECT TENDER RULE.

SUBSTANTIVE DUE PROCESS. A trend in American jurisprudence which uses the Due Process Clause of the Fourteenth Amendment to the Constitution not merely to prescribe the procedures which the state must invoke in order to impinge upon rights, but also to articulate the substance of those rights. Substantive Due Process has evolved from a concern to protect economic liberty to the modern court's willingness to protect the personal rights of autonomy and privacy.

SUBSTITUTE FATHER RULE. See MAN IN THE HOUSE RULE.

SUBVERSIVE ACTIVITIES. Under the Internal Security Act (1950) and the Communist Control Act (1954) any Communist action, Communist front or Communist-infiltrated organization must register with the United States government. Severe consequences follow registration which obliges the party and its fronts to list the names, aliases and addresses of their officers, members and contributors; compels those organizations to identify all broadcasts and publications as Communist in origin; removes the organization's tax exemptions; and forbids members to hold passports, government jobs, defense plant employment or labor union offices.

SUBVERSIVE ACTIVITIES CONTROL BOARD. An independent agency established by Congress in 1950 and abolished in 1973, the Board was created to investigate allegedly Communist organizations. The Board ordered several groups, including the Communist Party, to register. In *Communist Party v. Subversive Activities Control Board*, 367 U.S. 1 (1961), the Supreme Court upheld such registration of the Party. However, four years later, in *Albertson v. Subversive Activities Control Board*, 381 U.S. 910 (1965), the Court struck down an order requiring registration of individual Party members as violative of the protection against self-incrimination. Although the Board itself was later authorized to register individuals, its power was considerably weakened and it was dissolved.

SUCCESSOR EMPLOYER. A new employer who faces a pre-existing labor contract. This situation may arise through a corporate acquisition, merger, or otherwise assuming control of a business. Certain provisions of the Taft-Hartley Act, the National Labor Relations Act, and Title VII of the Civil Rights Act determine whether the new employer is bound by the pre-existing contract.

SUGAR ACT OF 1948. See JONES-COSTIGAN SUGAR ACT OF 1934.

SUGAR KING. See JONES-COSTIGAN SUGAR ACT OF 1934.

SUGARMAN PLAN. A proposal by the vice-chairman of the Civil Service Commission which would earmark up to twenty percent of civil service job vacancies for women, blacks, Hispanics and other minority groups who are under-represented in government.

SUIT TO QUIET TITLE. A lawsuit brought to establish clear title to real property.

SULLIVAN LAW. See PLAIN LANGUAGE LAW.

SUMMARY DEATH SENTENCE. See ISLAMIC REVOLUTIONARY COURTS.

SUMMARY JUDGMENT. A procedure generally initiated at the outset of a trial which asks the court to determine whether or not, as a matter of law, the moving party should prevail. In federal courts, summary judgment is governed by Rule 56 of the Federal Rules of Civil Procedure.

SUN DAY. See SOLAR ENERGY RESEARCH INSTITUTE.

SUNDAY CLOSING LAWS. See BLUE LAWS.

SUNDAY TRADING LAWS. See BLUE LAWS.

SUNDOWN PROBATION. An order by the court banishing a person from a given area—city, county or state. It is reminiscent of the Old West when the order by the sheriff was, "I want you out of here before the sun goes down."

SUNSET LAW. A statute first passed by Colorado in 1976 and since followed by a majority of American states. It requires newly created agencies of government to justify successfully their continued existence in periodic review of their activities or face summary extinction through failure of appropriations and thereby fade away into the sunset.

SUNSHINE LAW. A requirement that a government agency open its meetings and records to the spotlight of public participation and scrutiny on a theory that if the honest sun shines into its activities, the agency will not be able to conceal undesirable action, fraud or inefficiency through secrecy.

SUN YAT-SEN. See LONG MARCH FORWARD.

SUPER LAWYERS. See GOULDEN, JOSEPH.

SUPER POWERS. The U.S. and the U.S.S.R., each of whom has the nuclear capacity for the complete destruction not only of each other but also the entire world, and thereby to bring an end to human habitation on the planet Earth. This highlights the importance of the hot line which is an instantaneous and continuous direct telephone communication between the White House and Red Square to ensure that nuclear bombs are not unleashed in a holocaust by mistake by either side.

SUPERSESSION DOCTRINE. See PREEMPTIVE RIGHT DOCTRINE.

SUPERVENING IMPOSSIBILITY. See FORCE MAJEURE.

SUPERVENING PROHIBITION. An act by an administrative agency, a state, or a municipality which renders the party to an agreement unable to complete his contractual obligation or performance. A failure to perform due to a supervening prohibition is excused.

497

SUPPLEMENTAL AGREEMENT. In federal government contracting this term describes a contract modification that is accomplished by the mutual action of the parties.

SUPPLEMENTAL EDUCATIONAL OPPORTUNITY GRANTS. See FEDERAL COLLEGE-AID STATUTES.

SUPPLEMENTAL REGISTER. Provides trademark registration for purposes of international conventions and treaties which usually require that a trademark be registered in the owner's home country before it can be protected internationally. The supplemental register does not grant the trademark owner substantial benefits apart from the ability to take advantage of international conventions and treaties and to assert federal jurisdiction under Sections 32 and 39 of the Lanham Act, the Federal Trademark Statute. The supplemental register has little impact on domestic trademark law.

SUPPLEMENTARY CONVENTION ON THE ABOLITION OF SLAVERY, THE SLAVE TRADE, AND INSTITUTIONS AND PRACTICES SIMILAR TO SLAVERY. Convention which supplements the Slavery Convention of September, 1926 by requiring parties to that Convention to take all measures to bring about "the complete abolition of debt bondage, serfdom, involuntary marriage, transfer of women for money or other consideration, and exploitation of women." Ratified by eighty-seven states as of 1976, the Supplementary Convention entered into force on July 7, 1955.

SUPPLEMENTS TO WAGES AND SALARIES. Employer contributions for social insurance and other labor income. The latter includes items such as employer payments for private pension, health and welfare funds, compensation for injuries, directors' fees, and pay of the military reserves.

SUPPORT AND MAINTENANCE. Traditionally refers to the duty of a husband to maintain his wife in the manner to which she became accustomed during the marriage, including the obligation to provide such necessities as food, clothing, shelter, and usually medical care.

SUPPORT, INCORPORATED. A licensed collection agency specializing in obtaining support from spouses who are delinquent in making child support or alimony payments. It is tied to a national network of collection agencies and seeks to aid attorneys whose clients are having difficulty collecting their support.

SUPPORT TRUSTS (Maintenance Trusts). Trust arrangements designed to provide adequate and continuous support to the trust beneficiary. The trustee is directed to spend or distribute only so much on behalf of the trust beneficiary as is necessary to sustain the purpose of the trust. The most common Support Trusts are designed to provide for educational expenses or maintenance of an elderly person. Such a trust arrangement does not constitute a restraint on alienation because the trust beneficiary's interest is limited by its nature as a support interest.

SUPPRESSION OF EVIDENCE. Keeping evidence known by one party to a legal controversy from the other party. If the judge learns that a party is suppressing evidence, he may declare a mistrial, dismiss the action, or instruct the jury to suppress it. Suppression of evidence should be distinguished from the situation where the court excludes evidence on the ground that it was illegally obtained.

SUPRANATIONAL INSTITUTION. A functional federal organization of sovereign nations operating on a regional level. The term supranational was first used in Article 9 of the Paris Treaty creating the European Coal and Steel Community (E.C.S.C.).

SUPREMACY CLAUSE. The Supremacy Clause, contained in Article VI of the Constitution of the United States, states that the "Constitution, and the Laws of the United States which shall be made in Pursuance thereof; and all Treaties made, or which shall be made, under the authority of the United

States, shall be the Supreme Law of the Land; and the Judges in every State shall be bound thereby, any Thing in the Constitution or Laws of any State to the Contrary notwithstanding."

SUPREME COURT HISTORICAL SOCIETY. Established in 1975 to collect memorabilia and information associated with the history of the Supreme Court, in order to help the public understand the least known branch of government.

SUPREME COURT JUSTICE DISCLOSURE. Supreme Court Justices adopted an ethics code in 1973 which requires them to report gifts over $100 and income from outside work. Because Justices must avoid any appearance of a conflict of interest, most of them severely isolate their lives, and some avoid all outside contacts such as speaking engagements or honorary posts. Justices earn $72,500 a year ($75,000 for the Chief Justice), and are limited by law from accepting over $25,000 in outside income.

SUPREME COURT OF JUDICATURE. An English court created in 1873. It serves in two divisions: a court of original jurisdiction, called the High Court of Justice, and a court of appeal, called the Court of Appeal. The word "supreme" in its title is misleading because, unlike the United States Supreme Court, there is an appeal from this court to the Superior Appellate Jurisdiction of the House of Lords and Privy Council.

SUPREME COURT OF THE UNITED STATES. Article III, section 1, of the Constitution of the United States provides that "the judicial Power of the United States, shall be vested in one Supreme Court, and in such inferior Courts as the Congress may from time to time ordain and establish." The Supreme Court of the United States was created in accordance with this provision and by authority of the Judiciary Act of September 24, 1789. It was organized on February 2, 1790. The Supreme Court comprises the Chief Jus-

tice of the United States and such number of Associate Justices as may be fixed by Congress. Under that authority, and by virtue of the Act of June 25, 1948, the present number of Associate Justices is eight. Power to nominate the Justices is vested in the President of the United States, and appointments are made by and with the Advice and Consent of the Senate. Article III, section 1, of the Constitution further provides that "the Judges, both of the Supreme and Inferior Courts, shall hold their Offices during good Behavior, and shall, at stated Times, receive for their Services, a Compensation, which shall not be diminished during their Continuance in Office." A Justice may, if he so desires, retire at the age of 70, after serving for 10 years as a federal judge or at age 65 after 15 years of service. The officers of the Supreme Court are the Clerk, the Reporter of Decisions, the Marshal, and the Librarian, who are appointed by the Court to assist in the performance of its functions. The library is open to members of the Bar of the Court, attorneys for the various federal departments and agencies, and members of Congress. Only members of the Bar of the Court may practice before the Supreme Court. The term of the Court begins, by law, the first Monday in October of each year and continues as long as the business before the Court requires, usually until about the end of June. Six members constitute a quorum. Approximately 4,200 cases are passed upon in the course of a term. In addition, some 1,200 applications of various kinds are filed each year that can be acted upon by a single Justice. As of January 1, 1980, of the 101 Justices on the Court to date, 100 have been white, 90 have been Protestant, 6 have been Catholic, 5 have been Jews and none has been a woman.

SUPREME COURT REPORTS (Lawyer's Edition). One of the unofficial series of reports of the Supreme Court. The *United States Supreme Court Reports Lawyer's Edition* contains all of the decisions contained in the official *United States Reports* as well as many decisions not reported originally in the early official volumes. The *Lawyer's Edition* points out publishing errors in the official edition and also includes parallel statutory and case citations which are not included in the official edition. In the *Lawyer's Edition* case summaries precede the headnotes and the cases are often elaborately annotated in the manner of the *American Law Reports Annotated* (A.L.R.) published by the same firm.

SUPREME PONTIFF (The Pope). The spiritual head of the Roman Catholic Church and sovereign of the independent state of Vatican City. The term is the translation of the Pope's title of Pontifex Maximus, a Latin term which originally was the title of a high priest in the government of ancient Rome. The incumbent Pope, John Paul II (Cardinal Karol Wojtyla, Archbishop of Krakow, Poland) is the 264th Pontiff in a line which Roman Catholic doctrine claims traces back directly to the Apostle Peter, whom Catholics regard as the first Pope. John Paul II is the first non-Italian Pope since the Dutch Adrian VI, who reigned in 1522-1523, and is, of course, the first Pontiff from a Communist country. John Paul II took his name from his immediate predecessor John Paul I (Cardinal Albino Luciani, Patriarch of Venice) who reigned a mere 33 days after his election in late August, 1978. John Paul I was the first Pope to select an original name in several hundred years and the first Pope ever to select a double name. The name was selected as a tribute to John Paul's immediate predecessors, the much beloved John XXIII and the widely respected Paul VI, and as a pledge of continuity of the two Popes' policies. It has been said that the first policy statement of a new Pontiff is his choice of a name. If this is true it appears that John Paul II has pledged to continue the policies of his predecessors as well as paid tribute to the tragically short reign of John Paul I.

SURETY AGREEMENT. Provides that one person will pay the debt of another. In case of default on the debt, the surety stands in the shoes of the debtor.

SURETYSHIP AGREEMENT. A contract entered into between one who owes a debt or has incurred a liability and one who agrees to be answerable for that debt or liability. When the debt is discharged, the latter party (the surety) is entitled to indemnity from the debtor. The party to whom the debt is owed may pursue either the surety or the original debtor to obtain his remedy.

SURFACE MINING CONTROL AND RECLAMATION ACT OF 1977. A federal statute that attempted to control the ruinous effects of stripping coal from the land, an effort which the states largely had neglected. The Act combined stringent regulatory requirements for the mining industry with substantial money for the states to administer the program and to reclaim abandoned strip mines. Congress required in the first phase of the program that the states apply key federal environmental-protection standards and that both the states and the federal government conduct and enforce prohibited activities. Unfortunately, the law never was fully implemented.

SURNAME MARK. A trademark or part of a trade name which contains a surname. At common law a trademark or trade name which consisted of a personal name, a surname, first name, or both, was entitled to legal protection when it attained secondary meaning. Under the Lanham Act, the Federal Trademark statute, a surname mark can be registered if it becomes distinctive of the applicant's goods.

SURPLUS PROFITS TAX. See WINDFALL TAX.

SURROGATE PARTNER. A third party used by a sex therapist for sexual activity with a client as part of a professional treatment which may nonetheless constitute the crime of fornication or adultery in some states. A surrogate mother is a woman who agrees to bear the child of another.

SURROGATE'S COURT. A specialized court having limited jurisdiction over the administration of the estates of deceased persons and infants. In some states, this type of court is known as a probate court. In others, probate matters are handled by a chancery court in addition to its general equity jurisdiction. The presiding judicial officer of a surrogate's court is usually known as a surrogate. In some states, the surrogate need not have formal legal training although some familiarity with probate matters is required. In a probate court, the presiding judicial officer is known as a probate judge.

SURVIVING SPOUSE. Generally, the spouse who outlives the other. However, in the law, the term has come to describe a particular relationship of the survivor with the deceased. This relationship serves to establish certain rights of the survivor as prescribed by law to some or all of the property of the deceased as well as to various other benefits. As a general rule, a divorce which is final before the death of one spouse ends the marital relationship, so that the survivor will not be considered the surviving spouse for most purposes. Also, it has been held that one who murders his or her spouse is not considered a surviving spouse and thus cannot benefit by his or her crime. Some states also hold that a spouse who has committed acts constituting grounds for divorce cannot qualify as a surviving spouse and may be disinherited.

SUSPECT CLASSIFICATIONS. The notion of suspect classifications is a tool used in adjudication of cases under the Fourteenth Amendment's equal protection clause. The suspect classifications are race, illegitimacy and alienage. When a state enacts legislation which discriminates on the basis of one of these classifications, it must prove a compelling state interest to avoid unconstitutionality. Proof of a state interest sufficient to allow such discrimination is very difficult. Indeed, a compelling state interest has been demonstrated only once. In *Korematsu v. United States*, 323 U.S. 214 (1944), the Supreme Court upheld a military

order during World War II excluding all persons of Japanese ancestry from certain areas of the West Coast. The Court felt that the possibility of a Japanese invasion of the Pacific Coast, along with the possibility of Japanese-American collusion, justified the removal of the Japanese-Americans, or Nisei. Curfew orders affecting Japanese-Americans were upheld under the same rationale in *Hirabayashi v. United States*, 320 U.S. 81 (1943).

SUSPENDED SENTENCE. The court decision postponing the pronouncing of sentence upon a convicted person, or postponing the execution of a sentence that has been pronounced by the court. When the court suspends a sentence, it retains jurisdiction over the person, and may later set or execute a penalty. When a sentence is suspended the person is usually placed on probation. A violation of the conditions of probation may lead to revocation of probation and return to court for re-sentencing.

SUSPENSION OF WORK CLAUSE. In Department of Defense contracting, this clause requires that a contractor be compensated for government-caused delays of all or any part of the contract work for an unreasonable period. The compensation is to provide no allowance for profit.

SUTTER RULE. A Tax Court rule which provides that a taxpayer who entertains when he is not traveling away from home cannot deduct that portion of his own meal equal to what he would ordinarily have spent for his personal meal if he weren't entertaining. Generally, the Internal Revenue Service applies the Sutter Rule only to cases where a taxpayer claims deductions for substantial amounts of personal living expenses, but the Commissioner has not issued any guidelines as to what is "substantial."

SWALLOWING THE GUN. Reducing an armed robbery charge to unarmed robbery in plea bargaining.

S.W.A.P.O. (South West Africa People's Organization). Political oragnization founded in 1960 by Sam Nujomo to

501

end what it regards as illegal South African rule in South West Africa (Namibia). When peaceful efforts proved unsuccessful, the group turned to armed violence to achieve its goal. Although South African authorities have attempted to crush S.W.A.P.O., it continues to organize political meetings and boycotts. S.W.A.P.O. estimates that seventy percent of the Namibian people support the movement, despite government efforts to destroy it. Opponents of S.W.A.P.O. claim it is a Communist front supported by Russia.

S.W.A.T. (Special Weapons and Tactics). A specially trained elitist Army military group stationed in Fort Bragg, North Carolina to combat terrorists who engage in violent violations of the law. Some local police forces have similar law-enforcement units.

SWEARING CONTEST. A lawsuit in which each side produces expert witnesses who give conflicting professional opinions after they have been sworn to tell the truth and the jury must select which ones to believe in their decision of the case.

SWEETHEART CONTRACT. A collective bargaining agreement entered into as a result of collusion between an employer and a union; or any contract whereby a franchisee or subsidiary agrees to buy, sell or deal solely with a third-party supplier as a requirement of the franchisor or parent company.

SWEETHEART LOAN. The practice of a financial institution to give preferential treatment (which is unethical if not illegal) in the borrowing of money to an officer, director or important client. Former Budget Chief Bert Lance was a favorite beneficiary of this practice.

SWIFT v. TYSON (41 U.S. 1 (1842)). A celebrated Supreme Court case concerning the Rules of Decision Act, also known as Section 34 of the Federal Judiciary Act of 1789. The Act provided that "the laws of the several states, except where the Constitution, treaties, or statutes of the United States

shall otherwise provide, shall be regarded as rules of decisions in trials at common law in the courts of the United States in cases where they apply." The central issue in the case was whether the decisions of state courts were "the laws of the several states" and thus controlling in the federal courts. The Supreme Court declared they were not controlling, and held that federal courts were free to decide questions of substantive law for themselves. The ruling in *Swift* that state court decisions are not "laws" was attacked heavily in subsequent cases. Critics noted that the freedom of federal courts to make their own law led to inconsistent and inequitable results, Finally, in 1938, the Supreme Court acknowledged the need for uniformity in federal court decisions and dramatically overruled *Swift* in *Erie R.R. Co. v. Tompkins*, 304 U.S. 64 (1938), which established state law, including state court decisions, as the Rule of Decision in Diversity of Citizenship cases in federal courts.

SWINE FLU CLAIM AND LITIGATION REPORTER. A bi-weekly news service sold to lawyers who represent the hundreds of claimants suing the federal government for injuries or death arising out of the 1976 Swine-Flu immunization program. At a cost of $600 a year, the subscribers are supplied with technical information to assist them in arguing their cases, one of which involves a family in California with a one billion dollar claim against Uncle Sam. Although only six cases of Swine Flu fever were recorded, 535 persons developed a rare paralytic disease known as Guillain-Barré Syndrome, as a result of having been vaccinated against Swine Flu at the government's urging. President Gerald Ford pushed the panic button after a soldier died of Swine Flu in February, 1976 at Fort Dix. Some 20 million people died in an epidemic in 1919 which swept the world. In an attempt to inoculate every American, the federal government guaranteed reimbursement to anyone injured by taking the injection, thereby getting the manufacturers off the hook. In June, 1978, the government agreed to pay any claimant without the need to prove any negligence.

SYMINGTON AMENDMENT TO THE FOREIGN ASSISTANCE ACT. A A federal law that bars foreign aid to any nation developing nuclear weapons. In 1979, Pakistan became the first country against which the new rule was invoked.

SYMPATHY STRIKE (Sympathetic Strike). A work stoppage by employees not directly involved in a labor dispute who wish to give moral support, and demonstrate worker solidarity to bring additional pressure upon the employer involved.

SYNOD OF BISHOPS. A consultative body of 200 established by Pope Paul VI, after Ecumenical Council Vatican II in 1965, to foster joint decision-making between the Pope and the Bishops.

T

TAFT-HARTLEY ACT (1947). Sponsored by conservative Republicans, Senator Taft and Representative Hartley, the Taft-Hartley Act was designed to amend drastically the Wagner Act of 1935 which was the basic Federal Labor Relations Law. The Wagner Act proscribed unfair labor practices by employers, while the Taft-Hartley Act did the same for unions. A key section of the Act gives the President power to seek an injunction against any union whose strike imperils the "national health and safety." According to Labor Department statistics only the United Mine Workers have ever defied Taft-Hartley injunctions.

TAIL GATING. Following too closely behind the motor vehicle of another and thereby endangering the safety of both cars. Some states make Tail Gating a crime. The standard rule of thumb is to stay one car length behind a car for every ten miles of speed. An Illinois Appellate Court has held that the trial court should hear an $80,000 civil suit against a Tail Gating truck driver. The truck stayed within two feet of the plaintiff's back bumper at speeds of up to 75 miles per hour. Unfortunately for the truck driver, the car he was Tail Gating was driven by an attorney, who brought suit for causing him and his family severe emotional distress.

TAIWAN RELATIONS ACT OF 1979. A federal law intended to protect the Republic of China (Free China) from the People's Republic of China (Communist China). The Act states that the United States will consider any effort to determine the future of Taiwan by other than peaceful means "a threat to the peace and security of the Western Pacific area" and thus "of grave concern to the United States."

TAIWAN'S COORDINATION COUNCIL FOR NORTH AMERICAN AFFAIRS. An informal embassy in Washington, D.C., established after the United States severed diplomatic relations with the Republic of China. The Council performs a function similar to that of the American Institute in Paipei, which is staffed by 54 former American Foreign Service Officers.

TAKE-AWAYS. See GIVE-BACKS.

TAKE-IT-OR-LEAVE-IT CONTRACT (Adhesion Contract). An unfair contract arising when the parties have unequal bargaining power, as its name suggests. Such contracts are unenforceable.

TAKE-OVER BID. See TENDER OFFER.

TAKE THE FIFTH. The colloquial expression for invoking the privilege against self-incrimination guaranteed by the Fifth Amendment. When a defendant "Takes the Fifth," he may not be penalized for his failure to testify. *Spevack v. Klein*, 385 U.S. 511 (1967), for example, held that a lawyer who took the Fifth in a disciplinary proceeding could not be disbarred for asserting his constitutional privilege. Furthermore, in *Griffin v. California*, 380 U.S. 609 (1965), the Supreme Court held that when a defendant refuses to testify on grounds he may incriminate himself, neither the prosecution nor the Court may comment that the defendant's silence is proof of his guilt. In a recent case, however, *Lakeside v. Oregon*, 435 U.S. 333 (1978), the Court held that a jury may be instructed not to draw an adverse inference from the defendant's silence, despite the defendant's objection to such an instruction.

TAKING A WALK. Legislative parlance for the practice of a member of the assembly to pass instead of voting by registering "present" on a controversial proposal as a cop-out in an effort to avoid offending either the proponents or the opponents of the measure.

TAKING THE BACK DOOR. A Chinese term for black market or the swapping of ration coupons.

TANEY, ROGER. From 1836 to 1864, he was Chief Justice of the United States Supreme Court. State economic and commercial powers vis-à-vis the federal government became more well-defined during his tenure. This pattern culminated in 1852 with the *Dred Scott* case, in which the Court, in an opinion rendered by Taney, in effect gave Constitutional support to slavery. Under Taney, the Court became a less unified body than it had been previously: dissenting opinions were written with greater frequency, and the justices stopped living together during the term of the Court. Taney was elected as a conservative to the Maryland legislature in 1799, largely because of his father's influence with the landed gentry. His political persuasions changed, however, and he aligned himself with Andrew Jackson's Democrats in the 1820s. Although he gained a reputation as an effective advocate, he experienced extreme stage fright when he spoke in front of others.

T.A.P. FUND (Trans-Alaska Pipeline Liability Fund). A Fund established by Congress and financed by companies transporting oil through the Trans-Alaska Pipeline. The Fund is intended to pay for damages resulting from either oil spills along the pipeline, or from ships transporting oil from the pipeline terminal.

TAP THE EXCHANGE. See ASSOCIATION OF TRIAL LAWYERS OF AMERICA.

TARDIVE DYSKINESIA. Side effect from use of Thorazine and some other anti-psychotic medications. The patient suffers a loss of control over his tongue and mouth movements in addition to persistent dryness of the throat. In severe cases the victim is virtually unable to utter a distinctive word and begins to appear considerably more abnormal than his illness would indicate. Understandably, the condition causes the patient a great deal of frustration and loss of self esteem. The neurological side effects of Thorazine treatment, as evidenced by Tardive Dyskinesia, have led many civil libertarians to suggest that drug therapy be included as a form of care subject to the patient's right to refuse treatment.

TARGET SYSTEM. A new data bank computerized information retrieval system which is being developed by the Veterans Administration and would lead to massive invasions of the right to privacy by making confidential personal records available to unauthorized persons without the knowledge or consent of the veterans or their families.

TARIFF TAX. Duty imposed on merchandise which, in the course of trade, crosses international boundaries. Tariffs are imposed on most of the goods, not because the government needs or wants the revenue so derived, but so that consumers will be encouraged to buy domestic products. A Swiss watch, for example, may be as finely made as any in this country and at considerably less cost, but if a Tariff forces its price to a prohibitive level, the American watchmaker is protected.

T.A.R.P. (Transitional Air Research Project for Ex-Offenders). Experimental activity which tests the hypothesis that prison releasees who have adequate financial resources available to them when they re-enter society will be less involved in new criminal activity than similar releasees without such funds.

TASK FORCE FOR WOMEN'S EQUITY. A group appointed by the American Association of University Women in 1978 to work with college and university presidents to obtain the appointment of more women to their faculties in teaching and administrative positions, especially with tenure, in order to implement Title IX of the Federal Educational Amendments Law of 1972 which prohibits discrimination on the basis of sex to any educational institution which receives federal funds.

TATOL CO TREATY. An agreement between the United States and Mexico signed in 1977 in which the United States agreed not to store, deploy or possess any nuclear weapons in any of its Caribbean military bases located in Cuba, Puerto Rico, the Panama Canal Zone or the Virgin Islands.

TAX AID PROGRAM. Sponsored by the American Association of Retired Persons, this organization provides free professional tax advice to senior citizens.

TAXATION, ART OF (Latin—"taxare": to touch sharply). As one of Louis XIV's ministers put it, "the art of plucking the goose in such a way as to produce the largest amount of feathers with the least possible squawking." Taxes have been laid on nearly everything man could think of; from fireplaces to funerals; from whiskey to wigs. The Czar of Russia even levied an assessment on beards. And Americans hardly need be reminded that there was once a tax on tea. One of the oldest, most prevalent, and certainly the most effective of revenue-gathering devices is the income tax which is a tax on yearly net profits. In ancient Egypt this form of taxation exacted twenty percent of the output of land, spoken of in the Bible as "Pharaoh's fifth," which was not too difficult a measurement. As civilization progressed, however, income became easier to conceal and so harder to tax, with the result that treasurers developed some bizarre criteria for taxation. A Dutch tax on windows, for example, was designed to tax the wealthy; the philosophy apparently being that the more money one had, the larger his home and the more its windows. The chief result of this tax as might be supposed, was an architecture virtually devoid of fenestration. For this same reason the Greeks taxed doors, the French levied on fireplaces, and New York imposed a tax on wigs. Archeological evidence leads us to believe that the Egyptians of about 3,000 B.C. were the first to tax their fellow man, at least on any organized scale. An interesting note on this early tax is that it was assessed against the head of a household in an amount determined by the size of his family, which is to a degree true of our present income tax, the main difference being that while our taxes are decreased by deductions for dependents, the Egyptian's tax increased as his family grew. It might also be noted that many of this country's most infamous hoodlums were put away not for their more nefarious crimes, but because they had failed to pay some tax or other. Al Capone is the classic case in point.

TAXATION WITH REPRESENTATION. A non-profit non-partisan public interest taxpayers' lobby, founded in 1970. It is supported entirely by individual contributions. Contributors receive the *Taxation with Representation Newsletter* eight times each year. The group files regular lobby reports with Congress as required by law. It does not support any political party or candidate, nor does it participate in political campaigns.

TAX AUDIT. An Internal Revenue Service (I.R.S.) procedure randomly applied to the nation's taxpayers to keep the self-assessing tax system relatively honest. There are no published criteria for the selection of those who will be audited, but generally individuals with big incomes, large itemized deductions, or a disproportionate ratio of income to expenses can expect an audit. There are three types of audits. (1) In a Correspondence Audit, the taxpayer is asked to mail material to the local I.R.S. office. (2) In an Office Audit, that taxpayer must personally appear at the I.R.S. office. (3) In a Field Audit, an I.R.S. official examines the taxpayer's books and other relevant material at the taxpayer's home or business. Of the 88 million people who file income tax returns, more than 2 million annually will eventually receive a deceptively amiable but ominous form letter from the Internal Revenue Service that reads in part: "We are examining your federal income tax return for the above year(s) and find we need additional information." Translation: these taxpayers' returns for 1977 —or perhaps as far back as 1975—will be audited. Two out of three of those chosen will be assessed higher taxes, raising a total of $1.5 billion in otherwise lost Treasury revenues. A taxpayer who disagrees with a tax auditor's findings can appeal; first to the I.R.S. group supervisor, then to the agency's appellate division and, higher still, to a United States Tax Court.

TAX AVOIDANCE. The lawful attempt by a taxpayer to pay the tax collector only exactly what is due him and no more. Since the rules controlling the apportionment of income, gift or inheritance to taxes are complicated, it is possible for two honest persons to arrive at two different answers to the same tax question. Essentially the taxpayer who attempts to reduce his taxes to the minimum without resorting to deception, cheating, or omission is avoiding tax, but not evading it. Tax avoidance is thus the legitimate right of every taxpayer to plan his business and financial affairs so as to provide for the lowest applicable tax. This is the essence of a voluntary, self-assessment tax collection system which is unique in the world in its honest compliance by American citizens.

TAX-BASED INCOME POLICY. See T.I.P.

TAX BIBLE (Publication 17). A useful guide published annually by the Internal Revenue Service and distributed free of charge to assist taxpayers in the preparation of their returns.

TAX COURT. See UNITED STATES TAX COURT.

TAX COURT SMALL TAX CASE DIVISION. A federal agency which settles disputes with as little formality, expense or delay as possible for disputes about income, gift or estate taxes involving not more than $5,000 for any one year. You need to pay only $10 when you file the easy-to-complete petition form asking for a hearing which can be held by yourself without any need for the professional services of a lawyer.

TAX DIVORCE. A legal dissolution of a marriage shortly before December 31st, so that the couple may file separate tax returns for that year and thereby reduce their tax liability for that year. The couple usually remarries after January 1st, and may divorce again at the end of December.

TAX EVASION. A willful and unlawful attempt to reduce taxes by fraudulent means. The line between Tax Avoidance which is legal and Tax Evasion which is a crime, is sometimes blurry, but it is clear that acts of deception, cheating, and purposeful omission bring the taxpayer fully within the ambit of criminal evasion.

TAX FERRET. A person who receives a cash payment for information supplied to the federal government, which results in a recovery of money from those engaged in tax evasion. In 1977, $360,000 was paid to 483 persons, an average of $746 each, out of a total of 5,251 persons who filed claims for such awards. The informers are usually disgruntled, dismissed employees, irate divorcees or jealous neighbors. The rewards are based on a sliding scale that starts at 10 percent of the first $75,000 in taxes recovered, drops to 5 percent of the next $25,000 and to 1 percent of any additional amounts. The maximum award is $50,000 for any one case. The award itself is taxable income and other tax ferrets inform on those who have not reported and paid a tax on their tax ferret windfall.

TAX FRAUD. An attempt to evade or defeat any tax or to file a return that the taxpayer does not believe to be true and correct. It must be proven by clear and convincing evidence in civil cases and beyond a reasonable doubt in criminal cases. Congress has made tax fraud a serious crime, subject to a maximum sentence of five years' imprisonment and a $10,000 fine.

TAX-FREE HOUSING BONDS. Securities issued by cities to support the financing of low-cost housing for moderate-income families by providing mortgage money at several points less than the prevailing market rate.

TAX FREEDOM DAY. The day you start working for yourself. It was May 6th in 1978. Up until that day, Americans had been working just to cover their 1978 tax bills. The 1978 observance, the latest in the years on record, means Americans labored 126 eight-hour days to pay their 1978 federal, state and local taxes, compared with the 124 days it took in 1977. This year's late date points up the increasing tax bite since it was only February 9 in 1929. Putting it another way, over the year, in an eight-hour day, the average American in 1978 spent two hours and 45 minutes on the job to pay taxes. Of this, one hour and 46 minutes went to the federal government and 59 minutes to state and local governments.

TAX-FREE ROLLOVER. An exchange of property which is not taxable. Such exchanges include a like-kind exchange of property, a replacement for property which has been involuntarily converted, or similar types of transfers where the replacement property generally takes on the basis equal to the property transferred.

TAX HAVENS. Foreign countries, which offer investment incentives to attract capital from wealthy people and corporations in order to stimulate their local economy. In addition to having no taxes, these countries offer efficient and reliable banking facilities, good communications, sound legal counsel, political stability and a free flow of money. There are approximately thirty such tax havens, including Monaco, Liechtenstein, the Bahamas and Bermuda.

TAX INCENTIVE (Tax Rebate). A financial carrot offered by Uncle Sam to encourage participation in a program promoted by the government. For example, tax rebates are given to homeowners for installing insulation or solar energy and to companies for investing in ghetto areas.

TAX INCENTIVE PROGRAM. See T.I.P.

TAX INDEXING. A proposal to adjust the tax rates automatically to reflect any increase in inflation. In Canada, for example, where the system is successfully in operation, the tax rates for the coming year are announced in October, based on the increase in the official Consumer Price Index for the twelve-month period ending September 30. Both personal exemptions and tax brackets are automatically adjusted to reflect the change in prices—and the impact has been dramatic. Canada's five-year compounded inflation total of 52.1 percent raised personal exemptions for a family of four from $3,600 to $5,480 and the income level at which the 56 percent tax rate starts rose from $60,000 to $91,260.

TAX JEOPARDY ASSESSMENT. The awesome carte blanche power of Uncle Sam, acting through the Internal Revenue Service, to seize money and property of taxpayers who may owe taxes and might attempt to transfer their assets beyond reach.

TAX LOTTERY. The arbitrary selection by lot by the Internal Revenue Service of which Tax Returns it will subject to a routine tax audit.

TAX OPTION CORPORATIONS. See SUBCHAPTER S CORPORATIONS.

TAXPAYER COMPLIANCE MEASUREMENT PROGRAM. See T.C.M.P. AUDIT.

TAXPAYER PROTECTION AND RE-IMBURSEMENT ACT. A federal law proposed in 1979 by Senator Baucus, Democrat of Montana, which would reimburse taxpayers for the first time, for their attorney's fee in a case which they won against the government, where the government's position in the litigation was found to have been unreasonable.

TAXPAYER SUIT. A lawsuit brought by a taxpayer to prevent a certain expenditure of public money of which he disapproves. While taxpayer suits are common in most states, the federal courts have severely limited the ability of taxpayers to seek injunctions against federal expenditures. Early cases held that federal taxpayers do not have standing to challenge the use of federal funds because a taxpayer's interest is "too remote." In *Flast v. Cohen*, 292 U.S. 83 (1968), however, a taxpayer was given standing to challenge federal aid to parochial schools because a specific constitutional provision was involved.

TAX REBATE. See TAX INCENTIVE.

TAX REFUND. Cash paid by the government when there has been an overpayment of tax.

TAX REVOLT. For a good part of her colorful life, Vivien Kellems refused to pay income taxes on the grounds that they were unconstitutional. She was typical of those who rebelled against what they thought was illegal confiscation but, upon her death in 1975, Uncle Sam inexorably proceeded to collect his due from her estate, which, with back interest and penalties, came to a grand total of $816,949.97.

TAX RULING (Letter Ruling; Revenue Ruling). An official interpretation by the Internal Revenue Service (I.R.S.) of the tax law for the information and guidance of taxpayers. Most of the rulings are based on actual taxpayer cases. Generally, taxpayers may rely upon rulings in determining the tax treatment of their own transactions. However, since a ruling is predicated on a particular set of facts, taxpayers should be cautioned against assuming a like tax treatment unless their particular facts and circumstances are substantially the same. These rulings appear in the *Internal Revenue Bulletin*, which is published on a weekly basis.

TAX SHELTER. A business or enterprise which the taxpayer enters into for the purpose of transferring income to a lower tax bracket. Tax shelters may afford the taxpayer a temporary exclusion from taxable income as in stock options, accelerated deductions like rapid depreciation, or a special rate of tax, such as the lower rate of tax on corporate capital gains. For example, a motion picture tax shelter offers two tax advantages. First, the films may be depreciated over a short period of time. Second, borrowed funds, whose interest payments are tax deductible, may be used for the investment. Therefore, the taxpayer can offset his income with a large depreciation deduction, and at the same time not use any of his own income for the original investment. This method is especially advantageous if the taxpayer is able to secure a non-recourse loan without personal liability for repaying the debt. Typical tax shelters include: motion pictures, oil and gas, equipment leasing, cattle feeding and breeding, and real estate. One technique used in tax shelters is to deduct losses from such businesses in excess of the amount the taxpayer is actually "at risk." In other words, the taxpayer creates the form, but not the substance of assuming a risk which is tax deductible. The Tax Reform Act of 1976 was designed to plug such loopholes.

TAX SWAP. An exchange of property of the same kind, such as land for land, between two owners whose separate assets have increased in value. The swap enables each to obtain a property worth more than what he transfers without paying any capital gains tax on the increased value.

TAYLOR LAW (Public Employees Fair Employment Act). Legislation first passed in New York and since followed in other states. Basically it sets forth restraints and punishment for public employees, including teachers, who seek to improve their economic status by withholding their services, a right not denied other segments of our society. It does so through a penalty of loss of two days' pay for every day off the job as a result of a strike action. With respect to teachers, money lost by teachers becomes a financial windfall for school boards. While the Taylor Law also requires "good-faith" bargaining on the part of school boards, it sets forth no penalty provision for absence of such bargaining. A board of education that provokes a strike does so with the knowledge that not only will a profit be reaped, but there will also be no penalties for its actions. Never in the history of the Taylor Law has a school board member been fined or jailed.

T.C.A. (Terminal Control Area). A block of airspace surrounding an airport to which special flight rules apply. All student pilots are barred from any use of the space and all planes using the airport must be equipped with two-way radios and a device called a transponder which can be interrogated from the ground and automatically responds with the aircraft's identity and altitude. In September, 1978, 144 people were killed in a collision between a small private plane and a commercial jet above the San Diego, California airport. The Federal Aviation Administration admitted after an investigation that it had been lax in its responsibility to guard against mid-air accidents; in 1979 the F.A.A. promulgated the most sweeping changes in air traffic control rules in American history. Eleven new T.A.C.s were created, added radar guidance was given to all planes near major airports and airspace in which pilots may fly free of ground control was sharply restricted.

T.C.M.P. AUDIT (Taxpayer Compliance Measurement Program). A random selection by an Internal Revenue Service computer of some taxpayer returns for examination which is so detailed by nature that some commentators call it harassment.

T.C.O. See TERMINATION CONTRACTING OFFICER.

TEACHER'S BILL OF RIGHTS. Laws which establish procedures to hear complaints by those in the academic life and grant relief in appropriate cases, including collective bargaining on salaries, pensions, terms of employment and fringe benefits.

TEAMSTER BAR ASSOCIATION. Cynical term describing the numerous lawyers who were quickly hired and fired by Teamster's Union president Jimmy Hoffa in his defense against mounting governmental attacks on his management of the Union.

TEAPOT DOME SCANDALS. Secret leasing to private companies of United States oil reserves during the 1920s. The Scandals took their name from an odd-shaped Wyoming hill which resembled a teapot.

TEL LAW. Pre-taped information on over 80 legal topics available free to the public. Tel Law was created by California Bar Associations to provide ready access to legal information, and in its first year of operation 42,000 calls were made to the program.

TELEVISED TRIALS. Judicial proceedings where television and audio equipment are used for media coverage of the event. To avoid problems of media coverage, discussed in *Sheppard v. Maxwell*, 383 U.S. 902 (1966), jurors should be sequestered and media coverage should emphasize the factual presentation of the trial rather than editorial commentary.

TELEVISION INTOXICATION. A novel defense attempted in the murder trial of fifteen-year-old Ronald Zamora of Miami Beach. Defense Attorney Ellis Rubin invented the concept, suggesting that his client had been electronically brainwashed, that the normal conscience-infusing sources — parents, school, religion—had been supplanted by the tube. Claiming that the crime bore a remarkable resemblance to a contemporaneous episode of Kojak, Rubin attempted to call Telly Savalas, the show's star, as a defense witness. Ironically, the trial was the first to be televised under a Florida Supreme Court experiment allowing criminal trials to be broadcast. The defense failed and Zamora was convicted.

TELLER VOTE. A legislative vote whereby members pass a teller to be counted. Such a procedure is often used when it is important to get an accurate vote count, but legislators do not want to have their votes recorded. Teller votes are used in the House of Representatives, but now individual votes may be recorded if one-fifth of the quorum so requests.

TEMPLE BAR. An ancient gateway to the capital of the United Kingdom in London which has been the living symbol of the glory of the common law since the dawn of the Magna Carta in 1215.

TEMPORARY EMERGENCY COURT OF APPEALS. See SPECIAL COURTS OF THE UNITED STATES.

TEMPORARY LIVING ARRANGEMENT. See LINDSEY, BEN.

TEMPORARY RESTRAINING ORDER. See T.R.O.

TEMPORARY WORKER VISA. See H-1 VISA.

TENANCY BY THE ENTIRETY. A form of ownership of property, both real and personal, created by the conveyance of property to a husband and wife. Characterized by a right of survivorship, this tenancy is based on the unity of marriage and the common-law theory that husband and wife are one person. Therefore, each spouse owns the whole of the property and not merely a part. Property held by the entirety may be conveyed only with the consent of both spouses, and the ten-ancy continues for property so owned as long as both spouses live, unless the marriage is dissolved by divorce. The main advantage of such a form of ownership is that only joint creditors of both husband and wife can seize and sell the property in satisfaction of their claim.

TENANCY IN COMMON. A form of ownership of property, both real and personal, whereby two or more persons have undivided possession of the property while maintaining their individual interests in that property. There is no automatic right of survivorship among the tenants in common. The key to the tenancy in common is that of unity of possession or right of possession as between the various tenants. Therefore, no tenancy in common may exist as between a landowner and the owner of a stand of timber on the land, or between owners of separate and distinct parts of a building or tract of land. While one tenant in common may convey his undivided share in the tenancy to a third party without the consent of the other tenants, the general rule is that such a conveyance may not affect the interests of the other tenants.

TEN-B-FIVE (10-B-5). See RULE 10-B-5.

TENDER OFFER. Where an individual or group makes an offer to buy the stock belonging to the shareholders of a company over which they want to take control. Sections 13 and 14 of the Securities Exchange Act of 1934 regulate tender offers, requiring disclosure of material facts by the parties and prohibiting fraudulent acts and practices in connection with the offer.

TENDER YEARS PRESUMPTION (Maternal Preference). The traditional doctrine relied on by courts in child custody disputes, especially those involving infants. Under this presumption, absent substantial evidence to the contrary, the mother is deemed better qualified than the father to care for a young child. The tender years presumption replaced the early English rigid common law rule that the father had the absolute legal right to custody of all his children. The modern trend is towards abandoning the tender years presumption and to award custody solely on the basis of the best interest of the child. This trend may be explained by the growing rejection of sexual stereotypes in theories of child development and by a belief that the presumption deprives fathers of their right to equal protection under the Fourteenth Amendment. In some cases, when a judge is neutral between the parents, the result is a decision of joint custody, where the rights of the parents are equal.

10-K. A form that the Securities and Exchange Commission requires public corporations to file disclosing in detail their operating and financial results.

TEN MOST WANTED LIST. Americans love to rank people and events. So in 1950, J. Edgar Hoover, late Director of the F.B.I., and the International News Service, created a list of the 10 most desperate and brutal lawbreakers in the hope that the wide publicity given to them would lead to their arrest. To be included in this ever-changing elite group of the nation's top-most vicious criminals, one had to be a great threat to the community. Over 400 different fugitives have been so listed in the past and an average of 15 of them have been caught each year. Crime doesn't pay.

TENNESSEE VALLEY AUTHORITY. See T.V.A.

TEN-POINT MEN. Lawyers who specialize in settling personal-injury suits forwarded by other lawyers. They get their nickname because, for this service, they usually are paid 10 percent of the total settlement as a fee.

TERM CONTRACT. See COST-PLUS-FIXED FEE.

TERMINAL CONTROL AREA. See T.C.A.

TERMINATE WITH EXTREME PREJUDICE. Espionage term for assassination.

TERMINATION CONTRACTING OFFICER (T.C.O.). In federal government contracting this term refers to a contracting officer who is responsible for the settlement of terminated contracts.

TERMINATION FOR CONVENIENCE. This term refers to the ordered cessation of all or a portion of contractually required performance where the contractor is not at fault. These contractually authorized terminations are effected pursuant to a unilateral order of the contracting officer acting in the government's best interests.

TERMINATION OF CONTRACTS. See CONTRACT TERMINATION.

TERRA NULLIUS (Latin—no man's land). A territory which is the land of no nation. This legal status means that every country willing to do so may exercise its legal power on such land, in the same way it would exercise its power within its own boundaries. Under the international principle of effectiveness, any country can legally acquire a No Man's Land by taking effective and actual possession of it, thus expressing its Animus Occupandi (Latin —intent to occupy). The acquisition of territory by possession gives its beneficiary an absolute and sovereign right upon it. In 1858, for example, France thus proclaimed her sovereignty over the Clipperton Island on the basis of the Terra Nullius principle.

TERRELL, ROBERT H. See BLACK FEDERAL JUDGES.

TERRITORIAL ASYLUM. See POLITICAL REFUGEES.

TERRITORIAL SEA. See TWO-HUNDRED-MILE LIMIT; THREE-MILE LIMIT.

TERRITORIAL WATERS. A zone of water immediately adjacent to the coast of a sovereign country. As provided by the Geneva Conventions of 1958 and 1960, sovereignty of the coastal country extends to the territorial waters. Each country exerts jurisdiction over its territorial waters. The limits of territorial waters is, however, a subject of considerable international controversy, since the Geneva Convention failed to meet with the two-thirds vote necessary to establish a uniform limit for territorial waters. Countries usually recognize three miles as a minimum limit, but their maximum claims vary broadly, depending on fishing or mineral resources to protect, or on political reasons. Thus, a number of countries, including the United States, claim twelve miles of territorial waters, whereas others claim up to two hundred miles.

TERRORISM LIABILITY. Under the Warsaw Convention, airlines are absolutely liable for deaths and injuries to passengers caused by terrorist's attacks. A 1973 United States Court decision interpreted the Warsaw Convention to apply to injuries sustained by passengers preparing to embark, as well as those physically on board a plane.

TERRY v. OHIO. See STOP AND FRISK.

TESTAMENTARY CAPACITY. The capacity to make a will. It may be divided into two broad categories: 1) testamentary capacity as to status and age and 2) testamentary capacity as to mental ability. Without either kind of testamentary capacity, one cannot make a legally valid will. Although married women, aliens, convicts and Indians once could not pass real property by will, this disability has been removed in every state by the Married Women's Property Acts and other statutes. All states fix the testamentary age by statute, most at the age of 21. In order to have testamentary capacity as to mental ability, the testator must have sufficient mind and memory at the time of making his will to understand the nature of what he is doing, to comprehend generally the nature and extent of his estate which he intends to dispose of, and to recollect the objects of his bounty.

TESTAMENTARY TRANSFER. A disposition of property by gift which does not take effect or become complete until the donor dies.

TESTAMENTARY TRUST. A trust arrangement created under a last will and testament, as opposed to an express private trust, which takes effect by initiative of the trust settlor during his lifetime. To take effect, the testamentary trust must be in compliance with a properly executed will.

TESTATOR or TESTATRIX. A person who dies and leaves a will. A testator is a male and a testatrix, a female.

TEST-TUBE BABY (Embryo Transfer; In Vitro Fertilization). A birth which occurs after an egg was removed from a woman's ovary, placed in a laboratory culture medium (in a Petri dish and not a test tube) and exposed to a male sperm. After fertilization, the resulting conceptus is introduced into the mother's womb. A child is born nine months later. This is different from cloning which is the genetic reproduction of the same individual. The first such baby ever so born was in July 1978, in England. Since the sperm of the husband, Gilbert Brown, was used for an egg of his wife Lesley, there is no question as to the legitimacy of their child, Louise Joy. But suppose the egg of one woman is fertilized by the sperm of a stranger and then implanted into the womb of another woman. Whose child is it? Shades of Aldous Huxley's *Brave New World* and his Hatcheries and Conditioning Centers. The first such medical facility in the United States was established in Norfolk, Virginia, in January, 1980.

TEST 21. Employment test used by the federal service to screen applicants on verbal ability, vocabulary, and reading and comprehension. Attacked as discriminatory by Black applicants, the test was upheld by the Supreme Court as a neutral, legitimate attempt by the government to establish modest literacy requirements for government workers.

TEXAS MAFIA. An inner circle of powerful advisors to President Lyndon B. Johnson, who all hailed from the Lone Star State.

TEXTILE WORKERS UNION v. DARLINGTON CO. See RUNAWAY SHOP.

TEXTUALLY DEMONSTRABLE COMMITMENTS. Term first used in *Powell v. McCormack*, 395 U.S. 486 (1969), to describe a Separation of Powers concept based on the text of the Constitution. In *Powell* the Court refused to find a textually demonstrable commitment to the Congress of the power to exclude a person elected to that body who meets all the requirements for membership prescribed in the Constitution. The Court held that, at most, the Congress had a textually demonstrable commitment to judge only the qualifications set forth in the Constitution.

THATCHER, MARGARET (Iron Lady; Maggie). Britain's "Lady in Waiting." The first woman to become Britain's or Europe's Prime Minister, in the year 1979 in the reign of Elizabeth II. She was former Education Minister under Edward Heath and leader of the Conservative (Tory) Party.

THEATRE ENTERPRISES, INC. v. PARAMOUNT FILM DISTRIBUTING. See CONSCIOUS PARALLELISM.

THE COMPANY. In-house name for the Central Intelligence Agency.

THE HAGUE PEACE CONFERENCES. Convened in 1899 and 1907 at the initiative of Czar Nicholas II of Russia. Their purpose was to develop a Law of War (jus in bello) by submitting military actions to humanitarian and procedural rules, and to promote peace and disarmament by providing procedures for peacefully adjusting international disputes. The first Conference was attended by representatives of 24 countries, including the European countries, the United States, Japan, Mexico, Persia, China, Turkey and Siam. They failed to reach any agreement on disarmament, but three conventions on neutrality and military activities were signed. The second Conference involved 44 countries, including most South American countries. They signed eleven conventions on neutrality and the Law of Naval War. The Permanent Court of Arbitration was created although incompletely organized. However, the Conference failed to reach any agreement on the key question of arms limitation. The Conferences were to meet regularly to implement peace, but the session planned for 1915 could not meet because of the outbreak of war in 1914. Despite this obvious failure, the Hague Conferences constituted an important step in disarmament. Later, the Permanent Court of Arbitration codified the laws of war and neutrality.

THE HILL. See CAPITOL HILL.

THE SPIRIT OF THE LAWS. A classic written by Montesquieu, philosopher of the Enlightenment period of eighteenth-century France. Though an "Enlightenment" philosopher, Montesquieu could also aptly be called a deist and a natural law theorist. All of these strains in his thought are united in his chef-d'oeuvre, *The Spirit of the Laws* (L'Esprit des Lois) (1748). Montesquieu's over-arching credo is that there exists an original reason which is the author of nature, for "how can there be a greater absurdity than . . . that a blind fatality could have produced intelligent beings?" Second, there is an objective standard of right action, justice, which it is man's duty to enshrine in his civil laws. Most attempts to do this have, according to Montesquieu, resulted in governments belonging to one of three classes: republics (in which the people are sovereign), monarchies (the rule of princes through established laws), and despotisms (the arbitrary rule of one man). The sustaining principle of the first is civic virtue; of the second, honor; of the third, fear. Montesquieu mistrusted despotisms, calling them "monstrous" —yet he found republics only slightly more congenial, founded as they were on the political participation of the unreflective masses. It is safe to say that he believed that monarchies best harmonized the principles of political order and personal freedom. Strangely enough, his concepts of separation of powers and judicial review were accepted not by his native France or by common-law England, but by the United States.

THIN-SKULL DOCTRINE. Holds that a tortfeasor takes his victim as he finds him and is therefore legally responsible for unexpected injuries resulting from some peculiar trait of the victim. For example, assume that the defendant-driver's negligent operation of his automobile causes the plaintiff-bicyclist to be knocked down and scraped slightly. If the cyclist were a hemophiliac and bled to his death, the defendant would be held legally accountable to the full extent of the injury, even though another victim would have suffered only relatively inconsequential scrapes and bruises.

THIRD DEGREE INSTRUCTION. See ALLEN INSTRUCTION.

THIRD-PARTY BENEFICIARY. A non-party to a contract who benefits from the contract. Such benefit may be intended or incidental. If the contract names the third party, then the benefit is intended. An Intended Beneficiary can enforce a contract when his rights vest, i.e. when he has knowledge of the contract and assents to it. Thus, if Tom and John agree that Tom will pay John to mow Mike's lawn, Mike can enforce his rights under the contract once he knows about it and agrees to it. If Tom has entered into this contract to confer a gift on Mike, Mike is a Donee Beneficiary. When his rights vest, the Donee Beneficiary may sue John to enforce the contract, but not Tom. If, however, Tom has entered into the contract to repay a debt he owes Mike, then Mike is a Creditor Beneficiary. The Creditor Beneficiary may sue both Tom and John although he may collect only one satisfaction. If John fails to mow the lawn, Mike may also sue Tom on the original debt, and Tom may recover against John.

THIRD-PARTY DEFENDANT. See IMPLEADER RULE.

THIRD-PARTY PLAINTIFF. See IMPLEADER RULE.

THIRD-PARTY PRACTICE. The rules governing a defendant's right to join another party in the litigation for indemnification against any damages which the defendant must pay. This practice generally permits a defendant either to join the third party in the action against the defendant, or to institute a later, separate suit against the third party for damages which the defendant actually paid to the original plaintiff.

THIRD-PARTY SEARCH. Laws which forbid the government from surprise searches by law-enforcement officials, looking for evidence relating to a crime and from examination of records in the possession of third parties such as lawyers, doctors, accountants, banks or newspapers, without first having obtained a valid Subpoena Duces Tecum.

THIRD WORLD (Non-Aligned Countries). Consists of approximately one hundred neutral countries, most of which have gained political independence since the end of World War II. Though many of these countries are poor and economically underdeveloped, the Third World includes countries rich in natural resources, such as some of the oil-producing nations of the Mideast. During the past decade, the Non-Aligned Countries have held a series of conferences to protect and promote their own interests.

THIRD WORLD COUNTRY. See L.D.C.

THIRTEENTH JUROR. 1. An alternative member of the jury who is dismissed at the end of the case or replaces any juror who becomes ill during the course of the trial. 2. A retired person who regularly attends court trials as a spectator preferring the drama of real life for diversion instead of that of the T.V. soap opera. 3. A theory of appellate review which allows the reviewing judge to consider all the facts as well as the disputed issues of law in a case.

THIRTY-DAY RULE. Under Article 9 of the Uniform Commercial Code (U.C.C.), if immediate removal of goods to another state is contemplated at the time of the creation of a Purchase Money Security Interest, then the law of the other jurisdiction governs perfection. There is, however, a thirty-day grace period to perfect.

THIRTY-DAY TAX LETTER. Letter from the Internal Revenue Service to a taxpayer informing him of a tax discrepancy and the amount involved. The taxpayer is given thirty days within which he may come in and dispute the matter with the Commissioner if he wishes to do so. However, the letter is not required to respond.

THREE-JUDGE COURT. An ad hoc tribunal of special dignity which may replace the customary single-judge district court. Typically, at least one of the judges on a three-judge district court is a circuit judge. Cases tried in such courts may be appealed to the Supreme Court of the United States under the Expediting Act of 1903. The special three-judge district courts should be distinguished from the three-judge panels on circuit courts. The idea of a special three-judge district court in certain cases was embodied in law in a series of statutes beginning in 1903. The first such statute provided for a three-judge court in cases brought by the United States to enforce antitrust laws or to review orders of the Interstate Commerce Commission. In 1910, Congress again borrowed this device and applied it to suits where a temporary injunction was sought in federal court against the enforcement of state statutes by state officers. Three years later Congress extended the three-judge concept to restrain the enforcement of orders of state administrative boards and commissions. In 1925, suits requesting a permanent as well as temporary injunction were further required to be heard by a three-judge district court. Finally, in 1937, as part of President Roosevelt's court reform proposals, a three-judge district court was provided in actions for injunctions against allegedly unconstitutional Acts of Congress, ending the differences in court review of Acts of Congress as compared to state statutes or administrative orders. Chief Justice Warren Burger has recommended the abolition of three judge courts in order to reduce the workload of an already overburdened Supreme Court.

THREE-MILE LIMIT. At early common law, the distance over which a country extended its sovereign control in the territorial waters surrounding it. This length is said to have been chosen because that was how far a cannon shot would carry. Most nations have since expanded it to 12 miles and a few have gone as far as 200 miles, mainly to claim exclusive control over the valuable mineral and fishing rights. This is one of the major issues to be resolved by the Law of the Sea Conference.

THREE WICKED SISTERS. See WORKMEN'S COMPENSATION.

THRESHOLD TEST-BAN TREATY OF 1974. An international agreement that prohibits Russia and the United States from conducting any underground nuclear-weapon test having a yield exceeding 150 kilotons. While the Senate has not yet ratified it, both Russia and the United States are observing the terms of the Accord.

THROWBACK RULE. Provision of the Internal Revenue Code [§§ 665-667 (Subpart D of Part I of Subchapter J)] designed to include accumulations of trust income in the gross estate of the distributee-beneficiary. Before the adoption of the rule in 1954, trustees were wont, where a trust was in a lower bracket than the beneficiary, to pay the tax on the accumulated income, and then distribute the net income to the beneficiary. The 1954 rule was eviscerated by so many exceptions that this result was not effectively prevented. In 1969, Congress passed the Tax Reform Act, which eliminated the exceptions and subjected the beneficiary to a tax on the accumulated income. The 1976 Act continues this general trend, allowing only one exception to the Rule.

THROW-DOWN GUN. A weapon planted near the body of a criminal suspect by a member of a police force to justify a claim of self-defense.

TIME AND MATERIAL CONTRACT. This contractual arrangement provides for payment of the cost of material and a specified amount for each direct labor hour expended in contract performance. The fixed rate for labor hours includes direct and indirect wage costs plus profit.

TIME CHARTER. A contractual arrangement among a party wishing the services of a vessel, the charterer, and the vessel owner, to carry goods anywhere in the world or within agreed geographical limits, on as many voyages as may be accomplished within a fixed period of time. Although the vessel is manned and operated by the owner, the charterer determines the ports-of-call and the cargo carried. This form of charter arrangement is particularly useful where a charterer wishes to have a particular amount of vessel tonnage under his control without incurring the obligations of ownership.

TIME, INC. v. HILL (385 U.S. 374 (1967)). A Supreme Court case which held that the rule in *New York Times v. Sullivan*, 376 U.S. 254 (1964), regarding "knowledge of falsehood or reckless disregard to truth", is applicable to "false light" privacy actions. In a "false light" action the claim is that the disclosure invaded the plaintiff's privacy and held him up to a "false light." The claim, unlike one in defamation, need not allege injury to the reputation. The Court also held that newsworthiness would be a complete defense against a "true" privacy action.

TIME IS OF THE ESSENCE. The phrase used in contract to indicate that certain conditions must be fulfilled by a specified date.

TIME, PLACE OR MANNER RESTRICTION. The Supreme Court has held that it is not unconstitutional to regulate the time, place or manner of speech or assembly, provided the restrictions are justified "without reference to the content of the speech, that they serve a significant governmental interest, and that in so doing they leave open ample alternative channels for communication of the information."

TINKER v. DES MOINES. See MORATORIUM DAY.

T.I.P. (Tax-Based Income Policy; Tax Incentive Program). An innovative anti-inflation program urged by some economists. The T.I.P. would be alternatively used, either as a carrot or as a stick, to induce unions and companies to moderate wage and price increases by raising the taxes of a company which gave inflationary wage increases to its employees.

TITHE TAX. A form of tribute consisting of a tenth of a person's property or produce, connected politically with taxation, and religiously with the offering of first fruits to the deity. This custom was almost universal in the ancient world, and can be traced to Babylonia, Persia, Arabia, Egypt, Greece, Rome, and even to China. The tax probably originated in a tribute laid by a conqueror or ruler on his subjects; and it may be assumed that the custom of dedicating a tenth of the spoils of war to the gods led to a religious extension of the term. The earliest authentic example of anything like a law of the state enforcing payment of tithes occurs in the capitularies of Charlemagne at the end of the eighth or the beginning of the ninth century. Tithes were to be applied to the fabric of the church and the poor.

TITLE ABSTRACT. A brief summary of all recorded instruments with respect to title of real property. It shows all the mortgages or claims held on a particular piece of property, as well as all previous owners.

TITLE XVIII. See MEDICARE PROGRAM.

TITLE INSURANCE. Protects a purchaser of real estate against any defects in the legal title to that property. Such insurance protects only against defects unknown at the time of sale. A single premium is paid for the coverage, and it remains in effect until the property is sold again. In the event a defect is later discovered, the remedy of the insured is not possession of the property but a dollar indemnification up to the policy limits. Also, the Title Insurance Company agrees to defend the insured against any legal action arising out of the defect. Title insurance is wisely purchased by the overwhelming majority of people buying homes or real property because of the difficulty of ascertaining the various possible defects in title.

TITLE IX OF THE EDUCATION AMENDMENTS OF 1972. A federal law that prohibits schools from treating boys and girls differently because of sex. Schools cannot provide separate classes or activities for male and female students; deny students the right to take a particular course because of sex; apply different rules about physical appearance to boys and girls; make different disciplinary rules or enforce them differently on the basis of sex; refuse to let a female student take part in a class or activity because she is pregnant. (The school may, in some cases, require a pregnant student to get a doctor's approval for participation in a particular class.) Because of these rules, a school cannot force boys to cut their hair shorter than girls; it cannot prevent a girl from taking shop or a boy from taking home economics. There are some exceptions to the requirement for joint classes. Schools may, for example, provide separate classes for sex education; they also may separate students by sex within physical education for participation in contact sports. One of the most controversial sections of Title IX requires that a fair share of educational and athletic funds and facilities at American colleges and schools be given to females. While Title IX does not require equal funding for male and female athletic programs, it does require equal opportunity, which a college must provide by accommodating the recreational interests of both males and females. Less than full compliance may

risk a cutoff of federal educational monies.

T.L.A. (Temporary Living Arrangement). See LINDSEY, BEN.

TOKYO CONVENTION OF 1963 (Convention on Offenses and Certain Other Acts Committed on Board Aircraft). Addressed the international problem of skyjacking for the first time. With the increase of aircraft terrorism, this Convention was followed by the Hague Convention on Hijacking and the Montreal Convention for the Suppression of Unlawful Acts Against the Safety of Civil Aviation.

TOKYO ROUND. The third in a series of conferences among the industrial nations of Europe, Canada, Japan and the United States, which first began in Tokyo in 1973 and then concluded in Geneva, Switzerland, in 1979, under the sponsorship of G.A.T.T. Their goal was to stem the world's recession-borne tide of protectionism and leave the door open for a renewed expansion of international trade, mostly through tariff reduction or elimination, which the participants argued was vital to underpin the industrial nations' faltering efforts to climb back onto the plateau of faster growth and full employment. The first such series of Free Trade Conferences is called the Dillon Round (named after the then American Secretary of the Treasury) and the second is called the Kennedy Round (named after the then American President).

TOLL GATE TAX. Approximately 1,000 Puerto Rican subsidiaries of stateside corporations pay no federal income tax if they retain their profits in Puerto Rico; but when and if the money is repatriated to the United States, then a 10 percent Toll Gate Tax must be paid.

TOMBSTONE AD. Document utilized in the sale of shares of securities. The ad bears its bizarre name because it gives the prospective buyer only the bare essentials regarding the shares: the name of the security, its price, and the name of a person from whom a prospectus may be obtained. The tombstone ad is not to be considered as an offer to sell; rather, it serves to identify those prospective buyers who are sufficiently interested to warrant sending a prospectus. Under § 2(10) of the Securities Act, it may be used after the filing of the registration statement and before the statement becomes effective.

TOMPLAIN v. UNITED STATES. See SLIGHT EVIDENCE RULE.

TONKIN GULF RESOLUTION. On August 2, 1964, North Vietnamese patrol boats attacked the *U.S.S. Maddox* on the grounds that the American ship had intruded into North Vietnamese waters. Three days later American planes bombed North Vietnamese naval bases in what Secretary of Defense McNamara called a retaliatory action. On August 7, 1964 Congress approved a Joint Resolution assuring President Johnson of its full support "for all necessary measures" to protect American Armed Forces in Southeast Asia. And so, without a formal Declaration of War as required by the Constitution, began the longest war the United States ever engaged in and the only one it ever lost.

TONTINE POLICY. A life insurance contract named for its creator, the seventeenth-century Italian banker Lorenzo Tonti. In this type of policy a group of people make high premium payments over a prescribed period of years, with the payment of the accumulated funds withheld until the end of that period. The contract provides that only those who survive the entire period and keep their policy in force by the timely payment of premiums shall share in the distribution of funds. Almost all states have banned Tontine insurance plans due to the mysterious deaths of many persons who participated in them; most likely caused by the participant who discovers the identity of others in a Tontine program and takes steps to insure that they do not survive him.

TONTONS MACOUTES. Strong-arm ruffians of the Haitian government who terrorize the population through acts of violence, including murder, with complete impunity.

TORRENS SYSTEM. System of title registration of real property adopted by some states in which a certificate of title (much like an automobile registration document) must accompany all transfers of the property. The certificate of title reveals all mortgages and liens on the property, except certain court judgments or tax liens, and provides a ready reference for checking a title. Also under most state Torrens Systems registered property may never be adverse possessed.

TORTILLA CURTAIN. A twelve-mile fence erected across part of the 1,950-mile Mexican border by the U.S. Immigration and Naturalization Service to keep out the estimated one million Mexicans who enter the country illegally each year in search of employment in the land of the big PX.

TORTIOUS ACT. A civil injury to the person or property of another, as opposed to a crime which is an offense against the sovereign. Derived from the Latin torquere, "to twist," and the French tort, meaning "wrong," the term is broadly applied to any violation of a right, other than a Breach of Contract, for which the law affords a remedy in the form of a civil action for money damages or an injunction. A tort case concerns the compensation of losses suffered by individuals because of the unlawful or socially unreasonable conduct of others. While it is virtually impossible to identify satisfactorily any single principle which explains the group of legal wrongs labelled torts, almost all of the actions in this legal family fall into one of three categories: intentional torts, negligent torts and strict liability torts. The breadth of the concept is not to be underestimated. Courts have provided remedies for beating up one's neighbor, falling on a slippery sidewalk, stealing property, injuring reputation and failing to produce a product which lives up to its purchaser's expectations—all under the Law of Tort.

TOTTEN TRUST. Money deposited in a bank in trust for a designated third party. This transfer does not necessarily mean the trustee or depositor meant to create an irrevocable trust arrangement. On the contrary, the bank holds the money during the life of the depositor as a revocable trust arrangement. Upon death of the depositor, the bank will respect the presumption that an Irrevocable Trust was created as to the deposited funds for the named beneficiary.

T.O.V.A.L.O.P. (Tanker Owner's Voluntary Agreement Concerning Liability for Oil Pollution). A private agreement between most of the oil tanker owners in the world, under which they pledge either to clean up oil spilled by their tankers or to reimburse national governments for clean-up expenses.

TOWER OF LONDON. Oldest and most celebrated fortress, garrison and museum, located on the north bank of the Thames River in London, England. The White Tower, the oldest and central part of the fortress, built by William the Conqueror in 1078, was constructed of limestone from Caen in Normandy, which was whitewashed in medieval times. The other buildings were constructed mostly in the reign of Henry III (1216-1272). There are 13 towers on the inner wall along with many gardens covering about 18 acres of land. The most famous of these towers are the Bloody Tower, which held such famous prisoners as Lady Jane Grey and Sir Walter Raleigh, the Beauchamp Tower and the Wakefield Tower, which housed the British crown jewels and regalia, from the mid-19th Century until 1967, when they were moved to bomb-proof quarters in Waterloo Barracks. The outer wall had six towers and two bastions surrounded by a moat, drained in 1843. Although the Tower was used as a royal residence, its fame arises from the many historic persons who died there. Richard III allegedly murdered the "little Princes" there. Anne Boleyn and Catherine Howard, wives of Henry VIII, were beheaded in the Tower as well as prominent churchmen such as Lord Chancellor Sir Thomas More. Guy Fawkes, Archbishop Laud, and the Earl of Strafford

have been among other famous prisoners of the Tower. Also associated with the Tower are the 40 illustrious beefeaters or yeomen, pensioners whose duties are directly connected with ceremonial occasions.

T.P.L. See TRUST FOR PUBLIC LAND.

TRADE ACT OF 1974. See TRADE ADJUSTMENT ASSISTANCE.

TRADE ADJUSTMENT ASSISTANCE. Money paid by the federal government, pursuant to the Trade Act of 1974, to employees who have been laid off or have had their working hours reduced due to increased competitive imports from abroad. The benefits include job hunting help and up to 70 percent of a worker's former weekly wage.

TRADE LIBEL. See DISPARAGEMENT OF GOODS.

TRADEMARK ABANDONMENT. Occurs when use of a trademark has been discontinued intentionally or when the mark has lost its significance as an indication of origin, as defined by Section 45 of the Lanham Act (1946). However, lapse of time or mere disuse does not destroy the trademark right as a matter of law. To establish abandonment, one has to show not only acts indicating a practical abandonment, but an actual intent to abandon. Though lapse of time without use may be evidence from which an intent to abandon may be inferred, the strength of such inference depends upon the length and cause of discontinuance.

TRADEMARK FUNCTIONS. A trademark serves three purposes. First, the mark can demonstrate the origin and ownership of the product. This identification enables consumers to distinguish the goods of one manufacturer from the goods of another. Second, the mark denotes a particular standard of quality which is embodied in the product or service. The "guarantee" function does not assure the acceptability or safety of the product, but suggests consistent quality. Finally, trademarks function as advertising devices. Trademarks have a persuasive quality in that the repetition of a mark through advertising media creates demand for the product.

TRADEMARK INFRINGEMENT TEST. Common law test which asks whether the subsequent use is "confusingly similar" or whether there is a "likelihood of confusion" with the goods of the prior user. Some of the factors used in determining whether confusion is likely are: 1) the degree of similarity between the designation and the trademark or trade name in appearance, pronunciation of the words used, verbal translations of the pictures or designs involved, and suggestion; 2) the intent of the actor in adopting the designation; 3) the relation in use and manner of marketing between the goods or services marketed by the actor and those marketed by the other; and 4) the degree of care likely to be exercised by purchasers. Under the Lanham Act (1946) the test of infringement is similar. The Lanham Act requires a showing that the use by the alleged infringer be: 1) in commerce; 2) a reproduction, a counterfeit, copy, or colorable imitation of a registered mark; 3) used in connection with the sale, offering for sale, distribution or advertising of any goods or service; and 4) in such a way as to be likely to cause confusion, or to cause mistake, or to deceive.

TRADEMARK RECAPTURE. The process whereby a generic term which was once a trademark again assumes the status of a trademark. When a word becomes generic, it remains so unless an effort is made to recreate its distinctiveness. For example, this unusual phenomenon occurred to the "Singer" trademark. The United States Supreme Court in 1896 held that the word "Singer" had become a generic term for certain kinds of sewing machines. Over a half-century later, the 5th Circuit Court of Appeals held that the Singer Manufacturing Company had by the constant and exclusive use of the name "Singer" in designating sewing machines and other articles which it manufactured and sold, and by its constant advertising of the product, recaptured from the public domain the name "Singer." The mark had come to mean not only that the manufactured goods bearing that name were the goods of the Singer Company, but also that they were of superior quality. Trademark Recapture depends on factors such as the nature and extent of advertising, exclusivity of the use of the mark, and possible acquisition of a secondary meaning. Perhaps, too, a time span covering a few generations is needed to allow the loss of older, generic associations.

TRADEMARK SLOGANS. Phrases used in advertising and promotion which function as trademarks and are entitled to legal protection and federal registration. In order to be eligible for such protection, the slogan must signify the source of the goods or services and distinguish them from the goods or services of others. For example, "You are in good hands with Allstate" may be protected under law because it functions as a trademark which identifies the Allstate Insurance Company as the source of this service.

TRADEMARK STATUTES. Federal statutes which regulate the issuance and use of trademarks. Such laws were recommended by Thomas Jefferson when he was Secretary of State, but Congress did not heed his suggestion in the 1790s, probably because it deemed this area should be left to state regulation. However, in the nineteenth century Congress did move to regulate trademarks. The first Federal Trademark Statute, the Act of 1870, was held unconstitutional by the Supreme Court on the ground that it was not expressly limited to interstate or foreign commerce. The Act of 1881 was appropriately limited and continued in effect until it was replaced by the Act of 1905. The 1905 Act was supplanted in 1946 by the Lanham Act, which is today the basic Federal Trademark Statute. Because trademarks now have great social and economic importance, the Lanham Act has liberalized and expanded the concept of trademark infringement.

The Lanham Act provides the federal registration of a trademark and constitutes constructive notice of the registrant's claim of ownership, thus increasing the protection available to trademark owners. Although prior to registration the mark is protected by the common law, the owner acquires additional remedies and procedural rights by registering under the Lanham Act. The extraordinary growth of interstate commercial activity, population mobility, and advertising have made people aware of the importance of the Federal Trademark Statute.

TRADE NAME. A descriptive, geographical, or personal name, notation or symbol used by firms and associations engaged in trade or commerce. Trade names refer to corporate partnership or other names of a business, while goods or services produced by the business may have a trademark. For example, "Sterling Drug, Inc." is used as the trade name of the business which sells aspirin under the trademark, "Bayer." Generally speaking, the trademark is applicable to a commodity, while a trade name refers to a business. This distinction was adopted by the Supreme Court in *American Steel Foundries v. Robertson,* 262 U.S. 209 (1926). Both trade names and trademarks are protected in order to prevent and repair injury caused by confusing or deceptive use in trade.

TRADE REFORM ACT OF 1974. Federal legislation designed to reduce trade barriers by affording the President greater powers to negotiate reciprocal agreements. The more controversial provisions of the Act enable the President to use tariffs as a political lever. For example, the President is empowered to extend Most Favored Nation status to the Soviet Union for a period of eighteen months in order to secure a more lenient Soviet policy with respect to Jewish emigration. Conversely, the Act prohibited the extension of tariff preferences to member countries of O.P.E.C.

TRADE SCHOOLS. See BLUE RIBBON SCHOOLS.

TRADE SECRET. Any formula, plan, pattern, or compound, machine or process of manufacturing, or any device or compilation of information known only to its owner and selected employees. For example, the formula for Coca-Cola is a closely guarded trade secret. Trade secret protection is in some ways greater and in some respects less than that afforded by a patent privilege. The protection is greater in that it is not limited to a fixed number of years, nor does it require that the mark be the product of novelty and invention. On the other hand, the protection may be weaker in that it depends on the preservation of a secret.

TRANSACTIONAL IMMUNITY. Grant of immunity from prosecution. There are two types of immunity—Transactional and Use and Derivative Use. Transactional Immunity protects a person from prosecution for all crimes to which his testimony relates. Obviously this is very attractive and persons receiving it give comprehensive testimony in order to create the broadest immunity possible. Although the Supreme Court has held that Use and Derivative Use Immunity is legally sufficient to compel testimony, Transactional Immunity is sometimes granted to induce maximum cooperation.

TRANSFERRED INTENT. A doctrine in both tort law and criminal law which holds a defendant liable for injury to a person or object caused when the defendant attempted to injure another person or object. In effect, the defendant's intent is transferred from the intended victim to the actual victim. Thus, if John intends to kill Paul, but kills Tom instead, he is guilty of murdering Tom.

TRANSFER TAX (Convenience Tax). A state tax imposed on the transfer of an interest in real property. The transfer tax is paid by the party selling, leasing or assigning the property. If the transfer is between husband and wife or parent and child and the consideration paid was less than $100, or if the tax had been paid when the underlying contract was recorded or if the transaction is a mortgage, the tax generally need not be paid.

TRANSITORY ACTION. A cause of action in which the subject matter of the occurrence or injury involved has no necessary relation to any particular locality and thus could have arisen anywhere. The common-law rule is that a Transitory Action may be tried wherever the defendant may be subjected to personal jurisdiction. In contrast, a local action must be tried where the cause of action actually arose.

TRAYNOR, ROGER. A justice of the California Supreme Court from 1940-70, he felt that generalized, mechanical, legal rules had no durability. A philosophy that judge-made rules based on rationality were necessary to respond to a changing society guided Traynor. He was skeptical about rigid legal maxims and fashioned many innovative approaches to traditional problems arising in a rapidly-changing society. Not surprisingly he preferred judges to juries and contended that it was specious to say that courts did not make law. Traynor's greatest influence permeated tort law. He initiated the concept of strict liability, undermined the immunity defense in negligence cases, revised the landowner's duty of care to visitors on his property, and introduced the tort of intentional infliction of emotional distress.

TREASURY SHARES. Stock which has been repurchased or otherwise reacquired by the corporation and not yet cancelled. The corporation may return them to the status of unissued shares or eliminate them by reducing the number of authorized shares. Treasury Shares usually may not be voted or used to determine whether there has been shareholder approval. They do not participate in dividends or distribution of net assets upon liquidation. Where the original issuance complied with preemptive rights and requirements of adequate consideration received by the corporation, the reallotment of the shares is not subject to those restrictions.

TREAT 'EM RIGHT, WRIGHT. See TURN 'EM LOOSE, BRUCE.

TREATY RATIFICATION. See ADVICE and CONSENT.

TREATY TRADER AND INVESTOR VISA. See H-1 VISA.

TREBLE DAMAGES. In certain cases such as antitrust and trademark infringement, the successful plaintiff recovers three times the amount of his actual loss to deter that defendant and other prospective wrongdoers from engaging in such misconduct.

TRESPASS TO CHATTELS. A tort involving an intentional act by the defendant which results in an invasion of the owner's interest in his personal property. Two separate invasions are encompassed in the tort. Dispossession refers to conduct which amounts to an assertion of ownership rights inconsistent with those of the rightful owner. Theft and destruction are examples. Intermeddling refers to a lesser invasion which is not an assertion of ownership. Examples include throwing a stone at another's car or hitting a neighbor's dog.

TRESPASS TO LAND. A tort involving an intentional act by the defendant, causing an intrusion upon land which was in the plaintiff's possession. At common law, virtually any unauthorized entry onto another's land was considered a trespass since, as one English judge said, "the law bounds every man's property and is his fence." The modern trend is to award damages for injury to property caused by trespass only when the defendant has been negligent or was acting intentionally. The Supreme Court approved this trend in the famous Nitroglycerine Case in which the employees of a carrier used a hammer to open a box which was leaking nitroglycerine. The resulting explosion damaged the plaintiff's property, but the Supreme Court refused to award damages absent proof of negligent or intentional conduct.

TRIAL BY AMBUSH (Wear 'Em Down Tactic). Through a process called discovery, a party may delay endlessly by demanding often absurdly peripheral information "relating to" the lawsuit. The Wear 'Em Down philosophy is said to have been articulated by senior partner Bruce Bromley of the Wall Street firm of Cravath, Swaine & Moore in a speech before an appreciative audience of Stanford Law students 20 years ago: "I was born, I think, to be a protractor . . . I could take the simplest antitrust case and protract it for the defense almost to infinity . . . [one case] lasted 14 years . . . Despite 50,000 pages of testimony, there really wasn't any dispute about the facts. . . . We won that case, and, as you know, my firm's meter was running all the time—every month for 14 years."

TRIAL BY ORDEAL. An ancient form of trial, practiced in England until after the Norman period, in which an accused person was subjected to a physical test such as plunging the hand in boiling water or holding a hot iron. The result determined the guilt (hand burned) or innocence (hand did not burn) of the person and was thought to be the immediate judgment of God. It was a "heads I win, tails you lose" form of Justice.

TRIAL MARRIAGE. Suggested by some law reformers as an alternate form of institutionalized marriage which would legalize relationships of persons living together. Trial marriages would create minimal legal obligations and would be easily dissolved. Emphasis would be placed on whether the couple was compatible intellectually, emotionally and sexually. A more durable relationship could then be entered into by couples who were compatible, and by those who desired to raise children.

TRIAL OF THE TEMPLARS. The Order of the Temple was a military religious order, vowed to defend the holy Christian places against the Moslems. During the twelfth century the popularity of the crusades enabled the order to amass great wealth, and to fulfil an important function as bankers. However, in 1291 the Christians were driven out of Palestine, which caused the Templars'

role to be questioned. This situation left the order vulnerable to the attack of Philip IV of France, who, plagued by financial troubles, succumbed to the temptation to seize the Templars' wealth. In 1307, ostensibly at the request of the Inquisition, he suddenly caused the Templars in France to be arrested and charged with heretical crimes, including the denial of Christ, indecent reception ceremonies and idol worship. Pope Clement V, to whom the Templars were directly responsible, at first objected; but then in an attempt to assert his own authority he tried to take over the trial, instructing the other European rulers to arrest the Templars as well.

TRIALOGUE NEWSLETTER. See TRIALATERAL COMMISSION.

TRIANGLE PAPERS. See TRILATERAL COMMISSION.

TRIBUNAL OF WATERS (Tribunal De Las Aquas). Oldest court of justice in Europe composed of farmers in Valencia's irrigated plains, which mediates disputes among the 15,000 farmers who depend on the irrigation system to sustain their crops. The Tribunal of Waters began hearing such disputes ten centuries ago and continues to enforce equitable rules without any of the accoutrements of modern courts. If the Tribunal finds a farmer guilty, he may be forced to pay costs and penalties. Farmers generally pay promptly, as failure to do so will result in water being denied their land.

TRIGGER PRICE MECHANISM. A device used by the treasury department to set a minimum price at which imported goods may be sold to protect American manufacturers from unfair competition from abroad. If the foreign seller sets a sales price lower than that established by the treasury, the federal government may invoke the Anti-Dumping Law protection for the American producers.

TRILATERAL COMMISSION. Conceived by David Rockefeller, head of the Chase Manhattan Bank, in 1973, this is a group of approximately 250 scholars, statesmen, politicians, labor and business leaders, selected from the three of the world's principal industrialized areas of North America, Western Europe and Japan. It meets every nine months for the purpose of promoting closer international co-operation among the non-Communist industrial nations. President Carter and 17 of his foreign policy advisers were former members. Some conservative critics claim that it is a conspiracy to control, if not take over, the American government. Its first full time Director was Zbigniew Brzezinski, subsequently National Security Adviser to President Carter.

T.R.O. (Temporary Restraining Order). As its name suggests, a T.R.O. is intended to maintain the status quo between the parties while a court considers a motion for a preliminary injunction. A T.R.O. may not be granted for a period longer than ten days, and it may be renewed only once. It may be granted without notice if the movant shows that immediate and irreparable damage will occur before the opposing party can be notified or if reasonable efforts have been made to notify the opposing party. The movant is required also to give security to cover damages of the opposing party in the event the T.R.O. has been wrongfully issued.

TROIKA PRINCIPLE. An unaccepted Russian recommendation, named after the Russian three-horse snow sled, that the United Nations Secretary General's functions be divided among three persons—a capitalist, a communist and a neutral (whatever that is).

TRUE VALUE RULE. Requires that the consideration received by a corporation in exchange for the issuance of shares have a market value at the time of the issuance at least equal to the par value of the stock issued. This is now the minority rule, the liberal good faith rule having been adopted by a majority of courts. The True Value Rule ignores the inherent difficulties in the valuation of services and property. It does not take into account the fact that experts might differ as to value. Furthermore, it does not allow anticipated profits to serve as a basis for valuation.

TRUMAN DOCTRINE. Expounded in 1947 by President Harry S. Truman, this program was designed to end the growth of Communism in Southeastern Europe, especially in Greece and Turkey. The Truman Doctrine initiated a United States effort to contain Communism, which continued until Detente.

TRUMPED UP CHARGES (French—tromper: to deceive). Slang expression for trying to make a criminal case against an innocent victim where there is no basis at all for the allegation of guilt.

TRUST ARRANGEMENT. This is usually a private express agreement between the trust settlor, the trustee and the beneficiary in which the settlor places such money or property as he desires under the supervision of the trustee for the benefit of the beneficiary. Legal title in the trust property passes from the settlor to the trustee, and the beneficiary obtains an equitable or beneficial interest in the trust property being held by the trustee. Because the settlor relinquishes legal title in the trust property in favor of the trustee, only the beneficiary can sue the trustee to enforce the trust arrangement. Generally, a trust arrangement may be created for any purpose that is neither against the public welfare nor the law. An early trust was called a use. A use was not enforceable in court until the court of chancery first gave it legal sanction in England in the fifteenth century. With the enactment of the Statute of Uses in 1536, the modern trust was born. The use was no longer an equitable interest to be dealt with by the court of chancery, but a legal interest which could be enforced by the courts of common law.

TRUST BENEFICIARY. The person or group of persons for which a benefit such as money or property is held in trust. However, the law has seen many strange beneficiaries—such as a pet dog or horse—sometimes being paid thousands of dollars in food and lavish care by a trustee after their master dies.

TRUST-BUSTER. Term first applied to President Theodore Roosevelt in the early part of the twentieth century when he vigorously enforced the Anti-Trust Laws against various American giant corporations. It now applies to any government official who is deemed to be anti-big business.

TRUST CHARGE. The fee charged by a trust institution for the professional creation, supervision or administration of a trust, and more specifically, charges for duties performed by the trustee.

TRUST DISTRIBUTION. The actual apportionment of assets according to the terms of a trust arrangement. A distribution is to be distinguished from a disbursement, the latter being moneys paid to discharge a debt or expense.

TRUSTEE IN BANKRUPTCY. Representative of the bankruptcy estate, elected by creditors of the bankrupt debtor and confirmed by the bankruptcy court. The trustee's principal task is to liquidate the bankrupt's assets and distribute them to the creditors. As administrator of the estate, the trustee may contest the discharge of debts of the bankrupt, contest claims of a creditor, act in court to rescind a voidable transfer, or defend suits brought against the bankrupt.

TRUSTEESHIP COUNCIL. United Nations organ which regulates the administration of trust territories. At present, participating members of the Council are the United Kingdom, France, the Union of Soviet Socialist Republics, and the United States. The goals of the trusteeship system are to transform trust territories into independent countries or parts thereof. Of the original eleven trust territories, all except the Pacific Islands, administered by the United States, and Southwest Africa, have attained independent status.

TRUST ESTATE. The interest or right a trust beneficiary has in the trust property. The estate is held, however, by the legal owner of the trust property, the trustee.

TRUST FEE. The fixed compensation a qualified trust institution receives for its services. This fee is usually paid by the trust settlor and is distinguishable from the trust charge which compensates for the creation, supervision, or administration of the trust.

TRUST FOR PUBLIC LAND (T.P.L.). Established in California in 1973 by Huey Johnson, for non-profit land acquisition to protect urban open spaces and to fight inner city decay. T.P.L. buys eyesores such as empty lots, and transfers them to neighborhood land trusts which turn the property into community gardens or parks. The innovative program encourages self-sufficiency and pride of ownership among inner-city residents, as well as improving the quality of life in the city.

TRUST FOUNDATION. A collection of assets, usually established through donations and contributions, which are used for a wide variety of purposes such as education, medicine, religion and industry. One such famous American foundation is the Ford Foundation, which was founded in honor of Henry Ford, the American automotive giant.

TRUST GRANTEE. Generally, a person to whom property is transferred by deed or otherwise, or to whom property rights or interests in money are granted by a trust arrangement. Hence, the trustee and the beneficiary are both technically trust grantees of the trust settlor, the former being a direct grantee, the latter an indirect grantee.

TRUST GRANTOR (Trust Settlor). The party to a trust arrangement who transfers such properties and assets as he desires for the benefit of another by means of an express trust. Historically, this is accomplished by a written trust instrument which is witnessed, signed and recorded pursuant to the requirements of the Statute of Frauds.

TRUST GUARDIAN. A Trust institution or individual who is appointed by a court to act as a temporary trust trustee when circumstances such as death or incapacity render an existing trustee unable to perform.

TRUST INDENTURE ACT (1939). Requires that debt securities publicly offered for sale in significant amounts be issued under an indenture that meets certain statutory standards and has been duly qualified with the Security Exchange Commission (S.E.C.). These standards relate, among other things, to the eligibility, qualification and independence of trustees under the indenture in order to provide reasonable financial responsibility and to minimize conflicting interests.

TRUST INSTITUTION. A business, often affiliated with a bank, which specializes in initiating, supervising and dissolving trust arrangements. These institutions provide convenient, consolidated, and efficient services for the settlor, ranging from banking and investment to management and distribution of trust assets.

TRUST REFEREE. A qualified person appointed by a court to conduct hearings and to investigate a trustee's financial transactions and records, for evidence of improper conduct or other breaches of trust. The Referee then reports findings to the court and to the various interested parties.

TRUST PROPERTY. The corpus of a trust arrangement. Usually it is in the nature of money, such as proceeds from investments or bank funds. Trust property is commonly physical and tangible as opposed to conceptual or theoretical. However, one English case in the nineteenth century involved merely the written ideas of the settlor held in trust for his family as beneficiaries, to be read each year on the anniversary of his death by a designated trustee.

TRUST SETTLOR. One who creates a trust arrangement by giving something to a trustee to hold in beneficial interest for the trust beneficiary. Traditionally, this party to a trust arrangement is a wealthy parent or relative of the trust beneficiary who wants to give some asset, usually money, and still retain the control that an outright gift would preclude.

TRUST TRUSTEE. One who is responsible for the management and supervision of trust property. Generally, this term describes one who has legal title to property but holds it as a fiduciary for the benefit or use of another. Today, most trustees are not persons, but institutions which handle thousands of trusts in a professional capacity. In this way, a trust settlor can be confident his records will be managed without regard to an individual who might die or become incapacitated.

TRUTH IN LENDING ACT. A federal statute whose basic purpose is to assure that every customer who needs consumer credit is given meaningful information with respect to the cost of that credit. In most cases, the credit cost must be expressed in the dollar amount of finance charges, and as an annual percentage rate computed on the unpaid balance of the amount financed. Other relevant credit information must also be disclosed, so that the customer may compare the various credit terms available to him from different sources and avoid the uninformed use of credit. The Act further provides a customer the right, in certain circumstances, to cancel a credit transaction which involves a lien on his residence. The Truth in Lending Act was amended in 1970 to regulate the issuance, holder's liability, and fraudulent use of credit cards. New credit cards may be issued only in response to a request or application by the person who is to receive the card. Also, the liability to the cardholder for unauthorized use of a credit card is specifically limited to $50.00 if the cardholder has taken reasonable steps to notify the card issuer of the loss or theft. The Act also establishes penalties for the fraudulent use of credit cards in interstate or foreign commerce when the aggregate retail value is $5,000 or more. The Federal Trade Commission enforces the requirements of the Truth in Lending Act over finance companies, retailers, non-federal credit unions, and other creditors not specifically regulated by another government agency, as well as persons or their agents who issue credit cards.

TRUTH IN NEGOTIATIONS ACT. A federal law which requires prospective Department of Defense government procurement contractors to submit cost and pricing data prior to the negotiation of certain contract prices. In general, the Act requires contractors to submit and certify that such data is accurate, complete, and current prior to the award of any negotiated contract where the price is expected to exceed $100,000 and prior to the pricing of any contract modification (with respect to any contract) where the price is expected to exceed $100,000 unless the price is based on adequate price competition or on established catalog or market prices of commercial items sold in substantial quantities to the general public, or where the price has been set by law or regulation. Pursuant to the Act, the government reserves the right to unilaterally reduce the contract price by any amount it was increased as a result of defective data.

TRUTH IN SECURITIES ACT. See S.E.C.

TRUTH-IN-TAXATION LAW. Forces local governments to be candid about who's raising taxes and why. Pioneered by Carl Ogden of Florida, Truth-in-Taxation requires local governments to run a conspicuous quarter-page ad announcing that the City Council proposes to raise property taxes and setting a date for a public hearing on the proposal. These ads have become known as "The Death Notice" because most municipalities are reluctant to run them. Other states which have Florida-style Truth-in-Taxation laws include Hawaii, Virginia, and Maryland.

TRUTH IN TESTING LAW. The popular name for the Admissions Testing Law of 1979, which was passed by the New York State Legislature. A coalition of student and consumer organizations, including the New York Public Interest Research Group Inc., lobbied vigorously for the law on the ground that the standardized-testing industry operated with too much secrecy and that students were entitled to see the tests that play such an important role in their education and future careers. It was opposed by Gordon M. Ambach, the Commissioner of Education, and by representatives of the testing industry, who argued that financial and other costs would outweigh any education or consumer gains, and that there were other ways to provide greater accountability for the industry.

TSUNAMI INSURANCE. Coverage to protect against tidal wave action. Owners of property in flood and Tsunami zones generally are required by mortgage lenders to provide insurance covering flood and tidal wave damage.

TUCKER ACT. This is the federal legislation by which the Court of Claims and Federal District Courts, where the claim does not exceed $10,000, are granted jurisdiction to render judgments on any claim against the United States founded upon any express or implied contract with the United States. The jurisdiction is limited to obligations which the United States has voluntarily assumed by an express or implied promise to the contractor; it does not extend to quasi-contractual obligations which are imposed by law.

TUESDAY MASSACRE. The mass "voluntary" and unprecedented resignation on Tuesday, July 17, 1979, of all 34 Cabinet members and senior White House staff advisors of President Jimmy Carter in a dramatic attempt to re-establish his leadership. This is the first time in American history that such an event took place in the middle of a presidential term of office. Its effectiveness will be left to the judgment of future historians.

527

TURKEY FARM. A place where an incompetent government employee, who is protected by Civil Service status, is assigned. At a turkey farm unimportant work is performed and little damage can be done.

TURNCOAT WITNESS. An insider or fellow employee who testifies for the prosecution as state's evidence in a "white collar" crime in the hope of getting lenient treatment.

TURN 'EM LOOSE BRUCE. A Black Judge named Bruce Wright who was given this nickname by the New York City police. He not only criticized the criminal justice system as racist, but also tried to correct some of the injustices he perceived by setting low or no bail in many cases. That didn't please either the police or his colleagues, and in 1974—after four years on the bench—Wright was transferred to civil court. David Ross, the New York City Administrative Judge, said the transfer was the first step in a new rotational system designed to give judges a broader range of experience. But Wright charged that it was really the culmination of a campaign to force him into judicial conformity. With the help of the Center for Constitutional Rights, the National Conference of Black Lawyers, and the National Lawyers Guild, Judge Wright filed suit in the United States District Court for the Southern District of New York, alleging that his transfer violated the Fourteenth Amendment because it was motivated by displeasure with his criticism of the system, his bail decisions, and his race. Wright's suit received some unexpected assistance from the Criminal Courts Committee of the New York City Bar. In a report critical of the transfer, the Committee described meetings it had with Judge Ross, New York State Chief Judge Charles Breitel, Deputy New York City Administrative Judge Jawn Sandifer, and New York State Administrative Judge Richard Bartlett. In February, 1978, just as these judges were about to be called to court to explain their roles in Wright's transfer, Wright was transferred back to criminal court by Judge Ross.

TURNOVER ORDER. An order by a bankruptcy court, commanding someone in possession of property deemed by the court to be part of a bankrupt's estate, to surrender the property to the bankruptcy trustee. Typically, the property at issue has been the subject of a fraudulent transfer or a voidable preference on the part of the bankrupt.

TUSKEGEE STUDY. Initiated by the United States Public Health Service in the 1930s to determine the long-term effects of syphilis on men. Two groups of Black men in the Tuskegee, Alabama, area were used: one group had syphilis; the control group was disease free. The men were given health care for any ailment except syphilis. The study extended well into the 1960s. Therefore, even after penicillin was found to be a cure to syphilis, it was withheld from the subjects. The study so shocked the American people that in 1974 the Congress passed the National Research Act to prevent such abuses in medical experimentation with humans.

T.V.A. (Tennessee Valley Authority). A Government-owned corporation that conducts a unified program of resource development for the advancement of economic growth in the Tennessee Valley region. The Authority's activities include flood control, navigation development, electric power production, fertilizer development, recreation improvement, and forestry and wildlife development. While its power program is financially self-supporting, other programs are financed primarily by appropriations from Congress. The T.V.A. is the nation's largest and only federally owned utility (1977 sales: $1.96 billion). It was founded by President Franklin D. Roosevelt in 1933 as a daring experimental power and soil-reclamation project designed to be a model for regional development. During the depressed 1930s, the Seven-State South Eastern T.V.A., brought the cheap electricity and fertilizers and flood control that lifted the Tennessee

Valley from poverty to the brink of prosperity.

T.V.A. v. HILL. See ENDANGERED SPECIES ACT.

TWEED RING. Composed of William "Boss" Tweed, and several high New York City officials who embezzled millions of dollars from the city. The *New York Times* exposed some of Tweed's frauds when two city employees turned over copies of the Comptroller's books. A Committee of Seventy was convened to recover the stolen money. Although Tweed was convicted of 204 out of 220 counts in the indictments for forgery and larceny, the maximum penalty for any one count was $250 and a year in prison. Prosecutors argued that the sentence should be imposed cumulatively, while the defense maintained that Tweed could only be liable for the maximum on any one count. The judge compromised and imposed a sentence of one-half the cumulative amount (12 years and $12,750). The court of appeals reversed and Tweed was made to pay only $250 and a year in prison. Upon his release, however, Tweed was rearrested in a civil action brought under a new law allowing a state to sue for money stolen from the public treasury. Tweed was imprisoned for failure to meet a $3,000,000 bail. Confinement was rather pleasant there; Tweed was allowed daily drives in his carriage and visits to his mansion. On one such visit, Tweed escaped to a New Jersey farm, and via Cuba, to Spain where he was identified and extradited to New York. Tweed died in prison in 1878.

TWELFTH AMENDMENT (1804). Provides that the President and Vice President be elected by separate ballots. The Twelfth Amendment altered the older system whereby the candidate with the second highest number of Electoral College votes was declared Vice President. The Amendment was the result of the election of 1800, in which each party-pledged elector cast two votes. As a result, Thomas Jefferson, the Presidential candidate, was tied with his running mate, Aaron Burr.

The Amendment was intended to avoid such confusion.

TWELVE TABLETS. Promulgated about 450 B.C., they represent the beginning of Roman law. Political strife between the plebeians, or lower class, and the patricians, or upper class, gave rise to the Twelve Tablets. The plebeians complained that knowledge of the law was not available to them and that it was unfair for the law to be the preserve of patricians alone. Consequently, Roman representatives visited Greece to learn about law and then produced Twelve Tablets, which were displayed in the Roman Forum. The Twelve Tablets have been hailed as signalling the growth of written law as ushering in a closer equality between the classes, despite the fact that Emperor Gaius Caesar (Caligula) had the Tablets placed on a pillar so high that no citizen standing on the ground could read them. Nor has their significance been diminished even though they relied on rigid formalisms and oral formulas so that "What one shall have declared by tongue that shall be law." The Tablets were destroyed when the Gauls ransacked Rome in 390 B.C.

TWENTIETH AMENDMENT. See LAME DUCK AMENDMENT.

TWENTY-SIXTH AMENDMENT (1971). Lowered the voting age to eighteen. The Voting Rights Act of 1970 had already given eighteen-year-olds the right to vote, but in *Oregon v. Mitchell*, 400 U.S. 112 (1970) the Supreme Court declared that Congress could determine voting requirements for national elections only. During 1971, the required number of states hurriedly ratified the new amendment so that eighteen-year-olds could vote in the 1972 elections. During the ratification campaign, proponents argued that if eighteen-year-olds were old enough to be drafted, they were old enough to vote.

TWENTY-THIRD AMENDMENT (1961). Accorded the District of Columbia three electoral votes, enabling the people of the District to participate in presidential elections.

TWO-CHINA POLICY. The recognition of the People's Republic of China (Mainland Communist China) and the Republic of China (Taiwan) as separate independent sovereign Chinese countries.

TWO HUNDRED-MILE LIMIT. The claim of a coastal nation regarding the seaward limit of its jurisdiction as measured from a baseline generally describing the low-water mark along the coast. Such claims have taken serious forms, from a Two Hundred Mile Territorial Sea, limiting freedom of navigation and overflight, to a Two-Hundred Mile Fishing Conservation Zone, which generally excludes only foreign fishing vessels. Other claims have been asserted to an exclusive economic zone, preserving the right of exploration for an exploitation of the area's resources, both living and nonliving. Likewise, similar claims have been made regarding the width of the continental shelf, restricting access to the nonliving resources of that area. Whether or not any such claims are recognized by the international community depends upon the existence of bilateral and multilateral international treaties as well as customary international law. At this time there is no consensus of opinion regarding the acceptance of the Two-Hundred Mile Limit.

TWO PARTNER RULE. See N.S.M. CASE.

TWO-STEP FORMAL ADVERTISING. A Department of Defense method of contractor selection which combines aspects of formal advertising and negotiation. Under this system, in step one a procuring agency requests contractors to submit unpriced technical proposals. In step two, contractors who have submitted acceptable proposals are requested to submit bids under regular formal advertised procedures; however, each contractor competes on the basis of his own proposal.

TWO STRAWBERRIES CASE. Woman convicted in 1978, by a jury, of eating two strawberries in a grocery store without paying for them. The strawberries were valued at two cents. Sentenced to 18 months in prison and a $500 fine, her sentence was reduced after public outrage over the case.

TWO-TIER APPROACH. A method of analysis used in cases brought under the equal protection clause of the Fourteenth Amendment. Under this approach, in some cases the Supreme Court has used strict scrutiny which has, in fact, been fatal to the challenged statute. In other cases, the Court has employed minimal scrutiny, which has usually amounted to no more than questioning the rationality of the statute. The two areas in which the Court has employed the strict scrutiny test are suspect classifications and fundamental rights and interests.

TWO-TIER SCAM. A crime made possible after the Arab Oil Embargo of 1973 when the federal government fixed a price structure of $5.65 per barrel for "old" domestic oil already in production and $12.53 for "new" finds. Not unexpectedly, some unscrupulous dealers would buy oil at the lower price and sell it fraudulently at the higher price in violation of Federal Antiracketeering Statutes. Dozens of such crooks who made millions of dollars of illegal profits at the expense of consumers are now residing in jail.

TYING ARRANGEMENT. An agreement by a party to sell one product, the Tying Product, to another party, but only on the condition that the buyer also purchases a second product, the Tied Product. Usually the two products are related in use, but they need not be. A Tying Arrangement enables a seller who enjoys substantial power in one product market to gain undue advances in a separate product market. Such arrangements are specifically banned by the Clayton Act (1914) and are per se violations of the Sherman Act (1890).

U

U.C.C. (Uniform Commercial Code). A nine-article product of the Permanent Editorial Board, the American Law Institute, and the National Conference of Commissioners on Uniform State Law. Between 1957 and 1967 all states but Louisiana enacted the Code. However, many of the states have varied the original text. There are two major articles to the Code: Article 2 applies to the sale of goods, and Article 9 deals with the transfer or assignment of contractual rights. Article 2, which has made changes in traditional contract law, serves as a guideline for many courts in determining contractual transactions that do not completely pertain to the sale of goods. The relatively rapid national acceptance of the U.C.C. has been called the "most spectacular success story in American Law."

U.C.M.J. See UNIFORM CODE OF MILITARY JUSTICE.

U.G.M.A. See UNIFORM GIFTS TO MINORS ACT.

ULTIMATE ISSUE RULE. At common law, a witness could not testify concerning an ultimate issue in the case. Under modern law and the Federal Rules of Evidence, however, testimony may not be excluded on the ground that it goes to an ultimate issue.

ULTIMATE TRUST BENEFICIARY. The trust beneficiary who takes after the primary or principal beneficiary. An ultimate beneficiary is often included by the trust settlor to protect the trust arrangement from unforeseen catastrophe. A typical arrangement would be to X in trust for Y, at the date of Y's death to his youngest brother, Z.

ULTRA VIRES DOCTRINE (Latin— beyond the power). Generally the term concerns an action taken by a corporation beyond corporate purposes, as stated in the Articles of Incorporation. Such action may be invalid, depending upon the law in the state of incorporation. In the past, corporations were formed for limited purposes, and the charter clause which stated this purpose generally was strictly construed. An Ultra Vires act was beyond the corporation's power and thus illegal and void. Modern Enabling Acts provide that a corporation may be formed for any lawful purpose, and that an Ultra Vires act is not illegal if it is not a public wrong. Corporations today are substantially unlimited. Where the Ultra Vires Doctrine was once a principal concern to the corporate lawyer, such cases today are anachronisms. The corporation is aided, in these instances, by a more liberal interpretation of the purpose clause. Modern acts also grant wide-ranging implied powers. Typically, present statutory provisions abolish the Ultra Vires Doctrine except with respect to shareholder injunction suits against the corporation.

UMBRELLA LIABILITY POLICY. Insurance coverage protecting against claims of a catastrophic proportion. To qualify for such coverage, the insured must first purchase underlying liability insurance. When a loss occurs, the underlying insurance pays to the limits of its liability, with the Umbrella Liability Policy paying the excess, up to the limits of its liability, generally from one to five million dollars. Umbrella Liability Policies are carried by many professionals, such as doctors and dentists, well-to-do members of society, and large business firms, those against whom large judgments are likely to be obtained.

UMBRELLA RECEIVERSHIP (Equity Receivership). A proceeding developed by the federal courts which allows a corporation with financial problems to reorganize while it continues business operations. The purpose of such a receivership is to allow the corporation to preserve its viability. Umbrella receiverships developed when a creditor filed a creditor's bill in the federal district court, alleging imminent insolvency of the corporation. The bill cited the threat of creditor attachments and the subsequent dissection of corporate property. The lack of an adequate legal remedy pointed up the need for a receiver to preserve corporate assets for the benefit of all creditors. The corporation had to admit all allegations and join in the prayer for receivership. The resulting receivership, which protected the corporate property from the enforcement of claims of creditors, was given the name umbrella receivership. At a judicial sale the property was sold to the highest bidder, usually a creditor's committee, at a price sufficient to pay expenses and the pro rata shares of creditors not assenting to the purchase. The property was then conveyed to a new corporation, which would continue the business of the old corporation. The consenting creditors received securities in the new corporation as set out in the plan of reorganization. Shareholders of the old corporation might be required to contribute additional sums of money in order to receive an interest in the new business. Some shareholders, not given this opportunity, were denied any continuing interest. The prevailing rule as to shareholders was that they could not retain any interest under a reorganization plan which did not satisfy all creditor claims. Umbrella receiverships had many defects including costly and complex procedures which were not adequately supervised by the courts. In 1934, Section 77B of the Federal Bankruptcy Act prohibited the commencement of any further umbrella receiverships. Section 77B was replaced in 1938 by Chapter X of the Chandler Act.

U.N. (United Nations). An international organization established in accordance with a charter drafted by governments represented at the Conference on International Organization meeting at San Francisco. The charter was signed in 1945, and came into force the same year when the required number of ratifications and accessions had been made by the signatories. Amendments increasing membership of the Security Council and the Economic and Social Council came into effect in 1965. The United Nations now consists of 152 member countries of which 51 are founding members. The purposes of the United Nations set out in the charter are: to maintain international peace and security; to develop friendly relations among nations; to achieve international cooperation in solving international problems of an economic, social, cultural or humanitarian character and in promoting respect for human rights; and to be a center for harmonizing the actions of nations in the attainment of these common ends.

UNAUTHORIZED CAR USE. See JOY RIDING.

UNAUTHORIZED PRACTICE OF LAW. The prohibited offering of professional legal services by a person or organization not qualified to practice law.

UNBLESSED EVENT. See WRONGFUL LIFE.

UNCLE CHARLIE. The affectionate name given to any one of the five Federal Communication Commissioners by Citizen's Band radio operators.

UNCLEAN HANDS. See CLEAN HANDS.

UNCONSCIONABLE BARGAIN. An agreement accompanied by an inadequate consideration which indicates that one party has been taken advantage of by another.

U.N. CONVENTION ON THE PREVENTION AND PUNISHMENT OF THE CRIME OF GENOCIDE. A reaction against Nazi atrocities and mass murders of Jews during World War II, the Genocide Convention was unanimously adopted by the U.N. General Assembly on December 9, 1948 and came into force on January 12, 1951. Genocide is defined as "acts committed with intent to destroy, in whole or in part, a national, ethical, racial, or religious group." Killing, causing physical or mental harm, inflicting poor conditions of life, imposing birth control, and forcibly transferring children from one group to another, are made international crimes. The Convention provides for individual responsibility for acts of genocide or incitation to genocide. Persons charged with genocide are subject to trial by national or international courts, and are extraditable. However, no institutions for international enforcement have been established, and no one has thus far been charged with such a crime. Interpretation of the Convention may be effected by the International Court of Justice.

U.N.C.T.A.D. (United Nations Conference on Trade and Development). The world's largest annual meeting on wealth and poverty in which poor countries tell rich countries how to bridge the gap between them. It is an outgrowth of the Group of 77, formed in 1964, which now has 119 members of Less Developed Countries (L.D.C.s). In addition to foreign aid assistance, they seek higher prices for the raw materials they export, lower prices for the manufactured goods they import, a greater share in ocean natural resources and foreign investment.

UNDERDEVELOPED COUNTRY. See L.D.C.

UNDERGROUND ECONOMY. A form of illegal tax evasion in which people sell their services or goods for cash which they do not report as taxable income and therefore do not pay the tax which is due on the transaction. Millions of dollars of such unlawful transactions take place every day as a colossal rip-off on Uncle Sam (and on you and us).

UNDERWRITING AGREEMENT. An Agreement to purchase securities from an issuing corporation for the purpose of reselling them either directly or indirectly to the public. The Agreement with the corporation is usually one of two types: Best Effort Underwriters who sell as much stock as they are able to at a set price, but no fixed amount must be sold; or Firm Commitment Underwriters who agree to buy the shares to be issued at a certain price. Usually the principal underwriter makes an agreement with a group of underwriters who help sell the shares. He then gives those underwriters an agreed amount. Such a contract is called the Agreement Among. Such distributions are regulated by both the Securities Act of 1933 and the Securities Exchange Act of 1934.

UNDISTRIBUTED PROFITS. The portion of a corporation's profit remaining after taxes and dividends have been paid. It is one of the two main components of the corporate cash flow or gross retained earnings of the business. The second is Capital Consumption Allowances.

UNDOCUMENTED PERSON. See WET BACK.

U.N.D.P. (United Nations Development Program). An agency of the U.N. which provides technical and financial assistance to less developed countries (L.D.C.s).

UNDUE INFLUENCE. Any influence, whether physical or mental, which destroys the free will of a person and then substitutes the will of another. It is a form of fraud or constructive fraud designed to take advantage of another's weakness of mind, body or spirit. Modest persuasion, arguments, or advice appealing to understanding or affection are not Undue Influence. It is only where such persuasion, argument, or advice is accompanied by a fraudulent intent to overcome one's will that the influence can be said to be undue.

U.N.E.F. (United Nations Emergency Force). An international army with a peace-keeping vocation, the U.N.E.F. is under the exclusive authority of the U.N. The establishment of an armed force of its own does not, however, give the U.N. the power to use it as an enforcement means for all its decisions. The U.N.E.F. operates under very strict limitations, due to the need to maintain its international independence and authority. It is not meant to be a coercive force and is authorized to use arms only as a self-defense. Its vocation is mostly to play a "buffer" role, by representing a continuous U.N. presence, which attempts to separate combatants, and to allow a peaceful settlement of disputes. The U.N.E.F. operates only on territories where countries agree to their presence, and must withdraw upon demand of these countries. Essentially a neutral organization, the U.N.E.F. is formed of international personnel and owes allegiance only to the U.N. It must avoid any interference with internal affairs of the countries. The U.N.E.F. has intervened in several conflicts in the Congo, Cyprus, Egypt, and Lebanon. It was not, however, called upon in Vietnam, nor in most conflicts in Africa and Middle East.

UNEMANCIPATED MINOR. A minor child who is still under the control of his or her parents. A child may become emancipated or free of his or her parents' control even though still below the statutory age. There are no set procedures by which a child can become emancipated. However, enlistment in the armed forces, marriage, or becoming self-supporting are the types of things which traditionally affect the determination. The Unemancipated Minor is entitled to support from his or her parents. Another important effect of the status is that Unemancipated Minors often cannot be held liable on otherwise enforceable contracts.

U.N.E.S.C.O. (United Nations Educational and Scientific Organization). A specialized agency and charter member of the U.N. which promotes international co-operation in the fields of education, science, mass communications, and culture.

UNFAIR COMPETITION. Commercial dealings which involve deceit and dishonesty. In the nineteenth century the term applied only to misuse of a Trademark, but the courts have expanded its meaning to include other unfair business practices. Though the law of trademarks is well developed there is no specific federal statute which regulates unfair competition. Provisions of the Lanham Act (1946) protect foreign nationals who have treaties with the United States from false designations of origin and false descriptions of goods. However, generally the laws governing unfair competition stem from the common law of the individual states. Al-

though unfair competition depends on the particular facts and circumstances of each case, the following practices are commonly regarded as unfair: passing or palming-off one product for another; disparagement of goods; unauthorized use of trade secrets; simulation of a trade name; interference with the business growth of another; copyright infringement; obstruction of a competitor's suppliers or customers; unfair use of corporate stock; unfair use of imported products; and, bribery in competition.

UNFAIR LABOR PRACTICES. A conclusory legal term applied to actions by employers or employees which violate certain provisions of the National Labor Relations Act (N.L.R.A.). The term may refer to activities by an employer which abridge rights guaranteed to employees under the N.L.R.A. to band together to form unions, to bargain collectively, and to engage in certain concerted activities. For example, employer surveillance of employees through spies or informers has been found illegal. Interrogation, polling, or solicitation of employees under certain circumstances have been found to be unfair practices. However, the N.L.R.A. recognizes employer rights in this area and provides that mere expression of ideas and opinions is not a violation if they contain no threat of reprisal or force, and no promise of benefit. The term Unfair Labor Practices also refers to activities by union members or other employees which violate rights of other employees or competing unions. However, the N.L.R.A. clause defining unfair practices by unions does not include the word "interfere," which appears in the clause governing employer actions. Thus, courts have held that unions have greater freedom in organizing activities than do employers.

UNFAIR LABOR PRACTICE STRIKE. A work stoppage caused or prolonged by an unfair labor practice under the National Labor Relations Act.

UNICAMERAL LEGISLATURE. See BICAMERAL LEGISLATURE.

534

U.N.I.C.E.F. (United Children's Emergency Fund). A fund created by the U.N. General Assembly, and financed by voluntary contributions from countries and individuals, to provide emergency relief for children. It has now extended with great success its action to permanent programs of child welfare. The Fund was awarded the Nobel Peace Prize in 1965, in recognition of the remarkable help it provided for developing countries.

U.N.I.D.R.O.I.T. See INTERNATIONAL INSTITUTE FOR THE UNIFICATION OF PRIVATE LAW.

UNIFIED BAR ASSOCIATIONS. Establishment of a government-sanctioned, dues-paying organization of all lawyers admitted to practice in a state. Generally, the state legislature sets forth the structure and duties of the Unified Bar Association. In some states the statutes authorize the state's highest court to unify the Bar and to adopt rules providing the details of organization. In other states, members of the Bar apply directly to the highest court for the adoption of rules unifying the Bar. Finally, one state has initiated a unified Bar through constitutional amendment. Pursuant to a unified Bar scheme, an attorney must belong to the state's Unified Bar Association.

UNIFIED RATE. A tax rate structure adopted by the Tax Reform Act of 1976 concerning estate and gift taxation. Before the Tax Reform Act two different rate structures existed: one for estate tax purposes, the other for gift tax purposes. The Reform Act replaced this dual system with a unified rate structure, though separate estate and gift tax collection mechanisms were maintained. The unified rate reduces the incentive for lifetime giving which existed under the dual rate structure.

UNIFORM ANATOMICAL GIFT ACT. Permits donations of any portion or all of one's body to certain institutions or individuals for scientific advancement, research, therapy education or transplantation by anyone over a specified age and of sound mind.

UNIFORM CODE OF MILITARY JUSTICE (U.C.M.J.). A comprehensive federal statute enacted in 1950 which established a unified system of military criminal law applicable to all the Armed Forces of the United States. Based primarily on the Army's Articles of War, this Code provides the basic procedural and substantive framework of military justice. It attempts to assure that all persons accused of violating military law are treated with equality and accorded basic justice and fairness throughout the criminal proceedings. The U.C.M.J. establishes strict court martial procedures in order to safeguard the rights of the accused. Depending on the severity of the charge, a summary, special, or general court martial is invoked. Additionally, for judicial review of military decisions, the Code creates a court of military appeals composed of civilians and under the administration of the Department of Defense. The justification for a special military code lies in the differences between military and civilian life and the particular need for discipline in the former.

UNIFORM COMMERCIAL CODE. See U.C.C.

UNIFORM CONSUMER CREDIT CODE. A comprehensive consumer credit protection act, promulgated in 1968, and regulating disclosure in consumer credit sales and loans, credit advertising, maximum credit charges, home solicitation and remedies and penalties. Importantly, the Uniform Code provides that a buyer, lessee or debtor may not waive his rights under the Act. This provision does not forbid the settling of claims when the settlement terms are not unconscionable.

UNIFORM CRIME VICTIMS REPARATIONS ACT. Proposed law to provide state-financed payments to victims of violent crimes. The Uniform Act is merely a model which may be adopted in part or in whole by the various states that consider it. Under this proposal, victims would not be compensated for property damage, pain and suffering or inconvenience; and payments of compensated injuries from other sources would be deducted from the award. Guidelines are also provided for ceilings on personal injury awards.

UNIFORM JUDICIAL NOTICE OF FOREIGN LAW ACT. See FOREIGN PAY-OFF LAW.

UNIFORM MOTOR VEHICLE ACCIDENT REPARATIONS ACT. See NO-FAULT INSURANCE.

UNIFORM SIMULTANEOUS DEATH ACT. A statute enacted in a majority of states which provides that where the title to property depends upon the priority of death of two or more persons, and there is no sufficient evidence that the persons died other than simultaneously, the property of each shall be disposed of as if that person had survived the others. The Act further provides that if tenants by the entirety die simultaneously, the property so held shall be distributed one half as if one had survived, and one half as if the other had survived. This same provision applies to joint tenants, except where there are more than two owners. In that case, the property shall be divided evenly among the joint tenants. Where an insured and a beneficiary die simultaneously, the Act provides that the proceeds of the policy shall be distributed as if the insured survived the beneficiary. The Act applies only where there is insufficient evidence that the persons died other than simultaneously. Where there is sufficient evidence of survivorship, the normal rules of distribution apply.

UNIFORM STATE LAWS, NATIONAL CONFERENCE OF COMMISSIONERS. Created in 1892 to promote uniformity of legislation throughout the Union. The Conference has drafted over two hundred Uniform Laws on numerous subjects in many fields of social concern. Among the major acts drafted and approved are: 1) Uniform Commercial Code; 2) Uniform Narcotic Drug Act; 3) Uniform Criminal Extradition Act; 4) Uniform Probate Code; 5) Uniform Residential Landlord and Tenant Act; 6) Uniform Adoption Act; 7) Uniform Marriage and Divorce Act; and 8) Uniform Consumer Credit Code.

UNIFORM SYSTEM OF CITATION. See BLUE BOOK.

UNIFORM WAREHOUSE RECEIPTS ACT. Law stating that the warehouseman will be held liable for goods lost or injured because of his failure to exercise the same standard of reasonable care as would the owner of similar goods. But unless there is an agreement stating the correct procedure, the warehouseman will not be held liable for the loss or injury of the goods resulting from his lack of exercising due care.

UNILATERAL CONTRACT. An agreement which makes the promise of only one of the contracting parties subject to legal obligations.

UNINSURED MOTORIST COVERAGE. A type of automobile insurance coverage designed to protect the insured, his immediate family, and anyone else occupying an insured automobile against liability for the acts of a financially irresponsible motorist. Such coverage pays the amount which the insured would have recovered from the insurance company of an uninsured motorist or from a hit and run driver. Most states limit Uninsured Motorist Coverage to bodily injury only. Such coverage, compulsory in many states, is available in all but one state. The minimum amount of insurance is generally the same as required by the Financial Responsibility Laws of the state.

UNION LABEL. A tag, imprint, design or notice attached to an article as evidence that it was produced by "Union Labor."

UNION OF SOVIET SOCIALIST REPUBLICS. See U.S.S.R.

UNION SECURITY CLAUSE. A provision in a union contract which attempts to stabilize the position of a union with respect to an employer by requiring a degree of union membership. These range from maintenance of membership clauses which merely required continued membership by the employee once entered into, to closed shop clauses which allow an employer to hire only union members. The closed shop is illegal under the National Labor Relations Act. The union seeks such agreements to protect it against encroachment by rival unions or attempts by management to lure employees away and to assure a reliable source of funds for union activities.

UNION SHOP. An agreement, between a union and an employer, requiring membership in the union once employment has been obtained. The National Labor Relations Act requires that a 30-day grace period be granted to the employee after hiring before membership becomes mandatory. Recent case law holds that full-fledged membership cannot be required even under Union Shop agreements. Membership is compelled only to the extent of paying dues and initiation fees.

UNITED ARAB LEAGUE. A band of 21 Arab Nations and the Palestine Liberation Organization (P.L.O.) created in 1943 to promote their own interests in general and to destroy Israel in particular. Egypt, which had been the headquarters, withdrew from the League after signing the separate Peace Treaty with Israel in 1979, thereby shattering the dream of Arab unity in ending the 30-year war.

UNITED HOUSING v. FORMAN (420 U.S. 987 (1975)). A Supreme Court decision concerning securities regulation. Justice Powell, speaking for the majority of the Court, stated that shares in a government-subsidized apartment cooperative, which linked share ownership to the right to possess an apartment, were not subject to the Federal Securities Regulations. The case marks further federal court development of the concept of an investment security and the requirements for triggering Federal Disclosure Laws.

UNITED MINE WORKERS v. GIBBS. See PENDENT PARTIES.

UNITED NATIONS. See U.N.

UNITED NATIONS CHARTER OF 1945. This is not the usual Treaty for two reasons. First, because it is the legal basis for the formation of a worldwide international organization (the United Nations) for peace and security. And second, because nations have given it preeminence over all of their other treaties.

UNITED NATIONS CONFERENCE ON TRADE AND DEVELOPMENT. See U.N.C.T.A.D.

UNITED NATIONS CONVENTION ON THE CARRIAGE OF GOODS BY SEA. See HAMBURG RULES.

UNITED NATIONS COVENANTS ON HUMAN RIGHTS. International agreements signed by one third of the nations in the world but not the United States despite the recommendation of every American President since Truman that we ratify these civilized accords which promote the protection of human rights and monitor any violations.

UNITED NATIONS DECLARATION ON THE ELIMINATION OF ALL FORMS OF RACIAL DISCRIMINATION. Adopted by the United Nations General Assembly in 1973 to increase understanding among all races and to prevent deprivation of human rights. By supporting international measures which inform the world about racial discrimination, it seeks to end violations of the rights and freedoms proclaimed in the Universal Declaration of Human Rights. The International Convention on the Elimination of all Forms of Racial Discrimination, adopted by the General Assembly in 1965 and convened in 1969, is open to all United Nations Members and Specialized Agencies.

UNITED NATIONS DEVELOPMENT PROGRAM. See U.N.D.P.

UNITED NATIONS ECONOMIC AND SECURITY COUNCIL. See ECONOMIC AND SOCIAL COUNCIL.

UNITED NATIONS EDUCATIONAL, SCIENTIFIC AND CULTURAL ORGANIZATION. See U.N.E.S.C.O.

UNITED NATIONS GENERAL ASSEMBLY. See GENERAL ASSEMBLY.

UNITED NATIONS HIGH COMMISSIONER FOR REFUGEES (U.N.H.C.R.). Established by the U.N. General Assembly in 1951, it replaced the International Refugee Organization (I.R.O.). Its purpose is to afford temporary international protection for refugees pending countries' decisions about immigration, resettlement, assimilation, or repatriation. Influenced by the position of the United States, the U.N.H.C.R. leaves the final responsibility for caring of refugees and incurring financial expenses to asylum states. The U.N.H.C.R. does not provide for any solution to the problem of dual nationality.

UNITED NATIONS INTERNATIONAL COURT OF JUSTICE. See INTERNATIONAL COURT OF JUSTICE.

UNITED NATIONS MANDATE OF NOVEMBER 27, 1947. Action by this world agency which subsequently led to the creation in Palestine of the state of Israel which has been in a continuous war with the Arab world since its Declaration of Independence.

UNITED NATIONS SECURITY COUNCIL. See SECURITY COUNCIL.

UNITED NATIONS TRANSITION ASSISTANCE GROUP. See U.N.T.A.G.

UNITED NATIONS TRUST FUND FOR SOUTH AFRICA. Established in 1965 to assist victims of the apartheid policy in Zambia, Southern Rhodesia, and South Africa. The primary purpose of the Fund is to provide legal counsel and education. It is supported by volunteer contributions from concerned governments, organizations and individuals.

UNITED NATIONS TRUSTEESHIP COUNCIL. See TRUSTEESHIP COUNCIL.

UNITED STATES ASSAY OFFICE. See ASSAY OFFICE.

UNITED STATES ATTORNEY GENERAL. Head of the U.S. Department of Justice, and top legal officer in the executive branch of government. Under Article II of the Constitution, the office of Attorney General was created as the primary source of legal advice to the President and the executive departments. In addition to formal public opinions on legal matters and policies, the Attorney General and his subordinates also give constant oral counsel and write many informal letters and memoranda of advice. As head of the Department of Justice, the Attorney General is further responsible for the supervision and guidance of the many United States prosecutors and investigators including the Federal Bureau of Investigation. The Attorney General is an executive officer, not a legislative or judicial officer, therefore he does not decide questions of fact, sit as an arbitrator in disputes between government departments and private individuals, or review appeals from the decisions of public officials. Those judicial functions are handled by the Courts. More importantly, the Attorney General does not act as the legal advisor to Congress or to any of its committees. The formal opinions of the Attorney General are issued in the form of advisory opinions, which were first published in 1841. As expressions of legal opinion by the executive branch, these formal opinions are usually accorded great weight by the courts; only on a few occasions have any been overruled. It is important to note that the Attorney General does not actually represent the government in the Supreme Court—that function is the responsibility of the Solicitor General of the United States.

UNITED STATES COURTS OF APPEALS. Intermediate appellate courts created in 1891 to relieve the Supreme Court of considering all appeals in cases originally decided by the federal trial courts. Appellate courts are empowered to review all final decisions and certain interlocutory decisions of district courts, except in those very few situations where the law provides for direct review by the Supreme Court. They are also empowered to review and enforce orders of many federal administrative bodies, such as the Securities and Exchange Commission and the National Labor Relations Board. The decisions of the courts of appeals are final except as they are subject to discretionary review or appeal in the Supreme Court. The United States is divided into 11 judicial circuits, including the District of Columbia as a circuit, in each of which there is a United States Court of Appeals. Each of the 50 states is assigned to one of the circuits, and the territories are assigned variously to the First, Third, Fifth, and Ninth Circuits. At present each United States Court of Appeals has from three to fifteen permanent circuit judgeships (over 100 in all), depending upon the amount of judicial work in the circuit. The judge who is senior in commission and who has not reached his seventieth birthday is the chief judge. One of the Justices of the Supreme Court is assigned as circuit justice for each circuit. Each court of appeals usually hears cases in divisions consisting of three judges, but they may sit En Banc with all judges present. The Judges of the United States Courts of Appeals constitute the Judicial Council of each circuit and meet at least twice a year to consider the state of federal judicial business in the circuit and to "make all necessary orders for its effective and expeditious administration." In 1971, the Congress provided for appointment of a Circuit Executive for each circuit by the Circuit Council. The function of the Circuit Executive is to exercise, among other duties, administrative control of nonjudicial activities of the court of appeals of the circuit in which he is appointed. The chief judge of each circuit summons annually a judicial conference of all circuit and district judges in his circuit, and sometimes members of the bar, to discuss the business of the federal courts of the circuit. The chief judge of each circuit, a district judge from each circuit elected by the circuit and district judges of the circuit at their

annual Judicial Conference for a term of 3 years, the Chief Judge of the Court of Claims, and the Chief Judge of the Court of Customs and Patent Appeals serve as members of the Judicial Conference of the United States, of which the Chief Justice of the United States serves as chairman. This is the governing body for the administration of the federal judicial system as a whole.

UNITED STATES COURT OF CLAIMS. A specialized federal court established in 1855 which sits in Washington, D.C., and has nationwide jurisdiction to hear such claims against the United States as the Constitution or federal statutes permit. In some instances, its jurisdiction is concurrent with that of the federal district courts. Judgments from the United States Court of Claims are reviewable by the United States Supreme Court. The court of claims is currently composed of seven judges, who sit in divisions of three for individual cases. The court is generally empowered to hear most types of money claims against the United States, with the exception of tort claims which must be brought in federal district court under the Federal Tort Claims Act. During the first one hundred years of its eixstence, there was much doubt as to the status of the court of claims as a constitutional court under Article III of the United States Constitution or a legislative court under Article I. A 1962 decision of the Supreme Court, however, held that the court of claims was a constitutional court. Its judges were thus entitled to protected status under Article III and could also sit on mixed court panels with judges from the regular federal courts.

UNITED STATES COURT OF CUSTOMS AND PATENT APPEALS. A specialized federal court with nationwide jurisdiction to hear appeals from decisions of the United States Customs Court, as well as appeals from the United States Patent Office in patent and trademark cases. The Court was established by Congress in 1909 to review the customs litigation which was swamping the regular federal courts, particularly in the second circuit which includes the port of New York City. The Court consists of five judges, who normally sit in Washington, D.C. but may sit elsewhere if necessary. Its decisions are reviewable by the United States Supreme Court. In 1962, a Supreme Court decision held that the court of customs and patent appeals, as well as the United States Court of Claims were Constitutional courts and that the assignment of judges or retired judges of these courts to sit with regular federal courts, which are clearly constitutional, is valid.

UNITED STATES COURT OF MILITARY APPEALS. Final appellate tribunal to review court-martial convictions of all the armed services. It is exclusively an appellate criminal court, established in 1950. The court, consisting of three civilian judges appointed by the President, is called upon to exercise jurisdiction as to questions of law in all cases affecting a general or flag officer, or extending to death; in cases certified to the court by the judge advocates general of the armed services, and by the general counsel of the Department of Transportation, acting for the Coast Guard; and in cases petitioned by the accused who has received a sentence of a year or more confinement, and/or a punitive discharge. The court also exercises authority under the All Writs Act. In all of its cases, the decisions of the court are final and there is no further direct review. In addition, the court is required by law to work jointly with the judge advocates general of the armed services and the general counsel of the Department of Transportation and to report annually to the Congress on the progress of the military justice system under the Uniform Code of Military Justice, and to recommend improvements therein wherever necessary. It is the only military court of last resort in the world which is composed entirely of civilians.

UNITED STATES CUSTOMS COURT. A specialized federal court with limited jurisdiction to review the classification and rate of duty applicable to imported merchandise as determined by the several collectors of customs. The court was established in 1926, replacing the former Board of General Appraisers. It is composed of nine judges, sitting in groups of three to hear individual cases, or, in some instances, sitting alone. The customs court normally sits in New York City, but may go to any port within the United States to hear cases. Appeals from decisions of the customs court are heard by the United States Court of Customs and Patent Appeals.

UNITED STATES DISTRICT COURT. Trial courts with general federal jurisdiction. Each state has at least one district court, while some of the larger states have as many as four. There is also a United States District Court in the District of Columbia. Altogether there are 89 district courts in the 50 states, plus the one in the District of Columbia. In addition, the Commonwealth of Puerto Rico has a United States District Court with jurisdiction corresponding to that of district courts in the various states. At present, each district court has from one to 27 federal district judgeships, depending upon the amount of judicial work within its territory. Only one judge is usually required to hear and decide a case in a district court, but in some kinds of cases it is required that three judges be called together to comprise the court. In districts with more than one judge, the judge senior in commission who has not reached his seventieth birthday acts as the chief judge. There are altogether over 400 permanent district judgeships in the 50 states and 15 in the District of Columbia. There are six district judgeships in Puerto Rico. Except in certain territories, such as the Virgin Islands, district judges hold their offices during good behavior as provided by Article III, section 1, of the Constitution. However, Congress may create temporary judgeships with the provision that when a vacancy occurs in that office, such vacancy shall not be filled. Each district court has a clerk, a United States attorney, a United States marshal, one or more United States magistrates, referees in bankruptcy, probation officers, court reporters, and their assistants. Cases from the district court are reviewed by the United States Courts of Appeal except that injunction orders of special three-judge district courts, certain decisions holding acts of Congress unconstitutional, and certain criminal decisions may be appealed directly to the Supreme Court.

UNITED STATES EMERGENCY COURT OF APPEALS. A temporary federal court created during World War II to review orders of the Price Control Administration. The court did not have judges of its own but was manned by regular federal district and circuit court judges on special assignment. The emergency court routinely heard appeals from denials of protests against price and rent control orders during the war and post-war period. With the end of price controls after the war, there was no continuing need for such a court, and it was abolished, except for pending cases, in 1953.

UNITED STATES FLAG CARRIER. One of a certain class of air carriers holding a certificate of public convenience and necessity issued by the Civil Aeronautics Board and approved by the President. This certificate authorizes scheduled operations over distinct routes between the United States and one or more foreign countries. Some United States Flag Carriers conduct domestic flights (TWA) while some do not (PAN-AM).

UNITED STATES FOREIGN SERVICE. See FOREIGN SERVICE.

UNITED STATES GOVERNMENT DIRECTORY. A reference book which covers the major federal departments and agencies, focusing on those of primary significance in terms of the litigation they undertake and the regulations they issue.

UNITED STATES GOVERNMENT MANUAL. See GOVERNMENT MANUAL.

UNITED STATES INFORMATION AGENCY. See INTERNATIONAL COMMUNICATION AGENCY.

UNITED STATES INTELLIGENCE-GATHERING CENTERS. Hundreds of federal government agencies constitute the American intelligence community. The major ones are as follows: (1) Air Force Intelligence. Gathers intelligence of special interest to the Air Force, including bombing targets. (2) Army Intelligence. Gathers intelligence of special interest to the Army, including order of battle of potential foes. (3) Bureau of Intelligence and Research (Department of State). Gathers foreign political, economic and political-military data. (4) Central Intelligence Agency. Collects intelligence overseas, coordinates work of other agencies and disseminates intelligence. (5) Department of Energy. Monitors foreign nuclear-weapons tests and collects data on foreign energy matters. (6) Department of Defense Intelligence Agency. Provides military intelligence, primarily for Pentagon officials. (7) Department of the Treasury. Collects foreign financial information. (8) Drug Enforcement Administration (Department of Justice). Collects and disseminates intelligence on foreign and domestic narcotics traffic. (9) Federal Bureau of Investigation (Department of Justice). Keeps track of foreign spies and collects foreign intelligence in the United States. (10) National Reconnaissance Office. A hush-hush agency that operates the country's spy satellites. (11) National Security Agency. Monitors radio, telegraph and radar traffic of other countries, cracks foreign codes. (12) Office of Naval Intelligence. Gathers information on foreign ships.

UNITED STATES MARSHALS SERVICE. A corps of federal officers consisting of ninety-four marshals and some 1,700 deputies whose duties reflect all aspects of the complex society they serve. The scope and detail of their responsibilities have dramatically increased since the first thirteen United States marshals were appointed by

President George Washington in 1789. Under the authority of the Organized Crime Control Act of 1970, marshals protect witnesses to organized crime when their lives and those of their families are jeopardized by their testimony. Marshals provide physical security for federal courtrooms and personal protection for federal judges, jurors, and attorneys. Besides serving as officers of the court, marshals perform federal law-enforcement functions for the Attorney General. Included are civil disturbance or anti-terrorist activities of the Special Operations Group and numerous security programs in cooperation with other federal agencies. The United States Marshals Service maintains the custody of federal prisoners from the time of their arrest to their commitment or release and also transports federal prisoners as directed by the Bureau of Prisons.

UNITED STATES METRIC BOARD. See METRIC CONVERSION ACT OF 1975.

UNITED STATES PATENT OFFICE. Today a division of the Department of Commerce, the Patent Office dates from 1802 when an official in the Department of State was placed in charge of patents. Among its chief functions are the examination of patent applications and the granting of patents to deserving applicants. However, the Office has no jurisdiction over utilization, infringement, or enforcement of patents.

UNITED STATES RAILWAY ASSOCIATION. See CONSOLIDATED RAIL CORPORATION.

UNITED STATES REPORTS. The official edition of the cases decided by the United States Supreme Court. Prior to 1817 the *United States Reports* were published by private reporters. Since that time the cases have been reported by official reporters. Until 1874 the reports were cited by the name of the reporter. The seven reporters who served during this time period were Dallas, Cranch, Wheaton, Peters, Howard, Black and Wallace. The modern *United States Reports* bound volumes are preceded by advance sheets which have the same volume and page numbers as the subsequent bound volumes. Initially the decisions are printed as "slip" opinions when issued by the Court. These "slip" opinions are not indexed or headnoted. Most, but not all, per curiam opinions are printed in the United States Reports. More are printed in the two unofficial editions of Supreme Court decisions, the *United States Supreme Court Reporter* and the *United States Supreme Court Reports* (Lawyer's Edition). Opinions of Justices in chambers are printed in the private series but usually not in the official series. An example is Justice Douglas' stay of execution in the Rosenberg Case (1953).

UNITED STATES SECRET SERVICE. See SECRET SERVICE.

UNITED STATES STATUTES AT LARGE. Bound volumes, issued annually, which contain all public and private laws and concurrent resolutions enacted during a session of Congress, as well as reorganization plans, proposed and ratified amendments to the Constitution, and Presidential proclamations. They include finding aids, such as a legislative history with each public law and proposed or ratified constitutional amendment, a table of prior laws affected, and indexes.

UNITED STATES STEEL CORP. v. MULTISTATE TAX COMMISSION. See COMPACT CLAUSE.

UNITED STATES TAX COURT. A federal court with specialized jurisdiction over taxpayer petitions contesting deficiency determinations made by the Internal Revenue Service. The Tax Court was an independent agency in the executive branch of government until 1969, when a federal statute declared it to be a legislative court under Article I of the United States Constitution. Decisions of the Tax Court, other than small tax cases under section 957 of the Tax Reform Act (1969), are reviewable by the federal courts of appeals. The offices of the court and its sixteen judges are located in Washington, D.C., however trials may be conducted at various locations within the United States convenient to taxpayers.

UNITED STATES TEMPORARY EMERGENCY COURT OF APPEALS. A specialized federal court created by the 1971 amendments to the Economic Stabilization Act of 1970. A modified version of the United States Emergency Court of Appeals during World War II, this court is staffed by regular judges from other existing federal courts. The court has exclusive jurisdiction of all appeals from the district courts in cases arising out of the 1970 wage-price regulations, as well as exclusive jurisdiction to determine constitutional questions arising under the Act. Its judgments are reviewable by the Supreme Court. Even though many of the wage-price regulations are no longer in force, it is anticipated that the court will continue to function until its workload is depleted.

UNITED STATES TERRITORIAL COURTS. Pursuant to its authority to govern the territories, Congress has established district courts in the territories of Puerto Rico, Guam, and the Virgin Islands. Except in Puerto Rico, these federal courts have jurisdiction not only of the subjects described in the judicial article of the Constitution, but also of many local matters which within the states are decided in state courts. The district court of Puerto Rico, however, is classified like other "district courts" and is called a "court of the United States." It has the same jurisdiction as the 90 district courts in the states and the District of Columbia. There are six federal judges in Puerto Rico, one in Guam, and two in the Virgin Islands. The judges in these federal courts are appointed for terms of 8 years, except in Puerto Rico where the judges hold their offices for life during good behavior.

UNITED STATES v. BYRUM (404 U.S. 937 (1972)). A landmark case in the area of taxation of estates. The grantor transferred shares of stock to an irrevocable trust, and explicitly retained the right to vote the shares of the stock not listed on a stock exchange.

The court held that, under section 2036(a)(1) & (2) of the Internal Revenue Code, Byrum had retained neither the rights to possession and enjoyment nor the right to designate the persons who shall possess or enjoy the property or the income therefrom. Thus it ruled that the value of the stock was not to be included in Byrum's estate for income tax purposes. Congress was so incensed by Byrum that it passed an amendment to section 2036 which made a Byrum-styled transfer subject to taxation.

UNITED STATES v. DARBY (321 U.S. 100 (1941)). One of the early post-Lochner Era cases giving wider powers to the Congress under its exercise of the Commerce Power. In *Darby* the Supreme Court held that Congress has the power "(1) to prohibit the shipment in interstate commerce of lumber manufactured by employees whose wages are less than a prescribed minimum or whose weekly hours of labor are greater than the prescribed maximum, and (2) to prohibit the employment of workmen in the production of goods for interstate commerce at other than prescribed wages and hours." *Darby* is famous for its restrictive reading of the Tenth Amendment to the Constitution.

UNITED STATES v. E. C. KNIGHT CO. (156 U.S. 1 (1895)). A Supreme Court case that restricted congressional power to prevent corporate mergers under the Sherman Act. The Court distinguished between regulation of "commerce" which was allowable to Congress and regulation of "manufacture" which was not. The Court also distinguished between matters that have "direct" effects on interstate commerce which were subject to congressional regulation and those matters that have only an "indirect effect" and are not subject to congressional regulation.

UNITED STATES v. IRAN. Unanimous decision of the World Court on December 15, 1979, ordering Iran to release immediately the 50 American hostages illegally held in Teheran; to return the American Embassy and Consulates to American control; and to allow the Americans to leave Iran safely. Speaking for the 15 Judges of the Court, who represented a wide range of political systems and religions, England's Sir Humphrey Waldock concluded that Iran's action was a violation of both historic international law and two currently valid treaties between the countries.

UNITED STATES v. JONES. See SILVER PLATTER DOCTRINE.

UNITED STATES v. LUSTIG. See SILVER PLATTER DOCTRINE.

UNITED STATES v. McCALEB. See DRUG COURIER PROFILE.

UNITED STATES v. NIXON (418 U.S. 683 (1974)). This Supreme Court case denied President Nixon's defense of executive privilege relating to the White House tape recordings regarding the burglary at the Democratic National Headquarters Watergate offices. Chief Justice Burger, speaking for the Court, held that the generalized ground of executive privilege must yield to the fundamental demands of due process in the fair administration of criminal justice. Thus President Nixon had to comply with a subpoena and produce the recordings.

UNITED STATES v. SANTANA. See DOORWAY SEARCH CASE.

UNITED STATES v. SHREVEPORT GRAIN & ELEVATOR CO. See NON DELEGATION DOCTRINE.

UNITED TRANSPORTATION UNION v. STATE BAR OF MICHIGAN. See PREPAID LEGAL SERVICE PLAN.

UNITING FOR PEACE RESOLUTION. See GENERAL ASSEMBLY.

UNIT OF ACCOUNT OF THE EUROPEAN COMMUNITIES. Established by the European Monetary Agreement (E.M.A.) in 1955. The value of the Unit of Account is stated to be 0.88867088 Grammes of fine gold. It is used as a reference by all the European Communities, but remains dependent on the United States gold policy.

UNIVERSAL COPYRIGHT CONVENTION (U.C.C.). An international agreement whereby a foreign creator is exempt from the formalities otherwise required under Statutory Copyright. Thus, American citizens in signatory countries enjoy protection for their works which would be unavailable to them because neither Common Law Copyright nor the Federal Copyright Act has extraterritorial effect. The U.C.C. requires work to be marketed with the symbol "c" accompanied by the name of the copyright owner and the year of first publication. The symbol "c" is specified rather than any word or variation thereof because the symbol is recognized internationally. The original text of the U.C.C. was adopted at Geneva in 1952, and modifications, known as the Paris Text, were ratified in 1974. The United States became a party to the Convention effective September 16, 1955. As of January 1, 1976 sixty-nine nations had adopted the U.C.C.

UNIVERSAL DECLARATION OF HUMAN RIGHTS. Adopted by a unanimous resolution of the United Nations General Assembly in 1948, The Preamble recognizes the inherent dignity and equal rights of all peoples and that such rights are often disregarded. The Declaration urges nations through education to promote respect for human rights and freedoms and through progressive measures, national and international, to secure their universal and effective observance, both among the member countries and the territories under their jurisdiction. Since the Declaration has no legal force, the United Nations has encouraged countries to formulate their own comprehensive human rights regulations.

UNIVERSAL POSTAL UNION (U.P.U.). A specialized agency of the United Nations since 1947, its purpose is the integration of national postal services. First established in 1874 by the Berne Treaty, it includes provisions for standardization of national procedures and for uniform postage rates. A compensatory accounts system clears balances between member countries. The U.P.U. includes: (1) a Congress which meets every five years, (2) an Executive and Liaison Committee elected by the Congress, (3) a Consultative Committee on Postal Research, and (4) an International Bureau located at Berne. The U.P.U. represents, by its technical and political realizations, one of the most successful international organizations.

UNJUST ENRICHMENT. An equitable doctrine that prevents one person from benefiting unfairly from the loss of another. The party who is enriched at the expense of another is required to make restitution.

"UNLAWFUL ACT" MANSLAUGHTER. A killing caused by the performance of an unlawful act. This form of involuntary manslaughter, for example, includes killings caused during the commission of a felony that does not fall in the Felony-Murder Doctrine.

UNLAWFUL DETAINER. Detention of property without the consent of the owner. For example, a tenant may be guilty of Unlawful Detainer if he stays in his apartment after his lease expires, or if he defaults in rent payments and neither pays nor moves out when the landlord serves him with notice to leave.

UNMARKETABLE TITLE. See CLOUD ON TITLE.

U.N. RESOLUTION 242. A United Nations policy statement which calls for Israeli withdrawal from occupied territories but also assures the right of every country in the area to "live in peace within secure and recognized boundaries," but which does not explicitly acknowledge Israel's right to exist as a sovereign nation.

UNSECURED NOTE. A loan granted on the basis of a borrower's creditworthiness and signature; not secured by collateral.

U.N.T.A.G. (United Nations Transition Assistance Group). A team of civilians and soldiers sent to South West Africa to assist the mineral-rich former Territory of South Africa to become the independent sovereign nation of Namibia.

UNWED FATHERS' RIGHTS. The Supreme Court case, *Stanley v. Illinois,* 405 U.S. 645 (1972), strengthened unwed fathers' right to child custody when it held that an unwed father must have an opportunity to a hearing on whether or not he should assume custody of his illegitimate child if the mother dies. Some states also require an unwed father's consent to adoption of his illegitimate child, which raises problems if the father cannot be found or if he refuses to allow the mother to give the child up for adoption, but also refuses to take custody himself.

UP-OR-OUT. The practice of large metropolitan law firms to release associates who are not elected to partnership after the apprenticeship period of seven to nine years. The average rate of successful admission to the firm is one out of three.

UP SALT RIVER. An old political maxim meaning that a candidate has suffered a decisive defeat. Legend has it that a political candidate, some say Henry Clay, asked to be taken up one river to make a speech. Instead a boatman of different political persuasion took the politician up Salt River— contributing to his political defeat.

UP THE RIVER. See SING SING.

URBAN DEVELOPMENT ACTION GRANTS. Money awarded by the federal government through H.U.D. on a competitive basis to generate jobs by putting public funds into projects that have some private sector backing in urban areas that are economically depressed.

U.R.E.S.A. See R.U.R.E.S.A.

USAGE OF TRADE. Where the regularity of a custom is well recognized and is expected to be continued in the practice of similar business transactions that re-occur in certain geographic locales, vocations, or trades.

U.S. CODE CONGRESSIONAL AND ADMINISTRATIVE NEWS
(U.S.C.C.A.N.). Publishes the texts of enacted federal public laws and the committee reports on the more important enactments, as well as administrative regulations and executive orders. It is published fortnightly by the West Publishing Company when Congress is in session and monthly when it is not.

U.S. COMMISSIONERS. See FEDERAL MAGISTRATE.

USE AND DERIVATIVE USE IMMUNITY. Grant of immunity from prosecution. However, the Supreme Court has held that transactional immunity need not be granted to force testimony since Use and Derivative Use immunity is sufficient. Use and Derivative Use Immunity permits the bringing of an action against the person immunized, so long as the prosecution only uses evidence gathered prior to the person's giving of testimony.

U.S.S.R. (Union of Soviet Socialist Republics). A Union of 15 different ethnically based Republics, of which Russia is the most powerful not only because it is the largest in geographical area and population but also because it has the highest standard of living and education.

USURIOUS BARGAIN. A loan or other agreement which charges an unconscionable or exorbitant amount of interest. Generally such an agreement requires the borrower to pay interest in excess of a legal rate.

UTMOST RESISTANCE. The standard used to describe the resistance with which a woman must repel a rapist. The standard is relative and may not apply if a woman submits to an act of rape to avoid serious bodily injury to herself. However, critics of the utmost resistance doctrine have asserted that it places an unfair burden on rape victims.

V

V.A. (Veterans Administration). The third largest federal agency, with an annual budget of more than $19 billion and a work force of 224,000, the V.A. oversees federal programs for about 30 million veterans, including the G.I. Bill, pensions, loan guarantees, and medical services. On any given day, the 172 V.A. hospitals will have 80,000 patients; 12 percent of them will be Vietnam veterans. The V.A. also helps 20,000 veterans—90 percent of whom are Vietnam veterans—through outpatient rehabilitation training. The largest single group of disabled veterans is the physically disabled. The V.A. is headed by a disabled veteran, Max Cleland. When he became V.A. administrator in 1977 at the age of 35, he was the youngest in the V.A.'s history. He had lost both legs and his right arm in a grenade explosion in Vietnam in 1968 and had spent the next 18 months in military and V.A. hospitals.

V.A.C.A.B. (Veterans Administration Contract Appeals Board). See BOARDS OF CONTRACT APPEALS.

VACATE A JUDGMENT. To void a judgment or set it aside.

VALENTINE v. CHRESTENSEN. See COMMERCIAL SPEECH DOCTRINE.

V.A.L.I.D. (Virginia Legal Information Database). A computerized legal research program for opinions of the Attorney-General, the official state code and decisions of the Supreme Court of Virginia. It is available to legal personnel and lay persons throughout the state through the use of the database from "on line searches," a system known as On Line System of Computer Assisted Research.

VALUE ADDED TAX (V.A.T.). A European-styled sales tax levied on all manufacturers and some services. At each stage of production and distribution the tax is imposed on the value added by the producer or packager. As you might have guessed, the tax is added to the price the consumer

eventually pays for the item, so once again we've been had. Michigan became the first state to adopt a V.A.T. tax in 1976, and it has been favorably accepted there. Called the Single Business Tax because it has replaced a corporate income tax and several other business taxes, it is designed to bring greater stability and predictability to state revenues and to make Michigan more attractive to business investment.

VARIABLE RATE MORTGAGE. A real estate loan in which the monthly payment or the term of the loan, or a combination of the two, is adjusted from time to time as money-market conditions fluctuate. The adjustments are linked to an index, usually a major money-market interest rate, and sometimes a ceiling is placed on the rate. Moreover, with this type of mortgage some lenders will extend the period for paying off the loan, thus keeping the monthly payments lower.

V.A.S.C.A.R. (Visual Average Speed Computer And Recorder). Instrument which permits measurement of speed from a moving police car. Vascar is an improvement over its predecessor, Radar (Radio Direction and Ranging) because it enables a policeman to clock vehicles in front of, behind him, and even those crossing his path. It also can be used in inclement weather and at night.

V.A.T. See VALUE ADDED TAX.

VAUGHN'S LAW. No matter how many rooms there are in the motel, the fellow who starts up his car at 5 o'clock in the morning is always parked under your window. By Bill Vaughn of *The Kansas City Star*, in the *Reader's Digest*, July 1977.

VENIRE DE NOVO (Latin—to come anew). Today the term is generally used to refer to a new trial, though at early common law it referred to a second trial which was convened because the verdict of the first jury was defective on its face.

VERA INSTITUTE OF JUSTICE. A foundation established in 1961 to support research in the fields of court procedure, law enforcement and crime. Some of its highly successful projects have been in the fields of bail, calendar control, traffic court, alert systems and court employment.

VERSAILLES TREATY. A major Treaty of Peace signed at Versailles, France, on June 28, 1919, and brought into force January 10, 1920, ending World War I, following ratification by Germany and four of the principal allied and associated powers—Great Britain, France, Italy and Japan. The United States signed a separate Treaty of Peace with Germany in 1921, incorporating much of the Versailles Treaty by reference. The pre-Armistice agreement among the Allies of November 5, 1918, and the Armistice of November 11, 1918, with Germany were the foundation of the Treaty, which accepted President Woodrow Wilson's Fourteen Points as the basis for peace with the Allies modifying three points—the freedom of the seas, reparations and the status of the Hapsburg Empire, which by that time had broken up.

VERTICAL MERGER. A business union designed to achieve control of a product from production to distribution. Such a merger might be between a manufacturer and a retail outlet, or a manufacturer and a supplier of component parts.

VESTED INTEREST. A present right or title to an interest in property. Although the right to enjoyment or possession may be postponed until the future, such an interest may be alienated.

VESTED REMAINDER. A vested future interest in property.

VETERANS ADMINISTRATION. See V.A.

VICARIOUS LIABILITY (Imputed Negligence or Respondeat Superior) (Latin—let the superior give answer). Applies to the situation in which *A* is held liable for the negligent conduct of *B* which results in injury to *C*. Vicarious Liability is like Strict Liability in that *A* is held liable even though he is not at fault. However, the two actions are different in that Vicarious Liability depends on negligence, albeit not in *A*, while Strict Liability does not require negligence. The most common examples of holding *A* liable for *B*'s torts are found in the employment area, where the law quaintly refers to the parties involved as master and servant. The general rule is that the employer stands liable for the tortious acts of his employee which were committed within the course and scope of the employment. Thus if florist *A* hires driver *B* to deliver flowers and *B* negligently runs down *C* while making a delivery, *A* may be held liable. However, if *B* were to take the delivery van and a few friends off to a party without *A*'s permission, any subsequent accident would be *B*'s responsibility alone. The most frequently cited justification for Vicarious Liability is that an employee's actions are within the control of his employer. Therefore, it is deemed sensible to hold the employer liable. However, as the above example suggests, the law is willing to assume that *B*'s actions are under *A*'s control only to the point where such an assumption is reasonable. In addition to the control questions, the law recognizes that many employees are financially unable to compensate fully the victim of a serious accident. Since the employee is working for his employer's advantage, it seems fair to go to the latter's "Deep Pocket" to satisfy one of the costs of the enterprise. In addition to its master-servant context, Vicarious Liability is also at times imposed upon the owner of a car for a tort committed by its driver, upon persons engaged in a joint enterprise, and upon parents for the torts of their children.

VICTIM IMPACT STATEMENT. An official confidential document prepared by a probation officer and submitted to a judge for consideration before any sentence is imposed on a convicted criminal. It contains information on the financial, physical and psychological effect of the crime on the victim.

VICTIMLESS CRIMES. Offenses which are punishable by fine or imprisonment even though individual choice or mutual consent precludes the existence of a victim. Victimless Crimes do not involve harm to another's person or property. These activities are often thought of as deviant rather than illegal. They include drug offenses, drunkenness, gambling, prostitution, obscenity, vagrancy, riding a motorcycle without a helmet, homosexuality, consensual sodomy, incest, and fornication. Those who favor maintaining legal sanctions for Victimless Crimes contend that such crimes jeopardize society as a whole by weakening social values and norms. Proponents of decriminalization argue that Victimless Crimes represent a paternalistic attempt to legislate morality and that law enforcement resources should be used more efficiently in combatting more serious crimes. One of the earliest advocates of decriminalization was the Archbishop of Canterbury who recently asserted: "There is a sacred realm of privacy for every man . . . . where he makes his choice and decisions, fashions his character and directs his desires, a realm of his own essential rights and liberties, including, in the providence of God, liberty to go to the devil, into which the law, generally speaking, must not intrude." Sociologists claim that punishment for a Victimless Crime tends to increase the likelihood of victim-oriented crime on the theory that once an individual is labelled a criminal, he will engage in illicit activities with greater frequency in the future. One recent study found that decriminalization was favored as social-economic status and community size increased, that younger people preferred decriminalization more than older persons, and that men advocated decriminalization more often than women.

VICTIMOLOGY INDUSTRY. Growing awareness of the plight of victims of crimes which has spawned courses of study, international symposia, statistical studies sponsored by the Law Enforcement Assistance Administration, and scholarly articles in specialized journals. Victimology includes both the effect of crime on those directly injured—about 40 million people a year, as well as the secondary victims; i.e., those who depend on the income or the love of someone who is killed or incapacitated.

VICTIM WITNESS BUREAU. First established in 1974 under the sponsorship of the National District Attorneys Association and local community organizations, through a $1 million L.E.A.A. grant, and now found in over 100 cities throughout the country, this is a program to help victims of crimes and witnesses through the maze of legal proceedings. Besides providing general orientation, the system assists in cutting red tape, getting people to court through private transportation, having employers pay for the time spent in court, and counselling in general. It is designed to reduce the anxiety, trauma, hassles and inconvenience which victims and witnesses often suffer from in their participation in a criminal trial.

VIDEO TAPE DEPOSITIONS. The television taping of pretrial depositions which allows the court and jury to observe the demeanor of critical witnesses during the depositions. This is, of course, not possible when the traditional transcript of pre-trial depositions is used. Use of video process, permitted under the new Federal Rules of Civil Procedure and is growing increasingly popular, especially for a witness who may die before the trial or be killed to prevent him from testifying.

VIENNA CONVENTIONS. A series of international agreements by civilized nations governing diplomatic immunity, access to embassies and the inviolability of embassy territories, following conferences held in Vienna in the nineteenth Century.

VILLAGE OF ARLINGTON HEIGHTS v. METROPOLITAN DEVELOPMENT CORP. See EXCLUSIONARY ZONING.

VIRGINIA DECLARATION OF RIGHTS. Document embodying the Virginia Bill of Rights. Largely the handiwork of George Mason, the Vir-ginia Declaration was adopted on June 12, 1776 by the Colonial House of Burgesses meeting as a convention. The Declaration enshrines principles drawn from such sources as the Magna Carta, and has served as the model for the national Bill of Rights. It appears today, in practically its original form, in the state constitution.

VIRGINIA LEGAL INFORMATION DATABASE. See V.A.L.I.D.

VIRGINIA STATE BOARD OF PHARMACY v. VIRGINIA CITIZENS CONSUMERS COUNCIL, INC. See COMMERCIAL SPEECH DOCTRINE.

VIRGINIA SUPREME COURT. The highest state court of last resort in the United States which was the first to be composed completely of lawyers in the year 1779.

VISA PERMIT (Latin—seen). An endorsement stamped or attached to a passport by the receiving country certifying that the passport has been examined by an authority of the receiving country. Special use visas may be issued, such as the Diplomatic Visa, the Non-Immigrant Visa, and the Immigrant Visa. A Tourist Visa may be issued in some countries without a passport, permitting a person to enter for a stay of limited duration, provided he has shown satisfactory evidence of his citizenship or origin.

VISCOUNT ST. ALBANS. See BACON, FRANCIS.

VISITATION RIGHTS. Permit a noncustodial parent to spend time with his or her child. Visitation rights often cause problems for both parent and child. The right to see one's child is recognized by many courts as a fundamental right which often helps soften the impact of divorce and preserves the relationship between the noncustodial parent and the child. But visitation often prolongs the child's involvement in the trauma of a bitter divorce or custody proceeding and may be used as a way to harass the former spouse rather than as an attempt to retain closeness to the child. Courts and statute writers, aware of this dilemma, often deny visitation in the best interest of the child.

VIS MAJOR. See FORCE MAJEURE.

V.I.S.T.A. See VOLUNTEERS IN SERVICE TO AMERICA.

VISUAL AVERAGE SPEED COMPUTER AND RECORDER. See V.A.S.C.A.R.

VLANDIS v. KLINE. See CONCLUSIVE PRESUMPTION.

V.O.A. See VOICE OF AMERICA.

VOICE OF AMERICA (V.O.A.). The broadcasting service of the former U.S.I.A. and now I.C.A. It produces and broadcasts radio programs in English and foreign languages, and operates broadcasting and relay facilities to transmit these programs abroad. Programming includes news, detailed reports from correspondents on the scene and analysis of events from Washington, presentation of conflicting views, feature programs, and music.

VOIDABLE CONTRACT. Contractual obligations which are not fully legally operative and may be either avoided or validated.

VOIDABLE MARRIAGE. A marital union which may be declared a void marriage but which is as valid as a lawful marriage for all purposes until it is appropriately set aside. A proceeding to declare such a marriage void may be conducted only while both parties are living. Voidable grounds usually include impotence, fraud, duress or nonage.

VOIDABLE PREFERENCE. Payment or transfer of property to a creditor by a bankrupt debtor which favors or "prefers" that creditor over other creditors. A voidable preference is subject to revocation under a turnover order if the transfer of property occurred within four months of filing a debtor's bankruptcy petition, at a time when the debtor was insolvent, and the preferred creditor had reason to believe that the debtor was insolvent at the time of the transfer.

VOID FOR VAGUENESS DOCTRINE. A judicial doctrine, derived from the Fifth and Fourteenth Amendments, which requires that a criminal statute be declared invalid when it is so vague that men of common intelligence must guess at its meaning and will differ as to its application. The statute must be reasonably certain as to the persons within the scope of the statute, the conduct that is prohibited, and the sanctions which may be imposed. The Supreme Court has used three criteria in determining whether a statute is vague. The first is whether it gives fair notice to persons potentially subject to it. The statute need not be drafted with perfect precision, since such a standard is not possible when using the English language, but must set discernible limits. The second criterion is whether the statute adequately guards against discriminatory enforcement. Here, the court is concerned that uncertain statutory language will allow discriminatory enforcement to go undetected. Finally, the statute must provide sufficient "breathing space" for First Amendment freedoms. Thus, a statute will be struck down if, though not infringing on First Amendment rights, it "chills" the exercise of those rights by creating a fear that constitutionally protected conduct may yield punishment.

VOID LEGACY. At common law a gift is void if at the time of execution of the will the beneficiary is dead.

VOIR DIRE (French—to see and speak). Questioning of potential jury members by the court, lawyers or parties themselves if not represented by counsel. Voir Dire is intended to determine the suitability of prospective jurors to hear a particular case.

VOLENTI NON FIT INJURIA (Latin —the volunteer suffers no wrong). Expresses the doctrine that no legal wrong is done to one who consents.

VOLSTEAD ACT (Prohibition Amendment of 1919). An amendment to the federal Constitution which prohibited the sale, use, possession or manufacturing of alcoholic beverages. It is the only amendment ever repealed (in 1933).

VOLUNTARY APPEARANCE. The participation of an individual in a judicial or other formal proceeding, even though he has not been validly served process.

VOLUNTARY BAR ASSOCIATION. A private organization of lawyers who band together for social life and to further the goals and integrity of the legal profession. One does not have to belong in order to practice law.

VOLUNTARY MANSLAUGHTER. An intentional killing perpetrated while the accused was in an enraged state caused by a reasonable provocation. Such provocation is based on an objective standard and asks whether a reasonable man would have been provoked to kill in such a situation. There are four major settings in which the courts have found reasonable provocation to exist. First, the discovery of one's spouse engaged in adultery has been held a sufficient provocation. Although it has traditionally been required that the husband or wife actually see the act, some recent decisions have held that discovery after the act is sufficient. Second, an intentional killing during mutual combat or in response to a battery has been held to be manslaughter. However, the courts balance the provocation with the retaliatory force. Hence, a slight push is not deemed to be a sufficient provocation. Additionally, mutual combat may not be an adequate provocation if the defendant was the instigator. Third, an injury to a close relative may be a sufficient provocation. Examples are the battery of a wife or the rape of a daughter. Finally, some courts have held that an unlawful arrest is sufficient provocation. Thus a killing while resisting such an arrest would be manslaughter. Many states hold otherwise either through statutes or case law. Even if reasonable provocation exists, an intentional homicide will not be manslaughter unless the defendant himself was actually enraged. Thus the deliberate killer may not hide behind a plea of provocation. Additionally, the accused must kill while in the heat of passion or hot blood, before any cooling-off. Thus the killing of a spouse's paramour several days after discovering the adulterous relationship would probably be murder since there was a cooling-off period.

VOLUNTARY PETITION IN BANKRUPTCY. A petition filed in bankruptcy court, in which a person asks to be adjudged bankrupt. Along with the voluntary petition are filed lists of the petitioner's assets, liabilities, and creditors, and a fifty-dollar filing fee. An adjudication in bankruptcy follows automatically from the filing of the voluntary petition. The bankrupt must then surrender to the court all his property except certain exempt property. He may then apply for a discharge of debts which, if granted by the bankruptcy court, will relieve him of his legal obligations to pay his debts.

VOLUNTEERS IN SERVICE TO AMERICA (V.I.S.T.A.). An organization created by Congress in 1964 to strengthen local efforts to eliminate poverty and poverty-related human, social, and environmental problems in the United States and its territories. V.I.S.T.A. volunteer men and women are chosen from all ages and all walks of life, and receive pre-service and in-service training for their project assignments. Volunteers serve for up to 2 years, living and working among the needy in urban ghettos, small towns, and rural areas of poverty such as Appalachia, as well as with migrant workers, on Indian reservations, and in institutions for the mentally ill or handicapped. V.I.S.T.A. volunteers include skilled craftsmen and tradesmen, doctors, lawyers, architects, teachers, and business and liberal arts graduates. A growing number of V.I.S.T.A. volunteers are also recruited by the local sponsor for work in their own communities. The range of V.I.S.T.A. activities is as broad as the needs which are defined by the poor community. V.I.S.T.A. volunteers act as resource mobilizers and catalysts in education, day care, drug abuse, corrections, health, legal aid, architecture and city planning, and many other programs. Throughout their year of service, V.I.S.T.A.s train and equip the community to better solve their own problems after the V.I.S.T.A. volunteer has left.

VOTE OF CONFIDENCE. A test of political power in which a Chief Executive, such as the British Prime Minister, resigns if the legislature fails to approve a specific proposal. When a prime minister does not receive a vote of confidence, elections are held to form a new government.

VOTING RIGHTS. A right in voting shares to vote for the election of at least one corporate director. Usually each share has one vote. However, the Articles of Incorporation or state law may also require cumulative voting, class voting, or even disproportionate voting, where one class of shares has greater rights than another. A corporation may also issue some non-voting stock.

VOTING RIGHTS ACT. A series of three acts whereby Congress prohibited discriminatory practices used by the states to qualify voters. The 1965 Act banned the use of literacy tests and authorized federal registration of voters and jurisdictions where such tests had been used and where less than half of the eligible voters had registered or voted. The Act also authorized the Attorney General to test the validity of poll taxes. The following year, in *Harper v. Virginia State Board of Elections,* 383 U.S. 663 (1966), the Court declared such taxes unconstitutional. Two Voting Rights Acts in the 1970s have expanded the efforts of the federal government to assure that all eligible citizens enjoy the right to vote. In 1970 Congress extended the 1965 Act for another five years. In addition, the new Act lowered the voting age from twenty-one to eighteen, and prohibited the use of residency requirements exceeding

thirty days. In 1975 the Voting Rights Act was extended for seven years. The new Act also required bilingual ballots to guarantee the voting of minorities such as Spanish and Asian Americans.

VOTING TRUST. A trust created when shareholders transfer their voting shares to a voting trustee, who holds and votes the shares in accordance with the terms of the Voting Trust agreement. Only the right to vote the shares is vested in the trustee, not the full legal title. Voting Trusts are used to concentrate shareholder control in one or more persons who, primarily through the election of directors, can control corporate policies. They have become less popular in recent years since more effective methods of control exist. At common law, Voting Trusts were found to be illegal by many courts, but a majority of states now authorize such trusts by statute.

VOYAGE CHARTER. A contractual arrangement among a party wishing to engage the services of a vessel, the charterer, and the vessel owner, to carry a full cargo on a single voyage. Under this form of charter, the vessel is manned and operated by the owner. The most common form of maritime charter arrangement, a Voyage Charter, is useful in any commercial situation where the charterer desires to move a specific cargo between specific points.

W

W.A.C.L. (World Anti-Communist League). A private international organization created in 1967 with memberships in 80 countries dedicated to serve as a deterrent to the expansion of Marxism-Leninism.

WADE HEARINGS. Pretrial identification hearings conducted by a court when there is a substantial likelihood of irreparable misidentification of a defendant. For example, in a drug case where a defendant is identified by an undercover police officer twelve weeks after an alleged drug sale, the accused may request a Wade Hearing to establish that he was indeed correctly identified by the officer.

WAGE ASSIGNMENT. An agreement permitting a lender to collect a certain portion of a borrower's salary from his employer if payment is not made as specified in the credit contract.

WAGE EARNER PLAN. See CHAPTER XIII PROCEEDING.

WAGNER ACT. See TAFT-HARTLEY ACT.

WAGNER, GUSTAV FRANZ (Human Beast). A Nazi World War II criminal who confessed to complicity in the death of 300,000 victims in a Polish camp, named Sabibor, in 1942 and 1943. In 1979, the Supreme Court of Brazil ruled that the Statute of Limitations had expired on Wagner's crimes and turned down extradition requests from West Germany, Poland, Austria and Israel, so he was set free.

WAIT AND SEE DOCTRINE (Second Look Doctrine). Ameliorates the harsh effect of the Rule Against Perpetuities by considering the facts as they existed at the conclusion of the life estates to determine whether the interests actually vested within the period of perpetuities. In the case of the exercise of a special power or a general power of appointment, the court may consider the facts existing at the time of the appointment in determining the validity of the appointed assets.

WALL STREET LAWYER. An attorney practicing in the financial district of New York City as a member of a firm serving the interests of big business.

WALSH-HEALY PUBLIC CONTRACTS ACT. This federal law requires, pursuant to a government procurement clause, that supply contractors, in procurements over $10,000, if they are manufacturers of, or regular dealers in, the supplies procured, meet certain requirements. They must pay a certain minimum wage, observe maximum daily and weekly hour limits, conform to minimum age for employment standards, and insure that working conditions are sanitary and safe. The Act provides for liquidated damages, contract termination, and a three-year debarment from government contracts for violations.

W.A.R.C. (World Administrative Radio Conference). Held in Geneva, Switzerland, in 1979, under the sponsorship of I.T.U. The 60-member American delegation was chaired by Glen O. Robinson, Professor of Law, University of Virginia. One of the big controversies the United States will probably encounter is the reallocation of orbital space and frequencies for satellite broadcast communications. On this issue a major political difference exists between the United States and most other nations. The United States wants a so-called "flexible" assignment plan for all satellite frequencies, and does not want to assign frequencies in advance of demonstrated need. Most European countries, the Soviet Union, Third World countries and South America want a "fixed assignment system," which assigns frequencies and orbital space slots on an equitable basis, regardless of need or immediately planned use. Many stations are concerned they might be frozen out under a flexible assignment system. Another major problem facing the United States at the conference involved a domestic controversy between land mobile users and broadcasters on allocation of U.H.F. frequencies. Although most of these frequencies are now allocated to television broadcasters, land mobile users want more of the frequency band. This is a highly volatile domestic issue.

WAR CRIMES. Consist of four specific offenses—conspiring to wage wars of aggression; waging wars of aggression in violation of international treaties; violating the laws or customs of war by taking lives and property not justified by military necessity; and committing crimes against humanity such as enslavement and extermination. The term is used most frequently in connection with the trial at Nuremberg of German officers and Nazi leaders in 1945-47. The proceedings at Nuremberg were conducted by the International Military Tribunal (I.M.T.) composed of representatives from the Allied Countries. The Charter of the I.M.T. restricted the defense of following superior orders to mitigation of punishment, rather than allowing it to be relevant to the ultimate issue of guilt or innocence. Moreover, the Charter established procedural rules and the substantive crimes to be considered. It directed the United States, Russia, France, and Great Britain each to supply a chief prosecutor. Supreme Court Justice Robert H. Jackson represented the United States. Of the twenty-four original defendants, one committed suicide, one became seriously ill, and one not in the Allies' custody was tried in absentia. Three of the defendants were acquitted, eleven were sentenced to death, and the remainder were given prison terms ranging from ten years to life. Similarly, in 1961, Adolf Eichmann, Director of the Jewish Affairs Section of the Reich Security Head Office, was tried, convicted, and hanged for committing war crimes against the Jewish people during World War II. Unlike the Nuremberg proceedings, however, an Israeli court rather than an international tribunal heard Eichmann's case. The defendant had been kidnapped from Argentina in 1960 and brought to Israel. Both the Nuremberg hearings and the Eichman case have been criticized—the former because of the Ad Hoc character of the I.M.T., the latter because it relied on an Ex Post Facto crime and abduction of the accused to obtain a conviction. While war crimes have gained widespread exposure since World War II, perhaps their earliest historical antecedent lies in the defeat of the Athenian fleet at Aegospotomos by Lysander in 405 B.C. After his conquest, Lysander formed a Tribunal to decide the fate of his prisoners. And in the fifteenth century, Sir Peter of Hagenbach, the governor of an Upper Rhine city, was tried for heinous crimes by judges and knights under the auspices of the Holy Roman Empire. In more modern times, Napoleon Bonaparte was exiled to St. Helena under joint consent of his foes although the action was executive rather than judicial. This action serves as a precedent of international action for the treatment of a defeated enemy.

WARD, HORACE T. Appointed by President Carter in 1979 and sworn in as Georgia's first Black Federal District Court Judge in the same courtroom where he fought unsuccessfully in 1950 for admission as the first Black to apply to the University of Georgia Law School. He was graduated instead from Northwestern Law School, and served as a State Senator and State Judge before joining the federal judiciary.

WAREHOUSING AGENCIES. Purchasers of mortgage loans which are assembled into packages for resale to investors. Government agencies such as Ginny Mae, Fanny May and Freddy Mac are the major warehousing agencies.

WAREHOUSING CHILDREN. Institutionalizing children without providing proper medical care, counseling, education, or other services needed for their growth and development. Children are placed in state and private institutions because of physical and mental infirmities, because of delinquency, or simply because they have no parents or their parents cannot properly care for them. Some facilities lack the trained personnel and funds to adequately care for these children and, in effect, are "warehousing" them for a period of time until the child reaches majority or is placed out of the institution, sometimes to be institutionalized as an adult. Such practices are contrary to the assumption that these children are in need of specially-designed rehabilitative services, and in some cases, permits parents to escape the responsibility of raising their children.

WAR HAWKS. See CLAY, HENRY.

WARM BENCH. See HOT BENCH.

WAR POWERS ACT OF 1973. A federal law designed to limit the power of the President to commit American troops abroad. The Act provides that American armed forces may be sent into action only when Congress has declared war or specifically authorized their use. Although the President can act unilaterally in a national emergency, he must then report to Congress and withdraw the troops if Congress fails to act within a designated period of time. The War Powers Act represented the intention of Congress to avoid American military intervention except where such intervention was deemed necessary by the President and the legislature. Since the end of World War II, American Presidents, acting without Congressional approval, had deployed American troops abroad without Congressional consent, leading to the controversial Vietnamese war experience.

WARRANTY DEED. This form of a deed is most advantageous to the buyer of real property. A warranty deed gives the buyer five covenants: (1) that the buyer is seized of the property in fee simple and can convey the property; (2) that the buyer shall be guaranteed quiet enjoyment of the property; (3) that the property is free from encumbrances; (4) that the seller will do what is necessary to assure the buyer takes clear title to the property; and (5) that the seller will continue to warrant title to the property.

WARRANTY OF HABITABILITY. A provision in a lease in which the landlord agrees to be liable in damages to the tenant if the rental premises are not fit for reasonable human living conditions or are dangerous to the life, safety or health of the tenants.

WARREN COMMISSION REPORT. A government inquiry panel headed by then Chief Justice Earl Warren, which conducted an investigation of the assassination of President John F. Kennedy, in 1963. The Commission concluded that there was no conspiracy but that the accused assassin, Lee Harvey Oswald (who was himself assassinated by Jack Ruby a few days later), had acted alone in the murder.

WARREN COURT. A short-hand label for the Supreme Court when its Chief Justice was Earl Warren. The Court is perhaps characterized as "activist" be-cause of its tendency to read the Constitution in a manner conducive to overturning official conduct and legislation in order to establish individual rights. Its opponents, pointing to expansive construction of the First, Fourth, Fifth, and Sixth Amendments, claimed the Court violated separation of powers by "legislating" substantive rights.

WARREN, EARL (1891-1974). Chief Justice of the Supreme Court from 1953 to 1969, known primarily for his deep commitment to fairness and equality. The Warren Court issued such landmark decisions as *Brown v. Board of Education*, 347 U.S. 483 (1954), *Baker v. Carr*, 369 U.S. 186 (1962), and *Miranda v. Arizona*, 384 U.S. 436 (1966). Warren was criticized for judicial activism when his attempts to remedy inequality and injustice led the Court to promote reform where other branches of the government had failed to act. Prior to his appointment to the Court by President Eisenhower, Warren served as a county prosecutor, state Attorney General, and finally, Governor of California.

WARSAW CONVENTION. A relic of an International Treaty adopted by the United States in 1929 which drastically limits the liability of airlines to passengers or their estates for injuries arising out of international flights. It may be on its last legs unless the United States Senate passes the Montreal Protocol, formerly known as the Guatemala Protocol.

WARSAW PACT ORGANIZATION. Created by the Treaty of Friendship, Cooperation and Mutual Assistance, signed at Warsaw on May 14, 1955. The members are: Bulgaria, Czechoslovakia, German Democratic Republic, Hungary, Poland, Rumania, and the U.S.S.R. Since the 1962 Soviet-Chinese split, China, Albania, and Mongolia ceased to participate. A defensive alliance, the Pact was initiated by the Soviet Union as a direct military counterpart of N.A.T.O. It was also a reaction against the re-armament of West Germany and its participation in

N.A.T.O. Article 4 of the Pact provides for "immediate assistance," by all necessary means, to its members. It was the pretext for the Soviet invasion of Hungary in 1956, and of Czechoslovakia in 1968. The Pact provides for (1) a Political Consultative Committee, (2) a Permanent Commission, which sits in Moscow, and (3) for a joint command for the armed forces of the members. Unification of their armies has effectively been realized. A powerful military organization, the Warsaw Pact is theoretically open for membership to all states "willing to preserve peace," of whatever system they might be. In practice, however, it is limited to Eastern European States.

WASHINGTON, GEORGE. The Father of our Country who was the first in our history who specifically ordered his will to be drafted by a non-lawyer and his estate to be probated by non-lawyers. Obviously, he did not think much of the legal profession, which had the last word in the large fees attorneys earned to unscramble his estate.

WASHINGTON OF THE WEST. See SPANISH CONSPIRACY.

WASHINGTON WOMEN'S NETWORK. (W.W.N.). An unstructured group of high-ranking women who work for the federal government in Washington. They meet monthly for the purpose of recruiting women executives for federal positions and to share expertise and information with each other to foster their own careers. The informal sophisticated grapevine came into existence after the 1976 election.

WASH SALE. A financial transaction which occurs when a taxpayer sells stock or securities and, within a period of 30 days before or after the sale, acquires or contracts to acquire a similar or substantially similar property. A loss realized from such a sale is not allowed as a tax deduction. But a gain is recognized for tax purposes.

WASTING ASSETS. Assets such as coal mines which cannot be replenished and the life of which cannot be prolonged by repairs.

WASTING TRUST. A trust arrangement in which the principal trust property is an asset which is declining in quantity and value. A Wasting Trust may consist of oil and gas, timber, mines, a copyrighted book, or tangible personal property. Wasting Trust administration can be quite complicated, depending on whether or not the trust property is a natural resource. These trust arrangements are governed by statute in most states, and in the case of natural resources, by the Uniform and the Revised Uniform Principal and Income Acts.

WATERED STOCK. Shares of a corporation purchased with over-valued consideration. The term is derived from the practice of inducing livestock to drink large quantities of water before they are sold by weight. Although watered stock is often used to refer to bonus stock and discount stock, the concepts are distinguishable. Bonus stock results when the corporation receives no consideration in return for issuance of the stock. Discount stock occurs where the value received by the corporation is openly acknowledged to be less than the lawful consideration.

WATERGATE SPECIAL PROSECUTION FORCE (W.S.P.F.). Full-time staff of 174 who spent 7.7 million dollars and 28 months investigating various Watergate crimes. A report written by the W.S.P.F. on its activities is available from the Superintendent of Documents.

WATERGATE TAPES CASE. See UNITED STATES v. NIXON.

W.C.T.U. See NOBLE EXPERIMENT.

WEAR 'EM DOWN TACTIC. See TRIAL BY AMBUSH.

WEAVER, ROBERT C. First Black to hold a position in the Federal Cabinet as Secretary of the Department of Housing and Urban Development under President Lyndon B. Johnson.

WEBER CASE. See AFFIRMATIVE ACTION.

WEBSTER, DANIEL. Born in New Hampshire, "Black Dan" was a Whig statesman whose career embraced two terms in the House of Representatives (1813-1817, 1823-1827), two in the Senate (1827-1841, 1845-1850) and two stints as Secretary of State (under William Henry Harrison, 1841-1843 and under Millard Fillmore, 1850-1854). Yet for all his administrative and legislative gifts, Webster was perhaps the most polished constitutional lawyer of his day. He felt that a strong central government was essential for the emerging nation, and he fought the efforts of states' rights partisans to undermine federal sovereignty. Thus, in *McCulloch v. Maryland*, 4 Wheat. 316 (1819), he defended the constitutionality of the United States Bank, and argued that such a federal institution should be exempt from taxation by individual states. The same overarching credo found expression again when, in 1828, he supported a federally-imposed protective tariff despite the opposition of southern states (which, without much manufacturing, stood to gain nothing thereby). When South Carolina's Robert Y. Hayne offered votes to the western states in return for western support of a low tariff, Webster's eloquence reached its pinnacle. In his second reply to Hayne, Webster deprecated such self-serving alliances, predicting (correctly) that they would lead to war. After an unsuccessful run at the Presidency in 1836 (Martin Van Buren, a democrat, prevailed), Webster found his antipathy toward slavery butting heads with his respect for the rule of law. Though he sided with the northern states on the moral issue of slavery, he believed that the South had a constitutionally protected interest in slaves as property. Thus, in his famous Seventh of March address, Webster supported the Fugitive Slave Law, much to the horror of the abolitionists. His words mark the keystone of his thought: he supported the slave law, he said, "not as a Massachusetts man, nor as a northern man, but as an American."

WEBSTER, NOAH. A lawyer by training, he was unable to earn a comfortable living, began teaching, and went on to become a renowned lexicographer and writer. His first dictionary appeared in 1806. Webster sold copies by subscription as he travelled around the country on other business. In 1828, he published his most comprehensive work, *An American Dictionary of the English Language,* which took five months to prepare and contained 70,000 entries. Webster's writings went beyond dictionaries, including such varied titles as *On Raising Potatoes, Experiments Respecting Dew,* and *A Brief History of Epidemic & Pestilential Diseases,* in which he argued that yellow fever was caused by noxious vapors rising from openings in the earth. He was instrumental in procuring state and federal copyright laws and, in 1785, compiled the first reader in America.

WELFARE CHEAT. A person who accepts food stamps, unemployment checks or other welfare benefits knowing that they are being received in violation of law. Welfare cheats are subject to fine and imprisonment. The sardonic title of Welfare Queen was dubiously conferred on Arlene Otis, 30 years of age, mother of four children and a college student studying Criminal Justice at the University of Illinois at the time of her arrest in Chicago in May, 1978. She was charged with 613 different counts of theft and perjury for using four different names in addition to her own to obtain $150,839 dollars in Welfare checks to which she was not entitled. A month later the title passed to Barbara Williams, 32, who lived in a $170,000 mansion in Compton, California. She was accused of allegedly collecting $290,000 illegally.

WELFARE QUEEN. See WELFARE CHEATS.

WELFARE STATE. A system of government which assures that individual social and economic needs will be satisfied. By guaranteeing a minimum standard of living, a welfare state is said to provide "cradle to the grave security." Critics of such a concept charge that it destroys individual enterprise and this impedes social progress. Supporters, however, claim that the protection afforded by the welfare state is necessary to combat the poverty caused by industrialism. In the United States, the ever-expanding role of such programs as Social Security, Unemployment Insurance and Welfare may well be leading us down the road to a welfare state.

WESTERN EUROPEAN UNION (W.E.U.). Created on October 23, 1954, this consists of a series of agreements signed in London and Paris which modified the outdated Brussels Treaty Organization. It had seven members: Belgium, France, West Germany, Italy, Luxembourg, the Netherlands, and the United Kingdom. The W.E.U. was largely influenced by the failure of the European Defense Community (E.D.C.), as well as the creation of N.A.T.O. and the Council of Europe. A system of collective security and self-defense, the W.E.U. regards an attack on any of its members as an attack on all, and provides for a strong obligation of assistance among its signatories. The organization includes a Council of Foreign Ministers and an Assembly. It also provides for a close co-operation with N.A.T.O., giving it in fact the principal military role, as well as decisive responsibilities regarding military information and advice.

WESTERN RIVERS RULES OF THE ROAD. See RULES OF THE ROAD.

WESTLAW. See COMPUTER-ASSISTED LEGAL RESEARCH.

WEST VIRGINIA STATE BOARD OF EDUCATION v. BARNETTE. See FLAG SALUTE CASES.

WET BACK. Slang expression for an alien illegally in the United States who works, especially as a migratory farm laborer, and is subject to deportation if discovered. The term has its origin in that Mexicans swim across the Rio Grande River to gain illegal entry into the United States. Persons who aid Wet Backs are referred to as coyotes and their fees reach as high as $1,000, so desperate is the desire of the unemployed Mexican to come to the land of El Dorado. A "wet house" is a place which harbors Wet Backs from the police, usually at an exhorbitant rent.

WHARTON'S RULE. A judicial rule which prohibits convicting two participants in a crime of criminal conspiracy if the substantive crime requires two participants, such as adultery or incest. However, in most states, if a third person conspires with the participants, then all are guilty of conspiracy.

WHALEN v. ROE (429 U.S. 811 (1977)). A Supreme Court case involving a New York law that required physicians to report to the state the names and addresses of patients obtaining prescriptions for certain dangerous drugs. This information was recorded on a centralized computer file. In a unanimous decision, the Court reversed the ruling of a three-judge District Court which had held the law unconstitutional on the ground that it invaded constitutionally protected "zones of privacy." In a concurring opinion, Justice Brennan noted that limited reported requirements in the medical field "are familiar and are not regarded as an invasion of privacy."

WHIP 'EM IN THE STREETS PETE KREHEL. The crusading presiding judge of Northumberland County, Pennsylvania's eighth judicial district, who is concerned about rising crime rates, particularly among teenagers. His barbaric solution: a return to whipping posts and stocks. Krehel first proposed his idea in February of 1978 at a meeting of the Central Susquehanna Fraternal Order of Police. He would use the punishments primarily against first offenders found guilty of such offenses as shoplifting, purse-snatching, and minor vandalism. The purpose, the judge explained, is to humiliate juvenile delinquents into settling down. "What's going on," says Krehel, "is brazen action by youthful offenders who think they can get away with anything. If a kid vandalized a school, I'd have the father inflict the ten lashes. Maybe the juvenile would even turn around and say, 'Hey, Pop, why didn't you do this to me sooner? Now, you're humiliated, too!' " A return to the Dark Ages?

WHIP-STOCKING. See HOT OIL.

WHISKEY REBELLION. As a response to a 1791 law taxing distilled liquors, farmers in western Pennsylvania refused to pay the tax and hinted at secession. In 1794, George Washington called out the militia of four states to quell the uprising. The farm leaders fled, and the rebellion collapsed. Taxation was a volatile issue in western Pennsylvania, where distillation had become the most economical method of using surplus corn. For example, jugs of corn liquor often were utilized as a means of exchange in much the same way money was used.

WHISPERING CHARLIE. Soft-spoken but highly effective advocate, Charles Fahy, former Solicitor General of the United States and United States Circuit Judge, who died in 1979 at the age of 87.

WHISTLE BLOWER. An employee who makes public any gross abuse of power, serious error in judgment or criminal acts committed by a high management official in either private industry or government. A Whistle Blower is usually summarily fired or severely disciplined for his action. A former Pentagon analyst, A. Ernest Fitzgerald, is a noted Whistle Blower who disclosed to a congressional committee a $2 billion cost overrun on the C-5A transport plane. Fitzgerald was fired from his Air Force job, and fought a 7-year, $400,000 legal battle to regain his position as productivity manager.

WHITE CANE ACT. A statute in force in a majority of United States jurisdictions which protects the rights of visually handicapped individuals. A typical White Cane Act assures the legal rights of blind individuals to use guide dogs or white canes and holds a blind person responsible for damage caused by his guide dog. In addition, the Act requires non-discrimination in employment, except where sight is a bona fide employment qualification, and non-discrimination in housing, except that landlords are not expected to modify facilities for the benefit of blind persons. In *Lyons v. Grether*, 239 S.E.2d 103 (1977), the Supreme Court of Virginia held that a blind person has standing to sue for both compensatory and punitive damages for violations of the White Cane Act.

WHITE COLLAR CRIME. A non-legal term which refers to certain criminal acts, such as embezzlement and bribery, committed by persons of upper socioeconomic status in the course of their occupations. Such crimes often involve office workers and large corporations. Common examples are tax fraud, unfair labor practices, deceptive advertising, and anti-trust violations. Because this type of crime is usually handled administratively very differently from ordinary crime, law enforcement agencies have been criticized for their leniency with white collar offenders.

WHITE COLLAR DEFENSE BAR. Lawyers who specialize in defending high-ranking business and government officials in criminal cases.

WHITE CONSPIRACY. Racial tension caused by the movement of middle-class Whites into inner-city areas which displaces low-income Black families. Blacks often perceive redevelopment of inner city areas as a White conspiracy to force them out of the neighborhoods which Whites abandoned to them years before.

WHITE FLIGHT. Theory first proposed by Dr. James Coleman, sociologist from the University of Chicago, who concluded that massive court-ordered desegregation efforts actually defeat the purpose of increasing interracial contact by stimulating Whites to flee rapidly desegregated areas. For example, from 1973-1977, when Boston's racial problems peaked, more than 45 percent of the White students listed on the Boston School Department's records left the rolls. However, Dr. Christine Rossell, a political scientist from Boston University, has discredited the White Flight theory through statistical analysis which shows an initial decline in White population, but no long-term decline in the White population of racially integrated urban areas. Rossell's theory has become known as the "Rossell Snap Back Effect."

WHITE HOUSE. Official residence of the American President. The President of South Korea lives in the Blue House. Ten Downing Street is the home of the British Prime Minister. The Queen, of course, lives in Buckingham Palace. Red Square is for the Russians. This litany could go on and on and on, but you get the general picture.

WHITE HOUSE OFFICE OF TELE-COMMUNICATIONS POLICY. See NATIONAL TELECOMMUNICATIONS AND INFORMATION ADMINISTRATION.

WHITE PAPER. An official government report on a crucial controversial current issue which presents the official version of a situation and may even recommend corrective action or implementing legislation.

WHITE PRIMARY. A device used by Southern states to exclude Black political candidates. By denying Black access to the primaries, the Democratic Party was able to assure only White candidates were elected. In *Smith v. Allwright,* 321 U.S. 649 (1944), the Supreme Court declared that Blacks could not be excluded from primaries.

WHITE SLAVERY. Colloquial term used to describe interstate transportation of females for the purpose of prostitution. The Mann Act (1910) makes this a federal offense, with punishment set at $5,000 or five years in prison or both. The Act also includes enticing or coercing a female to cross state lines for any immoral purpose.

WHITE WARRIORS. A right wing, pro-government, business-sponsored underground vigilante terrorist group in Central America which takes the law into its own hands allegedly to protect the establishment. Its weapons of revenge include torture, kidnapping and assassination. The police accommodate them by looking the other way. This is the quickest way back to the jungle.

WHITE WEDNESDAY. Commemorates the weekday in June, 1978, when the Supreme Court, in a 5-4 decision, partially struck down the affirmative action program at the University of California at Davis and ordered the Medical School to admit Allan Bakke.

WIDOW'S GAP. That period of time when a wife whose husband dies is too young to qualify for Social Security benefits.

WILDCAT STRIKE. A work stoppage not authorized by a vote of the full union. These strikes may take the form of a walkout by a dissident group within a local, or a strike by a local not authorized by its parent union. Such work stoppages are outside the protection of Section 7 of the National Labor Relations Act, and therefore are illegal.

WILDE, OSCAR—TRIAL OF. Wilde was a flamboyant Irish author and wit who lived from 1854 to 1900. He began the aesthetic movement, which was both criticized and praised for its "art for art's sake" ideal. By 1891, Wilde had become intimate with Lord Alfred Douglas. Douglas' father, the Marquis of Queensberry, accused Wilde of engaging in homosexual practices. Wilde sued the Marquis of Queensberry for libel, and on losing the case was charged with homosexual offenses under the Criminal Law Amendment. He was found guilty and sentenced to two years in prison. Financially and physically broken he was released in 1897, he lived in France under the name Sebastian Melmoth until his death in 1900. His experience in prison inspired two works, *The Ballad of Reading Gaol* (1898), a poem published anonymously, and *De Profundis* (1905), a posthumously published apologia.

WILLIAM AND MARY COLLEGE OF LAW. The earliest American Law School, founded in 1779 by Thomas Jefferson, where the renowned chancellor George Wythe held the first American professorship of law. The next two professorships of law were founded by Harvard in 1817 and Yale in 1824.

WILLIAMS ACT. A federal law named after its sponsor which regulates corporate takeovers by governing tender offers in allowing them to go forward as soon as the offering company has made the required disclosures about its plans and the source of its funds with respect to the target company. The law favors neither side in an unfriendly takeover, where some state laws, which also have legislation on the subject, tip the balance of protection in favor of the incumbent management, thereby making takeovers more difficult to consummate.

WILMINGTON TEN. Nine Black men and one White woman convicted of firebombing a White-owned grocery store in Wilmington, N.C., during a violent racial civil-rights protest in 1971. The group's leader, Rev. Ben Chavis, denied any involvement in the arson, insisting that he advocated non-violent techniques. After an original jury of ten Blacks and two Whites was chosen, the prosecutor's illness forced a postponement. When the trial finally commenced, the District Attorney used his forty peremptory challenges to virtually exclude Blacks from the jury so that only two out of twelve jurors were Black. After the Ten were jailed in 1976, three key witnesses recanted their testimony, and one of those three later changed his mind and reaffirmed the truth of his original story. Under pressure from a number of influential citizens to pardon the Ten, North Carolina Governor James Hunt, in 1978, declared the trial fair, but reduced the sentences of all the defendants. His decision outraged activists on both sides of the issue, and prompted renewed requests for federal court review of the trial's fairness. The Wilmington Ten were prominent "political prisoners" in the United States during the 1970s, according to a report by Amnesty International.

WINDFALL TAX (Surplus Profits Tax). President Carter's recommendation in 1979 of a special 50 percent income tax on the added revenues made by American oil companies as a result of the decontrol of oil prices.

W.I.N. See A.V.O.L.

WISCONSIN v. YODER. See FREE EXERCISE CLAUSE.

WISE MEN. A group of former government officials and experienced outsiders from whom the President seeks advice in foreign policy crises.

WITCH HUNT. See COLD WAR.

WITHOUT BENEFIT OF CLERGY. The cohabitation of a man and woman as husband and wife without being legally married to each other. Once scandalous, it is now practiced openly by millions.

WITHOUT PREJUDICE. Used in a court judgment to indicate that there has been no decision on the merits of a case. The term, indicating that no rights or remedies of the parties have been affected, waived, or lost, is used in contemplation of a new suit on the same cause of action. The defendant may not raise the defense of Res Judicata as a bar to a further action. Conversely, dismissal of a suit With Prejudice is considered conclusive of the rights of the parties as if the case had been carried to a final adjudication adverse to the plaintiff.

WITHOUT RECOURSE. The phrase in a contract that relieves a party from personal liability in the event of non-payment.

WITH PREJUDICE. See WITHOUT PREJUDICE.

WITNESS SECURITY PROGRAM. Formally established after passage of the Organized Crime Control Act of 1970 to hasten the breakdown of "Omerta," the underworld code of silence. Under this program, a witness is given a new identity in exchange for his testimony against organized criminal groups, such as the Mafia. The 13 million dollar program has become so popular that almost twice a day the justice department creates a new personality, complete with fake Social Security

Card, driver's license, school record and job history. Less than a dozen of the two thousand participating witnesses have been assassinated. Although the justice department credits the program with three thousand convictions, it has come under bitter attack. Some critics cite the plight of merchants, investors and employers who, deceived by the justice department's fabricated credentials, have lost money by trusting criminals. Other critics question whether the government should adopt a program boldly dedicated to telling lies. Still others wonder whether the benefits of the program amount to improper inducements for the witnesses' testimony.

WOBBLIES. See INDUSTRIAL WORKERS OF THE WORLD.

WOLFENDEN REPORT. See ROYAL COMMISSION.

WOLFF v. McCONNELL (1974). See "GOOD TIME LOSS."

WOMAN'S LAWYER. Marvin M. Mitchelson, Beverly Hills counsel for Michelle Triola, who won her case against Lee Marvin in the first "palimony" recovery for a woman who has been living with a man out of wedlock. Author of gossipy *Made In Heaven, Settled In Court,* he was the lawyer for many wives against husbands such as Marlon Brando, Redd Foxx, Groucho Marx, Rod Steiger, Chevy Chase, Flip Wilson, Mick Jagger, Bob Dylan, James Mason and other Hollywood celebrities from whom he has extracted millions of dollars.

WOMEN IN THE LAW. Historically, the legal profession has relied on a number of legal and social rationales of dubious persuasiveness to prevent women from joining its ranks. A few early cases held that the exclusive use of male pronouns in state statutes authorizing entry to the Bar precluded the admission of women. Other cases used the rationale that married women could not enter binding contracts. Male attorneys and judges also argued that women by nature did not possess "legal minds," and that women had insufficient

physical stamina for the rigors of trial practice. However, the most frequent argument against admitting women to the legal profession was simply that women belonged in the home and not in the courtroom. But by 1890, a total of 135 women lawyers and law students practiced and studied in the United States. Many of these pioneering attorneys were married to lawyers, and received support in beginning their professions from their husbands. Women often practiced in partnership with their husbands or other relatives, including mothers and sisters. Other more independent attorneys moved alone to states which allowed women to practice law, primarily in the Midwest and the West. However, about one fifth of women attorneys during the late nineteenth century never practiced. Instead, they married, performed office duties, or entered other professions. Those who remained active generally maintained low profiles, appearing in court only to litigate domestic relations suits or to defend criminal cases. By 1920, all of the states had opened their Bar Associations to women lawyers, and women were permitted to join the A.B.A. Many law schools, however, would not admit women as students until many years later. Columbia first opened its doors to women in 1929, and Harvard refused to admit women as students until 1950, despite the fact that a woman had been a member of its law faculty. Notre Dame denied women admission until 1969, and the last holdout, Washington and Lee in Lexington, Virginia, finally admitted women in 1972. Despite these advances, thinly veiled sexism still exists among the old guard of the legal profession. As late as 1968, a well-known property casebook commented that "land, like woman, was meant to be possessed." Undeterred by such attitudes, however, women entered law schools in unprecedented numbers during the 1970s, comprising one fourth to one third of many law school entering classes.

WOMEN LAWYERS. Comprise about 9.3 percent of the nation's 441,000 practicing lawyers in 1978; whereas, in

1970, only 2.8 percent of the lawyers were women; and presently about 25 percent of all law school students are women. Some observers predict that law may become the first traditionally male profession to achieve full sexual integration. Women, however, are still under-represented in the ranks of the judiciary, on law school faculties, and as partners in private firms. For example, there are no women Supreme Court Justices, and of the 394 federal district court judges in 1979, only five are women. On law school faculties, Harvard is representative, with only three women out of 66 permanent faculty positions.

WOMEN'S AUXILIARY OF THE DECALOGUE SOCIETY OF LAWYERS. Three hundred wives of judges and lawyers of the Jewish faith who seek to cultivate public respect for the legal profession through the bestowing of Awards.

WOMEN'S CHRISTIAN TEMPERANCE UNION. See NOBLE EXPERIMENT.

WOMEN'S RIGHTS LAW REPORTER. Published by Rutgers Law School in New Jersey, this is the oldest legal periodical in the country focusing solely on the protection of women's legal rights, especially any form of sex-based discrimination.

WOODCOCK COMMISSION. Established by President Carter, in 1977, to investigate the fate of 697 Americans missing in action (MIA) after the Vietnam War. After a painstaking review, the Commission concluded that the fate of these men would probably remain a mystery. Critics of the Commission feel that the government has prematurely closed the file on men they so willingly sent to fight in Vietnam, and point to various rumors of American prisoners being sighted in that country.

WOOD, JOHN H., Jr. The first judge to be assassinated in the 200-year-old history of the American federal judiciary. Known as a tough judge on account of his stern sentencing of narcotics smugglers, the 63-year-old jurist was shot in the back in San Antonio, Texas, on May 29, 1979, just before he was to preside over a major drug conspiracy case.

WORDS AND PHRASES. A West Publishing Company case-finding tool which includes over 350,000 court definitions of legal and non-legal terms, arranged alphabetically by the words or phrases. To locate all American cases that have ever defined any word or phrase, an attorney need only turn to this 46-volume set.

WORDS OF LIMITATION. See WORDS OF PURCHASE.

WORDS OF PURCHASE. Words denoting who is to receive an estate. For example, in the phrase "to A and his heirs," "A" is the only word of purchase. The words "and his heirs" are words of limitation indicating the duration of the estate.

WORKER BEES. See KILLER BEES.

WORKING CAPITAL. See NET ASSETS.

WORKING WOMEN UNITED INSTITUTE (W.W.U.I.). New York-based organization to aid women facing sexual harassment on the job. "Harassment" is defined as coercion to provide sexual favors on penalty of losing one's job.

WORKMEN'S COMPENSATION. In force in every state, these statutory schemes hold an employer strictly liable for injuries to his employees arising out of his business. The statutes have abolished what have been called the three wicked sisters of the common law —the employer's defenses of Contributory Negligence, Assumption of Risk, and the Fellow Servant Rule. The abolition of these defenses has made it possible for the employee to be compensated for injuries resulting from unavoidable accidents and even for injuries caused by negligence of the employee himself. In contrast to the often complex litigation attending a common law suit in negligence, Workmen's Compensation claims require a finding merely that the workman and his injury fall within the coverage of the Act and a determination of what compensation shall be paid. Often the level of compensation is itself fixed by statute, further simplifying matters. New York enacted the first State Workmen's Compensation Plan in 1910, and by 1921 the great majority of states had followed its lead. When Hawaii passed its statute in 1963, the coverage was complete. The theory behind Workmen's Compensation is expressed in its original campaign slogan: "The cost of the product should bear the blood of the workman." That is, in a modern industrial society the costs of accidents should be treated as another of the economic costs of production. Rather than impose these costs on the unfortunate employee, the workmen's compensation scheme shifts them to the employer who will eventually pass them on to the consumer in the form of higher prices for his products.

WORK PRODUCT (Lawyer's Work Product). Interviews, statements, memoranda, correspondence, briefs, mental impressions, and personal beliefs and other work of a lawyer which constitute his preparation for a case. The term was first used in *Hickman v. Taylor*, 329 U.S. 495 (1947). In *Hickman* the Supreme Court held that a lawyer's work product was not subject to discovery by an opponent under the Federal Rules of Civil Procedure without a special showing of necessity by the opponent.

WORK-RELEASE. A furlough program that allows a prisoner to leave the prison unescorted each day of the working week to attend a job or study in the community with continuing residence in the institution.

WORK-TO-RULE ACTION (Slow Down). A practice by employees engaged in a labor dispute with an employer to meticulously abide by every working and safety regulation, thereby greatly decreasing production and causing tremendous inconvenience to the innocent public as a result of the Slow Down.

WORLD ADMINISTRATIVE RADIO CONFERENCE. See W.A.R.C.

WORLD ANTI-COMMUNIST LEAGUE. See W.A.C.L.

WORLD ASSOCIATION OF JUDGES (W.A.J.). Created in 1966 under the sponsorship of the World Peace Through Law Center, it has more than 15,000 judges from over 100 different countries throughout the world who seek to improve the administration of justice by expansion of the Rule of Law.

WORLD ASSOCIATION OF LAW PROFESSORS. See WORLD PEACE THROUGH LAW CENTER.

WORLD ASSOCIATION OF LAW STUDENTS. See WORLD PEACE THROUGH LAW CENTER.

WORLD ASSOCIATION OF LAWYERS. See WORLD PEACE THROUGH LAW CENTER.

WORLD BANK (International Bank for Reconstruction and Development). Headquartered in Washington, D.C., it is a multilateral international organization created by the United States and twenty-seven other nations in 1945. Its purposes are to assist in the reconstruction and development of its member countries by facilitating the investment of capital for productive purposes. When private capital is not available on reasonable terms, the Bank makes loans for productive purposes out of its own funds. As of 1976 the World Bank was lending 6,000 million dollars a year toward raising the living standard in developing countries. The Bank has two principal affiliates, the International Development Association (I.D.A.) founded in 1960 to assist particularly poor governments with 50 year, interest-free credits, as distinct from bank loans, and the International Finance Corporation (I.F.C.) which works specifically with loans in the private sector in developing countries; both are closely integrated with the World Bank and are administered by the same staff.

WORLD CITIZEN. See WORLD SERVICE AUTHORITY.

WORLD COURT. See INTERNATIONAL COURT OF JUSTICE.

WORLD ENVIRONMENT DAY. Designated by the United Nations Conference on the Human Environment (1972) in order to focus attention on environmental problems. World Environment Day is held annually on June fifth.

WORLD PEACE THROUGH LAW CENTER. Formed by Charles S. Rhyne, former president of the American Bar Association, and headquartered in Washington, D.C., the Center was formed in 1963 at a meeting of judges and lawyers from 120 nations in Athens, Greece. The Center is devoted to strengthening both the institutions, such as the International Court of Justice, and the Rules of Law that constitute the world's legal system. Its ultimate goal is to help provide a peaceful world order with justice for all through the cooperation and effort of the world's judiciary and law professions. It is organized into 10 sections concerned with areas of particular interest to the international legal community: (1) human rights; (2) multinational business law; (3) multinational taxation laws; (4) law and computer technology; (5) intellectual property; (6) criminal laws; (7) international legal education; (8) young lawyers and law students; (9) government lawyers; and (10) the Center Lay Associates. To date, the Center has held nine world conferences on four continents, with a total attendance of over 40,000. Participants have addressed a broad range of international issues including hijacking, terrorism, rights of refugees, the international monetary system, global trade, expanding the jurisdiction of the International Court of Justice, the environment, copyrights and patents, regulation of dangerous drugs, population controls, and multinational business law. New draft conventions on many of these subjects have been prepared by the Center's experts, committees, and sections, and formal resolutions have been adopted on many of these issues. Through the technique of the demonstration trial, the Center indicates the possibility for peaceful resolution of international disputes through legal process in the courts. The Ninth World Conference was sponsored by the Center in conjunction with its self-explanatory affiliated organization, the World Association of Judges, the World Association of Lawyers, the World Association of Law Professors, and the World Association of Law Students. Held in Madrid, Spain, the 1979 Conference had as its theme "The Law of International Cooperation: International Law of Economic Development and Law Relating to Relations Between Capitalist and Socialist Countries."

WORLD'S BEST LAWYER. Sir Lionel Luckoo, a criminal lawyer in Guyana, South America. As defense counsel in 229 murder cases, he obtained 229 acquittals.

WORLD SERVICE AUTHORITY. An organization founded by expatriate American Gary Davis which purports to issue world passports and travel orders. Recently convicted in France of issuing "world passports" to immigrant laborers who believed the documents allowed them to remain in France, Davis has met with singular lack of success in his role as the first self-proclaimed "world citizen."

WORLD'S LARGEST LAW FIRM. (1) Private: Baker and McKenzie, Chicago, Illinois, 450 attorneys. (2) Government: United States Army Judge Advocate General (J.A.G.) Corps, 1,600 attorneys.

WORLD TRADE PACT. Negotiated in Geneva between the United States under the leadership of Robert S. Strauss and the Common Market over a six year period ending in 1979, this agreement, under the sponsorship of G.A.T.T., consisted of (a) tariff cuts averaging 33 percent phased in over a number of years and (b) ten International Trade Codes designed to reduce or eliminate non-tariff barriers to world trade, named as follows: (1) Agricultural framework (including the creation of a G.A.T.T.

supervised International Agriculture Advisory Council); (2) Beef Agreement including the creation of an International Meat Council); (3) Commercial Counterfeiting; (4) Countervailing Steps; (5) Customs Valuation; (6) Dairy Products (including the creation of a G.A.T.T. sponsored International Dairy Products Council); (7) Government Procurement; (8) Import Safeguards; (9) Technical Barriers to Trade; and finally, (10) General Trade Rules.

WORTHIER TITLE DOCTRINE. The rule that heirs take by descent, rather than by will, when a testator devises to them precisely the same interest in property that they would inherit if he died intestate. This feudal doctrine was probably created to prevent a transferor from making his own heirs purchasers, thereby depriving the mesne lords of their incidents. Justice Cardozo, in the case of *Doctor v. Hughes,* 225 N.Y. 305, 122 N.E. 221 (1919), made it plain that the Doctrine no longer prohibits the transferor from creating a valid remainder in his heirs; it requires only that his intent to do so be "clearly expressed."

W.O.W.S.E.R. An acronym of the motto of an Australian reform group: We Only Want Social Evils Righted. The term describes a public crusade against minor vices.

WRAPAROUND MORTGAGE. Assumption by a lender of an existing loan and creation of a new loan at a higher interest rate. The new loan includes funds to cover payments for the old loan as well as additional funds needed by the borrower. The borrower makes payments on the new loan while the lender makes payments on the old loan. For example, a buyer with minimal down-payment funds may want a wraparound mortgage in which he makes out a loan of the purchase price to the seller and the seller continues to pay off his old mortgage from the proceeds of the buyer's payments.

WRIT OF ATTACHMENT. Generally, a judicial order which compels persons or property to be brought into the custody of the court. More specifically, it is a remedy for the collection of a debt, which directs the sheriff to take possession or control of specific property of the debtor out of which any judgment in the creditor's favor will ultimately be satisfied. The creditor's access to such a writ is limited by state-imposed restrictions. Some states allow for attachment only when the debtor seems predisposed to pack up his property and leave the jurisdiction. Further, certain kinds of property are expressly "exempted" from attachment.

WRIT OF CERTIORARI. The procedure of discretionary review by the Supreme Court of the United States in cases presenting important national issues. The Writ is directed at a lower court, informing such court to send up all materials on the case in question. A petition must be filed by the challenging party before the Writ can be issued. The petition must show that the Court has jurisdiction and that the case is of sufficient general significance to warrant Supreme Court review. Since the Judges Bill of 1925 sharply reduced appeals to the Supreme Court as a matter of right, the most common method of obtaining Supreme Court review has been by timely application for a Writ of Certiorari. The Supreme Court rules make clear that review by Writ of Certiorari "is not a matter of right, but of sound judicial discretion, and will be granted only where there are special and important reasons therefor." The decision to grant or deny a Petition for Certiorari is made by the entire Supreme Court. Under the well-settled Rule of Four, however, Certiorari is granted when at least four Justices vote for a grant. The Court considers the case even though five Justices may not deem it worthy of the Court's attention. Review by Writ of Certiorari should be distinguished from Appeals As A Matter Of Right, a more limited class of cases. Denial of Certiorari has no significance as to the merits of a case. The lower court's opinion stands. Disposition of an appeal, however, either by affirmance or by dismissal, is a disposition on the merits and thus binding on the court. However, Certiorari has the advantage of allowing the reviewing Court to look into all aspects of a case, not only those about which there is a question.

WRIT OF EXECUTION. Used to enforce a court judgment or decree.

WRIT OF MANDAMUS. A request to a court to direct some person, corporation, government official, or an inferior court to affirmatively carry out a specified ministerial duty. The Writ of Mandamus derives from the early common law, and is one of the Extraordinary Writs which courts are empowered to issue at their discretion. This power, however, has been exercised only in a limited number of cases, including the early landmark case of *Marbury v. Madison,* 5 U.S. 137 (1803). More recently, issuance of the Writ has been commonly sought in cases against federal officers. Since 1962, such cases have been governed by the Mandamus and Venue Act, a statute vesting in the federal district courts original jurisdiction over actions to compel a federal officer to perform his duty. Mandamus also has been frequently sought to require jury trial where it has been improperly denied in a lower court, or where a transfer of venue has been improperly granted or refused.

WRIT OF PROHIBITION. A request to a court to prohibit some person, government official, corporation, or an inferior court from carrying out a specified duty. One of the extraordinary writs at common law, the Writ of Prohibition is the functional twin of the Writ of Mandamus, which orders an individual affirmatively to perform some specified ministerial duty. Issuance of Writs of Prohibition, however, has been extremely rare, and has most commonly been sought to prevent federal officers from performing their duty on the Constitutional ground that such performance would violate the Federal Constitution.

WRONGFUL DEATH STATUTES. Legislation enacted by virtually every jurisdiction in the United States to provide a tort action for wrongfully causing the death of a person. At common law, although the criminal law would punish the tortfeasor who wrongfully took another's life, no civil remedy was available to the victim's survivors. Under such a scheme it was more beneficial financially to kill a man than to injure him. The first Wrongful Death Statute was Lord Campbell's Act in 1846. Modern statutes are of two general types. The first of these, the so-called Survival Statute, merely provides for the survival of any action which the decedent might have maintained had he lived and gives a cause of action to his estate for any damages it suffered due to his death. Under such a statute the decedent's estate would be entitled to collect for his pain and suffering, medical expenses and loss of his future net earnings. The second and more prevalent statute, the so-called "true" type, creates a new cause of action in favor of the surviving relatives but limits the recovery to their pecuniary loss. This latter statute restricts recovery to the value of the support, services and contributions which the survivors would have received from the decedent had he not been killed.

WRONGFUL LIFE (Wrongful Birth; Wrongful Conception; Unblessed Event). A new medical malpractice claim by parents who demand that the doctor pay the full cost of rearing their child through the age of 18 on the basis that the doctor (a) performed a negligent sterilization or gave incorrect birth control advice or (b) failed to inform them of a possible birth defect in their unborn child in time for them to have a lawful abortion. Damages requested have been for the expense of bearing the child, the expense of raising the child, pain and suffering in the bearing of the child, mental anguish, and loss of consortium.

W.S.P.F. See WATERGATE SPECIAL PROSECUTION FORCE.

W.W.N. See WASHINGTON WOMEN'S NETWORK.

W.W.U.I. See WORKING WOMEN UNITED INSTITUTE.

WYTHE, GEORGE. The first law professor in the United States. He was appointed to the faculty of the College of William and Mary in 1779 by Thomas Jefferson. The next two professorships of law in America were founded by Harvard University in 1817 and Yale University in 1824.

Y

YAOUNDE CONVENTIONS (1963 and 1969). Provided for associations between the European Economic Community (E.E.C.) and eighteen African states, as provided by Article 238 of the E.E.C. The Yaounde Conventions were replaced in 1975 by the Lome Convention.

YASSER ARAFAT. See P.L.O.

YATES CASE. Supreme Court case (*Yates v. United States*, 355 U.S. 66 (1957)), which held that teaching and advocating the abstract doctrine of forcible overthrow of the government was not punishable under the Smith Act if such action were "divorced from any effort to instigate action to that end."

YEAR-AND-A-DAY RULE. The doctrine which states that a person cannot be guilty of murder if the victim lives for a year and a day after the crime was committed. The rule originated several centuries ago when limited medical knowledge made it almost impossible to determine with the passage of time whether the defendant had actually caused the victim's death. Although most states still observe the rule, many have abandoned it in light of today's increased medical knowledge.

YELLOW-DOG CONTRACT. An agreement signed by an employee as a condition of employment which prevents him from joining or remaining a member of a labor union. The agreement requires the employee to quit his job if he joins a union. Known in the early 1800s as "iron-clad oaths," the more modern term was used later in the century as union organizing activities increased and union supporters sought to express more forcefully their contempt for this anti-union device and those who submitted to it. In *Adair v. United States*, 208 U.S. 161 (1908) the Supreme Court held unconstitutional a federal law prohibiting yellow dog contracts on interstate railroads. However, such contracts were made illegal by the passage of the Norris-LaGuardia Act in 1932.

YODER CASE. Supreme Court decision (Wisconsin v. Yoder, 406 U.S. 212 (1972)), upholding the right of members of the Amish sect in Minnesota not to send their children to high school.

YOUNG AMENDMENT. A federal law proposed by a Republican Congressman from Florida which would bar the World Bank and other international financing institutions from using any American funds in programs for Angola, Cambodia, Central African Empire, Cuba, Laos and Vietnam.

YOUNG PLAN. An agreement promulgated by American advisor Owen D. Young in 1928, which eased the terms under which Germany was to pay reparations levied against it by the Allies at the end of World War I.

YOUNGSTOWN SHEET AND TUBE CO. v. SAWYER (343 U.S. 579 (1952)). (The Steel Seizure Case). Landmark case in which the United States Supreme Court defined the limits of presidential power. During the Korean War, collective bargaining disputes arose between the steel companies and their employees. A massive strike by the United Steel Workers of America threatened to halt completely the production of steel, a material essential to the war effort. On the ground that the national security was in jeopardy, President Harry S. Truman ordered government seizure of the steel mills and further ordered the Secretary of Commerce to keep the mills running. In *Youngstown* the Court found no constitutional provision authorizing the President to take such action.

YOUTH CORRECTION ACT (Y.C.A.). A federal law designed to reduce criminality among youthful offenders between the ages of sixteen and twenty-two. Modeled on England's Borstal System, the Y.C.A. incorporates three features: (1) flexibility in choosing a rehabilitative treatment program; (2) separation of youthful offenders from adult criminals; and (3) careful control of the length of commitment and supervision of the release. Other protections of the Y.C.A. allow an offender to obtain a certificate setting aside his conviction record. The Supreme Court, in *Durst v. United States,* 434 U.S. 552 (1978), preserved the authority to impose a fine or order restitution, as well as to order rehabilitative measures under the Y.C.A.

YOUTH LAW CENTER. See CHILDREN'S RIGHTS MOVEMENT.

YOUTH RIGHTS CASE (1967). A landmark Supreme Court decision which held that in criminal proceedings, minors must be accorded the fundamentals of due process. The case, *In re Gault,* 387 U.S. 1 (1967), involved a fifteen-year-old who was arrested because of an alleged obscene phone call to a neighbor. The boy was placed in a children's detention home. His parents, who were at work, were not notified. A probation officer filed a juvenile delinquency petition, void of any statement of facts, but generally reciting that Gault was a "delinquent minor." The petition was not served on the Gaults before the hearing. The neighbor did not attend the hearing and no record was kept. At a second hearing, from which the neighbor was also absent, the boy was sentenced as a juvenile delinquent to the Arizona State Industrial School for the period of his minority, approximately six years. Under the Arizona Criminal Code, an adult committing the same offense would be subject to a maximum $50 fine or imprisonment for not more than two months. Reversing Gault's conviction, the Supreme Court held

that before a juvenile can be found guilty and convicted, he must be accorded the following due process rights: notice of the charges; right to counsel; right to confrontation and cross-examination of witnesses; privilege against self-incrimination; right to transcript of proceedings; and right to appellate review.

Z

ZABLOCKI v. REDHAIL. See PERMISSION TO MARRY STATUTE.

ZEBRA CROSSING. Named after the African animal of similar color, these are striped white lines painted on a black street surface to serve as a place for pedestrians to cross. Pedestrians have the right-of-way at such intersections and car drivers are guilty of a traffic violation if they do not yield to them.

ZENGER, JOHN PETER. His acquittal in 1735 for seditious libel is often considered the foundation of freedom of the press. William Cosby, the English Governor of New York, used his office to bolster his personal fortune by selling political appointments. Political opponents launched a newspaper, the *New York Weekly Journal,* to stir up criticism of Cosby. The paper was printed at Zenger's shop and contained sham advertisements criticizing Cosby as a substitute for political cartoons. One such ad requested the return of a lost dog, the description of which matched that of one of Cosby's aides. Cosby acted quickly against the *Journal.* He ordered four issues burned, proclaimed a reward for the discovery of its authors, and arrested Zenger. Zenger was charged with "printing and publishing seditious libels which tended to raise factions and tumults in New York, inflaming the minds of the people against the Government." When Zenger's attorneys were disbarred for insinuating that the judge in the case was a crony of Cosby, Andrew Hamilton became defense counsel. Largely as a result of Hamilton's advocacy, the jury acquitted

Zenger in only a few minutes. Ironically, on the night of his acquittal, Zenger remained in jail while Cosby's opponents celebrated with Hamilton.

ZERO BASED BUDGETING (Z.B.B.). Accounting method which forces state or federal agencies to justify every dollar in their budgets, rather than only the additional money they request. President Carter brought Zero Based Budgeting to the federal government, but it has resulted in few savings because 80 percent of the spending is preset by law and cannot be altered without further legislation.

ZONING VARIANCE. An exemption from the restrictions of a zoning statute or regulation. The exemption is generally granted by administrative action to protect landowners against undue hardship created by strict enforcement of the zoning statute.

ZOO THEORY. A deliberate and diabolical policy by a colonial power to subjugate and exploit the natives by keeping them in their natural primitive life style in a complete denial of all human rights.

ZURCHER v. STANFORD DAILY. See DRINAN BILL.

PART II

Quotations on the Law

A bad agreement is better than a good lawyer. *Italian proverb*

A fundamental point for the pacification of human society is juridical order. *Pope Pius XII*

A jury consists of 12 persons chosen to decide who has the better lawyer. *Robert Frost*

A law, in the literal and proper sense of the word, may be defined as a rule laid down for the guidance of an intelligent being by an intelligent being having power over him. *Austin*

A law is a rule of conduct, administered by those organs of a political society which it has ordained for that purpose, and imposed in the first instance at the will of the dominating political authority in that society in pursuance of the conception of justice which is held by that dominating political authority or by those to whom it has committed the task of making such rules. *Keeton*

A law is a rule to which men are obliged to make their moral actions conformable. *Rutherforth*

A law is properly that which reason in such sort defineth to be good that it must be done. *Hooker*

A lawyer is a learned gentleman who rescues your estate from your enemies and keeps it himself. *Lord Henry Brougham*

A lawyer without history is a mechanic, a mere working mason. *Sir Walter Scott*

All law has for its object to confirm and exalt into a system the exploitation of the workers by a ruling class. *Mikhail Bakunin*

Apologists for the profession contend that lawyers are as honest as other men, but this is not very encouraging. *Ferdinand Lundberg*

Charity begins at home, and justice begins next door. *Charles Dickens*

Equal justice under law all too often means unequal justice among lawyers. *Jerold Auerbach*

Every once in a while you meet a fellow in some honorable walk of life that was once admitted to the bar. *Kin Hubbard*

For forms of government let fools contest; whate'er is best administered is best. *Alexander Pope*

General propositions do not decide concrete cases. *Justice Oliver Wendell Holmes, Jr.*

God has not given laws to make out of right wrong, as the un-Christianlike lawyers do, who study law only for the sake of gain and profit. *Martin Luther*

God save us from a lawyer's etcetera. *French proverb*

God works wonders now and then; Behold! A lawyer, an honest man. *Benjamin Franklin*

How in God's name could so many lawyers get involved in something like Watergate. *Disbarred participant John Dean*

Human society has developed as the rule of law has spread from the family to the village, from the village to the tribe and then to the nation. Only as just and enforceable law has been accepted . . . has it been possible for people to live in peace and security with one another. *Julius K. Nyerere, President of Tanzania*

I don't want a lawyer to tell me what I cannot do; I hire him to tell me how to do what I want to do. *J. P. Morgan*

I find no pleasure in saying that the majority of lawyers who appear in court are so poorly trained that they are not properly performing their job and that their manners and their professional performance and their professional ethics offend a great many people. *Chief Justice Warren E. Burger*

If that be the law, then the law is an ass. *Charles Dickens*

If war is too important to be left to the generals, surely justice is too important to be left to lawyers. *Robert McKay, former dean of N.Y.U. Law School*

If we are to keep our democracy, there must be one commandment: Thou shalt not ration justice. *Learned Hand*

I have a high opinion of lawyers. With all their faults, they stack up well against those in every other occupation or profession. *Harrison Tweed*

In an unjust society the place of a just man is in jail. *Henry David Thoreau*

Injustice anywhere is a threat to justice everywhere. *Dr. Martin Luther King, Jr.*

I question not but there are many attorneys born with open and honest hearts; but I know not one that has had the least practice who is not selfish, trickish, and disingenuous. *William Shenstone*

I shall not rest until every German sees that it is a shameful thing to be a lawyer. *Adolf Hitler*

I think the law is really a humbug, and a benefit principally to the lawyers. *Henry David Thoreau*

I think we may class the lawyers in the natural history of monsters. *John Keats*

It is a horrible demoralizing thing to be a lawyer. You look for such low motives in everyone and everything. *Katherine T. Hinkson*

It is a secret worth knowing that lawyers rarely go to law themselves. *Moses Crowell*

It isn't the bad lawyers who are screwing up the justice system in this country—it's the good lawyers—if you have two competent lawyers on opposite sides, a trial that should take three days could easily last six month. *Art Buchwald*

It is the sad duty of politics to establish justice in a sinful world. *Reinhold Niebuhr*

It's the trade of lawyers to question everything, yield nothing and talk by the hour. *Thomas Jefferson*

I used to be a lawyer, but now I am a reformed character. *Woodrow Wilson*

I wanted to make it a law that only those lawyers and attorneys should receive fees who had won their cases. How much litigation would have been prevented by such a measure. *Napoleon Bonaparte*

I would be loathe to speak ill of any person who I do not know deserves it, but I am afraid he is an attorney. *Samuel Johnson*

Jurisprudence, as I look at it, is simply law in its most generalized part. Every effort to reduce a case to a rule is an effort of jurisprudence, although the name as used in English is confined to the broadest rules and most fundamental conceptions. One mark of a great lawyer is that he sees the application of the broadest rules. . . . If a man goes into law it pays to be a master of it, and to be a master of it means to look straight through all the dramatic incidents and to discern the true basis for prophecy. . . . *Justice Oliver Wendell Holmes, Jr.*

Justice is not settled by legislators and laws—it is in the soul; it cannot be varied by statutes, any more than love, pride, the attraction of gravity, can; it is immutable—it does not depend on majorities—majorities or what not, come at last before the same passionless and exact tribunal. *Walt Whitman*

Justice, though due to the accused, is due the accuser also. *Benjamin N. Cardozo*

Law as it exists in the modern community may be conveniently, although perhaps not comprehensively, defined as the sum total of all those rules of conduct for which there is state sanction. *Harlan Fiske Stone*

Law I define as a rule, prescribed by the sovereign of a society to his subjects, either in order to lay an obligation upon them of doing or omitting certain things, under punishment, or to leave them at liberty to act or not in other things just as they think proper and to secure to them, in this respect, the full enjoyment of their rights. *Burlamaqui*

Law, in its widest sense, is a rule imposed by one being upon itself or upon some other being. It is a rule (Latin—regula, from rego, to govern); a norm or standard of being or conduct determining the nature and attributes of a thing or regulating its actions or forbearances. It is imposed by a being possessing and exercising authority over itself or other beings, and enforcing obedience to the rule either by making its observances inevitable, or by attaching to its violation certain penalties. . . . Human law is a rule prescribed by man for his own government or that of other men. *Robinson*

Law in the objective sense of the term is a peaceable ordering of the external relations of men and their relations to each other. *Gareis*

Law is a body of authoritative guides to the decision of controversies which, as the courts are expected to, and hold themselves bound to, follow them, can serve as rules of conduct to the individual and as the bases of prediction to the counselor. *Roscoe Pound*

Law is a command proceeding from the supreme political authority of a state, and addressed to the persons who are the subjects of that authority. *Amos*

Law is a minimum ethics, that is to say, the whole combined requirements of morals, whose observance, at a given stage of social development, is absolutely indispensable. *Jellinek*

Law is a mode of regulating conduct by means of sanctions imposed by politically organized society. *Seagle*

Law is an attempt to solve the tensions and conflicts inherent in social life, not by arbitrary force or violence, but by an orderly and peaceful adjustment of the reasonable claims of individuals or groups. *Bodenheimer*

Law is a rule and measure of acts, whereby man is induced to act or is restrained from acting; for lex (law) is derived from ligare (to bind), because it binds one to act. Now the rule and measure of human acts is the reason.

. . . Law is an ordinance of reason, for the common good, promulgated by him who has care of the community. *St. Thomas Aquinas*

Law is a rule of action. *Clarke*

Law is a rule of civil conduct prescribed by the supreme power in a state, commanding what is right, and prohibiting what is wrong. *Sir William Blackstone*

Law is a rule of moral action obliging to that which is right. *Hugo Grotius*

Law is a system of social relationships which serves the interests of the ruling classes and hence is supported by their organized power, the state. *Russian Penal Code, Article 590*

Law is defined by two characteristics. It determines, in sovereign fashion, who shall be subject to it, and claims inviolability as long as it is in force. *Stammler*

Law is not a command or body of commands but consists of rules springing from the social standard of justice, or from the habits and customs from which that standard has itself been derived. *Carter*

Law is the conformity of social relations to the essence, the life, the destiny, of society as a whole, or conformity of the individual life to the social life. *Kashnitsa*

Law is the delimitation of the interests of different persons. *Korkunov*

Law is the general body of rules which are addressed by the rulers of a political community to the members of that society, and which are generally obeyed. *Markby*

Law is the highest reason, implanted in nature, which prescribes those things which ought to be done, and forbids the contrary. *Cicero*

Law is the power of an organized political society brought to bear through the judgment of officials, on matters subject to governmental control, as a result of following the processes provided by government. *Green*

Law is the sum of the compulsory rules in force in a state. *von Ihering*

QUOTATIONS

Law may be defined, provisionally, as the force or tendency, which makes for righteousness. *Jenks*

Law must be stable and yet it cannot stand still. *Roscoe Pound*

Law represents an attempt to realize in a given social environment the idea of justice (that is, a preliminary and essentially variable reconciliation of conflicting spiritual values embodied in a social structure), through multilateral imperative-attributive regulation based on a determined link between claims and duties; this regulation derives its validity from the normative facts which give a social guaranty of its effectiveness and can in certain cases execute its requirements by precise and external constraint, but does not necessarily presuppose it. *Gurvitch*

Law sharpens a man's mind by narrowing it. *Edmund Burke*

Laws, in their most general signification, are the necessary relations resulting from the nature of things. *Charles de Secondat de Montesquieu*

Lawyering is within the relatively narrow category of occupations where borderline dishonesty is fairly lucrative. In many instances, the very art of the lawyer is a sort of calculated disregard of the law or at least of ordinary notions of morality. *Eric Schnapper*

Lawyers are masters of a mysterious art form to which the layman is not privy, with mumbo jumbo going on. *Dean Sanford Kadish, University of California (Berkeley) Law School*

Lawyers are oppressors and robbers who did that which is not good among the people. *The Talmud*

Lawyers are paid to keep a dispute alive, to make everything technical. *Fred Dutton, White House Aide*

Lawyers have been known to wrest from reluctant juries triumphant verdicts of acquittal for their clients, even when those clients, as often happens, were clearly and unmistakably innocent. *Oscar Wilde*

Lawyers love to play games. *G. William Baab, Dallas lawyer*

Lawyers make a living out of trying to figure out what other lawyers have written. *Will Rogers*

Lawyers use the law as shoemakers use leather; rubbing it, pressing it, and stretching it with their teeth, all to the end of making it fit their purposes. *Louis XII*

Lawyers will as a rule advance quarrels rather than repress them. *Mahatma Gandhi*

Liberty burns brightly in dungeons. *George Gordon, Lord Byron*

Litigation takes the place of sex at middle age. *Gore Vidal*

Most lawyers who win a case advise their clients that "We have won." And when justice has frowned upon their cause that "You have lost." *Louis Nizer*

Nations can only secure their progress and social welfare through the rule of law, so the community of nations must strive to advance the cause of human welfare through obedience to rules of law. *S. Radhakrishnan, President of the Republic of India*

No other profession is more clearly connected with life than the law. It concerns the highest of all temporal interests of man; property, reputation, the peace of all families, the arbitration and peace of nations, liberty, life; and the very foundations of society. *Edmund Burke*

Of all those arts in which the wise excel, Nature's chief masterpiece is writing well. *John Sheffield*

Reason is the life of the law, nay, the common law itself is nothing else but reason. . . . The law is the perfection of reason. *Sir Edward Coke*

Short is the lawyer's life and shorter still his fame. Soon or late, oblivion awaits us all. *John W. Davis*

That is law, which all men ought to obey for many reasons, and especially because every law is an invention and gift of the gods, a resolution of wise men, a corrective of errors intentional and unintentional, a compact of the whole state, according to which all men who belong to the state ought to live. *Demosthenes*

That 150 lawyers [referring to Congress] should do business together ought not to be expected. *Thomas Jefferson*

The conventional conception of law to which lawyers and judges adhere most consistently is that the law is the aggregate of interrelated rules and principles of human conduct which are prescribed by the government (state) as potentially enforceable to the limit of its power. *Patterson*

The first thing we do, let's kill all the lawyers. *William Shakespeare*

The inn that shelters for the night is not the journey's end. The law, like the traveler, must be ready for the morrow. It must have a principle of growth. *Benjamin N. Cardozo*

The law at bottom can only be what the mass of the people actually does and tends to some extent to make other people do by means of governmental agencies. *Bentley*

The law, in its majestic equality, forbids the rich as well as the poor to sleep under bridges, to beg in the streets, and to steal bread. *Anatole France*

The law is a body of principles recognized and applied by the state in the administration of justice. Or, more shortly: The law consists of the rules recognized and acted on in courts of justice. *Salmond*

The law is a sort of hocus-pocus science. *Macklin*

The law is a very mischievous system designed not to achieve but to frustrate the truth. *Abraham Pomerantz, New York lawyer*

The law is not the place for the artist or poet. The law is the calling of thinkers. *Justice Oliver Wendell Holmes*

The law is the last result of human wisdom acting upon human experience for the benefit of the public. *Johnson*

The law is the source of light from which right and justice radiate. *Faisal, King of Saudi Arabia*

The law is the true embodiment of everything that's excellent. *Gilbert and Sullivan*

The lawless science of our law, that codeless myriad of precedent, that wilderness of single instances. *Alfred Lord Tennyson*

The law of the state or of any organized body of men is composed of the rules which the courts, that is, the judicial organs of that body, lay down for the determination of legal rights and duties. *Gray*

The lawyers know they are liars; they know they are known to be liars; and they feel it no disgrace to constantly practice falsehood and false pretense. From among these men we select our judges. *Edward Willis Scripps*

The legal process, because of its unbridled growth, has become a cancer which threatens the vitality of our forms of capitalism and democracy. *United States Deputy Attorney General Laurence Silberman*

The life of the law has not been logic, it has been experience. *Justice Oliver Wendell Holmes, Jr.*

The penalty for laughing in a courtroom is six months; if it were not for this penalty the jury would never hear the evidence. *H. L. Mencken*

The progressive establishment of the rule of law around the globe constitutes one of the major forces in the task of defending peace and raising the moral level of humanity. *Haile Selassie I, Emperor of Ethiopia*

The prophecies of what the courts will do in fact, and nothing more pretentious, are what I mean by the law. *Justice Oliver Wendell Holmes, Jr.*

The rule of law is an ideal to which we must continuously devote ourselves in order to protect freedom and justice, maintain world peace and promote human welfare. *Archbishop Makarios, President of the Republic of Cyprus.*

The science of law is, therefore, that organized examination of all the data that affect social conduct which will enable us to predict that evaluation in the sense of "ought" or "may" a judge will make of some conduct which is a little outside of the usual patterns. *Radin*

575